EIGHTH EDITION

Life-Span Development

John W. Santrock
UNIVERSITY OF TEXAS AT DALLAS

McGraw Hill

Boston Burr Ridge, IL Dubuque, IA Madison, WI New York San Francisco St. Louis
Bangkok Bogotá Caracas Kuala Lumpur Lisbon London Madrid Mexico City
Milan Montreal New Delhi Santiago Seoul Singapore Sydney Taipei Toronto

McGraw-Hill Higher Education

A Division of The McGraw-Hill Companies

LIFE-SPAN DEVELOPMENT, EIGHTH EDITION

This book is printed on acid-free paper.

1 2 3 4 5 6 7 8 9 0 VNH/VNH 0 9 8 7 6 5 4 3 2 1

ISBN 0–07–241434–0
ISBN 0–07–112153–6 (ISE)

Editorial director: *Jane E. Karpacz*
Senior sponsoring editor: *Rebecca H. Hope*
Senior developmental editor: *Sharon Geary*
Senior marketing manager: *Chris Hall*
Senior project manager: *Marilyn Rothenberger*
Lead production supervisor: *Sandra Hahn*
Coordinator of freelance design: *Michelle D. Whitaker*
Freelance cover/interior designer: *Diane Beasley*
Cover images: (top) © *Nasi Sakura/SuperStock;* (middle) © *Bruce Ayres/Stone;* (bottom) © *Aaron Strong/Stone*
Senior photo research coordinator: *Carrie K. Burger*
Photo research: *LouAnn K. Wilson*
Senior supplement producer: *David A. Welsh*
Media technology lead producer: *David Edwards*
Compositor: *GTS Graphics, Inc.*
Typeface: *10.5/12 Minion*
Printer: *Von Hoffmann Press, Inc.*

The credits section for this book begins on page C-1 and is considered an extension of the copyright page.

Library of Congress Cataloging-in-Publication Data

Santrock, John W.
Life-span development / John W. Santrock. — 8th ed.
p. cm.
Includes bibliographical references and indexes.
ISBN 0–07–241434–0
1. Developmental psychology. I. Title.
BF713 .S26 2002
155—dc21 2001018721
CIP

INTERNATIONAL EDITION ISBN 0–07–112153–6

www.mhhe.com

Online Learning Center

MULTIMEDIA

ABOUT THE BOOK

- **Table of Contents**
  Lists the entire TOC.
- **Overview**
  Provides a quick synopsis of the edition and the material covered.
- **What's New**
  Introduces the new features of the textbook.
- **Supplements**
  Click here to see a web version of the IM, including material for the 4 optional *Psychology,* sixth edition chapters.
- **Meet the Author**
  Click here to see a web version of the IM.

Welcome to the
Santrock: **Life-Span Development, eighth edition**
website:
www.mhhe.com/santrockld8

STUDENT RESOURCES

- **Table of Contents**
  Lists the entire TOC.
- **Overview**
  Provides a quick synopsis of the edition and the material covered.
- **What's New**
  Introduces the new features of the textbook.
- **Supplements**
  Click here to see a web version of the IM, including material for the 4 optional *Psychology,* sixth edition chapters.
- **Meet the Author**
  Click here to see a web version of the IM.

INSTRUCTOR'S RESOURCES

- **Table of Contents**
  Lists the entire TOC.
- **Overview**
  Provides a quick synopsis of the edition and the material covered.
- **What's New**
  Introduces the new features of the textbook.
- **Supplements**
  Click here to see a web version of the IM, including material for the 4 optional *Psychology,* sixth edition chapters.
- **Meet the Author**
  Click here to see a web version of the IM.

Preface

The Eighth Edition: A Major Revision

This, the eighth edition, is the first edition of this book in the twenty-first century, nearly 20 years after the first edition was published in 1983. When a book reaches its eighth edition, it typically generates two reactions from instructors:

1. The book must be successful to have lasted this long, and
2. The eighth edition likely is not much different from the seventh edition.

We acknowledge the accuracy of the first impression—more than half a million students have used previous editions. However, to instructors who might have the second perception of *Life-Span Development's* eighth edition, we optimistically challenge you to put it to the test. With the most extensive input from instructors, research experts, and students any edition of the book has ever received, the inclusion of many new topics, deletion of other topics, an extensive reworking, updating, and expansion of material on adolescence and adult development and aging, a new design, and line-by-line revision of material, *we are confident that you will find that the eighth edition of* Life-Span Development *is significantly different from the seventh edition and that you will be pleasantly surprised.*

> *"My impression is that John Santrock's text is the most comprehensive life-span text suitable for undergraduates now available. The 8th edition has been strengthened by giving greater coverage and depth to the 75 percent of the life span spent in adulthood and old age. There has been significant updating of material as well. . . . The coverage is comprehensive and up-to-date without heavy emphasis on transitory fads. . . . My enthusiasm for this book is high."*
>
> **K. Warner Schaie**
> **Pennsylvania State University**

> *"This edition of John Santrock's* Life-Span Development *is significantly better than the previous one. This is not just a new edition. It is a better textbook."*
>
> **Gary Allen**
> **University of South Carolina**

The Burrston House Story

Burrston House has very successfully developed textbooks for more than a decade and put their skills to work on the eighth edition of *Life-Span Development.* They conduct focus groups as well as extensive reviews of a book by having an unusually large number of instructors who teach the course provide *extremely detailed* reviews of every chapter. Essentially, they seek to discover what instructors want in a book for their course, so the author can revise the book accordingly. They then subject the manuscript to another extensive and exhaustive set of reviews in order to test the author's changes and to produce a foundation for further refinement in a final draft. A unique aspect of the Burrston House approach is that after reviewing an individual chapter, instructors grade the chapter from A to F in terms of how effectively the chapter meets their needs.

For *Life-Span Development,* reviewers initially evaluated the seventh edition and then subsequent drafts of the eighth edition. *The results were dramatic.* Many of the chapters in the seventh edition, especially the chapters on adulthood and aging, averaged in the B to B– range in terms of whether instructors believed they were appropriate for their life-span course. Virtually all of the final drafts of the chapters for the eighth edition were rated in the A range (and most in the very high A range), indicating that for a wide range of instructors they were outstanding and exactly what they were looking for in their course.

What Did We Learn?

From Instructors

What do most instructors really want from a life-span development text? To find out, we obtained detailed input from more than 40 instructors who teach the life-span course—some of whom had used previous editions of this book and a large number of whom have used other texts.

Expansion of Material on Adult Development and Aging

Instructors especially told us that most life-span texts don't give enough attention to adult development and aging. We took this seriously and significantly modified, expanded, and updated the material on adult development and aging in the eighth edition.

> *"John Santrock has made significant improvements in the coverage of adult development and aging in the 8th edition of his book. It is refreshing to see a developmental textbook that does not 'slack off' in the adulthood years. I appreciate your expanded coverage of adult development and I firmly believe others will too. Every chapter of the book has been improved, not just in adult development and aging, but in the entire book."*
>
> **Meredith Cohen**
> **University of Pittsburgh**

"The 8th edition is significantly improved. I am very pleased with the expanded coverage in the adult chapters."
Ava Craig
Sacramento City College

Balanced Coverage

Instructors said they want balanced coverage of all the life-span periods and of physical, cognitive, and socioeconomic development. We increased coverage of physical development in the chapters on early childhood, middle childhood, adolescence, and adulthood. We increased coverage of cognitive development in the chapters on adulthood. We modified coverage of socioemotional development to include more relevant topics.

"Santrock is broader and has more balanced coverage for each period of development than other books."
Ava Craig
Sacramento City College

"Santrock's text has balanced coverage of all domains—physical, cognitive, and socioemotional. And it is highly readable."
Jean Seitz
University of Memphis

The Most Contemporary Research

Every effort was made to infuse *Life-Span Development,* eighth edition, with the most up-to-date coverage of research that is available. To this end, every research area was carefully examined and new research was added where appropriate. For example, this new edition has more than 500 new citations from the twenty-first century alone. Also, to ensure that the research in every area of the text is very contemporary, a number of experts in different areas of life-span development served as consultants on the book. We will describe their efforts shortly. Also, later in the preface when we describe the main changes in each chapter, we will list the highlights of new research.

Level

Focus-group participants and reviewers told us that many texts on life-span development have become unnecessarily high-level and include too many details about research that go over their students' heads. Instructors encouraged us to include the latest research on life-span development, and we did, but in presenting the research, we made every effort to present it at a level that will challenge and interest students but not overwhelm them. Reviewers consistently informed us that the level of the research descriptions were just right for students taking their first course on life-span development.

Careers in Life-Span Development

Instructors and students told us that they would like to see more information about the range of careers in life-span development. To meet this need, descriptions of individuals in various careers in life-span development appear in every chapter. Students also will read about careers in life-span development in chapter 1.

Sensitivity to Gender and Ethnicity

Another effort we undertook was to be especially sensitive to coverage of gender and ethnicity issues—in the book's content, in the photographs chosen, and in the use of gender-neutral language. The Sociocultural Worlds of Development boxes that appear in many chapters capture how culture, ethnicity, and gender influence life-span development. Also, many new photographs that illustrate cultural and ethnic diversity were added to this new edition of the book. A diversity expert, Algea Harrison-Hale, evaluated the entire book to ensure that the text and photographs reflected a high standard of diversity.

An Exciting, Very Well-Written Book

Instructors also said they want a text that is exciting and well written. We worked very hard to make this book one that students will truly enjoy reading and studying.

"Santrock's text shows a deep appreciation for the mystery and beauty of development and life itself. I especially like the attention to diversity and to positive aging."
Nancy Rankin
University of New England

"Santrock's writing style makes his books. Other books in this area do not compare well in terms of the writing style used."
Jean Seitz
University of Memphis

"Santrock's writing is very nice, very readable, and overall quite engaging."
Debra Hollister
Valencia Community College

A Much Improved, Cleaner, Open, Dynamic Look

Instructors also told us that they wanted a life-span text that was not cluttered and busy. To this end, *Life-Span Development* underwent a major design overhaul. This included going from the previous edition's dense two-column design with lots of special features and boxes to a more open, one-column look with fewer boxes and special features in this new edition. Also, the colors used in the new edition are much brighter and more appealing for today's student.

Supplements with Exceptional Utility and Quality

Our extensive surveys of instructors and focus groups told us how important the "everyday" ancillaries, such as an Instructor's Resource Manual, the test bank, and transparencies/Power Point slides are. This came through loud and clear. Thus, we spent considerable time revamping these important supplements. We also extensively updated and expanded the technology ancillaries. The ancillaries are described further toward the end of the preface.

From Experts

What do experts in various areas of life-span development say is the most important research content to be included in an undergraduate text? To find out, we enlisted the input of thirteen leading world experts in different age ranges and different content areas.

No single author can possibly be an expert in all areas of life-span development. With research information on life-span development exploding in all age periods and content areas, input from a number of experts is an extremely valuable asset. Our experts provided detailed recommendations on new research to include in every period of the life span.

The experts for this book literally are a Who's Who in the field of life-span development. Their photographs and biographies appear on pages xxxii–xxxiii.

From Students

Not surprisingly, students told us they want a book that is exciting and well written and provides good learning aids, especially visual ones. They also want lots of Internet connections to further explore topics in the text that interest them. To that end, we have made a special effort to include high-interest topics that are personally relevant to students, clarify the writing with appropriate examples, and include extensive Internet connections.

Chapter-by-Chapter Changes

To illustrate some of the substantial content changes in the eighth edition of Life Span Development, let's briefly examine each of the twenty-one chapters. Virtually all of these changes were made in response to requests from instructors who teach the life-span course and leading research experts in life-span development.

CHAPTER 1 Introduction

Exploration of why life-span development is an important college course
Updated coverage of characteristics of the life-span perspective
Career biographies on a professor of human development and a child clinical psychologist
Expanded discussion of careers in life-span development

> *"This first chapter very clearly outlines the life-span perspective and the nature of development. It gives the reader a sense of breadth/depth of the issues."*
> **Patrick K. Ackles**
> **University of Illinois at Chicago**

CHAPTER 2 The Science of Life-Span Development

New figures diagonally displayed on page to illustrate the staircase-like nature of stage theories—Freud's, Piaget's, and Erikson's
New sections at the end of each set of theoretical perspectives describing strengths and weaknesses
Complete overhaul of coverage of the information-processing perspective
New section on Pavlov's classical conditioning theory
Completely rewritten methods section for improved clarity
New section on research journals
Career biographies on a director of human subjects protection and an educational psychologist

> *"Strenghts of this chapter include the strong theoretical approach and the extensive inclusion of the scientific approach."*
> **Ava Craig**
> **Sacramento City College**

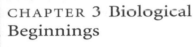

CHAPTER 3 Biological Beginnings

Extensively revised, updated discussion of evolution and life-span development
New coverage of mitosis and meiosis, including an easy-to-understand visual presentation of these processes
Reorganization of heredity section—the discussion of abnormalities now follows the discussion of genetic principles
New section on reproduction challenges and choices
The material on intelligence moved to the section on heredity-environment interaction
Extensively revised and updated coverage of heredity-environment interaction, including a discussion of Judith Harris' controversial book, *The Nurture Assumption*
Career biography on a genetic counselor

> *"This chapter is excellent and reflects the most important issues in the field of developmental psychobiology. . . . It is clearly written."*
> **Ross Thompson**
> **University of Nebraska–Lincoln**

CHAPTER 4 Prenatal Development and Birth

Dramatic new Images of Life-Span Development opening section: "Tanner Roberts' Birth: A Fantastic Voyage"
New section on cultural beliefs about pregnancy
Extensive reorganization of teratology section
New coverage of prescription and nonprescription drugs
Updated research on cocaine and prenatal development
New research on stress and pregnancy
New section on positive prenatal development
New section on the transition from fetus to newborn

> *"This chapter is extraordinarily well constructed, incorporating excellent examples, wonderful photographs, interesting boxes, and well-placed figures. Interesting and holds one's attention."*
> **Karla Miley**
> **Black Hawk College**

CHAPTER 5 Physical Development in Infancy

New Images of Life-Span Development opening section: "Bottle- and Breast-Feeding in Africa"

New material on shared sleeping
Updated, expanded coverage of SIDS
Extensively rewritten, updated discussion of breast-feeding
New section on perceptual-motor coupling and unification
Increased coverage of diversity

> *"The organization of this chapter is a strength and there are wonderful sections on motor development and perception."*
> **Ann Merriwether**
> **University of Michigan**

CHAPTER 6 Cognitive Development in Infancy

Extensive revision, reorganization, and updating of section on information processing
New section, "Learning and Remembering"
New section on conditioning; Rovee-Collier's research moved to this section
Extensively revised, updated discussion of memory in infancy
New coverage of Fagan Test of Infant Intelligence
New organization of language section; development now precedes biological, environmental influences
New research on poverty and language development
Motherese now discussed under topic of infant-directed speech
Career biography of an infant assessment specialist

> *"Santrock does a great job of presenting a number of important theoretical perspectives with thoughtful discussions of their strengths and weaknesses. The reorganization of the language development section is also a strength. This is a strong chapter."*
> **Meredith Cohen**
> **University of Pittsburgh**

CHAPTER 7 Socioemotional Development in Infancy

Extensive reorganization of chapter; emotional development is now the first main topic of the chapter (in the seventh edition, it was the last section)
Improved clarity of information about what emotions are
Updated coverage of goodness of fit and temperament
New material on phases of infant attachment
New coverage of Type D babies
New section on caregiving styles and attachment
New research on day care
Career biography on a day-care director

> *"This is an excellent chapter, as I had expected. It reflects the most important issues in the field of early socioemotional development and it is well-written and engaging with discussions of the central concerns for the field."*
> **Ross Thompson**
> **University of Nebraska–Lincoln**

CHAPTER 8 Physical and Cognitive Development in Early Childhood

New material on why some children are unusually short
Very recent research (1999, 2000) on the use of brain scans to document changes in the brain in early childhood
New discussion of handedness and brain hemispheres
Expanded, updated coverage of Vygotsky's theory
Extensive examination of applying Vygotsky's theory to education
New comparison of Piaget and Vygotsky, including a summary figure
New section on strategies, including recent research (Chen & Siegler, 2000)
More streamlined discussion of language development
Career biographies on a pediatric nurse, an early childhood educator, and a Head Start director

> *"This chapter is well organized with a nice flow and has really solid sections on Piaget and Vygotsky. Overall a very solid chapter."*
> **Ann Merriwether**
> **University of Michigan**

CHAPTER 9 Socioemotional Development in Early Childhood

New Images of Life-Span Development opening section: "Sarah and Her Developing Morality and Values"
Extensive reorganization of chapter; emotional and personality development now start the chapter, followed by families, peers, and TV
New discussion of emotional development in early childhood
Additional examples of parenting styles
New section on parenting, nature, and nurture, with very recent citations (2000)
New section on the fact that parenting takes time and effort, with very recent citations (2000)
Extensive revision and updating of discussion of divorce and children
New section on television and cognitive development
Increased coverage of diversity
Career biography on a child social worker

> *"Great chapter! I am impressed with how succinct yet comprehensive it is. Typically, I find more to criticize but found this chapter to be clearly written and up-to-date."*
> **Craig Hart**
> **Brigham Young University**

CHAPTER 10 Physical and Cognitive Development in Middle and Late Childhood

Updated research on how much exercise children are getting
Deletion of section on stress; reviewers believed it was inappropriate for this chapter
Considerable expansion of material on physical development, including new sections on accidents and injuries, obesity, and cancer

Very contemporary coverage of educational issues involving children with disabilities
Expanded, updated discussion of Piaget applied to education
Expanded, updated coverage of critical thinking
Expanded, updated exploration of metacognition
Updated coverage of Gardner's eight frames of mind
Updated, revised examination of reading
Updated, revised coverage of bilingualism
Career biographies on a child life specialist, a science museum curator and research specialist, a program supervisor for gifted and talented children, and a speech pathologist

> *"This chapter is a great chapter. The summary tables and graphic organizers are excellent. The section on children with disabilities is excellent. A great discussion of multiple intelligences."*
>
> **Gaby Vandergiessen**
> **Fairmont State College**

CHAPTER 11 Socioemotional Development in Middle and Late Childhood

Chapter restructured; emotional and personality development now precede contexts (families, peers, and schools)
New discussion of research on self-esteem
New section on developmental changes in emotion
Revised and updated examination of emotional intelligence
Revised, updated labeling and definitions of Kohlberg's stages
New material on strategies teachers and parents can use to increase children's prosocial behavior
New section with very up-to-date research on bullying
Extensively updated and expanded discussion of socioeconomic status and ethnicity in schools, including Jonathan Kozol's observations
Career biographies on a director for social emotional education, a school psychologist, and a child psychiatrist

> *"This chapter is extremely well written and does an excellent job of describing the socioemotional development of middle and late childhood for ethnic minority children. This chapter is an example of how texts should handle diversity issues."*
>
> **Algea Harrison-Hale**
> **Oakland University**

CHAPTER 12 Physical and Cognitive Development in Adolescence

Substantial increase in the amount of coverage given to puberty and physical changes
Extensive increase in coverage of adolescent sexuality
New section on body image
New section on STDs in adolescence
New section on cigarette smoking in adolescence
New section on adolescent health and adolescence as a critical juncture in health
New section on leading causes of death in adolescence
New section on information processing with a focus on decision making and critical thinking
New section on moral education
New section on service learning
Career biography on a high school guidance counselor

> *"A strength of the chapter now is the complete discussion of physical changes associated with puberty including sequence and sexual development."*
>
> **Krista Forrest**
> **University of Nebraska–Kearney**

CHAPTER 13 Socioemotional Development in Adolescence

Extensive reorganization of chapter; identity now is the first major chapter topic, followed by social contexts (families, peers, and culture) and problems/disorders
Drug abuse and eating disorders moved to previous chapter because of their physical connections
Updated, revised discussion of identity's components
Updated coverage of attachment in adolescence
Much-expanded exploration of dating, including developmental changes and emotional aspects
New coverage of immigration by ethnic minorities in the United States
New section on youth violence
Career biographies on a counseling psychologist and a health psychologist

> *"This chapter is concise, well stated, and readable. I liked the way identity formation is explained. A primary chapter strength is the ease with which students can read this information. The topics included also are a strength."*
>
> **Kathy Manuel**
> **Bossier Parish Community College**

CHAPTER 14 Physical and Cognitive Development in Early Adulthood

New Images of Life-Span Development opening section: "Flo Jo"
New introductory material on the criteria for becoming an adult and the new concept of "emerging adulthood" (Arnett, 2000)
New commentary about returning students
Updated, revised coverage of eating and weight, including new section on restrained eaters
New discussion of cigarette smoking
New section on sexually transmitted diseases
Completely rewritten and updated discussion of careers and work
New sections on values and careers, finding the right career, and work
Career biographies on a college/career counselor, a university professor, health psychology researcher, and university president, a university professor and researcher, and a clinical psychologist

"I liked this chapter a lot. It was well written and organized. I liked the outline and the way it flowed."

Renee Babcock
Central Michigan University

CHAPTER 15 Socioemotional Development in Early Adulthood

Substantial reorganization of chapter: Continuity and discontinuity now open chapter, intimacy now opens section on faces of love, friendship now follows affectionate love just before discussion of loneliness
Much-expanded coverage of continuity and discontinuity with a focus on longitudinal research studies on temperament and attachment
New section on female, male, and female-male friendships
New staircase visual presentation of stages in the family life cycle
Extensive revision, expansion, and updating of marital relationships, including Gottman's recent research
New section on the benefits of a good marriage
New section on cohabiting adults
Expanded coverage of remarried couples
New section on gay and lesbian couples
Career biographies on a clinical psychologist and a parent educator

CHAPTER 16 Physical and Cognitive Development in Middle Adulthood

New introductory material on baby-boom cohorts in middle age
Considerable expansion, revision, and very contemporary updating of material on physical changes in middle age
Recent research from the MacArthur Foundation Study of Mid-Life (Brim, 1999)
New sections on strength, joints, and bones; sleep; and health and social relationships
New section on mortality rates in middle age
New discussion of cross-cultural variations in menopause
Extensively revised and updated examination of hormone replacement therapy
Extensive expansion and updating of coverage of cognitive development in middle adulthood
New discussion of crystallized and fluid intelligence in middle age
New discussion of Schaie's Seattle Longitudinal Study of Intelligence in this chapter
Expanded coverage of information processing in middle age
New section on expertise
New section on career challenges and changes in middle age
Expanded and updated exploration of religion and meaning of life
New section on religion and health
Career biography on a pastoral counselor

"A major strength of the chapter by far is the expanded coverage of cognitive development in middle adulthood."

Meredith Cohen
University of Pittsburgh

CHAPTER 17 Socioemotional Development in Middle Adulthood

Extensive reorganization of chapter: adult personality theories now begin the chapter
Reorganization within personality theories for clearer presentation with two main types of theories now discussed: stage and life-events
New stand-alone section on midlife crisis
New research by the MacArthur Foundation documenting that midlife crises are exaggerated
Updated coverage of Costa and McCrae's Baltimore Longitudinal Study, including cross-cultural information
New research by Labouvie-Vief and others (2000) on developmental aspects of midlife personality traits
New research on divorce, marital happiness, and middle age
New section on parenting conceptions
Extensively expanded, updated coverage of intergenerational relationships
Career biography on a professor of human development and a researcher on families and women's issues

"This chapter is informative, well written, and insightful. It offers a nice blend of both theoretical and empirical scholarship and draws on a wide array of research evidence to provide students with a comprehensive overview of what we know about midlife development. This book offers an important life-span view of development."

Phyllis Moen
Cornell University

CHAPTER 18 Physical Development in Late Adulthood

Updated data on life expectancy in the United States, new data on African Americans, and new data on life expectancy around the world
New date on the percentage of older adults in different countries around the world
New data on life expectancy at 65
Updated, expanded coverage of research on centenarians
New material on the importance of thinking about age in terms of functional age rather than only in terms of chronological age
New, updated research on telomeres and aging, including photograph of telomeres
New research on neurogenesis
New section on physical appearance and aging
New section on touch and aging
More streamlined, clearer presentation of health treatment
Career biography on a geriatric nurse

> *"A very engaging chapter. Examples are really attention-getting. Some challenging areas (brain, theories of aging) are covered well at a very nice level for students. I love how this chapter presents such a positive view of aging and breaks down stereotypes."*
>
> Ann Merriwether
> University of Michigan

CHAPTER 19 Cognitive Development in Late Adulthood

New discussion of the decline in explicit memory in older adults
New section on memory beliefs, including recent research (2000)
New research on links between complex work and intellectual functioning in older adults (Schooler & others, 1999)
New research on links between exercise and thinking (Kramer & others, 1999)
Important new section, "Use It or Lose It"
Recent research on how cognitive training can remediate cognitive decline ([illegible] & others, 1999)
Updated, rewritten section on work
Extensive updating and expansion of material on dementias, Alzheimer's disease, and other afflictions
New section on the stages of Alzheimer's disease
New discussion of elder mistreatment
New research on praying and longevity

> *"I found this chapter to be very well written, clear, and organized. I enjoyed reading it very much and found it informative and enlightening. The section on memory is very good."*
>
> David Mitchell
> Loyola University–Chicago

CHAPTER 20 Socioemotional Development in Late Adulthood

New Images of Life-Span Development opening section: "Bob Cousy"
Major reorganization of chapter; expanded section "Theories of Socioemotional Development" now starts the chapter
Important new theory discussed in depth: Carstensen's socioemotional selectivity theory
New staircase figure showing personal investment of people at different points in adult development
Revised section with new title: "Older Adults in Society"
Recent research on older adults' friendships (Jerome & Wenger, 1999)
Revised, updated, clearer presentation of social support and social integration
Revised, updated, expanded coverage of successful aging with this now placed at the final section in the chapter
Career biography on a psychology professor and director of a women's studies program

> *"My list of positive reactions about this chapter could go on and on—I like the presentation on ageism, the succinct description of social theories of aging, and the great coverage of ethnicity, gender, and culture. What can I say—I like it all."*
>
> Karla Miley
> Black Hawk College

CHAPTER 21 Death and Grieving

New Images of Life-Span Development opening section: "Princess Diana's Death"
New discussion of the Natural Death Act and advanced directive
Revised, updated coverage of euthanasia
Recent research on physicians' attitudes about active euthanasia
Revised, clearer presentation of Kübler-Ross' theory
Recent research on healthy grieving and family communication
Recent research on the link between religion and mourning/funeral rituals
Biographies on a geropsychologist and a certified grief counselor

> *"This chapter offers an abundance of useful information on a variety of topics related to death, dying, and grief; [illegible] has made a diligent effort to discover and include updated material."*
>
> Robert Kastenbaum
> Arizona State University

Technology

An important new addition to the eighth edition of *Life-Span Development* is the presence of a large number of relevant Internet connections. In every chapter, labeled icons in the margins signal students that by going to the website for this book, they can connect with other websites to read further about a topic that interests them. There are 15 to 45 of these in every chapter. This allows for more in-depth exploration about the topic than is usually possible in the text itself.

Also, a new end-of-chapter feature called "Taking It to the Net" presents students with problem-solving exercises that require them to visit the websites listed.

Improved Instructor- and Student-Driven Pedagogy

Students not only should be challenged to study hard and think more deeply and productively about life-span development, they also should be provided with a pedagogical framework to help them learn more effectively. The learning and study aids we will describe next, some of which are unique to this text and many of which are new to this edition, have been class-tested with students and endorsed by them. As a consequence, we are more confident than ever before that your students will find this edition of *Life-Span Development* to be a very student-friendly book. Following are some of the new pedagogical features in this edition, descriptions and visuals of which can be found in this text's visual preface.

Careers in Life-Span Development

This new feature was especially encouraged by instructors and reviewers. One to five times in each chapter, students will read about real people in careers related to the content in that chapter. Each of these boxes describes the educational background of the individual and what her or his job entails. These boxes give students information about a wide range of careers in life-span development, helping them reflect on whether they might want to pursue one of these careers.

Cross-Linkages

Reviewers recommended that we provide more connections and links with material across chapters. To accomplish this, we created a new pedagogical feature that is unique to life-span development texts. The new *cross-linkages* refer students to the primary discussions of key concepts. Each time a key concept occurs in a chapter subsequent to its initial coverage, the page reference for its initial coverage is embedded in the text with a backward-pointing arrow.

Cognitive Maps

Instructor and student reviewers said they liked the cognitive map at the end of the chapter but thought that it also should be placed at the beginning of the chapter. We not only added an overall cognitive map of the chapter at the beginning of the chapter but, in addition, added mini cognitive maps, which are unique in life-span development texts, throughout the chapters. Students now get many visual looks at the organization of the material: Each chapter opens with a cognitive map of the entire chapter, then several times within the chapter they see mini cognitive maps that give them an ongoing visual picture of what they will be reading next, and finally at the end of the chapter, the overall cognitive map is presented again along with reminders to study the summary tables, which are page-referenced.

Revised Summary Tables

Summary tables have been a popular feature in *Life-Span Development.* However, reviewers recommended that we modify them in two ways: (1) make them shorter and less dense, and (2) use bullets to highlight important characteristics and descriptions of material. We made both of these changes and believe that the summary tables are now even more effective for helping students get a handle on important concepts as they go through each chapter.

Key People

At the recommendation of reviewers, we have added at the end of each chapter a page-referenced list of the most important theorists and researchers discussed in the chapter.

Acknowledgments

A project of this magnitude requires the efforts of a great many people. I owe special gratitude to Rebecca Hope, Senior Sponsoring Editor, and to Sharon Geary, Director of Development and Media, for their outstanding guidance and support. I also benefited enormously from Glenn Turner's extensive, detailed analysis and recommendations. Chris Hall, marketing manager, also made special contributions to the book's direction and presentation. Jane Vaicunas, Editorial Director, Thalia Dorwick, editorial vice president, and Bob McLaughlin, national sales manager, also deserve a great deal of thanks for their support of this book. I also want to give special thanks to Marilyn Rothenberger, Project Manager, and Wendy Nelson, copy editor, for their outstanding work on the book's production. I value not only the extraordinary, competent professional relationship I have with these individuals, but also their friendship.

General Text Reviewers

I also owe a special gratitude to the instructors who teach the life-span course and have provided detailed feedback about the book. Substantial changes in the eighth edition of *Life-Span Development* are based on their feedback. In this regard, I thank the following individuals.

User/Nonuser Pre-revision Reviewers

Saundra Y. Boyd, *Houston Community College*
Ann Brandt-Williams, *Glendale Community College*
Tom L. Day, *Weber State University*
Mary B. Eberly, *Oakland University*
Ramona O. Hopkins, *Brigham Young University*
Susan Horton, *Mesa Community College*
Kevin Keating, *Broward Community College*
Pete Peterson, *Johnson County Community College*
Robert Poresky, *Kansas State University*
Mark P. Rittman, *Cuyahoga Community College*
Nancy Sauerman, *Kirkwood Community College*
Elisabeth Shaw, *Texarkana College*
Donald M. Stanley, *North Harris College*

Focus Group Participants

Lilia Allen, *Charles County Community College*
Alice D. Beyrent, *Hesser College*
Stephanie Blecharczyk, *Keene State College*
Karyn Mitchell Boutin, *Massasoit Community College*
Lynne Andreozzi Fontaine, *Community College of Rhode Island*
Kathleen Corrigan Fuhs, *J. Sargeant Reynolds Community College*
Jean Berko Gleason, *Boston University*
Ester Hanson, *Prince George's Community College*
Stephen Werba, *The Community College of Baltimore County–Catonsville*
Linda B. Wilson, *Quincy College*

Eighth Edition Full-Manuscript Reviewers

Patrick K. Ackles, *Michigan State University*
Gary L. Allen, *University of South Carolina*
Renee L. Babcock, *Central Michigan University*
Meredith Cohen, *University of Pittsburgh*
Ava Craig, *Sacramento City College*

Debra Hollister, *Valencia Community College*
Heather Holmes-Lonergan, *Metropolitan State College of Denver*
Karla Miley, *Black Hawk College*
Nancy Rankin, *University of New England*
Jean A. Steitz, *The University of Memphis*

Eighth Edition Manuscript Chapter Reviewers

Doreen Arcus, *University of Massachusetts, Lowell*
Michelle Boyer-Pennington, *Middle Tennessee State University*
Diane Cook, *Gainesville College*
Darryl M. Dietrich, *College of St. Scholastica*
Dan Fawaz, *Georgia Perimeter College*
Dan Grangaard, *Austin Community College*
Rea Gubler, *Southern Utah University*
Laura Hanish, *Arizona State University*
Amanda W. Harrist, *Oklahoma State University*
Kathleen Day Hulbert, *University of Massachusetts, Lowell*
Kathryn French Iroz, *Utah Valley State College*
Kathy Manuel, *Bossier Parish Community College*
Allan Mayotte, *Riverland Community College*
Susan McClure, *Westmoreland Community College*
Dorothy H. McDonald, *Sandhills Community College*
Sharon McNeely, *Northeastern Illinois University*
Jessica Miller, *Mesa State College*
David B. Mitchell, *Loyola University*
Christopher Quarto, *Middle Tennessee State University*
Mark P. Rittman, *Cuyahogo Community College*
Gregory Smith, *University of Maryland*
Donald M. Stanley, *North Harris College*
Stacy D. Thompson, *Oklahoma State University*
Gaby Vandergiessen, *Fairmont State College*

Expert Consultants

As mentioned earlier in the preface, an extraordinary number of the world's leading experts on life-span development served as expert consultants for the eighth edition of *Life-Span Development.* Every chapter of the book benefited from their willingness to share their insights about the field of life-span development—what our state of knowledge is now and where it is going in the twenty-first century. Their biographies and photographs appear at the end of the preface.

Marc H. Bornstein, *National Institute of Child Health & Development*
Robert Kastenbaum, *Arizona State University*
Gisela Labouvie-Vief, *Wayne State University*
Phyllis Moen, *Cornell University*
Jean M. Mandler, *University of California–San Diego*
Barry M. Lester, *Women and Infant's Hospital*
K. Warner Schaie, *Pennsylvania State University*
Julia Graber, *Columbia University*
Toni Antonucci, *University of Michigan–Institute for Social Research*
Algea O. Harrison-Hale, *Oakland University*
Craig Hart, *Brigham Young University*
Ravenna Helson, *University of California–Berkeley*
Ross A. Thompson, *University of Nebraska–Lincoln*

Reviewers of Previous Editions

I also remain indebted to the following individuals who reviewed previous editions and whose suggestions have been carried forward into the current edition of the text:

Joanne M. Alegre, *Yavajai College*
Susan E. Allen, *Baylor University*
Frank R. Ashbury, *Valdosta State College*
Daniel R. Bellack, *Trident Technical College*
Helen E. Benedict, *Baylor University*
James A. Blackburn, *University of Wisconsin, Madison*
Belinda Blevin-Knabe, *University of Arkansas, Little Rock*
Donald Bowers, *Community College of Philadelphia*
Joan B. Cannon, *University of Lowell*
Kathleen Crowley-Long, *College of Saint Rose*
Margaret Sutton Edmonds, *University of Massachusetts, Boston*
Martha M. Ellis, *Collin County Community College*
Shirley Feldman, *Stanford University*
Linda E. Flickinger, *St. Claire Community College*
Tom Frangicetto, *Northhampton Community College*
J. Steven Fulks, *Utah State University*
Cathy Furlong, *Tulsa Junior College*
Duwayne Furman, *Western Illinois University*
David Goldstein, *Temple University*
Mary Ann Goodwyn, *Northeast Louisiana University*
Peter C. Gram, *Pensacola Junior College*
Michael Green, *University of North Carolina*
Sharon C. Hott, *Allegany Community College*
Stephen Hoyer, *Pittsburgh State University*
Kathleen Day Hulbert, *University of Lowell*
Seth Kalichman, *Loyola University*
Karen Kirkendall, *Sangamon State University*
Joseph C. LaVoie, *University of Nebraska at Omaha*
Jean Hill Macht, *Montgomery County Community College*
Salvador Macias, *University of South Carolina–Sumter*
Heather E. Metcalfe, *University of Windsor*
Teri M. Miller-Schwartz, *Milwaukee Area Technical College*
Martin D. Murphy, *University of Akron*
Malinda Muzi, *Community College of Philadelphia*
Gordon K. Nelson, *Pennsylvania State University*
Richard Pierce, *Pennsylvania State University–Altoona*
Susan Nakayama Siaw, *California State Polytechnical University*
Vicki Simmons, *University of Victoria*
Jon Snodgrass, *California State University–LA*
Donald Stanley, *North Dallas Community College*
James Turcott, *Kalamazoo Valley Community College*
B.D. Whetstone, *Birmingham Southern College*
Nancy C. White, *Reynolds Community College*
Lyn W. Wickelgren, *Metropolitan State College*
Ann M. Williams, *Luzerne County Community College*

Further Instructor Feedback

The quality of the text was also improved through the feedback I received over the years from many other colleagues. I would like to thank the following individuals for sharing their thoughts and suggestions for improving *Life-Span Development.*

Berkeley Adams, *Jamestown Community College*
Jack Busky, *Harrisburg Area Community College*
Jeri Carter, *Glendale Community College*
Vincent Castranovo, *Community College of Philadelphia*
Ginny Chappeleau, *Muskingum Area Technical College*
M.A. Christenberry, *Augusta College*
Cynthia Crown, *Xavier University*
Diane Davis, *Bowie State University*
Doreen DeSantio, *West Chester University*
Jill De Villiers, *Smith College*
Richard Ewy, *Penn State University*
Roberta Ferra, *University of Kentucky*
John Gat, *Humboldt State University*
Marvin Gelman, *Montgomery County College*
Rebecca J. Glare, *Weber State College*
Judy Goodell, *National University*
Robert Heavilin, *Greater Hartford Community College*
Sharon Holt, *Allegany Community College*
Erwin Janek, *Henderson State University*
James Jasper-Jacobsen, *Indiana University–Purdue*
Ursula Joyce, *St. Thomas Aquinas College*
Barbara Kane, *Indiana State University*
James L. Keeney, *Middle Georgia College*
Elinor Kinarthy, *Rio Hondo College*
A. Klingner, *Northwest Community College*
Jane Krump, *North Dakota State College of Science*
Joe LaVoie, *University of Nebraska*
Karen Macrae, *University of South Carolina*
Robert C. McGinnis, *Ancilla College*
Clara McKinney, *Barstow College*
Michael Newton, *Sam Houston State University*
Beatrice Norrie, *Mount Royal College*
Jean O'Neil, *Boston College*
David Pipes, *Caldwell Community College*
Bob Rainey, *Florida Community College*
H. Ratner, *Wayne State University*
Russell Riley, *Lord Fairfax Community College*
Clarence Romeno, *Riverside Community College*
Paul Roodin, *SUNY–Oswego*
Ron Russac, *University of North Florida*
Cynthia Scheibe, *Ithaca College*
Robert Schell, *SUNY–Oswego*
Owen Sharkey, *University of Prince Edward Island*
Donald Stanley, *North Harris Community College*
Barbara Thomas, *National University*
James Turcott, *Kalamazoo Valley Community College*
Stephen Truhon, *Winston-Salem State University*
Myron D. Williams, *Great Lakes Bible College*

Supplements

The eighth edition of *Life-Span Development* is accompanied by a comprehensive and fully integrated array of supplemental materials, both print and electronic, written specifically for instructors and students of life-span development. In addition, a variety of generic supplements are available to further aid in the teaching and learning of life-span psychology.

The supplements listed here may accompany Santrock, *Life-Span Development,* eighth edition. Please contact your McGraw-Hill representative for details concerning policies, prices, and availability, as some restrictions may apply.

For the Instructor

Once again, based on comprehensive and extensive feedback from instructors, we spent considerable time and effort in expanding and improving the ancillary materials.

Instructor's Manual

K. Laurie Dickson, Northern Arizona State University
Cynthia Jenkins, University of Texas, Dallas
This comprehensive manual has been fully revised to provide a variety of useful tools for both seasoned instructors and those new to the life-span development course. The Instructor's Manual provides a focused introductory section on teaching the life-span development course. This section covers helpful material for new instructors, including course-planning ideas, teaching tips, and teaching resources. Additionally, the new Total Teaching Package Outline begins each chapter and features a fully integrated outline to help instructors better use the many resources for the course. Instructors will find that all of the course resources available have been correlated to the main concepts in each chapter. Lecture suggestions, classroom activities, research projects, and critical thinking multiple-choice and essay exercises have been extensively revised, with new material and possible answers provided where appropriate. Classroom activities now provide logistics for required materials, such as accompanying handouts, varying group sizes, and time needed for completion. New features include greatly expanded chapter outlines and personal application projects where students can apply development topics to their own lives. Other features in the Instructor's Manual include comprehensive transparency, film, and video resources, updated URLs for useful Internet sites, and cognitive maps derived from the textbook that can be used for lecture aids.

Printed Test Bank

Angela Sadowski, Chaffey College
This comprehensive Test Bank has once again been extensively revised to include over 2,400 multiple-choice and short answer/brief essay questions for the text's 21 chapters. Each multiple-choice item is classified as factual, conceptual, or applied, as defined by Benjamin Bloom's taxonomy of educational objectives. Learning objectives have been added to this edition and are similarly included in both the Instructor's Manual and Study Guide. Test items are keyed to the learning objectives so that instructors can pinpoint areas in which students may have difficulty.

Study Guide

Anita Rosenfield, The DeVry Institute of Technology
The revised Study Guide has benefited from the author's experience in teaching courses in Student Success Strategies as well

as student feedback on what makes an effective study guide. The Study Guide provides a complete introduction for students on how best to use each of the various study aids plus invaluable strategies on setting goals, benefiting from class, reading for learning, taking tests, and memory techniques in the section "Being an Excellent Student." For each chapter, features include learning objectives from the Instructor's Manual and Text Bank and a chapter outline. A self-test section contains multiple-choice questions keyed to the learning objectives, matching sets on key people found in the text, comprehensive essays with suggested answers, and new word scramblers on key terms found in the text. In addition, new to this edition of the Study Guide are personal application projects and Internet exercises that complement the revised student research projects and allow for more effective student learning.

PowerPoint Slide Presentations

Cynthia Jenkins, University of Texas, Dallas
The chapter-by-chapter PowerPoint lectures were completely redone for this edition by one of the Instructor's Manual coauthors, Cynthia Jenkins. You will find great cohesiveness between the comprehensive lectures and the presentation of material in the text and in this manual, particularly in the use of the cognitive maps as an organizing feature.

Computerized Test Bank (Mac/IBM) CD-ROM

The computerized test bank contains all of the questions in the print test bank and is available in both Macintosh and Windows platforms. This CD-ROM provides a fully functioning editing feature that enables instructors to integrate their own questions, scramble items, and modify questions.

Overhead Transparencies

The overhead transparency package provides full-color acetates for use in the classroom. All of the images in this package are taken directly from the eighth edition of *Life-Span Development,* and they include key illustrations, tables, and charts that highlight key concepts in the course.

Instructor's Resource CD-ROM

This resourceful tool offers instructors the opportunity to customize McGraw-Hill materials to create their lecture presentations. Resources included for instructors include the Instructor's Manual Materials, PowerPoint presentation slides, and the Image Database for life-span development.

The McGraw-Hill Developmental Psychology Image Bank

This set of 200 full-color images was developed using the best selection of our human development art and tables and is available online for both instructors and students on the text's Online Learning Center.

Online Learning Center

The extensive website designed specifically to accompany Santrock, *Life-Span Development,* eighth edition, offers an array of resources for both instructor and student. For instructors, the website includes a full set of PowerPoint Presentations, hotlinks for the text's topical web links that appear in margins and for the Taking it to the Net exercises that appear at the end of each chapter. These resources and more can be found by logging on to the website at http://www.mhhe.com/santrockld8.

The AIDS Booklet

Frank D. Cox
This brief but comprehensive text has been recently revised to provide the most up-to-date information about acquired immune deficiency syndrome (AIDS).

The Critical Thinker

Richard Mayer and Fiona Goodchild of the University of California, Santa Barbara, use excerpts from introductory psychology textbooks to show students how to think critically about psychology.

Annual Editions–Developmental Psychology

Published by Dushkin/McGraw-Hill, this is a collection of articles on topics related to the latest research and thinking in human development. These editions are updated annually and contain helpful features including a topic guide, an annotated table of contents, unit overviews, and a topical index. An Instructor's Guide containing testing materials is also available.

Sources: Notable Selections in Human Development

This volume presents a collection of more than 40 articles, book excerpts, and research studies that have shaped the study of human development and our contemporary understanding of it. The selections are organized topically around major areas of study within human development. Each selection is preceded by a headnote that establishes the relevance of the article or study and provides biographical information of the author.

Taking Sides

This debate-style reader is designed to introduce students to controversial viewpoints on the field's most crucial issues. Each issue is carefully framed for the student, and the pro and con essays represent the arguments of leading scholars and commentators in their fields. An Instructor's Guide containing testing material is available.

For the Student

Student Study Guide

by Anita Rosenfield, DeVry Institutes
The revised Study Guide has benefited from the author's experience in teaching courses in Student Success Strategies as well as student feedback on what makes an effective study guide. The Study Guide provides a complete introduction for students in the sections "How to Use this Study Guide" and "Guide to Academic Success." For each chapter, features include learning objectives from the Instructor's Manual and a guided review for students with highlighted key terms. A self-test section contains an interactive workbook for students to complete the fill-in-the-blank format that corresponds to the main text chapters and sections. In addition, new to this edition of the Student Study Guide are research project ideas for students as well as crossword puzzles and Internet exercises for more effective student learning.

Making the Grade CD-ROM

This user-friendly CD-ROM gives students an opportunity to test their comprehension of the course material. Written specifically to accompany Santrock, *Life-Span Development,* eighth edition, this CD-ROM provides 25 multiple-choice questions for each chapter to help students further test their understanding of key concepts. Feedback is provided for each question's answer. In addition, the CD-ROM provides a Learning Assessment questionnaire to help students discover which type of learner they are, of the three types covered in the program.

Online Learning Center

The extensive website designed specifically to accompany Santrock, *Life-Span Development,* eighth edition, offers an array of resources for instructors and students. For students, the website includes interactive quizzing and exercises as well as hotlinks for the text's topical web links that appear in the margins and for the *Taking It to the Net* exercises that appear at the end of each chapter. These resources and more can be found by logging on to the website at
http://www.mhhe.com/santrockld8.

Guide to Life-Span Development for Future Educators

Guide to Life-Span Development for Future Nurses

These new course supplements help students apply the concepts of human development to education. They contain information, exercises, and sample tests designed to help students prepare for certification and understand human development from a professional perspective.

Resources for Improving Human Development

This informative booklet provides descriptions and contact information for organizations and agencies that can provide helpful information, advice, and support related to particular problems or issues in life-span development. Recommended books and journals are also described and included. The booklet is organized by chronological order of the periods of the life span.

Expert Consultants

K. Warner Schaie, Evan Pugh Professor of Human Development and Psychology and Director of the Penn State Gerontology Center, is regarded as one of the foremost scholars in the field of adult development and aging. Dr. Schaie holds a Ph.D. in psychology from the University of Washington. Since 1956, he has directed the Seattle Longitudinal Study, a major study of intellectual performance in several thousand older adults. He has found that most adults maintain their mental abilities well into their sixties, disproving scientists' earlier belief that intelligence peaks in adolescence and then steadily declines. He has also made substantial contributions to research methodology in adult development and aging. Dr. Schaie is a past president and council representative of the American Psychological Association's Division 20, and in 1992 received that Division's Distinguished Scientific Contributions award. He has also received the Kleemeier Award, 1987, for distinguished research contributions from the Gerontological Society of America; Method to Extend Research in Time (MERIT) Award from the National Institute on Aging, 1989; and an honorary doctorate from Friedrich-Schiller University, Jena, Germany, 1997. Dr. Schaie's research interests focus on cognitive and personality development from young adulthood to old age, influences of health on behavior, and studies of multigenerational adult families. He teaches research methods in the developmental sciences.

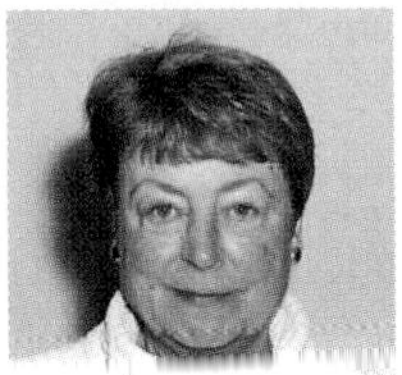

Jean Mandler is Research Professor of Cognitive Science at the University of California, San Diego. She obtained her undergraduate degree from Swarthmore College and her Ph.D. from Harvard University in 1956. She is a fellow of the American Academy of Arts and Sciences. Since 1965 she has taught at UCSD, first in the Department of Psychology and then as a founding member of the Department of Cognitive Science. She has been an active contributor to schema theory in cognitive psychology. In the past 15 years her research has concentrated on the foundations of mind, studying the origins of the conceptual system and declarative memory in infancy. Some of this work is summarized in a 1992 article in the *Psychological Review* entitled "How to Build a Baby" and in a book she is currently writing.

Marc H. Bornstein is Senior Investigator and Head of Child and Family Research at the National Institute of Child Health and Human Development. He received a B.A. from Columbia College and M.S. and Ph.D. degrees from Yale University. Bornstein was a J.S. Guggenheim Foundation Fellow. His awards include a Research Career Development Award from the National Institute of Child Health and Human Development, and a C.S. Ford Cross-Cultural Research Award from the Human Relations Area Files. Bornstein has held faculty positions at Princeton University and New York University, as well as a number of visiting fellowships. He co-authored *Development in Infancy* and *Perceiving Similarity and Comprehending Metaphor.* He is general editor of the *Crosscurrents in Contemporary Psychology Series* and is editor of *Child Development and Parenting: Science and Practice.* He is author of several children's books and puzzles in the *Child's World* series.

Ross A. Thompson is the Carl A. Happold Distinguished Professor of Psychology at the University of Nebraska. He received his B.A. from Occidental College in 1976, his M.A. from the University of Michigan in 1979, and the Ph.D. from the University of Michigan in 1981, when he also joined the faculty at the University of Nebraska. He is currently Associate Editor of *Child Development.* He is also Director of the Developmental Psychology Program, and a core faculty member of the Law-Psychology Program at the University of Nebraska–Lincoln (UNL). He has received the Boyd McCandless Young Scientist Award for Early Distinguished Achievement from the American Psychological Association and the Scholarship in Teaching Award and the Outstanding Research and Creative Activity Award from the University of Nebraska, and he is a lifetime member of the University of Nebraska Academy of Distinguished Teachers. His research interests include basic topics in developmental psychology (especially infant-parent attachment and parent-child relationships, the growth of conscience and emotional understanding, and emotion regulation) and the applications of developmental research to public policy problems concerning children and families. His books include *Preventing Child Maltreatment Through Social Support: A Critical Analysis* (Sage, 1995) and *Early Brain Development, the Media, and Public Policy* (University of Nebraska Press, forthcoming).

Craig H. Hart received his Ph.D. from Purdue University in 1987 and is Professor and Chair of the Marriage, Family, and Human Development Program in the School of Family Life at Brigham Young University. He was formerly an Associate Professor in the School of Human Ecology at Louisiana State University. Dr. Hart has authored and co-authored 40 scientific articles and has presented numerous papers at national and international conferences on parenting/familial linkages with children's social development and on developmentally appropriate practices in early childhood education. His articles have appeared in leading human development scientific journals such as *Child Development* and *Developmental Psychology,* and in early childhood education research journals including *Early Childhood Research Quarterly* and *Journal of Research in Childhood Education.* He has also written 13 book chapters and has published two edited books.

Algea O. Harrison-Hale is a Professor of Psychology at Oakland University in Rochester, Michigan. She completed her Ph.D. at the University of Michigan and is currently a leading national and international expert on ethnic minority children, youth, and families. Dr. Harrison-Hale has been a Visiting Scholar and Professor at University of Zimbabwe, Nanjing University, and Free University of Amsterdam, where she collaborated with colleagues on cross-cultural research projects. In cooperation with her international colleagues she has completed empirical investigations on the topics of social support, ethnic identification, and conflict resolutions. Her scholarly work has been supported with various awards, including Fullbright and Kellogg Foundation awards. Dr. Harrison-Hale has an extensive publication record in professional journals, and she has written numerous book chapters. She is also an active participant in professional and community organizations.

Julia Graber is an Assistant Professor in Psychology at the University of Florida. She received her doctorate in Developmental Psychology from Pennsylvania State University and a bachelor of science degree from Michigan State University. Dr. Graber's research has focused on the transitional aspects of adolescent development, with particular interest in the entry into adolescence and the transition from adolescence to adulthood. Her research has examined the development of psychopathology across the adolescent decade; the impact of pubertal timing on psychosocial functioning during adolescence and beyond; and stress reactivity and psychosocial development in childhood and adolescence. Dr. Graber is presently studying the biological, social, and psychological development of a diverse group of girls and boys as they make the transition from middle childhood into adolescence.

Gisela Labouvie-Vief is a Professor in the Department of Psychology, as well as the Chair of the Developmental Area, at Wayne State University. Her research interests center around cognition and social development in adulthood and later life. Labouvie-Vief's current research program focuses on how individuals describe themselves and their relationships at different stages in the life span. She is currently involved in a study in which individuals ranging in age from 10 to over 80 are assessed on aspects of self-development. Labouvie-Vief has published articles in journals such as *Psychology and Aging, Human Development, Journal of Personality and Social Psychology,* and the *Journal of Gerontology.* She has authored a number of chapters, including "Emotions in Later Life," in *Theories of Adult Development and Aging.*

Phyllis Moen is the Ferris Family Professor of Life Course Studies, and Professor of Human Development and of Sociology at Cornell University. She teaches and conducts research on life-course transitions and trajectories of workers and families, focusing on gender, aging, organizations, social change, and social policy. An underlying theme in her scholarship is the implications of the dramatic and interrelated social transformations in career path and employment, gender roles, the family, and longevity. Moen is founding director of Cornell's Bronfenbrenner Life Course Center, which addresses the impacts of these dramatic transformations on individual lives. She also created and directs the Cornell Employment and Family Careers Institute, which promotes understanding of career/life issues over the life course, and conducts research on retirement planning and transitions.

Ravenna Helson is Research Psychologist at the Institute of Personality and Social Research and Adjunct Professor in the Department of Psychology, University of California, Berkeley. She completed her Ph.D. at the University of California and after 3 years on the faculty at Smith College returned to Berkeley. In 1957 she began what became the Mils Longitudinal Study. The study began with women seniors who graduated from college shortly before the women's movement and the social changes of the 1960s, and has traced their lives for more than 40 years. Dr. Helson's work has been funded by the National Institute of Mental Health. She is the author of more than 100 articles and chapters in professional publications, concerned with various aspects and contexts of personality change, creativity, and adult development.

Toni C. Antonucci is a Professor in the Department of Psychology, as well as Senior Research Scientist of the Institute for Social Research at the University of Michigan, Ann Arbor. She holds a B.A. from Hunter College and an M.A. and Ph.D. from Wayne State University. She is currently involved in a research project with the Michigan Center for Urban African American Aging Research at the University of Michigan and Wayne State University focused on African American health inequalities over the life course. Other recent research includes *Aging in America: A Study of Three Cohorts,* a study that is examining whether there have been changes in the factors that predict and influence well-being, and whether these changes place the aging American disproportionately at risk. She has published articles in journals such as the *Journal of Gerontology: Social Sciences, Family Relations, Psychology and Aging,* the *Journal of Aging and Health,* and the *Journal of Marriage and the Family.*

Robert Kastenbaum, Professor of Gerontology at Arizona State University, has for many years focused on the limits of human understanding, endurance, and creativity, especially in life-threatening situations. In addition to his research, clinical, and educational activities, he has served as director of a geriatric hospital and co-founder of the National Caucus on Black Aging. Dr. Kastenbaum is editor of the *International Journal of Aging and Human Development* and *Omega: Journal of Death and Dying.* His books include *Death, Society, and Human Experience; The Psychology of Death; Defining Acts: Aging as Drama;* and *Dorian, Graying: Is Youth the Only Thing Worth Having?* His theater pieces often deal with themes of aging and death, as in the opera *Dorian* (premiered New York 1995; music by Herbert Deutsch). Robert Kastenbaum is widely recognized as one of the world's leading experts on death and dying.

Student Driven Pedagogy

BEGINNING OF CHAPTER

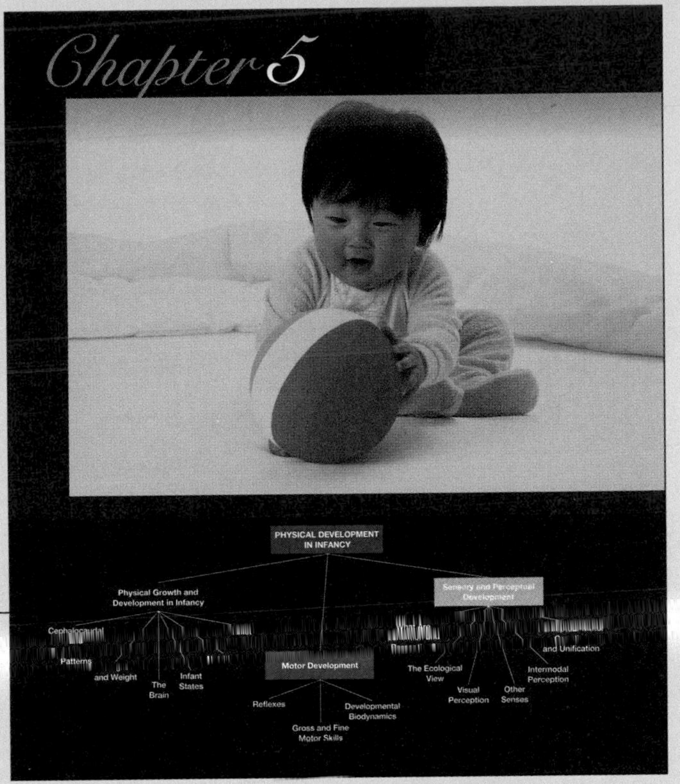

NEW!
Cognitive Map

This provides students with a visual overview of the entire chapter.

Quotations

These appear at the beginning of the chapter and occasionally in the margins to stimulate further thought about a topic.

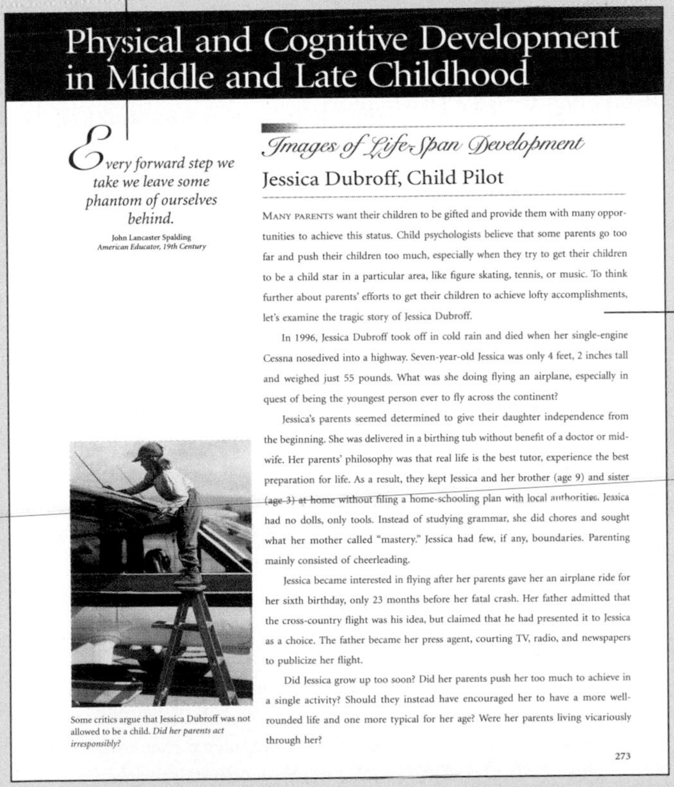

Physical and Cognitive Development in Middle and Late Childhood

Every forward step we take we leave some phantom of ourselves behind.

John Lancaster Spalding
American Educator, 19th Century

Images of Life-Span Development

Jessica Dubroff, Child Pilot

MANY PARENTS want their children to be gifted and provide them with many opportunities to achieve this status. Child psychologists believe that some parents go too far and push their children too much, especially when they try to get their children to be a child star in a particular area, like figure skating, tennis, or music. To think further about parents' efforts to get their children to achieve lofty accomplishments, let's examine the tragic story of Jessica Dubroff.

In 1996, Jessica Dubroff took off in cold rain and died when her single-engine Cessna nosedived into a highway. Seven-year-old Jessica was only 4 feet, 2 inches tall and weighed just 55 pounds. What was she doing flying an airplane, especially in quest of being the youngest person ever to fly across the continent?

Jessica's parents seemed determined to give their daughter independence from the beginning. She was delivered in a birthing tub without benefit of a doctor or midwife. Her parents' philosophy was that real life is the best tutor, experience the best preparation for life. As a result, they kept Jessica and her brother (age 9) and sister (age 3) at home without filing a home-schooling plan with local authorities. Jessica had no dolls, only tools. Instead of studying grammar, she did chores and sought what her mother called "mastery." Jessica had few, if any, boundaries. Parenting mainly consisted of cheerleading.

Jessica became interested in flying after her parents gave her an airplane ride for her sixth birthday, only 23 months before her fatal crash. Her father admitted that the cross-country flight was his idea, but claimed that he had presented it to Jessica as a choice. The father became her press agent, courting TV, radio, and newspapers to publicize her flight.

Did Jessica grow up too soon? Did her parents push her too much to achieve in a single activity? Should they instead have encouraged her to have a more well-rounded life and one more typical for her age? Were her parents living vicariously through her?

Some critics argue that Jessica Dubroff was not allowed to be a child. *Did her parents act irresponsibly?*

273

Images of Life-Span Development

Each chapter opens with a high-interest story that is linked to the chapter's content. Many of the chapter-opening stories are new in this edition.

WITHIN CHAPTER

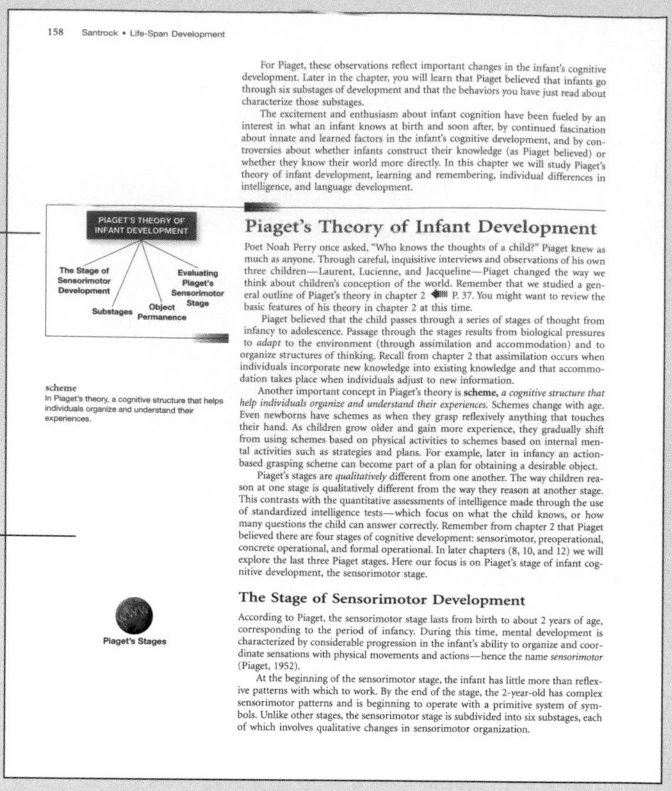

158 Santrock • Life-Span Development

For Piaget, these observations reflect important changes in the infant's cognitive development. Later in the chapter, you will learn that Piaget believed that infants go through six substages of development and that the behaviors you have just read about characterize those substages.

The excitement and enthusiasm about infant cognition have been fueled by an interest in what an infant knows at birth and soon after, by continued fascination about innate and learned factors in the infant's cognitive development, and by controversies about whether infants construct their knowledge (as Piaget believed) or whether they know their world more directly. In this chapter we will study Piaget's theory of infant development, learning and remembering, individual differences in intelligence, and language development.

PIAGET'S THEORY OF INFANT DEVELOPMENT

The Stage of Sensorimotor Development

Substages

Object Permanence

Evaluating Piaget's Sensorimotor Stage

Piaget's Theory of Infant Development

Poet Noah Perry once asked, "Who knows the thoughts of a child?" Piaget knew as much as anyone. Through careful, inquisitive interviews and observations of his own three children—Laurent, Lucienne, and Jacqueline—Piaget changed the way we think about children's conception of the world. Remember that we studied a general outline of Piaget's theory in chapter 2 ◀ P. 37. You might want to review the basic features of his theory in chapter 2 at this time.

Piaget believed that the child passes through a series of stages of thought from infancy to adolescence. Passage through the stages results from biological pressures to *adapt* to the environment (through assimilation and accommodation) and to organize structures of thinking. Recall from chapter 2 that assimilation occurs when individuals incorporate new knowledge into existing knowledge and that accommodation takes place when individuals adjust to new information.

scheme
In Piaget's theory, a cognitive structure that helps individuals organize and understand their experiences.

Another important concept in Piaget's theory is **scheme,** *a cognitive structure that help individuals organize and understand their experiences.* Schemes change with age. Even newborns have schemes as when they grasp reflexively anything that touches their hand. As children grow older and gain more experience, they gradually shift from using schemes based on physical activities to schemes based on internal mental activities such as strategies and plans. For example, later in infancy an action-based grasping scheme can become part of a plan for obtaining a desirable object.

Piaget's stages are *qualitatively* different from one another. The way children reason at one stage is qualitatively different from the way they reason at another stage. This contrasts with the quantitative assessments of intelligence made through the use of standardized intelligence tests—which focus on what the child knows, or how many questions the child can answer correctly. Remember from chapter 2 that Piaget believed there are four stages of cognitive development: sensorimotor, preoperational, concrete operational, and formal operational. In later chapters (8, 10, and 12) we will explore the last three Piaget stages. Here our focus is on Piaget's stage of infant cognitive development, the sensorimotor stage.

Piaget's Stages

The Stage of Sensorimotor Development

According to Piaget, the sensorimotor stage lasts from birth to about 2 years of age, corresponding to the period of infancy. During this time, mental development is characterized by considerable progression in the infant's ability to organize and coordinate sensations with physical movements and actions—hence the name *sensorimotor* (Piaget, 1952).

At the beginning of the sensorimotor stage, the infant has little more than reflexive patterns with which to work. By the end of the stage, the 2-year-old has complex sensorimotor patterns and is beginning to operate with a primitive system of symbols. Unlike other stages, the sensorimotor stage is subdivided into six substages, each of which involves qualitative changes in sensorimotor organization.

NEW!
Mini Cognitive Maps

These mini maps appear three to five times per chapter and provide students with a more detailed, visual look at the organization of the chapter.

NEW!
Single-Column Design

The previous edition of *Life-Span Development* had a dense, two-column format. Instructors and students told us to change this to a more open, one-column design. They said this makes the text material easier to read and allows the wider margins to be used for many pedagogical features, such as key term definitions and Internet sites.

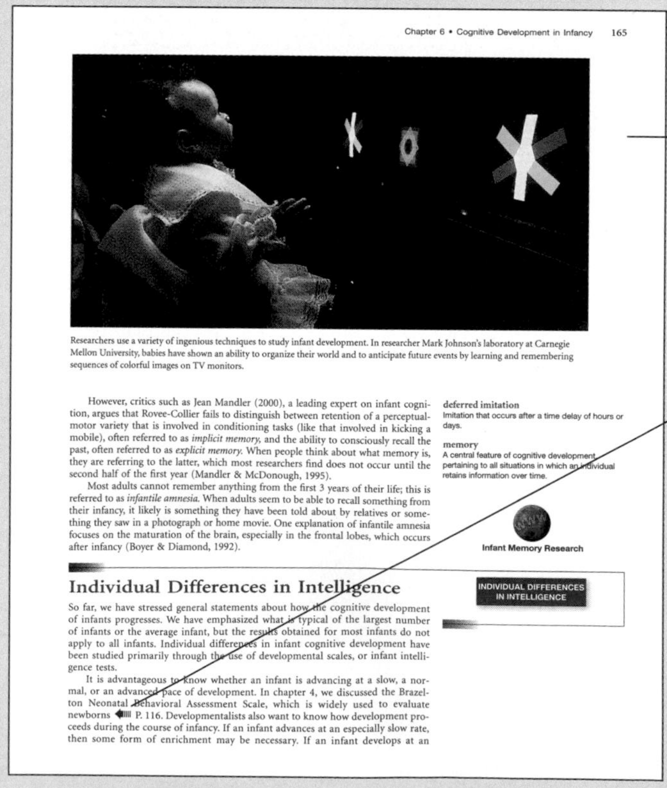

Chapter 6 • Cognitive Development in Infancy 165

Researchers use a variety of ingenious techniques to study infant development. In researcher Mark Johnson's laboratory at Carnegie Mellon University, babies have shown an ability to organize their world and to anticipate future events by learning and remembering sequences of colorful images on TV monitors.

However, critics such as Jean Mandler (2000), a leading expert on infant cognition, argues that Rovee-Collier fails to distinguish between retention of a perceptual-motor variety that is involved in conditioning tasks (like that involved in kicking a mobile), often referred to as *implicit memory,* and the ability to consciously recall the past, often referred to as *explicit memory.* When people think about what memory is, they are referring to the latter, which most researchers find does not occur until the second half of the first year (Mandler & McDonough, 1995).

deferred imitation
Imitation that occurs after a time delay of hours or days.

memory
A central feature of cognitive development pertaining to all situations in which an individual retains information over time.

Most adults cannot remember anything from the first 3 years of their life; this is referred to as *infantile amnesia.* When adults seem to be able to recall something from their infancy, it likely is something they have been told about by relatives or something they saw in a photograph or home movie. One explanation of infantile amnesia focuses on the maturation of the brain, especially in the frontal lobes, which occurs after infancy (Boyer & Diamond, 1992).

Infant Memory Research

Individual Differences in Intelligence

INDIVIDUAL DIFFERENCES IN INTELLIGENCE

So far, we have stressed general statements about how the cognitive development of infants progresses. We have emphasized what is typical of the largest number of infants or the average infant, but the results obtained for most infants do not apply to all infants. Individual differences in infant cognitive development have been studied primarily through the use of developmental scales, or infant intelligence tests.

It is advantageous to know whether an infant is advancing at a slow, a normal, or an advanced pace of development. In chapter 4, we discussed the Brazelton Neonatal Behavioral Assessment Scale, which is widely used to evaluate newborns ◀ P. 116. Developmentalists also want to know how development proceeds during the course of infancy. If an infant advances at an especially slow rate, then some form of enrichment may be necessary. If an infant develops at an

NEW!
Diversity Photos and Critical Thinking Captions

To improve the coverage of diversity, many more photos of ethnic minority individuals and individuals from other cultures are included. Also, most photos have a caption that ends with a critical thinking or knowledge question.

NEW!
Cross-Linkage

This system, unique to this text and new in this edition, refers students to the primary discussion of all key concepts. A specific page reference appears in the text with a backward-pointing arrow each time a key concept occurs in a chapter subsequent to its initial coverage.

Chapter 7 • Socioemotional Development in Infancy 195

In Sweden, mothers or fathers are given paid maternity or paternity leave for up to 9 months. Sweden and many other European countries have well-developed child care policies. To learn about these policies, see the Sociocultural Worlds of Development box. In Sweden, day care for infants under 1 year of age is usually not a major concern because one parent is on paid leave for child care.

Because the United States does not have a policy of paid leave for child care, day care in the United States has become a major national concern. The type of day care that young children receive varies extensively (Burchinal & others, 1996; Scarr, 2000). Many day-care centers house large groups of children and have elaborate facilities. Some are commercial operations; others are nonprofit centers run by churches, civic groups, and employers. Child care is frequently provided in private homes, at times by child care professionals, at others by mothers who want to earn extra money.

A special contemporary interest of researchers who study day care is the role of poverty (Huston, McLoyd, & Coll, 1994). In one study, day-care centers that served high-income children delivered better-quality care than did centers that served middle- and low-income children (Phillips & others, 1994). The indices of quality (such as teacher-child ratios) in subsidized centers for the poor were fairly good, but the quality of observed teacher-child interaction was lower than in high-income centers.

What constitutes a high-quality day-care program for infants? The demonstration program developed by Jerome Kagan and his colleagues (Kagan, Kearsley, & Zelazo, 1978) at Harvard University is exemplary. The day-care center included a pediatrician, a nonteaching director, and an infant-teacher ratio of 3 to 1. Teachers' aides assisted at the center. The teachers and aides were trained to smile frequently, to talk with the infants, and to provide them with a safe environment, which included many stimulating toys. No adverse effects of day care were observed in this project. More information about what to look for in a quality day-care center is presented in figure 7.5. Using such criteria, one study discovered that children who entered low-quality child care as infants were least likely to be socially competent in early childhood (less compliant, less self-controlled, less task-oriented, more hostile, and having more problems in peer interaction) (Howes, 1988). Unfortunately, children who come from families with few resources (psychological, social, and economic) are more likely to experience poor-quality day care than are children from more-advantaged backgrounds (Lamb, 1994).

Aware of the growing use of child care, the National Institute of Child Health and Human Development (NICHD) set out to develop a comprehensive, longitudinal study (a study that follows the same individuals over time, usually several years or more) that focuses on the child care experiences of children and their development (Peth-Pierce, 1998). The study began in 1991, and data were collected on a diverse sample of almost 1,400 children and

Critical Thinking

Characteristics of Competent Caregivers

MUCH OF the health and well-being of infants is in the hands of caregivers. Whether the caregivers are parents or day-care personnel, these adults play significant roles in children's lives. What are the characteristics of competent caregivers? For one thing, competent caregivers enjoy caregiving. They reflect these positive feelings as they interact with infants and children. Try to come up with a list of five other characteristics of competent caregivers.

CAREERS IN LIFE-SPAN DEVELOPMENT

Rashmi Nakhre, Day-Care Director

RASHMI NAKHRE has two master's degreees—one in psychology, the other in child development—and is director of the Hattie Daniels Day Care Center in Wilson, North Carolina. At a recent ceremony, "Celebrating a Century of Womeen," Rashmi received the Distinguished Women of North Carolina Award for 1999–2000.

Nakhre first worked at the day-care center soon after she arrived in the United States 25 years ago. She says that she took the job initially because she needed the money but "ended up falling in love with my job." Nakhre has turned the Wilson, North Carolina, day-care center into a model for other centers. The Center almost closed several years after Nakhre began working there because of financial difficulties. Nakhre played a major role in raising funds not only to keep it open but to improve it. The Center provides quality day care for the children of many Latino migrant workers.

Rashmi Nakre, day-care director, working with some of the children at her center.

Critical Thinking

These critical thinking boxes appear periodically in each chapter to challenge students to stretch their minds.

NEW!
Careers in Life-Span Development

This feature, appearing in each chapter, explores a variety of careers in the field of life-span development.

NEW!
Diversity Photos and Critical Thinking Captions

To improve the coverage of diversity, many more photos of ethnic minority individuals and individuals from other cultures are included. Also, most photos have a caption that ends with a critical thinking or knowledge question.

592 Santrock • Life-Span Development

so on—but it appears that older women do not necessarily become more masculine—assertive, dominant, and so on (Turner, 1982). Keep in mind that cohort effects are especially important to consider in areas like gender roles. As sociohistorical changes take place and are assessed more frequently in lifespan investigations, what were once perceived to be age effects may turn out to be cohort effects (Jacobs, 1994).

One study found that time spent in committed activities by older adults had shifted in opposite ways for women and men (Verbrugge, Gruber-Baldini, & Fozard, 1996). Between 1958 and 1992, older men decreased their time in paid work and spent more doing housework, home repairs, yardwork, shopping, and child care. By contrast, older women engaged in more paid work and decreased their time in housework.

Racism and Sexism A possible double jeopardy also faces many women—the burden of *both* ageism and sexism (Lopata, 1994). The poverty rate for older adult females is almost double that of older adult males. According to Congresswoman Mary Rose Oakar, the number one priority for midlife and older women should be economic security. She predicts that 25 percent of all women working today can expect to be poor in old age. Yet only recently has scientific and political interest in the aging woman developed. For many years, the aging woman was virtually invisible in aging research and in protests involving rights for the older adult (Markson, 1995). An important research and political agenda for the twenty-first century is increased interest in the aging and the rights of older adult women.

Not only is it important to be concerned about older women's double jeopardy of ageism and sexism, but special attention also needs to be devoted to female ethnic minority older adults. They face what could be described as triple jeopardy—ageism, sexism, and racism (Burton, 1996; Markides, 1995). More information about being female, ethnic, and old appears in the Sociocultural Worlds of Development box.

Culture

Old Age Across Cultures and Time

What factors are associated with whether the older adult are accorded a position of high status in a culture? Seven factors are most likely to predict high status for older adults in a culture (Sangree, 1989):

- Older persons have valuable knowledge.
- Older persons control key family/community resources.
- Older persons are permitted to engage in useful and valued functions as long as possible.
- There is role continuity throughout the life span.
- Age-related role changes involve greater responsibility, authority, and advisory capacity.
- The extended family is a common family arrangement in the culture, and the older person is integrated into the extended family.
- In general, respect for older adults is greater in collectivistic cultures (such as China and Japan), than in individualistic cultures (such as the United States). However, some researchers are finding that this collectivistic/individualistic difference in respect for older adults is not as strong as it used to be and that in some cases older adults in individualistic cultures receive considerable respect (Antonucci, Vandewater, & Lansford, 2000).

Cultures vary in the prestige they give to older adults. In the Navajo culture, older adults are especially treated with respect because of their wisdom and extensive life experiences. *What are some other factors that are linked with respect for older adults in a culture?*

86 Santrock • Life-Span Development

Sociocultural Worlds of Development

The Abecedarian Project

Each morning a young mother waited with her child for the bus that would take the child to school. The unusual part of this is that the child was only 2 months old and "school" was an experimental program at the University of North Carolina at Chapel Hill. There the child experienced a number of interventions designed to improve her intellectual development—everything from bright objects dangled in front of her eyes while she was a baby to language instruction and counting activities when she was a toddler (Wickelgren, 1999).

This child was part of the Abecedarian Intervention Program conducted by Craig Ramey and his associates (Ramey & Campell, 1984; Ramey & Ramey, 1998; Ramey, Ramey, & Lanzi, 2001). They randomly assigned 111 young children from low-income, poorly educated families either to an intervention group, which experienced full-time, year-round day care along with medical and social work services, or to a control group, which got medical and social benefits but no day care. The day-care program included gamelike learning activities aimed at improving language, motor, social, and cognitive skills. The success of the program in improving IQ was evident by the time the children were 3 years old, at which time the children in the experimental group showed normal IQs averaging 101, a 17-point advantage over the control group. Recent follow-up results suggest that the effects are long-lasting. More than a decade later, at age 15, children from the intervention group still maintained an IQ advantage of 5 points over the control group children (97.7 to 92.6) (Ramey & others, in press; Ramey, Campbell, & Ramey, in press). They also did better on standardized tests of reading and math, and they were less likely to be held back a year in school. The greatest IQ gains were in the children whose mothers had especially low IQs—below 70. At age 15, these children showed a 10-point IQ advantage over a group of children whose mothers had IQs below 70 but did not experience the day-care intervention.

Craig Ramey's research has documented that high-quality early educational day care can significantly raise the intelligence of young children from impoverished environments.

passive genotype-environment correlations
Correlations that exist when the natural parents, who are genetically related to the child, provide a rearing environment for the child.

evocative genotype-environment correlations
Correlations that exist when the child's genotype elicits certain types of physical and social environments.

active (niche-picking) genotype-environment correlations
Correlations that exist when children seek out environments they find compatible and stimulating.

Passive genotype-environment correlations *occur when biological parents, who are genetically related to the child, provide a rearing environment for the child.* For example, the parents might have a genetic predisposition to be intelligent and read skillfully. Because they read well and enjoy reading, they provide their children with books to read. The likely outcome is that their children, given their own inherited predispositions, will become skilled readers.

Evocative genotype-environment correlations *occur because a child's genotype elicits certain types of physical and social environments.* For example, active, smiling children receive more social stimulation than passive, quiet children do. Cooperative, attentive adolescents evoke more pleasant and instructional responses from the adults around them than uncooperative, distractible adolescents do. Athletically inclined youth tend to elicit encouragement to engage in school sports. As a consequence, these adolescents tend to be the ones who try out for sport teams and go on to participate in athletically oriented environments.

Active (niche-picking) genotype-environment correlations *occur when children and adolescents seek out environments they find compatible and stimulating.* Niche-picking refers to finding a niche or setting that is suited to one's abilities. Adolescents select from their surrounding environment some aspect that they respond to, learn about, or ignore. Their active selections of environments are related to their partic-

Sociocultural Worlds of Development

Life-Span Development gives special attention to cultural, ethnic, and gender worlds of individuals. Most chapters have a box that highlights the sociocultural dimensions of life-span development.

Key Terms Definitions

Key terms appear in boldface type with their definitions immediately following in italic type and they also appear nearby in the margin. This provides you with a clear understanding of important concepts.

NEW! Web Icons

Web icons appear a number of times in each chapter. They signal students to go to the website for Santrock's Life-Span Development, eighth edition, where they will find connecting links that provide additional information on the topic discussed in the text. The labels under the Internet icon appear as Web links at the Santrock website, under that chapter for easy access.

Chapter 10 • Physical and Cognitive Development in Middle and Late Childhood 285

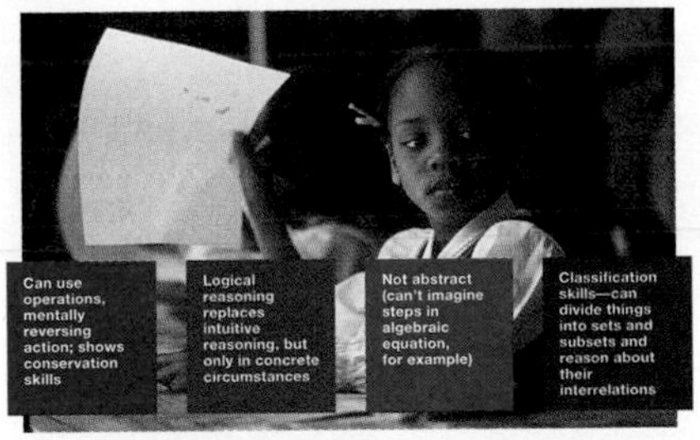

Can use operations, mentally reversing action; shows conservation skills
Logical reasoning replaces intuitive reasoning, but only in concrete circumstances
Not abstract (can't imagine steps in algebraic equation, for example)
Classification skills—can divide things into sets and subsets and reason about their interrelations

Figure 10.4
Characteristics of Concrete Operational Thought

B is intermediate in length, and C is the shortest. Does the child understand that, if A > B and B > C, then A > C? In Piaget's theory, concrete operational thinkers do, preoperational thinkers do not.

Piaget and Education

Piaget and Education Piaget was not an educator and never pretended to be. However, he provided a sound conceptual framework from which to view learning and education. Earlier, we examined some specific suggestions for classroom activities based on Piaget's stages. Following are some more general principles in Piaget's theory that can be applied to teaching (Elkind, 1976; Heuwinkel, 1996):

1. *Take a constructivist approach.* In a constructivist vein, Piaget emphasized that children learn best when they are active and seek solutions for themselves. Piaget opposed teaching methods which imply that children are passive receptacles. The educational implication of Piaget's view is that, in all subjects, students learn best by making discoveries, reflecting on them, and discussing them, rather than blindly imitating the teacher or doing things by rote.
2. *Facilitate rather than direct learning.* Effective teachers design situations that allow students to learn by doing. These situations promote students' thinking and discovery. Teachers listen, watch, and question students to help them gain better understanding. Don't just examine *what* students think and the product of their learning. Rather, carefully observe them as they find out *how* they think. Ask relevant questions to stimulate their thinking and ask them to explain their answers.
3. *Consider the child's knowledge and level of thinking.* Students do not come to class with empty heads. They have many ideas about the physical and natural world. They have concepts of space, time, quantity, and causality. These ideas differ from the ideas of adults. Teachers need to interpret what a student is saying and [illegible]
4. [illegible] by standardized tests. Math and language portfolios (which contain work in

We owe to Piaget the present field of cognitive development with its image of the developing child, who through its own active and creative commerce with its environment, builds an orderly succession of cognitive structures enroute to intellectual maturity.

John Flavell
Contemporary Developmental Psychologist, Stanford University

Summary Tables

Several times in each chapter, we review what has been discussed so far in that chapter by displaying the information in summary tables. This learning device helps students get a handle on material several times a chapter, so they don't have to wait until the end of a chapter and have too much information to digest.

Chapter 4 • Prenatal Development and Birth 107

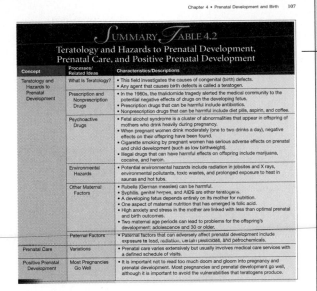

SUMMARY TABLE 4.2
Teratology and Hazards to Prenatal Development, Prenatal Care, and Positive Prenatal Development

Concept	Processes/ Related Ideas	Characteristics/Descriptions
Teratology and Hazards to Prenatal Development	What Is Teratology?	• This field investigates the causes of congenital (birth) defects. • Any agent that causes birth defects is called a teratogen.
	Prescription and Nonprescription Drugs	• In the 1960s, the thalidomide tragedy alerted the medical community to the potential negative effects of drugs on the developing fetus. • Prescription drugs that can be harmful include antibiotics. • Nonprescription drugs that can be harmful include diet pills, aspirin, and coffee.
	Psychoactive Drugs	• Fetal alcohol syndrome is a cluster of abnormalities that appear in offspring of mothers who drink heavily during pregnancy. • When pregnant women drink moderately (one to two drinks a day), negative effects on their offspring have been found. • Cigarette smoking by pregnant women has serious adverse effects on prenatal and child development (such as low birthweight). • Illegal drugs that can have harmful effects on offspring include marijuana, cocaine, and heroin.
	Environmental Hazards	• Potential environmental hazards include radiation in jobsites and X rays, environmental pollutants, toxic wastes, and prolonged exposure to heat in saunas and hot tubs.
	Other Maternal Factors	• Rubella (German measles) can be harmful. • Syphilis, genital herpes, and AIDS are other teratogens. • A developing fetus depends entirely on its mother for nutrition. • One aspect of maternal nutrition that has emerged is folic acid. • High anxiety and stress in the mother are linked with less than optimal prenatal and birth outcomes. • Two maternal age periods can lead to problems for the offspring's development: adolescence and 30 or older.
	Paternal Factors	• Paternal factors that can adversely affect prenatal development include exposure to lead, radiation, certain pesticides, and petrochemicals.
Prenatal Care	Variations	• Prenatal care varies extensively but usually involves medical care services with a defined schedule of visits.
Positive Prenatal Development	Most Pregnancies Go Well	• It is important not to read too much doom and gloom into pregnancy and prenatal development. Most pregnancies and prenatal development go well, although it is important to avoid the vulnerabilities that teratogens produce.

Positive Prenatal Development

In the previous section, we mainly examined what can go wrong with prenatal development. It is important to keep in mind that for most pregnancies, prenatal development does not go awry and development occurs along the positive path that we described at the beginning of the chapter (Lester, 2000). That said, it is still important for prospective mothers and those who are pregnant to avoid the vulnerabilities to fetal development that we have described.

At this point, we have discussed a number of ideas about teratology and hazards to prenatal development. To review these ideas, see summary table 4.2. Next, we will explore the birth process itself.

Chapter Review

The chapter review consists of a cognitive map of the entire chapter and a bulleted list of the summary tables, which are page-referenced with a backward-pointing arrow.

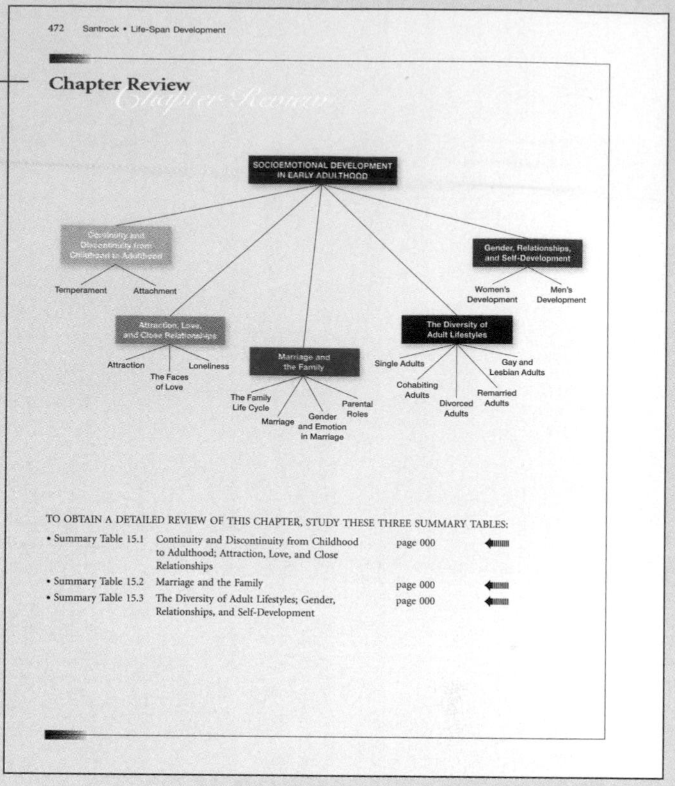

472 Santrock • Life-Span Development

Chapter Review

TO OBTAIN A DETAILED REVIEW OF THIS CHAPTER, STUDY THESE THREE SUMMARY TABLES:

- Summary Table 15.1 Continuity and Discontinuity from Childhood to Adulthood; Attraction, Love, and Close Relationships page 000
- Summary Table 15.2 Marriage and the Family page 000
- Summary Table 15.3 The Diversity of Adult Lifestyles; Gender, Relationships, and Self-Development page 000

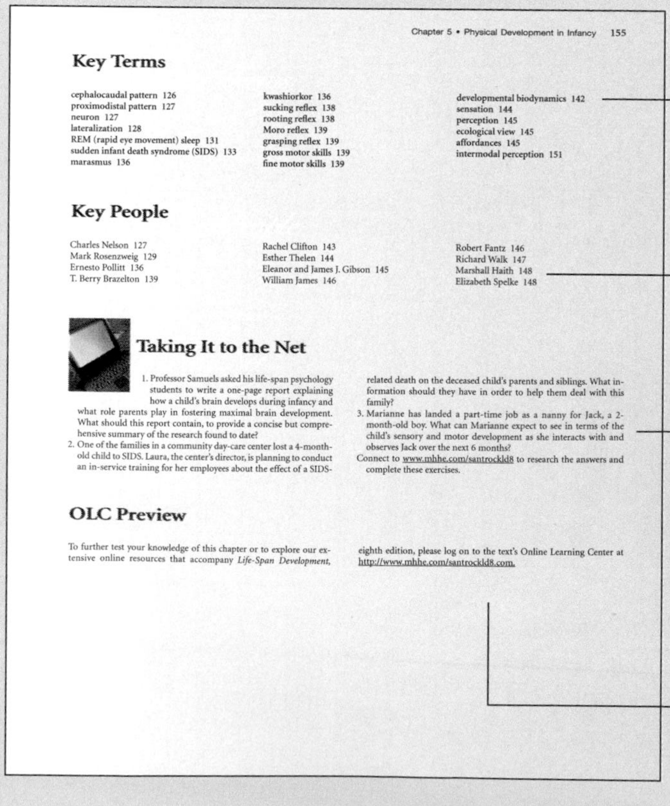

Chapter 5 • Physical Development in Infancy 155

Key Terms

cephalocaudal pattern 126
proximodistal pattern 127
neuron 127
lateralization 128
REM (rapid eye movement) sleep 131
sudden infant death syndrome (SIDS) 133
marasmus 136
kwashiorkor 136
sucking reflex 138
rooting reflex 138
Moro reflex 139
grasping reflex 139
gross motor skills 139
fine motor skills 139
developmental biodynamics 142
sensation 144
perception 145
ecological view 145
affordances 145
intermodal perception 151

Key People

Charles Nelson 127
Mark Rosenzweig 129
Ernesto Pollitt 136
T. Berry Brazelton 139
Rachel Clifton 143
Esther Thelen 144
Eleanor and James J. Gibson 145
William James 146
Robert Fantz 146
Richard Walk 147
Marshall Haith 148
Elizabeth Spelke 148

Taking It to the Net

1. Professor Samuels asked his life-span psychology students to write a one-page report explaining how a child's brain develops during infancy and what role parents play in fostering maximal brain development. What should this report contain, to provide a concise but comprehensive summary of the research found to date?
2. One of the families in a community day-care center lost a 4-month-old child to SIDS. Laura, the center's director, is planning to conduct an in-service training for her employees about the effect of a SIDS-related death on the deceased child's parents and siblings. What information should they have in order to help them deal with this family?
3. Marianne has landed a part-time job as a nanny for Jack, a 2-month-old boy. What can Marianne expect to see in terms of the child's sensory and motor development as she interacts with and observes Jack over the next 6 months?

Connect to www.mhhe.com/santrockld8 to research the answers and complete these exercises.

OLC Preview

To further test your knowledge of this chapter or to explore our extensive online resources that accompany *Life-Span Development,* eighth edition, please log on to the text's Online Learning Center at http://www.mhhe.com/santrockld8.com.

Key Terms

They are listed and page-referenced. Key terms also are defined and page-referenced in a comprehensive Glossary at the end of the book.

NEW! Key People

The most important theorists and researchers in the chapter are listed and page referenced.

NEW! Taking It to the Net

This presents students with questions to explore on the Internet that are related to the chapter. By going to the Santrock website under *Taking It to the Net,* students will be able to connect to other websites, where they can find information that will help them think more deeply about the questions posed.

NEW! OLC Preview

This directs you to the Online Learning Center for this book, where you will find many learning activities to improve your knowledge and understanding of the chapter.

Section 1

The Life-Span Developmental Perspective

All the world's a stage, And all the men and women merely players; They have their exits and their entrances, And one man in his time plays many parts . . .

William Shakespeare
English Playwright, 17th Century

This book is about human development—its universal features, its individual variations, its nature. Every life is distinct, a new biography in the world. Examining the shape of human development allows us to understand it better. Life-Span Development is about the rhythm and meaning of people's lives, about turning mystery into understanding, and about weaving a portrait of who each of us was, is, and will be. In Section 1, you will read two chapters: "Introduction" (chapter 1) and "The Science of Life-Span Development" (chapter 2).

Chapter 1

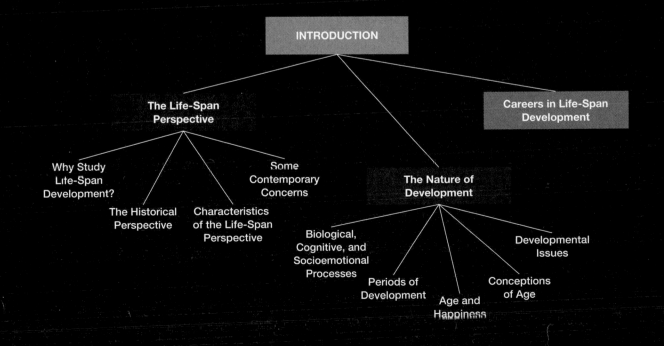

INTRODUCTION

- **The Life-Span Perspective**
  - Why Study Life-Span Development?
  - The Historical Perspective
  - Characteristics of the Life-Span Perspective
  - Some Contemporary Concerns
- **The Nature of Development**
  - Biological, Cognitive, and Socioemotional Processes
  - Periods of Development
  - Age and Happiness
  - Conceptions of Age
  - Developmental Issues
- **Careers in Life-Span Development**

We reach backward to our parents and forward to our children, and through their children to a future we will never see, but about which we need to care.

Carl Jung
Swiss Pyschiatrist, 20th Century

Images of Life-Span Development

How Did Ted Kaczynski Become Ted Kaczynski and Alice Walker Become Alice Walker?

THE INTELLECTUAL Ted Kaczynski sprinted through high school, not bothering with his junior year and making only passing efforts at social contact. Off to Harvard at age 16, Ted was a loner during his college years. One of his roommates at Harvard said that Ted had a special way of avoiding people by quickly shuffling by them and slamming the door behind him.

After obtaining his Ph.D. in mathematics at the University of Michigan, Kaczynski became a professor at the University of California at Berkeley. His colleagues there remember him as hiding from social circumstances—no friends, no allies, no networking.

After several years at Berkeley, Kaczynski resigned and moved to a rural area of Montana where he lived as a hermit in a crude shack for 25 years. Town residents described him as a bearded eccentric. Ted traced his own difficulties to growing up as a genius in a kid's body and sticking out like a sore thumb in his surroundings as a child. In 1996, he was arrested and charged with being the notorious Unabomber, America's most wanted killer who sent sixteen mail bombs in 17 years that left 23 people wounded and maimed, and 3 people dead. In 1998, he plead guilty to the offenses and was sentenced to life in prison.

Ted Kaczynski, the convicted Unabomber, traced his difficulties to growing up as a genius in a kid's body and not fitting in when he was a child.

Alice Walker won the Pulitzer Prize for her book *The Color Purple.* Like the characters in her book (especially the women), Walker overcame pain and anger to triumph and celebrate the human spirit.

A decade before Kaczynski allegedly mailed his first bomb, Alice Walker, who would later win a Pulitzer Prize for her book *The Color Purple,* spent her days battling racism in Mississippi. She had recently won her first writing fellowship, but rather than use the money to follow her dream of moving to Senegal, Africa, she put herself into the heart and heat of the civil rights movement. Walker grew up knowing the brutal effects of poverty and racism. Born in 1944, she was the eighth child of Georgia sharecroppers who earned $300 a year. When Walker was 8, her brother accidentally shot her in the left eye with a BB gun. By the time her parents got her to the hospital a week later (they had no car), she was blind in that eye and it had developed a disfiguring layer of scar tissue. Despite the counts against her, Walker went on to become an essayist, a poet, an award-winning novelist, a short-story writer, and a social activist who, like her characters (especially the women), has overcome pain and anger.

What leads one individual, so full of promise, to commit brutal acts of violence and another to turn poverty and trauma into a rich literary harvest? How can we attempt to explain how one individual can pick up the pieces of a life shattered by tragedy, such as a loved one's death, whereas another one seems to come unhinged by life's minor hassles? Why is it that some individuals are whirlwinds—successful in school, involved in a network of friends, and full of energy—while others hang out on the sidelines, mere spectators of life? If you have ever wondered what makes people develop, you have asked yourself the central question we explore in this book.

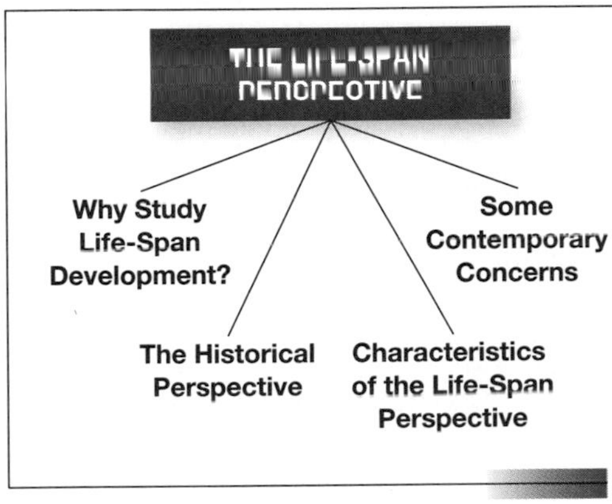

The Life-Span Perspective

The book is a window into the nature of human development—your own and that of every member of the human species. How might we benefit from examining our development?

Why Study Life-Span Development?

Perhaps you are or will be a parent or teacher. Responsibility for children is or will be a part of your everyday life. The more you learn about them, the better you can deal with them. Perhaps you hope to gain some insight into your own history—as an infant, a child, an adolescent, or a young adult. Perhaps you want to know more about what your life will be like as you grow through the adult years—as a middle-aged adult, as an adult in old age, for example. Or perhaps you just stumbled onto this course, thinking that it sounded intriguing and that the topic of the human life span would raise some provocative and intriguing issues about our lives as we grow and develop. Whatever your reasons, you will discover that the study of life-span development *is* provocative, *is* intriguing, and *is* filled with information about who we are, how we have come to be this way, and where our future will take us.

development
The pattern of change that begins at conception and continues through the life cycle.

This book is about **development,** *the pattern of movement or change that begins at conception and continues through the human life span.* Most development involves growth, although it also includes decline (as in death and dying). Later in the chapter we will explore the concept of development in greater detail.

Thus, in exploring development, we will examine the point in time when life begins until the time when it ends, at least life as we know it. You will see yourself as an infant, as a child, and as an adolescent, and be stimulated to think about how those years influenced the kind of individual you are today. And you will see yourself as a young adult, as a middle-aged adult, and as an adult in old age, and be stimulated to think about how your experiences today will influence your development through the remainder of your adult years.

Human development is the core of societal development and psychology is centrally relevant to it.

Cigdem Kagitcibasi
Contemporary Developmental Psychologist, Istanbul, Turkey

Life-span development also is an important course in many departments because it is linked with so many different areas of psychology. In many programs its importance is recognized by its being a required or core course. Neuroscience/biolog-

ical psychology, cognitive psychology, abnormal psychology, social psychology, and virtually all other areas of psychology can be connected with life-span development in terms of exploring how people develop in these areas. For example, how memory works is a key aspect of congnitive psychology. In this book you will read about how memory develops from the time individuals are infants through when they are older adults.

In thinking about the importance of studying life-span development, consider the following research findings:

- Massage therapy facilitates the growth and improves the immune system functioning of preterm infants (Dieter & others, 2001; Field, 1998).
- Secure attachment to parents in adolescence is linked with a host of positive outcomes for adolescents, such as positive peer relations and emotional well-being (Allen, Hauser, & Borman-Spurrell, 1996; Allen & Land, 2001).
- Scientists' ability to extend the life span of human cells in a test tube has implications for the potential expansion of the upper boundary of human life (Bodnar & others, 1998; Shay, 2000).

These are but a few of the thousands of research findings we will examine in this text that can improve our understanding of the human life span. *This is an exciting time of discovery in the field of life-span development.*

Before we further discuss the exciting new findings in this field, let's first turn the clock back and explore its historical development.

The Historical Perspective

Interest in children has a long and rich history, but interest in adults began to develop seriously only in the latter half of the twentieth century.

History of Childhood
Children's Issues
Children's Rights
UNICEF

Child Development

Throughout history, philosophers have speculated about the nature of children and how they should be reared. Three such philosophical views are based on the notions of original sin, tabula rasa, and innate goodness. In the **original sin view,** *especially advocated during the Middle Ages, children were perceived as being basically bad, born into the world as evil beings.* The goal of child rearing was salvation, which was believed to remove sin from the child's life. Toward the end of the seventeenth century, the **tabula rasa view** *was proposed by English philosopher John Locke. He argued that children are not innately bad. Instead they are like a "blank tablet," a "tabula rasa" as he called it. They acquire their characteristics through experience.* Locke believed that childhood experiences are important in determining adult characteristics. He advised parents to spend time with their children and help them become contributing members of society. In the eighteenth century, the **innate goodness view** *was presented by Swiss-born French philosopher Jean-Jacques Rousseau. He stressed that children are inherently good.* Rousseau said that because children are basically good, they should be permitted to grow naturally with little parental monitoring or constraint.

original sin view
Advocated during the Middle Ages, the belief that children were born into the world as evil beings and were basically bad.

tabula rasa view
The idea, proposed by John Locke, that children are like a "blank tablet."

innate goodness view
The idea, presented by Swiss-born philosopher Jean-Jacques Rousseau, that children are inherently good.

During the past century and a half, interest in the nature of children and ways to improve their well-being have continued to be important concerns of our society (Booth & Crouter, 2000; Graham, 2001). We now conceive of childhood as a highly eventful and unique period of life that lays an important foundation for the adult years and is highly differentiated from them. In most approaches to childhood, distinct periods are identified in which special skills are mastered and new life tasks are confronted. Childhood is no longer seen as an inconvenient "waiting" period during which adults must suffer the incompetencies of the young. We now value childhood as a special time of growth and change, and we invest great resources in caring for and educating our children. We protect them from the excesses of adult work through strict child labor laws. We treat their crimes against society under a special system of juvenile justice. And we have government provisions for helping them when ordinary family support systems fail or when families seriously interfere with the child's well-being.

Time Period	Average Life Expectancy (in years)
Prehistoric times	18
Ancient Greece	20
Middle Ages, England	33
1620, Massachusetts Bay Colony	35
19th century, England	41
1900, USA	47
1915, USA	54
1954, USA	70
1998, USA	77

Figure **1.1**

Human Life Expectancy at Birth from Prehistoric to Contemporary Times

As we see next, although development in childhood is important, a complete view of development requires that we also consider developmental changes in the adult years.

Life-Span Development Let's now examine the distinction between the traditional and life-span views of development, and the increased attention given to aging in the twentieth century.

Traditional and Life-Span Approaches The *traditional approach* to development emphasizes extensive change from birth to adolescence, little or no change in adulthood, and decline in late old age. Infancy is especially thought to be a time of considerable change, in the traditional approach. In contrast, the *life-span approach* emphasizes developmental change during adulthood as well as childhood (Salthouse, 2000).

The Twentieth Century Before the twentieth century, it took 5,000 years of human history to extend human life expectancy by 25 years of age (see figure 1.1). Then in the twentieth century alone, life expectancy increased by 30 years. Improvements in sanitation, nutrition, and medical knowledge led to this amazing increase in life expectancy. Today, for most individuals, childhood and adolescence represent only about one-fourth of their life span (Schaie, 2000; Schaie & Willis, 2001).

How much has the older adult population grown in the United States? Figure 1.2 reveals a dramatic increase in the over-65 age group since 1900 and projects continued increases through 2040. A significant increase also will occur in the number of individuals in the 85-and-over and in the 100-and-over age categories. Currently, fewer than 50,000 Americans are 100 years of age or older; in 2050, the projected number is more than 800,000. A baby girl born today has a 1-in-3 chance of living to be 100 years of age!

Although we are living longer, on the average, than we did in the past, the maximum life span of humans has not changed since the beginning of recorded history. The upper boundary of the life span is approximately 120 years, and, as indicated in figure 1.3, our only competition from other species for the maximum recorded life span is the Galápagos turtle.

For too long we believed that development was something that happened only to children. To be sure, growth and development are dramatic in the first two decades of life, but a great deal of change goes on in the next five or six decades of life, too. Consider these descriptions of adult development:

> The next five or six decades are every bit as important, not only to those adults who are passing through them but to their children, who must live with and understand parents and grandparents. The changes in body, personality, and abilities through these later decades is great. Developmental tasks are imposed by marriage and parenthood, by the waxing and waning of physical prowess and of some intellectual capacities, by the children's flight from the nest, by the achievement of an occupational plateau, and by retirement and the prospect of final extinction. Parents have always been fascinated by their children's development, but it is high time adults began to look objectively at themselves, to examine the systematic changes in their own physical, mental, and emotional qualities, as they pass through the life span, and to get acquainted with the limitations and assets they share with so many others of their age. (Sears & Feldman, 1973, pp. v–vi)

As the older population continues to increase in the twenty-first century, concerns are raised about the increasing number of older adults that will be without either a spouse or children (traditionally the main sources of support for older adults). In recent decades, American adults were less likely to be married, more likely to be childless, and more likely to be living alone than earlier in the twentieth century. As these individuals become older, their need for social relationships, networks, and supports is increasing at the same time as the supply is dwindling.

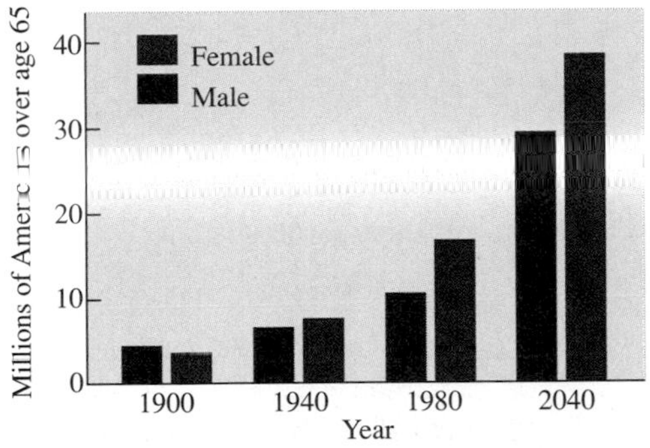

Figure **1.2**

The Aging of America

Millions of Americans over age 65 from 1900 to the present and projected to the year 2040.

Species (common name)	Maximum life span (years)
Human	120
Galápagos turtle	100+
Indian elephant	70
Chinese alligator	52
Golden eagle	46
Gorilla	39
Common toad	36
Domestic cat	27
Domestic dog	20
Vampire bat	13
House mouse	3

Figure **1.3**

Maximum Recorded Life Spans for Different Species

Characteristics of the Life-Span Perspective

In this book we take a life-span perspective on understanding development. What does it mean to adopt a life-span perspective? According to life-span development expert Paul Baltes (1987, 2000), the **life-span perspective** *involves these characteristic beliefs: Development is lifelong, multidimensional, multidirectional, plastic, contextual, multidisciplinary, and involves growth, maintenance, and regulation.*

life-span perspective
The view that development is lifelong, multidimensional, multidirectional, plastic, contextual, multidisciplinary, and involves growth, maintenance and regulation.

Development Is Lifelong Is early adulthood the endpoint of development? In the life-span perspective it is not; rather, no age period dominates development. Researchers increasingly study the experiences and psychological orientations of adults at different points in their development. Later in this chapter we will describe the age periods of development and their characteristics.

Exploring Aging Issues
National Aging Information Center
Global Resources on Aging

Development Is Multidimensional Development consists of biological, cognitive, and socioemotional dimensions (also later in the chapter, we will explore these key dimensions of life-span development). Even within a dimension, such as intelligence, there are many components, such as abstract intelligence, nonverbal intelligence, and social intelligence.

Development Is Multidirectional Some dimensions or components of a dimension increase in growth, others decrease. In language development, when one language (such as English) is acquired early in development, the capacity for acquiring second and third languages (such as French and Spanish) decreases later in development, especially after early childhood (Levelt, 1989). In socioemotional development, heterosexual individuals begin to have more relationships with opposite-sex peers during adolescence as they establish intimate relationships, while their relationships with same-sex peers might decrease (Hartup, 2000). In cognitive development, older adults might become wiser by being able to call on experience to guide their intellectual decision making (Baltes, 2000). However, they perform more poorly on tasks that require speed in processing information (Salthouse, 2000).

Development Is Plastic A key developmental research agenda is the search for plasticity and its constraints (Mauer, 2001; Taub, 2001). Plasticity involves the degree to which characteristics change or remain stable. For example, can intellectual skills still be improved through education for individuals in their seventies or eighties? Or might these intellectual skills be cast in stone by the time people are in their thirties and not be capable of further improvement? In one research study, the reasoning abilities of older adults were improved through retraining (Willis & Schaie, 1994). However, developmentalists debate how much plasticity people have at different points in their development; possibly we possess less capacity for change when we become old (Baltes, 2000; Craik & Salthouse, 2000). Later in the chapter we will discuss the issue of stability and change in development, which has close ties with the concept of plasticity.

CAREERS IN LIFE-SPAN DEVELOPMENT

K. Warner Schaie, Professor of Human Development

K. WARNER SCHAIE is a professor of human development and psychology at Pennsylvania State University, where he teaches and conducts research on adult development and aging. He also directs the Gerontology Center there. He is one of the pioneering psychologists who helped to create the life-span perspective. He is the author or editor of more than 25 books and more than 250 journal articles and book chapters on adult development and aging. Dr. Schaie conducted the Seattle Longitudinal Study of intellectual development, a major research investigation that revealed that many intellectual skills are maintained or even increase during the years of middle age.

Life-span developmentalist K. Warner Schaie *(right)* with two older adults who are actively using their cognitive skills.

Development Is Contextual The individual continually responds to and acts on contexts, which includes a person's biological makeup, physical environment, cognitive processes, historical contexts, social contexts, and cultural contexts. In the contextual view, individuals are thought of as changing beings in a changing world.

Baltes and other life-span developmentalists (Baltes, 2000; Baltes, Reese, & Lipsitt, 1980; Schaie, 1996, 2000) believe that three important sources of contextual influences are (1) normative age-graded influences, (2) normative-history graded influences, and (3) nonnormative life events.

Normative age-graded influences are biological and environmental influences that are similar for individuals in a particular age group. These influences include biological processes such as puberty and menopause. They also include sociocultural, environmental processes such as entry into formal education (usually at about age 6 in most cultures) and retirement (which takes place in the fifties and sixties in most cultures).

Adult Development and Aging
The Gerontological Society of America
Geropsychology Resources

Normative history-graded influences are common to people of a particular generation because of the historical circumstances they experience. Examples include economic changes (such as the Great Depression in the 1930s), war (such as World War II in the 1940s), the changing role of women, the technology revolution we currently are experiencing, and political upheaval and change (such as the decrease in hard-line communism in the 1990s and into the twenty-first century).

Nonnormative life events are unusual occurrences that have a major impact on the individual's life and usually are not applicable to many people. These events might include the death of a parent when a child is young, pregnancy in early adolescence, a disaster (such as a fire that destroys a home), or an accident. Nonnormative life events also can include positive events (such as winning the lottery or getting an unexpected career opportunity with special privileges). An important aspect of understanding the role of nonnormative life events is to focus on how people adapt to them.

Development Is Studied by a Number of Disciplines Psychologists, sociologists, anthropologists, neuroscientists, and medical researchers all study human development and share an interest in unlocking the mysteries of development through the life span. Examples of research questions that cut across disciplines include these:

- What constraints on intelligence are set by the individual's heredity and health status?
- How universal are cognitive and socioemotional changes?
- How do environmental contexts influence intellectual development?

Development Involves Growth, Maintenance, and Regulation Baltes and his colleagues (Baltes, 2000; Baltes, Staudinger, & Lindenberger, 1999) believe that the mastery of life often involves conflicts and competition among three goals of human development: growth, maintenance, and regulation.

As individuals age into middle and late adulthood, the maintenance and regulation of their capacities takes center stage away from growth. Thus, for many individuals, the goal is not to seek growth in intellectual capacities (such as memory) or physical capacities (such as physical strength), but to maintain those skills or minimize their deterioration. In Section 9, "Late Adulthood," we will discuss these ideas about maintenance and regulation in greater depth.

So far in this chapter we have explored why it is important to study life-span development, an historical perspective on life-span development, and the life-span perspective. As you will see next, the life-span perspective also addresses a number of contemporary concerns.

Some Contemporary Concerns

Consider some of the topics you read about every day in newspapers and magazines: genetic research, child abuse, homosexuality, mental retardation, parenting, intelligence, career changes, divorce, addiction and recovery, the increasing ethnic minority population, gender issues, midlife crises, stress and health, retirement, and aging. What life-span experts are discovering in each of these areas has direct and significant consequences for understanding children and adults and our decisions as a society about how they should be treated.

Health Links
Prevention Programs
AskERIC

An important theme of this textbook is to provide detailed, contemporary coverage of the roles that health and well-being, parenting and education, and sociocultural contexts play in life-span development.

Health and Well-Being Health and well-being have been important goals for just about everyone for most of human history. Asian physicians in 2600 B.C. and Greek physicians in 500 B.C. recognized that good habits are essential for good health. They did not blame the gods for illness or think that magic would cure it—they realized that people have some control over their health and well-being. A physician's role became that of a guide, assisting patients to restore a natural physical and emotional balance.

In the twenty-first century, we once again recognize the power of lifestyles and psychological states in health and well-being (Baum, Revenson, & Singer, 2001; Kennedy, 2001; Manuck & others, 2001; Melamed, Roth, & Fogel, 2001; Rosenstock, 2000; Weiss, 2000). In every chapter of this book, issues of health and well-being are integrated into our discussion of life-span development. They also are highlighted in the Internet connections that appear with World Wide Web icons throughout the book.

The topics on health and well-being we will discuss include these:

- Drug and alcohol use during pregnancy
- Genetic counseling
- Breast- versus bottle-feeding
- Early intervention
- School health programs
- At-risk adolescents
- Women's health issues
- Exercise
- Addiction and recovery
- Loneliness
- Adaptive physical skills in aging adults
- Coping with death

Parenting and Education We hear a lot about pressures on the contemporary family (Cowan, Powell, & Cowan, 1998; Ellis, 2000; Hetherington, 2000; Pruett & Jackson, 2001). We will evaluate many different issues related to family functioning and parenting. The topics involved in these issues include:

- Day care
- Working parents and latchkey children
- Effects of divorce on children

Careers in Life-Span Development

Luis Varga, Child Clinical Psychologist

LUIS VARGA is Director of the Clinical Child Psychology Internship Program and a professor in the Department of Psychiatry at the University of New Mexico Health Sciences Center. He also is Director of Psychology at the University of New Mexico Children's Psychiatric Hospital.

Luis obtained an undergraduate degree in psychology from St. Edwards University in Texas, a master's degree in psychology from Trinity University in Texas, and a Ph.D. in clinical psychology from the University of Nebraska–Lincoln.

His main interests are cultural issues and the assessment and treatment of children, adolescents, and families. He is motivated to find better ways to provide culturally responsive mental health services. One of his special interests is the treatment of Latino youth for delinquency and substance abuse. He recently co-authored (with Joan Koss-Chioino) *Working with Latino Youth* (Koss-Chioino & Vargas, 1999), which spells out effective strategies for improving the lives of at-risk Latino youth.

Luis Varga *(left)* conducting a child therapy session

Children
learn to love
when they are
loved

- The best way to parent
- Child maltreatment
- Support systems for families
- Marital relationships
- Intergenerational relations
- Aging parents

Another life-span concern is homelessness and the impact of this impoverished condition on children's development.

In the past decade the American educational system has come under attack (Freiberg & Driscoll, 2000; Johnson & others, 2002; Rogoff, Turkanis, & Bartlett, 2001; Spring, 1998). A national committee appointed by the Office of Education concluded that children are being poorly prepared for the increasingly complex future they will face. The educational topics we will explore include these:

- Variations in early childhood education
- Ethnicity, social class, and schools
- Programs to improve children's critical thinking
- School and family coordination
- Cooperative learning
- How to avoid stifling children's creativity
- Bilingual education
- The best schools for adolescents

Sociocultural Contexts The tapestry of American culture has changed dramatically in recent years. Nowhere is the change more dramatic than in the increasing ethnic diversity of America's citizens. This changing demographic tapestry promises not only the richness that diversity produces, but also difficult challenges in extending the American dream to all individuals.

context
The settings, influenced by historical, economic, social, and cultural factors, in which development occurs.

Sociocultural contexts include four important concepts: context, culture, ethnicity, and gender. A **context** *is the setting in which development occurs. This setting is influenced by historical, economic, social, and cultural factors.* Every person's development occurs against the backdrop of cultural contexts. These contexts or settings include homes, schools, peer groups, churches, cities, neighborhoods, university laboratories, the United States, Canada, China, Japan, Egypt, and many others. Each of these settings has meaningful historical, economic, social, and cultural legacies (Brislin, 2000; Rogoff, 2001; Triandis, 2000).

culture
The behavior patterns, beliefs, and all other products of a group that are passed on from generation to generation.

cross-cultural studies
Comparisons of one culture with one or more other cultures. These provide information about the degree to which children's development is similar, or universal, across cultures, and to the degree to which it is culture-specific

Culture *is the behavior patterns, beliefs, and all other products of a particular group of people that are passed on from generation to generation.* Culture results from the interaction of people over many years. A cultural group can be as large as the United States or as small as an African hunter-gatherer group. Whatever its size, the group's culture influences the behavior of its members (Cole, 1999; Kagitcibasi, 1996; Shiraev & Levy, 2001; Valsiner, 2000). For example, the United States is an achievement-oriented culture with a strong work ethic. However, recent comparisons of American and Japanese children showed that Japanese children are better at math, spend more time working on math at school, and do more math homework than American children (Stevenson, 1995, 2000; Stevenson & Hofer, 1999). **Cross-cultural studies** *involve a comparison of a culture with one or more other cultures. The comparison provides information about the degree to which development is similar, or universal, across cultures, or is instead culture-specific.*

The topics on culture that we will discuss include these:

- Child-care policy around the world
- Vygotsky's sociocultural cognitive theory
- Gender roles in Egypt and China
- Cross-cultural comparisons of secondary schools
- Marriage around the world
- Death and dying in different cultures

Ethnicity (the word *ethnic* comes from the Greek word for "nation") *is based on cultural heritage, nationality characteristics, race, religion, and language.* Not only is there diversity within a culture such as the United States, there also is diversity within each ethnic group. These groups include African Americans, Latinos, Asian Americans, Native Americans, Polish Americans, Italian Americans, and so on. Not all African Americans live in low-income circumstances. Not all Latinos are Catholics. Not all Native Americans are high school dropouts. It is easy to fall into the trap of stereotyping an ethnic group by thinking that all of its members are alike. A more accurate ethnic group portrayal is diversity (Eccles, 2001; McLoyd, 1998, 1999, 2000).

Among the ethnicity topics we will examine are these:

- Similarities, differences, and diversity
- Immigration
- Support systems for ethnic minority individuals
- Ethnicity and schooling
- Value conflicts
- Being old, female, and ethnic

Two Korean-born children on the day they became United States citizens. Asian American and Latino children are the fastest-growing immigrant groups in the United States. *How diverse are the students in this class on life-span that you now are taking? How are their experiences in growing up likely similar to or different than yours?*

Gender *is the sociocultural dimension of being female or male. Sex* refers to the biological dimension of being female or male. Few aspects of our development are more central to our identity and social relationships than gender (Crawford & Unger, 2000; Eagly, 2000; Paludi, 2001; Wood, 2001). Society's gender attitudes are changing. But how much? The gender-related topics we will discuss include these:

- The mother's role and the father's role
- Parental and peer roles in gender development
- Gender similarities and differences
- Femininity, masculinity, and androgyny
- Carol Gilligan's care perspective
- Gender communication patterns
- Family work
- Gender and aging

We will integrate the discussion of sociocultural contexts into each chapter. A "Sociocultural Worlds of Development" box also appears in most chapters. Turn to the first one now for a discussion of women's international struggle for equality. Next, we will explore another contemporary concern in life-span development—social policy.

ethnicity
A characteristic based on cultural heritage, nationality characteristics, race, religion, and language.

gender
The social dimension of being male or female.

social policy
A national government's course of action designed to influence the welfare of its citizens.

Social Policy

Social policy *is a national government's course of action designed to influence the welfare of its citizens.* A current trend is to conduct developmental research that will lead to effective social policy (Maccoby, 2001; Sanders, 2000; Zigler & Hall, 2000). When more than 20 percent of all children and more than half of all ethnic minority children are being raised in poverty, when 40 to 50 percent of all children can expect to spend at least 5 years in a single-parent home, when children and young adolescents are giving birth, when the use and abuse of drugs is widespread, when the specter of AIDS is present, and when the provision of health care for the elderly is inadequate, our nation needs revised social policy.

The shape and scope of social policy is strongly tied to our political system. Our country's policy agenda and the welfare of the nation's citizens are influenced by the values held by individual lawmakers, the nation's economic strengths and weaknesses, and partisan politics.

Marian Wright Edelman, president of the Children's Defense Fund, has been a tireless advocate of children's rights. Especially troublesome to Edelman (1995) are the indicators of social neglect that place the United States at or near the lowest rank for industrialized nations in the treatment of children. Edelman says that parenting and nurturing the next generation of children is our society's most important

WWW

Diversity

Social Policy

Trends in the Well-Being of Children and Youth

generational inequity
An aging society's being unfair to its younger members because older adults pile up advantages by receiving inequitably large allocations of resources.

SOCIOCULTURAL WORLDS OF DEVELOPMENT

Women's Struggle for Equality: An International Journey

WHAT ARE some of the educational, political, family, and psychological conditions of women around the world? They include the following (Culbertson, 1991):

Women and Education

The countries with the fewest women being educated are in Africa, where in some areas women are receiving no education at all. Canada, the United States, and Russia have the highest percentages of educated women. In developing countries, 67 percent of the women and 50 percent of the men over the age of 25 have never been to school. In 1985, 80 million more boys than girls were in primary and secondary educational settings around the world.

Women and Psychosocial Issues

Women around the world, in every country, experience violence, often from someone close to them. Partner abuse occurs in one of every six households in the United States, with the vast majority of the abuse being directed at women by men (Browne, 1993; Goodman & Quas, 2000). In a survey, "The New Woman Ethics Report," wife abuse was listed as number one among 15 of the most pressing concerns facing society today (Johnson, 1990). Although most countries around the world now have battered women's shelters, beating women continues to be accepted and expected behavior in some countries.

In a study of depression in high-income countries, women were twice as likely as men to be diagnosed as depressed (Nolen-Hoeksema, 1990). In the United States, from adolescence through adulthood, females are more likely than males to be depressed (Davison & Neale, 2000; McGrath, Kelly, & Rhodes, 1993). Many sociocultural inequities and experiences have contributed to the greater incidence of depression in females than males. Also, possibly more women are diagnosed with depression than actually have depression.

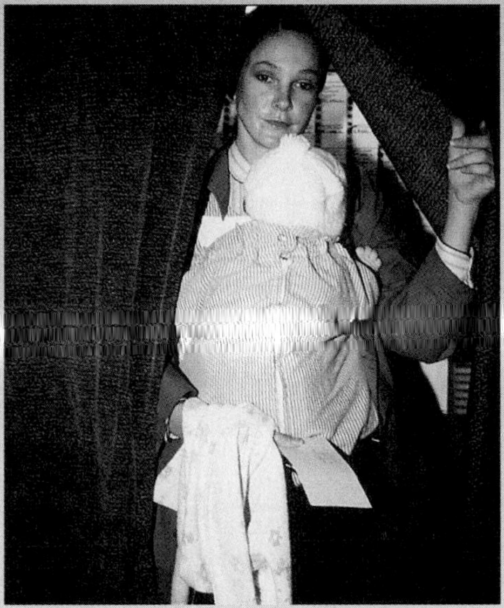

Around the world women too often are treated as burdens rather than assets in the political process. *What can be done to strengthen women's roles in the political process?*

Marian Wright Edelman, president of the Children's Defense Fund (shown here interacting with young children), has been a tireless advocate of children's rights and has been instrumental in calling attention to the needs of children. *What are some of these needs?*

function and that we need to take it more seriously than we have in the past. She points out that we hear a lot from politicians these days about "family values," but that when we examine our nation's policies for families, they don't reflect the politicians' words.

Our aging society and older persons' status in this society raise policy issues about the well-being of older adults. Special concerns are escalating health-care costs and the access of elderly to adequate health care.

Who should get the bulk of government dollars for improved well-being? Children? Their parents? The elderly? **Generational inequity,** *a social policy concern, is the condition in which an aging society is being unfair to its younger members. This occurs because older adults pile up advantages by receiving inequitably large allocations of resources, such as Social Security and Medicare.* Generational inequity raises questions about whether the young should have to pay for the old and whether an "advantaged" older population is using up resources that should go to disadvantaged children. The argument is that older adults are advantaged because they have publicly pro-

Summary Table 1.1
The Life-Span Perspective

Concept	Processes/ Related Ideas	Characteristics/Descriptions
Why Study Life-Span Development?	Reasons	• Responsibility for children is or will be a part of our everyday lives. The more we learn about children, the more we can better deal with them and assist them in becoming competent human beings. • Life-span development gives us insights about our development as adults as well.
	Defining Development	• Development is the pattern of movement or change that begins at conception and continues through the human life span. • Development includes growth and decline.
The Historical Perspective	Child Development	• Interest in children has a long and rich history. • In the Renaissance, philosophical views were prominent, including the notions of original sin, tabula rasa, and innate goodness.
	Life-Span Development and Aging	• The traditional approach emphasizes extensive change in childhood but stability in adulthood; the life-span perspective emphasizes that change is possible throughout the life span. • In the twentieth century alone, life expectancy has increased by 30 years.
Characteristics of the Life-Span Perspective	Baltes' View	• The life-span perspective involves these basic contentions: Development is lifelong, multidimensional, multidirectional, plastic, contextual, multidisciplinary, and involves growth, maintenance, and regulation.
Some Contemporary Concerns	Development and Well-being of Children and Adults	• Today, the development and well-being of children and adults capture the interest of the public, scientists, and policy makers. • Among the important contemporary concerns are family issues, parenting, education, sociocultural contexts, and social policy. • Three important sociocultural contexts are culture, ethnicity, and gender.

vided pensions, health care, food stamps, housing subsidies, tax breaks, and other benefits that younger groups do not have. While the trend of greater services for the elderly has been occurring, the percentage of children in poverty has been rising.

Bernice Neugarten (1988) says the problem should be viewed not as one of generational inequity, but rather as a major shortcoming of our broader economic and social policies. She believes we need to develop a spirit of support for improving the range of options for all people in our society. Also, it is important to keep in mind that children will one day become older adults and will in turn be supported by the efforts of their children (Williams & Nussbaum, 2000). If there were no Social Security system, many adult children would have to bear the burden of supporting their elderly parents and spend less of their resources on educating their children (Schaie, 2000).

At this point we have discussed a number of ideas about why we should study life-span development, a historical perspective on life-span development, the life-span perspective, and contemporary concerns. A review of these ideas is presented in Summary Table 1.1.

Earlier in the chapter we described Paul Baltes' view of the life-span perspective's characteristics. Next, we will further explore the nature of development, examining in greater detail some of the topics Baltes presented along with other ways of thinking about development.

Maggie Kuhn, founder of the Gray Panthers.

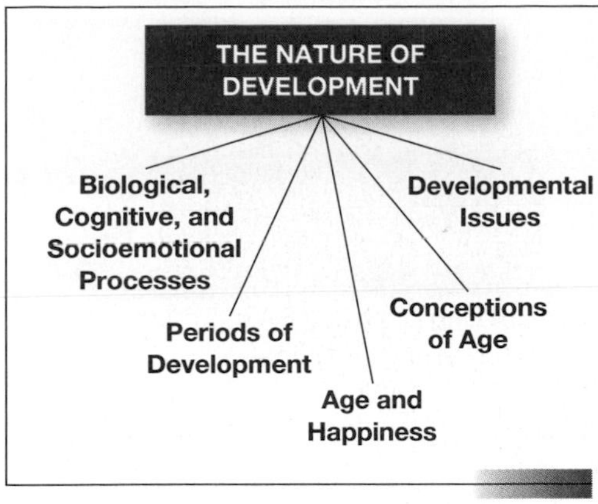

The Nature of Development

Each of us develops partly like all other individuals, partly like some other individuals, and partly like no other individuals. Most of the time, our attention is directed to an individual's uniqueness. But psychologists who study life-span development are drawn to our shared as well as our unique characteristics. As humans, we all have traveled some common paths. Each of us—Leonardo da Vinci, Joan of Arc, George Washington, Martin Luther King, Jr., you—walked at about 1 year, engaged in fantasy play as a young child, and became more independent as a youth. Each of us, if we live long enough, will experience hearing problems and the deaths of family members and friends.

At the beginning of the chapter, we defined *development* as the pattern of movement or change that begins at conception and continues through the life span. The pattern of movement is complex because it is the product of biological, cognitive, and socioemotional processes.

Biological, Cognitive, and Socioemotional Processes

biological processes
Changes in an individual's physical nature.

cognitive processes
Changes in an individual's thought, intelligence, and language.

socioemotional processes
Changes in an individual's relationships with other people, emotions, and personality.

Biological processes *involve changes in the individual's physical nature.* Genes inherited from parents, the development of the brain, height and weight gains, changes in motor skills, the hormonal changes of puberty, and cardiovascular decline all reflect the role of biological processes in development.

Cognitive processes *involve changes in the individual's thought, intelligence, and language.* Watching a colorful mobile swinging above the crib, putting together a two-word sentence, memorizing a poem, imagining what it would be like to be a movie star, and solving a crossword puzzle all reflect the role of cognitive processes in development.

Socioemotional processes *involve changes in the individual's relationships with other people, changes in emotions, and changes in personality.* An infant's smile in response to her mother's touch, a young boy's aggressive attack on a playmate, a girl's development of assertiveness, an adolescent's joy at the senior prom, and the affection of an elderly couple all reflect the role of the socioemotional processes in development.

Biological, cognitive, and socioemotional processes are inextricably intertwined. For example, consider a baby smiling in response to its mother's touch. This response depends on biological processes (the physical nature of touch and responsiveness to it), cognitive processes (being able to understand intentional acts), and socioemotional processes (the act of smiling often reflects a positive emotional feeling and smiling helps to connect us in positive ways with other human beings).

Also, in many instances biological, cognitive, and socioemotional processes are bidirectional. For example, biological processes can influence cognitive processes and vice versa. In section 9, "Late Adulthood," you will read about how poor health (a biological process) is linked to lower intellectual functioning (a cognitive process). You also will read about how positive thinking about the ability to control one's environment (a cognitive process) can have a powerful effect on an individual's health (a biological process).

Thus, although usually we will study the different processes (biological, cognitive, and socioemotional) in separate locations, keep in mind that you are examining the development of an integrated individual with a mind and body that are interdependent (see figure 1.4).

One's children's children's children. Look back to us as we look to you; we are related by our imaginations. If we are able to touch, it is because we have imagined each other's existence, our dreams running back and forth along a cable from age to age.

Roger Rosenblatt
American Writer, 20th Century

Periods of Development

For the purposes of organization and understanding, we commonly describe development in terms of periods. The most widely used classification of developmental periods involves the following sequence: prenatal period, infancy, early childhood, middle and late childhood, adolescence, early adulthood, middle adulthood, and late adulthood. Approximate age ranges are listed below for the periods to provide a general idea of when a period begins and ends.

The *prenatal period* is the time from conception to birth. It involves tremendous growth—from a single cell to an organism complete with brain and behavioral capabilities, produced in approximately a 9-month period.

Infancy is the developmental period extending from birth to 18 or 24 months. Infancy is a time of extreme dependence upon adults. Many psychological activities are just beginning—language, symbolic thought, sensorimotor coordination, and social learning, for example.

Early childhood is the developmental period extending from the end of infancy to about 5 or 6 years. This period is sometimes called the "preschool years." During this time, young children learn to become more self-sufficient and to care for themselves, develop school readiness skills (following instructions, identifying letters), and spend many hours in play with peers. First grade typically marks the end of early childhood.

Middle and late childhood is the developmental period extending from about 6 to 11 years of age, approximately corresponding to the elementary school years. This period is sometimes called the "elementary school years." The fundamental skills of reading, writing, and arithmetic are mastered. The child is formally exposed to the larger world and its culture. Achievement becomes a more central theme of the child's world, and self-control increases.

Adolescence is the developmental period of transition from childhood to early adulthood, entered at approximately 10 to 12 years of age and ending at 18 to 22 years of age. Adolescence begins with rapid physical changes—dramatic gains in height and weight, changes in body contour, and the development of sexual characteristics such as enlargement of the breasts, development of pubic and facial hair, and deepening of the voice. At this point in development, the pursuit of independence and an identity are prominent. Thought is more logical, abstract, and idealistic. More time is spent outside of the family.

Early adulthood is the developmental period beginning in the late teens or early twenties and lasting through the thirties. It is a time of establishing personal and economic independence, career development, and, for many, selecting a mate, learning to live with someone in an intimate way, starting a family, and rearing children.

Middle adulthood is the developmental period beginning at approximately 40 years of age and extending to about 60. It is a time of expanding personal and social involvement and responsibility; of assisting the next generation in becoming competent, mature individuals; and of reaching and maintaining satisfaction in a career.

Late adulthood is the developmental period beginning in the sixties or seventies and lasting until death. It is a time of adjustment to decreasing strength and health, life review, retirement, and adjustment to new social roles.

Life-span developmentalists increasingly distinguish between two age groups in late adulthood: the *young old,* or *old age* (65 to 74 years of age), and the *old old,* or *late old age* (75 years and older). Still others distinguish the *oldest old* (85 years and older) from younger older adults (Pearlin, 1994). Beginning in the sixties and extending to more than 100 years of age, late adulthood has the longest span of any period of development. Combining this lengthy span with the dramatic increase in the number of adults living to older ages, we will see increased attention given to differentiating the late adulthood period.

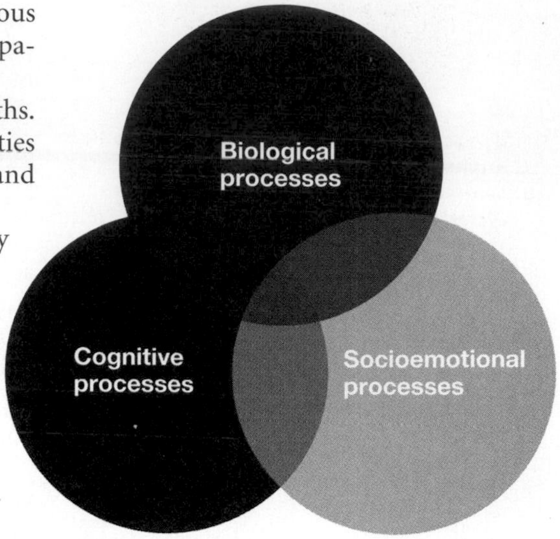

Figure **1.4**

Developmental Changes Are the Result of Biological, Cognitive, and Socioemotional Proceses

These processes are interwoven as individuals develop.

Critical Thinking

Asking Questions . . . What Is the Best Age to Be?

ASKING QUESTIONS reflects our active curiosity. Children—especially young children—are remarkable for their ability to ask questions. The favorite question of my granddaughter, Jordan, when she was 3½ years old was "Why?" and she used the word *why* relentlessly. As strong as question asking is early in our life, many of us ask fewer questions as adults.

Asking questions can help us engage in critical thinking about many domains of life-span development. Consider the question we asked in the text: "What is the best age to be?" Have you ever thought about this in any depth? It is an intriguing question, and one I always ask in the life-span development course I teach. Last year, one student spent about 10 minutes developing the argument that the best age to be is 28 years old. She stressed that at 28 a person is old enough to have experienced enough things in life to show maturity yet still be physically healthy and strong enough to fully enjoy life. Many other students, of course, did not agree and asked her questions, such as "If you are only 30 yourself, how do you know 28 is the best age?" and "Aren't there factors in many individuals' lives that might make a different age be the best age for them?"

Be curious. Ask questions. Ask yourself what is the best age to be. Ask your friends the same question and be sure to ask some people of different ages this question.

The periods of the human life span are shown in figure 1.5, along with the processes of development—biological, cognitive, and socioemotional. The interplay of these processes produces the periods of the human life span.

Age and Happiness

When individuals report how happy they are and how satisfied they are with their lives, no particular age group says they are happier or more satisfied than any other age group (Diener & others, 1999). In one study in eight Western European countries, there was no difference in the percentage of people who were satisfied with life at different ages: 78 percent of 15- to 24-year olds, 78 percent of 35- to 44-year-olds, and 78 percent of those 65 years and older (Ingelhart & Rabier, 1986). Similarly, slightly less than 20 percent of each of the age groups reported that they were "very happy."

Why might older people report just as much happiness and life satisfaction as younger people? Every period of the life span has its stresses, pluses and minuses, hills and valleys. Although adolescents must cope with developing an identity, feelings of insecurity, mood swings, and peer pressure, the majority of adolescents develop positive perceptions of themselves, feelings of competence about their skills, positive relationships with friends and family, and an optimistic view of their future. And while older adults face a life of reduced income, less energy, decreasing physical skills, and concerns about death, they are also less pressured to achieve and succeed, have more time for leisurely pursuits, and have accumulated many years of experience that help them adapt to their lives with a wisdom they may not have had in their younger years. Because growing older is a certain outcome of living, we can derive considerable pleasure from knowing that we are likely to be just as happy as older adults as when we were younger.

Conceptions of Age

In our description of the periods of the life span, we associated approximate age bands with the periods. However, life-span expert Bernice Neugarten (1988) believes we are rapidly becoming an age-irrelevant society. She says we are already familiar with the 28-year-old mayor, the 35-year-old grandmother, the 65-year-old father of a preschooler, the 55-year-old widow who starts a business, and the 70-year-old student. Neugarten stresses that choices and dilemmas do not spring forth at 10-year intervals. Decisions are not made and then left behind as if they were merely beads on a chain. Neugarten argues that most adulthood themes appear and reappear throughout the human life span. The issues of intimacy and freedom can haunt couples throughout their relationship. Feeling the pressure of time, reformulating goals, and coping with success and failure are not the exclusive property of adults of a particular age.

"How old would you be if you didn't know how old you were?"

Satchel Paige
American Baseball Pitcher, 20th Century

Neugarten's ideas raise questions about how age should be conceptualized. Some of the ways age has been conceptualized are as chronological age, biological age, psychological age, and social age (Hoyer, Rybash, & Roodin, 1999).

chronological age
The number of years that have elapsed since a person's birth; what is usually meant by "age."

biological age
A person's age in terms of biological health.

psychological age
An individual's adaptive capacities compared to those of other individuals of the same chronological age.

social age
Social roles and expectations related to a person's age.

nature-nurture issue
Nature refers to an organism's biological inheritance, *nurture* to environmental influences. The "nature" proponents claim biological inheritance is the most important influence on development; the "nurture" proponents claim that environmental experiences are the most important.

Chronological Age **Chronological age** *is the number of years that have elapsed since a person's birth. Many people consider chronological age synonymous with the concept of age.* However, some developmentalists argue that chronological age is not very relevant to understanding a person's psychological development (Botwinick, 1978). A person's age does not cause development. Time is a crude index of many events and experiences, and it does not cause anything.

Biological Age **Biological age** *is a person's age in terms of biological health.* Determining biological age involves knowing the functional capacities of a person's vital organ system. One person's vital capacities may be better or worse than those of others of comparable age. The younger the person's biological age, the longer the person is expected to live, regardless of chronological age.

Psychological Age **Psychological age** *is an individual's adaptive capacities compared to those of other individuals of the same chronological age.* Thus, older adults who continue to learn, are flexible, are motivated, control their emotions, and think clearly are engaging in more adaptive behaviors than their chronological agemates who do not continue to learn, are rigid, are unmotivated, do not control their emotions, and do not think clearly.

Social Age **Social age** *refers to social roles and expectations related to a person's age.* Consider the role of "mother" and the behaviors that accompany the role (Huyck & Hoyer, 1982). In predicting an adult woman's behavior, it may be more important to know that she is the mother of a 3-year-old child than to know whether she is 20 or 30 years old. We still have some expectations for when certain life events—such as getting married, having children, becoming a grandparent, and retiring—should occur. However, as Neugarten concluded, chronological age has become a less accurate predictor of these life events in our society.

From a life-span perspective, an overall age profile of an individual involves more than just chronological age. It also consists of biological age, psychological age, and social age (see figure 1.6). For example, a 70-year-old man (chronological age) might be in good physical health (biological age), be experiencing memory problems and not coping well with the demands placed on him by his wife's recent hospitalization (psychological age), and have a number of friends with whom he regularly golfs (social age).

Developmental Issues

The most important developmental issues include nature and nurture, continuity and discontinuity, and stability and change.

Nature and Nurture The **nature-nurture issue** *involves the debate about whether development is primarily influenced by nature or nurture.* Nature *refers to an organism's biological inheritance,* nurture *to its environmental experiences.* "Nature" proponents claim that the most important influence on development is biological inheritance. "Nurture" proponents claim that environmental experiences are the most important influence.

According to the nature advocates, just as a sunflower grows in an orderly way—unless defeated by an unfriendly environment—so does the human grow in an orderly way. The range of environments can be vast, but the nature approach argues that the genetic blueprint produces commonalities in growth and development. We walk before we talk, speak one word before

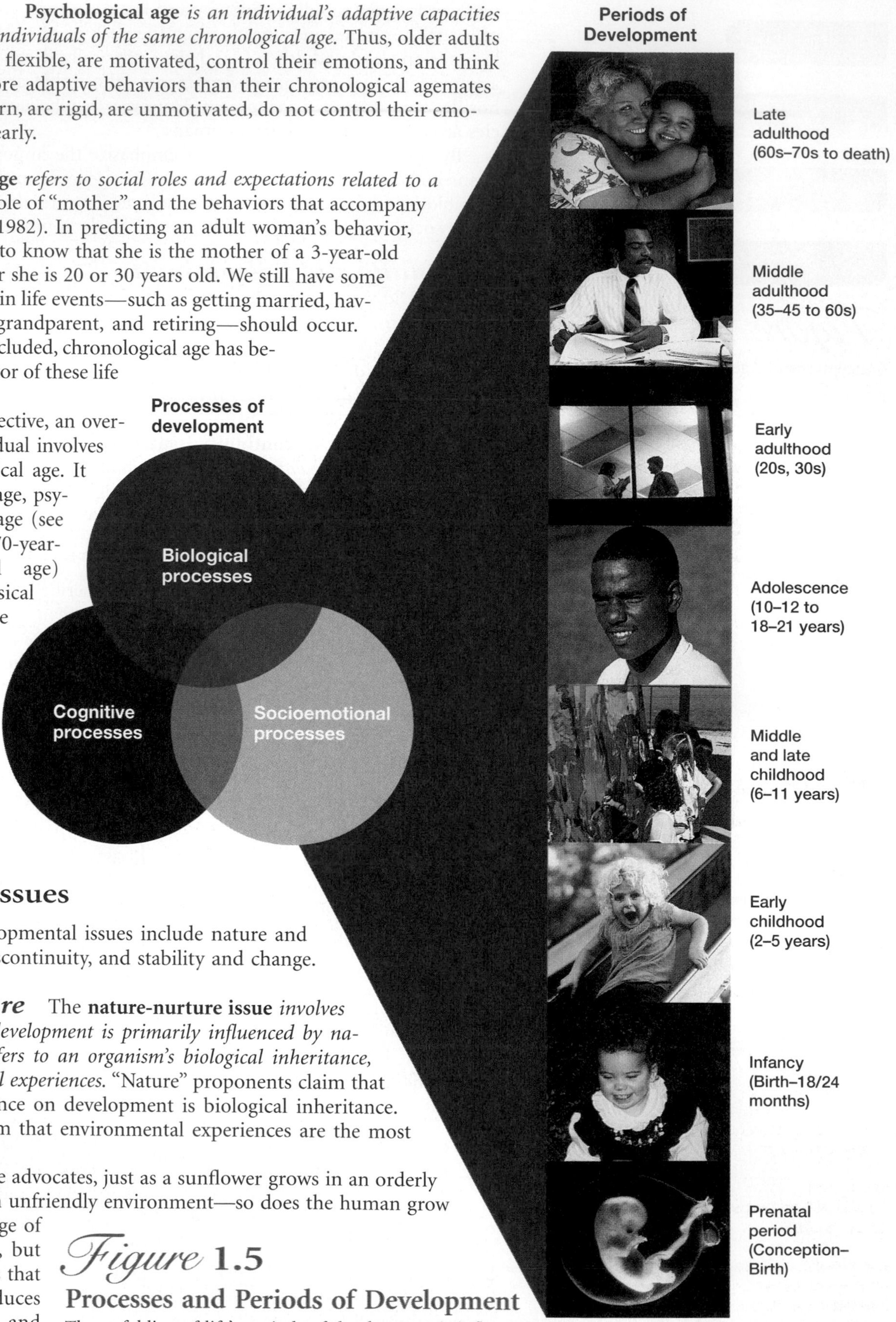

Figure **1.5**

Processes and Periods of Development

The unfolding of life's periods of development is influenced by the interaction of biological, cognitive, and socioemotional processes.

two words, grow rapidly in infancy and less so in early childhood, experience a rush of sexual hormones in puberty, reach the peak of our physical strength in late adolescence and early adulthood, and then physically decline. The nurture proponents acknowledge that extreme environments—those that are psychologically barren or hostile—can depress development. However, they believe that basic growth tendencies are genetically wired into humans.

By contrast, other psychologists emphasize the importance of nurture, or environmental experiences, in development. Experiences run the gamut from the individual's biological environment (nutrition, medical care, drugs, and physical accidents) to the social environment (family, peers, schools, community, media, and culture).

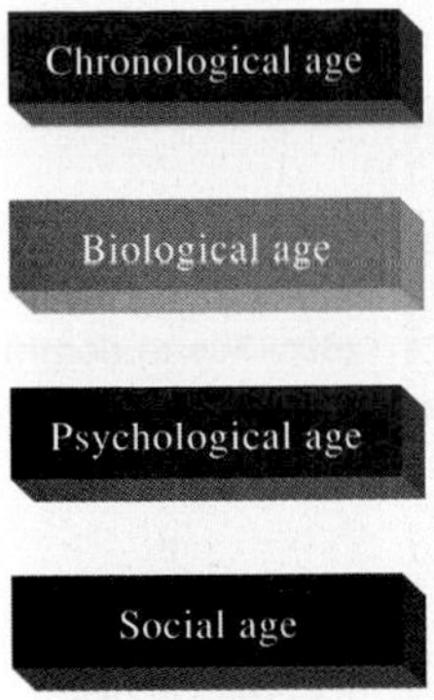

Figure **1.6**
Conceptions of Age

Continuity and Discontinuity

Think about your development for a moment. Did you become the person you are gradually, like the slow, cumulative way a seedling grows into a giant oak? Or did you experience sudden, distinct changes in your growth, like the way a caterpillar changes into a butterfly (see figure 1.7)? For the most part, developmentalists who emphasize nurture usually describe development as a gradual, continuous process. Those who emphasize nature often describe development as a series of distinct stages.

continuity-discontinuity issue
The issue regarding whether development involves gradual, cumulative change (continuity) or distinct stages (discontinuity).

The **continuity-discontinuity issue** *focuses on the extent to which development involves gradual, cumulative change (continuity) or distinct stages (discontinuity).* In terms of continuity, a child's first word, though seemingly an abrupt, discontinuous event, is actually the result of weeks and months of growth and practice. Puberty, though also seemingly an abrupt, discontinuous occurrence, is actually a gradual process occurring over several years.

In terms of discontinuity, each person is described as passing through a sequence of stages in which change is qualitatively rather than quantitatively different. As the oak moves from seedling to giant oak, it becomes *more* oak—its development is continuous. As the caterpillar changes to a butterfly, it is not just more caterpillar, it is a *different kind* of organism—its development is discontinuous. For example, at some point a child moves from not being able to think abstractly about the world to being able to. This is a qualitative, discontinuous change in development, not a quantitative, continuous change.

Stability and Change

stability-change issue
The issue of whether development is best described as involving stability or as involving change. This issue involves the degree to which we become older renditions of our early experience or instead develop into someone different from who we were at an earlier point in development.

Another important developmental topic is the **stability-change issue,** *which addresses whether development is best described by stability or by change. The stability-change issue involves the degree to which we become older renditions of our early experience or whether we develop into someone different from who we were at an earlier point in development.* Will the shy child who hides behind the sofa when visitors arrive be a wallflower at college dances, or will the child become a sociable, talkative individual? Will the fun-loving, carefree adolescent have difficulty holding down a 9-to-5 job as an adult or become a straitlaced, serious conformist?

The stability-change issue is linked with Paul Baltes' (1987, 2000) belief, which we discussed earlier, that plasticity or change is an important life-span issue. Recall that in the life-span perspective, plasticity or change is possible throughout the life span, although experts such as Baltes argue that older adults often show less capacity for change than younger adults.

One of the reasons adult development was so late in being studied was the predominant belief for many years that nothing much changes in adulthood. The major changes were believed to take place in childhood, especially during the first 5 years of life. Today, most developmentalists believe that some change is possible throughout the human life span, although they disagree, sometimes vehemently, about just how much change can take place, and how much stability there is. The important issue of stability and change in development will reappear on many occasions in our journey through the human life span.

An important dimension of the stability-change issue is the extent to which early experiences (especially in infancy) or later experiences are the key determinants of a

person's development. That is, if infants experience negative, stressful circumstances in their lives, can those experiences be overcome by later, more positive experiences? Or are the early experiences so critical, possibly because they are the infant's first, prototypical experiences, that they cannot be overridden by an enriched environment later in development?

The early-later experience issue has a long history and continues to be hotly debated among developmentalists (Cairns, 1998). Some believe that unless infants experience warm, nurturant caregiving in the first year or so of life, their development will never be optimal (Waters & others, 1995). Plato was sure that infants who were rocked frequently became better athletes. Nineteenth-century New England ministers told parents in Sunday sermons that the way they handled their infants would determine their children's future character. The emphasis on the importance of early experience rests on the belief that each life is an unbroken trail on which a psychological quality can be traced back to its origin (Kagan, 1992, 1998, 2000).

The early-experience doctrine contrasts with the later-experience view that, rather than a statuelike permanence after change in infancy, development continues to be like the ebb and flow of a river. The later-experience advocates argue that children are malleable throughout development and that later sensitive caregiving is just as important as earlier sensitive caregiving. A number of life-span developmentalists, who focus on the entire life span rather than only on child development, stress that too little attention has been given to later experiences in development (Baltes, Lindenberger, & Staudinger, 1998; Schaie & Willis, 2001; Willis & Reid, 1999). They argue that early experiences are important contributors to development, but no more important than later experiences. Jerome Kagan (2000) points out that even children who show the qualities of an inhibited temperament, which is linked to heredity, have the capacity to change their behavior. In his research, almost one-third of a group of children who had an inhibited temperament at 2 years of age were not unusually shy or fearful when they were 4 years of age.

People in Western cultures, especially those steeped in the Freudian belief that the key experiences in development are children's relationships with their parents in the first 5 years of life, have tended to support the idea that early experiences are more important than later experiences. But the majority of people in the world do not share this belief. For example, people in many Asian countries believe that experiences occurring after about 6 to 7 years of age are more important aspects of development than earlier experiences. This stance stems from the long-standing belief in Eastern cultures that children's reasoning skills begin to develop in important ways in the middle childhood years.

One recent book—*The Myth of the First Three Years*—supports the later experience argument (Bruer, 1999). The argument is made, based on the available research evidence, that learning and cognitive development do not occur only in the first 3 years of life but rather are lifelong. The author concludes that too many parents treat the first 3 years as if a switch goes off, after which further learning either does not take place or is greatly diminished. That is not to say experiences in the first 3 years are unimportant, but rather that later experiences are too. This book has been highly controversial, with early-experience advocates being especially critical of it (Bornstein, 2000).

Evaluating the Developmental Issues As we further consider these three salient developmental issues—nature and nurture, continuity and discontinuity, and stability and change—it is important to point out that most life-span developmentalists recognize that extreme positions on these issues are unwise. Development is not all nature or all nurture, not all continuity or all discontinuity, and not all stability or all change (Lerner, 1998). Both nature and nurture, continuity and discontinuity, stability and change characterize our development through the human life span. For example, in considering the nature-nurture issue, the key to development is the *interaction* of nature and nurture rather than either factor alone (Rutter, 2001). For instance, an individual's cognitive development is the

Figure **1.7**
Continuity and Discontinuity in Development
Is our development like that of a seedling gradually growing into a giant oak? Or is it more like that of a caterpillar suddenly becoming a butterfly?

What is the nature of the early and later experience issue in development?

result of heredity-environment interaction, not heredity or environment alone. (Much more about the role of heredity-environment interaction appears in chapter 3.)

Although most developmentalists do not take extreme positions on these three important issues, there is spirited debate regarding how strongly development is influenced by each of these factors (Appelbaum & Conger, 1996; Waters, 2001). Are girls less likely to do well in math because of their "feminine" nature, or because of society's masculine bias? How extensively can the elderly be trained to reason more effectively? How much, if at all, does our memory decline in old age? Can techniques be used to prevent or reduce the decline? For children who experienced a world of poverty, neglect by parents, and poor schooling in childhood, can enriched experiences in adolescence remove the "deficits" they encountered earlier in their development? The answers given by developmentalists to such questions depend on their stances regarding the issues of nature and nurture, continuity and discontinuity, and stability and change. The answers to these questions also influence public policy decisions about children, adolescents, and adults, and influence how we each live our lives as we go through the human life span.

Now that you have learned about the field of life-span development, you might be considering a career in this field. Let's explore what types of careers are available in life-span development.

CAREERS IN LIFE-SPAN DEVELOPMENT

Careers in Life-Span Development

A career in life-span development is one of the most rewarding vocations you can pursue. In such a career you can help individuals reach their full potential and function competently. Professionals who work in the field of life-span development often feel a sense of pride in their ability to contribute in meaningful ways to people's lives. At the end of this chapter you will find an appendix, "Exploring Careers in Life-Span Development," where you can find out some of the careers that are available in this field and read about what individuals currently in life-span careers have to say about them and the importance of this course you now are taking in life-span development.

Some of you might be quite sure about what you plan to make your life's work. Others of you might not have decided on a major yet and might be uncertain which career path you want to follow. Each of us wants to find a rewarding career and enjoy the work we do.

If you decide to pursue a career in life-span development, what options are available to you? Many. College and university professors teach courses in many different areas of life-span development, education, family development, nursing, and medicine. Counselors, clinical psychologists, nurses, pediatricians, and geriatric specialists help individuals of different ages cope more effectively with their lives and improve their health and well-being. Educators and teachers help individuals become more knowledgeable.

Although an advanced degree is not absolutely necessary in some areas of life-span development, you can expand your opportunities (and income) considerably by obtaining a graduate degree. Many careers in life-span development pay reasonably well. For example, psychologists earn well above the median salary in the United States. Also, by working in the field of life-span development you can guide people in improving their lives, understand yourself and others better, possibly advance the state of knowledge in the field, and have an enjoyable time while you are doing these things.

If you are considering a career in some area of life-span development, would you prefer to work with infants? children? adolescents? the elderly? As you go this term, try to spend some time with individuals of different ages. Observe their behavior. Talk with them about their lives. Think about whether you would like to work with people of this age in your life's work.

Another important aspect of exploring careers is to talk with individuals who work in various jobs. For example, if you have some interest in becoming a school counselor, call a school, ask to speak with the counselor, and set up an appointment to discuss their career. If you have an interest in becoming a nurse, think about whether you might prefer working with babies, adolescents, or the elderly. Call a

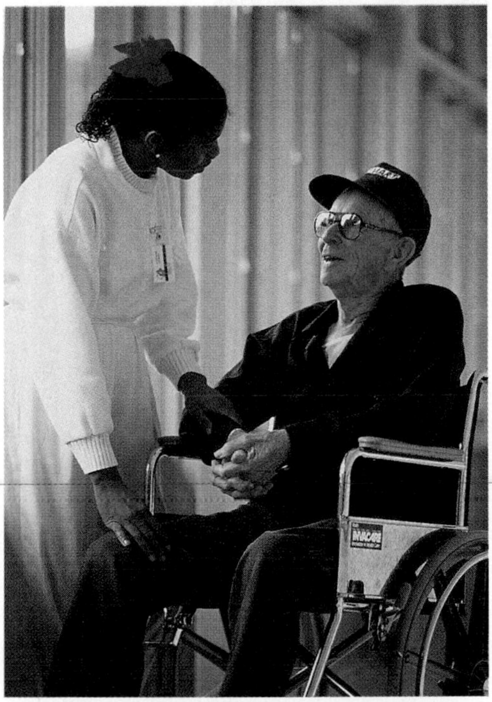

Nursing is but one of the many rewarding careers that involve life-span development. *What might be some others?*

Jobs/Careers	Degree	Education	Training	Description of Work
Audiologist	Undergraduate degree	Minimum 4 years	Courses and supervisory training in hearing science	Assess and identify presence and severity of hearing loss, as well as problems in balance
Child clinical psychologist or counseling psychologist	Ph.D or psy.D	5–7 years postundergraduate	Includes clinical training; involves a 1-year internship in a psychiatric hospital or mental health facility.	Diagnose problems, administer psychological tests, conduct psychotherapy
Child life specialist	Undergraduate degree	4 years of undergraduate study	Often trained in child development or education, but usually includes additional training in a child life program.	Work with children and their families before they are admitted to a hospital; monitor child patient's activities
Child psychiatrist	M.D.	7–9 years postundergraduate	Four years of medical school, plus an internship and residency in child psychiatry are required.	Similar to a clinical psychologist, but a psychiatrist can prescribe drugs whereas clinical psychologist cannot
Child welfare worker	Undergraduate degree is minimum	4 years minimum	Coursework and training in social work or human services.	Employed by the Child Protective Services Unit of each state to protect children's rights; monitor cases of child maltreatment
College/university professor in development, education, family development, nursing, social work	Ph.D. or master's degree	5–6 years for Ph.D. (or D.Ed.) postundergraduate; 2 years for master's degree postundergraduate	Take graduate courses, learn to conduct research, attend and present papers at professional meetings	Teach courses in child development, adolescence, adult development and aging, education, or nursing; conduct research; train undergraduates
Day-care supervisor	Varies by state	Varies by state	The Department of Public Welfare in many states publishes a booklet with the requirements for a day-care supervisor.	Direct day-care or preschool programs
Early childhood educator	Master's degree (minimum)	2 years of graduate work (minimum)	Coursework in early childhood education and practice in day-care or early childhood centers with supervised training.	Usually teach in community colleges that award a degree in early childhood education; train individuals for careers in day care
Elementary or secondary school teacher	Undergraduate degree (minimum)	4 years	Wide range of courses with a major or concentration in education.	Teach one or more subjects; prepare the curriculum; give tests, assign grades, and monitor students' progress
Family and consumer science educator	Undergraduate degree (minimum)	Four years or more	Coursework in a family and consumer education department; internship	Teaching in middle or high school about such topics as nutrition, relationships, sexuality, parenting, and human development
Gerontologist	Master's degree or Ph.D.	2–5 years postundergraduate	Coursework, research training in gerontology	Study the aging process, as well as impact of aging on government programs, social policy, and service delivery
Geriatric physician	M.D	7–9 years postundergraduate	Four years of medical school, plus a residency in geriatric medicine	Diagnose medical problems of the elderly, evaluate treatment options, and make recommendations for nursing care or other arrangements

continued

Figure **1.8** Jobs and Careers in Life-Span Development

Jobs/Careers	Degree	Education	Training	Description of Work
Geriatric nurse	R.N.	2–5 years	Courses in biological sciences, nursing care, and mental health in a school of nursing; supervised clinical training and in geriatric settings	Provide prevention and intervention for chronic and acute health problems in the elderly
Geropsychologist	Ph.D.	5–7 years postundergraduate	Includes clinical and research training, 1-yr internship, 1–2 yr post-doctoral training; license is usually required.	Provide intervention, assessment, and support for the elderly. Recommend interventions when needed.
Home health aide	No education required	——	Brief training session by agency	Provide direct services to the elderly in the elderly person's home; give assistance in basic self-care tasks
Medical social worker	M.S.W.	1–2 years postundergraduate	Undergraduate training in social work; graduate training in social work and supervised training in medical settings; state certification usually required	Coordinate a variety of support services to the elderly and their families when the elderly have a severe or long-term disability.
Pediatrician	M.D.	7–9 years of medical school	Four years of medical school, plus an internship and residency in pediatrics.	Monitor infants' and children's health, and treat their diseases; advise parents about infant and child development
Pediatric nurse	R.N.	2–5 years	Courses in biological sciences, nursing care, and pediatrics (often in a school of nursing); supervised clinical experiences in medical settings.	Monitor infants' and children's health, work to prevent disease or injury, help children achieve optimal health, and treat children with health deviations
Physical therapist	Undergraduate degree	Courses and training in physical therapy	Course work in physical therapy in a specialized program; state certification usually required	Work directly with individuals of all ages who have a physical disability to help them function as competently as possible. Consult with other professionals and coordinate services.
Preschool/kindergarten teacher	Usually undergraduate degree	4 years	Coursework in education with a specialization in early childhood education; state certification usually required.	Direct the activities of prekindergarten children, many of whom are 4 years old.
Therapeutic Recreation Specialist	Undergraduate degree minimum	4 years	Coursework in leisure studies with a concentration in therapeutic recreation. National certification usually required. Previous coursework in anatomy, special education, and psychology beneficial.	Maintain/improve quality of life for those with special needs through functional intervention, leisure education, and recreation participation. Work in hospitals, rehabilitation centers, local government agencies, and youth at risk programs among others.
Rehabilitation counselor	Master's degree or Ph.D.	2–5 years postgraduate	Coursework, clinical training, research in rehabilitation counseling	Provide rehabilitation to individuals who have impaired physical functioning.
School psychologist	Master's degree or Ph.D.	5–6 years of graduate work for Ph.D. or D.Ed.; 2 years for master's degree	Includes coursework and supervised training in school settings, usually in a department of educational psychology.	Usually, work with secondary school students, assisting them in educational and career planning; also see students who have school-related problems.

Summary Table 1.2
The Nature of Development and Careers in Life-Span Development

Concept	Processes/ Related Ideas	Characteristics/Descriptions
The Nature of Development	Biological, Cognitive, and Socioemotional Processes	• Development is influenced by an interplay of biological, cognitive, and socioemotional processes.
	Periods of Development	• The life span is commonly divided into the following periods of development: prenatal, infancy, early childhood, middle and late childhood, adolescence, early adulthood, middle adulthood, and late adulthood. • Some experts on life-span development, however, believe too much emphasis is placed on age; Neugarten believes we are moving toward a society in which age is a weaker predictor of development in adulthood.
	Age and Happiness	• In studies covering adolescence through old age, people report that they are not happier at one point in development than at others.
	Conceptions of Age	• We often think of age only in terms of chronological age. However, a full evaluation of age requires consideration of four dimensions of age: chronological, biological, psychological, and social.
	Developmental Issues	• The nature-nurture issue focuses on the extent to which development is mainly influenced by nature (biological inheritance) or nurture (experience). • Developmentalists describe development as continuous (gradual, a cumulative change) or as discontinuous (abrupt, a sequence of stages). • Is development best described as stable or changing? The stability-change issue focuses on the degree to which we become older renditions of our early experience or develop into someone different from who we were earlier in development. A special aspect of the stability-change issue is the extent to which development is determined by early versus later experiences. • Most developmentalists recognize that extreme positions on the nature-nurture, continuity-discontinuity, and stability-change issues are unwise. Despite this consensus, there is still spirited debate on these issues.
Careers in Life-Span Development	Many Options	• Careers in life-span development can be extremely rewarding. • These careers offer a number of options in the education, helping, and health professions.

hospital, ask to speak with the nursing department, and set up an appointment to speak with the nursing coordinator about a nursing career.

Something else that should benefit you is to work in one or more jobs related to your career interests while you are in college. Many colleges and universities have internships or work experiences for students who major in such fields as life-span development. In some instances, these opportunites are for course credit or pay. Take advantage of these opportunities. They can provide you with valuable experiences to help you decide if this is the right career area for you, and they can help you get into graduate school if you decide to go.

For brief descriptions of many jobs and careers in life-span development, see figure 1.8.

At this point we have discussed the nature of development and careers in life-span development. To review these ideas, see Summary Table 1.2. In the next chapter we will discuss the science of life-span development.

Careers in Life-Span Development
Exploring Psychology Careers
Nonacademic Careers in Psychology

Chapter Review

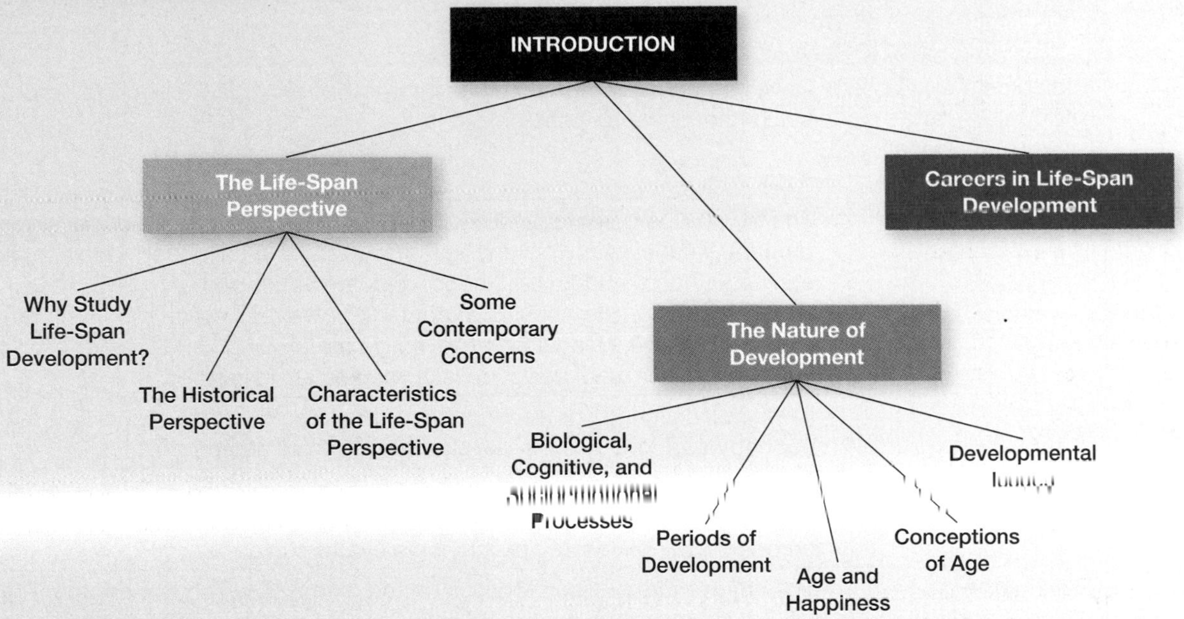

TO OBTAIN A DETAILED REVIEW OF THIS CHAPTER, STUDY THESE TWO SUMMARY TABLES:

- Summary Table 1.1 The Life-Span Perspective page 15
- Summary Table 1.2 The Nature of Development and Careers in Life-Span Development page 25

Key Terms

development 6
original sin view 7
tabula rasa view 7
innate goodness view 7
life-span perspective 9
context 12
culture 12
cross-cultural studies 12
ethnicity 13
gender 13
social policy 13
generational inequity 14
biological processes 16
cognitive processes 16
socioemotional processes 16
chronological age 18
biological age 18
psychological age 19
social age 19
nature-nurture issue 19
continuity-discontinuity issue 20
stability-change issue 20

Key People

John Locke
Jean-Jacques Rousseau
Paul Baltes
Marian Wright Edelman
Bernice Neugarten
Jerome Kagan

Taking It to the Net

1. Janice plans to join a small family practice group upon completion of her medical school pediatrician residency. Why should Janice, as a pediatrician, be involved in detecting and helping to prevent violence in the lives of her young patients?
2. Derrick has heard about a recent book that has stirred up a lot of controversy about the role of parents and peers in development. What is the book, what is its premise, and why has it generated so many strong feelings?
3. Carmen is completing her PhD in clinical psychology. She is interested in geropsychology. What are some of the areas in which geropsychologists might conduct research and practice?

Connect to www.mhhe.com/santrockld8 to research the answers and complete these exercises.

OLC Preview

To further test your knowledge of this chapter or to explore our extensive online resources that accompany *Life-Span Development,* eighth edition, please log on to the text's Online Learning Center at http://www.mhhe.com/santrockld8.com.

Chapter 2

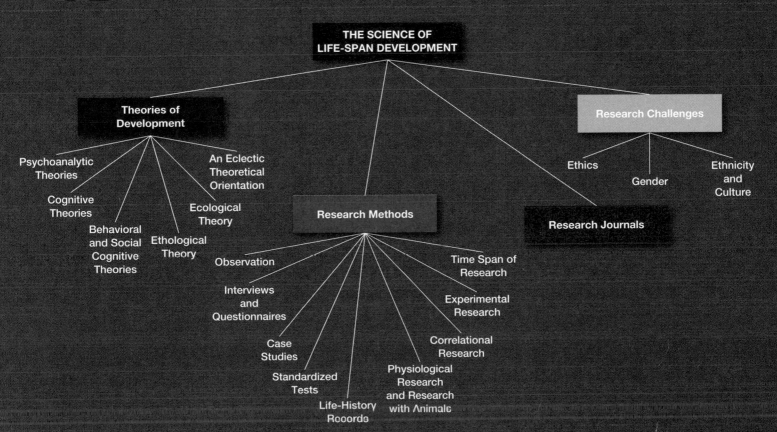

THE SCIENCE OF LIFE-SPAN DEVELOPMENT

- **Theories of Development**
  - Psychoanalytic Theories
  - Cognitive Theories
  - Behavioral and Social Cognitive Theories
  - Ethological Theory
  - Ecological Theory
  - An Eclectic Theoretical Orientation
- **Research Methods**
  - Observation
  - Interviews and Questionnaires
  - Case Studies
  - Standardized Tests
  - Life-History Records
  - Physiological Research and Research with Animals
  - Correlational Research
  - Experimental Research
  - Time Span of Research
- **Research Journals**
- **Research Challenges**
  - Ethics
  - Gender
  - Ethnicity and Culture

The Science of Life-Span Development

There is nothing quite so practical as a good theory.

Kurt Lewin
American Social Psychologist, 20th Century

Images of Life-Span Development

The Childhoods of Erikson and Piaget

IMAGINE THAT YOU have developed a major theory of development. What would influence someone such as you to construct this theory? A person interested in developing such a theory usually goes through a long university training program that culminates in a doctoral degree. As part of the training, the future theorist is exposed to many ideas about a particular area of life-span development, such as biological, cognitive, or socioemotional development. Another factor that could explain why someone develops a particular theory is that person's life experiences. Two important developmental theorists, whose views will be described later in the chapter, are Erik Erikson and Jean Piaget. Let's examine a portion of their lives as they were growing up to discover how their experiences might have contributed to the theories they developed.

Erik Homberger Erikson (1902–1994) was born near Frankfurt, Germany, to Danish parents. Before Erik was born, his parents separated, and his mother left Denmark to live in Germany. At age 3, Erik became ill, and his mother took him to see a pediatrician named Homberger. Young Erik's mother fell in love with the pediatrician, married him, and named Erik after his new stepfather.

Erik attended primary school from the ages of 6 to 10 and then the gymnasium (high school) from 11 to 18. He studied art and a number of languages rather than science courses, such as biology and chemistry. Erik did not like the atmosphere of formal schooling, and this was reflected in his grades. Rather than go to college at age 18, the adolescent Erikson wandered around Europe, keeping a diary about his experiences. After a year of travel through Europe, he returned to Germany and enrolled in art school, became dissatisfied, and enrolled in another. Later he traveled to Florence, Italy. Psychiatrist Robert Coles described Erikson at this time:

> To the Italians he was . . . the young, tall, thin Nordic expatriate with long, blond hair. He wore a corduroy suit and was seen by his family and friends as not odd or "sick" but as a wandering artist who was trying to come to grips with himself, a not unnatural or unusual struggle. (Coles, 1970, p. 15)

The second major theorist whose life we will examine is Jean Piaget. Piaget (1896–1980) was born in Neuchâtel, Switzerland. Jean's father was an intellectual who taught young Jean to think systematically. Jean's mother was also very bright. His father had an air of detachment from his mother, whom Piaget described as prone to frequent outbursts of neurotic behavior.

In his autobiography, Piaget detailed why he chose to study cognitive development rather than social or abnormal development:

> I started to forego playing for serious work very early. Indeed, I have always detested any departure from reality, an attitude which I relate to . . . my mother's poor health. It was this disturbing factor which at the beginning of my studies in psychology made me keenly interested in psychoanalytic and pathological psychology. Though this interest helped me to achieve independence and widen my cultural background, I have never since felt any desire to involve myself deeper in that particular direction, always much preferring the study of normalcy and of the workings of the intellect to that of the tricks of the unconscious. (Piaget, 1952a, p. 238)

These excerpts from Erikson's and Piaget's lives illustrate how personal experiences might influence the direction in which a particular theorist goes. Erikson's own wanderings and search for self contributed to his theory of identity development, and Piaget's intellectual experiences with his parents and schooling contributed to his emphasis on cognitive development.

Theories are part of the science of life-span development. Some individuals have difficulty thinking of life-span development as being a science in the same way that physics, chemistry, and biology are sciences. Can a discipline that studies how parents nurture children, whether watching TV long hours is linked with being overweight, and the factors involved in life satisfaction among older adults be equated with disciplines that study the molecular structure of a compound and how gravity works? Science is not defined by *what* it investigates, but by *how* it investigates. Whether you're studying photosynthesis, butterflies, Saturn's moons, or human development, it is the way you study that makes the approach scientific or not. Let's now explore the theories and methods that are at the heart of the science of life-span development.

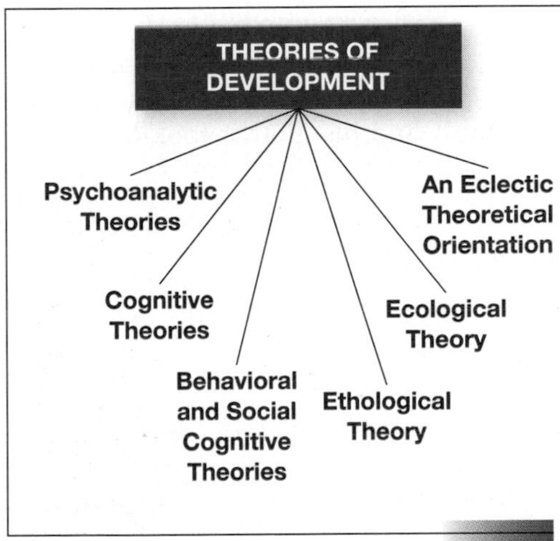

Theories of Development

As researchers formulate a problem to study, they often draw on *theories* and develop *hypotheses* (Miller, 2001). A **theory** *is an interrelated, coherent set of ideas that helps to explain and to make predictions.* **Hypotheses** *are specific assumptions and predictions that can be tested to determine their accuracy.* For example, a theory on mentoring might attempt to explain and predict why sustained support, guidance, and concrete experience make a difference in the lives of children from impoverished backgrounds. The theory might focus on children's opportunities to model the behavior and strategies of mentors, or it might focus on the effects of individual attention, which might be missing in the children's lives.

We will briefly explore five major theoretical perspectives on development: psychoanalytic, cognitive, behavioral and social cognitive, ethological, and ecological. You will read more about these theories at different points in later chapters in the book.

The diversity of theories makes understanding life-span development a challenging undertaking. Just when you think one theory has the correct explanation of life-span development, another theory crops up and makes you rethink your earlier conclusion. To keep from getting frustrated, remember that life-span development is a complex, multifaceted topic. No single theory has been able to account for all aspects of it. Each theory contributes an important piece to the life-span development puzzle. Although the theories sometimes disagree about certain aspects of life-span development, much of their information is complementary rather than contradictory. Together they let us see the total landscape of life-span development in all its richness.

theory
An interrelated, coherent set of ideas that helps to explain events and make predictions.

hypotheses
Specific assumptions and predictions that can be tested to determine their accuracy.

psychoanalytic theory
Development is primarily unconscious and heavily colored by emotion. Behavior is merely a surface characteristic. It is important to analyze the symbolic meanings of behavior. Early experiences are important in development.

In chapter 1, we described the three major processes involved in children's development: biological, cognitive, and socioemotional. The theoretical approaches that we will describe reflect these processes. Biological processes are very important in Freud's psychoanalytic and ethological theory, cognitive processes in Piaget's, Vygotsky's, information-processing, and social cognitive theories. Socioemotional processes are important in Freud's and Erikson's psychoanalytic theories, Vygotsky's sociocultural cognitive theory, behavioral and social cognitive theories, and ecological theory. To begin our exploration of theories of child development, we will examine the first of the theories proposed: psychoanalytic.

Psychoanalytic Theories

Psychoanalytic theory *describes development as primarily unconscious—that is, beyond awareness—and as heavily colored by emotion. Psychoanalytic theorists believe that behavior is merely a surface characteristic and that, to truly understand development, we have to analyze the symbolic meanings of behavior and the deep inner workings of the mind. Psychoanalytic theorists also stress that early experiences with parents extensively shape our development.* These characteristics are highlighted in the main psychoanalytic theory, that of Sigmund Freud.

Freud's Theory Freud (1856–1939) developed his ideas about psychoanalytic theory from work with mental patients. He was a medical doctor who specialized in neurology. He spent most of his years in Vienna, though he moved to London near the end of his career because of the Nazis' anti-Semitism.

Freud (1917) believed that personality has three structures: the id, the ego, and the superego. The *id* is the Freudian structure of personality that consists of instincts, which are an individual's reservoir of psychic energy. In Freud's view, the id is totally unconscious; it has no contact with reality. As children experience the demands and constraints of reality, a new structure of personality emerges—the *ego,* the Freudian structure of personality that deals with the demands of reality. The ego is called the executive branch of personality because it uses reasoning to make decisions. The id and the ego have no morality. They do not take into account whether something is right or wrong. The *superego* is the Freudian structure of personality that is the moral branch of personality. The superego takes into account whether something is right or wrong. Think of the superego as what we often refer to as our "conscience." You probably are beginning to sense that both the id and the superego make life rough for the ego. Your ego might say, "I will have sex only occasionally and be sure to take the proper precautions because I don't want the intrusion of a child in the development of my career." However, your id is saying, "I want to be satisfied; sex is pleasurable." Your superego is at work, too: "I feel guilty about having sex."

As Freud listened to, probed, and analyzed his patients, he became convinced that their problems were the result of experiences early in life. Freud believed that we go

Careers in Life-Span Development

Saundra Boyd, Community College Instructor

Saundra Boyd went back to graduate school after doing volunteer work, including teaching parenting skills with the American Red Cross and making decisions about allocations for United Way. Her interest in learning more about how parents rear children and determining which programs are effective in helping improve children's lives motivated her to obtain a doctorate in psychology, which she did at the University of Houston.

Saundra now teaches life-span development and other psychology courses in the Houston Community College system. She feels that teaching life-span development is like an extension of parent training, with the potential to communicate to the many students in her courses effective messages about parenting and helping children. She says that a number of her students tell her that they wish they had taken this course on life-span development before they had children of their own.

In the classroom, Saundra encourages students to relate life-span development to themselves and the people in their lives. She also challenges them to do something creative and become motivated to make this a better world in which to live.

In addition to teaching five classes a term, Saundra also counsels and advises students, manages a website, and serves on a number of committees. She also works with the Center for Healing Racism, where she has started a newsletter and website, served on the board of directors, facilitated workshops, and written grants to obtain funds for the center.

Saundra Boyd (in blue dress) in her community college class on life-span development.

Freud's Theory

Sigmund Freud, the pioneering architect of psychoanalytic theory. *How did Freud believe each individual's personality is organized?*

through five stages of psychosexual development, and that at each stage of development we experience pleasure in one part of the body more than in others ◀ P. 12. *Erogenous zones,* according to Freud, are parts of the body that have especially strong pleasure-giving qualities at particular stages of development.

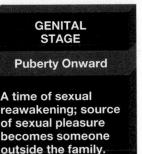

Freud thought that our adult personality is determined by the way we resolve conflicts between these early sources of pleasure—the mouth, the anus, and then the genitals—and the demands of reality. When these conflicts are not resolved, the individual may become fixated at a particular stage of development. *Fixation* occurs when the individual remains locked in an earlier developmental stage because needs are under- or overgratified. For example, a parent might wean a child too early, be too strict in toilet training the child, punish the child for masturbation, or "smother" the child with too much attention. Figure 2.1 illustrates the five Freudian stages.

ORAL STAGE
Birth to 1½ Yrs.
Infant's pleasure centers on the mouth.

ANAL STAGE
1½ to 3 Yrs.
Child's pleasure focuses on the anus.

PHALLIC STAGE
3 to 6 Yrs.
Pleasure focuses on the genitals.

LATENCY STAGE
6 Yrs. to Puberty
Child represses sexual interest and develops social and intellectual skills.

GENITAL STAGE
Puberty Onward
A time of sexual reawakening; source of sexual pleasure becomes someone outside the family.

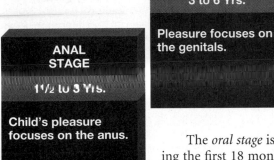

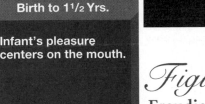

Figure **2.1**
Freudian Stages

The *oral stage* is the first Freudian stage of development, occurring during the first 18 months of life, in which the infant's pleasure centers around the mouth. Chewing, sucking, and biting are the chief sources of pleasure. These actions reduce tension in the infant.

The *anal stage* is the second Freudian stage of development, occurring between 1½ and 3 years of age, in which the child's greatest pleasure involves the anus or the eliminative functions associated with it. In Freud's view, the exercise of anal muscles reduces tension.

The *phallic stage* is the third Freudian stage of development, which occurs between the ages of 3 and 6; its name comes from the Latin word *phallus,* which means "penis." During the phallic stage, pleasure focuses on the genitals as both boys and girls discover that self-manipulation is enjoyable.

In Freud's view, the phallic stage has a special importance in personality development because it is during this period that the Oedipus complex appears. This name comes from Greek mythology, in which Oedipus, the son of the King of Thebes, unwittingly kills his father and marries his mother. The *Oedipus complex* according to Freudian theory, is the young child's development of an intense desire to replace the same-sex parent and enjoy the affections of the opposite-sex parent.

How is the Oedipus complex resolved? At about 5 to 6 years of age, children recognize that their same-sex parent might punish them for their incestuous wishes. To reduce this conflict, the child identifies with the same-sex parent, striving to be like him or her. If the conflict is not resolved, though, the individual may become fixated at the phallic stage.

The *latency stage* is the fourth Freudian stage of development, which occurs between approximately 6 years of age and puberty; the child represses all interest in sexuality and develops social and intellectual skills. This activity channels much of the child's energy into emotionally safe areas and helps the child forget the highly stressful conflicts of the phallic stage.

The *genital stage* is the fifth and final Freudian stage of development, occurring from puberty on. The genital stage is a time of sexual reawakening; the source of sexual pleasure now becomes someone outside of the family. Freud believed that unresolved con-

"So, Mr. Fenton . . . Let's begin with your mother."

flicts with parents reemerge during adolescence. When resolved, the individual is capable of developing a mature love relationship and functioning independently as an adult.

Freud's theory has undergone significant revisions by a number of psychoanalytic theorists (Eagle, 2000; Westin, 2000). Many contemporary psychoanalytic theorists place less emphasis on sexual instincts and more emphasis on cultural experiences as determinants of an individual's development. Unconscious thought remains a central theme, but most contemporary psychoanalysts believe that conscious thought makes up more of the mind than Freud envisioned. Next, we will explore the ideas of an important revisionist of Freud's ideas—Erik Erikson.

Erikson's Theory Erik Erikson (1902–1994) recognized Freud's contributions but believed that Freud misjudged some important dimensions of human development. For one, Erikson (1950, 1968) said we develop in *psychosocial* stages, in contrast to Freud's *psychosexual* stages. For Freud, the primary motivation for human behavior was sexual in nature, for Erikson it was social and reflected a desire to affiliate with other people. Erikson emphasized developmental change throughout the human life span, whereas Freud argued that our basic personality is shaped in the first five years of life. In **Erikson's theory,** *eight stages of development unfold as we go through the life span* (see figure 2.2). *Each stage consists of a unique developmental task that confronts individuals with a crisis that must be faced.* According to Erikson, this crisis is not a catastrophe but a turning point of increased vulnerability and enhanced potential. The more an individual resolves the crises successfully, the healthier development will be (Hopkins, 2000).

Trust versus mistrust is Erikson's first psychosocial stage, which is experienced in the first year of life. A sense of trust requires a feeling of physical comfort and a minimal amount of fear and apprehension about the future. Trust in infancy sets the stage for a lifelong expectation that the world will be a good and pleasant place to live.

Autonomy versus shame and doubt is Erikson's second stage of development, occurring in late infancy and toddlerhood (1–3 years). After gaining trust in their caregivers, infants begin to discover that their behavior is their own. They start to assert their sense of independence, or autonomy. They realize their *will.* If infants are restrained too much or punished too harshly, they are likely to develop a sense of shame and doubt.

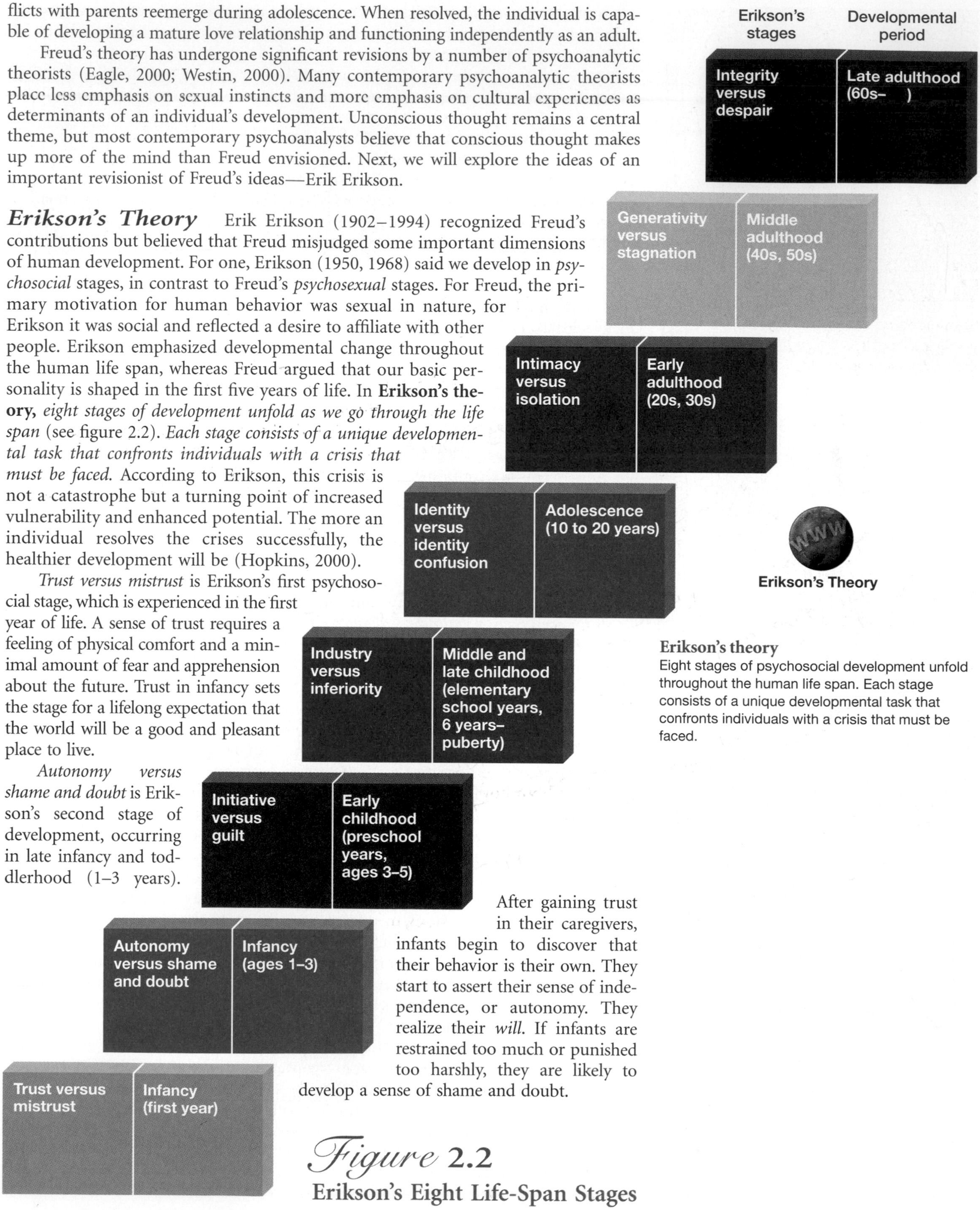

Figure **2.2**
Erikson's Eight Life-Span Stages

Erikson's Theory

Erikson's theory
Eight stages of psychosocial development unfold throughout the human life span. Each stage consists of a unique developmental task that confronts individuals with a crisis that must be faced.

Erik Erikson with his wife, Joan, an artist. Erikson generated one of the most important developmental theories of the twentieth century. *Which stage of Erikson's theory are you in? Does Erikson's description of this stage characterize you?*

Initiative versus guilt is Erikson's third stage of development, occurring during the preschool years. As preschool children encounter a widening social world, they are challenged more than when they were infants. Active, purposeful behavior is needed to cope with these challenges. Children are asked to assume responsibility for their bodies, their behavior, their toys, and their pets. Developing a sense of responsibility increases initiative. Uncomfortable guilt feelings may arise, though, if the child is irresponsible and is made to feel too anxious. Erikson has a positive outlook on this stage. He believes that most guilt is quickly compensated for by a sense of accomplishment.

Industry versus inferiority is Erikson's fourth developmental stage, occurring approximately in the elementary school years. Children's initiative brings them in contact with a wealth of new experiences. As they move into middle and late childhood, they direct their energy toward mastering knowledge and intellectual skills. At no other time is the child more enthusiastic about learning than at the end of early childhood's period of expansive imagination. The danger in the elementary school years is the development of a sense of inferiority—of feeling incompetent and unproductive. Erikson believes that teachers have a special responsibility for children's development of industry. Teachers should "mildly but firmly coerce children into the adventure of finding out that one can learn to accomplish things which one would never have thought of by oneself" (Erikson, 1968, p. 127).

Identity versus identity confusion is Erikson's fifth developmental stage, which individuals experience during the adolescent years. At this time, individuals are faced with finding out who they are, what they are all about, and where they are going in life. Adolescents are confronted with many new roles and adult statuses—vocational and romantic, for example. Parents need to allow adolescents to explore many different roles and different paths within a particular role. If the adolescent explores such roles in a healthy manner and arrives at a positive path to follow in life, then a positive identity will be achieved. If an identity is pushed on the adolescent by parents, if the adolescent does not adequately explore many roles, and if a positive future path is not defined, then identity confusion reigns.

Intimacy versus isolation is Erikson's sixth developmental stage, which individuals experience during the early adulthood years. At this time, individuals face the developmental task of forming intimate relationships with others. Erikson describes intimacy as finding oneself yet losing oneself in another. If the young adult forms healthy friendships and an intimate relationship with another individual, intimacy will be achieved; if not, isolation will result.

Generativity versus stagnation is Erikson's seventh developmental stage, which individuals experience during middle adulthood. A chief concern is to assist the younger generation in developing and leading useful lives—this is what Erikson means by generativity. The feeling of having done nothing to help the next generation is stagnation.

Integrity versus despair is Erikson's eighth and final stage of development, which individuals experience in late adulthood. This involves reflecting on the past and either piecing together a positive review or concluding that one's life has not been well spent. Through many different routes, the older person may have developed a positive outlook in most or all of the previous stages of development. If so, the retrospective glances will reveal a picture of a life well spent, and the person will feel a sense of satisfaction—integrity will be achieved. If the older adult resolved many of the earlier stages negatively, the retrospective glances likely will yield doubt or gloom—the despair Erikson talks about.

Erikson does not believe that the proper solution to a stage crisis is always completely positive. Some exposure or commitment to the negative end of the person's bipolar conflict is sometimes inevitable—you cannot trust all people under all circumstances and survive, for example. Nonetheless, in the healthy solution to a stage crisis, the positive resolution dominates. We will discuss Erikson's theory again on a number of occasions in the chapters on socioemotional development in this book.

Evaluating the Psychoanalytic Theories The contributions of psychoanalytic theories include their emphases on these factors:

- Early experiences play an important part in development.
- Family relationships are a central aspect of development.
- Personality can be better understood if it is examined developmentally.
- The mind is not all conscious; unconscious aspects of the mind need to be considered.
- Changes take place in the adulthood as well as the childhood years (Erikson).

These are some criticisms of psychoanalytic theories:

- The main concepts of psychoanalytic theories have been difficult to test scientfically.
- Much of the data used to support psychoanalytic theories come from individuals' reconstruction of the past, often the distant past, and are of unknown accuracy.
- The sexual underpinnings of development are given too much importance (especially in Freud's theory).
- The unconscious mind is given too much credit for influencing development.
- Psychoanalytic theories present an image of humans that is too negative (especially Freud).
- Psychoanalytic theories are culture- and gender-biased.

To read about such culture and gender bias, see the Sociocultural Worlds of Development box.

Cognitive Theories

Whereas psychoanalytic theories stress the importance of children's unconscious thoughts, cognitive theories emphasize their conscious thoughts. Three important cognitive theories are Piaget's cognitive development theory, Vygotsky's sociocultural cognitive theory, and the information-processing approach.

Piaget's theory will be covered in greater detail later in this book, when we discuss cognitive development in infancy, early childhood, middle and late childhood, and adolescence. Here we briefly present the main ideas of his theory.

Piaget's Cognitive Developmental Theory The famous Swiss psychologist Jean Piaget (1896–1980) proposed an important theory of cognitive development. **Piaget's theory** *states that children actively construct their understanding of the world and go through four stages of cognitive development.* Two processes underlie this cognitive construction of the world: organization and adaptation. To make sense of our world, we organize our experiences. For example, we separate important ideas from less important ideas. We connect one idea to another. But not only do we organize our observations and experiences, we also *adapt* our thinking to include new ideas because additional information furthers understanding. Piaget (1954) believed that we adapt in two ways: assimilation and accommodation.

Piaget's theory
Children actively construct their understanding of the world and go through four stages of cognitive development.

Assimilation *occurs when individuals incorporate new information into their existing knowledge.* **Accommodation** *occurs when individuals adjust to new information.* Consider a circumstance in which a 9-year-old girl is given a hammer and nails to hang a picture on the wall. She has never used a hammer, but from observation and vicarious experience she realizes that a hammer is an object to be held, that it is swung by the handle to hit the nail, and that it is usually swung a number of times. Recognizing each of these things, she fits her behavior into this information she already has (assimilation). However, the hammer is heavy, so she holds it near the top. She swings too hard and the nail bends, so she adjusts the pressure of her strikes. These adjustments reveal her ability to alter slightly her conception of the world (accommodation).

assimilation
In Piaget's theory, an individual's incorporation of new information into her or his existing knowledge.

accommodation
In Piaget's theory, an individual's adjustment to new information.

Piaget thought that assimilation and accommodation operate even in the very young infant's life. Newborns reflexively suck everything that touches their lips (assimilation), but, after several months of experience, they construct their understanding of the world differently. Some objects, such as fingers and the mother's breast, can be sucked, but others, such as fuzzy blankets, should not be sucked (accommodation).

OCIOCULTURAL WORLDS OF DEVELOPMENT

Cultural and Gender Bias in Freud's Theory

EDIPUS COMPLEX was one of Freud's most influential epts, involving early psychosexual relationships for r personality development. Freud's theory was devel-ped during the Victorian era of the late nineteenth cen-ury, when the male was dominant and the female was passive, and when sexual interests, especially the female's, were repressed.

Many psychologists believe Freud overemphasized behavior's biological determinants and did not give adequate attention to sociocultural influences. In particular, his view on the differences between males and females has a strong biological flavor and focuses on anatomical differences. That is, Freud argued that because they have a penis, boys develop a dominant, powerful personality, and that girls, because they do not have a penis, develop a submissive, weak personality. In basing his view of male/female differences in personality development on anatomical differences, Freud ignored the enormous impact of culture and experience in determining the personalities of the male and the female (Nolen-Hoeksema, 1998).

Three-quarters of a century ago, English anthropologist Bronislaw Malinowski (1927) observed the behavior of the Trobriand islanders of the Western Pacific. He found that the Oedipus complex is not universal but depends on cultural variations in families. The family pattern of the Trobriand islanders is different than in many cultures. In the Trobriand Islands, the biological father is not the head of the household. This role is reserved for the mother's brother, who acts as a disciplinarian. Thus, the Trobriand islanders tease apart the roles played by the same person in Freud's Vienna and in many other cultures. In Freud's view, this different family constellation should make no difference. The Oedipus complex should still emerge, in which the father is the young boy's hated rival for the mother's love. However, Malinowski found no indication of conflict between fathers and sons in the Trobriand islanders. However, he did observe some negative feelings directed by the boy toward the maternal uncle.

The first feminist-based criticism of Freud's theory was proposed by psychoanalytic theorist Karen Horney (1967). She developed a model of women with positive feminine qualities and self-evaluation. Her critique of Freud's theory included reference to a male-dominant society and culture. Rectification of the male bias in psychoanalytic theory continues today.

Karen Horney developed the first feminist-based criticism of Freud's theory. Horney's model emphasizes women's positive qualities and self-evaluation. *Where did Horney think Freud was off base?*

Horney's Theory
Piaget's Theory

Piaget also believed that we go through four stages in understanding the world (see figure 2.3). Each of the stages is age-related and consists of distinct ways of thinking. Remember, it is the *different* way of understanding the world that makes one stage more advanced than another; knowing *more* information does not make the child's thinking more advanced, in the Piagetian view. This is what Piaget meant when he said the child's cognition is *qualitatively* different in one stage compared to another (Vidal, 2000). What are Piaget's four stages of cognitive development like?

The *sensorimotor stage*, which lasts from birth to about 2 years of age, is the first Piagetian stage. In this stage, infants construct an understanding of the world by coordinating sensory experiences (such as seeing and hearing) with physical, motoric actions—hence the term *sensorimotor*. At the beginning of this stage, newborns have little more than reflexive patterns with which to work. At the end of the stage, 2-year-olds have complex sensorimotor patterns and are beginning to operate with primitive symbols.

The *preoperational stage,* which lasts from approximately 2 to 7 years of age, is the second Piagetian stage. In this stage, children begin to represent the world with words, images, and drawings. Symbolic thought goes beyond simple connections of sensory information and physical action. However, although preschool children can symbolically represent the world, according to Piaget, they still lack the ability to perform *operations,* the Piagetian term for internalized mental actions that allow children to do mentally what they previously did physically.

The *concrete operational stage,* which lasts from approximately 7 to 11 years of age, is the third Piagetian stage. In this stage, children can perform operations, and logical reasoning replaces intuitive thought as long as reasoning can be applied to specific or concrete examples. For instance, concrete operational thinkers cannot imagine the steps necessary to complete an algebraic equation, which is too abstract for thinking at this stage of development.

The *formal operational stage,* which appears between the ages of 11 and 15, is the fourth and final Piagetian stage. In this stage, individuals move beyond concrete experiences and think in abstract and more logical terms. As part of thinking more abstractly, adolescents develop images of ideal circumstances. They might think about what an ideal parent is like and compare their parents to this ideal standard. They begin to entertain possibilities for the future and are fascinated with what they can be. In solving problems, formal operational thinkers are more systematic, developing hypotheses about why something is happening the way it is, then testing these hypotheses in a deductive manner. We will further examine Piaget's cognitive developmental theory in chapters 6, 8, 10, 12, and 14.

SENSORIMOTOR STAGE
The infant constructs an understanding of the world by coordinating sensory experiences with physical actions. An infant progresses from reflexive, instinctual action at birth to the beginning of symbolic thought toward the end of the stage.
Birth to 2 years of age
PREOPERATIONAL STAGE
The child begins to represent the world with words and images. These words and images reflect increased symbolic thinking and go beyond the connection of sensory information and physical action.
2–7 years of age
CONCRETE OPERATIONAL STAGE
The child can now reason logically about concrete events and classify objects into different sets.
7–11 years of age
FORMAL OPERATIONAL STAGE
The adolescent reasons in more abstract, idealistic, and logical ways.
11 years of age through adulthood

Figure **2.3**
Piaget's Four Stages of Cognitive Development

Jean Piaget, the famous Swiss developmental psychologist, changed the way we think about the development of children's minds. *What are some key ideas in Piaget's theory?*

Vygotsky's Sociocultural Cognitive Theory

Like Piaget, Russian Lev Vygotsky (1896–1934) also believed that children actively construct their knowledge. **Vygotksy's theory** *is a sociocultural cognitive theory that emphasizes developmental analysis, the role of language, and social relations.* Vygotsky was born in Russia in the same year as Piaget, but he died much earlier, at the age of 37. Both Piaget's and Vygotsky's ideas remained virtually unknown to American scholars for many years, not being introduced to American audiences through English translations until the 1960s. In the past several decades, American psychologists and educators have shown increased interest in Vygotsky's (1962) views.

Three claims capture the heart of Vygotsky's view (Tappan, 1998): (1) the child's cognitive skills can be understood only when they are developmentally analyzed and interpreted, (2) cognitive skills are mediated by words, language, and forms of discourse, which serve as psychological tools for facilitating and transforming mental

Vygotksy's theory
A sociocultural cognitive theory that emphasizes developmental analysis, the role of language, and social relations.

There is considerable interest today in Lev Vygotsky's sociocultural cognitive theory of child development. *What were Vygotsky's three basic claims about children's development?*

Vygotsky's Theory

information-processing approach
The approach that emphasizes that individuals manipulate information, monitor it, and strategize about it. Central to information processing are the processes of memory and thinking.

activity, and (3) cognitive skills have their origins in social relations and are embedded in a sociocultural backdrop.

For Vygotsky, taking a developmental approach means that, in order to understand any aspect of the child's cognitive functioning, one must examine its origins and transformations from earlier to later forms. Thus, a particular mental act, such as using private speech (speech-to-self), cannot be viewed accurately in isolation but should be evaluated as a step in a gradual developmental process.

Vygotsky's second claim, that to understand cognitive functioning it is necessary to examine the tools that mediate and shape it, led him to believe that language is the most important of these tools. Vygotsky argued that, in early childhood, language begins to be used as a tool that helps the child plan activities and solve problems.

Vygotsky's third claim was that cognitive skills originate in social relations and culture. Vygotsky portrayed the child's development as inseparable from social and cultural activities. He believed that the development of memory, attention, and reasoning involves learning to use the inventions of society, such as language, mathematical systems, and memory strategies. In one culture, this might consist of learning to count with the help of a computer. In another, it might consist of counting on one's fingers or using beads.

Vygotsky's theory has stimulated considerable interest in the view that knowledge is *situated* and *collaborative* (Greeno, Collins, & Resnick, 1996; Kozulin, 2000; Rogoff, 1998). That is, knowledge is distributed among people and environments, which include objects, artifacts, tools, books, and the communities in which people live. This suggests that knowing can best be advanced through interaction with others in cooperative activities.

Within these basic claims, Vygotsky articulated unique and influential ideas about the relation between learning and development. In chapter 8, "Physical and Cognitive Development in Early Childhood," we will further explore Vygotsky's contributions to our understanding of children's development.

The Information-Processing Approach

The **information-processing approach** *emphasizes that individuals manipulate information, monitor it, and strategize about it. Central to this approach are the processes of memory and thinking.* According to the information-processing approach, individuals develop a gradually increasing capacity for processing information, which allows them to acquire increasingly complex knowledge and skills (Bjorklund & Rosenbaum, 2000; Chen & Siegler, 2000; Siegler, 2001). Unlike Piaget's cognitive developmental theory, the information-processing approach does not describe development as stagelike.

Although a number of factors stimulated the growth of the information-processing approach, none was more important than the computer, which demonstrated that a machine could perform logical operations. Psychologists began to wonder if the logical operations carried out by computers might tell us something about how the human mind works. They drew analogies to computers to explain the relation between cognition or thinking and the brain. The physical brain is said to be analogous to the computer's hardware, cognition is said to be analogous to its software. Although computers and software are not perfect analogies for brains and cognitive activities, the comparison contributed to our thinking about the mind as an active information-processing system.

Robert Siegler (1998), a leading expert on children's information processing, believes that thinking is information processing. He says that when individuals perceive, encode, represent, store, and retrieve information, they are thinking. Siegler especially thinks that an important aspect of development is to learn good strategies for processing information. For example, in becoming a better reader this might involve learning to monitor the key themes of the material being read.

Evaluating the Cognitive Theories

The contributions of cognitive theories include these:

- The cognitive theories present a positive view of development, emphasizing individuals' conscious thinking.

Summary Table 2.1
Psychoanalytic and Cognitive Theories

Concept	Processes/ Related Ideas	Characteristics/Descriptions
Psychoanalytic Theories	Freud's Theory	• Personality is made up of three structures—id, ego, and supergo. The conflicting demands of these structures produce anxiety. • Most of children's thoughts are unconscious. • Freud was convinced that problems develop because of early experiences. • Individuals go through five psychosexual stages—oral, anal, phallic, latency, and genital.
	Erikson's Theory	• His theory emphasizes these eight psychosocial stages of development: trust vs. mistrust, autonomy vs. shame and doubt, initiative vs. guilt, industry vs. inferiority, identity vs. identity confusion, intimacy vs. isolation, generativity vs. stagnation, and integrity vs. despair.
	Evaluating the Psychoanalytic Theories	• Their contributions include an emphasis on a developmental framework. • One criticism is that they lack scientific support.
Cognitive Theories	Piaget's Cognitive Developmental Theory	• Piaget proposed a cognitive developmental theory. • Children use the processes of organization and adaptation (assimilation and accomodation) to understand their world. • Children go through four cognitive stages: sensorimotor, preoperational, concrete operational, and formal operational.
	Vygotsky's Sociocultural Cognitive Theory	• His theory consists of three basic claims about development: (1) Cognitive skills need to be interpreted developmentally, (2) cognitive skills are mediated by language, and (3) cognitive skills have their origins in social relations and culture.
	The Information-Processing Approach	• This view emphasizes that individuals manipulate information, monitor it, and strategize about it. • The development of computers stimulated interest in this approach.
	Evaluating the Cognitive Theories	• Their contributions include an emphasis on the active construction of understanding. • One criticism is that they give too little attention to individual variations.

- The cognitive theories (especially Piaget's and Vygotsky's) emphasize the individual's active construction of understanding.
- Piaget's and Vygotsky's theories underscore the importance of examining developmental changes in children's thinking.
- The information-processing approach offers detailed descriptions of cognitive processes.

These are some criticisms of cognitive theories:

- There is skepticism about the pureness of Piaget's stages.
- The cognitive theories do not give adequate attention to individual variations in cognitive development.
- The information-processing approach does not provide an adequate description of development changes in cognition.
- Psychoanalytic theorists argue that the cognitive theories do not give enough credit to unconscious thought.

At this point we have studied a number of ideas about psychoanalytic and cognitive theories. A review of these ideas is presented in summary table 2.1. Next, we

continue our exploration of theories of development by examining behavioral and social cognitive theories.

Behavioral and Social Cognitive Theories

Behavioral and Social Cognitive Theories

Behaviorists essentially believe that scientifically we can study only what can be directly observed and measured. At about the same time as Freud was interpreting patients' unconscious minds through their early childhood experiences, Ivan Pavlov and John B. Watson were conducting detailed observations of behavior in controlled laboratory settings. Out of the behavioral tradition grew the belief that development is observable behavior that can be learned through experience with the environment. The three versions of the behavioral approach that we will explore are Pavlov's classical conditioning, Skinner's operant conditioning, and social cognitive theory.

Pavlov's Classical Conditioning In the early 1900s, Russian physiologist Ivan Pavlov (1927) knew that dogs innately salivate when they taste food. He became curious when he observed that dogs salivate to various sights and sounds before eating their food. For example, when an individual paired the ringing of a bell with the food, the bell ringing subsequently developed the ability to elicit the salivation of the dogs when it was presented by itself. Pavlov discovered the principle of *classical conditioning,* in which a neutral stimulus (in our example, ringing a bell) acquires the ability to produce a response originally produced by another stimulus (in our example, food).

In the 1920s, John Watson wanted to show that Pavlov's concept of classical conditioning could be applied to human beings. A little boy named Albert was shown a white rat to see if he was afraid of it. He was not. As Albert played with the rat, a loud nose was sounded behind his head. As you might imagine, the noise caused little Albert to cry. After only several pairings of the loud noise and the white rat, Albert begin to fear the rat even when the noise was not sounded (Watson & Raynor, 1920). Today, we could not ethically conduct such an experiment. Later in the chapter we will discuss the ethical precautions that must be taken in studying individuals.

B. F. Skinner was a tinkerer who liked to make new gadgets. The younger of his two daughters, Deborah, was raised in Skinner's enclosed Air-Crib, which he invented because he wanted to control her environment completely. The Air-Crib was sound-proofed and temperature controlled. Debbie, shown here as a child with her parents, is currently a successful artist, is married, and lives in London. *What do you think about Skinner's Air-Crib?*

Many of our fears—fear of the dentist from a painful experience, fear of driving from being in an automobile incident, fear of heights from falling off a high chair when we were infants, and fear of dogs from being bitten—can be learned through classical conditioning.

Skinner's Operant Conditioning In B. F. Skinner's (1938) *operant conditioning,* the consequences of a behavior produce changes in the probability of the behavior's occurrence. If a behavior is followed by a rewarding stimulus it is more likely to recur, but if a behavior is followed by a punishing stimulus it is less likely to recur. For example, when a person smiles at a child after the child has done something, the child is more likely to engage in the activity than if the person gives the child a nasty look.

For Skinner, such rewards and punishments shape individuals' development. For example, Skinner's approach argues that shy people learned to be shy because of the environmental experiences they had while growing up. It follows that rearranging environmental experiences can help a shy person become more socially oriented.

Social Cognitive Theory Some psychologists believe that the behaviorists basically are right when they say development is learned and is influenced strongly by environmental experiences. However, they believe that Skinner went too far in declaring that cognition is unimportant in understanding development. **Social cognitive theory** *is the view of psychologists who emphasize behavior, environment, and cognition as the key factors in development.*

social cognitive theory
The theory that behavior, environment, and person/cognitive factors are important in understanding development.

American psychologists Albert Bandura (1986, 1998, 2000) and Walter Mischel (1973, 1995) are the main architects of social cognitive theory's contemporary version, which Mischel (1973) initially labeled *cognitive* social learning theory. Both Bandura and Mischel believe that cognitive processes are important mediators of environment-behavior connections. Bandura's early research program focused heavily on observational learning, learning that occurs through observing what others do. Observational learning is also referred to as imitation or modeling. What is *cognitive* about observational learning in Bandura's view? Bandura (1925–) believes that people cognitively represent the behavior of others and then sometimes adopt this behavior themselves. For example, a young boy might observe his father's aggressive outbursts and hostile interchanges with people; when observed with his peers, the young boy's style of interaction is highly aggressive, showing the same characteristics as his father's behavior. A girl might adopt the dominant and sarcastic style of her teacher. When observed interacting with her younger brother, she says, "You are so slow. How can you do this work so slowly?" Social cognitive theorists believe that people acquire a wide range of such behaviors, thoughts, and feelings through observing others' behavior. These observations form an important part of life-span development.

Albert Bandura

Albert Bandura has been one of the leading architects of social cognitive theory. *What is the nature of his theory?*

Bandura's (1986, 1998, 2000) most recent model of learning and development involves behavior, the person, and the environment. As shown in figure 2.4, behavior, personal (and cognitive), and environmental factors operate interactively. Behavior can influence personal factors and vice versa. The person's cognitive activities can influence the environment, the environment can change the person's cognition, and so on.

Let's consider how Bandura's model might work in the case of a college student's achievement behavior. As the student diligently studies and gets good grades, her behavior produces positive thoughts about her abilities. As part of her effort to make good grades, she plans and develops a number of strategies to make her studying more efficient. In these ways, her behavior has influenced her thought and her thought has influenced her behavior. At the beginning of the term, her college made a special effort to involve students in a study skills program. She decided to join. Her success, along with that of other students who attended the program, has led the college to expand the program next semester. In these ways, environment influenced behavior, and behavior changed the environment. And the college administrators' expectations that the study skills program would work made it possible in the first place. The program's success has spurred expectations that this type of program could work in other colleges. In these ways, cognition changed the environment, and the environment changed cognition.

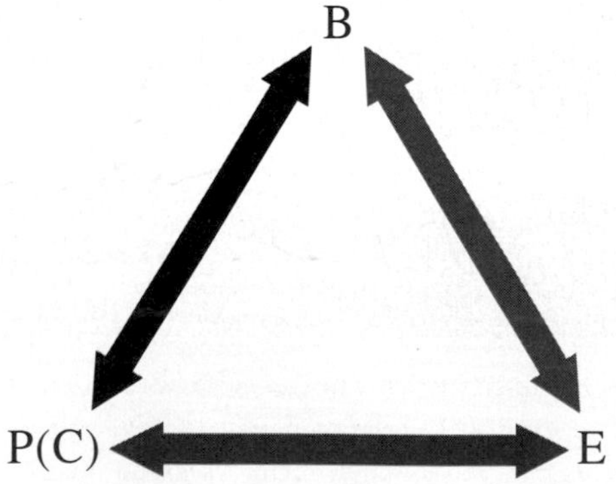

Figure **2.4**

Bandura's Social Cognitive Model

P(C) stands for personal and cognitive factors, *B* for behavior, and *E* for environment. The arrows reflect how relations between these factors are reciprocal rather than unidirectional.

Evaluating the Behavioral and Social Cognitive Theories

Contributions of behavioral and social cognitive theories include their emphases on these factors:

- The importance of scientific research
- The environmental determinants of behavior
- The importance of observational learning (Bandura)
- Person and cognitive factors (social cognitive theory)

These are some of the criticisms of the behavioral and social cognitive theories:

- Too little emphasis on cognition (Pavlov, Skinner)
- Too much emphasis on environmental determinants
- Inadequate attention to developmental changes
- Too mechanical and inadequate consideration of the spontaneity and creativity of humans

Behavioral and social cognitive theories emphasize the importance of environmental experiences in human development. Next we turn our attention to a theory that underscores the importance of biological foundations of development—ethological theory.

Ethological Theory

Sensitivity to different kinds of experience varies over the life span. The presence or absence of certain experiences at particular times in the life span influences individuals well beyond the time they first occur. Ethologists believe that most psychologists underestimate the importance of these special time frames in early development. Ethologists also stress the powerful roles that evolution and biological foundations play in development (Rosenzweig, 2000).

Ethology emerged as an important view because of the work of European zoologists, especially Konrad Lorenz (1903–1989). **Ethology** *stresses that behavior is strongly influenced by biology, is tied to evolution, and is characterized by critical or sensitive periods.*

ethology
An approach that stresses that behavior is strongly influenced by biology, tied to evolution, and characterized by critical or sensitive periods.

Working mostly with greylag geese, Lorenz (1965) studied a behavior pattern that was considered to be programmed within the birds' genes. A newly hatched gosling seemed to be born with the instinct to follow its mother. Observations showed that the gosling was capable of such behavior as soon as it hatched. Lorenz proved that it was incorrect to assume that such behavior was programmed in the animal. In a remarkable set of experiments, Lorenz separated the eggs laid by one goose into two groups. One group he returned to the goose to be hatched by her. The other group was hatched in an incubator. The goslings in the first group performed as predicted. They followed their mother as soon as they hatched. However, those in the second group, which saw Lorenz when they first hatched, followed him everywhere, as though he were their mother. Lorenz marked the goslings and then placed both groups under a box. Mother goose and "mother" Lorenz stood aside as the box lifted. Each group of goslings went directly to its "mother" (see figure 2.5). Lorenz called this process *imprinting,* the rapid, innate learning within a limited critical period of time that involves attachment to the first moving object seen.

WWW
Exploring Ethology

When imprinting studies go awry

The ethological view of Lorenz and the European zoologists forced American developmental psychologists to recognize the importance of the biological basis of behavior. However, the research and theorizing of ethology still seemed to lack some ingredients that would elevate it to the ranks of the other theories discussed so far in this chapter. In particular, there was little or nothing in the classical ethological view about the nature of social relationships across the human life span, something that any major theory of development must explain. Also, its concept of *critical period,* a fixed time period very early in development during which certain behaviors optimally emerge, seemed to be overdrawn. Classical ethological theory was weak in

Figure **2.5**
Konrad Lorenz, a pioneering student of animal behavior, is followed through the water by three imprinted greylag geese. Describe Lorenz's experiment with the geese. *Do you think his experiment would have the same results with human babies? Explain.*

stimulating studies with humans. Recent expansion of the ethological view has improved its status as a viable developmental perspective.

One of the most important applications of ethological theory to human development involves John Bowlby's (1969, 1989) theory of attachment. Bowlby argues that attachment to a caregiver over the first year of life has important consequences thoughout the life span. In his view, if this attachment is positive and secure, the individual will likely develop more positive in childhood and adulthood. If is negative and insecure, life-span development will likely not be optimal. In chapter 7, "Socioemotional Development in Infancy," we will explore the concept of infant attachment in much greater detail.

Urie Bronfenbrenner developed ecological theory, a perspective that is receiving increased attention. His theory emphasizes the importance of both micro and macro dimensions of the environment in which the child lives.

Evaluating Ethological Theory These are some of the contributions of ethological theory:

- Increased focus on the biological and evolutionary basis of development
- Use of careful observations in naturalistic settings
- Emphasis on sensitive periods of development

These are some criticisms of ethological theory:

- The concepts of critical and sensitive periods might be too rigid
- Too strong an emphasis on biological foundations
- Inadequate attention to cognition
- The theory has been better at generating research with animals than with humans

In addition to ethological theory, another theory that emphasizes the biological aspects of human development—evolutionary psychology—will be presented in chapter 3, "Biological Beginnings," along with views on the role of heredity in development. Also, we will examine a number of biological theories of aging in chapter 18, "Physical Development in Late Adulthood."

Ecological Theory

While ethological theory stresses biological factors, ecological theory emphasizes environmental factors. One ecological theory that has important implications for understanding life-span development was created by Urie Bronfenbrenner (1917–).

ecological theory
Bronfenbrenner's environmental system view of development, involving five environmental systems—microsystem, mesosystem, exosystem, macrosystem, and chronosystem. These emphasize the role of social contexts in development.

Ecological theory *is Bronfenbrenner's environmental system view of development. It consists of five environmental systems ranging from the fine-grained inputs of direct interactions with social agents to the broad-based inputs of culture. The five systems in Bronfenbrenner's ecological theory are the microsystem, mesosystem, exosystem, macrosystem, and chronosystem.* Bronfenbrenner's (1986, 1995, 2000; Bronfenbrenner & Morris, 1998) ecological model is shown in figure 2.6. The *microsystem* in Bronfenbrenner's ecological theory is the setting in which the individual lives. These contexts include the person's family, peers, school, and neighborhood ◀ P. 12. It is in the microsystem that the most direct interactions with social agents take place—with parents, peers, and teachers, for example. The individual is not viewed as a passive recipient of experiences in these settings, but as someone who helps to construct the settings. Bronfenbrenner points out that most research on sociocultural influences has focused on microsystems.

The *mesosystem* in Bronfenbrenner's ecological theory involves relations between microsystems or connections between contexts. Examples are the relation of family experiences to school experiences, school experiences to church experiences, and family experiences to peer experiences. For example, children whose parents have rejected them may

Critical Thinking

Imagine Growing Up Somewhere Else

IMAGINE WHAT it would be like to live in a culture that offered few choices compared to the Western world. Think about Communist China during the Cultural Revolution, where young rural people could not select their job or their mate and were not given the choice of migrating to the city. Imagine also living in a cultural context in the United States that is different from yours. For instance, if you live in a rural, suburban, or small-town area, what would your life be like if you lived in an inner city where most services have moved out, schools are inferior, poverty is extreme, and crime is common?

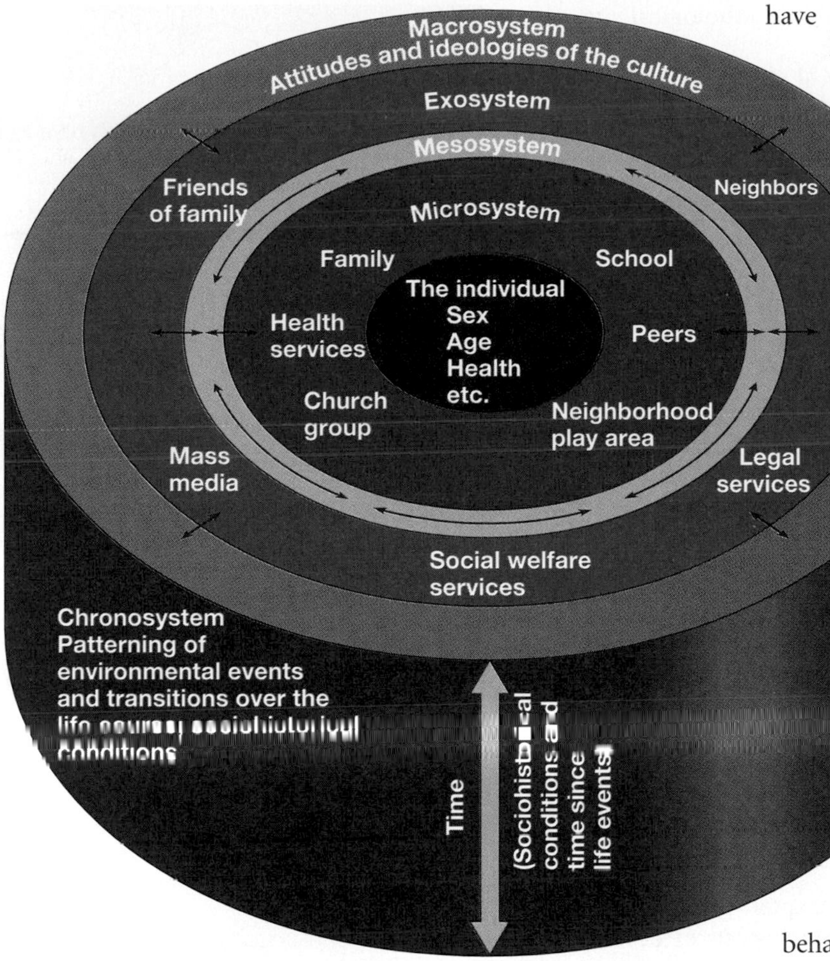

Figure 2.6
Bronfenbrenner's Ecological Theory of Development

Bronfenbrenner's ecological theory consists of five environmental systems: microsystem, mesosystem, exosystem, macrosystem, and chronosystem.

have difficulty developing positive relations with teachers. Developmentalists increasingly believe it is important to observe behavior in multiple settings—such as family, peer, and school contexts—to obtain a more complete picture of the individual's development (Booth & Dunn, 1996).

The *exosystem* in Bronfenbrenner's ecological theory is involved when experiences in another social setting—in which the individual does not have an active role—influence what the individual experiences in an immediate context. For example, work experiences can affect a woman's relationship with her husband and their child. The mother might receive a promotion that requires more travel, which might increase marital conflict and change patterns of parent-child interaction. Another example of an exosystem is the city government, which is responsible for the quality of parks, recreation centers, and library facilities for children and adolescents. Yet another example is the federal government through its role in the quality of medical care and support systems for the elderly.

The *macrosystem* in Bronfenbrenner's ecological theory involves the culture in which individuals live. Remember from chapter 1 that culture refers to the behavior patterns, beliefs, and all other products of a group of people that are passed on from generation to generation ◄ P. 12. Remember also that *cross-cultural studies*—the comparison of one culture with one or more other cultures—provide information about the generality of development.

The *chronosystem* in Bronfenbrenner's ecological theory involves the patterning of environmental events and transitions over the life course, as well as sociohistorical circumstances. For example, in studying the effects of divorce on children, researchers have found that the negative effects often peak in the first year after the divorce. The effects also are more negative for sons than for daughters (Hetherington, 1995). By 2 years after the divorce, family interaction is less chaotic and more stable. With regard to sociocultural circumstances, women today are much more likely to be encouraged to pursue a career than they were 20 or 30 years ago. In ways such as these, the chronosystem has a powerful impact on our development.

Bronfenbrenner (1995; Bronfenbrenner & Morris, 1998) recently added biological influences to his theory and now describes it as a bioecological theory. Nonetheless, ecological, environmental contexts still predominate in Bronfenbrenner's theory (Ceci, 2000).

Bronfenbrenner's Theory
Bronfenbrenner and a Multicultural Framework

Evaluating Ecological Theory

These are some of the contributions of ecological theory:

- A systematic examination of macro and micro dimensions of environmental systems
- Attention to connections between environmental settings (mesosystem)
- Consideration of sociohistorical influences on development (chronosystem)

These are some criticisms of ecological theory:

- Even with the added discussion of biological influences in recent years, there is still too little attention to biological foundations of development
- Inadequate attention to cognitive processes

An Eclectic Theoretical Orientation

An **eclectic theoretical orientation** *does not follow any one theoretical approach but, rather, selects and uses from each theory whatever is considered the best in it.* No single theory described in this chapter is indomitable or capable of explaining entirely the rich complexity of life-span development. Each of the theories has made important contributions to our understanding of development, but none provides a complete description and explanation. Psychoanalytic theory best explains the unconscious mind. Erikson's theory best describes the changes that occur in adult development. Piaget's, Vygotsky's, and the information-processing views provide the most complete description of cognitive development. The behavioral and social cognitive and ecological theories have been the most adept at examining the environmental determinants of development. The ethological theories have made us aware of biology's role and the importance of sensitive periods in development. It is important to recognize that, although theories are helpful guides, relying on a single theory to explain development is probably a mistake.

eclectic theoretical orientation
An approach that does not follow any one theoretical approach, but instead selects and uses whatever is considered the best in many different theories.

An attempt was made in this chapter to present five theoretical perspectives objectively. The same eclectic orientation will be maintained throughout the book. In this way, you can view the study of development as it actually exists—with different theorists making different assumptions, stressing different empirical problems, and using different strategies to discover information.

The theories that we have discussed were developed at different points in the twentieth century. To see when these theories were proposed, see figure 2.7.

These theoretical perspectives, along with research issues that were discussed in chapter 1 and methods that will be described shortly, provide a sense of development's scientific nature. Figure 2.8 compares the main theoretical perspectives in terms of how they view important developmental issues and the methods used to study life-span development.

In addition to the grand theories discussed in this chapter, which serve as general frameworks for thinking about and interpreting many aspects of development, there are many more "local" theories, or mini-models, that guide research in specific areas (Kuhn, 1998, Parke & Buriel, 1998). For example, in chapter 5 you will read

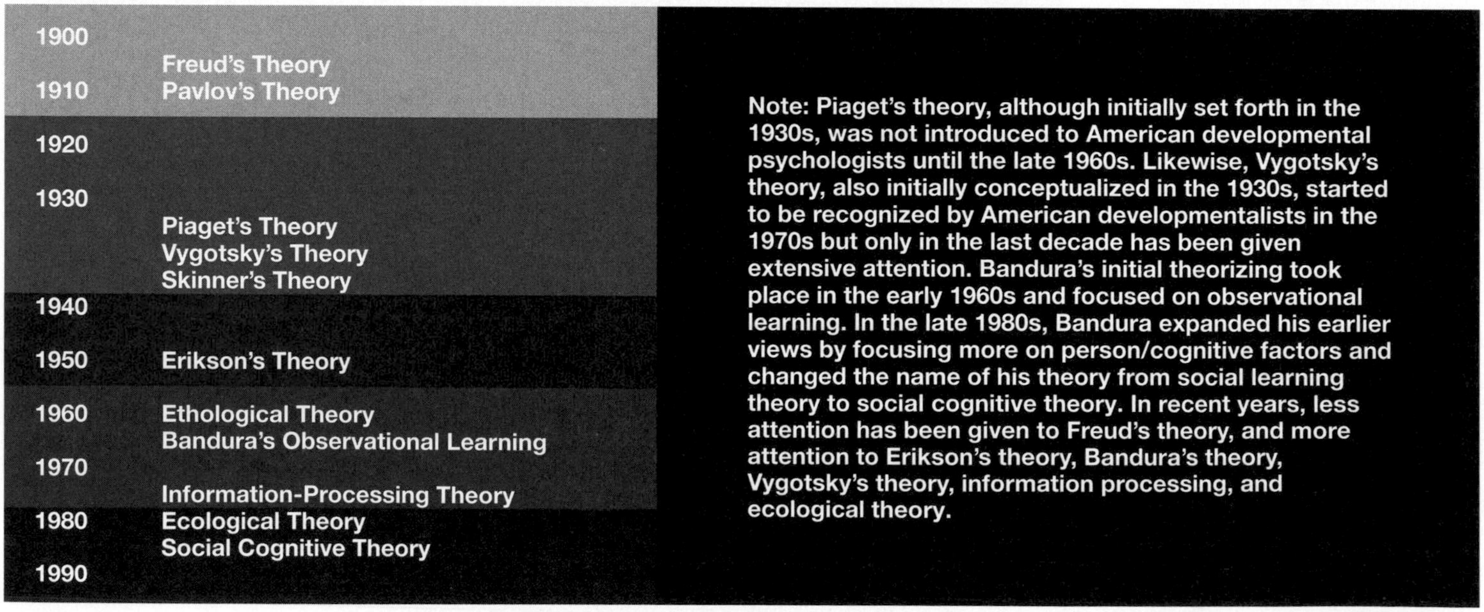

Figure 2.7
Time Line for Major Developmental Theories

Theory	Issues and methods		
	Continuity/discontinuity, early versus later experiences	*Biological and environmental factors*	*Importance of cognition*
Psychoanalytic	Discontinuity between stages—continuity between early experiences and later development; early experiences very important; later changes in development emphasized in Erikson's theory	Freud's biological determination interacting with early family experiences; Erikson's more balanced biological-cultural interaction perspective	Emphasized, but in the form of unconscious thought
Cognitive	Discontinuity between stages in Piaget's theory; continuity between early experiences and later development in Piaget's and Vygotsky's theory; no stages in Vygotsky's theory or information-processing approach	Piaget's emphasis on interaction and adaptation; environment provides the setting for cognitive structures to develop; information-processing view has not addressed this issue extensively but mainly emphasizes biological-environmental interaction	The primary determinant of behavior
Behavioral and social cognitive	Continuity (no stages); experience at all points of development important	Environment viewed as the cause of behavior in both views	Strongly deemphasized in the behavioral approach but an important mediator in social cognitive theory
Ethological	Discontinuity but no stages; critical or sensitive periods emphasized; early experiences very important	Strong biological view	Not emphasized
Ecological	Little attention to continuity/discontinuity; change emphasized more than stability	Strong environmental view	Not emphasized

Figure **2.8**

A Comparison of Theories and Issues in Life-Span Development

Summary Table 2.2
Behavioral and Social Cognitive Theories, Ethological Theory, Ecological Theory, and an Eclectic Theoretical Orientation

Concept	Processes/ Related Ideas	Characteristics/Descriptions
Behavioral and Social Cognitive Theories	Pavlov's Classical Conditioning	• A neutral stimulus acquires the ability to produce a response originally produced by another stimulus.
	Skinner's Operant Conditioning	• The consequences of a behavior produce changes in the probability of the behavior's occurrence.
	Social Cognitive Theory	• In Bandura's view, observational learning is a key aspect of life-span development. • Bandura emphasizes reciprocal interactions among the person (cognition), behavior, and environment.
	Evaluating the Behavioral and Social Cognitive Theories	• Contributions include an emphasis on scientific research. • One criticism is that they give inadequate attention to developmental changes.
Ethological Theory	Lorenz	• Imprinting and critical periods are key concepts.
	Evaluating Ethological Theory	• Contributions include a focus on the biological and evolutionary basis of development. • Criticisms include a belief that the critical and sensitive period concepts are too rigid.
Ecological Theory	Bronfenbrenner	• In Bronfenbrenner's theory, five environmental systems are important: microsystem, mesosystem, exosystem, macrosystem, and chronosystem.
	Evaluating Ecological Theory	• Contributions include a systematic examination of macro and micro dimensions of enviornmental systems. • One criticism is that it gives inadequate attention to biological and cognitive factors.
Eclectic Theoretical Orientation	Complexity, Specificity	• No single theory can explain the rich, complex nature of child development. Each of these theories has made a different contribution. • Many "local" theories, or mini-models, also guide research in specific areas of child development.

about the recently developed dynamic systems theory (Thelen & Smith, 1998), which offers an explanation of infant perceptual-motor development; you will also read about the old and new approaches to parent-adolescent relationships in chapter 13, theories of adult personality development in chapter 17, and social theories of aging in chapter 20.

The "micro" theories focus on a specific aspect or time frame of development, seeking precise explanations of that particular dimension. As you read the remaining chapters of this book, you will come across many of these more focused views. Together, the grand theories and the micro approaches give us a more complete view of how the fascinating journey of development unfolds.

At this point we have studied a number of ideas about the behavioral and social cognitive theories, ethological theory, ecological theory, and an eclectic theoretical orientation. A review of these ideas is presented in summary table 2.2. Next, we will explore the methods that scientists use to study life-span development.

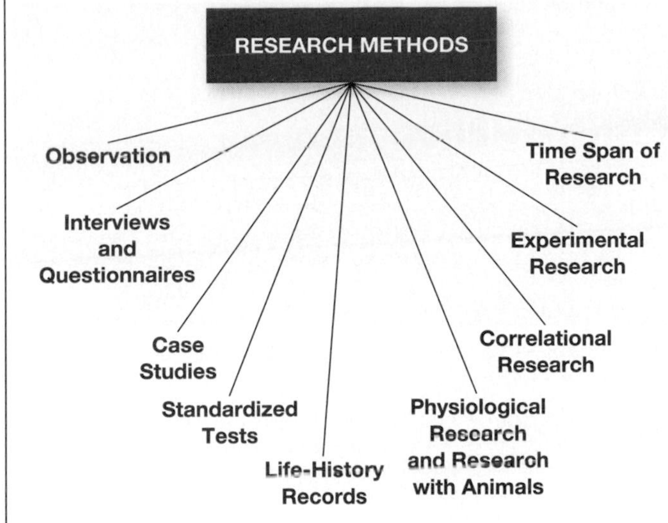

Research Methods

In addition to theories, the scientific study of development also involves research. We will begin our research inquiry with an overview of the measures researchers use to obtain information about development.

When researchers want to find out, for example, if cocaine taken by pregnant women will affect the fetus, if academic preschool programs place too much stress on young children, if watching a lot of MTV detracts from adolescents' learning in school, or if social support decreases depression in older adults, they can choose from many methods. We will discuss these methods separately, but recognize that ofen more than one is used in a single study.

Observation

Sherlock Holmes chided his assistant, Watson, "You see but you do not observe." We look at things all the time; however, casually watching two children interacting is not the same as the type of observation used in scientific studies. Scientific observation is highly systematic. It requires knowing what you are looking for, conducting observations in an unbiased manner, accurately recording and categorizing what you see, and effectively communicating your observations (Kerig & Lindahl, 2001; McBurney, 2001).

Science refines everyday thinking.

Albert Einstein
German-Born American Physicist, 20th Century

A common way to record observations is to write them down, often using shorthand or symbols. In addition, tape recorders, video cameras, special coding sheets, one-way mirrors, and computers increasingly are being used to make observations more efficient (Kerig & Lindahl, 2000).

Observations can be made in either laboratories or naturalistic settings (Hartmann & George, 1999). A **laboratory** *is a controlled setting from which many of the complex factors of the real world have been removed.* Some researchers conduct studies in laboratories at the colleges or universities where they teach. Although laboratories often help researchers gain more control over the behavior of the participants, laboratory studies have been criticized as being artificial. In **naturalistic observation,** *behavior is observed outside of a laboratory, in the so-called real world.* Researchers conduct naturalistic observations in classrooms, at home, at youth centers, at museums, in neighborhoods, in nursing homes, and in other settings.

laboratory
A controlled setting from which many of the complex factors of the real world have been removed.

naturalistic observation
Observations that take place out in the real world instead of in a laboratory.

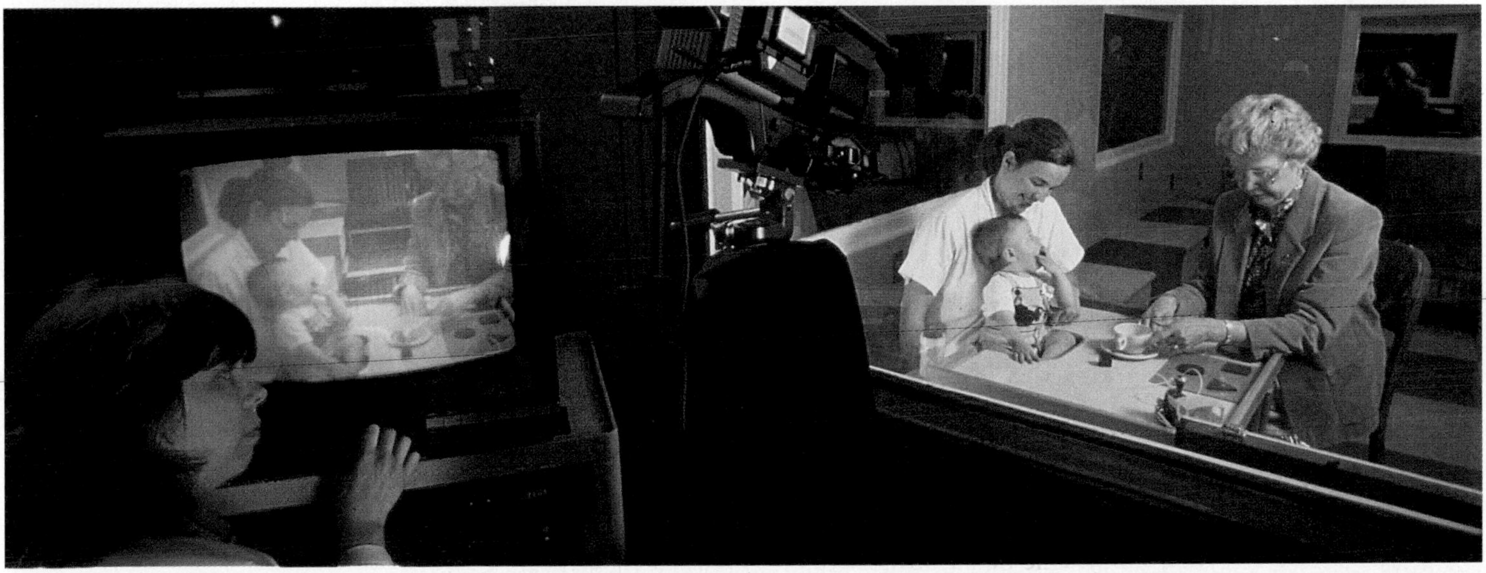

In this research study, mother-child interaction is being videotaped. Later, researchers will code the interaction using precise categories. *What methods other than observation might researchers use to study mothers and children?*

Interviews and Questionnaires

Sometimes the quickest and best way to get information about people is to ask them for it. Researchers use interviews and questionnaires (surveys) to find out about experiences, beliefs, and feelings. Most interviews take place face-to-face, although they can be done over the phone or via the Internet. **Questionnaires** *are usually given to individuals in printed form, and they are asked to fill them out. This can be done in person, by mail, or via the Internet.*

questionnaire
A method similar to a highly structured interview except that respondents read the questions and mark their answers on paper rather than respond verbally to the interviewer.

Good interviews and surveys involve concrete, specific, and unambiguous questions and a means of checking the authenticity of the respondents' replies. However, interviews and surveys are not without problems. One crucial limitation is that many individuals give socially desirable answers, responding in a way they think is most socially acceptable and desirable, rather than how they truly think or feel. For example, when asked whether they cheat on tests in school, some individuals may say that they don't, even though they do, because it is socially undesirable to cheat. Skilled interviewing techniques and questions that increase forthright responses are critical in obtaining accurate information.

Case Studies

A **case study** *is an in-depth look at an individual.* It often is used when unique aspects of a person's life cannot be duplicated, for either practical or ethical reasons. A case study provides information about an individual's fears, hopes, fantasies, traumatic experiences, upbringing, family relationships, health, and anything else that helps a psychologist understand that person's development.

case study
An in-depth look at an individual.

Although case studies provide dramatic, in-depth portrayals of people's lives, we need to exercise caution when generalizing from this information. The subject of a case study is unique, with a genetic makeup and experiences no one else shares. In addition, case studies involve judgments of unknown reliability, in that usually no check is made to see if other psychologists agree with the observations.

Standardized Tests

Standardized tests *are commercially prepared tests that assess individuals' performance in different domains.* Many standardized tests allow an individual's performance to be compared with the performance of others at the same age or grade level, in many cases on a national basis (Aiken, 2000; Walsh & Betz, 2001). Individuals might take a number of standardized tests, including tests that assess their intelligence, achievement, personality, career interests, and other skills. These tests could be for a variety of purposes, including providing outcome measures for research studies, information that helps psychologists and educators make decisions about an individual, and comparisons of individuals' performance across schools, states, and countries (Murphy & Davidshofer, 2001).

standardized tests
Tests that require people to answer a series of questions and that have two distinct features: (1) Usually the individual's score is totaled to yield a single score, or set of scores, that reflects something about the individual; (2) the individual's score is compared to the scores of a large group of similar people to determine how the individual responded relative to others.

Life-History Records

Life-history records *are records of information about a lifetime chronology of events and activities. They often involve a combination of data records on education, work, family, and residence.* These records may be generated by obtaining information from archival materials (public records or historical documents) or interviews with a respondent (which might include obtaining a life calendar from the person). Life calendars record the age (year and month) at which transitions occur in a variety of activity domains and life events, thus portraying an unfolding life course. In compiling life-history records, researchers increasingly use a wide array of materials, including written and oral reports from the subject, vital records, observation, and public documents (Clausen, 1993). One of the advantages of the multiple-materials approach is that information from varied sources can be compared and discrepancies sometimes can be resolved, resulting in a more accurate life-history record.

life-history records
Records of a lifetime chronology of events and activities; often a combination of data records on education, work, family, and residence.

Physiological Research and Research with Animals

Two additional methods that psychologists use to gather data are physiological research and research with animals. Research on the biological basis of behavior and technological advances continue to produce remarkable insights about development. For example, researchers have found that electrical stimulation of certain areas of the brain turns docile, mild-mannered people into hostile, vicious attackers. Higher concentrations of some hormones are associated with anger in adolescents (Dorn & Chrousos, 1996).

Since much physiological research cannot be carried out with humans, psychologists sometimes use animals (Suomi, 1996). Animal studies permit researchers to control their subjects' genetic background, diet, experiences during infancy, and many other factors (Drickamer, Vessey, & Mickle, 1996). In studying humans, psychologists treat these factors as random variation, or "noise," that may interfere with accurate results. In addition, animal researchers can investigate the effects of treatments (brain implants, for example) that would be unethical with humans. Moreover, it is possible to track the entire life span of some animals over a relatively short period of time. Laboratory mice, for instance, have a life span of approximately one year.

Correlational Research
Experimental Research

correlational research
Research whose goal is to describe the strength of the relation between two or more events or characteristics.

experimental research
Research involving experiments that permit the determination of cause. A carefully regulated procedure in which one or more of the factors believed to influence the behavior being studied are manipulated and all other factors are held constant.

Correlational Research

In **correlational research,** *the goal is to describe the strength of the relation between two or more events or characteristics.* Correlational research is useful because, the more strongly two events are correlated (related or associated), the more effectively we can predict one from the other (McMillan, 2000). For example, if researchers find that low-involved, permissive parenting is correlated with a child's lack of self-control, it suggests that low-involved, permissive parenting might be one source of the lack of self-control.

A caution is in order, however. *Correlation does not equal causation.* The correlational finding just mentioned does not mean that permissive parenting necessarily causes low self-control in children. It could mean that, but it also could mean that a child's lack of self-control caused the parents to simply throw up their arms in despair and give up trying to control the child. It also could mean that other factors, such as heredity or poverty, caused the correlation between permissive parenting and low self-control in children. Figure 2.9 illustrates these possible interpretations of correlational data.

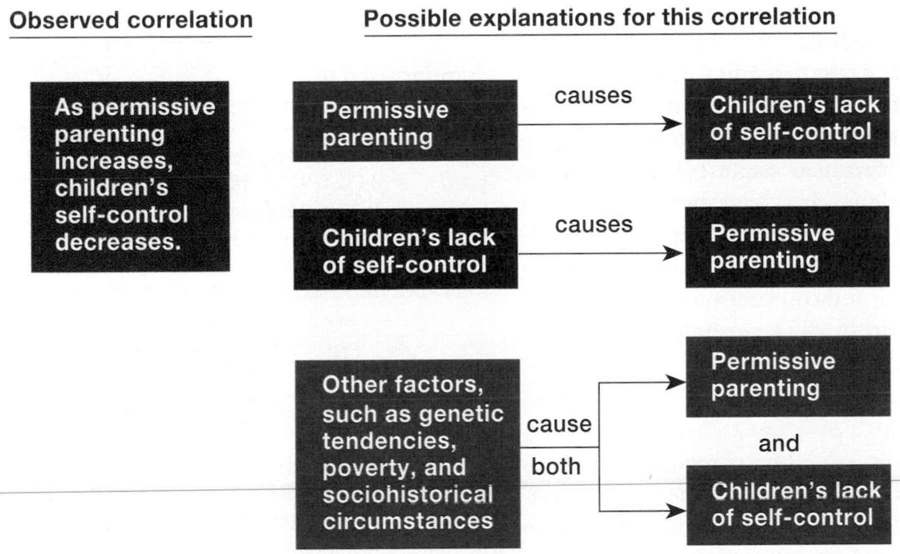

Figure **2.9**
Possible Explanations for Correlational Data
An observed correlation between two events cannot be used to conclude that one event caused the other. Some possibilities are that the second event caused the first event or that a third, unknown event caused the correlation between the first two events.

Experimental Research

Experimental research *allows researchers to determine the causes of behavior. They accomplish this task by performing an experiment, a carefully regulated procedure in which one or more of the factors believed to influence the behavior being studied are manipulated and all other factors are held constant. If the behavior under study changes when a factor is manipulated, we say the manipulated factor causes the behavior to change.* "Cause" is the event being manipulated. "Effect" is the

behavior that changes because of the manipulation. Experimental research is the only truly reliable method of establishing cause and effect. Because correlational research does not involve the manipulation of factors, it is not a dependable way to isolate cause (Kantowitz, Roediger, & Elmes, 2001).

Experiments involve at least one independent variable and one dependent variable. The **independent variable** *is the manipulated, influential, experimental factor.* The label "independent" indicates that this variable can be changed independently of any other factors. For example, suppose we want to design an experiment to study the effects of peer tutoring on children's achievement. In this example, the amount and type of peer tutoring could be independent variables. The **dependent variable** *is the factor that is measured in an experiment. It can change as the independent variable is manipulated.* The label *dependent* is used because this variable depends on what happens to the participants in an experiment as the independent variable is manipulated. In the peer tutoring study, achievement is the dependent variable. This might be assessed in a number of ways. Let's say in this study it is measured by scores on a nationally standardized achievement test.

independent variable
The manipulated, influential, experimental factor in an experiment.

dependent variable
The factor that is measured as the result of an experiment.

In experiments, the independent variable consists of differing experiences that are given to one or more experimental groups and one or more control groups. An **experimental group** *is a group whose experience is manipulated.* A **control group** *is a group that is treated in every way like the experimental group except for the manipulated factor.* The control group serves as the baseline against which the effects of the manipulated condition can be compared. In the peer tutoring study, we need to have one group of adolescents that gets peer tutoring (experimental group) and one that doesn't (control group).

experimental group
A group whose experience is manipulated in an experiment.

control group
A comparison group in an experiment that is treated in every way like the experimental group except for the manipulated factor.

random assignment
In experimental research, the assignment of participants to experimental and control groups by chance.

Another important principle of experimental research is **random assignment,** *which involves assigning participants to experimental and control groups by chance.* This practice reduces the likelihood that the experiment's results will be due to any preexisting differences between the groups. In our study of peer tutoring, random assignment greatly reduces the probability that the two groups will differ on such factors as age, family background initial achievement, intelligence, personality, and health.

To summarize the study of peer tutoring and achievement, children are randomly assigned to one of two groups: one (the experimental group) is given peer tutoring; the other (control group) is not. The independent variables consist of the differing experiences that the experimental and control groups receive. After the peer tutoring is completed, the adolescents are given a nationally standardized achievement test (dependent variable). Figure 2.10 illustrates the experimental research method applied to a different problem: the effects of aerobic exercise by pregnant women on their newborns' breathing and sleeping patterns.

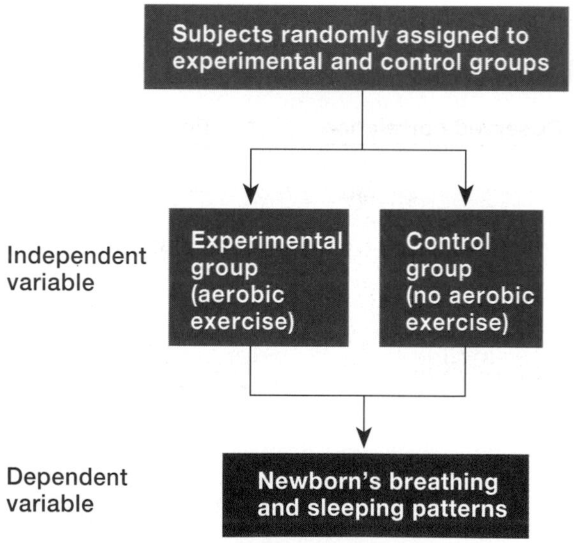

Figure **2.10**
Principles of the Experimental Strategy
The effects of aerobic exercise by pregnant women on their newborns' breathing and sleeping patterns.

Time Span of Research

A special concern of developmentalists is the time span of a research investigation (Miller, 1998). Studies that focus on the relation of age to some other variable are common in life-span development. We have several options: We can study different individuals of different ages and compare them; we can study the same individuals as they age over time; or we can use some combination of these two approaches.

Cross-Sectional Approach The **cross-sectional approach** *is a research strategy in which individuals of different ages are compared at one time.* A typical cross-sectional study might include a group of 5-year-olds, 8-year-olds, and 11-year-olds. Another might include a group of 15-year-olds, 25-year-olds, and 45-year-olds. The different groups can be compared with respect to a

cross-sectional approach
A research strategy in which individuals of different ages are compared at one time.

variety of dependent variables: IQ, memory, peer relations, attachment to parents, hormonal changes, and so on. All of this can be accomplished in a short time. In some studies data are collected in a single day. Even in large-scale cross-sectional studies with hundreds of subjects, data collection does not usually take longer than several months to complete.

The main advantage of the cross-sectional study is that the researcher does not have to wait for the individuals to grow up or become older. Despite its time efficiency, the cross-sectional approach has its drawbacks. It gives no information about how individuals change or about the stability of their characteristics. The increases and decreases of development—the hills and valleys of growth and development—can become obscured in the cross-sectional approach. For example, in a cross-sectional approach to perceptions of life satisfaction, average increases and decreases might be revealed. But the study would not show how the life satisfaction of individual adults waxed and waned over the years. It also would not tell us whether adults who had positive or negative perceptions of life satisfaction as young adults maintained their relative degree of life satisfaction as middle-aged or older adults.

longitudinal approach
A research strategy in which the same individuals are studied over a period of time, usually several years or more.

Longitudinal Approach The **longitudinal approach** *is a research strategy in which the same individuals are studied over a period of time, usually several years or more.* For example, if a study of life satisfaction were conducted longitudinally, the same adults might be assessed periodically over a 70-year time span—at the ages of 20, 35, 45, 65, and 90, for example.

Although longitudinal studies provide a wealth of information about such important issues as stability and change in development and the importance of early experience for later development, they are not without their problems (Raudenbush, 2001). They are expensive and time-consuming. The longer the study lasts, the more subjects drop out—they move, get sick, lose interest, and so forth. Subjects can bias the outcome of a study, because those who remain may be dissimilar to those who drop out. Those individuals who remain in a longitudinal study over a number of years may be more compulsive and conformity-oriented, for example, or they might have more stable lives.

sequential approach
A combined cross-sectional, longitudinal design.

Sequential Approach Sometimes developmentalists also combine the cross-sectional and longitudinal approaches to learn about life-span development (Schaie, 1993). The **sequential approach** *is the combined cross-sectional, longitudinal design. In most instances, this approach starts with a cross-sectional study that includes individuals of different ages. A number of months or years after the initial assessment, the same individuals are tested again—this is the longitudinal aspect of the design. At this later time, a new group of subjects is assessed at each age level.* The new groups at each level are added at the later time to control for changes that might have taken place in the original group—some might have dropped out of the study, or retesting might have improved their performance, for example. The sequential approach is complex, expensive, and time-consuming, but it does provide information that is impossible to obtain from cross-sectional or longitudinal approaches alone. The sequential approach has been especially helpful in examining cohort effects in life-span development, which we will discuss next.

cohort effects
Effects that are due to a person's time of birth or generation but not to age.

Cohort Effects **Cohort effects** *are due to a person's time of birth or generation but not to actual age* ◄ P. 10. For example, cohorts can differ in years of education, child-rearing practices, health, attitudes toward sex, religious values, and economic status (see figure 2.11). Cohort effects are important because they can powerfully affect the dependent measures in a study ostensibly concerned with age. Researchers have shown that cohort effects are especially important to investigate in the assessment of adult intelligence (Schaie, 1996). Individuals born at different points in time—such as 1920, 1940, and 1960—have had varying opportunities for education, while individuals born in earlier years have had less access.

a. b. c. d. e. f.

Figure **2.11**

Cohort Effects

Cohort effects are due to a person's time of birth or generation but not actually to age. Think for a moment about growing up in *(a)* the Roaring Twenties, *(b)* the Great Depression, *(c)* the 1940s and World War II, *(d)* the 1950s, *(e)* the late 1960s, and *(f)* today. *How might your development be different depending on which of these time frames has dominated your life? your parents' lives? your grandparents' lives?*

The mark of the historic is the nonchalance with which it picks up an individual and deposits him in a trend, like a house playfully moved in a tornado.

Mary McCarthy
American Author, 20th Century

Cross-sectional studies can show how different cohorts respond but they can confuse age changes and cohort effects. Longitudinal studies are effective in studying age changes but only within one cohort. With sequential studies, both age changes in one cohort can be examined and compared with age changes in another cohort.

A point that is important to make is that theories often are linked with a particular research method or methods. Thus, the particular research method(s) that

RESEARCH METHOD	THEORY
Observation	• All theories emphasize some form of observation. • Behavioral and social cognitive theories place the strongest emphasis on laboratory observation. • Ethological theory places the strongest emphasis on naturalistic observation.
Interview/ Survey	• Psychoanalytic and cognitive studies (Piaget, Vygotsky) often use interviews. • Behavioral and social cognitive, and ethological, theories are the least likely to use interview/survey.
Case Study	• Psychoanalytic theories (Freud, Erikson) are the most likely to use this method.
Standardized Test	• None of the theories discussed emphasize the use of this method.
Life-History Records	• This method is most likely to be advocated by ecological theory and psychoanalytic theories.
Physiological Research and Research with Animals	• None of theories discussed address physiological research to any significant degree. • Behavioral and ethological theories are the most likely to conduct animal research.
Correlational Research	• All of the theories use this research method, although psychoanalytic theories are the least likely to use it.
Experimental Research	• The behavioral and social cognitive theories, and the information-processing approach, are the most likely to use the experimental method. • Psychoanalytic theories are the least likely to use it.
Cross-Sectional/ Longitudinal/ Sequential Methods	• No theory described uses these methods more than any other. • The sequential method is the least likely to be used by any theory.

Figure 2.12
Connections of Research Methods to Theories

researchers use is associated with the researcher's theoretical approach. Figure 2.12 illustrates the connections between research methods and theories.

At this point we have studied a number of ideas about research methods. A review of these ideas is presented in summary table 2.3. Next, we will continue our exploration of the scientific foundations of life-span development by focusing on research journals.

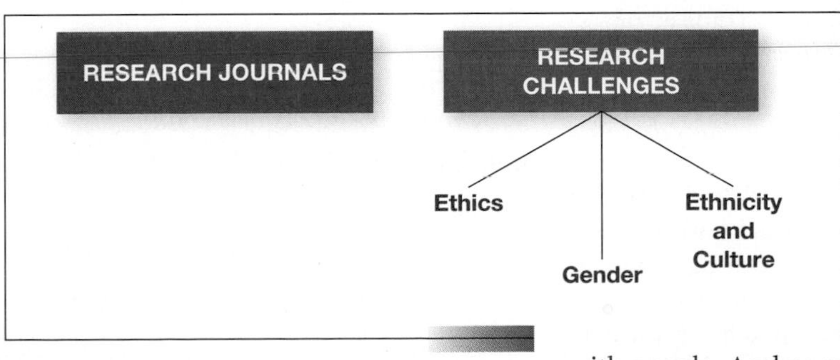

Research Journals

Regardless of whether you pursue a career in life-span development, psychology, or some related scientific field, you can benefit by learning about the journal process. Possibly as a student you will be required to look up original research in journals as part of writing a term paper. As a parent, teacher, or nurse you might want to consult journals to obtain information that will help you understand and work more effectively with people. And as an inquiring person, you might look up information in journals after you have heard or read something that piqued your curiosity.

Summary Table 2.3
Research Methods

Concept	Processes/ Related Ideas	Characteristics/Descriptions
Observation	Laboratory, Naturalistic	• Observations need to be conducted systematically. • Observations can be made in laboratories or in naturalistic settings.
Interviews and Questionnaires	Ask People for Information	• Most interviews take place face to face. • Most questionnaires (surveys) are given to individuals in printed form to be filled out.
Case Studies	Focus on Individual	• They represent an in-depth look at an individual. • Generalizing from a case study to other people is often not warranted.
Standardized Tests	Comparison of Individuals	• These are commercially prepared tests that assess performance in different domains.
Life-history Records	Chronology of Events	• They often involve a combination of data records on education, work, family and residence.
Physiological Research and Research with Animals	Physiological Research	• Physiological research provides information about the biological basis of behavior.
	Animal Studies	• Animal studies permit researchers to control genetic background, diet, experiences in infancy, and countless other factors.
Correlational Research	Relation, Not Cause	• The goal is to describe the relation between two or more events or characteristics. • Correlation does not equal causation.
Experimental Research	To Determine Cause	• This allows the determination of behavior's causes. • This involves examining the influence of at least one independent variable (the manipulated, influential, experimental factor) on one or more dependent variables (the measured factor). • Participants are randomly assigned to one or more experimental and one or more control groups.
Time Span of Research	Cross-Sectional	• Studying people all at one time.
	Longitudinal	• Studying the same people over time.
	Sequential Approach	• Combined cross-sectional, longitudinal design.
	Cohort Effects	• Effects due to time of birth or generation but not to chronological age.

A *journal* publishes scholarly and academic information, usually in a specific domain—like physics, math, sociology, or, in the case of our interest, life-span development. Scholars in these fields publish most of their research in journals, which are the source of core information in virtually every academic discipline.

Journal articles are usually written for other professionals in the specialized field of the journal's focus; therefore they often contain technical language and terms specific to the discipline that are difficult for nonprofessionals to understand. Most of you have already had one or more courses in psychology. You also will be learning a great deal more in this course about the specialized field of life-span development, which should improve your ability to understand journal articles in this field.

An increasing number of journals publish information about life-span development. Among the leading journals in life-span development are *Developmental Psychology, Child Development, Pediatric Nursing, Pediatrics, Journal of Gerontology, Infant*

Research journals are the core of information in virtually every academic discipline. Those shown here are among the increasing number of research journals that publish information about life-span development. *What are the main parts of a research arcticle that presents findings from original research?*

Behavior and Development, Journal of Research on Adolescence, Journal of Adult Development, Journal of Gerontological Nursing, Psychology and Aging, Human Development, and many others. Also, a number of journals that do not focus solely on development include articles on various aspects of human development. These journals include *Journal of Educational Psychology, Sex Roles, Journal of Cross-Cultural Psychology, Journal of Marriage and the Family,* and *Journal of Consulting and Clinical Psychology.*

In psychology and the field of life-span development, most journal articles are reports of original research. Many journals also include review articles that present an overview of different studies on a particular topic—such as intergenerational relationships, infant attachment, or adolescent depression.

Child Development
Developmental Psychology
Journal of Gerontology: Psychological Sciences

Many journals are highly selective about what they publish. Every journal has a board of experts who evaluate articles submitted for publication. Each submitted paper is accepted or rejected on the basis of such factors as its contribution to the field, theoretical relevance, methodological excellence, and clarity of writing (Leavitt, 2001). Some of the most prestigious journals reject as many as 80 to 90 percent of the articles that are submitted because they fail to meet the journal's standards.

Where do you find journals such as those we have listed? Your college or university library likely has one or more of them, and some public libraries also carry journals.

To help you understand the journals, let's examine the format followed by many of them. Their organization often takes this course: abstract, introduction, method, results, discussion, and references.

The *abstract* is a brief summary that appears at the beginning of the article. The abstract lets readers quickly determine whether the article is relevant to their interests and whether they want to read the entire article. The *introduction,* as its title suggests, introduces the problem or issue that is being studied. It includes a concise review of research relevant to the topic, theoretical ties, and one or more hypotheses to be tested. The *method* section consists of a clear description of the subjects evaluated in the study, the measures used, and the procedures that were followed. The method section should be sufficiently clear and detailed so that by reading it another researcher could repeat or replicate the study. The *results* section reports the analysis of the data collected. In most cases, the results section includes statistical analyses that are difficult for nonprofessionals to understand. The *discussion* section describes the author's conclusions, inferences, and interpretation of what was found. Statements are usually made about whether the hypotheses presented in the introduction were supported, limitations of the study, and suggestions for future research. The last part of the journal article, called *references,* includes bibliographic information for each source cited in the article. The references section is often a good source for finding other articles relevant to the topic you are interested in.

Research Challenges

Research on development poses a number of challenges. Some of the challenges involve the pursuit of knowledge itself. Others involve the effects of research on participants. Still others relate to a better understanding of the information derived from research studies.

Ethics

Researchers exercise considerable caution to ensure the well-being of individuals participating in a study. Most colleges have review boards that evaluate whether the research is ethical.

The code of ethics adopted by the American Psychological Association (APA) instructs researchers to protect participants from mental and physical harm. The best interests of the participants always must be kept foremost in the researcher's mind (Kimmel, 1996; Sieber, 2000). All participants, if they are old enough (typically 7 years or older), must give their informed consent to participate. If they are not old enough, their parents' or guardians' consent must be obtained. Informed consent means that the participants (and/or their parents/legal guardians) have been told what their participation will entail and any risks that might be involved. For example, if researchers want to study the effects of conflict in divorced families on children's self-esteem, the participants should be informed that in some instances discussion of a family's experiences might improve family relationships, but in other cases might raise unwanted family stress. After informed consent is given, participants retain the right to withdraw at any time (Jones, 2000).

Ethics

CAREERS IN LIFE-SPAN DEVELOPMENT

Tom Puglisi, Director of Human Subjects Protection

Tom Puglisi currently is Director of Policy and Assurance in the Federal Office for Human Research Protection (OHRP). He was trained as a life-span developmental psychologist and has always been interested in politics. Tom received a Congressional Science Fellowship and worked on aging issues in the House of Representatives. These contacts, along with 6 years' experience as chair of a human subjects Institutional Review Board (IRB), led him to be offered a position in what was then the Office for Protection from Research Risks (OPRR).

Over the years, Tom and his colleagues have been faced with making challenging and controversial decisions about such issues as informed consent for research on mental disorders, regulations governing pregnant women and fetuses in research, ethical issues regarding AIDS vaccine research, and the ramifications of surreptitious egg and embryo swapping by nationally recognized fertility researchers (now convicted on felony charges).

Tom says, "My training in life-span development has been invaluable in helping me understand the perspective of both the scientist-researcher and the research participant—perspectives that are critically important in making the judgments required in my present job of protecting human subjects."

Reflecting on his career, Tom Puglisi says, "I could not imagine a more fascinating and rewarding professional endeavor. I love my job and look forward every day to the never ending challenges that it presents" (*Psychological Science Agenda,* 1998).

CAREERS IN LIFE-SPAN DEVELOPMENT

Pam Reid, Educational and Developmental Psychologist

AS A CHILD, PAM REID played with chemistry sets, and at the university she was majoring in chemistry, planning on becoming a medical doctor. Because some of her friends signed up for a psychology course as an elective, she decided to join them. She was so intrigued by learning more about how people think, behave, and develop that she changed her major to psychology. She says, "I fell in love with psychology." Pam went on to obtain her Ph.D. in educational psychology.

Today, Pamela Trotman Reid is a professor of education and psychology at the University of Michigan. She is also a research scientist for the UM Institute for Research on Women and Gender. Her main interest is how children and adolescents develop social skills, and especially how gender, socioeconomic status, and ethnicity are involved in development. Because many psychological findings have been based on research with middle-socioeconomic-status non-Latino white populations, Pam believes it is important to study people from different ethnic groups. She stresses that by understanding the expectations, attitudes, and behavior of diverse groups, we enrich the theory and practice of psychology. Currently Pam is working with her graduate students on a project involving middle school girls. She is interested in why girls, more often than boys, stop taking classes in mathematics.

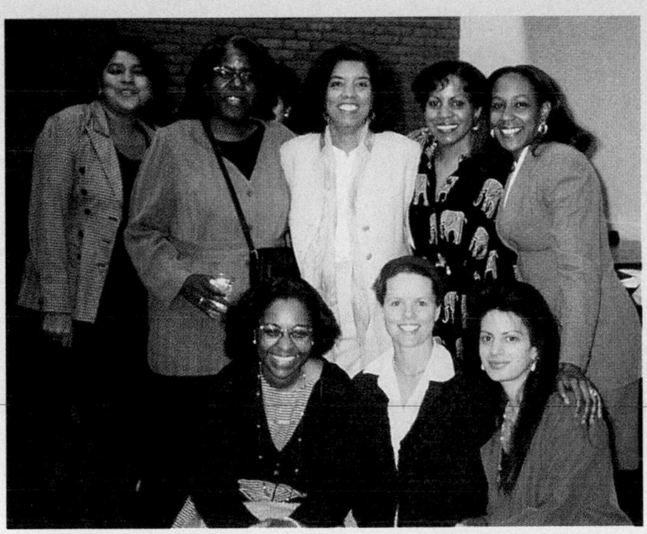

Pam Reid (back row, center) with graduate students she is mentoring at the University of Michigan.

Gender

Traditionally, science has been presented as nonbiased and value-free. However, many experts on gender believe that psychological research often has entailed gender bias (Anselmi, 1998; Doyle & Paludi, 1998) ◀ P. 13. They argue that for too long the female experience was subsumed under the male experience. For example, conclusions have been drawn routinely about females based on research conducted only with males.

Following are three broad questions that female scholars have raised regarding gender bias in psychological research (Tetreault, 1997):

- How might gender be a bias that influences the choice of theory, questions, hypotheses, participants, and research design?
- How might research on topics of primary interest to females, such as relationships, feelings, and empathy, challenge existing theory and research?
- How has research that heretofore has exaggerated gender differences between females and males influenced the way parents, teachers, and others think about and interact with female and male adolescents? For example, gender differences in mathematics often have been exaggerated and fueled by societal bias.

Ethnicity and Culture

More individuals from ethnic minority backgrounds need to be included in research (Graham, 1992) ◀ P. 13. Historically, ethnic minority individuals essentially have been ignored in research or simply have been viewed as variations from the norm or average. Their developmental and educational problems have been viewed as "confounds," or "noise" in data. Researchers have deliberately excluded these individuals from the samples they have selected to study (Ryan-Finn, Cauce, & Grove, 1995). Because ethnic minority individuals have been excluded from research for so long, there likely is more variation in the real lives of people than research studies have indicated (Stevenson, 1995, 1998, in press).

Researchers also have tended to practice what is called "ethnic gloss" when they select and describe ethnic minority samples (Trimble, 1989). *Ethnic gloss* is using an ethnic label, such as African American or Latino, in a superficial way that makes an ethnic group look more homogeneous than it really is. For example, a researcher might describe a sample as "20 Latinos and 20 Anglo Americans," when a more precise description of the Latino group would need to state, "The 20 Latino participants were Mexican Americans from low-income neighborhoods in the southwestern area of Los Angeles. Twelve were from homes in which Spanish is the dominant language spoken, 8 from homes in which English is

Summary Table 2.4
Research Journals and Research Challenges

Concept	Processes/ Related Ideas	Characteristics/Descriptions
Research Journals	Scholarly and Academic Information	• A journal publishes scholarly and academic information. • Most journal articles are reports of original research. • Most research journal articles follow this format: abstract, introduction, methods, results, discussion, and references.
Research Challenges	Ethics	• Researchers recognize that a number of ethical requirements have to be met when conducting studies. • The best interests of the participants always have to be kept in mind.
	Gender	• Every effort should be made to make research equitable for both females and males. • In the past, research often was biased against females.
	Ethnicity and Culture	• We need to include more individuals from ethnic minority backgrounds in life-span development research. • A special concern is ethnic gloss.

the main spoken language. Ten were born in the United States, 10 in Mexico. Ten described themselves as Mexican American, 5 as Mexican, 3 as American, 2 as Chicano, and 1 as Latino." Ethnic gloss can cause researchers to obtain samples of ethnic groups that either are not representative or conceal the group's diversity, which can lead to overgeneralization and stereotyping.

Also, historically, when researchers have studied ethnic minority individuals, they mainly have focused on their problems. It is important to study the problems, such as poverty, that ethnic minority individuals face, but it also is important to examine their strengths as well, such as their pride, self-esteem, improvised problem-solving skills, and extended family support systems. Fortunately, now, in the context of a more pluralistic view of our society, researchers are increasingly studying the positive dimensions of ethnic minority individuals (Swanson, 1997).

At this point we have discussed many ideas about research journals and research challenges. A review of these ideas is presented in summary table 2.4. Now that we have learned some basic ideas about the field of life-span development, including its scientific basis, in the next chapter we will turn our attention to the biological beginnings of human development.

Critical Thinking

Isn't Everyone a Psychologist?

EACH OF US has theories about human development, and it is hard to imagine how we could get through life without them. In this sense, we are all psychologists. However, the theories of psychology that we carry around and the way we obtain support for our theories are often quite different from the way psychologists go about theorizing and collecting data about an issue or topic (Stanovich, 1998).

Think for a few moments about your views of human development. How did you arrive at them? Might at least some of them be biased? Now think about what you have read about theories and methods in this chapter. How is our personal psychology of life-span development different from the scientific psychology of life-span development? Which one is more likely to be accurate? Why? Although our personal psychology and the scientific psychology of life-span development are often different, in what ways might they be similar?

Chapter Review

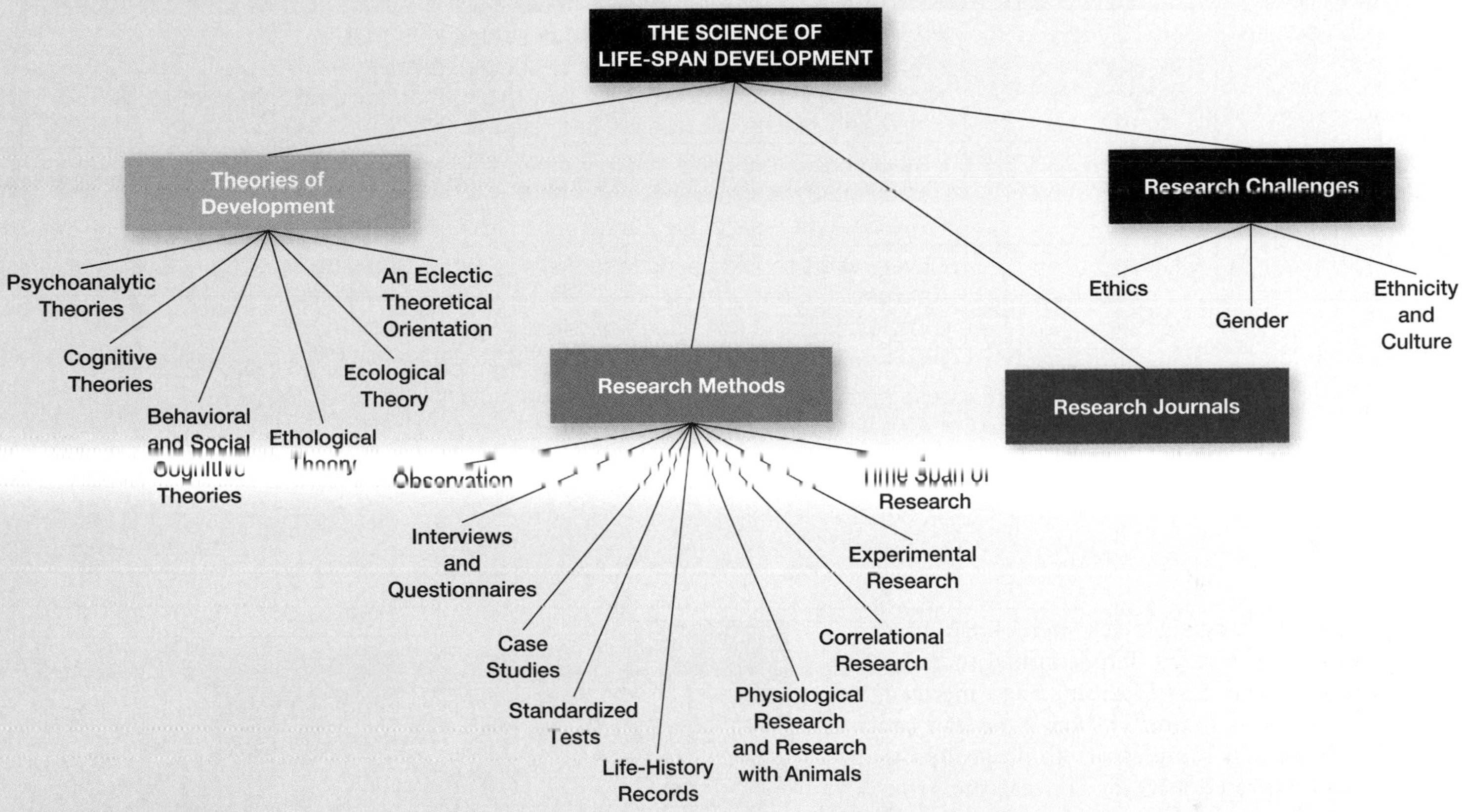

TO OBTAIN A DETAILED REVIEW OF THIS CHAPTER, STUDY THESE FIVE SUMMARY TABLES:

- Summary Table 2.1: Psychoanalytic and Cognitive Theories — page 39
- Summary Table 2.2: Behavioral and Social Cognitive Theories, Ethological Theory, Ecological Theory, and an Eclectic Theoretical Orientation — page 47
- Summary Table 2.3: Research Methods — page 55
- Summary Table 2.4: Research Journals and Research Challenges — page 59

Key Terms

theory 30
hypotheses 30
psychoanalytic theory 31
Erikson's theory 33
Piaget's theory 35
assimilation 35
accommodation 35
Vygotsky's theory 37
information-processing approach 38
social cognitive theory 40
ethology 42
ecological theory 43
eclectic theoretical orientation 45
laboratory 48
naturalistic observation 48
questionnaire 49
case study 49
standardized tests 49
life-history records 49
correlational research 50
experimental research 50
independent variable 51
dependent variable 51
experimental group 51
control group 51
random assignment 51
cross-sectional approach 51
longitudinal approach 52
sequential approach 52
cohort effects 52

Key People

Sigmund Freud 31
Erik Erikson 33
Jean Piaget 35
Karen Horney 36
Lev Vygotsky 37
Robert Siegler 38
Ivan Pavlov 40
B. F. Skinner 40
Albert Bandura 41
Walter Mischel 41
Konrad Lorenz 42
Urie Bronfenbrenner 43

Taking It to the Net

1. Like many students of lifespan psychology, Ymelda has a hard time with Freud's theory, insisting that it is "all about sex." Is that the extent of Freud's theoretical perspective?
2. Juan's lifespan psychology teacher asked the class to read about Albert Bandura's famous "Bobo" doll experiment and determine if there were any gender differences in the responses of boys and girls who (1) saw aggressive behavior rewarded and (2) who saw aggressive behavior punished. What should Juan's conclusions be?
3. Clarice wants to be a research psychologist, but being an animal lover is not sure that she could commit herself to research that might subject animals—even laboratory mice—to harm. According to the APA code of ethics, what obligations do research psychologists have to their research animals?

Connect to www.mhhe.com/santrockld8 to research the answers and complete these exercises.

OLC Preview

To further test your knowledge of this chapter or to explore our extensive online resources that accompany *Life-Span Development*, eighth edition, please log on to the text's Online Learning Center at http://www.mhhe.com/santrockld8.com.

Section 2

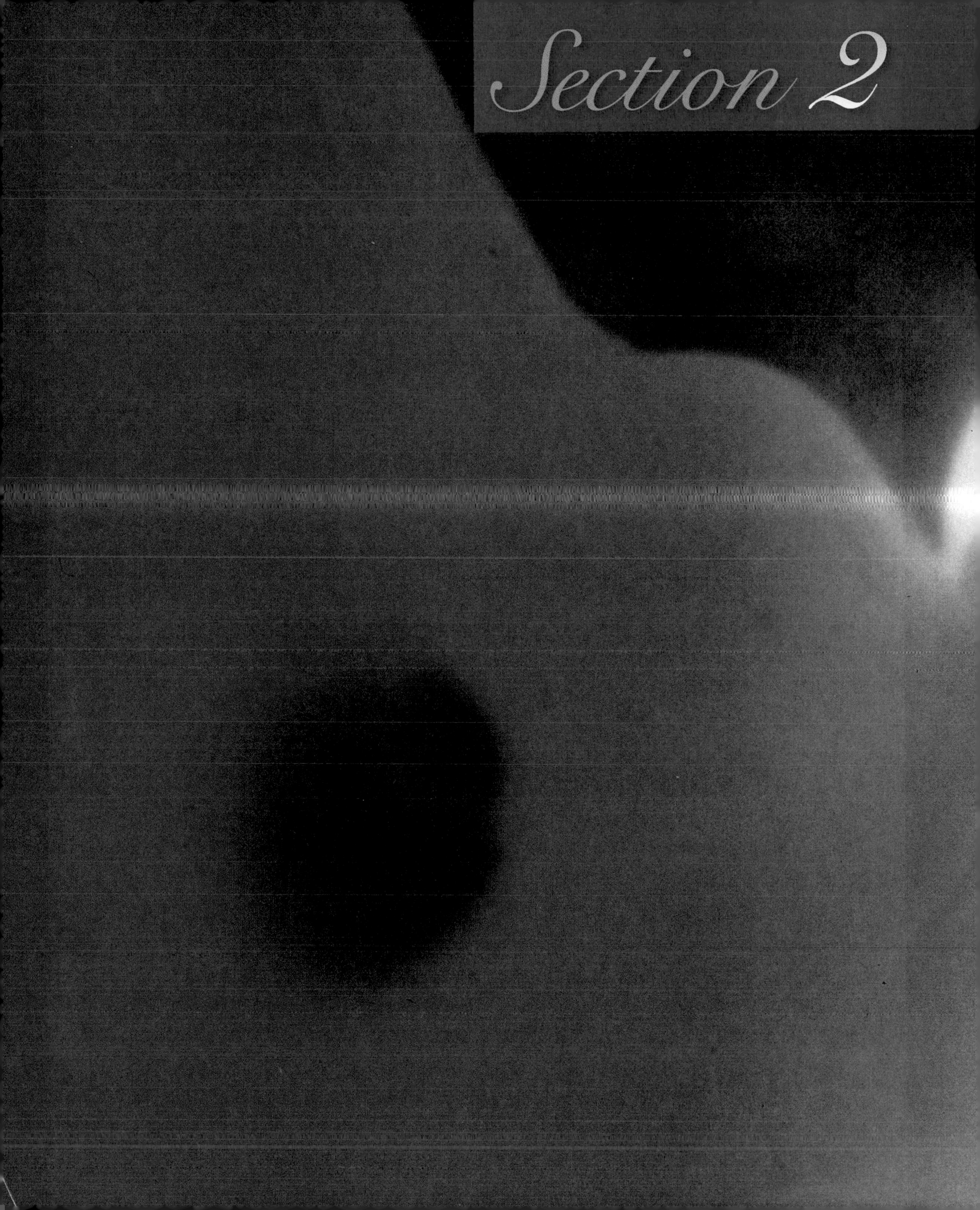

Beginnings

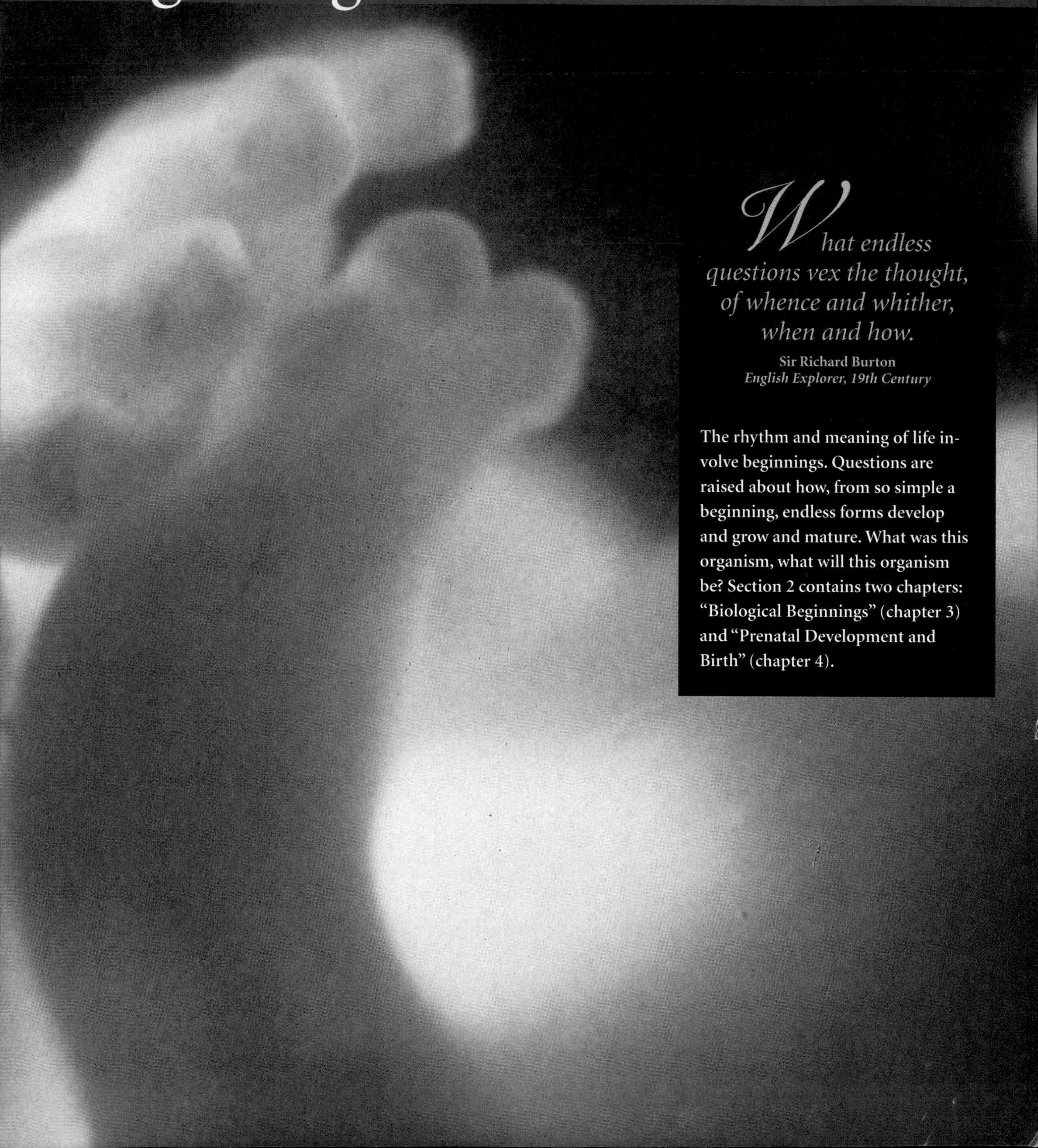

What endless questions vex the thought, of whence and whither, when and how.

Sir Richard Burton
English Explorer, 19th Century

The rhythm and meaning of life involve beginnings. Questions are raised about how, from so simple a beginning, endless forms develop and grow and mature. What was this organism, what will this organism be? Section 2 contains two chapters: "Biological Beginnings" (chapter 3) and "Prenatal Development and Birth" (chapter 4).

Chapter 3

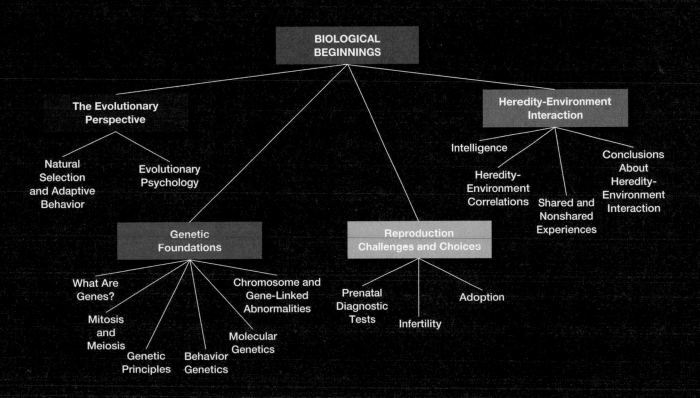

BIOLOGICAL BEGINNINGS

- The Evolutionary Perspective
  - Natural Selection and Adaptive Behavior
  - Evolutionary Psychology
- Genetic Foundations
  - What Are Genes?
  - Mitosis and Meiosis
  - Genetic Principles
  - Behavior Genetics
  - Molecular Genetics
  - Chromosome and Gene-Linked Abnormalities
- Reproduction Challenges and Choices
  - Prenatal Diagnostic Tests
  - Infertility
  - Adoption
- Heredity-Environment Interaction
  - Intelligence
  - Heredity-Environment Correlations
  - Shared and Nonshared Experiences
  - Conclusions About Heredity-Environment Interaction

There are one hundred and ninety-three living species of monkeys and apes. One hundred and ninety-two of them are covered with hair. The exception is the naked ape, self-named Homo sapiens.

Desmond Morris
British Zoologist, 20th Century

Images of Life-Span Development

The Jim and Jim Twins

JIM SPRINGER AND JIM LEWIS are identical twins. They were separated at 4 weeks of age and did not see each other again until they were 39 years old. Both worked as part-time deputy sheriffs, vacationed in Florida, drive Chevrolets, had dogs named Toy, and married and divorced women named Betty. One twin named his son James Allan, and the other named his son James Alan. Both liked math but not spelling, enjoyed carpentry and mechanical drawing, chewed their fingernails down to the nubs, had almost identical drinking and smoking habits, had hemorrhoids, put on 10 pounds at about the same point in development, first suffered headaches at the age of 18, and had similar sleep patterns.

Jim Lewis *(left)* and Jim Springer *(right)*.

But Jim and Jim have some differences. One wears his hair over his forehead, the other slicks it back and has sideburns. One expresses himself best orally; the other is more proficient in writing. But, for the most part, their profiles are remarkably similar.

Another pair, Daphne and Barbara, are called the "giggle sisters" because, after being reunited, they were always making each other laugh. A thorough search of their adoptive families' histories revealed no gigglers. And the identical sisters handled stress by ignoring it, avoided conflict and controversy whenever possible, and showed no interest in politics.

Two other female identical twin sisters were separated at 6 weeks and reunited in their fifties. Both had nightmares, which they describe in hauntingly similar ways: both dreamed of doorknobs and fishhooks in their mouths as they smothered to death! The nightmares began during early adolescence and stopped in the past 10 to 12 years. Both women were bed wetters until about 12 or 13 years of age, and they report educational and marital histories that are remarkably similar.

These sets of twins are part of the Minnesota Study of Twins Reared Apart, directed by Thomas Bouchard and his colleagues. They bring identical twins (identical genetically because they come from the same fertilized egg) and fraternal twins

(dissimilar genetically because they come from different fertilized eggs) from all over the world to Minneapolis to investigate their lives. The twins are given a number of personality tests, and detailed medical histories are obtained, including information about diet and smoking, exercise habits, chest X-rays, heart stress tests, and EEGs (brain-wave tests). The twins are interviewed and asked more than 15,000 questions about their family and childhood environment, personal interests, vocational orientation, values, and aesthetic judgments. They also are given ability and intelligence tests (Bouchard & others, 1990).

Critics of the Minnesota identical twins study point out that some of the separated twins were together several months prior to their adoption, that some of the twins had been reunited prior to their testing (in some cases, a number of years earlier), that adoption agencies often place twins in similar homes, and that even strangers who spend several hours together and start comparing their lives are likely to come up with some coincidental similarities (Adler, 1991). Still, even in the face of such criticism, the Minnesota study of identical twins indicates how scientists have recently shown an increased interest in the genetic basis of human development and that we need further research on genetic and environmental factors (Bouchard, 1995).

The examples of Jim and Jim, the giggle sisters, and the identical twins who had the same nightmares stimulate us to think about our genetic heritage and the biological foundations of our existence. Organisms are not like billiard balls, moved by simple, external forces to predictable positions on life's pool table. Environmental experiences and biological foundations work together to make us who we are. Our coverage of life's biological beginnings in this chapter focuses on evolution, genetic foundations, reproduction challenges and choices, and the interaction of heredity and environment.

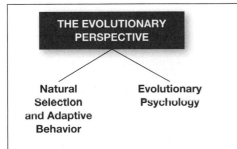

THE EVOLUTIONARY PERSPECTIVE

- Natural Selection and Adaptive Behavior
- Evolutionary Psychology

The Evolutionary Perspective

In evolutionary time, humans are relative newcomers to Earth, yet we have established ourselves as the most successful and dominant species. If we consider evolutionary time as a calendar year, humans arrived here in the last moments of December (Sagan, 1977). As our earliest ancestors left the forest to feed on the savannahs, and finally to form hunting societies on the open plains, their minds and behaviors changed. How did this evolution come about?

Natural Selection and Adaptive Behavior

WWW

Evolution

Evolution and Behavior

Natural selection is the evolutionary process that favors individuals of a species that are best adapted to survive and reproduce. To understand natural selection, let's return to the middle of the nineteenth century, when Charles Darwin was traveling around the world, observing many different species of animals in their natural surroundings. Darwin, who published his observations and thoughts in *On the Origin of Species* (1859), observed that most organisms reproduce at rates that would cause enormous increases in the population of most species and yet populations remain nearly constant. He reasoned that an intense, constant struggle for food, water, and resources must occur among the many young born each generation, because many of the young do not survive. Those that do survive pass on their genes to the next generation. Darwin believed that those who do survive to reproduce are probably superior in a number of ways to those who do not. In other words, the survivors are better adapted to their world than are the nonsurvivors (Enger & others, 1996). Over the course of many generations, organisms with the characteristics needed for survival would comprise a larger percentage of the population. Over many, many generations, this could produce a gradual modification of the whole population. If environmental conditions change, however, other characteristics might become favored by natural selection, moving the process in a different direction (Zubay, 1996).

To understand the role of evolution in behavior, we need to understand the concept of adaptive behavior. In evolutionary conceptions of psychology, *adaptive behavior* is behavior that promotes an organism's survival in the natural habitat. Adaptive behavior involves the organism's modification of its behavior to include its likelihood of survival. All organisms must adapt to particular places, climates, food sources, and ways of life. Natural selection designs adaptation to perform a certain function. An example of adaptation is an eagle's claws, designed by natural selection to facilitate predation. In the human realm, attachment is a system designed by natural selection to ensure an infant's closeness to the caregiver for feeding and protection from danger.

Humans, more than any other mammal, adapt to and control most types of environments. Because of longer parental care, humans learn more complex behavior patterns, which contribute to adaptation. *What are some other adaptive aspects of human behavior that might be tied to evolution?*

Evolutionary Psychology

Although Darwin introduced the theory of evolution by natural selection in 1859, his ideas about evolution only recently have emerged as a popular framework for explaining behavior. Psychology's newest approach, **evolutionary psychology,** *emphasizes the importance of adaptation, reproduction, and "survival of the fittest" in explaining behavior.* Evolution favors organisms that are best adapted to survive and reproduce in a particular environment. The evolutionary psychology approach focuses on conditions that allow individuals to survive or to fail. In this view, the evolutionary process of natural selection favors behaviors that increase organisms' reproductive success and their ability to pass their genes to the next generation (Bjorklund & Bering, 2001; Caporael, 2001; Geary & Bjorklund, 2000).

David Buss' (1995, 1999, 2000) ideas on evolutionary psychology have ushered in a whole new wave of interest in how evolution is involved in explaining human behavior. He believes that just as evolution shapes our physical features, such as body shape and height, it also pervasively influences how we make decisions, how aggressive we are, our fears, and our mating patterns.

Evolution and Life-Span Development According to life-span developmentalist Paul Baltes (1996; Baltes, Staudinger, & Lindenberger, 1999), the benefits of evolutionary selection decrease with age. As a result, older adults have a higher number of deleterious genes and dysfunctional gene expressions.

Why do the later years of life benefit less from the optimizing power of evolutionary selection pressure than the younger years? The main reason is reproductive fitness, which primarily extends from conception through the earlier part of adulthood. As a consequence, says Baltes, selection operates mainly during the first half of life. Also, given the much shorter life span in early human evolution, selection pressure could not function as often in the later years of life. Most individuals died before possible negative genetic attributes were activated or their negative consequences appeared.

A concrete example of a decrease in evolutionary selection benefits in older adults involves Alzheimer's disease, a progressive, irreversible brain disorder characterized by gradual deterioration. This disease typically does not appear until age 70 or older. Possibly diseases like Alzheimer's emerge in later life because evolutionary pressures based on reproductive fitness were not able to select against it.

While Baltes believes that the benefits of evolutionary selection decrease following the decline in reproductive capacity, he argues that the need for culture increases

evolutionary psychology
A contemporary approach that emphasizes that behavior is a function of mechanisms, requires input for activation, and is ultimately related to survival and reproduction.

Evolutionary Psychology
Handbook of Evolutionary Psychology
Evolutionary Psychology Resources

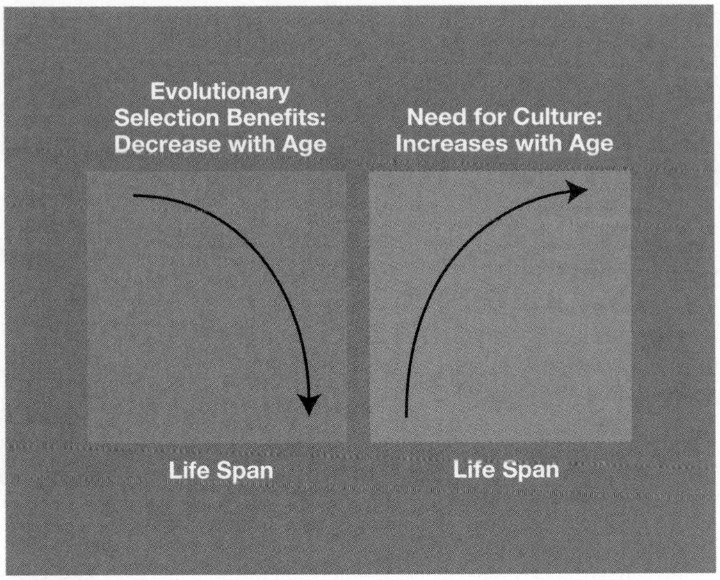

Figure **3.1**

Baltes' View of Evolution and Culture Across the Life Span

(see figure 3.1). Some of the cultural factors needed are cognitive skills, motivation, socialization, literacy, and medical technology. That is, as older adults weaken biologically, they need culture-based resources (material, social, economic, psychological). For example, for cognitive skills to continue into old age at comparable levels of performance to earlier in adulthood, cognitive support and training are needed (Hoyer, Rybash, & Roodin, 1999). And as we indicated in chapter 1, Baltes also stresses that a life-span shift in the allocation of resources takes place away from growth and toward maintenance and the regulation of loss.

Evaluating Evolutionary Psychology Albert Bandura (1998), whose social cognitive theory was described in chapter 2, recently addressed the "biologizing" of psychology and evolution's role in social cognitive theory ◀ P. 41. Bandura acknowledges the important influence of evolution on human adaptation and change. However, he rejects what he calls "one-sided evolutionism," which sees social behavior as the product of evolved biology. In the bidirectional view, evolutionary pressures created changes in biological structures for the use of tools, which enabled organisms to manipulate, alter, and construct new environmental conditions. Environmental innovations of increasing complexity produced, in turn, new selection pressures for the evolution of specialized biological systems for consciousness, thought, and language.

Human evolution gave us bodily structures and biological potentialities, not behavioral dictates. Having evolved, advanced biological capacities can be used to produce diverse cultures—aggressive, pacific, egalitarian, or autocratic. As American scientist Steven Jay Gould (1981) concluded, in most domains of human functioning, biology allows a broad range of cultural possibilities. And Russian American Theodore Dobzhansky (1977) reminds us that the human species has been selected for the ability to learn and plasticity—for the capacity to adapt to diverse contexts, not for biologically fixed behavior. Bandura (1998) points out that the pace of social change shows that biology does permit a range of possibilities.

At this point we have studied a number of ideas about the evolutionary perspective. A review of these ideas is presented in summary table 3.1. Next, we will continue our exploration of biological influences by examining heredity and reproduction.

Summary Table 3.1
The Evolutionary Perspective

Concept	Processes/ Related Ideas	Characteristics/Descriptions
Natural Selection and Adaptive Behavior	Natural Selection	• Natural selection is the process that favors the individuals of a species that are best adapted to survive and reproduce. • The process of natural selection was originally proposed by Charles Darwin.
	Adaptive Behavior	• In evolutionary theory, adaptive behavior is behavior that promotes the organism's survival in a natural habitat. • Biological evolution shaped human beings into a culture-making species.
Evolutionary Psychology	David Buss' View	• The view that adaptation, reproduction, and "survival of the fittest" are important in explaining behavior.
	Evolution and Life-Span Development	• According to Baltes, the benefits of evolutionary selection decrease with age mainly because of a decline in reproductive fitness. • While evolutionary selection benefits decrease with age, cultural needs increase.
	Evaluating Evolutionary Psychology	• Social cognitive theorist Albert Bandura acknowledges evolution's important role in human adaptation and change but argues for a bidirectional view that enables organisms to alter and construct new environmental conditions. • Biology allows for a broad range of cultural possibilities.

Genetic Foundations

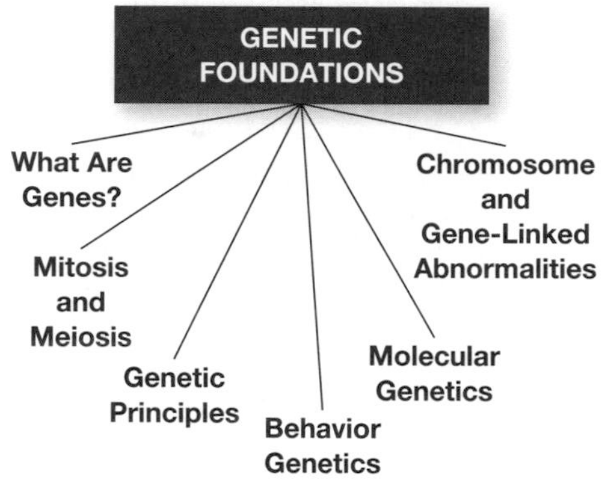

Every species must have a mechanism for transmitting characteristics from one generation to the next. This mechanism is explained by the principles of genetics. Each of us carries a genetic code that we inherited from our parents. This code is located within every cell in our bodies. Our genetic codes are alike in one important way—they all contain the human genetic code. Because of the human genetic code, a fertilized human egg cannot grow into an egret, eagle, or elephant.

What Are Genes?

Each of us began life as a single cell weighing about one twenty-millionth of an ounce! This tiny piece of matter housed our entire genetic code—information about who we would become. These instructions orchestrated growth from that single cell to a person made of trillions of cells, each containing a perfect replica of the original genetic code.

The nucleus of each human cell contains 46 **chromosomes,** *which are threadlike structures that come in 23 pairs, one member of each pair coming from each parent. Chromosomes contain the remarkable genetic substance deoxyribonucleic acid, or DNA.* **DNA** *is a complex molecule that contains genetic information.* DNA's "double helix" shape looks like a spiral staircase. **Genes,** *the units of hereditary information, are short segments composed of DNA. Genes act as a blueprint for cells to reproduce themselves and manufacture the proteins that maintain life.* Chromosomes, DNA, and genes can be mysterious. To help you turn mystery into understanding, see figure 3.2.

chromosomes
Threadlike structures that come in 23 pairs, one member of each pair coming from each parent. Chromosomes contain the genetic substance DNA.

DNA
A complex molecule that contains genetic information.

genes
Units of hereditary information composed of DNA. Genes act as a blueprint for cells to reproduce themselves and manufacture the proteins that maintain life.

Mitosis and Meiosis

Mitosis and meiosis are biological processes that are important in understanding how genes function.

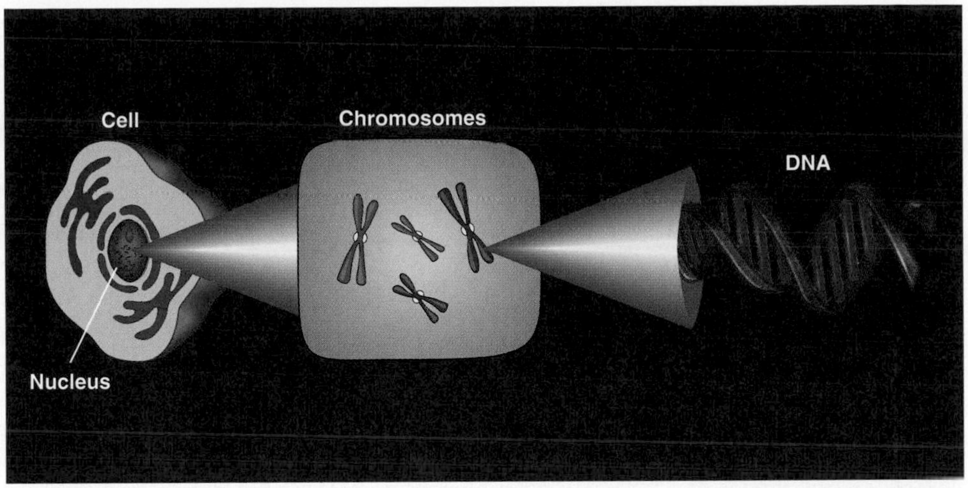

Figure 3.2

Cells, Chromosomes, Genes, and DNA

(*Left*) The body contains trillion of cells, which are the basic structural units of life. Each cell contains a central structure, the nucleus. (*Middle*) Chromosomes and genes are located in the nucleus of the cell. Chromosomes are made up of threadlike structures composed mainly of DNA molecules. (*Right*) A gene, which is a segment of DNA that contains the hereditary code. The structure of DNA is a spiraled double chain of molecules.

mitosis
The process by which each chromosome in a cell's nucleus duplicates itself.

meiosis
The process of cell doubling and separation of chromosomes in which each pair of chromosomes in a cell separates, with one member of each pair going into each gamete.

reproduction
The process that, in humans, begins when a female gamete (ovum) is fertilized by a male gamete (sperm).

zygote
A single cell formed through fertilization.

Mitosis *is the process by which each chromosome in the cell's nucleus duplicates itself.* The resulting 46 chromosomes move to the opposite sides of the cell, then the cell separates, and two new cells are formed with each now containing 46 chromosomes. Thus the process of mitosis allows DNA to duplicate itself.

A specialized division of chromosomes occurs during the formation of reproductive cells. **Meiosis** *is the process by which cells divide into gametes (testes/sperm in males, ovaries/eggs in females), which have half the genetic material of the parent cell.*

Figure 3.3 illustrates the basic transformations that occur during mitosis and meiosis. To understand the differences between mitosis and meiosis, remember that:

- In mitosis, the focus is on cell growth and repair, whereas meiosis involves sexual reproduction.
- In mitosis, the number of chromosomes present remains the same (the chromosomes copy themselves), whereas in meiosis, the chromosomes are halved.
- In mitosis, two daughter cells are formed; in meiosis four daughter cells are produced.

Each human gamete has 23 unpaired chromosomes. The process of human **reproduction** *begins when a female gamete (ovum) is fertilized by a male gamete (sperm)* (see figure 3.4). A **zygote** *is a single cell formed through fertilization.* In the zygote, two sets of unpaired chromosomes combine to form one set of paired chromosomes—one member of each pair from the mother and the other member from the father. In this manner, each parent contributes 50 percent of the offspring's heredity.

Genetic Principles

Genetic determination is a complex affair, and much is unknown about the way genes work (Lewis, 1999). But a number of genetic principles have been discovered, among them those of dominant-recessive genes, sex-linked genes, polygenically inherited characteristics, reaction range, and canalization.

According to the *dominant-recessive genes principle,* if one gene of a pair is dominant and one is recessive, the dominant gene exerts its effect, overriding the potential

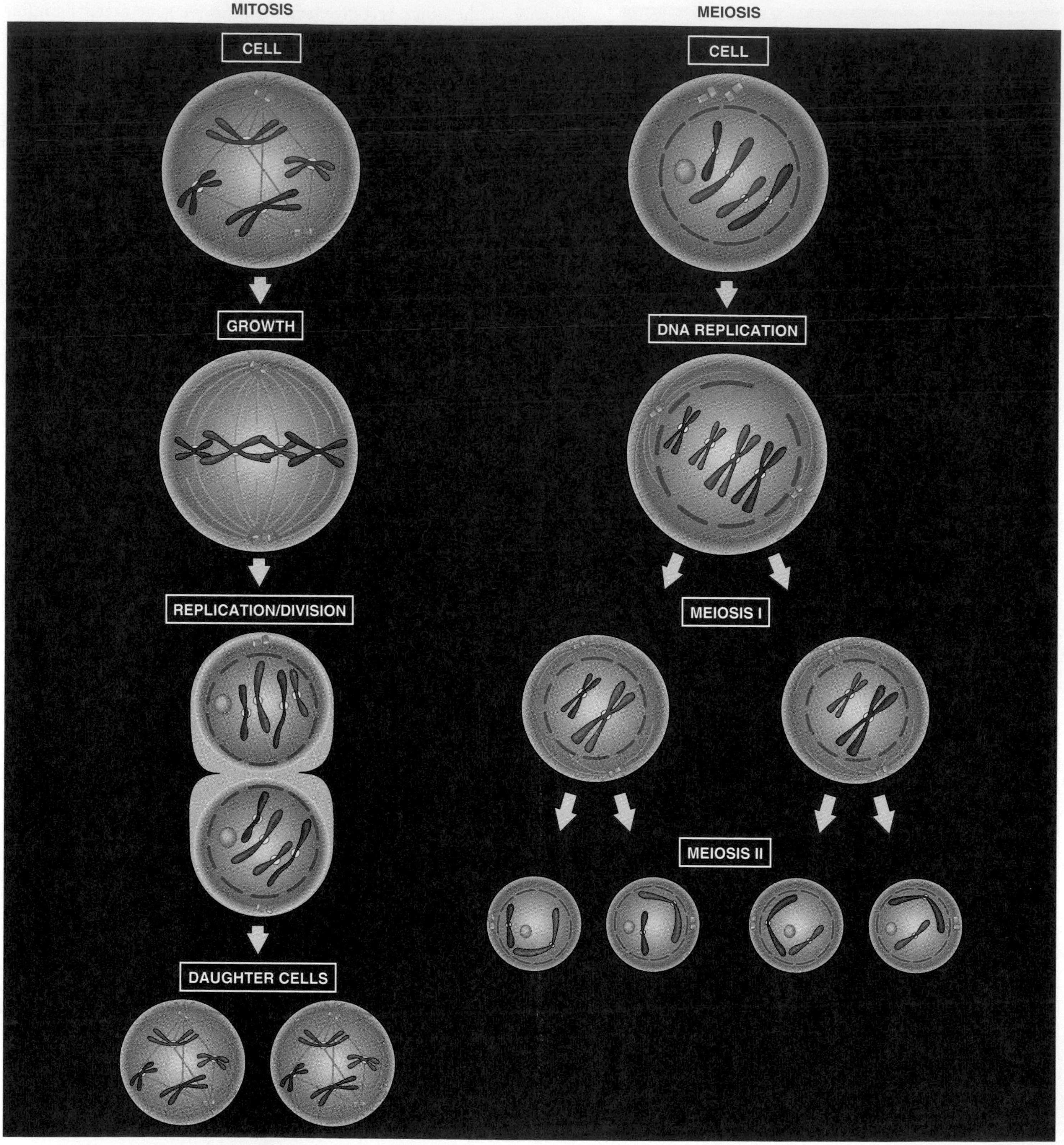

Figure **3.3 Mitosis and Meiosis**

The sequences on the left illustrate the basic transformations that take place in mitosis; those on the right illustrate those that take place in meiosis. In mitosis, the cell's nucleus duplicates itself. Notice in the third drawing from the top, on the left, how the chromosomes have moved to opposite sides and then in the fourth drawing how the cell has separated to form two daughter cells. In the meiosis transformations shown on the right side of the page, during meiosis I the chromosome pairs separate. During meiosis II, four daughter cells are formed. Note that the blue chromosomes were inherited from one parent, the red chromosomes from the other parent.

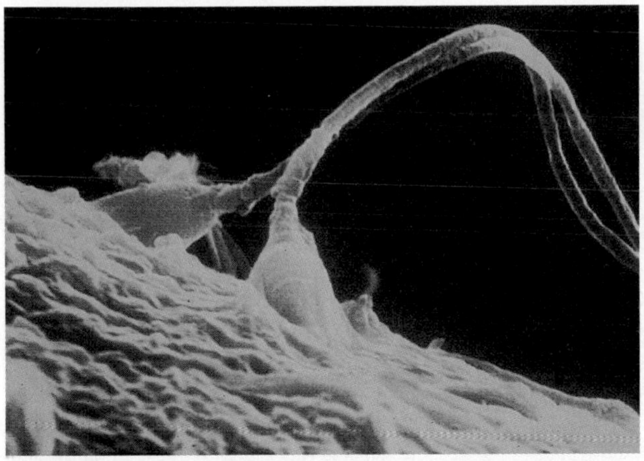

Figure **3.4**
Union of Sperm and Egg

Landmarks in the History of Genetics
Heredity Resources
Genetic Journals and News

genotype
A person's genetic heritage; the actual genetic material.

influence of the other, recessive gene. A recessive gene exerts its influence only if the two genes of a pair are both recessive. If you inherit a recessive gene for a trait from each of your parents, you will show the trait. If you inherit a recessive gene from only one parent, you may never know you carry the gene. Brown eyes, farsightedness, and dimples rule over blue eyes, nearsightedness, and freckles in the world of dominant-recessive genes. Can two brown-eyed parents have a blue-eyed child? Yes, they can. Suppose that in each parent the gene pair that governs eye color includes a dominant gene for brown eyes and a recessive gene for blue eyes. Since dominant genes override recessive genes, the parents have brown eyes, but both are carriers of blueness and pass on their recessive genes for blue eyes. With no dominant gene to override them, the recessive genes can make the child's eyes blue. Figure 3.5 illustrates the dominant-recessive genes principles.

For thousands of years, people wondered what determined whether we become male or female. Aristotle believed that the father's arousal during intercourse determines the offspring's sex. The more excited the father was, the more likely it would be a son, he reasoned. Of course, he was wrong, but it was not until the 1920s that researchers confirmed the existence of human sex chromosomes, 2 of the 46 chromosomes human beings normally carry. As we saw earlier, ordinarily females have two X chromosomes, and males have an X and a Y. (Figure 3.6 shows the chromosomal makeup of a male and a female.)

Genetic transmission is usually more complex than the simple examples we have examined thus far (Weaver & Hedrick, 1999). *Polygenic inheritance* is the genetic principle that many genes can interact to produce a particular characteristic. Few psychological characteristics are the result of single pairs. Most are determined by the interaction of many different genes. There are 50,000 or more genes, so you can imagine that possible combinations of these are staggering in number. Traits produced by this mixing of genes are said to be polygenically determined.

No one possesses all the characteristics that our genetic structure makes possible. A **genotype** *is the person's genetic heritage, the actual genetic material.* However,

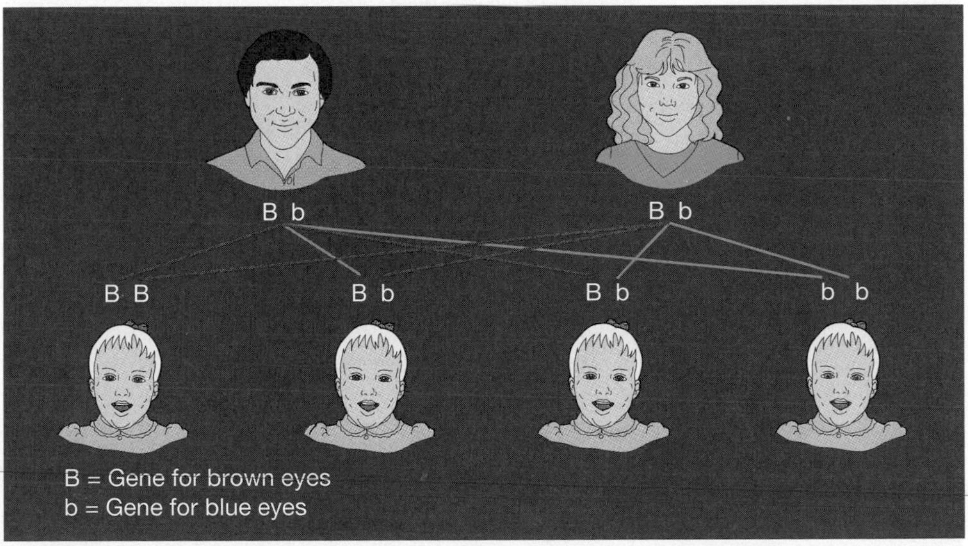

Figure **3.5**
How Brown-Eyed Parents Can Have a Blue-Eyed Child

Although both parents have brown eyes, each parent can have a recessive gene for blue eyes. In this example, both parents have brown eyes, but each parent carries the recessive gene for blue eyes. Therefore, the odds of their child having blue eyes is one in four—the probability the child will receive a recessive gene (*b*) from each parent.

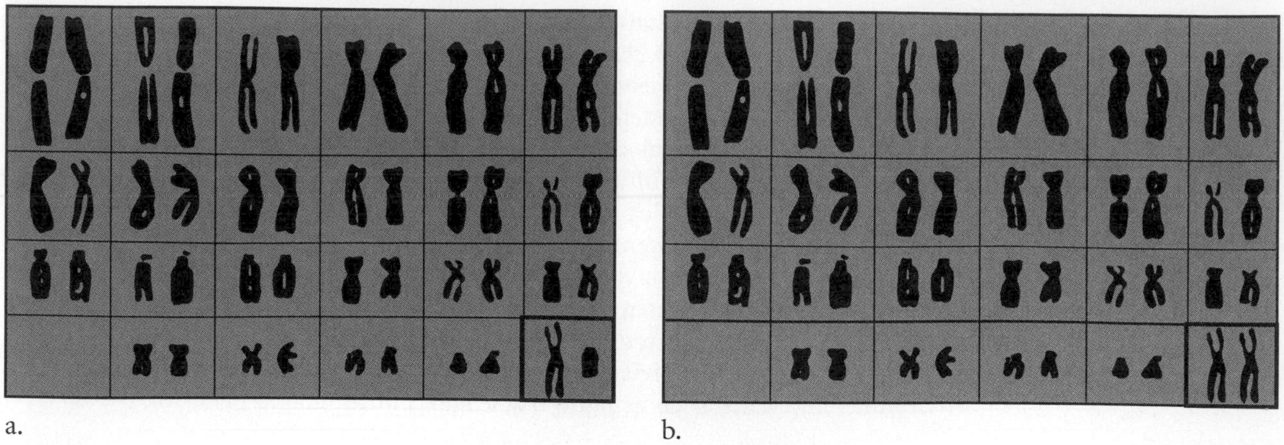

Figure 3.6

The Genetic Difference Between Males and Females

Set (*a*) shows the chromosome structure of a male, and set (*b*) shows the chromosome structure of a female. The last pair of 23 pairs of chromosomes is in the bottom right box of each set. Notice that the Y chromosome of the male is smaller than the X chromosome of the female. To obtain this kind of chromosomal picture, a cell is removed from a person's body, usually from the inside of the mouth. The chromosomes are stained by chemical treatment, magnified, and then photographed.

not all of this genetic material is apparent in our observed and measurable characteristics. A **phenotype** *is the way an individual's genotype is expressed in observed and measurable characteristics.* Phenotypes include physical traits (such as height, weight, eye color, and skin pigmentation) and psychological characteristics (such as intelligence, creativity, personality, and social tendencies).

For each genotype, a range of phenotypes can be expressed. Imagine that we could identify all of the genes that would make a person introverted or extraverted. Would measured introversion-extraversion be predictable from knowledge of the specific genes? The answer is no, because, even if our genetic model were adequate, introversion-extraversion is a characteristic shaped by experience throughout life. For example, parents may push an introverted child into social situations and encourage the child to become more gregarious.

To understand how introverted a child is, think about a series of genetic codes that predispose the child to develop in a particular way, and imagine environments that are responsive or unresponsive to this development. For instance, the genotype of some persons may predispose them to be introverted in an environment that promotes a turning inward of personality, yet, in an environment that encourages social interaction and outgoingness, these individuals may become more extraverted. However, it would be unlikely for the individual with this introverted genotype to become a strong extravert. The **reaction range** *is the range of possible phenotypes for each genotype, suggesting the importance of an environment's restrictiveness or richness* (see figure 3.7).

Sandra Scarr (1984) explains reaction range this way: each of us has a range of potential. For example, an individual with "medium-tall" genes for height who grows up in a poor environment may be shorter than average; however, in an excellent nutritional environment, the individual may grow up taller than average. No matter how well fed the person is, though someone with "short" genes will never be taller than average. Scarr believes that characteristics such as intelligence and introversion work the same way. That is, there is a range within which the environment can modify intelligence, but intelligence is not completely malleable. Reaction range gives us an estimate of how modifiable intelligence is.

Although some traits have a wide reaction range, others are somewhat immune to extensive changes in the environment. These characteristics seem to stay on a particular developmental course, regardless of the environmental assaults on them

phenotype
The way an individual's genotype is expressed in observed and measurable characteristics.

reaction range
The range of possible phenotypes for each genotype, suggesting the importance of an environment's restrictiveness or richness.

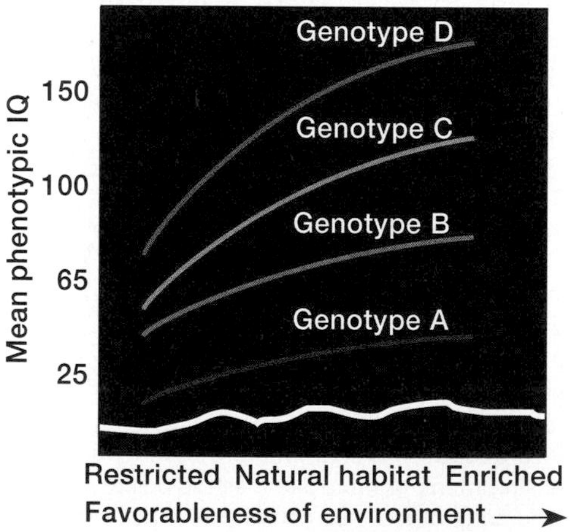

Figure 3.7

Responsiveness of Genotypes to Environmental Influences

Although each genotype responds favorably to improved environments, some are more responsive than others to environmental deprivation and enrichment.

canalization
The process by which characteristics take a narrow path or developmental course. Apparently, preservative forces help to protect a person from environmental extremes.

(Waddington, 1957). **Canalization** *is the term chosen to describe the narrow path, or developmental course, that certain characteristics take. Apparently, preservative forces help protect, or buffer, a person from environmental extremes.* For example, Jerome Kagan (1984) points to his research on Guatemalan infants who had experienced extreme malnutrition as infants yet showed normal social and cognitive development later in childhood.

Although the genetic influence of canalization exerts its power by keeping organisms on a particular developmental path, genes alone do not directly determine human behavior. Developmentalist Gilbert Gottlieb (1991, 2000; Gottlieb, Wahlsten, & Lickliter, 1998) points out that genes are an integral part of the organism but that their activity (genetic expression) can be affected by the organism's environment. For example, hormones that circulate in the blood make their way into the cell, where they influence the cell's activity. The flow of hormones themselves can be affected by environmental events, such as light, day length, nutrition, and behavior.

Behavior Genetics

behavior genetics
The study of the degree and nature of behavior's basis in heredity.

At the beginning of this chapter, in "Images of Life-Span Development," we described the Minnesota Study of Twins Reared Apart. Comparing twins reared apart is one of a number of methods used to examine heredity's influence on behavior. **Behavior genetics** *is the study of the degree and nature of behavior's hereditary basis.* Behavior geneticists assume that behaviors are jointly determined by the interaction of heredity and environment (Goldsmith, 1994; Rowe, 2001; Wahlsten, 2000).

twin study
A study in which the behavioral similarity of identical twins is compared with the behavioral similarity of fraternal twins.

To study the influence of heredity on behavior, behavior geneticists often use either twins or adoption situations. In the most common **twin study**, *the behavioral similarity of identical twins is compared with the behavioral similarity of fraternal twins. Identical twins* (called monozygotic twins) develop from a single fertilized egg that splits into two genetically identical replicas, each of which becomes a person. *Fraternal twins* (called dizygotic twins) develop from separate eggs and separate sperm, making them genetically no more similar than ordinary siblings. Although fraternal twins share the same womb, they are no more alike genetically than are nontwin brothers and sisters, and they may be of different sexes. By comparing groups of identical and fraternal twins, behavior geneticists capitalize on the basic knowledge that identical twins are more similar genetically than are fraternal twins (Mitchell, 1999; Plomin & DeFries, 1998; Scarr, 1996). In one twin study, 7,000 pairs of Finnish identical and fraternal twins were compared on the personality traits of extraversion and neuroticism (psychological instability) (Rose & others, 1998). On both of these personality traits, the identical twins were much more similar than the fraternal twins were, suggesting the role of heredity in both traits. However, several issues crop up as a result of twin studies. Adults might stress the similarities of identical twins more than those of fraternal twins, and identical twins might perceive themselves as a "set" and play together more than fraternal twins do. If so, observed similarities in identical twins could be environmentally influenced.

WWW
Behavior Genetics
Twin Research
Human Genome Project

adoption study
A study in which investigators seek to discover whether, in behavior and psychological characteristics, adopted children are more like their adoptive parents, who provided a home environment, or more like their biological parents, who contributed their heredity. Another form of the adoption study is to compare adoptive and biological siblings.

In an **adoption study,** *investigators seek to discover whether, in behavior and psychological characteristics, adopted children are more like their adoptive parents, who provided a home environment, or more like their biological parents, who contributed their heredity. Another form of the adoption study is to compare adoptive and biological siblings.* In one investigation, the educational levels attained by the biological parents were better predictors of the adopted chilren's IQ scores than were the IQs of the children's adopted parents (Scarr & Weinberg, 1983). Because of the genetic relation between the adopted children and their biological parents, the implication is that heredity influences children's IQ scores.

Molecular Genetics

Studies of behavior genetics do not focus on the molecular makeup of genes. Rather, behavior geneticists study the effects of heredity at a more global level by such methods as comparing the behavior of identical and fraternal twins.

Today, there is a great deal of enthusiasm about the use of molecular genetics to discover the specific locations on genes that determine an individual's susceptibility to many diseases and other aspects of health and well-being.

The term *genome* is used to describe the complete set of instructions for making an organism, the master blueprint for all cellular structures and activities for the life span of the organism. The human genome consists of tightly coiled threads of DNA.

The Human Genome Project, begun in the 1970s, has made stunning progress in mapping the human genome. For example, they have located the genes for Huntington disease (which causes the central nervous system to deteriorate), some forms of cancer, and many other diseases. Once these genetic markers are found, what next? One strategy is to find a healthy copy of the missing gene and transplant it into the affected cells. Another is to develop drugs that will alter the genetic makeup of the affected cells.

These athletes, many of whom have Down syndrome, are participating in a Special Olympics competition. Notice the distinctive facial features of the individuals with Down syndrome, such as round face and a flattened skull. *What causes Down syndrome?*

Chromosome and Gene-Linked Abnormalities

Let's examine some abnormalities that can occur in chromosomes and genes. As you will see, some of these abnormalities involve chromosomes, others harmful genes.

Chromosome Abnormalities When gametes are formed, the 46 chromosomes do not always divide evenly. In this case, the resulting sperm and ovum not having their normal 23 chromosomes. The most notable instances when this occurs involve Down syndrome and abnormalities of the sex chromosomes (see figure 3.8).

Genetic Disorders

Prenatal Testing and Down Syndrome

Name	Description	Treatment	Incidence
Down syndrome	Extra or altered 21st chromosome causes mild to severe retardation and physical abnormalities.	Surgery, early intervention, infant stimulation, and special learning programs	1 in 1,900 births at age 20 1 in 300 births at age 35 1 in 30 births at age 45
Klinefelter syndrome	An extra X chromosome causes physical abnormalities.	Hormone therapy can be effective	1 in 800 males
Fragile X syndrome	An abnormality in the X chromosome can cause mental retardation, learning disabilities, or short attention span.	Special education, speech and language therapy	More common in males than in females
Turner syndrome	A missing X chromosome in females can cause mental retardation and sexual underdevelopment.	Hormone therapy in childhood and puberty	1 in 3,000 female births
XYY syndrome	An extra Y chromosome can cause above-average height.	No special treatment required	1 in 1,000 male births

Figure **3.8**

Some Chromosome Abnormalities

Careers in Life-Span Development

Holly Ishmael, Genetic Counselor

Holly Ishmael is a genetic counselor at Children's Mercy Hospital in Kansas City. She obtained an undergraduate degree in psychology from Sarah Lawrence College and then a master's degree in genetic counseling from the same college.

Genetic counselors have specialized graduate degrees in the areas of medical genetics and counseling. They enter graduate school in these areas with undergraduate backgrounds from a variety of disciplines, including biology, genetics, psychology, public health, and social work. Genetic counselors, like Holly, work as members of a health-care team, providing information and support to families with birth defects or genetic disorders. They identify families at risk by analyzing inheritance patterns and explore options with the family. Genetic counselors may serve as educators and resource people for other health-care professionals and the public. Some genetic counselors also work in administrative positions or conduct research. Some genetic counselors, like Holly, become specialists in prenatal and pediatric genetics; others might specialize in cancer genetics or psychiatric genetic disorders.

Holly says, "Genetic counseling is a perfect combination for people who want to do something science-oriented, but need human contact and don't want to spend all of their time in a lab or have their nose in a book."

There are approximately thirty graduate genetic counseling programs in the United States. If you are interested in this profession, you can obtain further information from the National Society of Genetic Counselors at this website: *http://www.nsgc.org.*

Holly Ishmael (left) in a genetic counseling session.

Down Syndrome **Down syndrome** *is a chromosomally transmitted form of mental retardation, caused by the presence of an extra (47th) chromosome.* An individual with Down syndrome has a round face, a flattened skull, an extra fold of skin over the eyelids, a protruding tongue, short limbs, and retardation of motor and mental abilities. It is not known why the extra chromosome is present, but the health of the male sperm or female ovum may be involved (Davison, Gardiner, & Costa, 2001; MacLean, 2000). Women between the ages of 18 and 38 are less likely to give birth to a child with Down syndrome than are younger or older women. Down syndrome appears approximately once in every 700 live births. African American children are rarely born with Down syndrome. Some individuals have developed special programs to help children with Down syndrome. One such individual is Janet Marchese, adoptive mother of a baby with Down syndrome. She began putting the parents of children with Down syndrome together with couples who wanted to adopt them. Her adoption network has placed more than 1,500 children with Down syndrome and has a waiting list of couples who want to adopt.

Sex-Linked Chromosome Abnormalities Each newborn has at least one X chromosome. However, approximately 1 in every 500 infants either is missing a second X chromosome, or has an X chromosome that is combined with two more sex chromosomes. Three such sex-linked chromosomal disorders are Klinefelter syndrome, fragile X syndrome, and Turner syndrome (Baum, 2000).

Klinefelter syndrome *is a genetic disorder in which males have an extra X chromosome, making them XXY instead of XY.* Males with this disorder have undeveloped testes, and they usually have enlarged breasts and become tall. Klinefelter syndrome occurs approximately once in every 800 live male births.

Fragile X syndrome *is a genetic disorder that results from an abnormality in the X chromosome, which becomes constricted and often breaks.* Mental deficiency often is an outcome but its form may vary considerably (mental retardation, learning disability, short attention span) (Lewis, 1999). This disorder occurs more frequently in males than in females, possibly because the second X chromosome in females negates the disorder's negative effects (see figure 3.8).

Turner syndrome *is a chromosome disorder in females in which either an X chromosome is missing, making the person XO instead of XX, or the second X chromosome is partially deleted.* These females are short in stature and have a webbed neck. They might be infertile and have difficulty in mathematics, but their verbal ability is often facilitated. Turner syndrome occurs in approximately 1 of every 2,500 live females births.

The **XYY syndrome** *is a chromosomal disorder in which the male has an extra Y chromosome. Early interest in this syndrome involved the belief that the Y chromosome found in males contributed to male aggression and violence.* It was then reasoned that if a male had an extra Y chromosome he would likely be extremely aggressive and possibly develop a violent personality. However, researchers subsequently found that XYY males are no more likely to commit crimes than are XY males (Witkin & others, 1976).

Down syndrome
A chromosomally transmitted form of mental retardation, caused by the presence of an extra (47th) chromosome.

Klinefelter syndrome
A chromosomal disorder in which males have an extra X chromosome, making them XXY instead of XY.

Gene-Linked Abnormalities Not only can abnormalities be produced by an uneven number of chromosomes, they also can result from harmful genes (Croyle, 2000). More than 7,000 such genetic disorders have been identified, although most of them are rare.

Phenylketonuria (PKU) *is a genetic disorder in which the individual cannot properly metabolize an amino acid. Phenylketonuria is now easily detected, but, if it is left untreated, mental retardation and hyperactivity result.* The disorder is treated by diet to prevent an excess accumulation of phenylalanine, an amino acid. Phenylketonuria involves a recessive gene and occurs about once in every 10,000 to 20,000 live births. Phenylketonuria accounts for about 1 percent of institutionalized mentally retarded individuals, and it occurs primarily in Whites.

Sickle-cell anemia, *which occurs most often in African Americans, is a genetic disorder affecting the red blood cells.* A red blood cell is usually shaped like a disk, but in sickle-cell anemia, a change in a recessive gene modifies its shape to a hook-shaped "sickle." These cells die quickly, causing anemia and early death of the individual because of their failure to carry oxygen to the body's cells. About 1 in 400 African American babies is affected. One in 10 African Americans is a carrier, as is 1 in 20 Latin Americans (see figure 3.9).

Other genetic abnormalities include cystic fibrosis, diabetes, hemophilia, Huntington disease, spina bifida, and Tay-Sachs disease. Figure 3.10 provides further information about the genetic abnormalities we have discussed.

At this point we have explored a number of ideas about genetic foundations. To review these ideas, see Summary Table 3.2 on page 79.

Figure **3.9** Sickle-Cell Anemia

During a physical examination for a college football tryout, Jerry Hubbard, 32, learned that he carried the gene for sickle-cell anemia. Daughter Sara is healthy but daughter Avery (in the flowered dress) has sickle-cell anemia. *If you were a genetic counselor, would you recommend that this family have more children? Explain.*

Reproduction Challenges and Choices

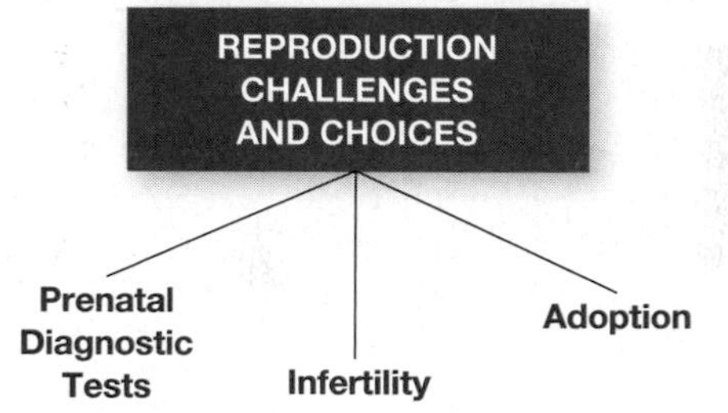

Earlier in this chapter we described the process of meiosis and how reproduction takes place. We also just examined a number of genetic abnormalities that can occur. Let's return to the topic of reproduction and explore some of it challenges and choices.

Prenatal Diagnostic Tests

Scientists have developed a number of tests to determine whether a fetus is developing normally, among them amniocentesis, ultrasound sonography, chorionic villus sampling, and the maternal blood test.

Amniocentesis is a prenatal medical procedure in which a sample of amniotic fluid is withdrawn by syringe and tested to discover if the fetus is suffering from any chromosomal or metabolic disorders (Tercyak & others, 2001). Amniocentesis is performed between the 12th and 16th weeks of pregnancy. The later amniocentesis is performed, the better its diagnostic potential. The earlier it is performed, the more useful it is in deciding whether a pregnancy should be terminated. There is a small risk of miscarriage when amniocentesis is performed; about 1 woman in every 200 to 300 miscarries after amniocentesis.

Ultrasound sonography is a prenatal medical procedure in which high-frequency sound waves are directed into the pregnant woman's abdomen. The echo from the sounds is transformed into a visual representation of the fetus's inner structures. This technique has been able to detect such disorders as microencephaly, a form of mental retardation involving an abnormally small brain. Ultrasound sonography is often used in conjunction with amniocentesis to determine the precise location of the fetus in the mother's abdomen (see figure 3.11 on p. 79). When ultrasound sonography is used five or more times, the risk of low birth weight may be increased.

fragile X syndrome
A genetic disorder involving an abnormality in the X chromosome, which becomes constricted and, often, breaks.

Turner syndrome
A chromosome disorder in females in which either an X chromosome is missing, making the person XO instead of XX, or the second X chromosome is partially deleted.

XYY syndrome
A chromosomal disorder in which males have an extra Y chromosome.

phenylketonuria (PKU)
A genetic disorder in which an individual cannot properly metabolize an amino acid. PKU is now easily detected but, if left untreated, results in mental retardation and hyperactivity.

sickle-cell anemia
A genetic disorder that affects the red blood cells and occurs most often in people of African descent.

Name	Description	Treatment	Incidence
Cystic fibrosis	Glandular dysfunction that interferes with mucus production; breathing and digestion are hampered, resulting in a shortened life span.	Physical and oxygen therapy, synthetic enzymes, and antibiotics; most individuals live to middle age.	1 in 2,000 births
Diabetes	Body does not produce enough insulin, which causes abnormal metabolism of sugar.	Early onset can be fatal unless treated with insulin.	1 in 2,500 births
Hemophilia	Delayed blood clotting causes internal and external bleeding.	Blood transfusions/ injections can reduce or prevent damage due to internal bleeding.	1 in 10,000 males
Huntington disease	Central nervous system deteriorates, producing problems in muscle coordination and mental deterioration.	Doesn't usually appear until age 35 or older; death likely 10 to 20 years after symptoms appear.	1 in 20,000 births
Phenylketonuria (PKU)	Metabolic disorder that, left untreated, causes mental retardation.	Special diet can result in average intelligence and normal life span.	1 in 14,000 births
Sickle-cell anemia	Blood disorder that limits the body's oxygen supply; it can cause joint swelling, sickle-cell crises; heart and kidney failure.	Penicillin, medication for pain, antibiotics, and blood transfusions.	1 in 400 African American children (lower among other groups)
Spina bifida	Neural tube disorder that causes brain and spine abnormalities.	Corrective surgery at birth, orthopedic devices, and physical/medical therapy.	2 in 1,000 births
Tay-Sachs disease	Deceleration of mental and physical development caused by an accumulation of lipids in the nervous system.	Medication and special diet are used, but death is likely by 5 years of age.	One in 30 American Jews is a carrier.

Figure **3.10**
Some Gene-Linked Abnormalities

Amniocentesis
Obstetric Ultrasound
Chorionic Villi Sampling
Genetic Counseling

As scientists have searched for more accurate, safer assessments of high-risk prenatal conditions, they have developed a new test. *Chorionic villi sampling* is a prenatal medical procedure in which a small sample of the placenta is removed at some point between the 8th and 11th weeks of pregnancy. Diagnosis takes approximately 10 days. Chorionic villi sampling allows a decision about abortion to be made near the end of the first trimester of pregnancy, a point when abortion is safer and less traumatic than after amniocentesis in the second trimester. Chorionic villi sampling has a slightly higher risk of miscarriage than amniocentesis and is linked with a slight risk of limb deformities. These techniques provide valuable information about the presence of birth defects, but they also raise issues pertaining to whether an abortion should be obtained if birth defects are present. Figure 3.12 on p. 80 shows how the procedures of amniocentesis and chorionic villi sampling are carried out.

The *maternal blood test (alpha-fetoprotein—AFP)* is a prenatal diagnostic technique that is used to assess blood alphaprotein level, which is associated with neural-

Summary Table 3.2
Genetic Foundations

Concept	Processes/ Related Ideas	Characteristics/Descriptions
What Are Genes?	Chromosomes, DNA	• The nucleus of each human cell contains 46 chromosomes, which are composed of DNA. • Genes are short segments of DNA and act as a blueprint for cells to reproduce and manufacture proteins that maintain life.
Mitosis and Meiosis	Mitosis	• Mitosis is the process by which each chromosome duplicates itself.
	Meiosis	• Genes are transmitted from parents to offspring by gametes, or sex cells. • Gametes are formed by the splitting of cells, a process called "meiosis." • Reproduction takes place when a female gamete (ovum) is fertilized by male gamete (sperm) to create a single-celled ovum.
Genetic Principles	From Dominant-Recessive to Canalization	• Genetic principles include those involving dominant-recessive genes, sex-linked genes, polygenic inheritance, genotype-phenotype influences, reaction range, and canalization.
Behavior Genetics	Behavior Genetics	• Behavior genetics is the field concerned with the degree and nature of behavior's hereditary basis.
	Range of Methods	• These include twin studies and adoption studies.
Molecular Genetics	The Human Genome Project	• The field of molecular genetics seeks to discover the precise locations of genes that determine an individual's susceptibility to various diseases and other aspects of health and well-being. • The Human Genome Project has made stunning progress in mapping the human genome.
Chromosome and Gene-Linked Abnormalities	Chromosome Abnormalities	• These occur when chromosomes do not divide evenly. • Down syndrome is the result of a chromosomal abnormality caused by the presence of a 47th chromosome. • Sex-linked chromosomal abnormalities include Klinefelter syndrome, fragile X syndrome, Turner syndrome, and XYY syndrome.
	Gene-Linked Abnormalities	• These involve harmful genes. • Gene-linked disorders include phenylketonuria (PKU) and sickle-cell anemia.

tube defects. This test is administered to women 14 to 20 weeks into pregnancy only when they are at risk for bearing a child with defects in the fromation of the brain and spinal cord.

Infertility

Approximately 10 to 15 percent of couples in the United States experience infertility, which is defined as the inability to conceive a child after 12 months of regular intercourse without contraception. The cause of infertility can rest with the woman or the man (Paseh, 2001). The woman may not be ovulating, she may be producing abnormal ova, her fallopian tubes may be blocked, or she may have a disease that prevents implantation of the ova. The man may produce too few sperm, the sperm may lack motility (the ability to move adequately), or he may have a blocked passageway. In one study, long-term use of cocaine by men was related to low sperm count, low motility, and a higher number of abnormally formed sperm (Bracken & others, 1990). Cocaine-related infertility appears to be reversible if users stop taking the drug for at least one year. In some

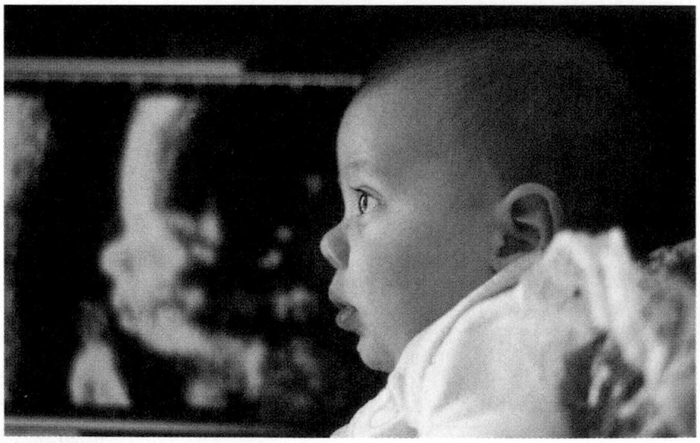

Figure 3.11 Ultrasound Sonography
A 6-month-old infant poses with the ultrasound sonography record taken 4 months into the baby's prenatal development. *What is ultrasound sonography?*

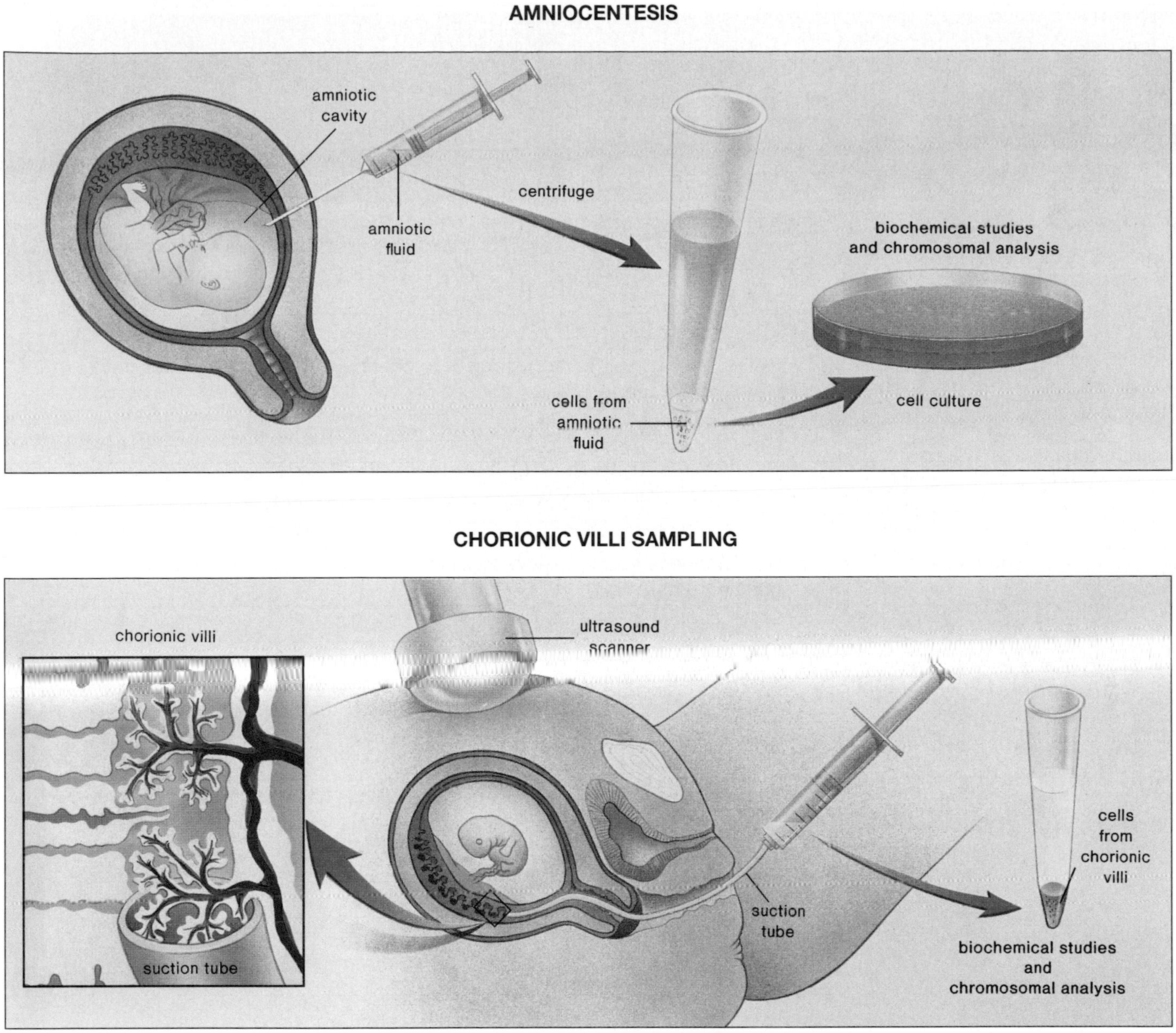

Figure **3.12**
Amniocentesis and Chorionic Villi Sampling

cases of infertility, surgery may correct the problem; in others, hormonal-based drugs may improve the probability of having a child. However, in some instances, fertility drugs have caused superovulation, producing three or more babies at a time. A summary of some of infertility's causes and solutions is presented in figure 3.13.

In the United States, more than 2 million couples seek help for infertility every year. Of those, about 40,000 try high-tech assisted reproduction. The five most common techniques are these:

WWW
Infertility Resources

- *In vitro fertilization (IVF).* An egg and a sperm are combined in a laboratory dish. If the egg is fertilized, the resulting embryo is transferred into the woman's uterus. The success rate is just under 20 percent.
- *Gamete intrafallopian transfer (GIFT).* A doctor inserts eggs and sperm directly into a woman's fallopian tube. The success rate is almost 30 percent.
- *Intrauterine insemination (IUI).* Frozen sperm—that of the husband or an unknown donor—is placed directly into the uterus, bypassing the cervix and upper vagina. The success rate is 10 percent.

MEN		
Problem	**Possible Causes**	**Treatment**
Low sperm count	Hormone imbalance, varicose vein in scrotum, possibly environmental pollutants	Hormone therapy, surgery, avoiding excessive heat
	Drugs (cocaine, marijuana, lead, arsenic, some steroids and antibiotics)	
	Y chromosome gene deletions	
Immobile sperm	Abnormal sperm shape Infection Malfunctioning prostate	None Antibiotics Hormones
Antibodies against sperm	Problem in immune system	Drugs

WOMEN		
Problem	**Possible Causes**	**Treatment**
Ovulation problems	Pituitary or ovarian tumor Underactive thyroid	Surgery Drugs
Antisperm secretions	Unknown	Acid or alkaline douche, estrogen therapy
Blocked fallopian tubes	Infection caused by IUD or abortion or by sexually transmitted disease	Surgical incision, cells removed from ovary and placed in uterus
Endometriosis (Tissue buildup in uterus)	Delayed parenthood until the thirties	Hormones, surgical incision

Figure **3.13**

Fertility Problems, Possible Causes, and Treatments

- *Zygote intrafallopian transfer (ZIFT)*. This involves a two-step procedure. First, eggs are fertilized in the laboratory. Then, any resulting zygotes are transferred to a fallopian tube. The success rate is approximately 25 percent.
- *Intracytoplasmic sperm injection (ICSI)*. A doctor uses a miscroscopic pipette to inject a single sperm from a man's ejaculate into an egg. The zygote is returned to the uterus. The success rate is approximately 25 percent.

The creation of families by means of the new reproductive technologies raises important questions about the psychological consequences for children. In one study, the family relationships and socioemotional development of children were investigated in four types of families—two created by the most widely used reproductive technologies (in vitro fertilization and donor insemination) and two control groups (families with a naturally conceived child and adoptive families) (Golombok & others, 1995). There were no differences between the four types of families on any of the measures of children's socioemotional development. The picture of families created by the new reproductive technologies was a positive one.

One consequence of fertility treatments is an increase in multiple births. Twenty-five to 30 percent of pregnancies achieved by fertility treatments—including in vitro

The McCaughey septuplets, born in 1998. *Why has there been such a dramatic increase in multiple births?*

fertilization—now result in multiple births. Though parents may be thrilled at the prospect of having children, they also face serious risks. Any multiple birth increases the likelihood that the babies will have life-threatening and costly problems, such as extremely low birthweight.

Adoption

Although surgery and fertility drugs can solve the infertility problem in some cases, another choice is to adopt a child. Adoption is the social and legal process by which a parent-child relationship is established between persons unrelated at birth. Researchers have found that adopted children and adolescents often show more psychological and school-related problems than nonadopted children (Brodzinsky & others, 1984; Brodzinsky, Lang, & Smith, 1995). Adopted adolescents are referred to psychological treatment two to five times as often as their nonadopted peers (Grotevant & McRoy, 1990).

In one recent large-scale study of 4,682 adopted adolescents and the same number of nonadopted adolescents, adoptees showed slightly lower levels of adjustment (Sharma, McGue, & Benson, 1996). However, adoptees actually showed higher levels of prosocial behavior. Also, the later adoption occurred, the more problems the adoptees had. Infant adoptees had the fewest adjustment difficultics; those adopted after they were 10 years of age had the most. Other research has documented that early adoption often has better outcomes for the child than later adoption. At age 6, children adopted from an orphanage in the first 6 months of their lives showed no lasting negative effects of their early experience. However, children from the orphanage who were adopted after they were 6 months of age had abnormally high levels of cortisol, indicating that their stress regulation had not developed adequately (Chisholm, 1998; Gunnar, in press).

These results have policy implications, especially for the thousands of children who are relegated to the foster care system after infancy. Most often, older children are put up for adoption due to parental abuse or neglect. The process of terminating the birth parents' parental rights can be lengthy. In the absence of other relatives, children are turned over to the foster care system, where they must wait for months or even years to be adopted. In the large-scale adoption study described earlier, increasingly negative effects occurred if a child was adopted above the age of 2, but the effects were even more deleterious when adoption took place after the age of 10 (Sharma, McGue, & Bensen, 1996).

A question that virtually every adoptive parent wants answered is, "Should I tell my adopted child that he or she is adopted? If so, when?" Most psychologists believe that adopted children should be told that they are adopted, because they will eventually find out anyway. Many children begin to ask where they came from when they are approximately 4 to 6 years of age. This is a natural time to begin to respond in simple ways to children about their adopted status. Clinical psychologists report that one problem that sometimes surfaces is the desire of adoptive parents to make life too perfect for the adoptive child and to present a perfect image of themselves to the child. The result too often is that adopted children feel that they cannot release any angry feelings and openly discuss problems in this climate of perfection (Warshak, 1997).

At this point, we have discussed a number of ideas about reproduction challanges and choices. A review of these ideas is presented in summary table 3.3. In our discussion of adoption, we indicated that children who are adopted later in their development often show more difficulties than those who are adopted very early in their lives. This finding suggests that the environment plays an important role in children's development.

Summary Table 3.3
Reproduction Challenges and Choices

Concept	Processes/ Related Ideas	Characteristics/Descriptions
Prenatal Diagnostic Tests	Range of Tests	• Amniocentesis, ultrasound sonography, chorionic villi sampling, and the maternal blood test are used to determine the presence of defects once pregnancy has begun.
	Genetic Counseling	• Genetic counseling has increased in popularity as couples desire information about their risk of having a child with defective characteristics.
Infertility	Degree of Problem	• Approximately 15 percent of U.S. couples have infertility problems, some of which can be corrected through surgery or fertility drugs.
	High-Tech Assisted Reproduction	• Methods include in vitro fertilization and other more recently developed techniques.
Adoption	Outcomes	• Adopted children and adolescents have more problems than their nonadopted counterparts. • When adoption occurs very early in development, the outcomes for the child are improved.

Heredity-Environment Interaction

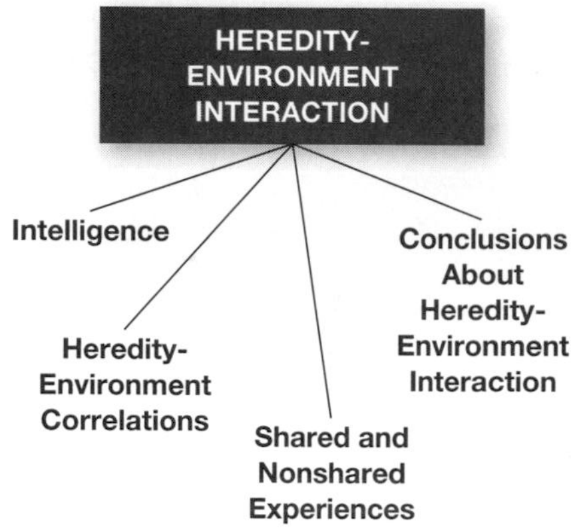

Heredity and environment interact to produce development (McGuire, 2001). To explore this interaction, we will focus on an important area of development—intelligence—and then explore many other aspects of heredity-environment interaction.

Intelligence

Arthur Jensen (1969) sparked a lively and, at times, hostile debate when he presented his thesis that intelligence is primarily inherited. Jensen believes that environment and culture play only a minimal role in intelligence. He examined several studies of intelligence, some of which involved comparisons of identical and fraternal twins. Remember that identical twins have identical genetic endowments, so their IQs should be similar. Fraternal twins and ordinary siblings are less similar genetically, so their IQs should be less similar. Jensen found support for his argument in these studies. Studies with identical twins produced an average correlation of .82; studies with ordinary siblings produced an average correlation of .50. Note the difference of .32. To show that genetic factors are more important than environmental factors, Jensen compared identical twins reared together with those reared apart; the correlation for those reared together was .89 and for those reared apart was .78 (a difference of only .11). Jensen argued that, if environmental influences are more important than genetic influences, then siblings reared apart, who experienced different environments, should have IQs much further apart.

Many scholars have criticized Jensen's work. One criticism concerns the definition of intelligence itself. Jensen believes that IQ as measured by standardized intelligence tests is a good indicator of intelligence. Critics argue that IQ tests tap only a narrow range of intelligence. Everyday problem solving, work, and social adaptability, say the critics, are important aspects of intelligence not measured by the traditional intelligence tests used in Jensen's sources. A second criticism is that most investigations of heredity and environment do not include environments that differ

radically. Thus, it is not surprising that many genetic studies show environment to be a fairly weak influence on intelligence.

Intelligence is influenced by heredity, but most developmentalists have not found as strong a relationship as Jensen found in his work. Other experts estimate heredity's influence on intelligence to be in the 50 percent range (Plomin, DeFries, & McClearn, 1990).

Two Views of *The Bell Curve*
Sternberg's Critique of *The Bell Curve*

The most recent controversy about heredity and intelligence focuses on the book *The Bell Curve: Intelligence and Class Structure in Modern Life* (1994) by Richard Herrnstein and Charles Murray. The authors argue that America is rapidly evolving a huge underclass of intellectually deprived individuals whose cognitive abilities will never match the future needs of most employers. The authors believe that members of this underclass, a large percentage of whom are African American, might be doomed by their shortcomings to welfare dependency, poverty, crime, and lives devoid of any hope of ever reaching the American dream.

Herrnstein and Murray believe that IQ can be quantitatively measured and that IQ test scores vary across ethnic groups. They point out that, in the United States, Asian Americans score several points higher than Whites, while African Americans score about 15 points lower than Whites. They also argue that these IQ differences are at least partly due to heredity and that government money spent on education programs such as Project Head Start is wasted, helping only the government's bloated bureaucracy.

Why do Herrnstein and Murray call their book *The Bell Curve?* A bell curve is a normal distribution graph, which has the shape of a bell—bulging in the middle and thinning out at the edges (see figure 3.14). Normal distribution graphs are used to

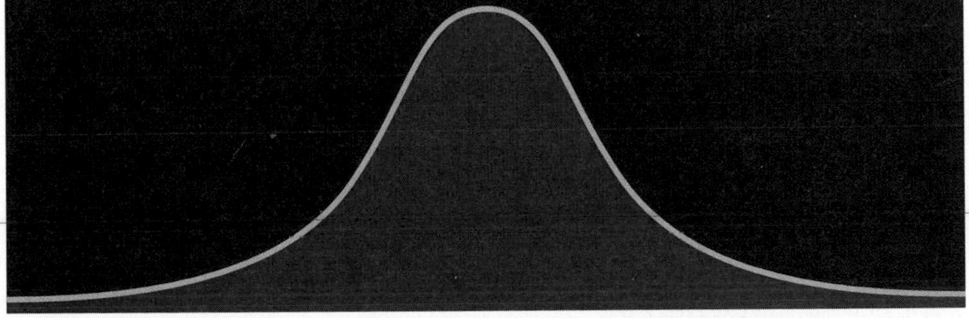

Figure **3.14**

The Bell Curve

The term *bell curve* is used to describe a normal distribution graph, a symmetrical shape that looks like a bell—bulging in the middle and thinning out at the edges.

represent large numbers of people, who are sorted according to a shared characteristic, such as weight, exposure to asbestos, taste in clothing, or IQ.

Herrnstein and Murray often refer to bell curves to make a point: that predictions about any individual based exclusively on the person's IQ are useless. Weak correlations between intelligence and job success have predictive value only when they are applied to large groups of people. Within such large groups, say Herrnstein and Murray, the pervasive influence of IQ on human society becomes apparent.

Significant criticisms have been leveled at *The Bell Curve*. Experts on intelligence generally agree that African Americans score lower than Whites on IQ tests. However, many of these experts raise serious questions about the ability of IQ tests to accurately measure a person's intelligence. Among the criticisms of IQ tests is that the tests are culturally biased against African Americans and Latinos. In 1971, the U.S. Supreme Court endorsed such criticisms and ruled that tests of general intelligence, in contrast to tests that solely measure fitness for a particular job, are discriminatory and cannot be administered as a condition of employment. Another criticism is that most investigations of heredity and environment do not include environments that differ radically.

Most experts today agree that the environment plays an important role in intelligence (Brody, 2000; Ceci & others, 1997; Di Lalla, 2000; Patrick, 2000; Sternberg, 2001; Sternberg & Grigorenko, 2001). This means that improving children's environments can raise their intelligence. Consider the experiences of twenty children in France who had been abandoned in infancy by their low-socioeconomic-status parents and subsequently adopted by upper-middle-socioeconomic-status parents (Schiff & others, 1982). These children all had biological siblings who remained with their biological mothers and were reared in impoverished circumstances. No factors that might have made the children who were adopted more genetically promising could be found. When tested in the elementary school years, the adopted children's IQs averaged 14 points higher than the IQs of their biological siblings. Children who remained with their biological mothers in impoverished conditions were four times more likely to do poorly in school. These results are consistent with other research that reveals that adoption into well-functioning middle-socioeconomic-status homes improves the cognitive functioning of children who previously have lived in impoverished environments (Skodak & Skeels, 1949; Scarr & Weinberg, 1978). To read further about the importance of environment in children's intelligence, see the Sociocultural Worlds of Development box.

Critical Thinking

The Nobel Prize Sperm Bank

IN THE 1980s, Dr. Robert Graham founded the Repository for Germinal Choice in Escondido, California, as a sperm bank for Nobel Prize winners and other bright individuals with the intent of producing geniuses. The sperm is available to women of "good stock" whose husbands are infertile, according to Graham.

What are the odds that the sperm bank will yield that special combination of factors required to produce a creative genius? Twentieth-century Irish-born British playwright George Bernard Shaw once told a story about a beautiful woman who wrote him, saying that, with her body and his mind, they could produce marvelous offspring. Shaw responded by saying that unfortunately, the offspring might get his body and her mind.

What do you think about the Nobel Prize sperm bank? Is it right to breed for intelligence? Does it raise visions of the German gene program of the 1930s and 1940s, in which the Nazis believed that certain traits are superior? They tried to breed children with such traits and killed people without them. Or does the sperm bank merely provide a social service for couples who cannot conceive a child, couples who want to maximize the probability that their offspring will have good genes?

Where do you stand on this controversial topic of breeding for intelligence? Do you think it is unethical? Can you see where it might bring hope for once childless couples?

Dr. Graham with the frozen sperm of a donor who has won a Nobel Prize.

Heredity-Environment Correlations

The notion of heredity-environment correlations involves the concept that individuals' genes influence the types of environments to which they are exposed. That is, individuals inherit environments that are related or linked to their genetic propensities (Plomin & others, 1994). Behavior geneticist Sandra Scarr (1993) described three ways that heredity and environment are correlated: passively, evocatively, and actively.

Abecedarian Project

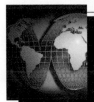

SOCIOCULTURAL WORLDS OF DEVELOPMENT

The Abecedarian Project

EACH MORNING a young mother waited with her child for the bus that would take the child to school. The unusual part of this is that the child was only 2 months old and "school" was an experimental program at the University of North Carolina at Chapel Hill. There the child experienced a number of interventions designed to improve her intellectual development—everything from bright objects dangled in front of her eyes while she was a baby to language instruction and counting activities when she was a toddler (Wickelgren, 1999).

This child was part of the Abecedarian Intervention Program conducted by Craig Ramey and his associates (Ramey & Campell, 1984; Ramey & Ramey, 1998; Ramey, Ramey, & Lanzi, 2001). They randomly assigned 111 young children from low-income, poorly educated families either to an intervention group, which experienced full-time, year-round day care along with medical and social work services, or to a control group, which got medical and social benefits but no day care. The day care program included gamelike learning activities aimed at improving language, motor, social, and cognitive skills. The success of the program in improving IQ was evident by the time the children were 3 years old, at which time the children in the experimental group showed normal IQs averaging 101, a 17-point advantage over the control group. Recent follow-up results suggest that the effects are long-lasting. More than a decade later, at age 15, children from the intervention group still maintained an IQ advantage of 5 points over the control group children (97.7 to 92.6) (Ramey & others, in press; Ramey, Campbell, & Ramey, in press). They also did better on standardized tests of reading and math, and they were less likely to be held back a year in school. The greatest IQ gains were in the children whose mothers had especially low IQs—below 70. At age 15, these children showed a 10-point IQ advantage over a group of children whose mothers had IQs below 70 but did not experience the day-care intervention.

Craig Ramey's research has documented that high-quality early educational day care can significantly raise the intelligence of young children from impoverished environments.

passive genotype-environment correlations Correlations that exist when the natural parents, who are genetically related to the child, provide a rearing environment for the child.

Passive genotype-environment correlations *occur when biological parents, who are genetically related to the child, provide a rearing environment for the child.* For example, the parents might have a genetic predisposition to be intelligent and read skillfully. Because they read well and enjoy reading, they provide their children with books to read. The likely outcome is that their children, given their own inherited predispositions, will become skilled readers.

evocative genotype-environment correlations Correlations that exist when the child's genotype elicits certain types of physical and social environments.

Evocative genotype-environment correlations *occur because a child's genotype elicits certain types of physical and social environments.* For example, active, smiling children receive more social stimulation than passive, quiet children do. Cooperative, attentive adolescents evoke more pleasant and instructional responses from the adults around them than uncooperative, distractible adolescents do. Athletically inclined youth tend to elicit encouragement to engage in school sports. As a consequence, these adolescents tend to be the ones who try out for sport teams and go on to participate in athletically oriented environments.

active (niche-picking) genotype-environment correlations Correlations that exist when children seek out environments they find compatible and stimulating.

Active (niche-picking) genotype-environment correlations *occur when children and adolescents seek out environments they find compatible and stimulating.* Niche-picking refers to finding a niche or setting that is suited to one's abilities. Adolescents select from their surrounding environment some aspect that they respond to, learn about, or ignore. Their active selections of environments are related to their partic-

According to Sandra Scarr, what are three ways that parents can contribute to genotype-environment correlations?

ular genotype. For example, attractive adolescents tend to seek out attractive peers. Adolescents who are musically inclined are likely to select musical environments in which they can successfully perform their skills.

Scarr believes that the relative importance of the three genotype-environment correlations changes as children develop from infancy through adolescence. In infancy, much of the environment that children experience is provided by adults. Thus, passive genotype-environment correlations are more common in the lives of infants and young children than they are for older children and adolescent who can extend their experiences beyond the family's influence and create their environments to a greater degree.

Shared and Nonshared Environmental Experiences

Behavior geneticists also believe that another way the environment's role in heredity-environment interaction can be carved up is to consider the experiences of children that are in common with those of other children living in the same home, as well as experiences that are not shared (Feinberg & Hetherington, 2001; Finkel, Whitfield, & McGue, 1995; Perusse, 1999; Turkheimer & Waldron, 2000). Behavior geneticist Robert Plomin (1993) has found that common rearing, or shared environment, accounts for little of the variation in children's personality or interests. In other words, even though two children live under the same roof with the same parents, their personalities are often very different.

Shared environmental experiences *are children's common experiences, such as their parents' personalities and intellectual orientation, the family's social class, and the neighborhood in which they live.* By contrast, **nonshared environmental experiences** *are a child's unique experiences, both within the family and outside the family, that are not shared with another sibling. Thus, experiences occurring within the family can be*

shared environmental experiences Children's common environmental experiences that are shared with their siblings, such as their parents' personalities and intellectual orientation, the family's social class, and the neighborhood in which they live.

nonshared environmental experiences The child's own unique experiences, both within the family and outside the family, that are not shared by another sibling. Thus, experiences occurring within the family can be part of the "nonshared environment."

part of the "nonshared environment." Parents often interact differently with each sibling, and siblings interact differently with parents (Hetherington, Reiss, & Plomin, 1994; Reiss & others, 2000). Siblings often have different peer groups, different friends, and different teachers at school.

Conclusions About Heredity-Environment Interaction

In sum, both genes and environment are necessary for a person to even exist. Without genes, there is no person; without environment, there is no person (Scarr & Weinberg, 1980). Heredity and environment operate together—or cooperate—to produce a person's intelligence, temperament, height, weight, ability to pitch a baseball, ability to read, and so on (Gottlieb, Wahlsten, & Lickliter, 1998; Kallio, 1999) P. 20. If an attractive, popular, intelligent girl is elected president of her senior class in high school, is her success due to heredity or to environment? Of course, the answer is both. Because the environment's influence depends on genetically endowed characteristics, we say the two factors *interact* (Mader, 1999).

The relative contributions of heredity and environment are not additive, as in such-and-such a percentage of nature, such-and-such a percentage of experience. That's the old view. Nor is it accurate to say that full genetic expression happens once, around conception or birth, after which we take our genetic legacy into the world to see how far it gets us. Genes produce proteins throughout the life span, in many different environments. Or they don't produce these proteins, depending on how harsh or nourishing those environments are

The emerging view is that many complex behaviors likely have some genetic loading that gives people a propensity for a particular developmental trajectory (Plomin & others, 2001). But the actual development requires more: an environment. And that environment is complex, just like the mixture of genes we inherit (Sternberg & Grigorenko, 2001). Environmental influences range from the things we lump together under "nurture" (such as parenting, family dynamics, schooling, and neighborhood quality) to biological encounters (such as viruses, birth complications, and even biological events in cells) (Greenough, 1997, 1999).

Imagine for a moment that there is a cluster of genes somehow associated with youth violence (this is hypothetical because we don't know of any such combination). The adolescent who carries this genetic mixture might experience a world of loving parents, regular nutritious meals, lots of books, and a series of masterful teachers. Or the adolescent's world might consist of parental neglect, a neighborhood where gunshots and crime are everyday occurrences, and inadequate schooling. In which of these environments are the adolescent's genes likely to manufacture the biological underpinnings of criminality? Also note that growing up with all of the "advantages" does not necessarily guarantee success. Adolescents from wealthy families might have access to books, excellent schools, travel, and tutoring. But they might take such opportunities for granted and fail to develop the motivation to learn and achieve. In the same way, "poor" or "disadvantaged" does not equal "doomed"; many impoverished adolescents make the best of the opportunities available to them and learn to seek out advantages that can help them improve their lives.

The most recent nature-nurture controversy erupted when Judith Harris (1998) published *The Nurture Assumption.* In this provocative book, she argued that what parents do does not make a difference in their children's and adolescents' behavior. Yell at them. Hug them. Read to them. Ignore them. Harris says it won't influence how they turn out. She argues that genes and peers are far more important than parents in children's and adolescents' development.

Harris is right that genes matter and she is right that peers matter, although her descriptions of peer influences do not take into account the complexity of peer con-

Genes and Parenting

"The interaction of heredity and environment is so extensive that to ask which is more important, nature or nurture, is like asking which is more important to a rectangle, height or width."

William Greenough
Contemporary Developmental Psychologist, University of Illinois at Urbana

What is the theme of Judith Harris' controversial book, The Nurture Assumption? *What is the nature of the controversy?*

Summary Table 3.4
Heredity-Environment Interaction

Concept	Processes/ Related Ideas	Characteristics/Descriptions
Intelligence	Heredity and Environment Controversy	• Herrnstein, Murray, and Jensen argue that intelligence is mainly due to heredity • Most experts today accept that the environment plays an important role in intelligence.
Heredity-Environment Correlations	Scarr's View	• Sandra Scarr argues that the environments parents select for their children depend on the parents' genotypes.
	Three Correlations	• Passive genotype-environment, evocative genotype-environment, and active (niche-picking) genotype-environment are three correlations. • Scarr believes the relative importance of the these three genotype-environment correlations changes as children develop.
Shared and Nonshared Environmental Experiences	Shared Experiences	• These refer to siblings' common experiences.
	Nonshared Experiences	• These refer to the child's unique experiences.
Conclusions About Heredity-Environment Interaction	Complexity	• Many complex behaviors have some genetic loading that gives people a propensity for a particular developmental trajectory. • Actual development also requires an environment and that environment is complex. • The interaction of heredity and environment is extensive.

texts and developmental trajectories (Hartup, 1999). In addition to not adequately considering peer complexities, Harris is wrong that parents don't matter. To begin with, in the early child years parents play an important role in selecting children's peers and indirectly influencing children's development (Baumrind, 1999). There is a huge parenting literature with many research studies documenting the importance of parents in children's development (Collins & others, 2000, 2001; Maccoby, 2000). We will discuss parents' important roles throughout this book.

Child development expert T. Berry Brazelton (1998) commented, "*The Nurture Assumption* is so disturbing it devalues what parents are trying to do. . . . Parents might say, 'If I don't matter, why should I bother?' That's terrifying and it's coming when children and youth need a stronger home base." Even Jerome Kagan (1998), a champion of biological influences on development, when commenting about Harris' book, concluded that whether children are cooperative or competitive, achievement-oriented or not, they are strongly influenced by their parents for better or for worse.

At this point we have discussed a number of ideas about heredity-environment interaction. To review these ideas see summary table 3.4. Earlier in this chapter we discussed some prenatal diagnostic tests. In the next chapter, we will explore prenatal development in greater depth, as well as the birth process.

The frightening part about heredity and environment is that we parents provide both.

Notebook of a Printer

Chapter Review

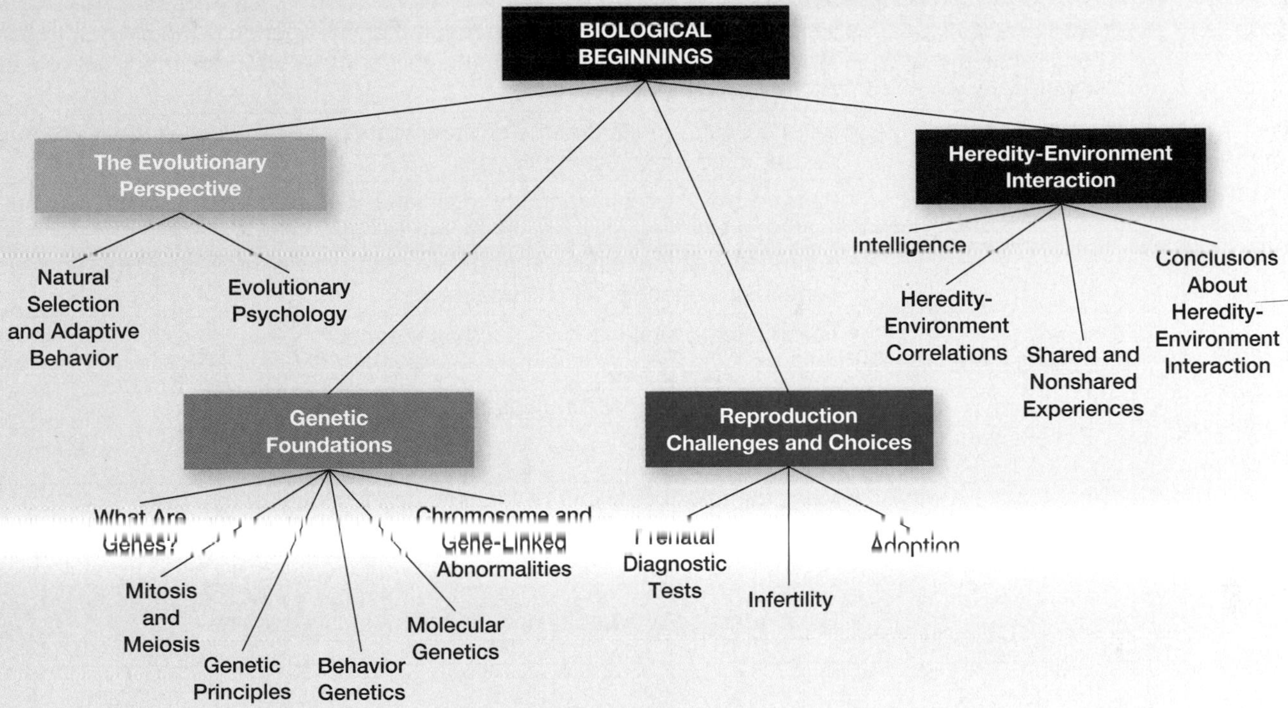

TO OBTAIN A DETAILED REVIEW OF THIS CHAPTER, STUDY THESE FOUR SUMMARY TABLES:

- Summary Table 3.1: The Evolutionary Perspective page 69
- Summary Table 3.2: Genetic Foundations page 79
- Summary Table 3.3: Reproduction Challenges and Choices page 83
- Summary Table 3.4: Heredity-Environment Interaction page 89

Key Terms

evolutionary psychology 67
chromosomes 69
DNA 69
genes 69
mitosis 70
meiosis 70
reproduction 70
zygote 70
genotype 72
phenotype 73
reaction range 73
canalization 74
behavior genetics 74
twin study 74
adoption study 74
Down syndrome 76
Klinefelter syndrome 76
fragile X syndrome 76
Turner syndrome 76
XYY syndrome 76
phenylketonuria (PKU) 77
sickle-cell anemia 77
passive genotype-environment correlations 86
evocative genotype-environment correlations 86
active (niche-picking) genotype-environment correlations 86
shared environmental experiences 87
nonshared environmental experiences 87

Key People

Thomas Bouchard 65
Charles Darwin 66
David Buss 67
Paul Baltes 67
Albert Bandura 68
Steven Jay Gould 68
Theodore Dobzhansky 68
Arthur Jensen 83
Richard Herrnstein and Charles Murray 84
Sandra Scarr 73
Craig Ramey 86
Robert Plomin 87
Judith Harris 88

Taking It to the Net

1. Ahmahl, a biochemistry major, is writing a psychology paper on the potential dilemmas that society and scientists may face as a result of the decoding of the human genome. What are some of the main issues or concerns that Ahmahl should address in his class paper?
2. Brandon and Katie are thrilled to learn that they are expecting their first child. They are curious about the genetic make-up of their unborn child and want to know (a) what disorders might be identified through prenatal genetic testing, and (b) which tests, if any, Katie should undergo to help determine this information?
3. Greg and Courtenay have three boys. They would love to have a girl. Courtenay read that there is a clinic in Virginia where you can pick the sex of your child. How successful are such efforts? Would you want to have this choice available to you?

Connect to www.mhhe.com/santrockld8 to research the answers and complete these exercises.

OLC Preview

To further test your knowledge of this chapter or to explore our extensive online resources that accompany *Life-Span Development*, eighth edition, please log on to the text's Online Learning Center at http://www.mhhe.com/santrockld8.com.

Chapter 4

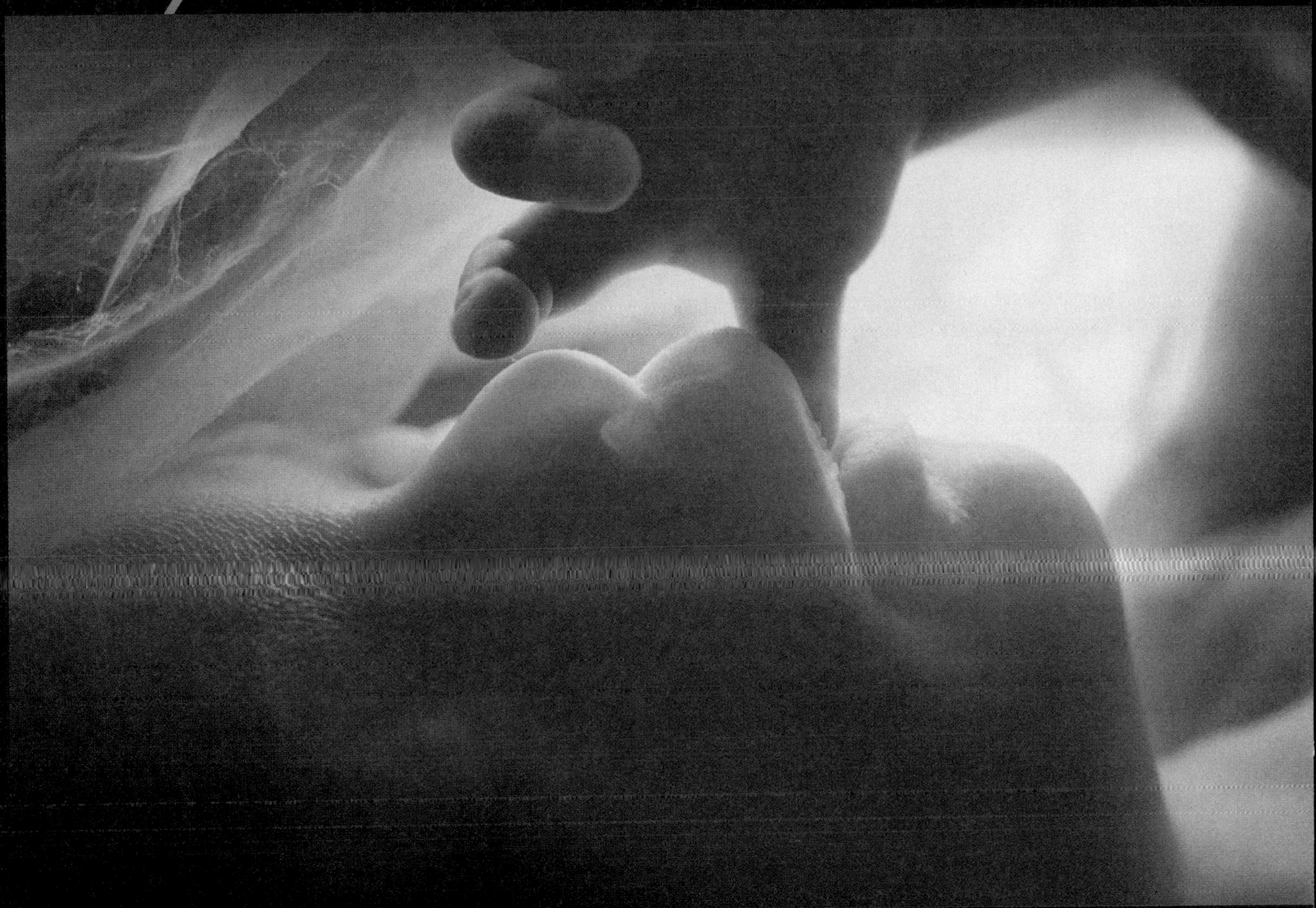

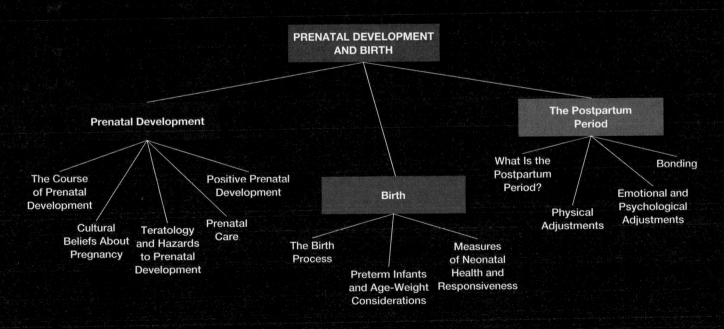

- **PRENATAL DEVELOPMENT AND BIRTH**
  - **Prenatal Development**
    - The Course of Prenatal Development
    - Cultural Beliefs About Pregnancy
    - Teratology and Hazards to Prenatal Development
    - Prenatal Care
    - Positive Prenatal Development
  - **Birth**
    - The Birth Process
    - Preterm Infants and Age-Weight Considerations
    - Measures of Neonatal Health and Responsiveness
  - **The Postpartum Period**
    - What Is the Postpartum Period?
    - Physical Adjustments
    - Emotional and Psychological Adjustments
    - Bonding

Prenatal Development and Birth

There was a star danced, and under that I was born.

William Shakespeare
English Playwright, 17th Century

Images of Life-Span Development

Tanner Roberts' Birth: A Fantastic Voyage

TANNER ROBERTS was born in a suite at St. Joseph's Medical Center in Burbank, California (Warrick, 1992). Let's examine what took place in the hours leading up to his birth. It is day 266 of his mother Cindy's pregnancy. She is in the frozen-food aisle of a convenience store and feels a sharp pain, starting in the small of her back and reaching around her middle, which causes her to gasp. For weeks, painless Braxton Hicks spasms (named for the gynecologist who discovered them) have been flexing her uterine muscles. But these practice contractions were not nearly as intense and painful as the one she just experienced. After 6 hours of irregular spasms, her uterus settles into a more predictable rhythm.

At 3 A.M., Cindy and her husband, Tom, are wide awake. They time Cindy's contractions with a stopwatch. The contractions are now only 6 minutes apart. It's time to call the hospital. At the hospital, Cindy goes to a labor-delivery suite. The nurse puts a webbed belt and fetal monitor around Cindy's middle to measure the labor. The monitor picks up the fetal heart rate. With each contraction of the uterine wall, Tanner's heartbeat jumps from its resting state of about 140 beats to 160–170 beats per minute. When the cervix is dilated to more than 4 centimeters, or almost half open, Cindy is given her first medication. As Demerol begins to drip in her veins, she becomes more relaxed. Tanner's heart rate dips to 130 and then 120.

Contractions are now coming every 3 to 4 minutes, each one lasting about 25 seconds. The Demerol does not completely obliterate Cindy's pain. She hugs her husband as the nurse urges her to "relax those muscles. Breathe deep. Relax. You are almost done."

Each contraction briefly cuts off Tanner's source of oxygen. However, the minutes of rest between each contraction resupply the oxygen and Cindy's deep breathing helps rush fresh blood to the fetal heart and brain.

At 8 A.M., Cindy's obstetrician arrives and determines that her cervix is almost completely dilated. Using a tool made for the purpose, he reaches into the birth canal and tears the membranes of the amnio sac, and about half a liter of clear fluid flows out. Contractions are now coming every 2 minutes, and each one is lasting a full minute.

By 9 A.M., the labor suite has been transformed into a delivery room. Tanner's body is compressed by his mother's contractions and pushes. As he nears his entrance into the world, the compressions help press the fluid from his lungs in preparation for his first breath.

Squeezed tightly in the birth canal, the top of Tanner's head emerges. His face is puffy and scrunched. Although fiercely squinting because of the sudden light, Tanner's eyes are open. Tiny bubbles of clear mucus are on his lips. Before any more of his body emerges, the obstetrician cradles Tanner's head and suctions his nose and mouth. Tanner takes his first breath, a large gasp followed by whimpering, and then a loud cry. Tanner's body is wet but only slightly bloody as the doctor lifts him onto his mother's abdomen. The umbilical cord, still connecting Tanner with his mother, slows and stops pulsating. The obstetrician cuts it, severing Tanner's connection to his mother's womb. Now Tanner's blood flows not to his mother's blood for nourishment, but to his own lungs, intestines, and other organs. This chapter chronicles the truly remarkable developments from conception through birth. Imagine . . . at one time you were an organism floating around in a sea of fluid in your mother's womb. Let's now explore what your development was like from the time you were conceived through the time you were born.

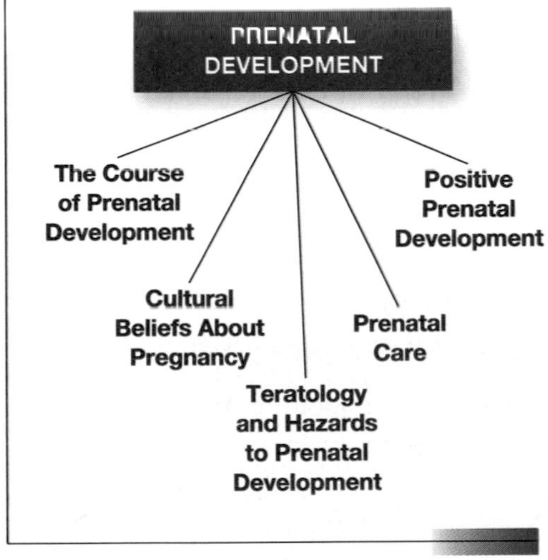

Prenatal Development

Imagine how Tanner Roberts came to be. Out of thousands of eggs and millions of sperm, one egg and one sperm united to produce him. Had the union of sperm and egg come a day or even an hour earlier or later, he might have been very different—maybe even of the opposite sex. Remember from chapter 3 that conception occurs when a single sperm cell from the male unites with an ovum (egg) in the female's fallopian tube in a process called fertilization. Remember also that the fertilized egg is called a zygote. By the time the zygote ends its 3- to 4-day journey through the fallopian tube and reaches the uterus, it has divided into approximately 12 to 16 cells.

The Course of Prenatal Development

Prenatal development is divided into three periods: germinal, embryonic, and fetal.

The Germinal Period

The **germinal period** *is the period of prenatal development that takes place in the first 2 weeks after conception. It includes the creation of the zygote, continued cell division, and the attachment of the zygote to the uterine wall.* By approximately 1 week after conception, the zygote is composed of 100 to 150 cells. The differentiation of cells has already commenced, as inner and outer layers of the organism are formed. The **blastocyst** *is the inner layer of cells that develops during the germinal period. These cells later develop into the embryo.* The **trophoblast** *is the outer layer of cells that develops during the germinal period. It later provides nutrition and support for the embryo. Implantation,* the attachment of the zygote to the uterine wall, takes place about 10 days after conception. Figure 4.1 illustrates some of the most significant developments during the germinal period.

germinal period
The period of prenatal development that takes place in the first 2 weeks after conception. It includes the creation of the zygote, continued cell division, and the attachment of the zygote to the uterine wall.

blastocyst
The inner layer of cells that develops during the germinal period. These cells later develop into the embryo.

trophoblast
The outer layer of cells that develops in the germinal period. These cells provide nutrition and support for the embryo.

The Embryonic Period

The **embryonic period** *is the period of prenatal development that occurs from 2 to 8 weeks after conception. During the embryonic period, the rate of cell differentiation intensifies, support systems for the cells form, and organs appear.* As the zygote attaches to the uterine wall, its cells form two layers. At this time, the name of the mass of cells changes from *zygote* to *embryo.* The embryo's *endoderm*

is the inner layer of cells, which will develop into the digestive and respiratory systems. The outer layer of cells is divided into two parts. The *ectoderm* is the outermost layer, which will become the nervous system, sensory receptors (ears, nose, and eyes, for example), and skin parts (hair and nails, for example). The *mesoderm* is the middle layer, which will become the circulatory system, bones, muscles, excretory system, and reproductive system. Every body part eventually develops from these three layers. The endoderm primarily produces internal body parts, the mesoderm primarily produces parts that surround the internal areas, and the ectoderm primarily produces surface parts.

embryonic period
The period of prenatal development that occurs 2 to 8 weeks after conception. During the embryonic period, the rate of cell differentiation intensifies, support systems for the cells form, and organs appear.

As the embryo's three layers form, life-support systems for the embryo mature and develop rapidly. These life-support systems include the placenta, the umbilical cord, and the amnion. The **placenta** *is a life-support system that consists of a disk-shaped group of tissues in which small blood vessels from the mother and the offspring interwine but do not join.* The **umbilical cord** *is a life-support system, containing two arteries and one vein, that connects the baby to the placenta.* Very small molecules—oxygen, water, salt, food from the mother's blood, as well as carbon dioxide and digestive wastes from the embryo's blood—pass back and forth between the mother and infant. Large molecules cannot pass through the placental wall; these include red blood cells and harmful substances, such as most bacteria, maternal wastes, and hormones. The mechanisms that govern the transfer of substances across the placental barrier are complex and are still not entirely understood (Rosenblith, 1992). Figure 4.2 provides an illustration of the placenta, the umbilical cord, and the nature of blood flow in the expectant mother and developing child in the uterus. The **amnion,** *a bag or an envelope that contains a clear fluid in which the developing embryo floats, is another important life-support system.* Like the placenta and umbilical cord, the amnion develops from the fertilized egg, not from the mother's own body. At approximately 16 weeks, the kidneys of the fetus begin to produce urine. This fetal urine remains the main source of the amniotic fluid until the third trimester, when some of the fluid is excreted from the lungs of the growing fetus. Although the amniotic fluid increases in volume tenfold from the 12th to the 40th week of pregnancy, it is also removed in various ways. Some is swallowed by the fetus, and some is absorbed through the

placenta
A life-support system that consists of a disk-shaped group of tissues in which small blood vessels from the mother and offspring intertwine.

umbilical cord
A life-support system containing two arteries and one vein that connects the baby to the placenta.

amnion
The life-support system that is a bag or envelope that contains a clear fluid in which the developing embryo floats.

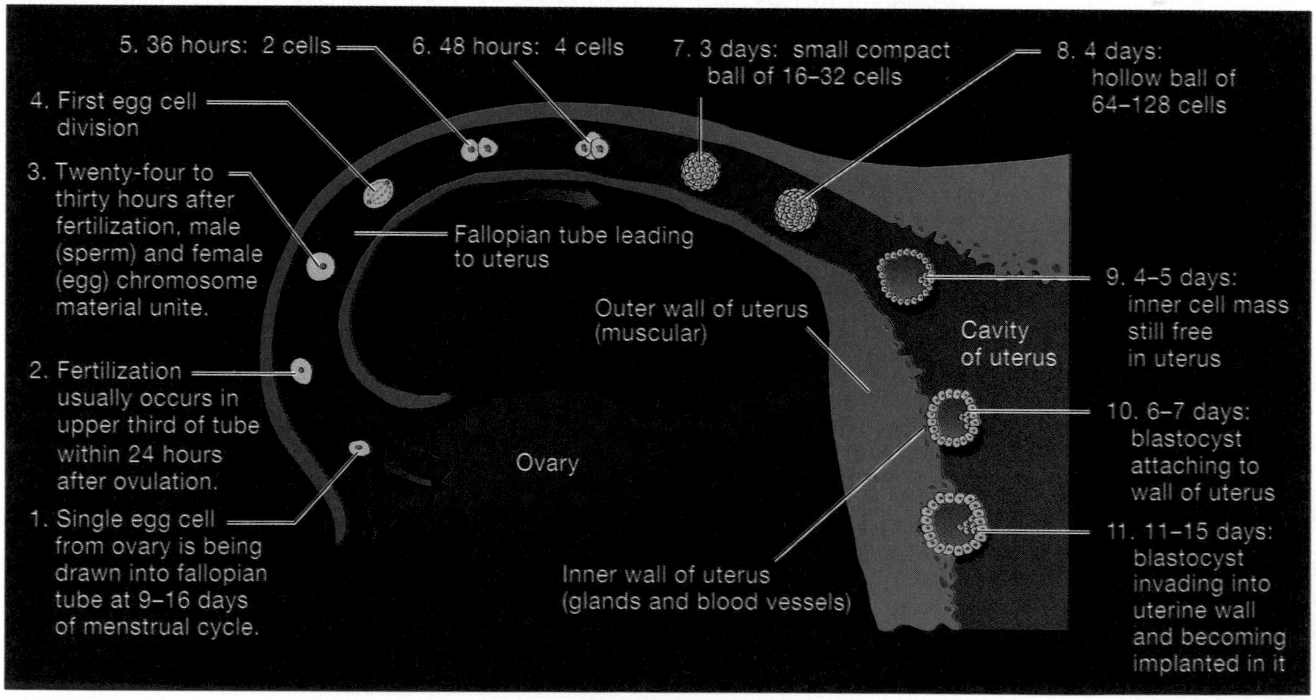

Figure **4.1**
Significant Developments in the Germinal Period

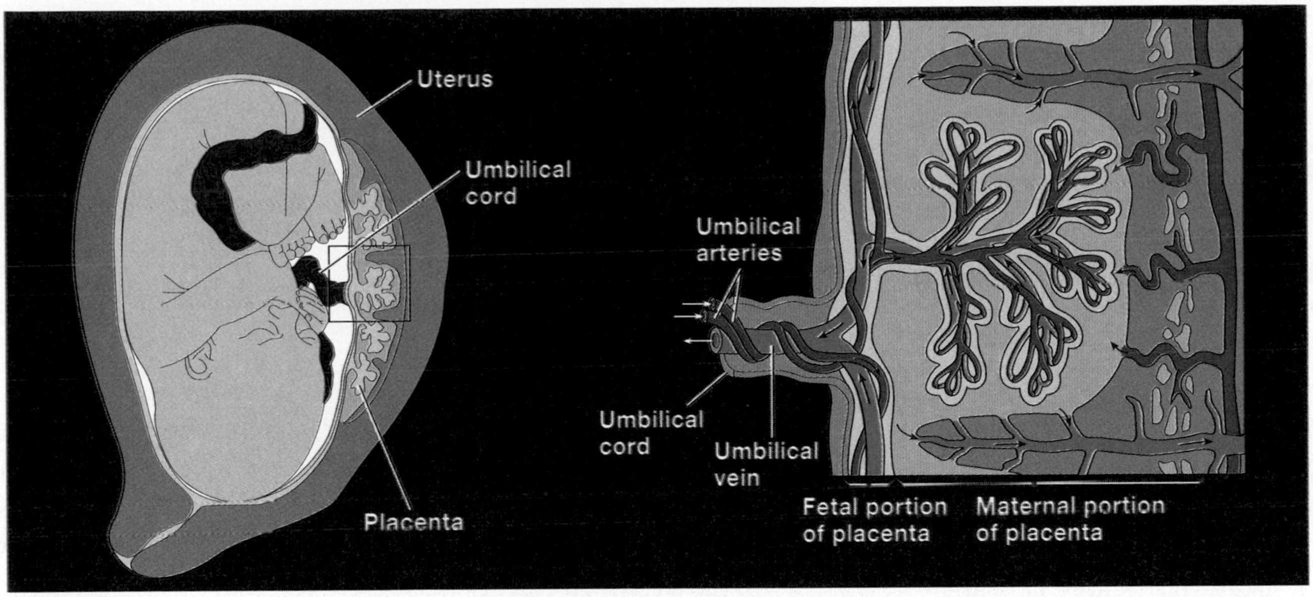

Figure **4.2**

The Placenta and the Umbilical Cord

Maternal blood flows through the uterine arteries to the spaces housing the placenta, and it returns through the uterine veins to maternal circulation. Fetal blood flows through the umbilical arteries into the capillaries of the placenta and returns through the umbilical veins to the fetal circulation. The exchange of materials takes place across the layer separating the maternal and fetal blood supplies, so the bloods never come into contact. *Note.* The area bound by the square is enlarged in the right half of the illustration. Arrows indicate the direction of blood flow.

organogenesis
Organ formation that takes place during the first 2 months of prenatal development.

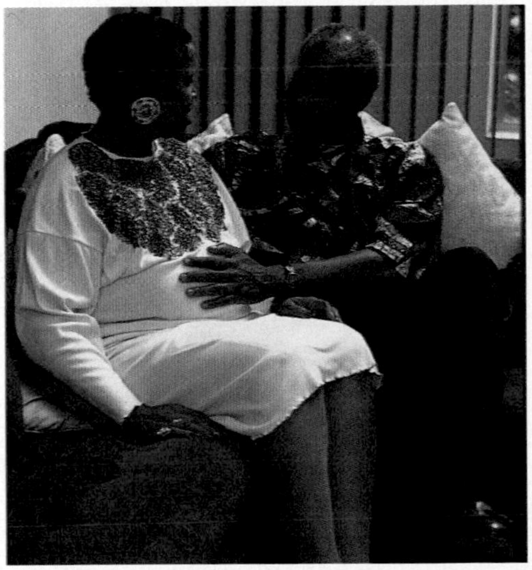

Lines of communication should be open between the expectant mother and her partner during pregnancy. *What are some examples of good partner communication during pregnancy?*

fetal period
The prenatal period of development that begins 2 months after conception and lasts for 7 months, on the average.

umbilical cord and the membranes covering the placenta. The amniotic fluid provides an environment that is temperature and humidity controlled, as well as shockproof.

Before most women even know they are pregnant, some important embryonic developments take place. In the third week, the neural tube that eventually becomes the spinal cord forms. At about 21 days, eyes begin to appear, and at 24 days the cells for the heart begin to differentiate. During the fourth week, the first appearance of the urogenital system is apparent, and arm and leg buds emerge. Four chambers of the heart take shape, and blood vessels surface. From the fifth to the eighth week, arms and legs differentiate further; at this time, the face starts to form but still is not very recognizable. The intestinal tract develops and the facial structures fuse. At 8 weeks, the developing organism weighs about 1/30 ounce and is just over 1 inch long. **Organogenesis** *is the process of organ formation that takes place during the first 2 months of prenatal development.* When organs are being formed, they are especially vulnerable to environmental changes. Later in the chapter, we will describe the environmental hazards that are harmful during organogenesis.

The Fetal Period The **fetal period** *is the prenatal period of development that begins 2 months after conception and lasts for 7 months, on the average.* Growth and development continue their dramatic course during this time. Three months after conception, the fetus is about 3 inches long and weighs about 1 ounce. It has become active, moving its arms and legs, opening and closing its mouth, and moving its head. The face, forehead, eyelids, nose, and chin are distinguishable, as are the upper arms, lower arms, hands, and lower limbs. The genitals can be identified as male or female. By the end of the fourth month, the fetus has grown to 6 inches in length and weighs 4 to 7 ounces. At this time, a growth spurt occurs in the body's lower parts. Prenatal reflexes are stronger; arm and leg movements can be felt for the first time by the mother.

By the end of the fifth month, the fetus is about 12 inches long and weighs close to a pound. Structures of the skin have formed—toenails and fingernails, for example. The fetus is more active, showing a preference for a particular position in the

womb. By the end of the sixth month, the fetus is about 14 inches long and already has gained another half pound to a pound. The eyes and eyelids are completely formed, and a fine layer of hair covers the head. A grasping reflex is present and irregular breathing movements occur. By the end of the seventh month, the fetus is about 16 inches long and has gained another pound, now weighing about 3 pounds. During the eighth and ninth months, the fetus grows longer and gains substantial weight—about another 4 pounds. At birth, the average American baby weighs 7 pounds and is about 20 inches long. In these last 2 months, fatty tissues develop, and the functioning of various organ systems—heart and kidneys, for example—steps up.

We have described a number of developments in the germinal, embryonic, and fetal periods. An overview of some of the main developments we have discussed and some more specific changes in prenatal development are presented in figure 4.3.

The history of man for nine months preceding his birth would, probably, be far more interesting, and contain events of greater moment than all three score and ten years that follow it.

Samuel Taylor Coleridge
English Poet, Essayist, 19th Century

First trimester (first 3 months)

	Conception to 4 weeks	8 weeks	12 weeks
Prenatal growth	• Is less than $1/10$ inch long • Beginning development of spinal cord, nervous system, gastrointestinal system, heart, and lungs • Amniotic sac envelops the preliminary tissues of entire body • Is called an "ovum"	• Is less than 1 inch long • Face is forming with rudimentary eyes, ears, mouth, and tooth buds • Arms and legs are moving • Brain is forming • Fetal heartbeat is detectable with ultrasound • Is called an "embryo"	• Is about 3 inches long and weighs about 1 ounce • Can move arms, legs, fingers, and toes • Fingerprints are present • Can smile, frown, suck, and swallow • Sex is distinguishable • Can urinate • Is called a "fetus"

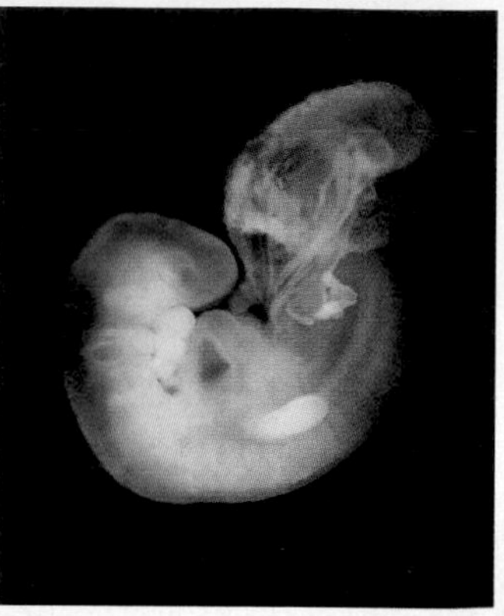

Second trimester (middle 3 months)

	16 weeks	20 weeks	24 weeks
Prenatal growth	• Is about $5\frac{1}{2}$ inches long and weighs about 4 ounces • Heartbeat is strong • Skin is thin, transparent • Downy hair (lanugo) covers body • Fingernails and toenails are forming • Has coordinated movements; is able to roll over in amniotic fluid	• Is 10 to 12 inches long and weighs $1/2$ to 1 pound • Heartbeat is audible with ordinary stethoscope • Sucks thumb • Hiccups • Hair, eyelashes, eyebrows are present	• Is 11 to 14 inches long and weighs 1 to $1\frac{1}{2}$ pounds • Skin is wrinkled and covered with protective coating (vernix caseosa) • Eyes are open • Meconium is collecting in bowel • Has strong grip

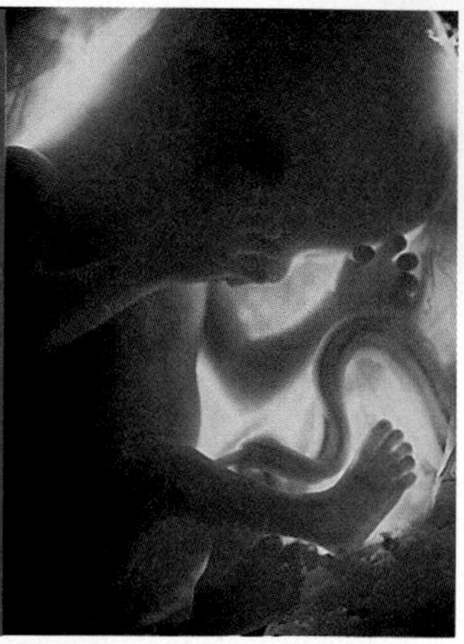

Third trimester (last 3 months)

	28 weeks	32 weeks	36 to 38 weeks
Prenatal growth	• Is 14 to 17 inches long and weighs $2\frac{1}{2}$ to 3 pounds • Is adding body fat • Is very active • Rudimentary breathing movements are present	• Is $16\frac{1}{2}$ to 18 inches long and weighs 4 to 5 pounds • Has periods of sleep and wakefulness • Responds to sounds • May assume birth position • Bones of head are soft and flexible • Iron is being stored in liver	• Is 19 inches long and weighs 6 pounds • Skin is less wrinkled • Vernix caseosa is thick • Lanugo is mostly gone • Is less active • Is gaining immunities from mother

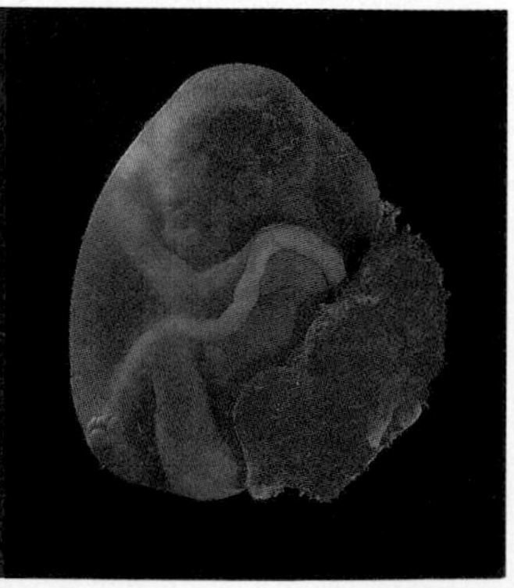

Figure **4.3**
The Three Trimesters of Prenatal Development

The Visible Embryo
The Trimesters

Notice in figure 4.4 that we have divided these changes into trimesters, or three equal time periods. The three trimesters are not the same as the three prenatal periods we have discussed—germinal, embryonic, and fetal. An important point that needs to be made is that the first time a fetus has a chance of surviving outside of the womb is the beginning of the third trimester (at about 7 months). Even when infants are born in the seventh month, they usually need assistance in breathing.

Cultural Beliefs About Pregnancy

Specific actions in pregnancy are often determined by cultural beliefs. Certain behaviors are expected if a culture views pregnancy as a medical condition, whereas other behaviors are expected if pregnancy is viewed as a natural occurrence. Prenatal care may not be a priority for expectant mothers who view pregnancy as a natural occurrence. It is important for health care providers to become aware of the health practices of various cultural groups, including health beliefs about pregnancy and prenatal development. Cultural assessment is an important dimension of providing adequate health care for expectant mothers from various cultural groups. Cultural assessment includes identifying the main beliefs, values, and behaviors related to pregnancy and childbearing. Among the important cultural dimensions are ethnic background, degree of affiliation with the ethnic group, patterns of decision making, religious preference, language, communication style, and common etiquette practices.

Health care practices during pregnancy are influenced by numerous factors, including the prevalence of traditional home care remedies and folk beliefs, the importance of indigenous healers, and the influence of professional health care workers. Many Mexican American mothers are strongly influenced by their mothers and older women in their culture, often seeking and following their advice during pregnancy. In Mexican American culture, the indigenous healer is called a *curandero.* In some Native American tribes, the medicine woman or man fulfills the healing role. Herbalists are often found in Asian cultures, and faith healers, root doctors, and spiritualists are sometimes found in African American culture. When health care providers come into contact with expectant mothers, they need to assess whether such cultural practices pose a threat to the expectant mother and the fetus. If they pose no threat, there is no reason to try to change them. On the other hand, if certain cultural practices do pose a threat to the health of the expectant mother or the fetus, the health care provider should consider a culturally sensitive way to handle the problem. For example, some Philippinos will not take any medication during pregnancy.

At this point we have studied a number of ideas about the course of prenatal development and cultural beliefs about pregnancy. A review of these ideas is presented in summary table 4.1. Next, we continue our exploration of prenatal development by discussing hazards to prenatal development.

Teratology and Hazards to Prenatal Development

Some expectant mothers carefully tiptoe about in the belief that everything they do and feel has a direct effect on their unborn child. Others behave casually, assuming that their experiences will have little effect. The truth lies somewhere between these two extremes. Although living in a protected, comfortable environment, the fetus is not totally immune to the larger world surrounding the mother (James & others, 1999; McFarlane, Parker, & Soeken, 1996). The environment can affect the child in many well-documented ways. Thousands of babies born deformed or mentally retarded every year are the result of events that occurred in the mother's life, as early as 1 or 2 months before conception.

teratogen
From the Greek word tera, meaning "monster." Any agent that causes a birth defect. The field of study that investigates the causes of birth defects is called teratology.

Exploring Teratology A **teratogen** *(the word comes from the Greek word* tera *meaning "monster") is any agent that causes a birth defect. The field of study that investigates the causes of birth defects is called teratology.* A specific teratogen (such as a drug) usually does not cause a specific birth defect (such as malformation of the

Summary Table 4.1
The Course of Prenatal Development and Cultural Beliefs About Pregnancy

Concept	Processes/ Related Ideas	Characteristics/Descriptions
The Course of Prenatal Development	The Germinal Period	• This is the period from conception until 10 to 14 days later. • A fertilized egg is called a zygote. • This period ends when the zygote attaches to the uterine wall.
	The Embryonic Period	• This is the period approximately 2 to 8 weeks after conception. • The embryo differentiates into three layers, life-support systems develop, and organ systems form (organogenesis).
	The Fetal Period	• This period lasts from about 2 months after conception until 9 months, or when the infant is born. • Growth and development continue their dramatic course, and organ systems mature to the point at which life can be sustained outside of the womb.
Cultural Beliefs About Pregnancy	Variations	• Specific actions in pregnancy are often determined by cultural beliefs. Certain behaviors are expected if a culture views pregnancy as a medical condition or a natural occurrence.

legs). So many teratogens exist that practically every fetus is exposed to at least some teratogens. For this reason, it is difficult to determine which teratogen causes which birth defect. In addition, it may take a long time for the effects of a teratogen to show up (Iannucci, 2000). Only about half of all potential effects appear at birth.

Health and Prenatal Development
Exploring Teratology
High-Risk Situations

Despite the many unknowns about teratogens, scientists have discovered the identity of some hazards to prenatal development and the particular point of fetal development at which they do their greatest damage (Brent & Fawcett, 2000; Schantz, 2000). As figure 4.4 shows, sensitivity to teratogens begins about 3 weeks after conception. The probability of a structural defect is greatest early in the embryonic period, because this is when organs are being formed. After organogenesis is complete, teratogens are less likely to cause anatomical defects. Exposure later, during the fetal period, is more likely to stunt growth or to create problems in the way organs function. The precision of organogenesis is evident; teratologists point out that the vulnerability of the brain is greatest at 15 to 25 days after conception, the eyes at 24 to 40 days, the heart at 20 to 40 days, and the legs at 24 to 36 days.

Prescription and Nonprescription Drugs Some pregnant women take prescription and nonprescription drugs without thinking about the possible effects on the fetus (Addis, Magrini & Mastroiacovo, 2001). Occasionally, a rash of deformed babies is born, bringing to light the damage drugs can have on a developing fetus. This happened in 1961, when many pregnant women took a popular tranquilizer, thalidomide, to alleviate their morning sickness. In adults, the effects of thalidomide are mild; in embryos, however, they are devastating. Not all infants were affected in the same way. If the mother took thalidomide on day 26 (probably before she knew she was pregnant), an arm might not grow. If she took the drug 2 days later, the arm might not grow past the elbow. The thalidomide tragedy shocked the medical community and parents into the stark realization that the mother does not have to be a chronic drug user for the fetus to be harmed. Taking the wrong drug at the wrong time is enough to physically handicap the offspring for life.

Prescription drugs that can function as teratogens include antibiotics, such as streptomycin and tetracycline; some depressants; certain hormones, such as progestin

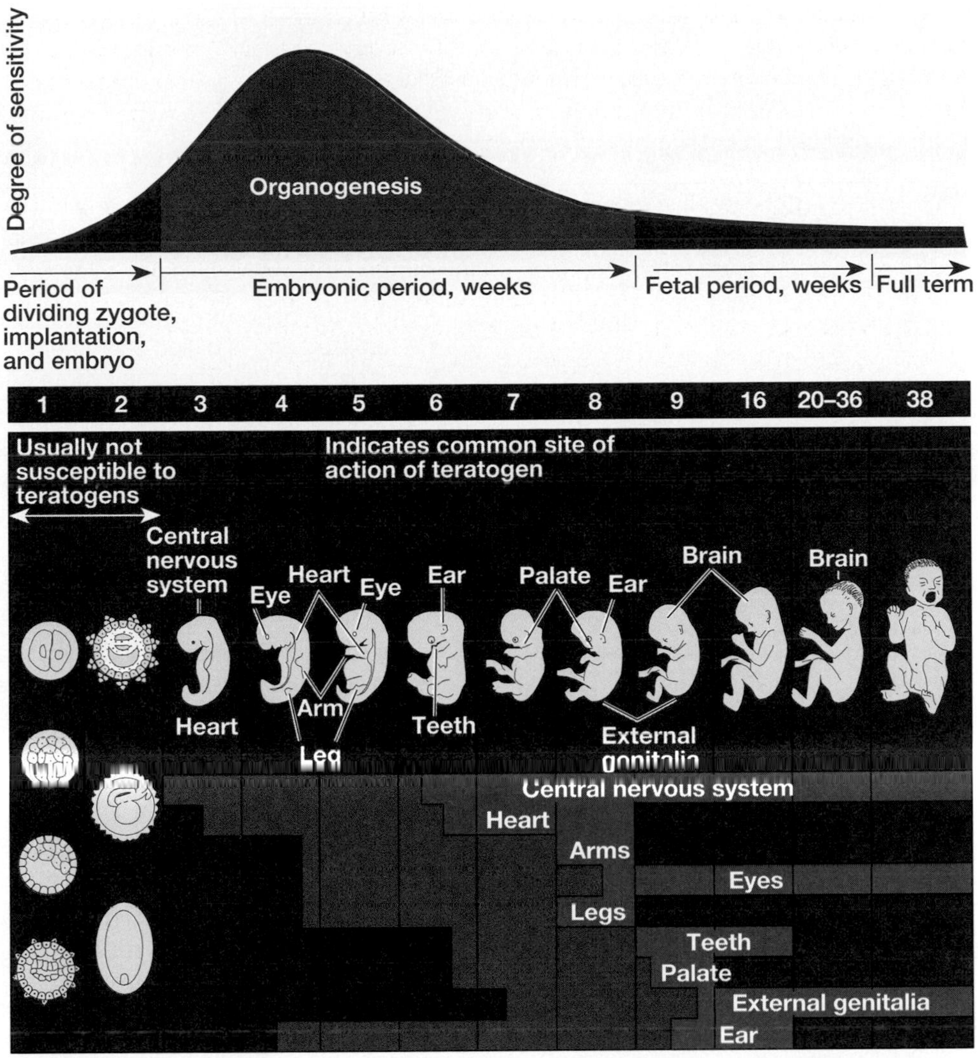

Figure **4.4**

Teratogens and the Timing of Their Effects on Prenatal Development

The danger of structural defects caused by teratogens is greatest early in embryonic development. This period of organogenesis lasts for about 6 weeks. Damage caused by teratogens during this period is represented by the red area. Later assaults by teratogens typically occur during the fetal period and, instead of structural damage, are more likely to stunt growth or cause problems of organ function.

and synthetic estrogen; and Accutane (which often is prescribed for acne) (Committee on Drugs, 2000).

Nonprescription drugs that can be harmful include diet pills, aspirin, and caffeine. Let's explore the research on caffeine. In a review of studies focused on caffeine consumption during pregnancy, it was concluded that a small increase in the risks for spontaneous abortion and low birthweight occurs for pregnant women consuming >150 mg caffeine per day (Fernandez & others, 1998). For example, in one recent study, pregnant women who drank caffeinated coffee were more likely have preterm deliveries and newborns with a lower birthweight compared to their counterparts who did not drink caffeinated coffee (Eskenazi & others, 1999). In this study, no effects were found for pregnant women who drank decaffeinated coffee. Taking into account such results, the Food and Drug Administration recommends that pregnant women either not consume caffeine or consume it only sparingly.

Psychoactive Drugs *Psychoactive drugs* are drugs that act on the nervous system to alter states of consciousness, modify perceptions, and change moods. A number of psychoactive drugs, including alcohol and nicotine, as well as illegal drugs such as cocaine, marijuana, and heroin have been studied to determine their links to prenatal and child development (Caulfield, 2001; Fogel, 2001).

Alcohol Heavy drinking by pregnant women can be devastating to offspring (Barr & Streissguth, 2001; Committee on Substance Abuse, 2000). **Fetal alcohol syndrome (FAS)** *is a cluster of abnormalities that appears in the offspring of mothers who drink alcohol heavily during pregnancy.* The abnormalities include facial deformities and defective limbs, face, and heart. Most of these children are below average in intelligence, and some are mentally retarded (Olson, 2000; Olson & Burgess, 1996). Although many mothers of FAS infants are heavy drinkers, many mothers who are heavy drinkers do not have children with FAS or have one child with FAS and other children who do not have it. Figure 4.5 shows a child with fetal alcohol syndrome. Although no serious malformations such as those produced by FAS are found in infants born to mothers who are moderate drinkers, in one study, the infants whose mothers drank moderately (one to two drinks a day) during pregnancy were less attentive and alert, with the effects still present at 4 years of age (Streissguth & others, 1984). In one recent study, prenatal alcohol exposure was a better predictor of adolescent alcohol use and its negative consequences than was family history of alcohol problems (Baer & others, 1998). And in another recent study, adults with fetal alcohol syndrome had a high incidence of mental disorders, such as depression or anxiety (Famy, Streissguth, & Unis, 1998).

fetal alcohol syndrome (FAS)
A cluster of abnormalities that appears in the offspring of mothers who drink alcohol heavily during pregnancy.

Nicotine Cigarette smoking by pregnant women can also adversely influence prenatal development, birth, and postnatal development. Fetal and neonatal deaths are higher among smoking mothers. There also are higher incidences of preterm births and lower birthweights (Wang & others, 2000) (see figure 4.6).

In one study, urine samples from 22 of 31 newborns of smoking mothers had substantial amounts of one of the strongest carcinogens (NNK) in tobacco smoke;

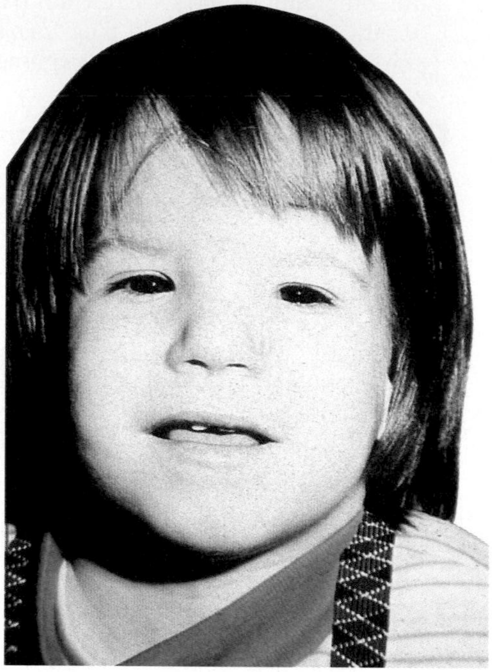

Figure **4.5**

Fetal Alcohol Syndrome

Notice the wide-set eyes, flat bones, and thin upper lip.

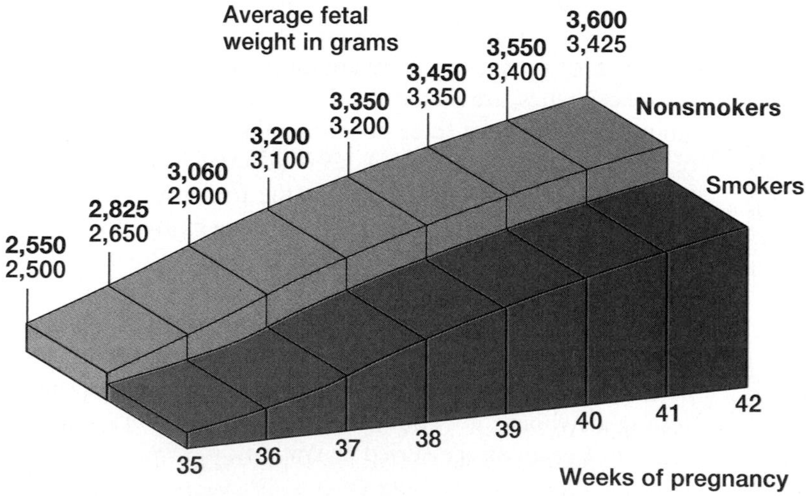

Figure **4.6**

The Effects of Smoking by Expectant Mothers on Fetal Weight

Throughout prenatal development, the fetuses of expectant mothers who smoke weigh less than the fetuses of expectant mothers who do not smoke.

Fetal Alcohol Syndrome
Smoking and Pregnancy

Critical Thinking

Intervention to Stop Pregnant Women from Smoking

SCIENTISTS HAVE KNOWN about the negative consequences of smoking for more than three decades, but they have made little progress in developing effective interventions to help pregnant women quit smoking or to keep young women from becoming addicted to smoking. What needs to be done to get pregnant women to not smoke? Consider the role of health care providers and their training, the role of insurance companies, and specific programs targeted at pregnant women.

the urine samples of the newborns whose mothers did not smoke did not contain the carcinogen (Lackmann & others, 1999). In another study, prenatal exposure to cigarette smoking was related to poorer language and cognitive skills at 4 years of age (Fried & Watkinson, 1990). Respiratory problems and sudden infant death syndrome (also known as crib death) are more common among the offspring of mothers who smoked during pregnancy (Schoendorf & Kiely, 1992). Intervention programs designed to get pregnant women to stop smoking can reduce some of smoking's negative behaviors, especially by raising birthweights (Chomitz, Cheung, & Lieberman, 1995; Lightwood, Phibbs, & Glantz, 1999).

Illegal Drugs Among the illegal drugs that have been studied to determine their effects on prenatal and child development are cocaine, marijuana, and heroin.

Cocaine With the increased use of cocaine in the United States, there is growing concern about its effects on the embryos, fetuses, and infants of pregnant cocaine users (Hurt & others, 1999). Cocaine use during pregnancy has recently attracted considerable attention because of possible harm to the developing embryo and fetus (Zeskind & others, 1999). The most consistent finding is that cocaine exposure during prenatal development is associated with reduced birthweight, length, and head circumference. Also, in one recent study, prenatal cocaine exposure was associated with impaired motor development at 2 years of age (Arendt & others, 1999).

Researchers increasingly are finding that fetal cocaine exposure is linked with impaired information processing (Singer, & others, 1999). In one study, prenatal cocaine exposure was moderately related to poor attentional skills through 5 years of age (Bandstra & others, 2000). In another study, prenatal cocaine exposure was related to impaired processing of auditory information after birth (Potter & others, 2000).

Although researchers are finding such deficits in children who are prenatally exposed to cocaine, caution in interpreting these findings is in order (Chavkin, 2001; Frank & others, 2001; Potter & others, 2000). Why? Because other factors (such as poverty, malnutrition, and other substance abuse) in the lives of pregnant women who use cocaine often cannot be ruled out as possible contributors to the negative effects on children (Kaugers & others, 2000). For example, cocaine users are more likely than nonusers to smoke cigarettes, use marijuana, drink alcohol, and take amphetamines. Teasing apart these potential influences from the effects of cocaine itself has not yet been adequately accomplished. Obtaining valid information about the frequency and type of drug use by mothers is complicated because many mothers fear prosecution and loss of child custody because of their drug use.

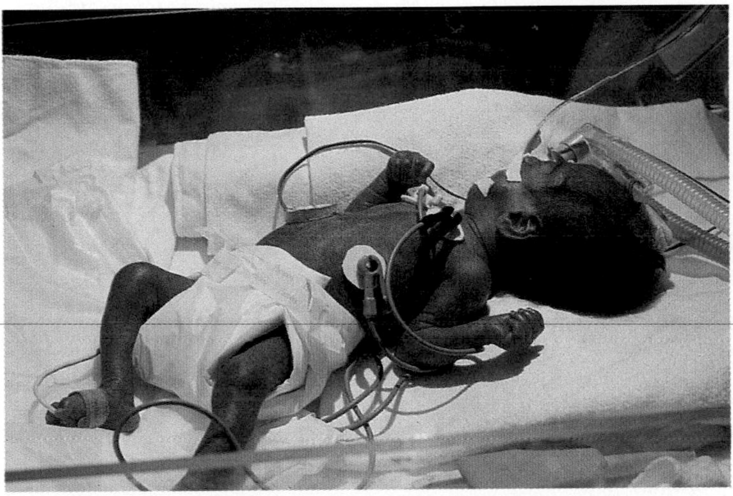

This baby was born addicted to cocaine because its mother was a cocaine addict. *What do we know about the effects of cocaine on children's development?*

Marijuana Marijuana use by pregnant women has detrimental effects on a developing fetus. Marijuana use by pregnant women is associated with increased tremors and startles among newborns and poorer verbal and memory development at 4 years of age (Fried & Watkinson, 1990).

Heroin It is well documented that infants whose mothers are addicted to heroin show several behavioral difficulties (Hans, 1989). The young infants of these mothers are addicted and show withdrawal symptoms characteristic of opiate abstinence, such as tremors, irritability, abnormal crying, disturbed sleep, and impaired motor control. Behavioral problems are still often present at the first birthday, and attention deficits

may appear later in the child's development. The most common treatment for heroin addicts, methadone, is associated with very severe withdrawal symptoms in newborns.

Environmental Hazards Radiation, chemicals, and other hazards in our modern industrial world can endanger the fetus (Grigorenko, 2001; Ostrea, Whitehall, & Laken, 2000). For instance, radiation can cause a gene mutation (an abrupt, permanent change in genetic material). Chromosomal abnormalities are higher among the offspring of fathers exposed to high levels of radiation in their occupations (Schrag & Dixon, 1985). Radiation from X rays also can affect the developing embryo and fetus, with the most dangerous time being the first several weeks after conception, when women do not yet know they are pregnant. It is important for women and their physicians to weigh the risk of an X ray when an actual or potential pregnancy is involved.

Environmental pollutants and toxic wastes are also sources of danger to unborn children. Researchers have found that various hazardous wastes and pesticides cause defects in animals exposed to high doses. Among the dangerous pollutants and wastes are carbon monoxide, mercury, and lead. Some children are exposed to lead because they live in houses in which lead-based paint flakes off the walls or near busy highways, where there are heavy automobile emissions from leaded gasoline. Researchers believe that early exposure to lead affects children's mental development (Markowitz, 2000). For example, in one study, 2-year-olds who prenatally had high levels of lead in their umbilical-cord blood performed poorly on a test of mental development (Bellinger & others, 1987).

Researchers also have found that manufacturing chemicals known as PCBs are harmful to prenatal development. In one study, the extent to which pregnant women ate PCB-polluted fish from Lake Michigan was examined, and subsequently their newborns were observed (Jacobson & others, 1984). The women who had eaten more PCB-polluted fish were more likely to have smaller, preterm infants who were more likely to react slowly to stimuli. And, in another study, prenatal exposure to PCBs was associated with problems in visual discrimination and short-term memory in 4-year-old children (Jacobson & others, 1992).

A current environmental concern involves women who spend long hours in front of computer monitors. The fear is that low-level electromagnetic radiation from the monitors might adversely affect their offspring, should these women become pregnant. Researchers have not found exposure to computer monitors to be related to miscarriage (Schnorr et al., 1991).

Yet another recent environmental concern for expectant mothers is prolonged exposure to heat in saunas or hot tubs that raises the mother's body temperature, creating a fever that endangers the fetus. The high temperature of a fever may interfere with cell division and may cause birth defects or even fetal death if the fever occurs repeatedly for prolonged periods of time. If the expectant mother wants to take a sauna or bathe in a hot tub, prenatal experts recommend that she take her oral temperature while she is exposed to the heat. When the expectant mother's body temperature rises a degree or more, she should get out and cool down. Ten minutes is a reasonable length of time for expectant mothers to spend in a sauna or hot tub, since the body temperature does not usually rise in this length of time. If the expectant mother feels uncomfortably hot in a sauna or hot tub, she should get out, even if she has been there only for a short time.

An explosion at the Chernobyl nuclear power plant in the Ukraine produced radioactive contamination that spread to surrounding areas. Thousands of infants were born with health problems and deformities as a result of the nuclear contamination, including this boy whose arm did not form. *Other than radioactive contamination, what are some other types of environmental hazards to prenatal development?*

Other Maternal Factors So far we have discussed a number of drugs that when taken by pregnant women can have harmful effects on prenatal and child development. We also have examined some environmental hazards that pregnant women may encounter that can be harmful. Here we will explore these other maternal factors that can affect prenatal and child development: infectious diseases, nutrition, emotional states and stress, and age.

Infectious Diseases Maternal diseases and infections can produce defects by crossing the placental barrier, or they can cause damage during the birth process itself (Iannucci, 2000). Rubella (German measles) is a maternal disease that can cause prenatal defects. A rubella outbreak in 1964–1965 resulted in 30,000 prenatal and

neonatal (newborn) deaths, and more than 20,000 affected infants were born with malformations, including mental retardation, blindness, deafness, and heart problems. The greatest damage occurs when mothers contract rubella in the third and fourth weeks of pregnancy, although infection during the second month is also damaging. Elaborate preventive efforts ensure that rubella will never again have the disastrous effects it had in the mid 1960s. A vaccine that prevents German measles is now routinely administered to children, and women who plan to have children should have a blood test before they become pregnant to determine if they are immune to the disease.

Syphilis (a sexually transmitted disease) is more damaging later in prenatal development—4 months or more after conception. Rather than affecting organogenesis, as rubella does, syphilis damages organs after they have formed. Damage includes eye lesions, which can cause blindness, and skin lesions. When syphilis is present at birth, other problems, involving the central nervous system and gastrointestinal tract, can develop. Most states require that pregnant women be given a blood test to detect the presence of syphilis.

Another infection that has received widespread attention recently is genital herpes. Newborns contract this virus when they are delivered through the birth canal of a mother with genital herpes. About one-third of babies delivered through an infected birth canal die; another one-fourth become brain damaged. If an active case of genital herpes is detected in a pregnant woman close to her delivery date, a cesarean section can be performed (in which the infant is delivered through an incision in the mother's abdomen) to keep the virus from infecting the newborn.

AIDS is a sexually transmitted disease that is caused by the human immunodeficiency virus (HIV), which destroys the body's immune system. In the early 1990s, before preventive treatments were available, 1,000 to 2,000 infants were born with HIV infection each year in the United States. Today, dramatic reductions in the transmission of AIDS from mothers to the fetus/newborn have occurred. Only about one-third as many cases of newborns with AIDS appear today as in the early 1990s. This decline is due to the increase in counseling and voluntary testing of pregnant women for HIV and the use of zidovudine (AZT) by infected women during pregnancy and delivery, and for the infant after birth (Bulterys, 2001; Centers for Disease Control and Prevention, 2000; Committee on Pediatric AIDS, 2000).

Pregnancy and HIV
Nutrition and Pregnancy
Exercise in Pregnancy
Later-Life Pregnancy

A mother can infect her offspring in three ways: (1) during gestation across the placenta, (2) during delivery through contact with maternal blood or fluids, and (3) postpartum (after birth) through breast-feeding. The transmission of AIDS through breast-feeding is especially a problem in many developing countries (Semba & Neville, 1999).

Babies born to HIV-infected mothers can be (1) infected and symptomatic (show AIDS symptoms), (2) infected but asymptomatic (not show AIDS symptoms), or (3) not infected at all. An infant who is infected and asymptomatic may still develop HIV symptoms up until 15 months of age.

Because the fetus depends entirely on its mother for nutrition, it is important for the pregnant woman to have good nutritional habits. In Kenya, this government clinic provides pregnant women with information about how their diet can influence the health of their fetus and offspring. *What might the information about diet be like?*

Nutrition A developing fetus depends completely on its mother for nutrition, which comes from the mother's blood. Nutritional status is not determined by any specific aspect of diet. Among the important factors are the total number of calories and appropriate levels of protein, vitamins, and minerals. The mother's nutrition even influences her ability to reproduce. In extreme instances of malnutrition, women stop menstruating, thus precluding conception. Children born to malnourished mothers are more likely to be malformed.

One aspect of maternal nutrition that has emerged as important is folic acid. The U.S. Public Health Service now recommends that pregnant women consume a minimum of

400 micrograms of folic acid per day (that is about twice the amount the average woman gets in one day). What is important about folic acid? A lack of folic acid is linked with neural tube defects in offspring, such as spina bifida. Orange juice and spinach are examples of foods rich in folic acid (Werler & others, 1996).

> *"There appears to be a clear link between stress during pregnancy and premature delivery."*
>
> Christine Dunkel-Schetter
> *Contemporary Psychologist, UCLA*

Emotional States and Stress Tales abound about how a pregnant woman's emotional state affects the fetus. For centuries it was thought that frightening experiences—such as a severe thunderstorm or a family member's death—leave birthmarks on the child or affect the child in more serious ways. Today we believe that the mother's stress can be transmitted to the fetus, but we have a better grasp of how this takes place (Monk & others, 2000). We now know that, when a pregnant woman experiences intense fears, anxieties, and other emotions, physiological changes occur—among them, changes in respiration and glandular secretions. For example, producing adrenaline in response to fear restricts blood flow to the uterine area and can deprive the fetus of adequate oxygen.

The mother's emotional state during pregnancy can influence the birth process too. An emotionally distraught mother might have irregular contractions and a more difficult labor, which can cause irregularities in the baby's oxygen supply or can produce irregularities after birth. Babies born after extended labor also may adjust more slowly to their world and be more irritable.

Maternal anxiety during pregnancy is related to less than optimal outcomes. Circumstances that are linked with maternal anxiety during pregnancy include marital discord, death of a husband, and unwanted pregnancy (Field, 1990).

In other research on stress, prenatal development, and birth, Christine Dunkel-Schetter and her colleagues (1998; Dunkel-Shetter & others, 2001) have found that women under stress are about four times as likely to deliver their babies prematurely than are their low-stress counterparts. In another study, maternal stress increased corticotrophin-releasing hormone (CRH) early in pregnancy (Hobel & others, 1999). This hormone is linked with stress. There also is a connection between stress and unhealthy behaviors, such as smoking, drug use, and poor prenatal care (Dunkel-Schetter, 1999). Further, researchers have found that pregnant women who are optimistic thinkers have less-adverse birth outcomes than pregnant women who are pessimistic thinkers (Loebel & Yali, 1999). Optimists believe that they have more control over the outcome of their pregnancy.

Maternal Age When the mother's age is considered in terms of possible harmful effects on the fetus and infant, two maternal ages are of special interest: adolescence and the thirties and beyond (James & others, 1999). Approximately 1 of every 5 births is to an adolescent; in some urban areas, the figure reaches as high as 1 in every 2 births. Infants born to adolescents are often premature (Ekwo & Moawad, 2000). The mortality rate of infants born to adolescent mothers is double that of infants born to mothers in their twenties. Although such figures probably reflect the mothers' immature reproductive system, they also may involve poor nutrition, lack of prenatal care, and low socioeconomic status. Prenatal care decreases the probability that a child born to an adolescent girl will have physical problems. However, adolescents are the least likely of women in all age groups to obtain prenatal assistance from clinics, pediatricians, and health services.

What are some of the risks for infants born to adolescent mothers?

Increasingly, women seek to establish their careers before beginning a family, delaying childbearing until their thirties. Down syndrome, a form of mental retardation, is related to the mother's age. A baby with Down syndrome rarely is born to a mother under the age of 30, but the risk increases after the mother reaches 30. By age 40, the probability is slightly over 1 in 100, and by age 50 it is almost 1 in 10. The risk also is higher before age 18.

Women also have more difficulty becoming pregnant after the age of 30. One study in a French fertility clinic focused on women whose husbands were sterile (Schwartz & Mayaux, 1982). To make it possible for the women to have a child, women were artificially inseminated once a month for 1 year. Each woman had 12 chances to become pregnant. Seventy-five percent of the women in their twenties

became pregnant, 62 percent of the women 31 to 35 years old became pregnant, and only 54 percent of the women over 35 years old became pregnant.

We still have much to learn about the role of the mother's age in pregnancy and childbirth. As women remain active, exercise regularly, and are careful about their nutrition, their reproductive systems may remain healthier at older ages than was thought possible in the past.

WWW

Reproductive Health Links
Exploring Pregnancy
Childbirth Classes
Prenatal Care
Health Care Providers

Paternal Factors So far, we have been considering maternal factors during pregnancy that can influence prenatal development and the development of the child. Might there also be some paternal factors that can have this influence? Men's exposure to lead, radiation, certain pesticides, and petrochemicals may cause abnormalities in sperm that lead to miscarriage or diseases, such as childhood cancer (Lindbohm, 1991; Trasler, 2000; Trasler & Doerkson, 2000). When fathers have a diet low in vitamin C, their offspring have a higher risk of birth defects and cancer (Fraga & others, 1991). Also, it has been speculated that, when fathers take cocaine, it may attach itself to sperm and cause birth defects, but the evidence for this is not yet strongly established. In some studies, chronic marijuana use has been shown to reduce testosterone levels and sperm counts, although the results have been inconsistent (Fields, 1998; Nahas, 1984).

The father's smoking during the mother's pregnancy also can cause problems for the offspring. In one investigation, the newborns of fathers who smoked during their wives' pregnancy were 4 ounces lighter at birth for each pack of cigarettes smoked per day than were the newborns whose fathers did not smoke during their wives' pregnancy (Rubin & others, 1986). In another study, in China, the longer the fathers smoked, the stronger the risk was for their children to develop cancer (Ji & others, 1997). In such studies, it is very difficult to tease apart prenatal and postnatal effects.

As is the case with older mothers, older fathers also may place their offspring at risk for certain birth defects. These include Down syndrome (about 5 percent of these children have older fathers), dwarfism, and Marfan's syndrome, which involves head and limb deformities.

Prenatal Care

Prenatal care varies enormously, but usually involves a package of medical care services in a defined schedule of visits. In addition to medical care, prenatal care programs often include comprehensive educational, social, and nutritional services (Nichols & Humenick, 2000; Shiono & Behrman, 1995).

Prenatal care usually includes screening that can reveal manageable conditions and/or treatable diseases that can affect the baby or the mother. The education an expectant woman receives about pregnancy, labor and delivery, and caring for the newborn can be extremely valuable, especially for first-time mothers. Prenatal care is also very important for women in poverty because it links them with other social services. The legacy of prenatal care continues after birth, because women who receive this type of care are more likely to seek preventive care for their infants (Bates & others, 1994).

Inadequate prenatal care can occur for a variety of reasons. These include the health care system, provider practices, and individual and social characteristics (Alexander & Korenbrot, 1995). In one national study, 71 percent of low-income women experienced problems obtaining prenatal care (U.S. General Accounting Office, 1987). Lack of transportation and child care, as well as financial difficulties, were commonly cited as barriers to getting prenatal care. Motivating positive attitudes toward pregnancy is also important. Women who have unplanned or unwanted pregnancies, or who have negative attitudes about being pregnant, are more likely to delay prenatal care or to miss appointments (Joseph, 1989).

Despite the advances made in prenatal care and technology in the United States, the availability of high-quality medical and educational services still needs much improvement. In some countries, especially in Scandinavia and Western Europe, more consistent, higher-quality prenatal care is provided than in the United States.

Early prenatal education classes focus on such topics as changes in the development of the fetus. Later classes focus on preparation for the birth and care of the newborn. *To what extent should fathers, as well as mothers, participate in these classes?*

Summary Table 4.2
Teratology and Hazards to Prenatal Development, Prenatal Care, and Positive Prenatal Development

Concept	Processes/ Related Ideas	Characteristics/Descriptions
Teratology and Hazards to Prenatal Development	What Is Teratology?	• This field investigates the causes of congenital (birth) defects. • Any agent that causes birth defects is called a teratogen.
	Prescription and Nonprescription Drugs	• In the 1960s, the thalidomide tragedy alerted the medical community to the potential negative effects of drugs on the developing fetus. • Prescription drugs that can be harmful include antibiotics. • Nonprescription drugs that can be harmful include diet pills, aspirin, and coffee.
	Psychoactive Drugs	• Fetal alcohol syndrome is a cluster of abnormalities that appear in offspring of mothers who drink heavily during pregnancy. • When pregnant women drink moderately (one to two drinks a day), negative effects on their offspring have been found. • Cigarette smoking by pregnant women has serious adverse effects on prenatal and child development (such as low birthweight). • Illegal drugs that can have harmful effects on offspring include marijuana, cocaine, and heroin.
	Environmental Hazards	• Potential environmental hazards include radiation in jobsites and X rays, environmental pollutants, toxic wastes, and prolonged exposure to heat in saunas and hot tubs.
	Other Maternal Factors	• Rubella (German measles) can be harmful. • Syphilis, genital herpes, and AIDS are other teratogens. • A developing fetus depends entirely on its mother for nutrition. • One aspect of maternal nutrition that has emerged is folic acid. • High anxiety and stress in the mother are linked with less than optimal prenatal and birth outcomes. • Two maternal age periods can lead to problems for the offspring's development: adolescence and 30 or older.
	Paternal Factors	• Paternal factors that can adversely affect prenatal development include exposure to lead, radiation, certain pesticides, and petrochemicals.
Prenatal Care	Variations	• Prenatal care varies extensively but usually involves medical care services with a defined schedule of visits.
Positive Prenatal Development	Most Pregnancies Go Well	• It is important not to read too much doom and gloom into pregnancy and prenatal development. Most pregnancies and prenatal development go well, although it is important to avoid the vulnerabilities that teratogens produce.

Positive Prenatal Development

In the previous section, we mainly examined what can go wrong with prenatal development. It is important to keep in mind that for most pregnancies, prenatal development does not go awry and development occurs along the positive path that we described at the beginning of the chapter (Lester, 2000). That said, it is still important for prospective mothers and those who are pregnant to avoid the vulnerabilities to fetal development that we have described.

At this point, we have discussed a number of ideas about teratology and hazards to prenatal development. To review these ideas, see summary table 4.2. Next, we will explore the birth process itself.

BIRTH

The Birth Process

Preterm Infants and Age-Weight Considerations

Measures of Neonatal Health and Responsiveness

Birth

As we saw in the opening story about Tanner Roberts, many changes take place during the birth of a baby. Let's further explore the birth process.

The Birth Process

To learn more about the birth process, we will examine the stages of birth, the transition from fetus to newborn, childbirth strategies, preterm infants and age-weight considerations, and measures of neonatal (newborn) health and responsiveness.

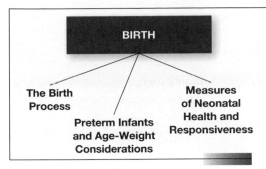

Preparing for Birth

Stages of Birth The birth process occurs in three stages. For a woman having her first child, the first stage lasts an average of 12 to 24 hours; it is the longest of the three stages. In the first stage, uterine contractions are 15 to 20 minutes apart at the beginning and last up to a minute. These contractions cause the woman's cervix to stretch and open. As the first stage progresses, the contractions come closer together, appearing every 2 to 5 minutes. Their intensity increases too. By the end of the first birth stage, contractions dilate the cervix to an opening of about 4 inches, so that the baby can move from the uterus to the birth canal.

The second birth stage begins when the baby's head starts to move through the cervix and the birth canal. It terminates when the baby completely emerges from the mother's body. This stage lasts approximately 1½ hours. With each contraction, the mother bears down hard to push the baby out of her body. By the time the baby's head is out of the mother's body, the contractions come almost every minute and last for about a minute.

Afterbirth is the third stage, at which time the placenta, umbilical cord, and other membranes are detached and expelled. This final stage is the shortest of the three birth stages, lasting only minutes.

We must respect this instant of birth, this fragile moment. The baby is between two worlds, on a threshold, hesitating . . .

Frederick Leboyer
French Obstetrician, 20th Century

The Transition from Fetus to Newborn Being born involves considerable stress for the baby. During each contraction, when the placenta and umbilical cord are compressed as the uterine muscles draw together, the supply of oxygen to the fetus is decreased. *Anoxia* is the condition in which the fetus/newborn has an insufficient supply of oxygen. Anoxia can cause brain damage. If the delivery takes too long, anoxia can develop.

The baby has considerable capacity to withstand the stress of birth. Large quantities of adrenaline and noradrenalin, hormones that are important in protecting the fetus in the event of oxygen deficiency, are secreted in stressful circumstances. These hormones increase the heart's pumping activity, speed up heart rate, channel blood flow to the brain, and raise blood-sugar level. Never again in life will such large amounts of these hormones be secreted. This circumstance underscores of how stressful it is to be born but also how prepared and adapted the fetus is for birth (Committee on Fetus and Newborn, 2000; Mishell, 2000; Von Beveren, 1999).

As we saw in the case of Tanner Roberts at the beginning of the chapter, the umbilical cord is cut immediately after birth, and the baby is on its own. Now 25 million little air sacs in the lungs must be filled with air. Until now, these air sacs have held fluid, but this fluid is rapidly expelled in blood and lymph. The first breaths may be the hardest ones at any point in the life span. Until now, oxygen came from the mother via the umbilical cord, but now the baby has to be self-sufficient and breathe on its own. The newborn's bloodstream is redirected through the lungs and to all parts of the body.

At the time of birth, the baby is covered with what is called *vernix caseosa,* a protective skin grease. This vernix consists of fatty secretions and dead cells, thought to function in protecting the baby's skin against heat loss before and during birth.

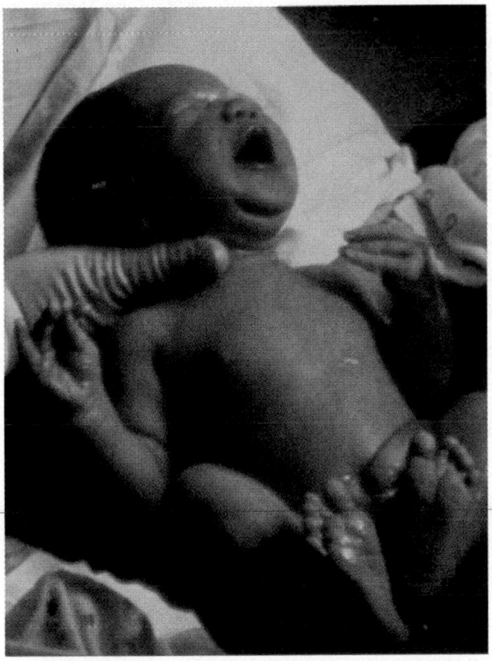

After the long journey of prenatal development, birth takes place. During birth the baby is on a threshold between two worlds. *What is the fetus/newborn transition like?*

After the baby and mother have met and become acquainted with each other, the baby is taken to be cleaned, examined, weighed, and evaluated. Later in the chapter, we will discuss several measures that are used to examine the newborn's health and responsiveness.

Childbirth Strategies
Childbirth Setting and Attendants
Midwifery
Doula
Fathers and Childbirth
Siblings and Childbirth

Childbirth Strategies Among the childbirth decisions that need to be made are what the setting will be and who the attendants will be, which childbirth technique will be used, and what the father's or sibling's role will be.

Childbirth Setting and Attendants In the United States, 99 percent of births take place in hospitals, and more over 90 percent are attended by physicians (Ventura & others, 1997). Many hospitals now have birthing centers, where fathers or birth coaches may be with the mother during labor and delivery. Some people believe this so-called alternative birthing center offers a good compromise between a technological, depersonalized hospital birth (which cannot offer the emotional experience of a home birth) and a birth at home (which cannot offer the medical backup of a hospital). A birthing room approximates a home setting as much as possible. The birthing room allows for a full range of birth experiences, from a totally unmedicated, natural birth to the most complex, medically intensive care. Some women with good medical histories and low risk for problem delivery choose a home delivery or a delivery in a freestanding birthing center, which is usually staffed by nurse-midwives.

doula
A caregiver who provides continuous physical, emotional, and educational support to the mother before, during, and just after childbirth.

Approximately 6 percent of women who deliver a baby in the United States are attended by a midwife (Ventura & others, 1997). Most midwives are nurses who have been specially trained in delivering babies (Webster & others, 1999).

In many countries around the world, babies are more likely to be delivered at home than they are in the United States. For example, in Holland, 35 percent of the babies are born at home, and more than 40 percent are delivered by midwives rather than doctors (Treffers & others, 1990).

In many countries, a doula attends a childbearing woman. *Doula* is a Greek word that means "a woman who helps." A **doula** *is a caregiver who provides continuous physical, emotional, and educational support for the mother before, during, and after childbirth.* Doulas remain with the mother throughout labor, assessing and responding to her needs. In one study, the mothers who received doula support reported less labor pain than the mothers who did not receive doula support (Klaus, Kennell, & Klaus, 1993). Doulas typically function as part of a "birthing team," serving as an adjunct to the midwife or the hospital obstetric staff (McGrath & others, 1999).

In the United States, most doulas work as independent providers hired by the expectant woman. Managed care organizations are increasingly offering doula support as a part of regular obstetric care. In many cultures, the practice of a knowledgeable woman helping a mother in labor is not officially labeled "doula" support but is simply an ingrained, centuries-old custom.

Methods of Delivery Among the methods of delivery are medicated, natural and prepared, and cesarean.

The American Academy of Pediatrics recommends the least possible medication during delivery (Hotchner, 1997). There are three basic kinds of drugs that are used

Careers in Life-Span Development

Linda Pugh, Perinatal Nurse

PERINATAL NURSES work with childbearing women to support health and growth during the childbearing experience. Linda Pugh, Ph.D., R.N.C., is a perinatal nurse on the faculty at The Johns Hopkins University School of Nursing. She is certified as an inpatient obstetric nurse and specializes in the care of women during labor and delivery. She teaches undergraduate and graduate students. In addition to educating professional nurses and conducting research, Dr. Pugh consults with hospitals and organizations about women's health issues.

Dr Pugh's research interests include nursing interventions with low-income breast-feeding women, discovering ways to prevent and ameliorate fatigue during childbearing, and using breathing exercises during labor.

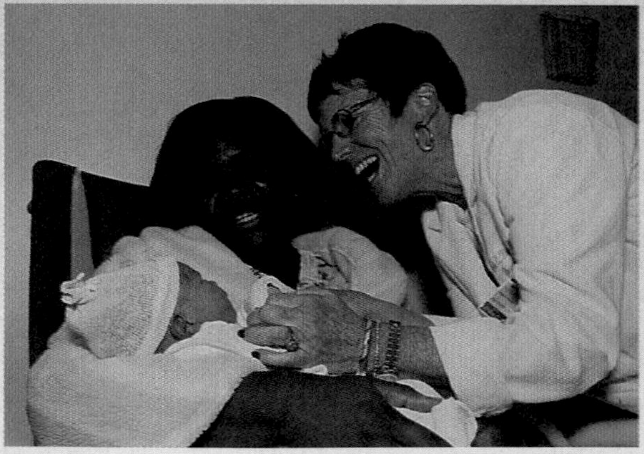

Linda Pugh (right), a perinatal nurse, with a mother and her newborn.

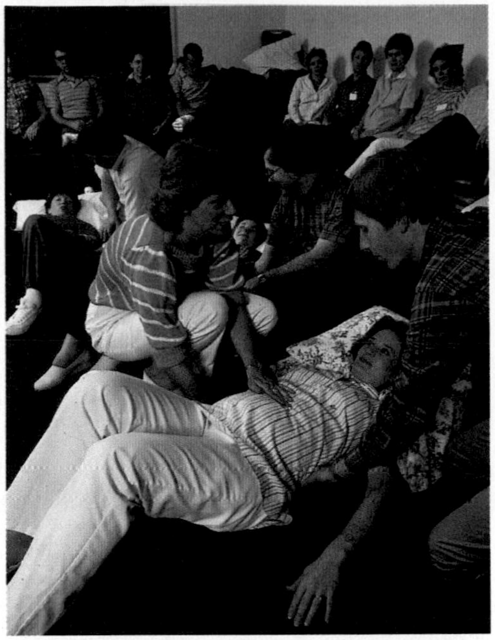

Many husbands, or coaches, take childbirth classes with their wives or friends as part of prepared or natural childbirth. This is a Lamaze training session. Lamaze training is available on a widespread basis in the United States and usually consists of six weekly classes. *What is the Lamaze method like?*

for labor: analgesia, anesthesia, and oxytocics. *Analgesia* is used to relieve pain. Analgesics include tranquilizers, barbiturates, and narcotics (such as Demerol). *Anesthesia* is used in late first-stage labor and during expulsion of the baby to block sensation in an area of the body or to block consciousness. There is a trend toward not using general anesthesia in normal births because it can be transmitted through the placenta to the fetus. However, an epidural anesthesia does not cross the placenta. An *epidural block* is regional anesthesia that numbs the woman's body from the waist down. Even this drug, thought to be relatively safe, has come under recent criticism because it is associated with fever, extended labor, and increased risk for cesarean delivery (Lieberman & others, 1997). *Oxytocics* are synthetic hormones that are used to stimulate contractions. Pitocin is the most commonly used oxytocic.

Predicting how a particular drug will affect an individual pregnant woman and the fetus is difficult. Though we have many commonalities as human beings, we also vary a great deal. Thus, a particular drug might have only a minimal effect on one fetus yet have a much stronger effect on another fetus. The drug's dosage also is a factor, with stronger doses of tranquilizers and narcotics given to decrease the mother's pain having a potentially more negative effect on the fetus than mild doses. It is important for the mother to assess her level of pain and be an important voice in the decision of whether she should receive medication or not.

Though the trend at one time was toward a natural childbirth without any medication, today the emphasis is on using some medication but keeping it to a minimum when possible. The emphasis today also is on broadly educating the pregnant woman so that she can be reassured and confident. Next, we will consider natural and prepared childbirth, which reflect this emphasis on education.

natural childbirth
Developed in 1914 by Dick-Read, this method attempts to reduce the mother's pain by decreasing her fear through education about childbirth and relaxation techniques during delivery.

Natural childbirth *was developed in 1914 by an English obstetrician, Grantley Dick-Read. It attempts to reduce the mother's pain by decreasing her fear through education about childbirth and by teaching her to use breathing methods and relaxation techniques during delivery.* Dick-Read also believed that the doctor's relationship with the mother is an important dimension of reducing her perception of pain. He said the doctor should be present during her active labor prior to delivery and should provide reassurance.

prepared childbirth
Developed by French obstetrician Ferdinand Lamaze, this childbirth strategy is similar to natural childbirth but includes a special breathing technique to control pushing in the final stages of labor and a more detailed anatomy and physiology course.

Prepared childbirth *was developed by French obstetrician Ferdinand Lamaze. This childbirth strategy is similar to natural childbirth but includes a special breathing technique to control pushing in the final stages of labor and a more detailed anatomy and physiology course.* The Lamaze method has become very popular in the United States. The pregnant woman's husband or a friend usually serves as a coach, who attends childbirth classes with her and helps her with her breathing and relaxation during delivery.

Many other prepared childbirth techniques also have been developed (Samuels & Samuels, 1996). They usually include elements of Dick-Read's natural childbirth or Lamaze's method, plus one or more new components. For instance, the Bradley method places special emphasis on the father's role as a labor coach. Virtually all of the prepared childbirth methods emphasize some degree of education, relaxation and breathing exercises, and support. In recent years, new ways of teaching relaxation have been offered, including guided mental imagery, massage, and meditation. In sum, the current belief in prepared childbirth is that, when information and support are provided, women *know* how to give birth.

WWW

Lamaze

Labor and Birth Resources

Cesarean Childbirth

breech position
The baby's position in the uterus that causes the buttocks to be the first part to emerge from the vagina.

In a *cesarean delivery,* the baby is removed from the mother's uterus through an incision made in her abdomen. This also is sometimes called a cesarean section. A cesarean section is usually performed if the baby is in a **breech position,** *which causes the baby's buttocks to be the first part to emerge from the vagina.* Normally, the crown of the baby's head comes through the vagina first, but in 1 of every 25 babies, the head does not come through first. Breech babies' heads are still in the uterus while the rest of their bodies are out, which can cause respiratory problems.

Cesarean deliveries also are performed if the baby is lying crosswise in the uterus, if the baby's head is too large to pass through the mother's pelvis, if the baby develops complications, or if the mother is bleeding vaginally.

The benefits and risks of cesarean sections continue to be debated (Growman, Peaceman, & Socol, 2000; Llewellyn-Jones, 1999; Lydon-Rochelle & others, 2000). Cesarean deliveries are safer than breech deliveries, but they involve a higher infection rate, longer hospital stay, and greater expense and stress that accompany any surgery.

Some critics believe that in the United States too many babies are delivered by cesarean section. More cesarean sections are performed in the United States than in any other country in the world. In the 1980s, births by cesarean section increased almost 50 percent in the United States, with almost one-fourth of babies delivered in this way. In the 1990s, the growing use of vaginal birth after a previous cesarean, greater public awareness, and peer pressure in the medical community led to some decline in cesarean sections.

Now that we have explored the stages of birth and childbirth strategies, it is important to consider how the birth process unfolds when babies are born preterm or low birthweight.

A "kilogram kid," weighing less than 2.3 pounds at birth. *What are some long-term outcomes for weighing so little at birth?*

Preterm Infants and Age-Weight Considerations

How can we distinguish between a preterm infant and a low-birthweight infant? What are the developmental outcomes for low-birthweight infants? Do preterm infants have a different profile from that of full-term infants? What conclusions can we reach about preterm infants?

Preterm and Low-Birthweight Infants An infant is full-term when it has grown in the womb for a full 38 to 42 weeks between conception and delivery. A **preterm infant** *is one who is born prior to 38 weeks after conception.* A **low-birthweight infant** *is born after a regular gestation period (the length of time between conception and birth) of 38 to 42 weeks but weighs less than 5½ pounds.* Both preterm and low-birthweight infants are considered high-risk infants (Barton, Hodgman, & Pavlova, 1999; Malloy, 1999; Shinwell, 2000).

preterm infant
An infant born prior to 38 weeks after conception.

low-birthweight infant
An infant born after a regular priod of gestation (the length of time between conception and birth) of 38 to 42 weeks but who weigh less than 51/2 pounds.

A short gestation period does not necessarily harm an infant. It is distinguished from retarded prenatal growth, in which the fetus has been damaged (Kopp, 1992). The neurological development of a short-gestation infant continues after birth on approximately the same timetable as if the infant still were in the womb (Koenigsberger, 2000). For example, consider an infant born after a gestation period of 30 weeks. At 38 weeks, approximately 2 months after birth, this infant shows the same level of brain development as a 38-week fetus who is yet to be born.

Some infants are born very early and have a precariously low birthweight. "Kilogram kids" weigh less than 2.3 pounds (which is 1 kilogram, or 1,000 grams) and are very premature.

There has been an increase in low-birthweight infants in the last two decades (Hall, 2000). The increase is thought to be due to the increasing number of adolescents having babies, the use of drugs, and poor nutrition.

Long-Term Outcomes for Low-Birthweight Infants Although most low-birthweight infants are normal and healthy, as a group they have more health and developmental problems than normal-birthweight infants (Chescheir & Hansen, 1999; Hack, Klein, & Taylor, 1995). The number and severity of these problems increase as birthweight decreases (Barton, Hodgman, & Pavlova, 1999; Kilbride, Thorstad, & Daily, 2000; Resnick & others, 2000; Saigal & others, 2000). With the improved survival rates for infants who are born very early and very small come increases in severe brain damage (Yu, 2000). Cerebral palsy and other forms of brain injury are highly correlated with brain weight—the lower the brain weight, the greater the like-

Neonatal Research
Preterm Infants
Low-Birthweight Infants
Exploring Low Birthweight
Touch Research Institute

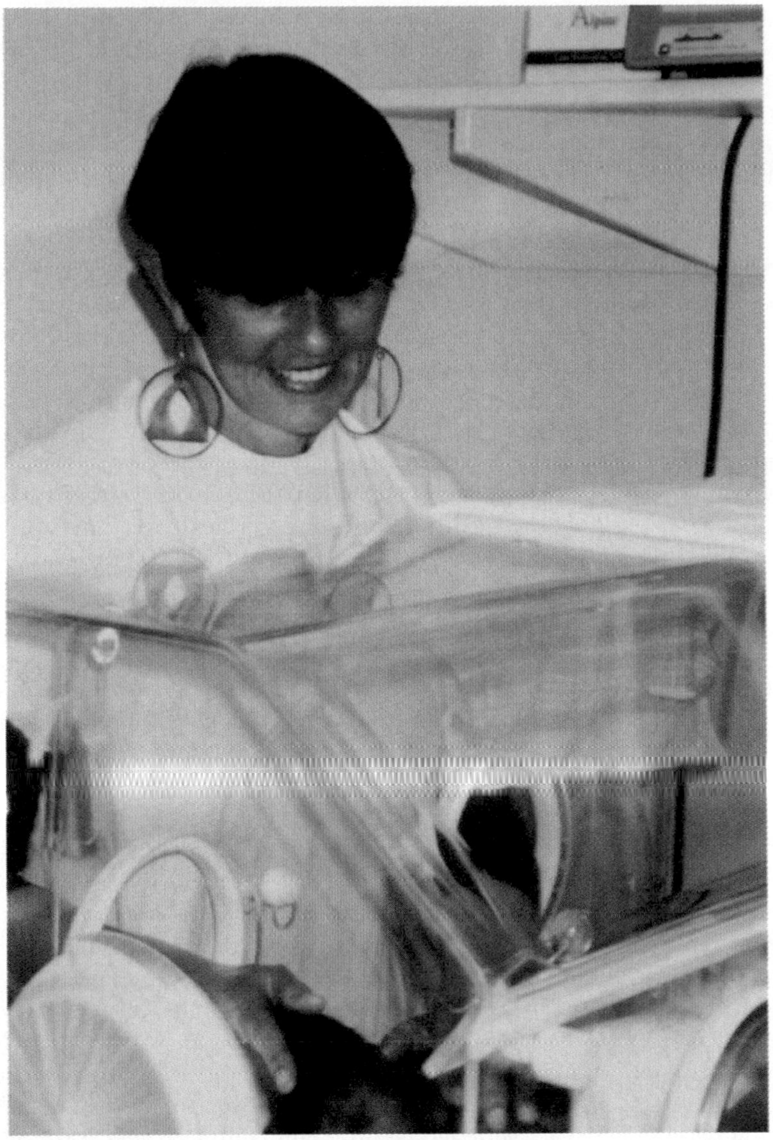

Shown here is Dr. Tiffany Field massaging a newborn infant. Dr. Field's research has clearly demonstrated the power of massage in improving the developmental outcome of at-risk infants. Under her direction, the Touch Research Institute in Miami, Florida, was developed to investigate the role of touch in a number of domains of health and well-being.

lihood of brain injury. Approximately 7 percent of moderately low-birthweight infants (3 pounds 5 ounces to 5 pounds 8 ounces) have brain injuries. This figure increases to 20 percent for the smallest newborns (1 pound 2 ounces to 3 pounds 5 ounces). Low-birthweight infants are also more likely than normal-birthweight infants to have lung or liver diseases.

At school age, children who were born low in birthweight are more likely than their normal-birthweight counterparts to have a learning disability, attention deficit disorder, or breathing problems such as asthma (Taylor, Klein, & Hack, 1994). Children born very low in birthweight have more learning problems and lower levels of achievement in reading and math than moderately low birthweight children. These problems are reflected in much higher percentages of low-birthweight children being enrolled in special education programs. Approximately 50 percent of all low-birthweight children are enrolled in special education programs.

Not all of these adverse consequences can be attributed solely to being born low in birthweight. Some of the less severe but more common developmental and physical delays occur because many low-birthweight children come from disadvantaged environments (Fang, Madhaven, & Alderman, 1999).

Some of the devastating effects of being born low in birthweight can be reversed (Blair & Ramey, 1996; Chescheir & Hansen, 1999; Shiono & Behrman, 1995). Intensive enrichment programs that provide medical and educational services for both the parents and the child have been shown to improve short-term developmental outcomes for low-birthweight children. Federal laws mandate that services for school-age children with a disability (which include medical, educational, psychological, occupational, and physical care) be expanded to include family-based care for infants. At present, these services are aimed at children born with severe congenital disabilities. The availability of services for moderately low birthweight children who do not have severe physical problems varies from state to state, but generally these services are not available.

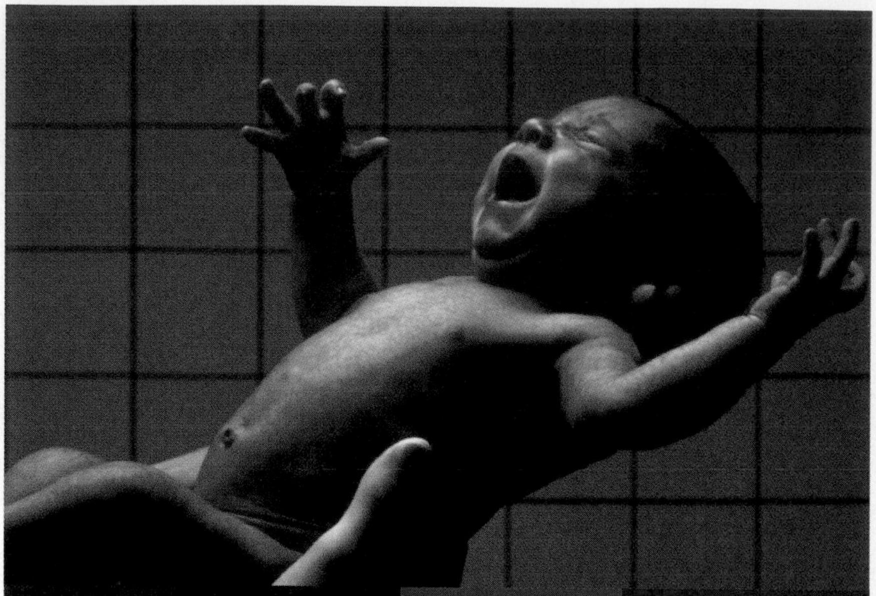

	0	1	2
Heart rate	Absent	Slow—less than 100 beats per minute	Fast—100–140 beats per minute
Respiratory effort	No breathing for more than one minute	Irregular and slow	Good breathing with normal crying
Muscle tone	Limp and flaccid	Weak, inactive, but some flexion of extremities	Strong, active motion
Body color	Blue and pale	Body pink but extremities blue	Entire body pink
Reflex irritability	No response	Grimace	Coughing, sneezing, and crying

Figure **4.7**
The Apgar Scale

Measures of Neonatal Health and Responsiveness

The **Apgar Scale** *is widely used to assess the health of newborns at 1 and 5 minutes after birth. The Apgar Scale evaluates infants' heart rate, respiratory effort, muscle tone, body color, and reflex irritability.* An obstetrician or a nurse does the evaluation and gives the newborn a score, or reading, of 0, 1, or 2 on each of these five health signs (see figure 4.7). A total score of 7 to 10 indicates that the newborn's condition is good. A score of 5 indicates there may be developmental difficulties. A score of 3 or below signals an emergency and indicates that the baby might not survive. The Apgar Scale is especially good at assessing the newborn's ability to respond to the stress of delivery, labor, and the new environment (Butterfield, 1999). The Apgar Scale also identifies high-risk infants who need resuscitation.

To evaluate the newborn more thoroughly, the **Brazelton Neonatal Behavioral Assessment Scale** *is performed within 24 to 36 hours after birth to evaluate the newborn's neurological development, reflexes, and reactions to people.* When the Brazelton is given, the newborn is treated as an active participant, and the score attained is based on the newborn's best performance. Sixteen reflexes, such as sneezing, blinking, and rooting, are assessed, along with reactions to circumstances, such as the infant's reaction to a rattle. (We will have more to say about reflexes in the next chapter, when we discuss physical development in infancy.) The examiner rates the newborn on each of 27 categories (see figure 4.8). As an indication of how detailed the ratings are, consider item 15: "cuddliness." Nine categories are involved in assessing this item, with infant behavior scored on a continuum that ranges from the

Apgar Scale
A widely used method to assess the health of newborns at 1 and 5 minutes after birth. The Apgar Scale evaluates infants' heart rate, respiratory effort, muscle tone, body color, and reflex irritability.

Brazelton Neonatal Behavioral Assessment Scale
A test given several days after birth to assess newborns' neurological development, reflexes, and reactions to people.

1. Response decrement to repeated visual stimuli
2. Response decrement to rattle
3. Response decrement to bell
4. Response decrement to pinprick
5. Orienting response to inanimate visual stimuli
6. Orienting response to inanimate auditory stimuli
7. Orienting response to inanimate visual and auditory stimuli
8. Orienting response to animate visual stimuli—examiner's face
9. Orienting response to animate auditory stimuli—examiner's voice
10. Orienting response to animate visual and auditory stimuli
11. Quality and duration of alert periods
12. General muscle tone—in resting and in response to being handled, passive, and active
13. Motor activity
14. Traction responses as the infant is pulled to sit
15. Cuddliness—responses to being cuddled by examiner
16. Defensive movements—reactions to a cloth over the infant's face
17. Consolability with intervention by examiner
18. Peak of excitement and capacity to control self
19. Rapidity of buildup to crying state
20. Irritability during examination
21. General assessment of kind and degree of activity
22. Tremulousness
23. Amount of startling
24. Lability of skin color—measuring autonomic lability
25. Lability of states during entire examination
26. Self-quieting activity—attempts to console self and control state
27. Hand-to-mouth activity

Figure **4.8**
The 27 Categories on the Brazelton Neonatal Behavioral Assessment Scale (NBAS)

infant's being very resistant to being held to the infant's being extremely cuddly and clinging. The Brazelton scale not only is used as a sensitive index of neurological competence in the week after birth, but it also is used widely as a measure in many research studies on infant development. In scoring the Brazelton scale, T. Berry Brazelton and his colleagues (Brazelton, Nugent, & Lester, 1987) categorize the 27 items into four categories—physiological, motoric, state, and interaction. They also classify the baby in global terms, such as "worrisome," "normal," or "superior," based on these categories (Nugent & Brazelton, 2000).

A very low Brazelton score can indicate brain damage, or it can reflect stress to the brain that may heal in time. However, if an infant merely seems sluggish in responding to social circumstances, parents are encouraged to give the infant attention and become more sensitive to the infant's needs. Parents are shown how the newborn can respond to people and how to stimulate such responses. Researchers have found that the social interaction skills of both high-risk infants and healthy, responsive infants can be improved through such communication with parents (Worobey & Belsky, 1982).

At this point we have studied a number of ideas about birth. A review of these ideas is presented in summary table 4.3. Next, we turn our attention to period after the birth of the baby—the postpartum period.

Summary Table 4.3
Birth

Concept	Processes/ Related Ideas	Characteristics/Descriptions
The Birth Process	Stages of Birth	• The first lasts about 12 to 24 hours for a woman having her first child. The cervix dilates to about 4 centimeters. • The second stage begins when the baby's head moves through the cervix and ends with the baby's complete emergence. • The third stage is afterbirth.
	The Transition from Fetus to Newborn	• Being born involves considerable stress for the baby, but the baby is well prepared and adapted to handle the stress. • Anoxia—insufficient oxygen supply to the fetus/newborn—is a potential hazard.
	Childbirth Strategies	• Considerations include the childbirth setting and attendants. In many countries, a doula attends a childbearing woman. • Methods of delivery include medicated, natural and prepared, and cesarean.
Preterm Infants and Age-Weight Considerations	Preterm and Low-Birthweight Infants	• Preterm infants are those born after an abnormally short time in the womb. • Infants who are born after a regular gestation period of 38 to 42 weeks but who weigh less than 5½ pounds are called low-birthweight infants.
	Long-Term Outcomes	• Although most low-birthweight infants are normal and healthy, as a group they have more health and developmental problems than normal-birthweight infants.
Measures of Neonatal Health and Responsiveness	Apgar Scale	• For many years, the Apgar Scale has been used to assess the newborn's health.
	Brazelton Neonatal Behavioral Assessment Scale	• This more recently developed scale is used for long-term neurological assessment. • Also assesses social responsiveness.

The Postpartum Period

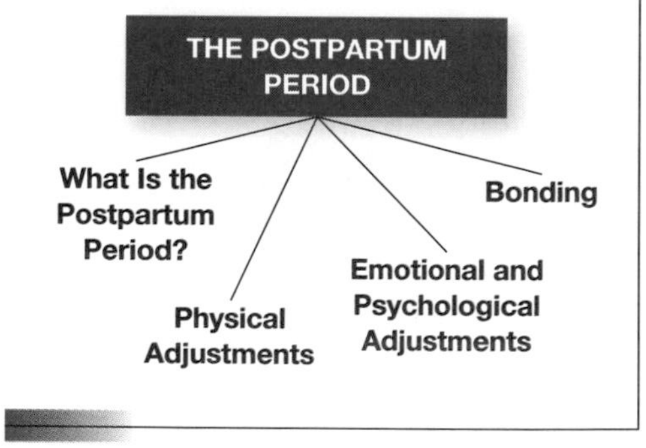

Many health professionals believe that the best postpartum care is family centered, using the family's resources to support an early and smooth adjustment to the newborn by all family members.

What Is the Postpartum Period?

The **postpartum period** *is the period after childbirth or delivery. It is a time when the woman's body adjusts, both physically and psychologically, to the process of childbearing. It lasts for about 6 weeks or until the body has completed its adjustment and has returned to a near prepregnant state.* Some health professionals refer to the postpartum period as the "fourth trimester." Though the time span of the postpartum period does not necessarily cover 3 months, the terminology of "fourth trimester" demonstrates the idea of continuity and the importance of the first several months after birth for the mother.

postpartum period
The period after childbirth when the mother adjusts, both physically and psychologically, to the process of childbirth. This period lasts for about 6 weeks or until her body has completed its adjustment and returned to a near prepregnant state.

The postpartum period is influenced by what preceded it. During pregnancy, the woman's body gradually adjusted to physical changes, but now it is forced to respond quickly. The method of delivery and circumstances surrounding the

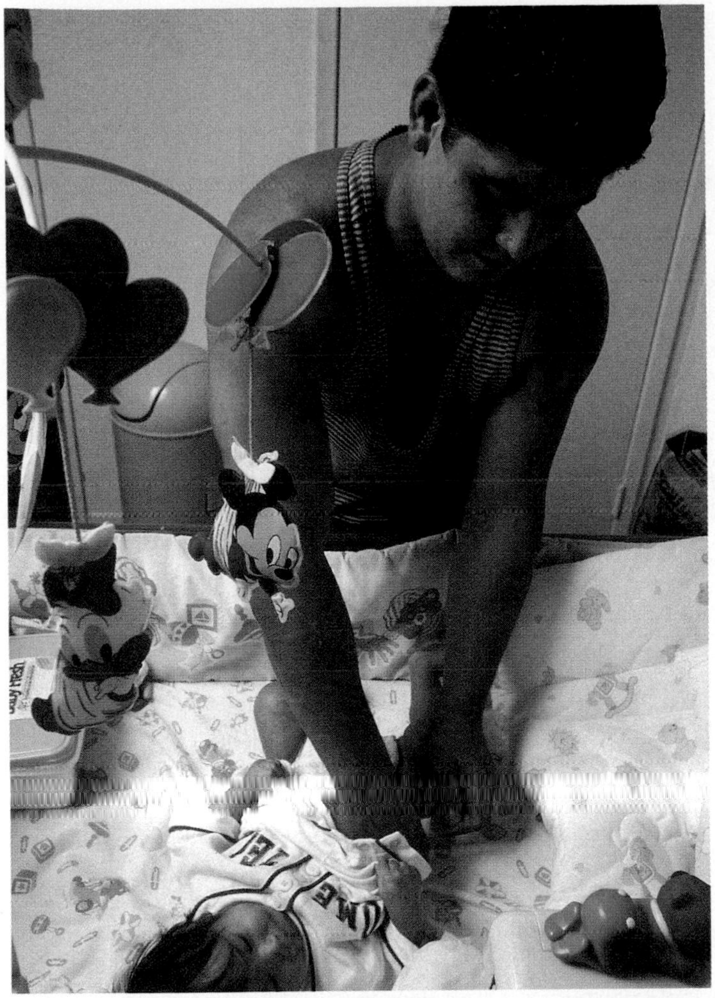

The postpartum period is a time of considerable adjustment and adaptation for both the mother and the father. Fathers can provide an important support system for mothers, especially in helping mothers care for young infants. *As part of supporting the mother, what kinds of tasks might the father of a newborn do?*

delivery affect the speed with which the woman's body readjusts during the postpartum period.

The postpartum period involves a great deal of adjustment and adaptation (Plackslin, 2000). The baby has to be cared for; the mother has to recover from childbirth; the mother has to learn how to take care of the baby; the mother needs to learn to feel good about herself as a mother; the father needs to learn how to take care of his recovering wife; the father needs to learn how to take care of the baby; and the father needs to learn how to feel good about himself as a father.

Physical Adjustments

The woman's body makes numerous physical adjustments in the first days and weeks after childbirth. She may have a great deal of energy or feel exhausted and let down. Most new mothers feel tired and need rest. Though these changes are normal, the fatigue can undermine the new mother's sense of well-being and confidence in her ability to cope with a new baby and a new family life.

Involution is the process by which the uterus returns to its prepregnant size five or six weeks after birth. Immediately following birth, the uterus weighs 2 to 3 pounds. By the end of 5 or 6 weeks, the uterus weighs 2 to 3½ ounces. Nursing the baby helps contract the uterus at a rapid rate.

After delivery, a woman's body undergoes sudden and dramatic changes in hormone production. When the placenta is delivered, estrogen and progesterone levels drop steeply and remain low until the ovaries start producing hormones again. The woman will probably begin menstruating again in 4 to 8 weeks if she is not breast-feeding. If she is breast-feeding, she might not menstruate for several months, though ovulation can occur during this time. The first several menstrual periods following delivery might be heavier than usual, but periods soon return to normal.

Some women and men want to resume sexual intercourse as soon as possible after the birth. Others feel constrained or afraid. A sore perineum (the area between the anus and vagina in the female), a demanding baby, lack of help, and extreme fatigue affect a woman's ability to relax and to enjoy making love. Physicians often recommend that women refrain from having sexual intercourse for approximately 6 weeks following the birth of the baby.

Postpartum Adjustment
Postpartum Resources

If the woman regularly engaged in conditioning exercises during pregnancy, exercise will help her recover her former body contour and strength during the postpartum period. With a caregiver's approval, the woman can begin some exercises as soon as one hour after delivery. In addition to recommending exercise in the postpartum period for women, health professionals also increasingly recommend that women practice the relaxation techniques they used during pregnancy and childbirth. Five minutes of slow breathing on a stressful day in the postpartum period can relax and refresh the new mother, as well as the new baby.

Emotional and Psychological Adjustments

bonding
Close contact, especially psysical, between parents and their newborn in the period shortly after birth.

Emotional fluctuations are common for mothers in the postpartum period. These emotional fluctuations may be due to any of a number of factors: hormonal changes, fatigue, inexperience or lack of confidence with newborn babies, or the extensive

CAREERS IN LIFE-SPAN DEVELOPMENT

Diane Stanford, Clinical Psychologist and Postpartum Expert

DIANE STANFORD has a doctorate in clinical psychology and never set out to become a specialist in women's health. For many years she had a private practice in clinical psychology with a focus on marital and family issues. Then she began collaborating with a psychiatrist whose clients included women with postpartum depression.

For the last 14 years, Diane has specialized in postpartum problems and other related aspects of female development, including infertility, pregnancy loss, and menopause.

Diane provides clients with practical advice that she believes helps women effectively cope with their problems. She begins by guiding them to think about concrete steps they can take to ease their emotional turmoil during this important postpartum transition. For example, new mothers may need help in figuring out ways to get partners and others to help with their infants. Or they may just need to be reassured that they can handle the responsibilities they face as parents.

After years of practicing on her own, Diane and a women's health nurse formed Women's Healthcare Partnership five years ago. In addition to the two partners, the staff now includes a full-time counselor in marriage and family relationships, and a social worker. Nurse educators, a dietician, and a fitness expert work on a consulting basis. Diane has also written *Post-partum survival guide* (1994), which reflects her strategies for helping women cope with postpartum issues (Clay, 2001).

Diane Stanford holding an infant of one of the mothers who comes to her for help in coping with postpartum issues.

time and demands involved in caring for a newborn. For some women, the emotional fluctuations decrease within several weeks after the delivery and are a minor aspect of their motherhood. For others, they are more long-lasting and can produce feelings of anxiety, depression, and difficulty in coping with stress (Murray & others, 1999). Mothers who have such feelings, even when they are getting adequate rest, may benefit from professional help in dealing with their problems. Following are some of the signs that can indicate a need for professional counseling about postpartum adaptation:

- Excessive worrying
- Depression
- Extreme changes in appetite
- Crying spells
- Inability to sleep

The father also undergoes considerable adjustment in the postpartum period, although in many cases he will be away at work all day, whereas the mother will be at home, at least in the first few weeks. One of the most common reactions of the husband is the feeling that the baby comes first and gets all of the attention. In some marriages, the man may have had that relationship with his wife and now feels that he has been replaced by the baby.

One strategy to help the man's postpartum reaction is for the parents to set aside some special time to be together with each other. The father's postpartum reaction

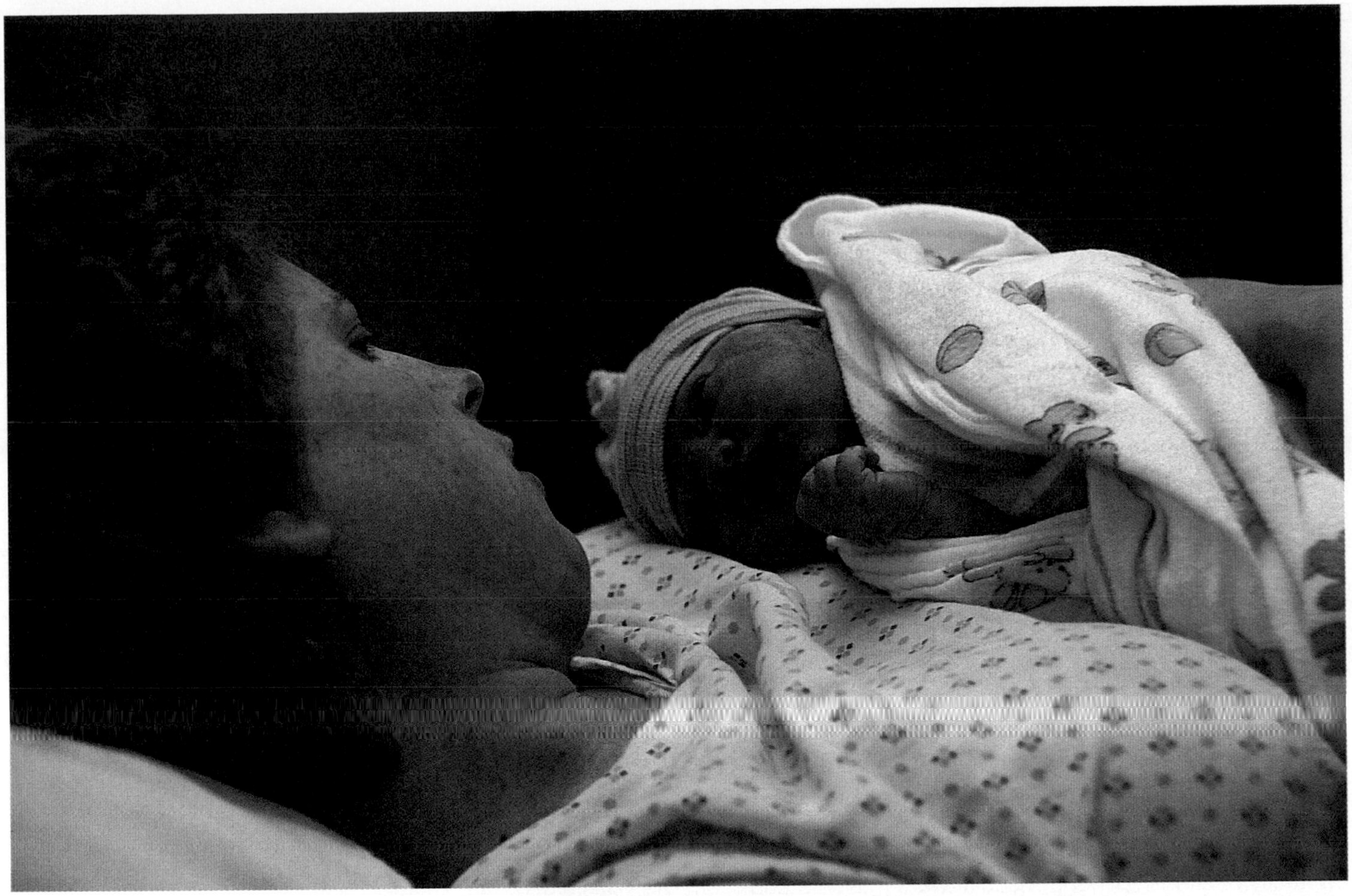

A mother bonds with her infant moments after it is born.
How critical is bonding for the development of social competence later in childhood?

also likely will be improved if he has taken childbirth classes with his wife and is an active participant in caring for the baby.

Important factors for both the mother and the father are the time and thought that go into being a competent parent of a young infant (Cowan & Cowan, 2000). It is important for both the mother and the father to become aware of the young infant's developmental needs—physical, psychological, and emotional. Both the mother and the father need to develop a sensitive, comfortable relationship with the baby.

Bonding

A special component of the parent-infant relationship is **bonding,** *the occurrence of close contact, especially physical, between parents and newborn in the period shortly after birth.* Some physicians believe that this period shortly after birth is critical in development. During this time, the parents and child need to form an important emotional attachment that provides a foundation for optimal development in years to come (Kennell & McGrath, 1999). Special interest in bonding came about when some pediatricians argued that the circumstances surrounding delivery often separate mothers and their infants, preventing or making difficult the development of a bond. The pediatricians further argued that giving the mother drugs to make her delivery less painful can contribute to the lack of bonding. The drugs can make the mother drowsy, thus interfering with her ability to

Summary Table 4.4
The Postpartum Period

Concept	Processes/ Related Ideas	Characteristics/Descriptions
What Is the Postpartum Period?	Key Features	• This is the period after childbirth or delivery. • The woman's body adjusts physically and psychologically to the process of childbearing. • It lasts for about 6 weeks or until the body has completed its adjustment.
Physical Adjustments	From Fatigue to Recovery	• These include fatigue, involution (the process by which the uterus returns to its prepregnant size 5 or 6 weeks after birth), hormonal changes, when to resume sexual intercourse, and exercises to recover body contour and strength.
Emotional and Psychological Adjustments	Mother	• Emotional fluctuations on the part of the mother are common in this period, and they can vary a a great deal from one mother to the next.
	Father	• The father also goes through a postpartum adjustment.
Bonding	What Is Bonding?	• This is the occurrence of close contact, especially physical, between parents and the newborn shortly after birth.
	Is There a Critical Period for Bonding?	• Early bonding has not been found to be critical in the development of a competent infant.

respond to and stimulate the newborn. Advocates of bonding also assert that preterm infants are isolated from their mothers to an even greater degree than are full-term infants, thereby increasing their difficulty in bonding.

Is there evidence that such close contact between mothers and newborns is critical for optimal development later in life? Although some research supports the bonding hypothesis (Klaus & Kennell, 1976), a body of research challenges the significance of the first few days of life as a critical period (Bakeman & Brown, 1980; Rode & others, 1981). Indeed, the extreme form of the bonding hypothesis—that the newborn must have close contact with the mother in the first few days of life to develop optimally—simply is not true.

Nonetheless, the weakness of the maternal-infant bonding research should not be used as an excuse to keep motivated mothers from interacting with their infants in the postpartum period. Such contact brings pleasure to many mothers. In some mother-infant pairs—including preterm infants, adolescent mothers, or mothers from disadvantaged circumstances—the practice of bonding may set in motion a climate for improved interaction after the mother and infant leave the hospital.

In recognition of the belief that bonding may have a positive effect on getting the parental-infant relationship off to a good start, many hospitals now offer a *rooming in* arrangement, in which the baby remains in the mother's room most of the time during its hospital stay. However, if parents choose not to use this rooming in arrangement, the weight of the research evidence suggests that it will not harm the infant emotionally (Lamb, 1994).

At this point, we have discussed a number of ideas about postpartum period. A review of these ideas is presented in summary table 4.4. Now that we have studied prenatal development and birth, in the next chapter we will turn our attention to the infant's physical development.

Chapter Review

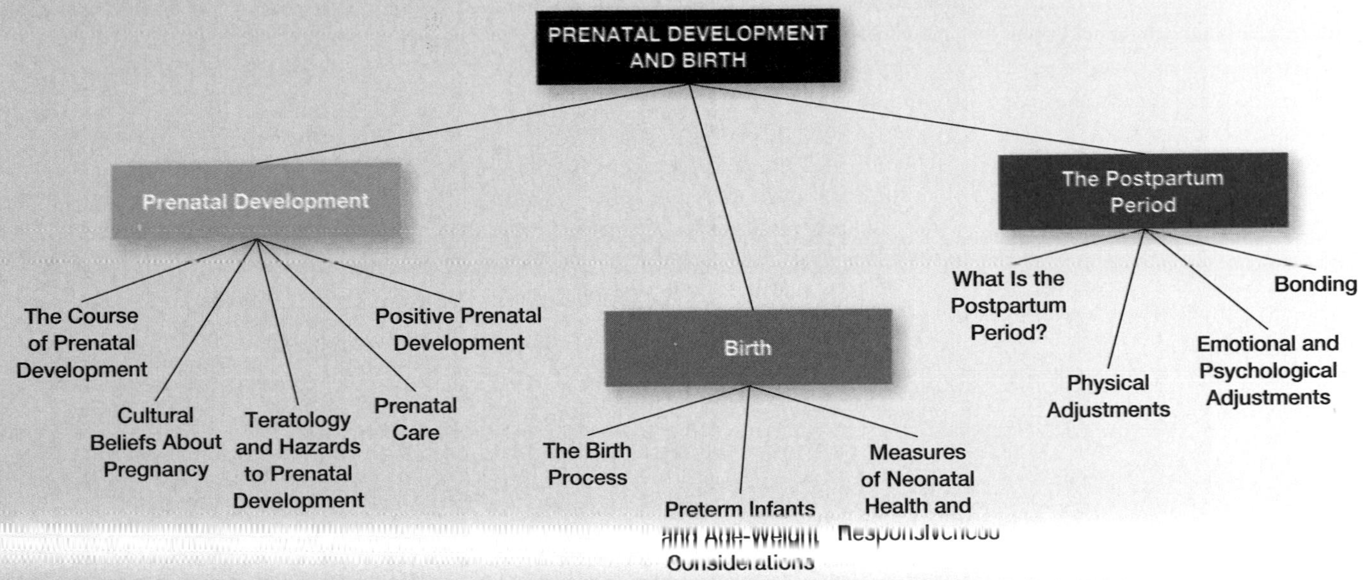

TO OBTAIN A MORE DETAILED REVIEW OF THIS CHAPTER, STUDY THESE FOUR SUMMARY TABLES:

- Summary Table 4.1 — The Course of Prenatal Development and Cultural Beliefs About Pregnancy — page 99
- Summary Table 4.2 — Teratology and Hazards to Prenatal Development — page 107
- Summary Table 4.3 — Birth — page 115
- Summary Table 4.4 — The Postpartum Period — page 119

Key Terms

germinal period 94
blastocyst 94
trophoblast 94
embryonic period 94
placenta 95
umbilical cord 95
amnion 95
organogenesis 96
fetal period 96
teratogen 98
fetal alcohol syndrome (FAS) 100
doula 109
natural childbirth 110
prepared childbirth 110
breech position 110
preterm infant 111
low-birthweight infant 111
Apgar Scale 113
Brazelton Neonatal Behavioral Assessment Scale 113
postpartum period 115
bonding 118

Key People

Christine Dunkel-Schetter 105
Grantley Dick-Read 110
Ferdinand Lamaze 110
T. Berry Brazelton 114

Taking It to the Net

1. Denise's sister, Doreen, is pregnant for the first time. Doreen is not particularly known for her healthy lifestyle. What particular things can Denise encourage Doreen to do in order to give birth to a healthy baby?
2. Sienne told her fiancé, Jackson, that he had better stop smoking before they begin trying to conceive a child. Why is Sienne concerned about Jackson's smoking and its effect on their children before they have even started planning their family?
3. Hannah, who gave birth to a healthy baby boy—her first child—two weeks ago, appears to her husband Sean to be sad, lethargic, and is having trouble sleeping. How can Sean determine if Hannah is just going through a natural period of post-baby "blues" or if she might be suffering from postpartum depression?

Connect to www.mhhe.com/santrockld8 to research the answers and complete these exercises.

OLC Preview

To further test your knowledge of this chapter or to explore our extensive online resources that accompany *Life-Span Development,* eighth edition, please log on to the text's Online Learning Center at http://www.mhhe.com/santrockld8.com.

Section 3

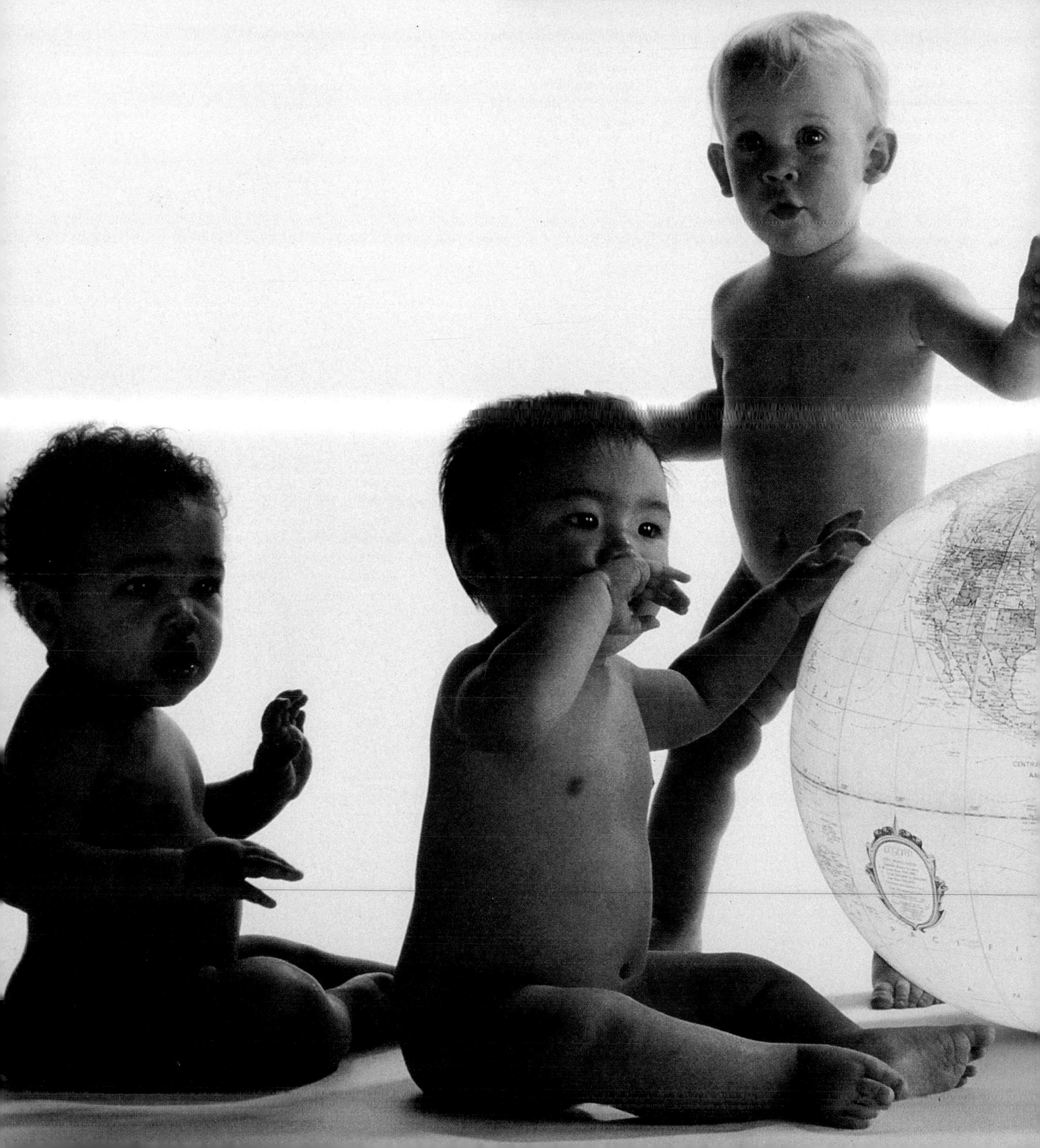

Infancy

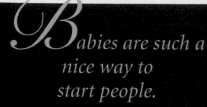

Babies are such a nice way to start people.

Don Herold
American Writer, 20th Century

As newborns, we were not empty-headed organisms. We had some basic reflexes, among them crying, kicking, and coughing. We slept a lot, and occasionally we smiled, although the meaning of our first smiles was not entirely clear. We ate and we grew. We crawled and then we walked, a journey of a thousand miles beginning with a single step. Sometimes we conformed, sometimes others conformed to us. Our development was a continuous creation of more complex forms. Our helpless kind demanded the meeting eyes of love. We juggled the necessity of curbing our will with becoming what we could will freely. Section 3 contains three chapters: "Physical Development in Infancy" (chapter 5), "Cognitive Development in Infancy" (chapter 6), and "Socioemotional Development in Infancy" (chapter 7).

Chapter 5

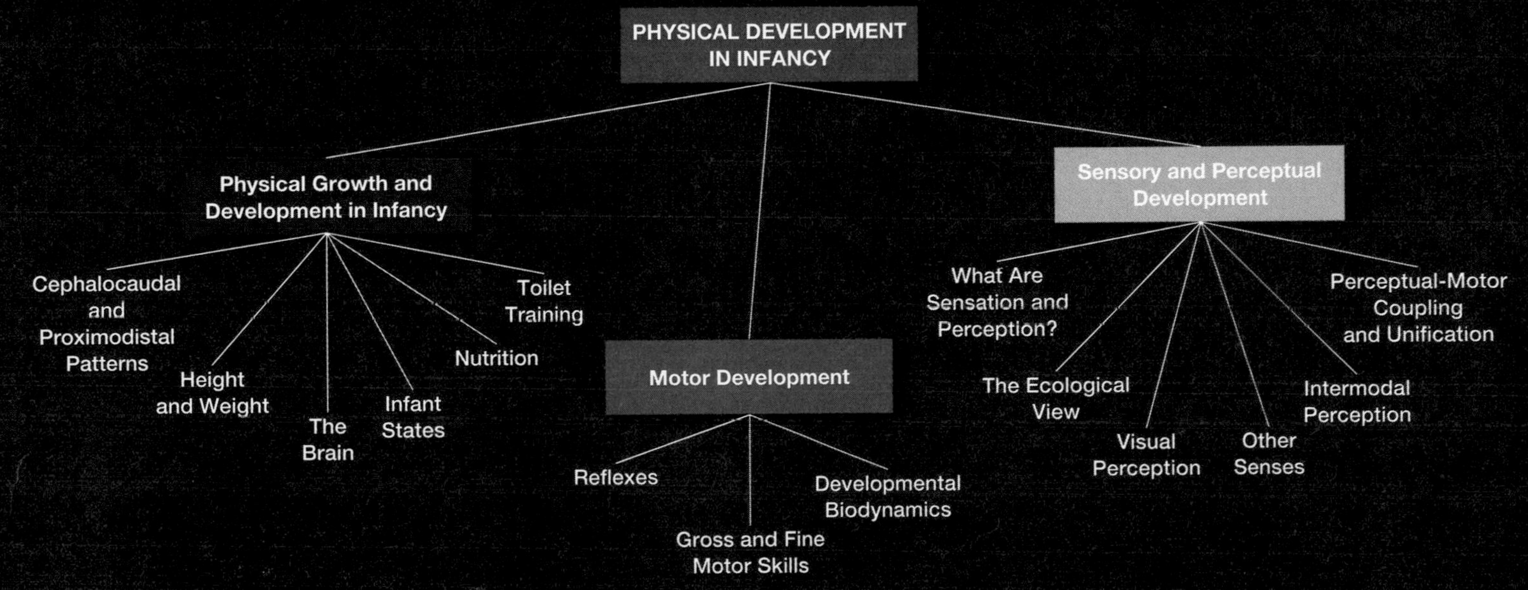

PHYSICAL DEVELOPMENT IN INFANCY
Physical Growth and Development in Infancy
Cephalocaudal and Proximodistal Patterns
Height and Weight
The Brain
Infant States
Nutrition
Toilet Training
Motor Development
Reflexes
Gross and Fine Motor Skills
Developmental Biodynamics
Sensory and Perceptual Development
What Are Sensation and Perception?
The Ecological View
Visual Perception
Other Senses
Intermodal Perception
Perceptual-Motor Coupling and Unification

Physical Development in Infancy

A baby is the most complicated object made by unskilled labor.

Anonymous

Images of Life-Span Development

Bottle- and Breast-Feeding in Africa

LATONYA IS A newborn baby in the African country of Ghana. The culture of the area in which she was born discourages breast-feeding. She has been kept apart from her mother and bottle-fed in her first days of infancy. Manufacturers of infant formula provide the hospital where she was born with free or subsidized milk powder. Her mother has been persuaded to bottle-feed rather than breast-feed her.

When her mother bottle-feeds Latonya, she overdilutes the milk formula with unclean water. Latonya's feeding bottles also have not been sterilized. Latonya starts getting sick, very sick. She dies before her first birthday.

By contrast, Ramona lives in the African country of Nigeria. Her mother is breast-feeding her. Ramona was born at a Nigerian hospital where a "baby-friendly" program had been initiated. In this program, babies are not separated from their mothers when they are born, and the mothers are encouraged to breast-feed them. The mothers are told of the perils that bottle-feeding can bring because of unsafe water and unsterilized bottles. They also are informed about the advantages of breast milk, which include its nutritious and hygienic qualities, its ability to immunize babies against common illnesses, and its role in reducing the mother's risk of breast and ovarian cancer. At 1 year of age, Ramona is very healthy.

For the past 10 to 15 years, the World Health Organization and UNICEF have been trying to reverse the trend toward bottle-feeding of infants, which emerged in many impoverished countries. They have instituted the "baby-friendly" program in many countries. They also have presuaded the International Association of Infant Formula Manufacturers to stop marketing their baby formulas to hospitals in countries where the governments support the baby-friendly initiatives. For the hospitals themselves, costs actually will be reduced as infant formula, feeding bottles, and separate nurseries become unnecessary.

For example, baby-friendly Jose Fabella Memorial Hospital in the Philippines already has reported saving 8 percent of its annual budget.

Hospitals play an important role in getting mothers to breast-feed their babies. For many years, maternity units were on the side of bottle-feeding babies and failed to give mothers adequate information about the benefits of breast-feeding. Fortunately, with the initiatives of the World Health Organization and UNICEF, that is beginning to change, but there still are many impoverished places in the world where the baby-friendly initiatives have not been implemented (Grant, 1993).

It is very important for infants to get a healthy start. In this chapter we will explore the following aspects of the infant's development: physical growth, motor development, and sensory and perceptual development.

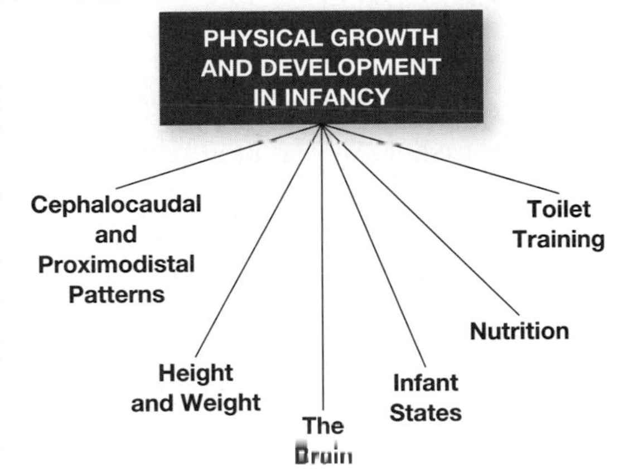

Physical Growth and Development in Infancy

Infants' physical development in the first 2 years of life is extensive (Caulfield, 2001). At birth, neonates have a gigantic head (relative to the rest of the body), which flops around uncontrollably. They also possess reflexes that are dominated by evolutionary movements. In the span of 12 months, infants become capable of sitting anywhere, standing, stooping, climbing, and usually walking. During the second year, growth decelerates, but rapid increases in such activities as running and climbing take place. Let's now examine in greater detail the sequence of physical development in infancy.

Cephalocaudal and Proximodistal Patterns

cephalocaudal pattern
The sequence in which the greatest growth occurs at the top—the head—with physical growth in size, weight, and feature differentiation gradually working from top to bottom.

The **cephalocaudal pattern** *is the sequence in which the greatest growth always occurs at the top—the head—with physical growth in size, weight, and feature differentiation gradually working its way down from top to bottom (for example, neck, shoulders, middle trunk, and so on)*. This same pattern occurs in the head area, because the top parts of the head—the eyes and brain—grow faster than the lower parts, such as the jaw. An extraordinary proportion of the total body is occupied by the head during prenatal development and early infancy (see figure 5.1). Later in the chapter you will see that sensory and motor development proceed according to the cephalocaudal principle. For example, infants see objects before they can control their trunk and they can use their hands long before they can they can crawl or walk.

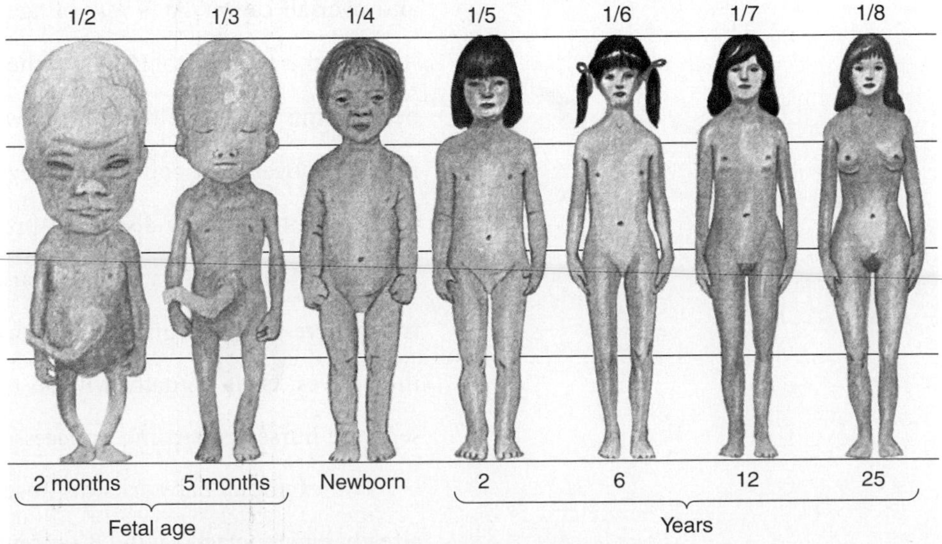

Figure **5.1**

Changes in Proportions of the Human Body During Growth

As individuals develop from infancy through adulthood, one of the most noticeable physical changes is that the head becomes smaller in relation to the rest of the body. The fractions listed refer to head size as a proportion of total body length at different ages.

The **proximodistal pattern** *is the sequence in which growth starts at the center of the body and moves toward the extremities.* An example of this is the early maturation of muscular control of the trunk and arms, as compared with that of the hands and fingers. Further, infants use their whole hand as a unit before they can control several fingers.

proximodistal pattern
The sequence in which growth starts at the center of the body and moves toward the extremities.

Height and Weight

The average North American newborn is 20 inches long and weighs 7½ pounds. Ninety-five percent of full-term newborns are 18 to 22 inches long and weigh between 5½ and 10 pounds.

In the first several days of life, most newborns lose 5 to 7 percent of their body weight before they learn to adjust to neonatal feeding. Once infants adjust to sucking, swallowing, and digesting, they grow rapidly, gaining an average of 5 to 6 ounces per week during the first month. They have doubled their birthweight by the age of 4 months and have nearly tripled it by their first birthday. Infants grow about 1 inch per month during the first year, reaching approximately 1½ times their birth length by their first birthday.

Infants' rate of growth is considerably slower in the second year of life. By 2 years of age, infants weigh approximately 26 to 32 pounds, having gained a quarter to half a pound per month during the second year; now they have reached about one-fifth of their adult weight. At 2 years of age, the average infant is 32 to 35 inches in height, which is nearly one-half of their adult height.

The Brain

As an infant walks, talks, runs, shakes a rattle, smiles, and frowns, changes in its brain are occurring. Consider that the infant began life as a single cell and nine months later was born with a brain and nervous system that contained approximately 100 billion nerve cells, or neurons. A **neuron** *is a nerve cell that handles information processing at the cellular level* (see figure 5.2). Indeed, at birth the infant probably has all of the neurons it will ever have.

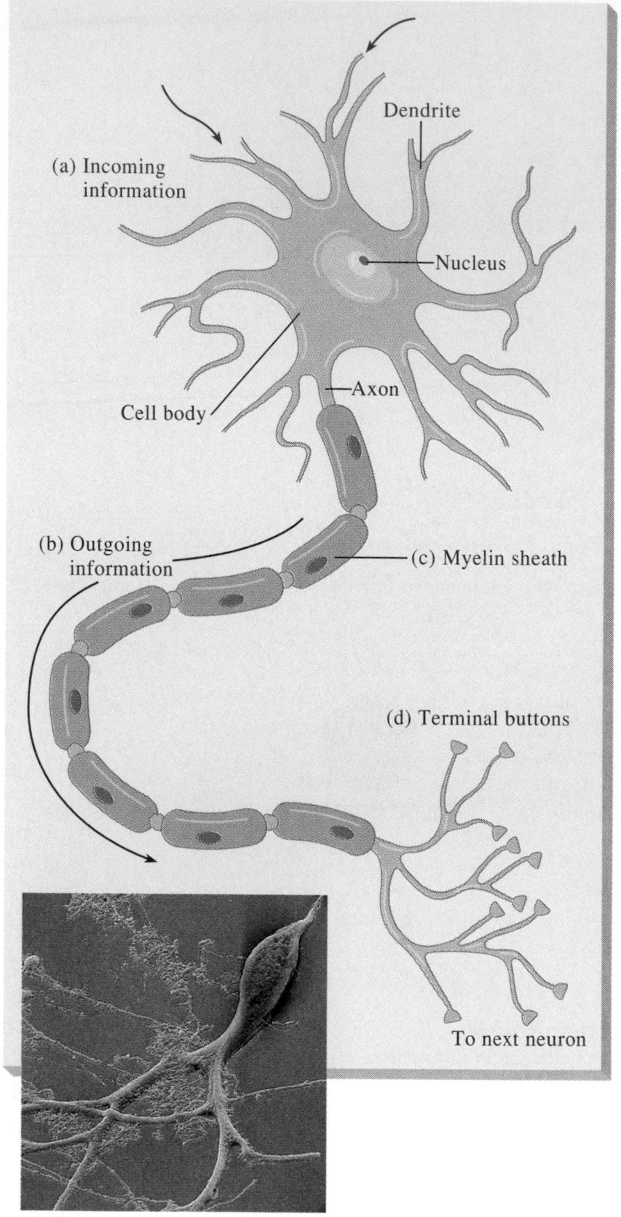

Figure **5.2**

The Neuron

(a) The dendrites of the cell body receive information from other neurons, muscles, or glands through the axon. *(b)* Axons transmit information away from the cell body. *(c)* A myelin sheath covers most axons and speeds information transmission. *(d)* As the axon ends, it branches out into terminal bottons. At the bottom left is an actual photograph of a neuron.

The Brain's Development Among the most dramatic changes in the brain in the first 2 years of life are the spreading connections of dendrites to each other. Figure 5.3 illustrates these changes.

A myelin sheath, which is a layer of fat cells, encases most axons (review figure 5.2). Not only does the myelin sheath insulate nerve cells, but it also helps nerve impulses travel faster. Myelination, the process of encasing axons with fat cells, begins prenatally and continues after birth. Myelination for visual pathways occurs rapidly after birth, being completed in the first 6 months. Auditory myelination is not completed until 4 or 5 years of age. Some aspects of myelination continue even into adolescence.

At birth, the newborn's brain is about 25 percent of its adult weight. By the second birthday, the brain is about 75 percent of its adult weight. However, the brain's areas do not mature uniformly. Some areas, such as the primary motor areas, develop earlier than others, such as the primary sensory areas.

Studying the brain's development in infancy is not as easy as it might seem, because even the latest brain-imaging technologies can't make out fine details and they can't be used on the babies. PET scans pose a radiation risk, and infants wriggle too much for an MRI (Marcus, Mulrine, & Wong, 1999).

However, one researcher who is making strides in finding out more about the brain's development in infancy is Charles Nelson (1999; deHaan & Nelson, 1999),

neuron
Nerve cell that handles information processing at the cellular level.

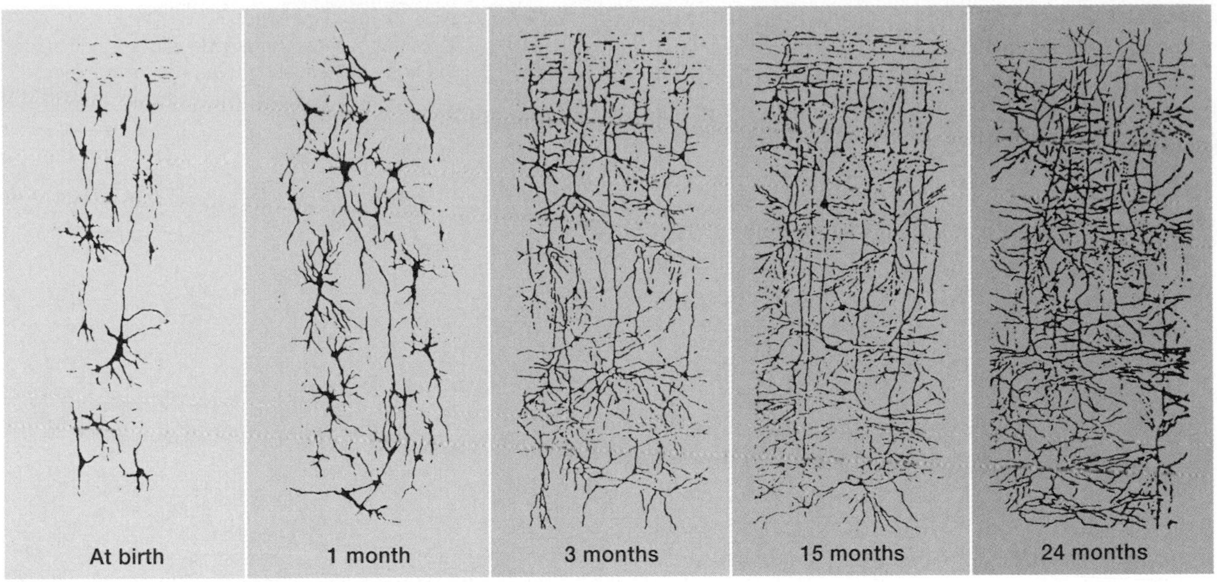

Figure **5.3**

The Development of Dendritic Spreading

Note the increase in connectedness between neurons over the course of the first 2 years of life

Neural Processes

lateralization
Specialization of function in one hemisphere of the cerebral cortex or the other.

some of whose research involves attaching up to 128 electrodes to a baby's scalp (see figure 5.4). He has found that even newborns produce distinctive brain waves that reveal they can distinguish their mother's voices from another woman's, even while they are asleep. In other research, Nelson has found that by 8 months of age babies can distinguish the picture of a wooden toy they were allowed to feel, but not see, from pictures of other toys. This achievement coincides with the development of neurons in the brain's hippocampus (an important structure in memory), allowing the infant to remember specific items and events.

The Brain's Hemispheres The cerebral cortex (the area of the brain with the highest level of function) is divided into two halves, or hemispheres (see figure 5.5). **Lateralization** *is specialization of function in one hemisphere of the cerebral cortex or the other.* There continues to be considerable interest in the degree to which each is involved in various aspects of thinking, feeling, and behavior.

The most extensive research on the brain's hemispheres has focused on language. At birth, the hemispheres already have started to specialize, with newborns showing greater electrical brain activity in the left hemisphere than the right hemisphere when they are listening to speech sounds (Hahn, 1987). A common misconception is that virtually all language processing is carried out in the left hemisphere. Speech and grammar are localized to the left hemisphere in most people; however, the understanding of such aspects of language as appropriate language use in different contexts and the use of metaphor and humor involves the right hemisphere. Thus, language in general does not occur exclusively in the brain's left hemisphere (Johnson, 1999, 2000).

In the media and public, the left hemisphere has been described as the exclusive location of logical thinking and the right hemisphere the exclusive location of creative thinking. However, most neuroscientists point out that complex functions, such as reading, performing music and creating art, involve both hemispheres. They believe labeling people as "left-brained" because they are logical thinkers and "right-brained" because they are creative thinkers does not correspond to the way the brain's hemispheres actually work. Such complex thinking in normal people is the outcome of communication between both sides of the brain.

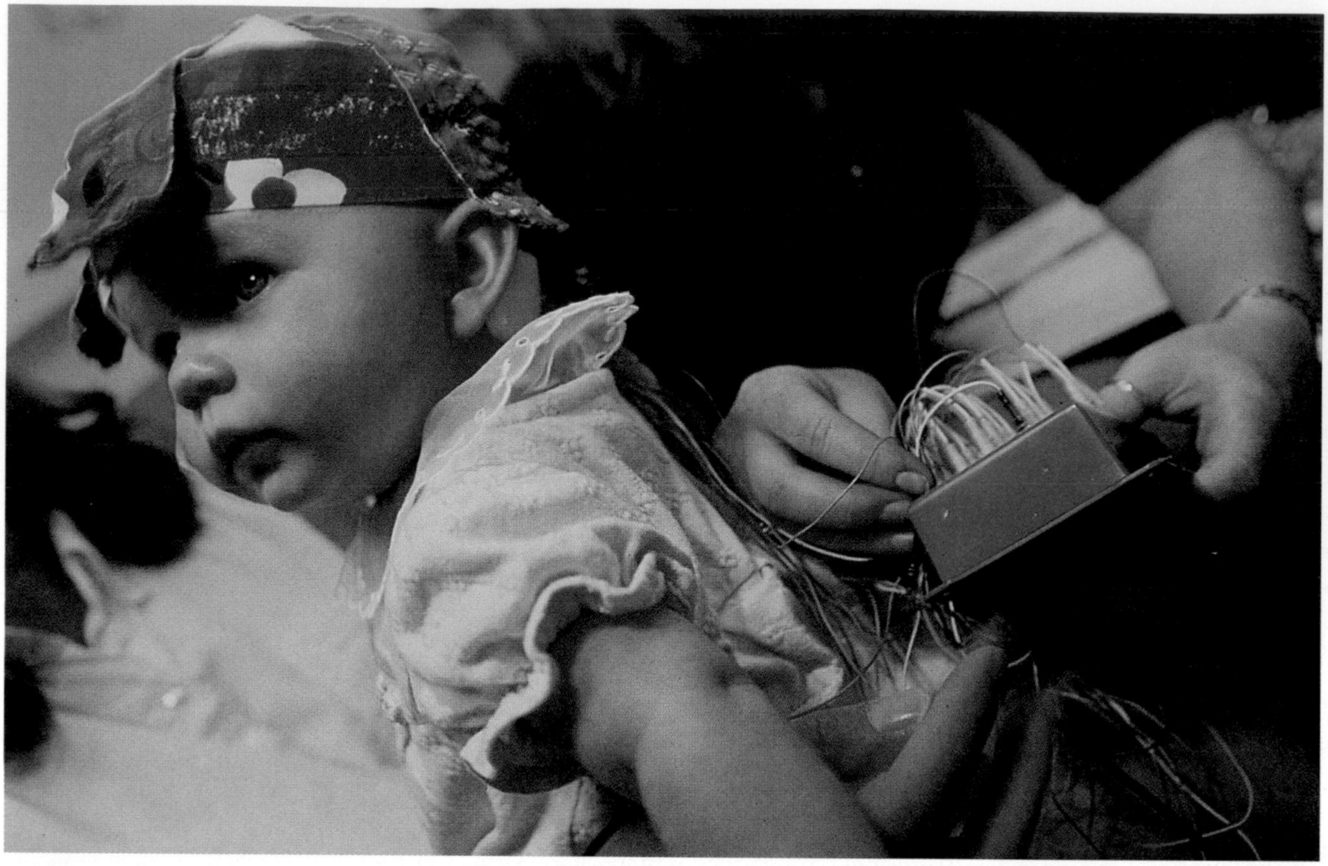

Figure 5.4
Measuring the Brain's Activity in Research on Infant Memory
In Charles Nelson's research, electrodes are attached to a baby's scalp to measure the brain's activity to determine its role in the development of an infant's memory. *Why is it so difficult to measure infants' brain activity?*

Early Experience and the Brain Until the middle of the twentieth century, scientists believed that the brain's development was determined almost exclusively by biological, hereditary factors. Researcher Mark Rosenzweig (1969) was curious about whether early experiences change the brain's development. He conducted a number of experiments with rats and other animals to investigate this possibility. Animals were randomly assigned to grow up in different environments. Animals in an enriched early environment lived in cages with stimulating features, such as wheels to rotate, steps to climb, levers to press, and toys to manipulate. In contrast, other animals had the early experience of growing up in standard cages or in barren, isolated conditions.

The results were stunning. The brains of the animals growing up in the enriched environment developed better than the brains of the animals reared in standard or isolated conditions. The brains of the "enriched" animals weighed more, had thicker layers, had more neuronal connections, and had higher levels of neurochemical activity.

Similar findings occurred when older animals were reared in vastly different environments, although the results were not as strong as for the younger animals. Such results give hope that enriching the lives of infants and young children who live in impoverished environments can produce positive changes in their development.

Depressed brain activity has recently been found in children who grow up in a deprived environment (Circhetti, 2001). As shown in figure 5.6, a child who grew up in the unresponsive and unstimulating environment of a Romanian orphanage showed considerably depressed brain activity compared to a normal child (Begley, 1997).

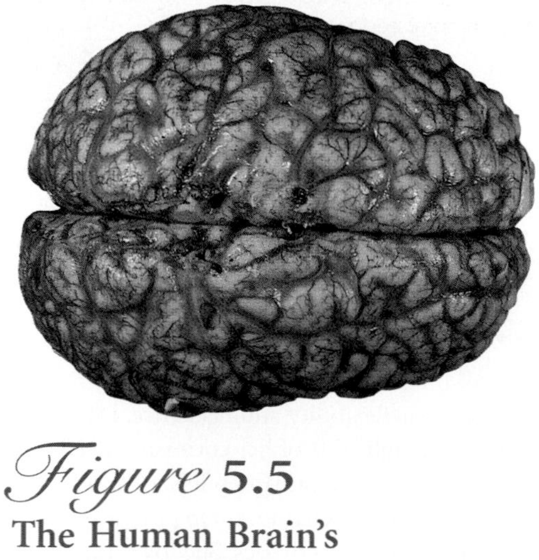

Figure 5.5
The Human Brain's Hemispheres
The two halves (hemispheres) of the human brain are clearly seen in this photograph.

Development of the Brain
Early Development of the Brain
Early Experience and the Brain

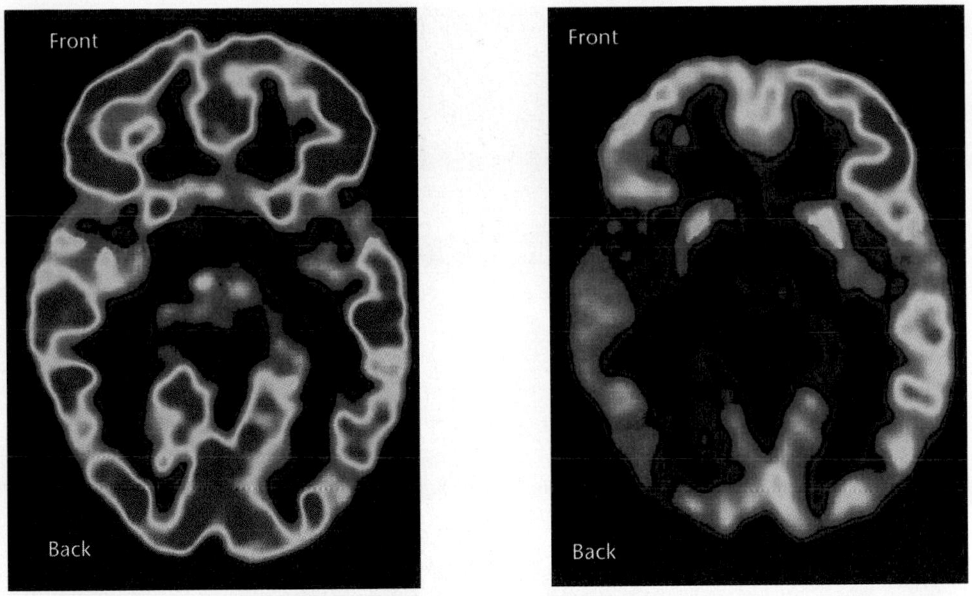

a. b.

Figure **5.6**

Early Deprivation and Brain Activity

These two photographs are PET (positron emission tomography) (which use radioactive tracers to image and analyze blood flow and metabolic activity in the body's organs) scans of the brains of *(a)* a normal child and *(b)* an institutionalized Romanian orphan who experienced substantial deprivation since birth. In PET scans, the highest to lowest brain activity is reflected in the colors of red, yellow, green, blue, and black, respectively. As can be seen, red and yellow show up to a much greater degree in the PET scan of the normal child than the deprived Romanian orphan.

Brandi Binder is evidence of the brain's hemispheric flexibility and resilience. Despite having the right side of her cortex removed because of a severe case of epilepsy, Brandi engages in many activities often portrayed as only "right-brain" activities. She loves music, math, and art, and is shown here working on one of her paintings. *What is the nature of the brains' lateralization?*

Scientists also now know that, starting shortly after birth, a baby's brain produces trillions more connections between neurons than it can possibly use. The brain eliminates connections that are seldom or never used. This pruning of brain connections continues at least until about 10 years of age.

The profusion of connections provides the growing brain with flexibility and resilience. Consider 13-year-old Brandi Binder, who developed such a severe case of epilepsy that surgeons at UCLA had to remove the right side of her cortex when she was 6. Binder lost virtually all the control she had established over muscles on the left side of her body, the side controlled by the right side of her brain, yet today, after years of therapy, ranging from leg lifts to math and music training, Binder is an A student. She loves music, math, and art—skills usually linked with the right side of the brain. Her recuperation is not 100 percent—for example, she never has regained the use of her left arm—but her recovery is remarkable and shows that if there is a way to compensate, the developing brain will find it.

Neuroscientists believe that what wires the brain—or rewires it, in the case of Brandi Binder—is repeated experience (Nash, 1997). Each time a baby tries to touch an attractive object or gazes intently at a face, tiny bursts of electricity shoot through the brain, knitting together neurons into circuits. The results are some of the behavioral milestones we discuss in this and other chapters. For example, at about 2 months of age, the motor-control centers of the brain develop to the point at which infants can suddenly reach out and grab a nearby object. At about 4 months, the neural connections necessary for depth perception begin to form. And at about 12 months the brain's speech centers are poised to produce one of infancy's magical moments: when the infant utters its first word.

In sum, neural connections are formed early in life. The infant's brain literally is waiting for experiences to determine how connections are made (Greenough, 1999,

Summary Table 5.1
Cephalocaudal and Proximodistal Patterns, Height and Weight, and the Brain

Concept	Processes/ Related Ideas	Characteristics/Descriptions
Cephalocaudal and Proximo- distal Patterns	Cephalocaudal	• Growth from the top down.
	Proximodistal	• Growth from the center out.
Height and Weight	Nature of Changes	• The average North American newborn is 20 inches long and weights 7½ pounds. • Infants grow about one inch per month in the first year and nearly triple their weight by their first birthday. • Infants' rate of growth slows in the second year.
The Brain	Development	• Dendritic spreading is dramatic in the first 2 years. • Myelination continues to develop in infancy and childhood.
	Hemispheres	• The cerebral cotex has two hemispheres (left, right). • Lateralization refers to specialization of function in one hemisphere or the other.
	Early Experience and the Brain	• The brains of animals growing up in enriched early environments develop better than those living in standard or isolated early environments.
		• Neural connections are formed early in life. Before birth, genes mainly direct neurons to locations. After birth, the inflowing stream of sights, sounds, smells, touches, language, and eye contact help shape the brain's neural connections.

2001; Johnson, 1999, 2000, 2001). Before birth, it appears that genes mainly direct how the brain establishes basic wiring patterns. Neurons grow and travel to distant places awaiting further instructions. After birth, environmental experiences are important in the brain's development. The inflowing stream of sights, sounds, smells, touches, language, and eye contact help shape the brain's neural connections (Black, 2001).

At this point we have studied a number of ideas about cephalocaudal and proximodistal patterns, height and weight, and the brain. A review of these ideas is presented in summary table 5.1. Next, we continue our exploration of physical development in infancy by discussing infant states.

Sleep that knits up the ravelled sleave of care. . . .

Balm of hurt minds, nature's second course. Chief nourisher in life's feast.

William Shakespeare
English Playwright, 17th Century

Infant States

Just as developmentalists chart infants' height and weight patterns, they also examine the infant states, or states of consciousness, the levels of awareness that characterize individuals.

Classification

One classification scheme describes eight infant states (Thoman & others, 1981):

1. *No* **REM (rapid eye movement) sleep,** *a recurring sleep stage during which vivid dreams commonly occur.* The infant's eyes are closed and still, and there is no motor activity other than occasional startle, rhythmic mouthing, or slight limb movement.
2. *Active sleep without REM.* The infant's eyes are closed and still; motor activity is present.
3. *REM sleep.* The infant's eyes are closed, although they may open briefly. Rapid eye movements can be detected through closed eyelids, and motor activity may or may not be present.

REM (rapid eye movement) sleep
A recurring sleep stage during which vivid dreams commonly occur.

4. *Indeterminate sleep*. This category is reserved for all transitional states that cannot fit the above codes.
5. *Drowsy*. The infant's eyes may be opening and closing but have a dull, glazed appearance. Motor activity is minimal.
6. *Inactive alert*. The infant is relatively inactive, although there may be occasional limb movements. The eyes are wide open and bright and shiny.
7. *Active awake*. The infant's eyes are open, and there is motor activity.
8. *Crying*. The infant's eyes can be open or closed, and motor activity is present. Agitated vocalizations are also present.

Using classification schemes such as the one just described, researchers have identified many aspects of infant development. One such aspect is the sleeping-waking cycle (Henderson & France, 1999; Ingersoll & Thoman, 1999). When we were infants, sleep consumed more of our time than it does now. Newborns sleep 16 to 17 hours a day, although some sleep more and others less. The range is from a low of about 10 hours to a high of about 21 hours, although the longest period of sleep is not always between 11 P.M. and 7 A.M. Although total sleep remains somewhat consistent for young infants, their sleep during the day does not always follow a rhythmic pattern. An infant might change from sleeping several long bouts of 7 or 8 hours to three or four shorter sessions only a few hours in duration. By about 1 month of age, most infants have begun to sleep longer at night, and, by about 4 months of age, they usually have moved closer to adultlike sleep patterns, spending their longest span of sleep at night and their longest span of waking during the day (Daws, 2000).

There are cultural variations in infant sleeping patterns. For example, in the Kipsigis culture in the African country of Kenya, infants sleep with their mothers at night and are permitted to nurse on demand (Super & Harkness, 1997). During the day they are strapped to their mother's backs, accompanying them on their daily rounds of chores and social activities. As a result, the Kipsigis infants do not sleep through the night until much later than American infants. During the first 8 months of postnatal life, Kipsigis infants rarely sleep longer than 3 hours at a stretch, even at night. This contrasts with American infants, many of whom begin to sleep up to 8 hours a night by 8 months of age.

REM Sleep Researchers are intrigued by the various forms of infant sleep. They are especially interested in REM sleep. Most adults spend about one-fifth of their night in REM sleep, and REM sleep usually appears about 1 hour after non-REM sleep. However, about one-half of an infant's sleep is REM sleep, and infants often begin their sleep cycle with REM sleep rather than non-REM sleep. By the time infants reach 3 months of age, the percentage of time they spend in REM sleep falls to about 40 percent, and no longer does REM sleep begin their sleep cycle. The large amount of REM sleep may provide infants with added self-stimulation, since they spend less time awake than do older children. REM sleep also might promote the brain's development in infancy. Figure 5.7 illustrates the average number of total hours spent in sleep and the amount of time spent in REM sleep, across the human life span. As can be seen, infants sleep far more than children and adults, and a much greater amount of time is taken up by REM sleep in infancy than at any other point in the life span.

Shared Sleeping There is considerable variation across cultures in newborns' sleeping arrangements. Sharing a bed with a mother is a common practice in many cultures, whereas in others newborns sleep in a crib, either in the same room as the parents or in a separate room. In the United States, sleeping in a crib in a separate room is the most frequent sleeping arrangement for an infant. In one cross-cultural study, American mothers said they have their infants sleep in a separate room to promote the infants' self-reliance and independence (Morelli & others, 1992). By contrast, Mayan mothers in rural Guatemala had infants sleep in their bed until the birth of a new sibling, at which time the infant would sleep with another family member or in a separate bed in the mother's room. The Mayan mothers believed that the co-sleeping arrangement with their infants enhances the closeness of their relation-

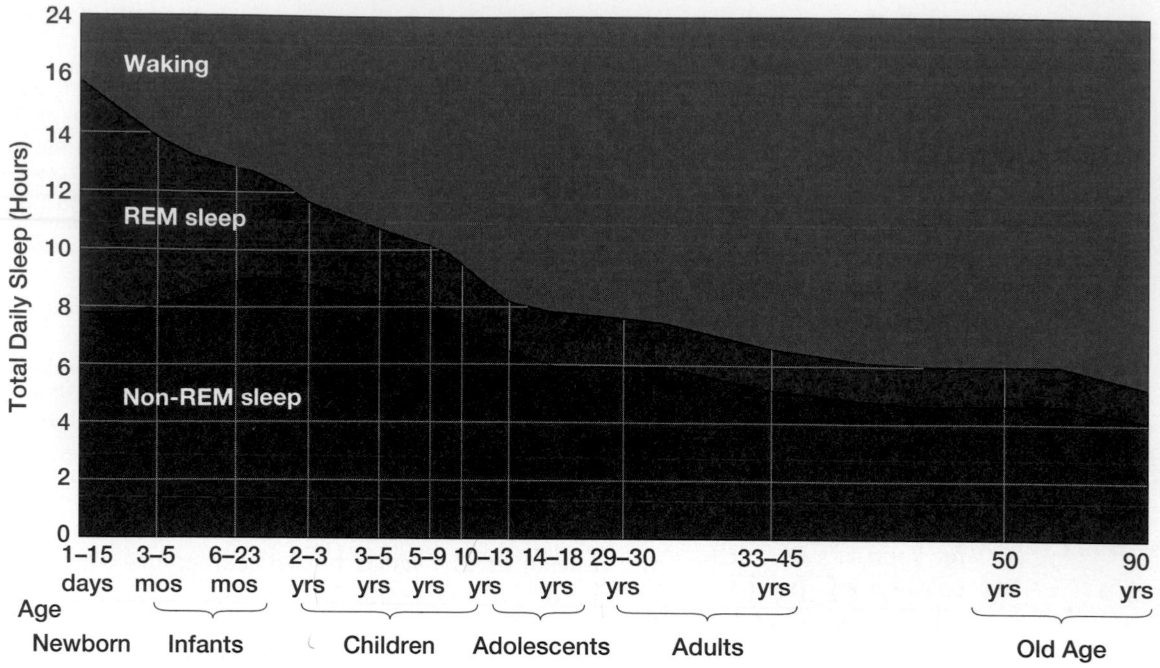

Figure **5.7**

Sleep Across the Human Life Span

ship with the infants and were shocked when told that American mothers have their baby sleep alone.

Some child experts believe there are benefits to shared sleeping, such as promoting breast-feeding, responding more quickly to the baby's cries, and detecting breathing pauses in the baby that might be dangerous (McKenna, Mosko, & Richard, 1997). However, the American Academy of Pediatrics Task Force on Infant Positioning and SIDS (1997; Cohen, 2000) recommended against shared sleeping. They argued that in some instances bed sharing might lead to sudden infant death syndrome (SIDS), as could be the case if a sleeping mother rolls over on her baby. Thus, shared sleeping remains a controversial issue, with some experts recommending it, others arguing against it.

SIDS **Sudden infant death syndrome (SIDS)** *is a condition that occurs when infants stop breathing, usually during the night, and suddenly dies without apparent cause.* The American Academy of Pediatrics has recommended since 1992 that infants be placed to sleep on their backs to reduce the risk of SIDS. Since that time, the frequency of prone sleeping has decreased from 70 percent to 20 percent of U.S. infants (American Academy of Pediatrics Task Force on Infant Sleep Position and SIDS, 2000). Some researchers now believe that an inability to swallow effectively in the prone sleeping position is an important reason SIDS occurs (Jeffery & others, 2000). Researchers have found that SIDS decreases when infants sleep on their backs rather than on their stomachs or sides (Skadberg, Morild, & Markesad, 1998; Smith & Hatterstey, 2000). However, SIDS still remains the highest cause of infant death in the United States with approximately 13 percent of all infant deaths due to SIDS. Risk of SIDS is highest at 4 to 6 weeks of age.

sudden infant death syndrome (SIDS) A condition that occurs when an infant stops breathing, usually during the night, and suddenly dies without an apparent cause.

SIDS

Unfortunately, at this time there is no definitive way to predict which infants will become the victims of SIDS. However, researchers have found the following regarding risk factors for SIDS (American Academy of Pediatrics Task Force on Infant Sleep Position and SIDS, 2000; Goldwater, 2001; Leach & others, 1999; Maas, 1998):

- Low-birthweight infants are 5 to 10 times more likely to die of SIDS than are their normal-weight counterparts.

- Twins and triplets, even at normal birthweight, are twice as likely to die of SIDS; after one twins dies, the surviving twin also has an increased risk of dying from SIDS.
- Infants whose siblings have died of SIDS are two to four times as likely to die of it.
- Six percent of infants with sleep apnea, a temporary cessation of breathing in which the airway is completely blocked, usually 10 seconds or longer, die of SIDS.
- African American and Eskimo infants are four to six times as likely as all others to die of SIDS.
- SIDS is more common in lower socioeconomic groups.
- SIDS is more common in infants who are passively exposed to cigarette smoke (Klonoff-Cohen & others, 1995; Pollack, 2001).
- Soft bedding is not recommended (Flick & others, 2001).

Careers in Life-Span Development

T. Berry Brazelton, Pediatrician

T. Berry Brazelton is America's best-known pediatrician as a result of his numerous books, television appearances, and newspaper and magazine articles about parenting and children's health. He takes a family-centered approach to child development issues and communicates with parents in easy-to-understand ways.

Brazelton founded the Child Development Unit at Boston Children's Hospital and created the Brazelton Neonatal Behavioral Assessment Scale, a widely used measure of the newborn's health and well-being (which you read about in chapter 4). He also has conducted a number of research studies on infants and children and has been president of the Society for Research in Child Development, a leading research organization.

T. Berry Brazelton, pediatrician, with a young child.

Nutrition

Our coverage of infant nutrition begins with information about nutritional needs and eating behavior, then turns to the issue of breast- versus bottle-feeding, and concludes with an overview of malnutrition.

Nutritional Needs and Eating Behavior

The importance of adequate energy and nutrient intake consumed in a loving and supportive environment during the infant years cannot be overstated (Dietz & Stern, 1999; Samour, Helm, & Lang, 2000; Tip, 1999). From birth to 1 year of age, human infants triple their weight and increase their length by 50 percent. Individual differences among infants in terms of their nutrient reserves, body composition, growth rates, and activity patterns make defining actual nutrient needs difficult. However, because parents need guidelines, nutritionists recommend that infants consume approximately 50 calories per day for each pound they weigh—more than twice an adult's requirement per pound.

Some years ago, controversy surrounded the issue of whether a baby should be fed on demand or on a regular schedule. Famous behaviorist John Watson (1928) argued that scheduled feeding is superior because it increases the child's orderliness. An example of a recommended schedule for newborns was 4 ounces of formula every six hours. In recent years, demand feeding—in which the timing and amount of feeding are determined by the infant—has become more popular.

Today, we have become extremely nutrition-conscious. Does the same type of nutrition that makes us healthy adults also make young infants healthy? Some affluent, well-educated parents almost starve their babies by feeding them the low-fat, low-calorie diet they eat themselves. Diets designed for adult weight loss and prevention of heart disease may actually retard growth and development in babies. Fat is very important for babies. Nature's food—breast milk—is not low in fat or calories. No child under the age of 2 should be consuming skim milk.

In one investigation, seven cases were documented in which babies 7 to 22 months of age were unwittingly undernourished by their health-conscious parents (Lifshitz & others, 1987). In some instances, the parents had

been fat themselves and were determined that their child was not going to be. The well-meaning parents substituted vegetables, skim milk, and other low-fat foods for what they called junk food. However, for growing infants, high-calorie, high-energy foods are part of a balanced diet.

Breast- Versus Bottle-Feeding Human milk, or alternative formula, is the baby's source of nutrients and energy for the first 4 to 6 months of life. For years, debate has focused on whether breast-feeding is better for the infant than bottle-feeding. The growing consensus is that breast-feeding is better for the baby's health (Blum, 2000; Bier & others, 1999; Eiger, 1992).

What are some of the benefits of breast-feeding? They include these benefits during the first 2 years of life and later (AAP Work Group on Breastfeeding, 1997; Eiger & Olds, 1999; London & others, 2000):

- Appropiate weight gain
- Fewer allergies (Arshad, 2001; Hoppu & others, 2001)
- Prevention or reduction of diarrhea, respiratory infections (such as pneumonia and bronchitis), bacterial and urinary tract infections, and otitis media (a middle ear infection) (AAP Work Group on Breastfeeding, 1997)
- Denser bones in childhood and adulthood (Gibson & others, 2000; Jones, Riley, & Dwyer, 2000)
- Reduced childhood cancer and reduced incidence of breast cancer in mothers and their female offspring (Bernier & others, 2000)
- Lower incidence of SIDS—in one study, for every month of exclusive breast-feeding, the rate of SIDS was cut in half (Fredrickson, 1993)
- Neurological and cognitive development (Brody, 1994)
- Visual acuity (Makrides & others, 1995)

Which women are least likely to breast-feed? They include mothers who work full time outside of the home, mothers under age 25, mothers without a high school education, African American mothers, and mothers in low-income circumstances (Ryan, 1997). In one study of of low income mothers in Georgia, interventions (such as counseling focused on the benefits of breast-feeding and free loan of a breast pump) increased the incidence of breast-feeding (Ahluwalia & others, 2000). Increasingly, mothers who return to work in the infant's first year of life use "pumping" in which they use a pump to extract breast milk that can be stored for later feeding of the infant when the mother is not present.

The American Pediatric Association strongly endorses breast-feeding throughout the first year of life (AAP Work Group on Breastfeeding, 1997). Are there circumstances when mothers should not breast-feed? Yes, they are (1) when the mother is infected with AIDS, which can be transmitted through her milk, or has another infectious disease, (2) if she has active tuberculosis, or (3) she is taking any drug that might not be safe for the infant (AAP Committee on Drugs, 1994; AAP Work Group on Breastfeeding, 1997).

Human milk, or an alternative formula, is a baby's source of nutrients for the first 4 to 6 months. The growing consensus is that breast-feeding is better for the baby's health, although controversy still swirls about the issue of breast- versus bottle-feeding. *Why is breast-feeding strongly recommended by pediatricians?*

Some women cannot breast-feed their infants because of physical difficulties; others feel guilty if they terminate breast-feeding early (Mozingo & others, 2000). They might worry that they are depriving their infants of important emotional and psychological

benefits. Some researchers have found that there are no psychological differences between breast-fed and bottle-fed infants (Ferguson, Harwood, & Shannon, 1987; Young, 1990).

marasmus
A wasting away of body tissues in the infant's first year, caused by severe protein-calorie deficiency.

kwashiorkor
A condition caused by a deficiency in protein in which the child's abdomen and feet become swollen with water.

Malnutrition in Infancy
Toilet Training

Malnutrition in Infancy

Marasmus *is a wasting away of body tissues in the infant's first year, caused by severe protein-calorie deficiency.* The infant becomes grossly underweight, and its muscles atrophy.

Kwashiorkor *is a condition caused by a deficiency in protein in which the child's abdomen and feet swell with water.* This disease usually appears between 1 to 3 years of age. Kwashiorkor makes children sometimes appear to be well-fed even though they are not. Kwashiorkor causes a child's vital organs to collect the nutrients that are present and deprive other parts of the body of them. The child's hair also becomes thin, brittle, and colorless. And the child's behavior often becomes listless.

The main cause of marasmus and kwashiorkor is early weaning from breast milk to inadequate nutrients, such as unsuitable and unsanitary cow's milk formula. Something that looks like milk but is not, usually a form of tapioca or rice, also might be used. In many of the world's developing countries, mothers used to breast-feed their infants for at least 2 years. To become more modern, they stopped breast-feeding much earlier and replaced it with bottle-feeding. Comparisons of breast-fed and bottle-fed infants in such countries as Afghanistan, Haiti, Ghana, and Chile document that the death rate of bottle-fed infants is as much as five times that of breast-fed infants (Grant, 1997).

Even if not fatal, severe and lengthy malnutrition is detrimental to physical, cognitive, and social development (Grantham-McGregor, Ani & Fernald, 2001; Mortimer, 1997). In some cases, even moderate malnutrition can produce subtle difficulties in development. In one investigation, two groups of extremely malnourished 1 year old South African infants were studied (Bayley, 1970). The children in one group were given adequate nourishment during the next 6 years; no intervention took place in the lives of the other group. After the seventh year, the poorly nourished group of children performed much worse on tests of intelligence than did the adequately nourished group. In yet another investigation, the diets of rural Guatemalan infants were associated with their social development at the time they entered elementary school (Barrett, Radke-Yarrow, & Klein, 1982). Children whose mothers had been given nutritious supplements during pregnancy and who themselves had been given more nutritious, high-calorie foods in their first 2 years of life were more active, more involved, more helpful with their peers, less anxious, and happier than their counterparts who had not been given nutritional supplements. The results suggest how important it is for parents to be attentive to the nutritional needs of their infants.

This Honduran child has kwashiorkor. Notice the tell-tale sign of kwashiorkor—a greatly expanded abdomen. *What are some other characteristics of kwashiorkor?*

In further research on early supplementary feeding and children's cognitive development, Ernesto Pollitt and his colleagues (1993) conducted a longitudinal investigation over two decades in rural Guatemala. They found that early nutritional supplements in the form of protein and increased calories can have positive long-term effects on cognitive development. The researchers also found that the relation of nutrition to cognitive performance is moderated both by the time period during which the supplement is given and by the sociodemographic context. For example, the children in the lowest socioeconomic groups benefited more than did the children in higher socioeconomic groups. Although there still was a positive nutritional influence when supplementation began after 2 years of age, the effect on cognitive development was less powerful. To read about a program that gives infants a healthy start in life, see the Sociocultural Worlds of Development box.

Toilet Training

In the North American culture, being toilet trained is a physical and motor skill that is expected to be attained by 3 years of age (Charlesworth, 1987). By the age of 3, 84 percent of children are dry throughout the day, and 66 percent are dry throughout the night. The ability to control elimination depends on both muscular maturation and motivation. Children must be able to control their muscles to eliminate at the

Sociocultural Worlds of Development

A Healthy Start

The Hawaii Family Support/Healthy Start Program began in 1985 (Allen, Brown, & Finlay, 1992). It was designed by the Hawaii Family Stress Center in Honolulu, which already for more than a decade had been making home visits to improve family functioning and reduce child abuse. Participation is voluntary. Families of newborns are screened for family risk factors, including unstable housing, histories of substance abuse, depression, parents' abuse as children, late or no prenatal care, fewer than 12 years of schooling, poverty, and unemployment. Early identification workers screen and interview new mothers in the hospital. They also screen families referred by physicians, nurses, and others. Because the demand for services outstrips available resources, only families with a substantial number of risk factors can participate.

Each new participating family receives a weekly visit from a family support worker. Each of the program's eight home visitors works with approximately 25 families at a time. The worker helps the family cope with any immediate crises, such as unemployment or substance abuse. The family also is linked directly with a pediatrician to ensure that the children receive regular health care. Infants are screened for developmental delays and are immunized on schedule. Pediatricians have been educated about the program. They are notified when a child is enrolled in Healthy Start and when a family at risk stops participating.

The Family Support/Healthy Start Program recently hired a child development specialist to work with families of children with special needs. And, in some instances, the program's male family support worker also visits a father to talk specifically about his role in the family. The support workers encourage parents to participate in group activities held each week at the program center located in a neighborhood shopping center.

Over time, parents are encouraged to assume more responsibility for their family's health and well-being. Families can participate in Healthy Start until the child is 5 and enters public school.

The Hawaii Family Support/Healthy Start Program provides overburdened families of newborns and young children many home-visitor services. This program has been very successful in reducing abuse and neglect in families. *What are some examples of the home-visitor services in this program?*

appropriate time, and they must want to eliminate in the toilet or potty, rather than in their pants (Maizels, Rosenbaum, & Keating, 1999).

In actuality, there are no data on the optimal time for toilet training, but developmentalists argue that, when it is initiated, it should be accomplished in a warm, relaxed, supportive manner. Many of today's parents begin toilet training of their infants at about 20 months to 2 years of age.

Many parents today are being encouraged to use a "readiness" approach to toilet training—that is, wait until children show signs that they are ready for toilet training. This contrasts with the argument of some developmentalists that delaying toilet training until the twos and threes can make it a battleground because many children at these ages are pushing so strongly for autonomy. Another argument is that late toilet training can be difficult for children who go to day care, because older children in diapers or training pants can be stigmatized by peers.

At this point we have studied a number of ideas about infant states, nutrition, and toilet training. A review of these ideas is presented in summary table 5.2. Next, we turn our attention to the infant's motor development.

Summary Table 5.2
Infant States, Nutrition, and Toilet Training

Concept	Processes/ Related Ideas	Characteristics/Descriptions
Infant States	Categorization	• One system has eight categories, including deep sleep, drowsy, alert and focused, and inflexibly focused. • Newborns usually sleep 16 to 17 hours a day. By 4 months of age, many American infants approach adultlike sleeping patterns.
	REM Sleep	• REM sleep—during which dreaming occurs—is present more in early infancy than in childhood and adulthood.
	Shared Sleeping	• Sleeping arrangements vary across cultures. In America, infants are more likely to sleep alone than in many other cultures.
	SIDS	• Sudden infant death syndrome (SIDS) is a condition that occurs when a sleeping infant suddenly stops breathing and dies without an apparent cause.
Nutrition	Nutritional Needs and Eating Behavior	• Infants need to consume about 50 calories per day for each pound they weigh. • The growing consensus is that breast-feeding is superior to bottle-feeding.
	Infant Malnutrition	• Severe infant malnutrition is still prevalent in many parts of the world. A special concern in industrialized countries is early weaning from breast milk, which can result in marasmus or kwashiorkor.
Toilet Training	Age at Attainment	• Toilet training is expected to be attained by about 3 years of age in North America. • Toilet training should be carried out in a relaxed, supportive manner.

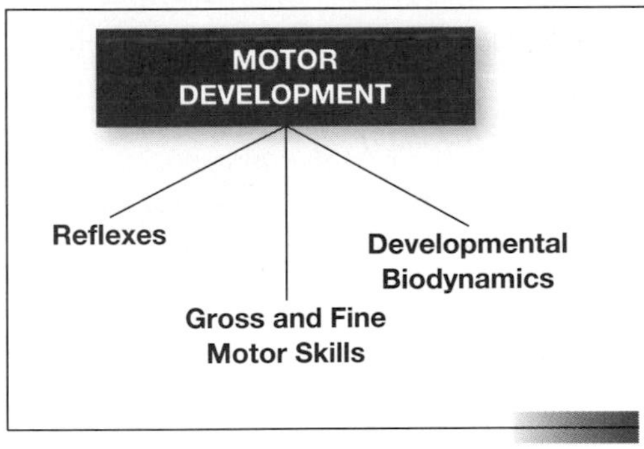

Motor Development

The study of motor development has seen a renaissance in the past decade. New insights are being made into the ways in which infants acquire motor skills. We will begin our exploration of motor development by examining reflexes and rhythmic movements, then turn our attention to gross and fine motor skills. To conclude, we will cover the fascinating field of developmental biodynamics, which is responsible for the awakened interest in the ways in which infants acquire motor skills.

Reflexes

The newborn is not an empty-headed organism. Among other things, it has some basic reflexes, which are genetically carried survival mechanisms. For example, the newborn has no fear of water, naturally holding its breath and contracting its throat to keep water out. Reflexes can serve as important building blocks for subsequent purposeful motor activity.

Reflexes govern the newborn's movements, which are automatic and beyond the newborn's control. They are built-in reactions to stimuli. In these reflexes, infants have adaptive responses to their environment before they have had the opportunity to learn. The **sucking reflex** *occurs when newborns automatically suck an object placed in their mouth. The sucking reflex enables newborns to get nourishment before they have associated a nipple with food.* The sucking reflex is an example of a reflex that is present at birth but later disappears. The **rooting reflex** *occurs when the infant's cheek is stroked or the side of the mouth is touched. In response, the infant turns its head toward the side that was touched in an apparent effort to find something to suck.* The sucking

sucking reflex
A newborn's built-in reaction of automatically sucking an object placed in its mouth. The sucking reflex enables the infant to get nourishment before it has associated a nipple with food.

rooting reflex
A newborn's built-in reaction that occurs when the infant's check is stroked or the side of the mouth is touched. In response, the infant turns its head toward the side that was touched, in an apparent effort to find something to suck.

and rooting reflexes disappear when the infant is 3 to 4 months old. They are replaced by the infant's voluntary eating. The sucking and rooting reflexes have survival value for newborn mammals, who must find the mother's breast to obtain nourishment.

The **Moro reflex** *is a neonatal startle response that occurs in response to a sudden, intense noise or movement. When startled, the newborn arches its back, throws back its head, and flings out its arms and legs. Then the newborn rapidly closes its arms and legs to the center of its body.* The Moro reflex is a vestige from our primate ancestry, and it also has survival value—it leads the newborn to grab for support while falling. This reflex, which is normal in all newborns, also tends to disappear at 3 to 4 months of age. Steady pressure on any part of the infant's body calms the infant after it has been startled. Holding the infant's arm flexed at the shoulder will quiet the infant.

Moro reflex
A neonatal startle response that occurs in reaction to a sudden, intense noise or movement. When startled, the newborn arches its back, throws its head back, and flings out its arms and legs. Then the newborn rapidly closes its arms and legs to the center of the body.

Some reflexes present in the newborn—coughing, blinking, and yawning, for example—persist throughout life. They are as important for the adult as they are for the infant. Other reflexes, though, disappear several months following birth, as the infant's brain functions mature, and voluntary control over many behaviors develops. The movements of some reflexes eventually become incorporated into more complex, voluntary actions. One important example is the **grasping reflex,** *which occurs when something touches the infant's palms. The infant responds by grasping tightly.* By the end of the third month, the grasping reflex diminishes, and the infant shows a more voluntary grasp, which is often produced by visual stimuli. For example, when an infant sees a mobile whirling above its crib, it may reach out and try to grasp it. As its motor development becomes smoother, the infant will grasp objects, carefully manipulate them, and explore their qualities.

grasping reflex
A neonatal reflex that occurs when something touches the infant's palms. The infant responds by grasping tightly.

An overview of the main reflexes we have discussed, along with others, is given in figure 5.8.

Sucking is an especially important reflex: it is the infant's route to nourishment. The sucking capabilities of newborns vary considerably. Some newborns are efficient at forceful sucking and obtaining milk; others are not as adept and get tired before they are full. Most newborns take several weeks to establish a sucking style that is coordinated with the way the mother is holding the infant, the way milk is coming out of the bottle or breast, and the infant's sucking speed and temperament.

The experiences of the first three years of life are almost entirely lost to us, and when we attempt to enter into a small child's world, we come as foreigners who have forgotten the landscape and no longer speak the native tongue.

Selma Fraiberg
Developmentalist and Child Advocate, 20th Century

A study by pediatrician T. Berry Brazelton (1956) involved observations of infants for more than a year to determine the incidence of their sucking when they were nursing and how their sucking changed as they grew older. Over 85 percent of the infants engaged in considerable sucking behavior unrelated to feeding. They sucked their fingers, their fists, and pacifiers. By the age of 1 year, most had stopped the sucking behavior.

Parents should not worry when infants suck their thumb, their fist, or even a pacifier. Many parents, though, do begin to worry when thumb sucking persists into the preschool and elementary school years. As much as 40 percent of children continue to suck their thumbs after they have started school (Kessen, Haith, & Salapatek, 1970). Most developmentalists do not attach a great deal of significance to this behavior and are not aware of parenting strategies that might contribute to it. Individual differences in children's biological makeup may be involved to some degree in the continuation of sucking behavior.

Gross and Fine Motor Skills

Gross motor skills *involve large muscle activities, such as moving one's arms and walking.* **Fine motor skills** *involve more finely tuned movements, such as finger dexterity.* Let's examine the changes in gross and fine motor skills in the first two years of life.

gross motor skills
Motor skills that involve large muscle activities, such as walking.

fine motor skills
Motor skills that involve more finely tuned movements, such as finger dexterity.

Gross Motor Skills

Ask any parents about their baby, and sooner or later you are likely to hear about one or more motor milestones, such as "Cassandra just learned to crawl," "Jesse is finally sitting alone," or "Shauna took her first step last week." It is no wonder that parents proudly announce such milestones. New motor

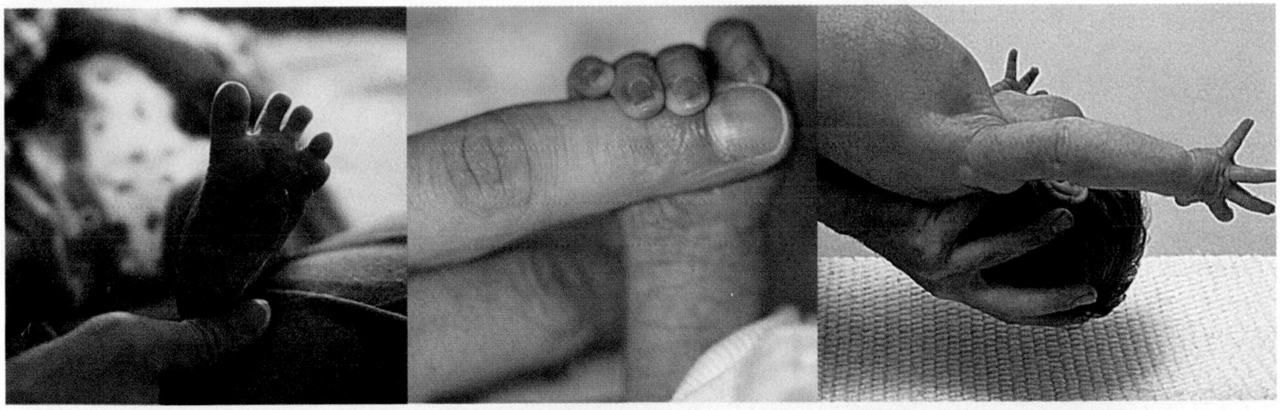

Babinski reflex | Grasping reflex | Moro reflex

Reflex	Stimulation	Infant's response	Developmental pattern
Blinking	Flash of light, puff of air	Closes both eyes	Permanent
Babinski	Sole of foot stroked	Fans out toes, twists foot in	Disappears after nine months to one year
Grasping	Palms touched	Grasps tightly	Weakens after three months, disappears after one year
Moro (startle)	Sudden stimulation, such as hearing loud noise or being dropped	Startles, arches back, throws head back, flings out arms and legs and then rapidly closes them to center of body	Disappears after three to four months
Rooting	Cheek stroked or side of mouth touched	Turns head, opens mouth, begins sucking	Disappears after three to four months
Stepping	Infant held above surface and feet lowered to touch surface	Moves feet as if to walk	Disappears after three to four months
Sucking	Object touching mouth	Sucks automatically	Disappears after three to four months
Swimming	Infant put face down in water	Makes coordinated swimming movements	Disappears after six to seven months
Tonic neck	Infant placed on back	Forms fists with both hands and usually turns head to the right (sometimes called the "fencer's pose" because the infant looks like it is assuming a fencer's position)	Disappears after two months

Figure **5.8**
Infant Reflexes

skills are the most dramatic and observable changes in the infant's first year of life. These motor progressions transform babies from being unable to even lift their heads to being able to grab things off the grocery store shelf, to chase the cat, and to participate actively in the family's social life (Thelen, 1995).

At birth, infants have no appreciable coordination of the chest or arms, but in the first month they can lift their head from a prone position. At about 3 months, infant can hold their chest up and use their arms for support after being in a prone position. At 3 to 4 months, infants can roll over, and at 4 to 5 months they can support some weight with their legs. At about 6 months, infants can sit

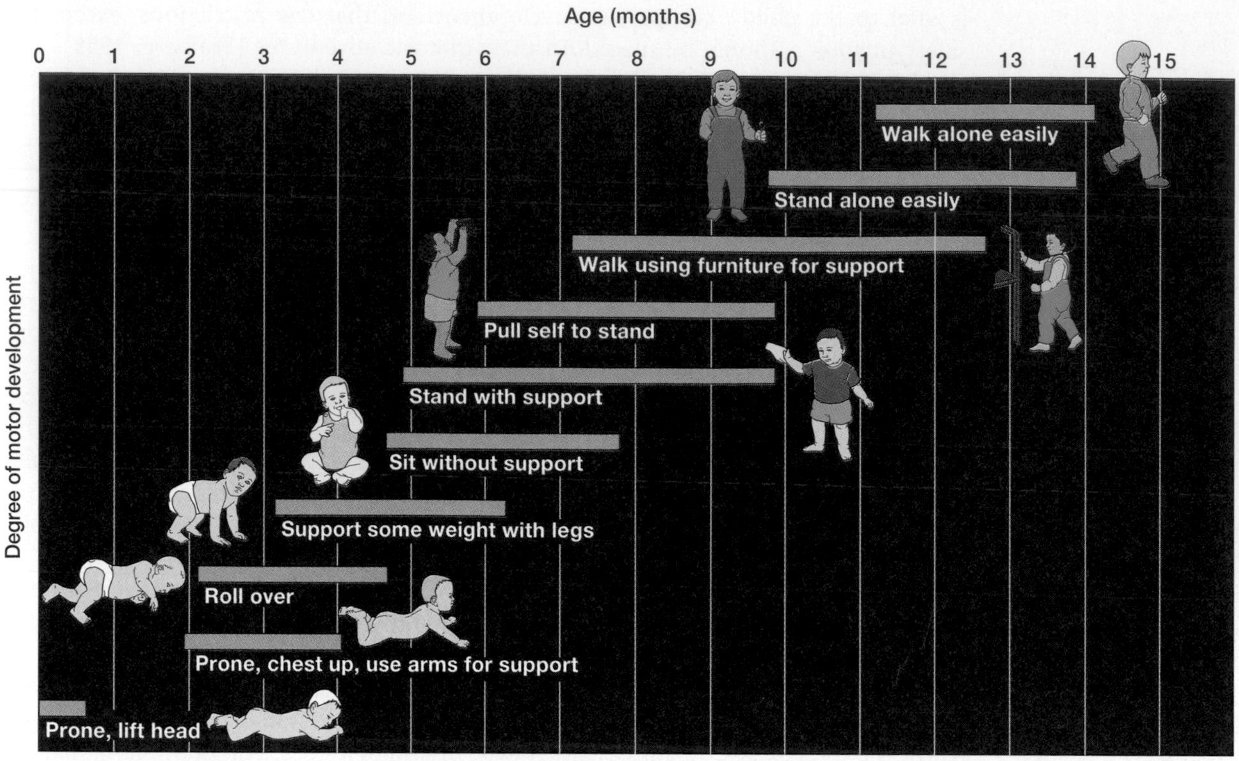

Figure **5.9**

Milestones in Gross Motor Development

without support, and by 7 to 8 months they can crawl and stand without support. At approximately 8 months, infants can pull themselves up to a standing position, at 10 to 11 months they can walk using furniture for support (this is called cruising), and at 12 to 13 months they can walk without assistance. A summary of the developmental accomplishments in gross motor skills during the first year is shown in figure 5.9. The actual month at which the milestones occur varies by as much as 2 to 4 months, especially among older infants. What remains fairly uniform, however, is the sequence of accomplishments. An important implication of these infant motor accomplishments is the increasing degree of independence they bring. Older infants can explore their environment more extensively and initiate social interaction with caregivers and peers more readily than when they were younger.

Although infants usually learn to walk about their first birthday, the neural pathways that control the leg alteration component of walking are in place from a very early age, possibly even at birth or before (Thelen, 2000). The clue for this belief is that infants engage in frequent alternating kicking movements throughout the first 6 months of life when they are lying on their backs. Also, when 1- to 2-month-olds are given support with their feet in contact with a motorized treadmill, they show well-coordinated, alternating steps.

If infants can produce forward stepping movements so early in their first year of life, why does it take them so long to learn to walk? The key skills in learning to walk appear to be stabilizing balance on one leg long enough to swing the other forward and shifting the weight without falling. This is a difficult biomechanical problem to solve, and it takes infants about a year to do it.

In the second year of life, toddlers become more motorically skilled and mobile. They are no longer content with being in a playpen and want to move all over the place. Child development experts believe that motor activity during the second year

WWW

Developmental Milestones

Physical Development in Infancy

A baby is an angel whose wings decrease as his legs increase.

French Proverb

is vital to the child's competent development and that few restrictions, except for safety purposes, should be placed on their motoric adventures (Fraiberg, 1959).

By 13 to 18 months, toddlers can pull a toy attached to a string, use their hands and legs to climb up a number of steps, and ride four-wheel wagons. By 18 to 24 months, toddlers can walk quickly or run stiffly for a short distance, balance on their feet in a squat position while playing with objects on the floor, walk backward without losing their balance, stand and kick a ball without falling, stand and throw a ball, and jump in place.

With the increased interest of today's adults in aerobic exercise and fitness, some parents have tried to give their infants a head start on becoming physically fit and physically talented. However, most pediatricians recommend against structured exercise classes for babies. They are seeing more bone fractures and dislocations and more muscle strains in babies now than in the past. They point out that, when an adult is stretching and moving an infant's limbs, it is easy to go beyond the infant's physical limits without knowing it.

The physical fitness classes for infants range from passive fare—with adults putting infants through the paces—to programs called "aerobic" because they demand crawling, tumbling, and ball skills. However, exercise for infants cannot be aerobic, because infants cannot exercise with enough intensity to achieve aerobic benefits.

In most cultures, infants are not exposed to structured physical fitness classes like the ones that are showing up in the United States. However, when parents or other caregivers provide babies with physical guidance by physically handling them in special ways (such as stroking, massaging, or stretching) or providing them with opportunities for exercise, the infants often attain motor milestones earlier than infants whose caregivers have not provided these physical activities. For example, Jamaican mothers expect their infants to sit and walk alone 2 to 3 months earlier than English mothers do (Hopkins & Westra, 1990). Also, Jamaican mothers regularly massage their infants and stretch their arms and legs, and this is linked with advanced motor development (Hopkins, 1991). Mothers in the Gusii culture of Kenya encourage vigorous movement in their babies (Hopkins & Westra, 1988).

Fine Motor Skills Infants have hardly any control over fine motor skills at birth, although they have many components of what later become finely coordinated arm, hand, and finger movements (Rosenblith, 1992). The onset of reaching and grasping marks a significant achievement in infants' functional interactions with their surroundings (McCarty & Ashmead, 1999). For many years it was believed that reaching for an object is visually guided—that is, the infant must continuously have sight of the hand and the target (White, Castle, & Held, 1964). However, in one study, Rachel Clifton and her colleagues (1993) demonstrated that infants do not have to see their own hands when reaching for an object. They concluded that, because the infants could not see their hand or arm in the dark in the experiment, proprioceptive (muscle, tendon, joint sense) cues, not sight of limb, guided the early reaching of the 4-month-old infants. The development of reaching and grasping becomes more refined during the first 2 years of life. Initially, infants show only crude shoulder and elbow movements, but later they show wrist movements, hand rotation, and coordination of the thumb and forefinger. The maturation of hand-eye coordination over the first 2 years of life is reflected in the improvement of fine motor skills. Figure 5.10 provides an overview of the development of fine motor skills in the first 2 years of life.

Developmental Biodynamics

Traditional views of motor development have chronicled the stagelike changes in posture and movement that characterize the first several years of life (Gesell, 1928; Shirley, 1933). In the past decade, advances in a number of domains have generated a new perspective on infant motor development. Rather than describing the ages at which various motor achievements are reached and explaining them as a result of brain and nervous-system maturation, the new perspective **developmental biodynamics** *seeks to explain how motor behaviors are assembled for perceiving and acting.* This

developmental biodynamics
The new perspective on motor development in infancy that seeks to explain how motor behaviors are assembled for perceiving and acting.

Birth to 6 months	
2 mo.	Holds rattle briefly
2 1/2 mo.	Glances from one object to another
3–4 mo.	Plays in simple way with rattle; inspects fingers; reaches for dangling ring; visually follows ball across table
4 mo.	Carries object to mouth
4–5 mo.	Recovers rattle from chest; holds two objects
5 mo.	Transfers object from hand to hand
5–6 mo.	Bangs in play; looks for object while sitting
6–12 months	
6 mo.	Secures cube on sight; follows adult's movements across room; immediately fixates on small objects and stretches out to grasp them; retains rattle
6 1/2 mo.	Manipulates and examines an object; reaches for, grabs, and retains rattle
7 mo.	Pulls string to obtain an object
7 1/2–8 1/2 mo.	Grasps with thumb and finger
8–9 mo.	Persists in reaching for toy out of reach on table; shows hand preference, bangs spoon; searches in correct place for toys dropped within reach of hands; may find toy hidden under cup
10 mo.	Hits cup with spoon; crude release of object
10 1/2–11 mo.	Picks up raisin with thumb and forefinger; pincer grasp; pushes car along
11–12 mo.	Puts three or more objects in a container
12–18 months	
	Places one 2-inch block on top of another 2-inch block (in imitation)
	Scribbles with a large crayon on large piece of paper
	Turns two to three pages in a large book with cardboard pages while sitting in an adult's lap
	Places three 1-inch cube blocks in a 6-inch diameter cup (in imitation)
	Holds a pencil and makes a mark on a sheet of paper
	Builds a four-block tower with 2-inch cube blocks (in imitation)
18–24 months	
	Draws an arc on piece of unlined paper with a pencil after being shown how
	Turns a doorknob that is within reach, using both hands
	Unscrews a lid put loosely on a small jar after being shown how
	Places large pegs in a pegboard
	Connects and takes apart a pop bead string of five beads
	Zips and unzips a large zipper after being shown how

Figure 5.10
The Development of Fine Motor Skills in Infancy

perspective is an outgrowth of developments in the neurosciences, biomechanics, and the behavioral sciences (Lockman & Thelen, 1993; Thelen, 2001). The research of Rachel Clifton and her colleagues (1993), which was described earlier, illustrates the developmental biodynamics view. They found that proprioceptive cues play an important role in early guided reaching. Their research shows how perception *and* action are linked in early manual skill development.

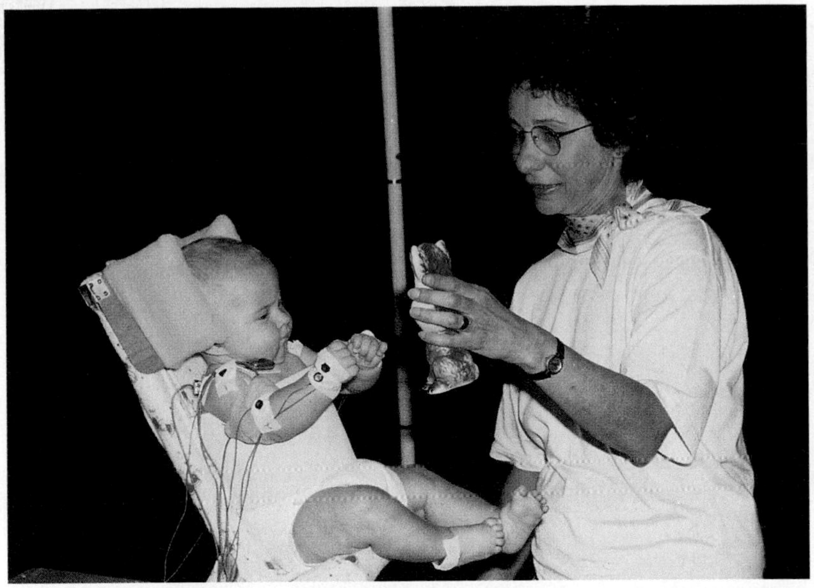

Esther Thelen is shown conducting an experiment to discover how infants learn to control their arms to reach and grasp for objects. A computer device is used to monitor the infant's arm movements and to track muscle patterns. Thelen's research is conducted from a developmental biodynamics perspective. *What is the nature of this perspective?*

The developmental biodynamics view of infant motor development has especially been advanced by the theorizing and research of Esther Thelen (1995, 2000). Following are some of the main concepts in her developmental biodynamics perspective.

The new view of motor development emphasizes the importance of exploration and selection in finding solutions to new task demands. This means that infants need to assemble adaptive patterns by modifying their current movement patterns. The first step is to get the infant into the "ball park" of the task demands—a tentative crawl or several stumbling steps. Then, the infant has to "tune" these configurations to make them smoother and more effective. Such tuning is achieved through repeated cycles of action and perception of the consequences of that action in relation to the goal.

The developmental biodynamics view contrasts with the traditional maturational view by proposing that even the universal milestones, such as crawling, reaching, and walking, are learned through a process of adaptation. Infants modulate their movement patterns to fit a new task by exploring and selecting various possible configurations. The assumption is that the infant is motivated by the new challenge—a desire to get a new toy into one's mouth or to cross the room to join other family members. It is the new task, the challenge of the context, not prescribed genetic instructions that represents the driving force for change.

At this point, we have discussed many ideas about motor development. To review these ideas see summary table 5.3. A key theme in the developmental biodynamics view we just evaluted is that perception and action are coupled when new skills are learned. Let's now explore the nature of the infant's perceptual development.

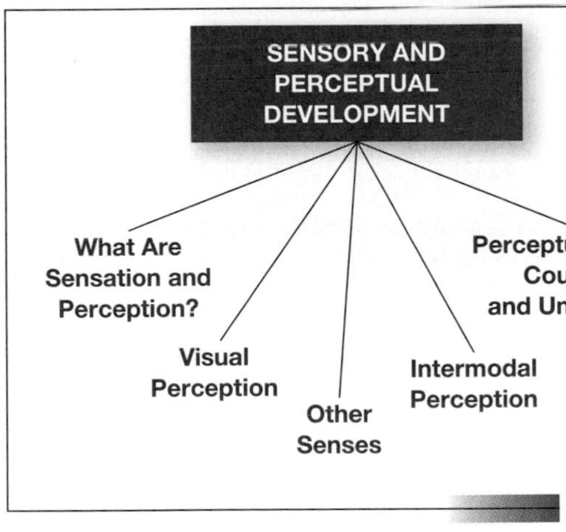

Sensory and Perceptual Development

What are sensation and perception? Can a newborn see? If so, what can it perceive? What about the other senses—hearing, smell, taste, touch, and pain? What are they like in the newborn, and how do they develop in infancy? Can an infant put together information from two different modalities, such as sight and sound, in perceiving its world? These are among the intriguing questions we will now explore.

What Are Sensation and Perception?

How does a newborn know that her mother's skin is soft rather than rough? How does a 5-year-old know what color his hair is? How does an 8-year-old know that summer is warmer than winter? How does a 10-year-old know that a firecracker is louder than a cat's meow? Infants and children "know" these things because of their senses. All information comes to the infant through the senses. Without vision, hearing, touch, taste, smell, and other senses, the infant's brain would be isolated from the world; the infant would live in dark silence, a tasteless, colorless, feelingless void.

sensation
The product of the interaction between information and the sensory receptors—the eyes, ears, tongue, nostrils, and skin.

Sensation *occurs when information interacts with sensory receptors—the eyes, ears, tongue, nostrils, and skin.* The sensation of hearing occurs when waves of pulsating air are collected by the outer ear and transmitted through the bones of the inner ear

Summary Table 5.3
Motor Development

Concept	Processes/ Related Ideas	Characteristics/Descriptions
Reflexes	Automatic Movements	• The newborn is no longer viewed as a passive, empty-headed organism. • Reflexes (automatic movements) govern the newborn's behavior. • For infants, sucking is an important means of obtaining nutrition.
Gross and Fine Motor Skills	Gross Motor Skills	• These involve large muscle activities, such as moving one's arms and walking. • A number of gross motor milestones occur in infancy.
	Fine Motor Skills	• These involve movements that are more finely tuned than gross motor skills. • A number of fine motor milestones occur in infancy.
Developmental Biodynamics	Nature of Ideas	• This approach seeks to explain how motor behaviors are assembled for perceiving and acting. • Emphasizes the importance of exploration and selection in finding solutions to new task demands. • A key theme is that perception and action are coupled when new skills are learned.

to the auditory nerve. The sensation of vision occurs as rays of light contact the eyes and become focused on the retina.

Perception *is the interpretation of what is sensed.* The information about physical events that contacts the ears may be interpreted as musical sounds, for example. The physical energy transmitted to the retinas may be interpreted as a particular color, pattern, or shape.

perception
The interpretation of what is sensed.

The Ecological View

Much of the research on perceptual development in infancy in the past several decades has been guided by the ecological view of Eleanor and James J. Gibson (E. J. Gibson, 1969, 1989, 2001; J. J. Gibson, 1966, 1979). They believe that we can directly perceive information that exists in the world around us: We do not have to build up representations of the world in our mind; information about the world is available out there in the environment. Thus, the **ecological view** *states that perception functions to bring organisms in contact with the environment and increase adaptation.* In ecological theory, perception is for action. Perception gives people such information as when to duck, when to turn their body through a narrow passageway, and when to put their hand up to catch something.

ecological view
The view that perception functions to bring organisms in contact with the environment and to increase adaptation.

The Gibsons believe that if complex things can be perceived directly, perhaps they can be perceived even by young infants. Thus, the ecological view has inspired investigators to search for the competencies that young infants possess. Of course, ecological theorists do not deny that perception develops as infants and children develop. In fact, the ecological theorists stress that, as perceptual processes mature, the child becomes more efficient at discovering the properties of objects available to the senses.

For the Gibsons, all objects have **affordances,** *which are opportunities for interaction offered by objects that are necessary to perform functional activities.* For example, adults immediately know when a chair is appropriate for sitting, a surface is for walking, or an object is within reach. We directly and accurately perceive these affordances by sensing information from the environment—such as the light or sound reflecting from the surfaces of the world—and from our own bodies through muscle receptors, joint receptors, skin receptors, and the like. The developmental question, though, is how these affordances are acquired. In one study, infants who were crawlers or walkers recognized the action-specific properties of surfaces (Gibson &

affordances
Opportunities for interaction offered by objects that are necessary to perform functional activities.

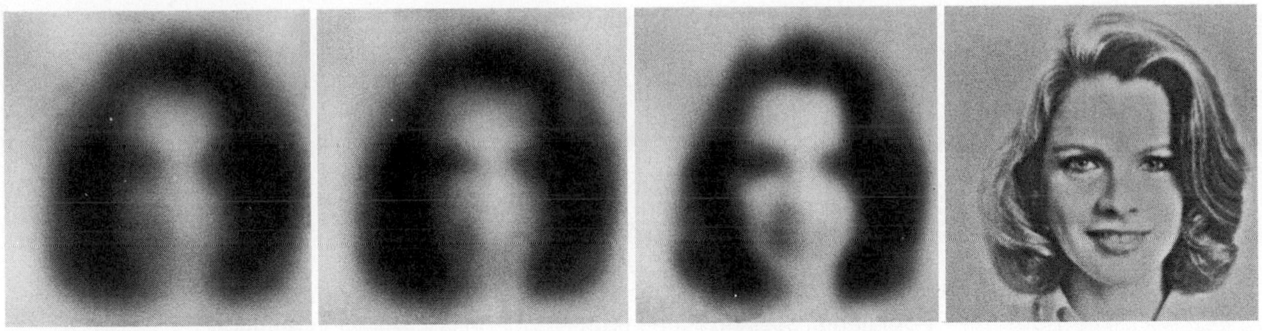

Figure 5.11

Visual Acuity During the First Months of Life

The four photographs represent a computer estimation of what a picture of a face looks like to a 1-month-old, 2-month-old, 3-month-old, and 1-year-old (which approximates that of an adult).

The infant is by no means as helpless as it looks and is quite capable of some very complex and important actions.

Herb Pick
Contemporary Developmental Psychologist, University of Minnesota

others, 1987). When faced with a rigid plywood surface or a squishy waterbed, crawlers crossed both without hesitating. The toddlers, however, stopped and explored the waterbed, then chose to crawl rather than walk across it. Note the coupling of perception and action to adapt to a particular task demand in the world.

In another study, infants who were learning to walk were more cautious when they were confronted with having to go down a steep slope than younger infants were (Adolph, 1997). The older infants perceived that a slope *affords* the possibility not only for faster locomotion but also for falling.

Visual Perception

Can newborns see? How does visual perception develop in infancy?

Visual Acuity and Color

Psychologist William James (1890/1950) called the newborn's perceptual world a "blooming, buzzing" confusion. Was James right? A century later, we can safely say that he was wrong. The infant's perception of visual information is far more advanced than was previously thought (Slater, 2001).

Just how well can infants see? The newborn's vision is estimated to be 20/400 to 20/800 on the well-known Snellan chart, with which you are tested when you have your eyes examined (Haith, 1991). This is about 10 to 30 times lower than normal adult vision (20/20). By 6 months of age, though, vision is 20/100 or better, and, by about the first birthday, the infant's vision approximates that of an adult (Banks & Salapatek, 1983). Figure 5.11 shows a computer estimation of what a picture of a face looks like to an infant at different points in development from a distance of about 6 inches.

Can newborns see color? At birth, babies can distinguish between green and red (Adams, 1989). An adultlike functioning in all three types (red, blue, green) of color-sensitive receptors (cones) is present by 2 months of age.

WWW

Perceptual Development
Newborns' Senses
Richard Aslin's Research
International Society on Infant Studies

Visual Preferences

Robert Fantz (1963) is an important pioneer in the study of visual perception in infants. Fantz made an important discovery that advanced the ability of researchers to investigate infants' visual perception: infants look at different things for different lengths of time. Fantz placed infants in a "looking chamber," which had two visual displays on the ceiling above the infant's head. An experimenter viewed the infant's eyes by looking through a peephole. If the infant was fixating on one of the displays, the experimenter could see the display's reflection in the infant's eyes. This allowed the experimenter to determine how long the infant looked at each display. In figure 5.12, you can see Fantz's looking chamber and the results of his experiment. The infants preferred to look at patterns rather than at color or brightness. For example, they preferred to look at a face, a piece of printed

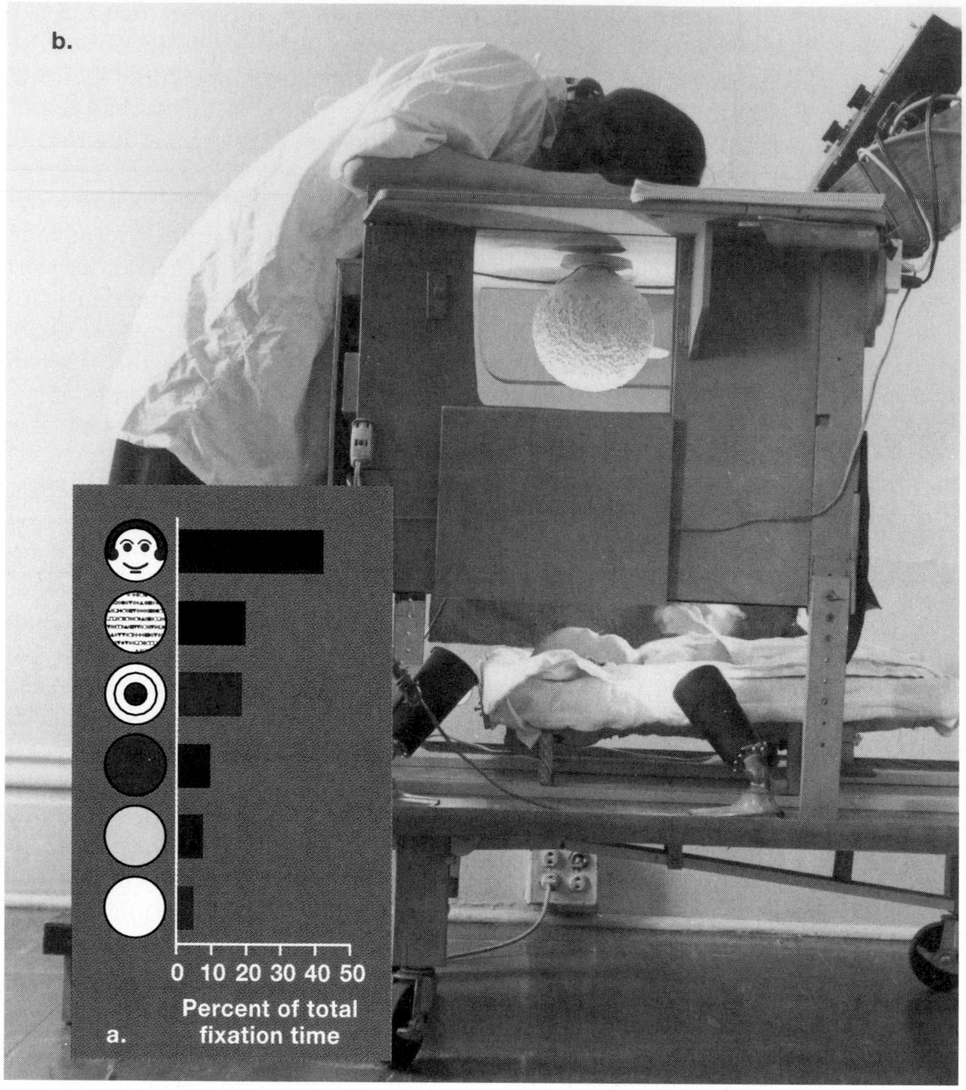

Figure 5.12

Fantz's Experiment on Infants' Visual Perception

(a) Infants 2 to 3 months old preferred to look at some stimuli more than others. In Fantz's experiment, infants preferred to look at patterns rather than at color or brightness. For example, they looked longer at a face, a piece of printed matter, or a bull's-eye than at red, yellow, or white discs. *(b)* Fantz used a "looking chamber" to study infants' perception of stimuli.

matter, or a bull's-eye longer than at red, yellow, or white discs. In another experiment, Fantz found that younger infants—only 2 days old—look longer at patterned stimuli, such as faces and concentric circles, than at red, white, or yellow discs. Based on these results, it is likely that pattern perception has an innate basis, or at least is acquired after only minimal environmental experience. The newborn's visual world is not the blooming, buzzing confusion William James imagined.

Depth Perception How early can infants perceive depth? To investigate this question, infant perception researchers Eleanor Gibson and Richard Walk (1960) conducted a classic experiment. They constructed a miniature cliff with a drop-off covered by glass. The motivation for this experiment arose when Gibson was eating a picnic lunch on the edge of the Grand Canyon. She wondered whether an infant looking over the canyon's rim would perceive the dangerous drop-off and back up. In their laboratory, Gibson and Walk placed infants on the edge of a visual cliff and had

Figure 5.13

Examining Infants' Depth Perception on the Visual Cliff

Eleanor Gibson and Richard Walk (1960) found that most infants would not crawl out on the glass, which indicated that they had depth perception.

Elizabeth Spelke's Research

their mothers coax them to crawl onto the glass (see figure 5.13). Most infants would not crawl out on the glass, choosing instead to remain on the shallow side, indicating that they could perceive depth. However, because the 6- to 14-month-old infants had extensive visual experience, this research did not answer the question of whether depth perception is innate.

Exactly how early in life does depth perception develop? Since younger infants do not crawl, this question is difficult to answer. Research with 2- to 4-month-old infants shows differences in heart rate when they are placed directly on the deep side of the visual cliff instead of on the shallow side (Campos, Langer, & Krowitz, 1970). However, an alternative interpretation is that young infants respond to differences in some visual characteristics of the deep and shallow cliffs, with no actual knowledge of depth.

Visual Expectations Infants not only see forms and figures at an early age but also develop expectations about future events in their world by the time they are 3 months of age. Marshall Haith and his colleagues (Canfield & Haith, 1991; Haith, Hazen, & Goodman, 1988) studied whether babies would form expectations about where an interesting picture would appear. The pictures were presented to the infants in either a regularly alternating sequence—such as left, right, left, right—or an unpredictable sequence—such as right, right, left, right. When the sequence was predictable, the 3-month-old infants began to anticipate the location of the picture, looking at the side on which it was expected to appear. The young infants formed this visual expectation in less than one minute. However, younger infants did not develop expectations about where a picture would be presented.

Elizabeth Spelke (1988, 1991) also has demonstrated that young infants form visual expectations. She placed babies before a puppet stage and showed them a series of unexpected actions—for example, a ball seemed to roll through a solid barrier, another seemed to leap between two platforms, and a third appears to hang in midair (Spelke, 1979) (see figure 5.14). Spelke measured the babies' looking times and recorded longer intervals for unexpected than expected actions. She concluded that, by 4 months of age, even though infants do not yet have the ability to talk about objects, move around objects, manipulate objects, or even see objects with high resolution, they can recognize where a moving object is when it has left their visual field and can infer where it should be when it comes into their sight again.

Other Senses

Considerable development also takes place in other sensory systems. We will explore development in hearing, touch and pain, smell, and taste.

Hearing Can the fetus hear? What is the newborn's hearing like? What types of auditory stimulation should be used with infants at different points in the first year?

In the last few months of pregnancy, the fetus can hear sounds: the mother's voice, music, and so on (Kisilevsky, 1995). Given that the fetus can hear sounds, two psychologists wanted to find out if listening to Dr. Seuss' classic story *The Cat in the Hat,* while still in the mother's womb, would produce a preference for hearing the story after birth (DeCasper & Spence, 1986). Sixteen pregnant women read *The Cat in the Hat* to their fetuses twice a day over the last 6 weeks of their pregnancies. When the babies were born, their mothers read *The Cat in the Hat* or a story with a different rhyme and pace, *The King, the Mice, and the Cheese* (which was not read to them during prenatal development). The infants sucked on a nipple in a different way when the mothers read *The Cat in the Hat,* suggesting that the infants recognized its pattern and tone (to which they had been exposed prenatally) (see figure 5.15).

Two important conclusions can be drawn from this investigation. First, it reveals how ingenious scientists have become at assessing the development not only of infants but of fetuses as well, in this case discovering a way to "interview" newborn babies who cannot yet talk. Second, it reveals the remarkable ability of an infant's brain to learn even before birth. However, conclusions from this study should not be overdrawn. It does not suggest that reading to an infant prenatally will produce a child who acquires language and cognitive development more repidly. Recall our discussion earlier in the chapter about lack of evidence for linkages between early enriched experiences and the brain's development.

Immediately after birth, infants can hear, although their sensory thresholds are somewhat higher than those of adults (Trehub & others, 1991). That is, a stimulus must be louder to be heard by a newborn than by an adult. Also, in one study, as infants aged from 8 to 28 weeks, they became more proficient at localizing sounds (Morrongiello, Fenwick, & Chance, 1990).

Babies are born into the world prepared to respond to the sounds of any human language. Even very young infants can discriminate subtle phonetic differences, such as those between the speech sounds of *ba* and *ga*. Young infants also will suck more on a nipple to hear a recording of their mother's voice than they will to hear the voice of an unfamiliar woman, and they will suck more to listen to their mother's native language than they will to listen to a foreign language (Mehler & others, 1988; Spence & DeCasper, 1987). And an interesting developmental change occurs during the first year: 6-month-old infants can discriminate phonetic sound contrasts from languages to which they have never been exposed, but they lose this discriminative ability by their first birthday, demonstrating that experience with a specific language is necessary for maintaining this ability (Werker & LaLonde, 1988).

Touch and Pain Do newborns respond to touch? Can newborns feel pain?

Figure 5.14

The Young Infant's Knowledge of the Perceptual World

A 4-month-old in Elizabeth Spelke's infant perception laboratory is tested to determine if it knows that an object in motion will not stop in midair.

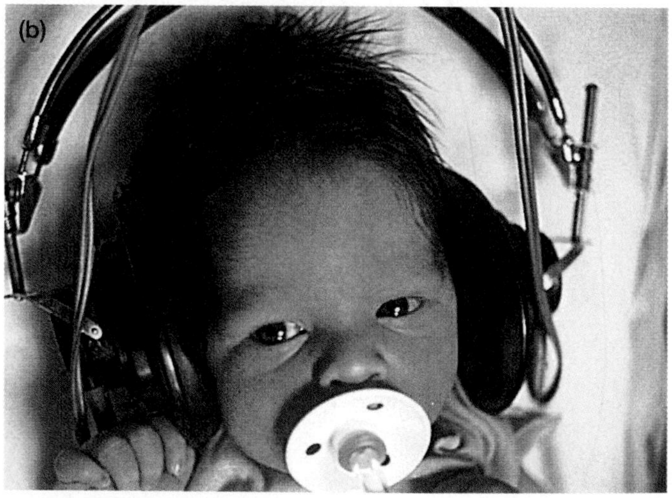

Figure 5.15

Hearing in the Womb

(a) Pregnant mothers read *The Cat in the Hat* to their fetuses during the last few months of pregnancy. *(b)* When they were born, the babies preferred listening to a recording of their mothers reading *The Cat in the Hat,* as evidenced by their sucking on a nipple that produced this recording, rather than another story, *The King, The Mice, and the Cheese.*

Touch Newborns respond to touch. A touch to the cheek produces a turning of the head, whereas a touch to the lips produces sucking movements. An important ability that develops in infancy is to connect information about vision with information about touch. One-year-olds clearly can do this, and it appears that 6-month-olds can, too (Acredolo & Hake, 1982). Whether still younger infants can coordinate vision and touch is yet to be determined.

Pain It once was thought that newborns are indifferent to pain, but we now know that is not true. The main research that has documented newborns' sensitivity to pain involves male infants' stressful reactions to being circumcised (Gunnar, Malone, & Fisch, 1987). For example, newborn males show a higher level of cortisol (an indicator of stress) after a circumcision than prior to the surgery. As a consequence, anesthesia now is used in some cases of circumcision (Taddio & others, 1997).

For many years, doctors have performed operations on newborns without anesthesia. This medical practice was accepted because of the dangers of anesthesia and the supposition that newborns do not feel pain. Recently, as researchers have convincingly demonstrated that newborns can feel pain, the long-standing practice of operating on newborns without anesthesia is being challenged.

Smell Newborns can differentiate odors. For example, by the expressions on their faces, they seem to indicate that they like the smell of vanilla and strawberry but do not like the smell of rotten eggs and fish (Steiner, 1979). In one investigation, young infants who were breast-fed showed a clear preference for smelling their mother's breast pad when they were 6 days old (MacFarlane, 1975) (see figure 5.16). However, when

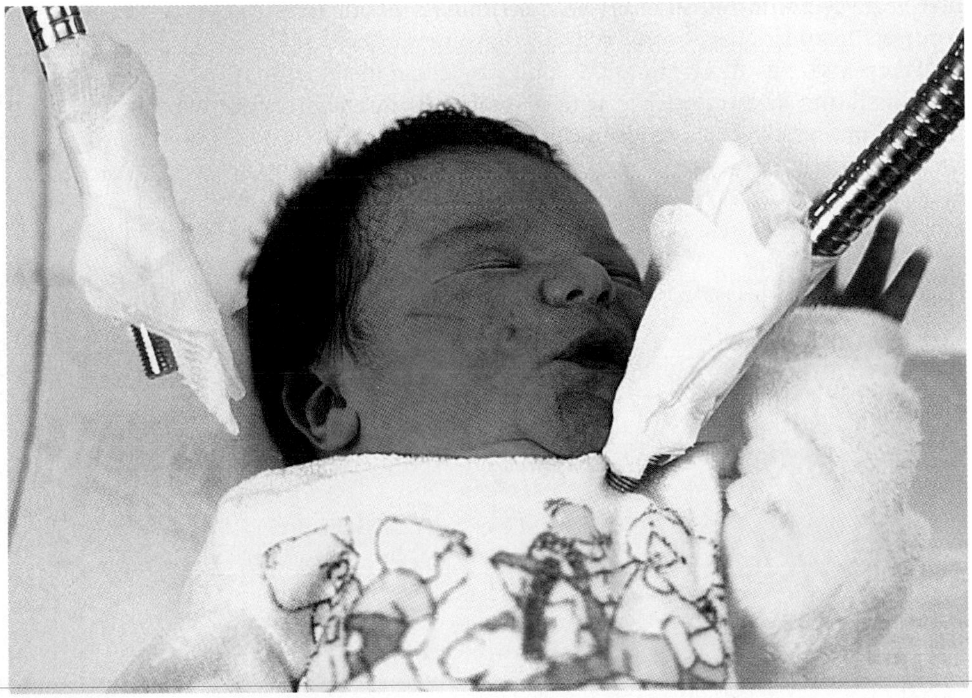

Figure **5.16**

Newborns' Preference for the Smell of Their Mother's Breast Pad

In the experiment by MacFarlane (1975), 6-day-old infants preferred to smell their mother's breast pad over a clean one that had never been used, but 2-day-old infants did not show the preference, indicating that this odor preference requires several days of experience to develop.

they were 2 days old, they did not show this preference (compared to a clean breast pad), indicating that they require several days of experience to recognize this odor.

Taste Sensitivity to taste might be present before birth. When saccharin was added to the amniotic fluid of a near-term fetus, increased swallowing was observed (Windle, 1940). In one study, even at only 2 hours of age, babies made different facial expressions when they tasted sweet, sour, and bitter solutions (Rosenstein & Oster, 1988) (see figure 5.17). At about 4 months of age, infants begin to prefer salty tastes, which as newborns they were averse to (Harris, Thomas, & Booth, 1990).

We have studied a number of different sensory modalities. In examining these different modalities, one topic that is of special interest involves determining what the best sensory stimulation is for the infant. Next we will focus on another intriguing aspect of infant perception—whether infants can engage in intermodal perception.

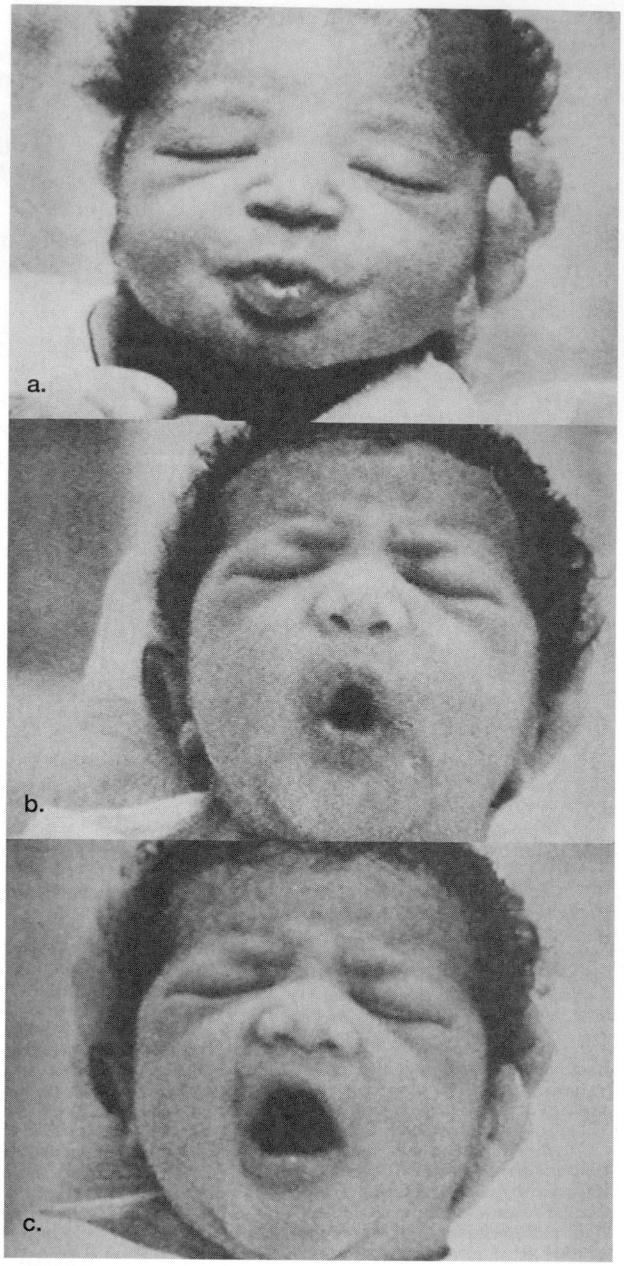

Figure **5.17**

Newborns' Facial Responses to Basic Tastes

Facial expressions elicited by (*a*) a sweet solution, (*b*) a sour solution, and (*c*) a bitter solution.

Intermodal Perception

Are young infants so competent that they can relate and integrate information through several senses? Imagine yourself playing basketball or tennis. You are experiencing many visual inputs: the ball coming and going, other players moving around, and so on. However, you are experiencing many auditory inputs as well the sound of the ball bouncing or being hit, the grunts and groans, and so on. There is good correspondence between much of the visual and auditory information: when you see the ball bounce, you hear a bouncing sound; when a player stretches to hit a ball, you hear a groan.

We live in a world of objects and events that can be seen, heard, and felt. When mature observers simultaneously look and listen to an event, they experience a unitary episode. All of this is so commonplace that it scarcely seems worth mentioning, but consider the task of very young infants with little practice at perceiving. Can they put vision and sound together as precisely as adults do?

Intermodal perception *is the ability to relate and integrate information about two or more sensory modalities, such as vision and hearing.* To test intermodal perception, Elizabeth Spelke (1979) showed 4-month-old infants two films simultaneously. In each film, a puppet jumped up and down, but in one of the films the sound track matched the puppet's dancing movements; in the other film, it did not. By measuring the infants' gaze, Spelke found that the infants looked more at the puppet whose actions were synchronized with the sound track, suggesting that they recognized the visual-sound correspondence. Young infants can also coordinate visual-auditory information involving people (Condry, Smuth & Spelke, 2001). In one study, as early as at 3½ months old, infants looked more at their mother when they also heard her voice and longer at their father when they also heard his voice (Spelke & Owsley, 1979).

Might auditory-visual relations be coordinated even in newborns? Newborns do turn their eyes and their head toward the sound of a voice or rattle when the sound is maintained for several seconds (Clifton & others, 1981), but the newborn can localize a sound and look at an object only in a crude way (Bechtold, Bushnell, & Salapatek, 1979). Improved accuracy at auditory-visual coordination likely requires a sharpening through experience with visual and auditory stimuli. Nonetheless, although at a crude level, auditory-visual intermodal perception appears to be present at birth, likely having evolutionary value.

intermodal perception
The ability to relate and integrate information about two or more sensory modalities, such as vision and hearing.

The development of perception and action is mutual and reciprocal. Improvements in coordinating actions demand greater perceptual differentiation; likewise, greater perceptual differentiation provides children with more precise information for coordinating their actions.

Bennett Bertenthal
Contemporary Developmental Psychologist, University of Chicago

In sum, crude exploratory forms of intermodal perception exist in newborns. These exploratory forms of intermodal perception become sharpened with experience in the first year of life. In the first 6 months, infants have difficulty forming mental representations that connect sensory input from different modes, but in the second half of the first year they show an increased ability to make this connection mentally. Thus, babies are born into the world with some innate abilities to perceive relations among sensory modalities, but their intermodal abilities improve considerably through experience. As with all aspects of development, in perceptual development, nature and nurture interact and cooperate.

Perceptual-Motor Coupling and Unification

For the most part our discussion of motor development and sensory/perceptual development have been isolated in this chapter. Indeed, the main thrust of research in many studies has been to discover how perception guides action. A less well studied but important issue is how action shapes perception. Motor activities might be crucial because they provide the means for exploring the world and learning about its properties. Only by moving one's eyes, head, hands, and arms and by traversing from one location to another can individuals fully experience their environment and learn to effectively adapt to it.

The distinction between perceiving and doing has been a time-honored tradition in psychology. However, a number of experts on perceptual and motor development question this distinction (Bornstein & Arterberry, 1999; Lochman, 2000; Pick, 1997; Thelen, 1995, 2000). For example, Esther Thelen (1995) argues that individuals perceive in order to move and move in order to perceive. Thus, there is an increasing belief that perceptual and motor development do not occur in isolation from one another but, rather, are coupled.

Babies are continually coordinating their movements with concurrent perceptual information to learn how to maintain balance, reach for objects in space, and locomote across various surfaces and terrains (Thelen, 2000). For example, in considering how infants are motivated to move by what they perceive, consider the sight of an attractive object across the room. In this situation, infants must perceive the cur-

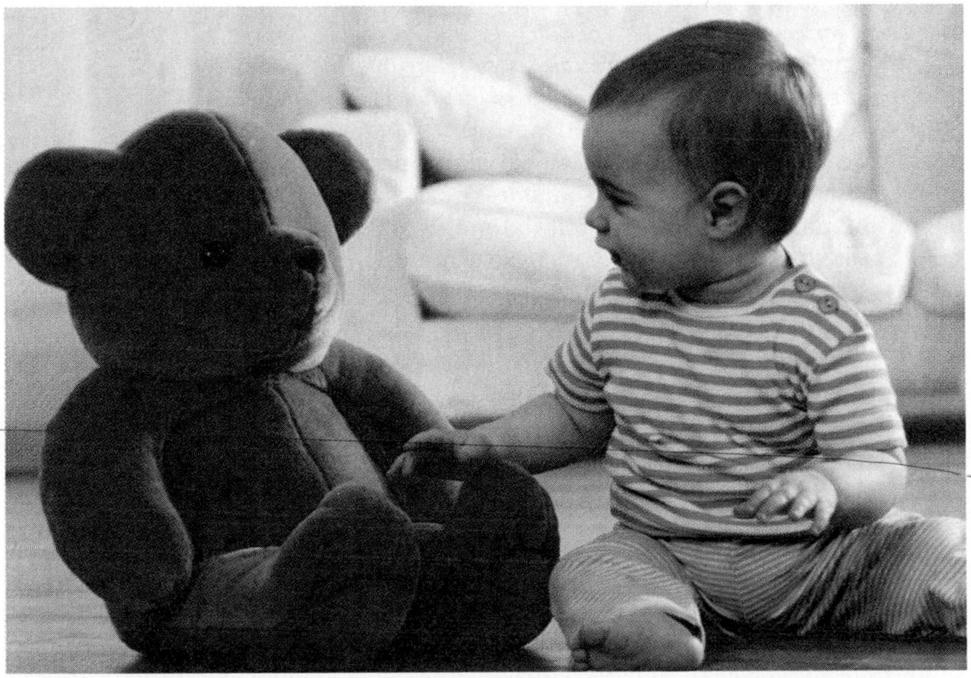

What are some examples of perceptual-motor coupling in infancy?

Summary Table 5.4
Sensory and Perceptual Development

Concept	Processes/ Related Ideas	Characteristics/Descriptions
What Are Sensation and Perception?	Sensation	• Sensation occurs when information interacts with the sensory receptors—the eyes, ears, tongue, nostrils, and skin.
	Perception	• This is the interpretation of what is sensed.
The Ecological View	Created by the Gibsons	• The view that perception functions to bring organisms in contact with the environment and increase adaptation.
Visual Perception	Visual Acuity and Color	• William James was wrong—the newborn's visual world is not a "blooming, buzzing confusion."
	Visual Preferences	• Newborns can see and can distinguish colors. • In Fantz's pioneering research, infants only 2 days old looked longer at patterned stimuli, such as faces, than at single-colored discs.
	Depth Perception	• A classic study by Gibson and Walk demonstrated through the use of the visual cliff that infants as young as 6 months of age have depth perception.
	Visual Expectations	• Haith has demonstrated that infants develop expectations about future events in their world by the time they are 3 months of age.
Other Senses	Hearing	• The fetus can hear several weeks before birth. • Immediately after birth, newborns can hear, although their sensory threshold is higher than that of adults.
	Touch and Pain	• Newborns respond to touch and can feel pain.
Intermodal Perception	Linking Sensory Modalities	• This is the ability to relate and integrate information about two or more sensory modalities, such as vision and hearing. • Spelke's research demonstrates that infants as young as 3 months of age can link visual and auditory stimuli.
Perceptual-Motor Coupling and Unification	Integration	• A time-honored belief in psychology has been that perceptual and motor development are distinct. • Increasingly, it is believed that perceptual-motor development is coupled and unified.

rent state of their bodies and learn how to use their limbs to get to the goal object. Although their movements at first are awkward and uncoordinated, babies soon learn to select patterns that are appropriate for reaching their goals. Equally important is the other part of the perception-action coupling: action educates perception. For example, watching an object while exploring it manually helps infants to visually discriminate its properties of texture, size, and hardness. Locomoting in the environment teaches babies how objects and people look from different perspectives, or whether surfaces will support their weight.

Also think about how often during each day you need to coordinate perceptual input with motor actions to accomplish what you want to do. For example, right now I am looking at my computer screen (perceiving) to make sure the words are appearing accurately as I am typing them (motorically).

At this point we have discussed a number of ideas about sensory and perceptual development. A review of these ideas is presented in summary table 5.4. In the next chapter, we will continue our exploration of infant development by focusing on cognitive changes.

Chapter Review

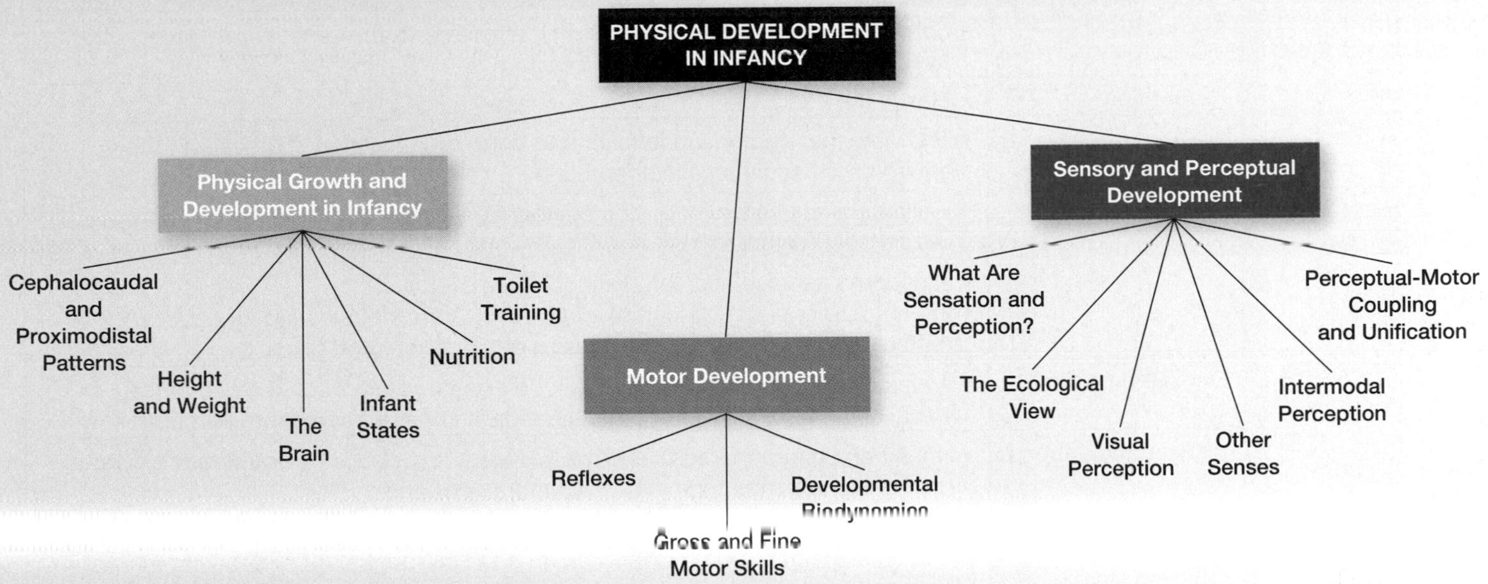

TO OBTAIN A DETAILED REVIEW OF THIS CHAPTER, STUDY THESE FOUR SUMMARY TABLES:

- Summary Table 5.1 Cephalocaudal and Proximodistal Patterns, Height and Weight, and the Brain page 131
- Summary Table 5.2 Infant States, Nutrition, and Toilet Training page 138
- Summary Table 5.3 Motor Development page 145
- Summary Table 5.4 Sensory and Perceptual Development page 153

Key Terms

cephalocaudal pattern 126
proximodistal pattern 127
neuron 127
lateralization 128
REM (rapid eye movement) sleep 131
sudden infant death syndrome (SIDS) 133
marasmus 136
kwashiorkor 136
sucking reflex 138
rooting reflex 138
Moro reflex 139
grasping reflex 139
gross motor skills 139
fine motor skills 139
developmental biodynamics 142
sensation 144
perception 145
ecological view 145
affordances 145
intermodal perception 151

Key People

Charles Nelson 127
Mark Rosenzweig 129
Ernesto Pollitt 136
T. Berry Brazelton 139
Rachel Clifton 143
Esther Thelen 144
Eleanor and James J. Gibson 145
William James 146
Robert Fantz 146
Richard Walk 147
Marshall Haith 148
Elizabeth Spelke 148

Taking It to the Net

1. Professor Samuels asked his life-span psychology students to write a one-page report explaining how a child's brain develops during infancy and what role parents play in fostering maximal brain development. What should this report contain to provide a concise but comprehensive summary of the research found to date?
2. One of the families in a community day-care center lost a 4-month-old child to SIDS. Laura, the center's director, is planning to conduct an in-service training for her employees about the effect of a SIDS-related death on the deceased child's parents and siblings. What information should they have in order to help them deal with this family?
3. Marianne has landed a part-time job as a nanny for Jack, a 2-month-old boy. What can Marianne expect to see in terms of the child's sensory and motor development as she interacts with and observes Jack over the next 6 months?

Connect to www.mhhe.com/santrockld8 to research the answers and complete these exercises.

OLC Preview

To further test your knowledge of this chapter or to explore our extensive online resources that accompany *Life-Span Development*, eighth edition, please log on to the text's Online Learning Center at http://www.mhhe.com/santrockld8.com.

Chapter 6

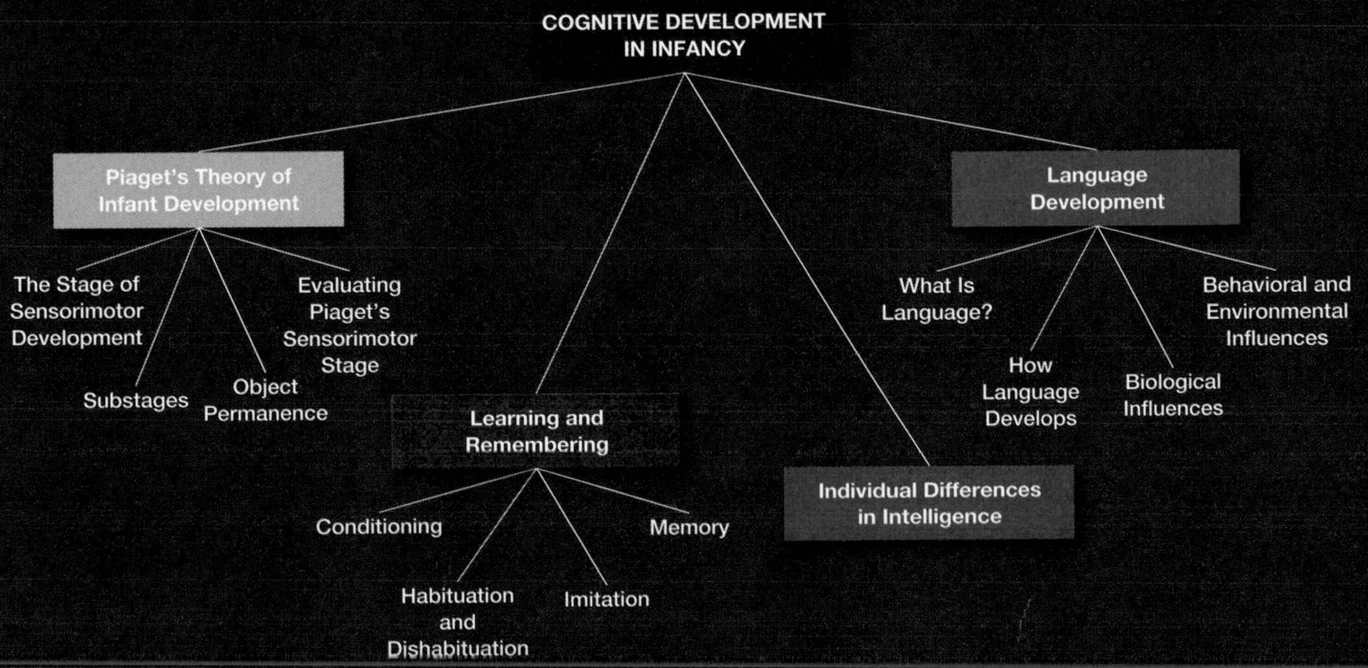
COGNITIVE DEVELOPMENT IN INFANCY
Piaget's Theory of Infant Development
The Stage of Sensorimotor Development
Substages
Object Permanence
Evaluating Piaget's Sensorimotor Stage
Learning and Remembering
Conditioning
Habituation and Dishabituation
Imitation
Memory
Individual Differences in Intelligence
Language Development
What Is Language?
How Language Develops
Biological Influences
Behavioral and Environmental Influences

Cognitive Development in Infancy

I wish I could travel by the road that crosses the baby's mind where Reason makes kites of her laws and flies them . . .

Rabindranath Tagore
Bengali Poet, Essayist, 20th Century

Images of Life-Span Development

Laurent, Lucienne, and Jacqueline

Jean Piaget, the famous Swiss psychologist, was a meticulous observer of his three children—Laurent, Lucienne, and Jacqueline. His books on cognitive development are filled with these observations. The following provide a glimpse of Piaget's observations of his children's cognitive development in infancy (Piaget, 1952).

- At 21 days of age, Laurent finds his thumb after three attempts; once he finds his thumb, prolonged sucking begins. But, when he is placed on his back, he doesn't know how to coordinate the movement of his arms with that of his mouth; his hands draw back, even when his lips seek them.
- During the third month, thumb sucking becomes less important to Laurent because of new visual and auditory interests. But, when he cries, his thumb goes to the rescue.
- Toward the end of Lucienne's fourth month, while she is lying in her crib, Piaget hangs a doll over her feet. Lucienne thrusts her feet at the doll and makes it move. Afterward, she looks at her motionless foot for a second, then kicks at the doll again. She has no visual control of her foot because her movements are the same whether she only looks at the doll or it is placed over her head. By contrast, she does have tactile control of her foot; when she tries to kick the doll and misses, she slows her foot movements to improve her aim.
- At 11 months, while seated, Jacqueline shakes a little bell. She then pauses abruptly so she can delicately place the bell in front of her right foot; then she kicks the bell hard. Unable to recapture the bell, she grasps a ball and places it in the same location where the bell was. She gives the ball a firm kick.
- At 1 year, 2 months, Jacqueline holds in her hands an object that is new to her: a round, flat box that she turns over and shakes; then she rubs it against her crib. She lets it go and tries to pick it up again. She succeeds only in touching it with her index finger, being unable to fully reach and grasp it. She keeps trying to grasp it and presses to the edge of her crib. She makes the box tilt up, but it nonetheless falls again. Jacqueline shows an interest in this result and studies the fallen box.
- At 1 year, 8 months, Jacqueline arrives at a closed door with a blade of grass in each hand. She stretches her right hand toward the doorknob but detects that she cannot turn it without letting go of the grass, so she puts the grass on the floor, opens the door, picks up the grass again, and then enters. But, when she wants to leave the room, things get complicated. She puts the grass on the floor and grasps the doorknob. Then she perceives that, by pulling the door toward her, she simultaneously chases away the grass that she had placed between the door and the threshold. She then picks up the grass and places it out of the door's range of movement.

For Piaget, these observations reflect important changes in the infant's cognitive development. Later in the chapter, you will learn that Piaget believed that infants go through six substages of development and that the behaviors you have just read about characterize those substages.

The excitement and enthusiasm about infant cognition have been fueled by an interest in what an infant knows at birth and soon after, by continued fascination about innate and learned factors in the infant's cognitive development, and by controversies about whether infants construct their knowledge (as Piaget believed) or whether they know their world more directly. In this chapter we will study Piaget's theory of infant development, learning and remembering, individual differences in intelligence, and language development.

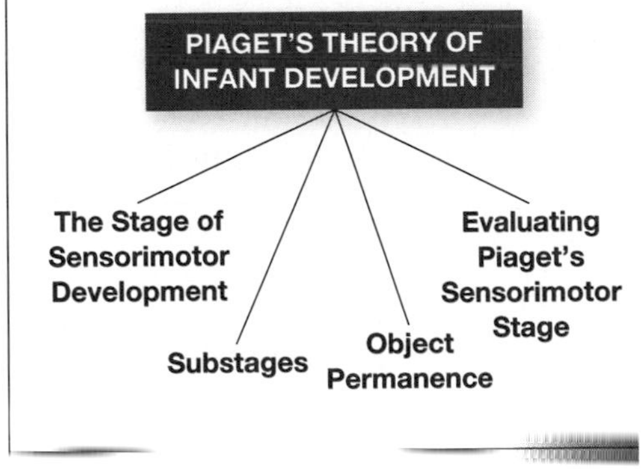

Piaget's Theory of Infant Development

Poet Noah Perry once asked, "Who knows the thoughts of a child?" Piaget knew as much as anyone. Through careful, inquisitive interviews and observations of his own three children—Laurent, Lucienne, and Jacqueline—Piaget changed the way we think about children's conception of the world. Remember that we studied a general outline of Piaget's theory in chapter 2 ◀ P. 35. You might want to review the basic features of his theory in chapter 2 at this time.

Piaget believed that the child passes through a series of stages of thought from infancy to adolescence. Passage through the stages results from biological pressures to adapt to the environment (through assimilation and accommodation) and to organize structures of thinking. Recall from chapter 2 that assimilation occurs when individuals incorporate new knowledge into existing knowledge and that accommodation takes place when individuals adjust to new information.

scheme
In Piaget's theory, a cognitive structure that helps individuals organize and understand their experiences.

Another important concept in Piaget's theory is **scheme,** *a cognitive structure that help individuals organize and understand their experiences.* Schemes change with age. Even newborns have schemes as when they grasp reflexively anything that touches their hand. As children grow older and gain more experience, they gradually shift from using schemes based on physical activities to schemes based on internal mental activities such as strategies and plans. For example, later in infancy an action-based grasping scheme can become part of a plan for obtaining a desirable object.

Piaget's stages are *qualitatively* different from one another. The way children reason at one stage is qualitatively different from the way they reason at another stage. This contrasts with the quantitative assessments of intelligence made through the use of standardized intelligence tests—which focus on what the child knows, or how many questions the child can answer correctly. Remember from chapter 2 that Piaget believed there are four stages of cognitive development: sensorimotor, preoperational, concrete operational, and formal operational. In later chapters (8, 10, and 12) we will explore the last three Piaget stages. Here our focus is on Piaget's stage of infant cognitive development, the sensorimotor stage.

The Stage of Sensorimotor Development

Piaget's Stages

According to Piaget, the sensorimotor stage lasts from birth to about 2 years of age, corresponding to the period of infancy. During this time, mental development is characterized by considerable progression in the infant's ability to organize and coordinate sensations with physical movements and actions—hence the name *sensorimotor* (Piaget, 1952).

At the beginning of the sensorimotor stage, the infant has little more than reflexive patterns with which to work. By the end of the stage, the 2-year-old has complex sensorimotor patterns and is beginning to operate with a primitive system of symbols. Unlike other stages, the sensorimotor stage is subdivided into six substages, each of which involves qualitative changes in sensorimotor organization.

Substages

Within a substage, there may be different schemes—sucking, rooting, and blinking in substage 1, for example. In substage 1, the schemes are basically reflexive. From substage to substage, the schemes change in organization. This change is at the heart of Piaget's description of the stages. The six substages of sensorimotor development are (1) simple reflexes; (2) first habits and primary circular reactions; (3) secondary circular reactions; (4) coordination of secondary circular reactions; (5) tertiary circular reactions, novelty, and curiosity; and (6) internalization of schemes.

Simple reflexes *is Piaget's first sensorimotor substage, which corresponds to the first month after birth. In this substage, the basic means of coordinating sensation and action is through reflexive behaviors. These include rooting and sucking, which the infant has at birth.* In substage 1, the infant exercises these reflexes. More important, the infant develops an ability to produce behaviors that resemble reflexes in the absence of obvious reflexive stimuli. The newborn may suck when a bottle or nipple is only nearby, for example. When the baby was just born, the bottle or nipple would have produced the sucking pattern only when placed directly in its mouth or touched to the lips. Reflexlike actions in the absence of a triggering stimulus are evidence that the infant is initiating action and is actively structuring experiences in the first month of life.

First habits and primary circular reactions *is Piaget's second sensorimotor substage, which develops between 1 and 4 months of age. In this substage, infants' reflexes evolved into adaptive schemes that are more refined and coordinated.* A *habit* is a scheme based on simple reflex, such as sucking, that has become completely separated from its eliciting stimulus. For example, an infant in substage 1 might suck when orally stimulated by a bottle or when visually shown the bottle. However, an infant in substage 2 might exercise the sucking scheme even when no bottle is present. A **primary circular reaction** *is a scheme based on the infant's attempt to reproduce an interesting or a pleasurable event that initially occurred by chance.* In a popular Piagetian example, a child accidentally sucks his fingers when they are placed near his mouth. Later, he searches for his fingers to suck them again, but the fingers do not cooperate in the search because the infant cannot coordinate visual and manual actions. Habits and circular reactions are stereotyped, in that the infant repeats them the same way each time.

Secondary circular reactions *is Piaget's third sensorimotor substage, which develops between 4 and 8 months of age. In this substage, the infant becomes more object-oriented or focused on the world, moving beyond preoccupation with the self in sensorimotor interactions.* By chance, the infant might shake a rattle. The infant will repeat this action for the sake of experiencing what it can do in the world. The infant imitates some simple actions of others, such as the baby talk or burbling of adults, and some physical gestures. However, these imitations are limited to actions the infant is already able to produce.

Coordination of secondary circular reactions *is Piaget's fourth sensorimotor substage, which develops between 8 and 12 months of age. In this substage, several significant changes take place that involve the coordination of schemes and intentionality.* Infants readily combine and recombine previously learned schemes in a *coordinated way.* They might look at an object and grasp it simultaneously, or they might visually inspect a toy, such as a rattle, and finger it simultaneously in obvious tactile exploration. Actions are even more outwardly directed than before. Related to this coordination is the second achievement—the presence of *intentionality,* the separation of means and goals in accomplishing simple feats. For example, infants might manipulate a stick (the means) to bring a desired toy within reach (the goal). They might knock over one block to reach and play with another one.

Tertiary circular reactions, novelty, and curiosity *is Piaget's fifth sensorimotor substage, which develops between 12 and 18 months of age. In this substage, infants become intrigued by the variety of properties that objects possess and by the many things they can make happen to objects.* A block can be made to fall, spin, hit another object,

simple reflexes
Piaget's first sensorimotor substage, which corresponds to the first month after birth. In this substage, the basic means of coordinating sensation and action is through reflexive behaviors, such as rooting and sucking, which the infant has at birth.

first habits and primary circular reactions
Piaget's second sensorimotor substage, which develops between 1 and 4 months of age. In this substage, infants' reflexes evolve into adaptive schemes that are more refined and coordinated.

primary circular reactions
A scheme based on the infant's attempt to reproduce an interesting or a pleasurable event that initially occurred by chance.

secondary circular reactions
Piaget's third sensorimotor substage, which develops between 4 and 8 months of age. In this substage, the infant becomes more object-oriented, or focused on the world, moving beyond preoccupation with the self in sensorimotor interactions.

coordination of secondary circular reactions
Piaget's fourth sensorimotor substage, which develops between 8 and 12 months of age. In this substage, several significant changes take place involving the coordination of schemes and intentionality.

tertiary circular reactions, novelty, and curiosity
Piaget's fifth sensorimotor substage, which develops between 12 and 18 months of age. In this substage, infants become intrigued by the variety of properties that objects possess and by the multiplicity of things they can make happen to objects.

and slide across the ground. Tertiary circular reactions are schemes in which the infant purposely explores new possibilities with objects, continually changing what is done to them and exploring the results. Piaget says that this stage marks the developmental starting point for human curiosity and interest in novelty. Previous circular reactions have been devoted exclusively to reproducing former events, with the exception of imitation of novel acts, which occurs as early as substage 4. The tertiary circular act is the first to be concerned with novelty.

internalization of schemes
Piaget's sixth and final sensorimotor substage, which develops between 18 and 24 months of age. In this substage, the infant's mental functioning shifts from a purely sensorimotor plane to a symbolic plane, and the infant develops the ability to use primitive symbols.

Internalization of schemes *is Piaget's sixth and final sensorimotor substage, which develops between 18 and 24 months of age. In this substage, the infant's mental functioning shifts from a purely sensorimotor plane to a symbolic plane, and the infant develops the ability to use primitive symbols.* For Piaget, a *symbol* is an internalized sensory image or word that represents an event. Primitive symbols permit the infant to think about concrete events without directly acting them out or perceiving them. Moreover, symbols allow the infant to manipulate and transform the represented events in simple ways. In a favorite Piagetian example, Piaget's young daughter saw a matchbox being opened and closed. Sometime later, she mimicked the event by opening and closing her mouth. This was an obvious expression of her image of the event. In another example, a child opened a door slowly to avoid disturbing a piece of paper lying on the floor on the other side. Clearly, the child had an image of the unseen paper and what would happen to it if the door opened quickly.

Sensorimotor Development

Object Permanence

object permanence
The Piagetian term for one of an infant's most important accomplishments: understanding that objects and events continue to exist, even when they cannot directly be seen, heard, or touched.

Object permanence *is the Piagetian term for one of an infant's most important accomplishments: understanding that objects and events continue to exist even when they cannot directly be seen, heard, or touched.* Imagine what thought would be like if you could not distinguish between yourself and your world. Your thought would be chaotic, disorganized, and unpredictable. This is what the mental life of a newborn is like, according to Piaget. There is no self-world differentiation and no sense of object permanence. By the end of the sensorimotor period, however, both are present.

The principal way that object permanence is studied is by watching an infant's reaction when an interesting object or event disappears (see figure 6.1). If infants show

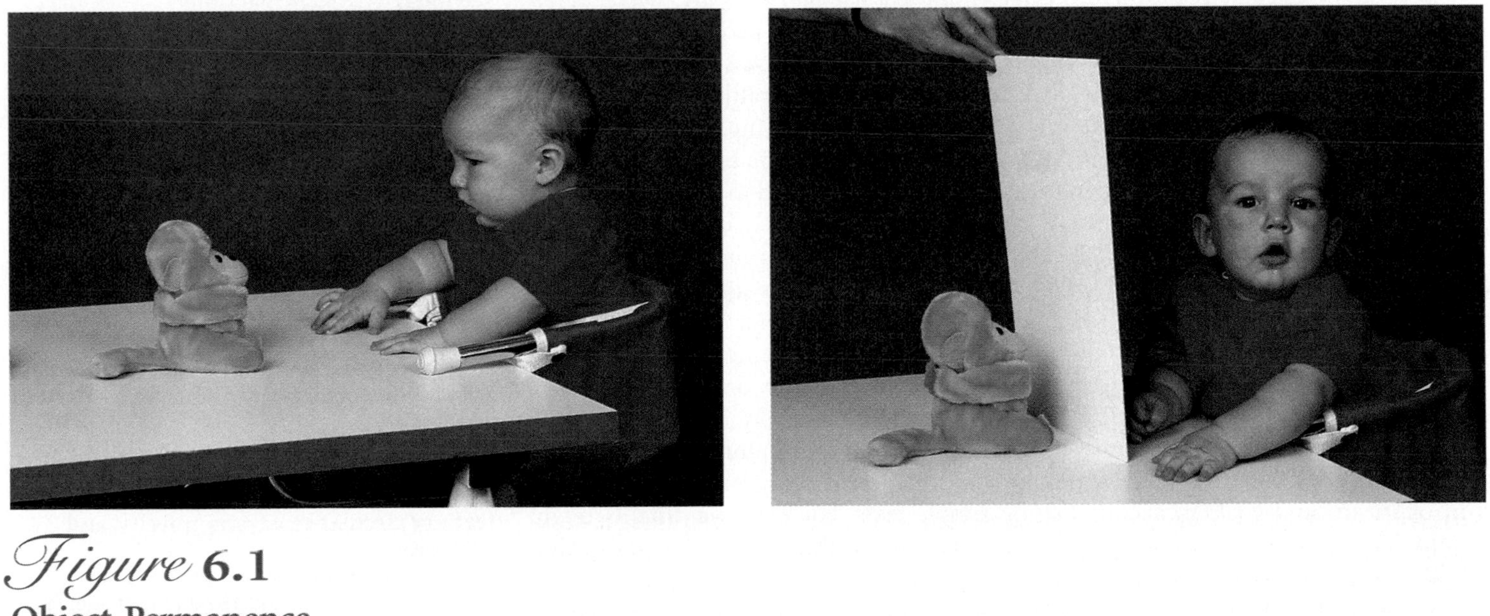

Figure **6.1**
Object Permanence
Piaget thought that object permanence is one of infancy's landmark cognitive accomplishments. For this 5-month-old boy, "out-of-sight" is literally out of mind. The infant looks at the toy monkey *(left)*, but, when his view of the toy is blocked *(right)*, he does not search for it. Several months later, he will search for the hidden toy monkey, reflecting the presence of object permanence.

no reaction, it is assumed they believe the object no longer exists. By contrast, if infants are surprised at the disappearance and search for the object, it is assumed they believe it continues to exist.

At this point we have discussed a number of characteristics of Piaget's stage of sensorimotor development. To help you remember the main characteristics of sensorimotor thought, turn to figure 6.2.

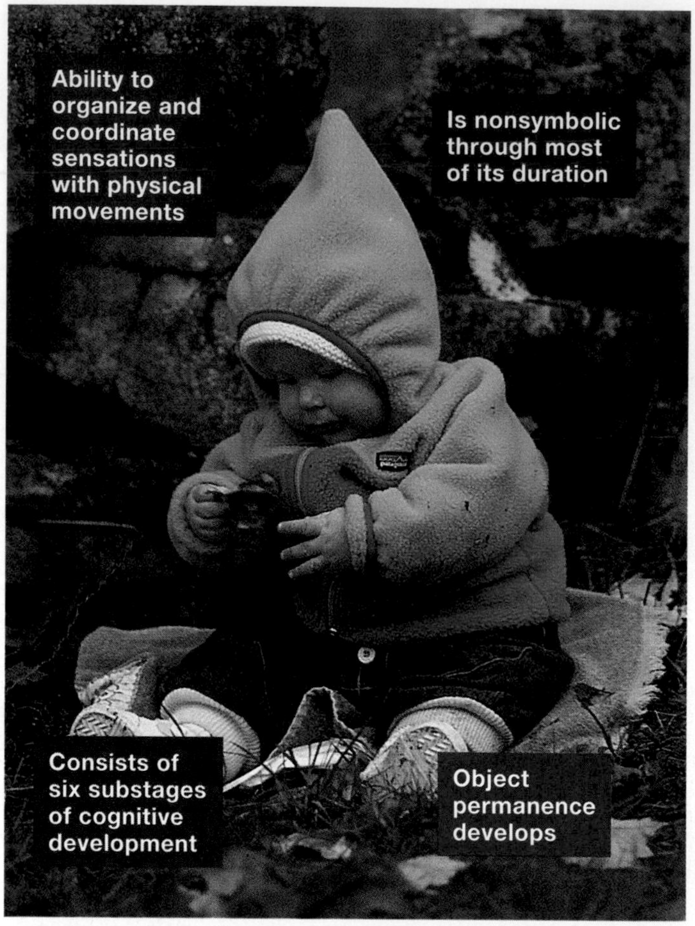

Figure **6.2**

The Main Characteristics of Sensorimotor Thought, According to Piaget

Evaluating Piaget's Sensorimotor Stage

Piaget opened up a whole new way of looking at infants by describing how their main task is to coordinate their sensory impressions with their motor activity. However, the infant's cognitive world is not as neatly packaged as Piaget portrayed it, and some of Piaget's explanations for the cause of change are debated.

Piaget constructed his view of infancy mainly by observing the development of his own three children. Few laboratory techniques were available at the time. In the past several decades, sophisticated experimental techniques have been devised to study infants, and there have been a large number of research studies on infant development. Much of the new research suggests that Piaget's view of sensorimotor development needs to be modified (Gounin-Decarie, 1996; Meltzoff & Moore, 1999). The two research areas that have led researchers to a somewhat different understanding of infant development are (1) perceptual development and (2) conceptual development.

Perceptual Development A number of theorists, such as Eleanor Gibson (1989) and Elizabeth Spelke (1991; Spelke & Newport, 1998), believe that infants' perceptual abilities are highly developed very early in development ◀IIII P. 145. For example, Spelke has demonstrated that infants as young as 4 months of age have intermodal perception—the ability to coordinate information from two or more sensory modalities, such as vision and hearing. Other research, by Renée Baillargeon (1995), documents that infants as young as 4 months expect objects to be substantial (in the sense that other objects cannot move through them) and permanent (in the sense that objects continue to exist when they are hidden). In sum, researchers believe that infants see objects as bounded, unitary, solid, and separate from their background, possibly at birth or shortly thereafter, but definitely by 3 to 4 months of age. Young infants still have much to learn about objects, but the world appears both stable and orderly to them and, thus, capable of being conceptualized. Infants are continually trying to structure and make sense of their world (Meltzoff & Gopnik, 1997).

Conceptual Development It is more difficult to study what infants are thinking about than to study what they see. Still, researchers have devised ways to assess whether or not infants are thinking. One strategy is to look for symbolic activity, such as using a gesture to refer to something. Piaget (1952) used this strategy to document infants' motor recognition. For example, he observed his 6-month-old daughter make a gesture when she saw a familiar toy in a new location. She was used to kicking at the toy in her crib. When she saw it across the room, she made a brief kicking motion. However, Piaget did not consider this to be true symbolic activity because it was a motor movement, not a purely mental act. Nonetheless, Piaget suggested that his daughter was referring to, or classifying, the toy through

her actions (Mandler, 1998). In a similar way, infants whose parents use sign language have been observed to start using conventional signs at about 6 to 7 months of age (Bonvillian, Orlansky, & Novack, 1983).

In summary, many of today's researchers believe that Piaget wasn't specific enough about how infants learn about their world and that infants are far more competent than Piaget envisioned (Lutz & Sternberg, 1999; Meltzoff, 2000). Recent research on infants' perceptual and conceptual development suggests that infants have more sophisticated perceptual abilities and can begin to think earlier than Piaget envisioned. These researchers believe that infants either are born with or acquire these abilities early in their development (Mandler, 1990, 1998).

WWW
Cognitive Milestones
Challenges to Piaget
Infant Cognition

Piaget's view is a general, unifying story of how biology and experience sculpt the infant's cognitive development: assimilation and accommodation always take the infant to higher ground through a series of substages. And for Piaget, the motivation for change is general, an internal search for equilibrium. However, like much of the modern world, today the field of infant cognition is very specialized. There are many researchers working on different questions, with no general theory emerging that can connect all of the different findings (Nelson, 1999). Their theories are local theories, focused on specific research questions, rather than grand theories like Piaget's (Kuhn, 1998). If there is a unifying theme, it is that investigators in infant development struggle with the big issue of nature and nurture.

At this point we have studied a number of ideas about Piaget's theory of infant development. To review these ideas, see summary table 6.1.

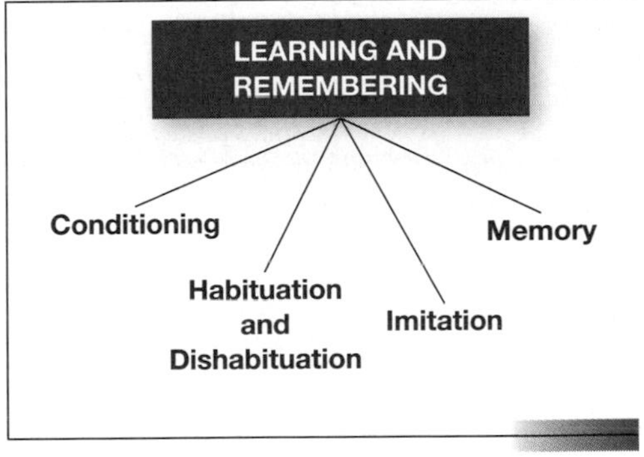

Learning and Remembering

Piaget viewed infants' and children's cognitive development in terms of stages. In this section, we will explore aspects of how infants learn and remember. The approaches we will look at here do not describe infant development in terms of stages.

Conditioning

In chapter 2, "The Science of Life-Span Development," we described both Pavlov's classical conditioning and Skinner's operant conditioning P. 40. Both classical conditioning and operant conditioning have been demonstrated to occur in infants.

Here we will examine some aspects of operant conditioning (in which the consequences of the behavior produce changes in the probability of the behavior's occurrence) in infants. For example, if an infant's behavior is followed by a rewarding stimulus, the behavior is likely to recur.

Operant conditioning has especially been helpful to researchers in their efforts to determine what infants perceive. For example, infants will suck faster on a nipple when the sucking behavior is followed by a visual display, music, or a human voice (Rovee-Collier, 1987).

Carolyn Rovee-Collier (1987) has demonstrated how infants can retain information from the experience of being conditioned. In a characteristic experiment, she places a 2½-month-old baby in a crib under an elaborate mobile. She then ties one end of a ribbon to the baby's ankle and the other end to the mobile. Subsequently, she observes as the baby kicks and makes the mobile move. The movement of the mobile is the reinforcing stimulus (which increases the baby's kicking behavior) in this experiment. Weeks later, the baby is returned to the crib, but its foot is not tied to the mobile. The baby kicks, suggesting that it has retained the information that if it kicks a leg, the mobile will move (see figure 6.3).

Summary Table 6.1
Piaget's Theory of Infant Development

Concept	Processes/ Related Ideas	Characteristics/Descriptions
Overview of Piaget's Theory	Cognitive Stages	• In Piaget's theory, there are four qualitative cognitive stages of development: sensorimotor, preoperational, concrete operational, and formal operational.
	Adaptation	• Assimilation, accommodation, and schemes are important concepts that are involved in the individual's adaptation.
The Stage of Sensorimotor Development	Basic Features	• The infant is able to organize and coordinate sensations with physical movements. • The stage lasts from birth to about 2 years of age and is nonsymbolic throughout, according to Piaget.
Substages	Six of Them	• Sensorimotor thought has six substages: simple reflexes; first habits and primary circular reactions; secondary circular reactions; coordination of secondary circular reactions; tertiary circular reactions, novelty, and curiosity; and internalization of schemes.
Object Permanence	An Important Infant Accomplishment	• This refers to the ability to understand that objects continue to exist even though the infant is no longer observing them.
Evaluating Piaget's Sensorimotor Stage	Contribution	• Piaget opened up a whole new way of looking at infant development in terms of coordinating sensory input with motoric actions.
	Needed Revision	• In the last three decades many research studies have suggested that revision of Piaget's view is needed.
	Perceptual and Conceptual Development	• In perceptual development, researchers have found that a stable and differentiated perceptual world is formed earlier than Piaget envisioned. • In conceptual development, researchers have found that memory and other forms of symbolic activity occur at least by the second half of the first year of life, much earlier than Piaget believed.

Habituation and Dishabituation

If a stimulus—a sight or sound—is presented to infants several times in a row, they usually pay less attention to it each time. This suggests they are bored with it. This is the process of **habituation**—*repeated presentation of the same stimulus, which causes reduced attention to the stimulus.* **Dishabituation** *is an infant's renewed interest in a stimulus.* Among the measures researchers use to study whether habituation is occurring are sucking behavior (sucking behavior stops when the young infant attends to a novel object), heart and respiration rates, and the length of time the infant looks at an object. Newborn infants can habituate to repetitive stimulation in virtually every stimulus modality—vision, hearing, touch, and so on (Rovee-Collier, 1987). However, habituation becomes more acute over the first three months of life.

habituation
Repeated presentation of the same stimulus, which causes reduced attention to the stimulus.

dishabituation
An infant's renewed interest in a stimulus.

Habituation can be used to tell us much about infants' perception, such as the extent to which they can see, hear, smell, taste, and experience touch. Habituation also can be used to tell whether infants recognize something they have previously experienced. The extensive assessment of habituation in recent years has resulted in its use as a measure of an infant's maturity and well-being. Infants who have brain damage or have suffered birth traumas, such as lack of oxygen, do not habituate well and might later have developmental and learning problems.

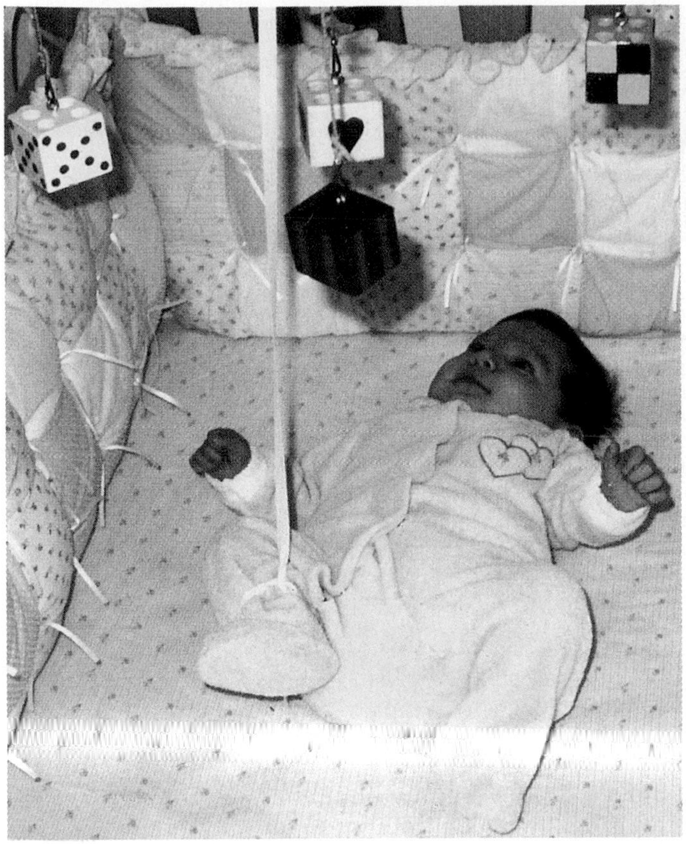

Figure 6.3
The Technique Used in Rovee-Collier's Investigation of Infant Memory
In Rovee-Collier's experiment, operant conditioning was used to demonstrate that infants as young as 2½ months of age can retain information from the experience of being conditioned.

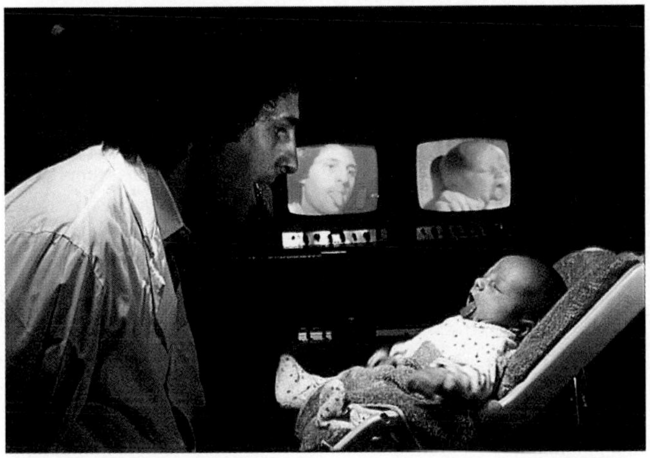

Figure 6.4
Infant Imitation
Infant development researcher Andrew Meltzoff protrudes his tongue in an attempt to get the infant to imitate his behavior.

A knowledge of habituation and dishabituation can benefit parent-infant interaction. Infants respond to changes in stimulation. If stimulation is repeated often, the infant's response will decrease to the point that the infant no longer responds to the parent. In parent-infant interaction, it is important for parents to do novel things and to repeat them often until the infant stops responding. The wise parent senses when the infant shows an interest and that many repetitions of the stimulus may be necessary for the infant to process the information. The parent stops or changes behaviors when the infant redirects her attention (Rosenblith, 1992).

Imitation

Can infants imitate someone else's emotional expressions? If an adult smiles, will the baby follow with a smile? If an adult protrudes her lower lip, wrinkles her forehead, and frowns, will the baby show a saddened look? If an adult opens his mouth, widens his eyes, and raises his eyebrows, will the baby follow suit? Can infants only a few days old do these things?

Infant development researcher Andrew Meltzoff (1992; Meltzoff, 1999, 2000; Meltzoff & Moore, 1999) has conducted numerous studies of infants' imitative abilities. He believes infants' imitation abilities are biologically based, because infants can imitate a facial expression within the first few days after birth. This occurs before they have had the opportunity to observe social agents in their environment protrude their tongues and engage in other behaviors. He also emphasizes that the infant's imitative abilities are not like what ethologists conceptualize as a hardwired, reflexive, innate releasing mechanism but, rather, involve flexibility, adaptability, and intermodal perception. In Meltzoff's observations of infants in the first 72 hours of life, the infants gradually displayed a full imitative response of an adult's facial expression, such as protruding the tongue or opening the mouth wide (see figure 6.4).

Not all experts on infant development accept Meltzoff's conclusions that newborns are capable of imitation. Some say that these babies were engaging in little more than automatic responses to a stimulus.

Meltzoff also has studied **deferred imitation,** *which occurs after a time delay of hours or days.* In one study, Meltzoff (1988) demonstrated that 9-month-old infants could imitate actions that they had seen performed 24 hours earlier. Each action consisted of an unusual gesture—such as pushing a recessed button in a box (which produced a beeping sound). Piaget believed that deferred imitation doesn't occur until about 18 months of age. Meltzoff's research suggested that it occurs much earlier.

Memory

Memory *is a central feature of cognitive development that involves the retention of information over time.* Sometimes information is retained only for a few seconds, and at other times it is retained for a lifetime.

Can infants remember? Some infant researchers, such as Carolyn Rovee-Collier, argue that infants as young as 2 to 6 months of age can remember some experiences through 1½ to 2 years of age (Rovee-Collier, 2001; Rovee-Collier, Hartshorn, & DiRubbio, 1999).

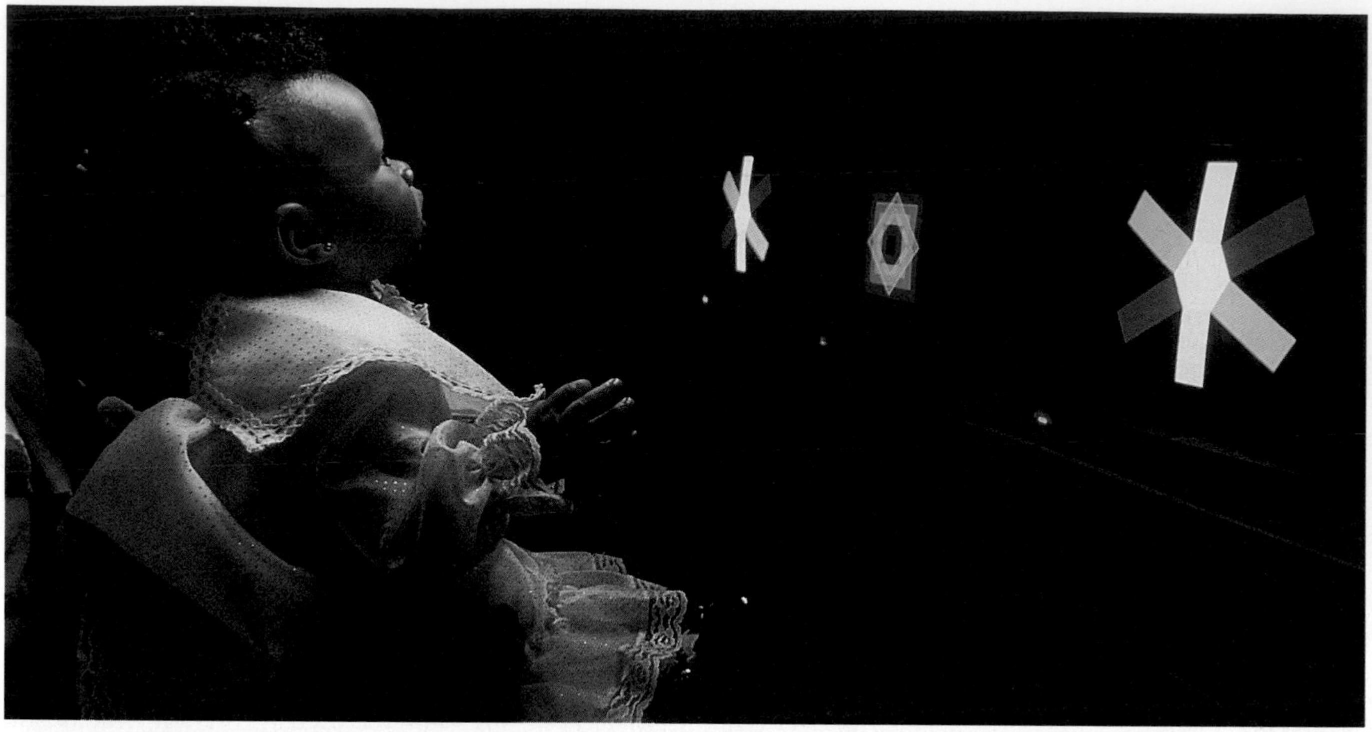

Researchers use a variety of ingenious techniques to study infant development. In researcher Mark Johnson's laboratory at Carnegie Mellon University, babies have shown an ability to organize their world and to anticipate future events by learning and remembering sequences of colorful images on TV monitors.

However, critics such as Jean Mandler (2000), a leading expert on infant cognition, argues that Rovee-Collier fails to distinguish between retention of a perceptual-motor variety that is involved in conditioning tasks (like that involved in kicking a mobile), often referred to as *implicit memory,* and the ability to consciously recall the past, often referred to as *explicit memory.* When people think about what memory is, they are referring to the latter, which most researchers find does not occur until the second half of the first year (Mandler & McDonough, 1995).

Most adults cannot remember anything from the first 3 years of their life; this is referred to as *infantile amnesia.* When adults seem to be able to recall something from their infancy, it likely is something they have been told about by relatives or something they saw in a photograph or home movie. One explanation of infantile amnesia focuses on the maturation of the brain, especially in the frontal lobes, which occurs after infancy (Boyer & Diamond, 1992).

deferred imitation
Imitation that occurs after a time delay of hours or days.

memory
A central feature of cognitive development, pertaining to all situations in which an individual retains information over time.

Infant Memory Research

Individual Differences in Intelligence

INDIVIDUAL DIFFERENCES IN INTELLIGENCE

So far, we have stressed general statements about how the cognitive development of infants progresses. We have emphasized what is typical of the largest number of infants or the average infant, but the results obtained for most infants do not apply to all infants. Individual differences in infant cognitive development have been studied primarily through the use of developmental scales, or infant intelligence tests.

It is advantageous to know whether an infant is advancing at a slow, a normal, or an advanced pace of development. In chapter 4, we discussed the Brazelton Neonatal Behavioral Assessment Scale, which is widely used to evaluate newborns P. 114. Developmentalists also want to know how development proceeds during the course of infancy. If an infant advances at an especially slow rate, then some form of enrichment may be necessary. If an infant develops at an

Critical Thinking

Comparing Piaget's Approach with the Individual Differences Approach

Piaget worked in the Paris laboratory of Alfred Binet, who, with Theophile Simon, developed the first intelligence test. Piaget was more intrigued by children's incorrect responses to items than by their correct responses. For Piaget, studying *what* children *know* was merely a beginning to discovering developmental changes in *how* children *think.*

In thinking about Piaget's theory and the individual differences approach, consider whether an older infant's intelligence is just quantitatively different from a younger infant's intelligence or qualitatively different. How would Piaget have answered this question?

advanced pace, parents may be advised to provide toys that stimulate cognitive growth in slightly older infants.

The infant testing movement grew out of the tradition of IQ testing of older children. However, the measures that assess infants are necessarily less verbal than IQ tests that assess the intelligence of older children. The infant developmental scales contain far more perceptual motor items. They also include measures of social interaction.

The most important early contributor to the developmental testing of infants was Arnold Gesell (1934). He developed a measure that was used as a clinical tool to help sort out potentially normal babies from abnormal ones. This was especially useful to adoption agencies, which had large numbers of babies awaiting placement. Gesell's examination was used widely for many years. It is still frequently used by pediatricians in their assessment of normal and abnormal infants. The current version of the Gesell test has four categories of behavior: motor, language, adaptive, and personal-social. The **developmental quotient (DQ)** *is an overall developmental score that combines subscores in motor, language, adaptive, and personal-social domains in the Gesell assessment of infants.* However, overall scores on tests like the Gesell do not correlate highly with IQ scores obtained later in childhood. This is not surprising, because the items on the developmental scales are considerably less verbal than the items on intelligence tests given to older children.

developmental quotient (DQ)
An overall developmental score that combines subscores in motor, language, adaptive, and personal-social domains in the Gesell assessment of infants.

Bayley Scales of Infant Development
Scales developed by Nancy Bayley, which are widely used in the assessment of infant development.The current version has three components: a mental scale, a motor scale, and an infant behavior profile.

The **Bayley Scales of Infant Development,** *developed by Nancy Bayley, are widely used in the assessment of infant development. The current version has three components: a mental scale, a motor scale, and an infant behavior profile.* Unlike Gesell, whose scales were clinically motivated, Bayley (1969) wanted to develop scales that could assess infant behavior and predict later development. The early version of the Bayley scales covered only the first year of development. In the 1950s, the scales were extended to assess older infants. In 1993, the Bayley-II was published, with updated norms for diagnostic assessment at a younger age.

Because our discussion in this chapter centers on the infant's cognitive development, our primary interest is in Bayley's mental scale. It includes assessment of the following:

- Auditory and visual attention to stimuli
- Manipulation, such as combining objects or shaking a rattle
- Examiner interaction, such as babbling and imitation
- Relation with toys, such as banging spoons together
- Memory involved in object permanence, as when the infant finds a hidden toy
- Goal-directed behavior that involves persistence, such as putting pegs in a board
- Ability to follow directions and knowledge of objects' names, such as understanding the concept of "one"

How well should a 6-month-old perform on the Bayley mental scale? The 6-month-old infant should be able to vocalize pleasure and displeasure, persistently search for objects that are just out of immediate reach, and approach a mirror that is placed in front of the infant by the examiner. How well should a 12-month-old perform? By 12 months of age, the infant should be able to inhibit behavior when commanded to do so, imitate words the examiner says (such as *Mama*), and respond to simple requests (such as "Take a drink").

The Fagan Test of Infant Intelligence is increasingly being used (Fagan, 1992). This test focuses on the infant's ability to process information, including encoding the attributes of objects, detecting similarities and differences between objects, forming mental representations, and retrieving these representations.

WWW

Bayley Scales of Infant Development

Zero to Three

The Fagan Test of Infant Intelligence estimates babies' intelligence by comparing the amount of time they look at a new object with the amount of time they spend looking at a familiar object. This test elicits similar performances from infants in different cultures and is correlated with measures of intelligence in older children.

Tests of infant intelligence have been valuable in assessing the effects of malnutrition, drugs, maternal deprivation, and environmental stimulation on the development of infants. However, they have met with mixed results in predicting later intelligence. Global developmental quotient or IQ scores for infants have not been good predictors of childhood intelligence. However, specific aspects of infant intelligence are related to specific aspects of childhood intelligence. For example, in one study, infant language abilities as assessed by the Bayley test predicted language, reading, and spelling ability at 6 to 8 years of age (Siegel, 1989). Infant perceptual motor skills predicted visuospatial, arithmetic, and fine motor skills at 6 to 8 years of age. These results indicate that an item analysis of infant scales like Bayley's can provide information about the development of specific intellectual functions.

The explosion of interest in infant development has produced many new measures, especially using tasks that evaluate the way infants process information. Evidence is accumulating that measures of habituation and dishabituation predict intelligence in childhood (McCall & Carriger, 1993). Less cumulative attention by an infant in the habituation situation and greater amounts of attention in the dishabituation situation reflect more efficient information processing. Both types of attention—decrement and recovery—when measured in the first 6 months of infancy, are related to higher IQ scores on standardized intelligence tests given at various times between infancy and adolescence. In sum, more precise assessments of the infant's cognition with information-processing tasks involving attention have led to the conclusion that continuity between infant and childhood intelligence is greater than was previously believed.

It is important, however, not to go too far and think that the connections between early infant cognitive development and later childhood cognitive development are so strong that no discontinutiy takes place. Rather than asking whether cognitive development is continuous *or* discontinuous, perhaps we should be examining the ways cognitive development is both continuous and discontinuous. Some important changes in cognitive development take place after infancy, changes that underscore the discontinuity of cognitive development. We will describe these changes in cognitive development in subsequent chapters, which focus on later periods of development.

At this point we have studied a number of ideas about learning and remembering and individual differences in intelligence. A review of these ideas is presented in summary table 6.2. Next, we will explore another key dimension of the infant's development: language.

Careers in Life-Span Development

Toosje Thyssen VanBeveren, Infant Assessment Specialist

Toosje Thyssen VanBeveren is a developmental psychologist at the University of Texas Medical Center in Dallas. She has a master's degree in child clinical psychology and a Ph.D. in human development.

Her main current work is in a program called New Connections. This 12-week program is a comprehensive intervention for young children (0 to 6 years of age) who were affected by substance abuse prenatally and for their caregivers.

In the New Connections program, Toosje conducts assessments of infants' developmental status and progress, identifying delays and deficits. She might refer the infants to a speech, physical, or occupational therapist and monitor the infants' therapeutic services and developmental progress. Toosje trains the program staff and encourages them to use the exercises she recommends. She also discusses the child's problems with the primary caregivers, suggests activities they can carry out with their children, and assists them in enrolling their infants in appropriate programs.

During her graduate work at the University of Texas at Dallas, Toosje was author John Santrock's teaching assistant in his undergraduate course on life-span development for 4 years. As a teaching assistant, she attended classes, graded exams, counseled students, and occasionally gave lectures. Each semester, Toosje returns to give a lecture on prenatal development and infancy in the life-span class. Toosje also teaches part-time in the psychology department at UT-Dallas. She teaches an undergraduate course, "The Child in Society" and a graduate course, "Infant Development."

In Toosje's words, "My days are busy and full. The work is often challenging. There are some disappointments but mostly the work is enormously gratifying."

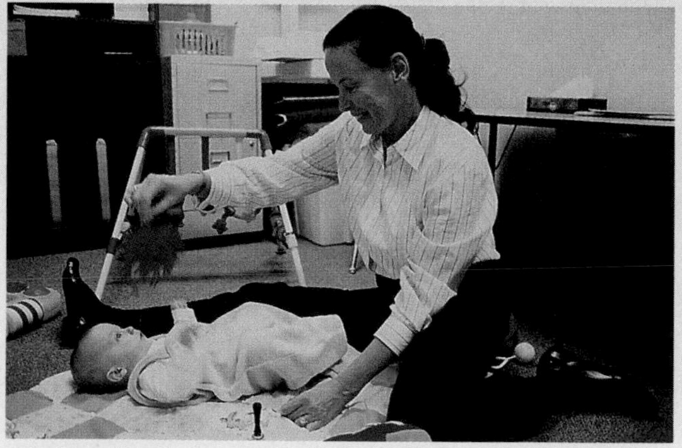

Toosje Thyssen VanBeveren conducting an infant assessment.

Summary Table 6.2
Learning and Remembering, and Individual Differences in Intelligence

Concept	Processes/ Related Ideas	Characteristics/Descriptions
Learning and Remembering	Conditioning	• Both classical and operant conditioning occur in infants. • Operant conditioning techniques have especially been useful to researchers in demonstrating infants' perception and retention of information about perceptual-motor actions.
	Habituation and Dishabituation	• Habituation is the repeated presentation of the same stimulus, causing reduced attention to the stimulus. • If a different stimulus is presented and the infant pays attention to it, dishabituation is occurring. • Newborn infants can habituate, but habituation becomes more acute over the first three months of infancy.
	Memory	• Memory is the retention of information over time. • Infants as young as 2 months of age can retain information about perceptual-motor actions. However, many experts argue that what we commonly think of as memory (consciously remembering the past) does not occur until the second half of the first year of life.
	Imitation	• Meltzoff has shown that newborns can match their behaviors (such as protruding their tongue) to a model. • His research also shows that deferred imitation occurs as early as 9 months of age.
Individual Differences in Intelligence	History	• Developmental scales for infants grew out of the tradition of IQ testing of older children. These scales are less verbal than IQ tests. • Gesell was an early developer of an infant test. His scale is still widely used by pediatricians; it provides a developmental quotient (DQ).
	Bayley Scales	• These are the developmental scales most widely used today; developed by Nancy Bayley, they consist of a motor scale, a mental scale, and an infant behavior profile.
	Fagan Test of Infant Intelligence	• Increasingly used, this test assesses how effectively the infant processes information.
	Conclusions About Infant Tests and Continuity in Mental Development	• Global infant intelligence measures are not good predictors of childhood intelligence. • However, specific aspects of infant intelligence, such as information-processing tasks involving attention, have been better predictors of childhood intelligence, especially in a specific area. • There is both continuity and discontinuity between infant cognitive development and cognitive development later in childhood.

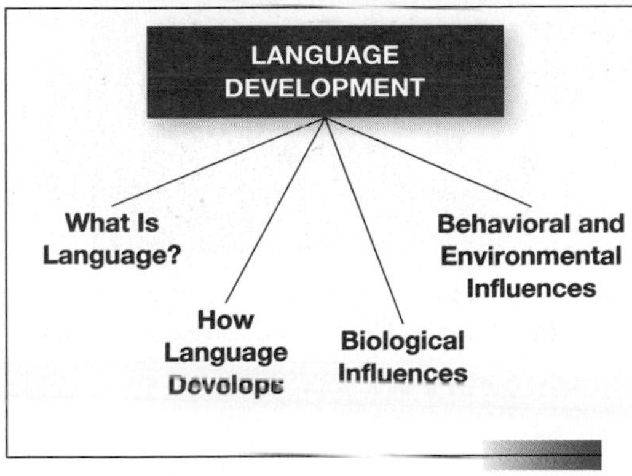

Language Development

In 1799, a nude boy was observed running through the woods in France. The boy was captured when he was 11 years old. He was called the Wild Boy of Aveyron and was believed to have lived in the woods alone for 6 years. When found, he made no effort to communicate. Even after a number of years, he never learned to communicate effectively. Sadly, a modern-day wild child named Genie was discovered in Los Angeles in 1970. Despite intensive intervention, Genie never acquired more than a primitive form of language. Both cases—the Wild Boy of

Aveyron and Genie—raise questions about the biological and environmental determinants of language, topics that we will examine in greater detail later in this chapter. First, though, we need to define what language is.

What Is Language?

Language *is a form of communication, whether spoken, written, or signed, that is based on a system of system of symbols.* Think how important language is in our everyday lives. We need language to speak with others, listen to others, read, and write. Our language enables us to describe past events in detail and to plan for the future. Language lets us pass down information from one generation to the next and create a rich cultural heritage.

language
A system of symbols used to communicate with others. In humans language is characterized by infinite generativity and rule systems.

All human languages have some common characteristics. These include infinite generativity and organizational rules. **Infinite generativity** *is the ability to produce an endless number of meaningful sentences using a finite set of words and rules.* This quality makes language a highly creative enterprise.

infinite generativity
An individual's ability to generate an infinite number of meaningful sentences using a finite set of words and rules, which makes language a highly creative enterprise.

How Language Develops

In the first few months of life, infants show a startle response to sharp noises. Then, at 3 to 6 months, they begin to show an interest in sounds, they play with saliva, and they respond to voices. During the next 3 to 6 months, infants begin to babble, emitting such sounds as "goo-goo" and "ga-ga." The start of babbling is determined mainly by biological maturation, not reinforcement, hearing, or caregiver-infant interaction. Even deaf babies babble for a time (Lenneberg, Rebelsky, & Nichols, 1965). The purpose of the baby's earliest communication is to attract attention from parents and others in the environment. Infants engage the attention of others by making or breaking eye contact, by vocalizing sounds, and by performing manual actions, such as pointing. All of these behaviors involve the aspect of language we have called pragmatics.

At approximately 6 to 9 months, infants begin to understand their first words. **Receptive vocabulary** *refers to the words an individual understands.* Its growth increases dramatically in the second year, from an average of 12 words understood at the first birthday to an estimated 300 words or more understood at the second birthday. At approximately 9 to 12 months, infants first begin to understand instructions, such as "Wave bye-bye."

receptive vocabulary
The words an individual understands.

So far, we have not mentioned *spoken* vocabulary, which begins when the infant utters its first word. This is a milestone anticipated by every parent. This event usually occurs at about 10 to 15 months of age. Many parents view the onset of language development as coincident with this first word. However, as we have seen, some significant language milestones have already occurred. The infant's spoken vocabulary rapidly increases once the first word is spoken (Dapretto, 1999). It reaches an average of 200 to 275 words by the age of 2.

Around the world, young children learn to speak in two-word utterances, in most cases, at about 18 to 24 months of age. *What are some examples of these two-word utterances?*

A child's first words include those that name important people *(dada),* familiar animals *(kitty),* vehicles *(car),* toys *(ball),* food *(milk),* body parts *(eye),* clothes *(hat),* household items *(clock),* and greeting terms *(bye).* These were the first words of babies 50 years ago. They are the first words of babies today. At times it is hard to tell what these one-word utterances mean. One possibility is that they stand for an entire sentence in the infant's mind. Because of the infant's limited cognitive or linguistic skills, possibly only one

holophrase hypothesis
The hypothesis that a single word can be used to imply a complete sentence; infants' first words characteristically are holophrastic.

Children pick up words as pigeons peas.

John Ray
English Naturalist, 17th Century

WWW

Language Milestones
The Naming Explosion
Brain and Language Development

telegraphic speech
The use of short and precise words to communicate; young children's two- and three-word utterances characteristically are telegraphic.

In the wild, chimps communicate through calls, gestures, and expressions, which evolutionary psychologists believe might be the roots of true language. *How strong is biology's role in language?*

word comes out instead of the whole sentence. The **holophrase hypothesis** *states that a single word can be used to imply a complete sentence. Infants' first words characteristically are holophrastic.*

By the time children are 18 to 24 months of age, they usually utter two-word statements. During this two-word stage, they quickly grasp the importance of expressing concepts and of the role that language plays in communicating with others. To convey meaning with two-word utterances, the child relies heavily on gesture, tone, and context. The wealth of meaning children can communicate with a two-word utterance includes the following (Slobin, 1972):

- Identification: "See doggie."
- Location: "Book there."
- Repetition: "More milk."
- Nonexistence: "Allgone thing."
- Negation: "Not wolf."
- Possession: "My candy."
- Attribution: "Big car."
- Agent-action: "Mama walk."
- Action-direct object: "Hit you."
- Action-indirect object: "Give Papa."
- Action-instrument: "Cut knife."
- Question: "Where ball?"

These examples are from children whose first language is English, German, Russian, Finnish, Turkish, or Samoan. Although these two-word sentences omit many parts of speech, they are remarkably succinct in conveying many messages. In fact, in every language, a child's first combinations of words have this economical quality. **Telegraphic speech** *is the use of short and precise words to communicate. Young children's two- and three-word utterances characteristically are telegraphic.* When we send a telegram, we try to be short and precise, excluding any unnecessary words. As a result, articles, auxiliary verbs, and other connectives usually are omitted. Of course, telegraphic speech is not limited to two-word phrases. "Mommy give ice cream" and "Mommy give Tommy ice cream" also are examples of telegraphic speech. As children leave the two-word stage, they move rather quickly into three-, four-, and five-word combinations.

Biological Influences

The strongest evidence for the biological basis of language is that children all over the world reach language milestones at about the same time developmentally and in about the same order. This occurs despite the vast variation in the language input they receive. For example, in some cultures, adults never talk to children under 1 year of age, yet these infants still acquire language. Also, there is no other convincing way to explain how *quickly* children learn language than through biological foundations.

With these thoughts in mind, let's now explore these questions about biological influences on language: How strongly is language influenced by biological evolution? Are humans biologically wired to learn language?

Biological Evolution Estimates vary as to how long ago humans acquired language—about 100,000 years ago. In evolutionary time, then, language is a very recent acquisition. A number of experts believe that biological evolution undeniably shaped humans into linguistic creatures (Chomsky, 1957). The brain, nervous system, and vocal apparatus of our predecessors changed over hundreds of thousands of years. Physically equipped to do so, *Homo sapiens* went beyond grunting and shrieking to develop abstract speech. Language clearly gave humans an enormous edge over other animals and increased the chances of survival (Pinker, 1994).

Biological Prewiring Linguist Noam Chomsky (1957) believes humans are biologically prewired to learn language at a certain time and in a certain way. He said that children are born into the world with a **language acquisition device (LAD),** *a biological endowment that enables the child to detect certain language categories, such as phonology, syntax, and semantics.* The LAD is a theoretical construct that flows from evidence about the biological basis of language.

Is there evidence for the existence of a LAD? Supporters of the LAD concept cite the uniformity of language milestones across languages and cultures, biological substrates for language, and evidence that children create language even in the absence of well-formed input. With regard to the last argument, most deaf children are the offspring of hearing parents. Some of these parents choose not to expose their deaf child to sign language, in order to motivate the child to learn speech while providing the child with a supportive social environment. Susan Goldin-Meadow (1979) has found that these children develop spontaneous gestures that are not based on their parents' gestures.

MIT linguist Noam Chomsky. *What is Chomsky's view of language?*

language acquisition device (LAD)
A biological endowment, hypothesized by Chomsky, that enables the child to detect certain language categories, such as phonology, syntax, and semantics.

Behavioral and Environmental Influences

Behaviorists view language as just another behavior, such as sitting, walking, and running. They argue that language represents chains of responses (Skinner, 1957) or imitation (Bandura, 1977). But many of the sentences we produce are novel; we have hot heard them or spoken them before. For example, a child hears the sentence "The plate fell on the floor" and then says, "My mirror fell on the blanket," after dropping the mirror on the blanket. The behavioral mechanisms of reinforcement and imitation cannot completely explain this.

While spending long hours observing parents and their young children, child language researcher Roger Brown (1973) searched for evidence that parents reinforce their children for speaking in grammatical ways. He found that parents sometimes smile and praise their children for sentences they like. However, they also reinforce sentences that are ungrammatical. Brown concluded that no evidence exists to document that reinforcement is responsible for language's rule systems.

Another criticism of the behavioral view is that it fails to explain the extensive orderliness of language. The behavioral view predicts that vast individual differences should appear in children's speech development because of each child's unique learning history. But, as we have seen, a compelling fact about language is its structure and ever-present rule systems. All infants coo before they babble. All toddlers produce one-word utterances before two-word utterances. All state sentences in the active form before they state them in a passive form.

However, we do not learn language in a social vacuum. Most children are bathed in language from a very early age (Fernald, 2001; Hart & Risley, 1995). We need this early exposure to language to acquire competent language skills (Snow, 1999). The Wild Boy of Aveyron did not learn to communicate effectively after living in social isolation for years. Genie's language is rudimentary, even after years of extensive training.

Today most language acquistion researchers believe that children from a wide variety of cultural contexts acquire their native language without explicit teaching (Clark, 2000). In some cases, they do so without apparent encouragement. Thus, there appear to be very few aids that are necessary for learning a language. However, the support and involvement of caregivers and teachers greatly facilitate a child's language learning (Berko-Gleason, 2000; Dewey, 1999; Hoff-Ginsberg & Lerner, 1999). Of special concern are children who grow up in poverty-infested areas and are not exposed to guided participation in language.

In a study conducted by Betty Hart and Todd Risley (1995), the language environments and language development of children from middle-income professional and welfare backgrounds were observed. All of the children developed normally in terms of learning to talk and acquiring all of the forms of English and basic vocabulary. However, there were enormous differences in the sheer amount of language the children were exposed to and the level of the children's language development. For

example, in a typical hour, the middle-income professional parents spent almost twice as much time communicating with their children as the welfare parents did. The children from the middle-income professional families heard about 2,100 words an hour, their child counterparts in welfare families only 600 words an hour. The researchers estimated that by 4 years of age, the average welfare family child would have 13 million fewer words of cumulative language experience than the child in the average middle-income professional family. Amazingly, some of the 3-year-old children from middle-class professional families had a recorded vocabulary that exceeded the recorded vocabulary of some of the welfare parents!

infant-directed speech
Speech often used by parents (in which case it sometimes is called "parentese") and other adults when they talk to babies. It has a higher than normal pitch and involves the use of simple words and sentences.

An intriguing aspect of the environment in the young child's acquisition of language is called **infant-directed speech.** *This type of speech often is used by parents (in which case it sometimes is called "parentese") and other adults when they talk to babies. It has a higher than normal pitch and involves the use of simple words and sentences.* It is hard to talk this way when not in the presence of a baby, but as soon as you start talking to a baby, you immediately shift into it. Much of this is automatic and something adults often are unaware that they are even doing. Infant-directed speech has the important functions of capturing the infant's attention and maintaining communication. When parents are asked why they use infant-directed speech when talking to their baby, they point out that it is designed to teach their baby to talk. Older child peers and siblings also might use infant-directed speech or "baby talk" when communicating with an infant.

WWW
Communicating with Babies
Babbling

Are there strategies other than infant-directed speech that adults use to enhance the child's acquisition of language? Four candidates are recasting, echoing, expanding, and labeling. *Recasting* is rephrasing something the child has said in a different way, perhaps turning it into a question. For example, if the child says, "The dog was barking," the adult can respond by asking, "When was the dog barking?" The effects of recasting fit with suggestions that "following in order to lead" helps a child learn language. That is, letting a child initially indicate an interest and then proceeding to elaborate that interest—commenting, demonstrating, and explaining—improve

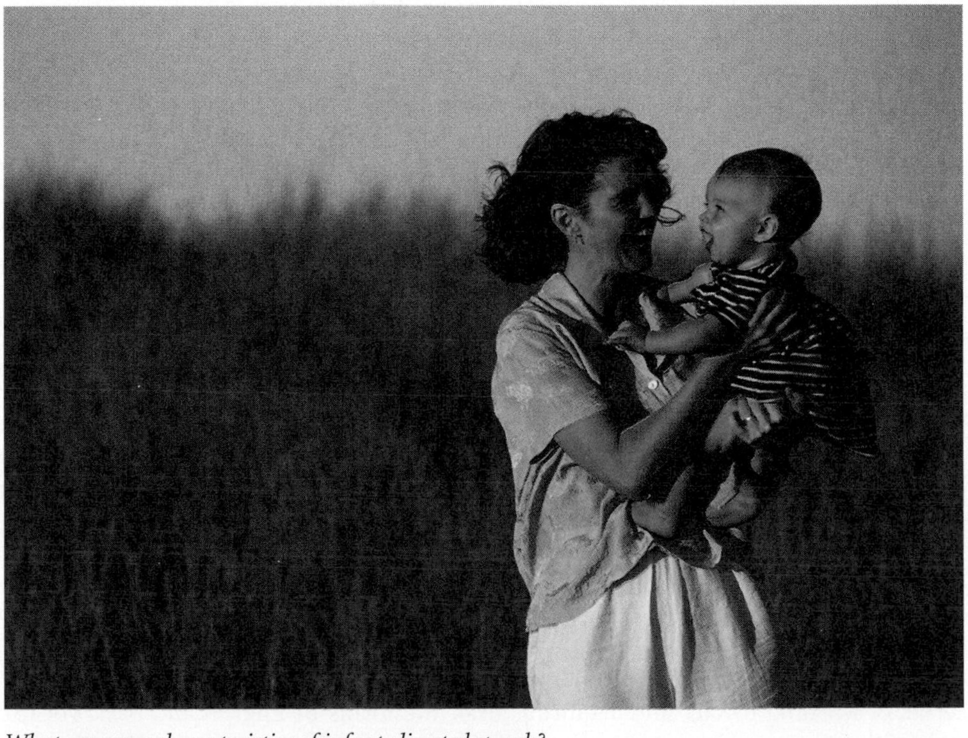

What are some characteristics of infant-directed speech?

Summary Table 6.3
Language Development

Concept	Processes/ Related Ideas	Characteristics/Descriptions
What Is Language?	A Form of Communication	• Language is a form of communication, whether spoken, written, or signed, that is based on a system of symbols.
	Infinite Generativity	• This is the ability to produce an endless number of meaningful sentences using a finite set of words and rules.
How Language Develops	Some Developmental Milestones	• Among the milestones in infant language development are babbling (3 to 6 months), first words understood (6 to 9 months), the growth of receptive vocabulary (reaches 300 or more words at age 2), first instructions understood (9 months to 1 year), first word spoken (10 to 15 months), and the growth of spoken vocabulary (reaches 200 to 275 words at age 2). At 18 to 24 months of age, infants often speak in two-word utterances.
Biological Influences	Strongest Evidence	• That children all over the world reach language milestones at about the same time developmentally despite vast variation in language input.
	Biological Evolution	• In evolution, language clearly gave humans an enormous edge over other animals and increased their chance of survival.
	Biological Prewiring	• Chomsky proposed the concept of language acquisition device (LAD) that flows from the evidence about the biological foundations of language.
Behavioral and Environmental Influences	The Behavioral View	• This view—that language reinforcement and imitation are the factors in language acquisition—has not been supported.
	Environmental Influences	• Among the ways that adults teach language to children are infant-directed speech, recasting, echoing, expanding, and labeling. • Parents should talk extensively with an infant, especially about what the baby is attending to. Talk primarily should be live talk, not mechanical talk.

communication and help language acquisition. In contrast, an overly active, directive approach to communicating with the child may be harmful.

Echoing is repeating what a child says, especially if it is an incomplete phrase or sentence. *Expanding* is restating, in a linguistically sophisticated form, what a child has said. *Labeling* is identifying the names of objects. Young children are forever being asked to identify the names of objects. Roger Brown (1986) identified this as "the great word game" and claimed that much of the early vocabulary acquired by children is motivated by this adult pressure to identify the words associated with objects.

The strategies just described—recasting, echoing, expanding, and labeling—are used naturally and in meaningful conversations. Parents do not (and should not) use any deliberate method to teach their children to talk. Even for children who are slow in learning language, the experts agree that intervention should occur in natural ways, with the goal of being able to convey meaning.

At this point, we have discussed a number of ideas about language development. To review these ideas, see summary table 6.3. In the next chapter, we will continue our coverage of infant development by focusing on the infant's socioemotional development.

Chapter Review

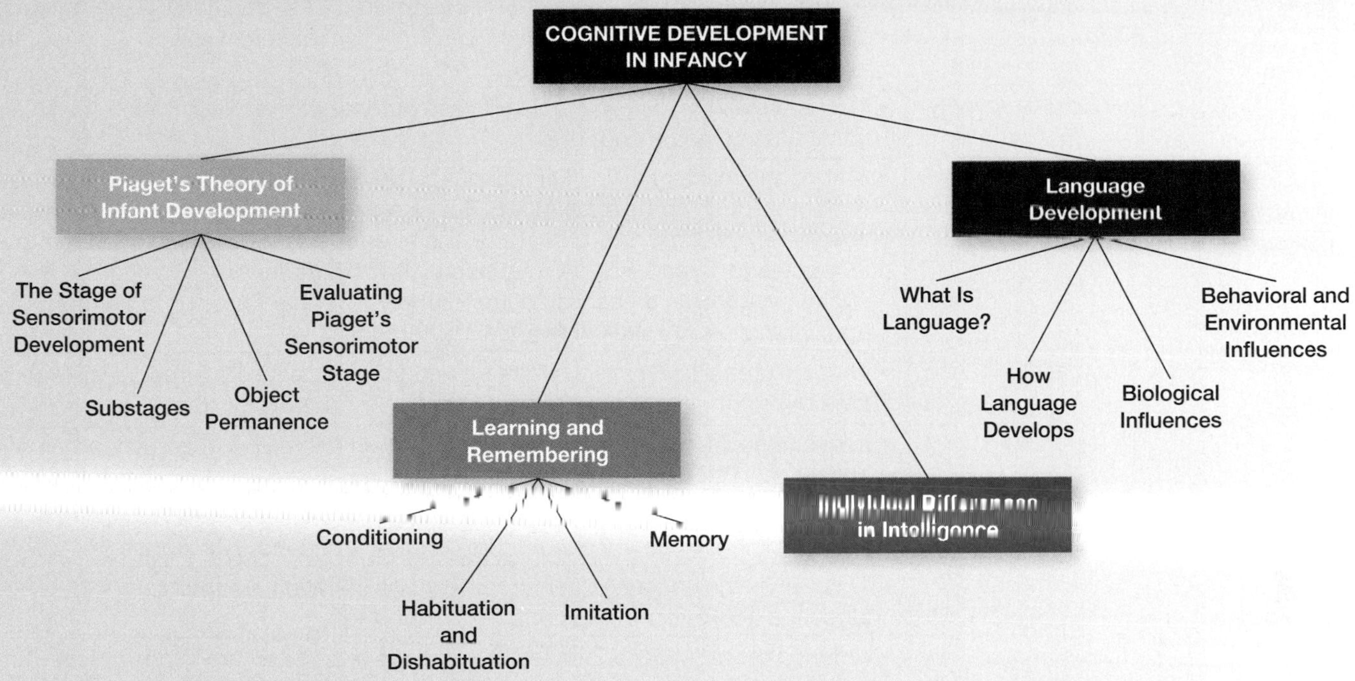

TO OBTAIN A DETAILED REVIEW OF THIS CHAPTER, STUDY THESE THREE SUMMARY TABLES:

- Summary Table 6.1 Piaget's Theory of Infant Development page 163
- Summary Table 6.2 Learning and Remembering, and Individual Differences in Intelligence page 168
- Summary Table 6.3 Language Development page 173

Key Terms

scheme 158
simple reflexes 159
first habits and primary circular reactions 159
primary circular reactions 159
secondary circular reactions 159
coordination of secondary circular reactions 159
tertiary circular reactions, novelty, and curiosity 159
internalization of schemes 160
object permanence 160
habituation 163
dishabituation 163
deferred imitation 164
memory 164
developmental quotient (DQ) 166
Bayley Scales of Infant Development 166
language 169
infinite generativity 169
receptive vocabulary 169
holophrase hypothesis 170
telegraphic speech 170
language acquisition device (LAD) 171
infant-directed speech 172

Key People

Jean Piaget 158
Eleanor Gibson 161
Elizabeth Spelke 161
Renée Baillargeon 161
Carolyn Rovee-Collier 162
Andrew Meltzoff 164
Jean Mandler 165
Arnold Gesell 166
Nancy Bayley 166
Noam Chomsky 171
Roger Brown 171
Betty Hart and Todd Risley 171

Taking It to the Net

1. Miller must make a 15-minute class presentation on an important theorist who has significantly contributed to our understanding of human development. If Miller were to select Piaget, what types of information (written, spoken, visual) should she include in this presentation to her class?
2. Jerri works in an infant day care center that serves mothers who are participating in a welfare-to-work program, advising the mothers about nutrition. What do these mothers need to know about the effect of poor nutrition on their child's cognitive development?
3. Eric is worried that his one year-old-cousin, Matthew, whom he often baby-sits, is not on track with his language development as compared to his niece Rita. By this age, what are some of the language-related milestones or tasks than an average child usually has achieved?

Connect to www.mhhe.com/santrockld8 to research the answers and complete these exercises.

OLC Preview

To further test your knowledge of this chapter or to explore our extensive online resources that accompany *Life-Span Development*, eighth edition, please log on to the text's Online Learning Center at http://www.mhhe.com/santrockld8.com.

Chapter 7

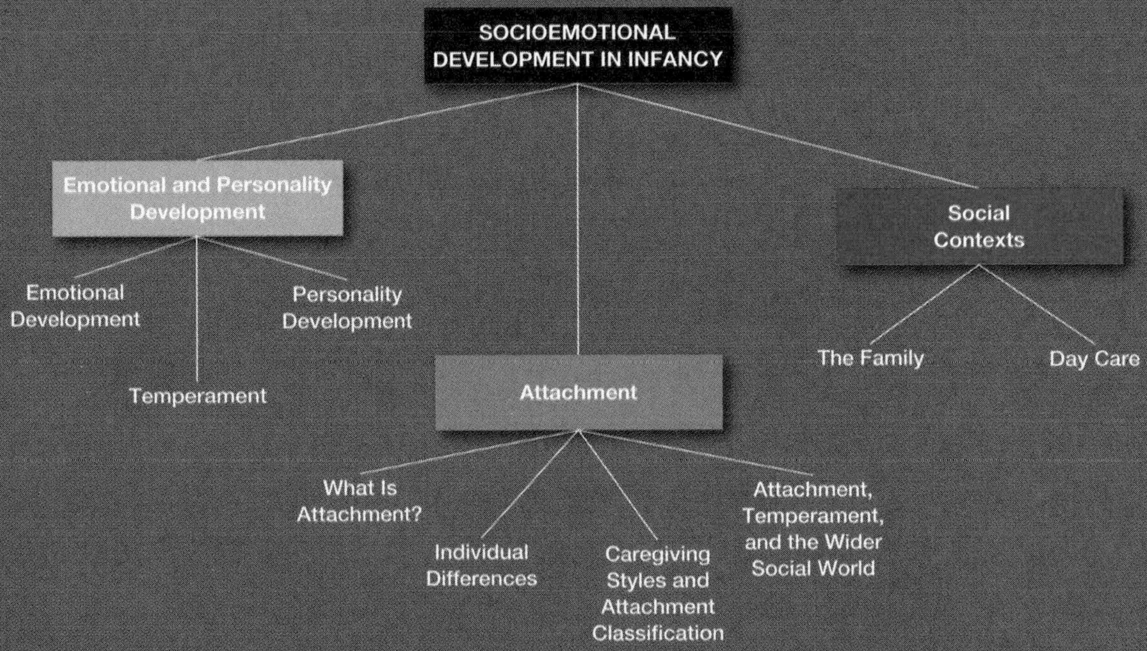
SOCIOEMOTIONAL DEVELOPMENT IN INFANCY
Emotional and Personality Development
Emotional Development
Temperament
Personality Development
Attachment
What Is Attachment?
Individual Differences
Caregiving Styles and Attachment Classification
Attachment, Temperament, and the Wider Social World
Social Contexts
The Family
Day Care

Socioemotional Development in Infancy

We never know the love of our parents until we have become parents.

Henry Ward Beecher
American Writer, 19th Century

Images of Life-Span Development

The Story of Tom's Fathering

TOM IS A 1-year-old infant who is being reared by his father during the day. His mother works full-time at her job away from home, and his father is a writer who works at home; they prefer this arrangement over putting Tom in day care. Tom's father is doing a great job of caring for him. Tom's father keeps Tom nearby while he is writing and spends lots of time talking to him and playing with him. From their interactions, it is clear that they genuinely enjoy each other.

Tom's father is a far cry from the emotionally distant, conformist, traditional-gender-role fathers of the 1950s. He looks to the future and imagines the Little League games Tom will play in and the many other activities he can enjoy with Tom. Remembering how little time his own father spent with him, he is dedicated to making sure that Tom has an involved, nurturing experience with his father. Of course, not all fathers in the 1950s behaved like Tom's father and not all fathers today are as emotionally involved with their children as Tom is.

Many fathers are spending more time with their infants.

When Tom's mother comes home in the evening, she spends considerable time with him. Tom shows a positive attachment to both his mother and his father. His parents have cooperated and successfully juggled their careers and work schedules to provide 1-year-old Tom with excellent child care.

In the previous two chapters, you read about how the infant perceives, learns, and remembers. Infants also are socioemotional beings, capable of displaying emotions and initiating social interaction with people close to them.

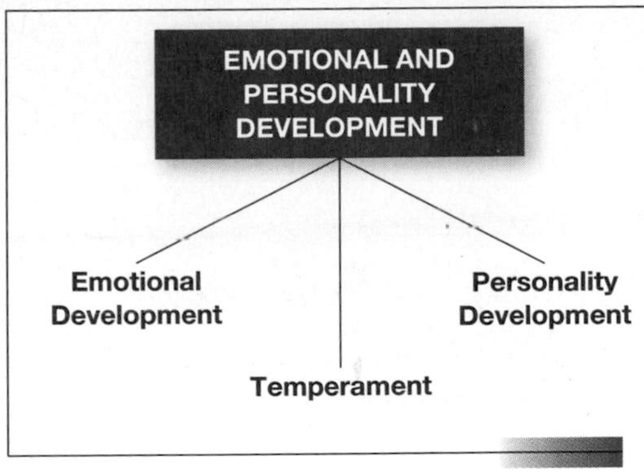

Emotional and Personality Development

Anyone who has been around infants for even a brief period of time detects that they are emotional beings. Not only do we notice infants' expressions of emotions, but we sense that they vary in their temperament—with some being shy and others outgoing, some active and others much less so. Let's further explore these and other aspects of emotional and personality development in infants.

Emotional Development

Infants can express a number of emotions. We will explore what these are and how they develop, but first we need to define *emotion.*

Defining Emotion Defining *emotion* is difficult because it is not easy to tell when a child or an adult is in an emotional state. Is a child in an emotional state when her heart beats fast, her palms sweat, and her stomach churns? Or is she in an emotional state when she smiles or grimaces? The body and face play important roles in understanding children's emotion. However, psychologists debate how important each is in determining whether a child is in an emotional state. For our purposes, we will define **emotion** *as feeling, or affect, that can involve physiological arousal (a fast heartbeat, for example), conscious experience (thinking about being in love with someone, for example), and behavioral expression (a smile or grimace, for example).* Psychologists debate which of these components is the most important aspect of emotion and how they mix to produce emotional experiences (Cacioppo & Gardner, 1999; Izard, 2000).

emotion
Feeling or affect, that can involve physiological arousal (a fast heartbeat, for example), conscious experience (thinking about being in love with someone, for example), and behavioral expression (a smile or grimace, for example).

When we think about children's emotions, a few dramatic feelings, such as rage, fear, and glorious joy, usually spring to mind. But emotions can be subtle as well—the feeling a mother has when she holds her baby, the mild irritation of boredom, and the uneasiness of being in a new situation.

Blossoms are scattered by the wind
And the wind cares nothing, but
The blossoms of the heart
No wind can touch.

Youshida Kenko
Buddhist Monk, 14th Century

An important aspect of emotional development is emotional regulation (Eisenberg, 2001; Posner, 1999; Saarni, Mumme, & Campos, 1998). During the first year of life, the infant gradually develops an ability to inhibit, or minimize, the intensity and duration of emotional reactions. At the same time, infants acquire a greater diversity of emotional responses. Examples of early emotional regulation are infants' soothing themselves by sucking or their withdrawing from excessive stimulation. Equally important is caregivers' assisting infants in learning how to regulate their emotions by attending to their distress and providing them with comfort.

Affect in Parent-Child Relationships Emotions are the first language with which parents and infants communicate before the infant acquires speech (Maccoby, 1992). Infants react to their parents' facial expressions and tone of voice. In return, parents "read" what the infant is trying to communicate, responding appropriately when their infants are either distressed or happy. Sensitive, responsive parents help their infants grow emotionally, whether the infants respond in distressed or happy ways (Campos, 2001).

Exploring Emotion
International Society for Research on Emotions

The initial aspects of infant attachment to parents are based on emotion-linked interchanges, as when an infant cries and the caregiver sensitively responds. By the end of the first year, a mother's facial expression—either smiling or fearful—influences whether an infant will explore an unfamiliar environment. And, when children hear their parents quarreling, they often react with distress and inhibit their play (Cummings, 1987). Exceptionally well-functioning families often include humor in their interactions, sometimes making each other laugh and developing light, pleasant mood states to defuse conflicts. And, when a positive mood has been induced in the child, the child is more likely to comply with a parent's directions.

Infant and adult affective communicative capacities make possible coordinated infant-adult interactions (Thompson, 1999). The face-to-face interactions of even 3-month-old infants and their adults are bidirectional (mutually regulated). This coordination has led to characterizations of the mother-infant interaction as "reciprocal" or "synchronous." These terms are attempts to capture the quality of interaction when all is going well.

Emotional expression	Approximate time of emergence
Interest, neonatal smile (a sort of half smile that appears spontaneously for no apparent reason),* startled response,* distress,* disgust	Present at birth
Social smile	4 to 6 weeks
Anger, surprise, sadness	3 to 4 months
Fear	5 to 7 months
Shame/shyness	6 to 8 months
Contempt, guilt	2 years

* These expressions are precursors of the social smile and the emotions of surprise and sadness, which appear later. No evidence exists to suggest that they are related to inner feelings when they are observed in the first few weeks of life.

Figure **7.1**

The Development Course of the Facial Expression of Emotions

Developmental Timetable of Emotions To determine whether infants are actually expressing a particular emotion, we need a system for measuring emotions. Carroll Izard (1982) developed such a system. The **Maximally Discriminative Facial Movement Coding System (MAX)** *is Izard's system of coding infants' facial expressions related to emotion. Using MAX, coders watch slow-motion and stop-action videotapes of infants' facial reactions to stimuli.* Among the stimulus conditions are giving an infant an ice cube, putting tape on the backs of the infant's hands, handing the infant a favorite toy and then taking it away, separating the infant from the mother and then reuniting them, having a stranger approach the infant, restraining the infant's head, placing a ticking clock next to the infant's ear, popping a balloon in front of the infant's face, and giving the infant camphor to sniff and lemon rind and orange juice to taste.

Based on Izard's classification system, interest, distress, and disgust are present at birth; a social smile appears at about 4 to 6 weeks; anger, surprise, and sadness emerge at about 3 to 4 months; fear is displayed at about 5 to 7 months; shame and shyness are displayed at about 6 to 8 months; and contempt and guilt don't appear until 2 years of age. A summary of the approximate timetable for the emergence of facial expression of emotions is shown in figure 7.1.

Maximally Discriminative Facial Movement Coding System (MAX) Izard's system of coding infants' facial expressions related to emotions. Using MAX, coders watch show-motion and stop-action videotapes of infants' facial reactions to stimuli.

Crying Crying is the most important mechanism newborns have for communicating with their world. This is true for the first cry, which tells the mother and

What are some developmental changes in emotion during infancy? What are some different types of crying that infants display?

Infant Crying

doctor the baby's lungs have filled with air. Cries also may tell physicians and researchers something about the central nervous system.

basic cry
A rhythmic pattern usually consisting of a cry, a briefer silence, a shorter inspiratory whistle that is higher pitched than the main cry, and then a brief rest before the next cry.

anger cry
A cry similar to the basic cry, with more excess air forced through the vocal chords (associated with exasperation or rage).

pain cry
A sudden appearance of loud crying without preliminary moaning and a long initial cry followed by an extended period of breath holding.

Babies don't have just one type of cry. They have at least three. The **basic cry** *is a rhythmic pattern that usually consists of a cry, followed by a briefer silence, then a shorter inspiratory whistle that is somewhat higher in pitch than the main cry, then another brief rest before the next cry.* Some infancy experts believe that hunger is one of the conditions that incite the basic cry. The **anger cry** *is a variation of the basic cry. However, in the anger cry, more excess air is forced through the vocal cords.* The **pain cry,** *which is stimulated by high-intensity stimuli, differs from other types of cries. A sudden appearance of loud crying without preliminary moaning and a long initial cry followed by an extended period of breath holding characterize the pain cry.*

Most parents, and adults in general, can determine whether an infant's cries signify anger or pain (Zeskind, Klein, & Marshall, 1992). Parents also can distinguish the cries of their own baby better than those of a strange baby. There is little consistent evidence to support the idea that mothers and females, but not fathers and males, are innately programmed to respond nurturantly to an infant's crying.

To soothe or not to soothe—should a crying baby be given attention and soothed, or does this spoil the infant? Many years ago, famous behaviorist John Watson (1928) argued that parents spend too much time responding to infant crying. As a consequence, he said, parents are actually rewarding infant crying and increasing its incidence. More recently, by contrast, infancy experts Mary Ainsworth (1979) and John Bowlby (1989) stress that you can't respond too much to infant crying in the first year of life. They believe that the caregiver's quick, comforting response to the infant's cries is an important ingredient in the development of secure attachment. In one of Ainsworth's studies, the mothers who responded quickly to their infants when they cried at 3 months of age had infants who cried less later in the first year of life (Bell & Ainsworth, 1972). On the other hand, behaviorist Jacob Gerwirtz (1977) found that a caregiver's quick, soothing response to crying increased subsequent crying.

He who binds himself to joy
Does the winged life destroy;
But he who kisses the joy as it
Flies lives in eternity's sun rise.

William Blake
English Poet, 19th Century

Controversy, then, still characterizes the issue of whether parents should respond to an infant's cries (Lewis & Ramsay, 1999). However, developmentalists increasingly argue that an infant cannot be spoiled in the first year of life, which suggests that parents should soothe a crying infant rather than be unresponsive; in this manner, infants will likely develop a sense of trust and secure attachment to the caregiver in the first year of life.

reflexive smile
A smile that does not occur in response to external stimuli. It happens during the month after birth, usually during irregular patterns of sleep, not when the infant is in an alert state.

social smile
A smile is response to an external stimulus, which, early in development, typically is in response to a face.

Smiling Smiling is another important communicative affective behavior of the infant. Two types of smiling can be distinguished in infants—one reflexive, the other social. A **reflexive smile** *does not occur in response to external stimuli. It appears during the first month after birth, usually during irregular patterns of sleep, not when the infant is in an alert state.* By contrast, a **social smile** *occurs in response to an external stimulus, which, early in development, typically is in response to a face.* Social smiling does not occur until 2 to 3 months of age (Emde, Gaensbauer, & Harmon, 1976), although some researchers believe that infants grin in response to voices as early as 3 weeks of age (Sroufe & Waters, 1976). The power of the infant's smiles was appropriately captured by British attachment theorist John Bowlby (1969): "Can we doubt that the more and better an infant smiles the better he is loved and cared for? It is fortunate for their survival that babies are so designed by nature that they beguile and enslave mothers."

stranger anxiety
An infant's fear and wariness of strangers; it needs to appear in the second half of the first year of life.

Stranger Anxiety The most frequent expression of an infant's fear involves **stranger anxiety,** *in which an infant shows a fear and wariness of strangers.* This tends to appear in the second half of the first year of life. There are individual variations in stranger anxiety, with not all infants showing distress when they encounter a stranger. Stranger anxiety usually emerges gradually, first appearing at about 6 months of age in the form of wary reactions. By age 9 months, the fear of strangers

Summary Table 7.1
Emotional Development

Concept	Processes/ Related Ideas	Characteristics/Descriptions
Defining Emotion	Feeling, Affect	• Emotion is feeling or affect that involves a mixture of physiological arousal and overt behavior. • Self-regulation is an important aspect of emotion.
Affect in Parent-Infant Relationships	Communication	• Emotions are the way that parents and infants communicate before the infant acquires speech. • Infant and adult affective communicative capacities make possible coordinated infant-adult interaction.
Developmental Timetable of Emotions	Izard's Coding System	• Izard developed the Maximally Discriminative Facial Coding System (MAX) for coding infants' emotional expressions. • Interest, distress, and disgust are present at birth; a social smile appears at about 4 to 6 weeks; anger, surprise, and sadness emerge at about 3 to 4 months; fear is displayed at about 5 to 7 months; shame and shyness emerge at about 6 to 8 months; and contempt and guilt appear at about 2 years of age.
Crying	Types of Cries	• Babies have at least three types of cries—basic cry, anger cry, and pain cry. • Most parents, and adults in general, can tell whether an infant's cry signifies anger or pain.
	Response to Crying	• There is controversy about whether babies should be soothed when crying. • An increasing number of development researchers support Bowlby and Ainsworth's belief that infant crying should be responded to immediately in the first year of life.
Smiling	Types of Smiling	• Two types of smiles can be distinguished in infants: reflexive and social.
Stranger Anxiety	Developmental Changes and Contexts	• Stranger anxiety involves an infant's fear and wariness of strangers, which tend to appear in the second half of the first year of life, intensifying toward the end of the first year. • A number of factors influence stranger anxiety, such as the social context and the characteristics of the stranger.

is often more intense and continues to escalate through the infant's first birthday (Emde, Gaensbauer, & Harmon, 1976).

A number of factors can influence whether an infant shows stranger anxiety, including the social context and the characteristics of the stranger. In terms of the social context, infants show less stranger anxiety when they are in familiar settings. For example, in one study, 10-month-olds showed little stranger anxiety when they met a stranger in their own home but much greater fear when they encountered a stranger in a research laboratory (Sroufe, Waters, & Matas, 1974). Also, infants show less stranger anxiety when they are sitting on their mothers' laps than when placed in an infant seat several feet away from their mothers (Bohlin & Hagekull, 1993). Thus, it appears that, when infants have a sense of security, they are less likely to show stranger anxiety.

Who the stranger is and how the stranger behaves also influence stranger anxiety in infants. Infants are less fearful of child strangers than adult strangers. They also are less fearful of friendly, outgoing, smiling strangers than of passive, unsmiling strangers (Bretherton, Stolberg, & Kreye, 1981).

At this point we have studied a number of ideas about emotional development in infancy. To review these ideas, see summary table 7.1.

Infant Temperament

Temperament

Infants show different emotional responses. One infant might be cheerful and happy much of the time; another baby might cry a lot and more often display a negative mood. These behaviors reflect differences in their temperament (Halpern & Brand, 1999). Let's explore a definition of temperament, the ways in which it can be classified, and the implications of temperamental variations for parenting.

temperament
An individual's behavioral style and characteristic way of emotional response.

Defining and Classifying Temperament **Temperament** *is an individual's behavioral style and characteristic way of emotional response.* Developmentalists are especially interested in the temperament of infants.

A widely debated issue is just what the key dimensions of temperament are. Psychiatrists Alexander Chess and Stella Thomas (Chess & Thomas, 1977; Thomas & Chess, 1991) believe there are three basic types, or clusters, of temperament—easy, difficult, and slow to warm up.

easy child
A child who is generally in a positive mood, who quickly establishes regular routines in infancy, and who adapts easily to new experiences.

difficult child
A child who tends to react negatively and cry frequently, who engages in irregular daily routines, and who is slow to accept new experiences.

slow-to-warm-up child
A child who has a low activity level, is somewhat negative, shows low adaptability, and displays a low intensity mood.

1. An **easy child** *is generally in a positive mood, quickly establishes regular routines in infancy, and adapts easily to new experiences.*
2. A **difficult child** *tends to react negatively and cry frequently, engages in irregular daily routines, and is slow to accept new experiences.*
3. A **slow-to-warm-up child** *has a low activity level, is somewhat negative, shows low adaptability, and displays a low intensity of mood.*

Various dimensions make up these three basic clusters of temperament. In their longitudinal investigation, Chess and Thomas found that 40 percent of the children they studied could be classified as easy, 10 percent as difficult, and 15 percent as slow to warm up (35 percent did not fit any of the three patterns). Researchers have found that these three basic clusters of temperament are moderately stable across the childhood years.

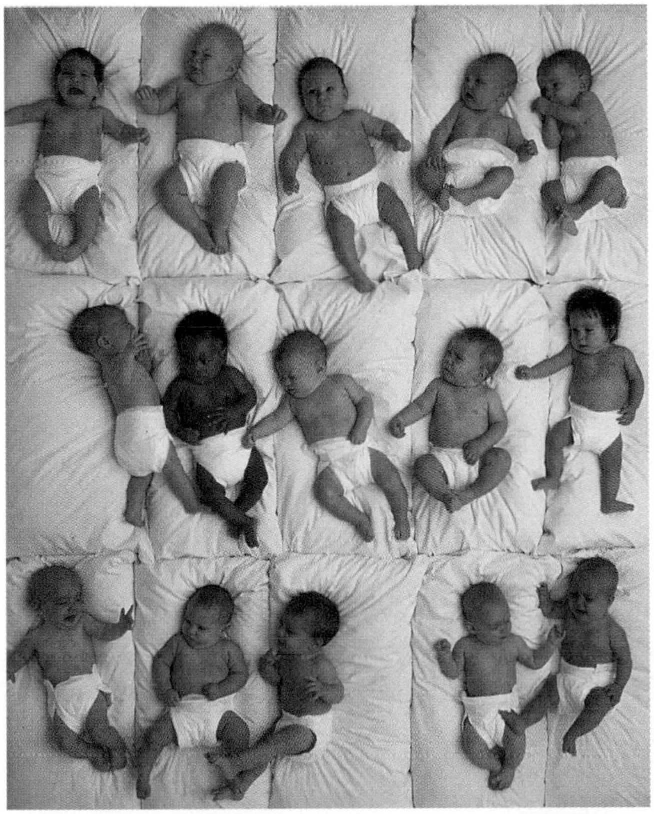
What are some ways that developmentalists have classified infants' temperaments? Which classification makes the most sense to you, based on your observations of infants?

New classifications of temperament continue to be forged (Bornstein, 2000; Lemery & others, 1999; Rothbart, 1999; Thompson, 1999; Wachs & Kohnstamm, 2001). In a recent review of temperament, Mary Rothbart and John Bates (1998) concluded that, based on current research, the best framework for classifying temperament involves a revision of Chess and Thomas' categories of easy, difficult, and slow to warm up. The general classification of temperament now focuses more on (1) positive affect and approach (much like the personality trait of extraversion/introversion), (2) negative affectivity, and (3) effortful control (self-regulation).

A number of scholars conceive of temperament as a stable characteristic of newborns, which comes to be shaped and modified by the child's later experiences. This raises the question of heredity's role in temperament (Goldsmith, 1988). Twin and adoption studies have been conducted to answer this question (Plomin & others, 1994). The researchers have found a heritability index in the range of .50 to .60, suggesting a moderate influence of heredity on temperament. However, the strength of the association usually declines as infants become older (Goldsmith & Gottesman, 1981). This finding supports the belief that temperament becomes more malleable with experience. Alternatively, it may be that, as a child becomes older, behavior indicators of temperament are more difficult to spot.

Goodness of Fit *Goodness of fit* refers to the match between a child's temperament and the environmental demands the child must cope with (Bates, 2001; Matheny & Phillips, 2001). Goodness of fit can be important to the child's adjustment. For example, consider an active child who is made to sit still for long pe-

riods of time or lives in a small apartment. Consider also a slow-to-warm-up child who is abruptly pushed into new situations on a regular basis. Such lacks of fit between the child's temperament and these environmental demands can produce adjustment problems for the child. In our discussion of parenting and the child's temperament, many of the recommendations involve consideration of goodness of fit.

What are some good strategies for parents to adopt when responding to their infant's temperament?

Parenting and the Child's Temperament

Many parents don't become believers in temperament's importance until the birth of their second child. Many parents view the first child's behavior as being solely a result of how they socialized the child. However, management strategies that worked with the first child might not be as effective with the second child. Problems experienced with the first child (such as those involved in feeding, sleeping, and coping with strangers) might not exist with the second child, but new problems might arise. Such experiences strongly suggest that nature as well as nurture influence the child's development, that children differ from each other from very early in life, and that these differences have important implications for parent-child interaction (Kwak & others, 1999).

What are the implications of temperamental variations for parenting? Although answers to this question necessarily are speculative because of the incompleteness of the research literature, the following conclusions were reached by temperament experts Ann Sanson and Mary Rothbart (1995):

- *Attention to and respect for individuality.* An important implication of taking children's individuality seriously is that it becomes difficult to generate prescriptions for "good parenting," other than possibly specifying that parents need to be sensitive and flexible. Parents need to be sensitive to the infant's signals and needs. A goal of parenting might be accomplished in one way with one child and in another way with another child, depending on the child's temperament.

Some temperament characteristics pose more parenting challenges than others, at least in modern Western societies. Children's proneness to distress, as exhibited by frequent crying and irritability, can contribute to the emergence of avoidant or coercive parental responses. In one research study, though, extra support and training for mothers of distress-prone infants improved the quality of mother-infant interaction (van den Boom, 1989).

Parents might react differently to a child's temperament, depending on whether the child is a girl or a boy and on the culture in which they live (Kerr, 2001). For example, in one study, mothers were more responsive to the crying of irritable girls than to the crying of irritable boys (Crockenberg, 1986). Also, an active temperament might be valued in some cultures (such as the United States) but not in other cultures (such as China). Parents should respect each child's temperament, rather than try to fit all children into the same mold.

- *Structuring the child's environment.* Crowded, noisy environments can pose greater problems for some children (such as a "difficult child") than others (such as an "easygoing" child). We might also expect that a fearful, withdrawing child would benefit from slower entry into new contexts.
- *The "difficult child" and packaged parenting programs.* Some books and programs for parents focus specifically on temperament (Cameron, Hansen, & Rosen, 1989; Turecki & Tonner, 1989). These programs usually focus on children with "difficult" temperaments. Acknowledgment that some children are harder to

parent is often helpful, and advice on how to handle particular difficult temperament characteristics can also be useful.

However, weighted against these potential advantages are several disadvantages. Whether a particular characteristic is difficult depends on its fit with the environment, whereas the notion of difficult temperament suggests that the problem rests solely with the child. To label a child "difficult" also has the danger of becoming a self-fulfilling prophecy. If a child is identified as "difficult," the labeling may maintain that categorization.

Children's temperament needs to be taken into account when considering caregiving behavior (Kochanska, 1999). Research does not yet allow for many highly specific recommendations, but, in general, caregivers should (1) be sensitive to the individual characteristics of the child, (2) be flexible in responding to these characteristics, and (3) avoid negative labeling of the child.

Personality Development

We have explored some important aspects of emotional development and temperament, which reveal individual variations in infants. Let's now examine the individual characteristics of the infant that often are thought of as central to personality development: trust and the development of self and independence.

Trust According to Erik Erikson (1968), the first year of life is characterized by the trust-versus-mistrust stage of development ◄ P. 33. Following a life of regularity, warmth, and protection in the mother's womb, the infant faces a world that is less secure. Erikson believes that infants learn trust when they are cared for in a consistent, warm manner. If the infant is not well fed and kept warm on a consistent basis, a sense of mistrust is likely to develop.

Trust versus mistrust is not resolved once and for all in the first year of life. It arises again at each successive stage of development. There are both hope and danger in this. Children who enter school with a sense of mistrust may trust a particular teacher who has taken the time to make herself trustworthy. With this second chance, children overcome their early mistrust. By contrast, children who leave infancy with a sense of trust can still have their sense of mistrust activated at a later stage, perhaps if their parents are separated or divorced under conflicting circumstances.

Self Development in Infancy
Seeking Independence

The Developing Sense of Self and Independence Individuals carry with them a sense of who they are and what makes them different from

Reprinted with special permission of North America Syndicate.

everyone else. They cling to this identity and begin to feel secure in the knowledge that this identity is becoming more stable. Real or imagined, this sense of self is a strong motivating force in life. When does the individual begin to sense a separate existence from others?

The Self Infants are not "given" a self by their parents or the culture. Rather, they find and construct selves. Studying the self in infancy is difficult mainly because infants are unable to describe with language their experiences of themselves.

To determine whether infants can recognize themselves, psychologists have used mirrors. In the animal kingdom, only the great apes learn to recognize their reflection in the mirror, but human infants accomplish this feat by about 18 months of age. How does the mirror technique work? The mother puts a dot of rouge on her infant's nose. The observer watches to see how often the infant touches its nose. Next, the infant is placed in front of a mirror, and observers detect whether nose touching increases. In two independent investigations in the second half of the second year of life, infants recognized their own image and coordinated the image they saw with the actions of touching their own body (Amsterdam, 1968; Lewis & Brooks-Gunn, 1979).

Erikson believed that autonomy versus shame and doubt is the key developmental theme of the toddler years. *What are some good strategies for parents to use with their toddler?*

Independence Not only does the infant develop a sense of self in the second year of life, but independence also becomes a more central theme in the infant's life. The theories of Margaret Mahler and Erik Erikson have important implications for both self-development and independence. Mahler (1979) believes that the child goes through a separation and then an individuation process. Separation involves the infant's movement away from the mother. Individuation involves the development of self.

Erikson (1968), like Mahler, believed that independence is an important issue in the second year of life. Erikson describes the second stage of development as the stage of autonomy versus shame and doubt. Autonomy builds on the infant's developing mental and motor abilities. At this point in development, not only can infants walk, but they can also climb, open and close, drop, push and pull, and hold and let go. Infants feel pride in these new accomplishments and want to do everything themselves, whether it is flushing a toilet, pulling the wrapping off a package, or deciding what to eat. It is important for parents to recognize the motivation of toddlers to do what they are capable of doing at their own pace. Then they can learn to control their muscles and their impulses themselves. But when caregivers are impatient and do for toddlers what they are capable of doing themselves, shame and doubt develop. Every parent has rushed a child from time to time. It is only when parents consistently overprotect toddlers or criticize accidents (wetting, soiling, spilling, or breaking, for example) that children develop an excessive sense of shame and doubt about their ability to control themselves and their world.

Erikson also believed that the stage of autonomy versus shame and doubt has important implications for the development of independence and identity during adolescence. The development of autonomy during the toddler years gives adolescents the courage to be independent individuals who can choose and guide their own future.

At this point, we have studied a number of ideas about the infant's temperament and personality development. A review of these ideas is presented in summary table 7.2. Next, we will focus on another important aspect of infants' socioemotional development—their attachment to a caregiver.

SUMMARY TABLE 7.2
Temperament and Personality Development

Concept	Processes/ Related Ideas	Characteristics/Descriptions
Temperament	Defining and Classifying Temperament	• Temperament is an individual's behavioral style and characteristic way of emotional responding. Developmentalists are especially interested in the temperament of infants. • Chess and Thomas classified infants as (1) easy, (2) difficult, or (3) slow to warm up. • Recent classifications focus more on (1) positive affect and approach, (2) negative affectivity, and (3) effortful control.
	Goodness of Fit	• This refers to the match between a child's temperament and the environmental demands the child must cope with. Goodness of fit can be an important aspect of a child's adjustment.
	Parenting and the Child's Temperament	• Although research evidence is sketchy at this point in time, some general recommendations are that caregivers should (1) be sensitive to the individual characteristics of the child, (2) be flexible in responding to these characteristics, and (3) avoid negative lableling of the child.
Personality Development	Trust	• Erikson argued that the first year is characterized by the crisis of trust versus mistrust. His ideas about trust have much in common with Ainsworth's concept of secure attachment.
	The Developing Sense of Self and Independence	• At some point in the second half of the second year of life, the infant develops a sense of self. • Independence becomes a central theme in the second year of life. Mahler argues that the infant separates herself from her mother and then develops individuation. Erikson stressed that the second year of life is characterized by the stage of autonomy versus shame and doubt.

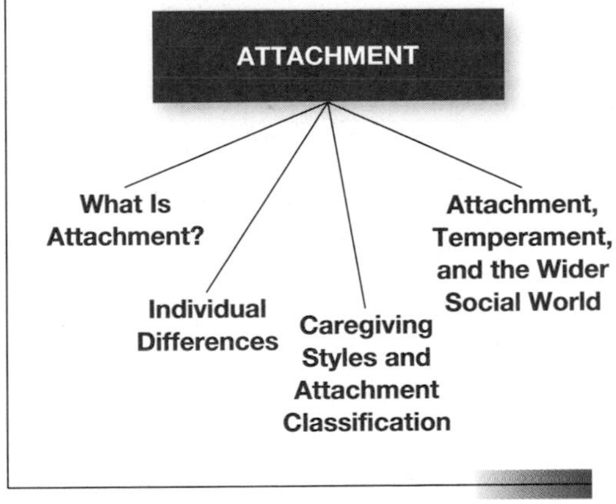

Attachment

A small curly-haired girl named Danielle, 12 months old, begins to whimper. After a few seconds, she begins to wail. The psychologist observing Danielle is conducting a research study on the nature of attachment between infants and their mothers. Subsequently, the mother reenters the room, and Danielle's crying ceases. Quickly, Danielle crawls over to where her mother is seated and reaches out to be held. This situation is one of the main ways that psychologists study the nature of attachment during infancy.

What Is Attachment?

In everyday language, attachment is a relationship between two individuals who feel strongly about each other and do a number of things to continue the relationship. Many pairs of people are attached: relatives, lovers, a teacher and student. In the language of developmental psychology, though, attachment is often restricted to a relationship between particular social figures and a particular phenomenon that is thought to reflect unique characteristics of the relationship. In this case, the developmental period is infancy, the social figures are the infant and one or more adult caregivers, and the phenomenon is a bond (Bowlby, 1969, 1989). To summarize, **attachment** *is a close emotional bond between the infant and the caregiver.*

attachment
A close emotional bond between an infant and a caregiver.

There is no shortage of theories about infant attachment. Freud believed that infants become attached to the person or object that provides oral satisfaction. For most infants, this is the mother, since she is most likely to feed the infant.

Is feeding as important as Freud thought? A classic study by Harry Harlow and Robert Zimmerman (1959) reveals that the answer is no (see figure 7.2). These researchers evaluated whether feeding or contact comfort was more important to infant attachment. Infant monkeys were removed from their mothers at birth and reared for 6 months by surrogate (substitute) "mothers." One of the mothers was made of wire, the other of cloth. Half of the infant monkeys were fed by the wire mother, half by the cloth mother. Periodically, the amount of time the infant monkeys spent with either the wire or the cloth monkey was computed. Regardless of whether they were fed by the wire or the cloth mother, the infant monkeys spent far more time with the cloth mother. This study clearly demonstrated that feeding is not the crucial element in the attachment process and that contact comfort is important.

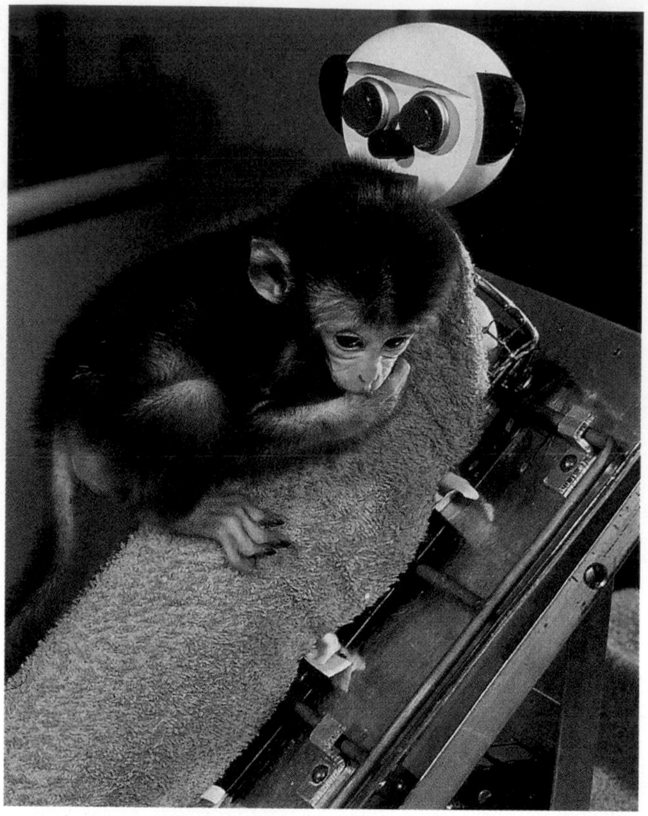

Figure 7.2

Harlow's Classic "Contact Comfort" Study

Regardless of whether they were fed by a wire mother or by a cloth mother, the infant monkeys overwhelmingly preferred to be in contact with the cloth mother, demonstrating the importance of contact comfort in attachment.

Harry Harlow

Erik Erikson (1968) believed that the first year of life is the key time frame for the development of attachment. Recall his proposal—also discussed in chapter 2—that the first year of life represents the stage of trust versus mistrust ◀ P. 33. A sense of trust requires a feeling of physical comfort and a minimal amount of fear and apprehension about the future. Trust in infancy sets the stage for a lifelong expectation that the world will be a good and pleasant place to be. Erikson also believed that responsive, sensitive parenting contributes to an infant's sense of trust.

The ethological perspective of British psychiatrist John Bowlby (1969, 1989) also stresses the importance of attachment in the first year of life and the responsiveness of the caregiver. Bowlby believes that an infant and its primary caregiver form an attachment. He argues that the newborn is biologically equipped to elicit attachment behavior (Weizmann, 2000). The baby cries, clings, coos, and smiles. Later, the infant crawls, walks, and follows the mother. The infant's goal is to keep the primary caregiver nearby.

Attachment does not emerge suddenly but rather develops in a series of phases, moving from a baby's general preference for human beings to a partnership with primary caregivers. Following are four such phases based on Bowlby's conceptualization of attachment (Schaffer, 1996):

Phase 1:	Birth to 2 months	Infants instinctively direct their attachment to human figures. Strangers, siblings, and parents are equally likely to elicit smiling or crying from the infant.
Phase 2:	2 to 7 months	Attachment becomes focused on one figure, usually the primary caregiver, as the baby gradually learns to distinguish familiar from unfamiliar people.
Phase 3:	7 to 24 months	Specific attachments develop. With increased locomotor skills, babies actively seek contact with regular caregivers, such as the mother or father.
Phase 4:	24 months on	A goal-corrected partnership is formed in which children become aware of others' feelings, goals, and plans and begin to take these into account in forming their own actions.

Individual Differences

secure attachment
The infant uses a caregiver as a secure base from which to explore the environment. Ainsworth believes that secure attachment in the first year of life provides an important foundation for psychological development later in life.

Strange Situation
An observational measure of infant attachment that requires the infant to move through a series of introductions, separations, and reunions with the caregiver and an adult stranger in a prescribed order.

Although attachment to a caregiver intensifies midway through the first year, isn't it likely that some babies have a more positive attachment experience than others? Mary Ainsworth (1979) thinks so. She says that, in **secure attachment,** *infants use the caregiver, usually the mother, as a secure base from which to explore the environment. Ainsworth believes that secure attachment in the first year of life provides an important foundation for psychological development later in life.* The caregiver's sensitivity to the infant's signals increases secure attachment (DeWolff & van IJzendoorn, 1997). The securely attached infant moves freely away from the mother but processes her location through periodic glances. The securely attached infant responds positively to being picked up by others and, when put back down, freely moves away to play. An insecurely attached infant, by contrast, avoids the mother or is ambivalent toward her, fears strangers, and is upset by minor, everyday separations.

Ainsworth created the **Strange Situation,** *an observational measure of infant attachment that requires the infant to move through a series of introductions, separations, and reunions with the caregiver and an adult stranger in a prescribed order* (see figure 7.3). In using the Strange Situation, researchers hope that their observations will provide them with information about the infant's motivation to be near the caregiver and the degree to which the caregiver's presence provides the infant with security and confidence. For example, when in the presence of their caregiver, securely attached infants explore the room and examine toys that have been placed in it. When the caregiver departs, securely attached infants might mildly protest, and

Episode	Persons Present	Duration of Episode	Description of Setting
1	Caregiver, baby, and observer	30 seconds	Observer introduces caregiver and baby to experimental room, then leaves. (Room contains many appealing toys scattered about.)
2	Caregiver and baby	3 minutes	Caregiver is nonparticipant while baby explores; if necessary, play is stimulated after 2 minutes.
3	Stranger, caregiver, and baby	3 minutes	Stranger enters. First minute: stranger is silent. Second minute: stranger converses with caregiver. Third minute: stranger approaches baby. After 3 minutes caregiver leaves unobtrusively.
4	Stranger and baby	3 minutes or less	First separation episode. Stranger's behavior is geared to that of baby.
5	Caregiver and baby	3 minutes or more	First reunion episode. Caregiver greets and/or comforts baby, then tries to settle the baby again in play. Mother then leaves, saying "bye-bye."
6	Baby alone	3 minutes or less	Second separation episode.
7	Stranger and baby	3 minutes or less	Continuation of second separation. Stranger enters and gears behavior to that of baby.
8	Caregiver and baby	3 minutes	Second reunion episode. Caregiver enters, greets baby, then picks baby up. Meanwhile stranger leaves unobtrusively.

Figure **7.3**

The Ainsworth Strange Situation

Mary Ainsworth (right) developed the Strange Situation to assess whether infants are securely or insecurely attached to their caregiver. The episodes involved in the Ainsworth Strange Situation are described above.

What is the nature of secure and insecure attachment?

when the caregiver returns these infants reestablish positive interaction with her, perhaps by smiling or climbing on her lap. Subsequently, the securely attached infant often resumes playing with the toys in the room.

Three types of insecurely attached infants have been described. **Insecure avoidant babies** *show insecurity by avoiding the mother.* In the Strange Situation, these babies engage in little interaction with the caregiver, often display distress by crying when she leaves the room, usually do not reestablish contact with her on her return, and may even turn their back on her at this point. If contact is established, the infant usually leans away or looks away. **Insecure resistant babies** *might cling to the caregiver then resist her by fighting against the closeness, perhaps by kicking or pushing away.* In the Strange Situation, these babies often cling anxiously to the caregiver and don't explore the playroom. When the caregiver leaves, they often cry loudly and push away if she tries to comfort them on her return. **Disorganized babies** *show insecurity in being disorganized and disoriented.* In the Strange Situation, these babies might appear dazed, confused, and fearful. To be classified as disorganized, strong patterns of avoidance and resistance must be shown or certain select behaviors, such as extreme fearfulness around the caregiver, must be present.

insecure avoidant babies
Babies that show insecurity by avoiding the caregiver.

insecure resistant babies
Babies that might cling to the caregiver, then resist her by fighting against the closeness, perhaps by kicking or pushing away.

disorganized babies
Babies that show insecurity by being disorganized and disoriented.

Although the Strange Situation has been used in a large number of studies of infant attachment, some critics believe that the isolated, controlled events of the setting might not necessarily reflect what would happen if infants were observed with their caregiver in a natural environment. The issue of using controlled, laboratory assessments versus naturalistic observations is widely debated in child development circles.

If early attachment to a caregiver is important, it should relate to a child's social behavior later in development. Researchers have found that for some children, early attachments seem to foreshadow later functioning (Schneider, Atkinson & Tardif, 2001; Sroufe, Egeland, & Carlson, 1999). For other children, there is little continuity (Thompson, 2000). Consistency in caregiving over a number of years is likely an important factor in connecting early attachment and the child's functioning later in development.

Caregiving Styles and Attachment Classification

Attachment is defined as a close emotional bond between the infant and caregiver. Is the parent's caregiving style linked with this close emotional bond called attachment? Securely attached babies have caregivers who are sensitive to their signals and are consistently available to respond to their infants' needs (Gao, Elliot, & Waters, 1999; Main, 2000). These caregivers often let their babies have an active part in determining the onset and pacing of interaction in the first year of life.

How do the caregivers of insecurely attached babies interact with them? Caregivers of avoidant babies tend to be unavailable or rejecting (Berlin & Cassidy, 2000). They often don't respond to their babies' signals and have little physical contact with them. When they do interact with their babies, they may behave in an angry and irritable way toward them. Caregivers of ambivalent-resistant babies tend to be inconsistently available to their babies (Cassidy & Berlin, 1994). That is, sometimes they respond to their babies' needs, and sometimes they don't. In general, they tend not to be very affectionate with their babies and show little synchrony when interacting with them. Caregivers of disorganized babies often neglect or physically abuse their babies (Barnett, Ganiban, & Cicchetti, 1999; Main & Solomon, 1990). In some cases,

Forming a Secure Attachment
Attachment Research

In the Hausa culture, siblings and grandmothers provide a significant amount of care for infants. *Might this influence the nature of attachment in this culture?*

these caregivers also have depression (Field, 1992; Levy, 1999). Later in the chapter, we will have more to say about child abuse.

Attachment, Temperament, and the Wider Social World

Not all research reveals the power of infant attachment to predict subsequent development. In one longitudinal study, attachment classification in infancy did not predict attachment classification at 18 years of age (Lewis, 1997). In this study, the best predictor of attachment classification at 18 was the occurrence of parent divorce in intervening years.

Thus, not all developmentalists believe that attachment in infancy is the only path to competence in life. Indeed, some developmentalists believe that too much emphasis is placed on the importance of the attachment bond in infancy. Jerome Kagan (1987, 2000), for example, believes that infants are highly resilient and adaptive; he argues that they are evolutionarily equipped to stay on a positive developmental course, even in the face of wide variations in parenting. Kagan and others stress that genetic and temperament characteristics play more important roles in a child's social competence than the attachment theorists, such as Bowlby, Ainsworth, and Sroufe, are willing to acknowledge (Chaudhuri & Williams, 1999; Young & Shahinfar, 1995). For example, infants may have inherited a low tolerance for stress. This, rather than an insecure attachment bond, may be responsible for their inability to get along with peers.

Also, researchers have found cultural variations in attachment. German and Japanese babies often show different patterns of attachment than American babies. German babies are more likely than American babies to be categorized as avoidant, possibly because caregivers encourage them to be more independent (Grossmann & others, 1985). Japanese babies are more likely than American babies to be categorized as resistant-ambivalent. This may have more to do with the Ainsworth Strange Situation as a measure of attachment than with attachment insecurity itself. Japanese mothers rarely let anyone unfamiliar with their babies care for them. Thus, the Ainsworth Strange Situation might create considerably more stress for Japanese infants than for American infants, who are more accustomed to separation from their mothers (Takahashi, 1990). Even though there are cultural variations in attachment classification, the most frequent classification in very culture studied so far is secure attachment (van IJzendoorn & Kroonenberg, 1988).

Another criticism of attachment theory is that it ignores the diversity of socializing agents and contexts that exists in an infant's world. In some cultures, infants show attachments to many people. Among the Hausa (who live in Nigeria), both grandmothers and siblings provide a significant amount of care for infants (Harkness & Super, 1995). Infants in agricultural societies tend to form attachments to older siblings, who are assigned a major responsibility for younger siblings' care. The attachments formed by infants in group care in Israeli kibbutzim provide another challenge to the singular attachment thesis.

Researchers recognize the importance of competent, nurturant caregivers in an infant's development (Maccoby, 1999). At issue, though, is whether or not secure attachment, especially to a single caregiver, is critical (Rosen & Burke, 1999; Thompson, 2000).

At this point we have discussed a number of ideas about attachment. To review these ideas see summary table 7.3.

Summary Table 7.3
Attachment

Concept	Processes/ Related Ideas	Characteristics/Descriptions
What Is Attachment?	Close Emotional Bond	• Attachment is a close emotional bond between the infant and caregiver. • Feeding is not an important aspect of attachment, although contact comfort and trust are.
	Bowlby's View	• Bowlby's ethological theory stresses that the caregiver and the infant instinctively trigger attachment. • Attachment develops in four phases.
Individual Differences	Ainsworth's View	• Securely attached babies use the caregiver, usually the mother, as a secure base from which to explore the environment. • Three types of insecure attachment are avoidant, resistant, and disorganized. • Ainsworth argued that secure attachment in the first year of life is optimal for development. • She created the Strange Situation, an observational measure of attachment.
Caregiving Styles and Attachment Classifications	Linkages	• Caregivers of secure babies are sensitive to the babies' signals and are consistently available to meet their needs. • Caregivers of avoidant babies tend to be unavailable or rejecting. • Caregivers of ambivalent-rejecting babies tend to be inconsistently available to their babies and usually are not very affectionate. • Caregivers of disorganized babies often neglect or physically abuse their babies.
Attachment, Temperament, and the Wider Social World	Biological Factors	• Some critics argue that attachment theorists have not given adequate attention to genetics and temperament.
	Social Factors	• Other critics stress that they have not adequately taken into account the diversity of social agents and contexts. • Cultural variations in attachment have been found, but in all cultures studied to date secure attachment is the most common classification.

Social Contexts

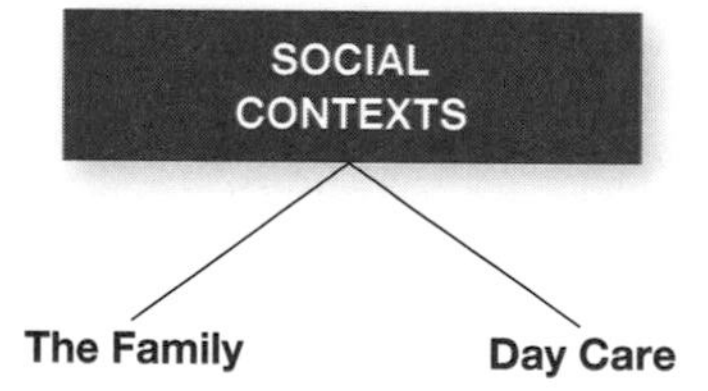

Now that we have explored the infant's emotional and personality development and attachment, let's examine the social contexts in which these occur. We will begin by studying a number of aspects of the family and then turn to a social context in which infants increasingly spend time—day care.

The Family

Most of us began our lives in families and spent thousands of hours during our childhood interacting with our parents. Some of you are already parents; others of you may become parents. What is the transition to parenthood like?

The Transition to Parenthood When people become parents through pregnancy, adoption, or stepparenting, they face disequilibrium and must adapt (Egeren, 1999; Klitzing, Simoni, & Burgin, 1999). Parents want to develop a strong attachment with their infant, but they still want to maintain strong attachments to their spouse and friends, and possibly continue their careers. Parents ask themselves how this new being will change their lives. A baby places new restrictions on partners; no

The Transition to Parenting

longer will they be able to rush out to a movie on a moment's notice, and money may not be readily available for vacations and other luxuries. Dual-career parents ask, "Will it harm the baby to place her in day care? Will we be able to find responsible baby-sitters?"

In a longitudinal investigation of couples from late pregnancy until 3½ years after the baby was born, couples enjoyed more positive marital relations before the baby was born than after (Cowan & others, 1995). Still, almost one-third showed an increase in marital satisfaction. Some couples said that the baby had both brought them closer together *and* moved them farther apart. They commented that being parents enhanced their sense of themselves and gave them a new, more stable identity as a couple. Babies opened men up to a concern with intimate relationships, and the demands of juggling work and family roles stimulated women to manage family tasks more efficiently and pay attention to their personal growth.

At some point during the early years of the child's life, parents face the difficult task of juggling their roles as parents and as self-actualizing adults. Until recently in our culture, nurturing our children and having a career were thought to be incompatible. Fortunately, we have come to recognize that the balance between caring and achieving, nurturing and working—although difficult to manage—can be accomplished (Hoffman & Youngblood, 1999).

reciprocal socialization
Socialization that is bidirectional; children socialize parents, just as parents socialize children.

Reciprocal Socialization For many years, socialization between parents and children was viewed as a one-way process: children were considered to be the products of their parents' socialization techniques. Today, however, we view parent-child interaction as reciprocal (Hartup & Laursen, 1999; Schaffer, 1996). **Reciprocal socialization** *is socialization that is bidirectional. That is, children socialize parents just as parents socialize children.* For example, the interaction of mothers and their infants is symbolized as a dance or a dialogue in which successive actions of the partners are closely coordinated. This coordinated dance or dialogue can assume the form of mutual synchrony (each person's behavior depends on the partner's previous behavior) (Feldman, Greenbaum, & Yirmiya, 1999). Or it can be reciprocal in a more precise sense. The actions of the partners can be matched, as when one partner imitates the other or when there is mutual smiling.

When reciprocal socialization has been studied in infancy, mutual gaze, or eye contact, plays an important role in early social interaction. In one investigation, the mother and infant engaged in a variety of behaviors while they looked at each other. By contrast, when they looked away from each other, the rate of such behaviors dropped considerably (Stern & others, 1977). In sum, the behaviors of mothers and infants involve substantial interconnection, mutual regulation, and synchronization.

scaffolding
Parental behavior that supports children's efforts, allowing them to be more skillful than they would be if they relied only on their own abilities.

Scaffolding *is parental behavior that supports children's efforts, allowing them to be more skillful than they would be if they were to rely only on their own abilities.* Caregivers provide a positive, reciprocal framework in which they and their children interact. Parents' efforts to time interactions in such a way that the infant experiences turn-taking with the parents illustrates an early parental scaffolding behavior. For example, in the game peek-a-boo, mothers initially cover their babies. Then they remove the covering, and finally they register "surprise" at the reappearance. As infants become more skilled at peek-a-boo, pat-a-cake, and so big, there are other caregiver games that exemplify scaffolding and turn-taking sequences. In one study, infants who had more extensive scaffolding experiences with their parents (especially in the form of turn-taking) were more likely to engage in turn-taking when they interacted with their peers (Vandell & Wilson, 1988). Scaffolding is not confined to parent-infant interaction but can be used by parents to support children's achievement-related efforts in school by adjusting and modifying the amount and type of support that best suits the child's level of development.

The Family as a System As a social system, the family can be thought of as a constellation of subsystems defined in terms of generation, gender, and role (Kreppner, 2001; Minuchin, 2001). Divisions of labor among family members de-

fine particular subunits, and attachments define others. Each family member is a participant in several subsystems. Some are dyadic (involving two people), some polyadic (involving more than two people). The father and child represent one dyadic subsystem, the mother and father another. The mother-father-child represent one polyadic subsystem, the mother and two siblings another.

An organizational scheme that highlights the reciprocal influences of family members and family subsystems is shown in figure 7.4 (Belsky, 1981). As the arrows in the figure show, marital relations, parenting, and infant behavior and development can have both direct and indirect effects on each other. An example of a direct effect is the influence of the parents' behavior on the child. An example of an indirect effect is how the relationship between the spouses mediates the way a parent acts toward the child (McHale, Lauretti, & Kuerston-Hogan, 1999). For example, marital conflict might reduce the efficiency of parenting, in which case marital conflict would be an indirect effect on the child's behavior.

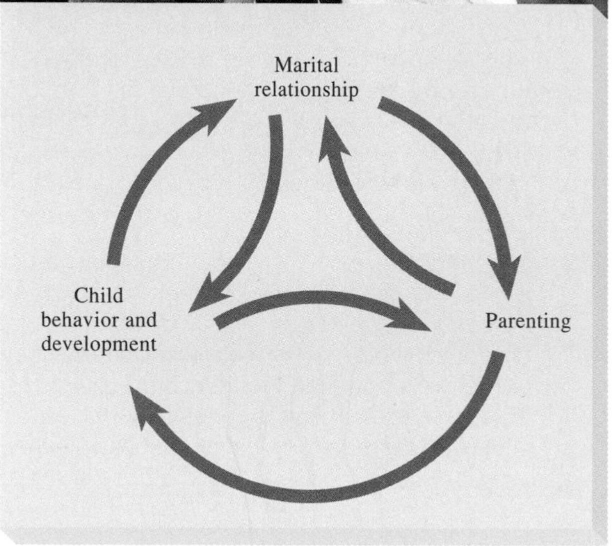

Figure **7.4**

Interaction Between Children and Their Parents: Direct and Indirect Effects

Maternal and Paternal Infant Caregiving Can fathers take care of infants as competently as mothers can? Observations of fathers and their infants suggest that fathers have the ability to act sensitively and responsively with their infants (Parke, 1995, 2000, 2001). The strongest evidence of the plasticity of male caregiving abilities is based on male primates, which are notoriously low in their interest in offspring. When forced to live with infants whose female caregivers are absent, the adult male competently rears the infants. Remember, however, that, although fathers can be active, nurturant, involved caregivers with their infants, many do not choose to follow this pattern (Eggebeen & Knoester, 2001; Silverstein, 2001).

Do fathers behave differently toward infants than mothers do? Maternal interactions usually center around child care activities—feeding, changing diapers, bathing. Paternal interactions are more likely to include play. Fathers engage in more rough-and-tumble play. They bounce infants, throw them up in the air, tickle them, and so on (Lamb, 1986, 2000; Lamb & others, 1999). Mothers do play with infants, but their play is less physical and arousing than that of fathers.

In stressful circumstances, do infants prefer their mother or father? In one study, 20 12-month-olds were observed interacting with their parents (Lamb, 1977). With both parents present, the infants preferred neither their mother nor their father. The same was true when the infants were alone with the mother or the father. However, the entrance of a stranger, combined with boredom and fatigue, produced a shift in the infants' social behavior toward the mother. In stressful circumstances, then, infants show a stronger attachment to the mother.

In one recent study, fathers were interviewed about their caregiving responsibilities when their children were 6, 15, 24, and 36 months of age (NICHD Early Child Care Research Network, 2000). A subset was videotaped during father-child play at 6 and 36 months. Caregiving activities (such as bathing, feeding, and dressing the child, and taking the child to day care) and sensitivity during play interactions (such as being responsive to the child's signals and needs, and expressing positive feelings) with their children were predicted by several factors. Fathers were more involved in caregiving when they worked fewer hours and mothers worked more hours, when fathers and mothers were younger, when mothers reported greater marital intimacy, and when the children were boys. Fathers who had less-traditional child-rearing beliefs and reported more marital intimacy were more sensitive during play.

Might the nature of parent-infant interaction be different in families that adopt nontraditional gender roles? This question was investigated by Michael Lamb and his colleagues (1982). They studied Swedish families in which the

Family Resources
Maternal Resources
The Fatherhood Project

Sociocultural Worlds of Development
Child Care Policy Around the World

Sheila Kammerman (1989, 2000a, b) has conducted extensive examinations of parental leave policies around the world. Parental leaves were first enacted as maternity policies more than a century ago to protect the physical health of working women at the time of childbirth. More recently, child rearing, parental, and paternity leaves were created in response not only to the needs of working women (and parents), but also because of concern for the child's well being. The European Union (EU) mandated a paid 14-week maternity leave in 1992 and a three-month parental leave in 1998.

Across cultures, policies vary in eligibility criteria, leave duration, benefit level, and the extent to which parents take advantage of these policies. The European policies just mentioned lead the way in creating new standards of parental leave. The United States is alone among advanced industrialized countries in the briefness of parental leave granted and among the few countries with unpaid leave (Australia and New Zealand are the others).

There are five different types of parental leave from employment:

- *Maternity Leave.* In some countries the pre-birth leave is compulsory as is a 6- to 10-week leave following birth.
- *Paternity Leave.* This is usually much briefer than maternity leave. It may be especially important when a second child is born and the first child requires care.
- *Parental Leave.* This is a gender-neutral leave that usually follows a maternity leave and allows either women or men to take advantage of the leave policy and share it or choose which of them will use it.
- *Child Rearing Leave.* In some countries, this is a supplement to a maternity leave or a variation on a parental leave. A child rearing leave is usually longer than a maternity leave and is typically paid at a much lower level.
- *Family Leave.* This covers reasons other than the birth of a new baby and can allow time off from employment to care for an ill child or other family members, time to accompany a child to school for the first time, or time to visit a child's school.

Sweden has one of the most extensive leave policies. Paid for by the government at 80 percent of wages, one year of parental leave is allowed (including maternity leave). Maternity leave may begin 60 days prior to expected birth of the baby and ends six weeks after birth. Another six months of parental leave can be used until the child's eighth birthday (Kammerman, 2000a). Virtually all eligible mothers take advantage of the leave policy and approximately 75 percent of eligible fathers take at least some part of the leave they are allowed. In addition, employed grandparents now also have the right to take time off to care for an ill grandchild.

Spain is an example of a relatively poor country that still provides substantial parental leave. Spain allows a 16-week paid maternity leave (paid at 100 percent of wages) at childbirth with up to 6 weeks prior to childbirth allowed. Fathers are permitted two days of leave.

The provision of day care in most developing countries has improved. In some locations in India, mobile day-care centers have provided intensive integrated child services to young children in slum settlements. *What are some of the most important ingredients of quality day care in any culture?*

fathers were the primary caregivers of their firstborn, 8-month-old infants. The mothers were working full-time. In all observations, the mothers were more likely to discipline, hold, soothe, kiss, and talk to the infants than were the fathers. These mothers and fathers dealt with their infants differently, along the lines of American fathers and mothers following traditional gender roles. Having fathers assume the primary caregiving role did not substantially alter the way they interacted with their infants. This may be for biological reasons or because of deeply ingrained socialization patterns in cultures.

Day Care

Many parents worry whether day care will adversely affect their children. They fear that day care will reduce their infants' emotional attachment to them, retard the infants' cognitive development, fail to teach them how to control anger, and allow them to be unduly influenced by their peers. How extensive is day care? Are the worries of these parents justified?

Today far more young children are in day care than at any other time in history; about 2 million children currently receive formal, licensed day care, and more than 5 million children attend kindergarten. Also, uncounted millions of children are cared for by unlicensed baby-sitters.

In Sweden, mothers or fathers are given paid maternity or paternity leave for up to 9 months. Sweden and many other European countries have well-developed child care policies. To learn about these policies, see the Sociocultural Worlds of Development box. In Sweden, day care for infants under 1 year of age is usually not a major concern because one parent is on paid leave for child care.

Because the United States does not have a policy of paid leave for child care, day care in the United States has become a major national concern. The type of day care that young children receive varies extensively (Burchinal & others, 1996; Scarr, 2000). Many day-care centers house large groups of children and have elaborate facilities. Some are commercial operations; others are nonprofit centers run by churches, civic groups, and employers. Child care is frequently provided in private homes, at times by child care professionals, at others by mothers who want to earn extra money.

A special contemporary interest of researchers who study day care is the role of poverty (Chase-Lansdale, Coley, & Grining, 2001; Huston, McLoyd, & Coll, 1994; Tout & Schmidt, 2001). In one study, day-care centers that served high-income children delivered better-quality care than did centers that served middle- and low-income children (Phillips & others, 1994). The indices of quality (such as teacher-child ratios) in subsidized centers for the poor were fairly good, but the quality of observed teacher-child interaction was lower than in high-income centers.

What constitutes a high-quality day-care program for infants? The demonstration program developed by Jerome Kagan and his colleagues (Kagan, Kearsley, & Zelazo, 1978) at Harvard University is exemplary. The day-care center included a pediatrician, a nonteaching director, and an infant-teacher ratio of 3 to 1. Teachers' aides assisted at the center. The teachers and aides were trained to smile frequently, to talk with the infants, and to provide them with a safe environment, which included many stimulating toys. No adverse effects of day care were observed in this project. More information about what to look for in a quality day-care center is presented in figure 7.5. Using such criteria, one study discovered that children who entered low-quality child care as infants were least likely to be socially competent in early childhood (less compliant, less self-controlled, less task-oriented, more hostile, and having more problems in peer interaction) (Howes, 1988). Unfortunately, children who come from families with few resources (psychological, social, and economic) are more likely to experience poor-quality day care than are children from more-advantaged backgrounds (Lamb, 1994).

Aware of the growing use of child care, the National Institute of Child Health and Human Development (NICHD) set out to develop a comprehensive, longitudinal study (a study that follows the same individuals over time, usually several years or more) that focuses on the child care experiences of children and their development (Burchinal, 2001; Owen, 2001; Peth-Pierce, 1998). The study began in 1991, and data were collected on a diverse sample of almost

Critical Thinking

Characteristics of Competent Caregivers

MUCH OF the health and well-being of infants is in the hands of caregivers. Whether the caregivers are parents or day-care personnel, these adults play significant roles in children's lives. What are the characteristics of competent caregivers? For one thing, competent caregivers enjoy caregiving. They reflect these positive feelings as they interact with infants and children. Try to come up with a list of five other characteristics of competent caregivers.

CAREERS IN LIFE-SPAN DEVELOPMENT

Rashmi Nakhre, Day-Care Director

RASHMI NAKHRE has two master's degreees—one in psychology, the other in child development—and is director of the Hattie Daniels Day Care Center in Wilson, North Carolina. At a recent ceremony, "Celebrating a Century of Women," Rashmi received the Distinguished Women of North Carolina Award for 1999–2000.

Nakhre first worked at the day-care center soon after she arrived in the United States 25 years ago. She says that she took the job initially because she needed the money but "ended up falling in love with my job." Nakhre has turned the Wilson, North Carolina, day-care center into a model for other centers. The Center almost closed several years after Nakhre began working there because of financial difficulties. Nakhre played a major role in raising funds not only to keep it open but to improve it. The Center provides quality day care for the children of many Latino migrant workers.

Rashmi Nakhre, day-care director, working with some of the children at her center.

What constitutes quality child care? The following recommendations were made by the National Association for the Education of Young Children (1986). They are based on a consensus arrived at by experts in early childhood education and child development. It is especially important for parents to meet the adults who will care for their child. They are responsible for every aspect of the program's operation.

1. The adult caregivers
   - The adults should enjoy and understand how infants and young children grow.
   - There should be enough adults to work with a group and to care for the individual needs of children. The recommended ratios of adult caregivers for children of different ages are as follows (Kontos & Wilcox-Herzog, 1997):

Age of children	Adult:children ratio
0–1 Year	1:3
1–2 Years	1:5
2–3 Years	1:6
3–4 Years	1:8
4–5 Years	1:10

   - Caregivers should observe and record each child's progress and development.
2. The program activities and equipment
   - The environment should foster the growth and development of young children working and playing together.
   - A good center should provide appropriate and sufficient equipment and play materials and make them readily available.
   - Infants and children should be helped to increase their language skills and to expand their understanding of the world.
3. The relation of staff to families and the community
   - A good program should consider and support the needs of the entire family. Parents should be welcome to observe, discuss policies, make suggestions, and work in the activities of the center.
   - The staff in a good center should be aware of and contribute to community resources. The staff should share information about community recreational and learning opportunities with families.
4. The design of the facility and the program to meet the varied demands of infants and young children, their families, and the staff
   - The health of children, staff, and parents should be protected and promoted. The staff should be alert to the health of each child.
   - The facility should be safe for children and adults.
   - The environment should be spacious enough to accommodate a variety of activities and equipment. More specifically, there should be a minimum of 35 square feet of usable playroom floor space indoors per child and 75 square feet of play space outdoors per child.

Figure 7.5
What Is High-Quality Day Care?

Summary Table 7.4
Social Contexts

Concept	Processes/ Related Ideas	Characteristics/Descriptions
The Family	The Transition to Parenthood	• This requires considerable adaptation and adjustment on the part of parents.
	Reciprocal Socialization	• Children socialize parents just as parents socialize children. • Mutual regulation and scaffolding are important aspects of reciprocal socialization.
	The Family as a System	• Belsky's model describes direct and indirect effects.
	Maternal and Paternal Infant Caregiving	• The mother's primary role when interacting with the infant is caregiving; the father's is playful interaction.
Day Care	A Basic Need of the American Family	• Day care has become a basic need of the American family. More children are in day care now than at any earlier point in history. • The quality of day care is uneven, and day care remains a controversial topic. Quality day care can be achieved and seems to have few adverse affects on children.
	NICHD study	• In the NICHD child-care study, infants from low-income families were found to receive the lowest quality of care. Also, higher quality of child care was linked with fewer child problems.

1,400 children and their families at 10 locations across the United States. Researchers are assessing children over seven years of their lives using multiple methods (trained observers, interviews, questionnaires, and testing) and measuring many facets of children's development, including physical health, cognitive development, and socioemotional development. Following are some of the results of this extensive study to date:

- The infants from low-income families were more likely to receive low-quality child care than were their higher-income counterparts. Quality of care was based on such characteristics as group size, child–adult ratio, physical environment, caregiver characteristics (such as formal education, specialized training, and child care experience), and caregiver behavior (such as sensitivity to children).
- Child care in and of itself neither adversely affected nor promoted the security of infants' attachments to their mothers. Certain child care conditions, in combination with certain home environments, did increase the probability that infants would be insecurely attached to their mothers. The infants who received either poor quality of care or more than 10 hours per week of care or were in more than one setting in the first 15 months of life, were more likely to be insecurely attached, but only if their mothers were less sensitive in responding to them.
- Child care quality, especially sensitive and responsive attention from caregivers, was linked with fewer child problems. The higher the quality of child care over the first three years of life (more positive language stimulation and interaction between the child and the provider), the greater the child's language and cognitive abilities. No cognitive benefits were found for the children in the exclusive care of their mother.

We have studied many ideas about social contexts. An overview of these ideas is presented in summary table 7.4.

National Child Care Information Center

NICHD Study of Early Child Care

We have all the knowledge necessary to provide absolutely first-rate child care in the United States. What is missing is the commitment and the will.

Edward Zigler
Contemporary Developmental Psychologist, Yale University

Chapter Review

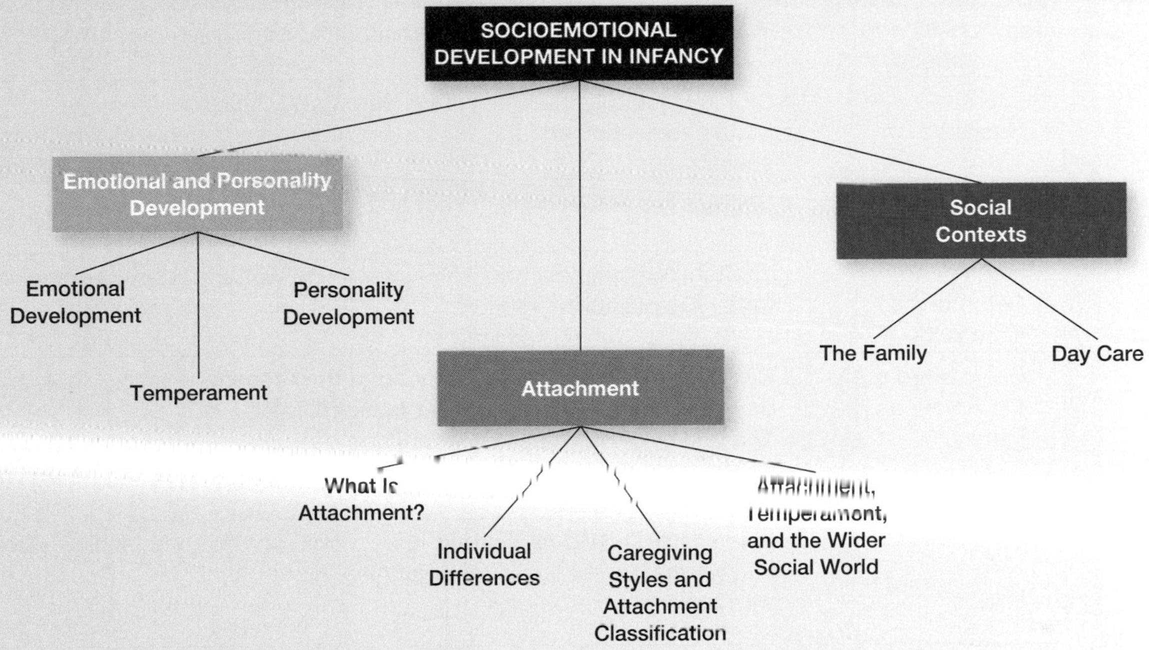

TO OBTAIN A DETAILED REVIEW OF THIS CHAPTER, STUDY THESE FOUR SUMMARY TABLES:

- Summary Table 7.1 Emotional Development page 181
- Summary Table 7.2 Temperament and Personality Development page 186
- Summary Table 7.3 Attachment page 191
- Summary Table 7.4 Social Contexts page 197

Key Terms

emotion 178
Maximally Discriminative Facial Movement Coding System (MAX) 179
basic cry 180
anger cry 180
pain cry 180
reflexive smile 180
social smile 180
stranger anxiety 180
temperament 182
easy child 182
difficult child 182
slow-to-warm-up child 182
attachment 186
secure attachment 188
Strange Situation 188
insecure avoidant babies 189
insecure resistant babies 189
disorganized babies 189
reciprocal socialization 192
scaffolding 192

Key People

Carroll Izard 179
John Watson 180
Mary Ainsworth 180
John Bowlby 180
Jacob Gewirtz 180
Alexander Chess and Stella Thomas 182
Mary Rothbart and John Bates 182
Erik Erikson 184
Margaret Mahler 185
Harry Harlow and Robert Zimmerman 187
Jerome Kagan 190

Taking It to the Net

1. Catherine is conducting a class for new parents at a local clinic. What advice should Catherine give the parents about how parenting practices can affect a child's inborn temperament?
2. Peter and Rachel are adopting a three-month old infant. What are some practical things they can do to help insure that their child develops a healthy attachment bond with them, in spite of not being with them in the first few months of life?
3. Veronica is anxious about choosing the best day care center for her child. What are the main things she should consider as she visits the facilities on her list?

Connect to www.mhhe.com/santrockld8 to research the answers and complete these exercises.

OLC Preview

To further test your knowledge of this chapter or to explore our extensive online resources that accompany *Life-Span Development,* eighth edition, please log on to the text's Online Learning Center at http://www.mhhe.com/santrockld8.com.

Section 4

Early Childhood

You are troubled at seeing him spend his early years doing nothing. What! Is it nothing to be happy? Is it nothing to skip, to play, to run about all day long? Never in his life will he be so busy as now.

Jean-Jacques Rousseau
Swiss-Born Philosopher, 18th Century

In early childhood, our greatest untold poem was being only 4 years old. We skipped and ran and played all day long, never in our lives so busy, busy being something we had not quite grasped yet. Who knew our thoughts, which we worked up into small mythologies all our own? Our thoughts and images and drawings took wings. The blossoms of our heart, no wind could touch. Our small world widened as we discovered new refuges and new people. When we said "I," we meant something totally unique, not to be confused with any other. Section Four consists of two chapters: "Physical and Cognitive Development in Early Childhood" (chapter 8) and "Socioemotional Development in Early Childhood" (chapter 9).

Chapter 8

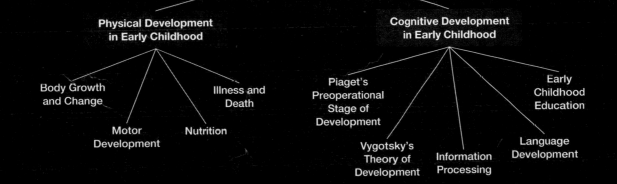

PHYSICAL AND COGNITIVE DEVELOPMENT IN EARLY CHILDHOOD

- **Physical Development in Early Childhood**
  - Body Growth and Change
  - Motor Development
  - Nutrition
  - Illness and Death
- **Cognitive Development in Early Childhood**
  - Piaget's Preoperational Stage of Development
  - Vygotsky's Theory of Development
  - Information Processing
  - Language Development
  - Early Childhood Education

Physical and Cognitive Development in Early Childhood

The greatest person ever known Is one all poets have outgrown; The poetry, innate, untold, Of being only four years old.

Christopher Morley
American Novelist, 20th Century

Images of Life-Span Development

Teresa Amabile and Her Creativity

TERESA AMABILE remembers that, when she was in kindergarten, she rushed in every day, excited and enthusiastic about getting to the easel and playing with all those bright colors and big paint brushes. Children also had free access to a clay table with all kinds of art materials on it. Teresa remembers going home every day and telling her mother she wanted to draw, paint, and play with crayons.

Teresa's kindergarten experience, unfortunately, was the high point of her artistic interest. The next year, she entered a traditional elementary school and things began to change. Instead of Teresa's having free access to art materials every day, art became just another subject, something she had for an hour and a half every Friday afternoon.

Week after week, all through elementary school, it was the same art class. According to Teresa, her elementary school art classes were very restricted and demoralizing. She recalls being given small reprints of painting masterpieces, a different one each week. For example, one week in the second grade, children were presented with Leonardo da Vinci's *Adoration of the Magi.* This was meant for art appreciation, but that's not how the teacher used it. Instead, the children were told to take out their art materials and try to copy the masterpiece. For Teresa, and the other children, this was an exercise in frustration. She says that young elementary school children do not have the skill development even to make all those horses and angels fit on the page, let alone make them look like the masterpiece. Teresa easily could tell that she was not doing well at what the teacher asked her to do.

The children were not given any help in developing their skills. Also, the teacher graded the children on the art they produced, adding evaluation pressure to the situation. Teresa was aware at that time that her motivation for doing artwork was being completely destroyed. She no longer wanted to go home and paint at the end of the day.

Teresa Amabile eventually obtained her Ph.D. in psychology and became one of the leading researchers on creativity. Her hope is that more elementary schools will not crush children's enthusiasm for creativity, the way hers did. So many young children, like Teresa, are excited about exploring and creating, but, by the time they reach the third or fourth grade, many don't like school, let alone have any sense of pleasure in their own creativity (Goleman, Kaufman, & Ray, 1993).

Children make considerable strides in physical and cognitive development in early childhood. After briefly charting some of the developmental milestones in body growth and motor development, we will explore health and illness in early childhood. Then we will study many different facets of young children's cognitive worlds.

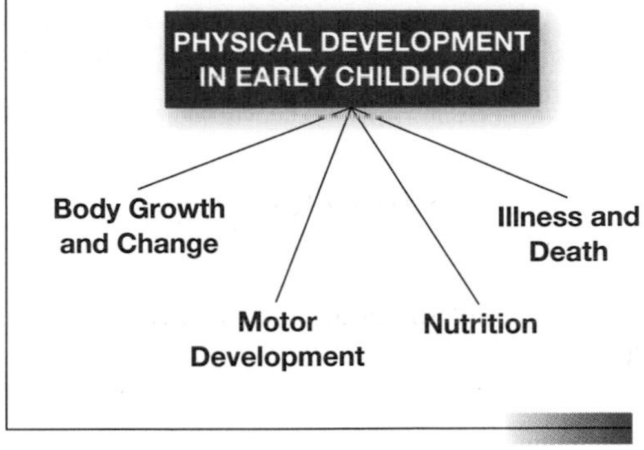

Physical Development in Early Childhood

Remember from chapter 5 that an infant's growth in the first year is rapid and follows cephalocaudal and proximodistal patterns ◀ P. 126. Around their first birthday, most infants begin to walk. During an infant's second year, the growth rate begins to slow down, but both gross and fine motor skills progress rapidly. The infant develops a sense of mastery through increased proficiency in walking and running. Improvement in fine motor skills—such as being able to turn the pages of a book one at a time—also contributes to the infant's sense of mastery in the second year. The growth rate continues to slow down in early childhood. Otherwise, we would be a species of giants.

Body Growth and Change

Body growth and change in early childhood involve height and weight, as well as the brain.

Preschool Growth and Development

Height and Weight

The average child grows 2½ inches in height and gains between 5 and 7 pounds a year during early childhood. As the preschool child grows older, the percentage of increase in height and weight decreases with each additional year. Girls are only slightly smaller and lighter than boys during these years, a difference that continues until puberty. During the preschool years, both boys and girls slim down as the trunks of their bodies lengthen. Although their heads are still somewhat large for their bodies, by the end of the preschool years most children have lost their top-heavy look. Body fat also shows a slow, steady decline during the preschool years. The chubby baby often looks much leaner by the end of early childhood. Girls have more fatty tissue than boys; boys have more muscle tissue.

The bodies of 5-year-olds and 2-year-olds are different. Notice how the 5-year-old not only is taller and weighs more, but also has a longer trunk and legs than the 2-year-old. *What might be some other physical dfferences in 2- and 5-year-olds?*

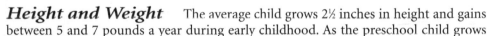

Growth patterns vary individually. Think back to your preschool years. This was probably the first time you noticed that some children were taller than you, some shorter; some were fatter, some thinner; some were stronger, some weaker. Much of the variation is due to heredity, but environmental experiences are involved to some extent. A review of the height and weight of children around the world concluded that the two most important contributors to height differences are ethnic origin and nutrition (Meredith, 1978). The urban, middle socioeconomic status, and firstborn children were taller than rural, lower socioeconomic status, and later-born children. The children whose mothers smoked during pregnancy were half an inch shorter than the children whose mothers did not smoke

during pregnacy. In the United States, African American children are taller than White children.

Why are some children unusually short? The culprits are congenital factors (genetic or prenatal problems), physical problems that develop in childhood, or emotional difficulties. For an example of a congenital factor, preschool children whose mothers smoked regularly during pregnancy are shorter than their counterparts whose mothers did not smoke. The physical problem of being chronically sick can make a child shorter than age-mates who are rarely sick. And regarding emotional difficulties, children who have been physically abused or neglected might not secrete adequate growth hormone, which can restrict their physical growth. In many cases, children with growth problems can be treated with hormones. Usually this treatment is directed at the pituitary gland, located at the base of the brain, which secretes growth-related hormones.

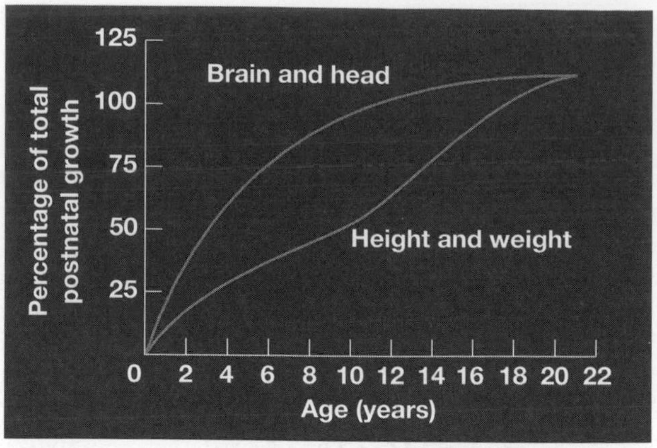

Figure **8.1**

Growth Curves for the Head and Brain and for Height and Weight

The more rapid growth of the brain and head can easily be seen. Height and weight advance more gradually over the first two decades of life.

The Brain One of the most important physical developments during early childhood is the continuing development of the brain and nervous system (Byrnes, 2001). Though the brain continues to grow in early childhood, it does not grow as rapidly as in infancy. By the time children have reached 3 years of age, the brain is three-quarters of its adult size. By age 5, the brain has reached about nine-tenths of its adult size.

The brain and the head grow more rapidly than any other part of the body. The top parts of the head, the eyes, and the brain grow faster than the lower portions, such as the jaw. Figure 8.1 reveals how the growth curve for the head and brain advances more rapidly than the growth curve for height and weight. At 5 years of age, when the brain has attained approximately 90 percent of its adult weight, the 5-year-old's total body weight is only about one-third of what it will be when the child reaches adulthood.

Some of the brain's increase in size is due to the increase in the number and size of nerve endings within and between areas of the brain. These nerve endings continue to grow at least until adolescence. Some of the brain's increase in size also is due to the increase in **myelination,** *in which nerve cells are covered and insulated with a layer of fat cells. This has the effect of increasing the speed of information traveling through the nervous system.* Some developmentalists believe myelination is important in the maturation of a number of children's abilities. For example, myelination in the areas of the brain related to hand-eye coordination is not complete until about 4 years of age. Myelination in the areas of the brain related to focusing attention is not complete until the end of the middle or late childhood.

myelination
The process in which the nerve cells are covered and insulated with a layer of fat cells, which increases the speed at which information travels through the nervous system.

Until recently, scientists have not had adequate technology to detect and map sensitive changes in the human brain as it develops. However, the creation of sophisticated brain-scanning techniques is allowing better detection of these changes (Blumenthal & others, 1999). Using these techniques, scientists recently have discovered that children's brains undergo dramatic anatomical changes between the ages of 3 and 15 (Thompson & others, 2000). By repeatedly obtaining brain scans of the same children for up to 4 years, they have found that children's brains experience rapid, distinct spurts of growth. The amount of brain material in some areas can nearly double in as little as a year, followed by a drastic loss of tissue as unneeded cells are purged and the brain continues to reorganize itself. The scientists found that the overall size of the brain did not increase dramatically from age 3 to 15. However, what did dramatically change were local patterns within the brain.

Researchers have found that from 3 to 6 years of age the most rapid growth takes place in the frontal lobe areas involved in planning and organizing new actions, and in maintaining attention to tasks. From age 6 through puberty, the most growth takes place in the temporal and parietal lobes, especially areas that play major roles in language and spatial relations.

Now that we have discussed some important growth changes in young children and in their brains, let's turn our attention their motor development.

Motor Development

Running as fast as you can, falling down, getting right back up and running just as fast as you can . . . building towers with blocks . . . scribbling, scribbling, and scribbling some more . . . cutting paper with scissors. During you preschool years, you probably developed the ability to perform all of these activities.

All the sun long I was running . . .

Dylan Thomas
Welsh Poet and Writer, 20th Century

Gross Motor Skills The preschool child no longer has to make an effort simply to stay upright and to move around. As children move their legs with more confidence and carry themselves more purposefully, moving around in the environment becomes more automatic.

At 3 years of age, children enjoy simple movements, such as hopping, jumping, and running back and forth, just for the sheer delight of performing these activities. They take considerable pride in showing how they can run across a room and jump all of 6 inches. The run-and-jump will win no Olympic gold medals, but for the 3-year-old the activity is a source of considerable pride and accomplishment.

At 4 years of age, children are still enjoying the same kind of activities, but they have become more adventurous. They scramble over low jungle gyms as they display their athletic prowess. Although they have been able to climb stairs with one foot on each step for some time, they are just beginning to be able to come down the same way.

At 5 years of age, children are even more adventuresome than when they were 4. It is not unusual for self-assured 5-year-olds to perform hair-raising stunts on practically any climbing object. Five-year-olds run hard and enjoy races with each other and their parents. A summary of development in gross motor skills during early childhood is shown in figure 8.2.

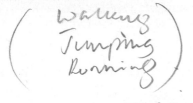

Development Milestones

You probably have arrived at one important conclusion about preschool children: they are very, very active. Indeed, 3-year-old children have the highest activity level of any age in the entire human life span. They fidget when they watch television. They fidget when they sit at the dinner table. Even when they sleep, they move around quite a bit. Because of their activity level and the development of large muscles, especially in the arms and legs, preschool children need daily exercise.

Fine Motor Skills At 3 years of age, children are still emerging from the infant ability to place and handle things. Although they have had the ability to pick

37–48 months	49–60 months	61–72 months
Throws ball underhanded (4′)	Bounces and catches ball	Throws ball (44′ boys; 25′ girls)
Pedals tricycle 10′	Runs 10′ and stops	Carries a 16-pound object
Catches large ball	Pushes/pulls a wagon/doll buggy	Kicks rolling ball
Completes forward somersault (aided)	Kicks 10″ ball toward target	Skips alternating feet
Jumps to floor from 12″	Carries 12-pound object	Roller skates
Hops three hops with both feet	Catches ball	Skips rope
Steps on footprint pattern	Bounces ball under control	Rolls ball to hit object
Catches bounced ball	Hops on one foot four hops	Rides two-wheel bike with training wheels

Figure **8.2**

The Development of Gross Motor Skills in Early Childhood

The skills are listed in the approximate order of difficulty within each age period.

up the tiniest objects between their thumb and forefinger for some time, they are still somewhat clumsy at it. Three-year-olds can build surprisingly high block towers, each block placed with intense concentration but often not in a completely straight line. When 3-year-olds play with a form board or a simple jigsaw puzzle, they are rather rough in placing the pieces. Even when they recognize the hole a piece fits into, they are not very precise in positioning the piece. They often try to force the piece in the hole or pat it vigorously.

By 4 years of age, children's fine motor coordination has improved substantially and become much more precise. Sometimes 4-year-old children have trouble building high towers with blocks because, in their desire to place each of the blocks perfectly, they may upset those already stacked. By age 5, children's fine motor coordination has improved further. Hand, arm, and body all move together under better command of the eye. Mere towers no longer interest the 5-year-old, who now wants to build a house or a church, complete with steeple, though adults might still need to be told what each finished projects is meant to be. A summary of the development of fine motor skills in early childhood is shown in figure 8.3.

37–48 months

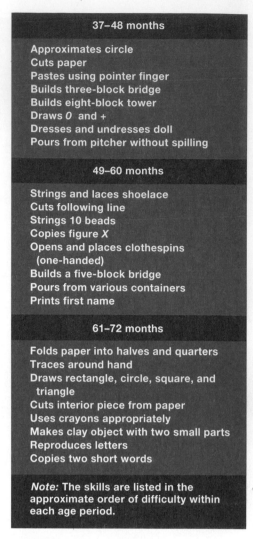

- Approximates circle
- Cuts paper
- Pastes using pointer finger
- Builds three-block bridge
- Builds eight-block tower
- Draws *O* and +
- Dresses and undresses doll
- Pours from pitcher without spilling

49–60 months

- Strings and laces shoelace
- Cuts following line
- Strings 10 beads
- Copies figure *X*
- Opens and places clothespins (one-handed)
- Builds a five-block bridge
- Pours from various containers
- Prints first name

61–72 months

- Folds paper into halves and quarters
- Traces around hand
- Draws rectangle, circle, square, and triangle
- Cuts interior piece from paper
- Uses crayons appropriately
- Makes clay object with two small parts
- Reproduces letters
- Copies two short words

Note: The skills are listed in the approximate order of difficulty within each age period.

Figure **8.3**
The Development of Fine Motor Skills in Early Childhood

Handedness For centuries, left-handers have suffered unfair discrimination in a world designed for right-handers. For many years, teachers forced all children to write with their right hand, even if they had a left-hand tendency. Fortunately, today most teachers let children write with the hand they favor.

Some children are still discouraged from using their left hand, even though many left-handed individuals have become very successful. Their ranks include Leonardo da Vinci, Benjamin Franklin, and Pablo Picasso. Each of these famous men was known for his imagination of spatial layouts, which may be stronger in left-handed individuals. Left-handed athletes also are often successful. Since there are fewer left-handed athletes, the opposition is not as accustomed to the style and approach of "lefties." Their tennis serve spins in the opposite direction, their curve ball in baseball swerves the opposite way, and their left foot in soccer is not the one children are used to defending against. Left-handed individuals also do well intellectually. In an analysis of the Scholastic Achievement Test (SAT) scores of more than 100,000 students, 20 percent of the top-scoring group was left-handed, which is twice the rate of left-handedness found in the general population (Bower, 1985). Clearly, many left-handed people are competent in a wide variety of human activities, ranging from athletic skills to intellectual accomplishments.

Preference for one hand is linked with the dominance of one brain hemisphere over the other in carrying out motor performance. Because most of the neural fibers cross over from one side of the brain to the other side of the body, right-handed individuals have a dominant left hemisphere. About 90 percent of individuals fall into this category—right-handed with the left hemisphere dominant for motor performance.

When does hand preference develop? Adults usually notice a child's hand preference during early childhood, but researchers have found handedness tendencies in the infant years. Even newborns have some preference for one side of their body over the other. In one study, 65 percent of the infants turned their head to the right when they were lying on their stomach in the crib (Michel, 1981). Fifteen percent preferred to face toward the left. These preferences for the right or left were related to later handedness. At about 7 months of age, infants prefer grabbing with one hand or the other, and this is also related to later handedness (Ramsay, 1980). By 2 years of age, about 10 percent of children favor their left hand. Many preschool children, though, use both hands, with a clear hand preference not completely distinguished until later in development. Some children use one hand for writing and drawing, and

Today, most teachers let children write with the hand they favor. *What are the main reasons children become left- or right-handed?*

Summary Table 8.1
Body Growth and Change, and Motor Development

Concept	Processes/ Related Ideas	Characteristics/Descriptions
Body Growth and Change	Height and Weight	• The average child grows 2½ inches in height and gains between 5 and 7 pounds a year during early childhood. Growth patterns vary individually, though. • Some children are unusually short because of congenital problems, a physical problem that develops in childhood, or emotional problems.
	The Brain	• By age 5, the brain has reached nine-tenths of its adult size. • Some of its increase in size is due to increases in the number and size of nerve endings, some to myelination. • Recently, researchers have found that changes in local patterns in the brain occur from 3 to 15 years of age. These changes often involve spurts of brain activity. From 3 to 6 years of age, the most rapid growth occurs in the frontal lobes; from 6 to puberty, the most substantial changes take place in the temporal and parietal lobes, especially those areas involving language and spatial relations. • Increasing brain maturation contributes to improved cognitive abilities.
Motor Development	Gross Motor Skills	• They increase dramatically during early childhood. • Children become increasingly adventuresome as their gross motor skills improve. • Young children's lives are extremely active, more active than at any other point in the life span.
	Fine Motor Skills	• They also improve substantially during early childhood.
	Handedness	• At one point, all children were taught to be right-handed. In today's world, the strategy is to allow children to use the hand they favor. • Left-handed children are as competent in motor skills and intellect as right-handed children. • Both genetic and environmental explanations of handedness have been given.

Handedness
Child Health Guide

the other hand for throwing a ball. My oldest daughter, Tracy, confuses the issue even further. She writes left-handed and plays tennis left-handed, but she plays golf right-handed. During early childhood, her handedness was still somewhat in doubt. My youngest daughter, Jennifer, was left-handed from early in infancy.

What is the origin of hand preference? Genetic inheritance and environmental experiences have been proposed as causes. In one study, a genetic interpretation was favored. The handedness of adopted children was not related to the handedness of their adoptive parents but was related to the handedness of their biological parents (Carter-Saltzman, 1980).

At this point we have studied many ideas about body growth and change, and motor development in early childhood. To review these ideas, see summary table 8.1.

Nutrition

Four-year-old Bobby is on a steady diet of double cheeseburgers, french fries, and chocolate milkshakes. Between meals, he gobbles up candy bars and marshmallows. He hates green vegetables. Only a preschooler, Bobby already has developed poor

nutritional habits. What are a preschool child's energy needs? What is a preschooler's eating behavior like?

Energy Needs

Feeding and eating habits are important aspects of development during early childhood. What children eat affects their skeletal growth, body shape, and susceptibility to disease. Recognizing that nutrition is important for the child's growth and development, the federal government provides money for school lunch programs. An average preschool child requires 1,700 calories per day.

Energy requirements for individual children are determined by the **basal metabolism rate (BMR),** *which is the minimum amount of energy a person uses in a resting state.* Energy needs of individual children of the same age, sex, and size vary. Reasons for these differences remain unexplained. Differences in physical activity, basal metabolism, and the efficiency with which children use energy are among the candidates for explanation.

basal metabolism rate (BMR)
The minimum amount of energy a person uses in a resting state.

Spinach: Divide into little piles. Rearrange again into new piles. After five or six maneuvers, sit back and say you are full.

Delia Ephron
American Writer and Humorist, 20th Century

Eating Behavior

Caregivers' special concerns involve the appropriate amount of fat in young children's diets (Troiano & Flegal, 1998). While some health-conscious parents may be providing too little fat in their infants' and children's diets, other parents are raising their children on diets in which the percentage of fat is far too high. Our changing lifestyles, in which we often eat on the run and pick up fast-food meals, contribute to the increased fat levels in children's diets. Most fast-food meals are high in protein, especially meat and dairy products. But the average American child does not need to be concerned about getting enough protein. What must be of concern is the vast number of young children who are being weaned on fast foods that are not only high in protein but also high in fat. Eating habits become ingrained very early in life; unfortunately, it is during the preschool years that many poeple get their first taste of fast food (Poulton & Sexton, 1996). The American Heart Association recommends that the daily limit for calories from fat should be approximately 35 percent, and many fast-food meals have fat content that is too high for good health.

This would be a better world for children if parents had to eat the spinach.

Groucho Marx
American Comedian, 20th Century

Being overweight can be a serious problem in early childhood (Behrman, Kliegman, & Jenson, 2000). Consider Ramón, a kindergartner who always begs to stay inside to help during recess. His teachers noticed that Ramón never joins the running games the small superheroes play as they propel themselves around the playground. Ramón is an overweight 4-year-old boy. Except for extreme cases of obesity, overweight preschool children are usually not encouraged to lose a great deal of weight but to slow their rate of weight gain so that they will grow into a more normal weight for their height by thinning out as they grow taller. Prevention of obesity in children includes helping children and parents see food as a way to satisfy hunger and nutritional needs, not as proof of love or as a reward for good behavior (Hill & Trowbridge, 1998). Snack foods should be low in fat, simple sugars, and salt, as well as high in fiber. Routine physical activity should be a daily occurrence. The child's life should be centered around activities, not meals (Kohl & Hobbs, 1998).

Exploring Childhood Obesity
Helping an Overweight Child
Preschoolers' Health
Harvard Center for Children's Health

Illness and Death

What are the leading causes of death in young children in the United States? How pervasive is death in young children around the world?

The United States

If a pediatrician stopped practicing 50 years ago and observed the illness and health of young children today, the sight might seem to be more science fiction than medical fact (Elias, 1998). The story of children's health in the past 50 years is a shift toward prevention and outpatient care.

CAREERS IN LIFE-SPAN DEVELOPMENT

Barbara Deloin, Pediatric Nurse

BARBARA DELOIN is a pediatric nurse in Denver, Colorado. She practices nursing in the Pediatric Oral Feeding Clinic and is involved in research as part of an irritable infant study for the Children's Hospital in Denver. She also is on the faculty of nursing at the Colorado Health Sciences Center. Barbara previously worked in San Diego where she was coordinator of the Child Health Program for the County of San Diego.

Her research interests focus on children with special health-care needs, especially high-risk infants and children and promoting positive parent-child experiences. She recently was elected president of the National Association of Pediatric Nurse Associates and Practitioners for the 2000–2001 term.

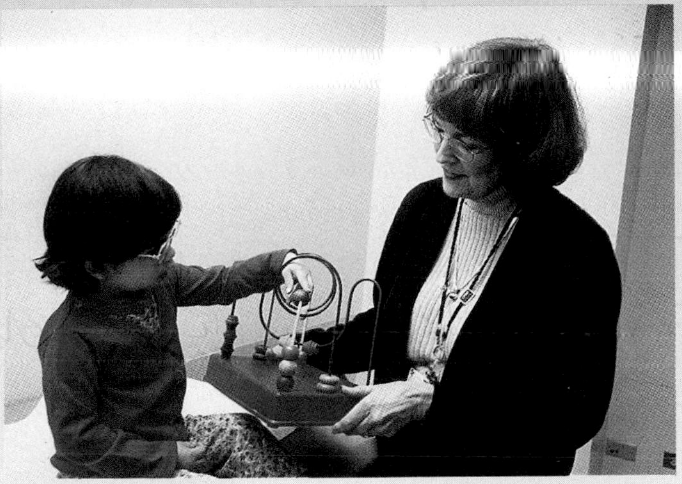

Barbara Deloin, working with a child with special health-care needs.

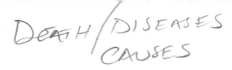

In recent decades, vaccines have nearly eradicated disabling bacterial meningitis and have become available to prevent measles, rubella, mumps, and chicken pox. From 1950 to the present, there has been a dramatic decline in deaths of children under the age of 5 from birth immaturity, birth defects, accidents, cancer, homicide, and heart disease. The disorders still most likely to be fatal during early childhood today are birth defects, cancer, and heart disease. Although the dangers of many diseases for children have been greatly diminished, it still is important for parents to keep young children on an immunization schedule.

Accidents are the leading cause of death in young children (National Center for Health Statistics, 1999). Motor vehicle accidents, drowning, falls, and poisoning are high on the list of causes of death in young children.

A special concern about children's illness and health is exposure to parental smoking. Exposure to tobacco smoke increases children's risk for developing a number of medical problems, including pneumonia, bronchitis, middle ear infections, burns, and asthma. It also may lead to cancer in adulthood (AAP Committee on Environmental Health, 1997). Because of such findings, most experts on children's health recommend that children be raised in a smoke-free environment.

Of special concern in the United States is the poor health status of many young children from low-income families (Karns, 2001). Approximately 11 million preschool children in the United States are malnourished. Their malnutrition places their health at risk. Many have less resistance to diseases, including minor ones, such as colds, and major ones, such as influenza.

The State of Illness and Health of the World's Children

A special concern is the state of children's illness and health in developing countries around the world. One death of every three in the world is the death of a child under the age of 5 (Grant, 1997). Every week, more than a quarter of a million children die in developing countries in a quiet carnage of infection and undernutrition. The leading cause of childhood death in the world is dehydration and malnutrition as a result of diarrhea. Millions of children killed by diarrhea every year could be saved if parents had available a low-cost breakthrough known as **oral rehydration therapy (ORT)**. *This treatment involves a range of techniques designed to prevent dehydration during episodes of diarrhea by giving the child fluids by mouth.*

oral rehydration therapy (ORT)
Treatment to prevent dehydration during episodes of diarrhea by giving fluids by mouth.

Most child malnutrition and deaths could now be prevented by parental actions that are almost universally affordable and based on knowledge that is already available. Making sure that parents know they can improve their children's health by adequate birth spacing, care during pregnancy, breast-feeding, immunization, special feeding before and after illness, and regular checkups of the children's weight can overcome many causes of malnutrition and poor growth (Radford, 2001).

At this point we have studied a number of ideas about nutrition and illness and and death in young children. To review these ideas, see summary table 8.2. Now that we have explored young children's physical development, let's turn our attention to their cognitive development.

A simple child
That lightly draws its breath,
What should it know of death?

William Wordsworth
English Poet, 19th Century

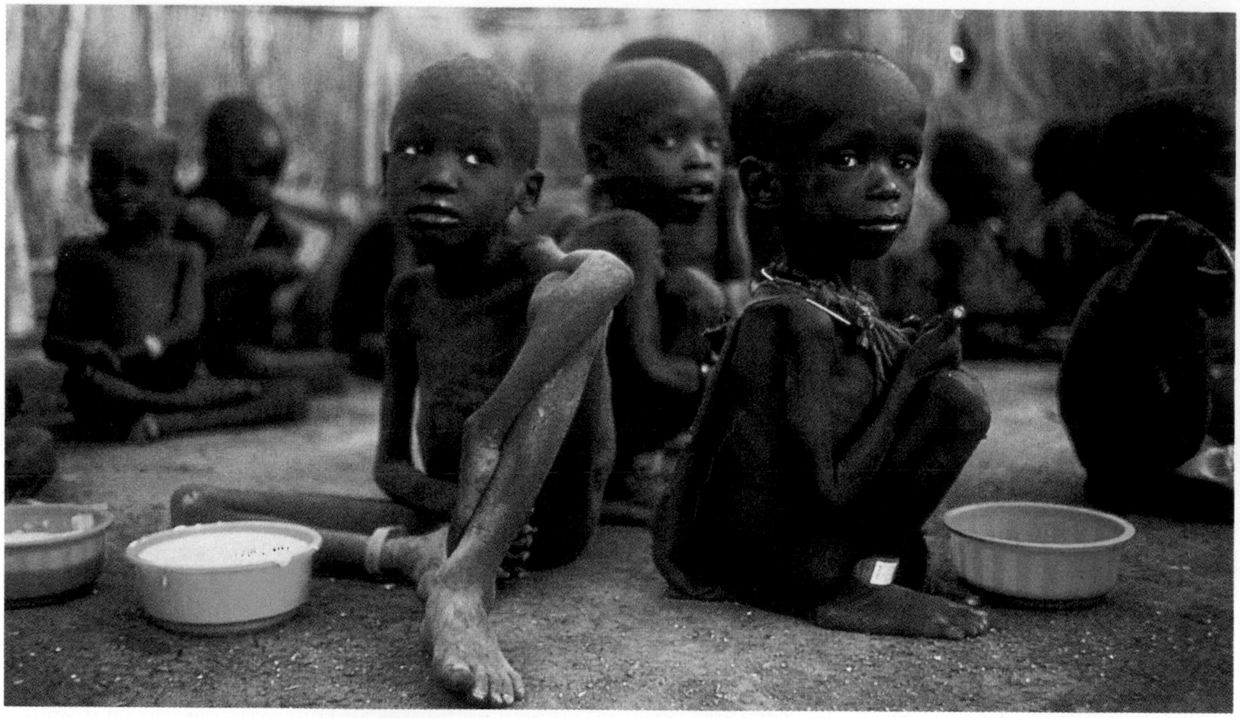

Ten percent of all children born in Bangladesh die before reaching the age of 5 from dehydration and malnutrition brought about by diarrhea. *What can be done about this?*

Summary Table 8.2
Nutrition; Illness and Death

Concept	Processes/ Related Ideas	Characteristics/Descriptions
Nutrition	Energy Needs	• They increase as children go through the childhood years. • Energy requirements vary according to basal metabolism, rate of growth, and level of activity.
	Eating Behavior	• A special concern is that too many young children are being raised on diets that are too high in fat. • The child's life should be centered around activities, not meals.
Illness and Death	The United States	• In recent decades, vaccines have virtually eradicated many diseases that once were responsible for the deaths of many young children. • The disorders still most likely to be fatal for young children are birth defects, cancer, and heart disease. • Accidents are the leading cause of death in young children. A special concern is the poor health status of many young children in low-income families. They often have less resistance to disease, including colds and influenza, than do their higher-socioeconomic status counterparts.
	Illness and Health in the World's Children	• One of every three deaths in the world is that of a child under 5. Every week, more than a quarter of a million children die in developing countries. • The most frequent cause of children's death is diarrhea. Oral rehydration therapy can be used to prevent death from diarrhea. • Most child malnutrition and death could be prevented by parental actions that are affordable and based on knowledge available today.

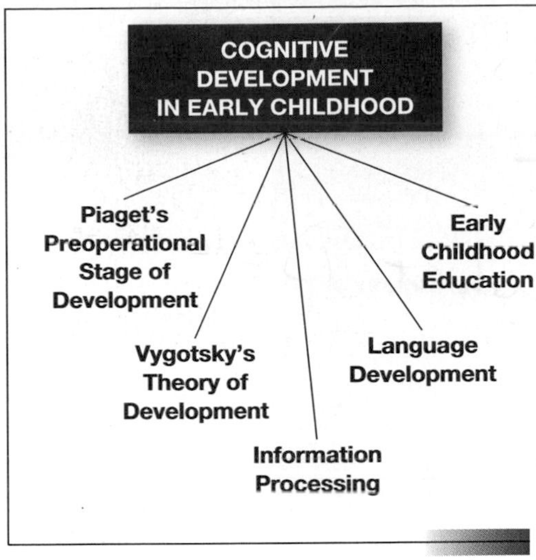

Cognitive Development in Early Childhood

The cognitive world of the preschool child is creative, free, and fanciful. Preschool children's imagination works overtime, and their mental grasp of the world improves. Our coverage of cognitive development in early childhood focuses on Piaget's stage of preoperational thought, information processing, language development, Vygotsky's theory of development, and early childhood education.

Piaget's Preoperational Stage of Development

What characterizes preoperational thought? What happens during the substages of symbolic function and intuitive thought?

Remember from chapter 6 that, during Piaget's sensorimotor stage of development, the infant progresses in the ability to organize and coordinate sensations and perceptions with physical movements and actions ◀ P. 158. What kinds of changes take place in the preoperational stage?

The preoperational stage stretches from approximately 2 to 7 years of age. It is a time when stable concepts are formed, mental reasoning emerges, egocentrism begins strongly and then weakens, and magical beliefs are constructed. Preoperational thought is anything but a convenient waiting period for concrete operational thought. However, the label *preoperational* emphasizes that the child at this stage does not yet think in an operational way. What are operations? **Operations** *are internalized sets of actions that allow the child to do mentally what before she did physically.* For example, mentally adding and subtracting numbers are examples of operations.

operations
In Piaget's theory, an internalized set of actions that allows a child to do mentally what she formerly did physically.

Thought in the preoperational stage is flawed and not well organized. Preoperational thought is the beginning of the ability to reconstruct at the level of thought what has been established in behavior. Preoperational thought also involves a transition from primitive to more sophisticated use of symbols. Preoperational thought can be divided into two substages: the symbolic function substage and the intuitive thought substage.

Symbolic Function Substage The **symbolic function substage** *is the first substage of preoperational thought, occurring roughly between the ages of 2 and 4. In this substage, the young child gains the ability to mentally represent an object that is not present.* The ability to engage in such symbolic thought is called symbolic function, and it vastly expands the child's mental world. Young children use scribbled designs to represent people, houses, cars, clouds, and so on. Other examples of symbolism in early childhood are language and the prevalence of pretend play. In sum, the ability to think symbolically and to represent the world mentally predominates in this early substage of preoperational thought (DeLoache, 2001). However, although young children make distinct progress during this substage, their thought still has several important limitations, two of which are egocentrism and animism.

symbolic function substage
Piaget's first substage of preoperational thought, in which the child gains the ability to mentally represent an object that is not present (between 2 and 4 years of age).

Egocentrism *is a salient feature of preoperational thought. It is the inability to distinguish between one's own perspective and someone else's perspective.* The following telephone conversation between 4-year-old Mary, who is at home, and her father, who is at work, typifies Mary's egocentric thought:

egocentrism
The inability to distinguish between one's own perspective and someone else's (salient feature of the first substage of preoperational thought).

Father: Mary, is Mommy there?
Mary: (Silently nods)
Father: Mary, may I speak to Mommy?
Mary: (Nods again silently)

Mary's response is egocentric in that she fails to consider her father's perspective before replying. A nonegocentric thinker would have responded verbally.

Piaget and Barbel Inhelder (1969) initially studied young children's egocentrism by devising the three mountains task (see figure 8.4). The child walks around the model of

Symbolic Thinking

the mountains and becomes familiar with what the mountains look like from different perspectives, and they can see that there are different objects on the mountains. The child is then seated on one side of the table on which the mountains are placed. The experimenter moves a doll to different locations around the table, at each location asking the child to select, from a series of photos, the one photo that most accurately reflects the view the doll is seeing. Children in the preoperational stage often pick their view from where they are sitting, rather than the doll's view. Perspective-taking does not develop uniformly in preschool children, who frequently show perspective skills on some tasks but not others.

Animism, *another limitation within preoperational thought, is the belief that inanimate objects have "lifelike" qualities and are capable of action.* A young child might show animism by saying, "That tree pushed the leaf off, and it fell down," or "The sidewalk made me mad; it made me fall down." A young child who uses animism fails to distinguish the appropriate occasions for using human and nonhuman perspectives.

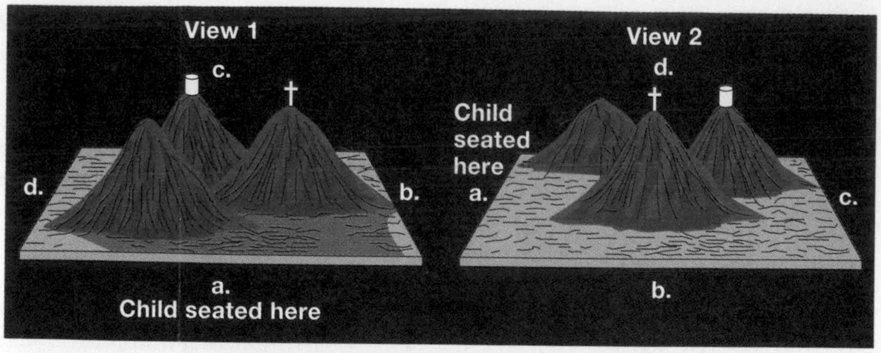

Figure **8.4**

The Three Mountains Task

View 1 shows the child's perspective from where he or she is sitting. View 2 is an example of the photograph the child would be shown, mixed in with others from different perspectives. To correctly identify this view, the child has to take the perspective of a person sitting at spot (*b*). Invariably, a preschool child who thinks in a preoperational way cannot perform this task. When asked what a view of the mountains looks like from position (*b*), the child selects a photograph taken from location (*a*), the child's view at the time.

Possibly because young children are not very concerned about reality, their drawings are fanciful and inventive. Suns are blue, skies are yellow, and cars float on clouds in their symbolic, imaginative world. One 3½-year-old looked at a scribble he had just drawn and described it as a pelican kissing a seal (see figure 8.5a). The symbolism is simple but strong, like abstractions found in some modern art. As Picasso commented, "I used to draw like Raphael but it has taken me a lifetime to draw like young children." In the elementary school years, a child's drawings become more realistic, neat, and precise (see figure 8.5b). Suns are yellow, skies are blue, and cars travel on roads (Winner, 1986).

animism
The belief that inanimate objects have "lifelike" qualities and are capable of action.

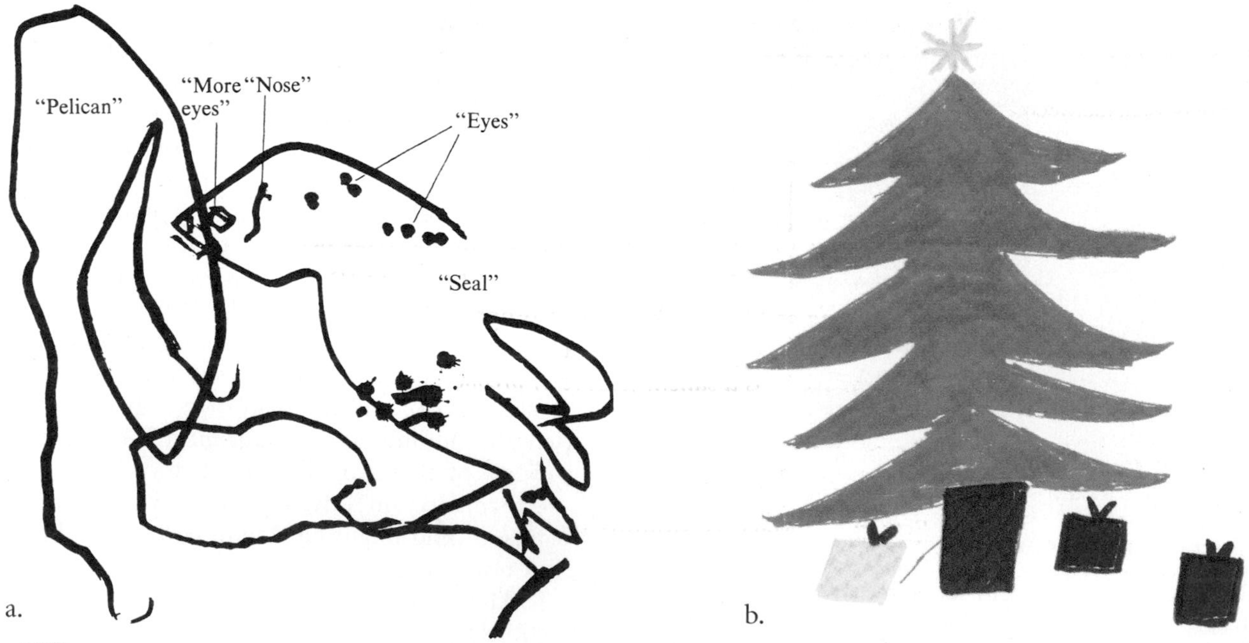

Figure **8.5** **The Symbolic Drawings of Young Children**

(*a*) A 3½-year-old's symbolic drawing. Halfway into this drawing, the 3½-year-old artist said it was "a pelican kissing a seal." (*b*) This 11-year-old's drawing is neater and more realistic but also less inventive.

Intuitive Thought Substage

Tommy is 4 years old. although he is starting to develop his own ideas about the world he lives in, his ideas are still simple, and he is not very good at thinking things out. He has difficulty understanding events he knows are taking place but which he cannot see. His fantasized thoughts bear little resemblance to reality. He cannot yet answer the question "What if . . . ?" in any reliable way. For example, he has only a vague idea of what would happen if a car were to hit him. He also has difficulty negotiating traffic because he cannot do the mental calculations necessary to estimate whether an approaching car will hit him when he crosses the road.

intuitive thought substage
Piaget's second substage of preoperational thought, in which children begin to use primitive reasoning and want to know the answers to all sorts of questions (between 4 and 7 years of age).

centration
The focusing of attention on one characteristic to the exclusion of all others.

conservation
In Piaget's theory, awareness that altering an object's or a substance's appearance does not change its basic properties.

The **intuitive thought substage** *is the second substage of preoperational thought, occurring between approximately 4 and 7 years of age. In this substage, children begin to use primitive reasoning and want to know the answers to all sorts of questions.* Piaget called this time period *intuitive* because, on the one hand, young children seem so sure about their knowledge and understanding, yet they are so unaware of how they know what they know. That is, they say they know something but know it without the use of rational thinking.

One characteristic of preoperational thought is **centration**—*the focusing, or centering, of attention on one characteristic to the exclusion of all others.* Centration is most clearly evidenced in young children's lack of **conservation**—*awareness that altering an object's or a substance's appearance does not change its basic properties.* To adults, it is obvious that a certain amount of liquid stays the same, regardless of a container's shape. But this is not at all obvious to young children. Instead, they are struck by the height of the liquid in the container. In the conservation task—Piaget's most famous test—a child is presented with two identical beakers, each filled to the same level with liquid (see figure 8.6). The child is asked if these beakers have the same amount of liquid, and she usually says yes. Then the liquid from one beaker is poured into a third beaker, which is taller and thinner than the first two. The child is then asked if the amount of liquid in the tall, thin beaker is equal to that which remains in one of the original beakers. Children who are less than 7 or 8 years old usually say no and justify their answers in terms of the differing height or width of the beakers. Older children usually answer yes and justify their answers appropriately ("If you poured the milk back, the amount would still be the same").

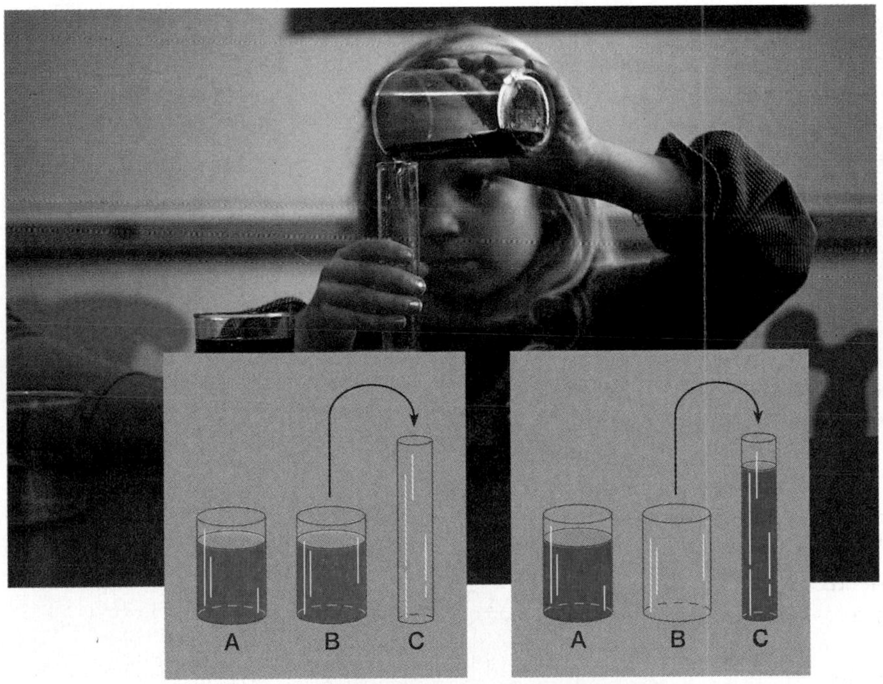

a. b.

Figure **8.6**

Piaget's Conservation Task

The beaker test is a well-known Piagetian test to determine whether a child can think operationally—that is, can mentally reverse actions and show conservation of the substance. *(a)* Two identical beakers are presented to the child. Then, the experimenter pours the liquid from B into C, which is taller and thinner than A or B. *(b)* The child is asked if these beakers (A and C) have the same amount of liquid. The preoperational child says no. When asked to point to the beaker that has more liquid, the preoperational child points to the tall, thin beaker.

In Piaget's theory, failing the conservation of liquid task is a sign that children are at the preoperational stage of cognitive development. Passing this test is a sign that they are at the concrete operational stage. In Piaget's view, the preoperational child fails to show conservation not only of liquid but also of number, matter, length, volume, and area (figure 8.7 portrays several of these). Children often vary in their performance on different conservation tasks. Thus, a child might be able to conserve volume but not number.

The child's inability to mentally reverse actions is an important characteristic of preoperational thought. For example, in the conservation of matter shown in figure 8.7, preoperational children say that the longer shape has more clay because they assume that "longer is more." Pre-

Type of conservation	Initial presentation	Manipulation	Preoperational child's answer
Number	Two identical rows of objects are shown to the child, who agrees they have the same number.	One row is lengthened and the child is asked whether one row now has more objects.	Yes, the longer row.
Matter	Two identical balls of clay are shown to the child. The child agrees that they are equal.	The experimenter changes the shape of one of the balls and asks the child whether they still contain equal amounts of clay.	No, the longer one has more.
Length	Two sticks are aligned in front of the child. The child agrees that they are the same length.	The experimenter moves one stick to the right, then asks the child if they are equal in length.	No, the one on the top is longer.

Figure **8.7**

Some Dimensions of Conservation: Number, Matter, and Length

operational children cannot mentally reverse the clay-rolling process to see that the amount of clay is the same in both the shorter ball shape and the longer stick shape.

Some developmentalists do not believe Piaget was entirely correct in his estimate of when children's conservation skills emerge. For example, Rochel Gelman (1969) showed that, when the child's attention to relevant aspects of the conservation task is improved, the child is more likely to conserve. Gelman has also demonstrated that attentional training on one dimension, such as number, improves the preschool child's performance on another dimension, such as mass. Thus, Gelman believes that conservation appears earlier than Piaget thought and that attention is especially important in explaining conservation.

Yet another characteristic of preoperational children is that they ask a barrage of questions. Children's earliest questions appear around the age of 3, and by the age of 5 they have just about exhausted the adults around them with "why" questions. The child's questions yield clues about mental development and reflect intellectual curiosity. These questions signal the emergence of the child's interest in reasoning and figuring out why things are the way they are. Following are some samples of the questions children ask during the questioning period of 4 to 6 years of age (Elkind, 1976):

- "What makes you grow up?"
- "What makes you stop growing?"
- "Why does a lady have to be married to have a baby?"
- "Who was the mother when everybody was a baby?"
- "Why do leaves fall?"
- "Why does the sun shine?"

At this point we have discussed a number of characteristics of preoperational thought. To help you remember these characteristics, see figure 8.8.

"I still don't have all the answers, but I'm beginning to ask the right questions."

More symbolic than sensorimotor thought
Inability to engage in operations; can't mentally reverse actions; lacks conservation skills
Egocentric (inability to distinguish between own perspective and someone else's)
Intuitive rather than logical

Figure 8.8
Characteristics of Preoperational Thought

WWW
Vygotsky on Language and Thought
Vygotsky: Revolutionary Scientist

Vygotsky's Theory of Development

In chapter 2, we described the basic principles of Vygotsky's theory (Tappan, 1998): (1) the child's cognitive skills can be understood only when they are developmentally analyzed and interpreted, (2) cognitive skills are mediated by words, language, and forms of discourse, which serve as psychological tools for facilitating and transforming mental activity, and (3) cognitive skills have their origins in social relations and are embedded in a sociocultural background ◄ P. 37. Here we expand on Vygotsky's theory of development, beginning with his unique ideas about the zone of proximal development.

zone of proximal development (ZPD)
Vygotsky's term for tasks too difficult for children to master alone but that can be mastered with assistance.

The Zone of Proximal Development

The **zone of proximal development (ZPD)** *is Vygotsky's term for the range of tasks too difficult for a child to master alone but which can be learned with the guidance and assistance of adults or more skilled children.* Thus, the lower limit of the ZPD is the level of problem solving reached by the child working independently. The upper limit is the level of additional responsibility the child can accept with the assistance of an able instructor (see figure 8.9). Vygotsky's emphasis on the ZPD underscores his belief in the importance of social influences, especially instruction, on children's cognitive development. An example of the ZPD is an adult helping a child put together a jigsaw puzzle.

The ZPD captures the child's cognitive skills that are in the process of maturing and can be accomplished only with the assistance of a more skilled person (Panofsky, 1999). Vygotsky (1962) called these the "buds" or "flowers" of development, to distinguish them from the "fruits" of development, which the child already can accomplish independently.

scaffolding
In cognitive development, Vygotsky used this term to describe the changing support over the course of a teaching session, with the more skilled person adjusting guidance to fit the child's current performance level.

Scaffolding

In chapter 7, we discussed the concept of scaffolding in socioemotional development. Here we describe its role in cognitive development. Closely linked to the idea of zone of proximal development is the concept of **scaffolding.** *Scaffolding means changing the level of support. Over the course of a teaching session, a more skilled person (teacher or more advanced peer of the child) adjusts the amount of guidance to fit the student's current performance level.* When the task the student is

learning is new, the more skilled person may use direct instruction. As the student's competence increases, less guidance is given.

Dialogue is an important tool of scaffolding in the zone of proximal development (John-Steiner & Mahn, 1996; Tappan, 1998). Vygotsky viewed children as having rich but unsystematic, disorganized, and spontaneous concepts. These meet with the skilled helper's more systematic, logical, and rational concepts. As a result of the meeting and dialogue between the child and the skilled helper, the child's concepts become more systematic, logical, and rational. For example, a dialogue might take place between a teacher and a child when the teacher uses scaffolding to help the child understand a concept like "transportation."

Language and Thought Vygotsky (1962) believed that young children use language not only for social communication but also to plan, guide, and monitor their behavior in a self-regulatory fashion. The use of language for self-regulation is called inner speech or private speech. For Piaget private speech is egocentric and immature, but for Vygotsky it is an important tool of thought during the early childhood years.

Vygotsky believed that language and thought initially develop independently of each other and then merge. He said that all mental functions have external, or social, origins. Children must use language to communicate with others before they can focus inward on their own thoughts. Children also must communicate externally and use language for a long period of time before the transition from external to internal speech takes place. This transition period occurs between the ages of 3 and 7 years of age and involves talking to oneself. After a while, the self-talk becomes second nature to children, and they can act without verbalizing. When this occurs, children have internalized their egocentric speech in the form of inner speech, which becomes their thoughts. Vygotsky believed that children who use a lot of private speech are more socially competent than those who don't. He argued that private speech represents an early transition in becoming more socially communicative.

Vygotsky's view challenged Piaget's ideas on language and thought. Vygotsky said that language, even in its earliest forms, is socially based. By contrast, Piaget emphasized young children's egocentric and nonsocial speech. For Vygotsky, when young children talk to themselves, they are using language to govern their behavior and guide themselves. Piaget believed that such self-talk reflects immaturity. However, researchers have found support for Vygotsky's view of the positive role of private speech in children's development (Winsler, Diaz, & Montero, 1997).

Evaluating and Comparing Vygotsky's and Piaget's Theories Vygotsky's theory came later than Piaget's theory, so it has not yet been evaluated as thoroughly. However, Vygotsky's theory already has been embraced by many teachers and has been successfully applied to education. His view of the importance of sociocultural influences on children's development fits with the current belief that it is important to evaluate the contextual factors in learning (Gojdamaschko, 1999). However, criticisms of his theory also have emerged. For example, some critics say he overemphasizes the role of language in thinking.

We already have mentioned several comparisons of Vygotsky's and Piaget's theories, such as Vygotsky's emphasis on the importance of inner speech in development and Piaget's view that such speech is immature. We also said earlier that both Vygotsky's and Piaget's theories are constructivist, emphasizing that children actively construct knowledge and understanding, rather than being passive receptacles.

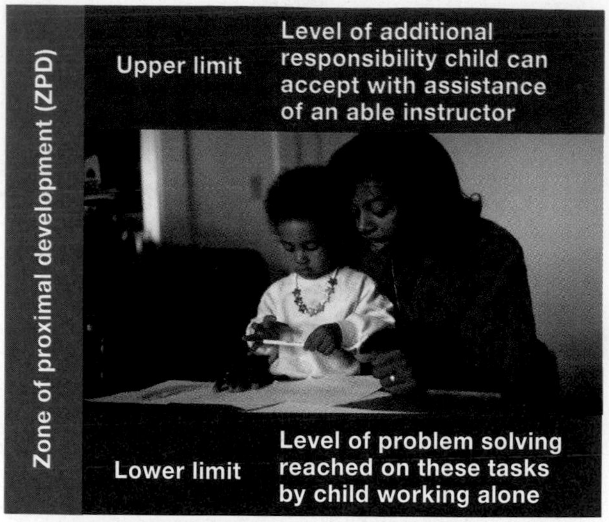

Figure **8.9**

Vygotsky's Zone of Proximal Development

Vygotsky's zone of proximal development has a lower limit and an upper limit. Tasks in the ZPD are too difficult for the child to perform alone. They require assistance from an adult or a skilled child. As children experience the verbal instruction or demonstration, they organize the information in their existing mental structures, so they can eventually perform the skill or task alone.

Lev Vygotsky (1896–1934), shown here with his daughter, believed that children's cognitive development is advanced through social interaction with skilled individuals embedded in a sociocultural backdrop. *How is Vygotsky's theory different from Piaget's?*

social constructivist approach An approach that emphasizes the social contexts of learning and that knowledge is mutually built and constructed. Vygotsky's theory reflects this approach.

Although both theories are constructivist, Vygotsky's is a **social constructivist approach,** *which emphasizes the social contexts of learning and that knowledge is mutually built and constructed.* Piaget's theory does not have this social emphasis. The following analogies reflect the differing degree of social emphasis in the theories. Moving from Piaget to Vygotsky, the conceptual shift is from the individual to collaboration, social interaction, and sociocultural activity (Rogoff, 1998). For Piaget, children construct knowledge by transforming, organizing, and reorganizing previous knowledge. For Vygotsky, children construct knowledge through social interaction with others (Hogan & Tudge, 1999). The implication of Piaget's theory for teaching is that children need support to explore their world and discover knowledge. The main implication of Vygotsky's theory for teaching is that students need many opportunities to learn with the teacher and more skilled peers. In both Piaget's and Vygotsky's theories, teachers serve as facilitators and guides, rather than as directors and molders of learning. Figure 8.10 compares Vygotsky's and Piaget's theories.

Teaching Strategies Based on Vygotsky's Theory

Following are some ways that Vygotsky's theory can be incorporated in the classroom:

1. *Use the child's zone of proximal development in teaching.* Teaching should begin toward the zone's upper limit, where the child is able to reach the goal only through close collaboration with the instructor. With adequate continuing instruction and practice, the child organizes and masters the behavioral sequences required to perform the target skill. As the instruction continues, the performance transfers from the teacher to the child. The teacher gradually reduces the explanations, hints, and demonstrations until the student is able to perform the skill alone. Once the goal is achieved, it may become the foundation for the development of a new ZPD.
2. *Use scaffolding.* Look for opportunities to use scaffolding when children need help with self-initiated learning activities (Elicker, 1996). Also use scaffolding to help children move to a higher level of skill and knowledge. Offer just enough assistance. You might ask, "What can I do to help you?" Or simply observe the child's intentions and attempts, smoothly providing support when needed. When the child hesitates, offer encouragement. And encourage the child to practice the skill. You may watch and appreciate the child's practice or offer support when the child forgets what to do.
3. *Use more-skilled peers as teachers.* Remember that it is not just adults that Vygotsky believed are important in helping children learn important skills. Children also benefit from the support and guidance of more-skilled children.
4. *Monitor and encourage children's use of private speech.* Be aware of the developmental change from externally talking to oneself when solving a problem during the preschool years to privately talking to oneself in the early elementary school years. In the elementary school years, encourage children to internalize and self-regulate their talk to themselves.
5. *Assess the child's ZPD, not IQ.* Like Piaget, Vygotsky did not believe that formal, standardized tests are the best way to assess children's learning. Rather, Vygotsky argued that assessment should focus on determining the child's zone of proximal development. The skilled helper presents the child with tasks of varying difficulty to determine the best level at which to begin instruction. The ZPD is a measure of learning potential. IQ, also a measure of learning potential, emphasizes that intelligence is a property of the child. By contrast, ZPD emphasizes that learning is interpersonal. It is inappropriate to say that the child *has* a ZPD. Rather, a child *shares* a ZPD with a more skilled individual.

In Vygotsky's theory, an important point is that children need to learn the skills that will help them do well in their culture. Vygotsky believed that this should be accomplished through interaction with more-skilled members of the culture, such as this Mexican-American girl learning to read with the guidance of her mother. *What are some other ways that skilled members of a society can interact with young children?*

Topic	Vygotsky	Piaget
Constructivism	Social constructivist	Cognitive constructivist
Stages	No general stages of development proposed	Strong emphasis on stages (sensorimotor, preoperational, concrete operational, and formal operational)
Key processes	Zone of proximal development, language, dialogue, tools of the culture	Schema, assimilation, accommodation, operations, conservation, classification, hypothetical-deductive reasoning
Role of language	A major role; language plays a powerful role in shaping thought	Language has a minimal role; cognition primarily directs language
View on education	Education plays a central role, helping children learn the tools of the culture.	Education merely refines the child's cognitive skills that already have emerged.
Teaching implications	Teacher is a facilitator and guide, not a director; establish many opportunities for children to learn with the teacher and more-skilled peers	Also views teacher as a facilitator and guide, not a director; provide support for children to explore their world and discover knowledge

Figure **8.10**

Comparison of Vygotsky's and Piaget's Theories

6. *Transform the classroom with Vygotskian ideas.* What does a Vygotskian classroom look like? The Kamehameha Elementary Education Program (KEEP) is based on Vygotsky's theory (Tharp, 1994). The zone of proximal development is the key element of instruction in this program. Children might read a story and then interpret its meaning. Many of the learning activities take place in small groups. All children spend at least 20 minutes each morning in an activity setting called "Center One." In this context, scaffolding is used to improve children's literary skills. The instructor asks questions, responds to students' queries, and builds on the ideas that

"Can we hurry up and get to the test? My short-term memory is better than my long-term memory."

students generate. Thousands of low-income children have attended KEEP public schools in Hawaii, on an Arizona Navajo Indian reservation, and in Los Angeles. Compared with a control group of non-KEEP children, the KEEP children participate more actively in classroom discussion, are more attentive in class, and have higher reading achievement (Tharp & Gallimore, 1988).

Piaget's cognitive development theory and Vygotsky's sociocultural cognitive theory have provided important insights about the way young children think and how this thinking changes developmentally. Next, we will explore a third major view on children's thinking—information processing.

Information Processing

Not only can we study the stages of cognitive development that young children go through, as Piaget did, but we can also study the different cognitive processes of young children's mental worlds. Two important aspects of preschool children's thoughts are attention and memory. What are the limitations and advances in attention and memory during the preschool years?

Attention

In chapter 6, we discussed attention in the context of habituation, which is something like being bored ◀ P. 163. In habituation, the infant becomes disinterested in a stimulus and no longer attends to it. Habituation involves a decrement in attention. Dishabituation is the recovery of attention. The importance of these aspects of attention in infancy for the preschool years was underscored by research showing that both decrement and recovery of attention, when measured in the first 6 months of infancy, were associated with higher intelligence in the preschool years (Bornstein & Sigman, 1986).

Although the infant's attention has important implications for cognitive development in the preschool years, the child's ability to pay attention changes significantly during the preschool years. The toddler wanders around, shifts attention from one activity to another, and seems to spend little time focused on any one object or event. By comparison, the preschool child might be observed watching television for a half hour. In one study, young children's attention to television in the natural setting of the home was videotaped (Anderson & others, 1985). Ninety-nine families comprising 460 individuals were observed for 4,672 hours. Visual attention to television dramatically increased during the preschool years.

One deficit in attention during the preschool years concerns those dimensions that stand out, or are *salient,* compared with those that are relevant to solving a problem or performing well on a task. For example, a problem might have a flashy, attractive clown that presents the directions for solving a problem. Preschool children are influenced strongly by the features of the task that stand out, such as the flashy, attractive clown. After the age of 6 or 7, children attend more efficiently to the dimensions of the task that are relevant, such as the directions for solving a problem. Developmentalists believe this change reflects a shift to cognitive control of attention, so that children act less impulsively and reflect more.

Memory

Memory is a central process in children's cognitive development; it involves the retention of information over time. Conscious memory comes into play as early as 7 months of age, although children and adults have little or no memory of events experienced before the age of 3 ◀ P. 165. Among the interesting questions about memory in the preschool years are those involving short-term memory.

short-term memory
The memory component in which individuals retain information for 15 to 30 seconds, assuming there is no rehearsal.

Short-Term Memory

In **short-term memory,** *individuals retain information for up to 15 to 30 seconds, assuming there is no rehearsal.* Using rehearsal (repeating information after it has been presented), we can keep information in short-term mem-

There are some positive aspects to television's influence on children, however. For one, television presents children with a world that is different from the one in which they live. It exposes children to a wider variety of viewpoints and information than they might get from only their parents, teachers, and peers. And some television programs have educational and developmental benefits (Anderson & others, 2001; Wright & others, 2001). One of television's major programming attempts to educate children is *Sesame Street.* It is designed to teach children both cognitive and social skills. The program began in 1969 and is still going strong. *Sesame Street* demonstrates that education and entertainment can work well together (Wright, 1995). Through *Sesame Street,* children experience a world of learning that is both exciting and entertaining (Fisch & Traglio, 2001).

"Mrs. Horton, could you stop by school today?"

Amount of Television Watching by Children

Just how much television do young children watch? They watch a lot, and they seem to be watching more all the time. In the 1950s, 3-year-old children watched television for less than 1 hour a day; 5-year-olds watched just over 2 hours a day. But, in the 1970s, preschool children watched television for an average of 4 hours a day; elementary school children watched television for a long as 6 hours a day (Friedrich & Stein, 1973). In the 1990s, children are averaging 11 to 28 hours of television per week, which is more than for any other activity except sleep.

As shown in figure 9.6, considerably more children in the United States than their counterparts in other developed countries watch television for long periods. For example, seven times as many 9-year-olds in the United States as their counterparts in Switzerland watch television more than 5 hours a day.

A special concern is the extent to which children are exposed to violence and aggression on television. Up to 80 percent of the prime-time shows include violent acts, including beatings, shootings, and stabbings. The frequency of violence increases on the Saturday morning cartoon shows, which average more than 25 violent acts per hour.

Effects of Television on Children's Aggression and Prosocial Behavior

What are the effects of television violence on children's aggression? Does television merely stimulate a child to go out and buy a *Star Wars* ray gun, or can it trigger an attack on a playmate? When children grow up, can television violence increase the likelihood they will violently attack someone?

In one longitudinal study, the amount of violence viewed on television at age 8 was significantly related to the seriousness of criminal acts performed as an adult (Huesmann, 1986). In another study, long-term exposure to television violence was significantly

WWW

Children's Television Workshop

Television and Violence

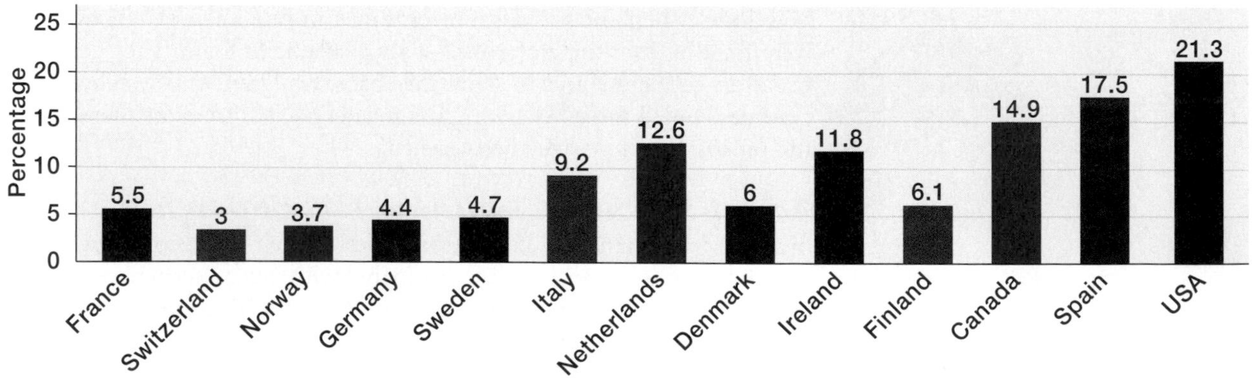

Figure **9.6**

Percentage of 9-Year-Old Children Who Report Watching More Than Five Hours of Television per Weekday

Critical Thinking: Developing Parental Guidelines for Children's TV Viewing

MANY PARENTS do not carefully monitor their children's TV viewing and do not discuss the content of TV shows with them. Develop a series of guidelines that you would recommend to parents that you believe would help them make television a more positive influence in their children's lives. Consider such factors as the child's age, the child's activities other than TV, the parents' patterns of interaction with their children, and types of television shows.

related to the likelihood of aggression in 1,565 12- to 17-year-old boys (Belson, 1978). Boys who watched the most aggression on television were the most likely to commit a violent crime, swear, be aggressive in sports, threaten violence toward another boy, write slogans on walls, or break windows. These studies are *correlational,* so we cannot conclude from them that television violence is *associated with* aggressive behavior. In one experiment, children were randomly assigned to one of two groups: one watched television shows taken directly from violent Saturday morning cartoon offerings on 11 different days; the second group watched television cartoon shows with all of the violence removed (Steur, Applefield, & Smith, 1971). The children were then observed during play at their preschool. The preschool children who saw the TV cartoon shows with violence kicked, choked, and pushed their playmates more than did the preschool children who watched nonviolent TV cartoon shows. Because the children were randomly assigned to the two conditions (TV cartoons with violence versus nonviolent TV cartoons), we can conclude that exposure to TV violence *caused* the increased aggression in the children in this investigation.

Some critics argue that the effects of television violence do not warrant the conclusion that TV violence causes aggression (Freedman, 1984). However, many experts argue that TV violence can induce aggressive or antisocial behavior in children (Murray, 2000; Strasburger, 1995). Of course, television is not the *only* cause of aggression. There is no *one* single cause of any social behavior. Aggression, like all other social behaviors, has a number of determinants.

Children need to be taught critical viewing skills to counter the adverse effects of television violence. In one study, elementary school children were randomly assigned to either an experimental or a control group (Huesmann & others, 1983). In the experimental group, children assisted in making a film to help children who had been fooled or harmed by television. The children also composed essays that focused on how television is not like real life and why it is bad to imitate TV violence or watch too much television. In the control group, the children received no training in critical viewing skills. The children who were trained in critical viewing skills developed more negative attitudes about TV violence and reduced their aggressive behavior.

Television also can teach children that it is better to behave in positive, prosocial ways than in negative, antisocial ways. Aimee Leifer (1973) demonstrated that television is associated with prosocial behavior in young children. She selected a number of episodes from the television show *Sesame Street* that reflected positive social interchanges. She was especially interested in situations that taught children how to use their social skills. For example, in one interchange, two men were fighting over the amount of space available to them. They gradually began to cooperate and to share the space. Children who watched these episodes copied these behaviors, and in later social situations they applied the prosocial lessons they had learned.

Children in Switzerland watch less television than children in other industrialized nations. *What effects might this have on their development?*

Television and Cognitive Development Children bring various cognitive skills and abilities to their television viewing experience (Rabin & Dorr, 1995). Compared with older children, preschoolers and young children comprehend less central content and more incidental content, and have difficulty making inferences about content. These youngest viewers have difficulty representing television content and often fill in their incomplete representations with stereotypes and familiar scripts derived from their limited general knowledge of television and the world. They usually are not aware that some content is intended to sell them toys and breakfast cereal, rather than to entertain and inform them. Older children have a better understanding in all of these areas, but

ory for a much longer period. One method of assessing short-term memory is the memory-span task. If you have taken an IQ test, you were probably exposed to one of these tasks. You simply hear a short list of stimuli—usually digits—presented at a rapid pace (one per second, for example). Then you are asked to repeat the digits. Research with the memory-span task suggests that short-term memory increases during early childhood. For example, in one investigation, memory span increased from about 2 digits in 2- to 3-year-old children to about 5 digits in 7-year-old children, yet, between 7 and 13 years of age, memory span increased only by 1½ digits (Dempster, 1981). Keep in mind, though, the individual differences in memory span, which is why IQ and various aptitude tests are used.

Why are there differences in memory span because of age? Rehearsal of information is important; older children rehearse the digits more than younger children. Speed and efficiency of processing information are important, too, especially the speed with which memory items can be identified. For example, in one study, children were tested on their speed at repeating words presented orally (Case, Kurland, & Goldberg, 1982). Speed of repetition was a powerful predictor of memory span. Indeed, when the speed of repetition was controlled, the 6-year-olds' memory spans were equal to those of young adults.

The speed-of-processing explanation highlights an important point in the information-processing perspective. That is, the speed with which a child processes information is an important aspect of the child's cognitive abilities.

How Accurate Are Young Children's Long-Term Memories? In chapter 6, we saw that most of infants' memories are fragile and, for the most part, short-lived—except for their memory of perceptual-motor actions, which can be substantial (Mandler, 2000). Does their memory become more accurate when they grow into the early childhood years? Yes, it does. Young children can remember a great deal of information if they are given appropriate cues and prompts (Hamond & Fivush, 1991). Sometimes the memories of preschoolers seem to be erratic, but these memory inconsistencies might be to some degree the result of inadequate prompts and cues.

Children's Eyewitness Testimony

Currently there is controversy over whether young children should be allowed to testify in court (Bruck & Ceci, 1999; Eisen, Quas & Goodman, 2001). Increasingly, young children are being allowed to testify, especially if they are the only witnesses to abuse, a crime, and so forth. Young children can be led, under certain circumstances, to incorporate false suggestions into their accounts of even intimate body touching by adults (Hyman & Loftus, 2001). Because of the possibility that they can be led into saying something false, young children should be interviewed by a neutral professional.

Strategies In chapter 2, we mentioned that an especially important aspect of the information-processing approach is the use of good strategies P. 38. What are strategies? They consist of using deliberate mental activities to improve the processing of information. For example, rehearsing information and organizing it are two typical strategies that older children and adults use to remember more effectively. Do young children use rehearsal and organization to remember? For the most part, they do not (Miller & Seier, 1994).

Do young children use any strategies at all? Problem-solving strategies in young children were the focus of research by Zhe Chen and Robert Siegler (2000). They placed young children at a table where an attractive toy was placed too far away for the child to reach it (they were not allowed to crawl on the table). On the table, between the child and the toy, were six potential tools (see figure 8.11). Only one of them was likely to be useful in obtaining the toy. After initially assessing the young

Four-year old Jennifer Royal was the only eyewitness to one of her playmate's being shot to death. She was allowed to testify in open court and the clarity of her statements helped to convict the gunman. *What are some issues involved in whether young children should be allowed to testify in court?*

Figure **8.11**

The Toy-Retrieval Task in the Study of Young Children's Problem-Solving Strategies

The child needed to choose the target tool (in this illustration, the toy rake) to pull in the toy (in this case, the turtle).

children's attempts to obtain the toy on their own, the experimenters either modeled how to obtain the toy (using the appropriate tool) or gave the child a hint (telling the child to use the particular tool). These 2-year-olds learned the strategy and subsequently mapped the strategy onto new problems. Admittedly, this is a rather simple problem-solving strategy—selecting the best tool to use to obtain a desired toy—but it does document that children as young as 2 years of age can learn a strategy.

The Young Child's Theory of Mind

Theory of mind *refers to individuals' thoughts about how mental processes work.* Even young children are curious about the nature of the human mind, and developmentalists have shown a flurry of interest in children's thoughts about what the human mind is like (Flavell, 1999; Wellman, 1997, 2000, 2001).

Children's developing knowledge of the mind includes (Flavell, Miller, & Miller, 1993, 2001) the awareness that

- The mind exists
- The mind has connections to the physical world
- The mind can represent objects and events accurately or inaccurately
- The mind actively interprets reality and emotions

theory of mind
Individuals' thoughts about how mental processes work.

Becoming Aware That the Mind Exists One of the child's first developmental acquisitions about the mind is knowing that such a thing as a mind even exists. By the age of 2 or 3, children refer to needs, emotions, and mental states—"I need my Mommy," "Tom feels bad," and "I forgot my doll." They also use intentional action or desire words, such as *wants to.* Cognitive terms such as *know, remember,* and *think* usually appear after perceptual and emotional terms but often are used by the age of 3. Later, children make finer distinctions between such mental phenomena as guessing versus knowing, believing versus fantasizing, and intending versus not on purpose.

Understanding Cognitive Connections to the Physical World At about 2 or 3 years of age, children develop the knowledge that people can be "cognitively connected" to objects and events in the external world. They understand that people can see them, hear them, like them, want them, fear them, and so on. By their awareness of the connections among stimuli, mental states, and behavior, young children possess a rudimentary mental theory of human action. On the input side, 2-year-olds sometimes hide objects, so that another person cannot see them, which involves manipulating stimuli to produce a certain perceptual state in another person. On the output side (mind to behavior), older 2-year-old children can predict action and emotional expression based on desires, as when comprehending that a child wants a cookie, tries to get one, and is happy if successful. However, 2-year-olds cannot predict actions based on beliefs. For instance, Ann wants to find her toy but can't find it in one location. Children predict she would be sad and look for it in another location, but they don't know that Ann's beliefs about possible locations influence where she will look.

In addition to inferring connections from stimuli to mental states, or from mental states to behavior or emotion, 3-year-olds can often infer mental states from behavior. When children use spontaneous language, they sometimes explain action

by referring to mental causes. For example, a 3-year-old explains that he has paint on his hands because he thought his hands were paper. This gives new meaning to the term *finger painting!* In sum, children acquire knowledge about links between stimuli, mental states, and behavior fairly early in their development.

Young children also develop an understanding that the mind is separate from the physical world. They know that the mind is different from rocks, roller skates, and even the head. For example, a 3-year-old is told that one boy has a cookie and that another boy is thinking about a cookie. The 3-year-old knows which cookie can be seen by others, touched, eaten, shared, and saved for later. Three-year-olds also know that they can fantasize about things that don't exist, such as Martians, ghosts, and dragons.

Detecting Accuracies/Inaccuracies of the Mind Children also develop an understanding that the mind can represent objects and events accurately or inaccurately. Understanding of false beliefs usually appears in 4- or 5-year-old children, but not 3-year-olds. Consider the following story acted out for children with dolls. A boy places some chocolate in a blue cupboard and then goes out to play. While he is outside, his mother moves the chocolate to a green cupboard. When the boy returns and wants the chocolate, the subject is asked where the boy will look for it. Three-year-olds usually say, "The green cupboard," where the chocolate actually is, even though the boy had no way of knowing the chocolate had been moved. Thus, 3-year-olds do not understand that a person acts on the basis of what he or she believes to be true, rather than what they themselves know to be true. By contrast, 4- and 5-year-old children usually understand false beliefs.

Understanding the Mind's Active Role in Emotion and Reality Finally, children also develop an understanding that the mind actively mediates the interpretation of reality and the emotion experienced. The shift from viewing the mind as passive to viewing it as active appears in children's knowledge that prior experiences influence current mental states, which in turn affect emotions and social inferences. In the elementary school years, children change from viewing emotions as caused by external events without any mediation by internal states to viewing emotional reactions to an external event as influenced by a prior emotional state, experience, or expectations. For example, 6-year-old children do not understand that a child would be sad or scared when his friends suggest they ride bikes if that child previously was almost hit by a car while riding his bike.

In summary, young children are very curious about the human mind (Wellman, 2000). By the age of 3, they turn some of their thoughts inward and understand that they and others have internal mental states. Beginning at about 3 years of age, children also show an understanding that the internal desires and beliefs of a person can be connected to that person's actions. Young children also know that they cannot physically touch thoughts, they believe that a person has to see an object to know it, and they grasp that their mental image of an object represents something that exists in the world.

CAREERS IN LIFE-SPAN DEVELOPMENT

Helen Schwe, Developmental Psychologist and Toy Designer

HELEN SCHWE obtained a Ph.D. from Stanford University in developmental psychology. She now spends her days talking with computer engineers and designing "smart" toys for children. Smart toys are designed to improve children's problem-solving and symbolic thinking skills.

During graduate school Helen worked part-time for Hasbro Toys, testing its children's software on preschoolers. Her first job after graduate school was with Zowie Entertainment, which recently was purchased by LEGO.

While with Zowie and now LEGO, Helen helped to design the pirate game called "Redbeard's Pirate Quest" and many other toys for children. Helen says that even in a toy's most primitive stage of development, you see children's creativity in responding to challenges and their joy when they solve a problem. Along with conducting experiments and focus groups at different stages of a toy's development, Helen also helps assess the age-appropriateness of a toy. Most of her current work focuses on 3- to 5-year-old children. (Schlegel, 2000).

Helen Schwe, a developmental psychologist, with some of the toys she designed.

Summary Table 8.3
Piaget's Preoperational Stage of Development, Vygotsky's Theory of Development, and Information Processing

Concept	Processes/ Related Ideas	Characteristics/Descriptions
Piaget's Preoperational Stage of Development	Definition	• This is the beginning of the ability to reconstruct at the level of thought what has been established in behavior, and a transition from primitive to more sophisticated use of symbols. • The child does not yet think in an operational way.
	Symbolic Function Substage	• This substage occurs between 2 and 4 years of age and is characterized by symbolic thought, egocentrism, and animism.
	Intuitive Thought Substage	• This substage stretches from 4 to 7 years of age. It is called intuitive because children seem so sure about their knowledge yet are so unaware of how they know what they know. • The preoperational child lacks conservation and asks a barrage of questions.
Vygotsky's Theory of Development	Zone of Proximal Development	• This is Vygotsky's term for the range of tasks too difficult for children to master alone but which can be learned with the guidance and assistance of adults and more skilled children.
	Scaffolding	• This involves changing support over the course of a teaching session, with the more skilled person adjusting guidance to fit the student's current performance level.
	Language and Thought	• Vygotsky believed that language plays a key role in guiding cognition.
	Evaluating and Comparing Vygotsky's and Piaget's Theories	• Vygotsky's theory has increasingly been applied to education. • Comparisons of Vygotsky's and Piaget's theories involve constructivism, metaphors for learning, stages, key processes, role of language, views on education, and teaching implications. Vygotsky's theory is social constructivist, Piaget's cognitive constructivist.
	Teaching Strategies	• These focus on using the child's zone of proximal development, using scaffolding and more skilled peers as teachers, monitoring and encouraging children's use of private speech, assessing the child's ZPD rather than IQ, and transforming the classroom with Vygotskian ideas.
Information Processing	Attention	• The child's attention dramatically improves during early childhood. • One deficit in attention in early childhood is that the child attends to the salient rather than the relevant features of a task.
	Memory	• Significant improvement in short-term memory occurs during early childhood. • With good probes and prompts, young children's long-term memories can be accurate, although young children can be led into developing false memories.
	Strategies	• Young children usually don't use strategies to remember, but they can learn rather simple problem-solving strategies.
	The Young Child's Theory of Mind	• Young children develop thoughts about how mental processes work. These include that the mind exists, has connections to the physical world, can represent objects and events, and actively interprets reality and emotion.

At this point we have studied many ideas about Piaget's preoperational stage of development, Vygotsky's theory of development, and information processing. To review these ideas, see summary table 8.3.

Language Development

Language Development
Language Growth
Pragmatic Language

Young children's understanding sometimes gets way ahead of their speech. One 3-year-old, laughing with delight as an abrupt summer breeze stirred his hair and tickled his skin, commented, "It did winding me!" Adults would be understandably perplexed if a young child ventured, "Anything is not to break, only plates and glasses," when she meant, "Nothing is breaking except plates and glasses." Many of the oddities of young children's language sound like mistakes to adult listeners. However, from the children's point of view, they are not mistakes. They represent the way young children perceive and understand their world at that point in their development.

As children go through the early childhood years, their grasp of the rule systems that govern language increase. These rule systems include morphology (the meaningfulness of words or parts of words), semantics (the meanings of phrases and sentences), and pragmatics (rules of conversation).

As children move beyond two-word utterances, they know morphology rules. Children begin using the plurals and possessive forms of nouns (such as *dogs* and *dog's*). They put appropriate endings on verbs (such as *-s* when the subject is third-person singular, *-ed* for the past tense, and *-ing* for the present progressive tense). They use prepositions (such as *in* and *on*), articles (such as *a* and *the*), and various forms of the verb *to be* (such as "I *was* going to the store"). Some of the best evidence for changes in children's use of morphological rules occurs in their overgeneralizations of the rules. Have you ever heard a preschool child say "foots" instead of "feet," or "goed" instead of "went"? If you do not remember having heard such oddities, talk to some parents who have young children, or to the young children themselves. You will hear some interesting errors in the use of morphological rule endings.

In a classic experiment, Jean Berko (1958) presented preschool children and first-grade children with cards such as the one shown in figure 8.12. Children were asked to look at the card while the experimenter read aloud the words on the card. Then the children were asked to supply the missing word. This might sound easy, but Berko was interested not just in the children's ability to recall the right word but also in their ability to say it "correctly" (with the ending that was dictated by morphological rules). "Wugs" would be the correct response for the card in figure 8.12.

Although the children's answers were not perfect, they were much better than chance. Moreover, the children demonstrated their knowledge of morphological rules, not only with the plural forms of nouns ("There are two wugs") but with possessive forms of nouns and the third-person singular and past-tense forms of verbs. What makes Berko's study impressive is that most of the words were fictional, created for the experiment. Thus, the children could not base their responses on remembering past instances of hearing the words. Instead, they were forced to rely on *rules.*

Regarding semantics, as children move beyond the two-word stage, their knowledge of meanings also rapidly advances. The speaking vocabulary of a 6-year-old child ranges from 8,000 to 14,000 words. Assuming that word learning began when the child was 12 months old, this translates into a rate of 5 to 8 new word meanings a day between the ages of 1 and 6. After 5 years of word learning, the 6-year-old child does not slow down. According to some estimates, the average child of this age is moving along at the awe-inspiring rate of 22 words a day! How would you fare if you were given the task of learning 22 new words every day? It is truly miraculous how quickly children learn language.

Although there are many differences between a 2-year-old's language and a 6-year-old's language, none are more dramatic than those pertaining to pragmatics—rules of conversation (Ninio & Snow, 1996). A 6-year-old is simply a much better conversationalist than a 2-year-old. What are

This is a wug.
Now there is another one.
There are two of them.
There are two ______.

Figure **8.12**

Stimuli in Berko's Study of Young Children's Understanding of Morphological Rules

In Jean Berko's (1958) study, young children were presented cards, such as this one with a "wug" on it. Then the children were asked to supply the missing word; in supplying the missing word, they had to say it correctly too. "Wugs" is the correct response here.

some of the improvements in pragmatics that are made in the preschool years? At about 3 years of age, children improve in their ability to talk about things that are not physically present. That is, they improve their command of the characteristic of language known as "displacement." One way displacement is revealed is in games of pretend. Although a 2-year-old might know the word *table,* he is unlikely to use this word to refer to an imaginary table that he pretends is standing in front of him. But a child over 3 probably has this ability, even if she does not always use it. There are large individual differences in preschoolers' talk about imaginary people and things.

child-centered kindergarten
Education that involves the whole child by considering both the child's physical, cognitive, and social development and the child's needs, interests, and learning styles.

Early Childhood Education

There are many variations in the ways young children are educated. First we will explore the child-centered kindergarten, then we will turn our attention to developmentally appropriate and inappropriate education, whether preschool is necessary, and education for children who are disadvantaged.

Careers in Life-Span Development

Anita Marie Hitchcock, Early Childhood Educator

ANITA MARIE HITCHCOCK teaches kindergarten in Santa Rosa, Florida. She was awarded the 1998 Teacher of the Year Award in her community.

Anita believes it is important for teachers to find that "something special" in every child and let the child know how terrific he or she is in some way. In her class of 28 kindergartners, she has one legally blind child, two with learning disabilities, a child with only one ear, nine children with missing teeth, a child who reads above the fourth-grade level, and children with lots of other differences. Anita encourages students to focus on positive aspects in themselves and others.

One recent class nominated her as State Teacher of the Year and had this to say about her:

"She always has a smile on her face and never frowns. She teaches us how to help each other. We get to play with toys, learn about bugs, and have fun centers. She reads books to us and is a good story teller. She loves us and we love her."

Anita Marie Hitchcock (left) and some of her happy kindergartners.

The Child-Centered Kindergarten

Kindergarten programs vary a great deal (Roopnarine & Johnson, 2000). Some approaches place more emphasis on young children's social development, others on their cognitive development. Some experts on early childhood education believe that the curriculum of too many of today's kindergarten and preschool programs place too much emphasis on achievement and success, putting pressure on young children too early in their development (Charlesworth, 1996; Elkind, 1988). Placing such heavy emphasis on success is not what kindergartens were originally intended to do. In the 1840s, Friedrich Froebel's concern for quality education for young children led to the founding of the kindergarten—literally, "a garden for children." The founder of the kindergarten understood that, like growing plants, children require careful nurturing. Unfortunately, too many of today's kindergartens have forgotten the importance of careful nurturing for our nation's young children (Driscoll, 2000; Golbeck, 2001; Trawick-Smith, 2000).

In the **child-centered kindergarten,** *education involves the whole child and includes concern for the child's physical, cognitive, and social development.* Instruction is organized around the child's needs, interests, and learning styles. The process of learning, rather than what is learned, is emphasized (White & Coleman, 2000). Each child follows a unique developmental pattern, and young children learn best through firsthand experiences with people and materials. Play is extremely important in the child's total development. *Experimenting, exploring, discovering, trying out, restructuring, speaking,* and *listening* are all words that describe excellent kindergarten programs. Such programs are closely attuned to the developmental status of 4- and 5-year-old children. They are based on a state of being, not on a state of becoming.

The Montessori Approach Montessori schools are patterned after the educational philosophy of Maria Montessori, an Italian physician-turned-educator,

who crafted a revolutionary approach to young children's education at the beginning of the twentieth century (Wentworth, 1999). Her work began in Rome with a group of children who were mentally retarded. She was successful in teaching them to read, write, and pass examinations designed for normal children. Some time later, she turned her attention to poor children from the slums of Rome and had similar success in teaching them. Her approach has since been adopted extensively in private nursery schools in the United States.

Early Childhood Education
Reggio Emilia

The **Montessori approach** *is a philosophy of education in which children are given considerable freedom and spontaneity in choosing activities. They are allowed to move from one activity to another as they desire.* The teacher acts as a facilitator rather than a director of learning. The teacher shows the child how to perform intellectual activities, demonstrates interesting ways to explore curriculum materials, and offers help when the child requests it.

Montessori approach
An educational philosophy in which children are given considerable freedom and spontaneity in choosing activities and are allowed to move from one activity to another as they desire.

Some developmentalists favor the Montessori approach, but others believe that it neglects children's social development (Chattin-McNichols, 1992). For example, while Montessori fosters independence and the development of cognitive skills, it deemphasizes verbal interaction between the teacher and child and peer interaction. Montessori's critics also argue that it restricts imaginative play.

Developmentally Appropriate and Inappropriate Practices in the Education of Young Children It is time for number games in a kindergarten class at the Greenbrook School in South Brunswick, New Jersey. With little prodding from the teacher, 23 five- and 6-year-old children fetch geometric puzzles, playing cards, and counting equipment from the shelves lining the room. At one round table, some young children fit together brightly colored shapes. One girl forms a hexagon out of triangles. Other children gather around her to count up how many parts were needed to make the whole. After about half an hour, the children prepare for story time. They put away their counting equipment and sit in a circle around one young girl. She holds up a giant book about a character named Mrs. Wishywashy, who insists on giving the farm animals a bath. The children recite the whimsical lines, clearly enjoying one of their favorite stories. The hallway outside the kindergarten is lined with drawings depicting the children's own interpretations of the book. After the first reading, volunteers act out various parts of the book. There is not one bored face in the room.

This is not reading, writing, and arithmetic the way most individuals remember it. A growing number of educators and psychologists believe that preschool and young elementary school children learn best through active, hands-on teaching methods such as games and dramatic play (Slentz & Krogh, 2001). They know that children develop at varying rates and that schools need to allow for these individual differences (Henninger, 1999; Jalongo & Isenberg, 2000; Krogh & Slentz, 2001). They also believe that schools should focus on improving children's social development, as well as their cognitive development. Educators refer to this type of schooling as **developmentally appropriate practice,** *which is based on knowledge of the typical development of children within an age span (age appropriateness) as well as the uniqueness of the child (individual appropriateness).* Developmentally appropriate practice contrasts with developmentally inappropriate practice, which ignores the concrete, hands-on approach to learning. Direct teaching largely through abstract paper-and-pencil activities presented to large groups of young children is believed to be developmentally inappropriate.

developmentally appropriate practice
Education that focuses on the typical developmental patterns of children (age appropriateness) and the uniqueness of each child (individual appropriateness).

One of the most comprehensive documents addressing the issue of developmentally appropriate practice in early childhood programs is the position statement by the National Association for the Education of Young Children (NAEYC) (Bredekamp, 1987, 1997; National Association for the Education of Young Children, 1986). This document represents the expertise of many of the foremost experts in the field of early childhood education. In figure 8.13 you can examine some of the NAEYC recommendations for developmentally appropriate practice. In one study, the children who attended developmentally appropriate kindergartens displayed more appropriate classroom behavior and had better conduct records and better work and

NAEYC
High/Scope: Active Learning

Component	Appropriate practice	Inappropriate practice
Language development, literacy, and cognitive development	Children are provided many opportunities to see how reading and writing are useful before they are instructed in letter names, sounds, and word identification. Basic skills develop when they are meaningful to children. An abundance of these activities is provided to develop language and literacy: listening to and reading stories and poems; taking field trips; dictating stories; participating in dramatic play; talking informally with other children and adults; and experimenting with writing.	Reading and writing instruction stresses isolated skill development, such as recognizing single letters, reading the alphabet, singing the alphabet song, coloring within predefined lines, and being instructed in correct formation of letters on a printed line.
	Children develop an understanding of concepts about themselves, others, and the world around them through observation, interaction with people and real objects, and the seeking of solutions to concrete problems. Learning about math, science, social studies, health, and other content areas is integrated through meaningful activities.	Instruction stresses isolated skill development through memorization. Children's cognitive development is seen as fragmented in content areas, such as math or science, and times are set aside for each of these.
Physical development	Children have daily opportunities to use large muscles, including running, jumping, and balancing. Outdoor activity is planned daily so children can freely express themselves.	Opportunity for large muscle activity is limited. Outdoor time is limited because it is viewed as interfering with instructional time, rather than as an integral part of the children's learning environment.
	Children have daily opportunities to develop small muscle skills through play activities, such as puzzles, painting, and cutting.	Small motor activity is limited to writing with pencils, coloring predrawn forms, and engaging in similar structured lessons.
Aesthetic development and motivation	Children have daily opportunities for aesthetic expression and appreciation through art and music. A variety of art media are available.	Art and music are given limited attention. Art consists of coloring predrawn forms or following adult-prescribed directions.
	Children's natural curiosity and desire to make sense of their world are used to motivate them to become involved in learning.	Children are required to participate in all activities to obtain the teacher's approval; to obtain extrinsic rewards, such as stickers or privileges; or to avoid punishment.

Figure **8.13** NAEYC Recommendations for Developmentally

Component	Appropriate practice	Inappropriate practice
Curriculum goals	Experiences are provided in all developmental areas—physical, cognitive, social, and emotional.	Experiences are narrowly focused on cognitive development without recognition that all areas of the child's development are interrelated.
	Individual differences are expected, accepted, and used to design appropriate activities.	Children are evaluated only against group norms, and all are expected to perform the same tasks and achieve the same narrowly defined skills.
	Interactions and activities are designed to develop children's self-esteem and positive feelings toward learning.	Children's worth is measured by how well they conform to rigid expectations and perform on standardized tests.
Teaching strategies	Teachers prepare the environment for children to learn through active exploration and interaction with adults, other children, and materials.	Teachers use highly structured, teacher-directed lessons almost exclusively.
	Children select many of their own activities from among a variety the teacher prepares.	The teacher directs all activity deciding what children will do and when.
	Children are expected to be mentally and physically active.	Children are expected to sit down, be quiet, and listen or do paper-and-pencil tasks for long periods of time. A major portion of time is spent passively sitting, watching, and listening.
Guidance of socioemotional development	Teachers enhance children's self-control by using positive guidance techniques, such as modeling and encouraging expected behavior, redirecting children to a more acceptable activity, and setting clear limits.	Teachers spend considerable time enforcing rules, punishing unacceptable behavior, demeaning children who misbehave, making children sit and be quiet, and refereeing disagreements.
	Children are provided many opportunities to develop social skills, such as cooperating, helping, negotiating, and talking with the person involved to solve interpersonal problems.	Children work individually at desks and tables most of the time and listen to the teacher's directions to the total group.

Appropriate and Inappropriate Education

Critical Thinking

Observing Children in Preschool and Kindergarten

TO LEARN ABOUT children, there is no substitute for interacting with them and observing them. Try to visit at least one preschool and one kindergarten. When I was trying to develop a meaningful idea for a master's thesis some years ago, my advisor suggested that I spend several weeks at different Head Start programs in Miami, Florida. The experience was invaluable and contributed significantly to my further pursuit of a career in the field of child development.

When you conduct your observations, consider whether the programs meet the criteria of developmentally appropriate education. Are the programs play- and child-centered or academics-centered?

study habits in the first grade than did the children who attended developmentally inappropriate kindergartens (Hart & others, 1993, 1998).

A special worry of early childhood educators is that the back-to-basics movement that has recently characterized educational reform is filtering down to kindergarten. Another worry is that many parents want their children to go to school earlier than kindergarten for the purpose of getting a "head start" in achievement.

How common are programs that use developmentally appropriate practice? Unfortunately, as few as one-third to one-fifth of all early childhood programs follow this educational strategy. Even fewer elementary schools do. Child-initiated activities, divergent questioning, and small-group instruction are the exception rather than the rule (Dunn & Kontos, 1997).

Does Preschool Matter? According to child developmentalist David Elkind (1988), parents who are exceptionally competent and dedicated and who have both the time and the energy can provide the basic ingredients of early childhood education in their home. If parents have the competence and resources to provide young children with a variety of learning experiences and exposure to other children and adults (possibly through neighborhood play groups), along with opportunities for extensive play, then home schooling may sufficiently educate young children. However, if parents do not have the commitment, the time, the energy, and the resources to provide young children with an environment that approximates a good early childhood program, then it *does* matter whether a child attends preschool. In this case, the issue is not whether preschool is important but whether home schooling can closely duplicate what a competent preschool program can offer.

We should always keep in mind the unfortunate idea of early childhood education as an early start to ensure that the participants will finish early or on top in an educational race. Elkind (1988) points out that perhaps the choice of the phrase *head start* for the education of disadvantaged children was a mistake. "Head Start program" does not imply a race. Not surprisingly, when middle socioeconomic status parents heard that low-income children were getting a "head start," they wanted a head start for their own young children. In some instances, starting children in formal academic training too early can produce more harm than good. In Denmark, where reading instruction follows a language experience approach and formal instruction is delayed until the age of 7, illiteracy is virtually nonexistent. By contrast, in France, where state-mandated formal instruction in reading begins at age 5, 30 percent of the children have reading problems. Education should not be stressful for young children. Early childhood education should not be solely an academic prep school.

Preschool is rapidly becoming a norm in early childhood education. Twenty-three states already have legislation pending to provide schooling for 4-year-old children, and there are already many private preschool programs. The increase in public preschools underscores the growing belief that early childhood education should be a legitimate component of public education. There are dangers, though. According to Elkind (1988), early childhood education is often not well understood at higher levels of education. The danger is that public preschool education for 4-year-old children will become little more than a downward extension of traditional elementary education. This is already occurring in preschool programs in which testing, workbooks, and group drills are imposed on 4- and 5-year-old children.

Researchers are already beginning to document some of the stress that increased academic pressure can bring to young children. In one study, Diane Burts and her colleagues (1989) compared the frequencies of stress-related behaviors observed in

young children in classrooms with developmentally appropriate instructional practices with those of children in classrooms with developmentally inappropriate instructional practices. They found that the children in the developmentally inappropriate classrooms exhibited more stress-related behaviors than the children in the developmentally appropriate classrooms. In another study, children in a highly academically oriented early childhood education program were compared with children in a low academically oriented early childhood education program (Hirsch-Pasek & others, 1989). No benefits appeared for children in the highly academically oriented early childhood education program, but some possible harmful effects were noted. Higher test anxiety, less creativity, and a less positive attitude toward school characterized more of the children who attended the highly academic program than who attended the low academic program.

In most Japanese preschools, surprisingly little emphasis is put on academic instruction. In one study, 300 Japanese and 210 American preschool teachers, child development specialists, and parents were asked about various aspects of early childhood education (Tobin, Wu, & Davidson, 1989). Only 2 percent of the Japanese respondents listed "to give children a good start academically" as one of their top three reasons for a society to have preschools. In contrast, over half the American respondents chose this as one of their top three choices. To prepare children for successful careers in first grade and beyond, Japanese schools do not teach reading, writing, and mathematics but, rather, such skills as persistence, concentration, and the ability to function as a member of a group. The vast majority of young Japanese children are taught to read at home by their parents. *Are many American preschools becoming too academically oriented? Explain.*

Education for Children Who Are Disadvantaged For many years, children from low-income families did not receive any education before they entered the first grade. In the 1960s, an effort was made to try to break the cycle of poverty and poor education for young children in the United States through compensatory education. **Project Head Start** *is a compensatory education program designed to provide children from low-income families the opportunity to acquire the skills and experiences important for success in school.* Project Head Start began in the summer of 1965, funded by the Economic Opportunity Act, and it continues to serve disadvantaged children today.

Initially, Project Head Start consisted of many different types of preschool programs in different parts of the country. Little effort was made to find out whether some programs worked better than others, but it eventually became apparent that some programs did work better than others. **Project Follow Through** *was implemented in 1967 as an adjunct to Project Head Start. In Project Follow Through, different types of educational programs were devised to determine which programs were the most effective. In the Follow Through programs, the enriched programs were carried through the first few years of elementary school.*

Were some Follow Through programs more effective than others? Many of the variations were able to produce the desired effects in children. For example, children in academically oriented, direct-instruction approaches did better on achievement tests and were more persistent on tasks than were children in the other approaches. Children in affective education approaches were absent from school less often and showed more independence than children in other approaches. Thus, Project Follow Through was important in demonstrating that variation in early childhood education does have significant effects in a wide range of social and cognitive areas (Stallings, 1975).

The effects of early childhood compensatory education continue to be studied, and recent evaluations support the positive influence on both the cognitive and social worlds of disadvantaged young children (Reynolds, 1999; Schweinhart, 1999). Of special interest are the long-term effects such intervention might produce. Model

Project Head Start
Compensatory education designed to provide children from low-income families the opportunity to acquire the skills and experiences important for school success.

Project Follow Through
An adjunct to Project Head Start, in which the enrichment programs are carried through the first few years of elementary school.

Head Start Resources
Poverty and Learning
Early Childhood Care and Education Around the World

CAREERS IN LIFE-SPAN DEVELOPMENT

Yolanda Garcia, Director of Children's Services/Head Start

YOLANDA GARCIA has worked in the field of early childhood education and family support for three decades. She has been the director of the Children's Services Department for the Santa Clara, California, County Office of Education since 1980. As director, she is responsible for managing child development programs for 2,500 three- to five-year-old children in 127 classrooms. Her training includes two master's degrees, one in public policy and child welfare from the University of Chicago and another in educational administration from San Jose State University.

Yolanda has served on many national advisory committees that have resulted in improvements in the staffing of Head Start programs. Most notably, she served on the Head Start Quality Committee that recommended the development of Early Head Start and revised performance standards for Head Start programs. Yolanda currently is a member of the American Academy of Science Committee on the Integration of Science and Early Childhood Education.

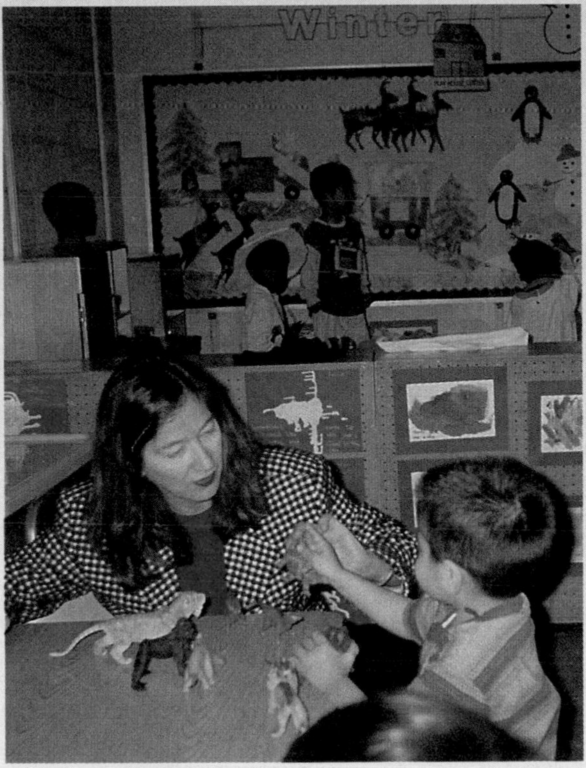

Yolanda Garcia, Director of Children's Services/Head Start, working with some Head Start children in Santa Clara, California.

preschool programs lead to lower rates of placement in special education, dropping out of school, grade retention, delinquency, and use of welfare programs. Such programs might also lead to higher rates of high school graduation and employment. For every dollar invested in high-quality, model preschool programs, taxpayers receive about $1.50 in return by the time the participants reach the age of 20. The benefits include savings on public school education (such as special-education services), tax payments on additional earnings, reduced welfare payments, and savings in juvenile justice system costs. Predicted benefits benefits over a lifetime are much greater to the taxpayer, a return of $5.73 on every dollar invested.

In one study, the researchers pooled the findings from 11 different investigations of well-executed, competent preschool programs (Lazar & others, 1982). Outcome measures assessed when the children were 9–19 years of age included indicators of school competence (such as special education and grade retention), abilities (as measured by standardized intelligence and achievement tests), attitudes and values, and impact on the family. The results indicated substantial benefits of competent preschool education with low-income children on all four dimensions investigated. In sum, ample evidence indicates that well-designed and well-implemented early childhood education programs with low-income children are successful.

Although educational intervention in impoverished children's lives is important, Head Start programs are not all created equal. One estimate is that 40 percent of the 1,400 Head Start programs are of questionable quality (Zigler & Styfco, 1994). More attention needs to be given to developing consistently high-quality Head Start programs (Bronfenbrenner, 1995). One high-quality early childhood education program (although not a Head Start program) is the Perry Preschool program in Ypsilanti, Michigan, a 2-year preschool program that includes weekly home visits from program personnel. In an analysis of the long-term effects of the program, as young adults the Perry Preschool children have higher high school graduation rates, more are in the workforce, fewer need welfare, crime rates are lower among them, and there are fewer teen pregnancies than in a control group from the same background who did not get the enriched early childhood education experience (Weikart, 1993).

Too many young children go to substandard early childhood programs (Morrison, 2000; Zigler & Finn-Stevenson, 1999). In a report by the Carnegie Corporation (1996), four out of five early childhood programs did not meet quality standards. Early childhood education should encourage adequate preparation for learning, varied learning activities, trusting relationships between adults and children, and increased parental involvement.

At this point we have studied a number of ideas about language development and early childhood education. To review these ideas, see summary table 8.4. In the next chapter, we will continue to explore early childhood by turing our attention to socioemotional development.

Summary Table 8.4
Language Development and Early Childhood Education

Concept	Processes/ Related Ideas	Characteristics/Descriptions
Language Development	Language's Rules	• Young children increase their grasp of language's rule systems. These include morphology, semantics, and pragmatics. Berko's classic experiment demonstrated that young children understand morphological rules.
Early Childhood Education	The Child-Centered Kindergarten	• The child-centered kindergarten involves education of the whole child, with emphasis on individual variation, the process of learning, and the importance of play in development.
	The Montessori Approach	• The Montessori approach is another well-known strategy for early childhood education.
	Developmentally Appropriate and Inappropriate Practices in the Education of Young Children	• Developmentally appropriate practice focuses on the typical patterns of children (age appropriateness) and the uniqueness of each child (individual appropriateness). • Such practice contrasts with developmentally inappropriate practice, which ignores the concrete, hands-on approach to learning.
	Does Preschool Matter?	• A special concern is the view that education is a race and that an early academic start in preschool will help children win the race. • Critics argue that too many preschools are academically oriented and stressful for young children.
	Education for Children Who Are Disadvantaged	• Compensatory education has tried to break through the poverty cycle through programs like Head Start and Project Follow Through. • Model programs have been shown to have positive effects on children from poverty backgrounds.

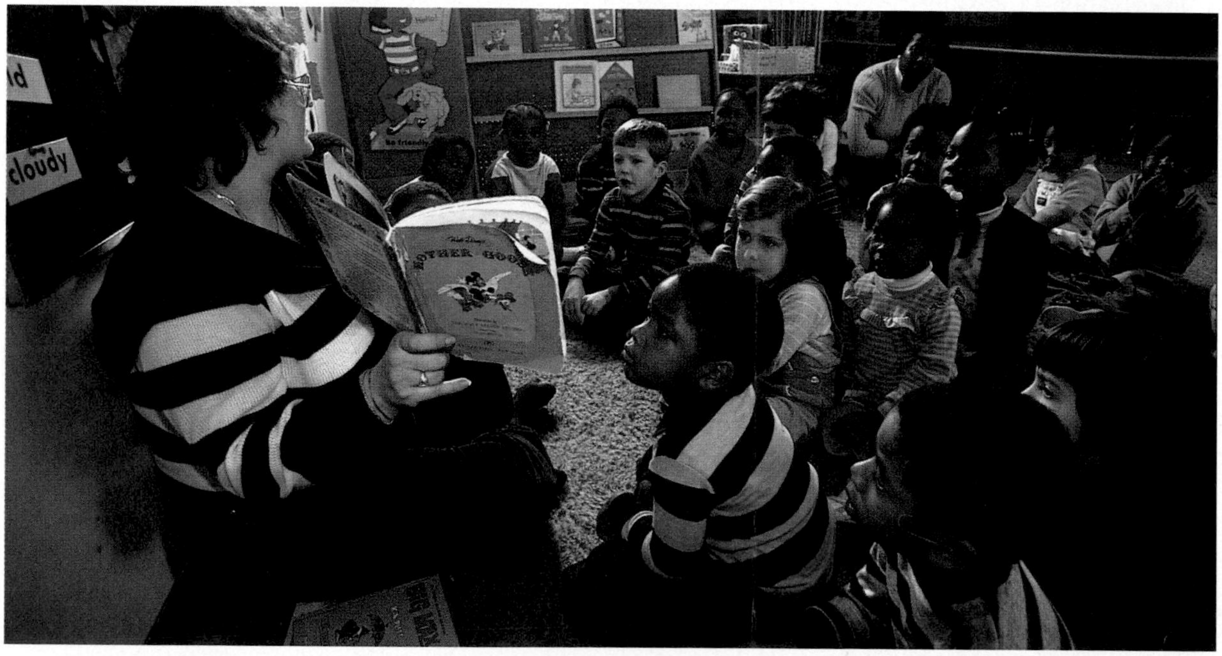

These preschool children are attending a Head Start program, a national effort to provide children from low-income families the opportunity to experience an enriched environment. *What have researchers found about the effects of Head Start on children's development?*

Chapter Review

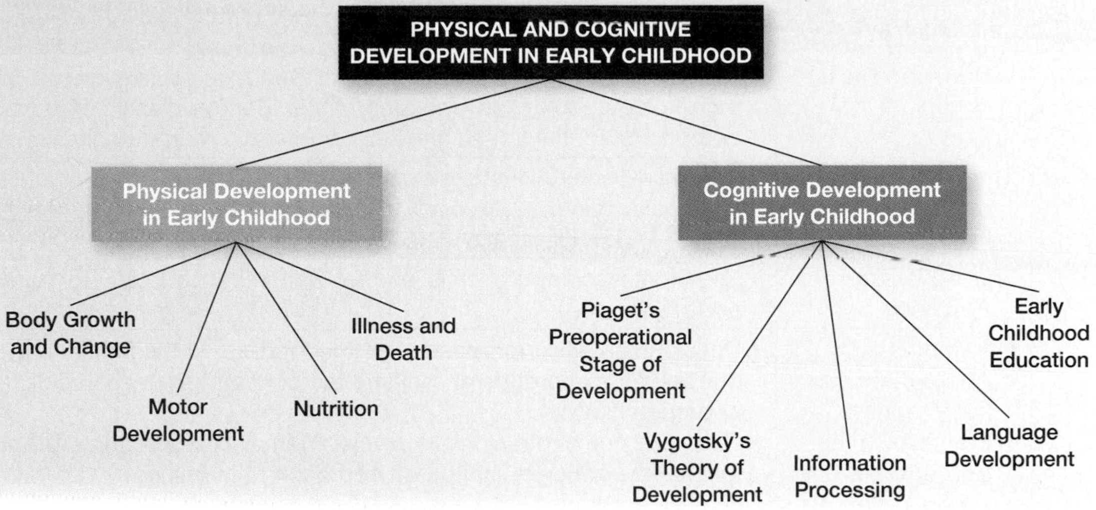

TO OBTAIN A DETAILED REVIEW OF THIS CHAPTER, STUDY THESE FOUR SUMMARY TABLES:

- Summary Table 8.1 Body Growth and Change, and Motor Development page 208
- Summary Table 8.2 Nutrition; Illness and Death page 211
- Summary Table 8.3 Piaget's Preoperational State of Development, Vygotsky's Theory of Development, and Information Processing page 224
- Summary Table 8.4 Language Development and Early Childhood Education page 233

Key Terms

myelination 205
basal metabolism rate (BMR) 209
oral rehydration therapy (ORT) 210
operations 212
symbolic function substage 212
egocentrism 212
animism 213
intuitive thought substage 214
centration 214
conservation 214
zone of proximal development (ZPD) 216
scaffolding 216
social constructivist approach 218
short-term memory 220
theory of mind 222
child-centered kindergarten 226
Montessori approach 227
developmentally appropriate practice 227
Project Head Start 231
Project Follow Through 231

Key People

Teresa Amabile 203
Jean Piaget 212
Barbel Inhelder 212
Rochel Gelman 215
Lev Vygtosky 216
Zhe Chen and Robert Siegler 221
Jean Berko 225
Maria Montessori 226
David Elkind 230

Taking It to the Net

1. Professor Issacson has asked his students to try and place Piaget's theories in the context of contemporary research. What should students know about how Piaget's theories stack up in relation to recent research findings?
2. Alexander is majoring in elementary education. He wants to know if any of Vygotsky's theories have found their way into the elementary school classroom. What will he discover?
3. Karen, who is working in a prosecutor's office for her senior internship, has been asked to write a memo on the suggestibility of child witnesses and how likely a jury is to believe a child's testimony in court cases. How can she find information for the memo that provides research-based facts as well as guidelines for dealing with child witnesses that will be helpful for the procecutors?

Connect to www.mhhe.com/santrockld8 to research the answers and complete these exercises.

OLC Preview

To further test your knowledge of this chapter or to explore our extensive online resources that accompany *Life-Span Development*, eighth edition, please log on to the text's Online Learning Center at http://www.mhhe.com/santrockld8.com.

Chapter 9

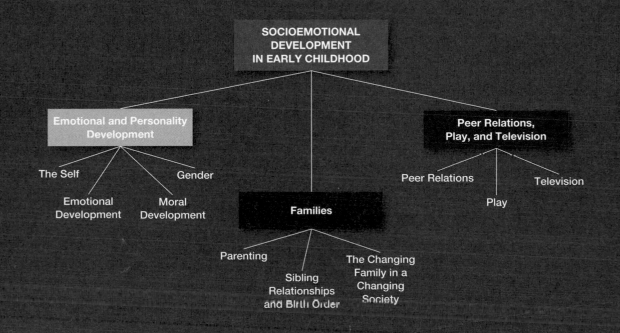

SOCIOEMOTIONAL DEVELOPMENT IN EARLY CHILDHOOD

- **Emotional and Personality Development**
  - The Self
  - Emotional Development
  - Moral Development
  - Gender
- **Families**
  - Parenting
  - Sibling Relationships and Birth Order
  - The Changing Family in a Changing Society
- **Peer Relations, Play, and Television**
  - Peer Relations
  - Play
  - Television

Socioemotional Development in Early Childhood

Let us play, for it is yet day 'And we cannot go to sleep; 'Besides, in the sky the little birds fly 'And the hills are all covered with sheep.'

William Blake
English Poet, 19th Century

Images of Life-Span Development

Sara and Her Developing Sense of Morality and Values

LIKE MANY CHILDREN, Sara Newland loves animals. When she was just 4 years old, she turned that love into social activism. During a trip to the zoo, she learned about the plight of an endangered species and became motivated to help. With her mother's assistance, Sara baked cakes and cookies and sold them on the sidewalk near her apartment building in New York City. She was elated when she raised $35, which she promptly mailed to the World Wildlife Fund. A few weeks later, her smiles turned into tears when the fund wrote Sara asking for more money. Sara was devastated because she thought she had taken care of the animal problem. Her mother told Sara that the endangered species problem and many others are so big that they require continual help from lots of people. That explanation apparently worked because Sara, now 9 years old, helps out at an inner-city child care center and regularly takes meals to homeless people in her neighborhood (Kantrowitz, 1991). Sara tells her friends not to be scared of homeless people. She says that some people wonder why she gives to them, then says, "If everyone gave food to them, they would all have decent meals."

Sensitive parents can make a difference in encouraging young children's sense of morality and values. Some experts on moral development believe that a capacity for goodness is present from the start, which reflects the "innate goodness" view of the child, which we discussed in chapter 1. But many developmentalists also believe that parents must nurture that goodness, just as they help their children become good readers, musicians, or athletes.

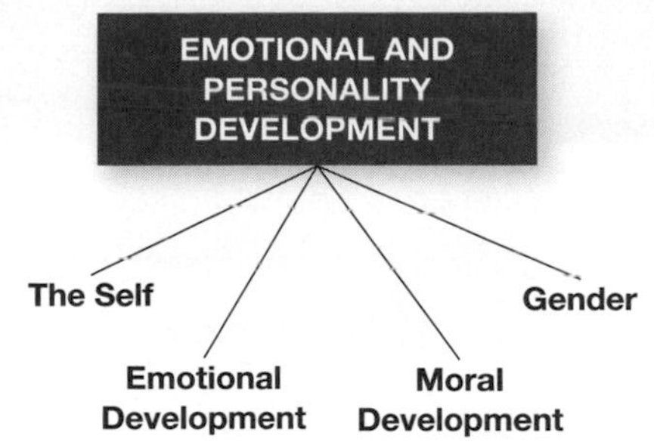

Emotional and Personality Development

In the story that opened the chapter, Sara displayed a positive sense of morality through her motivation to help an endangered species and the homeless. Let's further explore young children's moral development and other aspects of their emotional and personality development, beginning with the self.

The Self

We learned in chapter 7 that toward the end of the second year of life children develop a sense of self P. 185. During early childhood, some important developments in the self take place. Among these developments are facing the issue of initiative versus guilt and enhancing self-understanding.

Initiative Versus Guilt According to Erik Erikson (1968), the psychosocial stage that characterizes early childhood is *initiative versus guilt.* By now, children have become convinced that they are a person of their own; during early childhood, they must discover what kind of person they will become. They intensely identify with their parents, who most of the time appear to them to be powerful and beautiful, although often unreasonable, disagreeable, and sometimes even dangerous. During early childhood, children use their perceptual, motor, cognitive, and language skills to make things happen. They have a surplus of energy that permits them to forget failures quickly and to approach new areas that seem desirable—even if they seem dangerous—with undiminished zest and some increased sense of direction. On their own *initiative,* then, children at this stage exuberantly move out into a wider social world.

The great governor of initiative is *conscience.* Children now not only feel afraid of being found out, but they also begin to hear the inner voice of self-observation, self-guidance, and self-punishment (Bybee, 1999). Their initiative and enthusiasm may bring them not only rewards but also punishments. Widespread disappointment at this stage leads to an unleashing of guilt that lowers the child's self-esteem.

Whether children leave this stage with a sense of initiative that outweighs their sense of guilt depends in large part on how parents respond to their children's self-initiated activities. Children who are given the freedom and opportunity to initiate motor play, such as running, bike riding, sledding, skating, tussling, and wrestling, have their sense of initiative supported. Initiative is also supported when parents answer their children's questions and do not deride or inhibit fantasy or play activity. In contrast, if children are made to feel that their motor activity is bad, that their questions are a nuisance, and that their play is silly and stupid, then they often develop a sense of guilt over self-initiated activities that may persist through life's later stages (Elkind, 1970).

self-understanding
The child's cognitive representation of self, the substance and content of the child's self-conceptions.

Self-Understanding **Self-understanding** *is the child's cognitive representation of self, the substance and content of the child's self-conceptions.* For example, a 5-year-old girl understands that she is a girl, has blond hair, likes to ride her bicycle, has a friend, and is a swimmer. An 11-year-old boy understands that he is a student, a boy, a football player, a family member, a video-game lover, and a rock music fan. A child's self-understanding is based on the various roles and membership categories that define who children are. Though not the whole of personal identity, self-understanding provides its rational underpinnings (Damon & Hart, 1992).

The rudimentary beginning of self-understanding begins with self-recognition, which takes place by approximately 18 months of age. Since children can verbally communicate their ideas, research on self-understanding in childhood is not limited to visual self-recognition, as it was during infancy. Mainly by interviewing children, researchers have probed children's conceptions of many aspects of self-understanding (Moore & Lemmon, 2001). These include mind and body, self in relation to others,

and pride and shame in self. In early childhood, children usually conceive of the self in physical terms. Most young children think the self is part of their body, usually their head. Young children usually confuse self, mind, and body. Because the self is a body part for them, they describe it along many material dimensions, such as size, shape, and color. Young children distinguish themselves from others through many different physical and material attributes. Says 4-year-old Sandra, "I'm different from Jennifer because I have brown hair and she has blond hair." Says 4-year-old Ralph, "I am different from Hank because I am taller, and I am different from my sister because I have a bicycle."

Researchers also believe that the *active dimension* is a central component of the self in early childhood (Keller, Ford, & Meacham, 1978). If we define the category *physical* broadly enough, we can include physical actions as well as body image and material possessions. For example, preschool children often describe themselves in terms of such activities as play. In sum, in early childhood, children frequently think of themselves in terms of a physical self or an active self.

Emotional Development

Children, like adults, experience many emotions during the course of a day. At times, children also try to make sense of other people's emotional reactions and feelings.

Developmental Timetable of Young Children's Emotion Language and Understanding Among the most important changes in emotional development in early childhood are the increased use of emotion language and the understanding of emotion (Kuebli, 1994). Preschoolers become more adept at talking about their own and others' emotions. Between 2 and 3 years of age, children considerably increase the number of terms they use to describe emotion (Ridgeway, Waters, & Kuczaj, 1985). However, in the preschool years, children are learning more than just the "vocabulary" of emotion terms, they also are learning about the causes and consequences of feelings (Denham, 1998).

Emotion has taught humankind to reason.

Marquis de Vauvenargues
French Moralist, 18th Century

At 4 to 5 years of age, children show an increased ability to reflect on emotions. In this developmental time frame, they also begin to understand that the same event can elicit different feelings in different people. Moreover, they show a growing awareness about controlling and managing emotions to meet social standards (Bruce, Olen, & Jensen, 1999). A summary of the characteristics of young children's emotion language and understanding is shown in figure 9.1.

Approximate age of child	Description
2–3 years	Increase emotion vocabulary most rapidly Correctly label simple emotions in self and others and talk about past, present, and future emotions Talk about the causes and consequences of some emotions and identify emotions associated with certain situations Use emotion language in pretend play
4–5 years	Show increased capacity to reflect verbally on emotions and to consider more complex relations between emotions and situations Understand that the same event may call forth different feelings in different people and that feelings sometimes persist long after the events that caused them Demonstrate growing awareness about controlling and managing emotions in accord with social standards

Figure **9.1**
Some Characteristics of Young Children's Emotion Language and Understanding

Summary Table 9.1
The Self and Emotional Development

Concept	Processes/ Related Ideas	Characteristics/Descriptions
The Self	Initiative vs. Guilt	• Erikson believed that early childhood is a period when development involves resolving the conflict of initiative versus guilt.
	Self-Understanding	• While a rudimentary form of self-understanding occurs at about 18 months in the form of self-recognition, in early childhood the physical and active self emerges.
Emotional Development	Developmental Timetable of Young Children's Emotion Language and Understanding	• Preschoolers become more adept at talking about their own and others' emotions. • Two- and 3-year-olds considerably increase the number of terms they use to describe emotion and learn more about the causes and consequences of feelings. • At 4 to 5 years of age, children show an increased ability to reflect on emotions and understand that a single event can elicit different emotions in different people. They also show a growing awareness about controlling and managing emotions to meet social standards.

As this point we have discussed a number of ideas about the self and emotional development. To review these ideas see summary table 9.1.

Moral Development

Increasingly, theorists and researchers are conceptualizing and studying moral development in terms of its emotional underpinnings. As we will see next, emotion (or feeling) is believed to be one of moral development's three main components.

moral development
Development regarding rules and conventions about what people should do in their interactions with other people.

What Is Moral Development?

Moral development *involves the development of thoughts, feelings, and behaviors regarding standards of right and wrong.* Moral development has an *intrapersonal* dimension (a person's basic values and sense of self) and an interpersonal dimension (a focus on what people should do in their interactions with other people) (Walker, 1996: Walker & Pitts, 1998). The intrapersonal dimension regulates a person's activities when she or he is not engaged in social interaction. The interpersonal dimension regulates people's social interactions and arbitrates conflict. Let's now further explore some basic ideas about moral thoughts, feelings, and behaviors.

heteronomous morality
The first stage of moral development, in Piaget's theory, occurring from approximately 4 to 7 years of age. Justice and rules are conceived of as unchangeable properties of the world, removed from the control of people.

autonomous morality
The second stage of moral development in Piaget's theory, displayed by older children (about 10 years of age and older). The child becomes aware that rules and laws are created by people and that, in judging an action, one should consider the actor's intentions as well as the consequences.

Piaget's View of How Children's Moral Reasoning Develops

Interest in how the child thinks about moral issues was stimulated by Jean Piaget (1932). He extensively observed and interviewed children from the age of 4 to 12. He watched them play marbles, seeking to learn how they used and thought about the game's rules. He also asked children questions about ethical rules—theft, lies, punishment, and justice, for example. Piaget concluded that children think in two distinctly different ways about morality, depending on their developmental maturity. **Heteronomous morality** *is the first stage of moral development, in Piaget's theory, occurring from approximately 4 to 7 years of age. Justice and rules are conceived of as unchangeable properties of the world, removed from the control of people.* **Autonomous morality** *is the second stage of moral development, in Piaget's theory, displayed by older children (about 10 years of age and older). The child becomes aware that rules and laws are created by people and that, in judging an action, one should consider the actor's in-*

tentions as well as the consequences. Children 7 to 10 years of age are in a transition between the two stages, showing some features of both.

Let's consider Piaget's two stages of moral development further. The heteronomous thinker judges the rightness or goodness of behavior by considering the consequences of the behavior, not the intentions of the actor. For example, the heteronomous thinker says that breaking 12 cups accidentally is worse than breaking 1 cup intentionally while trying to steal a cookie. For the moral autonomist, the reverse is true. The actor's intentions assume paramount importance. The heteronomous thinker also believes that rules are unchangeable and are handed down by all-powerful authorities. When Piaget suggested that new rules be introduced into the game of marbles, the young children resisted. They insisted that the rules had always been the same and could not be altered. By contrast, older children—who were moral autonomists—accepted change and recognized that rules are merely convenient, socially agreed-upon conventions, subject to change by consensus.

The heteronomous thinker also believes in **imminent justice,** *the concept that, if a rule is broken, punishment will be meted out immediately.* The young child believes that the violation is connected in some automatic way to the punishment. Thus, young children often look around worriedly after committing a transgression, expecting inevitable punishment. Older children, the moral autonomists, recognize that punishment is socially mediated and occurs only if a relevant person witnesses the wrongdoing and that, even then, punishment is not inevitable.

imminent justice
The concept that, if a rule is broken, punishment will be meted out immediately.

Piaget argued that, as children develop, they become more sophisticated in thinking about social matters, especially about the possibilities and conditions of cooperation. Piaget believed that this social understanding comes about through the mutual give-and-take of peer relations. In the peer group, where all members have similar power and status, plans are negotiated and coordinated, and disagreements are reasoned about and eventually settled. Parent-child relations, in which parents have the power and the child does not, are less likely to advance moral reasoning, because rules are often handed down in an authoritarian way. Later, in chapter 11, we will discuss another highly influential cognitive view of moral development, that of Lawrence Kohlberg.

Moral Behavior

The study of moral behavior has been influenced by behavioral and social cognitive theories ◀ P. 40. The processes of reinforcement, punishment, and imitation are used to explain children's moral behavior. When children are rewarded for behavior that is consistent with laws and social conventions, they are likely to repeat that behavior. When models who behave morally are provided, children are likely to adopt their actions. And, when children are punished for immoral behavior, those behaviors are likely to be reduced or eliminated. However, because punishment may have adverse side effects, it needs to be used judiciously and cautiously.

Another important point needs to be made about the social cognitive view of moral development. Moral behavior is influenced extensively by the situation. What children do in one situation is often only weakly related to what they do in other situations. A child might cheat in math class but not in English class; a child might steal a piece of candy when others are not present but not steal it when they are present. More than half a century ago, morality's situational nature was observed in a comprehensive study of thousands of children in many different situations—at home, at school, and at church, for example. The totally honest child was virtually nonexistent; so was the child who cheated in all situations (Hartshorne & May, 1928–1930).

Social cognitive theorists also believe that the ability to resist temptation is closely tied to the development of self-control. Children must overcome their impulses toward something they want that is prohibited. To achieve this self-control, they must learn to be patient and to delay gratification. Social cognitive theorists believe that cognitive factors are important in the child's development of self-control. For example, in one study, children's cognitive transformations of desired objects helped them become more patient (Mischel & Patterson, 1976). Preschool children were asked to do a boring task. Close by was an exciting mechanical clown who tried to persuade

Childhood innocence

the children to come play with him. The children who had been trained to say to themselves, "I'm not going to look at Mr. Clown when Mr. Clown says to look at him" controlled their behavior and continued working on the dull task much longer than those who did not instruct themselves.

Moral Feelings In chapter 2, we discussed Sigmund Freud's psychoanalytic theory ◀ P. 31. It describes the *superego* as one of the three main structures of personality—the id and ego being the other two. In Freud's classical psychoanalytic theory, the child's superego—the moral branch of personality—develops as the child resolves the Oedipus conflict and identifies with the same-sex parent in the early childhood years. Among the reasons children resolve the Oedipus conflict is the fear of losing their parents' love and of being punished for their unacceptable sexual wishes toward the opposite-sex parent. To reduce anxiety, avoid punishment, and maintain parental affection, children form a superego by identifying with the same-sex parent. Through their identification with the same-sex parent, children internalize the parents' standards of right and wrong that reflect societal prohibitions. And the child turns inward the hostility that was previously aimed externally at the same-sex parent. This inwardly directed hostility is now felt self-punitively as guilt, which is experienced unconsciously (beyond the child's awareness). In the psychoanalytic account of moral development, the self-punitiveness of guilt is responsible for keeping the child from committing transgressions. That is, children conform to societal standards to avoid guilt.

Positive feelings, such as empathy, contribute to the child's moral development. *Empathy* is reacting to another's feelings with an emotional response that is similar to the other's feelings. Although empathy is experienced as an emotional state, it often has a cognitive component. The cognitive component is the ability to discern another's inner psychological states, or what is called "perspective taking." Young infants have the capacity for some purely empathic responses, but for effective moral action children need to learn how to identify a wide range of emotional states in others. They also need to learn to anticipate what kinds of action will improve another person's emotional state.

What is moral is what you feel good after and what is immoral is what you feel bad after.

Ernest Hemingway
American Author, 20th Century

We have seen that classical psychoanalytic theory emphasizes the power of unconscious guilt in moral development. However, other theorists, such as Martin Hoffman and William Damon, emphasize the role of empathy. Today, many child developmentalists believe that both positive feelings, such as empathy, sympathy, admiration, and self-esteem, as well as negative feelings, such as anger, outrage, shame, and guilt, contribute to the child's moral development (Eisenberg, 2000; Eisenberg & others, in press; Roberts & Strayer, 1996). When strongly experienced, these emotions influence children to act in accord with standards of right and wrong. Emotions such as empathy, shame, guilt, and anxiety over other people's violation of standards are present early in development and undergo developmental change throughout childhood and beyond (Damon, 2000; Damon & Hart, 1992). These emotions provide a natural base for the child's acquisition of moral values, both orienting children toward moral events and motivating children to pay close attention to such events. But moral emotions do not operate in a vacuum to build the child's moral awareness, and they are not sufficient in themselves to generate moral responsiveness. They do not give the "substance" of moral regulation—the actual rules, values, and standards of behavior that children need to understand and act on. Moral emotions are inextricably interwoven with the cognitive and social aspects of children's development (Damon, 2000).

Gender

So far in this chapter, we have studied the self, emotional development, and moral development. Another important dimension of young children's socioemotional development is gender.

Gender Resources

What Is Gender?

While sex refers to the biological dimension of being male or female, **gender** *refers to the social and psychological dimensions of being male or female.* Two aspects of gender bear special mention—gender identity and gender role. **Gender identity** *is the sense of being male or female, which most children acquire by the time they are 3 years old.* **Gender role** *is a set of expectations that prescribe how females or males should think, act, and feel.*

gender
The social and psychological dimension of being male or female.

gender identity
The sense of being male or female, which most children acquire by the time they are 3 years old.

gender role
A set of expectations that prescribes how females or males should think, act, and feel.

Biological Influences

It was not until the 1920s that researchers confirmed the existence of human sex chromosomes, the genetic material that determines our sex. In chapter 3, you learned that humans normally have 46 chromosomes arranged in pairs. The 23rd pair may have two X chromosomes to produce a female, or it may have an X and a Y chromosome to produce a male.

Just as chromosomes are important in understanding biological influences, so are hormones. The two main classes of sex hormones are estrogens and androgens. *Estrogens,* such as estradiol, influence the development of female physical sex characteristics. *Androgens,* such as testosterone, promote the development of male physical sex characteristics. In the first few weeks of gestation, female and male embryos look alike. Male sex organs start to differ from female sex organs when XY chromosomes in the male embryo trigger the secretion of androgens. Low levels of androgens in the female embryo allow the normal development of female sex organs.

Some biological approaches to gender address the differences between the brains of females and those of males (Eisenberg, Martin, & Fabes, 1996). One approach focuses on the corpus callosum, the massive band of fibers that connects the brain's two hemispheres. Other approaches emphasize variations in the left and right hemispheres of the brains of males and females. At present, these are controversial views. What we do know is that the brains of females and males are far more similar than they are different. We also know that the brain has considerable plasticity and that experiences can modify its growth.

In gender development, however, biology is not completely destiny. When gender attitudes and behavior are at issue, children's socialization experiences matter a great deal (Eccles, 2000).

Social Influences

In our culture, adults discriminate between the sexes shortly after the infant's birth. The "pink and blue" treatment might be applied to boys and girls before they leave the hospital. Soon afterward, differences in hairstyles, clothes, and toys become obvious. Adults and peers reward these differences throughout development. And boys and girls learn gender roles through imitation, or observational learning, by watching what other people say and do. In recent years, the idea that parents are the critical socializing agents in gender-role development has come under fire. Parents are only one of many sources through which the individual learns gender roles (Beal, 1994; Fagot, Rodgers, & Leinbach, 2000). Culture, schools, peers, the media, and other family members are others, yet it is important to guard against swinging too far in this direction because—especially in the early years of development—parents are important influences on gender development.

Psychoanalytic and Social Cognitive Theories

Two prominent theories address the way children acquire masculine and feminine attitudes and behaviors from their parents. The **psychoanalytic theory of gender** *stems from*

psychoanalytic theory of gender
A theory deriving from Freud's view that the preschool child develops a sexual attraction to the opposite-sex parent, by approximately 5 or 6 years of age renounces this attraction because of anxious feelings, and subsequently identifies with the same-sex parent, unconsciously adopting the same-sex parent's characteristics.

Children need models rather than critics.

Joseph Joubert
French Essayist, 19th Century

Freud's view that the preschool child develops a sexual attraction to the opposite-sex parent. At 5 or 6 years of age the child renounces this attraction because of anxious feelings. Subsequently, the child identifies with the same-sex parent, unconsciously adopting the same-sex parent's characteristics. However, today many child developmentalists do not believe gender development proceeds on the basis of identification, at least not in terms of Freud's emphasis on childhood sexual attraction. Children become gender-typed much earlier than 5 or 6 years of age, and they become masculine or feminine even when the same-sex parent is not present in the family.

social cognitive theory of gender
A theory that emphasizes that children's gender development occurs through the observation and imitation of gender behavior and through the rewards and punishments children experience for gender-appropriate and inappropriate behavior.

The **social cognitive theory of gender** *emphasizes that children's gender development occurs through observation and imitation of gender behavior, and through the rewards and punishments children experience for gender-appropriate and -inappropriate behavior.* Unlike identification theory, social cognitive theory argues that sexual attraction to parents is not involved in gender development. (A comparison of the psychoanalytic and social cognitive views is presented in figure 9.2.) Parents often use rewards and punishments to teach their daughters to be feminine ("Karen, you are being a good girl when you play gently with your doll") and their sons to be masculine ("Keith, a boy as big as you is not supposed to cry"). Peers also extensively reward and punish gender behavior. And, by observing adults and peers at home, at school, in the neighborhood, and on television, children are widely exposed to a myriad of models who display masculine and feminine behavior. Critics of the social cognitive view argue that gender development is not as passively acquired as it indicates. Later, we will discuss the cognitive views of gender development, which stress that children actively construct their gender world.

WWW

Fathers and Sons

Theory	Processes	Outcome
Freud's psychoanalytic theory	Sexual attraction to opposite-sex parent at 3–5 years of age; anxiety about sexual attraction and subsequent identification with same-sex parent at 5–6 years of age	Gender behavior similar to that of same-sex parent
Social cognitive theory	Rewards and punishments of gender-appropriate and -inappropriate behavior by adults and peers; observation and imitation of models' masculine and feminine behavior	Gender behavior

Figure **9.2**

A Comparison of the Psychoanalytic and Social Cognitive Views of Gender Development

Parents influence their children's development by action and example.

Parental Influences Parents, by action and by example, influence their children's gender development. Both mothers and fathers are psychologically important in children's gender development. Mothers are more consistently given responsibility for nurturance and physical care. Fathers are more likely to engage in playful interaction and to be given responsibility for ensuring that boys and girls conform to existing cultural norms. And, whether or not they have more influence on them, fathers are more involved in socializing their sons than their daughters. Fathers seem to play an especially important part in gender-role development. They are more likely than mothers to act differently toward sons and daughters. Thus, they contribute more to distinctions between the genders (Huston, 1983).

Many parents encourage boys and girls to engage in different types of play and activities (Fagot, Leinbach, & O'Boyle, 1992). Girls are more likely to be given dolls to play with during childhood. When old enough, they are more likely to be assigned baby-sitting duties. Girls are encouraged to be more nurturant and emotional than boys. Fathers are more likely to engage in aggressive play with their sons than with their daughters.

Peer Influences Parents provide the earliest discrimination of gender roles in development. Before long, though, peers join the societal process of responding to and modeling masculine and feminine behavior. Children who play in sex-appropriate activities tend to be rewarded for doing so by their peers. Those who play in cross-sexed activities tend to be criticized by their peers or left to play alone. Children show a clear preference for being with and liking same-sex peers (Maccoby,

1993, 1998). This tendency usually becomes stronger during the middle and late childhood years. After extensive observations of elementary school playgrounds, two researchers characterized the play settings as "gender school." They said that boys teach one another the required masculine behavior and enforce it strictly (Luria & Herzog, 1985). Girls also pass on the female culture and congregate mainly with one another. Individual "tomboy" girls can join boys' activities without losing their status in the girls' groups; however, the reverse is not true for boys, reflecting our society's greater pressure for boys to conform to a traditional male role than for girls to conform to a traditional female role.

In childhood, boys and girls tend to gravitate toward others of their own sex. Boys' and girls' groups develop distinct cultures with different agendas.

Eleanor Maccoby
Contemporary Developmental Psychologist, Stanford University

Peer demands for conformity to gender roles become especially intense during adolescence. Although there is greater social mixing of males and females during early adolescence, in both formal groups and in dating, peer pressure is strong for the adolescent boy to be the very best male possible and for the adolescent girl to be the very best female possible.

School and Teacher Influences In certain ways, both girls and boys might receive an education that is not fair (Sadker & Sadker, 1994)—for example:

- Girls' learning problems are not identified as often as boys' are.
- Boys are given the lion's share of attention in schools.
- Girls start school testing higher in every academic subject than boys yet graduate from high school scoring lower on the SAT exam.
- Boys are most often at the top of their classes, but they also are most often at the bottom as well—more likely to fail a class, miss promotion, or drop out of school.
- Pressure to achieve is more likely to be heaped on boys than on girls.

Cognitive Influences Developmentalists also recognize the important role that cognitive factors play in gender.

As reflected in this tug-of-war battle between boys and girls, the playground in elementary school is like going to "gender school." Elementary school children show a clear preference for being with and liking same-sex peers. *Think back to when you were in elementary school. How much did you prefer being with peers who were the same sex as you?*

cognitive developmental theory of gender The theory that children's gender typing occurs after they have developed a concept of gender. Once they consistently conceive of themselves as male or female, children often organize their world on the basis of gender.

Cognitive Developmental Theory In the **cognitive developmental theory of gender,** *children's gender typing occurs after they have developed a concept of gender. Once they consistently conceive of themselves as male or female, children often organize their world on the basis of gender.* In this view, children use physical and behavioral clues to differentiate gender roles and to gender-type themselves early in their development. Initially proposed by Lawrence Kohlberg (1966), this theory argues that gender development proceeds in the following way. A child realizes, "I am a girl. I want to do girl things. Therefore, the opportunity to do girl things is rewarding." Kohlberg said that gender constancy develops at about 6 or 7 years of age in concert with the development of children's conservation and categorization skills. After children consistently conceive of themselves as female or male, they begin to organize their world on the basis of gender, such as selecting same-sex models to imitate.

gender schema theory The theory that an individual's attention and behavior are guided by an internal motivation to conform to gender-based sociocultural standards and stereotypes.

Gender Schema Theory A *schema* is a cognitive structure, a network of associations that organizes and guides an individual's perceptions. A *gender schema* organizes the world in terms of female and male. **Gender schema theory** *states that an individual's attention and behavior are guided by an internal motivation to conform to gender-based sociocultural standards and stereotypes.* Gender schema theory suggests that "gender typing" occurs when individuals are ready to encode and organize information along the lines of what is considered appropriate or typical for males and females in a society (Martin, 2000; Rodgers, 2000; Sokal & Seifert, 2001). Whereas Kohlberg's cognitive developmental theory argues that a particular cognitive prerequisite—gender constancy—is necessary for gender typing, *gender constancy* refers to the understanding that sex remains the same even though activities, clothing, and hair style might change (Ruble, 2000). Gender schema theory states that a general readiness to respond to and categorize information on the basis of culturally defined gender roles fuels children's gender-typing activities. A comparison of the cognitive developmental and gender schema theories is presented in figure 9.3.

Theory	Processes	Emphasis
Cognitive developmental theory	Development of gender constancy, especially around 6–7 years of age, when conservation skills develop; after children develop ability to consistently conceive of themselves as male or female, children often organize their world on the basis of gender, such as selecting same-sex models to imitate	Cognitive readiness facilitates gender identity
Gender schema theory	Sociocultural emphasis on gender-based standards and stereotypes; children's attention and behavior are guided by an internal motivation to conform to these gender-based standards and stereotypes, allowing children to interpret the world through a network of gender-organized thoughts	Gender schemas reinforce gender behavior

Figure 9.3
The Development of Gender Behavior According to the Cognitive Developmental and Gender Schema Theories of Gender Development

Researchers have shown that the appearance of gender constancy in children is related to their level of cognitive development, especially the acquisition of conservation skills. This supports the cognitive developmental theory of gender (Serbin & Sprafkin, 1986). They also have shown that young children who are pregender-constant have more gender-role knowledge than the cognitive developmental theory of gender predicts (which supports gender schema theory) (Carter & Levy, 1988). Today, gender schema theorists acknowledge that gender constancy is one important aspect of gender-role development, but they stress that other cognitive factors—such as gender schema—are also important.

At this point, we have studied a number of ideas about moral development and gender. To review these ideas, see summary table 9.2. In our discussion of emotional development, moral development, and gender, we explored ways that parents and peers contribute to these important aspects of development. Next, we will focus more closely on such social contexts of development in early childhood.

Summary Table 9.2
Moral Development and Gender

Concept	Processes/ Related Ideas	Characteristics/Descriptions
Moral Development	What Is Moral Development?	• Moral development concerns rules and regulations about what people should do in their interactions with others. • Developmentalists study how children think, behave, and feel about such rules and regulations.
	Piaget's View	• Piaget distinguished between the heteronomous morality of younger children and the autonomous morality of older children.
	Moral Behavior	• Moral behavior is emphasized by behavioral and social cognitive theorists. • They believe there is considerable situational variability in moral behavior and that self-control is an important aspect of understanding children's moral behavior.
	Moral Feelings	• Freud's psychoanalytic theory emphasizes the importance of feelings with regard to the development of the superego, the moral branch of personality, which develops through the Oedipus conflict and identification with the same-sex parent. In Freud's view, children conform to societal standards to avoid guilt. • Positive emotions, such as empathy, also are an important aspect of understanding moral feelings. • In Damon's view, both positive and negative emotions contribute to children's moral development.
Gender	What Is Gender?	• Gender is the social dimension of being male or female. • Gender identity is acquired by 3 years of age for most children. • A gender role is a set of expectations that prescribes how females or males should think, act, and feel.
	Biological Influences	• The 23rd pair of chromosomes may have two X chromosomes to produce a female, or one X and one Y chromosome to produce a male. • The two main classes of sex hormones are estrogens, which are dominant in females, and androgens, which are dominant in males. • Some biological approaches focus on differences between the brains of females and males. • Biology is not completely destiny in gender development; children's socialization experiences matter a great deal.
	Social Influences	• Both psychoanalytic theory and social cognitive theory emphasize the adoption of parents' gender characteristics. • Peers are especially adept at rewarding gender-appropriate behavior. • There is still concern about gender imbalance in education.
	Cognitive Influences	• Both cognitive developmental and gender schema theories emphasize the role of cognition in gender development.

Families

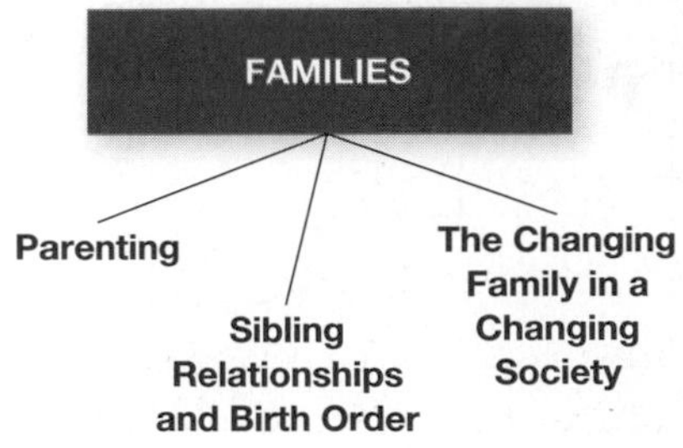

In chapter 7, we learned that attachment is an important aspect of family relationships during infancy P. 186. Remember that some experts believe attachment to a caregiver during the first several years of life is the key ingredient in the child's socioemotional development. We also learned that other experts believe secure attachment has been overemphasized and that the child's temperament, other social agents and contexts, and the complexity of the child's social world are also important in

There's no vocabulary for love within a family, love that's lived in but not looked at, love within the light of which all else is seen, the love within which all other love finds speech. This love is silent.

T. S. Eliot
American-Born English Poet, 20th Century

determining the child's social competence and well-being ◀ P. 190. Some developmentalists also emphasize that the infant years have been overdramatized as determinants of life-span development. They argue that social experiences in the early childhood years and later deserve more attention than they have sometimes been given.

In this chapter, we will discuss early childhood experiences beyond attachment. We will explore the different types of parenting styles, sibling relationships, and the ways in which more children are now experiencing socialization in a greater variety of family structures than at any other point in history. Keep in mind, as we discuss these aspects of families, the importance of viewing the family as a system of interacting individuals who reciprocally socialize and mutually regulate each other.

Parenting

An important dimension of parenting is the styles parents use when they interact with their children.

Parenting Styles

Parents want their children to grow into socially mature individuals, and they may feel frustrated in trying to discover the best way to accomplish this. Developmentalists have long searched for the ingredients of parenting that promote competent socioemotional development (Brooks, 1999). For example, in the 1930s, John Watson argued that parents are too affectionate with their children. In the 1950s, a distinction was made between physical and psychological discipline. Psychological discipline, especially reasoning, was emphasized as the best way to rear a child. In the 1970s and beyond, the dimensions of competent parenting have become more precise (Lerner, 2000).

Parenting

Especially widespread is the view of Diana Baumrind (1971). She believes parents should be neither punitive nor aloof. Rather, they should develop rules for their children and be affectionate with them. She emphasizes four types of parenting that are associated with different aspects of the child's socioemotional development: authoritarian, authoritative, neglectful, and indulgent.

authoritarian parenting
A restrictive punitive style in which parents exhort the child to follow their directions and to respect work and effort. The authoritarian parent places firm limits and controls on the child and allows little verbal exchange. Authoritarian parenting is associated with children's social incompetence.

Authoritarian parenting *is a restrictive, punitive style in which parents exhort the child to follow their directions and to respect work and effort. The authoritarian parent places firm limits and controls on the child and allows little verbal exchange. Authoritarian parenting is associated with children's social incompetence.* For example, an authoritarian parent might say, "You do it my way or else. There will be no discussion!"

Authoritarian parents also might spank the child frequently, enforce rules rigidly but not explain them, and show rage toward the child. Children of authoritarian parents often are unhappy, fearful, and anxious about comparing themselves with others, fail to initiate activity, and have weak communication skills.

Authoritative parenting *encourages children to be independent but still places limits and controls on their actions. Extensive verbal give-and-take is allowed, and parents are warm and nurturant toward the child. Authoritative parenting is associated with children's social competence.* An authoritative parent might put his arm around the child in a comforting way and say, "You know you should not have done that. Let's talk about how you can handle the situation better next time." Authoritative parents show pleasure and support of children's constructive behavior. They also expect mature, independent, and age-appropriate behavior of children. Children whose parents are authoritative are often cheerful, self-controlled and self-reliant, achievement-oriented, maintain friendly relations with peers, cooperate with adults, and cope well with stress.

How are authoritarian and authoritative parenting different? Authoritarian parents are especially punitive, authoritative parents are not. Authoritarian parents set strict rules without any input from their children and don't explain the rules adequately. Authoritative parents allow verbal give-and-take interchanges with children when developing rules for them. They also clearly explain the rules to the children. Authoritarian parents usually don't show warmth toward their children. Authoritative parents nurture their children. Authoritarian parents typically don't show pleasure toward their children when they accomplish something. Authoritative parents do.

Critical Thinking

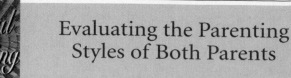

Evaluating the Parenting Styles of Both Parents

In our discussion of parenting styles, authoritative parenting was associated with social competence in children. In some cases, though, a child's parents differ in their parenting styles. Consider all four styles of parenting—authoritarian, authoritative, neglectful, and indulgent—on the parts of the mother and the father. A best case is when both parents are authoritative. What might the effects on the child be if the father is authoritarian and the mother is indulgent, or the father is authoritarian and the mother is authoritative, and so on? Is it better for the child if both parents have the same parenting style, even if the styles both are authoritarian, both indulgent, or both neglectful, or is it better for the child to have at least one authoritative parent when the other parent is authoritarian, indulgent, or neglectful?

In thinking about parenting styles, consider also what style or styles your father and mother used in rearing you. Were they both authoritative; one authoritarian, the other indulgent; and so on? What effects do you think their parenting styles had on your development?

Neglectful parenting *is a style in which the parent is very uninvolved in the child's life. It is associated with children's social incompetence, especially a lack of self-control.* This parent cannot answer the question "It is 10 P.M.—do you know where your child is?" Children whose parents are neglectful develop the sense that other aspects of the parents' lives are more important than they are. These children tend to be socially incompetent. Many have poor self-control and don't handle independence well. They frequently have low self-esteem, are immature, and may be alienated from the family. In adolescence, they may show patterns of truancy and delinquency.

Indulgent parenting *is a style of parenting in which parents are highly involved with their children but place few demands or controls on them. Indulgent parenting is associated with children's social incompetence, especially a lack of self-control.* Such parents let their children do what they want. The result is that the children never learn to control their own behavior and always expect to get their way. Some parents deliberately rear their children in this way because they believe the combination of warm involvement and few restraints will produce a creative, confident child. One boy I knew had parents who deliberately reared him in an indulgent manner. He moved his parents out of their bedroom suite and took it over for himself. He is now 18 years old and has not learned to control his behavior. When he can't get something he wants, he still throws temper tantrums. As you might expect, he is not popular with his peers. Children whose parents are indulgent rarely learn respect for others and have difficulty controlling their behavior. They might be aggressive, domineering, and noncompliant.

The four classifications of parenting just discussed involve combinations of acceptance and responsiveness on the one hand and demand and control on the other. How these dimensions combine to produce authoritarian, authoritative, neglectful, and indulgent parenting is shown in figure 9.4.

Child Abuse

Unfortunately, parenting sometimes leads to the abuse of infants and children. Child abuse is an increasing problem in the United States. Estimates of

authoritative parenting
A parenting style in which parents encourage their children to be independent but still place limits and controls on their actions. Extensive verbal give-and-take is allowed, and parents are warm and nurturant toward the child. Authoritative parenting is associated with children's social competence.

neglectful parenting
A style of parenting in which the parent is very uninvolved in the child's life; it is associated with children's social incompetence, especially a lack of self-control.

indulgent parenting
A style of parenting in which parents are highly involved with their children but place few demands or controls on them. Indulgent parenting is associated with children's social incompetence, especially a lack of self-control.

	Accepting, responsive	Rejecting, unresponsive
Demanding, controlling	Authoritative	Authoritarian
Undemanding, uncontrolling	Indulgent	Neglectful

Figure **9.4**

Classification of Parenting Styles

The four types of parenting styles (authoritative, authoritarian, indulgent, and neglectful) involve the dimensions of acceptance and responsiveness, on the one hand, and demand and control on the other. For example, authoritative parenting involves being both accepting/responsive and demanding/controlling.

its incidence vary, but some authorities say that as many as 500,000 children are physically abused every year. Laws in many states now require doctors and teachers to report suspected cases of child abuse, yet many cases go unreported, especially those of battered infants.

Child abuse is such a disturbing circumstance that many people have difficulty understanding or sympathizing with parents who abuse or neglect their children. Our response is often outrage and anger directed at the parent. This outrage focuses our attention on parents as bad, sick, monstrous, sadistic individuals who cause their children to suffer. Experts on child abuse believe that this view is too simple and deflects attention away from the social context of the abuse and parents' coping skills. It is especially important to recognize that child abuse is a diverse condition, that it is usually mild to moderate in severity, and that it is only partially caused by the individual personality characteristics of parents (Field, 2000). The most common kind of abuser is not a raging, uncontrolled physical abuser but an overwhelmed single mother in poverty who neglects the child.

The Multifaceted Nature of Abuse Whereas the public and many professionals use the term *child abuse* to refer to both abuse and neglect, developmentalists increasingly use the term *child maltreatment* (Cicchetti, 2001). This term does not have quite the emotional impact of the term *abuse* and acknowledges that maltreatment includes several different conditions. Among the different types of maltreatment are physical and sexual abuse; the fostering of delinquency; lack of supervision; medical, educational, and nutritional neglect; and drug or alcohol abuse. In one large survey, approximately 20 percent of the reported cases involved abuse alone, 46 percent neglect alone, 23 percent both abuse and neglect, and 11 percent sexual abuse (American Association for Protecting Children, 1986).

Severity of Abuse The concern about child abuse began with the identication of "battered child syndrome," which continues to be associated with severe, brutal injury for several reasons. First, the media tend to underscore the most bizarre and vicious incidents. Second, much of the funding for child abuse prevention, identification, and treatment depends on the public's perception of the horror of child abuse and the medical profession's lobby for funds to investigate and treat abused children and their parents. The emphasis is often on the worst cases. These horrific cases do exist and are indeed terrible. However, they make up only a small minority of maltreated children. Less than 1 percent of maltreated children die. Another 11 percent suffer life-threatening, disabling injuries (American Association for Protecting Children, 1986). By contrast, almost 90 percent suffer temporary physical injuries. These milder injuries, though, are likely to be experienced repeatedly in the context of daily hostile family exchanges. Similarly, neglected children, who suffer no physical injuries, often experience extensive, long-term psychological harm.

Child maltreatment involves grossly inadequate and destructive aspects of parenting.

Dante Cicchetti
Contemporary Developmental Psychologist, University of Rochester

The Cultural Context of Abuse The extensive violence that takes place in the American culture is reflected in the occurrence of violence in the family. A regular

diet of violence appears on television screens, and parents often resort to power assertion as a disciplinary technique. In China, where physical punishment is rarely used to discipline children, the incidence of child abuse is reported to be very low. In the United States, many abusing parents report that they do not have sufficient resources or help from others. This may be a realistic evaluation of the situation experienced by many low-income families, who do not have adequate preventive and supportive services.

Community support systems are especially important in alleviating stressful family situations, thereby helping prevent child abuse. An investigation of the support systems in 58 counties in New York State revealed a relation between the incidence of child abuse and the absence of support systems available to the family (Garbarino, 1976). Both family resources—relatives and friends, for example—and such formal community support systems as crisis centers and child abuse counseling were associated with a reduction in child abuse.

CAREERS IN LIFE-SPAN DEVELOPMENT

Debby Troopy, Child Social Worker

DEBBY TROOPY has been a child social worker for 10 years. She says, "I can't really see myself doing anything else. It emotionally drains me some days but I continue to think about the impact I can make."

Child Protective Services in Dallas, where Debbie works, removes children from homes where they are being abused or neglected, provides counseling services, and engages in parent training.

Family Influences To understand abuse in the family, the interactions of all family members need to be considered, regardless of who actually performs the violent acts against the child (Margolin, 1994). For example, even though the father may be the one who physically abuses the child, contributions by the mother, the child, and siblings also should be evaluated. Many parents who abuse their children come from families in which physical punishment was used. These parents view physical punishment as a legitimate way of controlling the child's behavior. Physical punishment may be a part of this sanctioning.

Were parents who abuse children abused by their own parents? About one-third of parents who were abused themselves when they were young abuse their own children (Cicchetti & Toth, 1998). Thus, some, but not a majority, of parents are locked into an intergenerational transmission of abuse. Mothers who break out of the intergenerational transmission of abuse often have at least one warm, caring adult in their background, have a close, positive marital relationship, and have received therapy (Egeland, Jacobvitz, & Sroufe, 1988).

Child Abuse Prevention Network
International Aspects of Child Abuse
National Clearinghouse on Child Abuse and Neglect

Developmental Consequences of Abuse Among the developmental consequences of child maltreatment are poor emotion regulation, attachment problems, problems in peer relations, difficulty in adapting to school, and other psychological problems (Rogosch & others, 1995; Shank & Cicchetti, 2001). Difficulties in initiating and modulating positive and negative affect have been observed in maltreated infants (Cicchetti, Ganiban, & Barnett, 1991). Maltreated infants also may show excessive negative affect or blunted positive affect.

Not only do maltreated infants show insecure patterns of attachment, but they also might show a form of attachment not often found in normal children. As we saw earlier in the chapter, maltreated children tend to display an attachment pattern referred to as *disorganized,* which involves high avoidance and high resistance (Main & Solomon, 1990). In one study, the disorganized attachment pattern was found in 80 percent of the maltreated infants observed (Carlson & others, 1989).

Maltreated children appear to be poorly equipped to develop successful peer relations, due to their aggressiveness, avoidance, and aberrant responses to both distress and positive approaches from peers (Bolger & Patterson, 2001; Mueller & Silverman, 1989). Two patterns of social behavior are common in maltreated children. Sometimes maltreated children show excessive physical and verbal aggression, while at other times maltreated children show a pattern of avoidance. These patterns have been described in terms of "fight or flight."

Critical Thinking

Developing a Model of Intervention for Maltreating Families

WHAT IS THE BEST way to help maltreated children? Intervention with maltreating families is difficult because of the multiple risk factors involved and the difficulty in getting such families to deal with the chaos in their lives. Poverty, intellectual and educational limitations, social isolation, and mental disorders are but a few of the factors that make it difficult to involve these families in effective treatment. With these limitations in mind, develop a model of intervention that you believe would benefit maltreated children and their families. Think about ways that therapists could assist families, about educational programs, and about recreational and activity possibilities.

Parenting is a very important profession, but no test of fitness for it is ever imposed in the interest of children.

George Bernard Shaw
Irish Playwright, 20th Century

Maltreated children's difficulties in establishing effective relationships may show up in their interactions with teachers. Maltreated children might expect teachers to be unresponsive or unavailable, based on their relationships with their parents. For maltreated children, dealing with fears about abuse and searching for security in relationships with adults can take precedence over performing competently at academic tasks.

Being physically abused has been linked with children's anxiety, personality problems, depression, conduct disorder, and delinquency (Toth, Manley, & Cicchetti, 1992). Later, during the adult years, maltreated children show increased violence toward other adults, dating partners, and marital partners, as well as increased substance abuse, anxiety, and depression (Malinosky-Rummell & Hansen, 1993). In sum, maltreated children are at risk for developing a wide range of problems and disorders.

Parenting: Nature and Nurture In chapter 3, "Biological Beginnings," we examined Judith Harris' (1998) argument that parents don't matter much in children's development, rather what matters are heredity and peer relations P. 88. We presented some general arguments refuting Harris' belief that parents don't matter. Here we explore some more specific research that documents the importance of parenting in children's, while at the same time acknowledging that heredity cannot be ignored.

Two types of recent studies are especially effective in disentangling children's heredity and their rearing experiences (Collins & others, 2000): (1) studies of the effects of rearing experiences on the behavior of children who differ in temperament, and (2) studies that compare the effects of high- and low-risk environments on children of different vulnerability.

In a longitudinal study, mothers' use of gentle childrearing techniques that deemphasized high degrees of control was more effective with temperamentally fearful children than with bolder, more exploratory children in promoting the development of children's conscience (Kochanska, 1999). Although only a few studies have examined the moderating effects of parenting on links between temperament and later adjustment, the evidence suggests that parenting moderates these associations (Rothbart & Bates, 1998).

Another way to examine links between parenting and child behavior is to study risk and resiliency in children. For example, researchers have found that children who showed early developmental problems because of risk factors such as low-birthweight problems subsequently showed better adjustment when authoritative parenting was used (Werner & Smith, 1992).

Studies of interventions with parents also can demonstrate whether parenting plays an important role in children's development (Collins & others, 2000). In one study, training low-income mothers to respond sensitively to their infants both modified the negative responses of the mothers to infant irritability and reduced the extent of avoidant attachment in distress-prone infants (Van den Boom, 1990). In another study, parents' participation in 16-week discussion groups on effective parenting just prior to their children's entry into kindergarten resulted in better school adjustment and higher academic achievement than children whose parents attended discussion groups without the effective parenting emphasis (Cowan & Cowan, 1998).

As with other areas of life-span development, the evidence on the role of parenting is that neither heredity alone nor environment alone is responsible for children's development. Interactions between heredity and environment determine children's development, and as part of this interaction, parenting does matter, as do heredity and peer relations (Vandell, 2000) P. 87.

Good Parenting Takes Time and Effort In today's society, there is an unfortunate theme which suggests that parenting can be done quickly and with little or no convenience (Sroufe, 2000). One example of this involves playing Mozart CDs in the hope that they will enrich infants' and young children's brains. Some of these parents might be thinking "I don't have enough time to spend with my children so I'll just play these intellectual CDs and then they won't need me as much." Judith Harris' book *The Nurture Assumption* (which states that heredity and peer relations are the key factors in children's development) fits into this theme that parents don't need to spend much time with their children. Why did it become so popular? To some degree some people who don't spend much time with their children saw it as supporting their neglect and reducing their guilt.

One-minute bedtime stories also are now being marketed successfully for parents to read to their children (Walsh, 2000). Most of these are brief summaries of longer stories. There are one-minute bedtime bear books, puppy books, and so on. These parents know it is good for them to read with their children, but they don't want to spend a lot of time doing it.

What is wrong with these quick-fix approaches to parenting? Good parenting takes a lot of time and a lot of effort. You can't do it in a minute here and a minute there. You can't do it with CDs.

Now that we have studied parenting, let's turn our attention to another aspect of many children's family life: relationships with siblings.

Sibling Relationships and Birth Order

What are sibling relationships like? How extensively does birth order influence behavior?

Sibling Relationships Any of you who have grown up with siblings probably have a rich memory of aggressive, hostile interchanges. But sibling relationships also have many pleasant, caring moments. Children's sibling relationships include helping, sharing, teaching, fighting, and playing. Children can act as emotional supports, rivals, and communication partners (Carlson, 1995). More than 80 percent of American children have one or more siblings (brothers or sisters). Because there are so many possible sibling combinations, it is difficult to generalize about sibling influences. Among the factors to consider are the number of siblings, the ages of siblings, birth order, age spacing, the sex of siblings, and whether sibling relationships are different from parent-child relationships.

Big sisters are the crab grass in the lawn of life.

Charles Schulz
American Cartoonist, 20th Century

Birth Order Birth order is a special interest of sibling researchers. When differences in birth order are found, they usually are explained by variations in interactions with parents and siblings associated with the unique experiences of being in a particular position in the family. This is especially true in the case of the firstborn child (Teti & others, 1993). Parents have higher expectations for firstborn children than for later-born children. They put more pressure on them for achievement and responsibility. They also interfere more with their activities (Rothbart, 1971).

Given the differences in family dynamics involved in birth order, it is not surprising that firstborns and later-borns have different characteristics (J. L. Rodgers, 2000). Firstborn children are more adult-oriented, helpful, conforming, anxious, and self-controlled than their siblings. Parents give more attention to firstborns and this is related to firstborns' nurturant behavior (Stanhope & Corter, 1993). Parental demands and high standards established for firstborns result in these children's excelling in academic and professional endeavors. Firstborns are overrepresented in *Who's Who* and Rhodes scholars, for example. However, some of the same pressures placed on firstborns for high achievement may be the reason they also have more guilt, anxiety, and difficulty in coping with stressful situations, as well as higher admission to child guidance clinics.

The one-child family is becoming much more common in China because of the strong motivation to limit the population growth in the People's Republic of China. The policy is still new, and its effects on children have not been fully examined. *In general, what have researchers found the only child to be like?*

What is the only child like? The popular conception is that the only child is a "spoiled brat," with such undesirable characteristics as dependency, lack of self-control, and self-centered behavior. But researchers present a more positive portrayal of the only child, who often is achievement-oriented and displays a desirable personality, especially in comparison with later-borns and children from large families (Falbo & Poston, 1993; Jiao, Ji, & Jing, 1996).

Keep in mind, though, that birth order by itself often is not a good predictor of behavior. When factors such as age spacing, sex of the siblings, heredity, temperament, parenting styles, peer influences, school influences, sociocultural factors, and so forth are taken into account, they often are more important in determining a child's behavior than birth order.

The Changing Family in a Changing Society

Children are growing up in a greater variety of family structures than ever before. Many mothers spend the greatest part of their day away from their children, even their infants. More than one of every two mothers with a child under the age of 5 is in the labor force; more than two of every three with a child from 6 to 17 years of age is. And the increasing number of children growing up in single-parent families is staggering. As shown in figure 9.5, the United States has the highest percentage of single-parent families, compared with virtually all other countries. If current trends continue, by the year 2000 one in every four children also will have lived a portion of his or her life in a stepparent family.

WWW

Working Parents

Family and the Workplace

Working Parents Because household operations have become more efficient and family size has decreased in America, it is not certain that when both parents work outside the home, children receive less attention than children in the past whose mothers were not employed. Outside employment—at least for parents with school-age children—might simply be filling time previously taken up by added

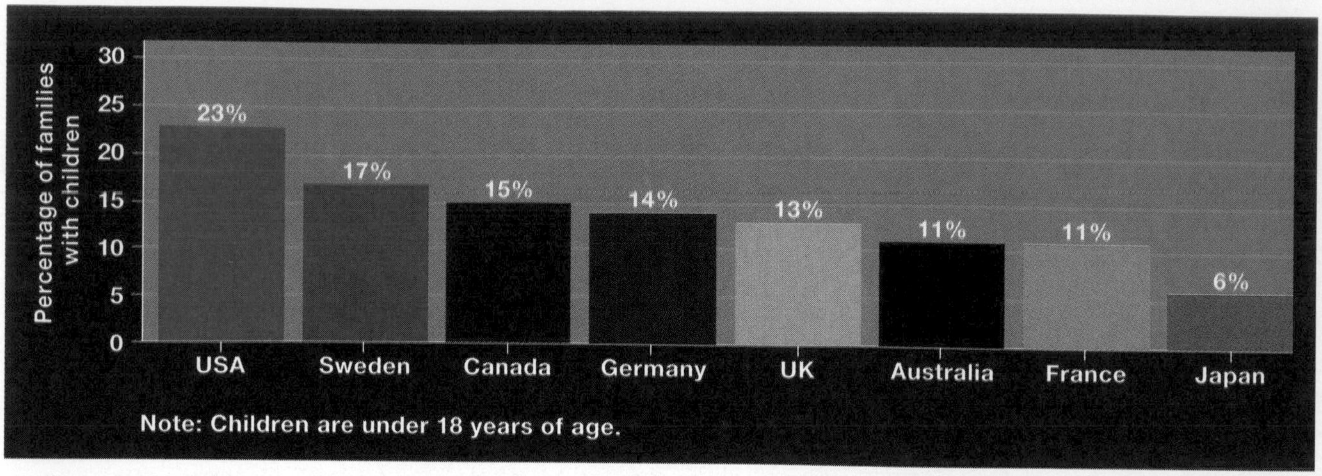

Figure 9.5
Single-Parent Families in Different Countries

household burdens and more children. It also cannot be assumed that, if the mother did not go to work, the child would benefit from the time freed up by streamlined household operations and smaller families. Mothering does not always have a positive effect on the child. The educated, nonworking mother may overinvest her energies in her children. This can foster an excess of worry and discourage the child's independence. In such situations, the mother may give more parenting than the child can profitably handle.

As Lois Hoffman (1989) commented, maternal employment is a part of modern life. It is not an aberrant aspect of it but a response to other social changes. It meets needs that cannot be met by the previous family ideal of a full-time mother and homemaker. Not only does it meet the parents' needs, but in many ways it may be a pattern better suited to socializing children for the adult roles they will occupy. This is especially true for daughters, but it is also true for sons. The broader range of emotions and skills that each parent presents is more consistent with this adult role. Just as his father shares the breadwinning role and the child-rearing role with his mother, so the son, too, may be more willing to share these roles. The rigid gender stereotyping perpetuated by the divisions of labor in the traditional family is not appropriate for the demands that will be made on children of either sex as adults.

The needs of the growing child require the mother to loosen her hold on the child. This task may be easier for the working woman, whose job is an additional source of identity and self-esteem. Overall, researchers have found no detrimental effects of maternal employment on children's development (Gottfried, Gottfried, & Bathurst, 1995; Hoffman & Youngblade, 1999; Richards & Duckett, 1994). For example, in one longitudinal study, no link between maternal employment and children's development from infancy to age 12 was found (Gottfried, Gottfried, & Bathurst, 1995).

A common experience of working mothers (and working fathers) is feeling guilty about being away from their children. The guilt can be triggered by missing their child, worry that their child is missing them, concern about the implications of working (such as whether the child is receiving good child care), and worry about the long-term effects of working (such as whether they are jeopardizing the child's future). To reduce guilt, the guilt needs to be acknowledged. Pediatrician T. Berry Brazelton (1983) believes that parents respond to guilt either by admitting it and working through it or by denying it and rationalizing it away. The

In Japan, only 6% of children live in single-parent families, compared to 23% in the United States. *What might explain this difference?*

latter tendency is not recommended. Working parents' guilt can also be reduced if they pay closer attention to how their children are doing.

Effects of Divorce on Children These are the questions that we will explore that focus on the effects of divorce: Are children better adjusted in intact, never divorced families than in divorced families? Should parents stay together for the sake of their children? How much do parenting skills matter in divorced families? What factors are involved in the child's individual risk and vulnerability in a divorced family? What role does socioeconomic status play in the lives of children in divorced families?

Children's Adjustment in Divorced Families Most researchers agree that children from divorced families show poorer adjustment than their counterparts in nondivorced families (Amato & Keith, 1991). Those that have experienced multiple divorces are at greater risk. Children in divorced families are more likely than children in nondivorced families to have academic problems, to show externalized problems (such as acting out and delinquency) and internalized problems (such as anxiety and depression), to be less socially responsible, to have less competent intimate relationships, to drop out of school, to become sexually active at an early age, to take drugs, to associate with antisocial peers, and to have low self-esteem (Conger & Chao, 1996).

Although there is a consensus that children from divorced families show these adjustment problems to a greater extent than do children from nondivorced families, there is less agreement about the size of the effects (Hetherington, Bridges, & Insabella, 1998). Some researchers report that the divorce effects are modest and have become smaller as divorce has become more commonplace in society (Amato & Keith, 1991). However, others argue that approximately 20 to 25 percent of children in divorced families have these types of adjustment problems, in contrast to only 10 percent of children in nondivorced families, which is a notable two-fold increase (Hetherington & Jodl, 1994). Nonetheless, the majority of children in divorced families do not have these problems (Hetherington, 1999, 2000). The weight of the research evidence underscores that most children competently cope with their parents' divorce but that significantly more children from divorced families have adjustment problems (20 to 25 percent) than children from nondivorced families (10 percent).

Should Parents Stay Together for the Sake of Their Children? Whether parents should stay in an unhappy or conflicted marriage for the sake of their children is one of the most commonly asked questions about divorce (Hetherington, 1999, 2000). If the stresses and disruptions in family relationships associated with an unhappy, conflictual marriage that erode the well-being of children are reduced by the move to a divorced, single-parent family, divorce can be advantageous. However, if the diminished resources and increased risks associated with divorce also are accompanied by inept parenting and sustained or increased conflict, not only between the divorced couple but also between the parents, children, and siblings, the best choice for the children would be for an unhappy marriage to be retained. These are

"ifs," and it is difficult to determine how these will play out when parents either remain together in an acrimonious marriage or become divorced.

Children and Divorce
Divorce and Family Ties
Divorce Resources
Father Custody

How Much Do Family Processes Matter in Divorced Families? Family processes matter a lot (Emery, 1999). When divorced parents' relationship with each other is harmonious and when they use authoritative parenting, the adjustment of children improves (Hetherington, Bridges, & Insabella, 1998). A number of researchers have shown that a disequilibrium, which includes diminished parenting skills, occurs in the year following the divorce but that, by two years after the divorce, restablization has occurred and parenting skills have improved (Hetherington, 1989). About one-fourth to one-third of children in divorced families, compared with 10 percent in nondivorced families, become disengaged from their families, spending as little time as possible at home and in interaction with family members (Hetherington & Jodl, 1994). This disengagement is higher for boys than girls in divorced families. However, if there is a caring adult outside the home, such as a mentor, the disengagement may be a positive solution to a disrupted, conflicted family circumstance.

What Factors Are Involved in the Child's Individual Risk and Vulnerability in a Divorced Family? Among the factors involved in the child's risk and vulnerability are the child's adjustment prior to the divorce, as well as the child's personality and temperament, gender, and custody situation. Children whose parents later divorce show poorer adjustment before the breakup (Amato & Booth, 1996). When antecedent levels of problem behaviors are controlled, differences in the adjustment of children in divorced and nondivorced families are reduced (Cherlin & others, 1991).

Personality and temperament also play a role in children's adjustment in divorced families. Children who are socially mature and responsible, who show few behavioral problems, and who have an easy temperament are better able to cope with their parents' divorce. Children with a difficult temperament often have problems in coping with their parents' divorce (Hetherington, 1999).

Earlier studies reported gender differences in response to divorce, with divorce being more negative for girls than boys in mother custody families. However, more recent studies have shown that gender differences are less pronounced and consistent than was previously believed. Some of the inconsistency may be due to the increase in father custody, joint custody, and increased involvement of noncustodial fathers, especially in their sons' lives.

In recent decades, an increasing number of children have lived in father custody and joint-custody families (Maccoby, 1999). What is their adjustment like, compared with that of children in mother custody families? Although there have been few thorough studies of the topic, there appear to be few advantages of joint custody over custody by one parent (Hetherington, Bridges, & Insabella. 1998). Some studies have shown that boys adjust better in father custody families, girls in mother custody familes, while other studies have not. In one study, the adolescents in father custody families had higher rates of delinquency, believed to be due to less competent monitoring by the fathers (Maccoby & Mnookin, 1992).

What Role Does Socioeconomic Status Play in the Lives of Children in Divorced Families? Custodial mothers experience the loss of about one-fourth to one-half of their predivorce income, in comparison with a loss of only one-tenth by custodial fathers (Emery, 1999). This income loss for divorced mothers is accompanied by increased workloads, high rates of job instability, and residential moves to less desirable neighborhoods with inferior schools.

Cultural, Ethnic, and Socioeconomic Variations in Families

Cultures vary on a number of issues involving families, such as what the father's

What are some characteristics of families within different ethnic groups?

role in the family should be, the extent to which support systems are available to families, and the ways in which children should be disciplined. Although there are cross-cultural variations in parenting (Whiting & Edwards, 1988), in one study of parenting behavior in 186 cultures around the world, the most common pattern was a warm and controlling style, one that was neither permissive nor restrictive (Rohner & Rohner, 1981). The investigators commented that the majority of cultures have discovered, over many centuries, a "truth" that only recently emerged in the Western world—namely, that children's healthy social development is most effectively promoted by love and at least some moderate parental control.

Families within different ethnic groups in the United States differ in their size, structure, composition, reliance on kinships networks, and levels of income and education (Parke & Buriel, 1998). Large and extended families are more common among minority groups than among the White majority. For example, 19 percent of Latino families have three or more children, compared with 14 percent of African American and 10 percent of White families. African American and Latino children interact more with grandparents, aunts, uncles, cousins, and more-distant relatives than do White children.

Single-parent families are more common among African Americans and Latinos than among White Americans. In comparsion with two-parent households, single parents often have more limited resources of time, money, and energy. African American and Latino parents also are less educated and more likely to live in low-income circumstances than their White counterparts. Still, many impoverished African American and Latino families raise competent children.

Some aspects of home life can help protect ethnic minority children from injustice. The community and the family can filter out destructive racist messages, and parents can present alternative frames of reference to those presented by the majority. The extended family also can serve as an important buffer to stress (McAdoo, 1999; Wakschlag, Chase-Lansdale, & Brooks-Gunn, 1996).

In America and most Western cultures, differences have been found in child rearing among different socioeconomic groups. Low-income parents often place a high value on external characteristics, such as obedience and neatness. By contrast, middle- and upper-income families frequently place a high value on internal characteristics, such as self-control and delay of gratification. Middle- and upper-income parents are more likely to explain something, praise, use reasoning to accompany their discipline, and ask their children questions. By contrast, low-income parents are more likely to use physical punishment and criticize their children (Hoff-Ginsburg & Tardif, 1995).

There also are socioeconomic differences in the way that parents think about education (Lareau, 1996). Middle- and upper-income parents more often think of education as something that should be mutually encouraged by parents and teachers. By contrast, low-income parents are more likely to view education as the teacher's job. Thus, increased school-family linkages especially can benefit students from low-income families.

At this point we have studied many aspects of families. To review these ideas, see summary table 9.3.

Family Diversity

Summary Table 9.3
Families

Concept	Processes/ Related Ideas	Characteristics/Descriptions
Parenting	Parenting Styles	• Authoritarian, authoritative, neglectful, and indulgent are four main parenting styles. • Authoritative parenting is the style most often associated with children's social competence.
	Child Abuse	• An understanding of child abuse requires information about cultural, familial, and community influences. • Sexual abuse of children is now recognized as a more widespread problem than was believed in the past. • Child maltreatment places the child at risk for a number of developmental problems.
	Parenting: Nature and Nurture	• Some critics, such as Judith Harris, have argued that heredity and peer relations, rather than parenting, are the key factors in children's development. • Contemporary parenting research documents that parenting plays an important role in children's development, while acknowledging the contributions of heredity and peer relations as well.
	Good Parenting Takes Time and Effort	• In today's society, an unfortunate theme is that parenting can be done quickly. However, good parenting takes extensive time and effort.
Sibling Relationships and Birth Order	Sibling Relationship	• Siblings interact with each order in positive and negative ways.
	Birth Order	• Birth order is related in certain ways to child characteristics, but some critics argue that birth order is not a good predictor of behavior.
The Changing Family in a Changing Society	Working Parents	• There is no indication that both parents working full-time outside the home has negative long-term effects on children.
	Effects of Divorce on Children	• Understanding the effects of divorce on children involves understanding adjustment, whether parents should stay together for the sake of the children, how much family processes matter, and socioeconomic status.
	Cultural, Ethnic, and Sociocultural Variations in Families	• Authoritative parenting is the most widely used style around the world. • Cultures vary on a number of issues regarding families. • African American and Latino children are more likely than White American children to live in single-parent families and larger families and to have extended family connections. • Higher-income families are more likely to use discipline that encourages internalization; low-income families, discipline that focuses on external characteristics.

Peer Relations, Play, and Television

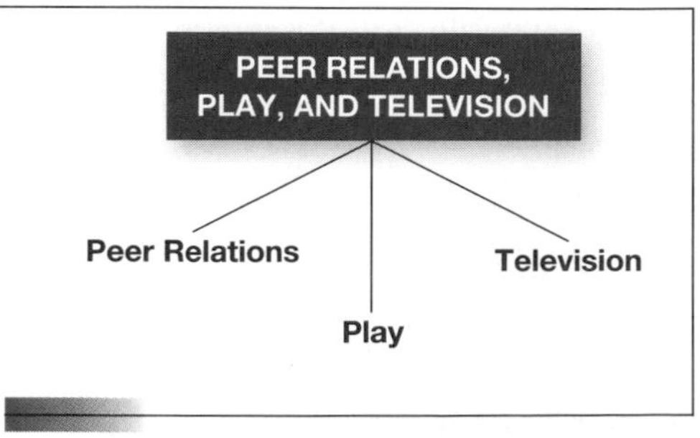

The family is an important social context for children's development. However, children's development also is strongly influenced by what goes on in other social contexts, such as peer relations, play, and television.

Peer Relations

As children grow older, peer relations consume an increasing amount of their time. What is the function of a child's peer group?

Peers are children of about the same age or maturity level. Same-age peer interaction fills a unique role in our culture. Age grading would occur even if schools were not age graded and children were left alone to determine the composition of their own societies. One of the most important functions of the peer group is to provide a source of information and comparison about the world outside the family. Children receive feedback about their abilities from their peer group. Children evaluate what they do in terms of whether it is better than, as good as, or worse than what other children do. It is hard to do this at home because siblings are usually older or younger.

Are peers necessary for development? When peer monkeys who have been reared together are separated, they become depressed and less advanced socially (Suomi, Harlow, & Domek, 1970). The human development literature contains a classic example of the importance of peers in social development. Anna Freud (Freud & Dann, 1951) studied six children from different families who banded together after their parents were killed in World War II. Intensive peer attachment was observed. The children formed a tightly knit group, dependent on one another and aloof with outsiders. Even though deprived of parental care, they neither became delinquent nor developed serious mental disorders.

Peer Relations

Thus, good peer relations can be necessary for normal social development. Special concerns focus on children who are withdrawn and aggressive (Coie, 1999; Ladd, 1999). Withdrawn children who are rejected by peers and/or victimized and feeling lonely are at risk for depression. Children who are aggressive with their peers are at risk for developing a number of problems, including delinquency and dropping out of school. We will have much more to say about peer relations in chapter 11, "Socioemotional Development in Middle and Late Childhood."

Play

An extensive amount of peer interaction during childhood involves play. Although peer interaction can involve play, social play is but one type of play. *Play* is a pleasurable activity that is engaged in for its own sake. Our coverage of play includes its functions, Parten's classic study of play, and types of play.

Play's Functions Play is essential to the young child's health. As today's children move into the twenty-first century and continue to experience pressure in their lives, play becomes even more crucial (VanHoorn & others, 1999). Play increases affiliation with peers, releases tension, advances cognitive development, increases exploration, and provides a safe haven in which to engage in potentially dangerous behavior. Play increases the probability that children will converse and interact with each other. During this interaction, children practice the roles they will assume later in life (Sutton-Smith, 2000).

And that park grew up with me; that small world widened as I learned its secret boundaries, as I discovered new refuges in the woods and jungles: hidden homes and lairs for the multitudes of imagination, for cowboys and Indians. . . . I used to dawdle on half holidays along the bent and devon-facing seashore, hoping for gold watches or the skull of a sheep or a message in a bottle to be washed up by the tide.

Dylan Thomas
Welsh Poet, 20th Century

According to Freud and Erikson, play is an especially useful form of human adjustment, helping the child master anxieties and conflicts. Because tensions are relieved in play, the child can cope with life's problems. Play permits the child to work off excess physical energy and to release pent-up tensions. *Play therapy* allows the child to work off frustrations. Through play therapy, the therapist can analyze the child's conflicts and ways of coping with them. Children may feel less threatened and be more likely to express their true feelings in the context of play.

Piaget (1962) believed that play advances children's cognitive development. At the same time, he said that children's cognitive development *constrains* the way they play. Play permits children to practice their competencies and acquired skills in a relaxed, pleasurable way. Piaget thought that cognitive structures need to be exercised, and play provides the perfect setting for this exercise. For example, children who have just learned to add or multiply begin to play with numbers in different ways as they perfect these operations, laughing as they do so.

Vygotsky (1962), whose developmental theory was discussed in chapter 8, also believed that play is an excellent setting for cognitive development. He was especially

Mildred Parten classified play into six categories. *Study this photograph. Which of Parten's categories are reflected in the behavior of the children?*

interested in the symbolic and make-believe aspects of play, as when a child substitutes a stick for a horse and rides the stick as if it were a horse. For young children, the imaginary situation is real. Parents should encourage such imaginary play, because it advances the child's cognitive development, especially creative thought.

Daniel Berlyne (1960) described play as exciting and pleasurable in itself because it satisfies our exploratory drive. This drive involves curiosity and a desire for information about something new or unusual. Play is a means whereby children can safely explore and seek out new information—something they might not otherwise do. Play encourages this exploratory behavior by offering children the possibilities of novelty, complexity, uncertainty, surprise, and incongruity.

Parten's Classic Study of Play Many years ago, Mildred Parten (1932) developed an elaborate classification of children's play. Based on observations of children in free play at nursery school, Parten arrived at these play categories:

1. **Unoccupied play** *is not play as it is commonly understood. The child may stand in one spot, look around the room, or perform random movements that do not seem to have a goal.* In most nursery schools, unoccupied play is less frequent than other forms of play.
2. **Solitary play** *occurs when the child plays alone and independently of others.* The child seems engrossed in the activity and does not care much about anything else that is happening. Two- and 3-year-olds engage more frequently in solitary play than older preschoolers do.
3. **Onlooker play** *occurs when the child watches other children play.* The child may talk with other children and ask questions but does not enter into their play behavior. The child's active interest in other children's play distinguishes onlooker play from unoccupied play.
4. **Parallel play** *occurs when the child plays separately from others, but with toys like those the others are using or in a manner that mimics their play.* The older

unoccupied play
Play in which the child is not engaging in play as it is commonly understood and might stand in one spot, look around the room, or perform random movements that do not seem to have a goal.

solitary play
Play in which the child plays alone and independently of others.

onlooker play
Play in which the child watches other children play.

parallel play
Play in which the child plays separately from others, but with toys like those the others are using or in a manner that mimics their play.

children are, the less frequently they engage in this type of play. However even older preschool children engage in parallel play quite often.

associative play
Play that involves social interaction with little or no organization.

5. **Associative play** *occurs when play involves social interaction with little or no organization.* In this type of play, children seem to be more interested in each other than in the tasks they are performing. Borrowing or lending toys and following or leading one another in line are examples of associative play.

cooperative play
Play that involves social interaction in a group with a sense of group identity and organized activity.

6. **Cooperative play** *involves social interaction in a group with a sense of group identity and organized activity.* Children's formal games, competition aimed at winning, and groups formed by the teacher for doing things together are examples of cooperative play. Cooperative play is the prototype for the games of middle childhood. Little cooperative play is seen in the preschool years.

Play

Types of Play Parten's categories represent one way of thinking about the different types of play. However, today researchers and practitioners who are involved with children's play believe other types of play are important in children's development. Whereas Parten's categories emphasize the role of play in the child's social world, the contemporary perspective on play emphasizes both the cognitive and the social aspects of play. Among the most widely studied types of children's play today are sensorimotor and practice play, pretense/symbolic play, social play, constructive play, and games (Bergin, 1988). We will consider each of these types of play in turn.

sensorimotor play
Behavior engaged in by infants to derive pleasure from exercising their existing sensorimotor schemas.

Sensorimotor and Practice Play **Sensorimotor play** *is behavior engaged in by infants to derive pleasure from exercising their existing sensorimotor schemas.* The development of sensorimotor play follows Piaget's description of sensorimotor thought, which we discussed in chapter 6. Infants initially engage in exploratory and playful visual and motor transactions in the second quarter of the first year of life. At 9 months of age, infants begin to select novel objects for exploration and play, especially those that are responsive, such as toys that make noise or bounce. At 12 months of age, infants enjoy making things work and exploring cause and effect. At this point in development, children like toys that perform when they act on them.

In the second year, infants begin to understand the social meaning of objects, and their play reflects this awareness. And 2-year-olds may distinguish between exploratory play that is interesting but not humorous and "playful" play, which has incongruous and humorous dimensions. For example, a 2-year-old might "drink" from a shoe or call a dog a "cow." When 2-year-olds find these deliberate incongruities funny, they are beginning to show evidence of symbolic play and the ability to play with ideas.

practice play
Play that involves repetition of behavior when new skills are being learned or when physical or mental mastery and coordination of skills are required for games or sports. Sensorimotor play, which often involves practice play, is primarily confined to infancy, while practice play can be engaged in throughout life.

Practice play *involves the repetition of behavior when new skills are being learned or when physical or mental mastery and coordination of skills are required for games or sports. Sensorimotor play, which often involves practice play, is primarily confined to infancy, while practice play can be engaged in throughout life.* During the preschool years, children often engage in play that involves practicing various skills. Estimates indicate that practice play constitutes one-third of the preschool child's play activities but less than one-sixth of the elementary school child's play activities (Rubin, Fein, & Vandenberg, 1983). Practice play contributes to the development of the coordinated motor skills needed for later game playing. While practice play declines in the elementary school years, practice play activities such as running, jumping, sliding, twirling, and throwing balls or other objects are frequently observed on the playgrounds at elementary schools. These activities appear similar to the earlier practice play of the preschool years, but practice play in the elementary school years differs from earlier practice play because much of it is ends- rather than means-related. That is, elementary school children often engage in practice play for the purpose of improving the motor skills needed to compete in games or sports.

In the sun that is young once only
Time let me play.

Dylan Thomas
Welsh Poet, 20th Century

pretense/symbolic play
Play in which the child transforms the physical environment into a symbol.

Pretense/Symbolic Play **Pretense/symbolic play** *occurs when the child transforms the physical environment into a symbol.* Between 9 and 30 months of age, children increase their use of objects in symbolic play. They learn to transform objects—substituting them for other objects and acting toward them as if they were

these other objects. For example, a preschool child treats a table as if it were a car and says, "I'm fixing the car," as he grabs a leg of the table.

Many experts on play consider the preschool years the "golden age" of symbolic/pretense play that is dramatic or sociodramatic in nature (Fein, 1986). This type of make-believe play often appears at about 18 months of age and reaches a peak at 4 to 5 years of age, then gradually declines. In the early elementary school years, children's interests often shift to games. In one observational study of nine children, at 4 years of age the children spent more than 12 minutes per hour in pretend play (Haight & Miller, 1993). In this study, a number of parents agreed with Piaget and Vygotsky that pretending helps develop children's imaginations.

Social Play **Social play** *is play that involves social interaction with peers.* Parten's categories, described earlier, are oriented toward social play. Social play with peers increases dramatically during the preschool years. In addition to general social play with peers and group pretense or sociodramatic play, another form of social play is rough-and-tumble play. The movement patterns of rough-and-tumble play are often similar to those of hostile behavior (running, chasing, wrestling, jumping, falling, hitting). However, in rough-and-tumble play these behaviors are accompanied by signals, such as laughter, exaggerated movement, and open rather than closed hands, that indicate that this is play.

social play
Play that involves social interactions with peers.

Constructive Play **Constructive play** *combines sensorimotor and practice repetitive activity with symbolic representation of ideas. Constructive play occurs when children engage in self-regulated creation or construction of a product or a problem solution.* Constructive play increases in the preschool years as symbolic play increases and sensorimotor play decreases. In the preschool years, some practice play is replaced by constructive play. For example, instead of moving their fingers around and around in finger paint (practice play), children are more likely to draw the outline of a house or a person in the paint (constructive play). Some researchers have found that constructive play is the most common type of play during the preschool years (Rubin, Maioni, & Hornung, 1976). Constructive play is also a frequent form of play in the elementary school years, both in and out of the classroom. Constructive play is one of the few playlike activities allowed in work-centered classrooms. For example, having children create a play about a social studies topic involves constructive play. Whether children consider such activities to be play usually depends on whether they get to choose whether to do it (it is play) or whether the teacher imposes it (it is not play), as well as whether it is enjoyable (it is play) or not (it is not play) (King, 1982).

constructive play
Play that combines sensorimotor/practice repetitive activity with symbolic representation of ideas. Constructive play occurs when children engage in self-regulated creation or construction of a product or a problem solution.

Constructive play also can be used in the elementary school years to foster academic skill learning, thinking skills, and problem solving. Many educators plan classroom activities that include humor, encourage playing with ideas, and promote creativity (Bergin, 1988). Educators also often support the performance of plays, the writing of imaginative stories, the expression of artistic abilities, and the playful exploration of computers and other technological equipment. However, distinctions between work and play frequently become blurred in the elementary school classroom. Think of constructive play as a midway point between play and work.

Games **Games** *are activities engaged in for pleasure. They include rules and often competition with one or more individuals.* Preschool children may begin to participate in social game play that involves simple rules of reciprocity and turn taking. However, games take on a much stronger role in the lives of elementary school children. In one study, the highest incidence of game playing occurred between 10 and 12 years of age (Eiferman, 1971). After age 12, games decline in popularity. They often are replaced by practice play, conversations, and organized sports (Bergin, 1988).

games
Activities engaged in for pleasure that include rules and often competition with one or more individuals.

In the elementary years, games feature the meaningfulness of a challenge. This challenge is present if two or more children have the skills required to play and understand the rules of the game. Among the types of games children engage in are steady or constant games, such as tag, which are played consistently; recurrent or cyclical games, such as marbles and hopscotch, which seem to follow cycles of popularity and

decline; sporadic games, which are rarely played; and one-time games, such as hula hoop contests, which rise to popularity once and then disappear.

In sum, play is a multidimensional, complex concept. It ranges from an infant's simple exercise of a newfound sensorimotor talent to a preschool child's riding a tricycle to an older child's participation in organized games. Children's play also can involve combinations of the play categories we have described. For example, social play can be sensorimotor (rough-and-tumble), symbolic, and constructive.

Television

Television and Children

Few developments in society in the second half of the twentieth century had a greater impact on children than television (Bryant & Bryant, 2001; Comstock & Scharrar, 1999; Murray, 2000). Many children spend more time in front of the television set than they do with their parents. Although it is only one of the many mass media that affect children's behavior, television is the most influential. The persuasive capabilities of television are staggering (Kotler, Wright, & Huston, 2001). The 20,000 hours of television watched by the time the average American adolescent graduates from high school are greater than the number of hours spent in the classroom.

Television's Many Roles Television can have a negative influence by taking children away from homework, making them passive learners, teaching them stereotypes, providing them with violent models of aggression, and presenting them with unrealistic views of the world. However, television can have a positive influence on children's development by presenting motivating educational programs, increasing their information about the world beyond their immediate environment, and providing models of prosocial behavior (Clifford, Gunter, & McAleer, 1995).

Television has been called many things, not all of them good. Depending on one's point of view, it may be a "window on the world," the "one-eyed monster," or the "boob tube." Television has been attacked as one of the reasons scores on national achievement tests in reading and mathematics are lower now than in the past. Television, it is claimed, attracts children away from books and schoolwork. In one study, children who read printed materials, such as books, watched television less than those who did not read (Huston, Seigle, & Bremer, 1983). Furthermore, critics argue, television trains children to become passive learners. Rarely, if ever, does television require active responses from the observer.

Television is a medium of entertainment which permits millions of people to listen to the same joke at the same time, and yet remain lonesome.

T. S. Eliot
American-Born English Poet, 20th Century

Television also is said to deceive. That is, it teaches children that problems are resolved easily and that everything always comes out right in the end. For example, TV detectives usually take only 30 to 60 minutes to sort through a complex array of clues to reveal the killer. And they *always* find the killer! Violence is a way of life on many shows, where it is all right for police to use violence and to break moral codes in their fight against evildoers. The lasting results of violence are rarely brought home to the viewer. A person who is injured suffers for only a few seconds. In real life, the person might need months or years to recover, or might not recover at all, yet one out of every two first-grade children says that the adults on television are like adults in real life.

A special concern is how ethnic minorities are portrayed on television (Dates & Stroman, 2001; Greenberg & Brand, 1994). Ethnic minorities have historically been underrepresented and misrepresented on television. Ethnic minority characters—whether African American, Latino, Asian American, or Native American—have traditionally been presented as less dignified and less positive than White characters. In one study, character portrayals of ethnic minorities were examined during heavy children's viewing hours (weekdays 4 to 6 P.M. and 7 to 11 P.M.) (Williams & Condry, 1989). The percentage of White characters far exceeded the actual percentage of Whites in the United States. The percentage of African American, Latino, and Asian American characters fell short of the population statistics. Latino characters were especially underrepresented. Only 0.6 percent of the characters were Latino, while the Latino population in the United States is 6.4 percent of the total U.S. population. Minorities tended to hold lower-status jobs and were more likely than Whites to be cast as criminals or victims.

Summary Table 9.4
Peer Relations, Play, and Television

Concept	Processes/ Related Ideas	Characteristics/Descriptions
Peer Relations	Peer Group Function	• Peers are powerful socialization agents. • Peers are children who are of about the same age or maturity level. • Peers provide a source of information and comparison about the world outside the family.
Play	Play's Functions	• Play's functions include affiliation with peers, tension release, advances in cognitive development, exploration, and provision of a safe haven.
	Parten's Classic Study of Play	• Parten developed the categories of unoccupied, solitary, onlooker, parallel, associative, and cooperative play.
	Types of Play	• The contemporary perpective on play emphasizes both the cognitive and the social aspects of play. • Among the most widely studied aspects of children's play today are sensorimotor play, practice play, pretense/symbolic play, social play, constructive play, and games.
Television	Television's Many Roles	• Television can have both negative influences (such as turning children into passive learners and presenting them with aggressive models) and positive influences (such as presenting motivating educational programs and providing models of prosocial behavior) on childrens's development.
	Amount of Television Watched by Children	• Children watch huge amounts of television.
	Effects of Television on Children's Aggression and Prosocial Behavior	• TV violence is not the only cause of children's aggression, but it can induce aggression. • Prosocial behavior on TV is associated with increased positive behavior by children.
	Television and Cognitive Development	• Children's cognitive skills influence their TV-viewing experiences. • Television veiwing is negatively related to children's creativity and verbal skills.

they still process television information less effectively than adults do. Children's greater attention to television and their less complete and more distorted understanding of what they view suggest that they may miss some of the positive aspects of television and be more vulnerable to its negative aspects.

How does television influence children's creativity and verbal skills? Television is negatively related to children's creativity (Williams, 1986). Also, because television is primarily a visual modality, verbal skills—especially expressive language—are enhanced more by aural or print exposure (Beagles-Roos & Gat, 1983). Educational programming for young children can promote creativity and imagination, possibly because it has a slower pace, and auditory and visual modalities are better coordinated (Anderson & others, 2001). Newer technologies, especially interactive television, hold promise for motivating children to learn and become more exploratory in solving problems (Singer, 1993).

At this point we have discussed a number of ideas about peers, play, and television. To review these ideas, see summary table 9.4. This concludes our examination of early childhood. In the next section, we will turn our attention to development in middle and late childhood.

Chapter Review

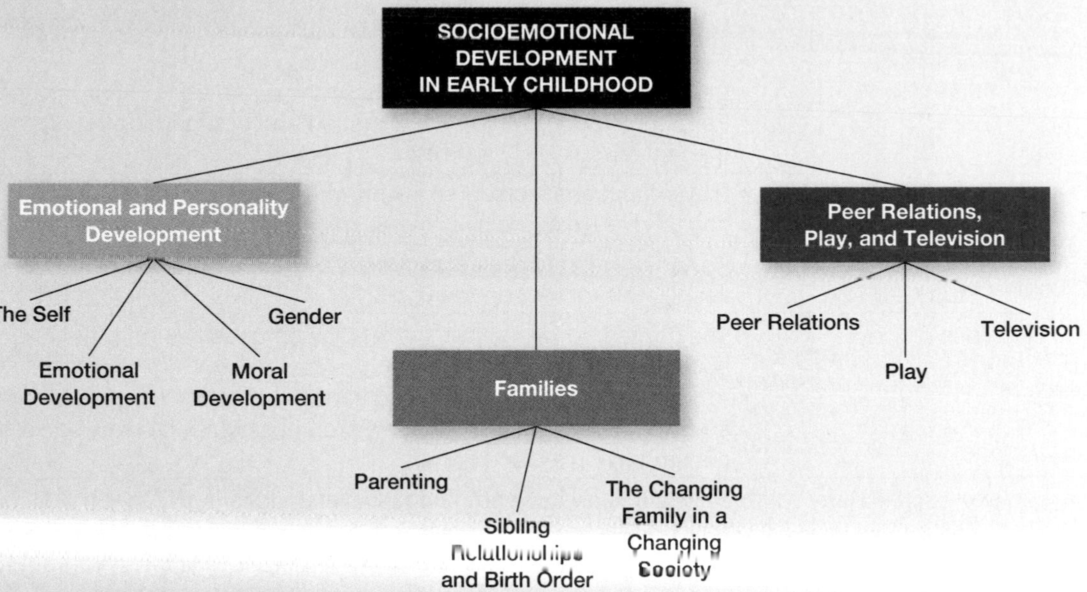

TO OBTAIN A DETAILED REVIEW OF THIS CHAPTER, STUDY THESE FOUR SUMMARY TABLES:

- Summary Table 9.1 The Self and Emotional Development page 240
- Summary Table 9.2 Moral Development and Gender page 247
- Summary Table 9.3 Families page 259
- Summary Table 9.4 Peer Relations, Play, and Television page 267

Key Terms

self-understanding 238
moral development 240
heteronomous morality 240
autonomous morality 240
imminent justice 241
gender 243
gender identity 243
gender role 243
psychoanalytic theory of gender 243
social cognitive theory of gender 244
cognitive developmental theory of gender 246
gender schema theory 246
authoritarian parenting 248
authoritative parenting 249
neglectful parenting 249
indulgent parenting 249
unoccupied play 261
solitary play 261
onlooker play 261
parallel play 261
associative play 262
cooperative play 262
sensorimotor play 262
practice play 262
pretense/symbolic play 262
social play 263
constructive play 263
games 263

Key People

Erik Erikson 238
Jean Piaget 240
Sigmund Freud 242
Martin Hoffman 242
William Damon 242
Lawrence Kohlberg 246
John Watson 248
Diana Baumrind 248
Lois Hoffman 255
Anna Freud 260
Lev Vygotsky 260
Daniel Berlyne 261
Mildred Parten 261

Taking It to the Net

1. A social worker spoke to a psychology class about how children with serious developmental delays and disabilities are more prone to being abused by their parents than are children without disabilities. What are the general risk factors for abuse for all children and how they are compounded for children with disabilities?
2. Karen's mother is concerned about how to best help her daughter, Teresa, whose husband has abandoned her and their five-year-old son. What are some of the challenges that Teresa may have to face and how can her mother help her through this difficult time?
3. Jonathan and Diedre want to shield their children from the violence on television, but they are not sure how to go about it—other than by not allowing any television viewing at all. What recommendations does the APA have for parents?

Connect to www.mhhe.com/santrockld8 to research the answers and complete these exercises.

OLC Preview

To further test your knowledge of this chapter or to explore our extensive online resources that accompany *Life-Span Development,* eighth edition, please log on to the text's Online Learning Center at http://www.mhhe.com/santrockld8.com.

Section 5

Middle and Late Childhood

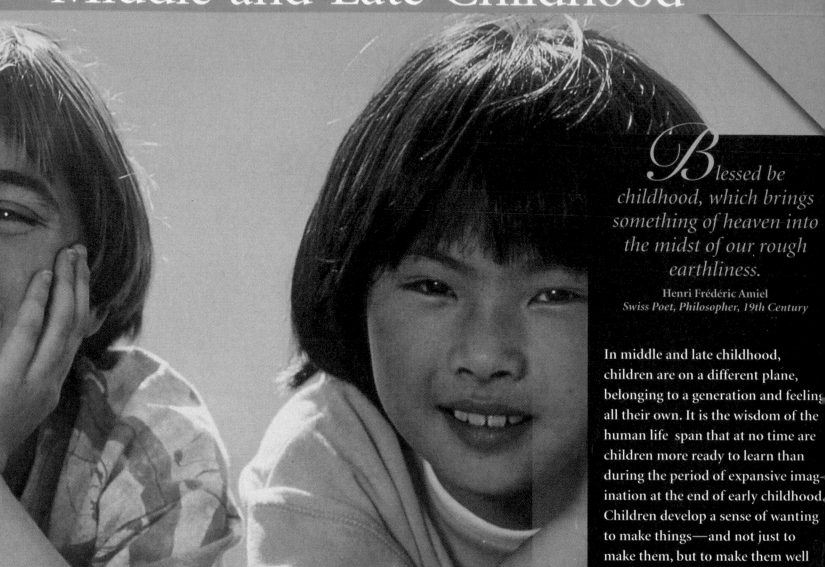

Blessed be childhood, which brings something of heaven into the midst of our rough earthliness.

Henri Frédéric Amiel
Swiss Poet, Philosopher, 19th Century

In middle and late childhood, children are on a different plane, belonging to a generation and feeling all their own. It is the wisdom of the human life span that at no time are children more ready to learn than during the period of expansive imagination at the end of early childhood. Children develop a sense of wanting to make things—and not just to make them, but to make them well and even perfectly. Their thirst is to know and to understand. They are remarkable for their intelligence and for their curiosity. Their parents continue to be important influences in their lives, but their growth also is shaped by successive choirs of friends. They don't think much about the future or about the past, but they enjoy the present moment. Section 5 consists of two chapters, "Physical and Cognitive Development in Middle and Late Childhood" (chapter 10) and "Socioemotional Development in Middle and Late Childhood" (chapter 11).

Chapter 10

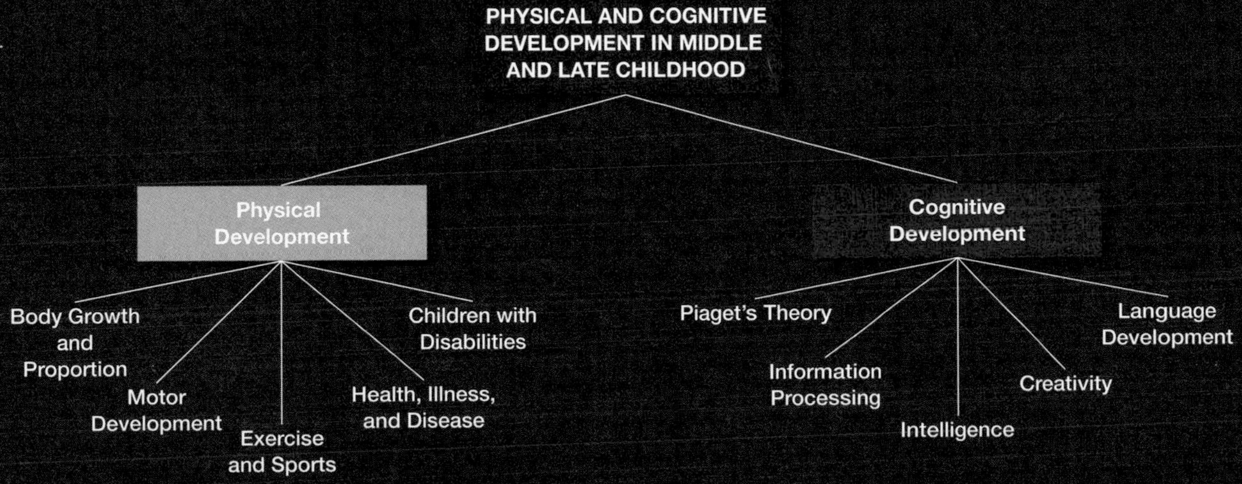
PHYSICAL AND COGNITIVE DEVELOPMENT IN MIDDLE AND LATE CHILDHOOD
Physical Development
Body Growth and Proportion
Motor Development
Exercise and Sports
Health, Illness, and Disease
Children with Disabilities
Cognitive Development
Piaget's Theory
Information Processing
Intelligence
Creativity
Language Development

Physical and Cognitive Development in Middle and Late Childhood

Every forward step we take we leave some phantom of ourselves behind.

— John Lancaster Spalding
American Educator, 19th Century

Images of Life-Span Development

Jessica Dubroff, Child Pilot

MANY PARENTS want their children to be gifted and provide them with many opportunities to achieve this status. Child psychologists believe that some parents go too far and push their children too much, especially when they try to get their children to be a child star in a particular area, like figure skating, tennis, or music. To think further about parents' efforts to get their children to achieve lofty accomplishments, let's examine the tragic story of Jessica Dubroff.

In 1996, Jessica Dubroff took off in cold rain and died when her single-engine Cessna nosedived into a highway. Seven-year-old Jessica was only 4 feet, 2 inches tall and weighed just 55 pounds. What was she doing flying an airplane, especially in quest of being the youngest person ever to fly across the continent?

Jessica's parents seemed determined to give their daughter independence from the beginning. She was delivered in a birthing tub without benefit of a doctor or midwife. Her parents' philosophy was that real life is the best tutor, experience the best preparation for life. As a result, they kept Jessica and her brother (age 9) and sister (age 3) at home without filing a home-schooling plan with local authorities. Jessica had no dolls, only tools. Instead of studying grammar, she did chores and sought what her mother called "mastery." Jessica had few, if any, boundaries. Parenting mainly consisted of cheerleading.

Jessica became interested in flying after her parents gave her an airplane ride for her sixth birthday, only 23 months before her fatal crash. Her father admitted that the cross-country flight was his idea, but claimed that he had presented it to Jessica as a choice. The father became her press agent, courting TV, radio, and newspapers to publicize her flight.

Did Jessica grow up too soon? Did her parents push her too much to achieve in a single activity? Should they instead have encouraged her to have a more well-rounded life and one more typical for her age? Were her parents living vicariously through her?

Some critics argue that Jessica Dubroff was not allowed to be a child. *Did her parents act irresponsibly?*

Later in this chapter, we will explore the real nature of giftedness in children. This chapter is about physical and cognitive development in middle and late childhood. To begin, we will explore some changes in physical development, including children's sports and whether some parents become overinvolved.

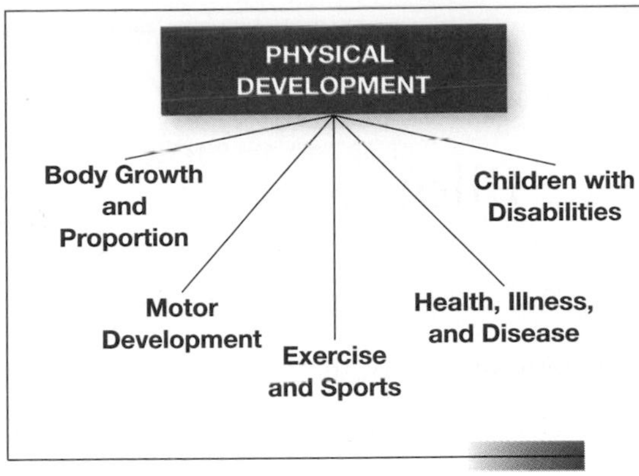

Physical Development

How do children's bodies change in middle and late childhood?

Body Growth and Proportion

The period of middle and late childhood involves slow, consistent growth. This is a period of calm before the rapid growth spurt of adolescence. During the elementary school years, children grow an average of 2 to 3 inches a year until, at the age of 11, the average girl is 4 feet, 10¼ inches tall, and the average boy is 4 feet, 9 inches tall. During the middle and late childhood years, children gain about 5 to 7 pounds a year. The weight increase is due mainly to increases in the size of the skeletal and muscular systems, as well as the size of some body organs. Muscle mass and strength gradually increase as "baby fat" decreases. The loose movements and knock knees of early childhood give way to improved muscle tone. The increase in muscular strength is due to heredity and to exercise. Children also double their strength capabilities during these years. Because of their greater number of muscle cells, boys are usually stronger than girls.

Proportional changes are among the most pronounced physical changes in middle and late childhood. Head circumference, waist circumference, and leg length decrease in relation to body height (Wong, 1997). A less noticeable physical change is that bones continue to ossify during middle and late childhood but yield to pressure and pull more than mature bones.

Motor Development

During middle and late childhood, children's motor development becomes much smoother and more coordinated than it was in early childhood. For example, only one child in a thousand can hit a tennis ball over the net at the age of 3, yet by the age of 10 or 11 most children can learn to play the sport. Running, climbing, skipping rope, swimming, bicycle riding, and skating are just a few of the many physical skills elementary school children can master. And, when mastered, these physical skills are a source of great pleasure and accomplishment for children. In gross motor skills involving large activity, boys usually outperform girls.

As children move through the elementary school years, they gain greater control over their bodies. Physical action is essential for them to refine their developing motor skills. *What are some of the main changes in body growth and proportion in middle and late childhood?*

As children move through the elementary school years, they gain greater control over their bodies and can sit and attend for longer periods of time. However, elementary school children are far from having physical maturity, and they need to be active. Elementary school children become more fatigued by long periods of sitting than by running, jumping, or bicycling. Physical action is essential for these children to refine their developing skills, such as batting a ball, skipping rope, or balancing on a beam. An important principle of practice for elementary school children, therefore, is that they should be engaged in *active,* rather than passive, activities.

Increased myelinization of the central nervous system is reflected in the improvement of fine motor skills

during middle and late childhood. Children's hands are used more adroitly as tools. Six-year-olds can hammer, paste, tie shoes, and fasten clothes. By 7 years of age, children's hands have become steadier. At this age, children prefer a pencil to a crayon for printing, and reversal of letters is less common. Printing becomes smaller. At 8 to 10 years of age, the hands can be used independently with more ease and precision. Fine motor coordination develops to the point at which children can write rather than print words. Letter size becomes smaller and more even. At 10 to 12 years of age, children begin to show manipulative skills similar to the abilities of adults. The complex, intricate, and rapid movements needed to produce fine-quality crafts or to play a difficult piece on a musical instrument can be mastered. Girls usually outperform boys in fine motor skills.

Children's advances in motor development in middle and late childhood enable them to participate in many sports activities. Let's explore what children's sport are like.

Exercise and Sports

How much exercise do children get? What are children's sports like?

Exercise Are children getting enough exercise? In a 1997 national poll, only 22 percent of children in grades 4 through 12 were physically active for 30 minutes every day of the week (Harris, 1997). Their parents said their children were too busy watching TV, spending time on the computer, or playing video games to exercise much.

In this poll, only 34 percent attended daily physical education classes and 23 percent didn't have P.E. at all. Boys were more physically active at all ages than girls.

Some ways to get children to exercise more include these:

- Offer more physical activity programs run by volunteers at school facilities.
- Improve physical fitness activities in schools (Committee on School Health, 2000).
- Have children plan community and school activities that really interest them.
- Encourage families to focus more on physical activity and parents to exercise more (in the national poll more than 50 percent of the parents engaged in no vigorous physical activities on a regular basis).

Sports Sports have become an integral part of American culture. Thus, it is not surprising that more and more children become involved in sports every year. Both in public schools and in community agencies, children's sports programs that involve baseball, soccer, football, basketball, swimming, gymnastics, and other activities have grown to the extent that they have changed the shape of many children's lives.

Participation in sports can have both positive and negative consequences for children. Children's participation in sports can provide exercise, opportunities to learn how to compete, self-esteem, and a setting for developing peer relations and friendships. However, sports also can have negative outcomes for children: the pressure to achieve and win, physical injuries, a distraction from academic work, and unrealistic expectations for success as an athlete (Cheng & others, 2000; Committee on Sports Medicine and Fitness, 2000). Few people challenge the value of sports for children when conducted as part of a school physical education or intramural program. However, some critics question the appropriateness of highly competitive, win-oriented sports teams in schools and communities.

There is a special concern for children in high-pressure sports settings involving championship play with accompanying media publicity. Some clinicians and child developmentalists believe such activities not only put undue stress on the participants but also teach children the wrong values—namely, a win-at-all-costs philosophy. The possibility of exploiting children through highly organized, win-oriented sports programs is an ever present danger. Overly ambitious parents, coaches, and community boosters can unintentionally create a highly stressful atmosphere in children's sports (Wolff, 1993). When parental, agency, or community prestige becomes the central focus of the child's participation in sports, the danger of exploitation is

Six-year-old Zhang Liyin *(third from left)* hopes to someday become an Olympic gymnastics champion. Attending the sports school is considered an outstanding privilege; only 260,000 of China's 200 million children are given this opportunity. *What positive and negative outcomes might children experience from playing sports? Are some sports programs, such as China's sports schools, too intense for children? Should children experience a more balanced life? Is there too much emphasis on sports in the United States?*

clearly present. Programs oriented toward such purposes often require long and arduous training sessions over many months and years, frequently leading to sports specialization at too early an age. In such circumstances, adults often transmit a distorted view of the role of the sport in the child's life, communicating to the child that the sport is the most important aspect of the child's existence.

Health, Illness, and Disease

For the most part, middle and late childhood is a time of excellent health. Disease and death are less prevalent in this period than in others in childhood and adolescence.

WWW
Child Health
Child Health Guide

Accidents and Injuries The most common cause of severe injury and death in middle and late childhood is motor vehicle accidents, either as a pedestrian or as a passenger (Wong, 1997). The use of safety-belt restraints is important in reducing the severity of motor vehicle injuries (Bolen, Bland, & Sacks, 1999). The school-age child's motivation to ride a bicycle increases the risk of accidents. Other serious injuries involve skateboards, roller skates, and other sports equipment.

Most accidents occur in or near the child's home or school. The most effective prevention strategy is to educate the child about the hazards of risk taking and improper use of equipment. Appropriate safety helmets, protective eye and mouth shields, and protective padding are recommended for children who engage in active sports. Physically active school-age children are more susceptible to fractures, strains, and sprains than are their less active counterparts (Furnival, Street, & Schunk, 1999). Also, boys are more likely than girls to experience these injuries.

Obesity Slightly more than one-fifth of children are overweight, and 10 percent are obese. Girls are more likely than boys to be obese. Obesity is less common

in African American than in White children during childhood, but during adolescence this reverses. Obesity at 6 years of age results in approximately a 25 percent probability that the child will be obese as an adult; obesity at age 12 results in approximately a 75 percent chance that the adolescent will be obese as an adult.

Consequences of Obesity in Children We already have mentioned an important consequence of obesity in children: 25 percent of obese children become obese adults, and 75 percent of obese young adolescents become obese adults. Obesity also is a risk factor for many medical and psychological problems (Hill & Trowbridge, 1998). Obese children can develop pulmonary problems, such as sleep apnea (which we discussed in chapter 6, involving upper airway obstruction). Hip problems also are common in obese children. Obese children also are prone to have high blood pressure and elevated blood cholesterol levels. Low self-esteem and depression also are common outgrowths of obesity. Furthermore, obese children often are excluded from peer groups.

Treatment of Obesity No evidence supports the use of surgical procedures in obese children. They should be used only when obesity is life-threatening (Klish, 1998). Diets only moderately deficient in calories are more successful over the long term than are those involving extreme deprivation of calories. Exercise is believed to be an extremely important component of a successful weight-loss program for overweight children. Exercise increases the child's lean body mass, which increases the child's resting metabolic rate. This results in more calories being burned in the resting state. Many experts on childhood obesity recommend a treatment that involves a combination of diet, exercise, and behavior modification. In a typical behavior modification program, children are taught to monitor their own behavior, keeping a food diary while attempting to lose weight. The diary should record not only the type and amount of food eaten but also when, with whom, and where it was eaten. That is, do children eat in front of the TV, by themselves, or because they are angry or depressed? A diary identifies behaviors that need to be changed.

Cancer

Cancer is the second leading cause of death (with injuries the leading cause) in children 5 to 14 years of age. Three percent of all children's deaths in this age period are due to cancer. In the 15 to 24 age group, cancer accounts for 13 percent of all deaths. Currently, 1 in every 330 children in the United States develops cancer before the age of 19. Morever, the incidence of cancer in children is increasing (Neglia & others, 2001).

Child cancers have a different profile from adult cancers. Adult cancers attack mainly the lungs, colon, breast, prostate, and pancreas. Child cancers mainly attack the white blood cells (leukemia), brain, bone, lymph system, muscles, kidneys, and nervous system. All are characterized by an uncontrolled proliferation of abnormal cells.

As indicated in figure 10.1, the most common cancer in children is leukemia, a cancer of the tissues that make blood cells. In leukemia, the bone marrow makes an abundance of white blood cells that don't function properly. They invade the marrow and crowd out normal cells,

WWW

Overweight Children
Heart Smart
Diseases and Illnesses
Medical Links
Cancer in Children

CAREERS IN LIFE-SPAN DEVELOPMENT

Sharon McLeod, Child Life Specialist

SHARON MCLEOD is a child life specialist who is clinical director of the Child Life and Recreational Therapy Department at the Children's Hospital Medical Center in Cincinnati.

Under Sharon's direction, the goals of the Child Life Department are to promote children's optimal growth and development, reduce the stress of health care experiences, and provide support to child patients and their families. These goals are accomplished through therapeutic play and developmentally appropriate activities, educating and psychologically preparing children for medical procedures, and serving as a resource for parents and other professionals regarding child development and health care issues.

In Sharon's view, "Human growth and development, coping theory, and play provide the foundation for the profession of child life. My most beneficial moments as a student were during my fieldwork and internship when I experienced hands-on theories and concepts learned in courses."

Sharon McLeod, child life specialist, working with a child at Children's Hospital Medical Center in Cincinnati.

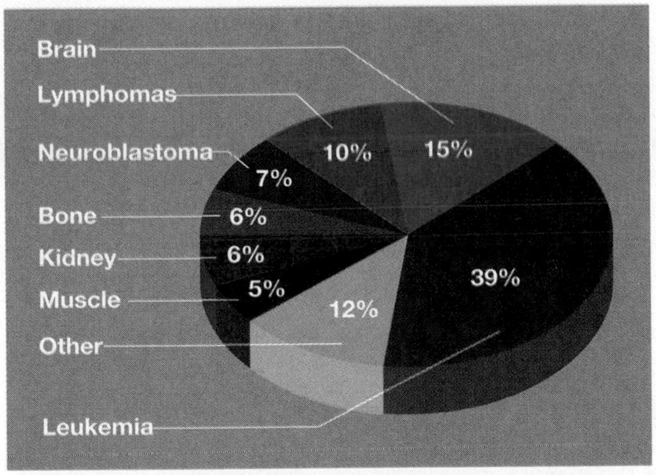

Figure **10.1**
Types of Cancer in Children

making the child susceptible to bruising and infection. Lymphomas arise in the lymph system. Childhood lymphomas spread to the central nervous system and bone marrow.

At this point, we have studied a number of ideas about body growth and proportion, motor development, exercise and sports, and health, illness, and disease. To review these ideas see summary table 10.1. Next, we will read about children with disabilities.

Children with Disabilities

The elementary school years are a time when children with disabilities become more sensitive about their differentness and how it is perceived by others.

Who Are Children with Disabilities?

Approximately 10 percent of all children in the United States receive special education or related services (Reschly, 1996). Figure 10.2 shows the approximate percentages of children with various disabilities who receive special education services (U.S. Department of Education, 1996). Within this group, a little more than half have a learning disability. Substantial percentages of children also have speech or language impairments (21 percent of those with disabilities), mental retardation (12 percent), and serious emotional disturbance (9 percent).

Educators now prefer to speak of "children with disabilities" rather than "disabled children" to emphasize the person, not the disability (Culatta & Tompkins, 1999). The term *handicapping conditions* is still used to describe impediments to the learning and functioning of individuals with a disability that have been imposed by society. For example, when children who use a wheelchair do not have adequate access to a bathroom, transportation, and so on, this is referred to as a handicapping condition.

Exploring Disabilities
Learning Disabilities
Learning Disabilities Association

Learning Disabilities

Children with a **learning disability** *(1) are of normal intelligence or above, (2) have difficulties in at least one academic area and usually several, and (3) have a difficulty that is not attributable to any other diagnosed problem or disorder.* The global concept of learning disabilities includes problems in listening, concentrating, speaking, thinking.

learning disability
A disability that involves (1) having normal intelligence or above, (2) having difficulties in at least one academic area and usually several, and (3) having no other problem or disorder, such as mental retardation, that can be determined as causing the difficulty.

About three times as many boys as girls are classified as having a learning disability (U.S. Department of Education, 1996). Among the explanations for this gender difference are a greater biological vulnerability of boys, as well as referral bias (boys are more likely to be referred by teachers for treatment because of their disruptive, hyperactive behavior).

The most common problem that characterizes children with a learning disability involves reading (Kamphaus, 2000; Torgesen, 1999; Willcott & others, 2001). Such children especially show problems with phonological skills (these involve being able to understand how sounds and letters match up to make words). **Dyslexia** *is a category that is reserved for individuals who have a severe impairment in their ability to read and spell.*

dyslexia
A category of learning disabilities involving a severe impairment in the ability to read and spell.

Children with a learning disability often have difficulties in handwriting, spelling, or composition. Their writing may be extremely slow, their writing products may be virtually illegible, and they may make numerous spelling errors because of their inability to match up sounds and letters.

Many interventions have focused on improving the child's reading ability (Johnson & Slomka, 2000; Lyon & Moats, 1997). For example, in one study, instruction in phonological awareness at the kindergarten level had positive effects on reading development when the children reached the first grade (Blachman & others, 1994).

Unfortunately, not all children who have a learning disability that involves reading problems have the benefit of appropriate early intervention. Most children whose

Summary Table 10.1
Body Growth and Proportion; Motor Development; Exercise and Sports; Health, Illness, and Disease

Concept	Processes/ Related Ideas	Characteristics/Descriptions
Body Growth and Proportion	Skeletal and Muscular Systems	• The period of middle and late childhood involves slow, consistent growth. During this period, children grow an average of 2 to 3 inches a year. Muscle mass and strength gradually increase. • Among the most pronounced changes are decreases in head circumference, waist circumference, and leg length in relation to body height.
Motor Development	Smoother and More Coordinated	• During the middle and late childhood years, motor development becomes much smoother and more coordinated. • Children gain greater control over their bodies and can sit and attend for longer periods of time. However, their lives should be activity-oriented and very active. • Increased myelination of the central nervous system is reflected in improved motor skills. • Improved fine motor skills appear in the form of handwriting development. • Boys are usually better at gross motor skills, girls at fine motor skills.
Exercise and Sports	Exercise	• Most American children do not get nearly enough exercise.
	Sports	• Children's participation in sports can have positive or negative consequences.
Health, Illness, and Disease	Accidents and Injuries	• The most common cause of severe injury and death in childhood is motor vehicle accidents, with most occurring at or near the child's home or school.
	Obesity	• Slightly more than one-fifth of children are overweight, and 10 percent are obese. • Treatment of obesity focuses mainly on diet, exercise, and behavior modification.
	Cancer	• Cancer is the second leading cause of death in children (after accidents). • Childhood cancers have a different profile from adult cancers—they usually already have spread to other parts of the body and they typically are of a different type. • Leukemia is the most common childhood cancer.

reading disability is not diagnosed until the third grade or later and who receive standard interventions fail to show noticeable improvement (Lyon, 1996). However, intensive instruction over a period of time by a competent teacher can remediate the deficient reading skills of many children. For example, in one study, 65 severely dyslexic children were given 65 hours of individual instruction in addition to group instruction in phonemic awareness and thinking skills (Alexander & others, 1991). The intensive intervention significantly improved the dyslexic children's reading skills.

ADHD

Attention Deficit Hyperactivity Disorder **Attention deficit hyperactivity disorder (ADHD)** *is a disability in which children consistently show one or more of the following characteristics over a period of time: (1) inattention, (2) hyperactivity, and (3) impulsivity.* Children who are inattentive have difficulty focusing on any one thing and may get bored with a task after only a few minutes. Children who are hyperactive show high levels of physical activity, almost always seeming to be in

attention deficit hyperactivity disorder (ADHD)
A disability in which children consistently show one or more of the following characteristics: (1) inattention, (2) hyperactivity, and (3) impulsivity.

Disability	Total	Percent of total
Specific learning disabilities	2,513,977	51.1
Speech or language impairments	1,023,665	20.8
Mental retardation	570,855	11.6
Serious emotional disturbance	428,168	8.7
Multiple disabilities	89,646	1.8
Hearing impairments	65,56	1.3
Orthopedic impairments	60,604	1.2
Other health impairments	106,5098	2.2
Visual impairments	24,877	0.5
Autism	22,780	0.5
Deaf-blindness	1,331	0.0
Traumatic brain injury	7,188	0.1
All disabilities	4,915,168	100.0

Note: The figures represent children with a disability who received special education services in a recent school year. Children with multiple disabilities also have been counted under various single disabilities.

Figure **10.2**

The Diversity of Children Who Have a Disability

motion. Children who are impulsive have-difficulty curbing their reactions and don't do a good job of thinking before they act. Depending on the characteristics that children with ADHD display, they can be diagnosed as (1) ADHD with predominantly inattention, (2) ADHD with predominantly hyperactivity/impulsivity, or (3) ADHD with both inattention and hyperactivity/ impulsivity (Whalen, 2000).

The U.S. Office of Education figures on children with a disability shown in figure 10.2 include children with ADHD in the category of children with specific learning disabilities, an overall category that comprises slightly more than one-half of all children who receive special education services. The number of children diagnosed and treated for ADHD has increased substantially, by some estimates doubling in the 1990s. The disorder occurs as much as four to nine times more in boys than in girls. There is controversy about the increased diagnosis of ADHD (Terman & others, 1996), however. Some experts attribute the increase mainly to heightened awareness of the disorder. Others are concerned that many children are being diagnosed without undergoing extensive professional evaluation based on input from multiple sources.

Definitive causes of ADHD have not been found. For example, scientists have not been able to identify cause-related sites in the brain. However, a number of causes have been proposed, such as low levels of certain neurotransmitters (chemical messengers in the brain), prenatal and postnatal abnormalities, and environmental toxins, such as lead. Heredity also may play a role, as 30 to 50 percent of children with ADHD have a sibling or parent who has the disorder (Woodrich, 1994).

Students with ADHD have a failure rate in school that is two to three times that of other students. About one-half of students with ADHD have repeated a grade by adolescence and more than one-third eventually drop out of school.

Many experts recommend a combination of academic, behavioral, and medical interventions to help students with ADHD learn and adapt more effectively (Appalachia Educational Laboratory, 1998; Rapport & Chung, 2000; Rapport & others, 2001; Whalen, 2001). This intervention requires cooperation and effort on the part of the parents of students with ADHD, school personnel (teachers, administrators, special educators, and school psychologists), and healthcare professionals (Guyer, 2000).

It is estimated that about 85 to 90 percent of students with ADHD are taking stimulant medication such as Ritalin to control their behavior (Tousignant, 1995). A child should be given medication only after a complete assessment that includes a physical examination.

Ritalin is a stimulant; in most individuals it speeds up the nervous system and behavior. However, in many children with ADHD it has the opposite effect, slowing down their nervous system and behavior, although scientists are still not sure why these drugs work in such opposite ways for children with ADHD and those who do not have the disorder (Johnson & Leung, 2001).

The use of Ritalin and other stimulants to treat ADHD continues to be controversial. Critics argue that physicians are too quick to prescribe Ritalin, especially for mild cases of ADHD, and that long-term studies of the effects of Ritalin on children with ADHD have not been conducted to determine possible negative effects.

Educational Issues The legal requirement that schools serve all children with a disability is fairly recent. Beginning in the mid 1960s to mid 1970s, legislatures, the federal courts, and the United States Congress laid down special educational rights for children with disabilities. Prior to that time, most children with a

disability were either refused enrollment or inadequately served by schools. In 1975, *Public Law 94-142,* the Education for All Handicapped Children Act, required that all students with disabilities be given a free, appropriate public education and be provided the funding to help implement this education.

In 1990, Public Law 94-142 was renamed the *Individuals with Disabilities Education Act (IDEA).* The IDEA spells out broad mandates for services to all children with disabilities. These include evaluation and eligibility determination, appropriate education and the individualized education plan (IEP), and the least restrictive environment (LRE) (Martin, Martin, & Terman, 1996).

The IDEA requires that students with disabilities have an **individualized education plan (IEP),** *a written statement that spells out a program specifically tailored for the student with a disability. In general, the IEP should be (1) related to the child's learning capacity, (2) specially constructed to meet the child's individual needs and not merely a copy of what is offered to other children, and (3) designed to provide educational benefits.*

Under the IDEA, a child with a disability must be educated in the **least restrictive environment (LRE).** *This means a setting that is as similar as possible to the one in which children who do not have a disability are educated.* This provision of the IDEA has given a legal basis to making an effort to educate children with a disability in the regular classroom (Crockett & Kaufmann, 1999). The term used to describe the education of children with a disability in the regular classroom used to *be mainstreaming.* However, that term has been replaced by the term **inclusion,** *which means educating a child with special education needs full-time in the general school program.* Today, **mainstreaming** *means educating a student with special education needs partially in a special education classroom and partially in a regular classroom.*

Critical Thinking

Reflecting on Learning Disabilities

THINK BACK on your own schooling and how students with learning disabilities either were or were not diagnosed. Were you aware of such individuals in your classes? Were they helped by teachers and/or specialists? You may know one or more people now who have a learning disability. Interview them about their school experiences. Ask them what they believe could have been done better to help with their disability.

individualized education plan (IEP)
A written statement that spells out a program tailored to a child with a disability. The plan should be (1) related to the child's learning capacity, (2) specially constructed to meet the child's individual needs and not merely a copy of what is offered to other children, and (3) designed to provide educational benefits.

least restrictive environment (LRE)
The concept that a child with a disability must be educated in a setting that is as similar as possible to the one in which children who do not have a disability are educated.

inclusion
Educating a child with special education needs full-time in the regular classroom.

mainstreaming
Educating a child with special education needs partially in a special education classroom and partially in a regular classroom.

Many children with ADHD show impulsive behavior, such as this child who is jumping out of his seat and throwing a paper airplane at other children. *How would you handle this situation if you were a teacher and this were to happen in your classroom?*

Public Law 94-142 mandates free, appropriate education for all children. *What are the aspects of this education?*

SOCIOCULTURAL WORLDS OF DEVELOPMENT

Family-Centered and Culture-Centered Approaches to Working with a Child Who Has a Disability

BEST PRACTICES in service delivery to children who are disabled or at risk for disabilities are moving toward a family-focused or family-centered approach (Lynch & Hanson, 1993). This approach emphasizes the importance of partnerships between parents and disability professionals and shared decision making in assessment, intervention, and evaluation. It also underscores the belief that services for children must be offered in the context of the entire family and that the entire family system is the partner and the client, not just the child (Lyytinen & others, 1994).

At the same time as services are becoming more family focused, the families served by many intervention programs are becoming increasingly diverse. Many families are characterized by attitudes, beliefs, values, customs, languages, and behaviors that are unfamiliar to interventionists. It is not uncommon for interventionists in some locations to work with families from as many as ten different cultures or more. In a large school district, as many as fifty languages may be spoken.

Who are these interventionists who work with children who have a disability or are at risk for one? They include educators, nurses, speech and language specialists, audiologists, occupational and physical therapists, physicians, social workers, and psychologists. Regardless of the agency, program, service, setting, or professional discipline, having the attitudes and skills that facilitate effective cross-cultural interactions is needed for competent intervention.

Ideally, families in need of services for their children receive assistance from professionals who are knowledgeable and competent in their discipline, who speak the same language as family members, and have the ability to establish rapport and work in partnership with family members to implement interventions for the child and family. However, the current match between many professionals and the families whom they serve is not perfect. This does not mean, though, that families cannot receive high-quality assistance. It simply means that interventionists need to be especially sensitive to the importance of developing cross-cultural competence and learning how to respond in sensitive and appropriate ways.

Education of Children Who Are Exceptional
Inclusion

Not long ago, it was considered appropriate to educate children with disabilities outside the regular classroom. However, today, schools must make every effort to provide inclusion for children with disabilities (Dettmer, Dyck & Thurston, 2002; Heward, 2000; Walther-Thomas & others, 2000). These efforts can be very costly financially and very time-consuming in terms of faculty effort.

The principle of least restrictive environment compels schools to examine possible modifications of the regular classroom before moving the child with a disability to a more restrictive placement (Hallahan & Kaufman, 2000). Also, regular classroom teachers often need specialized training to help some children with a disability, and state educational agencies are required to provide such training (Vaughn, Bos, & Schumm, 2000).

Many legal changes regarding children with disabilities have been extremely positive. Compared with several decades ago, far more children today are receiving competent, specialized services. For many children, inclusion in the regular classroom, with modifications or supplemental services, is appropriate (Kochhar, West, & Taymans, 2000; Turnbull & others, 1999). However, some experts believe that separate programs may be more effective and appropriate for children with disabilities (Martin, Martin, & Terman, 1996). To read further about children with disabilities, see the Sociocultural Worlds of Development box.

At this point, we have studied a number of ideas about children with disabilities. A review of these ideas is pre-

CAREERS IN LIFE-SPAN DEVELOPMENT

Myla Burgess, Learning Disabilities Specialist

MYLA BURGESS is a learning disabilities specialist in Chesterfield County, North Carolina. She has a master's degree in education from the University of North Carolina at Greensboro. Myla believes that children with learning disabilities need to know that the expectations held for them are no different from those for regular students. She works in a team-teaching approach with regular classroom teachers, stressing learning strategies that can benefit not just students with learning disabilities but all students. Myra especially focuses on helping these students improve their reading skills (Hallahan & Kauffman, 1997).

SUMMARY TABLE 10.2
Children with Disabilities

Concept	Processes/ Related Ideas	Characteristics/Descriptions
Who Are Children with Disabilities?	Their Identity	• An estimated 10 percent of U.S. children with a disability receive special education services. Slightly more than 50 percent of these students are classified as having a learning disability (in the federal government classification, this includes attention deficit/hyperactivity disorder (ADHD)). • The term *children with disabilities* is now used instead of the term *disabled children.*
Learning Disabilities	Their Nature	• Children with a learning disability are of normal intelligence or above, have difficulties in at least one academic area and usually several, and have a difficulty that is not attributable to another diagnosed problem or disorder. • The most common learning disability in children involves reading. Dyslexia is a severe impairment in the ability to read and spell.
Attention Deficit Hyperactivity Disorder	Three Areas	• ADHD is a disability in which children consistently show problems in one or more of these areas: inattention, hyperactivity, and impulsivity.
	Intervention Strategies	• Many experts recommend a combination of academic, behavioral, and medical interventions to help students with ADHD learn and adapt more effectively.
Educational Issues	Historical Background	• Beginning in the mid 1960s to mid 1970s, the educational rights for children with disabilities were laid down. • In 1975, Public Law 94-142, the Education for All Handicapped Children Act required that all children be given a free, appropriate public education. • In 1990, Public Law 94-142 was renamed the Individuals with Disabilities Education Act (IDEA).
	Appropriate Education and the Individualized Education Plan (IEP)	• An IEP consists of a written plan that spells out a program tailored to a child with a disability.
	Least Restrictive Environment (LRE)	• This concept, which is contained in the IDEA, states that children with disabilities must be educated in a setting that is as similar as possible to the one in which children without disabilities are educated. • The term *inclusion* means educating children with disabilities full-time in the regular classroom.

sented in summary table 10.2. Next, we will turn our attention to children's cognitive development in middle and late childhood.

Cognitive Development

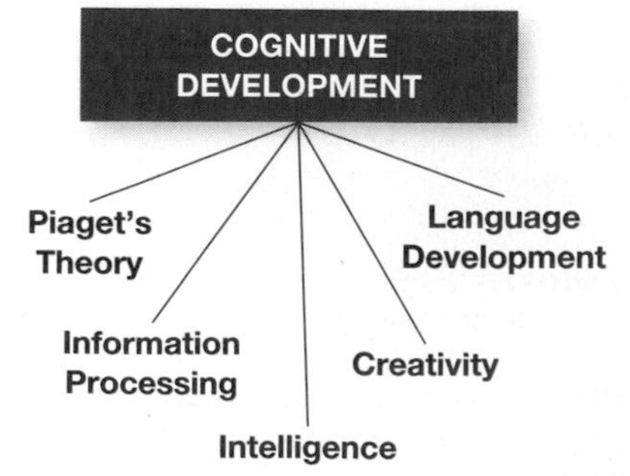

Our coverage of children's cognitive development focuses on Piaget's theory, information processing, intelligence, creativity, and language development.

Piaget's Theory

According to Piaget (1952), the preschool child's thought is preoperational P. 212. Preoperational thought involves the formation of stable concepts, the emergence of mental reasoning, the prominence of egocentrism, and the construction of magical

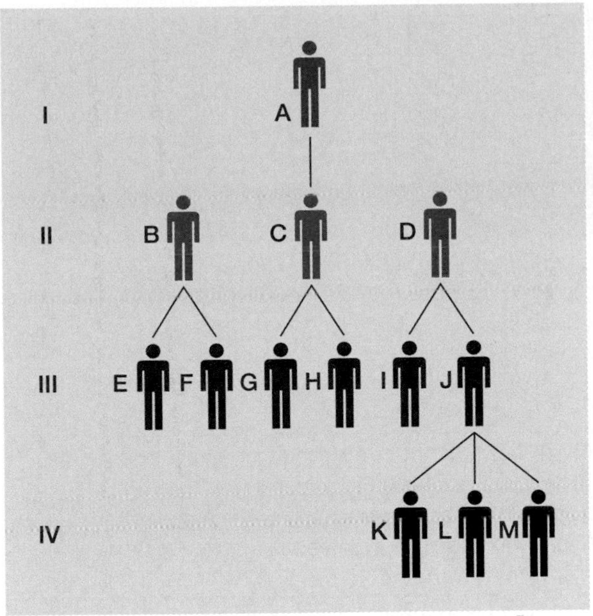

Figure 10.3

Classification: An Important Ability in Concrete Operational Thought

A family tree of four generations (I to IV): The preoperational child has trouble classifying the members of the four generations; the concrete operational child can classify the members vertically, horizontally, and obliquely (up and down and across). For example, the concrete operational child understands that a family member can be a son, a brother, and a father, all at the same time.

belief systems. Thought during the preschool years is still flawed and not well organized. Piaget believed that concrete operational thought does not appear until about the age of 7, but, as we learned in chapter 8, Piaget may have underestimated some of the cognitive skills of preschool children. For example, by carefully and cleverly designing experiments on understanding the concept of number, it was demonstrated that some preschool children show conservation, a concrete operational skill (Gelman, 1972). In chapter 8, we explored concrete operational thought by describing the preschool child's flaws in thinking about such concrete operational skills as conservation and classification; here we will cover the characteristics of concrete operational thought again, this time emphasizing the competencies of elementary school children. We will also consider applications of Piaget's ideas to children's education and an evaluation of Piaget's theory.

Remember that, according to Piaget, concrete operational thought is made up of operations—mental actions that allow children to do mentally what they had done physically before P. 212. Concrete operations are also mental actions that are reversible. In the well-known test of reversibility of thought involving conservation of matter, the child is presented with two identical balls of clay. The experimenter rolls one ball into a long, thin shape; the other remains in its original ball shape. The child is then asked if there is more clay in the ball or in the long, thin piece of clay. By the time children reach the age of 7 or 8, most answer that the amount of clay is the same. To answer this problem correctly, children have to imagine that the clay ball is rolled out into a long, thin strip and then returned to its original round shape. This type of imagination involves a reversible mental action. Thus, a concrete operation is a reversible mental action on real, concrete objects. Concrete operations allow the child to coordinate several characteristics rather than focus on a single property of an object. In the clay example, the preoperational child is likely to focus on height *or* width. The concrete operational child coordinates information about both dimensions.

Many of the concrete operations Piaget identified focus on the way children reason about the properties of objects. One important skill that characterizes the concrete operational child is the ability to classify or divide things into different sets or subsets and to consider their interrelationships. An example of the concrete operational child's classification skills involves a family tree of four generations (see figure 10.3) (Furth & Wachs, 1975). This family tree suggests that the grandfather (A) has three children (B, C, and D), each of whom has two children (E through J), and that one of these children (J) has three children (K, L, and M). A child who comprehends the classification system can move up and down a level (vertically), across a level (horizontally), and up and down and across (obliquely) within the system. The concrete operational child understands that person J can at the same time be father, brother, and grandson, for example. A summary of the characteristics of concrete operational thought is shown in figure 10.4.

Some Piagetian tasks require children to reason about relations between classes. One such task is **seriation,** *the concrete operation that involves ordering stimuli along a quantitative dimension (such as length).* To see if students can serialize, a teacher might haphazardly place eight sticks of different lengths on a table. The teacher then asks the students to order the sticks by length. Many young children end up with two or three small groups of "big" sticks or "little" sticks, rather than a correct ordering of all eight sticks. Another mistaken strategy they use is to evenly line up the tops of the sticks but ignore the bottoms. The concrete operational thinker simultaneously understands that each stick must be longer than the one that precedes it and shorter than the one that follows it.

Another aspect of reasoning about the relations between classes is **transitivity.** *This involves the ability to logically combine relations to understand certain conclusions.* In this case, consider three sticks (A, B, and C) of differing lengths. A is the longest,

seriation
The concrete operation that involves ordering stimuli along a quantitative dimension (such as length).

transitivity
In concrete operational thought, a mental concept that underlies the ability to logically combine relations to understand certain conclusions. It focuses on reasoning about the relations between classes.

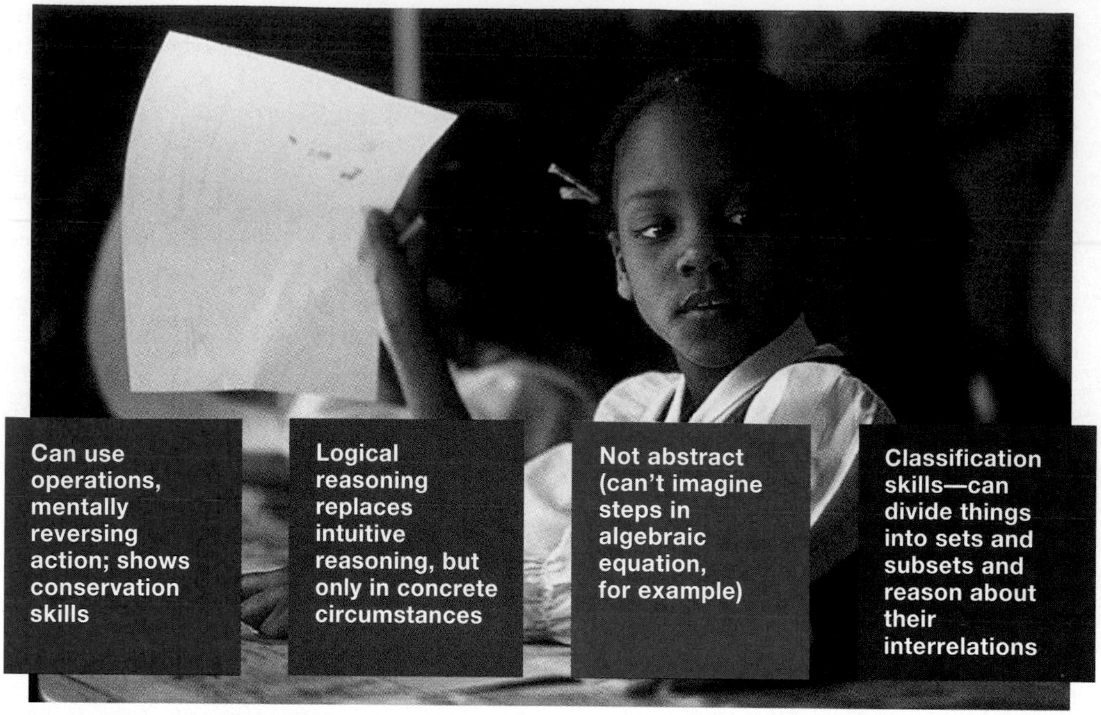
Can use operations, mentally reversing action; shows conservation skills
Logical reasoning replaces intuitive reasoning, but only in concrete circumstances
Not abstract (can't imagine steps in algebraic equation, for example)
Classification skills—can divide things into sets and subsets and reason about their interrelations

Figure **10.4**

Characteristics of Concrete Operational Thought

B is intermediate in length, and C is the shortest. Does the child understand that, if A > B and B > C, then A > C? In Piaget's theory, concrete operational thinkers do; preoperational thinkers do not.

Piaget and Education

Piaget and Education Piaget was not an educator and never pretended to be. However, he provided a sound conceptual framework from which to view learning and education. Earlier, we examined some specific suggestions for classroom activities based on Piaget's stages. Following are some more general principles in Piaget's theory that can be applied to teaching (Elkind, 1976; Heuwinkel, 1996):

1. *Take a constructivist approach.* In a constructivist vein, Piaget emphasized that children learn best when they are active and seek solutions for themselves. Piaget opposed teaching methods which imply that children are passive receptacles. The educational implication of Piaget's view is that, in all subjects, students learn best by making discoveries, reflecting on them, and discussing them, rather than blindly imitating the teacher or doing things by rote.
2. *Facilitate rather than direct learning.* Effective teachers design situations that allow students to learn by doing. These situations promote students' thinking and discovery. Teachers listen, watch, and question students to help them gain better understanding. Don't just examine *what* students think and the product of their learning. Rather, carefully observe them as they find out *how* they think. Ask relevant questions to stimulate their thinking and ask them to explain their answers.
3. *Consider the child's knowledge and level of thinking.* Students do not come to class with empty heads. They have many ideas about the physical and natural world. They have concepts of space, time, quantity, and causality. These ideas differ from the ideas of adults. Teachers need to interpret what a student is saying and respond in a mode of discourse that is not too far from the student's level.
4. *Use ongoing assessment.* Individually constructed meanings cannot be measured by standardized tests. Math and language portfolios (which contain work in

We owe to Piaget the present field of cognitive development with its image of the developing child, who through its own active and creative commerce with its environment, builds an orderly succession of cognitive structures enroute to intellectual maturity.

John Flavell
Contemporary Developmental Psychologist, Stanford University

Jean Piaget, at age 27, the main architect of the field of cognitive development. *What are some of his main contributions?*

progress as well as finished products), individual conferences in which students discuss their thinking strategies, and students' written and verbal explanations of their reasoning can be used to evaluate progress.

5. *Promote the student's intellectual health.* When Piaget came to lecture in the United States, he was asked, "What can I do to get my child to a higher cognitive stage sooner?" He was asked this question so often here compared with other countries that he called it the American question. For Piaget, children's learning should occur naturally. Children should not be pushed and pressured into achieving too much too early in their development, before they are maturationally ready. Some parents spend long hours every day holding up large flash cards with words on them to improve their baby's vocabulary. In the Piagetian view, this is not the best way for infants to learn. It places too much emphasis on speeding up intellectual development, involves passive learning, and will not work.
6. *Turn the classroom into a setting of exploration and discovery.* What do actual classrooms look like when the teachers adopt Piaget's views. Several first- and second-grade math classrooms provide some good examples (Kamii, 1985, 1989). The teachers emphasize students' own exploration and discovery. The classrooms are less structured than what we think of as a typical classroom. Workbooks and predetermined assignments are not used. Rather, the teachers observe the students' interests and natural participation in activities to determine what the course of learning will be. For example, a math lesson might be constructed around counting the day's lunch money or dividing supplies among students. Often, games are prominently used in the classroom to stimulate mathematical thinking. For example, a version of dominoes teaches children about even-numbered combinations. A variation on tic-tac-toe involves replacing *X*s and *O*s with numbers. Teachers encourage peer interaction during the lessons and games because students' different viewpoints can contribute to advances in thinking.

Evaluating Piaget's Theory

What were Piaget's main contributions? Has his theory withstood the test of time?

Piaget with his wife and three children; he often used his observations of his children to provide examples of his theory.

Contributions Piaget was a giant in the field of developmental psychology, the founder of the present field of children's cognitive development. Psychologists owe him a long list of masterful concepts of enduring power and fascination: assimilation, accommodation, object permanence, egocentrism, conservation, and others. Psychologists also owe him the current vision of children as active, constructive thinkers (Vidal, 2000).

Piaget also was a genius when it came to observing children ◀ P. 158. His careful observations showed us inventive ways to discover how children act on and adapt to their world. Piaget showed us some important things to look for in cognitive development, such as the shift from preoperational to concrete operational thinking. He also showed us how children need to make their experiences fit their schemas (cognitive frameworks) yet simultaneously adapt their schemas to experience. Piaget also revealed how cognitive change is likely to occur if the context is structured to allow gradual movement to the next higher level and that a concept does not emerge suddenly, fully-blown but, rather, through a series of partial accomplishments that lead to increasingly comprehensive understanding (Haith & Benson, 1998).

Criticisms Piaget's theory has not gone unchallenged. Questions are raised about estimates of children's competence at different developmental levels; stages; the training of children to reason at higher levels; and culture and education.

- *Estimates of children's competence.* Some cognitive abilities emerge earlier than Piaget thought. For example, as previously noted, some aspects of object permanence emerge earlier than he believed. Even 2-year-olds are nonegocentric

An outstanding teacher and education in the logic of science and mathematics are important cultural experiences that promote the development of operational thought. *Might Piaget have underestimated the roles of culture and schooling in children's cognitive development?*

in some contexts. Conservation of number has been demonstrated as early as age 3, although Piaget did not think it emerged until 7. Young children are not as uniformly "pre" this and "pre" that (precausal, preoperational) as Piaget thought. Other cognitive abilities also can emerge later than Piaget thought. Many adolescents still think in concrete operational ways or are just beginning to master formal operations. Even many adults are not formal operational thinkers. In sum, recent theoretical revisions highlight more cognitive competencies of infants and young children and more cognitive shortcomings of adolescents and adults (Flavell, Miller, & Miller, 1993).

- *Stages.* Piaget conceived of stages as unitary structures of thought. Thus, his theory assumes developmental synchrony; that is, various aspects of a stage should emerge at the same time. However, some concrete operational concepts do not appear in synchrony. For example, children do not learn to conserve at the same time they learn to cross-classify. Thus, most contemporary developmentalists agree that children's cognitive development is not as stagelike as Piaget thought.
- *Training children to reason at higher levels.* Some children who are at one cognitive stage (such as preoperational) can be trained to reason at a higher cognitive stage (such as concrete operational). This poses a problem for Piaget's theory. He argued that such training is only superficial and ineffective, unless the child is at a maturational transition point between the stages (Gelman & Williams, 1998).
- *Culture and education.* Culture and education exert stronger influences on children's development than Piaget believed (Gelman & Brenneman, 1994). The age at which children acquire conservation skills is related to the extent to which their culture provides relevant practice. An outstanding teacher and education in the logic of math and science can promote concrete and formal operational thought.

Still, some developmental psychologists believe we should not throw out Piaget altogether. These **neo-Piagetians** *argue that Piaget got some things right but that his theory needs considerable revision. In their revision of Piaget, more emphasis is given to*

neo-Piagetians
Developmentalists who have elaborated on Piaget's theory, believing that children's cognitive development is more specific in many respects than Piaget thought.

Memory Links
Strategies
Learning Technologies

Our life is what our thoughts make it.

Marcus Aurelius, Meditations
Roman Emperor, 2nd Century

how children process information through attention, memory, and strategy use (Case, 1987, 1999; Lewis, 2001). They especially believe that a more accurate vision of children's thinking requires more emphasis on strategies, the speed at which children process information, the particular cognitive task involved, and the division of cognitive problems into smaller, more precise steps (Case & Mueller, 2001; Demetriou, 2001).

Information Processing

Among the changes in information processing during middle and late childhood are those involving memory, critical thinking, and metacognition. Remember also, from chapter 8, that the attention of most children improves dramatically during middle and late childhood and that at this time children attend more to the task-relevant features of a problem than to the salient features P. 220.

Memory

In chapter 8, we concluded that short-term memory increases considerably during early childhood but after the age of 7 does not show as much increase P. 224. Is the same pattern found for **long-term memory,** *a relatively permanent and unlimited type of memory?* Long-term memory increases with age during middle and late childhood.

long-term memory
A relatively permanent type of memory that holds huge amounts of information for a long period of time.

If we know anything at all about long-term memory, it is that long-term memory depends on the learning activities individuals engage in when learning and remembering information (Intons-Peterson, 1996; Pressley, 1996). **Control processes** *are cognitive processes that do not occur automatically but require work and effort. They are under the learner's conscious control and can be used to improve memory. They are also appropriately called strategies.*

control processes
Cognitive processes that do not occur automatically but require work and effort. These processes are under the learner's conscious control and can be used to improve memory. They are also appropriately called strategies.

One research study found extensive variations in strategy instruction (Moely, Santulli, & Obach, 1995). Some teachers did try to help students with their memory and study strategies, but, overall, strategy instruction was low across a broad range of activities. Strategy instruction was most likely to occur in teaching math and problem solving.

In addition to strategies, the characteristics of the child influence memory. Apart from the obvious variable of age, many characteristics of the child determine the effectiveness of memory. These characteristics include attitude, motivation, and health. However, the characteristic that has been examined the most thoroughly is the child's previously acquired knowledge. What the child knows has a tremendous effect on what the child remembers. In one investigation, 10-year-old chess experts remembered chessboard positions much better than did adults who did not play much chess (Chi, 1978). However, the children did not do as well as the adults when both groups were asked to remember a group of random numbers; the children's expertise in chess gave them superior memories, but only in chess.

Critical Thinking Resources
Schools for Thought

Critical Thinking

Currently, both psychologists and educators have considerable interest in critical thinking, although it is not an entirely new idea (Gardner, 1999; Runco, 1999). Famous educator John Dewey (1933) proposed a similar idea when he talked about the importance of getting students to think reflectively.

Critical thinking *involves grasping the deeper meaning of ideas, keeping an open mind about different approaches and perspectives, and deciding for oneself what to believe or do.* In this book, the inserts called Adventures for the Mind, which appear in every chapter, challenge you to think critically about a topic or an issue related to the discussion.

critical thinking
Thinking that involves grasping the deeper meaning of ideas, keeping an open mind about different approaches and perspectives, and deciding for oneself what to believe or do.

Jacqueline and Martin Brooks (1993, 1999) lament that so few schools really teach students to think critically and develop a deep understanding of concepts. For example, many high school students read *Hamlet* but don't think deeply about it, never transforming their prior notions of power, greed, and relationships. Deep understanding occurs when students are stimulated to rethink their prior ideas.

In Brooks and Brooks' view, schools spend too much time on getting students to give a single correct answer in an imitative way, rather than encouraging them to expand their thinking by coming up with new ideas and rethinking earlier conclusions. They

Careers in Life-Span Development

Laura Martin, Science Museum Educator and Research Specialist

After taking a psychology course as an undergraduate, Laura Martin obtained a master's degree from Bank Street College of Education in New York. Laura then worked as a teacher of young children for several years. That experience challenged her to learn more about how children think, so she applied to graduate school in child development and eventually obtained her Ph.D. from the University of California–San Diego. She later returned to Bank Street College and orchestrated projects on technology and learning. Then Laura joined Children's Television Workshop, which produces *Sesame Street,* as research director. Later, she became Vice President for Productions Research at Children's Television Workshop.

Interesting opportunities continued to be presented to her including offers from a software developer, the government, and colleges. She took a job as a science museum education and research specialist at the Arizona Science Center. At the center, she conceptualizes exhibits and researches whether the layout designs are communicating effectively. She organizes programs, classes, and resources. She says that as she does these things, her education and training in child development are extremely helpful.

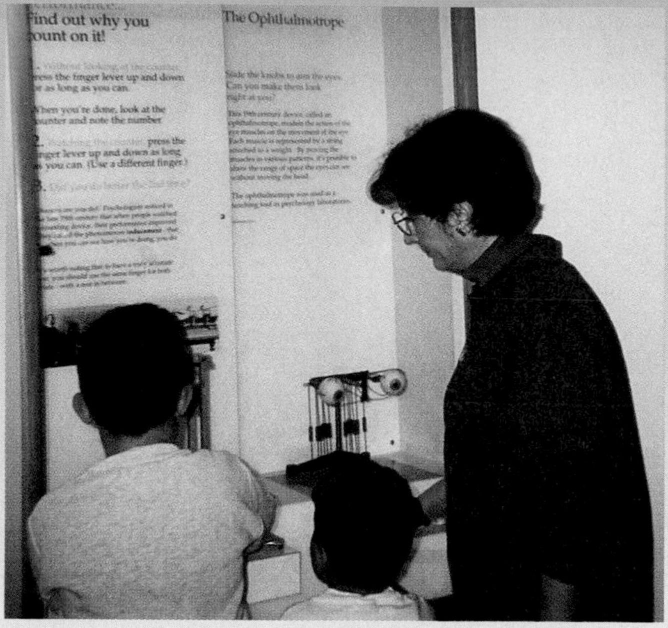

Laura Martin with children at the Arizona Science Center.

believe that too often teachers ask students to recite, define, describe, state, and list, rather than to analyze, infer, connect, synthesize, criticize, create, evaluate, think, and rethink.

Brooks and Brooks point out that many successful students complete their assignments, do well on tests, and get good grades, yet they don't ever learn to think critically and deeply. They believe our schools turn out students who think too superficially, staying on the surface of problems rather than stretching their minds and becoming deeply engaged in meaningful thinking.

Metacognition **Metacognition** *is cognition about cognition, or knowing about knowing* (Flavell, 1999; Flavell & Miller, 1998). One expert on children's thinking, Deanna Kuhn (1999), believes that metacognition should be a stronger focus of efforts to help children become better critical thinkers, especially at the middle school and high school levels. She distinguishes between first-order cognitive skills that enable children to know about the world (these have been the main focus of critical thinking programs) and second-order cognitive skills—*meta-knowing skills*—that entail knowing about one's own (and others') knowing.

metacognition
Cognition about cognition, or knowing about knowing.

The majority of developmental studies classified as "metacognitive" have focused on metamemory, or knowledge about memory (DeMarie, Abshier & Ferron, 2001). This includes general knowledge about memory, such as knowing that recognition tests are easier than recall tests. It also encompasses knowledge about one's own memory, such as a student's ability to monitor whether she has studied enough for a test that is coming up next week.

By 5 or 6 years of age, children usually know that familiar items are harder to learn than unfamiliar ones, that short lists are easier than long ones, that recognition is easier than recall, and that forgetting is more likely to occur over time (Lyon & Flavell, 1993). However, in other ways young children's metamemory is limited.

SUMMARY TABLE 10.3
Piaget's Theory, and Information Processing

Concept	Processes/ Related Ideas	Characteristics/Descriptions
Piaget's Theory	Concrete Operational Thought and Education	• Concrete operational thought involves operations, conservation, classification, seriation, and transitivity. Thought is not as abstract as later in development. • Piaget's ideas have been applied extensively to education.
	Contributions and Criticisms	• We owe Piaget the field of cognitive development; he was a genius at observing children. • Critics question his estimates of competence at different developmental levels, his stages concept, and other ideas. Neo-Piagetians believe that children's cognition is more specific than Piaget thought.
Information Processing	Memory	• Long-term memory increases in middle and late childhood. • Control processes, also called strategies, can be used by children to improve their memory.
	Critical Thinking	• Critical thinking involves grasping the deeper meaning of ideas, having an open mind, and deciding for oneself what to believe or do. • A special concern is the lack of emphasis on critical thinking in many schools.
	Metacognition	• Metacognition is cognition about cognition, or knowing about knowing. • Most metacognitive studies have focused on metamemory. • Pressley believes the key to education is helping students learn a rich repertoire of strategies.

They don't understand that related items are easier to remember than unrelated ones and that remembering the gist of a story is easier than remembering information verbatim (Kreutzer, Leonard, & Flavell, 1975). By the fifth grade, students understand that gist recall is easier than verbatim recall. Young children also have an inflated opinion of their memory abilities. For example, in one study a majority of young children predicted that they would be able to recall all 10 items on a list of 10 items. When tested for this, none of the young children managed this feat (Flavell, Friedrichs, & Hoyt, 1970). As they move through the elementary school years, children give more realistic evaluations of their memory skills (Schneider & Pressley, 1997).

In the view of Michael Pressley (Pressley, 1983; McCormick & Pressley, 1997), the key to education is helping students learn a rich repertoire of strategies that result in solutions of problems. Good thinkers routinely use strategies and effective planning to solve problems. Good thinkers also know when and where to use strategies (metacognitive knowledge about strategies). Understanding when and where to use strategies often results from the learner's monitoring of the learning situation.

Summarizing and getting the "gist" of what an author is saying are important strategies for improving one's reading skills. Planning, organizing, rereading, and writing multiple drafts are good strategies for improving writing skills.

At this point we have examined a number of ideas about Piaget's theory and information processing. To review these ideas, see summary table 10.3. Next, we will continue to explore cognition in middle and late childhood by focusing on intelligence and creativity.

Intelligence

Twentieth-century English novelist Aldous Huxley said that children are remarkable for their curiosity and intelligence. What did Huxley mean when he used the word *intelligence?*

What Is Intelligence? Intelligence is one of our most prized possessions, yet it is a concept that even the most intelligent people have not been able to agree on. Unlike such characteristics as height, weight, and age, intelligence cannot be directly measured. You can't peel back a student's scalp and observe the intelligence going on inside. You can evaluate students' intelligence only *indirectly,* by studying the intelligent acts they generate. For the most part, intelligence tests have been relied on to provide an estimate of a student's intelligence (Kail & Pelligrino, 1985).

Some experts describe intelligence as problem-solving skills. Others describe it as the ability to adapt to and learn from life's everyday experiences. Combining these ideas, we can arrive at a definition of **intelligence** *as problem-solving skills and the ability to adapt to and learn from life's everyday experiences.*

Interest in intelligence has often focused on individual differences and assessment. **Individual differences** *are the stable, consistent ways in which people are different from each other.* We can talk about individual differences in personality or any other domain, but it is in the domain of intelligence that the most attention has been directed at individual differences. For example, an intelligence test purports to inform us about whether a student can reason better than others who have taken the test.

Robert J. Sternberg recalls being terrified of taking IQ tests as a child. He says that he literally froze when the time came to take such tests. Even as an adult, Sternberg stings with humiliation when he recalls being in the sixth grade and taking an IQ test with fifth-graders. Sternberg eventually overcame his anxieties about IQ tests. He not only began performing better on them but at age 13 he even devised his own IQ test and began using it to assess classmates—that is, until the school principal found out and scolded him. Sternberg became so fascinated by intelligence that he made its study one of his lifelong pursuits. Later in the chapter, we will discuss his theory of intelligence. To begin, though, let's go back in time and examine the first intelligence test.

intelligence
Problem-solving skills and the ability to learn from and adapt to the experiences of everyday life.

individual differences
The stable, consistent ways that people are different from each other.

mental age (MA)
Binet's measure of an individual's level of mental development, compared with that of others.

intelligence quotient (IQ)
A person's mental age divided by chronological age, multiplied by 100.

normal distribution
A symmetrical distribution with most cases falling in the middle of the possible range of scores and a few scores appearing toward the extremes of the range.

The Binet Tests In 1904, the French Ministry of Education asked psychologist Alfred Binet to devise a method of identifying children who were unable to learn in school. School officials wanted to reduce crowding by placing students who did not benefit from regular classroom teaching in special schools. Binet and his student Theophile Simon developed an intelligence test to meet this request. The test is called the 1905 Scale. It consisted of 30 questions on topics ranging from the ability to touch one's ear to the ability to draw designs from memory and define abstract concepts.

Binet developed the concept of **mental age (MA),** *an individual's level of mental development relative to others.* Not much later, in 1912, William Stern created the concept of **intelligence quotient (IQ),** *a person's mental age divided by chronological age (CA), multiplied by 100.* That is IQ = MA/CA × 100. If mental age is the same as chronological age, then the person's IQ is 100. If mental age is above chronological age, then IQ is more than 100. If mental age is below chronological age, then IQ is less than 100.

The Binet test has been revised many times to incorporate advances in the understanding of intelligence and intelligence tests. These revisions are called the Stanford-Binet tests (Stanford University is where the revisions have been done). By administering the test to large numbers of people of different ages from different backgrounds, researchers have found that scores on the Stanford-Binet approximate a normal distribution (see figure 10.5). A **normal distribution** *is symmetrical, with a majority of the scores falling in the middle of the possible range of scores and few scores appearing toward the extremes of the range.*

What is intelligence? Might intelligence be reflected in this child's adaptation to her inability to walk?

The current Stanford-Binet is administered individually to people from the age of 2 through the adult years. It includes a variety of items, some of which require verbal responses, others nonverbal responses. For example, items that reflect a 6-year-old's

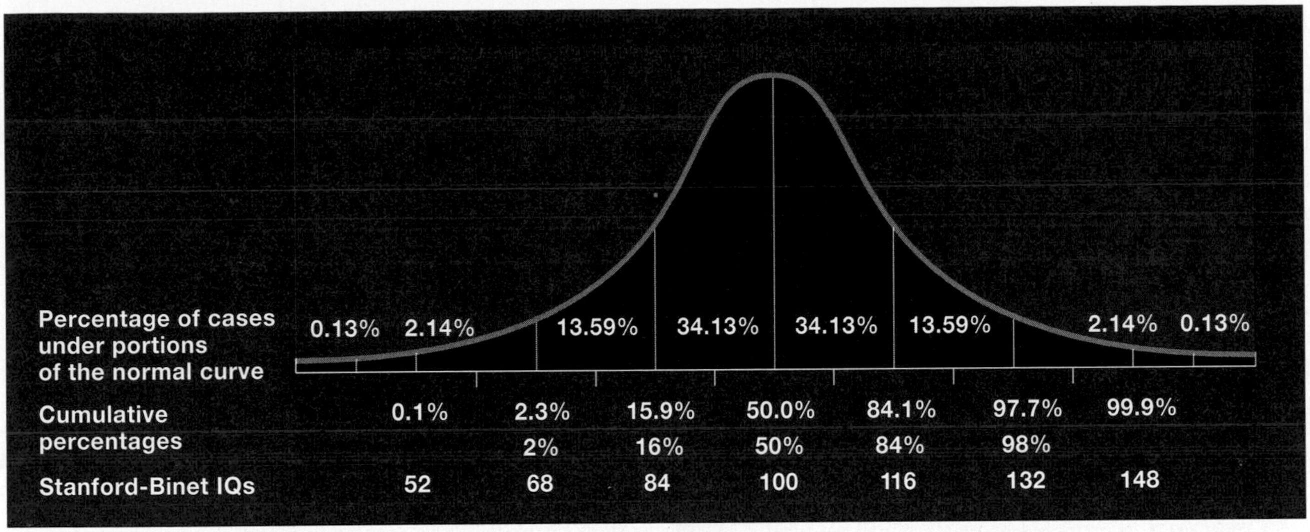

Figure **10.5**

The Normal Curve and Stanford-Binet IQ Scores

The distribution of IQ scores approximates a normal curve. Most of the population falls in the middle range of scores. Notice that extremely high and extremely low scores are very rare. Slightly more than two-thirds of the scores fall between 84 and 116. Only about 1 in 50 individuals has an IQ of more than 132, and only about 1 in 50 individuals has an IQ of less than 68.

performance on the test include the verbal ability to define at least six words, such as *orange* and *envelope,* as well as the nonverbal ability to trace a path through a maze. Items that reflect an average adult's intelligence include defining such words as *disproportionate* and *regard,* explaining a proverb, and comparing idleness and laziness.

The fourth edition of the Stanford-Binet was published in 1985. One important addition to this version was the analysis of the individual's responses in terms of four content areas: verbal reasoning, quantitative reasoning, abstract/visual reasoning, and short-term memory. A general composite score is still obtained to reflect overall intelligence. The Stanford-Binet continues to be one of the most widely used tests to assess a student's intelligence (Naglieri, 2000).

The Wechsler Scales Another set of widely used tests to assess students' intelligence is called the Wechsler scales, developed by David Wechsler. They include the Wechsler Preschool and Primary Scale of Intelligence-Revised (WPPSI-R) to test children 4 to 6½ years of age; the Wechsler Intelligence Scale for Children (WISC-III) for children and adolescents 6 to 16 years of age; and the Wechsler Adult Intelligence Scale (WAIS-III).

Not only do the Wechsler scales provide an overall IQ, but they also yield verbal and performance IQs. Verbal IQ is based on six verbal subscales, performance IQ on five performance subscales. This allows the examiner to quickly see patterns of strengths and weaknesses in different areas of the student's intelligence. Several of the Wechsler subscales are shown in figure 10.6.

Types of Intelligence Is it more appropriate to think of a child's intelligence as a general ability or as a number of specific abilities? Binet focused on a child's general intelligence. The IQ concept developed by William Stern was designed to capture this overall intellectual ability. Wechsler believed it was important to describe both a child's general intelligence and specific

Critical Thinking

Should Parents Be Testing Their Own Child's IQ?

A CD-ROM, *Children's IQ and Achievement Test,* now lets parents test their child's IQ and how he or she is performing in relation to his or her grade in school. The company that make the CD-ROM says that it helps to get parents involved in a constructive way with children's education.

What might be some problems with parents giving their children an IQ test? In constructing your answer, consider whether intelligence is much more than just IQ, whether parents can objectively test their own child, and other cautions.

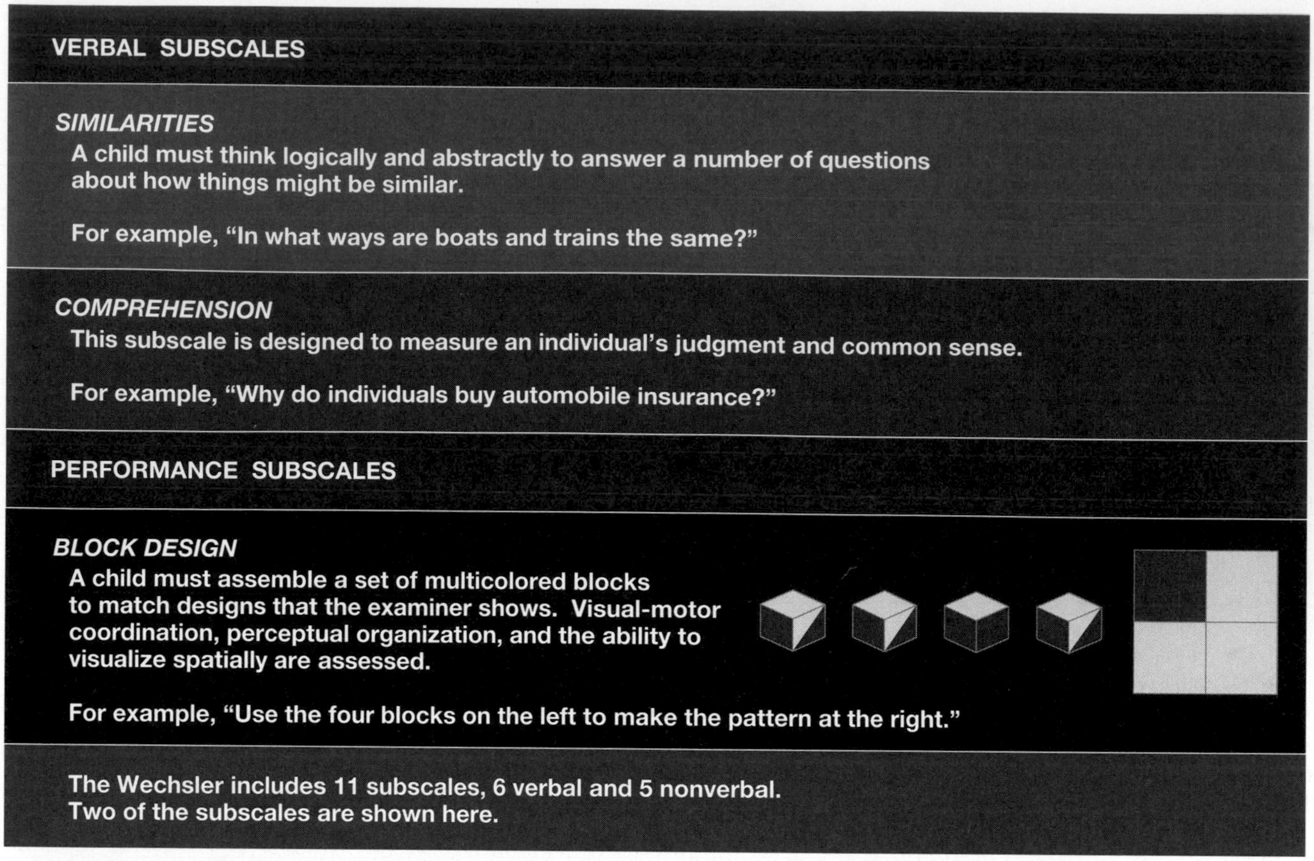

VERBAL SUBSCALES
SIMILARITIES
A child must think logically and abstractly to answer a number of questions about how things might be similar.
For example, "In what ways are boats and trains the same?"
COMPREHENSION
This subscale is designed to measure an individual's judgment and common sense.
For example, "Why do individuals buy automobile insurance?"
PERFORMANCE SUBSCALES
BLOCK DESIGN
A child must assemble a set of multicolored blocks to match designs that the examiner shows. Visual-motor coordination, perceptual organization, and the ability to visualize spatially are assessed.
For example, "Use the four blocks on the left to make the pattern at the right."
The Wechsler includes 11 subscales, 6 verbal and 5 nonverbal. Two of the subscales are shown here.

Figure **10.6**

Sample Subscales of the Wechsler Intelligence Scale for Children

verbal and performance intelligences. This built on the ideas of Charles Spearman (1927), who said that people have both a general intelligence, which he called *g*, and specific types of intelligence, which he called *s*. As early as the 1930s, L. L. Thurstone (1938) said people have seven of these specific abilities, which he called primary abilities: verbal comprehension, number ability, word fluency, spatial visualization, associative memory, reasoning, and perceptual speed. More recently, the search for specific types of intelligence has heated up (Brody, 2000).

Sternberg's Triarchic Theory Robert J. Sternberg (1986) developed the **triarchic theory of intelligence,** *which states that intelligence comes in three forms: analytical, creative, and practical.*

triarchic theory of intelligence Sternberg's theory that intelligence consists of componential intelligence, experiential intelligence, and contextual intelligence.

Analytical intelligence involves the ability to analyze, judge, evaluate, compare, and contrast. Creative intelligence consists of the ability to create, design, invent, originate, and imagine. Practical intelligence focuses on the ability to use, apply, implement, and put into practice. Some children are equally high in all three areas; others do well in only one or two of the areas. Consider three children:

- Ann, who scores high on traditional intelligence tests, such as the Stanford-Binet, and is a star analytical thinker (Analytical)
- Todd, who does not have the best test scores but has an insightful and creative mind (Creative)
- Art, who is street-smart and has learned to deal in practical ways with his world, although his scores on traditional intelligence tests are low (Practical)

WWW

Sternberg's Theory

Sternberg (1999), says that children with different triarchic patterns "look different" in school. Students with high analytic ability tend to be favored in conventional

"You're wise, but you lack tree smarts."

schooling. They often do well in direct instruction classes, in which the teacher lectures and gives students objective tests. They often are considered to be "smart" students, who get good grades, show up in high-level tracks, do well on traditional tests of intelligence and the SAT, and later get admitted to competitive colleges.

Children who are high in creative intelligence are often not in the top rung of their class. Sternberg says that many teachers have expectations about how assignments should be done, and creatively intelligent students may not conform to those expectations. Instead of giving conformist answers, they give unique answers, for which they might get reprimanded or marked down. No teacher wants to discourage creativity, but Sternberg believes that too often a teacher's desire to improve students' knowledge depresses creative thinking.

Like children high in creative intelligence, children who are practically intelligent often do not relate well to the demands of school. However, many of these children do well outside of the classroom's walls. They may have excellent social skills and good common sense. As adults, some become successful managers, entrepreneurs, or politicians, yet they have undistinguished school records.

Gardner's Eight Frames of Mind Howard Gardner (1983, 1993, 1999) believes there are eight types of intelligence. These are described below, followed by examples of the types of vocations in which they are reflected as strengths (Campbell, Campbell, & Dickinson, 1999):

- *Verbal skills:* the ability to think in words and to use language to express meaning (authors, journalists, speakers)
- *Mathematical skills:* the ability to carry out mathematical operations (scientists, engineers, accountants)
- *Spatial skills:* the ability to think three-dimensionally (architects, artists, sailors)
- *Bodily-kinesthetic skills:* the ability to manipulate objects and be physically skilled (surgeons, craftspeople, dancers, athletes)
- *Musical skills:* Sensitivity to pitch, melody, rhythm, and tone (composers, musicians, and sensitive listeners)
- *Interpersonal skills:* the ability to understand and effectively interact with others (teachers, mental health professionals)
- *Intrapersonal skills:* the ability to understand oneself and effectively direct one's life (theologians, psychologists)
- *Naturalist skills:* the ability to observe patterns in nature and understand natural and human-made systems (farmers, botanists, ecologists, landscapers)

The Key School in Indianapolis immerses students in activities that closely resemble Gardner's frames of mind (Goleman, Kaufman, & Ray, 1993). Each day, every student is exposed to materials that are designed to stimulate a range of human abilities, including art, music, computing, language skills, math skills, and physical games. In addition, attention is given to students' understanding of themselves and others.

Evaluating the Multiple Intelligence Approaches Sternberg's and Gardner's approaches have much to offer. They have stimulated teachers to think more broadly about what makes up children's competencies. And they have motivated educators to develop programs that instruct students in multiple domains. These approaches also have contributed to the interest in assessing intelligence and classroom learning in innovative ways that go beyond conventional standardized and paper-and-pencil memory tasks (Torff, 2000). One way this assessment is carried out is by evaluating students' learning portfolios.

WWW

Multiple Intelligence Links

Multiple Intelligences and Education

Children in the Key School form "pods," in which they pursue activities of special interest to them. Every day, each child can choose from activities that draw on Gardner's eight frames of mind. The school has pods that range from gardening to architecture to gliding to dancing. *What are are some of the main ideas of Gardner's theory and its application to education?*

Some critics say that classifying musical skills as a main type of intelligence is off base. They ask whether there are possibly other skill domains that Gardner has left out. For example, there are outstanding chess players, prizefighters, writers, politicians, physicians, lawyers, ministers, and poets, yet we do not refer to chess intelligence, prizefighter intelligence, and so on. Other critics say that the research base to support the three intelligences of Sternberg and the eight intelligences of Gardner as the best ways to categorize intelligence has not yet been developed.

Controversies and Issues in Intelligence The field of intelligence has its controversies. In chapter 3, "Biological Beginnings," we discussed Robert Graham's Nobel Prize Sperm Bank, which offers the sperm of Nobel Prize winners free of charge to intelligent women whose husbands are infertile ◀ P. 79. Critics say that breeding for intelligence is unethical. In reply, Graham says that the sperm bank provides a social service for couples who cannot conceive a child. Also in chapter 3 we discussed the controversial issue of how extensively intelligence is due to heredity or environment ◀ P. 83. We concluded that intelligence is due to an interaction of heredity and environment (Sternberg & Grigorenko, 2001). Here, we will focus on several more issues, involving ethnicity and culture, as well as the use and misuse of intelligence tests.

Ethnicity and Culture In the United States, children from African American and Latino families score below children from White families on standardized intelligence tests. Most comparisons have focused on African Americans and Whites. On the average, African American schoolchildren score 10 to 15 points lower than do White

"You can't build a hut, you don't know how to find edible roots and you know nothing about predicting the weather. In other words, you do terribly on our I.Q. test."

American schoolchildren (Neisser & others, 1996). Keep in mind that this figure of 10 to 15 points lower represents an average score. Many African American children score higher than many White children. Estimates are that 15 to 25 percent of all African American schoolchildren score higher than half of all White schoolchildren.

Are these differences based on heredity or environment? The consensus is environment (Brooks-Gunn, Klebanov, & Duncan, 1996). For example, in recent decades, as African Americans have experienced improved social, economic, and educational opportunities, the gap between White and African American children on conventional intelligence tests has narrowed (Jones, 1984). Between 1977 and 1996, as African Americans gained more educational opportunities, the gap between their SAT scores and those of their White counterparts shrank 23 percent (College Board, 1996). Also, when children from disadvantaged African American families are adopted by more advantaged middle-SES families, their scores on intelligence tests become closer to the national average for middle-SES children than to the national average for children from low-income families (Scarr & Weinberg, 1983).

Many of the early tests of intelligence were culturally biased, favoring urban children over rural children, children from middle-SES families over children from low-income families, and White children over minority children (Miller-Jones, 1989). The standards for the early tests were almost exclusively based on White middle-SES children. And some of the items were culturally biased. For example, one item on an early test asked what you should do if you find a 3-year-old in the street. The correct answer was "Call the police." However, children from impoverished inner-city families might not choose this answer if they have had bad experiences with the police. Children living in rural areas might not have police nearby. The contemporary versions of intelligence tests attempt to reduce such cultural bias.

Cultural Bias and Testing

Even if the content of test items is appropriate, another problem can characterize intelligence tests. Since many items are verbal, minority groups may encounter problems in understanding the language of the items. Consider Gregory Ochoa. When he was in high school, he and his classmates were given an IQ test. Gregory looked at the test questions and didn't understand many of the words. Spanish was spoken at his home, and his English was not very good. Several weeks later, Gregory was placed in a "special" class. Many of the other students in the special class had names such as Ramirez and Gonzales. The special class was for students who were mentally retarded. Gregory lost interest in school and eventually dropped out. He joined the Navy, where he took high school courses and earned enough credits to attend college. He graduated from San Jose City College as an honor student, continued his education, and became a professor of social work at the University of Washington in Seattle.

culture-fair tests
Tests that are designed to be free of cultural bias.

Culture-fair tests *are tests of intelligence that are intended to be free of cultural bias.* Two types of culture-fair tests have been devised. The first includes items that are familiar to children from all socioeconomic and ethnic backgrounds, or items that at least are familiar to the children taking the test. For example, a child might be asked how a bird and a dog are different, on the assumption that all children have been exposed to birds and dogs. The second type of culture-fair test has no verbal questions. Figure 10.7 shows a sample question from the Raven Progressive Matrices Test. Even though tests such as the Raven Progressive Matrices are designed to be culture-fair, people with more education still score higher than those with less education do.

These attempts to produce culture-fair tests remind us that conventional intelligence tests probably are culturally biased, yet the effort to create a truly culture-fair test has not yielded a successful alternative. It also is important to consider that what is viewed as intelligent in one culture may not be thought of as intelligent in another (Lonner, 1990; Serpell, 2000). In most Western cultures, children are considered intel-

ligent if they are both smart (have considerable knowledge and can solve verbal problems) and fast (can process information quickly). By contrast, in the Buganda culture in Uganda, children who are wise, slow in thought, and say the socially correct thing are considered intelligent. And, in the widely dispersed Caroline Islands, one of the most important dimensions of intelligence is the ability to navigate by the stars.

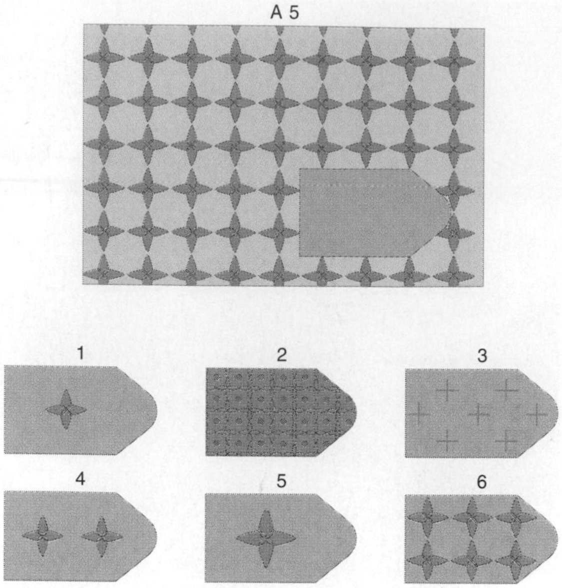

Figure **10.7**

Sample Item from the Raven Progressive Matrices Test

Individuals are presented with a matrix arrangement of symbols, such as the one at the top of this figure, and must then complete the matrix by selecting the appropriate missing symbol from a group of symbols.

The Use and Misuse of Intelligence Tests Psychological tests are tools. Like all tools, their effectiveness depends on the knowledge, skill, and integrity of the user. A hammer can be used to build a beautiful kitchen cabinet, or it can be used as a weapon of assault. Like a hammer, psychological tests can be used for positive purposes, or they can be badly abused. Following are some cautions about IQ that can help you avoid the pitfalls of using information about a child's intelligence in negative ways.

- A special concern is that the scores on an IQ test easily can lead to stereotypes and expectations about students. Sweeping generalizations are too often made on the basis of an IQ score. Imagine that you are in the teacher's lounge the day after school has started in the fall. You mention a student—Johnny Jones—and another teacher remarks that she had Johnny in class last year. She comments that he was a real dunce and mentions he scored 83 on an IQ test. How hard is it to ignore this information as you go about teaching your class? Probably difficult. But it is important that you not develop the expectation that, because Johnny scored low on an IQ test, it is useless to spend much time teaching him. An IQ test should always be considered a measure of current performance. It is not a measure of fixed potential. Maturational changes and enriched environmental experiences can advance a student's intelligence.
- Another concern about IQ tests occurs when they are used as the main or sole characteristic of competence. A high IQ is not the ultimate human value. As we have seen in this chapter, it is important to consider not only students' intellectual competence in such areas as verbal skills but also their creative and practical skills.
- Especially be cautious in interpreting the meaningfulness of an overall IQ score. In evaluating a child's intelligence, it is wiser to think of intelligence as consisting of a number of domains. Keep in mind the different types of intelligence described by Sternberg and Gardner. Remember that, by considering the different domains of intelligence, you can find that every child has at least one or more strengths.

WWW **Mental Retardation**

The Extremes of Intelligence Intelligence tests have been used to discover indications of mental retardation or intellectual giftedness, the extremes of intelligence. At times, intelligence tests have been misused for this purpose. Keeping in mind the theme that an intelligence test should not be used as the sole indicator of mental retardation or giftedness, we will explore the nature of these intellectual extremes.

Mental Retardation The most distinctive feature of mental retardation is inadequate intellectual functioning. Long before formal tests were developed to assess intelligence, the mentally retarded were identified by a lack of age-appropriate skills in learning and caring for themselves. Once intelligence tests were developed, numbers were assigned to indicate degree of mental retardation. It is not unusual to find two retarded people with the same low IQ, one of whom is married, employed, and involved in the community and the other requiring constant supervision in an institution. These differences in social competence led psychologists to include deficits in adaptive behavior in their definition of mental retardation (Baumeister, 2000; Hodapp & Zigler, 1999). **Mental retardation** *is a condition of limited mental ability in*

mental retardation
A condition of limited mental ability in which an individual has a low IQ, usually below 70 on a traditional test of intelligence, and has difficulty adapting to everyday life.

Figure **10.8**

A Child with Down Syndrome

What causes a child to develop Down syndrome? In which major classification of mental retardation does the condition fall?

which an individual has a low IQ, usually below 70 on a traditional intelligence test, and has difficulty adapting to everyday life. About 5 million Americans fit this definition of mental retardation.

There are several classifications of mental retardation. About 89 percent of the mentally retarded fall into the mild category, with IQs of 55 to 70. About 6 percent are classified as moderately retarded, with IQs of 40 to 54; these people can attain a second-grade level of skills and may be able to support themselves as adults through some types of labor. About 3.5 percent of the mentally retarded are in the severe category, with IQs of 25 to 39; these individuals learn to talk and engage in very simple tasks but require extensive supervision. Less than 1 percent have IQs below 25; they fall into the profoundly mentally retarded classification and need constant supervision (Drew & Hardman, 2000).

Mental retardation can have an organic cause, or it can be social and cultural in origin. **Organic retardation** *is mental retardation caused by a genetic disorder or by brain damage;* organic *refers to the tissues or organs of the body, so there is some physical damage in organic retardation.* Down syndrome, one form of mental retardation, occurs when an extra chromosome is present in an individual's genetic makeup (see figure 10.8) ◀ P. 75. It is not known why the extra chromosome is present, but it may involve the health or age of the female ovum or male sperm. Most people who suffer from organic retardation have IQs that range between 0 and 50.

Cultural-familial retardation *is a mental deficit in which no evidence of organic brain damage can be found; individuals' IQs range from 50 to 70.* Psychologists suspect that such mental deficits result from the normal variation that distributes people along the range of intelligence scores above 50, combined with growing up in a below-average intellectual environment. Children who are familially retarded can be detected in schools, where they often fail, need tangible rewards (candy rather than praise), and are highly sensitive to what others—both peers and adults—want from them. However, as adults, the familially retarded are usually invisible, perhaps because adult settings don't tax their cognitive skills as sorely. It may also be that the familially retarded increase their intelligence as they move toward adulthood.

organic retardation
Mental retardation that involves some physical damage and is caused by a genetic disorder or brain damage.

cultural-familial retardation
Retardation that is characterized by no evidence of organic brain damage, but the individual's IQ is between 50 and 70.

gifted
Having above-average intelligence (an IQ of 120 or higher) and/or superior talent for something.

Giftedness

There have always been people whose abilities and accomplishments outshine others'—the whiz kid in class, the star athlete, the natural musician.

What Is Giftedness?

People who are **gifted** *have above-average intelligence (an IQ of 120 or higher) and/or superior talent for something.* When it comes to programs for the gifted, most school systems select children who have intellectual superiority and academic aptitude. Children who are talented in the visual and performing arts (arts, drama, dance), athletics, or other special aptitudes tend to be overlooked.

Until recently giftedness and emotional distress were thought to go hand in hand. English novelist Virginia Woolf suffered from severe depression, for example, and eventually committed suicide. And Sir Isaac Newton, Vincent van Gogh, Ann Sexton, Socrates, and Sylvia Plath all had emotional problems. However, these are the exception rather than the rule; in general, no relation between giftedness and mental disorder has been found. Recent studies support the conclusion that gifted people tend to be more mature, have fewer emotional problems than others, and grow up in a positive family climate (Davidson, 2000; Feldman, 2001).

Characteristics of Gifted Children

Lewis Terman (1925) conducted an extensive study of 1,500 children whose Stanford-Binet IQs averaged 150. A popular myth is that gifted children are maladjusted, but Terman found in his study that

Children Who Are Gifted
Gifted Education

they were not only academically gifted but also socially well adjusted. Many of these gifted children went on to become successful doctors, lawyers, and professors, and scientists.

Ellen Winner (1996) recently described three criteria that characterize gifted children, whether in art, music, or academic domains:

1. *Precocity.* Gifted children are precocious. They begin to master an area earlier than their peers. Learning in their domain is more effortless for them than for ordinary children. In most instances, these gifted children are precocious because they have an inborn high ability in a particular domain or domains.
2. *Marching to their own drummer.* Gifted children learn in a qualitatively different way than ordinary children. One way that they march to a different drummer is that they need minimal help, or scaffolding, from adults to learn. In many instances, they resist any kind of explicit instruction. They also often make discoveries on their own and solve problems in unique ways.
3. *A passion to master.* Gifted children are driven to understand the domain in which they have high ability. They display an intense, obsessive interest and an ability to focus. They are not children who need to be pushed by their parents. They motivate themselves, says Winner.

As a 10-year-old, Alexandra Nechita recently burst onto the child prodigy scene. She paints quickly and impulsively on large canvases, some as large as 5 feet by 9 feet. It is not unusual for her to complete several of these large paintings in a week's time. Her paintings—in the modernist tradition—sell for up to $80,000 apiece. When she was only 2 years of age, Alexandra colored in coloring books for hours. She had no interest in dolls or friends. Once she started school, she would start painting as soon as she got home. And she continues to paint—relentlessy and passionately. It is, she says, what she loves to do.

CAREERS IN LIFE-SPAN DEVELOPMENT

Sterling Jones, Supervisor of Gifted and Talented Education

STERLING JONES is program supervisor for gifted and talented children in the Detroit Public School System. Sterling has been working with children who are gifted for more than three decades. He believes that students' mastery of skills mainly depends on the amount of time devoted to instruction and the length of time allowed for learning. Thus, he believes that many basic strategies for challenging children who are gifted to develop their skills can be applied to a wider range of students than once believed. He has rewritten several pamphlets for use by teachers and parents, including *How to Help Your Child Succeed* and *Gifted and Talented Education for Everyone.*

Sterling has udergraduate and graduate degrees from Wayne State University and taught English for a number of years before becoming involved in the program for gifted children. He also has written materials on African Americans, such as *Voices from the Black Experience,* that are used in the Detroit schools.

Sterling Jones with some of the children in the gifted program in the Detroit Public School System.

Creativity

Creativity *is the ability to think in novel and unusual ways and to come up with unique solutions to problems.* Thus, intelligence and creativity are not the same thing. This was recognized in Sternberg's account of intelligence earlier in this chapter and by J. P. Guilford (1967). Guilford distinguished between **convergent thinking,** *which produces one correct answer and is characteristic of the kind of thinking required on conventional intelligence tests,* and **divergent thinking,** *which produces many different answers to the same question and is more characteristic of creativity.* For example, a typical item on a conventional intelligence test is "How many quarters will you get in return for 60 dimes?" By contrast, the following question has many possible answers: "What image comes to mind when you hear the phrase 'Sitting alone in a dark room' or 'Can you think of some unique uses for a paper clip?' "

Are intelligence and creativity related? Although most creative children are quite intelligent, the reverse is not necessarily true. Many highly intelligent children (as measured by high scores on conventional intelligence tests) are not very creative. And,

creativity
The ability to think in novel and unusual ways and to come up with unique solutions to problems.

convergent thinking
Thinking that produces one correct answer and is characteristic of the kind of thinking tested by standardized intelligence tests.

divergent thinking
Thinking that produces many answers to the same question and is characteristic of creativity.

if Sternberg were to have his way, creative thinking would become part of a broader definition of intelligence.

An important goal is to help children become more creative. What are the best strategies for accomplishing this goal?

brainstorming
A technique in which individuals are encouraged to come up with ideas in a group, play off each other's ideas, and say practically whatever comes to mind.

- *Have children engage in brainstorming and come up with as many ideas as possible.* **Brainstorming** *is a technique in which children are encouraged to come up with creative ideas in a group, play off each other's ideas, and say practically whatever comes to mind.* Children are usually told to hold off from criticizing others' ideas at least until the end of the brainstorming session. Whether in a group or individually, a good creativity strategy is to come up with as many new ideas as possible. Famous twentieth-century Spanish artist Pablo Picasso produced more than 20,000 works of art. Not all of them were masterpieces. The more ideas children produce, the better their chance of creating something unique (Rickards, 1999; Runco, 2000). Creative children are not afraid of failing or getting something wrong. They may go down twenty dead-end streets before they come up with an innovative idea. They recognize that it's okay to win some and lose some. They are willing to take risks, just as Picasso was.

Never to be cast away are the gifts of the gods, magnificent.

Homer
Greek Poet, 9th Century B.C.

- *Provide children with environments that stimulate creativity.* Some settings nourish creativity; others depress it. People who encourage children's creativity often rely on their natural curiosity. They provide exercises and activities that stimulate children to find insightful solutions to problems, rather than asking a lot of questions that require rote answers. Adults also encourage creativity by taking children to locations where creativity is valued. Howard Gardner (1993) believes that science, discovery, and children's museums offer rich opportunities to stimulate children's creativity.

Teresa Amabile's Reserach
Csikszentmihalyi's Ideas
Harvard Project Zero

- *Don't overcontrol.* Teresa Amabile (1993) says that telling children exactly how to do things leaves them feeling that any originality is a mistake and any exploration is a waste of time. Letting children select their interests and supporting their inclinations are less likely to destroy their natural curiosity than dictating which activities they should engage in (Csikszentmihalyi, 2000). Amabile also believes that, when adults constantly hover over children, the children feel they are being watched while they are working. When children are under constant surveillance, their creative risk-taking and adventurous spirit wane. Another strategy that can harm creativity is to have grandiose expectations for a child's performance and expect the child to do something perfectly, according to Amabile.
- *Encourage internal motivation.* The excessive use of prizes, such as gold stars, money, or toys, can stifle creativity by undermining the intrinsic pleasure children derive from creative activities. Creative children's motivation is the satisfaction generated by the work itself. Competition for prizes and formal evaluations often undermine intrinsic motivation and creativity (Amabile & Hennessey, 1992).
- *Foster flexible and playful thinking.* Creative thinkers are flexible and play with problems, which gives rise to a paradox. Although creativity takes effort, the effort goes more smoothly if students take it lightly. In a way, humor can grease the wheels of creativity (Goleman, Kaufman, & Ray, 1993). When children are joking around, they are more likely to consider unusual solutions to problems. Having fun helps disarm the inner censor that can condemn a child's ideas as off-base. As one clown named Wavy Gravy put it, "If you can't laugh about it, it just isn't funny anymore."
- *Introduce children to creative people.* You may not know a clown named Wavy Gravy whom you can ask to stimulate a child's creativity, but it is a good strategy to think about the identity of the most creative people in your community. Teachers can invite these people to their classrooms and ask them to describe what helps them become creative or to demonstrate their creative skills. A writer, poet, musician, scientist, and many others can bring their props and productions to the class, turning it into a theater for stimulating students' creativity. Poet Richard Lewis (1997) visits classrooms in New York City. He brings with him only the

Summary Table 10.4
Intelligence and Creativity

Concept	Processes/ Related Ideas	Characteristics/Descriptions
What Is Intelligence?	More Than Just Verbal Ability	• Intelligence consists of verbal ability, problem-solving skills, and the ability to adapt to and learn from life's everyday experiences. • Interest in intelligence often focuses on individual differences and assessment.
	The Binet Tests	• Binet and Simon developed the first intelligence test. • Binet developed the concept of mental age and Stern created the concept of IQ as MA/CA X 100. • The Stanford-Binet approximates a normal distribution.
	The Wechsler Scales	• They are widely used to assess intelligence and yield an overall IQ, as well as verbal and performance IQs.
	Types of Intelligence	• Spearman proposed that people have a general intelligence (g) and specific types of intelligence (s).
	Sternberg's Triarchic Theory	• Sternberg proposed that intelligence comes in three main forms: analytical, creative, and practical.
	Gardner's Eight Frames of Mind	• Gardner believes there are eight types of intelligence: verbal, math, spatial, movement, self insight, insight about others, musical skills, and naturalist skills.
	Evaluating the Multiple Intelligence Approaches	• They have expanded our conception of intelligence. • Critics argue that the research base for these approaches is not well established.
Controversies and Issues	Sometimes Intelligence Tests Are Misused	• These include ethnicity and culture, and the use and misuse of intelligence tests.
Extremes of Intelligence	Mental Retardation	• Involves low IQ and problems in adapting to everyday life. • One classification consists of organic or cultural-familial.
	Giftedness	• A gifted child has above-average intelligence and/or superior talent for something. • Terman contributed to our understanding that gifted children are not more maladjusted than nongifted children. • Three characteristics of gifted children are precocity, individuality, and a passion to master.
Creativity	Novel, Unusual, Unique	• Creativity is the ability to think in novel and unusual ways and to come up with unique solutions to problems. • Guilford distinguished between convergent and divergent thinking. • A number of strategies can be used to encourage children's creative thinking, including brainstorming.

glassy spectrum that a shining marble holds. He lifts it above his head, so that every student can see its colored charms. He asks, "Who can see something playing inside?" Then he asks students to write about what they see. One student named Snigdha wrote that she sees the rainbow rising, the sun moving a lot, and the sun sleeping with the stars. She also wrote that she sees the rain dropping on the ground, stems breaking, apples falling from trees, and wind blowing the leaves.

At this point we have discussed a number of ideas about intelligence and creativity. To review these ideas see summary table 10.4. Next, we will continue our exploration of important changes in middle and late childhood by focusing on language development.

Children's reading is a complex process. *What kinds of information-processing skills are involved?*

Language Development

As children develop during middle and late childhood, changes in their vocabulary and grammar take place. Reading assumes a prominent role in their language world. An increasingly important consideration is bilingualism.

Vocabulary and Grammar

During middle and late childhood, a change occurs in the way children think about words. They become less tied to the actions and perceptual dimensions associated with words, and they become more analytical in their approach to words. For example, when asked to say the first thing that comes to mind when they hear a word, such as *dog,* preschool children often respond with a word related to the immediate context of a dog. A child might associate *dog* with a word that indicates its appearance *(black, big)* or to an action associated with it *(bark, sit).* Older children more frequently respond to *dog* by associating it with an appropriate category *(animal)* or to information that intelligently expands the context *(cat, veterinarian).* The increasing ability of elementary school children to analyze words helps them understand words that have no direct relation to their personal experiences. This allows children to add more abstract words to their vocabulary. For example, *precious stones* can be understood by understanding the common characteristics of *diamonds* and *emeralds.* Also, children's increasing analytic abilities allow them to distinguish between such similar words as *cousin* and *nephew* or *city, village,* and *suburb.*

Children make similar advances in grammar. The elementary school child's improvement in logical reasoning and analytical skills helps in the understanding of such constructions as the appropriate use of comparatives *(shorter, deeper)* and subjectives ("If you were president, . . ."). By the end of the elementary school years, children can usually apply many of the appropriate rules of grammar.

Reading

What are some approaches to teaching children how to read? Education and language experts continue to debate how children should be taught to read. The debate focuses on the whole-language approach versus the basic-skill-and-phonetics approach. The **whole-language approach** *stresses that reading instruction should parallel children's natural language learning. Reading materials should be whole and meaningful.* That is, in early reading instruction, children should be presented with materials in their complete form, such as stories and poems. In this way, say the whole-language advocates, children learn to understand language's communicative function.

whole-language approach
An approach to reading instruction based on the idea that instruction should parallel children's natural language learning. Reading materials should be whole and meaningful.

In the whole-language approach, reading is integrated with other skills and subjects. Reading should be connected with listening and writing skills. Although there are variations in whole-language programs, most share the premise that reading should be integrated with other skills and subjects, such as science and social studies, and that it should focus on real-world, relevant material. Thus, a class might read newspapers, magazines, or books, then write about them and discuss them.

By contrast, the **basic-skills-and-phonetics approach** *emphasizes that reading instruction should teach phonetics and its basic rules for translating written symbols into sounds. Early reading instruction should involve simplified materials.* Only after they have learned phonological rules should children be given complex reading materials, such as books and poems.

basic-skills-and-phonetics approach
An approach to reading instruction that stresses phonetics and basic rules for translating symbols into sounds. Early reading instruction should involve simplified materials.

Advocates of the basic-skills-and-phonetics approach often point to low reading achievement scores occurring as an outgrowth of the recent emphasis on holistic, literature-based instruction and the consequent lack of attention to basic skills and phonetics (Baumann & others, 1998). In California, a task force has recommended that children's reading skills be improved by pursuing a balanced approach, which includes teaching phonemic awareness (sounds in words), phonics, and other decoding skills.

WWW
Reading Research
Reading
Children's Literature

The term *balanced instruction* is now being used to refer to combinations of reading approaches (Freppon & Dahl, 1998). However, *balance* often means different things

to different researchers and teachers. For some, *balanced* means a primary emphasis on phonics instruction with minimal whole-language emphasis; for others, the reverse.

Which approach is best? Researchers have not been able to document consistently that one approach is better than the other. There is very strong evidence that the decoding skills involved in recognizing sounds and words are important in becoming a good reader. A good strategy is to work with kindergarten and first-grade students on developing phonemic awareness, which involves recognizing that separate sounds make up words and that combining these sounds can make words. If students have not developed this phonemic awareness early in school, their literacy will still benefit if it is taught to them later in school (Pressley, 1996). Some critics believe that, because of the prominence of the whole-language approach, some teacher training programs have not adequately instructed future teachers in phonics and other structural rules of language.

There is also good evidence that students in the early years of school benefit from the whole-language approach of being immersed in a natural world of print (Graham & Harris, 1994). This approach helps them understand the purpose of learning to read and builds on their early home experiences with books and language.

Some experts believe that a combination of the two approaches should be followed (Freppon & Dahl, 1998; Spear-Swerling & Sternberg, 1994). In sum, there is every reason to believe that students learn to read best when they are exposed to both whole-language experiences and decoding skills. Indeed, a combination of whole-language and phonics approaches also recently was recommended by a national panel of experts after reviewing the research evidence on the effectiveness of reading approaches (National Research Council, 1999).

In sum, balance, eclecticism, and common sense characterize the reading and language arts instructional practices of many elementary school teachers. As educational psychologist David Berliner (1997) commented, teachers often are not extremist on the whole-language–phonics issue. They tend to be pragmatists, using what works.

CAREERS IN LIFE-SPAN DEVELOPMENT

Sharla Peltier, Speech Pathologist

SHARLA PELTIER is a speech pathologist in Manitoulin, Ontario, Canada. A speech pathologist is a health professional who works with individuals with communication disorders. Sharla works with Native American children in the First Nation Schools. She conducts screening for speech/language and hearing problems and assesses infants as young as 6 months as well as school-aged children. She works closely with community health nurses to identify hearing problems.

Diagnosing problems is only about half of what Sharla does in her work. She especially enjoys treating speech/language and hearing problems. She conducts parent training sessions to help parents understand and help with their children's language problem. As part of this training, she guides parents in improving their communication skills with their children.

Sharla Peltier conducting speech therapy with a Native American child.

Bilingualism Octavio's parents moved to the United States one year before he was born. They do not speak English fluently and always have spoken to Octavio in Spanish. At age 6, Octavio has just entered the first grade in San Antonio. He speaks no English. What is the best way to teach Octavio?

As many as 10 million children in the United States come from homes in which English is not the primary language. Often, like Octavio, they live in a community in which English is the main form of communication. To be successful, they have to master the English language.

Bilingual education, *which has been the preferred strategy of schools for the past two decades, aims to teach academic subjects to immigrant children in their native languages (most often Spanish) while slowly and simultaneously adding English instruction.* Researchers have found that bilingualism does not interfere with performance in either language (Hakuta & Garcia, 1989; Oller, 1999). Indeed, researchers have demonstrated that bilingulism has a positive effect on children's cognitive development. Children who are fluent in two languages perform better

bilingual education
An educational approach whose aim is to teach academic subjects to immigrant children in their native languages (most often Spanish) while gradually adding English instruction.

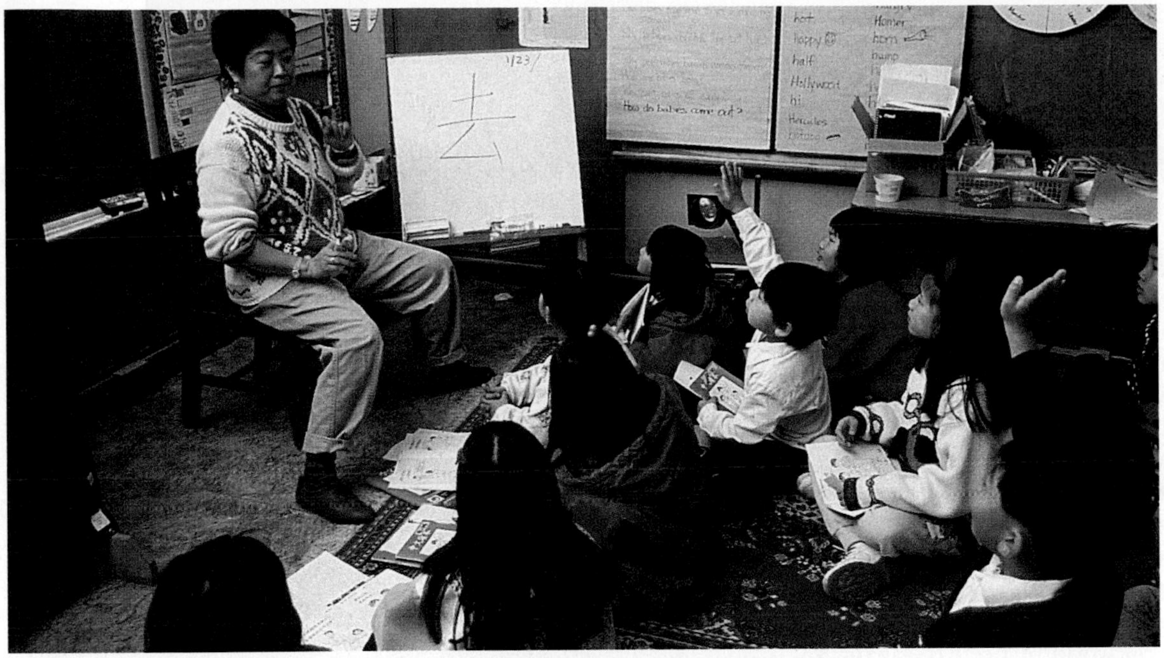

A first- and second-grade bilingual English-Cantonese teacher instructing students in Chinese in Oakland, California. *What is the nature of bilingual education?*

than their single language counterparts on tests of attentional control, concept formation, analytical reasoning, cognitive flexibility, and cognitive complexity (Bialystok, 1999). They also are more conscious of spoken and written language structure and better at noticing errors of grammar and meaning, skills that benefit their reading ability (Bialystok, 1993, 1997).

A common fear is that early exposure to English will lead to children's loss of their native language. In recent studies of Latino American children, there was no evidence of a loss in Spanish proficiency (productive language, receptive language, and language complexity) for children attending a bilingual preschool (Rodriquez & others, 1995; Winsler & others, 1999). Children who attended bilingual preschool, compared to those who remained at home, showed significant and parallel gains in both English and Spanish.

Researchers have found that bilingual children in a number of countries (such as Canada, Israel, Singapore, and Switzerland) do better than monolingual children on tests of intelligence (Lambert & others, 1993). Based on these findings, a Canadian program was developed to immerse English-speaking children in French for much of their early elementary school education in Quebec. Their English does not appear to have been harmed and their math scores, aptitude scores, and appreciation of French culture have benefited.

Bilingual Education
Multilingual Multicultural Research

Proponents of bilingual education argue that teaching immigrants in their native language values their family and community culture and increases their self-esteem, thus making their academic success more likely. By contrast, critics stress that, in actual practice, bilingual education harms immigrant children by failing to instruct them adequately in English, which will leave them behind in the workplace. In rebuttal, supporters of bilingual education say it aims to teach English. Some states recently have passed laws declaring English to be their official language, creating conditions in which schools are not obligated to teach minority children in languages other than English (Rothstein, 1998). In California, in 1998 voters repealed bilingualism altogether. Supporters of the appeal claimed that most Spanish-speaking voters opposed bilingual education, though polling after the election did not bear out this contention. Ironically, test scores released shortly after the election revealed that the scores of children in bilingual programs in several large school districts were higher on average than scores of native-English speaking children.

Summary Table 10.5
Language Development

Concept	Processes/ Related Ideas	Characteristics/Descriptions
Vocabulary and Grammar	Changes	• Children become more analytical and logical in their approach to words and grammar.
Reading	Whole-Language and Basic-Skills-and-Phonics Approaches	• Current debate focuses on the whole language approach versus basic skills-and-phonics approach. • Many experts today recommend a balance of these two approaches in teaching children to read.
Bilingualism	Its Nature	• Bilingual education aims to teach academic subjects to immigrant children in their native languages (most often in Spanish) while gradually adding English instruction. • Researchers have found that bilingualism does not interfere with performance in either language. • Success in learning a second language is greater in childhood than in adolescence.

Is it better to learn a second language as a child or as an adult? Adults make faster initial progress but their eventual success in the second language is not as great as children's. For example, in one study Chineses and Korean adults who immigrated to the United States at different ages were given a test of grammatical knowledge (Johnson & Newport, 1989). Those who began learning English from 3 to 7 years of age scored as well as native speakers on the test, but those whose arrived in the United States (and started learning English) in later childhood or adolescence had lower test scores. Children's ability to pronounce a second language with the correct accent also decreases with age, with an especially sharp decline occurring after the age of about 10 to 12 (Asher & Garcia, 1969). Adolescents and adults can become competent at a second language but this is a more difficult task than learning it as a child.

The United States is one of the few countries in the world in which most students graduate from high school knowing only their own language. For example, in Russia schools have 10 grades, called forms, which roughly correspond to the 12 grades in American schools. Children begin school at age 7 in Russia and begin learning English in the third form. Because of the emphasis on teaching English in Russian schools, most Russian citizens under the age of 40 today are bilingual, able to speak at least some English in addition to their native language.

Following are some recommendations for working with linguistically and culturally diverse children (National Association for the Education of Young Children, 1996):

- Recognize that all children are cognitively, linguistically, and emotionally connected to the language and culture of their home.
- Understand that second-language learning can be difficult. It takes time to become linguistically competent in any language. Although verbal proficiency in a second language can be attained in 2 to 3 years, the skills needed to understand academic content through reading and writing can take 4 or more years. Children who do not become proficient in their second language after 2 or 3 years usually are not proficient in their first language either.
- Recognize that children can and will acquire the use of English even when their home language is respected.

At this point we have discussed a number of ideas about how language develops in middle and late childhood and about bilingualism. A summary of these ideas is presented in summary table 10.5.

Chapter Review

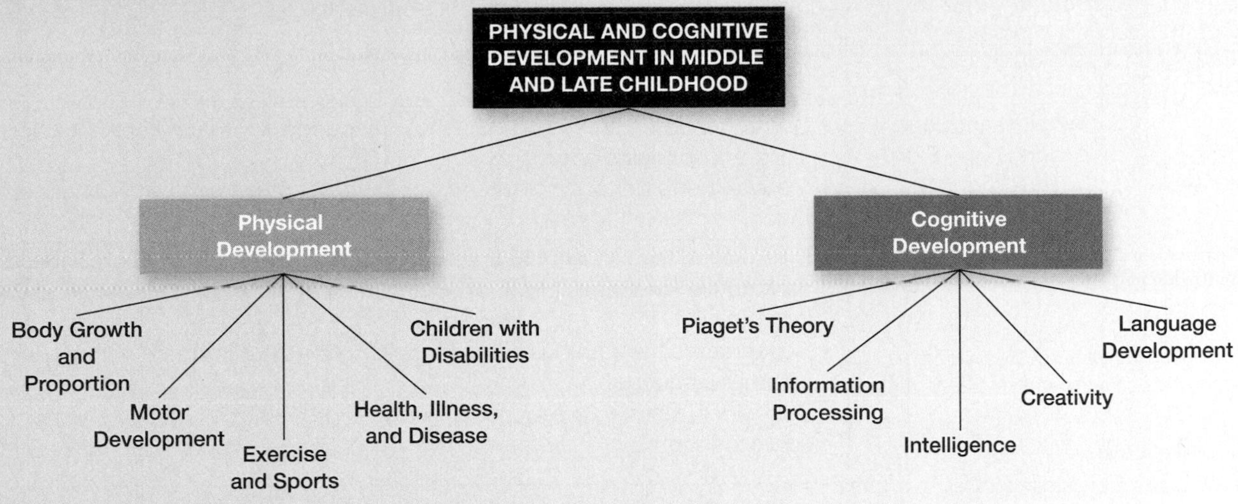

TO OBTAIN A DETAILED REVIEW OF THIS CHAPTER, STUDY THESE FIVE SUMMARY TABLES:

- Summary Table 10.1 Body Growth and Proportion; Motor Development; Exercise and Sports; Health, Illness, and Disease — page 279
- Summary Table 10.2 Children with Disabilities — page 283
- Summary Table 10.3 Piaget's Theory, and Information Processing — page 290
- Summary Table 10.4 Intelligence and Creativity — page 301
- Summary Table 10.5 Language Development — page 305

Key Terms

learning disability 278
dyslexia 278
attention deficit hyperactivity disorder (ADHD) 279
individualized education plan (IEP) 281
least restrictive environment (LRE) 281
inclusion 281
mainstreaming 281
seriation 284
transitivity 284
neo-Piagetians 287
long-term memory 288
control processes 288
critical thinking 288
metacognition 289
intelligence 291
individual differences 291
mental age (MA) 291
intelligence quotient (IQ) 291
normal distribution 291
triarchic theory of intelligence 293
culture-fair tests 296
mental retardation 297
organic retardation 298
cultural-familial retardation 298
gifted 298
creativity 299
convergent thinking 299
divergent thinking 299
brainstorming 300
whole-language approach 302
basic-skills-and-phonics approach 302
bilingual education 303

Key People

Jean Piaget 283
John Dewey 288
Jacqueline and Martin Brooks 288
Deanna Kuhn 289
Michael Pressley 290
Alfred Binet 291
Theophile Simon 291
William Stern 291
David Wechsler 292
Charles Spearman 293
L. L. Thurstone 293
Robert J. Sternberg 293
Howard Gardner 294
Lewis Terman 298
Ellen Winner 299
J. P. Guilford 299
Teresa Amabile 300

Taking It to the Net

1. Clarence wants to teach his fifth-grade students good diet, nutritional, and exercise habits. What lessons can they be taught now that will benefit them later in life?
2. Eric's parents are upset to hear that their fourth grader may have dyslexia. Eric's father voices his concern that people will think his son is stupid to Eric's teacher. What should Eric's teacher inform these parents about the nature and causes of dyslexia?
3. Elise was doing research for a report on intelligence theories. She ran across an online article that suggested a new dimension of intelligence, the "g factor" which she had never heard before. What is the g factor and how does it relate to other concepts of intelligence?

   Connect to www.mhhe.com/santrockld8 to research the answers and complete these exercises.

OLC Preview

To further test your knowledge of this chapter or to explore our extensive online resources that accompany *Life-Span Development,* eighth edition, please log on to the text's Online Learning Center at http://www.mhhe.com/santrockld8.com.

Chapter 11

SOCIOEMOTIONAL DEVELOPMENT IN MIDDLE AND LATE CHILDHOOD

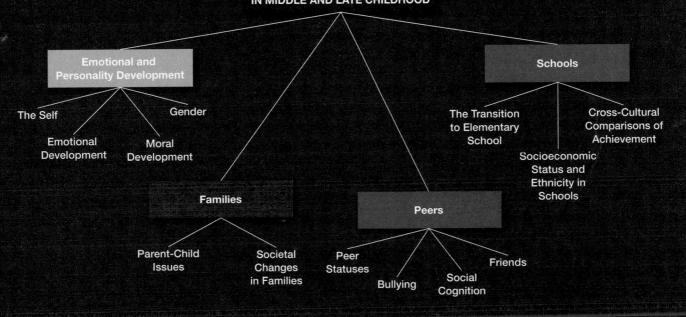

- **Emotional and Personality Development**
  - The Self
  - Emotional Development
  - Moral Development
  - Gender
- **Families**
  - Parent-Child Issues
  - Societal Changes in Families
- **Peers**
  - Peer Statuses
  - Bullying
  - Social Cognition
  - Friends
- **Schools**
  - The Transition to Elementary School
  - Socioeconomic Status and Ethnicity in Schools
  - Cross-Cultural Comparisons of Achievement

Socioemotional Development in Middle and Late Childhood

Children are busy becoming something they have not quite grasped yet, something which keeps changing. . . .

Alastair Reid
American Poet, 20th Century

Images of Life-Span Development

The Stories of Lafayette and Pharoah: The Tragedy of Poverty and Violence

ALEX KOTLOWITZ (1991) followed the lives of two brothers, 10-year-old Lafayette and 7-year-old Pharoah, for two years. The boys lived in an impoverished housing project in Chicago. Their father had a drug habit and had trouble holding down a job.

Kotlowitz approached their mother, LaJoe, about the possibility of writing a book about Lafayette, Pharoah, and other children in the neighborhood. She liked the idea but hesitated. She then commented, "But you know, there are no children around here. They've seen too much to be children."

Over the two years, Lafayette and Pharoah struggled with school, resisted the lure of gangs, and mourned the deaths of friends. All the time they wondered why they were living in such a violent place and hoped they could get out.

Their older brother, 17-year-old Terrence, was a drug user. Lafayette told one of his friends, "You grow up 'round it. There are a lot of people in the projects who say they're not gonna do drugs, that they're not gonna drop out of school, that they won't be on the streets. But they're doing it now. Never say never. But I say never. My older brother didn't set a good example for me, but I'll set a good example for my younger brother."

A few days later, police arrested Terrence as a robbery suspect. They handcuffed him in the apartment in front of Lafayette and Pharoah. Pharoah told his mother, "I'm just too young to understand how life really is."

Several months later, shooting erupted in the housing complex, and their mother herded Lafayette and Pharoah into the hallway, where they crouched along the walls to avoid stray bullets. Lafayette said to his mother, "If we don't get away, someone's gonna end up dead. I feel it." Shortly thereafter, a 9-year-old friend of the boys was shot in the back of the head as he walked into his building just across the street. The bullet had been meant for someone else.

Poverty, stress, and violence were constants where Lafayette and Pharoah lived. There were so many shootings that many of them didn't even make the newspaper. Both boys wanted to move to a safe, quiet neighborhood, but their mother struggled just to make ends meet in the projects.

How might the stress of poverty and violence affect children's development? How might it affect the parent-child relationship? Although these kinds of circumstances are often harmful to children, might some children be resilient in the face of such stressors and have positive outcomes in life?

Some children triumph over life's adversities (Wilson & Gottman, 1996). Norman Garmezy (1985, 1993) has studied resilience amid disadvantage for many years. He concluded that three factors help children become resilient to stress and disadvantage: (1) good cognitive skills, especially attention, which helps children focus on tasks, such as school work; (2) a family—even if enveloped in poverty—characterized by warmth, cohesion, and a caring adult, such as a grandparent who takes responsibility in the absence of responsive parents or in the presence of intense marital conflict; and (3) external support, such as a teacher, a neighbor, a mentor, a caring agency, or a church. In one longitudinal study of resilient individuals from birth to 32 years of age in Kuaia, these three factors were present in their lives (Werner, 1989).

Later in this chapter we will focus on some of the strategies that can be used in schools to help children like Lafayette and Pharoah who live in impoverished conditions. To begin, though, we will explore children's emotional and personality development in middle and late childhood.

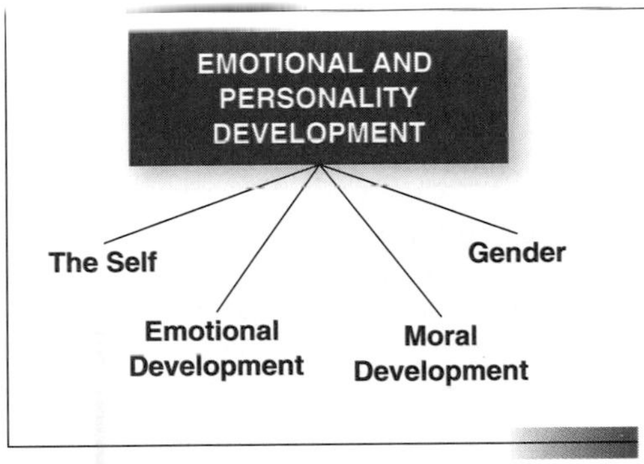

Emotional and Personality Development

In chapter 9, we discussed the development of the self, emotional development, moral development, and gender in early childhood ◀ P. 238. Here, we will focus on these important dimensions of children's development in middle and late childhood.

The Self

What is the nature of the child's self-understanding and self-esteem in the elementary school years?

Know yourself.

Socrates
Greek Philosopher, 5th Century B.C.

The Development of Self-Understanding In middle and late childhood, self-understanding increasingly shifts from defining oneself through external characteristics to defining oneself through internal characteristics. Elementary school children are also more likely to define themselves in terms of social characteristics and social comparisons (Harter, 1999). This theme of self-definition will be discussed shortly.

In middle and late childhood, children not only recognize differences between inner and outer states but also are more likely to include subjective inner states in their definition of self. For example, in one study, second-grade children were much more likely than younger children to name psychological characteristics (such as preferences or personality traits) in their self-definition and were less likely to name physical characteristics (such as eye color or possessions) (Aboud & Skerry, 1983). For example, 8-year-old Todd included in his self-description, "I am smart and I am popular." Ten-year-old Tina says about herself, "I am pretty good about not worrying most of the time. I used to lose my temper, but I'm better about that now. I also feel proud when I do well in school."

In addition to the increase of psychological characteristics in self-definition during the elementary school years, the *social aspects* of the self also increase at this point in development. In one investigation, elementary school children often included

references to social groups in their self-descriptions (Livesly & Bromley, 1973). For example, some children referred to themselves as Girl Scouts, as Catholics, or as someone who has two close friends.

Children's self-understanding in the elementary school years also includes increasing reference to *social comparison.* At this point in development, children are more likely to distinguish themselves from others in comparative rather than in absolute terms. That is, elementary-school-age children are no longer as likely to think about what I do or do not do but are more likely to think about what I can do *in comparison with others.* This developmental shift provides an increased tendency to establish one's differences from others as an individual.

It is difficult to make people miserable when they feel worthy of themselves.

Abraham Lincoln
American President, 19th Century

Self-Esteem and Self-Concept

High self-esteem and a positive self-concept are important characteristics of children's well-being (Harter, 1999).

What Are Self-Esteem and Self-Concept?

Self-esteem *refers to global evaluations of the self. Self-esteem is also referred to as self-worth or self-image.* For example, a child may perceive that she is not merely a person but a *good* person. Of course, not all children have an overall positive image of themselves. **Self-concept** *refers to domain-specific evaluations of the self.* Children can make self-evaluations in many domains of their lives—academic, athletic, appearance, and so on. In sum, *self-esteem* refers to global self-evaluations, *self-concept* to more domain-specific evaluations.

self-esteem
The global evaluative dimension of the self. Self-esteem is also referred to as self-worth or self-image.

self-concept
Domain-specific evaluations of the self.

Investigators have not always made clear distinctions between self-esteem and self-concept, sometimes using the terms interchangeably or not precisely defining them. The distinction between self-esteem as global self-evaluation and self-concept as domain-specific self-evaluation should help you keep the terms straight.

Research on Self-Esteem

One research area explores whether self-esteem fluctuates from day to day or remains stable. Most research studies have found it to be stable at least across a month or so of time (Baumeister, 1993; Tesser, 2000). Self-esteem can change, especially in response to transitions in life. For example, when children go from elementary school to middle school, their self-esteem usually drops (Hawkins & Berndt. 1985).

As children grow through the elementary years, they increasingly engage in social comparison with their peers. This can lower their self-esteem when they evaluate themselves in a less favorable light than their peers (Damon & Hart, 1988; Harter, 1998).

Another research issue involves whether low self-esteem is linked with developmental problems. One area where the research has been consistent is depression—low self-esteem is related to depression (Harter, 1998).

An important point needs to be made about much of the research on self-esteem: It is correlational rather than experimental. Remember from chapter 2, "The Science of Life-Span Development," that correlation does not equal causation. Thus, if a correlational study finds an association between self-esteem and depression, depression might cause low self-esteem or low self-esteem might cause depression.

Increasing Children's Self-Esteem

Four ways children's self-esteem can be improved are through (1) identification of the causes of low self-esteem and the domains of competence important to the self, (2) emotional support and social approval, (3) achievement, and (4) coping (see figure 11.1).

Identifying children's sources of self-esteem—that is, competence in domains important to the self—is critical to improving self-esteem. Susan Harter (1990) points out that the self-esteem enhancement programs of the 1960s, in which self-esteem itself was the target and individuals were encouraged to simply feel good about themselves, were ineffective. Rather, Harter believes that intervention must occur at the level of the *causes* of self-esteem if the individual's self-esteem is to improve significantly. Children have the highest self-esteem when they perform competently in domains that are important to them. Therefore, children should be

Figure **11.1**
Four Key Aspects of Improving Self-Esteem

encouraged to identify and value areas of competence. These areas might include academic skills, athletic skills, physical attractiveness, and social acceptance.

Emotional support and social approval in the form of confirmation from others also powerfully influence children's self-esteem. Some children with low self-esteem come from conflicted families or conditions in which they experienced abuse or neglect—situations in which support was unavailable. In some cases, alternative sources of support can be implemented either informally through the encouragement of a teacher, a coach, or another significant adult or, more formally, through programs such as Big Brothers and Big Sisters. While peer approval becomes increasingly important during adolescence, both adult and peer support are important influences on the adolescent's self-esteem.

Achievement also can improve children's self-esteem (Bednar, Wells, & Peterson, 1995). For example, the straightforward teaching of real skills to children often results in increased achievement and, thus, in enhanced self-esteem. Children develop higher self-esteem because they know the important tasks to achieve goals, and they have experienced performing them or similar behaviors. The emphasis on the importance of achievement in improving self-esteem has much in common with Bandura's cognitive social cognitive concept of *self-efficacy,* which refers to individuals' beliefs that they can master a situation and produce positive outcomes.

Self-esteem also is often increased when children face a problem and try to cope with it, rather than avoid it. If coping rather than avoidance prevails, children often face problems realistically, honestly, and nondefensively. This produces favorable self-evaluative thoughts, which lead to the self-generated approval that raises self-esteem. The converse is true of low self-esteem. Unfavorable self-evaluations trigger denial, deception, and avoidance in an attempt to disavow that which has already been glimpsed as true. This process leads to self-generated disapproval as a form of feedback to the self about personal adequacy.

Industry Versus Inferiority In chapter 2, we described Erik Erikson's eight stages of human development P. 34. His fourth stage, industry versus inferiority, appears during middle and late childhood. The term *industry* expresses a dominant theme of this period: children become interested in how things are made and how they work. It is the Robinson Crusoe age, in that the enthusiasm and minute detail Crusoe uses to describe his activities appeal to the child's budding sense of industry. When children are encouraged in their efforts to make, build, and work—whether building a model airplane, constructing a tree house, fixing a bicycle, solving an addition problem, or cooking—their sense of industry increases. However, parents who see their children's efforts at making things as "mischief" or "making a mess" encourage children's development of a sense of inferiority.

Children's social worlds beyond their families also contribute to a sense of industry. School becomes especially important in this regard. Consider children who are slightly below average in intelligence. They are too bright to be in special classes but not bright enough to be in gifted classes. They fail frequently in their academic efforts, developing a sense of inferiority. By contrast, consider children whose sense of industry is derogated at home. A series of sensitive and committed teachers may revitalize their sense of industry (Elkind, 1970).

Emotional Development

In chapter 9, we saw that preschoolers become more adept at talking about their own and others' emotions P. 239. They also show a growing awareness about controlling and managing emotions to meet social standards. Further developmental changes characterize emotion in middle and late childhood (Rubin, 2000; Saarni, 1999).

Developmental Changes Following are some important developmental changes in emotions during the elementary school years (Kuebli, 1994; Wintre & Vallance, 1994):

- An increased ability to understand such complex emotions as pride and shame (Kuebli, 1994). These emotions become more internalized and integrated with a sense of personal responsibility.
- Increased understanding that more than one emotion can be experienced in a particular situation
- An increased tendency to take into fuller account the events leading to emotional reactions
- Marked improvements in the ability to suppress or conceal negative emotional reactions
- The use of self-initiated strategies for redirecting feelings

Emotional Intelligence Both Sternberg's and Gardner's views, which were discussed in chapter 10, include categories of social intelligence P. 293. In Sternberg's theory the category is called "practical intelligence" and in Gardner's theory the categories are "insights about self" and "insights about others." However, the greatest interest in recent years in the social aspects of intelligence has focused on the concept of emotional intelligence. The concept of **emotional intelligence** *initially was proposed in 1990 as a form of social intelligence that involves the ability to monitor one's own and others' feelings and emotions, to discriminate among them, and to use this information to guide one's thinking and action* (Salovy & Mayer, 1990). However, the main interest in emotional intelligence was ushered in with the publication of Daniel Goleman's book *Emotional Intelligence* (1995). Goleman believes that when it comes to predicting an individual's competence, IQ as measured by standardized intelligence tests matters less than emotional intelligence. In Goleman's view, emotional intelligence involves these four main areas:

- *Developing emotional self-awareness* (such as the ability to separate feelings from actions)

emotional intelligence
A form of social intelligence that involves the ability to monitor one's own and others' feelings and emotions, to discriminate among them, and to use this information to guide one's thinking and action.

Emotional Intelligence

CAREERS IN LIFE-SPAN DEVELOPMENT

Jonathan Cohen, Director, Center for Social and Emotional Education

JONATHAN COHEN has worked at many jobs related to children's educational, mental health and development over the last 25 years. He has been a teacher, a school psychologist and program developer as well as a child clinical psychologist and psychoanalyst in private practice. Today, he believes that what is especially important for schools and parents is to purposively and effectively promote children's social-emotional competencies, or what is sometimes referred to as "social and emotional intelligences."

Jonathan obtained a Ph.D. in clinical psychology and then worked at Cornell Medical Center, Sloan Kettering Cancer Center, and the Columbia University Mental Health Clinic. Jonathan co-founded the Project for Social Emotional Learning at Teachers College, Columbia University, which a year later became the Center for Social and Emotional Education, a nonprofit center in New York City. The mission of the Center is to train and educate parents, educators, and youth workers to promote children's social-emotional skills, knowledge and values that result in social-emotional literacy. Through award-winning books, videotapes, a website (www.csee.net), annual conferences, and summer institutes, the Center is now working with thousands of educators and school-based mental health professionals in America and abroad.

Jonathan also supervises graduate students in education and clinical psychology at Columbia University and other training centers.

Jonathan Cohen (standing) talking with colleagues at the Center for Social and Emotional Education at Columbia University.

- *Managing emotions* (such as being able to control anger)
- *Reading emotions* (such as taking the perspective of others)
- *Handling relationships* (such as the ability to solve relationship problems)

Some schools have begun to develop programs that are designed to help children with their emotional lives. For example, one private school near San Francisco, the Nueva School, has a class in what is called "self science." The subject in self science is feelings—the child's own and those involved in relationships. Teachers speak to real issues, such as hurt over being left out, envy, and disagreements that could disrupt into a schoolyard battle. The list of the contents for self science matches up with many of Goleman's components of emotional intelligence. The topics in self science include:

- Having self-awareness (in the sense of recognizing feelings and building a vocabulary for them); seeing the links between thoughts, feelings, and reactions.
- Knowing if thoughts or feelings are ruling a decision
- Seeing the consequences of alternative choices
- Applying these insights to decisions about such issues as drugs, smoking, and sex
- Recognizing strengths and weaknesses, and seeing oneself in a positive but realistic light
- Managing emotions; realizing what is behind a feeling (such as the hurt that triggers anger); learning ways to handle anxieties, anger, and sadness
- Taking responsibility for decisions and actions, as well as following through on commitments
- Understanding that empathy, understanding others' feelings, and respecting differences in how people feel about things are key dimensions of getting along in the social world
- Recognizing the importance of relationships and learning how to be a good listener and question asker; being assertive rather than passive or aggressive; learning how to cooperate, resolve conflicts, and negotiate

Names for these classes range from "social development" to "life skills" to "social and emotional learning." Their common goal is to raise every child's emotional competence as part of regular education, rather than focus on emotional skills as something to be taught only remedially to children who are faltering and are identified as "troubled."

At this point we have studied a number of ideas about the self and emotional development. To review these ideas see summary table 11.1. Next, we will continue to explore socioemotional development in middle and late childhood by examining moral development.

Moral Development

Remember from chapter 9 our description of Piaget's view of moral development ◄ P. 240. Piaget believed that younger children are characterized by heteronomous morality but that, by 10 years of age, they have moved into a higher stage called

SUMMARY TABLE 11.1
The Self and Emotional Development

Concept	Processes/ Related Ideas	Characteristics/Descriptions
The Self	The Development of Self-Understanding	• The internal self, the social self, and the socially comparative self become more prominent in middle and late childhood.
	Self-Esteem, and Self-Concept	• *Self-esteem* refers to global evaluations of the self; self-esteem is also referred to as self-worth or self-image. *Self-concept* refers to domain-specific self-evaluations. • Four ways to increase children's self-esteem are (1) identification of the causes of low self-esteem, (2) emotional support and social approval, (3) achievement, and (4) coping.
	Industry vs. Inferiority	• Erikson's fourth stage, occurring in the elementary school years.
Emotional Development	Developmental Changes	• Among these are increased understanding of such complex emotions as pride and shame, increased understanding that more than one emotion can be experienced in a particular situation, increased tendency to take into account the events leading up to an emotional reaction, improved ability to suppress and conceal emotions, and the ability to use self-initiated strategies to redirect emotions.
	Emotional Intelligence	• A form of social intelligence that involves the ability to monitor one's own and others' feelings and emotions, to discriminate among them, and to use this information to guide one's own thinking and action. • Goleman believes emotional intelligence involves four main areas: emotional self-awareness, managing emotions, reading emotions, and handling relationships.

"autonomous" morality. According to Piaget, older children consider the intentions of the individual, believe that rules are subject to change, and are aware that punishment does not always follow a wrongdoing.

A second major perspective on moral development was proposed by Lawrence Kohlberg. Kohlberg acknowledged that Piaget's cognitive stages of development (especially preoperational, concrete operational, and formal operational) serve as the underpinnings for his theory. However, Kohlberg believed there was more to moral development than Piaget's stages. Kohlberg especially emphasized the importance of opportunities to take the perspective of others and experiencing conflict between one's current stage of moral thinking and the reasoning of someone at a higher stage.

Kohlberg's Theory of Moral Development Kohlberg stressed that moral development is based primarily on moral reasoning and unfolds in stages (Kohlberg, 1958, 1976, 1986). Kohlberg arrived at his view after 20 years of using a unique interview with children. In the interview, children are presented with a series of stories in which characters face moral dilemmas. The following is the most well-known Kohlberg dilemma:

Kohlberg's Theory

> In Europe a woman was near death from a special kind of cancer. There was one drug that the doctors thought might save her. It was a form of radium that a druggist in the same town had recently discovered. The drug was expensive to make, but the druggist was charging ten times what the drug cost him to make. He paid $200 for the radium and charged $2,000 for a small dose of the drug. The sick woman's husband, Heinz, went to everyone he knew to borrow the money, but he could only get together $1,000 which is half of what

it cost. He told the druggist that his wife was dying and asked him to sell it cheaper or let him pay later. But the druggist said, "No, I discovered the drug, and I am going to make money from it." So Heinz got desperate and broke into the man's store to steal the drug for his wife. (Kohlberg, 1969, p. 379)

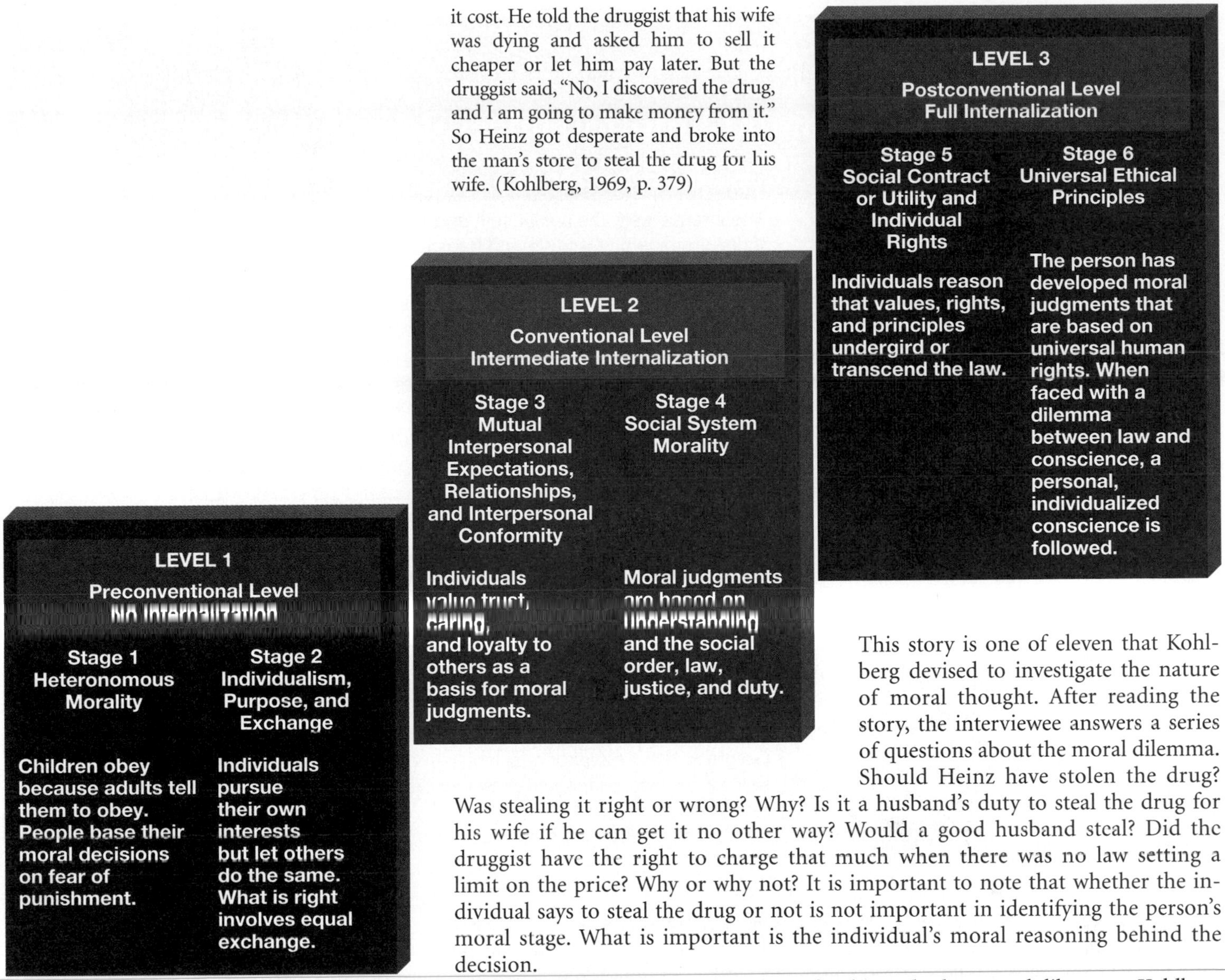
LEVEL 1
Preconventional Level
No Internalization
Stage 1
Heteronomous Morality
Children obey because adults tell them to obey. People base their moral decisions on fear of punishment.
Stage 2
Individualism, Purpose, and Exchange
Individuals pursue their own interests but let others do the same. What is right involves equal exchange.
LEVEL 2
Conventional Level
Intermediate Internalization
Stage 3
Mutual Interpersonal Expectations, Relationships, and Interpersonal Conformity
Individuals value trust, caring, and loyalty to others as a basis for moral judgments.
Stage 4
Social System Morality
Moral judgments are based on understanding and the social order, law, justice, and duty.
LEVEL 3
Postconventional Level
Full Internalization
Stage 5
Social Contract or Utility and Individual Rights
Individuals reason that values, rights, and principles undergird or transcend the law.
Stage 6
Universal Ethical Principles
The person has developed moral judgments that are based on universal human rights. When faced with a dilemma between law and conscience, a personal, individualized conscience is followed.

Figure **11.2**

Kohlberg's Three Levels and Six Stages of Moral Development

This story is one of eleven that Kohlberg devised to investigate the nature of moral thought. After reading the story, the interviewee answers a series of questions about the moral dilemma. Should Heinz have stolen the drug? Was stealing it right or wrong? Why? Is it a husband's duty to steal the drug for his wife if he can get it no other way? Would a good husband steal? Did the druggist have the right to charge that much when there was no law setting a limit on the price? Why or why not? It is important to note that whether the individual says to steal the drug or not is not important in identifying the person's moral stage. What is important is the individual's moral reasoning behind the decision.

From the answers interviewees gave for this and other moral dilemmas, Kohlberg hypothesized three levels of moral development, each of which is characterized by two stages. A key concept in understanding moral development is **internalization,** *the developmental change from behavior that is externally controlled to behavior that is controlled by internal standards and principles.* As children and adolescents develop, their moral thoughts become more internalized. Let's look further at Kohlberg's three levels of moral development (see figure 11.2)

internalization
The developmental change from behavior that is externally controlled to behavior that is controlled by internal standards and principles.

preconventional reasoning
The lowest level in Kohlberg's theory of moral development. The individual shows no internalization of moral values—moral reasoning is controlled by external rewards and punishment.

Kohlberg's Level 1: Preconventional Reasoning

Preconventional reasoning *is the lowest level in Kohlberg's theory of moral development. At this level, the individual shows no internalization of moral values—moral reasoning is controlled by external rewards and punishments.*

- Stage 1. *Heteronomous morality* is the first stage in Kohlberg's theory. At this stage, moral thinking is often tied to punishment. For example, children and adolescents obey adults because adults tell them to obey.
- Stage 2. *Individualism, instrumental purpose, and exchange* is the second Kohlberg stage of moral development. At this stage, individuals pursue their own interests but also let others do the same. Thus, what is right involves an equal exchange. People are nice to others so that they will be nice to them in return.

Kohlberg's Level 2: Conventional Reasoning

Conventional reasoning *is the second, or intermediate, level in Kohlberg's theory of moral development. At this level, internalization is intermediate. Individuals abide by certain standards (internal), but they are the standards of others (external), such as parents or the laws of society.*

- Stage 3. *Mutual interpersonal expectations, relationships, and interpersonal conformity* is Kohlberg's third stage of moral development. At this stage, individuals value trust, caring, and loyalty to others as a basis of moral judgements. Children and adolescents often adopt their parents' moral standards at this stage, seeking to be thought of by their parents as a "good girl" or a "good boy."
- Stage 4. *Social systems morality* is the fourth stage in Kohlberg's theory of moral development. At this stage, moral judgments are based on understanding the social order, law, justice, and duty. For example, adolescents may say that, for a community to work effectively, it needs to be protected by laws that are adhered to by its members.

Lawrence Kohlberg, the architect of a provocative cognitive developmental theory of moral development. *What is the nature of his theory?*

conventional reasoning
The second, or intermediate, level in Kohlberg's theory of moral development. Internalization is intermediate. Individuals abide by certain standards (internal), but they are the standards of others (external), such as parents or the laws of society.

postconventional reasoning
The highest level in Kohlberg's theory of moral development. Morality is completely internalized.

Kohlberg's Level 3: Postconventional Reasoning

Postconventional reasoning *is the highest level in Kohlberg's theory of moral development. At this level, morality is completely internalized and is not based on others' standards. The individual recognizes alternative moral courses, explores the options, and then decides on a personal moral code.*

- Stage 5. *Social contract or utility and individual rights* is the fifth Kohlberg stage. At this stage, individuals reason that values, rights, and principles undergird or transcend the law. A person evaluates the validity of actual laws and social systems can be examined in terms of the degree to which they preserve and protect fundamental human rights and values.
- Stage 6. *Universal ethical principles* is the sixth and highest stage in Kohlberg's theory of moral development. At this stage, the person has developed a moral standard based on universal human rights. When faced with a conflict between law and conscience, the person will follow conscience, even though the decision might involve personal risk.

Kohlberg believed that these levels and stages occur in a sequence and are age related: Before age 9, most children reason about moral dilemmas in a preconventional way; by early adolescence, they reason in more conventional ways. Most adolescents reason at stage 3, with some signs of stages 2 and 4. By early adulthood, a small number of individuals reason in postconventional ways. In a 20-year longitudinal investigation, the uses of stages 1 and 2 decreased (Colby & others, 1983). Stage 4, which did not appear at all in the moral reasoning of 10-year-olds, was reflected in 62 percent of the moral thinking of 36-year-olds. Stage 5 did not appear until age 20 to 22 and never characterized more than 10 percent of the individuals. Thus, the moral stages appeared somewhat later than Kohlberg initially envisioned, and the higher stages, especially stage 6, were extremely elusive. Recently, stage 6 was removed from the Kohlberg moral judgment scoring manual, but it still is considered to be theoretically important in the Kohlberg scheme of moral development. A review of data from forty-five studies in twenty-seven diverse world cultures provided support for the universality of Kohlberg's first four stages, although there was more cultural diversity at stages 5 and 6 (Snarey, 1987).

Critical Thinking

Exploring Your Moral Thinking

WHAT DO YOU think about the following circumstances?

- A man who had been sentenced to serve 10 years for selling a small amount of marijuana walked away from a prison camp six months after he was there. Twenty-five years later he was caught. He is now in his 50s and has been a model citizen. Should he be sent back to prison? Why or why not? At which Kohlberg stage should your response be placed?
- A young woman who had been in a tragic accident is "brain dead" and has been kept on life support systems for four years without ever regaining consciousness. Should the life support systems be removed? Explain your response. At which Kohlberg stage should your response be placed?

Carol Gilligan is shown with some of the students she has interviewed about the importance of relationships in a female's development. *What is Gilligan's view of moral development?*

Kohlberg's Critics Kohlberg's provocative theory of moral development has not gone unchallenged (Lapsley, 1996; Rest, 1999). The criticisms involve the link between moral thought and moral behavior, inadequate consideration of culture's role and the family's role in moral development, and underestimation of the care perspective.

Moral Thought and Moral Behavior Kohlberg's theory has been criticized for placing too much emphasis on moral thought and not enough emphasis on moral behavior. Moral reasons can sometimes be a shelter for immoral behavior. Bank embezzlers and presidents endorse the loftiest of moral virtues when commenting about moral dilemmas, but their own behavior may be immoral. No one wants a nation of cheaters and thieves who can reason at the postconventional level. The cheaters and thieves may know what is right yet still do what is wrong.

Culture and Moral Development Yet another criticism of Kohlberg's view is that it is culturally biased (Banks, 1993; Miller, 1995). A review of research on moral development in 27 countries concluded that moral reasoning is more culture-specific than Kohlberg envisioned and that Kohlberg's scoring system does not recognize higher level moral reasoning in certain cultural groups (Snarey, 1987). Examples of higher level moral reasoning that would not be scored as such by Kohlberg's system are values related to communal equity and collective happiness in Israel, the unity and sacredness of all life forms in India, and the relation of the individual to the community in New Guinea. These examples of moral reasoning would not be scored at the highest level in Kohlberg's system because they do not emphasize the individual's rights and abstract principles of justice. One study assessed the moral development of 20 adolescent male Buddhist monks in Nepal (Huebner, Garrod, & Snarey, 1990). The issue of justice, a basic theme in Kohlberg's theory, was not of paramount importance in the monks' moral views, and their concerns about the prevention of suffering and the role of compassion are not captured by Kohlberg's theory. In sum, although Kohlberg's approach does capture much of the moral reasoning voiced in various cultures around the world, as we have just seen, there are some important moral concepts in particular cultures that his approach misses or misconstrues (Walker, 1996).

Family Processes and Moral Development Kohlberg believed that family processes are essentially unimportant in children's moral development. He argued that parent-child relationships are usually power-oriented and provide children with little opportunity for mutual give and take or perspective taking. Rather, Kohlberg said that such opportunities are more likely to be provided by children's peer relations (Brabeck, 2000).

A number of developmentalists now believe that Kohlberg likely underestimated the contribution of family relationships to moral development. They emphasize that inductive discipline, which involves the use of reasoning and focuses children's attention on the consequences of their actions for others, positively influences moral development (Hoffman, 1970). They also stress that parents' moral values influence children's developing moral thoughts (Gibbs, 1993).

Gender and the Care Perspective Carol Gilligan (1982, 1992, 1996) believes that Kohlberg's theory of moral development does not adequately reflect relationships and concern for others. The **justice perspective** *is a moral perspective that focuses on the rights of the individual; individuals stand alone and independently make*

justice perspective
A moral perspective that focuses on the rights of the individual; individuals independently make moral decisions.

moral decisions. Kohlberg's theory is a justice perspective. By contrast, the **care perspective** *is a moral perspective that views people in terms of their connectedness with others and emphasizes interpersonal communication, relationships with others, and concern for others. Gilligan's theory is a care perspective.* According to Gilligan, Kohlberg greatly underplayed the care perspective in moral development. She believes that this may have happened because he was a male, because most of his research was with males rather than females, and because he used male responses as a model for his theory.

care perspective
The moral perspective of Carol Gilligan, that views people in terms of their connectedness with others and emphasizes interpersonal communication, relationships with others, and concern for others.

Gilligan's Care Perspective

In extensive interviews with girls from 6 to 18 years of age, Gilligan and her colleagues found that girls consistently interpret moral dilemmas in terms of human relationships and base these interpretations on listening and watching other people (Gilligan, 1992, 1996). According to Gilligan, girls have the ability to sensitively pick up different rhythms in relationships and often are able to follow the pathways of feelings. Gilligan believes that girls reach a critical juncture in their development when they reach adolescence. Usually around 11 to 12 years of age, girls become aware that their intense interest in intimacy is not prized by the male-dominated culture, even though society values women as caring and altruistic. The dilemma is that girls are presented with a choice that makes them look either selfish or selfless. Gilligan believes that, as adolescent girls experience this dilemma, they increasingly silence their "distinctive voice." Researchers have found support for Gilligan's claim that females' and males' moral reasoning often centers around different concerns and issues (Galotti, Kozberg, & Farmer, 1990). However, one of Gilligan's initial claims—that traditional Kohlbergian measures of moral development are biased against females—has been extensively disputed. For example, most research studies using the Kohlberg stories and scoring system do not find sex differences (Walker, 1991). Thus, the strongest support for Gilligan's claims comes from studies that focus on items and scoring systems pertaining to close relationships, pathways of feelings, sensitive listening, and the rhythm of interpersonal behavior.

While females often articulate a care perspective and males a justice perspective, the gender difference is not absolute, and the two orientations are not mutually exclusive (Lyons, 1990). For example, in one study, 53 of the 80 females and males showed either a care or a justice perspective, but 27 subjects used both orientations, with neither predominating (Gilligan & Attanucci, 1988).

Contextual variations influence whether girls silence their "voice." In one study, Susan Harter and her colleagues (Harter, Waters, & Whitesell, 1996) found evidence for a refinement of Gilligan's position in that "feminine" girls reported lower levels of voice in public contexts (at school with teachers and classmates) but not in more private interpersonal relationships with close friends and parents. However, "androgynous" girls reported a strong voice in all contexts. Harter and her colleagues also found that adolescent girls who buy into societal messages that females should be seen and not heard are at most risk for problems in self development. The greatest self liabilities occurred for females who not only lacked a "voice" but who also emphasized the importance of appearance. In focusing on their outer selves, these girls face formidable challenges in meeting the punishing cultural standards of attractiveness.

Every man takes care that his neighbor shall not cheat him. But a day comes when he begins to care that he does not cheat his neighbor. Then all goes well.

Ralph Waldo Emerson
American Poet, Essayist, 20th Century

Prosocial Behavior and Altruism

Children's moral behavior can involve negative, antisocial acts—such as lying, cheating, and stealing—or it can involve their *prosocial behavior*—the positive aspects of moral behavior, such as showing empathy to someone or behaving altruistically. While Kohlberg's and Gilligan's theories have focused primarily on the cognitive, thinking aspects of moral development, the study of prosocial moral behavior has placed more emphasis on its behavioral aspects.

Altruism *is an unselfish interest in helping someone else.* Human acts of altruism are plentiful—the hardworking laborer who places $5 in a Salvation Army kettle; rock concerts to feed the hungry, help farmers, and fund AIDS research; the child who takes in a wounded cat and cares for it, and so on.

altruism
Unselfish interest in helping another person.

William Damon (1988) described a developmental sequence of children's altruism, especially of sharing. Most sharing during the first three years of life is done not

for empathy reasons, but for the fun of the social play ritual or out of mere imitation. Then, at about 4 years of age, a combination of empathic awareness and adult encouragement produces a sense of obligation on the part of the child to share with others. This obligation forces the child to share, even though the child may not perceive this as the best way to have fun. Most 4-year-olds are not selfless saints, however. Children believe they have an obligation to share but do not necessarily think they should be as generous to others as they are to themselves. Neither do their actions always support their beliefs, especially when the object of contention is a coveted one. What is important developmentally is that the child has developed an internal belief that sharing is an obligatory part of a social relationship and that this involves a question of right and wrong. However, a preschool child's sense of reciprocity constitutes not a moral duty but, rather, a pragmatic means of getting one's way. Despite their shortcomings, these ideas about justice formed in early childhood set the stage for giant strides that children make in the years that follow.

By the start of the elementary school years, children genuinely begin to express more objective ideas about fairness. These notions about fairness have been used throughout history to distribute goods and to resolve conflicts. They involve the principles of equality, merit, and benevolence. *Equality* means that everyone is treated the same. *Merit* means giving extra rewards for hard work, a talented performance, or other laudatory behavior. *Benevolence* means giving special consideration to individuals in a disadvantaged condition. Equality is the first of these principles used regularly by elementary school children. It is common to hear 6-year-old children use the word *fair* as synonymous with *equal* or *same.* By the mid to late elementary school years, children also believe that equity means special treatment for those who deserve it—the principles of merit and benevolence.

Missing from the factors that guide children's altruism is one that many adults might expect to be the most influential of all: the motivation to obey adult authority figures. Surprisingly, a number of studies have shown that adult authority has only a small influence on children's sharing. For example, when Nancy Eisenberg (1982) asked children to explain their own altruistic acts, they mainly gave empathic and pragmatic reasons for their spontaneous acts of sharing. Not one of the children referred to the demands of adult authority. Parental advice and prodding certainly foster standards of sharing, but the give-and-take of peer requests and arguments provides the most immediate stimulation of sharing. Parents may set examples that children carry into peer interaction and communication, but parents are not present during all of their children's peer exchanges. The day-to-day construction of fairness standards is done by children in collaboration and negotiation with each other. Over the course of many years and thousands of encounters, children's understanding of altruism deepens. With this conceptual elaboration, which involves such notions as equality, merit, benevolence, and compromise, come a greater consistency and generosity in children's sharing behavior (Damon & Hart, 1992).

What can parents and teachers do to promote children's altruism and prosocial behavior? Figure 11.3 provides a number of effective strategies.

Gender

WWW
Gender Stereotyping

In chapter 9, we discussed the biological, congnitive, and social influences on gender development ◀ P. 243. Gender is such a pervasive aspect of a individuals's identity that we will further consider its role in children's development here. Among the gender-related topics we will examine are gender stereotypes, similarities, and difference; and gender-role classification.

gender stereotypes
Broad categories that reflect our impressions and beliefs about females and males.

Gender Stereotypes

Gender stereotypes *are broad categories that reflect our general impressions and beliefs about females and males.* All stereotypes, whether they are based on gender, ethnicity, or other groupings, refer to an image of what the typical member of a particular social category is like. The world is extremely complex. Every day we are confronted with thousands of different stimuli. The use of

Alice Honig and Donna Wittmer (1994, 1996) provided the following recommendations for teachers and parents that focus on promoting children's prosocial behavior.

Value and emphasize consideration of other's needs.

This results in children's engaging in more helping activities. Nel Noddings (1992) explains the morality of caring as one of teaching children to feel for others, which leads to empathy and concern.

Model prosocial behaviors.

Children imitate what adults do. For example, an adult who comforts children in times of stress is likely to observe other children imitating her comforting behaviors with other peers. When parents or teachers yell at children, they likely will observe more incidences of children yelling at others.

Label and identify prosocial and antisocial behaviors.

Often go beyond just saying, "That's good" or "That's nice" to a child. Be specific in identifying prosocial behaviors. Say, "You are being very helpful" or "You gave him a tissue. That was very nice of you because he needed to wipe his nose."

Attribute positive social behaviors to each child.

Attributing positive intentions, such as "You shared because you like to help others," increases children's prosocial behavior.

Notice and positively encourage prosocial behaviors, but don't overuse external rewards.

Commenting on positive behaviors and attributing positive characteristics to children rather than using external rewards helps children internalize prosocial responses.

Facilitate perspective taking and understanding others' feelings.

Helping children notice and respond to others' feelings can increase their consideration of others (Mecca, 1996).

Use positive discipline strategies.

Reason with children when they do something wrong. If a child is too aggressive and harms another child, point out the consequences of the child's behavior for the victim. Avoid harsh, punitive behavior with the child. Redirect antisocial actions to more acceptable actions.

Actively lead discussions on prosocial interactions.

Set up discussion sessions and let children evaluate how goods and benefits are distributed justly among people with varying needs, temperaments, talents, and troubles.

Develop class and school projects that foster altruism.

Let children come up with examples of projects they can engage in that will help others. These projects might include cleaning up the schoolyard, writing as pen pals to children in troubled lands, collecting toys or food for individuals in need, and making friends with older adults during visits to a nursing home.

Use technology to promote prosocial behavior.

Videotape children who behave prosocially to increase sharing. In one study, third-grade children viewed videotapes of themselves and models in sharing situations (Devoe & Sherman, 1978). This strategy increased sharing immediately, and more sharing was still observed one week later.

Invite moral mentors to visit the class.

Recruit and involve moral mentors in the classroom. Invite people who have contributed altruistically to better the lives of others in the community. In one classroom, a teacher invited a high school swimming star who spends time helping children with a disability to talk with her class.

Figure 11.3

Strategies Teachers and Parents Can Use to Increase Children's Prosocial Behavior

What are little boys made of?
Frogs and snails
And puppy dogs' tails.
What are little girls made of?
Sugar and spice
And all that's nice

J. O. Halliwell
English Author, 19th Century

stereotypes is one way we simplify this complexity. If we simply assign a label (such as *soft*) to someone, we then have much less to consider when we think about the individual. However, once labels are assigned, they are remarkably difficult to abandon, even in the face of contradictory evidence.

How widespread is feminine and masculine stereotyping? According to a far-ranging study of college students in 30 countries, stereotyping of females and males is pervasive (Williams & Best, 1982). Males were widely believed to be dominant, independent, aggressive, achievement-oriented, and enduring, while females were widely believed to be nurturant, affiliative, less esteemed, and more helpful in times of distress. Other research continues to find that gender stereotyping is pervasive (Plant & others, 2000; Spence & Buckner, 2000).

In a subsequent study, women and men who lived in more highly developed countries perceived themselves as more similar than women and men who lived in less developed countries (Williams & Best, 1989). In the more highly developed countries, the women were more likely to attend college and be gainfully employed. Thus, as sexual equality increases, male and female stereotypes, as well as actual behavioral differences, may diminish. In this study, the women were more likely to perceive similarity between the sexes than the men were (Williams & Best, 1989). And the sexes were perceived more similarly in the Christian than in the Muslim societies.

Gender Similarities and Differences Let's now examine some of the differences between the sexes, keeping in mind that (a) the differences are averages—not all females versus all males; (b) even when differences are reported, there is considerable overlap between the sexes, and (c) the differences may be due primarily to biological factors, sociocultural factors, or both. First, we will examine physical differences, and then we will turn to cognitive and socioemotional differences.

Physical Similarities and Differences From conception on, females have a longer life expectancy than males, and females are less likely than males to develop physical or mental disorders. Estrogen strengthens the immune system, making females more resistant to infection, for example. Female hormones also signal the liver to produce more "good" cholesterol, which makes females' blood vessels more elastic than males'. Testosterone triggers the production of low-density lipoprotein, which clogs blood vessels. Males have twice the risk of coronary disease as females. Higher levels of stress hormones cause faster clotting in males, but also higher blood pressure than in females. Women have about twice the body fat of men, most concentrated around breasts and hips. In males, fat is more likely to go to the abdomen. On the average, males grow to be 10 percent taller than females. Male hormones promote the growth of long bones; female hormones stop such growth at puberty.

Similarity was the rule rather than the exception in a study of metabolic activity in the brains of females and males (Gur & others, 1995). The exceptions involved areas of the brain that involve emotional expression and physical expression, which are more active in females. However, there are many physical differences between females and males. Are there as many cognitive differences?

Cognitive Similarities and Differences In a classic review of gender differences, Eleanor Maccoby and Carol Jacklin (1974) concluded that males have better math and visuospatial skills (the kinds of skills an architect needs to design a building's angles and dimensions), while females have better verbal abilities. More recently, Maccoby (1987) revised her conclusion about several gender dimensions. She said that the accumulation of research evidence now suggests that verbal differences between females and males have virtually disappeared but that the math and visuospatial differences still exist. Another analysis found that males outperform females in spatial tasks (Voyer, Voyer, & Bryden, 1995).

Some experts in gender, such as Janet Shibley Hyde (1993), believe that the cognitive differences between females and males have been exaggerated. For example, Hyde points out that there is considerable overlap in the distributions of female and

male scores on math and visuospatial tasks. Figure 11.4 shows that, although males outperform females on visuospatial tasks, female and male scores overlap substantially. Thus, though the *average* score for males is higher than the *average* score for females, many females have higher scores on visuospatial tasks than most males do. Similarly, the claim that "males outperform females in math" does not mean that all males outperform all females. Rather, it means that the *average* score for males is higher than the *average* score for females (Hyde & Plant, 1995).

In a recent national study by the Department of Education (2000), boys did slightly better than girls at math and science. Overall, though, girls were far superior students. An alarming gender gap that appeared in this study involved basic literacy: Girls performed much better than boys in reading and writing. For example, the writing skills of eighth-grade girls were comparable to the writing skills of eleventh-grade boys. The same study reported a similar finding regarding Great Britain: that boys seriously lag behind girls in overall academic skills.

In the Department of Education (2000) study, girls and boys took similar math and science courses in high school. However, another recent study found that, although girls were as likely as boys to use computers for surfing the Internet and for e-mail, they were far less likely to go into careers in technology and science (American Association of University Women, 2000). Only 28 percent of computer science undergraduate degrees were awarded to women. Girls represent only 17 percent of those who take the Advanced Placement Test in Computer Science.

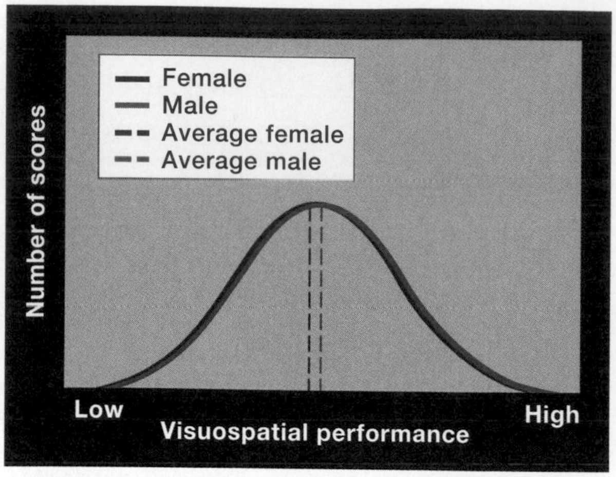

Figure **11.4**

Visuospatial Ability of Males and Females

Notice that, although an average male's visuospatial ability is higher than an average female's, the overlap between the sexes is substantial. Not all males have better visuospatial ability than all females—the substantial overlap indicates that, although the average score of males is higher, many females outperform many males on such tasks.

Socioemotional Similarities and Differences Two areas of socioemotional development in which gender similarities and differences have been studied extensively are aggression and the self-regulation of emotion.

One of the most consistent gender differences is that boys are more aggressive than girls. Another is that boys are more active than girls. The aggression differences is especially pronounced when children are provoked. Both biological and environmental factors have been proposed to account for gender differences in aggression. Biological factors include heredity and hormones. Environmental factors include cultural expectations, adult and peer models, and social agents who reward aggression in boys and punish aggression in girls.

An important skill is to be able to regulate and control your emotions and behavior. Males usually show less self-regulation than females (Eisenberg, Martin, & Fabes, 1996), and this low self-control can translate into behavioral problems. In one study, children's low self-regulation was linked with greater aggression, the teasing of others, overreaction to frustration, low cooperation, and inability to delay gratification (Block & Block, 1980).

Earlier in the chapter, we discussed Carol Gilligan's belief that many females are more sensitive about relationships and have better relationship skills than males do. In chapter 15, "Socioemotional Development in Early Adulthood," we will further explore this area of gender.

If you are going to generalize about women, you will find yourself up to here in exceptions.

Dolores Hitchens
American Mystery Writer, 20th Century

Gender Controversy Our coverage of gender similarities and differences reveals some areas in which gender differences are substantial and others in which they are small or nonexistent. Controversy swirls about such similarities and differences. Alice Eagly (1996, 2000) argues that the belief that gender differences are small or nonexistent is rooted in a feminist commitment to gender similarity and is seen as a route to political equality. Many feminists fear that gender differences will be interpreted as deficiencies on the part of females and will be seen as biologically based. They argue that such conclusions could revive traditional stereotypes that females are innately inferior to males (Crawford & Unger, 2000). Eagly responds to such criticisms by saying that a large body of research on gender now exists and reveals

Critical Thinking

Rethinking the Words We Use in Gender Worlds

SEVERAL DECADES AGO, the word *dependency* was used to describe the relational orientation of femininity. Dependency took on negative connotations for females—for instance, that females can't take care of themselves and males can. Today, the term *dependency* is being replaced by the term *relational abilities,* which has much more positive connotations (Caplan & Caplan, 1999). Rather than being thought of as dependent, women are now more often described as skilled in forming and maintaining relationships. Make up a list of words that you associate with masculinity and a list of words you associate with femininity. Do these words have any negative connotations for males or females? For the words that do have negative connotations, think about replacements for them that have more positive connotations.

stronger gender differences than feminists acknowledge. This controversy is evidence that negotiating the science and politics of gender is not an easy task.

Gender-Role Classification

Not very long ago, it was accepted that boys should grow up to be masculine and girls to be feminine, that boys are made of "frogs and snails" and girls are made of "sugar and spice and all that is nice." Let's further explore such gender classifications of boys and girls as "masculine" and "feminine."

What Is Gender-Role Classification?

In the past, a well-adjusted boy was supposed to be independent, aggressive, and powerful. A well-adjusted girl was supposed to be dependent, nurturant, and uninterested in power. The masculine characteristics were considered to be healthy and good by society; the feminine characteristics were considered undesirable.

In the 1970s, as both females and males become dissatisfied with the burdens imposed by their stereotypic roles, alternatives to femininity and masculinity were proposed. Instead of describing masculinity and femininity as a continuum in which more of one means less of the other, it was proposed that individuals could have both masculine and feminine traits. This thinking led to the development of the concept of **androgyny,** *the presence of masculine and feminine characteristics in the same person* (Bem, 1977; Spence & Helmreich, 1978). The androgynous boy might be assertive (masculine) and nurturant (feminine). The androgynous girl might be powerful (masculine) and sensitive to others' feelings (feminine). In one recent study it was confirmed that societal changes are leading females to be more assertive (Spence & Buckner, 2000).

androgyny
The presence of masculine and feminine characteristics in the same individual.

To be meek, patient, tactful, modest, honorable, brave, is not to be either manly or womanly, it is to be humane.

Jane Harrison
English Writer, 20th Century

Measures have been developed to assess androgyny. One of the most widely used measures is the Bem Sex-Role Inventory. To see whether you gender-role classification is masculine, feminine, or androgynous, see figure 11.5.

Gender experts, such as Sandra Bem, argue that androgynous individuals are more flexible, competent, and mentally healthy than their masculine or feminine counterparts. To some degree, though, deciding on which gender-role classification is best depends on the context involved. For example, in close relationships, feminine and androgynous orientations might be more desirable because of the expressive nature of close relationships. However, masculine and androgynous orientations might be more desirable in traditional academic and work settings because of the achievement demands in these contexts.

A special concern involves adolescent boys who adopt a strong masculine role. Researchers have found that high-masculinity adolescent boys often engage in problem behaviors, such as delinquency, drug abuse, and unprotected sexual intercourse (Pleck, 1995). Many of these boys, who present themselves as virile, macho, and aggressive, also do poorly in school. Too many adolescent males base their manhood on the caliber of gun they carry or the number of children they have fathered (Sullivan, 1991).

Androgyny and Education

Can and should androgyny be taught to students? In general, it is easier to teach androgyny to girls than to boys and easier to teach it before the middle school grades. For example, in one study, a gender curriculum was put in place for one year in the kindergarten, fifth, and ninth grades (Guttentag & Bray, 1976). It involved books, discussion materials, and classroom exercises with an androgynous bent. The program was most successful with the fifth-graders, least successful with the ninth-graders. The ninth-graders, especially the boys, showed a

WWW
Androgyny

The following items are from the Bem Sex-Role Inventory. To find out whether you score as androgynous, first rate yourself on each item, on a scale from 1 (never or almost never true) to 7 (always or almost always true).

1. self-reliant	21. reliable	41. warm
2. yielding	22. analytical	42. solemn
3. helpful	23. sympathetic	43. willing to take a stand
4. defends own beliefs	24. jealous	44. tender
5. cheerful	25. has leadership abilities	45. friendly
6. moody	26. sensitive to the needs of others	46. aggressive
7. independent	27. truthful	47. gullible
8. shy	28. willing to take risks	48. inefficient
9. conscientious	29. understanding	49. acts as a leader
10. athletic	30. secretive	50. childlike
11. affectionate	31. makes decisions easily	51. adaptable
12. theatrical	32. compassionate	52. individualistic
13. assertive	33. sincere	53. does not use harsh language
14. flatterable	34. self-sufficient	54. unsystematic
15. happy	35. eager to soothe hurt feelings	55. competitive
16. strong personality	36. conceited	56. loves children
17. loyal	37. dominant	57. tactful
18. unpredictable	38. soft-spoken	58. ambitious
19. forceful	39. likable	59. gentle
20. feminine	40. masculine	60. conventional

Scoring

(a) Add up your ratings for items 1, 4, 7, 10, 13, 16, 19, 22, 25, 28, 31, 34, 37, 40, 43, 46, 49, 52, 55, and 58. Divide the total by 20. That is your masculinity score.

(b) Add up your ratings for items 2, 5, 8, 11, 14, 17, 20, 23, 26, 29, 32, 35, 38, 41, 44, 47, 50, 53, 56, and 59. Divide the total by 20. That is your femininity score.

(c) If your masculinity score is above 4.9 (the approximate median for the masculinity scale), and your femininity score is above 4.9 (the approximate femininity median), then you would be classified as androgynous on Bem's scales.

Figure **11.5**

The Bem Sex-Role Inventory: Are You Androgynous?

boomerang effect, in which they had more traditional gender-role attitudes after the year of androgynous instruction than before it.

Despite such mixed findings, the advocates of androgyny programs believe that traditional sex-typing is harmful for all students and especially has prevented many girls from experiencing equal opportunity. The detractors argue that androgynous educational programs are too value-laden and ignore the diversity of gender roles in our society.

Gender-Role Transcendence Some critics of androgyny say enough is enough and that there is too much talk about gender. They believe that androgyny is less of a panacea than originally envisioned (Doyle & Paludi, 1998). An alternative is **gender-role transcendence,** *the view that when an individual's competence is at issue, it should be conceptualized in terms of the person, rather than on the basis of masculinity, femininity, or androgyny* (Pleck, 1983). That is, we should think about ourselves as people; not as masculine, feminine, or androgynous. Parents should rear their children to be competent boys and girls, not masculine, feminine, or androgynous, say the gender-role critics. They believe such gender-role classification leads to too much stereotyping.

gender-role transcendence
The belief that, when an individual's competence is at issue, it should not be conceptualized on the basis of masculinity, femininity, or androgyny but, rather, on a personal basis.

Gender in Context The concept of gender-role classification involves a personality-traitlike categorization of a person. However, it may be helpful to think of personality in terms of person-situation interaction rather than personality traits alone.

In Egypt near the Aswan Dam, women are returning from the Nile River, where they have filled their water jugs. *How might gender-role socialization for girls in Egypt compare with that in the United States?*

Thus, in our discussion of gender-role classification, we describe how different gender roles might be more appropriate, depending on the context, or setting, involved.

To see the importance of considering gender in context, let's examine helping behavior and emotion. The stereotype is that females are better than males at helping. But it depends on the situation. Females are more likely than males to volunteer their time to help children with personal problems and to engage in caregiving behavior. However, in situations in which males feel a sense of competence and involve danger, males are more likely than females to help (Eagly & Crowley, 1986). For example, a male is more likely than a female to stop and help a person stranded by the roadside with a flat tire.

"She is emotional; he is not"—that is the master emotional stereotype. However, like differences in helping behavior, emotional differences in males and females depend on the particular emotion involved and the context in which it is displayed (Shields, 1991). Males are more likely to show anger toward strangers, especially male strangers, when they feel they have been challenged. Males also are more likely to turn their anger into aggressive action. Emotional differences between females and males often show up in contexts that highlight social roles and relationships. For example, females are more likely to discuss emotions in terms of relationships, and they are more likely to express fear and sadness.

Gender and Culture

The importance of considering gender in context is nowhere more apparent than when examining what is culturally prescribed behavior for females and males in different countries around the world (Gibbons, 2000). While there has been greater acceptance of androgyny and similarities in male and female behavior in the United States, in many countries gender roles have remained gender-specific. For example, in Egypt in the division of labor between Egyptian males and females is dramatic. Egyptian males are socialized and schooled to work in the public sphere, females in the private world of home and child rearing. The Islamic religion, which predominates in Egypt, dictates that the man's duty is to provide for his family and the woman's is to care for her family and household. Any deviations from this traditionally masculine and feminine behavior are severely disapproved of. China also has been a male-dominant culture. Although women have made some strides in China, the male role is still dominant. Androgynous behavior and gender equity are not what most males in China want to see happen.

At this point, we have studied a number of ideas about moral development and gender in middle and late childhood. To review these ideas, see summary table 11.2. Next, we will explore how social contexts influence development in middle and late childhood, beginning with the family.

Summary Table 11.2
Moral Development and Gender

Concept	Processes/ Related Ideas	Characteristics/Descriptions
Moral Development	Kohlberg's Theory	• Kohlberg developed a provocative theory of moral reasoning with three levels—preconventional, conventional, and postconventional—and six stages (two at each level). Increased internalization characterizes movement to levels 2 and 3. • Criticisms of Kohlberg's theory include the claims that Kohlberg overemphasizes cognition and underemphasizes behavior, underestimates culture's role as well as the family's role, and inadequately considers the care perspective (Gilligan).
	Prosocial Behavior and Altruism	• Prosocial behavior involves positive moral behaviors. • Altruism is an unselfish interest in helping someone else. • Damon described a developmental sequence of altruism.
Gender	Stereotypes, Similarities, and Differences	• Gender stereotypes are widespread around the world. • A number of physical differences exist between females and males. • Some experts, such as Hyde, argue that cognitive differences between females and males have been exaggerated. • In terms of socioemotional differences, males are more aggressive and active than females, while females regulate their emotions better. • Currently, there is controversy about how similar or different females and males are in a number of areas.
	Gender-Role Classification	• This focuses on how masculine, feminine, or androgvnous an individual is. In the past, competent males were supposed to be masculine, females were supposed to be feminine. • Androgyny means having both masculine and feminine characteristics. • Of special concern are adolescents who adopt a strong masculine role. • Some experts believe that too much attention is given to gender in our society and that instead we should pursue gender-role transcendence.
	Gender in Context	• This view states that the best way to conceptualize gender is not as a traitlike category but as a person-situation concept in terms of gender in context. • Although androgyny and multiple gender roles are often available for American children to choose from, in many countries around the world, rigid, traditional gender roles are still in place.

Families

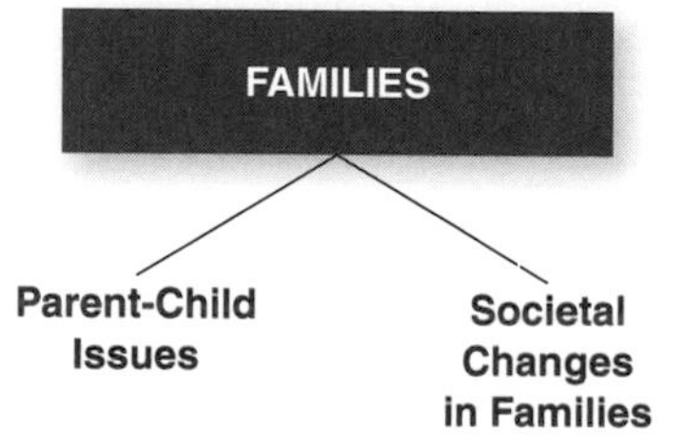

As children move into the middle and late childhood years, parents spend considerably less time with them. In one study, parents spent less than half as much time with their children aged 5 to 12 in caregiving, instruction, reading, talking, and playing as when the children were younger (Hill & Stafford, 1980). This drop in parent-child interaction may be even more extensive in families with little parental education. Although parents spend less time with their children in middle and late childhood than in early childhood, parents continue to be extremely important socializing agents in their children's lives. What are some of the most important parent-child issues in middle and late childhood?

Parent-Child Issues

Parent-child interactions during early childhood focus on such matters as modesty, bedtime regularities, control of temper, fighting with siblings and peers, eating behavior

School-Family Linkages

and manners, autonomy in dressing, and attention seeking. While some of these issues—fighting and reaction to discipline, for example—are carried forward into the elementary school years, many new issues have appeared by the age of 7 (Maccoby, 1984). These include whether children should be made to perform chores and, if so, whether they should be paid for them; how to help children learn to entertain themselves, rather than relying on parents for everything; and how to monitor children's lives outside the family in school and peer settings.

School-related matters are especially important for families during middle and late childhood. School-related difficulties are the number one reason that children in this age group are referred for clinical help. Children must learn to relate to adults outside the family on a regular basis—adults who interact with the child much differently than parents. During middle and late childhood, interactions with adults outside the family involve more formal control and achievement orientation.

Discipline during middle and late childhood is often easier for parents than it was during early childhood; it may also be easier than during adolescence. In middle and late childhood, children's cognitive development has matured to the point where it is possible for parents to reason with them about resisting deviation and controlling their behavior. By adolescence, children's reasoning has become more sophisticated, and they may be less likely to accept parental discipline. Adolescents also push more strongly for independence, which contributes to parenting difficulties. Parents of elementary school children use less physical discipline than do parents of preschool children. By contrast, parents of elementary school children are more likely to use deprivation of privileges, appeals directed at the child's self-esteem, comments designed to increase the child's sense of guilt, and statements indicating to the child that he or she is responsible for his or her actions.

During middle and late childhood, some control is transferred from parent to child, although the process is gradual and involves *coregulation* rather than control by either the child or the parent alone. The major shift to autonomy does not occur until about the age of 12 or later. During middle and late childhood, parents continue to exercise general supervision and exert control, while children are allowed to engage in moment-to-moment self-regulation. This coregulation process is a transition period between the strong parental control of early childhood and the increased relinquishment of general supervision of adolescence.

During this coregulation, parents should:

- Monitor, guide, and support children at a distance
- Effectively use the times when they have direct contact with their children
- Strengthen in their children the ability to monitor their own behavior, to adopt appropriate standards of conduct, to avoid hazardous risks, and to sense when parental support and contact are appropriate

Life changes in parents also influence the nature of parent-child interaction in middle and late childhood; parents become more experienced in child rearing. As child-rearing demands are reduced in middle and late childhood, mothers are more likely to consider returning to a career or beginning a new career. Marital relationships change, as less time is spent in child rearing and more time is spent in career development, especially for mothers.

Societal Changes in Families

As we discussed in chapter 9, increasing numbers of children are growing up in divorced and working-mother families ◀ P. 254. But there are several other major shifts in the composition of family life that especially affect children in middle and late childhood. Parents are divorcing in greater numbers than ever before, but many of them remarry. It takes time for parents to marry, have children, get divorced, and then remarry. Consequently, there are far more elementary and secondary school children than infant or preschool children living in stepfamilies.

Stepfamilies The number of remarriages involving children has grown steadily in recent years, although the rate of remarriage actually has declined as the divorce rate has increased in the past several decades. Also, divorces occur at a 10 percent higher rate in remarriages than in first marriages (Cherlin & Furstenberg, 1994). As a result of their parents' successive marital transitions, about half of all children whose parents divorce will have a stepparent within four years of parental separation.

How does living in a stepfamily influence a child's development?

As in divorced families, children in stepfamilies have more adjustment problems than their counterparts in nondivorced families (Hetherington, Bridges, & Insabella, 1998). The adjustment problems of stepfamily children are much like those of children in divorced families—academic problems, externalizing and internalizing problems, lower self-esteem, early sexual activity, delinquency, and so on (Anderson & others, 1999). There is an increase in adjustment problems of children in newly remarried families (Hetherington & Clingempeel, 1992). Early adolescence seems to be an especially difficult time in which to have a remarriage occur, possibly because it exacerbates normal early adolescent concerns about autonomy, identity, and sexuality (Hetherington, 1993). Restabilization may take longer in stepfamilies, up to five years or more, than in divorced families, which often occurs in one to two years.

Boundary ambiguity, *the uncertainty in stepfamilies about who is in or out of the family and who is performing or responsible for certain tasks in the family system,* can present problems in stepfamilies. In the early stages of remarriage, stepfathers have been described as behaving like polite strangers, trying to win over their stepchildren by reducing negative behaviors and trying to control them less than do fathers in nondivorced families (Bray & Berger, 1993; Bray, Berger, & Boethel, 1999). In longer established stepfamilies, a distant, disengaged parenting style predominates for stepfathers, although conflict can remain high between stepfather and children. Stepmothers have a more difficult time integrating themselves into stepfamilies than do stepfathers. Children's relationships with custodial parents (biological father in stepmother families, biological mother in stepfather families) tend to be better than with stepparents (Santrock, Sitterle, & Warshak, 1988). Also, children in complex (or blended) stepfamilies (in which both parents bring offspring from previous marriages to live in the newly constituted stepfamily) show more adjustment problems than do children in simple stepfamilies (in which only one parent brings offspring into the stepfamily (Hetherington, 1993; Santrock & Sitterle, 1987).

boundary ambiguity
The uncertainty in stepfamilies about who is in or out of the family and who is performing or responsible for certain tasks in the family system.

Stepfamilies
Stepfamily Resources
Stepfamily Support

Latchkey Children We concluded in chapter 9 that when both parents work outside the home it does not necessarily have negative outcomes for their children P. 255. However, a certain subset of children from dual-earner families deserves further scrutiny: latchkey children. These children typically do not see their parents from the time they leave for school in the morning until about 6 or 7 P.M. They are called "latchkey" children because they are given the key to their home, take the key to school, and then use it to let themselves into the home while their parents are still at work. Latchkey children are largely unsupervised for two to four hours a day during each school week. During the summer months, they might be unsupervised for entire days, 5 days a week.

In one study, researchers interviewed more than 1,500 latchkey children (Long & Long, 1983). They concluded that a slight majority of these children had had negative latchkey experiences. Some latchkey children may grow up too fast, hurried by the responsibilities placed on them. How do latchkey children handle the lack of limits and structure during the latchkey hours? Without limits and parental supervision, latchkey children find their way into trouble more easily, possibly stealing,

vandalizing, or abusing a sibling. Ninety percent of the juvenile delinquents in Montgomery County, Maryland, are latchkey children. Joan Lipsitz (1983), in testifying before the Select Committee on Children, Youth, and Families, called the lack of adult supervision of children in the after-school hours one of today's major problems. Lipsitz called it the "three-to-six o'clock problem" because it was during this time that the Center for Early Adolescence in North Carolina, when Lipsitz was director, experienced a peak of referrals for clinical help. And, in a 1987 national poll, teachers rated the latchkey children phenomenon the number one reason that children have problems in schools (Harris, 1987).

While latchkey children may be vulnerable to problems, the experiences of latchkey children vary enormously, as do the experiences of all children with working parents (Belle, 1999). Parents need to give special attention to the ways in which their latchkey children's lives can be effectively monitored. Variations in latchkey experiences suggest that parental monitoring and authoritative parenting help the child cope more effectively with latchkey experiences, especially in resisting peer pressure (Galambos & Maggs, 1989; Steinberg, 1986). In one study, attending a formal after-school program that included academic, recreational, and remedial activities was associated with better academic achievement and social adjustment, in comparison with other types of after-school care (such as informal adult supervision or self-care) (Posner & Vandell, 1994). Practitioners and policymakers recommend that after-school programs have warm and supportive staff, a flexible and relaxed schedule, multiple activities, and opportunities for positive interactions with staff and peers (Pierce, Hamm, & Vandell, 1997; Vandell & Pierce, 1999).

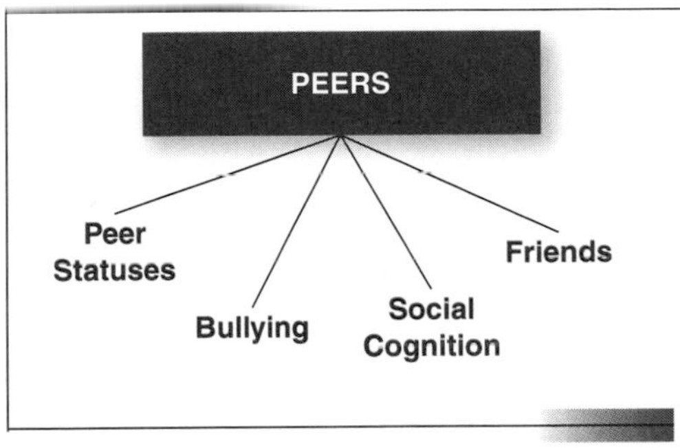

Peers

During middle and late childhood, children spend an increasing amount of time in peer interaction. As they interact with peers, children can acquire one of several peer statuses.

Peer Statuses

Children often think, "What can I do to get all of the kids at school to like me?" or "What's wrong with me? Something must be wrong, or I would be more popular." What makes a child popular with peers? **Popular children** *are frequently nominated as a best friend and are rarely disliked by their peers.* Researchers have found that popular children give out reinforcements, listen carefully, maintain open lines of communication with peers, are happy, act like themselves, show enthusiasm and concern for others, and are self-confident without being conceited (Hartup, 1983).

popular children
Children who are frequently nominated as a best friend and are rarely disliked by their peers.

neglected children
Children who are infrequently nominated as a best friend but are not disliked by their peers.

rejected children
Children who are infrequently nominated as a best friend and are actively disliked by their peers.

controversial children
Children who are frequently nominated both as someone's best friend and as being disliked.

Developmentalists have distinguished among three types of children who have a different peer status than popular children: those who are neglected, those who are rejected, and those who are controversial (Ladd, 1999; Wentzal & Asher, 1995). **Neglected children** *are infrequently nominated as a best friend but are not disliked by their peers.* **Rejected children** *are infrequently nominated as someone's best friend and are actively disliked by their peers.* **Controversial children** *are frequently nominated both as someone's best friend and as being disliked.*

Rejected children often have more serious adjustment problems later in life than do neglected children (Dishion & Li, 1996; Kupersmidt & Patterson, 1993). For example, in one study, 112 fifth-grade boys were evaluated over a period of seven years until the end of high school (Kupersmidt & Coie, 1990). The key factor in predicting whether rejected children would engage in delinquent behavior or drop out of school later during adolescence was aggression toward peers in elementary school.

Not all rejected children are aggressive. Although aggression and its related characteristics of impulsiveness and disruptiveness underlie rejection about half the time, approximately 10 to 20 percent of rejected children are shy.

An important question to ask is how neglected children and rejected children can be trained to interact more effectively with their peers. The goal of training pro-

grams with neglected children is often to help them attract attention from their peers in positive ways and to hold their attention by asking questions, by listening in a warm and friendly way, and by saying things about themselves that relate to the peers' interests. They also are taught to enter groups more effectively.

The goal of training programs with rejected children is often to help them listen to peers and "hear what they say" instead of trying to dominate peer interactions. Rejected children are trained to join peers without trying to change what is taking place in the peer group. Children may need to be motivated to use these strategies by being persuaded that they work effectively and are satisfying. In some programs, children are shown videotapes of appropriate peer interaction; then they are asked to comment on them and to draw lessons from what they have seen. In other training programs, popular children are taught to be more accepting of neglected or rejected peers.

Bullying

Significant numbers of students are victimized by bullies (Slee & Taki, 1999; Smith & others, 1999). In one survey of bullying in South Carolina middle schools, 1 of every 4 students reported that they had been bullied several times in a 3-month period; 1 in 10 said they were chronically bullied (at least once a week) (Institute for Families in Society, 1997).

Reducing Bullying

Victims of bullying have been found to have certain characteristics. In one recent study, victims of bullies had parents who were intrusive and demanding but low in responsiveness with their children (Ladd & Kochenderfer, in press). This study also found that parent-child relationships characterized by intense closeness were linked with higher levels of peer victimization in boys. Overly close and emotionally intense relationships between parents and sons might not foster assertiveness and independence. Rather, they might foster self-doubts and worries that are perceived as weaknesses when expressed in male peer groups. In another study, both bullying and victim behavior were linked to parent-child relationships (Olweus, 1980). Bullies' parents were more likely to be rejecting, authoritarian, or permissive about their son's aggression, whereas victims' parents were more likely to be anxious and overprotective.

Another recent study found that third- and sixth-grade boys and girls who experienced internalizing problems (such as being anxious and withdrawn), physical weakness, and peer rejection increasingly were victimized over time (Hodges & Perry, 1999). Yet another study found that the relation between internalizing problems and victimization was reduced by a protective friendship (Hodges & others, 1999).

Victims of bullies can suffer both short-term and long-term effects (Limber, 1997). Short-term they can become depressed, lose interest in schoolwork, or even avoid going to school. The effects of bullying can persist into adulthood. A recent longitudinal study of male victims who were bullied during childhood found that in their twenties they were more depressed and had lower self-esteem than their counterparts who had not been bullied in childhood (Olweus, in press). Bullying also can indicate a serious problem for the bully as well as the victim. In the study just mentioned, about 60 percent of the boys who were identified as bullies in middle school had at least one criminal conviction (and about one-third had three or more convictions) in their twenties, a far higher percentage than for nonbullies. To reduce bullying, teachers can do the following (Limber, 1997):

- Get older peers to serve as monitors for bullying and intervene when they see it taking place.
- Develop schoolwide rules and sanctions against bullying and post them throughout the school.
- Form friendship groups for adolescents who are regularly bullied by peers.
- Incorporate the message of the antibullying program into church, school, and other community activities where adolescents are involved.

Some children who are highly aggressive turn into juvenile delinquents and some become violent youth. We will discuss juvenile delinquency and violent youth in chapter 13, "Socioemotional Development in Adolescence." Next, we will turn our attention to the role of social cognition in peer relations. In part of this discussion, we will explore ideas about reducing the aggression of children in their peer encounters.

Social Cognition

Social Cognition

Social cognitions involves thoughts about social matters. Children's social cognitions about their peers become increasingly important for understanding peer relationships in middle and late childhood. Of special interest are the ways in which children process information about peer relations and their social knowledge (Dodge, 2000).

A boy accidentally trips and knocks a peer's soft drink out of his hand. The peer misinterprets the encounter as hostile, which leads him to retaliate aggressively against the boy. Through repeated encounters of this kind, other peers come to perceive the aggressive boy as habitually acting in inappropriate ways. Kenneth Dodge (1983) argues that children go through five steps in processing information about their social world. They decode social cues, interpret, search for a response, select an optimal response, and enact. Dodge has found that aggressive boys are more likely to perceive another child's actions as hostile when the child's intention is ambiguous. And when aggressive boys search for cues to determine a peer's intention, they respond more rapidly, less efficiently, and less reflectively than do nonaggressive children. These are among the social cognitive factors believed to be involved in the nature of children's conflicts.

Social knowledge is also involved in children's ability to get along with peers. An important part of children's social life involves knowing what goals to pursue in poorly defined or ambiguous situations. Social relationship goals, such as how to initiate and maintain a social bond, are also important. Children need to know what scripts to follow to get other children to be their friends. For example, as part of the script for getting friends, it helps to know that saying nice things, regardless of what the peer does or says, will make the peer like the child more.

From a social cognitive perspective, children who are maladjusted do not have adequate social cognitive skills to interact effectively with others. One investigation explored the possibility that children who are maladjusted do not have the social cognitive skills necessary for positive social interaction (Asarnow & Callan, 1985). Boys with and without peer adjustment difficulties were identified, and their social cognitive skills were assessed. Boys without peer adjustment problems generated more alternative solutions to problems, proposed more assertive and mature solutions, gave less intense aggressive solutions, showed more adaptive planning, and evaluated physically aggressive responses less positively than did boys with peer adjustment problems.

The world of peers is one of varying acquaintances; children interact with some children they barely know and with friends for hours every day. it is to the latter—friends—that we now turn.

A man's growth is seen in the successive choirs of his friends.

Ralph Waldo Emerson
American Poet, Essayist, 19th Century

Friends

Friendships

"My best friend is nice. She is honest and I can trust her. I can tell her my innermost secrets and know that nobody else will find out about them. I have other friends, but she is my best friend. We consider each other's feelings and don't want to hurt each other. We help each other out when we have problems. We make up funny names for people and laugh our selves silly. We make lists of which boys we think are the ugliest, which are the biggest jerks, and so on. Some of these things we share with other friends, some we don't." This is a description of a friendship by a 10-year-old girl. It

reflects the belief that children are interested in specific peers—not just any peers. They want to share concerns, interests, information, and secrets with them.

Why are children's friendships important? They serve six functions: companionship, stimulation, physical support, ego support, social comparison, and intimacy/affection (Gottman & Parker, 1987). Concerning companionship, friendship provides children with a familiar partner and playmate, someone who is willing to spend time with them and join in collaborative activities. Concerning stimulation, friendship provides children with interesting information, excitement, and amusement. Concerning physical support, friendship provides time, resources, and assistance. Concerning ego support, friendship provides the expectation of support, encouragement, and feedback, which helps children maintain an impression of themselves as competent, attractive, and worthwhile individuals. Concerning social comparison, friendship provides information about where the child stands vis-à-vis others and whether the child is doing OK. Concerning intimacy and affection, friendship provides children with a warm, close, trusting relationship with another individual in which self-disclosure takes place (Rose & Asher, 1999) (see figure 11.6).

Figure **11.6**
Functions of Children's Friendships

Willard Hartup (1996, 2000; Hartup & Laursen, 1999; Hartup & Stevens, 1997) has studied peer relations and friendship for more than three decades. He recently concluded that friends can be cognitive and emotional resources from childhood through old age. Friends can foster self-esteem and a sense of well-being. Although having friends can be a developmental advantage, not all friendships are alike. People differ in the company they keep—that is, who their friends are. Developmental advantages occur when children have friends who are socially skilled and supportive. However, it is not developmentally advantageous to have coercive and conflict-ridden friendships (Berndt, 1999).

Hold a true friend with both hands.

Nigerian Proverb

Two of friendship's most common characteristics are intimacy and similarity. **Intimacy in friendships** *is self-disclosure and the sharing of private thoughts.* Research reveals that intimate friendships may not appear until early adolescence (Berndt & Perry, 1990). Also, throughout childhood, friends are more similar than dissimilar in terms of age, sex, race, and many other factors. Friends often have similar attitudes toward school, similar educational aspirations, and closely aligned achievement orientations. Friends like the same music, the same kind of clothes, and the same kind of leisure activities.

intimacy in friendships
Self-disclosure and the sharing of private thoughts.

At this point we have studied a number of ideas about families and peers. To review these ideas, see summary table 11.3. Next, we will continue our exploration of social contexts in children's development by focusing on schools.

Summary Table 11.3
Families and Peers

Concept	Processes/ Related Ideas	Characteristics/Descriptions
Families	Parent-Child Issues	• Parents spend less time with children during middle and late childhood, including less time in caregiving, instruction, reading, talking, and playing. Nonetheless, parents still are powerful and important socializing agents during this period. • New parent-child issues emerge, and discipline changes. Control is more coregulatory.
	Societal Changes in Families	• Like in divorced families, children living in stepfamilies have more adjustment problems than their counterparts in nondivorced families. • Latchkey children may become vulnerable when they are not monitored by adults in the after-school hours.
Peers	Peer Statuses	• Popular children are frequently nominated as a best friend and are rarely disliked by their peers. • Neglected children are infrequently nominated as a best friend but are not disliked by their peers. • Rejected children are infrequently nominated as a best friend and are actively disliked by peers. • Controversial children are frequently nominated both as someone's best friend and as being disliked. • Rejected children are at risk for a number of problems.
	Bullying	• Significant numbers of students are bullied, and this can result in short-term and long-term negative effects for the victim.
	Social Cognition	• Social information-processing skills and social knowledge are two important dimensions of social cognition in peer relations.
	Friends	• Children's friendships serve six functions: companioship, stimulation, physical support, ego support, social comparison, and intimacy/affection. • Intimacy and similarity are common characteristics of friendships.

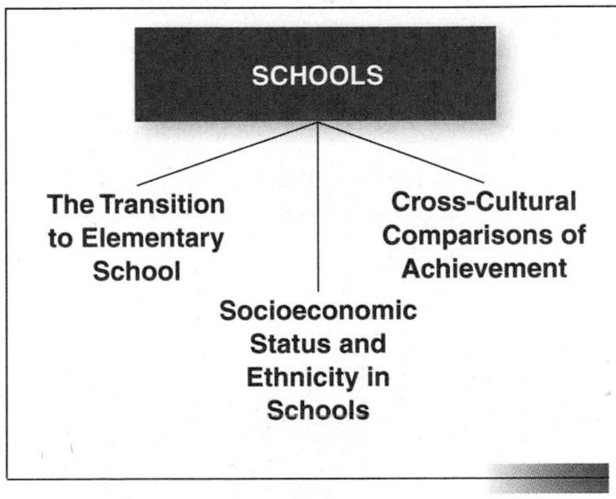

Schools

It is justifiable to be concerned about the impact of schools on children: By the time students graduate from high school, they have spent 10,000 hours in the classroom. Children spend many years in schools as members of a small society in which there are tasks to be accomplished, people to be socialized and socialized by, and rules that define and limit behavior, feelings, and attitudes.

The Transition to Elementary School

For most children, entering the first grade signals a change from being a "homechild" to being a "schoolchild"—a situation in which new roles and obligations are experienced. Children take up a new role (being a student), interact and develop relationships with new significant others, adopt new reference groups, and develop new standards by which to judge themselves. School provides children with a rich source of new ideas to shape their sense of self.

A special concern about children's early school experiences is emerging. Evidence is mounting that early schooling proceeds mainly on the basis of negative feedback. For example, children's self-esteem in the latter part of elementary school is lower

WWW

ERIC Clearinghouse on Teachers
Elementary Education
Pathways to School Improvement

than it is in the earlier part, and older children rate themselves as less smart, less good, and less hardworking than do younger ones (Blumenfeld & others, 1981).

In school as well as out of school, children's learning, like children's development, is *integrated* (National Association for the Education of Young Children, 1988). One of the main pressures on elementary teachers has been the need to "cover the curriculum." Frequently, teachers have tried to do so by tightly scheduling discrete time segments for each subject. This approach ignores the fact that children often do not need to distinguish learning by subject area. For example, they advance their knowledge of reading and writing when they work on social studies projects; they learn mathematical concepts through music and physical education (Katz & Chard, 1989). A curriculum can be facilitated by providing learning areas in which children plan and select their activities. For example, the classroom may include a fully equipped publishing center, complete with materials for writing, illustrating, typing, and binding student-made books; a science area, with animals and plants for observation and books to study; and other similar areas. In this type of classroom, children learn reading as they discover information about science; they learn writing as they work together on interesting projects. Such classrooms also provide opportunities for spontaneous play, recognizing that elementary school children continue to learn in all areas through unstructured play, either alone or with other children.

Let's examine two elementary school classrooms (Katz & Chard, 1989). In one, children spent an entire morning making identical pictures of traffic lights. The teacher made no attempt to get the children to relate the pictures to anything else the class was doing. In the other class, the children were investigating a school bus. They wrote to the district's school superintendent and asked if they could have a bus parked at their school for a few days. They studied the bus, discovered the functions of its parts, and discussed traffic rules. Then, in the classroom, they built their own bus out of cardboard. The children had fun, but they also practiced writing, problem solving, and even some arithmetic. When the class had their parents' night, the teacher was ready with reports on how each child was doing. However, all that the parents wanted to see was the bus because their children had been talking about it at home for weeks. Many contemporary education experts believe that this is the kind of education all children deserve. That is, they believe that children should be active, constructivist learners and taught through concrete, hands-on experience (Bonk & Cunningham, 1999).

Socioeconomic Status and Ethnicity in Schools

Children from low-income, ethnic minority backgrounds have more difficulties in school than do their middle-socioeconomic status, White counterparts. Why? Critics argue that schools have not done a good job of educating low-income, ethnic minority students to overcome the

CAREERS IN LIFE-SPAN DEVELOPMENT

Donna Smith, School Psychologist

DONNA SMITH is a school psychologist with the Cape Slattery School District in the state of Washington. After studying psychology at Brigham Young University and teaching elementary school and English as a second language, she trained as an educational specialist at Seattle University to become a school psychologist.

Donna has been working for the past 7 years at the elementary school and high school on the Neah Bay Makah Indian Reservation. One of her responsibilities is assessing children's needs for special education and other services. Although she performs a limited amount of direct counseling herself, she often works with counselors and others who provide a range of needed services.

The Makah tribe has been relatively isolated from mainstream culture until recently, compared with other Native American groups. One positive result of this is that the Makah community still provides kinds of support that do not exist in non-Native school settings. For example, when a traumatic incident occurs (for example, when a young boy disappears in the woods and is never found), tribal elders will come to the school to talk with the children and share their own experiences to help them through the difficult emotions of the situation.

The Makah people still believe that "it takes a village to raise a child." Although there are many family problems in the community, there is also the added resource that not only a parent but also a caring aunt, grandmother, or grandfather frequently becomes available to help a child with a problem.

Donna greatly values her role as the facilitator of a team approach of teachers and other professionals designing individual education programs for students. "Working with teams," she says, "is a positive and powerful part of my job."

Donna Smith counseling a student.

I touch the future. I teach.

Christa McAuliffe
American Educator and Astronaut, 20th Century

Urban Education and Children in Poverty

Interview with Jonathan Kozol

Diversity and Education

barriers to their achievement (Scott-Jones, 1995). Let's further explore the roles of socioeconomic status and ethnicity in schools.

The Education of Students from Low Socioeconomic Backgrounds

Many children in poverty face problems at home and at school that present barriers to their learning (Phillips & others, 1999; Wertheimer, 1999). At home, they might have parents who don't set high educational standards for them, who are incapable of reading to them, and who don't have enough money to pay for educational materials and experiences, such as books and trips to zoos and museums. They might be malnourished and live in areas where crime and violence are a way of life (Ceballo, 1999; DuRant, 1999).

Many of the schools that children from impoverished backgrounds attend have fewer resources than do the schools in higher-income neighborhoods (Shade, Kelly, & Oberg, 1997). Schools in low-income areas are more likely to have more students with lower achievement test scores, lower graduation rates, and smaller percentages of students going to college. And they are more likely to have young teachers with less experience than do schools in higher-income neighborhoods. In some instances, though, federal aid has provided a context for improved learning in schools located in low-income areas.

Schools in low-income areas also are more likely to encourage rote learning, while schools in higher-income areas are more likely to work with children to improve their thinking skills (Spring, 1998). Thus far too many schools in low-income neighborhoods provide students with environments that are not conducive to effective learning, and many of the schools' buildings and classrooms are old, crumbling, and poorly maintained.

Jonathan Kozol (1991) vividly described some of the problems that children of poverty face in their neighborhood and at school in *Savage Inequalities.* Following are some of his observations in one inner-city area. East St. Louis, Illinois, which is 98 percent African American, has no obstetric services, no regular trash collection, and few jobs. Nearly one third of the families live on less than $7,500 a year, and 75 percent of its population lives on welfare of some form. Blocks upon blocks of housing consist of dilapidated, skeletal buildings. Residents breathe the chemical pollution of nearby Monsanto Chemical Company. Raw sewage repeatedly backs up into homes. Lead from nearby smelters poisons the soil. Child malnutrition and fear of violence are common. The problems of the streets spill over into the schools, where sewage also backs up from time to time. Classrooms and hallways are old and unattractive, athletic facilities inadequate. Teachers run out of chalk and paper, the science labs are 30 to 50 years out of date, and the school's heating system has never worked correctly. A history teacher has 110 students but only 26 books.

Kozol says that anyone who visits places like East St. Louis, even for a brief time, comes away profoundly shaken. After all, these are innocent children who have done nothing wrong. Kozol's interest was in describing what life is like in the nation's inner-city neighborhoods and schools, which are predominantly African American and Latino. However, as indicated earlier, there are many non-Latino White children who live in poverty, although they often are in suburban or rural areas. Kozol argues that many inner-city schools are still segregated, are grossly underfunded, and do not provide adequate opportunities for children to learn effectively.

In his book *Savage Inequalities,* Jonathan Kozol *(above)* vividly portrayed the problems that children of proverty face in their neighborhood and at school. *What are some of these problems?*

One recent trend in antipoverty programs is to conduct two-generational intervention (Huston, 1999; McLoyd, 1998, 1999, 2000). This involves providing both services for children (such as educational day care or preschool education) and services for parents (such as adult education, literacy training, and job skill training). Recent evaluations of the two-generational programs suggest that they have more positive effects on parents than they do on children (St. Pierre, Layzer, & Barnes, 1996). Also discouraging for children is that, when the two-generational programs show benefits, they are more likely to be in the form of health benefits than cognitive gains.

Ethnicity in Schools School segregation is still a factor in the education of children of color in the United States (Simons, Finlay, & Yang, 1991). Almost one third of all African American and Latino students attend schools in which 90 percent or more of the students are from minority groups.

The school experiences of students from different ethnic groups vary considerably (Hollins & Oliver, 1999; Nelson-LeGall & Kelly, 2001). African American and Latino students are much less likely than non-Latino White or Asian American students to be enrolled in academic, college preparatory programs and are much more likely to be enrolled in remedial and special education programs. Asian American students are far more likely than other ethnic minority groups to take advanced math and science courses in high school. African American students are twice as likely as Latinos, Native Americans, or Whites to be suspended from school. Ethnic minorities of color constitute the majority in 23 of the 25 largest school districts in the United States, a trend that is increasing (Banks, 1995, 1997). However, 90 percent of the teachers in America's schools are non-Latino White, and the percentage of minority teachers is projected to decrease even further in the coming years.

American anthropologist John Ogbu (1989) proposed the view that ethnic minority students are placed in a position of subordination and exploitation in the American educational system. He believes that students of color, especially African Americans and Latinos, have inferior educational opportunities, are exposed to teachers and school administrators who have low academic expectations for them, and encounter negative stereotypes of ethnic minority groups (Ogbu & Stern, 2001). In one study of middle schools in predominantly Latino areas of Miami, Latino and White teachers rated African American students as having more behavioral problems than African American teachers rated the same students as having (Zimmerman & others, 1995).

Multicultural Education

Like Ogbu, educational psychologist Margaret Beale Spencer (1990) says that a form of institutional racism permeates many American schools. That is, well-meaning teachers, acting out of misguided liberalism, fail to challenge children of color to achieve. Such teachers prematurely accept a low level of performance from these children, substituting warmth and affection for high standards of academic success.

Following are some strategies for improving relationships among ethnically diverse students (Santrock, in press).

- *Turn the class into a jigsaw classroom.* When Eliot Aronson was a professor at the University of Texas at Austin, the school system contacted him for ideas on how to reduce the increasing racial tension in classrooms. Aronson (1986) developed the concept of "jigsaw classroom," in which students from different cultural backgrounds are placed in a cooperative group in which they have to construct, different parts of a project to reach a common goal. Aronson used the term *jigsaw* because he saw the technique as much like a group of students cooperating to put different pieces together to complete a jigsaw puzzle. How might this work? Consider a class of students, some White, some African American, some Latino, and some Asian American. The lesson to be learned by the groups focuses on the life of Joseph Pulitzer. The class might be broken up into groups of six students each, with the groups being as equal as possible

Sociocultural Worlds of Development

The Global Lab

Traditionally, students have learned within the walls of their classroom and interacted with their teacher and other students in the class. With advances in telecommunications, students can learn from and with teachers and students around the world. The teachers and students might be from schools in such diverse locations as Warsaw, Tokyo, Istanbul, and a small village in Israel.

The Global Laboratory Project is one example that has capitalized on advances in telecommunications (Schrum & Berenfeld, 1997). It consists of science investigations that involve environmental monitoring, sharing data via telecommunication hookups, and placing local findings in a global context. In an initial telecommunications meeting, students introduced themselves and described their schools, communities, and study locations. The locations included Moscow, Russia; Warsaw, Poland; Kenosha, Wisconsin; San Antonio, Texas; Pueblo, Colorado; and Aiken, South Carolina. This initial phase was designed to help students develop a sense of community and become familiar with their collaborators from around the world. As their data collection and evaluation evolved, students continued to communicate with their peers worldwide and to learn more not only about science but also about the global community.

Classrooms or schools also can use fax machines to link students from around the country and world (Cushner, McClelland, & Safford, 1996). Fax machines transfer artwork, poetry, essays, and other materials to other students in locations as diverse as Europe, Asia, Africa, and South America. Students also can communicate the same day with pen pals through e-mail, where once it took weeks for a letter to reach someone in a faraway place. An increasing number of schools also use videotelephone technology in foreign language instruction. Instead of simulating a French café in a typical French language class. American students might talk with French students who have placed a videotelephone in a French café in their country.

Such global technology projects can go a long way toward reducing American students' ethnocentric beliefs. The active building of connections around the world through telecommunications gives students the opportunity to experience others' perspectives, better understand other cultures, and reduce prejudice.

Global technology projects can help students become less ethnocentric. *What is the nature of some of these projects?*

in terms of ethnic composition and achievement level. The lesson about Pulitzer's life is divided into six parts, with each part given to a member of each six-person group. The parts might be paragraphs from Pulitzer's biography, such as how the Pulitzer family came to the United States, Pulitzer's childhood, and his early work. All the students in each group are given an allotted time to study their parts. Then the groups meet, and each member tries to teach a part to the group. Learning depends on the students' interdependence and cooperation in reaching the same goal. Sometimes the jigsaw classroom strategy is referred to as creating a superordinate goal or common task for students. Team sports, drama productions, and music performances are examples of contexts in which students cooperatively participate to reach a superordinate goal.

- *Use technology to foster cooperation with students from around the world.* The Sociocultural Worlds of Development box illustrates how to do this.
- *Encourage students to have positive personal contact with diverse other students.* Contact alone does not do the job of improving relationships with diverse

others. For example, busing ethnic minority students to predominantly White schools, or vice versa, has not reduced prejudice or improved interethnic relations (Minuchin & Shapiro, 1983). What matters is what happens after children get to school. Especially beneficial in improving interethnic relations is sharing one's worries, successes, failures, coping strategies, interests, and other personal information with people of other ethnicities. When this happens, people are seen more as individuals than as a heterogeneous cultural group.

- *Encourage students to engage in perspective taking.* Exercises and activities that help students see others' perspectives can improve interethnic relations. This helps students "step into the shoes" of peers who are culturally different and feel what it is like to be treated in fair or unfair ways (Cushner, McClelland, & Safford, 1996).
- *Help students think critically and be emotionally intelligent when cultural issues are involved.* Students who think in narrow ways are prejudiced. Students who learn to think critically and deeply about interethnic relations are likely to decrease their prejudice. Becoming more emotionally intelligent includes understanding the causes of one's feelings, managing anger, listening to what others are saying, and being motivated to share and cooperate.
- *Reduce bias.* Teachers can reduce bias by displaying images of children from diverse ethnic and cultural groups, selecting play materials and classroom activities that encourage cultural understanding, helping students resist stereotyping, and working with parents (Derman-Sparks, 1989).
- *View the school and community as a team to help support teaching efforts.* James Comer (1988; Comer & others, 1996) believes that a community, team approach is the best way to educate children. Three important aspects of the Comer Project for Change are (1) a governance and management team that develops a comprehensive school plan, assessment strategy, and staff development plan; (2) a mental health or school support team; and (3) a parent's program. Comer believes that the entire school community should have a cooperative rather than an adversarial attitude. The Comer program is currently operating in more than 600 schools in 26 states.
- *Be a competent cultural mediator.* Teachers can play a powerful role as a cultural mediator by being sensitive to racist content in materials and classroom interactions, learning more about different ethnic groups, being sensitive to children's ethnic attitudes, viewing students of color positively, and thinking of positive ways to get parents of color more involved as partners with teachers in educating children (Banks, 1997; Cushner, 1999).

CAREERS IN LIFE-SPAN DEVELOPMENT

James Comer, Child Psychiatrist

JAMES COMER grew up in a low-income neighborhood in East Chicago, IN, and credits his parents with leaving no doubt about the importance of education. He obtained a BA degree from Indiana University. He went on to obtain a medical degree from Howard University College of Medicine, a Master of Public Health degree from the University of Michigan School of Public Health, and psychiatry training at the Yale University School of Medicine's Child Study Center. He currently is the Maurice Falk Professor of Child Psychiatry at the Yale University Child Study Center and an associate dean at the Yale University Medical School. During his years at Yale, Comer has concentrated his career on promoting a focus on child development as a way of improving schools. His efforts in support of healthy development of young people are known internationally.

Dr. Comer, perhaps, is best known for the founding of the School Development Program in 1968, which promotes the collaboration of parents, educators, and community to improve social, emotional, and academic outcomes for children. His concept of teamwork is currently improving the educational environment in more than 500 schools throughout America.

James Comer *(left)* is shown with some of the inner-city African American children who attend a school that became a better learning environment because of Comer's intervention.

Asian grade schools intersperse studying with frequent periods of activities. This approach helps children maintain their attention and likely makes learning more enjoyable. Shown here are Japanese fourth-graders making wearable masks. *What are some differences in the way children in many Asian countries are taught compared to children in the United States?*

"We [the United States] accept performances in students that are nowhere near where they should be."

Harold Stevenson
Contemporary Developmental Psychologist, University of Michigan

Cross-Cultural Comparisons of Achievement

American children are more achievement oriented than their counterparts in many countries. However, in the past decade, the poor performance of American children in math and science has become well publicized. For example, in one cross-national comparison of the math and science achievement of 9- to 13-year-old students, the United States finished 13th (out of 15) in science and 15th (out of 16) in math achievement (Educational Testing Service, 1992). In this study, Korean and Taiwanese students placed first and second, respectively.

Harold Stevenson's (1995, 2000, Stevenson & Hofer, 1999) research explores reasons for the poor performance of American students. Stevenson and his colleagues have completed five cross-cultural comparisons of students in the United States, China, Taiwan, and Japan. In these studies, Asian students consistently outperform American students. And, the longer the students are in school, the wider the gap becomes between Asian and American students—the lowest difference is in the first grade, the highest in the eleventh grade (the highest grade studied).

To learn more about the reasons for these large cross-cultural differences, Stevenson and his colleagues spent thousands of hours observing in classrooms, as well as interviewing and surveying teachers, students, and parents. They found that the Asian teachers spent more of their time teaching math than did the American teachers. For example, more than one fourth of total classroom time in the first grade was spent on math instruction in Japan, compared with only one tenth of the time in the U.S. first-grade classrooms. Also, the Asian students were in school an average of 240 days a year, compared with 178 days in the United States.

In addition to the substantially greater time spent on math instruction in the Asian schools than the American schools, differences were found between the Asian and American parents. The American parents had much lower expectations for their

Summary Table 11.4
Schools

Concept	Processes/ Related Ideas	Characteristics/Descriptions
The Transition to Elementary School	Members of a Small Society	• Children spend more than 10,000 hours in the classroom as members of a small society in which there are tasks to be accomplished, people to be socialized and socialized by, and rules that define and limit behavior. • A special concern is that early schooling proceeds mainly on the basis of the negative feedback to children.
Socioeconomic Status and Ethnicity in Schools	Socioeconomic Status	• Children in poverty face problems at home and at school that present barriers to their learning. • Schools in low-income neighborhoods often have fewer resources, have less experienced teachers, and are more likely to encourage rote learning rather than thinking skills.
	Ethnicity	• The school experiences of students from different ethnic groups vary considerably. • It is important for teachers to have positive expectations for and challenge children of color to achieve. • Among the strategies teachers can follow for improving relations among ethnically diverse students are to turn the classroom into a jigsaw classroom, to encourage positive personal contact among ethnically diverse students, to stimulate perspective taking, to reduce bias, to view the school and the community as a team, and to be a competent cultural mediator.
Cross-Cultural Comparisons of Achievement	American Versus Asian Children	• American children are more achievement-oriented than children in many other countries, but are less achievement-oriented than many children in Asian countries such as China, Taiwan, and Japan.

children's education and achievement than did the Asian parents. Also, the American parents were more likely to believe that their children's math achievement was due to innate ability; the Asian parents were more likely to say that their children's math achievement was the consequence of effort and training. The Asian students were more likely to do math homework than were the American students, and the Asian parents were far more likely to help their children with their math homework than were the American parents (Chen & Stevenson, 1989).

Critics of the cross-national comparisons argue that, in many comparisons, virtually all U.S. children are being compared with a "select" group of children from other countries, especially in the secondary school comparisons. Therefore, they conclude, it is no wonder that American students don't fare so well. That criticism holds for some international comparisons. However, even when the top 25 percent of students in different countries were recently compared, U.S. students move up some, but not a lot (Mullis, 1999).

At this point we have studied a number of ideas about schools. To review these ideas see summary table 11.4. In the next section of the book, we will explore development during the adolescent years, beginning with Chapter 12, Physical and Cognitive Development in Adolescence.

Chapter Review

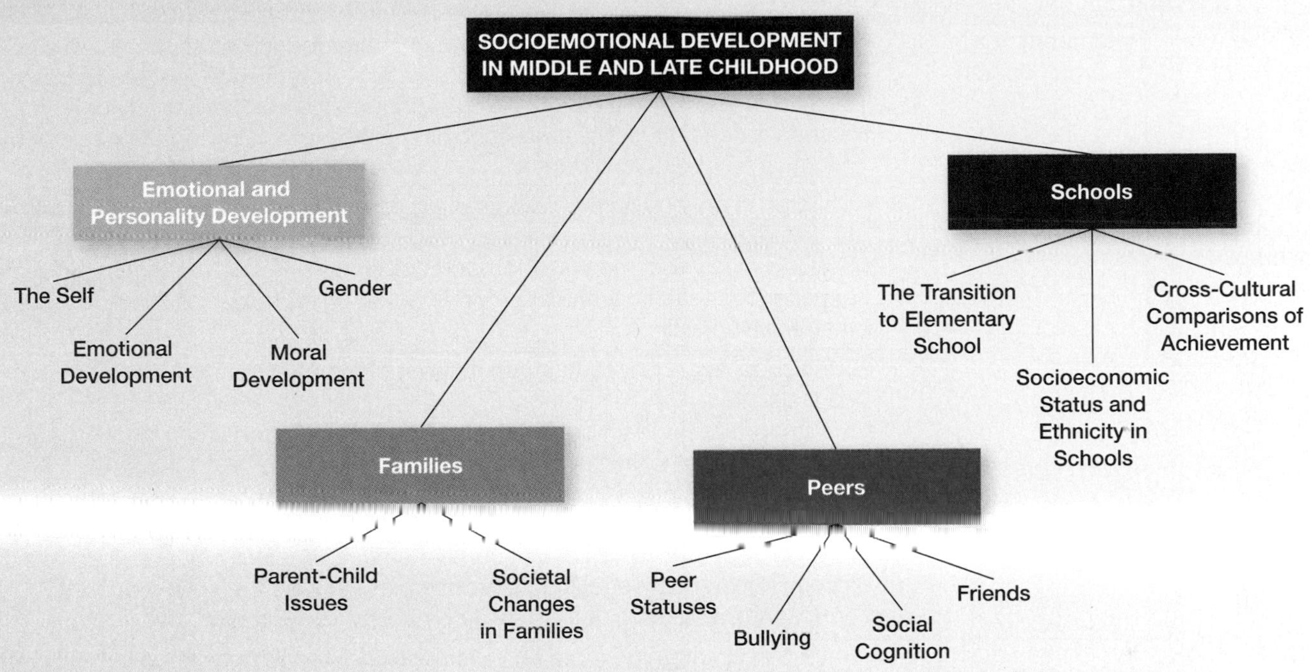

TO OBTAIN A DETAILED REVIEW OF THIS CHAPTER, STUDY THESE FOUR SUMMARY TABLES:

- Summary Table 11.1 The Self and Emotional Development page 315
- Summary Table 11.2 Moral Development and Gender page 327
- Summary Table 11.3 Families and Peers page 334
- Summary Table 11.4 Schools page 341

Key Terms

self-esteem 311
self-concept 311
emotional intelligence 313
internalization 316
preconventional reasoning 316
conventional reasoning 317
postconventional reasoning 317
justice perspective 318
care perspective 319
altruism 319
gender stereotypes 320
androgyny 324
gender-role transcendence 325
boundary ambiguity 329
popular children 330
neglected children 330
rejected children 330
controversial children 330
intimacy in friendships 333

Key People

Susan Harter 311
Erik Erikson 313
Daniel Goleman 313
Lawrence Kohlberg 315
Carol Gilligan 318
William Damon 319
Nancy Eisenberg 320
Eleanor Maccoby 322
Carol Jacklin 322
Janet Shibley Hyde 322
Alice Eagly 323
Sandra Bem 324
Joan Lipsitz 330
Kenneth Dodge 332
Willard Hartup 333
Jonathan Kozol 336
John Ogbu 337
Margaret Beale Spencer 337
Eliot Aronson 337
Harold Stevenson 340

Taking It to the Net

1. Nancy, a third-grade teacher, overheard a talk show discussion on emotional intelligence. She has seen several books on the subject in the local library but was unaware of its impact on learning. What is emotional intelligence and how can Nancy and her students' parents facilitate this type of development in children?
2. Alex is having difficulty understanding Kohlberg's theories on moral reasoning and is worried about the upcoming exam in class. What strengths and weaknesses should Alex focus on in his exam preparation and what impact has the Kohlberg research had on the understanding of human development?
3. Frank is researching the latest information on bullying after his younger brother told him of his recent experiences with bullies at his junior high school. What information is available on the prevalence of bullying, the make-up of the children who bully, and why this type of behavior is increasing?

Connect to www.mhhe.com/santrockld8 to research the answers and complete these exercises.

OLC Preview

To further test your knowledge of this chapter or to explore our extensive online resources that accompany *Life-Span Development*, eighth edition, please log on to the text's Online Learning Center at www.mhhe.com/santrockld8.com.

Section 6

Adolescence

"Who are you?" asked the caterpillar. Alice replied rather shyly, "I—I hardly know, sir, just at present—at least I know who I was when I got up this morning, but I must have changed several times since then."

Lewis Carroll
English Writer, 19th Century

Adolescents feel like they will live forever. At times, they are sure that they know everything. They clothe themselves with rainbows and go brave as the zodiac, flashing from one end of the world to the other in both mind and body. In many ways, today's adolescents are privileged, wielding unprecedented economic power. At the same time, they move through a seemingly endless preparation for life. They try on one face after another, seeking to find a face of their own. In their most pimply and awkward moments, they become acquainted with sex. They play furiously at "adult games" but are confined to the society of their own peers. They want their parents to understand them. Their generation of young people is the fragile cable by which the best and the worst of their parents' generation is transmitted to the present. In the end, there are only two lasting bequests parents can leave youth, one being roots, the other wings. Section Six contains two chapters: "Physical and Cognitive Development in Adolescence" (chapter 12) and "Socioemotional Development in Adolescence" (chapter 13).

Chapter 12

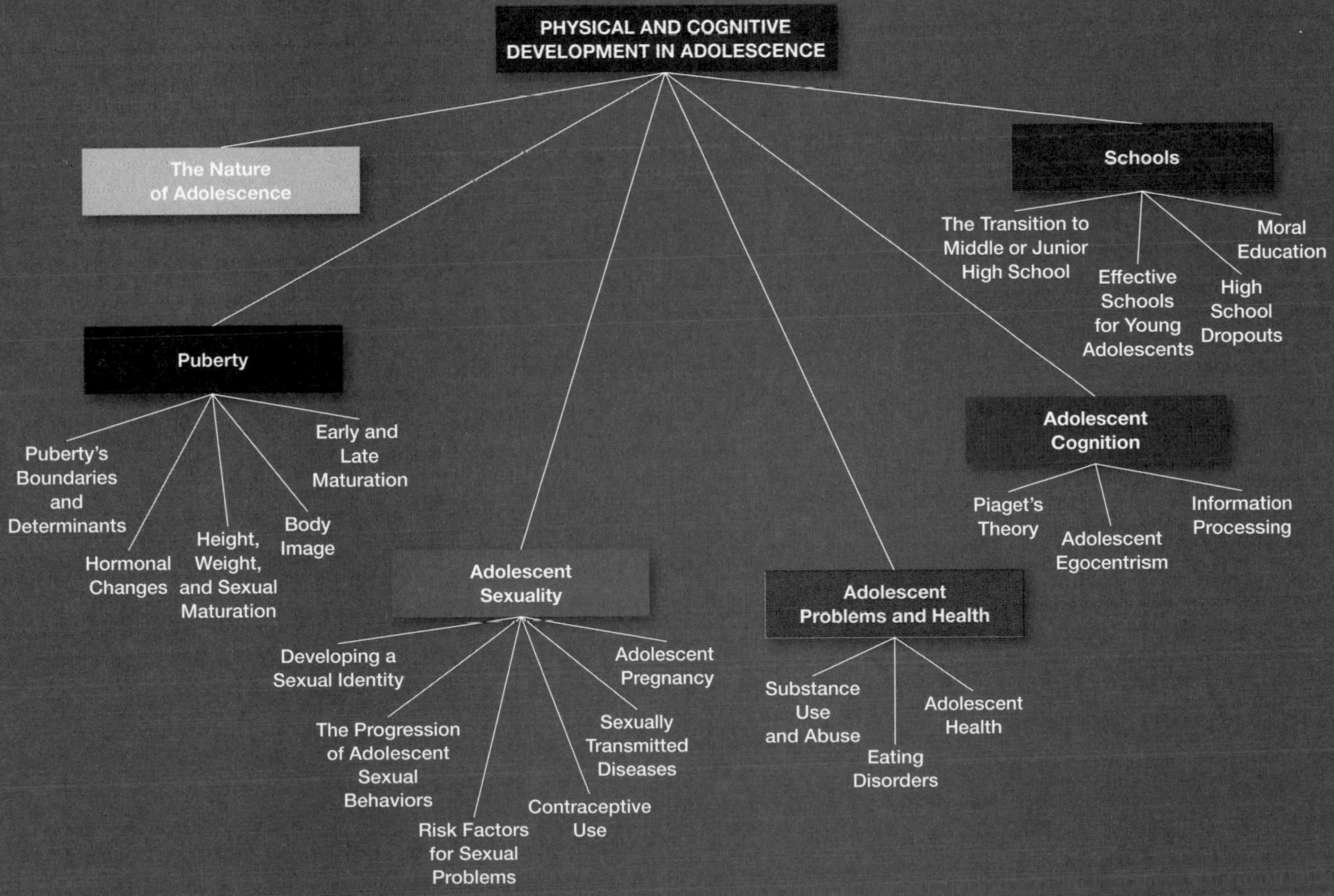

PHYSICAL AND COGNITIVE DEVELOPMENT IN ADOLESCENCE
The Nature of Adolescence
Puberty
Puberty's Boundaries and Determinants
Hormonal Changes
Height, Weight, and Sexual Maturation
Body Image
Early and Late Maturation
Adolescent Sexuality
Developing a Sexual Identity
The Progression of Adolescent Sexual Behaviors
Risk Factors for Sexual Problems
Contraceptive Use
Sexually Transmitted Diseases
Adolescent Pregnancy
Adolescent Problems and Health
Substance Use and Abuse
Eating Disorders
Adolescent Health
Adolescent Cognition
Piaget's Theory
Adolescent Egocentrism
Information Processing
Schools
The Transition to Middle or Junior High School
Effective Schools for Young Adolescents
High School Dropouts
Moral Education

Physical and Cognitive Development in Adolescence

In youth, we clothe ourselves with rainbows, and go brave as the zodiac.

Ralph Waldo Emerson
American Poet, Essayist, 19th Century

Images of Life-Span Development

The Best of Times and the Worst of Times for Today's Adolescents

IT IS BOTH the best of times and the worst of times for adolescents. Their world possesses powers and perspectives inconceivable 50 years ago: computers, longer life expectancies, the entire planet accessible through television, satellites, air travel. So much knowledge, though, can be chaotic and dangerous. School curricula have been adapted to teach new topics: AIDS, adolescent suicide, drug and alcohol abuse, incest. The hazards of the adult world—its sometimes fatal temptations—descend upon children and adolescents so early that their ideals may be shattered.

Crack, for example, is far more addictive and deadly than marijuana, the drug of an earlier generation. Strange fragments of violence and sex flash out of the television set and lodge in the minds of youth. The messages are powerful and contradictory. Rock videos suggest orgiastic sex. Public health officials counsel safe sex. Jerry Springer conducts seminars on exotic drugs, transsexual surgery, serial murders. Television pours a bizarre version of reality into the imaginations of adolescents (Morrow, 1988).

Adolescence is not a time of rebellion, crisis, pathology, and deviance. A far more accurate vision of adolescence is of a time of evaluation, of decision making, of commitment, of carving out a place in the world. Most of the problems of today's youth are not with the youth themselves. What adolescents need is access to a range of legitimate opportunities and to long-term support from adults who care deeply about them.

In this chapter, we will focus on the physical and cognitive development of adolescents. This includes the many changes of puberty, adolescent sexuality, some adolescent problems and health, how adolescents think, and their schooling.

THE NATURE OF ADOLESCENCE

The Nature of Adolescence

As in the development of children, genetic, biological, environmental, and social factors interact in adolescent development. Also, continuity and discontinuity characterize adolescent development. The genes inherited from parents still influence thought and behavior during adolescence, but inheritance now interacts with the social conditions of the adolescent's world—with family, peers, friendships, dating, and school experiences ◀ P. 69. An adolescent has experienced thousands of hours of interaction with parents, peers, and teachers in the past 10 to 13 years of development. Still new experiences and developmental tasks appear during adolescence. Relationships with parents take a different form, moments with peers become more intimate, and dating occurs for the first time, as do sexual exploration and possibly intercourse. The adolescent's thoughts are more abstract and idealistic. Biological changes trigger a heightened interest in body image. Adolescence, then, has both continuity and discontinuity with childhood.

Today's adolescents face demands and expectations, as well as risks and temptations, that appear to be more numerous and complex than those faced by adolescents only a generation ago. Nonetheless, contrary to the popular stereotype of adolescents as highly stressed and incompetent, the vast majority of adolescents successfully negotiate the path from childhood to adulthood. By some criteria, today's adolescents are doing better than their counterparts from a decade or two earlier. Today, more adolescents complete high school, especially African American adolescents. The majority of adolescents today have positive self-concept and positive relationships with others.

A cross-cultural study by Daniel Offer and his colleagues (1988) supported the contention that most adolescents have positive images of themselves and contradicted the stereotype that most adolescents have problems or are disturbed in some way. The self-images of adolescents around the world were sampled—in the United States, Australia, Bangladesh, Hungary, Israel, Italy, Japan, Taiwan, Turkey, and West Germany. A healthy self-image characterized at least 73 percent of the adolescents studied. They appeared to be moving toward adulthood with a healthy integration of previous experiences, self-confidence, and optimism about the future. Although there were some differences among the adolescents, they were happy most of the time, they enjoyed life, they perceived themselves as able to exercise self-control, they valued work and school, they expressed confidence about their sexual selves, they expressed positive feelings toward their families, and they felt they had the capability to cope with life's stresses: not exactly a storm-and-stress portrayal of adolescence.

Public attitudes about adolescence emerge from a combination of personal experience and media portrayals, neither of which produce an objective picture of how normal adolescents develop (Feldman & Elliott, 1990). Some of the readiness to assume the worst about adolescents likely involves the short memories of adults. Many adults measure their current perceptions of adolescents by their memories of their own adolescence. Adults may portray today's adolescents as more troubled, less respectful, more self-centered, more assertive, and more adventurous than they were.

However, in matters of taste and manners, the young people of every generation have seemed radical, unnerving, and different from adults—different in how they look, in how they behave, in the music they enjoy, in their hairstyles, and in the clothing they choose. It is an enormous error, though, to confuse adolescents' enthusiasm for trying on new identities and enjoying moderate amounts of outrageous behavior with hostility toward parental and societal standards. Acting out and boundary testing are time-honored ways in which adolescents move toward accepting, rather than rejecting, parental values.

Although the majority of adolescents experience the transition from childhood to adulthood more positively than is portrayed by many adults and the media, too many adolescents today are not provided with adequate opportunities and support to become competent adults. In many ways, today's adolescents are presented with a less stable environment than adolescents of a decade or two ago. High divorce rates, high adolescent pregnancy rates, and increased geographic mobility of families contribute to this lack of

WWW

Practical Resources and Research

Adolescent Issues

Profile of America's Youth

Trends in the Well-Being of America's Youth

stability in adolescents' lives. Today's adolescents are exposed to a complex menu of lifestyle options through the media, and, although the adolescent drug rate is beginning to show signs of decline, the rate of adolescent drug use in the United States is higher than that of any other country in the industrialized Western world. Many of today's adolescents face these temptations, as well as sexual activity, at increasingly young ages.

Our discussion underscores an important point about adolescents: they do not make up a homogeneous group (Galambos & Tilton-Weaver, 1996). Most adolescents negotiate the lengthy path to adult maturity successfully, but too large a group does not. Ethnic, cultural, gender, socioeconomic, age, and lifestyle differences influence the actual life trajectory of every adolescent. Different portrayals of adolescence emerge, depending on the particular group of adolescents being described.

Now that we have considered some historical views of adolescents and have evaluated today's adolescents, let's turn our attention to the ways in which adolescents develop physically. We will begin with the dramatic changes of puberty.

Puberty

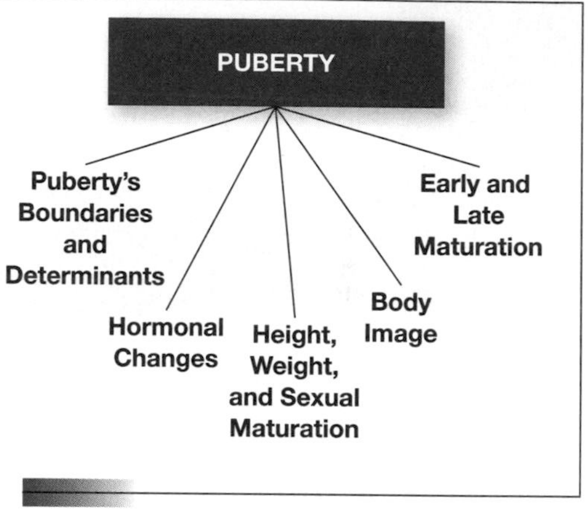

One father remarked that the problem with his teenage son was not that he grew, but that he did not know when to stop growing. As we will see, there is considerable variation in the timing of the adolescent growth spurt.

Puberty's Boundaries and Determinants

Puberty can be distinguished from adolescence. For most of us, puberty has ended long before adolescence is exited, although puberty is the most important marker of the beginning of adolescence. What is puberty? **Puberty** *is a period of rapid physical maturation involving hormonal and bodily changes that occur primarily during early adolescence.*

Imagine a toddler displaying all the features of puberty—a 3-year-old girl with fully developed breasts or a boy just slightly older with a deep voice. That is what we would see by the year 2250 if the age at which puberty arrives kept getting younger at its present pace. In Norway, **menarche**—*a girl's first menstruation*—occurs at just over 13 years of age, compared to 17 years of age in the 1840s. In the United States—where children mature up to a year earlier than children in European countries—the average age of menarche has been declining an average of about 4 months per decade for the past century. Fortunately, however, we are unlikely to see pubescent toddlers, since what has happened in the past century is likely the result of a higher level of nutrition and health. The available information suggests that menarche began to occur earlier at about the time of the Industrial Revolution, a period associated with increased standards of living and advances in medical science (Petersen, 1979).

puberty
A period of rapid skeletal and sexual maturation that occurs mainly in early adolescence.

menarche
First menstruation.

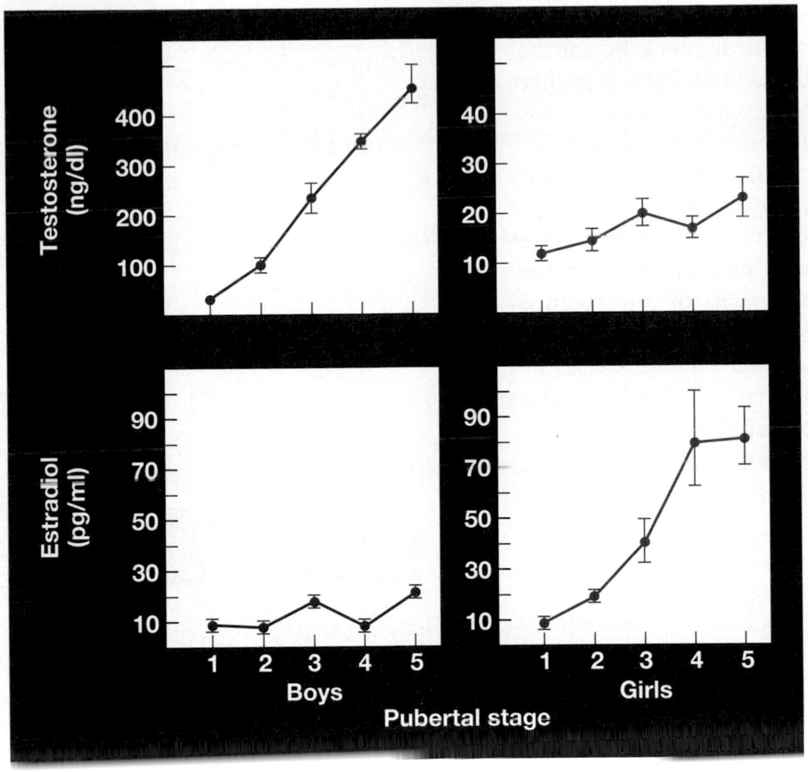

Figure **12.1**

Hormone Levels by Sex and Pubertal Stage for Testosterone and Estradiol

The five stages range from the early beginning of puberty (stage 1) to the most advanced stage of puberty (stage 5).

Genetic factors also are involved in puberty. Puberty is not simply an environmental accident. As indicated earlier, while nutrition, health, and other factors affect puberty's timing and variations in its makeup, the basic genetic program is wired into the nature of the species (Plomin, 1993).

Another key factor in puberty's occurrence is body mass, as was mentioned earlier. Menarche occurs at a relatively consistent weight in girls. A body weight approximating 106 ± 3 pounds can trigger menarche and the end of the pubertal growth spurt. For menarche to begin and continue, fat must make up 17 percent of the girl's body weight. Both teenage anorexics whose weight drops dramatically and female athletes in certain sports (such as gymnastics) may become amenorrheic (having an absence or suppression of menstrual discharge).

In summary, puberty's determinants include nutrition, health, heredity, and body mass. So far, our discussion of puberty has emphasized its dramatic changes. Keep in mind, though, that puberty is not a single, sudden event. We know when a young boy or girl is going through puberty, but pinpointing its beginning and its end is difficult. Except for menarche, which occurs rather late in puberty, no single marker heralds puberty. For boys, the first whisker or first wet dream is an event that could mark its appearance, but both may go unnoticed.

Hormonal Changes

Behind the first whisker in boys and the widening of hips in girls is a flood of **hormones,** *powerful chemical substances secreted by the endocrine glands and carried through the body by the bloodstream.* The endocrine system's role in puberty involves the interaction of the hypothalamus, the pituitary gland, and the gonads (sex glands). The **hypothalamus** *is a structure in the higher portion of the brain that monitors eating, drinking, and sex.* The **pituitary gland** *is an important endocrine gland that controls growth and regulates other glands.* The **gonads** *are the sex glands—the testes in males, the ovaries in females.* How does this hormonal system work? The pituitary sends a signal via *gonadotropins* (hormones that stimulate the testes or ovaries) to the appropriate gland to manufacture the hormone. Then the pituitary gland, through interaction with the hypothalamus, detects when the optimal level of hormones is reached and responds by maintaining gonadotropin secretion.

hormones
Powerful chemical substances secreted by the endocrine glands and carried through the body by the bloodstream.

hypothalamus
A structure in the higher portion of the brain that monitors eating, drinking, and sex.

pituitary gland
An important endocrine gland that controls growth and regulates other glands.

gonads
The sex glands—the testes in males and the ovaries in females.

Behind the first whisker in boys and widening of hips in girls is a flood of hormones, powerful chemical substances secreted by the endocrine glands and carried through the body by the bloodstream. The concentrations of certain hormones increase dramatically during adolescence (Dorn & Lucas, 1995; Susman & others, 1995). *Testosterone* is a hormone associated in boys with the development of genitals, an increase in height, and a change in voice. *Estradiol* is a hormone associated in girls with breast, uterine, and skeletal development. In one study, testosterone levels increased eighteenfold in boys but only twofold in girls during puberty; estradiol increased eightfold in girls but only twofold in boys (Nottelmann & others, 1987) (see figure 12.1).

Note that both testosterone and estradiol are present in the hormonal makeup of both boys and girls but that testosterone dominates in male pubertal development, estradiol in female pubertal development.

The same influx of hormones that puts hair on a male's chest and imparts curvature to a female's breast may contribute to psychological development in adolescence (Dorn & Lucas, 1995). In one study of 108 normal boys and girls ranging in

age from 9 to 14, a higher concentration of testosterone was present in boys who rated themselves more socially competent (Nottelmann & others, 1987). In another study, of 60 normal boys and girls in the same age range, girls with higher estradiol levels expressed more anger and aggression (Inoff-Germain & others, 1988). However, hormonal effects by themselves do not account for adolescent development. For example, in one study, social factors accounted for two to four times as much variance as did hormonal factors in young adolescent girls' depression and anger (Brooks-Gunn & Warren, 1989). Also, behavior and moods can affect hormones (Paikoff, Buchanan, & Brooks-Gunn, 1991). Stress, eating patterns, exercise, sexual activity, tension, and depression can activate or suppress various aspects of the hormonal system. In sum, the hormone-behavior link is complex.

One additional aspect of the pituitary gland's role in development still needs to be described. Not only does the pituitary gland release gonadotropins that stimulate the testes and ovaries, but through interaction with the hypothalamus the pituitary gland also secretes hormones that either directly lead to growth and skeletal maturation or produce such growth effects through interaction with the *thyroid gland,* located in the neck region.

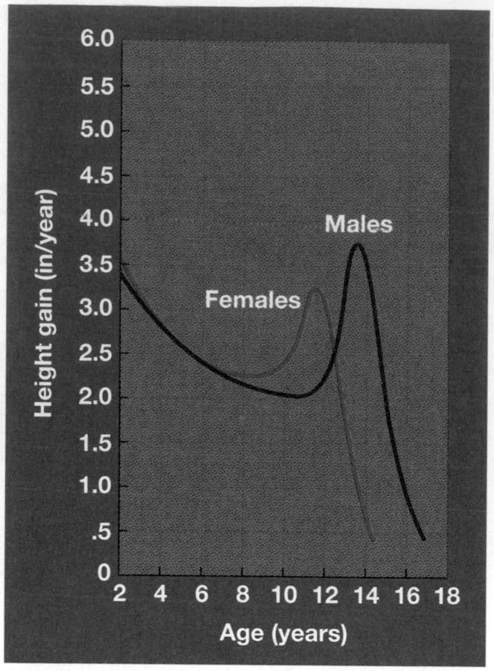

Figure **12.2**

Pubertal Growth Spurt

On the average, the growth spurt that characterizes pubertal change occurs two years earlier for girls ($10\frac{1}{2}$) than for boys ($12\frac{1}{2}$).

Biological Changes

Height, Weight, and Sexual Maturation

Among the most noticeable physical changes during puberty are increases in height and weight, as well as sexual maturation.

Height and Weight

As indicated in figure 12.2, the growth spurt occurs approximately two years earlier for girls than for boys (Abbassi, 1998). The mean beginning of the growth spurt in girls in 9 years of age; for boys, it is 11 years of age. The peak rate of pubertal change occurs at 11.5 years for girls and 13.5 years for boys. During their growth spurt, girls increase in height about $3\frac{1}{2}$ inches per year, boys about 4 inches.

Boys and girls who are shorter or taller than their peers before adolescence are likely to remain so during adolescence. In our society, there is a stigma attached to short boys. At the beginning of the adolescent period, girls tend to be as tall as or taller than boys of their age, but by the end of the middle school years most boys have caught up or, in many cases, have even surpassed girls in height. And, even though height in the elementary school years is a good predictor of height later in adolescence, there is still room for the individual's height to change in relation to the height of his or her peers. As much as 30 percent of the height of late adolescence is unexplained by height in the elementary school years.

The rate at which adolescents gain weight follows approximately the same developmental timetable as the rate at which they gain height. Marked weight gains coincide with the onset of puberty. During early adolescence, girls tend to outweigh boys, but, just as with height, by about age 14 boys begin to surpass girls.

Sexual Maturation

Think back to the onset of your puberty. Of the striking changes that were taking place in your body, what was the first change that occurred? Researchers have found that male pubertal characteristics develop in this order: increase in penis and testicle size, appearance of straight public hair, minor voice change, first ejaculation (which usually occurs through masturbation or a wet dream), appearance of kinky pubic hair, onset of maximum growth, growth of hair in armpits, more detectable voice changes, and growth of facial hair. Three of the most noticeable areas of sexual maturation in boys are penis elongation, testes development, and growth of facial hair. The normal range and average age of development for these sexual characteristics, along with height spurt, are shown in figure 12.3.

What is the order of appearance of physical changes in females? First, either the breasts enlarge or public hair appears. Later, hair appears in the armpits. As these changes occur, the female grows in height, and her hips become wider than her shoulders. Her first menstruation comes rather late in the pubertal cycle. Initially, her menstrual cycles

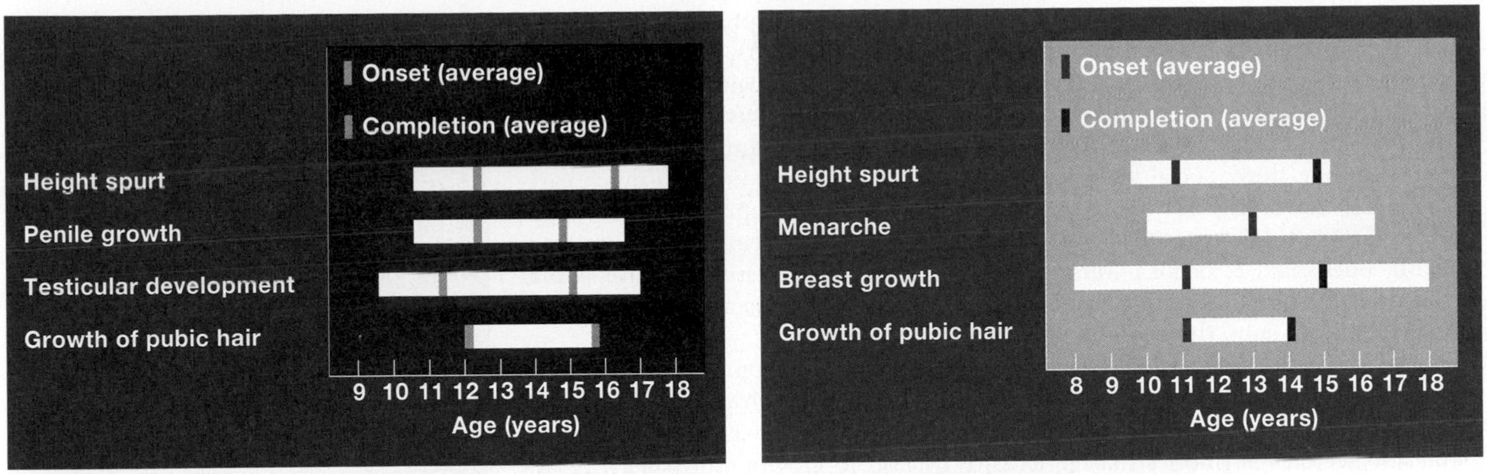

Figure **12.3**

Normal Range and Average Development of Sexual Characteristics in Males and Females

may be highly irregular. For the first several years, she might not ovulate every menstrual cycle. Some girls do not become fertile until 2 years after the period begins. No voice changes comparable to those in pubertal males occur in pubertal females. By the end of puberty, the female's breasts have become more fully rounded. Two of the most noticeable aspects of female pubertal change are public hair and breast development. Figure 12.3 shows the normal range and average development of these sexual characteristics and also provides information about menarche and height gain.

Adolescents show a strong preoccupation with their changing bodies and develop individual images of what their bodies are like. Adolescent boys, as well as adolescent girls, rate body build as one of the most important dimensions of physical attractiveness. *Think back to when you were going through puberty. What was your body image like?*

Individual Variation in Puberty The pubertal sequence may begin as early as 10 years of age or as late as 13½ for most boys. It may end as early as 13 years or as late as 17 years for most boys. The normal range is wide enough that, given two boys of the same chronological age, one might complete the pubertal sequence before the other one has begun it. For girls, the age range of the first menstrual period is even wider. Menarche is considered within a normal range if it appears between the ages of 9 and 15.

Body Image

One psychological aspect of physical change in puberty is certain: adolescents are preoccupied with their bodies and develop individual images of what their bodies are like. Perhaps you looked in the mirror on a daily and sometimes even hourly basis to see if you could detect anything different about your changing body. Preoccupation with one's body image is strong throughout adolescence, but it is especially acute during puberty, a time when adolescents are more dissatisfied with their bodies than in late adolescence (Wright, 1989).

There are gender differences in adolescents' perceptions of their bodies. In general, girls are less happy with their bodies and have more negative body images, compared with boys, throughout puberty (Brooks-Gunn &

Paikoff, 1993). Also, as pubertal change proceeds, girls often become more dissatisfied with their bodies, probably because their body fat increases, while boys become more satisfied as they move through puberty, probably because their muscle mass increases (Gross, 1984).

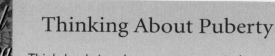

> **Critical Thinking**
>
> ### Thinking About Puberty
>
> Think back to when you were entering puberty. Were you an early maturer or a late maturer, or did you enter puberty "on time"? How do you think it affected your experiences during early adolescence? Has it had any lasting effects on your development?

Early and Late Maturation

Some of you entered puberty early, others late, and yet others on time. When adolescents nature earlier or later than their peers, might they perceive themselves differently? In the Berkeley Longitudinal Study some years ago, early-maturing boys perceived themselves more positively and had more successful peer relations than did their late-maturing counterparts (Jones, 1965). The findings for early-maturing girls were similar but not as strong as for boys. When the late-maturing boys were in their thirties, however, they had developed a stronger sense of identity than the early-maturing boys had (Peskin, 1967). Possibly this occurred because the late-maturing boys had more time to explore life's options or because the early-maturing boys continued to focus on their advantageous physical status instead of on career development and achievement.

More recent research confirms, though, that at least during adolescence it is advantageous to be an early-maturing rather than a late-maturing boy (Simmons & Blyth, 1987). The more recent findings for girls suggest that early-maturing girls experience more problems in school but also more independence and popularity with boys. The time that maturation is assessed also is a factor. In the sixth grade, early-maturing girls show greater satisfaction with their figures than do late-maturing girls, but by the tenth grade late-maturing girls are more satisfied (Simmons & Blyth, 1987). The reason for this is that, in late adolescence, early-maturing girls are shorter and stockier, whereas late-maturing girls are taller and thinner. Late-maturing girls in late adolescence have bodies that more closely approximate the current American ideal of feminine beauty—tall and thin.

In the past decade, an increasing number of researchers have found that early maturation increases girls' vulnerability to a number of problems (Brooks-Gunn & Paikoff, 1993). Early-maturing girls are more likely to smoke, drink, be depressed, have an eating disorder, request earlier independence from their parents, and have older friends; and their bodies are likely to elicit responses from males that lead to earlier dating and earlier sexual experiences. In one study, the early-maturing girls had lower educational and occupational attainment in adulthood (Stattin & Magnusson, 1990). Apparently as a result of their social and cognitive immaturity, combined with early physical development, early-maturing girls are easily lured into problem behaviors, not recognizing the possible long-term effects of these on their development (Petersen, 1993; Sarigiani & Petersen, 2000).

Some researchers now question whether the effects of puberty are as strong as once believed (Petersen, 1993). Puberty affects some adolescents more strongly than others and some behaviors more strongly than others. Body image, dating interest, and sexual behavior are affected by pubertal change. The recent questioning of puberty's effects suggests that, in terms of overall development and adjustment in the human life span, pubertal variations (such as early and late maturation) are less dramatic than is commonly thought. In thinking about puberty's effects, keep in mind that an adolescent's world involves cognitive and socioemotional changes, as well as physical changes. As with all periods of development, these processes work in concert to produce who we are in adolescence.

At this point we have studied a number of ideas about the nature of adolescence and puberty. A review of these ideas is presented in summary table 12.1. In our exploration of puberty, we explored the substantial changes in sexual maturation that occur. Next, we will further examine many aspects of the adolescent's changing sexuality.

SUMMARY TABLE 12.1
The Nature of Adolescence and Puberty

Concept	Processes/ Related Ideas	Characteristics/Descriptions
The Nature of Adolescence	Today's Youth	• Many stereotypes of adolescents are too negative. Most adolescents today successfully negotiate the path from childhood to adulthood. • Too many of today's adolescents are not provided with adequate opportunities and support to become competent adults. • It is important to view adolescents as a heterogeneous group because a different portrayal emerges, depending on the particular set of adolescents being described.
Puberty	Puberty's Boundaries and Determinants	• Puberty is a rapid change to physical maturation involving hormonal and bodily changes that occur primarily during early adolescence. • Puberty's determinants include nutrition, health, heredity, and body mass.
	Hormonal Changes	• The endocrine system's influence on puberty involves an interaction of the hypothalamus, the pituitary gland, and the gonads (sex glands). • Testosterone plays a key role in the pubertal development of males. • Estradiol plays a key role in the pubertal development of females. • Research has documented a link between hormonal levels and the adolescent's behavior.
	Height, Weight, and Sexual Maturation	• The initial onset of pubertal growth occurs on the average at 9½ years for girls and 11½ years for boys, reaching a peak change at 11½ for girls and 13½ for boys. Girls grow an average of 3½ inches per year during pubertal change, boys 4 inches. • Sexual maturation is a predominant feature of pubertal change and includes a number of changes in physical development. • Individual variation in puberty is extensive.
	Body Image	• Adolescents show considerable interest in their body image. • Young adolescents are more preoccupied and less satisfied with their body image than are late adolescents. • Girls have more negative body images throughout puberty than boys do.
	Early and Late Maturation	• Early maturation favors boys, at least during adolescence. As adults, though, late-maturing boys achieve more successful identities. • Researchers are increasingly finding that early-maturing girls are vulnerable to many problems. • Some researchers now question whether puberty's effects are as strong as once believed.

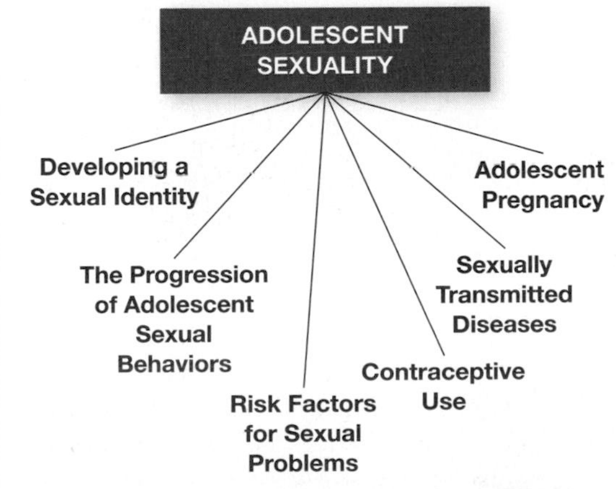

Adolescent Sexuality

Adolescence is a time of sexual exploration and experimentation, of sexual fantasies and realities, of incorporating sexuality into one's identity. Adolescents have an almost insatiable curiosity about sexuality's mysteries. They think about whether they are sexually attractive, how do to sex, and what the future holds for their sexual lives. The majority of adolescents eventually manage to develop a mature sexual identity, but for most there are times of vulnerability and confusion along life's sexual journey.

Adolescence is a bridge between the asexual child and the sexual adult (Feldman, 1999). Every society gives some attention to adolescent sexuality. In some societies, adults clamp down and protect adolescent females from males by chaperoning them. Other societies promote very early marriage. Yet

other societies, such as the United States, allow some sexual experimentation, although there is controversy about just how far sexual experimentation should be allowed to go.

An important point to keep in mind as you read about adolescent sexuality is that sexual development and interest are normal aspects of adolescent development and that the majority of adolescents have healthy sexual attitudes and engage in sexual practices that will not compromise their development (Feldman, 1999). In our discussion of adolescent sexuality, we will focus on developing a sexual identity, the progression of adolescent sexual behaviors, risk factors for sexual problems, contraceptive use, sexually transmitted diseases, and adolescent pregnancy. In chapter 14, "Physical and Cognitive Development in Early Adulthood," we will further explore these important aspects of sexuality: heterosexuality and homosexuality, sexually transmitted diseases, and forcible sexual behavior and sexual harassment.

Sexual arousal emerges as a new phenomena in adolescence and it is important to view sexuality as a normal aspect of adolescent development.

Shirley Feldman
Contemporary Developmental Psychologist, Stanford University

Developing a Sexual Identity

Mastering emerging sexual feelings and forming a sense of sexual identity is multifaceted (Brooks-Gunn & Graeber, 1999; Graeber, Brooks-Gunn, & Galen, 1999). This lengthy process involves learning to manage sexual feelings (such as sexual arousal and attraction), developing new forms of intimacy, and learning the skills to regulate sexual behavior to avoid undesirable consequences. Developing a sexual identity also involves more than just sexual behavior. It includes interfaces with other developing identities. Sexual identities emerge in the context of physical factors, social factors, and cultural factors, with most societies placing constraints on the sexual behavior of adolescents.

An adolescent's sexual identity involves an indication of sexual orientation (homosexual, heterosexual, bisexual), and it also involves activities, interests, and styles of behavior (Buzwell & Rosenthal, 1996). For example, some adolescents have a high anxiety level about sex, others a low level. Some adolescents are strongly aroused sexually, others less so. Some adolescents are very active sexually, others are virgins. Some adolescents are sexually inactive because of a strong religious upbringing, others go to church regularly and it does not inhibit their sexual activity (Thorton & Canburn, 1989).

Although the development of gay or lesbian identity has been widely studied in adults, few researchers have investigated the gay or lesbian identity (often referred to as the coming-out process) in adolescents.

In one recent comprehensive survey of adolescent sexual orientation in almost 35,000 junior and senior high school students in Minnesota, 4.5 percent reported predominantly homosexual attractions (Remafedi & others, in press). Homosexual identities, attractions, and behaviors increased with age. More than 6 percent of the 18-year-olds said they had predominantly homosexual attractions. How many of these youths later become gay is not known, although it is widely accepted that many adolescents who engage in homosexual behavior in adolescence do not continue the practice into adulthood.

One of the harmful aspects of the stigmatization of homosexuality is the self-devaluation engaged in by gay individuals (Patterson, 1995; Savin-Williams & Rodriguez, 1993). One common form of self-devaluation is called *passing,* the process of hiding one's real social identity. Passing strategies include giving out information that hides one's homosexual identity or avoiding one's true sexual identity. Passing behaviors include lying to others and saying, "I'm straight and attracted to opposite-sex individuals." Such defenses against self-recognition are heavily entrenched in our society. Without adequate support, and with fear of stigmatization, many gay and lesbian youth return to the closet and then reemerge at a safer time later, often in college. A special concern is the lack of support gay adolescents receive from parents, teachers, and counselors (Davis & Stewart, 1997). We will discuss homosexuality, as well as heterosexuality, in greater depth in chapter 14, "Physical and Cognitive Development in Early Adulthood."

One important aspect of developing a sexual indentity involves sexual orientation. These two individuals have chosen a homosexual orientation. *What are some of the stigmas that adolescents who are homosexual face?*

What is the progression of sexual behaviors in adolescence?

The Progression of Adolescent Sexual Behaviors

Adolescents engage in a rather consistent progression of sexual behaviors (DeLamater & MacCorquodale, 1979). Necking usually comes first, followed by petting. Next comes intercourse, or, in some cases, oral sex, which has increased substantially in adolescence in recent years. In one recent study, 452 individuals 18 to 25 years of age were asked about their own past sexual experiences (Feldman, Turner, & Araujo, 1999). The following progression of sexual behaviors occurred: kissing preceded petting which preceded sexual intercourse and oral sex (Feldman, Turner, & Araujo, 1999). Male adolescents reported engaging in these sexual behaviors approximately 1 year earlier than female adolescents.

The following information from a national survey of adolescents further reveals the timing of their sexual activities (Alan Guttmacher Institute, 1998):

- Most young adolescents have not had sexual intercourse: 8 in 10 girls and 7 in 10 boys are virgins at age 15.
- The probability that adolescents will have sexual intercourse increases steadily with age, but 1 in 5 individuals have not yet had sexual intercourse by age 19.
- Initial sexual intercourse occurs in the mid- to late adolescent years for a majority of teenagers, about 8 years before they marry.
- The majority of adolescent females' first voluntary sexual partner are younger, the same age, or no more than 2 years older; 27 percent are 3 to 4 years older; and 12 percent are 5 or more years older.

In some areas of the United States, the percentages of sexually active young adolescents even may be greater. In an inner-city area of Baltimore, 81 percent of the males at age 14 said that they already had engaged in sexual intercourse. Other surveys in inner-city, low-income areas also reveal a high incidence of early sexual intercourse (Clark, Zabin, & Hardy, 1984).

In sum, by the end of adolescence the majority of adolescents have had sexual intercourse. Male, African American, and inner-city adolescents report being the most sexually active (Feldman, Turner, & Araujo, 1999). Although sexual intercourse can be a meaningful experience for older, mature adolescents, many adolescents are not emotionally prepared to handle sexual experiences, especially in early adolescence. In one study, the earlier in adolescence boys and girls engaged in sexual intercourse, the more likely they were likely to show adjustment problems (Bingham & Crockett, 1996).

Risk Factors for Sexual Problems

While most adolescents become sexually active at some point during adolescence, some adolescents engage in sex at early ages (before age 16) and experience a number of partners over time. These adolescents are the least effective users of contraception and are at risk for early, unintended pregnancy and for sexually transmitted diseases. Early sexual activity is also linked with other risky behaviors such as excessive drinking, drug use, delinquency, and school-related problems (Dryfoos, 1990). Also, adolescents who live in low-income neighborhoods often are more sexually active and have higher adolescent pregnancy rates than adolescents who live in more affluent circumstances. And as we saw earlier, African American adolescents engage in sexual activities at an earlier age than other ethnic groups, while Asian American adolescents have the most restrictive sexual timetable.

Contraceptive Use

Sexual activity is a normal activity necessary for procreation, but it involves considerable risks if appropriate safeguards are not taken. There are two kinds of risks that youth encounter: unintended/unwanted pregnancy and sexually transmitted diseases. Both of these risks can be reduced significantly by using contraception and barriers (such as condoms). Gay and lesbian youth who do not experiment with heterosexual intercourse are spared the risk of pregnancy, but, like their heterosexual peers, they still face the risk of sexually transmitted diseases.

> *Even though U.S. adolescents do not show significantly different patterns of sexual activity compared to adolescents in many industrialized countries, they contracept less consistently and effectively.*
>
> P. Lindsay Chase-Lansdale
> *Contemporary Developmental Psychologist, Northwestern University*

The good news is that adolescents are increasing their use of contraceptives. Adolescent girls' contraceptive use at first intercourse rose from 48 percent to 65 percent during the 1980s (Forrest & Singh, 1990). By 1995, use at first intercourse reached 78 percent, with two-thirds of that figure involving condom use. A sexually active adolescent who does not use contraception has a 90 percent chance of pregnancy within 1 year (Alan Guttmacher Institute, 1998). The method adolescent girls use most frequently is the pill (44 percent), followed by the condom (38 percent). About 10 percent use an injectable contraception, 4 percent use withdrawal, and 3 percent use an implant (Alan Guttmacher Institute, 1998). Approximately one-third of adolescent girls who rely on condoms also take the pill or practice withdrawal.

Although adolescent contraceptive use is increasing, many sexually active adolescents still do not use contraceptives, or they use them inconsistently. Sexually active younger adolescents are less likely than older adolescents to take contraceptive precautions. Younger adolescents are more likely to use a condom or withdrawal, whereas older adolescents are more likely to use the pill or a diaphragm. In one study, adolescent females reported changing their behavior in the direction of safer sex practices more than did adolescent males (Rimberg & Lewis, 1994).

Sexually Transmitted Diseases

Sexually transmitted diseases (STDs) *are contracted primarily through sexual contact, which is not limited to sexual intercourse. Oral-genital and anal-genital contact also can transmit STDs.*

sexually transmitted diseases (STDs) Diseases that are contracted primarily through sexual contact, which is not limited to sexual intercourse. Oral-genital and anal-genital contact also can transmit STDs.

Every year more than 3 million American adolescents (about one-fourth of those who are sexually experienced) acquire an STD (Alan Guttmacher Institute, 1999). In a single act of unprotected sex with an infected partner, a teenager girl has a 1 percent risk of getting HIV, a 30 percent risk of acquiring genital herpes, and a 50 percent chance of contracting gonorrhea (Glei, 1999). Chlamydia (which can spread by sexual contact and infects the genitals of both sexes) is more common among adolescents than among young adults. In some areas, as many as 25 percent of sexually active adolescents have contracted chlamydia (Donovan, 1993). In one recent cross-cultural study of sixteen developed countries, the incidence of chlamydia was high among adolescents in all of the countries (Panchaud & others, 2000). Adolescents also have a higher incidence of gonorrhea than young adults.

In chapter 14, "Physical and Cognitive Development in Early Adulthood," we will study sexually transmitted diseases in more depth. Earlier we mentioned that when adolescents are sexually active and do not use contraception, one possible outcome is adolescent pregnancy. Let's further explore the nature of adolescent pregnancy.

WWW

The Alan Guttmacher Institute

Adolescent Pregnancy

Teen Pregnancy Prevention Initiative

Adolescent Pregnancy

They are from different ethnic groups and from different places, but their circumstances have the same stressfulness. Each year more than 500,000 American teenagers become pregnant, and more than 70 percent of them are unmarried (Child Trends, 1996). They represent a flaw in America's social fabric. Far too many become pregnant in their early or middle adolescent years. More than 200,000 females in the United States have a child before their eighteenth birthday. As one 17-year-old Los Angeles mother of a 1-year-old son said, "We are children having children."

Despite the rise in the teenage birth rate in the 1980s, the rate is lower now than it was in the 1950s and 1960s. What is different now, though, is the steady rise in births to unmarried teenagers.

How does the adolescent pregnancy rate in the United States compare with other developed countries? In one recent study of 46 countries, Russia had the highest adolescent pregnancy rate with the United States not far behind (Singh & Darroch, 2000). The lowest adolescent pregnancy rate, in the Netherlands, was six times lower than in the United States. Why is the adolescent pregnancy rate so low in the Netherlands? Most adolescents in the Netherlands would not think of having sex without effective contraception.

Although the adolescent pregnancy rate in the United States is still very high, it began to decline slightly in the 1990s (U.S. Department of Health and Human Services, 1998). Since 1990, the sharpest drop in adolescent pregnancy has occurred in 15- to 17-year-old African Americans. Fear of sexually transmitted diseases (especially AIDS), school/community health center health classes, and a greater hope for the future are the likely reasons for this decrease.

Consequences of Adolescent Pregnancy

The consequences of America's high adolescent pregnancy rate are cause for great concern. Adolescent pregnancy creates health risks for both the offspring and the mother. Infants born to adolescent mothers are more likely to have low birthweights—a prominent factor in

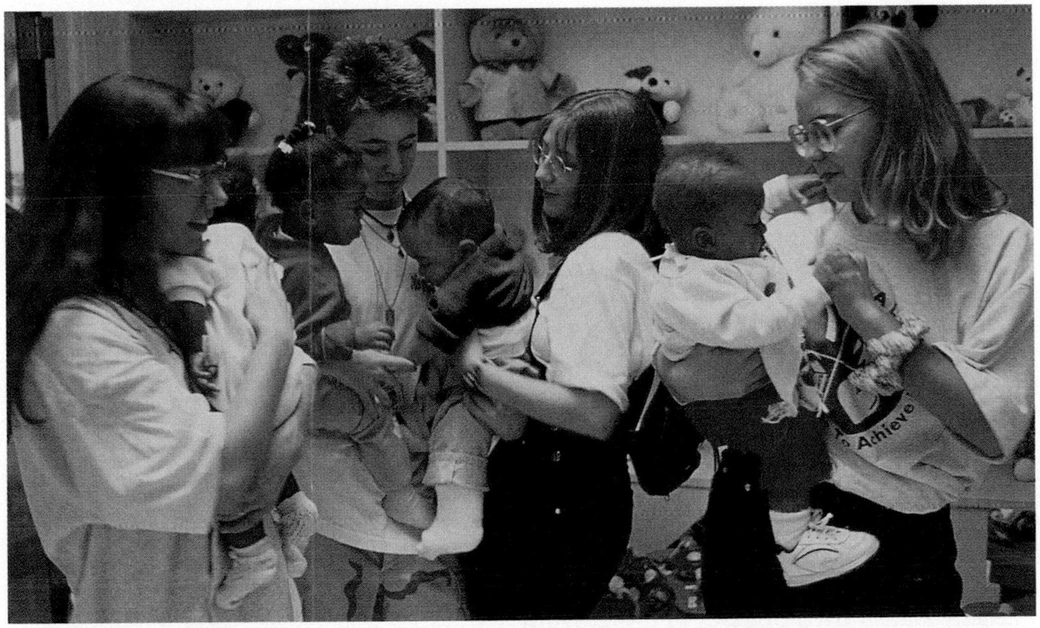

These are not adolescent mothers, but rather adolescents who are participating in the Teen Outreach Program (TOP) which engages adolescents in volunteer community service. These adolescent girls are serving as volunteers in a day-care center for crack babies. Researchers have found that such volunteer experiences can reduce the rate of adolescent pregnancy. *What are some other strategies for reducing adolescent pregnancy?*

infant mortality—as well as neurological problems and childhood illness (Dryfoos, 1990). Adolescent mothers often drop out of school. However, often it is not pregnancy alone that leads to negative consequences for an adolescent mother and her offspring (Brooks-Gunn & Paikoff, 1997; Feldman, 1999; Leadbetter & Way, 2001). Adolescent mothers are more likely to come from low-income backgrounds (Hoffman, Foster, & Furstenberg, 1993). Many adolescents mothers also were not good students before they became pregnant. Also keep in mind that not every adolescent female who bears a child lives a life of poverty and low achievement. Thus, while adolescent pregnancy is a high risk circumstance and in general adolescents who do not become pregnant fare better than those who don't, some adolescent mothers do well in school and have positive outcomes (Ahn, 1994; Whitman, Barkowski, & Keogh, 2001). Serious, extensive efforts are needed to help pregnant adolescents and young mothers enhance their educational and occupational opportunities. Adolescent mothers also need extensive help in obtaining competent day care and in planning for the future.

Reducing Adolescent Pregnancy Recommendations for reducing the high rate of adolescent pregnancy include (1) sex education and family planning, (2) access to contraceptive methods, (3) the life options approach, (4) broad community involvement and support, and (5) abstinence, especially for young adolescents.

One strategy for reducing adolescent pregnancy, called the Teen Outreach Program (TOP), focuses on engaging adolescents in volunteer community service and stimulates discussions that help adolescents appreciate the lessons they learn through volunteerism. In one study, 695 adolescents in grades 9 to 12 were randomly assigned to either a Teen Outreach group or a control group (Allen & others, 1997). They were assessed both at program entry and at program exit 9 months later. The rate of pregnancy was substantially lower for the Teen Outreach adolescents. These adolescents also had a lower rate of school failure and academic suspension.

At this point we have discussed a number of ideas about sexual development in adolescence. A review of these ideas is presented in summary table 12.2 on the following page. In our examination of adolescent sexual development, we examined the problem of adolescent pregnancy. Next, we will explore another major problem in adolescence: substance use and abuse.

Adolescent Problems and Health

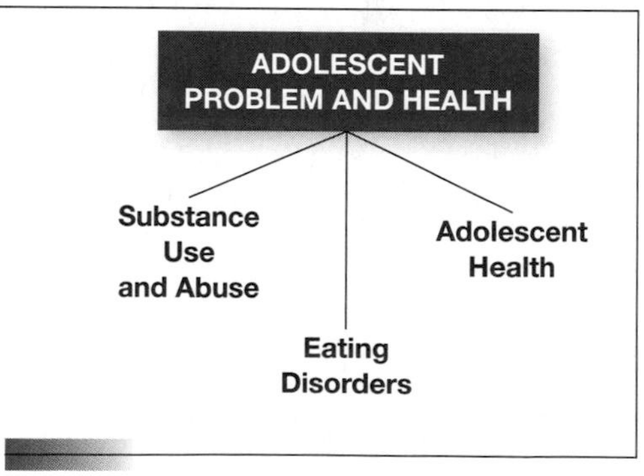

Problems that can develop in adolescence include substance use and abuse, and eating disorders. We will discuss these problems here, then in the next chapter explore the adolescent problems of juvenile delinquency, depression, and suicide. Also in this section we will examine adolescent health.

Substance Use and Abuse

The 1960s and 1970s were a time of marked increases in the use of illicit drugs. During the social and political unrest of those years, many youth turned to marijuana, stimulants, and hallucinogens. Increases in alcohol consumption by adolescents also were noted (Robinson & Greene, 1988). More precise data about drug use by adolescents have been collected in recent years. Each year since 1975, Lloyd Johnston, Patrick O'Malley, and Gerald Bachman (2000), working at the Institute of Social Research at the University of Michigan, have carefully monitored drug use by America's high school seniors in a wide range of public and private high schools. From time to time, they also sample the drug use of younger adolescents and adults.

Drug use among U.S. secondary school students declined in the 1980s but began to increase in the early 1990s and peaked in the mid 1990s (Johnston, O'Malley, & Bachman, 2000). Drugs that reached peak use levels by adolescents in the mid 1990s included inhalants, hallucinogens (such as LSD), marijuana, and amphetamines.

Summary Table 12.2
Adolescent Sexuality

Concept	Processes/ Related Ideas	Characteristics/Descriptions
Developing a Sexual Identity	Multifaceted	• Mastering emerging sexual feelings and forming a sense of sexual identity are multifaceted. • An adolescent's sexual identity involves sexual orientation, activities, interests, and styles of behavior.
The Progression of Adolescent Sexual Behaviors	Starts with Necking	• The progression of sexual behaviors is typically this: necking, petting, sexual intercourse, oral sex. • National data indicate that by age 19, 4 of 5 individuals have had sexual intercourse.
Risk Factors for Sexual Problems	Early Sexual Activity to Poverty	• These include early sexual activity, having a number of sexual partners, not using contraception, engaging in other at-risk behaviors such as heavy drinking and delinquency, living in a low-income neighborhood, and ethnicity.
Contraceptive Use	Increasing	• Adolescents are increasing their use of contraceptives, but large numbers still do not use contraceptives. • Young adolescents and those from low-income backgrounds are less likely to use contraceptives than older, middle-income adolescents.
Sexually Transmitted Diseases (STDs)	A Sexual Problem	• STDs are contacted primarily through sexual contact. More than 1 in 4 sexually active adolescents has an STD.
Adolescent Pregnancy	Incidence	• More than 5,000 American adolescents become pregnant every year. • Eight of 10 are unintended. • The only bright spot in these statistics is that the rate of adolescent pregnancy is declining somewhat. • America's adolescent pregnancy rate is among the highest in the Western world.
	Consequences of Adolescent Pregnancy	• Adolescent pregnancy increases health risks for both the mother and the offspring. • Adolescent mothers are more likely to drop out of school and have lower-paying jobs as adults than adolescent girls who do not bear children. • It is important to remember that often it is not pregnancy alone that places adolescents at risk. Adolescent mothers often come from low-income circumstances and were not doing well in school prior to their pregnancy.
	Reducing Adolescent Pregnancy	• Strategies include sex education and family planning, access to contraception, life options, community involvement and support, and abstention.

Figure 12.4 shows the trends in overall drug use by American high school seniors since 1975.

With only a few exceptions, drug use by American adolescents held steady in 1999. One bright spot in the 1999 and 2000 data was a drop in the use of crack cocaine among adolescents. Cigarette smoking among younger adolescents continued to decline in 1999. However, the use of anabolic steroids by male adolescents increased in 1999, believed to be the result of baseball home run king Mark McGwire's reported use of steroids (Johnston, O'Malley, & Bachman, 1999).

There are a number of "club drugs," so labeled because they are popular at night clubs and all-night dance parties called "raves." The main club drugs are Ecstasy and Rohypnol. Ecstasy is a metamphetamine, but it also has hallucinogenic properties. In

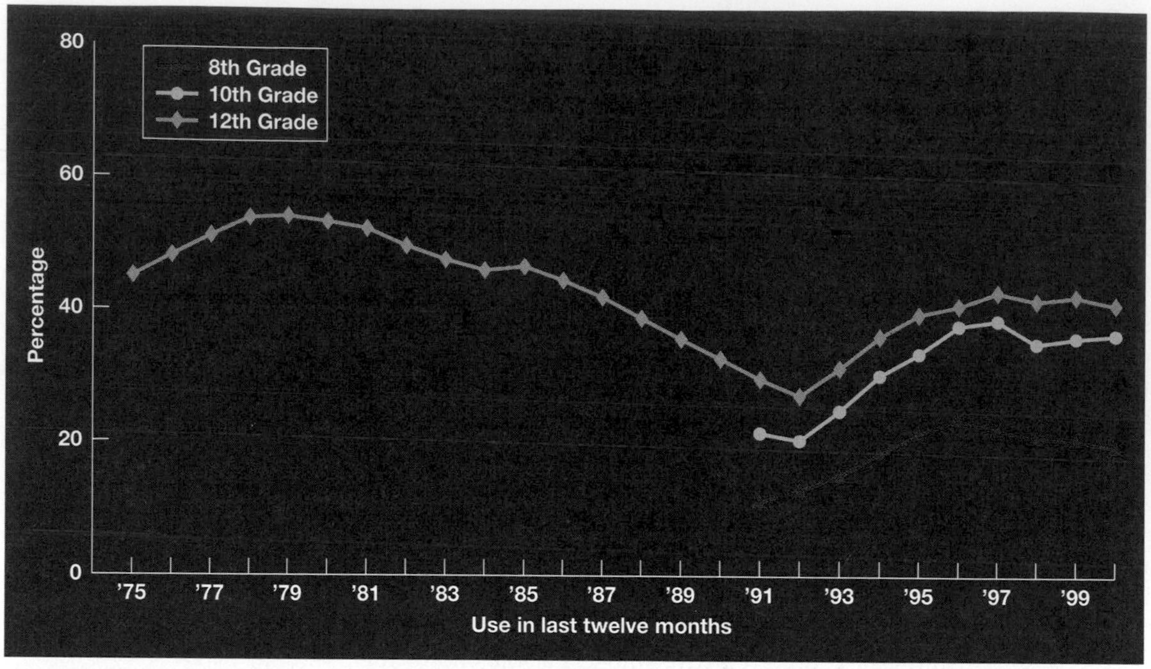

Figure **12.4**

Trends in Drug Use by U.S. Eighth-, Tenth-, and Twelfth-Grade Students

This graph shows the percentage of U.S. eighth-, tenth-, and twelfth-grade students who reported having taken an illicit drug in the last 12 months, over the period 1975 to 1999.

1999 and 2000, Ecstasy use rose sharply among adolescents (Johnston, O'Malley, & Bachman, 2000). Eight percent of the twelfth-graders and 5 percent of the tenth-graders said they had used Ecstasy in the last year. Rohypnol has been called a "date rape drug" because it can induce amnesia of events that occurred while under its influence. The drug is surreptitiously slipped into the drink of a victim, who then is raped. Fortunately, only about 1 percent of high school seniors report having used this drug (Johnston, O'Malley, & Bachman, 2000).

Even with the recent leveling off in drug use, the United States still has the highest rate of adolescent drug use of any industrialized nation. Also, the University of Michigan study likely underestimated the percentage of adolescents who take drugs, because it does not include high school dropouts, who have a higher rate of drug use than do students who are still in school. Johnston, Bachman, and O'Malley (1998) believe that "generational forgetting" contributed to the rise of adolescent drug use in the 1990s: adolescents tended to have less belief that drugs are dangerous.

Alcohol Alcohol is the drug most widely used by adolescents in our society. For them, it has produced many enjoyable moments and many sad ones as well. Alcoholism is the third leading killer in the United States, with more than 13 million people classified as alcoholics, many of whom established their drinking habits during adolescence. Each year, approximately 25,000 people are killed and 1.5 million injured by drunk drivers. In 65 percent of the aggressive male acts against females, the offender is under the influence of alcohol (Goodman & others, 1986). In numerous instances of drunken driving and assaults on females, the offenders are adolescents.

What is the pattern of alcohol consumption among adolescents?

How extensive is alcohol use by adolescents? Alcohol use by high school seniors has gradually declined. Monthly use declined from 72 percent in 1980 to 50 percent in 2000 (Johnston, O'Malley, & Bachman, 2000). The prevalence of drinking five or more drinks in a row in a 2-week interval fell from 41 percent in 1980 to 32 percent in 2000. However, data from college students show little drop in alcohol use and an increase in heavy drinking. Heavy drinking at parties among college males is common and is becoming more common (Wechsler, 2000).

Cigarette Smoking Smoking begins primarily during childhood and adolescence. One study found that, once young adolescents begin to smoke cigarettes, the addictive properties of nicotine make it extremely difficult for them to stop (Melby & Vargas, 1996).

The good news is that cigarette smoking is decreasing. In the national survey by the Institute of Social Research, the percentage of high school seniors who are current cigarette smokers continued to gradually decline in 2000 (Johnston, O'Malley, & Bachman, 2000). Cigarette smoking peaked in 1997 among high school seniors and since then has been gradually declining. Among high school seniors, a decline from 36.5 percent in 1997 to 31 percent in 2000 occurred regarding smoking one or more cigarettes in the past 30 days. Among eighth- and tenth-graders, the decline was even greater. However, despite these recent improvements, approximately one-third of America's youth are active smokers at the end of high school.

Cigarette Brands and Adolescents

Adolescent Substance Use

Anorexia Nervosa

The devastating effects of early smoking were brought home in a recent research study that found that smoking in the adolescent years causes permanent genetic changes in the lungs and forever increases the risk of lung cancer, even if the smoker quits (Weincke & others, 1999). Such damage was much less likely among smokers in the study who started in their twenties. One of the remarkable findings in the study was that the early age of onset of smoking was more important in predicting the genetic damage than how much the individuals smoked.

The Roles of Development, Parents, and Peers Most adolescents become drug users at some point in their development, whether limited to alcohol, caffeine, and cigarettes or extended to marijuana, cocaine, and hard drugs. A special concern involves adolescents using drugs as a way of coping with stress, which can interfere with the development of competent coping skills and responsible decision making. Researchers have found that drug use in childhood or early adolescence has more detrimental long-term effects on the development of responsible, competent behavior than when drug use occurs in late adolescence (Newcomb & Bentler, 1988). When they use drugs to cope with stress, many young adolescents enter adult roles of marriage and work prematurely, without adequate socioemotional growth, and experience greater failure in adult roles.

How early are adolescents beginning drug use? National samples of eighth- and ninth-grade students were included for the first time in 1991 in the Institute for Social Research survey of drug use (Johnston, O'Malley, & Bachman, 1992). Early in the drug use increase in the United States (late 1960s, early 1970s), drug use was much higher among college students than among high school students, who in turn had much higher rates of drug use than middle or junior high school students. However, today the rates for college and high school students are similar, and the rates for young adolescents are not as different from those for older adolescents as might be anticipated.

Parents, peers, and social support play important roles in preventing adolescent drug abuse (Dishion, 2001; Durlak, 2000; Johnson & others, 1996; Pentz, 1994; Reifman, 2001). Positive relationships with parents and others are important in reducing adolescents' drug use (Brody & Ge, 2001; Emshoff & others, 1996). In one study, social support (which consisted of good relationships with parents, siblings, adults, and peers) during adolescence substantially reduced drug abuse (Newcomb & Bentler, 1988). In another study, the adolescents were most likely to take drugs

when both of their parents took drugs (such as tranquilizers, amphetamines, alcohol, or nicotine) and when their peers took drugs (Kandel, 1974).

Substance abuse is a serious problem in adolescence. As we see next, eating disorders also can become serious problems in adolescents, especially for females.

Eating Disorders

Two eating disorders that may appear in adolescence are anorexia nervosa and bulimia nervosa.

Anorexia Nervosa

Anorexia nervosa *is an eating disorder that involves the relentless pursuit of thinness through starvation.* Anorexia nervosa eventually can lead to death. Three main characteristics of persons with anorexia nervosa are these (Davison & Neale, 2000):

- Weighing less than 85 percent of what is considered normal for their age and height.
- Having an intense fear of gaining weight. The fear does not decrease with weight loss.
- Having a distorted image of their body shape. Even when they are extremely thin, they see themselves as too fat. They never think they are thin enough, especially in the abdomen, buttocks, and thighs. They usually weigh themselves frequently, often take their body measurements, and gaze critically at themselves in mirrors.

Anorexia nervosa has become an increasing problem for adolescent girls and young adult women. *What are some possible causes of anorexia nervosa?*

Anorexia nervosa typically begins in the early to middle teenage years, often following an episode of dieting and the occurrence of some type of life stress (Kahn & Golden, 2001). It is about ten times more likely in females than in males. When anorexia nervosa does occur in males, the symptoms and other characteristics (such as family conflict) are usually similar to those reported by females who have the disorder (Olivardia & others, 1995).

anorexia nervosa
An eating disorder that involves the relentless pursuit of thinness through starvation.

Most anorexics are White adolescent or young adult females from well-educated, middle- and upper-income families that are competitive and high-achieving. They set high standards, become stressed about not being able to reach the standards, and are intensely concerned about how others perceive them (Striegel-Moore, Silberstein, & Rodin, 1993). Unable to meet these high expectations, they turn to something they can control: their weight.

The fashion image in the American culture that emphasizes "thin is beautiful" contributes to the incidence of anorexia nervosa. This image is reflected in the saying "You never can be too rich or too thin." The media portrays thin as beautiful in their choice of fashion models, which many adolescents girls want to emulate.

Bulimia Nervosa

Anorexics control their eating by restricting it. Most bulimics cannot. **Bulimia nervosa** *is an eating disorder in which the individual consistently follows a binge-and-purge eating pattern.* The bulimic goes on an eating binge and then purges by self-inducing vomiting or using a laxative. Most binge-purge eaters are female in their late teens or early twenties. As with anorexics, most bulimics are preoccupied with food, have a strong fear of becoming overweight, and are depressed or anxious (Davison & Neale, 2000). Unlike anorexia nervosa, the binge-and-purging of bulimia nervosa occurs within a normal weight range, which means that it often is difficult to detect (Mizes & Miller, 2000; Orbanic, 2001).

bulimia nervosa
An eating disorder in which the individual consistently follows a binge-and-purge pattern.

Although many people binge and purge occasionally and some experiment with it, for a person to be considered to have a serious bulimic disorder, the episodes must occur at least twice a week for 3 months. Many bulimics once were somewhat overweight and began binging and purging during an episode of dieting (Schwitzer & others, 2001).

This concludes our discussion of adolescent problems in this chapter. However, in the next chapter we will explore these additional adolescent problems: juvenile delinquency, youth violence, depression, and suicide. Let's now turn our attention to the role of adolescence in the development of health.

Adolescent Health

Adolescent Health Attitudes and Behavior

National Longitudinal Study of Adolescent Health

Adolescent Health

How important is adolescence in the development of health? What are the leading causes of death in adolescence?

Adolescence: A Critical Juncture in Health

Adolescence is a critical juncture in the adoption of behaviors relevant to health (Maggs, Schulenberg, & Hurrelmann, 1997; Roth & Brooks-Gunn, 2000; Spear & Kolbok, 2001). Many of the factors linked to poor health habits and early death in the adult years begin during adolescence.

The early formation of healthy behavioral patterns, such as eating foods low in fat and cholesterol and engaging in regular exercise, not only has immediate health benefits but contributes to the delay or prevention of major causes of premature disability and mortality in adulthood—heart disease, stroke, diabetes, and cancer (Jessor, Turbin, & Costa, 1998, in press).

In a recent comparison of adolescent health behavior in 28 countries, U.S. adolescents exercised less and ate more junk food than adolescents in most other countries (World Health Organization, 2000). Just two-thirds of U.S. adolescents exercised at least twice a week, compared to 80 percent or more of adolescents in Ireland, Austria, Germany, and the Slovak Republic. U.S. adolescents were more likely to eat fried food and less likely to eat fruits and vegetables than adolescents in most other countries studied. U.S. adolescents' eating choices were similar to those of adolescents in England. Eleven-year-olds in the United States were as likely as European 11-year-olds to smoke, but by age 15 U.S. adolescents were less likely to smoke.

Many health experts believe that improving adolescent health involves far more than trips to a doctor's office when sick. The health experts increasingly recognize that whether adolescents will develop a health problem or be healthy is primarily based on their behavior. The goals are to (1) reduce adolescents' *health-compromising behaviors*, such as drug abuse, violence, unprotected sexual intercourse, and dangerous driving, and (2) increase *health-enhancing behaviors*, such as eating nutritiously, exercising, and wearing seat belts.

Leading Causes of Death in Adolescence

Medical improvements have increased the life expectancy of today's adolescents compared to their counterparts who lived earlier in the twentieth century. Still, life-threatening factors continue to exist in adolescents' lives.

The three leading causes of death in adolescence are accidents, suicide, and homicide. More than half of all deaths in adolescents ages 10 to 19 are due to accidents, and most of those involve motor vehicles, especially for older adolescents. Risky driving habits, such as speeding, tailgating, and driving under the influence of alcohol or other drugs, may be more important causes of these accidents than is lack of driving experience. In about 50 percent of the motor vehicle fatalities involving an adolescent, the driver has a blood alcohol level of 0.10 percent, twice the level needed to be "under the influence" in some states. A high rate of intoxication is also often present in adolescents who die as pedestrians or while using recreational vehicles.

Suicide accounts for 6 percent of the deaths in the 10-to-14 age group, a rate of 1.3 per 100,000 population. In the 15-to-19 age group, suicide accounts for 12 percent of deaths or 9 per 100,000 population. Since the 1950s, the adolescent suicide rate has tripled. We will discuss suicide further in the next chapter.

Homicide also is a leading cause of death in adolescence. Homicide is especially high among African American male adolescents, who are three times more likely to be killed by guns than by natural causes (Simons, Finlay, & Yang, 1991).

At this point we have discussed many ideas about adolescent problems and health. To review these ideas, see summary table 12.3. Now that we have examined physical development in adolescence, let's turn our attention to the cognitive changes that characterize adolescence.

Summary Table 12.3
Adolescent Problems and Health

Concept	Processes/ Related Ideas	Characteristics/Descriptions
Substance Use and Abuse	Trends in Overall Drug Use	• The 1960s and 1970s were times of marked increase in the use of illicit drugs. • Drug use began to decline in the 1980s, increased in the mid 1990s, and then declined in the late 1990s. • The United States has the highest adolescent drug use rate of any industrialized nation.
	Alcohol	• Alcohol is a depressant and is the most widely used drug by adolescents. • Alcohol abuse is a major adolescent problem.
	Cigarette Smoking	• Most individuals who smoke cigarettes began this habit in childhood or adolescence. Adolescent cigarette smoking recently has declined, but approximately one-third of high school seniors still smoke cigarettes.
	The Roles of Development, Parents, and Peers	• Drug use in childhood or early adolescence has more detrimental long-term effects than drug use that begins in late adolescence. • Parents and peers can provide important supportive roles in preventing adolescent drug abuse.
Eating disorders	Anorexia Nervosa	• The relentless pursuit of thinness through starvation.
	Bulimia Nervosa	• The individual consistently follows a binge-and-purge pattern of eating.
Adolescent Health	Adolescence: A Critical Juncture in Health	• Adolescence is an important time in the development of healthy or unhealthy health patterns. • Compared to adolescents in most other countries, U.S. adolescents exercise less and eat more junk food. • Health goals for adolescents include reducing health-compromising behaviors and increasing health-enhancing behaviors.
	Leading Causes of Death in Adolescence	• In order, they are accidents, suicide, and homicide.

Adolescent Cognition

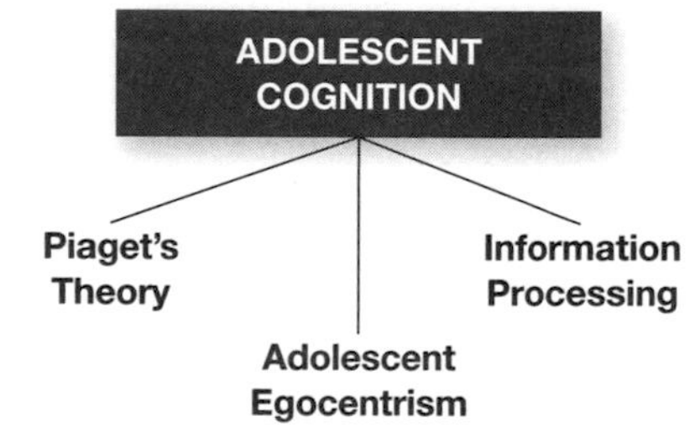

Adolescents' developing power of thought opens up new cognitive and social horizons. Let's examine what their developing power of thought is like, beginning with Piaget's theory.

Piaget's Theory

What are Jean Piaget's ideas about cognitive development in adolescence? To answer this question, we will study Piaget's stage of formal operational thought P. 35.

Most significantly, formal operational thought is more *abstract* than concrete operational thought. Adolescents are no longer limited to actual, concrete experiences as anchors for thought. They can conjure up make-believe situations, events that are purely hypothetical possibilities or strictly abstract propositions, and can try to reason logically about them.

The abstract quality of the adolescent's thought at the formal operational level is evident in the adolescent's verbal problem-solving ability. Whereas the concrete operational thinker needs to see the concrete elements A, B, and C to be able to make the logical inference that, if A = B and B = C, then A = C, the formal operational thinker can solve this problem merely through verbal presentation.

> *The thoughts of youth are long, long thoughts.*
>
> Henry Wadsworth Longfellow
> *American Poet, 19th Century*

Another indication of the abstract quality of adolescents' thought is their increased tendency to think about thought itself. One adolescent commented, "I began thinking about why I was thinking what I was. Then I began thinking about why I was thinking about what I was thinking about what I was." If this sounds abstract, it is, and it characterizes the adolescent's enhanced focus on thought and its abstract qualities.

Accompanying the abstract nature of formal operational thought in adolescence is thought full of idealism and possibilities. While children frequently think in concrete ways, or in terms of what is real and limited, adolescents begin to engage in extended speculation about ideal characteristics—qualities they desire in themselves and in others. Such thoughts often lead adolescents to compare themselves with others in regard to such ideal standards. And, during adolescence, the thoughts of individuals are often fantasy flights into future possibilities. It is not unusual for the adolescent to become impatient with these newfound ideal standards and to become perplexed over which of many ideal standards to adopt.

At the same time that adolescents think more abstractly and idealistically, they also think more logically. Adolescents begin to think more as a scientist thinks, devising plans to solve problems and systematically testing solutions. This type of problem solving has an imposing name. **Hypothetical-deductive reasoning** *is Piaget's formal operational concept that adolescents have the cognitive ability to develop hypotheses, or best guesses, about ways to solve problems, such as an algebraic equation. Then they systematically deduce, or conclude, which is the best path to follow in solving the equation.* By contrast, children are more likely to solve problems in a trial-and-error fashion.

hypothetical-deductive reasoning
Piaget's formal operational concept that adolescents have the cognitive ability to develop hypotheses, or best guesses, about ways to solve problems, such as an algebraic equation.

One example of hypothetical-deductive reasoning involves a modification of the familiar game Twenty Questions. Individuals are shown a set of 42 color pictures, displayed in a rectangular array (six rows of seven pictures each) and are asked to determine which picture the experimenter has in mind (that is, which is "correct"). The subjects are allowed to ask only questions to which the experimenter can answer yes or no. The object of the game is to select the correct picture by asking as few questions as possible. Adolescents who are deductive hypothesis testers formulate a plan and test a series of hypotheses, which considerably narrows the field of choices. The most effective plan is a "halving" strategy (*Q:* Is the picture in the right half of the array? *A:* No. *Q:* OK. Is it in the top half? And so on.). A correct halving strategy guarantees the answer in seven questions or less. By contrast, concrete operational thinkers may persist with questions that continue to test some of the same possibilities that previous questions could have eliminated. For example, they may ask whether the correct picture is in row 1 and are told that it is not. Later, they ask whether the picture is *x,* which is in row 1.

Thus, formal opertional thinkers test their hypotheses with judiciously chosen questions and tests. By contrast, concrete operational thinkers often fail to understand the relation between a hypothesis and a well-chosen test of it, stubbornly clinging to ideas that already have been discounted.

Piaget believed that formal operational thought is the best description of how adolescents think. A summary of the characteristics of formal operational thought is shown in figure 12.5. As we will see next, though, formal operational thought is not a homogeneous stage of development.

Some of Piaget's ideas on formal operational thought are being challenged (Kuhn, 2000; Overton & Byrnes, 1991). There is much more individual variation in formal operational thought than Piaget envisioned. Only about one in three young adolescents is a formal operational thinker. Many American adults never become formal operational thinkers, and neither do many adults in other cultures. Education in the logic of science and

Critical Thinking

Piaget, Children, Adolescents, and Political Conventions

SUPPOSE AN 8-year-old and a 16-year-old are watching a political convention on television. In view of where each child is likely to be in terms of Piaget's stages of cognitive development, how would their perceptions of the proceedings likely differ? What would the 8-year-old "see" and comprehend? What Piagetian changes would these differences reflect?

Abstract
Adolescents think more abstractly than children. Formal operational thinkers can solve abstract algebraic equations, for example.
Idealistic
Adolescents often think about what is possible. They think about ideal characteristics of themselves, others, and the world.
Logical
Adolescents begin to think more like scientists, devising plans to solve problems and systematically testing solutions. Piaget called this type of logical thinking "hypothetical-deductive reasoning."

Figure **12.5**

Characteristics of Formal Operational Thought

Adolescents begin to think in more abstract, idealistic, and logical ways than when they were children.

mathematics is an important cultural experience that promotes the development of formal operational thinking.

Also, for adolescents who become formal operational thinkers, assimilation (incorporating new information into existing knowledge) dominates the initial development of formal operational thought, and the world is perceived subjectively and idealistically. Later in adolescence, as intellectual balance is restored, these individuals accommodate (adjust to new information) to the cognitive upheaval that has occurred.

In addition to thinking more logically, abstractly, and idealistically, which characterize Piaget's formal operational thought stage, in what other ways does adolescent cognition change? One important way involves adolescent egocentrism.

The error of youth is to believe that intelligence is a substitute for experience, while the error of age is to believe that experience is a substitute for intelligence.

Lyman Bryson
American Author, 20th Century

Adolescent Egocentrism

"Oh, my gosh! I can't believe it. Help! I can't stand it!" Tracy desperately yells. "What is wrong? What is the matter?" her mother asks. Tracy responds, "Everyone in here is looking at me." The mother queries, "Why?" Tracy says, "Look, this one hair just won't stay in place," as she rushes to the rest room of the restaurant. Five minutes later, she returns to the table in the restaurant after she has depleted an entire can of hair spray.

During a conversation between two 14-year-old girls, the one named Margaret says, "Are you kidding, I won't get pregnant." And, 13-year-old Adam describes himself, "No one understand me, particularly my parents. They have no idea of what I am feeling."

Adolescent egocentrism *is the heightened self-consciousness of adolescents.* David Elkind (1976) believes that adolescent egocentrism can be dissected into two types

adolescent egocentrism
The heightened self-consciousness of adolescents.

imaginary audience
Adolescents' belief that others are as interested in them as they themselves are; attention-getting behavior motivated by a desire to be noticed, visible, and "on stage."

personal fable
The part of adolescent egocentrism that involves an adolescent's sense of uniqueness and invincibility.

of social thinking—imaginary audience and personal fable. The notion of **imaginary audience** *involves adolescents' belief that others are as interested in them as they themselves are, as well as attention-getting behavior—attempts to be noticed, visible, and "on stage."* Tracy's comments and behavior that we described in the first paragraph of this section reflect the imaginary audience. Another adolescent might think that others are as aware of a small spot on his trousers as he is, possibly knowing that he has masturbated. Another adolescent, an eighth-grade girl, walks into her classroom and thinks that all eyes are riveted on her complexion. Adolescents especially sense that they are "on stage" in early adolescence, believing they are the main actors and all others are the audience.

According to Elkind, the **personal fable** *is the part of adolescent egocentrism involving an adolescent's sense of uniqueness and invincibility.* The comments of Margaret and Adam, mentioned earlier, reflect the personal fable. Adolescents' sense of personal uniqueness makes them feel that no one can understand how they really feel. For example, an adolescent girl thinks that her mother cannot possibly sense the hurt she feels because her boyfriend has broken up with her. As part of their effort to retain a sense of personal uniqueness, adolescents might craft a story about the self that is filled with fantasy, immersing themselves in a world that is far removed from reality. Personal fables frequently show up in adolescent diaries.

Adolescents also often show a sense of invincibility, believing that they themselves will never suffer the terrible experiences (such as deadly car wrecks) that can happen to other people. This sense of invincibility likely is involved in the reckless behavior of some adolescents, such as drag racing, drug use, suicide, and having sexual intercourse without using contraceptives or barriers against STDs.

Information Processing

Two of the most important aspects of changes in information processing in adolescence involve decision making and critical thinking.

Many adolescent girls spend long hours in front of the mirror, depleting cans of hair-spray, tubes of lipstick, and jars of cosmetics. *How might this behavior be related to changes in adolescent cognitive and physical development?*

Decision Making Adolescence is a time of increased decision making—about the future, which friends to choose, whether to go to college, which person to date, whether to have sex, whether to buy a car, and so on (Byrnes, 1997; Galotti & Kozberg, 1996; Kuhn, 2000). How competent are adolescents at making decisions? In some reviews, older adolescents are described as more competent than younger adolescents, who, in turn, are more competent than children (Keating, 1990). Compared to children, young adolescents are more likely to generate options, to examine a situation from a variety of perspectives, to anticipate the consequences of decisions, and to consider the credibility of sources.

The ability to make competent decisions does not guarantee that they will be made in everyday life, where breadth of experience often comes into play (Jacobs & Potenza, 1990; Keating, 1990). For example, driver-training courses improve adolescents' cognitive and motor skills to levels equal to, or sometimes superior to, those of adults. However, driver training has not been effective in reducing adolescents' high rate of traffic accidents (Potvin, Champagne, & Laberge-Nadeau, 1988). An important research agenda is to study the ways adolescents make decisions in practical situations.

Another strategy is for parents to involve their adolescents in appropriate decision-making activities. In one study of more than 900 young adolescents and a subsample of their parents, adolescents were more likely to participate in family decision making when they perceived themselves as in control

of what happens to them and if they thought that their input would have some bearing on the outcome of the decision-making process (Liprie, 1993).

Critical Thinking Adolescence is an important transitional period in the development of critical thinking (Keating, 1990). Among the cognitive changes that allow improved critical thinking in adolescence are:

- Increased speed, automaticity, and capacity of information processing, which free cognitive resources for other purposes
- More breadth of content knowledge in a variety of domains
- Increased ability to construct new combinations of knowledge
- A greater range and more spontaneous use of strategies or procedures for applying or obtaining knowledge, such as planning, considering alternatives, and cognitive monitoring

Although driver-training courses can improve adolescents' cognitive and motor skills related to driving, these courses have not been effective in reducing adolescents' high rate of traffic accidents. *Why might this be so?*

Although adolescence is an important period in the development of critical-thinking skills, if a solid basis of fundamental skills (such as literacy and math skills) is not developed during childhood, such critical-thinking skills are unlikely to mature in adolescence ◄ P. 288. For the subset of adolescents who lack such fundamental skills, potential gains in adolescent thinking are not likely.

In one recent study of fifth-, eighth-, and eleventh-graders, critical thinking increased with age but still only occurred in 43 percent of even the eleventh-graders, and many adolescents showed self-serving biases in their reasoning (Klaczynski & Narasimham, 1998).

At this point we have discussed a number of ideas about cognitive development in adolescence. To review these ideas, see summary table 12.4. Next, we will turn our attention to schools and their effects on adolescent development.

Schools

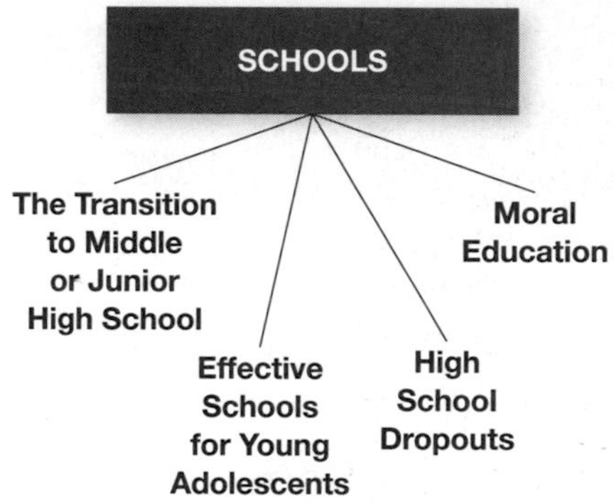

The impressive changes in adolescents' cognition lead us to examine the nature of schools for adolescents. In chapter 11, we discussed different ideas about the effects of schools on children's development ◄ P. 334. Here, we will focus more exclusively on the nature of secondary schools. Questions we will look at include these: What is the transition from elementary to middle or junior high school like? What are effective schools for young adolescents?

The Transition to Middle or Junior High School

The emergence of junior high schools in the 1920s and 1930s was justified on the basis of the physical, cognitive, and social changes that characterize early adolescence, as well as the need for more schools for the growing student population. Old high schools became junior high schools, and new regional high schools were built. In most systems, the ninth grade remained a part of the high school in content, although physically separated from it in a 6-3-3 system. Gradually, the ninth grade was restored to the high school, as many school systems developed middle schools that include the seventh and eighth grades, or sixth, seventh, and eighth grades. The creation of middle schools was influenced by the earlier onset of puberty in recent decades.

One worry of educators and psychologists is that junior high and middle schools have simply become watered-down versions of high schools, mimicking their curricular and extracurricular schedules. The critics argue that unique curricular and extracurricular activities reflecting a wide range of individual differences in biological and psychological development in early adolescence should be incorporated into

SUMMARY TABLE 12.4
Adolescent Cognition

Concept	Processes/ Related Ideas	Characteristics/Description
Piaget's Theory	Formal Operational Thought	• Abstractness and idealism, as well as hypothetical-deductive reasoning, are highlighted in formal operational thought. • Formal operational thought involves the ability to reason about what is possible and hypothetical, as opposed to what is real, and the ability to reflect on one's own thoughts. • Formal operational thought occurs in two phases—an assimilation phase, in which reality is overwhelmed (early adolescence), and an accommodation phase, in which intellectual balance is restored through a consolidation of formal operational thought (middle years of adolescence).
	Variations	• Individual variation is extensive, and Piaget did not give this adequate attention. • Many young adolescents are not formal operational thinkers but, rather, are consolidating their concrete operational thought.
Adolescent Egocentrism	Imaginary Audience and Personal Fable	• Elkind proposed that adolescents, especially young adolescents, develop an egocentrism that involves both the construction of an imaginary audience (the belief that others are as preoccupied with the adolescent as the adolescent is) and a personal fable (a sense of personal uniqueness and invulnerability).
Information Processing	Decision Making	• Adolescence is a time of increased decision making. • The ability to make competent decisions does not guarantee that such decisions will be made in everyday life, where breadth of experience comes into play.
	Critical Thinking	• Adolescence is an important transitional period in critical thinking because of such cognitive changes as increased speed, automaticity, and capacity of information processing; more breadth of content knowledge; increased ability to construct new combinations of knowledge; and a greater range and spontaneous use of strategies.

our junior high and middle schools. The critics also stress that many high schools foster passivity rather than autonomy and that schools should create a variety of pathways for students to achieve an identity.

The transition to middle school or junior high school from elementary schools interests developmentalists because, even though it is a normative experience for virtually all children, the transition can be stressful (Eccles, 2000; Seidman, 2000). Why? The transition takes place at a time when many changes—in the individual, in the family, and in school—are occurring simultaneously. These changes include puberty and related concerns about body image; the emergence of at least some aspects of formal operational thought, including accompanying changes in social cognition; increased responsibility and independence in association with decreased dependency on parents; change from a small, contained classroom structure to a larger, more impersonal school structure; change from one teacher to many teachers and from a small, homogeneous set of peers to a larger, more heterogeneous set of peers; and an increased focus on achievement and performance and their assessment. This list includes a number of negative, stressful features, but there can be positive aspects to the transition. Students are more likely to feel grown up, have more subjects from which to select, have more opportunities to spend time with peers and to locate compatible friends, and enjoy increased independence from direct parental monitoring, and they may be more challenged intellectually by academic work.

WWW

Schools for Adolescents

National Center for Education Statistics

United States Department of Education

Middle Schools

The transition from elementary to middle or junior high school occurs at the same time as a number of other developmental changes. *What are some of these other developmental changes?*

When students make the transition from elementary school to middle or junior high school, they experience the **top-dog phenomenon,** *the circumstance of moving from the top position (in elementary school, being the oldest, biggest, and most powerful students in the school) to the lowest position (in middle or junior high school, being the youngest, smallest, and least powerful students in the school).* Researchers who have charted the transition from elementary to middle or junior high school find that the first year of middle or junior high school can be difficult for many students (Hawkins & Berndt, 1985). For example, in one study of the transition from sixth grade in an elementary school to the seventh grade in a junior high school, adolescents' perceptions of the quality of their school life plunged in the seventh grade (Hirsch & Rapkin, 1987). In the seventh grade, the students were less satisfied with school, were less committed to school, and liked their teachers less. The drop in school satisfaction occurred regardless of how academically successful the students were.

top-dog phenomenon
The circumstance of moving from the top position in elementary school to the lowest position in middle or junior high school.

Effective Schools for Young Adolescents

What makes a successful middle school? Joan Lipsitz (1984) and her colleagues searched the nation for the best middle schools. Extensive contacts and observations were made. Based on the recommendations of education experts and observations in schools in different parts of the United States, four middle schools were chosen for their outstanding ability to educate young adolescents. What were these middle schools like? The most striking feature was their willingness and ability to adapt all school practices to their students' individual differences in physical, cognitive, and social development. The schools took seriously the knowledge we have developed about young adolescents. This seriousness was reflected in the decisions about different aspects of school life. For example, one middle school fought to keep its schedule of minicourses on Friday, so that every student could be with friends and pursue personal interests. Two other middle schools expended considerable energy on a complex school organization, so that small groups of students worked with small groups of teachers who could vary the tone and pace of the school day, depending on the students' needs. Another middle school developed an advisory scheme, so that each student had daily contact with an adult who was willing to listen, explain, comfort,

What does education often do? It makes a straight-cut ditch of a free, meandering brook.

Henry David Thoreau
American Poet, Essayist, 19th Century

Careers in Life-Span Development

Armando Ronquillo, High School Counselor/College Advisor

Armando Ronquillo is a high school counselor and college advisor at Pueblo High School, which is in a low-socioeconomic-status area in Tucson, Arizona. More than 85 percent of the students have a Latino background. Armando was named top high-school counselor in the state of Arizona for the year 2000. He has especially helped to increase the number of Pueblo High School students who go to college.

Armando has an undergraduate degree in elementary and special education, and a master's degree in counseling. He counsels the students on the merits of staying in school and on the lifelong opportunities provided by a college education. Armando guides students in obtaining the academic preparation that will enable them to go to college, including how to apply for financial aid and scholarships. He also works with parents to help them understand that "their child going to college is not only doable but also affordable."

Armando works with students on setting goals and planning. He has students plan for the future in terms of 1-year (short-term), 5-year (mid-range), and 10-plus-year (long-term) time periods. Armando says he does this "to help students visualize how the educational plans and decisions they make today will affect them in the future." He also organizes a number of college campus visitations for students from Pueblo High School each year.

Armando Ronquillo, counseling a Latina high school student about college.

and prod the adolescent. Such school policies reflect thoughtfulness and personal concern about individuals who have compelling developmental needs.

Another aspect of the effective middle schools was that early in their existence—the first year in three of the schools and the second year in the fourth school—they emphasized the importance of creating an environment that was positive for adolescents' social and emotional development. This goal was established not only because such environments contribute to academic excellence but also because social and emotional development were valued as intrinsically important in adolescents' schooling.

Recognizing that the vast majority of middle schools do not approach the excellent schools described by Joan Lipsitz (1984), in 1989 the Carnegie Corporation issued an extremely negative evaluation of our nation's middle schools. In the report, "Turning Points: Preparing American Youth for the 21st Century," the conclusion was put forth that most young adolescents attend massive, impersonal schools, learn from seemingly irrelevant curricula, trust few adults in school, and lack access to health care and counseling. The Carnegie Corporation (1989) report recommended the following:

- Develop smaller "communities" or "houses" to lessen the impersonal nature of large middle schools.
- Lower student-to-counselor ratios from several hundred-to-1 to 10-to-1.
- Involve parents and community leaders in schools.
- Develop curricula that produce students who are literate, understand the sciences, and have a sense of health, ethics, and citizenship.
- Have teachers team teach in more flexibly designed curriculum blocks that integrate several disciplines, instead of presenting students with disconnected, rigidly separated 50-minute segments.
- Boost students' health and fitness with more in-school programs and help students who need public health care to get it.

In sum, middle schools throughout the nation need a major redesign if they are to be effective in educating adolescents for becoming competent adults in the twenty-first century.

High School Dropouts

For many decades, dropping out of high school has been viewed as a serious educational and societal problem. By leaving high school before graduating, many dropouts take with them educational deficiencies that severely curtail their economic and social well-being throughout their adult lives.

In the last half of the twentieth century, high school dropout rates declined overall (Digest of Education Statistics, 1999). For example, in the 1940s, more than half of American youth did not finish high school. Today, only 11.8 percent of individuals in the United States have not finished high school. More than 90 percent of White non-Latino youth graduate from high school in the United States today. The African

American dropout rate has been cut in half in the last 30 years—from 28 percent in 1970 to less than 14 percent today. However, the Latino dropout rate has not followed suit—today it is at 30 percent, virtually the same as it was in 1975. The highest dropout rate in the United States, though, occurs for Native American youth—only about 10 percent finish their high school education.

Students drop out of schools for many reasons (Jacobs, Garnier, & Weisner, 1996). In one study, almost 50 percent of the dropouts cited school-related reasons for leaving school, such as not liking school or being expelled or suspended (Rumberger, 1995). Twenty percent of the dropouts (but 40 percent of the Latino students) cited economic reasons for leaving school. One-third of the female students dropped out for personal reasons, such as pregnancy or marriage.

Not only is the school drop out rate of Latinos a concern, so is their low rate of going to college. In one recent study, African-American adolescents were more likely to have U.S.-born, college-educated parents while Latino adolescents were more likely to have immigrant parents with a high school education or less (Cooper & others, 2001). In this study, resources and challenges across social worlds (parents' and teachers' help and siblings' challenges) were positively linked with adolescents' higher grade point average, eligibility, and admission to more prestigious colleges.

In another recent study, it was concluded that U.S. schools are especially doing a poor job of meeting the needs of America's fastest-growing minority population—Latinas (Ginorio & Huston, 2001). The study focused on how Latinas' futures—or "possible selves"—are influenced by their families' culture, peers, teachers, and media. In the investigation, many high school counselors viewed success as "going away to college" yet some Latinas, because of family responsibilities, believe it is important to stay close to home. The high school graduation rate for Latinas lags behind that for girls of any other ethnic minority group. Latinas also are less likely to take the SAT exam than other ethnic group females. Thus, a better effort needs to be made at encouraging Latinas' academic success and involving the Latina adolescent's family in the process of college preparation.

Are American secondary schools different from those in other countries? To read about this, see the Sociocultural Worlds of Development box.

These adolescents participate in the "I Have a Dream" (IHAD) program, a comprehensive, long-term dropout prevention program that has been very successful. Local IHAD projects around the country "adopt" entire grades (usually the third or fourth) from public elementary schools, or corresponding age-cohorts from public housing developments. These children—"Dreamers"—are then provided with a program of academic, social, cultural, and recreational activities throughout their elementary, middle school, and high school years.

Reducing the Dropout Rate

High School Education

Moral Development and Education

Moral Education

In previous chapters we discussed various aspects of moral development, including Piaget's theory in chapter 9, "Socioemotional Development in Early Childhood," and Kohlberg's theory in chapter 11, "Socioemotional Development in Middle and Late Childhood." Here we will focus on the cognitive approach to moral education, which is based on Kohlberg's theory.

The Hidden Curriculum More than 60 years ago, educator John Dewey (1933) recognized that, even when schools do not have specific programs in moral education, they provide moral education through a "hidden curriculum." The **hidden curriculum** *is conveyed by the moral atmosphere that is a part of every school.* The moral atmosphere is created by school and classroom rules, the moral orientation of teachers and school administrators, and text materials. Teachers serve as models of ethical or unethical behavior. Classroom rules and peer relations at

hidden curriculum
Dewey's concept that every school has a pervasive moral atmosphere, even if it doesn't have a program of moral education.

Sociocultural Worlds of Development

Cross-Cultural Comparisons of Secondary Schools

Secondary schools in different countries share a number of features, but differ on others (Cameron & others, 1983). Let's explore the similarities and differences in secondary schools in six countries: Australia, Brazil, Germany, Japan, Russia, and the United States.

Most countries mandate that children begin school at 6 to 7 years of age and stay in school until they are 14 to 17 years of age. Brazil requires students to go to school only until they are 14 years of age, while Russia mandates that students stay in school until they are 17. Germany, Japan, Australia, and the United States require school attendance until 15 to 16 years of age.

Most secondary schools around the world are divided into two or more levels, such as middle school (or junior high school) and high school. However, Germany's schools are divided according to three educational ability tracks: (1) The main school provides a basic level of education, (2) the middle school gives students a more advanced education, and (3) the academic school prepares students for entrance to a university. German schools, like most European schools, offer a classical education, which includes courses in Latin and Greek.

Japanese secondary schools have an entrance exam, but secondary schools in the other five countries do not. Only Australia and Germany have comprehensive exit exams.

The United States is the only country in the world in which sports are an integral part of the public school system. Only a few private schools in other countries have their own sports teams, sports facilities, and highly organized sports events.

Curriculum is often similar in secondary schools in different countries, although there are some differences in content and philosophy. For example, at least until recently, the secondary schools in Russia have emphasized the preparation of students for work. The "labor education program," which is part of the secondary school curriculum, includes vocational training and on-the-job experience. The idea is to instill in youth a love for manual work and a positive attitude about industrial and work organizations. Russian students who are especially gifted—academically, artistically, or athletically—attend special schools where they are encouraged to develop their talents and are trained to be the very best in their vocation. With the breakup of the Soviet Union, it will be interesting to follow what changes in education take place in Russia.

In Brazil, students are required to take Portuguese (the native language) and four foreign languages (Latin, French, English, and Spanish). Brazil requires these languages because of the country's international character and emphasis on trade and commerce. Seventh-grade students in Australia take courses in sheep husbandry and weaving, two areas of economic and cultural interest in the country. In Japan, students take a number of Western courses in addition to their basic Japanese courses; these courses include Western literature and languages (in addition to Japanese literature and language), Western physical education (in addition to Japanese martial arts classes), and Western sculpture and handicrafts (in addition to Japanese calligraphy). The Japanese school year is also much longer than that of other countries (225 days versus 180 days in the United States, for example).

The juku, or "cramming school," is available to Japanese children and adolescents in the summertime and after school. It provides coaching to help them improve their grades and their entrance exam scores for high schools and universities. The Japanese practice of requiring an entrance exam for high school is a rarity among the nations of the world.

school transmit attitudes about cheating, lying, stealing, and consideration of others. And, through its rules and regulations, the school administration infuses the school with a value system.

Character Education

Character education *is a direct approach that involves teaching students a basic moral literacy to prevent them from engaging in immoral behavior and doing harm to themselves or others.* The argument is that such behaviors as lying, stealing, and cheating are wrong, and students should be taught this throughout their education. Every school should have an explicit moral code that is clearly communicated to students. Any violations of the code should be met with sanctions (Bennett, 1993). Instruction in specified moral concepts, such as cheating, can take the form of example and definition, class discussions and role playing, or rewarding students for proper behavior.

character education
A direct approach to moral education that involves teaching students a basic moral literacy to prevent them from engaging in immoral behavior and doing harm to themselves and others.

Some character education movements are the Character Education Partnership, the Character Education Network, the Aspen Declaration on Character Education, and the publicity campaign "Character Counts." Among the books that promote character education are William Bennett's (1993) *The Book of Virtues* and William Damon's (1995) *Greater Expectations.*

The Character Counts Coalition, which represents almost 100 organizations and 40 million Americans, recommends that children be taught six core values (Myers, 2000):

- Be trustworthy
- Treat people with respect
- Be responsible
- Be fair
- Be caring
- Be a good citizen

Values Clarification

Values clarification *means helping people clarify what their lives are for and what is worth working for.* In this approach, students are encouraged to define their own values and understand the values of others. Values clarification differs from character education in that students are not told what their values should be.

values clarification
An approach to moral education that emphasizes helping people clarify what their lives are for and what is worth working for. Students are encouraged to define their own values and to understand the values of others.

In the following values clarification exercise, students are asked to select from among 10 people the 6 who should be allowed to enter a safe shelter because a third world war has broken out (Johnson, 1990):

> You work for a government agency in Washington and your group has to decide which six of the following ten people will be admitted to a small fallout shelter. Your group has only 20 minutes to make the decision. These are your choices:
>
> - A 30-year-old male bookkeeper
> - The bookkeeper's wife, who is 6 months pregnant
> - A second-year African American male medical student who is a political activist
> - A 42-year-old male who is a famous historian-author
> - A Hollywood actress who is a singer and dancer
> - A female biochemist
> - A 54-year-old male Rabbi
> - A male Olympic athlete who is good in all sports
> - A female college student
> - A policeman with a gun

In this type of values clarification exercise, there are no right or wrong answers. The clarification of values is left up to the individual student. Advocates of values clarification say it is value-free. However, critics argue that is controversial content offends community standards. They also say that, because of its relativistic nature, values clarification undermines accepted values and fails to stress right behavior.

Shown here is an adolescent who has volunteered to work in the National Helpers Network. This program gives students an opportunity to participate in service learning. Among the services provided are helping with environmental concerns, improving neighborhoods, and tutoring. Students also participate in weekly seminars that encourage them to reflect on their active involvement in the community. For more information about the National Helpers Network, call 212-679-7461

cognitive moral education
An approach to moral education based on the belief that students should develop such values as democracy and justice as their moral reasoning develops; Kohlberg's theory has been the basis of a number of cognitive moral education programs.

Cognitive Moral Education **Cognitive moral education** *is a concept based on the belief that students should learn to value such things as democracy and justice as their moral reasoning develops.* Lawrence Kohlberg's theory, which we discussed in chapter 11, has been the basis for a number of cognitive moral education programs ◄ P. 315. In a typical program, high school students meet in a semester-long course to discuss a number of moral issues. The instructor acts as a facilitator, rather than as a director, of the class. The hope is that students will develop more advanced notions of such concepts as cooperation, trust, responsibility, and community. Toward the end of his career, Kohlberg (1986) recognized that the moral atmosphere of the school is more important than he initially envisioned. For example, in one study, a semester-long moral education class based on Kohlberg's theory was successful in advancing moral thinking in there democratic schools, but not in three authoritarian schools (Higgins, Power, & Kohlberg, 1983).

service learning
A form of education that promotes social responsibility and service to the community.

Service Learning **Service learning** *is a form of education that promotes social responsibility and service to the community.* In service learning, students might engage in tutoring, help the elderly, work in a hospital, assist at a day-care center, or clean up a vacant lot to make a play area. An important goal of service learning is for students to become less self-centered and more motivated to help others (Waterman, 1997).

Service learning takes education out into the community (Levesque & Prosser, 1996). One eleventh-grade student worked as a reading tutor for students from low-income homes who had reading skills well below their grade levels. She commented that, until she did the tutoring, she didn't realize how many students had not experienced the same opportunities she had had when she was growing up. An especially rewarding moment was when one young girl told her, "I want to learn to read like you do so I can go to college when I grow up." Thus, service learning can benefit not only the students but also the recipients of their help.

Service Learning

It is one of the beautiful compensations of life that no one can sincerely try to help another without helping himself.

Charles Warner
American Novelist, 19th Century

Researchers have found that service learning benefits students in a number of ways:

- Their grades improve, they become more motivated, and they set more goals (Johnson & others, 1998).

Summary Table 12.5
Schools

Concept	Processes/ Related Ideas	Characteristics/Descriptions
Transition to Middle or Junior High School	Top-Dog Phenomenon	• The emergence of junior highs in the 1920s and 1930s was justified on the basis of physical, cognitive, and social changes in early adolescence and the need for more schools in response to a growing student population. Middle schools have become more popular in recent years and coincide with puberty's earlier arrival. • The transition to middle or junior high school coincides with many social, familial, and individual changes in the adolescent's life. The transition involves moving from the top-dog to the lowest position.
Effective Schools for Young Adolescents	Socioemotional and Cognitive Emphasis	• Successful schools for young adolescents take individual differences in development seriously, show a deep concern for what is known about early adolescence, and emphasize social and emotional development as much as intellectual development. • In 1989, the Carnegie Corporation recommended a major redesign of middle schools.
High School Dropouts	General Improvement in Rates	• The dropout rate overall declined considerably in the last half of the twentieth century. The dropout rates for Latino and Native American youth are still very high.
Moral Education	The Hidden Curriculum	• The hidden curriculum involves the belief that every school has a moral atmosphere.
	Character Education	• Character education is a direct education approach that advocates teaching students a basic moral literacy.
	Values Clarification	• Values clarification emphasizes helping students clarify what their lives are for and what is worth working for.
	Cognitive Moral Education	• Cognitive moral education states that students should develop such values as democracy and justice as their moral reasoning develops. Kohlberg's theory has been the basis of a number of cognitive moral education programs.
	Service Learning	• Service learning involves educational experiences that promote social responsibility and service to the community. Researchers have found that service learning benefits students in a number of ways.

- Their self-esteem improves (Hamburg, 1997).
- They become less alienated (Calabrese & Schumer, 1986).
- They increasingly reflect on society's political organization and moral order (Yates, 1995).

Required community service has increased in high schools. In one survey, 15 percent of the nation's largest school districts had such a requirement (National and Community Service Coalition, 1995). Even though required community service has increased in high schools, in another survey of 40,000 adolescents, two thirds said they had never done any volunteer work to help other people (Benson, 1993). The benefits of service learning, for both the volunteer and the recipient, suggest that more adolescents should be required to participate in such programs.

At this point we have studied a number of ideas about schools for adolescents. To review these ideas, see summary table 12.5. In the next chapter we will continue to explore adolescent development by focusing on socioemotional changes.

Chapter Review

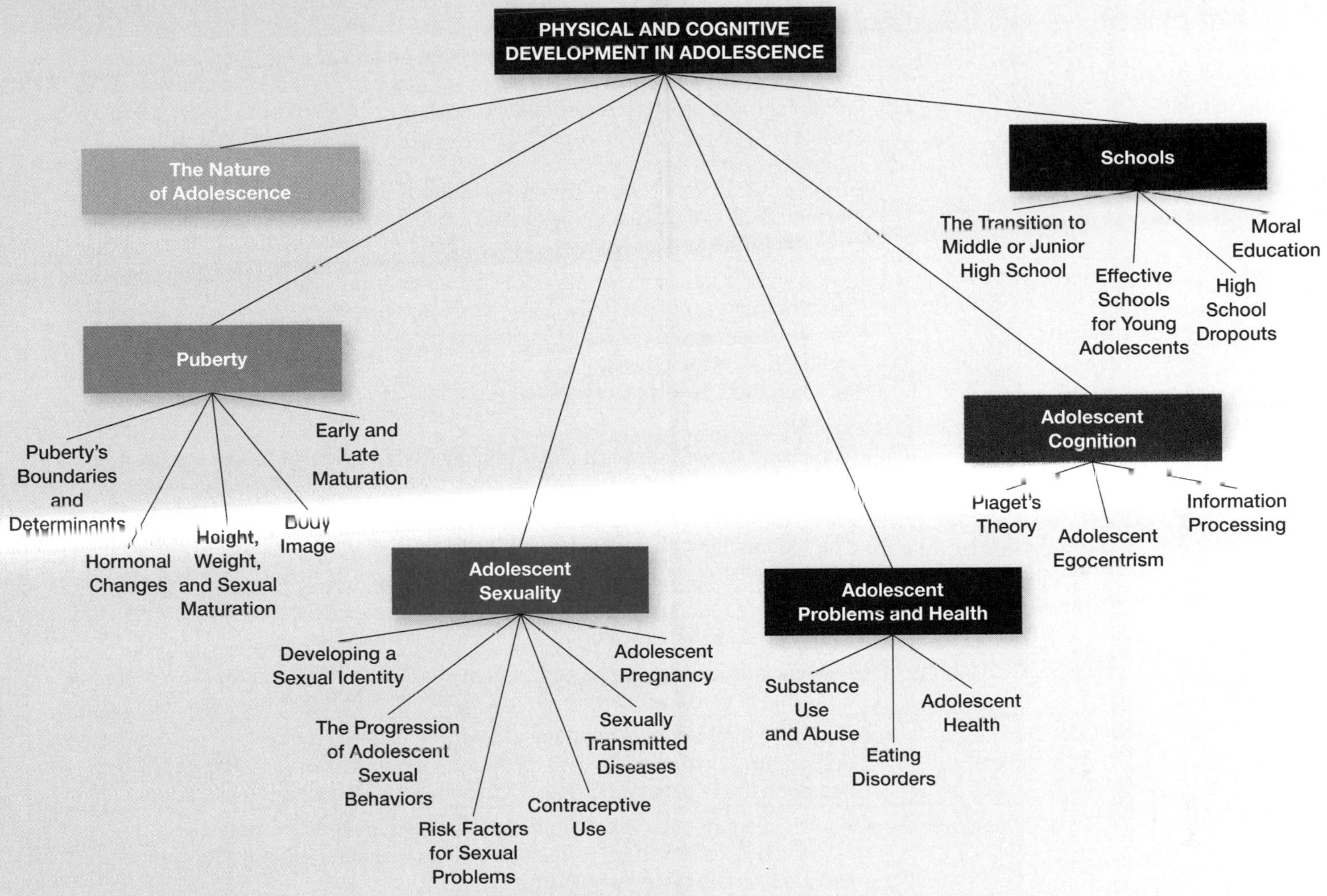

TO OBTAIN A DETAILED REVIEW OF THIS CHAPTER, STUDY THESE FIVE SUMMARY TABLES:

- Summary Table 12.1 — The Nature of Adolescence and Puberty — page 354
- Summary Table 12.2 — Adolescent Sexuality — page 360
- Summary Table 12.3 — Adolescent Problems and Health — page 365
- Summary Table 12.4 — Adolescent Cognition — page 370
- Summary Table 12.5 — Schools — page 377

Key Terms

puberty 349
menarche 349
hormones 350
hypothalamus 350
pituitary gland 350
gonads 350
sexually transmitted diseases (STDs) 357
anorexia nervosa 363
bulimia nervosa 363
hypothetical-deductive reasoning 366
adolescent egocentrism 367
imaginary audience 368
personal fable 368
top-dog phenomenon 371
hidden curriculum 373
character education 375
values clarification 375
cognitive moral education 376
service learning 376

Key People

Lloyd Johnston, Patrick O'Malley, & Gerald Bachman 359
Jean Piaget 365
David Elkind 367
Joan Lipsitz 372
Lawrence Kohlberg 376

Taking It to the Net

1. Sharon wonders why so much of the talk about adolescent pregnancy focuses on the girl's motivation and behavior. What about the guys, she wonders. What are the risk factors that account for teenage pregnancy
2. Jared is the student member of his high school's substance abuse awareness educational forum. He has been asked to address the incoming freshman on the latest statistics about teen use of tobacco, marijuana, cocaine, heroin, alcohol, and methamphetamine. What information should his report focus on to best educate the group?
3. Mrs. Rice, an elementary school principal, wants to help prepare her fourth-grade students for transition to middle-school. What can parents, teachers, and students do to prepare for a smooth transition and cause the least amount of upheaval for the child?

Connect to www.mhhe.com/santrockld8 to research the answers and complete these exercises.

OLC Preview

To further test your knowledge of this chapter or to explore our extensive online resources that accompany *Life-Span Development,* eighth edition, please log on to the text's Online Learning Center at http://www.mhhe.com/santrockld8.com.

Chapter 13

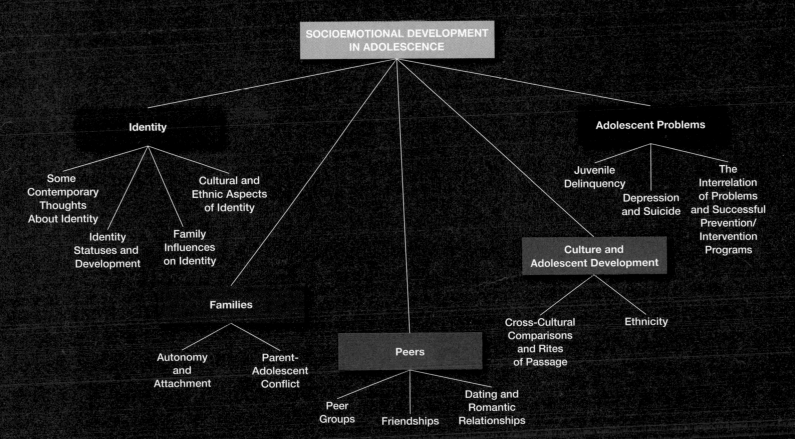

SOCIOEMOTIONAL DEVELOPMENT IN ADOLESCENCE

- **Identity**
  - Some Contemporary Thoughts About Identity
  - Identity Statuses and Development
  - Family Influences on Identity
  - Cultural and Ethnic Aspects of Identity
- **Families**
  - Autonomy and Attachment
  - Parent-Adolescent Conflict
- **Peers**
  - Peer Groups
  - Friendships
  - Dating and Romantic Relationships
- **Culture and Adolescent Development**
  - Cross-Cultural Comparisons and Rites of Passage
  - Ethnicity
- **Adolescent Problems**
  - Juvenile Delinquency
  - Depression and Suicide
  - The Interrelation of Problems and Successful Prevention/Intervention Programs

Socioemotional Development in Adolescence

In case you're worried about what's going to become of the younger generation, it's going to grow up and start worrying about the younger generation.

Roger Allen
Contemporary American Author

Images of Life-Span Development

A 15-Year-Old Girl's Self-Description

HOW DO ADOLESCENTS describe themselves? How would you have described yourself when you were 15 years old? What features would you have emphasized? The following is a self-portrait of one 15-year-old girl:

> What am I like as a person? Complicated! I'm sensitive, friendly, outgoing, popular, and tolerant, though I can also be shy, self-conscious, and even obnoxious. Obnoxious! I'd *like* to be friendly and tolerant all of the time. That's the kind of person I *want* to be, and I'm disappointed when I'm not. I'm responsible, even studious now and then, but on the other hand, I'm a goof-off, too, because if you're too studious, you won't be popular. I don't usually do that well at school. I'm a pretty cheerful person, especially with my friends, where I can even get rowdy. At home I'm more likely to be anxious around my parents. They expect me to get all A's. It's not fair! I worry about how I probably *should* get better grades. But I'd be mortified in the eyes of my friends. So I'm usually pretty stressed-out at home, or sarcastic, since my parents are always on my case. But I really don't understand how I can switch so fast. I mean, how can I be cheerful one minute, anxious the next, and then be sarcastic? Which one is the *real* me? sometimes, I feel phony, especially around boys. Say I think some guy might be interested in asking me out. I try to act different, like Madonna. I'll be flirtatious and fun-loving. And then everybody, I mean *everybody* else is looking at me like they think I'm totally weird. Then I get self-conscious and embarrassed and become radically introverted, and I don't know who I really am! Am I just trying to impress them or what? But I don't really care what they think anyway. I don't *want* to care, that is. I just want to know what my close friends think. I can be my true self with my close friends. I can't be my real self with my parents. They don't understand me. What do *they* know about what it's like to be a teenager? They still treat me like I'm still a kid. At least at school people treat you more like you're an adult. That gets confusing, though. I mean, which am I, a kid or an adult? it's scary, too, because I don't have any idea what I want to be when I grow up. I mean, I have lots of *ideas.* My friend Sheryl and I talk about whether we'll be stewardesses, or teachers, or nurses, veterinarians, maybe mothers, or actresses. I know I *don't* want to be a waitress or a secretary. But how do you decide all of this? I really don't know. I mean, I think about it a lot, but I can't resolve it. There are days when I wish I could just become immune to myself. (Harter, 1990)

This self-description eflects the increased interest in self-portrayal and search for an identity in adolescence. Let's now explore the nature of identity development in adolescence.

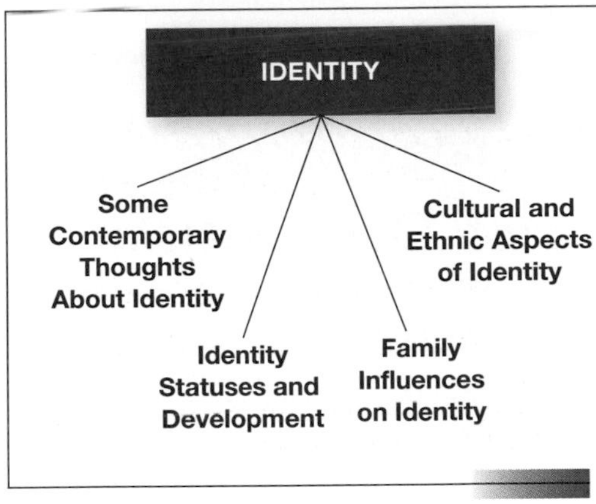

Identity

By far the most comprehensive and provocative story of identity development has been told by Erik Erikson. As you may remember from chapter 2, identity versus identity confusion is the fifth stage in Erikson's eight stages of the life span, occurring at about the same time as adolescence ◀ P. 33. It is a time of being interested in finding out who one is, what one is all about, and where one is headed in life.

During adolescence, worldviews become important to the individual, who enters what Erikson (1968) calls a "psychological moratorium," a gap between the security of childhood and the autonomy of adulthood. Adolescents experiment with the numerous roles and identities they draw from the surrounding culture. Youth who successfully cope with these conflicting identities during adolescence emerge with a new sense of self that is both refreshing and acceptable (Moshman, 1999). Adolescents who do not successfully resolve this identity crisis are confused, suffering what Erikson calls "identity confusion." This confusion takes one of two courses: the individuals withdraw, isolating themselves from peers and family, or they lose their identity in the crowd.

Identity is a self-portrait composed of many pieces. These pieces include:

- The career and work path a person wants to follow (vocational/career identity)
- Whether a person is conservative, liberal, or a middle-of-the roader (political identity)
- A person's spiritual beliefs (religious identity)
- Whether a person is single, married, divorced, and so on (relationship identity)
- The extent to which the person is motivated to achieve and is intellectual (achievement, intellectual identity)
- Whether a person is heterosexual, homosexual, or bisexual (sexual identity)
- Which part of the world or country a person is from and how intensely the person identifies with his/her cultural heritage (cultural/ethnic identity)
- The kind of things a person likes to do, which can include sports, music, hobbies, and so on (interest)
- The individual's personality characteristics (such as being introverted or extraverted, anxious or calm, friendly or hostile, and so on) (personality)
- The individual's body image (physical identity)

Identity Development
The Society for Research on Identity Development
Identity Development in Literature

Some Contemporary Thoughts About Identity

Contemporary views of identity development suggest several important considerations. First, identity development is a lengthy process; in many instances, it is a more gradual, less cataclysmic transition than Erikson's term *crisis* implies. Second, identity development is extraordinarily complex.

Identity formation neither begins nor ends with adolescence. It begins with the appearance of attachment, the development of a sense of self, and the emergence of independence in infancy, and it reaches its final phase with a life review and integration in old age. What is important about identity in adolescence, especially late adolescence, is that for the first time physical development, cognitive development, and social development advance to the point at which the individual can sort through and synthesize childhood identities and identifications to construct a viable pathway toward adult maturity. Resolution of the identity issue at adolescence does not mean that identity will be stable through the remainder of one's life. A person who develops a healthy identity is flexible, adaptive, and open to changes in society, in relationships, and in careers. This openness assures numerous reorganizations of identity features throughout the life of the person who has achieved identity.

"Who are you?" said the caterpillar. Alice replied rather shyly, "I—I hardly know, sir, just at present—at least I know who I was when I got up this morning, but I must have changed several times since then."

Lewis Carroll
English Writer, 19th Century

Identity formation does not happen neatly, and it usually does not happen cataclysmically. At the bare minimum, it involves commitment to a vocational direction, an ideological stance, and a sexual orientation. Synthesizing the identity components can be a long, drawn-out process, with many negations and affirmations of various roles and faces (Marcia, 1996). Identities are developed in bits and pieces. Decisions are not made once and for all but have to be made again and again. And the decisions may seem trivial at the time: whom to date, whether or not to break up, whether or not to have intercourse, whether or not to take drugs, whether to go to college after high school or get a job, which major to choose, whether to study or whether to play, whether or not to be politically active, and so on. Over the years of adolescence, the decisions begin to form a core of what the individual is all about as a person—what is called "identity" (Arboleda, 1999).

Once formed, an identity furnishes individuals with a historical sense of who they have been, a meaningful sense of who they are now, and a sense of who they might become in the future.

James Marcia
Contemporary Canadian, Developmental Psychologist

Identity Statuses and Development

Canadian psychologist James Marcia (1980, 1994) analyzed Erikson's theory of identity development and concluded that four identity statuses, or modes of resolution, appear in the theory: identity diffusion, identity foreclosure, identity moratorium, and identity achievement. The extent of an adolescent's commitment and crisis is used to classify him or her, according to one of the four identity statuses. **Crisis** *is defined as a period of identity development during which the adolescent is choosing among meaningful alternatives.* Most researchers now use the term *exploration* rather than *crisis,* although, in the spirit of Marcia's original formulation, we will use the term *crisis.* **Commitment** *is defined as the part of identity development in which adolescents show a personal investment in what they are going to do.*

Identity diffusion *is Marcia's term for adolescents who have not yet experienced a crisis (that is, they have not yet explored meaningful alternatives) or made any commitments.* Not only are they undecided about occupational and ideological choices, but they are also likely to show little interest in such matters. **Identity foreclosure** *is the term Marcia uses to describe adolescents who have made a commitment but have not experienced a crisis.* This occurs most often when parents hand down commitments to their adolescents, more often than not in an authoritarian manner. In these circumstances, adolescents have not had adequate opportunities to explore different approaches, ideologies, and vocations on their own. **Identity moratorium** *is the term Marcia uses to describe adolescents who are in the midst of a crisis, but their commitments are either absent or only vaguely defined.* **Identity achievement** *is Marcia's term for adolescents who have undergone a crisis and have made a commitment.* Marcia's four statuses of identity are summarized in figure 13.1.

Let's explore some examples of Marcia's identity statuses. A 13-year-old adolescent has neither begun to explore her identity in any meaningful way nor made an identity commitment, so she is *identity diffused.* An 18-year-old boy's parents want him to be a medical doctor so he is planning on majoring in premedicine in college

crisis
Marcia's term for a period of identity development during which the adolescent is choosing from among meaningful alternatives.

commitment
Marcia's term for the part of identity development in which adolescents show a personal investment in what they are going to do.

identity diffusion
Marcia's term for adolescents who have not yet experienced a crisis (explored meaningful alternatives) or made any commitments.

identity foreclosure
Marcia's term for adolescents who have made a commitment but have not experienced a crisis.

identity moratorium
Marcia's term for adolescents who are in the midst of a crisis, but their commitments are either absent or vaguely defined.

identity achievement
Marcia's term for adolescents who have undergone a crisis and have made a commitment.

	Identity status			
Position on occupation and ideology	Identity moratorium	Identity foreclosure	Identity diffusion	Identity achievement
Crisis	Present	Absent	Absent	Present
Commitment	Absent	Present	Absent	Present

Figure **13.1**
Marcia's Four Statuses of Identity

Critical Thinking

Exploring Your Identity

THINK DEEPLY about your exploration and commitment in the areas listed below. For each area, check whether your identity status is diffused, foreclosed, moratorium, or achieved.

IDENTITY COMPONENT	IDENTITY STATUS: Diffused	Foreclosed	Moratorium	Achieved
Vocational (Career)				
Political				
Religious				
Relationship				
Achievement				
Sexual				
Gender				
Ethnic/Cultural				
Interests				
Personality				
Physical				

If you checked "diffused" or "foreclosed" for any area, take some time to think about what you need to do to move into a moratorium identity status in those areas. How much has your identity in each of the areas listed changed in recent years?

and really has not adequately explored any other options, so he is *identity foreclosed.* Nineteen-year-old Sasha is not quite sure what life paths she wants to follow, but she recently went to the counseling center at her college to find out about different careers, so she is in *identity moratorium* status. Twenty-one-year-old Marcelo extensively explored a number of different career options in college, eventually getting his degree in science education, and is looking forward to his first year of teaching high school students, so he is *identity achieved.* Our examples of identity statuses have focused on the career dimension, but remember that the whole of identity is made up of a number of dimensions.

Young adolescents are primarily in Marcia's identity diffusion, foreclosure, or moratorium status. At least three aspects of the young adolescent's development are important in identity formation: young adolescents must establish confidence in parental support, develop a sense of industry, and gain a self-reflective perspective on their future. Some researchers believe the most important identity changes take place in the college years, rather than earlier in adolescence. For example, Alan Waterman (1992) has found that, from the years preceding high school through the last few years of college, the number of individuals who are identity achieved increases, along with a decrease in those who are identity diffused. College upperclassmen are more likely than college freshmen or high school students to be identity achieved. Many young adolescents are identity diffused. These developmental changes are especially true in regard to vocational choice. For religious beliefs and political ideology, fewer college students have reached the identity achieved status, with a substantial number characterized by foreclosure and diffusion. Thus, the timing of identity may depend on the particular role involved, and many college students are still wrestling with ideological commitments.

Many identity status researchers believe that a common pattern of individuals who develop positive identities is to follow what are called "MAMA" cycles of *m*oratorium-*a*chiever-*m*oratorium-*a*chiever. These cycles may be repeated throughout life. Personal, family, and societal changes are inevitable, and, as they occur, the flexibility and skill required to explore new alternatives and develop new commitments are likely to facilitate an individual's coping skills.

As long as one keeps searching, the answers come.

Joan Baez
American Folk Singer, 20th Century

Family Influences on Identity

Parents are important figures in the adolescent's development of identity. In studies that relate identity development to parenting styles, democratic parents, who encourage adolescents to participate in family decision making, foster identity achievement. Autocratic parents, who control the adolescent's behavior without giving the adolescent an opportunity to express opinions, encourage identity foreclosure. Permissive parents, who provide little guidance to adolescents and allow them to make their own decisions, promote identity diffusion (Enright & others, 1980).

In addition to doing studies on parenting styles, researchers have also examined the role of individuality and connectedness in the development of identity. The presence of a family atmosphere that promotes both individuality and connectedness is important in the adolescent's identity development (Cooper & Grotevant, 1989). **Individuality** *consists of two dimensions; self-assertion, the ability to*

individuality
According to Cooper and her colleagues, individuality consists of two dimensions: self-assertion (the ability to have and communicate a point of view) and separateness (the use of communication patterns to express how one is different from others).

have and communicate a point of view, and separateness, the use of communication patterns to express how one is different from others. **Connectedness** *also consists of two dimensions: mutuality, sensitivity to, and respect for others' views, and permeability—openness to others' views.* In general, research findings reveal that identity formation is enhanced by family relationships that are both individuated, which encourages adolescents to develop their own point of view, and connected, which provides a secure base from which to explore the widening social worlds of adolescence. To further evaluate identity development, see Adventures for the Mind.

connectedness
According to Cooper and her colleagues, connectedness consists of two dimensions: mutuality (sensitivity to and respect for others' views) and permeability (openness to others' views).

Cultural and Ethnic Aspects of Identity

Erikson was especially sensitive to the role of culture in identity development. He points out that, throughout the world, ethnic minority groups have struggled to maintain their cultural identities while blending into the dominant culture (Erikson, 1968). Erikson said that this struggle for an inclusive identity, or identity within the larger culture, has been the driving force in the founding of churches, empires, and revolutions throughout history.

Cultural Identity in Canada
Exploring Ethnic Identities
An Adolescent Talks About Ethnic Identity
Ethnic Identity Research

For ethnic minority individuals, adolescence is often a special juncture in their development (Bat-Chava & others, 1997; Kurtz, Cantu, & Phinney, 1996; Phinney, 2000, Spencer & Dornbusch, 1990; Swanson, Spencer, & Petersen, 1998). Although children are aware of some ethnic and cultural differences, most ethnic minority individuals consciously confront their ethnicity for the first time in adolescence. In contrast to children, adolescents have the ability to interpret ethnic and cultural information, to reflect on the past, and to speculate about the future (Wong, 1997).

Jean Phinney (1996) defined **ethnic identity** *as an enduring, basic aspect of the self that includes a sense of membership in an ethnic group and the attitudes and feelings related to that membership.* Thus, for adolescents from ethnic minority groups, the process of identity formation has an added dimension due to exposure to alternative sources of identification—their own ethnic group and the mainstream or dominant culture. Researchers have found that ethnic identity increases with age and that higher levels of ethnic identity are linked with more positive attitudes not only toward one's own ethnic group but toward members of other ethnic groups as well (Phinney, Ferguson, & Tate, 1997). Many ethnic minority adolescents have bicultural identities—identifying in some ways with their ethnic minority group, in other ways with the majority culture (Phinney & Devich-Navarro, 1997).

ethnic identity
An enduring, basic aspect of the self that includes a sense of membership in an ethnic group and the attitudes and feelings related to that membership.

The ease or difficulty with which ethnic minority adolescents achieve healthy identities depends on a number of factors (Phinney & Rosenthal, 1992). Many ethnic minority adolescents have to confront issues of prejudice and discrimination, and barriers to the fulfillment of their goals and aspirations.

In one investigation, ethnic identity exploration was higher among ethnic minority than among White American college students (Phinney & Alipuria, 1990). In this same investigation, ethnic minority college students who had thought about and resolved issues involving their ethnicity had higher self-esteem than did their ethnic minority counterparts who had not. In another investigation, the ethnic identity development of Asian American, African American, Latino, and White American tenth-grade students in Los Angeles was studied (Phinney, 1989). Adolescents from each of the three ethnic minority groups faced a similar need to deal with their ethnic-group

Researcher Margaret Beale Spencer, shown here talking with adolescents, believes that adolescence is often a critical juncture in the identity development of ethnic minority individuals. Most ethnic minority individuals consciously confront their ethnicity for the first time in adolescence. *What factors influence whether ethnic minority adolescents will develop a healthy identity?*

> *Many ethnic minority youth must bridge "multiple worlds" in constructing their identities.*
>
> Catherine Cooper
> *Contemporary Developmental Psychologist, University of California–Santa Cruz*

identification in a predominantly White American culture. In some instances, the adolescents from the three ethnic minority groups perceived different issues to be important in their resolution of ethnic identity. For Asian American adolescents, pressures to achieve academically and concerns about quotas that make it difficult to get into good colleges were salient issues. Many African American adolescent females discussed their realization that White American standards of beauty (especially hair and skin color) did not apply to them; African American adolescent males were concerned with possible job discrimination and the need to distinguish themselves from a negative societal image of African American male adolescents. For Latino adolescents, prejudice was a recurrent theme, as was the conflict in values between their Latino culture heritage and the majority culture.

The contexts in which ethnic minority youth live influence their identity development (Spencer, 1999). Many ethnic minority youth in the United States live in low-income urban settings where support for developing a positive identity is absent. Many of these youth live in pockets of poverty, are exposed to drugs, gangs, and criminal activities, and interact with other youth and adults who have dropped out of school and/or are unemployed. In such settings, effective organizations and programs for youth can make important contributions to developing a positive identity.

One study focused on sixty youth organizations that involved 24,000 adolescents over a period of 5 years (Heath & McLaughlin, 1993). They found that these organizations were especially good at building a sense of ethnic pride in inner-city ethnic youth. Heath & McLaughlin (1993) believe that many inner-city youth have too much time on their hands, too little to do, and too few places to go. Inner-city youth want to participate in organizations that nurture them and respond positively to their needs and interests. Organizations that perceive youth as fearful, vulnerable, and lonely, but also frame them as capable, worthy, and eager to have a healthy and productive life contribute in positive ways to the identity development of ethnic minority youth.

Gender and Identity Development

In Erikson's (1968) classic discussion of identity development, the division of labor between the sexes was reflected in his assertion that males' aspirations were mainly oriented toward career and ideological commitments, while females' were centered around marriage and childbearing. In the 1960s, and 1970s, researchers found support for Erikson's assertion about gender differences in identity. For example, vocational concerns were more central to the identity of males, and affiliative concerns were more important in the identity of females. However, in the past two decades, as females have developed stronger vocational interests, sex differences are turning into sex similarities.

Some investigators believe the order of stages proposed by Erikson is different for females and males. One view is that for males identity formation precedes the stage of intimacy, while for females intimacy precedes identity. These ideas are consistent with the belief that relationships and emotional bonds are more important concerns of females, while autonomy and achievement are more important concerns of males (Gilligan, 1990). In one study, the development of a clear sense of self by adolescent girls was related to their concerns about care and response in relationships (Rogers, 1987).

The task of identity exploration may be more complex for females than for males, in that females may try to establish identities in more domains than males. In today's world, the options for females have increased and thus may at times be confusing and conflicting, especially for females who hope to successfully integrate family and career roles (Archer, 1994).

At this point we have studied a number of ideas about identity development. To review these ideas, see summary table 13.1. In our coverage of identity development we discussed the role of families. Next, we will further examine the nature of parent-adolescent relationships.

Summary Table 13.1
Identity

Concept	Processes/ Related Ideas	Characteristics/Descriptions
Exploring Identity	Erikson's Theory	• Erikson's theory is the most comprehensive view of identity development. Identity vs. identity confusion is the fifth stage in Erikson's theory. • Identity is a self-portrait composed of many pieces.
Some Contemporary Thoughts About Identity	Complexity of Adolescence	• Identity development is extraordinarily complex. • For the first time in development, during adolescence, individuals are physically, cognitively, and socially mature enough to synthesize their lives and pursue a path toward adult maturity.
Identity Statuses and Development	Marcia's View	• He proposed that four statuses of identity exist, based on a combination of conflict and commitment: diffusion, foreclosure, moratorium, and achievement.
	Development	• Some experts believe the main identity changes take place in late adolescence or youth. • Individuals often follow "moratorium-achievement-moratorium-achievement" cycles.
Family Influences on Identity	Their Nature	• Both individuation and connectedness in parent-adolescent relationships are linked with progress in adolescent identity development.
Cultural and Ethnic Aspects of Identity	Culture and Ethnicity	• Erikson argued that throughout the world ethnic minority groups have struggled to maintain their cultural identities while blending into the majority culture. • Adolescence is often a special juncture in ethnic minority identity development.
	Gender	• Erikson's theory argues for gender differences in identity, but some researchers have found gender similarities rather than differences. Others argue that relationships are more central in the identity development of females than of males.

Families

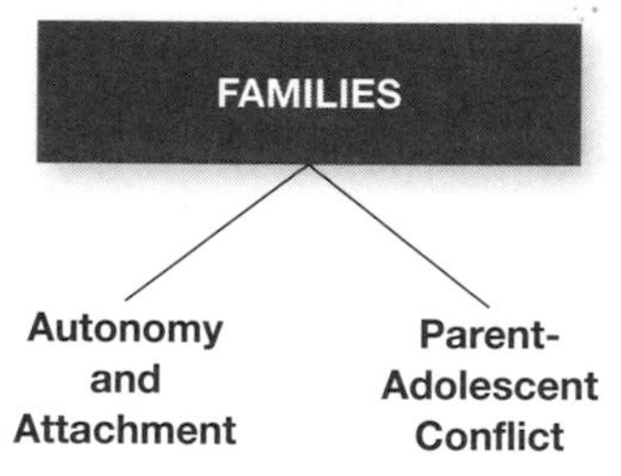

In chapter 11, we discussed how, during middle and late childhood, parents spend less time with their children than in early childhood P. 327. Discipline involves an increased use of reasoning and deprivation of privileges, and there is a gradual transfer of control from parents to children but still within the boundary of coregulation. One of the most important issues and questions that need to be raised about family relationships in adolescence is, What is the nature of autonomy and attachment?

Autonomy and Attachment

The adolescent's push for autonomy and responsibility puzzles and angers many parents. Parents see their teenager slipping from their grasp. They may have an urge to take stronger control as the adolescent seeks autonomy and responsibility. Heated emotional exchanges may ensue, with either side calling names, making threats, and doing whatever seems necessary to gain control. Parents may seem frustrated because they *expect* their teenager to heed their advice, to want to spend time with the family, and to grow up to do what is right. Most parents anticipate that their teenager will have some difficulty adjusting to the changes that adolescence brings, but few parents can imagine and predict just how strong an adolescent's desires will be to

spend time with peers or how much adolescents will want to show that it is they—not their parents—who are responsible for their successes and failures.

The ability to attain autonomy and gain control over one's behavior in adolescence is acquired through appropriate adult reactions to the adolescent's desire for control (Keener & Boykin, 1996; Urberg & Wolowicz, 1996). At the onset of adolescence, the average individual does not have the knowledge to make appropriate or mature decisions in all areas of life. As the adolescent pushes for autonomy, the wise adult relinquishes control in those areas in which the adolescent can make reasonable decisions but continues to guide the adolescent to make reasonable decisions in areas in which the adolescent's knowledge is more limited. Gradually, adolescents acquire the ability to make mature decisions on their own.

Recall from chapter 7 that one of the most widely discussed aspects of socioemotional development in infancy is secure attachment to caregivers. In the past decade, researchers have explored whether secure attachment also might be an important concept in adolescents' relationships with their parents (Cassidy & Shaver, 1999). For example, Joseph Allen and his colleagues (Allen & Hauser, 1994; Allen & Kuperminc, 1995) found that securely attached adolescents were less likely than those who were insecurely attached to engage in problem behaviors, such as juvenile delinquency and drug abuse. In other research, securely attached adolescents had better peer relations than their insecurely attached counterparts (Cassidy, 1999; Kobak, 1999; Laible, Carlo, & Raffaeli, 2000).

Parent-Adolescent Relationships
Parenting Today's Adolescents
Parent-Adolescent Conflict

Parent-Adolescent Conflict

While attachment to parents remains strong during adolescence, the connectedness is not always smooth. Early adolescence is a time when conflict with parents escalates beyond childhood levels. This increase may be due to a number of factors: the biological changes of puberty, cognitive changes involving increased idealism and logical reasoning, social changes focused on independence and identity, maturational changes in parents, and expectations that are violated by parents and adolescents. The adolescent compares her parents to an ideal standard and then criticizes their flaws. A 13-year-old girl tells her mother, "That is the tackiest-looking dress I have ever seen. Nobody would be caught dead wearing that." The adolescent demands logical explanations for comments and discipline. A 14-year-old boy tells his mother, "What do you mean I have to be home at 10 P.M. because it's the way we do things around here? Why do we do things around here that way? It doesn't make sense to me."

Many parents see their adolescent changing from a compliant child to someone who is noncompliant, oppositional, and resistant to parental standards. When this happens, parents tend to clamp down and put more pressure on the adolescent to conform to parental standards. Parents often expect their adolescents to become mature adults overnight, instead of understanding that the journey takes 10 to 15 years. Parents who recognize that this transition takes time handle their youth more competently and calmly than those who demand immediate conformity to adult standards. The opposite tactic—letting adolescents do as they please without supervision—is also unwise.

When I was a boy of 14, my father was so ignorant I could hardly stand to have the man around. But when I got to be 21, I was astonished at how much he had learnt in 7 years.

Mark Twain
American Writer and Humorist, 20th Century

In one study, Reed Larson and Marsye Richards (1994) had mothers, fathers, and adolescents carry electronic pagers for a week and report their activities and emotions at random times. The result was a portrait of the hour-by-hour emotional realities lived by families with adolescents. Differences between the fast-paced daily realities lived by each family member created considerable potential for misunderstanding and conflict. Because each family member was often attending to different priorities, needs, and stressors, their realities were often out of sync. Even when they wanted to shared leisure activity, their interests were at odds. One father said that his wife liked to shop, his daughter liked to play video games, and he liked to stay home. Although the main theme of this work was the hazards of contem-

porary life, some of the families with adolescents were buoyant, and their lives were coordinated.

Conflict with parents increases in early adolescence, but it does not reach the tumultuous proportions G. Stanley Hall envisioned at the beginning of the twentieth century (Holmbeck, 1996; Holmbeck, Paikoff, & Brooks-Gunn, 1995). Rather, much of the conflict involves the everyday events of family life, such as keeping a bedroom clean, dressing neatly, getting home by a certain time, and not talking forever on the phone. The conflicts rarely involve major dilemmas, such as drugs and delinquency.

It is not unusual to hear parents of young adolescents ask, "Is it ever going to get better?" Things usually do get better as adolescents move from early to late adolescence. Conflict with parents often escalates during early adolescence, remains somewhat stable during the high school years, and then lessens as the adolescent reaches 17 to 20 years of age. Parent-adolescent relationships become more positive if adolescents go away to college than if they stay at home and go to college (Sullivan & Sullivan, 1980).

The everyday conflicts that characterize parent-adolescent relationships may actually serve a positive developmental function. These minor disputes and negotiations facilitate the adolescent's transition from being dependent on parents to becoming an autonomous individual. For example, in one study, adolescents who expressed disagreement with their parents explored identity development more actively than did adolescents who did not express disagreement with their parents (Cooper & others, 1982). As previously mentioned, one way for parents to cope with the adolescent's push for independence and identity is to recognize that adolescence is a 10- to 15-year transitional period in the journey to adulthood, rather than an overnight accomplishment. Recognizing that conflict and negotiation can serve a positive developmental function can tone down parental hostility too. Understanding parent-adolescent conflict, though, is not simple (Conger & Ge, 1999).

In sum, the old model of parent-adolescent relationships suggested that as adolescents mature they detach themselves from parents and move into a world of autonomy apart from parents. The old model also suggested that parent-adolescent conflict is intense and stressful throughout adolescence. The new model emphasizes that parents serve as important attachment figures and support systems as adolescents explore a wider, more complex social world. The new model also emphasizes that, in most families, parent-adolescent conflict is moderate rather than severe and that the everyday negotiations and minor disputes are normal and can serve the positive developmental function of helping the adolescent make the transition from childhood dependency to adult independence (see figure 13.2).

Still, a high degree of conflict characterizes some parent-adolescent relationships. One estimate of the proportion of parents and adolescents who engage in prolonged, intense, repeated, unhealthy conflict is about one in five families (Montemayor, 1982). While this figure represents a minority of adolescents, it indicates that 4 to 5 million American families encounter serious, highly stressful parent-adolescent conflict. And this prolonged, intense conflict is associated with a number of adolescent problems—movement out of the home, juvenile delinquency, school dropout, pregnancy and early marriage, membership in religious cults, and drug abuse (Brook & others, 1990).

It should be pointed out that in some cultures there is less parent-adolescent conflict than in others. American psychologist Reed Larson (1999) recently spent 6 months in India studying middle socioeconomic status adolescents and their

Critical Thinking

Age Trends in the Parents of Adolescents and Parent-Adolescent Relationships

In the future, many parents of adolescents will be older because many people are delaying marriage and childbearing. How do you think this will affect the nature of parent-adolescent relationships? Do you think the parents of adolescents who are in their fifties and sixties will be more strict or more permissive than parents who are in their late thirties and forties?

It is not enough for parents to understand children. They must accord children the privilege of understanding them.

Milton Sapirstein
American Psychiatrist, 20th Century

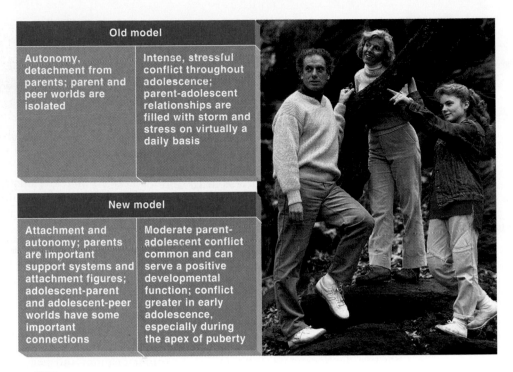

Old model	
Autonomy, detachment from parents; parent and peer worlds are isolated	Intense, stressful conflict throughout adolescence; parent-adolescent relationships are filled with storm and stress on virtually a daily basis

New model	
Attachment and autonomy; parents are important support systems and attachment figures; adolescent-parent and adolescent-peer worlds have some important connections	Moderate parent-adolescent conflict common and can serve a positive developmental function; conflict greater in early adolescence, especially during the apex of puberty

Figure 13.2

Old and New Models of Parent-Adolescent Relationships

families. He observed that in India there seems to be little parent-adolescent conflict and that many families likely would be described as "authoritarian" in Baumrind's categorization. Larson also observed that in India adolescents do not go through a process of breaking away from their parents and that parents choose their youths' marital partners.

Reengaging Families with Adolescents

Families as Asset Builders

We have seen that parents play very important roles in adolescent development. Although adolescents are moving toward independence, they still need to stay connected with families (Roth & Brooks-Gunn, 2000). In the National Longitudinal Study on Adolescent Health (Council of Economic Advisors, 2000) of more than 12,000 adolescents, those who did not eat dinner with a parent five or more days a week had dramatically higher rates of smoking, drinking, marijuana use, getting into fights, and initiation of sexual activity.

Competent adolescent development is most likely to happen when adolescents have parents who (Small, 1990):

- Show them warmth and mutual respect
- Demonstrate sustained interest in their lives
- Recognize and adapt to their cognitive and socioemotional development
- Communicate expectations for high standards of conduct and achievement
- Display constructive ways of dealing with problems and conflict

These ideas coincide with Diana Baumrind's (1971, 1991) authoritative parenting style, which we discussed in chapter 9, "Socioemotional Development in Early Childhood."

At this point, we have studied many ideas about families in adolescence. To review these ideas, see summary table 13.2. Next, we will continue our exploration of the social contexts in which adolescents develop.

Summary Table 13.2
Families

Concept	Processes/ Related Ideas	Characteristics/Descriptions
Autonomy and Attachment	Autonomy	• Many parents have a difficult time handling the adolescent's push for autonomy, even though the push is one of the hallmarks of adolescence.
	Attachment	• Adolescents do not simply move into a world isolated from parents; attachment to parents increases the probability that an adolescent will be socially competent.
Parent-Adolescent Conflict	Its Nature	• Increases in early adolescence. • The conflict is usually moderate rather than severe and the increased conflict may serve the positive developmental function of promoting autonomy and identity. • A subset of adolescents experiences high parent-adolescent conflict, which is linked with negative outcomes.

Peers

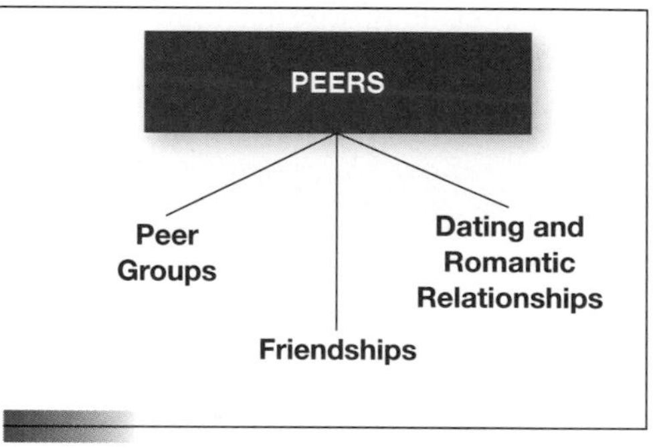

In chapter 11, we discussed how children spend more time with their peers in middle and late childhood than in early childhood ◀ P. 330. We also found that friendships become more important in middle and late childhood and that popularity with peers is a strong motivation for most children. Advances in cognitive development during middle and late childhood also allow children to take the perspective of their peers and friends more readily, and their social knowledge of how to make and keep friends increases.

Imagine you are back in junior or senior high school, especially during one of your good times. Peers, friends, cliques, dates, parties, and clubs probably come to mind. Adolescents spend huge chunks of time with peers, more than in middle and late childhood.

Peer Groups

How much pressure is there to conform to peers during adolescence? Consider the following statement made by an adolescent girl:

> Peer pressure is extremely influential in my life. I have never had very many friends, and I spend quite a bit of time alone. The friends I have are older. The closest friend I have had is a lot like me in that we are both sad and depressed a lot. I began to act even more depressed than before when I was with her. I would call her up and try to act even more depressed than I was because that is what I thought she liked. In that relationship, I felt pressure to be like her.

Each of you, individually, walkest with the tread of a fox, but collectively ye are geese.

Solon
Greek Poet, Statesman, 6th Century B.C.

Conformity to peer pressure in adolescence can be positive or negative. Teenagers engage in all sorts of negative conformity behavior—use seedy language, steal, vandalize, and make fun of parents and teachers. However, a great deal of peer conformity is not negative and consists of the desire to be involved in the peer world, such as dressing like friends and wanting to spend large amounts of time with members of a clique. Such circumstances may involve prosocial activities as well, as when clubs raise money for worthy causes.

Adolescent Peer Relationships
Peer Pressure
Youth Connections

Young adolescents conform more to peer standards than children do. Investigators have found that, around the eighth and ninth grades, conformity to peers—especially

Most adolescents conform to the mainstream standards of their peers. However, the rebellious or anticonformist adolescent reacts counter to the mainstream peer group's expectations, deliberately moving away from the actions or beliefs this group advocates.

to their antisocial standards—peaks (Leventhal, 1994). At this point, adolescents are most likely to go along with a peer to steal hubcaps off a car, draw graffiti on a wall, or steal cosmetics from a store counter.

Cliques Allegiance to cliques can exert powerful control over the lives of adolescents (Tapper, 1996). Group identity often overrides personal identity. The leader of a group may place a member in a position of considerable moral conflict by asking, in effect, "What's more important, our code or your parents'?" or "Are you looking out for yourself, or the members of the group?" Such labels as *brother* and *sister* sometimes are adopted and used in the members' conversations with each other. These labels symbolize the bond between the members and suggest the high status of group membership.

Think about your high school years. What were the cliques, and which one were you in? Although the names of cliques change, we could go to almost any high school in the United States and find three to six well-defined cliques or crowds. In one study, six peer group structures emerged: populars, unpopulars, jocks, brains, druggies, and average students (Brown & Mounts, 1989). The proportion of students in these cliques was much lower in multi-ethnic schools because of the additional existence of ethnically based crowds.

In one study, clique membership was associated with adolescent self-esteem (Brown & Lohr, 1987). The cliques included jocks (athletically oriented), populars (well-known students who led social activities), normals (middle-of-the-road students who made up the masses), druggies or toughs (known for illicit drug use or other delinquent activities), and nobodies (low in social skills or intellectual abilities). The self-esteem of the jocks and the populars was highest, whereas that of the nobodies was lowest. One group of adolescents not in a clique had self-esteem equivalent to that of the jocks and the populars; this group was the independents, who indicated that clique membership was not important to them. Keep in mind that these data are correlational; self-esteem could increase an adolescent's probability of becoming a clique member, just as clique membership could increase the adolescent's self-esteem.

Adolescent Groups Versus Children Groups Children groups differ from adolescent groups in several important ways. The members of children groups often are friends or neighborhood acquaintances, and their groups usually are not as formalized as many adolescent groups. During the adolescent years, groups tend to include a broader array of members. In other words, adolescents other than friends or neighborhood acquaintances often are members of adolescent groups. Try to recall the student council, honor society, or football team at your junior high school. If you were a member of any of these organizations, you probably remember that they were made up of many people you had not met before and that it was a more heterogeneous group than your childhood peer groups. For example, peer groups in adolescence are more likely to have a mixture of individuals from different ethnic groups than are peer groups in childhood.

Friendships

Harry Stack Sullivan (1953) was the most influential theorist to discuss the importance of adolescent friendships, and his ideas have withstood the test of time. He argued that there is a dramatic increase in the psychological importance and inti-

macy of close friends during early adolescence. In contrast to other psychoanalytic theorists' narrow emphasis on the importance of parent-child relationships, Sullivan contended that friends also play important roles in shaping children's and adolescents' well-being and development. In terms of well-being, he argued that all people have a number of basic social needs, including the need for tenderness (secure attachment), playful companionship, social acceptance, intimacy, and sexual relations. Whether or not these needs are fulfilled largely determines our emotional well-being. For example, if the need for playful companionship goes unmet, then we become bored and depressed; if the need for social acceptance is not met, we suffer a lowered sense of self-worth. Developmentally, friends become increasingly depended on to satisfy these needs during adolescence; thus, the ups-and-downs of experiences with friends increasingly shape adolescents' state of well-being. In particular, Sullivan believed that the need for intimacy intensifies during early adolescence, motivating teenagers to seek out close friends. He felt that, if adolescents fail to forge such close friendships, they experience painful feelings of loneliness, coupled with a reduced sense of self-worth.

What changes take place in friendship during the adolescent years?

Research findings support many of Sullivan's ideas. For example, adolescents report disclosing intimate and personal information to their friends more often than do younger children (Buhrmester & Furman, 1987). Adolescents also say they depend more on friends than on parents to satisfy their needs for companionship, reassurance of worth, and intimacy (Furman & Buhrmester, 1992). In one study, daily interviews with 13- to 16-year-old adolescents over a 5-day period were conducted to find out how much time they spent engaged in meaningful interactions with friends and parents (Buhrmester & Carbery, 1992). Adolescents spent an average of 103 minutes per day in meaningful interactions with friends, compared with just 28 minutes per day with parents. In addition, the quality of friendship is more strongly linked to feelings of well-being during adolescence than during childhood. Teenagers with superficial friendships, or no close friendships at all, report feeling lonelier and more depressed, and they have a lower sense of self-esteem than do teenagers with intimate friendships (Yin, Buhrmester, & Hibbard, 1996). In another study, friendship in early adolescence was a significant predictor of self-worth in early adulthood (Bagwell, Newcomb, & Bukowski, 1994).

Although most adolescents develop friendships with individuals who are close to their own age, some adolescents become best friends with younger or older individuals. A common fear, especially among parents, is that adolescents who have older friends will be encouraged to engage in delinquent behavior or early sexual behavior. Researchers have found that adolescents who interact with older youths do engage in these behaviors more frequently, but it is not known whether the older youth guide younger adolescents toward deviant behavior or whether the younger adolescents were already prone to deviant behavior before they developed the friendship with the older youth (Billy, Rodgers, & Udry, 1984).

Dating and Romantic Relationships

Adolescents spend considerable time either dating or thinking about dating, which has gone far beyond its original courtship function to become a form of recreation, a source of status and achievement, and a setting for learning about close relationships. One function of dating, though, continues to be mate selection.

Dating and Romantic Relationships
Teen Chat

Types of Dating and Developmental Changes In their early romantic relationships, many adolescents are not motivated to fulfill attachment or even sexual needs. Rather, early romantic relationships serve as a context for

What are dating relationships like in adolescence?

He who would learn to fly one day must first learn to stand and walk and climb and dance: one cannot fly into flying.

Friedrich Nietzsche
German Philosopher, 19th Century

adolescents to explore how attractive they are, how they should romantically interact with someone, and how all of this looks to the peer group (Brown, in press). Only after adolescents acquire some basic competencies in interacting with romantic partners does the fulfillment of attachment and sexual needs become central functions of these relationships (Furman & Wehner, in press).

In their early exploration of romantic relationships, today's adolescents often find comfort in numbers and begin hanging out together in heterosexual groups. Sometimes they just hang out at someone's house or get organized enough to get someone to drive them to a mall or a movie (Peterson, 1997). A special concern is early dating and "going with" someone, which is associated with adolescent pregnancy and problems at home and school (Downey & Bonica, 1997).

Yet another form of dating recently has been added. *Cyberdating* is dating over the Internet (Thomas, 1998). One 10-year-old girl posted this ad on the Net:

> Hi! I'm looking for a Cyber Boyfriend! I'm 10. I have brown hair and brown eyes. I love swimming, playing basketball, and think kittens are adorable!!!

Cyberdating is especially becoming popular among middle school students. By the time they reach high school and are able to drive, dating usually has evolved into a more traditional real-life venture. Adolescents need to be cautioned about the potential hazards of cyberdating and not really knowing who is on the other end of the computer connection.

dating scripts
The cognitive models that adolescents and adults use to guide and evaluate dating interactions.

Dating Scripts **Dating scripts** *are the cognitive models that guide individuals' dating interactions.* In one study, first dates were highly scripted along gender lines (Rose & Frieze, 1993). The males followed a proactive dating script, the females a reactive one. The male's script involved initiating the date (asking for and planning it), controlling the public domain (driving and opening doors), and initiating sexual interaction (making physical contact, making out, and kissing). The female's script focused on the private domain (concern about appearance, enjoying the date), participating in the structure of the date established by the male (being picked up, having doors opened), and responding to his sexual overtures. These gender differences give males more power in the initial stage of a dating relationship.

In another study, male and female adolescents brought different motivations to the dating experience (Feiring, 1996). The 15-year-old girls were more likely to describe romance in terms of interpersonal qualities, the boys in terms of physical

attraction. The young adolescents frequently mentioned the affiliative qualities of companionship, intimacy, and support as positive aspects of romantic relationships, but not love and security. Also, the young adolescents described physical attraction more in terms of cute, pretty, or handsome than in sexual terms (such as being a good kisser). Possibly the failure to discuss sexual interests was due to the adolescents' discomfort in talking about such personal feelings with an unfamiliar adult.

Emotion and Romantic Relationships The strong emotions of romantic relationships can thrust adolescents into a world in which things are turned upside down and ordinary reality recedes from view (Larson, Clore, & Wood, in press). One 14-year-old reports that he is so in love he can't think about anything else. A 15-year-old girl is enraged by the betrayal of her boyfriend. She is obsessed with ways to get back at him. The daily fluctuations in the emotions of romantic relationships can make the world seem almost surreal. Although the strong emotions of romance can have disruptive effects on adolescents, they also provide a source for possible mastery and growth. Learning to manage these strong emotions can give adolescents a sense of competence.

Romantic relationships often are involved in an adolescent's emotional experiences. In one study of ninth to twelth graders, girls gave real and fantasized heterosexual relationships as the explanation for more than one third of their strong emotions and boys gave this reason for 25 percent of their strong emotions (Wilson-Shockley, 1995). Strong emotions were attached far less to school (13%), family (9%), and same-sex peer relations (8%). The majority of the emotions were reported as positive, but a substantial minority (42%), were reported as negative, including feelings of anxiety, anger, jealousy, and depression.

Sociocultural Contexts and Dating The sociocultural context exerts a powerful influence on adolescent's dating patterns. Values and religious beliefs of people various cultures often dictate the age at which dating begins, how much freedom in dating is allowed, whether dates must be chaperoned by adults or parents, and the roles of males and females in dating. For example, Latino and Asian American cultures have more conservative standards regarding adolescent dating than does the Anglo-American culture. Dating may be a source of cultural conflict for many immigrants and their families who have come from cultures in which dating begins at a late age, little freedom in dating is allowed, dates are chaperoned, and adolescent girl dating is especially restricted. Next, we will further explore the culture's role in adolescent socioemotional development.

Culture and Adolescent Development

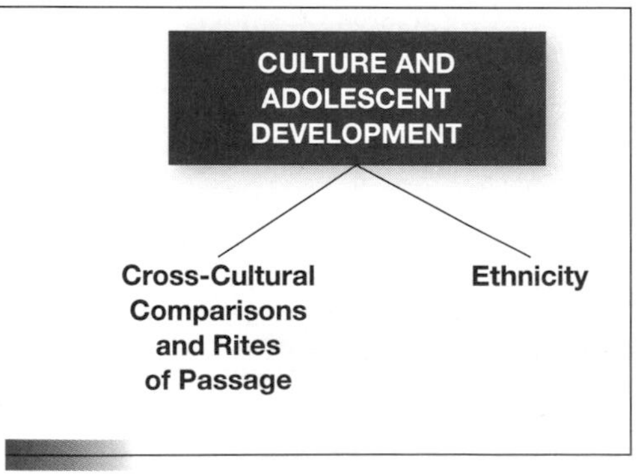

We live in an increasingly diverse world, one in which there is increasing contact between adolescents from different cultures and ethnic groups. (We will explore these questions in this section.) How do adolescents vary cross-culturally? What rites of passage do adolescents experience? What is the nature of ethnic minority adolescents and their development?

Cross-Cultural Comparisons and Rites of Passage

Ideas about the nature of adolescents and orientation toward adolescents may vary from culture to culture and within the same culture over different time periods (Whiting, 1989). For example, some cultures (such as the Mangaian culture in the South Sea islands) have more permissive attitudes toward adolescent sexuality than the American culture, and some cultures (the Ines Beag culture off the coast of Ireland, for example) have more conservative attitudes toward adolescent sexuality than the American culture. Over the course of the twentieth century, attitudes toward sexuality—especially for females—have become more permissive in the American culture.

Early in this century, overgeneralizations about the universal aspects of adolescents were made based on data and experience in a single culture—the middle-class culture of the United States. For example, it was believed that adolescents everywhere went through a period of "storm and stress," characterized by self-doubt and conflict. However, when Margaret Mead visited the island of Samoa, she found that the adolescents of the Samoan culture were not experiencing much stress.

cross-cultural studies
The comparison of a culture with one or more other cultures, which provides information about the degree to which development is similar (universal) across cultures or the degree to which it is culture-specific.

As we discovered in chapter 1, **cross-cultural studies** *involve the comparison of a culture with one or more other cultures, which provides information about the degree to which development is similar, or universal, across cultures, or the degree to which it is culture-specific.* The study of adolescence has emerged in the context of Western industrialized society, with the practical needs and social norms of this culture dominating thinking about adolescents. Consequently, the development of adolescents in Western cultures has evolved as the norm for all adolescents of the human species, regardless of economic and cultural circumstances. This narrow viewpoint can produce erroneous conclusions about the nature of adolescents. One variation in the experiences of adolescents in different cultures is whether the adolescents go through a rite of passage.

rite of passage
A ceremony or ritual that marks an individual's transition from one status to another. Most rites of passage focus on the transition to adult status.

Some societies have elaborate ceremonies that signal the adolescent's move to maturity and achievement of adult status. A **rite of passage** *is a ceremony or ritual that marks an individual's transition from one status to another. Most rites of passage focus on the transition to adult status.* In many primitive cultures, rites of passage are the avenue through which adolescents gain access to sacred adult practices, to knowledge, and to sexuality. These rites often involve dramatic practices intended to facilitate the adolescent's separation from the immediate family, especially the mother. The transformation is usually characterized by some form of ritual death and rebirth, or by means of contact with the spiritual world. Bonds are forged between the adolescent and the adult instructors through shared rituals, hazards, and secrets to allow the adolescent to enter the adult world. This kind of ritual provides a forceful and discontinuous entry into the adult world at a time when the adolescent is perceived to be ready for the change.

Africa has been the location of many rites of passage for adolescents, especially sub-Saharan Africa. Under the influence of Western culture, many of the rites are disappearing today, although some vestiges remain. In locations where formal education is not readily available, rites of passage are still prevalent.

Changing Contexts

Do we have such rites of passage for American adolescents? We certainly do not have universal formal ceremonies that mark the passage from adolescence to adulthood. Certain religious and social groups do have initiation ceremonies that indicate that an advance in maturity has been reached—the Jewish bar mitzvah, the Catholic confirmation, and social debuts, for example. School graduation ceremonies come the closest to being culturewide rites of passage in the United States. The high school graduation ceremony has become nearly universal for middle-class adolescents and increasing numbers of adolescents from low-income backgrounds. Nonetheless, high school graduation does not result in universal changes; many high school graduates continue to live with their parents, continue to be economically dependent on them, and continue to be undecided about career and lifestyle matters. Another rite of passage for increasing numbers of American adolescents is sexual intercourse (Halonen & Santrock, 1999). By 19 years of age, 4 out of 5 American adolescents have had sexual intercourse.

Now that we have discussed the importance of a global perspective in understanding adolescence and the nature of rites of passage, we will turn our attention to the development of ethnic minority adolescents in the United States.

Ethnicity

Earlier in this chapter, we explored the identity development of ethnic minority adolescents. Here we will examine other aspects of ethnicity, beginning with difficulty of separating ethnicity and socioeconomic influences. First, we will examine the nature

These Congolese Kota boys painted their faces as part of a rite of passage to adulthood. *What kinds of rites of passage do American adolescents have?*

of ethnicity and socioeconomic status; second, we will examine the nature of differences and diversity; third, we will study the aspects of value conflicts, assimilation, and pluralism.

Ethnicity and Socioeconomic Status Much of the research on ethnic minority adolescents has failed to tease apart the influences of ethnicity and socioeconomic status. Ethnicity and socioeconomic status can interact in ways that exaggerate the influence of ethnicity because ethnic minority individuals are overrepresented in the lower socioeconomic levels of American society. Consequently, researchers too often have given ethnic explanations of adolescent development that were largely due to socioeconomic status rather than ethnicity. For example, decades of research on group differences in self-esteem failed to consider the socioeconomic status of African American and White children and adolescents. When African American adolescents from low-income backgrounds are compared with White adolescents from middle-income backgrounds, the differences are often large but not informative because of the confounding of ethnicity and socioeconomic status (Scott-Jones, 1995).

Although some ethnic minority youth are from middle-income backgrounds, economic advantage does not entirely enable them to escape their ethnic minority status (Spencer & Dornbusch, 1990). Middle-income ethnic minority youth still encounter much of the prejudice, discrimination, and bias associated with being a

member of an ethnic minority group. Often characterized as a "model minority" because of their strong achievement orientation and family cohesiveness, Japanese Americans still experience stress associated with ethnic minority status (Sue, 1990). Even though middle-income ethnic minority adolescents have more resources available to counter the destructive influences of prejudice and discrimination, they still cannot completely avoid the pervasive influence of negative stereotypes about ethnic minority groups.

Not all ethnic minority families are poor. However, poverty contributes to the stressful life experiences of many ethnic minority adolescents. Thus, many ethnic minority adolescents experience a double disadvantage: (1) prejudice, discrimination, and bias because of their ethnic minority status and (2) the stressful effects of poverty.

Consider the flowers of a garden: though differing in kind, colour, form and shape, yet inasmuch as they are refreshed by the waters of one spring, revived by the breath of one wind, invigorated by the rays of one sun, this diversity increases their charm, and adds to their beauty. . . . How unpleasing to the eye if all the flowers and plants, the leaves and blossoms, the fruits, the branches and the trees of that garden were all of the same shape and colour! Diversity of hues, form and shape, enriches and adorns the garden. . . .

Àbud'l-Bahá
Persian Baha'i Religious Leader, 20th Century

Differences and Diversity

There are legitimate differences between various ethnic minority groups, as well as between ethnic minority groups and the majority White group. Recognizing and respecting these differences are important aspects of getting along with others in a multicultural world. Historical, economic, and social experiences produce differences in ethnic groups (Coll, Meyer, & Brillion, 1995). Individuals living in a particular ethnic or cultural group adapt to the values, attitudes, and stresses of that culture. Their behavior, while possibly different from yours, is, nonetheless, often functional for them. It is important for adolescents to take the perspective of individuals from ethnic and cultural groups that are different from theirs and think, "If I were in their shoes, what kind of experiences might I have had?" "How would I feel if I were a member of their ethnic or cultural group?" "How would I think and behave if I had grown up in their world?" Such perspective taking often increases an adolescent's empathy and understanding of individuals from ethnic and cultural groups different from their own.

Another important dimension to continually keep in mind when studying ethnic minority adolescents is their diversity (Burton & Allison, 1995; Wilson, 2000). Ethnic minority groups are not homogeneous; they have different social, historical, and economic backgrounds. For example, Mexican, Cuban, and Puerto Rican immigrants are all Latinos, but they migrated for different reasons, came from varying socioeconomic backgrounds in their native countries, and experience different rates and types of employment in the United States. The federal government now recognizes the existence of 511 *different* Native American tribes, each having a unique ancestral background with differing values and characteristics. Asian Americans include the Chinese, Japanese, Filipinos, Koreans, and Southeast Asians, each group having a distinct ancestry and language. As an indication of the diversity of Asian Americans, they not only show high educational attainments but also include a high proportion of individuals with no education whatsoever. For example, 90 percent of Korean American males graduate from high school, but only 71 percent of Vietnamese American males do.

Relatively high rates of minority immigration are contributing to the growth in the proportion of ethnic minorities in the U.S. population (McLoyd, 1998, 2000). Because immigrants often experience stressors uncommon to or less prominent among longtime residents (such as language barriers, dislocations and separations from support networks, dual struggle to preserve identity and to acculturate, and changes in SES status), adaptions in intervention programs may be required to achieve optimal cultural sensitivity when working with adolescents and their immigrant families.

Although the U.S. immigrant population has been growing, psychologists have been slow to study these families. In one recent study, the cultural values and intergenerational value discrepancies in immigrant (Vietnamese, Armenian, and Mexican) and non-immigrant families (African American and European American) were studied (Phinney, Ong, & Madden, in press). Family obligations were endorsed more by parents than adolescents in all groups, and the intergenerational value discrepancy generally increased with time in the United States.

Migration and Ethnic Relations

Immigration and Ethnicity: Research Centers

Immigrant Families

Value Conflicts, Assimilation, and Pluralism Stanley Sue (1990) believes that value conflicts are often involved when individuals respond to ethnic issues. These value conflicts have been a source of considerable controversy. According to Sue, without properly identifying the assumptions and effects of the conflicting values, it is difficult to resolve ethnic minority issues. Let's examine one of these value conflicts, assimilation versus pluralism, to see how it might influence an individual's response to an ethnic minority issue.

Assimilation *is the absorption of ethnic minority groups into the dominant group, which often means the loss of some or virtually all of the behavior and values of the ethnic minority group.* Individuals who adopt an assimilation stance usually advocate that ethnic minority groups become more American. By contrast, **pluralism** *is the coexistence of distinct ethnic and cultural groups in the same society. Individuals who adopt a pluralistic stance usually advocate that cultural differences be maintained and appreciated* (Leong, 2000).

Sue believes that one way to resolve value conflicts about sociocultural issues is to conceptualize or redefine them in innovative ways. For example, in the assimilation/pluralism conflict, rather than assume that assimilation is necessary for the development of functional skills, one strategy is to focus on the fluctuating criteria defining those skills considered to be functional; another is to consider the possibility that developing functional skills does not prevent the existence of pluralism. For instance, the classroom instructor might use multicultural examples when teaching social studies and still be able to discuss both culturally universal and culturally specific approaches to American and other cultures. To read about two programs that provide support for ethnic minority youth, see the Sociocultural Worlds of Development box.

At this point we have studied a number of ideas about peers and culture in adolescence. To review these ideas see summary table 13.3. Next, we will explore some problems and disorders in adolescence.

CAREERS IN LIFE-SPAN DEVELOPMENT

Teresa LaFromboise, Counseling Psychologist

TERESA LAFROMBOISE is a professor of counseling psychology at Stanford University. She obtained her Ph.D. from the University of Oklahoma. Teresa is a descendent of the Miami tribe.

She is interested in finding out more about ways to improve the social skills of bicultural individuals. She recently completed a study on the impact of a culturally tailored life-skills curriculum on American Indian high school students' knowledge, beliefs, and ability to intervene in suicidal situations. The life-skills curriculum developed for this study is now being used on reservations in Northern Wisconsin for the prevention of teenage pregnancy, violence, and AIDS.

Teresa is a past president of the Society for Indian Psychologists and also a past president of the Society for the Study of Ethnic Minority Issues (a division of the American Psychological Association).

assimilation
The absorption of ethnic minority groups into the dominant group, which often involves the loss of some or virtually all of the behavior and values of the ethnic minority group.

pluralism
The coexistence of distinct ethnic and cultural groups in the same society. Individuals with a pluralistic stance usually advocate that cultural differences be maintained and appreciated.

Adolescent Problems

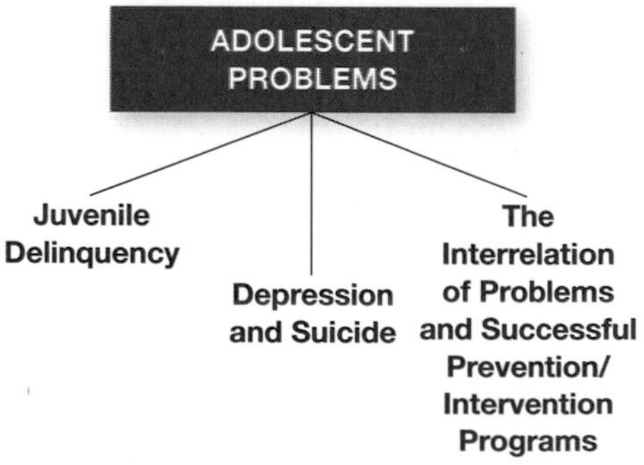

In chapter 12, we described these adolescent problems: Substance abuse, sexually transmitted diseases, and eating disorders. Here, we will examine the problems of juvenile delinquency, depression, and suicide.

Juvenile Delinquency

The label **juvenile delinquent** *is applied to an adolescent who breaks the law or engages in behavior that is considered illegal.* Like other categories of disorders, juvenile delinquency is a broad concept; legal infractions range from littering to murder. Because the adolescent technically becomes a juvenile delinquent only after being judged guilty of a crime by a court of law, official records do not accurately reflect the number of illegal acts juvenile delinquents commit. Estimates of the number of juvenile delinquents in the United States are sketchy, but FBI statistics indicate that at least 2 percent of all youth are involved in juvenile court cases.

Arrests of adolescent males for delinquency still are much higher than for adolescent females. However, the juvenile delinquency rate of females has increased substantially in the last several decades (Office of Juvenile Justice and Prevention, 1999). This is especially true for adolescent females committing violent crimes.

juvenile delinquent
An adolescent who breaks the law or engages in behavior that is considered illegal.

SOCIOCULTURAL WORLDS OF DEVELOPMENT

El Puente and Quantum

EL PUENTE, which means "the bridge," was opened in New York City in 1983 because of community dissatisfaction with the health, education, and social services youth were receiving (Simons, Finlay, & Yang, 1991). El Puente emphasizes five areas of youth development health, education, achievement, personal growth, and social growth.

El Puente is located in a former Roman Catholic church on the south side of Williamsburg in Brooklyn, a neighborhood made up primarily of low-income Latino families, many of which are far below the poverty line. Sixty-five percent of the residents receive some form of public assistance. The neighborhood has the highest school dropout rate for Latinos in New York City and the highest felony rate for adolescents in Brooklyn.

When the youth, ages 12 through 21, first enroll in El Puente, they meet with counselors and develop a four-month plan that includes the programs they are interested in joining. At the end of four months, the youth and staff develop a plan for continued participation. Twenty-six bilingual classes are offered in such subjects as the fine arts, theater, photography, and dance. In addition, a medical and fitness center, GED night school, and mental health and social services centers are a part of El Puente.

El Puente is funded through state, city, and private organizations and serves about 300 youth. The program has been replicated in Chelsea and Holyoke, Massachusetts, and two other sites in New York are being developed.

The Quantum Opportunities Program, funded by the Ford Foundation, was a 4-year, year-around mentoring effort. The students were entering the ninth grade at a high school with high rates of poverty, were minorities, and came from families that received public assistance. Each day for four years, mentors provided sustained support, guidance, and concrete assistance to their students.

The Quantum program required students to participate in (1) academic-related activities outside school hours, including reading, writing, math, science, social studies, peer tutoring, and computer skills training; (2) community service projects, including tutoring elementary school students, cleaning up the neighborhood, and volunteering in hospitals, nursing homes, and libraries; and (3) cultural enrichment and personal development activities, including life skills training and college and job planning. In exchange for their commitment to the program, students were offered financial incentives that encouraged participation, completion, and long-range planning. A stipend of $1.33 was given to students for each hour they participated in these activities. For every 100 hours of education, service, or development activities, students received a bonus of $100. The average cost per participant was $10,600 for the 4 years, which is one half the cost of 1 year in prison.

An evaluation of the Quantum project compared the mentored students with a nonmentored control group. Sixty-three percent of the mentored students graduated from high school, but only 42 percent of the control group did; 42 percent of the mentored students are currently enrolled in college, but only 16 percent of the control group are. Further, the control-group students were twice as likely as the mentored students to receive food stamps or welfare, and they had more arrests. Such programs clearly have the potential to overcome the intergenerational transmission of proverty and its negative outcomes.

These adolescents participate in the programs of El Puente, located in a predominantly low-income Latino neighborhood in Brooklyn, New York. *Which areas of youth development does the El Puente program stress?*

SUMMARY TABLE 13.3
Peers and Culture

Concept	Processes/ Related Ideas	Characteristics/Descriptions
Peers	Peer Groups	• The pressure to conform to peers is strong during adolescence, especially during the eighth and ninth grades. • There are usually three to six well-defined cliques in every secondary school. Membership in certain cliques—especially jocks and populars—is associated with increased self-esteem. Independents also show high self-esteem. • Children groups are less formal, less heterogeneous, and less heterosexual than adolescent groups.
	Friendships	• Harry Stack Sullivan was the most influential theorist to discuss the importance of friendships. He argued that there is a dramatic increase in the psychological importance and intimacy of close friends in early adolescence.
	Dating and Romantic Relationships	• Dating takes on added importance in adolescence, and it can have many functions. Younger adolescents often begin to hang out together in heterosexual groups. A special concern is early dating, which is linked with developmental problems. • Male dating scripts are proactive, those of females reactive. • Emotions are heavily involved in adolescent dating and romantic relationships. • Culture can exert a powerful influence on adolescent dating.
Culture and Adolescent Development	Cross-Cultural Comparisons and Rites of Passage	• As in other periods of development, culture influences adolescents' development. • Ceremonies mark an individul's transition from one status to another, especially into adulthood. In primitive cultures, rites of passage are often well defined. In contemporary America, rites of passage to adulthood are ill-defined.
	Ethnicity	• Much of the research on ethnic minority adolescents has not teased apart the influences of ethnicity and social class. Because of this failure, too often researchers have given ethnic explanations that were largely due to socioeconomic factors. While not all ethnic minority families are poor, poverty contributes to the stress of many ethnic minority adolescents. • There are legitimate differences between many ethnic groups, as well as between ethnic groups and the White majority. Recognizing these differences is an important aspect of getting along with others in a diverse, multicultural world. Too often, differences between ethnic groups and the White majority have been interpreted as deficits on the part of the ethnic minority group. • Another important dimension of ethnic minority groups is their diversity. Ethnic minority groups are not homogeneous; they have different social, historical, and economic backgrounds. Failure to recognize diversity and individual variations results in the stereotyping of an ethnic minority group. • Value conflicts are often involved when individuals respond to ethnic issues. One prominent value conflict involves assimilation versus pluralism.

Delinquency rates among African Americans, other minority groups, and lower socioeconomic status youth are especially high in proportion to the overall population of these groups. However, such groups have less influence over the judicial decision-making process in the United States and, therefore, may be judged delinquent more readily than their White, middle socioeconomic status counterparts.

One issue in juvenile justice is whether an adolescent who commits a crime should be tried as an adult. In a recent study, trying adolescent offenders as adults increased rather than reduced their crime rate (Myers, 1999). The study evaluated

Office of Juvenile Justice and Delinquency Prevention

Justice Information Center

Preventing Crime

Careers in Life-Span Development

Rodney Hammond, Health Psychologist

When Rodney Hammond went to college at the University of Illinois in Champaign-Urbana, he had not decided on a major. To help finance his education, he took a part-time job in a child development research program sponsored by the psychology department. In this job, he observed inner-city children in contexts designed to improve their learning. He saw firsthand the contributions psychology can make and knew then that he wanted to be a psychologist.

Rodney Hammond went on to obtain a doctorate in school and community psychology with a focus on children's development. Today, he trains psychologists at Wright State University in Ohio and directs a program funded by federal and state agencies to prevent homicide and violence among ethnic minority youth. Rodney calls himself a "health psychologist," although when he went to graduate school, training for that profession did not exist as it does now. He and his associates teach at-risk youth how to use social skills to manage conflict effectively and to recognize situations that could become violent. They have shown in their research that with this intervention many youth are less likely to become juvenile delinquents. Hammond's message to undergraduates: "If you are interested in people and problem solving, psychology is a great way to combine the two."

Rodney Hammond, counseling an adolescent girl about the risks of adolescence and how to effectly cope with them.

more than 500 violent youths in Pennsylvania, which has adopted a "get tough" policy. Although these 500 offenders had been given harsher punishment than a comparison group retained in juvenile court, they were more likely to be rearrested—and rearrested more quickly—for new offenses once they were returned to the community. This suggests that the price of short-term public safety attained by prosecuting juveniles as adults might increase the number of criminal offenses over the long run.

Causes of Delinquency What causes delinquency? Many causes have been proposed, including heredity, identity problems, community influences, and family experiences. Erik Erikson (1968), for example, believes that adolescents whose development has restricted them from acceptable social roles or has made them feel they cannot measure up to the demands placed on them may choose a negative identity. Adolescents with a negative identity may find support for their delinquent image among their peers, reinforcing the negative identity. For Erikson, delinquency is an attempt to establish an identity, although a negative one.

Although delinquency is less exclusively a phenomenon of lower socioeconomic status (SES) than it was in the past, some characteristics of the lower-class culture might promote delinquency. The norms of many lower-SES peer groups and gangs are antisocial, or counterproductive, to the goals and norms of society at large. Getting into and staying out of trouble are prominent features of life for some adolescents in low-income neighborhoods. Adolescents from low-income backgrounds may sense that they can gain attention and status by performing antisocial actions. Being "tough" and "masculine" are high-status traits for lower-SES boys, and these traits are often measured by the adolescent's success in performing and getting away with delinquent acts. A community with a high crime rate also lets the adolescent observe many models who engage in criminal activities. These communities may be characterized by poverty, unemployment, and feelings of alienation toward the middle class. Quality schooling, educational funding, and organized neighborhood activities may be lacking in these communities.

Family support systems are also associated with delinquency (Feldman & Weinberger, 1994). Parents of delinquents are less skilled in discouraging antisocial behavior and in encouraging skilled behavior than are parents of nondelinquents. Parental monitoring of adolescents is especially important in determining whether an adolescent becomes a delinquent (Patterson, DeBaryshe, & Ramsey, 1989). Family discord and inconsistent and inappropriate discipline are also associated with delinquency, as are relations. Having delinquent peers greatly increases the risk of becoming delinquent. A summary of the antecedents of delinquency is presented in figure 13.3.

Youth Violence In the late 1990s, a series of school shootings gained national attention. In April 1999, two Columbine High School (in Littleton, Colorado) stu-

Antecedent	Association with delinquency	Description
Identity	Negative identity	Erikson believes delinquency occurs because the adolescent fails to resolve a role identity.
Self-control	Low degree	Some children and adolescents fail to acquire the essential controls that others have acquired during the process of growing up.
Age	Early initiation	Early appearance of antisocial behavior is associated with serious offenses later in adolescence. However, not every child who acts out becomes a delinquent.
Sex	Males	Boys engage in more antisocial behavior than girls do, although girls are more likely to run away. Boys engage in more violent acts.
Expectations for education and school grades	Low expectations and low grades	Adolescents who become delinquents often have low educational expectations and low grades. Their verbal abilities are often weak.
Parental influences	Monitoring (low), support (low), discipline (ineffective)	Delinquents often come from families in which parents rarely monitor their adolescents, provide them with little support, and ineffectively discipline them.
Peer influences	Heavy influence, low resistance	Having delinquent peers greatly increases the risk of becoming delinquent.
Socioeconomic status	Low	Serious offenses are committed more frequently by lower-class males.
Neighborhood quality	Urban, high crime, high mobility	Communities often breed crime. Living in a high-crime area, which also is characterized by poverty and dense living conditions, increases the probability that a child will become a delinquent. These communities often have grossly inadequate schools.

Figure **13.3**
The Antecedents of Juvenile Delinquency

dents, Eric Harris (18) and Dylan Klebold (17) shot and killed 12 students and a teacher, wounded 23 others, and then killed themselves. In May 1998, slightly-built Kip Kinkel strode into a cafeteria at Thurston High School in Springfield, Oregon, and opened fire on his fellow students, murdering two and injuring many others. Later that day, police went to Kip's home and found his parents lying dead on the floor, also victims of Kip's violence.

Is there any way psychologists can predict whether a youth will turn violent? It's a complex task, but researchers have pieced together some clues (Cowley, 1998). Violent youth are overwhelmingly male, and many are driven by feelings of powerlessness. Violence seems to infuse these youth with a sense of power.

Small-town shooting sprees attract attetention, but youth violence is far greater in poverty-infested areas of inner cities. Urban poverty fosters powerlessness and rage, and many inner-city neighborhoods provide almost daily opportunities to observe violence. Many urban youth who live in poverty also lack adequate parent involvement and supervision.

James Garbarino (1999) says there is a lot of ignoring that goes on these kinds of situations. Parents often don't want to acknowledge what might be a very upsetting

Common parenting weaknesses in the families of antisocial boys include a lack of supervision, poor disciplining skills, limited problem-solving abilities, and a tendency to be uncommunicative with sons.

Gerald Patterson
Contemporary American Psychologist, University of Oregon

A recent, special concern in low-income areas is escalating gang violence. *What are some possible reasons for youth violence?*

Youth who kill often have a distorted perspective on what is right and wrong. This distorted perspective can become a self-justifying rationale for violence.

James Garbarino
Contemporary Developmental Psychologist, Cornell University

Violence and Gangs
Prevention of Youth Violence
Lost Boys

reality. Harris and Klebold were members of the "Trenchcoat Mafia" clique of Columbine outcasts. The two even had made a video for a school video class the previous fall that depicted them walking down the halls at the school shooting other students. Allegations were made that a year earlier the sheriff's department had been given information that Harris had bragged openly on the Internet that he and Klebold had built four bombs. Kip Kinkel had an obsession with guns and explosives, a history of abusing animals, and a nasty temper when crossed. When police examined his room, they found two pipe bombs, three larger bombs, and bomb-making recipes Kip had downloaded from the Internet. Clearly, some signs were present in these students' lives to suggest that they had some serious problems, but it is still very difficult to predict whether youth like these will act on their anger and sense of powerlessness to commit murder.

Garbarino (1999) has interviewed a number of youth killers. He concludes that nobody really knows precisely why a tiny minority of youth kill but that it might be a lack of a spiritual center. In the youth killers he interviewed, Garbarino often found a spiritual or emotional emptiness in which the youth sought meaning in the dark side of life.

Some interventions can reduce or prevent youth violence (Carnegie Council on Adolescent Development, 1995). Efforts at prevention should include developmentally appropriate schools, supportive families, and youth and community organizations. At a more specific level, one promising strategy for preventing youth violence is the teaching of conflict management as part of health education in elementary and middle schools. To build resources for such programs, the Carnegie Foundation is supporting a national network of violence prevention practitioners based at the United States Department of Education, linked with a national research center on youth violence at the University of Colorado.

Dylan Klebold. *What are some of the reasons psychologists give to explain why youths like Dylan Klebold kill?*

ITEMS

Date

HATFIELD LRC
CHARGED - SELF ISSUE

format: Year-MM-DD
2006-03-21

Issued at:
15:45

Veronica Boateng

DUE DATE:
2006-04-27 21:45:00

TITLE:Developing child

ITEM:4403592611

Please note that the date is in
the American format: year-month-day.

Final year students must return all
loans and pay any outstanding debts
before leaving the university.
Continuing students should remember
to return or renew their loans before

These are some of the Oregon Social Learning Center's recommendations for reducing youth violence (Walker, 1998):

- *Recommit to raising children safely and effectively.* This includes engaging in parenting practices that have been shown to produce healthy, well-adjusted children. Such practices include consistent, fair discipline that is not harsh or severly punitive, careful monitoring and supervision, positive family management techniques, involvement in the child's daily life, daily debriefings about the child's experiences, and teaching problem-solving strategies.
- *Make prevention a reality.* Too often lip service is given to prevention strategies without investing in them at the necessary levels to make them effective.
- *Give more support to schools, which are struggling to educate a population that includes many at-risk children.*
- *Forge effective partnerships among families, schools, social service systems, churches, and other agencies to create the socializing experiences that will provide all youth with the opportunity to develop in positive ways.*

Depression and Suicide

What is the nature of depression in adolescence? What causes an adolescent to commit suicide?

Adolescent Depression
Suicide

Depression

Depression is more likely to occur in adolescence than in childhood. Also, adolescent girls consistently have higher rates of depression than adolescent boys. (Ka Itiala-Heino & others, 2001). Among the reasons for this sex difference are that

- Females tend to ruminate in their depressed mood and amplify it.
- Females' self-images, especially their body images, are more negative than males'.
- Females face more discrimination than males do.

Certain family factors place adolescents at risk for developing depression. These include having a depressed parent, emotionally unavailable parents, parents who have high marital conflict, and parents with financial problems.

Poor peer relationships also are associated with adolescent depression. Not having a close relationship with a best friend, having less contact with friends, and experiencing peer rejection all increase depressive tendencies in adolescents.

The experience of difficult changes or challenges also is associated with depressive symptoms in adolescence (Compas & Grant, 1993), and parental divorce increases depressive symptoms in adolescents. Also, when adolescents go through puberty at the same time as they move from elementary school to middle or junior high school, they report being depressed more than do adolescents who go through puberty after the school transition.

Depression is more likely to occur in adolescence than in childhood, and female adolescents are more likely than male adolescents to be depressed. *What are some possible reasons adolescents become depressed?*

Suicide

Suicide is a common problem in our society. Its rate has tripled in the past 30 years in the United States; each year, about 25,000 people take their own lives. Beginning with the 15-year-old age group, the suicide rate begins to rise rapidly.

Suicide is now the third leading cause of death in 15- to 24-year-olds (Shneidman, 1996). Males are about three times as likely to commit suicide as females are; this may be because of their choice of more active methods for attempting suicide—shooting, for example. By contrast,

Critical Thinking

Why Is a Course of Risk Taking in Adolescence Likely to Have More Serious Consequences Today Than in the Past?

THE WORLD IS dangerous and unwelcoming for too many of America's teenagers, especially those from low-income families, neighborhoods, and schools. Many adolescents are resilient and cope with the challenges of adolescence without too many setbacks. Others struggle unsuccessfully to find jobs, are written off as losses by their schools, become pregnant before they are ready to become parents, or risk their health through drug abuse. Adolescents in virtually every era have been risk takers, testing limits and making shortsighted judgments. But why are the consequences of choosing a course of risk taking possibly more serious today than they have ever been?

females are more likely to use passive methods, such as sleeping pills, which are less likely to produce death. Although males commit suicide more frequently, females attempt it more frequently (Levinsohn & others, 2001).

Homosexual adolescents are especially vulnerable to suicide. Suicide attempts have been found to consistently be six to seven times higher for homosexual than for heterosexual adolescents over the last 40 years (Ferguson, Horwood, & Beautrais, 1999; Herrill, 1999).

Distal, or earlier, experiences often are involved in suicide attempts as well. The adolescent might have a long-standing history of family instability and unhappiness. Just as a lack of affection and emotional support, high control, and pressure for achievement by parents during childhood are related to adolescent depression, such combinations of family experiences are also likely to show up as distal factors in suicide attempts. The adolescent might also lack supportive friendships.

Just as genetic factors are associated with depression, they are also associated with suicide. The closer a person's genetic relationship to someone who has committed suicide, the more likely that person is to also commit suicide.

What is the psychological profile of the suicidal adolescent? Suicidal adolescents often have depressive symptoms (American Academy of Pediatrics, 2000; Gadpaille, 1996). Although not all depressed adolescents are suicidal, depression is the most frequently cited factor associated with adolescent suicide. A sense of hopelessness, low self-esteem, and high self-blame are also associated with adolescent suicide (Harter & Marold, 1992; Harter & Whitesell, 2001).

The Interrelation of Problems and Successful Prevention/Intervention Programs

We have described some of the major adolescent problems in this chapter and the preceding chapter: substance abuse; juvenile delinquency; school-related problems, such as dropping out of school; adolescent pregnancy and sexually transmitted diseases; depression; and suicide ◄ P. 356.

The most at-risk adolescents have more than one problem. Researchers are increasingly finding that problem behaviors in adolescence are interrelated (Tubman & Windle, 1995). For example, heavy substance abuse is related to early sexual activity, lower grades, dropping out of school, and delinquency. Early initiation of sexual activity is associated with the use of cigarettes and alcohol, the use of marijuana and other illicit drugs, lower grades, dropping out of school; and delinquency. Delinquency is related to early sexual activity, early pregnancy, substance abuse, and dropping out of school. As many as 10 percent of all adolescents in the United States have serious multiple-problem behaviors (for example, adolescents who have dropped out of school, are behind in their grade level, are users of heavy drugs, regularly use cigarettes and marijuana, and are sexually active but do not use contraception). Many, but not all, of these very high-risk youth "do it all." Another 15 percent of adolescents participate in many of these behaviors but with slightly lower frequency and less deleterious consequences. These high-risk youth often engage in two- or three-problem behaviors (Dryfoos, 1990).

In addition to understanding that many adolescents engage in multiple-problem behaviors, it also is important to develop programs that reduce adolescent problems.

In a review of the programs that have been successful in preventing or reducing adolescent problems, adolescence researcher Joy Dryfoos (1990) described the common components of these successful programs:

Youth Risk Behaviors
Treating Adolescent Problems

There is no easy path leading out of life, and few are the easy ones that lie within it.

Walter Savage Landor
English Poet, 19th Century

Summary Table 13.4
Adolescent Problems

Concept	Processes/ Related Ideas	Characteristics/Descriptions
Juvenile Delinquency	Its Nature	• A juvenile delinquent is an adolescent who breaks the law or engages in conduct that is considered illegal. • Heredity, identity problems, community influences, and family experiences have been proposed as causes of juvenile delinquency. • An increasing concern is the high rate of violence among youth.
Depression and Suicide	Depression	• Adolescents have a higher rate of depression than children. • Female adolescents are more likely to have mood and depressive disorders than male adolescents are.
	Suicide	• Adolescent suicide in the United States has tripled since the 1950s. • Both proximal and distal factors are likely involved in suicide's causes.
The Interrelation of Problems and Successful Prevention/ Intervention Programs	Interrelation	• Researchers are increasingly finding that problem behaviors in adolescence are interrelated.
	Prevention/ Intervention	• Dryfoos found a number of common components in programs designed to prevent or reduce adolescent problems: They provide individual attention to high risk adolescents, they develop community-wide intervention, and they include early identification and intervention.

1. *Intensive individualized attention.* In successful programs, high-risk children are attached to a responsible adult, who gives the child attention and deals with the child's specific needs. This theme occurs in a number of programs. In a successful substance-abuse program, a student assistance counselor is available full-time for individual counseling and referral for treatment.
2. *Communitywide multiagency collaborative approaches.* The basic philosophy of communitywide programs is that a number of different programs and services have to be in place. In one successful substance-abuse program, a communitywide health promotion campaign has been implemented that uses local media and community education, in concert with a substance-abuse curriculum in the schools.
3. *Early identification and intervention.* Reaching children and their families before children develop problems, or at the beginning of their problems, is a successful strategy. One preschool program serves as an excellent model for the prevention of delinquency, pregnancy, substance abuse, and dropping out of school. Operated by the High Schope Foundation in Ypsilanti, Michigan, the Perry Preschool has had a long-term positive impact on its students. This enrichment program, directed by David Weikart, serves disadvantaged African American children. They attend a high-quality two-year preschool program and receive weekly home visits from program personnel. Based on official police records, by age 19, individuals who had attended the Perry Preschool program were less likely to have been arrested and reported fewer adult offenses than a control group. The Perry Preschool students also were less likely to drop out of school, and teachers rated their social behavior as more competent than that of a crowd group who had not receive the enriched preschool experience.

At this point, we have discussed many ideas about adolescent problems. To review these ideas, see summary table 13.4. This concludes our coverage of adolescence. In the next section of the book, we will continue our journey through the human life span by exploring development in early adulthood.

Chapter Review

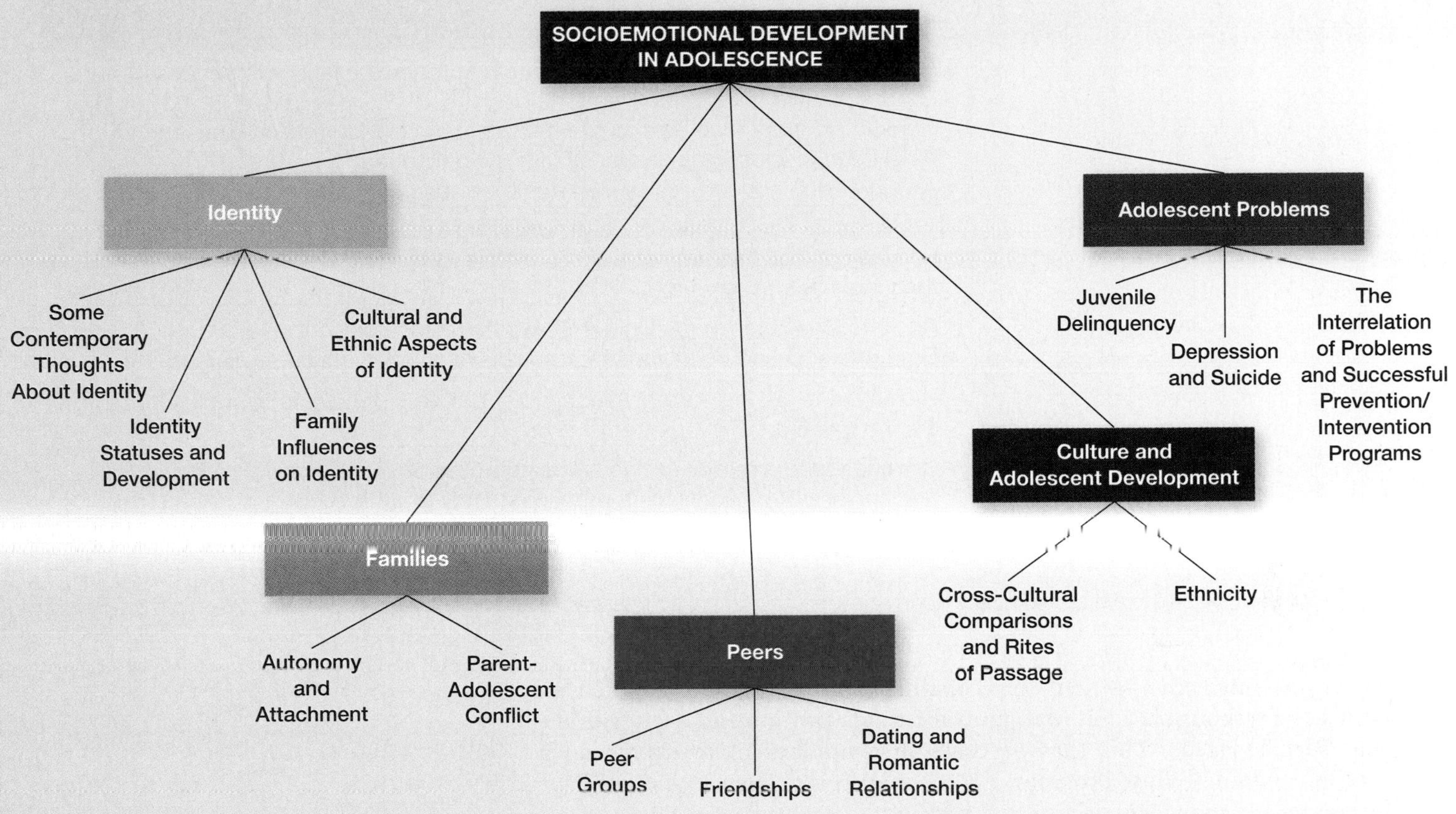

TO OBTAIN A DETAILED REVIEW OF THIS CHAPTER, STUDY THESE FOUR SUMMARY TABLES:

- Summary Table 13.1 Identity page 387
- Summary Table 13.2 Families page 391
- Summary Table 13.3 Peers and Culture page 401
- Summary Table 13.4 Adolescent Problems page 407

Key Terms

crisis 383
commitment 383
identity diffusion 383
identity foreclosure 383
identity moratorium 383
identity achievement 383
individuality 384
connectedness 385
ethnic identity 385
dating scripts 394
cross-cultural studies 396
rite of passage 396
assimilation 399
pluralism 399
juvenile delinquent 399

Key People

Erik Erikson 382
James Marcia 383
Alan Waterman 384
Reed Larson and Marsye Richards 388
G. Stanley Hall 389
Harry Stack Sullivan 392
Stanley Sue 399
Joy Dryfoos 406

Taking It to the Net

1. What is your ethnic identity? How would you define the term "ethnic identity" and the ways in which ethnic minority teens achieve their identities?
2. Fourteen-year-old Denise, an only child, and her mother, Doris, always had a great relationship—until recently. Now it seems that they are constantly arguing. Doris is trying to understand what is going on with her daughter. How can she tell if Denise's behavior is normal for a 14-year-old?
3. The local school board wants to try to prevent violent and tragic incidents like those in Littleton, Colorado and Springfield, Oregon. It has asked its principals and teachers to study an APA publication that identifies warning signs of violence and suggests interventions. What will they learn from it and how can they try and prevent similar situations in their own school district if possible?

Connect to www.mhhe.com/santrockld8 to research the answers and complete these exercises.

OLC Preview

To further test your knowledge of this chapter or to explore our extensive online resources that accompany *Life-Span Development,* eighth edition, please log on to the text's Online Learning Center at http://www.mhhe.com/santrockld8.com.

Section 7

Early Adulthood

How many roads must a man walk down before you call him a man?

Bob Dylan
American Folk Singer, 20th Century

Early adulthood is a time for work and a time for love, sometimes leaving little time for anything else. For some of us, finding our place in adult society and committing to a more stable life take longer than we imagine. We still ask ourselves who we are and wonder if it isn't enough just to be. Our dreams continue and our thoughts are bold, but at some point we become more pragmatic. Sex and love are powerful passions in our lives—at times angels of light, at others fiends of torment. And we possibly will never know the love of our parents until we become parents ourselves. Section 7 contains to chapters: "Physical and Cognitive Development in Early Adulthood" (chapter 14) and "Socioemotional Development in Early Adulthood" (chapter 15).

Chapter 14

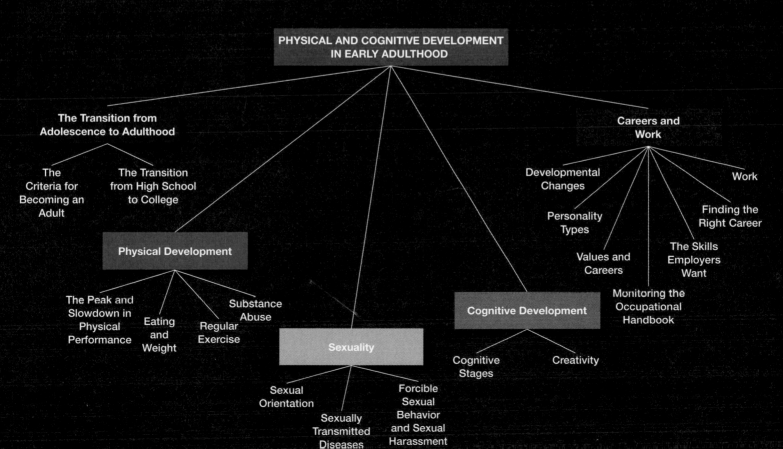

PHYSICAL AND COGNITIVE DEVELOPMENT IN EARLY ADULTHOOD

- **The Transition from Adolescence to Adulthood**
  - The Criteria for Becoming an Adult
  - The Transition from High School to College
- **Physical Development**
  - The Peak and Slowdown in Physical Performance
  - Eating and Weight
  - Regular Exercise
  - Substance Abuse
- **Sexuality**
  - Sexual Orientation
  - Sexually Transmitted Diseases
  - Forcible Sexual Behavior and Sexual Harassment
- **Cognitive Development**
  - Cognitive Stages
  - Creativity
- **Careers and Work**
  - Developmental Changes
  - Personality Types
  - Values and Careers
  - Monitoring the Occupational Handbook
  - The Skills Employers Want
  - Finding the Right Career
  - Work

Physical and Cognitive Development in Early Adulthood

Whatever you can do, or dream you can, begin it. Boldness has genius, power, and magic.

Johann Wolfgang von Goethe
German playwright and novelist, 19th century

Images of Life-Span Development

Flo Jo

FLORENCE GRIFFITH JOYNER, also known as "Flo Jo," smashed Olympic and world records in the 100-meter and 200-meter dashes at 28 years of age. This was especially unusual because earlier sprint champions were in their early twenties. Through better weight training, eating habits, and remarkable self-discipline, Flo Jo was able to accomplish her track goals at an age at which many thought such achievements were impossible.

"When you have been second best for so long, you can either accept it or try to become the best. I made the decision to try to be the best"—Florence Griffith Joyner, Olympic gold medalist

In college, Flo Jo had to juggle many aspects of her life to be successful. In addition to being a full-time college student, she also worked and commuted to school. Nonetheless, she not only became the NCAA champion in the 200 meters but she also managed to achieve high grades.

Flo Jo grew up in poverty in the Watts area in Los Angeles. She never forgot her past and frequently gave back to the community. She often returned to speak to children and urged them to place academics ahead of athletics in their lives.

Florence Griffith Joyner unfortunately died an early death at the age of 38, apparently as the result of a seizure. A book she wrote prior to her death was later published (Griffith-Joyner & Hanc, 1999). In it, she talked about the importance of finding a career that you like and making a deep commitment to be the best you can be in life and work.

In this chapter, we will explore many aspects of physical and cognitive development in early adulthood. These include some of the areas that were so important in Flo Jo's life: seeking to reach peak physical performance, achieving, finding the right career match, and juggling roles. However, we will begin where we left off in the last major section of the book, "Adolescence," and address the transition from adolescent to adulthood.

THE TRANSITION FROM ADOLESCENCE TO ADULTHOOD

- The Criteria for Becoming an Adult
- The Transition from High School to College

The Transition from Adolescence to Adulthood

As the Bob Dylan quotation at the opening of Section Seven says, "How many roads must a man walk down before you call him a man?" When does an adolescent become an adult? In chapter 12, we saw that it is not easy to tell when a girl or boy enters adolescence ◀ P. 348. Many developmentalists, though, believe the task of determining adolescence's beginning is easier than determining its end and adulthood's beginning. Although no consensus exists as to when adolescence is left behind and adulthood is entered, some criteria have been proposed.

The Criteria for Becoming an Adult

In terms of age, recall from chapter 1 that we said the period of early adulthood is entered in the late teens or early twenties and lasts through the thirties ◀ P. 17. As many individuals make the transition from adolescence to adulthood, they face a complex and challenging world of work with highly specialized tasks. During this period, their income is often low and sporadic and they might change residences periodically. Marriage and a family are increasingly being delayed until the mid twenties or later. This period of extended economic and personal temporariness might last from 2 to 8 years or even longer.

The age range from 18 to 25 recently has been labeled "emerging adulthood" by Jeffrey Arnett (2000). He says that during this time frame in their lives, individuals have left the dependency of childhood but have not yet entered the enduring responsibilities of adulthood. They are a point when they are exploring a variety of possible directions in what they want to do with their lives, especially in the areas of work and love.

The most widely recognized marker of entry into adulthood is the occasion when an individual first takes a more or less permanent, full-time job. This usually happens when individuals finish school—high school for some, college for others, postgraduate training for others. However, criteria for determining when an individual has left adolescence and entered adulthood are not clear-cut. Economic independence may be considered a criterion of adulthood. However, developing this independence is often a long, drawn-out process rather than an abrupt one. Increasingly, college graduates are returning to live with their parents as they attempt to get their feet on the ground economically. In one study, adolescents often cited taking responsibility for oneself and independent decision making as identifying the onset of adulthood (Scheer & Unger, 1994). And in another study, more than 70 percent of college students said that being an adult means accepting responsibility for the consequences of one's actions, deciding on one's own beliefs and values, and establishing a relationship with parents as an equal adult (Arnett, 1995).

Although change characterizes the transition from adolescence to adulthood, keep in mind that considerable continuity still glues these periods together (Bachman & others, 1996). Consider the data collected in a longitudinal study of more than 2,000 males from the time they were in the tenth grade until 5 years after high school (Bachman, O'Malley, & Johnston, 1978). Some of the males dropped out, others graduated from high school. Some took jobs after graduating from high school, others went to college. Some were employed, others were unemployed. The dominant picture of the males as they went through this 8-year period was stability rather than change. For example, the tenth-graders who had the highest self-esteem were virtually the same individuals who had the highest self-esteem 5 years after high school. A similar patterning was found for achievement orientation. Those who were the most achievement oriented in the tenth grade remained the most achievement oriented 8 years later. Some environmental changes produced differences in this transition period. For example, marriage reduced drug use, unemployment increased it. Success in college and career increased achievement orientation; less education and poor occupational performance diminished achievement orientation.

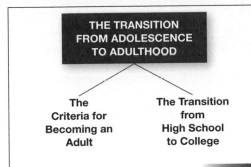

The Transition from High School to College

Just as the transition from elementary school to middle or junior high school involves change and possible stress, so does the transition from high school to college ◄ P. 369. In many instances, there are parallel changes in the two transitions. Going from being a senior in high school to being a freshman in college replays the top-dog phenomenon of transferring from the oldest and most powerful group of students to the youngest and least powerful group of students that occurred earlier as adolescence began. For many of you, the transition from high school to college was not very long ago.

Transition to College

The American College Freshman

The transition from high school to college involves movement to a larger, more impersonal school structure; interaction with peers from more diverse geographical and sometimes more diverse ethnic backgrounds; and increased focus on achievement and its assessment.

But, as with the transition from elementary to middle or junior high school, the transition from high school to college can involve positive features. Students are more likely to feel grown up, have more subjects from which to select, have more time to spend with peers, have more opportunities to explore different lifestyles and values, enjoy greater independence from parental monitoring, and be challenged intellectually by academic work (Santrock & Halonen, 1999).

However, today's college students experience more stress and are more depressed than in the past, according to a national study of more than 300,000 freshmen at more than 500 colleges and universities (Sax & others, 2000). In 2000, 28 percent (up from 16 percent in 1985) said they frequently "felt overwhelmed with what I have to do." And college freshmen in 2000 indicated that they felt more depressed than their counterparts from the 1980s had indicated. The pressure to succeed in college, get a great job, and make lots of money were pervasive concerns of these students.

The United States is becoming a more educated country. In 1998, 24 percent of the population over 25 years and old had completed 4 years or more years of college, compared with only 17 percent in 1980 (U.S. Department of Education. 1999). Total college enrollment is expected to increase in the next decade as increasing numbers of high school graduates pursue higher education. In the last several decades, there has been a dramatic increase in the number of individuals who attend community colleges rather than 4-year colleges, and the community college movement continues to expand.

What is college attendance like around the world? Canada has the largest percentage of 18- to 21-year-olds enrolled in college (41%), followed by Belgium (40%), France (36%), the United States (35%), Ireland (31%), and New Zealand (25%) (U.S. Department of Education, 1999). The greatest percentage increase in college attendance is taking place in Africa—128 percent from 1980 through 1996.

These figures do not include the many returning students who in the United States make up an increasing percentage of the college population. Returning students either did not go to college right out of high school or went to college, dropped out, and now have returned. More than one of every five full-time college students today is a returning student, and about two-thirds of part-time college students are (Sax & others, 2000). Many

Careers in Life-Span Development

Grace Leaf, College/Career Counselor

Grace Leaf is a counselor at Spokane Community College in Washington. She has a master's degree in educational leadership and is working toward a doctoral degree in educational leadership at Gonzaga University in Washington. Her job involves teaching orientation for international students, conducting individual and group advising, and doing individual and group career planning. Grace tries to connect students with goals and values and help them design an educational program that fits their needs and visions.

Grace Leaf, counseling college students at Spokane Community College about careers.

The transition from high school to college often involves positive as well as negative features. In college, students are likely to feel grown up, be able to spend more time with peers, have more opportunities to explore different lifestyles and values, and enjoy greater freedom from parental monitoring. However, college involves a larger, more impersonal school structure and an increased focus on achievement and its assessment. *What was your transition to college like?*

returning students have to balance their course work with commitments to a partner, children, job, and community responsibilities. Despite the many challenges that returning students face, they bring many strengths to campus, such as life experiences that can be applied to a wide range of issues and topics.

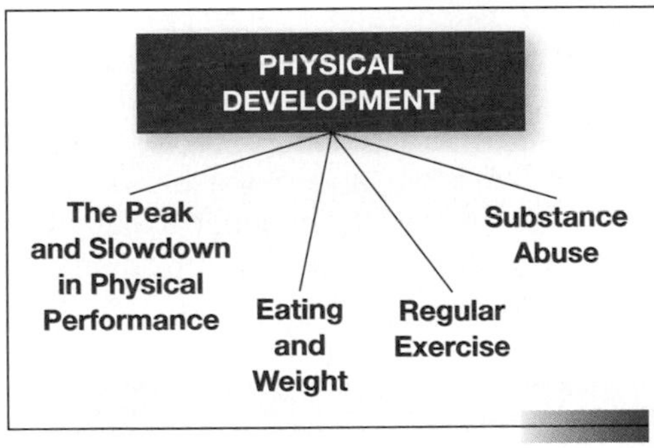

Physical Development

For most individuals physical status not only reaches its peak in early adulthood, it also begins to decline during this period. Interest in health has increased among young adults, with special concerns about diet, weight, exercise, and addiction.

The Peak and Slowdown in Physical Performance

Most of us reach our peak physical performance under the age of 30, often between the ages of 19 and 26. This peak of physical performance occurs not only for the average young adult, but for outstanding athletes as well. Even though athletes as a group keep getting better than their predecessors—running faster, jumping higher, and lifting more weight—the age at which they reach their peak performance has remained virtually the same (Schultz & Curnow, 1988). However, as you saw in Images of Life-Span Development at the beginning of the chapter some individuals such as Florence Griffith Joyner have been able to extend the "biological window" of peak performance to an older age in early adulthood.

Most swimmers and gymnasts reach their peak performance in their late teens. Golfers and marathon runners tend to peak in their late twenties. In other areas of athletics, peak performance is often in the early to mid twenties.

Not only do we reach our peak physical performance during early adulthood, but during this time we are also the healthiest. Few young adults have chronic health problems, and they have fewer colds and respiratory problems than when they were children. Most college students know what it takes to prevent illness and promote health. In one study, college students' ranking of health-protective activities—nutri-

tion, sleep, exercise, watching one's weight, and so on—virtually matched that of licensed nurses (Turk, Rudy, & Salovey, 1984).

Although most college students know what it takes to prevent illness and promote health, they don't fare very well when it comes to applying this information to themselves. In one study, college students reported that they probably would never have a heart attack or drinking problem, but that other college students would (Weinstein, 1984). The college students also said no relation exists between their risk of heart attack and how much they exercise, smoke, or eat meat or high-cholesterol food such as eggs, even though they correctly recognized that factors such as family history influence risk. Many college students, it seems, have unrealistic, overly optimistic beliefs about their future health risks.

In early adulthood, few individuals stop to think about how their personal lifestyles will affect their health later in their adult lives. As young adults, many of us develop a pattern of not eating breakfast, not eating regular meals, and relying on snacks as our main food source during the day, eating excessively to the point where we exceed the normal weight for our age, smoking moderately or excessively, drinking moderately or excessively, failing to exercise, and getting by with only a few hours of sleep at night. These poor personal lifestyles were associated with poor health in one investigation of 7,000 individuals from the ages of 20 to 70 (Belloc & Breslow, 1972). In the Berkeley Longitudinal Study—in which individuals were evaluated over a period of 40 years—physical health at age 30 predicted life satisfaction at age 70, more so for men than women (Mussen, Honzik, & Eichorn, 1982).

There are some hidden dangers in the peaks of performance and health in early adulthood. Young adults can draw on physical resources for a great deal of pleasure, often bouncing back easily from physical stress and abuse. However, this can lead them to push their bodies too far. The negative effects of abusing one's body may not show up in the first part of early adulthood, but they probably will surface later in early adulthood or in middle adulthood (Csikszentmihalyi & Rathunde, 1998).

Not only do we reach our peak in physical performance during early adulthood, but it is during this age period that we also begin to decline in physical performance. Muscle tone and strength usually begin to show signs of decline around the age of 30. Sagging chins and protruding abdomens may also begin to appear for the first time. The lessening of physical abilities is a common complaint among the just-turned-thirties. Says one 30-year-old, "I played tennis last night. My knees are sore and my lower back aches. Last month, it was my elbow that hurt. Several years ago it wasn't that way. I could play all day and not be sore the next morning." Sensory systems show little change in early adulthood, but the lens of the eye loses some of its elasticity and becomes less able to change shape and focus on near objects. Hearing peaks in adolescence, remains constant in the first part of early adulthood, and then begins to decline in the last part of early adulthood. And in the mid to late twenties, the body's fatty tissue increases.

After thirty, a body has a mind of its own.

Bette Midler
American Actress, 20th Century

The health profile of our nation's young adults can be improved by reducing the incidence of certain healthimpairing lifestyles, such as overeating, and by engaging in health-improving lifestyles that include good eating habits, exercising regularly, and not abusing drugs.

Eating and Weight

In earlier chapters, we explored obesity in childhood (chapters 8 and 10) and examined the eating disorders of anorexia nervosa and bulimia nervosa in adolescence (chapter 12) ◀ Pp. 209, 277, and 363. Now, we will turn our attention to obesity in the adult years and the extensive preoccupation that many adults have with dieting.

Obesity Obesity is a serious and pervasive problem. Let's explore its pervasiveness and costs, as well as the roles that heredity, set point and metabolism, and environmental factors play in its development.

Obesity
Heredity and Obesity

Pervasiveness and Costs Approximately one-third of the American population are overweight enough to be at increased health risk, and the prevalence of obesity has risen 8 percent in the 1990s (Friedman & Brownell, 1998). Obesity often becomes more common with increased age, especially among women.

The health care costs linked to obesity are estimated to be $46 billion per year. Obesity is associated with increased risk of hypertension, diabetes, and cardiovascular disease (Stunkard, 2000).

Heredity Until recently, the genetic component of obesity had been underestimated by scientists. Some individuals do inherit a tendency to be overweight. Researchers have documented that animals can be inbred to have a propensity for obesity (Blundell, 1984). Further, identical human twins have similar weights, even when they are reared apart. Estimates of the variance in body mass that can be explained by heredity range from 25 to 70 percent.

Set Point and Metabolism The amount of stored fat in your body is an important factor in your *set point,* the weight maintained when no effort is made to gain or lose weight. Fat is stored in what are called adipose cells. When these cells are filled, you do not get hungry. When people gain weight—because of genetic predisposition, childhood eating patterns, or adult overeating—the number of their fat cells increases, and they might not be able to get rid of them. A normal-weight individual has 30 to 40 billion fat cells. An obese individual has 80 to 120 billion fat cells. Some scientists have proposed that these fat cells can shrink but might not go away.

basal metabolism rate (BMR) The minimal amount of energy a person uses in a resting state.

Another factor in weight is **basal metabolism rate (BMR),** *the minimal amount of energy an individual uses in a resting state.* BMR varies with age and sex. Rates decline precipitously during adolescence and then more gradually in adulthood; they also are slightly higher for males than females (see figure 14.1). Many people gradually increase their weight over many years (Wing & Polley, 2001). To some degree the weight gain can be due to a declining basal metabolism rate.

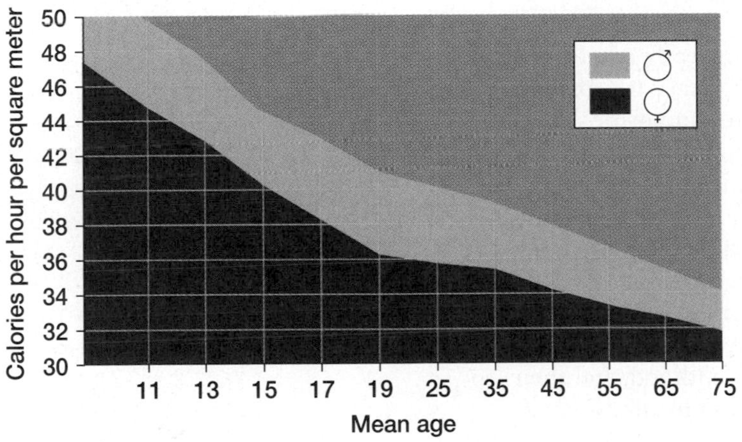

Figure **14.1**

Changes in Basal Metabolism Rate with Age

BMR varies with age and sex. Rates are usually higher for males and decline proportionately with age for both sexes.

Environmental Factors The human gustatory system and taste preferences developed at a time when reliable food sources were scarce. Our earliest ancestors probably developed a preference for sweets, because ripe fruit, which is a concentrated source of sugar (and calories), was so accessible. Today many people still have a "sweet tooth," but unlike our ancestors' ripe fruit that contained sugar *plus* vitamins and minerals, the soft drinks and candy bars we snack on today often fill us with empty calories.

Strong evidence of the environment's influence on weight is the doubling of the rate of obesity in the United States since 1900. This dramatic increase in obesity likely is due to greater availability of food (especially food high in fat), energy-saving devices, and declining physical activity. Obesity is six times more prevalent among women with low incomes than among women with high incomes. Americans also are more obese than Europeans and people in many other areas of the world.

Dieting

Let's explore the diet scene in America, restrained eating, whether diets work, the role of exercise in losing weight, and the potential harm and benefits of dieting.

Why People Are Getting Fatter

The Diet Scene Many divergent interests are involved in the topic of dieting. These include the public, health professionals, policy makers, the media, and the pow-

erful diet and food industries. On one side are the societal norms that promote a very lean, aesthetic body. This ideal is supported by $30 billion a year in sales of diet books, programs, videos, foods, and pills. On the other side are health professionals and a growing minority of the press. Although they recognize the alarmingly high rate of obesity, they are frustrated by high relapse rates and the obsession with excessive thinness that can lead to chronic dieting and serious health risks (Brownell, 2000; Brownell & Rodin, 1994).

Restrained Eating One area related to dieting that psychologists have studied is restrained eating. Too many people live their lives as one big long diet, interrupted by occasional hot fudge sundaes or chocolate chip cookies. **Restrained eaters** *are individuals who chronically restrict their food intake to control their weight.* Restrained eaters are often on diets, are very conscious of what they eat, and tend to feel guilty after splurging on sweets. An interesting characteristic of restrained eaters is that when they stop dieting, they tend to binge eat—that is, eat large quantities of food in a short time (McFarlane, Polivy, & Herman, 1998).

restrained eaters
Individuals who chronically restrict their food intake to control their weight. Restrained eaters are often on diets, are very conscious of what they eat, and tend to feel guilty after splurging on sweets.

Do Diets Work? Although many Americans regularly embark on a diet, few are successful in keeping weight off long-term. Some critics argue that all diets fail (Wooley & Garner, 1991). However, the weight of the evidence is that some individuals who go on diets do lose weight and maintain the loss (Brownell & Cohen, 1995). How often this occurs and whether some diet programs work better than others are still open questions.

Exercise What we do know about losing weight is that the most effective programs include an exercise component. Exercise not only burns up calories, but continues to elevate the person's metabolic rate for several hours *after* the exercise. Also, exercise lowers a person's set point for weight, which makes it easier to maintain a lower weight (Bennett & Gurin, 1982).

Dieting: Harm or Benefit? Dieting is a pervasive concern of many Americans, but the population is not uniform and many people who are on diets should not be. A 10 percent reduction in body weight might produce striking benefits for an older, obese, hypertensive man but be unhealthy for a female college student who is not overweight. The pressure to be thin, and thus diet, is greatest among young women, yet they do not have the highest risk of obesity.

Even when diets do produce weight loss, they can place the dieter at risk for other health problems. One main concern focuses on weight cycling (commonly called "yo-yo dieting"), in which the person is in a recurring cycle of dieting and weight gain (Wadden & others, 1996). Researchers have found a link between frequent changes in weight and chronic disease (Brownell & Rodin, 1994). Also, liquid diets and other very-low calorie strategies are related to gall bladder damage.

With these problems in mind, when overweight people diet and maintain their weight loss, they do become less depressed and reduce their risk for a number of health-impairing disorders (Christensen, 1996).

CAREERS IN LIFE-SPAN DEVELOPMENT

Judith Rodin, University Professor, Health Psychology Researcher, and University President

JUDITH RODIN has conducted numerous research studies, especially in the area of eating behavior and women's health. She obtained her Ph.D in psychology at the University of Pennsylvania and went on to teach and conduct research at Yale University. Her book *Body Traps* (Rodin, 1992) focuses on her belief that the American culture has unhealthy views of women's health, especially in its emphasis on extreme thinness as an ideal body build.

Judith Rodin returned to the University of Pennsylvania to become its president. In doing so, she became the first female to become president of an Ivy League university.

Judith Rodin (center) talking with college students at the University of Pennsylvania.

Regular Exercise

In 1961, President John F. Kennedy offered the following message: "We are under-exercised as a nation. We look instead of play. We ride instead of walk. Our existence deprives us of the minimum of physical activity essential for healthy living." Without question, people are jogging, cycling, and aerobically exercising more today than in 1961, but far too many of us are still couch potatoes. **Aerobic exercise** *is sustained exercise—jogging, swimming, or cycling, for example—that stimulates heart and lung activity.*

aerobic exercise
Sustained exercise (such as jogging, swimming, or cycling) that stimulates heart and lung activity.

Aerobic Institute
Women and Exercise

The main focus of exercise's effects on health has involved preventing heart disease. Most health experts recommend that you should try to raise your heart rate to 60 percent of your maximum heart rate. Your maximum heart rate is calculated as 220 minus your age multiplied by 0.6, so if you are 20, you should aim for an exercise heart rate of 120 ($220 - 20 = 200 \times 0.6 = 120$). If you are 45, you should aim for an exercise heart rate of 105 ($220 - 45 = 175 \times 0.6 = 105$).

People in some occupations get more vigorous exercise than those in others. For example, longshoremen have about half the risk of fatal heart attacks as co-workers like crane drivers and clerks who have physically less demanding jobs. Further, elaborate studies of 17,000 male alumni of Harvard University found that those who exercised strenuously on a regular basis had a lower risk of heart disease and were more likely to still be alive in their middle adulthood years than their more sedentary counterparts (Lee, Hsieh, & Paffenbarger, 1995; Paffenbarger & others, 1986). Based on such findings, some health experts conclude that, regardless of other risk factors (smoking, high blood pressure, overweight, heredity), if you exercise enough to burn more than 2,000 calories a week, you can cut your risk of heart attack by an impressive two-thirds (Sherwood, Light, & Blumenthal, 1989). Burning up 2,000 calories a week through exercise requires a lot of effort, far more than most of us are willing to expend. To burn 300 calories a day, through exercise, you would have to do one of the following: swim or run for about 25 minutes, walk for 45 minutes at about 4 miles an hour, or participate in aerobic dancing for 30 minutes.

What role does exercise play in losing weight?

Many experts recommend that adults engage in 30 minutes or more of moderate-intensity physical activity on most, preferably all, days of the week. However, only about one-fifth of adults are active at these recommended levels of physical activity. Examples of the physical activities that qualify as moderate or vigorous are listed in figure 14.2.

Researchers have found that exercise benefits not only physical health, but mental health as well (King, 2000; Leith, 1998). In particular, exercise improves self-concept and reduces anxiety and depression (Moses & others, 1989).

Research on the benefits of exercise suggests that both moderate and intense activities produce important physical and psychological gains (Thayer & others, 1996). Some people enjoy rigorous, intense exercise. Others enjoy more moderate exercise routines. The enjoyment and pleasure we derive from exercise added to its aerobic benefits make exercise one of life's most important activities.

Substance Abuse

In chapter 12, "Physical and Cognitive Development in Adolescence," we explored the nature of substance abuse in adolescence ◄ P. 359. Let's now examine the extent of substance abuse in college students and young adults.

Alcohol Almost half of U.S. college students say they drink heavily (Johnston, O'Malley, & Bachman, 1996). The effects of heavy drinking take their toll on them. In a national survey of drinking patterns on 140 campuses, almost half of the binge drinkers reported problems that included (Wechsler & others, 1994):

- missing classes,
- physical injuries,
- troubles with policy, and
- having unprotected sex.

For example, binge-drinking college students were 11 times more likely to fall behind in school, 10 times more likely to drive after drinking, and twice as likely to have unprotected sex than college students who did not binge drink.

In one recent study of 14,000 college students, approximately 40 percent engaged in binge drinking at least once in the 2 weeks before they were surveyed (Wechsler & others, 2000). In this study, binge drinking was defined as having five or more drinks in a row for men and four or more drinks in a row for women. Also, the percentage of frequent binge drinkers (those who consumed these amounts more than once a week) increased from 20 percent in 1993 to 23 percent in 1999. In this study, almost 20 percent of college students said they do not drink at all, the same as in 1997 but an increase from 15 percent in 1993.

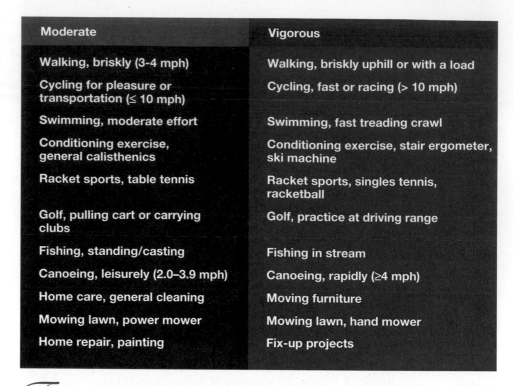

Moderate	Vigorous
Walking, briskly (3-4 mph)	Walking, briskly uphill or with a load
Cycling for pleasure or transportation (≤ 10 mph)	Cycling, fast or racing (> 10 mph)
Swimming, moderate effort	Swimming, fast treading crawl
Conditioning exercise, general calisthenics	Conditioning exercise, stair ergometer, ski machine
Racket sports, table tennis	Racket sports, singles tennis, racketball
Golf, pulling cart or carrying clubs	Golf, practice at driving range
Fishing, standing/casting	Fishing in stream
Canoeing, leisurely (2.0–3.9 mph)	Canoeing, rapidly (≥4 mph)
Home care, general cleaning	Moving furniture
Mowing lawn, power mower	Mowing lawn, hand mower
Home repair, painting	Fix-up projects

Figure **14.2**
Moderate and Vigorous Physical Activities

Fortunately, by the time individuals reach their mid twenties, many have reduced their use of alcohol and drugs. That is the conclusion reached by Jerald Bachman (1997) in a longitudinal analysis of more than 33,000 individuals. They were evaluated from the time they were high school seniors through their twenties. Following are some of the main findings in the study.

- College students drink more than youths who end their education after high school.
- Those who don't go to college smoke more.
- Singles use marijuana more than married individuals.
- Drinking is heaviest among singles and divorced individuals. Becoming engaged, married, or even remarried quickly brings down alcohol use.

Thus, living arrangements and marital status are key factors in alcohol and drug use rates during the twenties.

Clearinghouse for Drug Information
Alcoholism
Smoking/Tobacco Control
Smoking Cessation

Cigarette Smoking Converging evidence from a number of studies underscores the dangers of smoking or being around those who do (Millis, 1998; Pomerleaw, 2000). For example, smoking is linked to 30 percent of cancer deaths, 21 percent of heart disease deaths, and 82 percent of chronic pulmonary disease deaths. Secondhand smoke is implicated in as many as 9,000 lung cancer deaths a year (Sandler & others, 1989). Children of smokers are at special risk for respiratory and middle-ear diseases.

Fewer people smoke today than in the past, and almost half of all living adults who ever smoked have quit. The prevalence of smoking in men has dropped from over 50 percent in 1965 to about 25 percent today. However, more than 50 million Americans still smoke cigarettes today. And recently cigar smoking, with risks similar to those of cigarette smoking, has increased.

Quitting smoking is not easy. Nicotine, the active drug in cigarettes, is a stimulant that increases the smoker's energy and altertness, a pleasurable and reinforcing

Critical Thinking

Do You Abuse Drugs?

RESPOND yes or no to the following items:

Yes No

___ ___ I have gotten into problems because of using drugs.

___ ___ Using alcohol or other drugs has made my college life unhappy at times.

___ ___ Drinking alcohol or taking other drugs has been a factor in my losing a job.

___ ___ Drinking alcohol or taking other drugs has interfered with my studying for exams.

___ ___ Drinking alcohol or taking drugs has jeopardized my academic performance.

___ ___ My ambition is not as strong since I've been drinking a lot or taking drugs.

___ ___ Drinking or taking drugs has caused me to have difficulty sleeping.

___ ___ I have felt remorse after drinking or taking drugs.

___ ___ I crave a drink or other drugs at a definite time of the day.

___ ___ I want a drink or another drug the next morning.

___ ___ I have had a complete or partial loss of memory as a result of drinking or using other drugs.

___ ___ Drinking or using other drugs is affecting my reputation.

___ ___ I have been in the hospital or another institution because of my drinking or taking drugs.

College students who responded yes to items similar to these on the Rutgers Collegiate Abuse Screening Test were more likely to be substance abusers than those who answered no. If you responded yes to just 1 of the 13 items on this screening test, consider going to your college health or counseling center for further screening.

experience (Seidman, Rosecan, & Role, 1999). Nicotine also stimulates neurotransmitters that have a calming or pain-reducing effect. Nicotine substitutes, such as nicotine gum and the nicotine patch, have shown good success rates in helping smokers quit (Eissenberg, Stitzer, & Hennigfield, 1999). They work on the principle of supplying small amounts of nicotine to diminish the intensity of withdrawal. The behavior modification technique of *stimulus control,* in which the smoker is sensitized to smoking cues, also has been used effectively in getting some individuals to stop smoking. For example, the smoker might associate a morning cup of coffee or a social drink with smoking. Stimulus control strategies help the smoker to avoid these cues or learn to substitute other behaviors for smoking. Some smokers just go "cold turkey" and quit smoking, although this strategy usually has a higher success rate with lighter than with heavier smokers.

Addiction **Addiction** *is a pattern of behavior characterized by an overwhelming involvement with using a drug and securing its supply.* This can occur despite adverse consequences associated with the use of the drug. There is a strong tendency to relapse after quitting or withdrawal. Withdrawal symptoms consist of significant changes in physical functioning and behavior. Depending on the drug, these symptoms might include insomnia, tremors, nausea, vomiting, cramps, elevation of heart rate and blood pressure, convulsions, anxiety, and depression when a physically dependent person stops taking the drug. Experts on drug abuse use the term *addiction* to describe either a physical or psychological dependence on the drug or both (Pinger & others, 1998).

Controversy continues about whether addictions are diseases (Ray & Ksir, 1999). The **disease model of addiction** *describes addictions as biologically based, lifelong diseases that involve a loss of control over behavior and require medical and/or spiritual treatment for recovery.* In the disease model, addiction is either inherited or bred into a person early in life. Current or recent problems or relationships are not believed to be causes of the disease. Once involved in the disease, you can never completely rid yourself of it, according to this model. The disease model has been strongly promoted and supported by the medical profession and Alcoholics Anonymous (AA) (Humphreys, 2000).

In contrast to the disease model of addiction, which focuses on biological mechanisms, some psychologists believe that understanding addiction requires that it be placed in context as part of people's lives, their personalities, their relationships, their environments, and their perspectives. In this **life-process model of addiction,** *addiction is not a disease but rather a habitual response and a source of gratification or security that can be understood only in the context of social relationships and experiences.* Each of these views of addiction—the disease model and the nondisease, life-process model—has its supporters.

About one-third of alcoholics recover whether they are in a treatment program or not. This figure was found in a long-term study of 700 individuals over 50 years and has consistently been found by other researchers as well (Vaillant, 1992). There is a "one-third rule" for alcoholism: by age 65, one-third are dead or in terrible shape, one-third are abstinent or drinking socially, and one-third are

addiction
A pattern of behavior characterized by an overwhelming involvement with using a drug and securing its supply.

disease model of addiction
The view that addictions are biologically based, lifelong diseases that involve a loss of control over behavior and require medical and/or spiritual treatment for recovery.

life-process model of addiction
The view that addiction is not a disease but rather a habitual response and a source of gratification and security that can be understood only in the context of social relationships and experiences.

Summary Table 14.1
The Transition from Adolescence to Adulthood; Physical Development

Concept	Processes/ Related Ideas	Characteristics/Descriptions
The Transition from Adolescence to Adulthood	The Criteria for Becoming an Adult	• During the transition, there is often personal and economic temporariness. • Two criteria for adult status are economic independence and independent decision making.
	The Transition from High School to College	• There is both continuity and change in the transition, and the transition can involve both positive and negative features. An increasing number of college students are returning students.
Physical Development	The Peak and Slowdown in Physical Performance	• Peak physical status is often reached between 18 and 30 years of age. There is a hidden hazard in this time period—bad health habits are often formed then. • Toward the latter part of early adulthood, a detectable slowdown in physical development is apparent for most individuals.
	Eating and Weight	• Obesity is a serious problem, with about one-third of Americans overweight enough to be at increased health risk. • Heredity, set point, and basal metabolism are biological factors involved in obesity. Environmental factors and culture influence obesity. • Many divergent interests are involved in the topic of dieting. Restrained eating is an important dieting topic. • Most diets don't work long-term. For those that do, exercise is usually an important component. Dieting can be harmful; however, when overweight people diet and maintain their weight loss, it can have positive effects.
	Regular Exercise	• Both moderate and intense exercise produce important physical and psychological gains, such as lowered risk of heart disease and lowered anxiety.
	Substance Abuse	• Although some reduction in alcohol use has occurred among college freshmen, binge drinking is still a major concern. By the mid twenties a reduction in drug use often takes place. • A number of strategies, such as nicotine substitutes, have shown some success in getting smokers to quit but quitting is difficult because of the addictive properties of nicotine. • Two strategies for intervening in addictions are the disease model and the and the life-process model, each of which has supporters.

still trying to beat their addiction. A positive outcome and recovery from alcoholism are predicted by certain factors: (1) a strong negative experience related to drinking, such as a serious medical emergency or condition; (2) finding a substitute dependency to compete with alcohol abuse, such as meditation, exercise, or overeating (which of course has its own negative health consequences); (3) having new social supports (such as a concerned, helpful employer or a new marriage); and (4) joining an inspirational group, such as a religious organization or AA (Vaillant, 1992).

At this point we have studied a number of ideas about the transition from adolescence to adulthood, and about physical development in early adulthood. To review these ideas, see summary table 14.1. So far we have seen that proper nutrition, regular exercise, and not engaging in substance abuse are healthy aspects of life in early adulthood. As we will see next, so is sound sexual decision making.

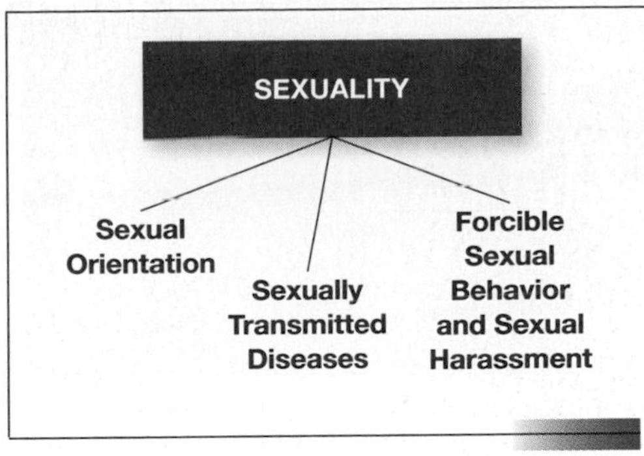

Sexuality

We do not need sex for everyday survival the way we need food and water, but we do need it for the survival of the species. What is the nature of heterosexuality and homosexuality in the human species?

Sexual Orientation

Let's now explore sexual orientation and various aspects of heterosexual and homosexual attitudes and behaviors.

Heterosexual Attitudes and Behavior In a well-designed, comprehensive study of American's sexual patterns. Robert Michael and his colleagues (1994) interviewed nearly 3,500 people from 18 to 50 years of age who were randomly selected, a sharp contrast from earlier samples that were based on unrepresentative groups of volunteers.

Some of the key findings from the 1994 survey (see figure 14.3):

- Americans tend to fall into three categories: One-third have sex twice a week or more, one-third a few times a month, and one-third a few times a year or not at all.
- Married couples have sex the most and also are the most likely to have orgasms when they do. Figure 14.3 portrays the frequency of sex for married and noncohabitating individuals in the past year.
- Most Americans do not engage in kinky sexual acts. When asked about their favorite sexual acts, the vast majority (96 percent) said that vaginal sex was "very" or "somewhat" appealing. Oral sex was in third place, after an activity that many have not labeled a sexual act—watching a partner undress.
- Adultery is clearly the exception rather than the rule. Nearly 75 percent of the married men and 85 percent of the married women indicated that they have never been unfaithful.
- Men think about sex far more than women do—54 percent of the men said they think about it every day or several times a day, whereas 67 percent of the women said they think about it only a few times a week or a few times a month.

In sum, one of the most powerful messages in the 1994 survey was that Americans' sexual lives are more conservative than previously believed. Although 17 percent of the men and 3 percent of the women said they have had sex with at least 21 partners, the overall impression from the survey was that sexual behavior is ruled by marriage and monogamy for most Americans.

Homosexual Attitudes and Behavior Until the end of the nineteenth century, it was generally believed that people were either heterosexual or homosexual. Today, it is more accepted to view sexual orientation along a continuum from exclusive heterosexuality to exclusive homosexuality rather than as an either/or proposition (see figure 14.4). Some individuals are also *bisexual,* being sexually attracted to people of both sexes. In the Sex in America survey, 2.7 percent of the men and 1.3 percent of the women reported that they had had homosexual sex in the past year (Michael & others, 1994).

Why are some individuals homosexual and others heterosexual? Speculation about this question has been extensive (Herek, 2000). Homosexuals and heterosexuals have similar physiological responses during sexual arousal and seem to be aroused by the same types of tactile stimulation.

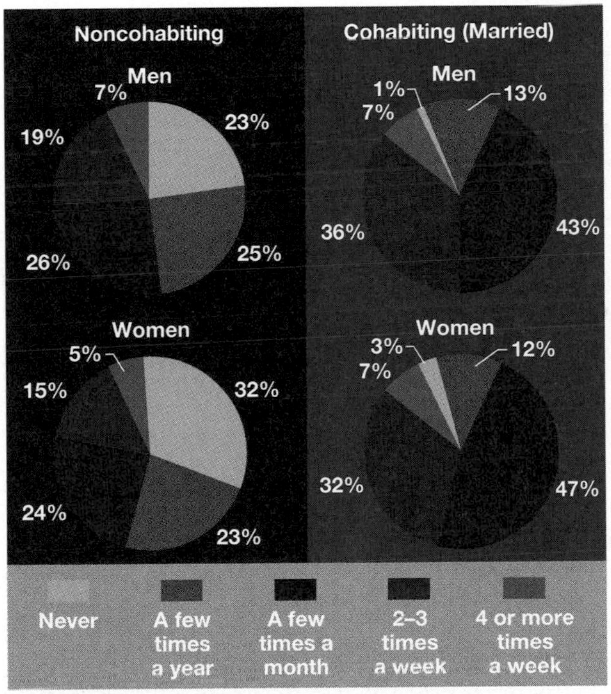

Figure **14.3**

The Sex in America Survey

Percentages show noncohabiting and cohabiting (married) males' and females' responses to the question "How often have you had sex in the past year?"

Investigators find no differences between homosexuals and heterosexuals in a wide range of attitudes, behaviors, and adjustments (Bell, Weinberg, & Mammersmith, 1981). Homosexuality once was classified as a mental disorder, but both the American Psychiatric Association and the American Psychological Association discontinued this classification as a mental disorder in the 1970s.

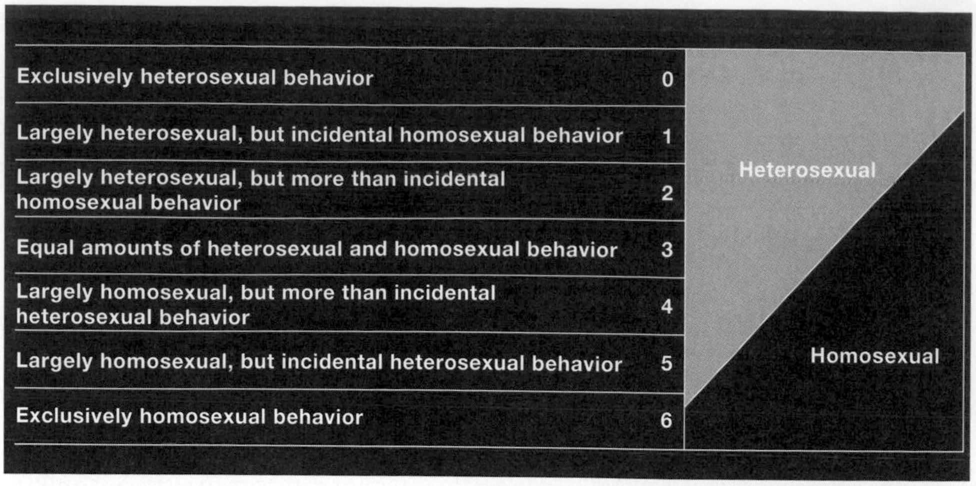

Exclusively heterosexual behavior 0
Largely heterosexual, but incidental homosexual behavior 1
Largely heterosexual, but more than incidental homosexual behavior 2
Equal amounts of heterosexual and homosexual behavior 3
Largely homosexual, but more than incidental heterosexual behavior 4
Largely homosexual, but incidental heterosexual behavior 5
Exclusively homosexual behavior 6
Heterosexual
Homosexual

Figure **14.4**

The Continuum of Sexual Orientation

The continuum ranges from exclusive heterosexuality, which Kinsey and associates (1948) rated as 0, to exclusive homosexuality (6). People who are about equally attracted to both sexes (ratings 2 to 4) are bisexual.

Recently, researchers have explored the possible biological basis of homosexuality (D'Auqelli, 2000; Gladue, 1994). The results of hormone studies have been inconsistent. If male homosexuals are given male sex hormones (androgens), their sexual orientation doesn't change. Their sexual desire merely increases. A very early prenatal critical period might influence sexual orientation. In the second to fifth months after conception, exposure of the fetus to hormone levels characteristic of females might cause the individual (male or female) to become attracted to males (Ellis & Ames, 1987). If this critical-period hypothesis turns out to be correct, it would explain why clinicians have found that sexual orientation is difficult, if not impossible, to modify.

WWW

Human Sexuality
American Sexual Behavior
Lesbian and Gay Issues

With regard to anatomical structures, neuroscientist Simon LeVay (1991) found that an area of the hypothalamus that governs sexual behavior is twice as large (about the size of a grain of sand) in heterosexual males as in homosexual males. This area was found to be about the same size in homosexual males and heterosexual females. Critics of this research point out that many of the homosexuals in the study had AIDS and suggest that their brains could have been altered by the disease.

An individual's sexual orientation—homosexual, heterosexual, or bisexual—is most likely determined by a combination of genetic, hormonal, cognitive, and environmental factors (Baldwin & Baldwin, 1998). Most experts on homosexuality believe that no one factor alone causes homosexuality and that the relative weight of each factor can vary from one individual to the next. In effect, no one knows exactly why some individuals are homosexual. Scientists have a clearer picture of what does not cause homosexuality. For example, children raised by gay or lesbian parents or couples are no more likely to be homosexual than are children raised by heterosexual parents (Patterson, 1995). There also is no evidence that male homosexuality is caused by a dominant mother or a weak father, or that female homosexuality is caused by girls choosing male role models.

How can gays and lesbians adapt to a world in which they are a minority? According to psychologist Laura Brown (1989), gays and lesbians experience life as a minority in a dominant, majority culture. For lesbian women and gay men, developing a *bicultural identity* creates new ways of defining themselves. Brown believes that gays and lesbians adapt best when they don't define themselves in polarities, such as trying to live in an encapsulated gay or lesbian world completely divorced from the majority culture or completely accepting the dictates and bias of the majority culture. Balancing the demands of the two cultures—the minority gay/lesbian culture and the majority heterosexual culture—can often lead to more effective coping for homosexuals, says Brown.

What likely determines an individual's sexual preference?

Sexually Transmitted Diseases

sexually transmitted diseases (STDs)
Diseases that are contracted primarily through sex.

Sexually transmitted diseases (STDs) *are diseases that are contracted primarily through sexual contact. This contact is not limited to vaginal intercourse but includes oral-genital and anal-genital contact as well. STDs are an in-increasing health problem.* Among the main STDs individuals can get are bacterial infections (such as gonorrhea and syphilis), chlamydia, and two STDs caused by viruses—genital herpes and AIDS (acquired immune deficiency syndrome).

gonorrhea
Reported to be one of the most common STDs in the United States, this sexually transmitted disease is caused by a bacterium called gonococcus, which thrives in the moist mucous membranes lining the mouth, throat, vagina, cervix, urethra, and anal tract. This disease is commonly called the "drip" or the "clap."

Gonorrhea

Gonorrhea *is a sexually transmitted disease that is commonly called the "drip" or the "clap." It is reported to be one of the most common STDs in the United States and is caused by a bacterium from the gonococcus family, which thrives in the moist mucous membranes lining the mouth, throat, vagina, cervix, urethra, and anal tract.* The bacterium is spread by contact between the infected moist membranes of one individual and the membranes of another.

Gonorrhea can be successfully treated in its early stages with penicillin or other antibiotics. Although the incidence of gonorrhea has declined, more than 500,000 cases are still reported annually (Centers for Disease Control and Prvention, 1999).

syphilis
A sexually transmitted disease caused by the bacterium Treponema pallidum, a spirochete.

Syphilis

Syphilis *is a sexually transmitted disease caused by the bacterium* Treponema pallidum, *a member of the spirochete family.* The spirochete needs a warm, moist environment to survive, and it is transmitted by penile-vaginal, oral-genital, or anal contact. It can also be transmitted from a pregnant woman to her fetus after the fourth month of pregnancy. If the mother is treated before this time with penicillin, the syphilis will not be transmitted to the fetus.

In its early stages, syphilis can be effectively treated with penicillin. In its advanced stages, syphilis can cause paralysis or even death. Approximately 100,000 cases of syphilis are reported in the United States each year.

chlamydia
The most common STD. Named for Chlamydia trachomitis, an organism that spreads by sexual contact and infects the genitals of both sexes.

Chlamydia

Chlamydia, *the most common of all sexually transmitted diseases, is named for* Chlamydia trachomitis, *an organism that spreads by sexual contact and infects the genital organs of both sexes.* Although fewer individuals have heard of chlamydia than have heard of gonorrhea and syphilis, its incidence is much higher (Morris, Warren, & Aral, 1993). About 4 million Americans are infected with chlamydia each year. About 10 percent of all college students have chlamydia. This STD is highly infectious, and women run a 70 percent risk of contracting it in a single sexual encounter. The male risk is estimated at between 25 and 50 percent.

WWW

CDC National Prevention Network

American Social Health Association

Sexually Transmitted Diseases Resources

Males with chlamydia often get treatment because of noticeable symptoms in the genital region; however, females are asymptomatic. Therefore, many females go untreated and the chlamydia spreads to the upper reproductive tract where it can cause pelvis inflammatory disease (PID). The resultant scarring of tissue in the fallopian tubes can result in infertility or in ectopic pregnancies (tubal pregnancies), or a pregnancy in which the fertilized egg is implanted outside the uterus. One-quarter of females who have PID become infertile; multiple cases of PID increase the rate of infertility to half. Some researchers suggest that chlamydia is the number one preventable cause of female infertility.

We now turn to two STDs that are caused by viruses—herpes genitalis and acquired immune deficiency syndrome (AIDS). Neither of these STDs is curable.

genital herpes
A sexually transmitted disease caused by a large family of viruses of different strains. These strains also produce other, nonsexually transmitted diseases such as chicken pox and mononucleosis.

Genital Herpes

Genital herpes *is a sexually transmitted disease caused by a large family of viruses with many different strains. These strains produce other, nonsexually transmitted diseases such as chicken pox and mononucleosis.* Three to 5 days after contact, itching and tingling can occur, followed by an eruption of sores and blisters. The attacks can last up to 3 weeks and may recur in a few weeks or a few years.

Although drugs such as acyclovir can be used to alleviate symptoms, there is no known cure for herpes. Therefore, people infected with herpes often experience severe emotional distress in addition to the considerable physical discomfort. The virus can be transmitted through nonlatex condoms and foams, making infected individuals reluctant about sex, angry about the unpredictability of their lives, and fearful that they won't be able to cope with the pain of the next attack. For these reasons, support groups for victims of herpes have been established.

HIV Info Web

HPV

HPV *is a virus (human papillomavirus) that causes warts on people. A few types of the virus cause warts on the genitals.* They can be as large as nickels or so small that they cannot be seen. There are more than a million new cases of HPV each year in the United States.

The most common way to contract HPV is by having sex with or touching the genitals of someone who already has the virus. Women with HPV are at a higher risk for cervical cancer.

HPV can be treated by physicians. The warts can be frozen off or burned off with a laser. Although the warts can be removed, it generally is believed that once acquired, HPV does not go away.

HPV
A virus (human papillomavirus) that causes warts on people. A few types of the virus cause warts on the genitals.

AIDS
Acquired immune deficiency syndrome, a primarily sexually transmitted disease caused by the HIV virus, which destroys the body's immune system.

AIDS

No single STD has had a greater impact on sexual behavior, or created more public fear in the last several decades than AIDS. **AIDS** *is a sexually transmitted disease that is caused by the human immunodeficiency virus (HIV), which destroys the body's immune system.* A person who has contracted HIV is vulnerable to germs that a normal immune system could destroy.

Of the AIDS cases reported through the end of 1999 in the United States, 82 percent were men, 18 percent were women. Overall, 47 percent of the AIDS cases were gay men, 25 percent were injection drug users, 10 percent were persons infected heterosexually, and 2 percent were individuals infected through blood or blood products (Centers for Disease Control and Prevention, 2000). In the 1990s in the United States, there was a trend of increasing rates of AIDS in women and in African Americans and Latinos.

Because of education and the development of more-effective drug treatments, deaths due to AIDS have begun to decline in the United States (Centers for Disease Control and Prevention, 2000). Use of potent multidrug combinations has been shown to suppress HIV to low levels for an extended period of time (Davey & others, 2000; Kelly, 2000). However, in some locations around the world AIDS is increasing. For example, in Africa more than 4 million had AIDS in 2000. To put this in perspective, a total of 733,000 cases of AIDS had been reported to the Centers for Disease Control and Prevention (2000) by the end of 1999 in the United States.

Experts say that AIDS can be transmitted only by (Kalichman, 1996)

- sexual contact,
- sharing hypodermic needles,
- blood transfusion (which in the last few years has been tightly monitored), or
- other direct contact of cuts or mucous membranes with blood and sexual fluids.

Critical Thinking

Sexual Behavior and Moral Choices: Privacy and Protection

CAROLINE CONTRACTED genital herpes from her boyfriend, whom she had been dating for the past 3 years. After breaking off that relationship and spending some time on her own, Caroline began dating Charles. Before becoming sexually involved with him, Caroline told Charles about her herpes infection, thinking that it was the right thing to do. Charles seemed accepting of the news, but soon after the discussion he began treating Caroline differently. He became distant and cold toward her, and eventually broke off their relationship saying that it "just wasn't working." Caroline firmly believed it was because she had told him about the herpes.

Caroline later met Jeff, whom she really liked and wanted to start dating. As they became closer to developing a sexual relationship, Caroline felt that she should tell Jeff about the herpes, but she was afraid that he also would abandon her. She thought that if she arranged it so that they never had sexual contact when she had herpes blisters (the time when infecting someone else is most likely to occur), she could protect him. She also thought that if they used latex condoms for protection, he would be safe, even though condoms can break.

Would Caroline not telling Jeff be acceptable to you, even if she acted to protect him? If Jeff should know, in what ways would it be best to tell him? If Caroline did tell Jeff, and he did end their relationship, would telling him have been a mistake? Does Jeff have a right to know? Does Caroline have a right to privacy?

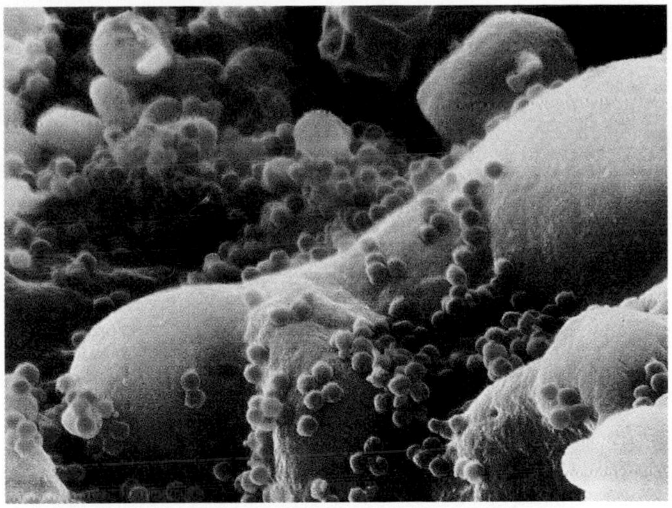

HIV attacking the body's immune system. Each blue sphere is an HIV virus.

Remember that it is not who you are, but what you do, that puts you at risk for getting HIV. *Anyone* who is sexually active or uses intravenous drugs is at risk. *No one* is immune. Once an individual is infected, the prognosis is likely illness and death. The only safe behavior is abstinence from sex, which is not perceived as an option by most individuals. Beyond abstinence, there is only safer behavior, such as sexual behavior without exchange of semen, vaginal fluids, or blood, and sexual intercourse with a condom.

Just asking a date about his or her sexual behavior does not guarantee protection from AIDS and other sexually transmitted diseases. For example, in one investigation, 655 college students were asked to answer questions about lying and sexual behavior (Cochran & Mays, 1990). Of the 422 respondents who said they were sexually active, 34 percent of the men and 10 percent of the women said they had lied so their partner would have sex with them. Much higher percentages—47 percent of the men and 60 percent of the women—said they had been lied to by a potential sexual partner. When asked what aspects of their past they would be most likely to lie about, more than 40 percent of the men and women said they would understate the number of their sexual partners. Twenty percent of the men, but only 4 percent of the women, said they would lie about their results from an AIDS blood test.

Center for AIDS Prevention Studies

HIV/STD Education

Signs of HIV Infection in Females

Protecting Against STDs What are some good strategies for protecting against AIDS and other sexually transmitted diseases? They include these:

- *Know your and your partner's risk status.* Anyone who has had previous sexual activity with another person might have contracted an STD without being aware of it. Spend time getting to know a prospective partner before you have sex. Use this time to inform the other person of your STD status and inquire about your partner's. Remember that many people lie about their STD status.
- *Obtain medical examinations.* Many experts recommend that couples who want to begin a sexual relationship should have a medical checkup to rule out STDs before they engage in sex. If cost is an issue, contact your campus health service or a public health clinic.
- *Have protected, not unprotected, sex.* When correctly used, latex condoms help to prevent many STDs from being transmitted. Condoms are most effective in preventing gonorrhea, syphilis, chlamydia, and AIDS. They are less effective against the spread of herpes.
- *Don't have sex with multiple partners.* One of the best predictors of getting an STD is having sex with multiple partners. Having more than one sex partner elevates the likelihood that you will encounter an infected partner.

What are some good strategies for protecting against AIDS and other sexually transmitted diseases? How effectively have you practiced these strategies?

Forcible Sexual Behavior and Sexual Harassment

Too often, sexual behavior becomes forcible and is engaged in against another person's will. Also, concern about sexual harassment has increased in recent years.

Rape

Rape *is forcible sexual intercourse with a person who does not give consent.* Legal definitions of rape differ from state to state. For example, in some states, husbands are not prohibited from forcing their wives to have intercourse, although this has been challenged in several states. Because of difficulties involved in reporting rape, the actual incidence is not easily determined. It appears that rape occurs most often in large cities, where it has been reported that 8 of every 10,000 women 12 years and older are raped each year. Nearly 200,000 rapes are reported each year in the United States.

rape
Forcible sexual intercourse with a person who does not consent to it.

An increasing concern is **date or acquaintance rape,** *which is coercive sexual activity directed at someone with whom the individual is at least casually acquainted.* Date rape is an increasing problem on college campuses (Rosen & Stith, 1995). As many as two-thirds of college males admit to fondling females against their will and one-half admit to forced sexual activity.

date or acquaintance rape
Coercive sexual activity directed at someone with whom the perpetrator is at least casually acquainted.

Why is rape so pervasive in the American culture? Among the causes given are that males are socialized to be sexually aggressive, to regard women as inferior beings, and to view their own pleasure as the most important objective. Researchers have found the following common characteristics among rapists: aggression enhances the offender's sense of power or masculinity; rapists are angry at women generally; and they want to hurt and humiliate the victim (Browne & Williams, 1993).

Rape is a traumatic experience for the victim and those close to her (Koss & Boeschen, 1998). The rape victim initially feels shock and numbness, and is often acutely disorganized. Some women show their distress through words and tears, other show more internalized suffering. As victims strive to get their lives back to normal, they may experience depression, fear, and anxiety for months or years. Sexual dysfunctions, such as reduced sexual desire and an inability to reach orgasm, occur in 50 percent of rape victims (Sprei & Courtois, 1988). Many rape victims make changes in their lifestyle—such as moving to a new apartment or refusing to go out at night. A woman's recovery depends on both her coping abilities and her psychological adjustment prior to the assault. Social support from parents, boyfriend or husband and others close to her are important factors in recovery, as is the availability of professional counseling, which sometimes is obtained through a rape crisis center (Allison & Wrightsman, 1993).

Although most victims of rape are women, male rape does occur. Men in prisons are especially vulnerable to rape, usually by heterosexual males who use rape as a means of establishing their dominance and power. Though it might seem impossible for a man to be raped by a woman, a man's erection is not completely under his voluntary control, and some cases of male rape by women have been reported (Sarrel & Masters, 1982). Although male victims account for fewer than 5 percent of all rapes, the trauma that males suffer is just as great as that experienced by females.

Sexual Harassment

Women encounter sexual harassment in many different forms—from sexist remarks and covert physical contact (patting, brushing against their bodies) to blatant propositions and sexual assaults (Fitzgerald, 2000; Ogoski, 2001; Paludi, 1998). Literally millions of women experience such sexual harassment each year in work and educational settings. Sexual harassment can result in serious psychological consequences for the victim. Sexual harassment is a manifestation of power and domination of one person over another. The elimination of such exploitation requires the development of work and academic environments that are compatible with the needs of women workers and students, providing them with equal opportunities to develop a career and obtain an education in a climate free of sexual harassment (Marks & Nelson, 1993). Sexual harassment of men by women does occur, but to a far less extent than the sexual harassment of women by men.

WWW
Sexual Assault
Sexual Harassment

Summary Table 14.2
Sexuality

Concept	Processes/ Related Ideas	Characteristics/Descriptions
Sexual Orientation	Heterosexual Attitudes and Behavior	• Describing sexual practices in America always has been challenging. The 1994 Sex in America Survey was a major improvement over the earlier Kinsey survey. • In the 1994 survey, Americans' sexual lives were portrayed as more conservative than in the earlier surveys.
	Homosexual Attitudes and Behavior	• It generally is accepted to view sexual orientation along a continuum from exclusively heterosexual to exclusively homosexual. • An individual's sexual preference likely is the result of a combination of genetic, hormonal, cognitive, and environmental factors.
Sexually Transmitted Diseases	Common STDs	• Also called STDs, sexually transmitted diseases are contracted primarily through sexual contact. • Gonorrhea, syphilis, chlamydia, genital herpes, and HPV are among the most common STDs.
	AIDS	• The STD that has received the most attention in the last several decades is AIDS (acquired immune deficiency syndrome), which is caused by HIV, a virus that destroys the body's immune system.
	Protecting Against STDs	• Some good strategies for protecting against AIDS and other STDs are to (1) know your and your partner's risk status, (2) obtain medical examinations, (3) have protected, not unprotected, sex, and (4) not have sex with multiple partners.
Forcible Sexual Behavior and Harassment	Rape	• Rape is forcible sexual intercourse with a person who does not give consent. Rape usually produces traumatic reactions in its victims.
	Sexual Harassment	• This occurs when one person uses his or her power over another individual in a sexual manner.

At this point we have discussed a number of ideas about sexuality. To review these ideas, see summary table 14.2. Now that we have examined the transition from adolescence to adulthood, physical development, and sexuality, we will turn our attention to the cognitive changes that take place in early adulthood.

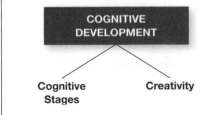

COGNITIVE DEVELOPMENT

Cognitive Stages — **Creativity**

Cognitive Development

To explore the nature of cognition in early adulthood, we will focus on issues related to cognitive stages and creative thinking.

Cognitive Stages

Are young adults more advanced in their thinking than adolescents? Let's explore what Piaget and others have said about this intriguing question.

Piaget's View Piaget believed that an adolescent and an adult think qualitatively in the same way. That is, Piaget argued that formal operational thought (more logical, abstract, and idealistic than the concrete operational thinking of 7- to 11-year-olds) is entered in early adolescence at approximately 11 to 15 years of age P. 365.

Piaget did believe that young adults are more *quantitatively* advanced in their thinking in the sense that they have more knowledge than adolescents. He also believed, as do information-processing psychologists, that adults especially increase their knowledge in a specific area, such as a physicist's understanding of physics or a financial analyst's knowledge about finance.

Some developmentalists believe it is not until adulthood that many individuals consolidate their formal operational thinking. That is, they may begin to plan and hypothesize about intellectual problems in adolescents, but they become more systematic and sophisticated at this as young adults. Nonetheless, many adults do not think in formal operational ways at all (Keating, 1980).

Realistic and Pragmatic Thinking Other developmentalists believe that the idealism that Piaget described as part of formal operational thinking decreases in early adulthood. This especially occurs as young adults move into the world of work and face the constraints of reality (Labouvie-Vief, 1986).

A related perspective on adult cognitive change was proposed by K. Warner Schaie (1977). He concluded that it is unlikely that adults go beyond the powerful methods of scientific thinking characteristic of the formal operational stage. However, Schaie argued that adults do progress beyond adolescents in their *use* of intellect. For example, he said that in early adulthood individuals often switch from acquiring knowledge to applying knowledge. This especially occurs as individuals pursue long-term career goals and attempt to achieve success in their work.

Reflective and Relativistic Thinking William Perry (1970) also described some changes in cognition that take place in early adulthood. He said that adolescents often view the world in terms of polarities—right/wrong, we/they, good/bad. As youth move into adulthood, they gradually move away from this type of absolute thinking as they become aware of the diverse opinions and multiple perspectives of others. Thus, in Perry's view, the *absolute, dualistic thinking* (either/or) of adolescence gives way to the *reflective, relativistic thinking* of adulthood.

As we see next, some theorists have pieced together some of these different aspects of thinking and proposed a new qualitative stage of cognitive development.

Is There a Fifth, Postformal Stage? **Postformal thought** *is qualitatively different from Piaget's formal operational thought. Postformal thought involves understanding that the correct answer to a problem requires reflective thinking and can vary from one situation to another, and that the search for truth is often an ongoing, never-ending process. Also part of the fifth stage is the belief that solutions to problems need to be realistic and that emotion and subjective factors can influence thinking* (Kitchener & King, 1981; Kramer, Kahlbaugh, & Goldston, 1992). Researchers have found that young adults are more likely to engage in this postformal thinking than adolescents are (Commons & others, 1989).

postformal thought
A form of thought, proposed as a fifth stage, that is qualitatively different from Piaget's formal operational thought. It involves understanding that the correct answer to a problem can require reflective thinking, that the correct answer can vary from one situation to another, and that the search for truth is often an ongoing, never-ending process. It also involves the belief that solutions to problems need to be realistic and that emotion and subjective factors can influence thinking.

As young adults engage in more reflective judgment when solving problems, they might think deeply about many aspects of politics, their career and work, relationships, and other areas of life (Labouvie-Vief & Diehl, 1999). They might understand that what might be the best solution to a problem at work (with a co-worker or boss) might not be the best solution at home (with a romantic partner). Many young adults also become more skeptical about there being a single truth and often are not willing to accept an answer as final. They also often recognize that thinking can't just be abstract but rather has to be realistic and pragmatic. And many young adults understand that emotions can play a role in thinking—for example, that one likely thinks more clearly in a calm, collected state than in an angry, highly aroused state.

How strong is the research evidence for a fifth, postformal stage of cognitive development? The fifth stage is controversial, and some critics argue that the research evidence has yet to be provided to document it as clearly a qualitatively more advanced stage than formal operational thought.

The horse is here to stay, but the automobile is only a novelty—a fad.

President of the Michigan Savings Bank advising Henry Ford not to invest in Ford Motor Company

Heavier-than-air flying machines are impossible.

Lord Kelvin
British scientist, 1895

Video won't be able to hold on to any market it captures after the first six months. People will soon get tired of staring at a plywood box every night.

Darryl Zanuck, head of 20th Century Fox movie studios, commenting on television in 1946

Creativity

In chapter 10, "Physical and Cognitive Development in Middle and Late Childhood," we studied creativity in children P. 299. The strategies for being creative in adulthood are essentially the same as in childhood. Here we focus on the issue of whether creativity might decline at some point in adulthood and explore Mihaly Csikszentmihalyi's ideas about how to lead a more creative life.

Adult Developmental Changes At the age of 30, Thomas Edison invented the phonograph, Hans Christian Anderson wrote his first volume of fairy tales, and Mozart composed *The Marriage of Figaro.* One early study of creativity found that individuals' most creative products were generated in their thirties and that 80 percent of the most important creative contributions were completed by age fifty (Lehman, 1960). More recently, researchers have found that creativity does peak in adulthood and then decline, but that the peak often occurs in the forties. However, qualifying any conclusion about age and creative accomplishments are (1) the magnitude of the decline in productivity, (2) contrasts across creative domains, and (3) individual differences in lifetime output (Simonton, 1996).

Even though a decline in creative contributions is often found in the fifties and later, the decline is not as great as commonly thought. An impressive array of creative accomplishments occur in late adulthood. Benjamin Franklin invented bifocal lens when he was 78 years old; Goethe completed *Faust* when he was in his eighties. And one of the most remarkable examples of creative accomplishment in late adulthood can be found in the life of Henri Chevreul. After a distinguished career as a physicist, Chevreul switched fields in his nineties to become a pioneer in gerontological research. He published his last research paper just a year prior to his death at the age of 103!

U.S. Poet Laureate Mark Strard says that in his most creative moments he loses a sense of time and becomes absorbed in what he is doing. In this state, he feels he is dismantling meaning and remaking it. Strand comments that he can't stay in this absorbed frame of mind for an entire day. It comes and goes. His attention coils and uncoils. His focus sharpens and softens. When an idea clicks, he focuses intensely, transforming the idea into a vivid verbal image that communicates its essence to the reader.

Nina Holton, a leading contemporary sculptor, turns playfully wild germs of ideas into stunning sculptures. She says that sculpture is a combination of wonderful, unique ideas and a lot of hard work. She comments that when she is introduced to people they often say, "It must be so exciting and wonderful being a sculptor." Holton loves her work, but says that most people see only its creative side, not the hard work.

Jonas Salk, who invented the polio vaccine, says that his best ideas come to him at night when he suddenly wakes up. After about five minutes of visualizing problems he had thought about the day before, he begins to see an unfolding, as if a poem, painting, story, or concept is about to take form. Salk also believes that many creative ideas are generated through conversations with others who have open, curious minds and positive attitudes. Salk's penchant for seeing emergent possibilities often brought him in conflict with people who had orthodox opinions.

Any consideration of decline in creativity with age requires consideration of the domain involved. In such fields as philosophy and history, older adults often show as much creativity as when they were in their thirties and forties. By contrast, in such fields as lyric poetry, abstract math, and theoretical physics, the peak of creativity is often reached in the twenties or thirties.

There also is extensive individual variation in the lifetime output of creative individuals. Typically, the most productive creators in any field are far more prolific than their least productive counterparts. The contrast is so extreme that the top 10 percent of creative producers frequently account for 50 percent of the creative output in a particular domain. For instance, only sixteen composers account for half of the music regularly performed in the classical repertoire.

Csikszentmihalyi's Ideas Mihaly Csikszentmihalyi (pronounced ME-high CHICK-sent-me-high-ee) (1995) interviewed 90 leading figures in art, business, government, education, and science to learn how creativity works. He discovered that creative people regularly experience a state he calls *flow,* a heightened state of pleasure we experience when we are engaged in mental and physical challenges that absorb us. Csikszentmihalyi (1997, 2000) believes everyone is capable of achieving flow. Based on his interviews with some of the most creative people in the world, the first step toward a more creative life is cultivating your curiosity and interest. How can you do this?

- *Try to be surprised by something every day.* Maybe it is something you see, hear, or read about. Become absorbed in a lecture or a book. Be open to what the world is telling you. Live is a stream of experiences. Swim widely and deeply in it, and your life will be richer.
- *Try to surprise at least one person every day.* In a lot of things you do, you have to be predictable and patterned. Do something different for a change. Ask a question you normally would not ask. Invite someone to go to a show or a museum you never have visited.
- *Write down each day what surprised you and how you surprised others.* Most creative people keep a diary, notes, or lab records to ensure that their experience is not fleeting or forgotten. Start with a specific task. Each evening record the most surprising event that occurred that day and your most surprising action. After a few days, reread your notes and reflect on your past experiences. After a few weeks, you might see a pattern of interest emerging in your notes, one that might suggest an area you can explore in greater depth.
- *When something sparks your interest, follow it.* Usually when something captures your attention, it is short-lived—an idea, a song, a flower. Too often we are too busy to explore the idea, song, or flower further. Or we think these areas are none of our business because we are not experts about them. Yet the world is our business. We can't know which part of it is best suited to our interests until we make a serious effort to learn as much about as many aspects of it as possible.

Careers in Life-Span Development

Mihaly Csikszentmihalyi, University Professor and Researcher

Mihaly Csikszentmihalyi, born in Hungary and a professor at the University of Chicago for many years, currently is a professor at Claremont Graduate School in California. Csikszentmihalyi has had a special interest in adolescents, initially conducting a number of research studies on what they do in their lives, the contexts in which they spend their time, and the people with whom they interact, and how they are feeling. He developed what is known as the experience sampling technique (the "beeper" technique) in which researchers give participants an electronic pager and contact them at random times, asking them a series of questions.

Csikszentmihalyi developed the concept of "flow"—the mental and emotional state people are in when they deeply enjoy what they are doing. Currently he is one of the main architects of changing psychology's focus from the negative to the positive, believing that for too long the field has studied the dark side of life and that it is high time psychologists started focusing more on the good aspects of people—things like optimistic thinking, being altruistic, having good relationships, and being creative.

He has conducted a study of highly creative people in different walks of life—business, the arts, science—to discover what they are thinking, feeling, and doing when they come up with their most creative insights (Csikszentmihalyi, 1995). One thing he found was that certain settings are more likely to stimulate creativity than others. *When and where do you get your most creative thoughts?*

Mihaly Csikszentmihalyi, in the setting where he gets his most creative ideas.

Csikszentmihalyi

Summary Table 14.3
Cognitive Development

Concept	Processes/ Related Ideas	Characteristics/Descriptions
Congnitive Stages	Piaget's View	• Formal operational thought, entered at age 11 to 15 is Piaget's final cognitive stage. Piaget did say that adults are quantitatively more knowledgeable than adolescents but that adults do not enter a new, qualitatively different stage.
	Realistic and Pragmatic Thinking	• Some experts argue that the idealism of Piaget's formal operational stage declines in young adults, replaced by more realistic, pragmatic thinking.
	Reflective and Relativistic Thinking	• Perry said that adolescents often engage in dualistic, absolute thinking, while young adults are more likely to engage in reflective, relativistic thinking.
	Is There a Fifth, Postformal Stage?	• Postformal thought is qualitatively different from Piaget's formal operational thought. It involves understanding that the correct answer might require reflective thinking and might vary from one situation to another, and that the search for truth is often never-ending. Also, the postformal stage includes the understanding that solutions to problems often need to be realistic and that emotion and subjective factors can be involved in thinking.
Creativity	Adult Developmental Changes	• Creativity peaks in adulthood, often in the forties, and then declines. However, (a) the magnitude of the decline is often slight; (b) the creativity-age link varies by domain; and (c) there is extensive individual variation in lifetime creative output.
	Csikszentmihalyi's Ideas	• Based on interviews with leading experts in different domains, Csikszentmihalyi charted the way creative people go about living a creative life, such as waking up every morning with a mission and spending time in settings that stimulate their creativity.

- *Wake up in the morning with a specific goal to look forward to.* Creative people wake up eager to start the day. Why? Not necessarily because they are cheerful, enthusiastic types but because they know that there is something meaningful to accomplish each day, and they can't wait to get started.
- *Take charge of your schedule.* Figure out which time of the day is your most creative time. Some of us are more creative late at night, others early in the morning. Carve out some time for yourself when your creative energy is at its best.
- *Spend time in settings that stimulate your creativity.* In Csikszentmihalyi's (1995) research, he gave people an electronic pager and beeped them randomly at different times of the day. When he asked them how they felt, they reported the highest levels of creativity when walking, driving, or swimming. I (your author) do my most creative thinking when I'm jogging. These activities are semi-automatic in that they take a certain amount of attention while leaving some time free to make connections among ideas. Another setting in which highly creative people report coming up with novel ideas is the sort of half-asleep, half-awake state we are in when we are deeply relaxed or barely awake.

At this point we have studied a number of ideas on cognitive development in early adulthood. To review these ideas, see summary table 14.3. Next, we turn to the final main section in this chapter as we explore some very important aspects of early adulthood: career development and work.

Careers and Work

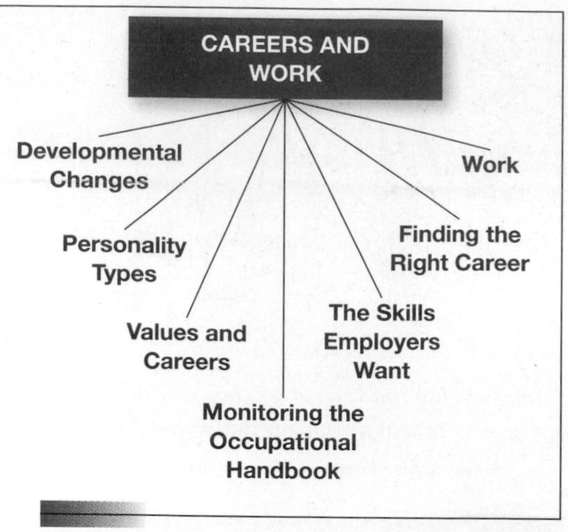

At age 21, Thomas Smith graduated from college and accepted a job as a science teacher at a high school in Boston. At age 26, Mary Lou Hernandez graduated from medical school and took a job as an intern at a hospital in Los Angeles. At age 20, Barbara Breck finished her training at a vocational school and went to work as a computer programmer for an engineering firm in Chicago. Earning a living, choosing an occupation, establishing a career, and developing in a career—these are important themes of early adulthood.

Developmental Changes

Many children have idealistic fantasies about what they want to be when they grow up. For example, young children might want to be a superhero, a sports star, or a movie star. In the high school years, they often have begun to think about careers on a somewhat less idealistic basis. In their late teens and early twenties, their career decision making has usually turned more serious as they explore different career possibilities and zero in on the career they want to enter. In college, this often means choosing a major or specialization that is designed to lead to work in a particular field. By their early and mid twenties, many individuals have completed their education or training and started to enter a full-time occupation. From the mid twenties through the remainder of early adulthood, individuals often seek to establish their emerging career in a particular field. They may work hard to move up the career ladder and improve their financial standing.

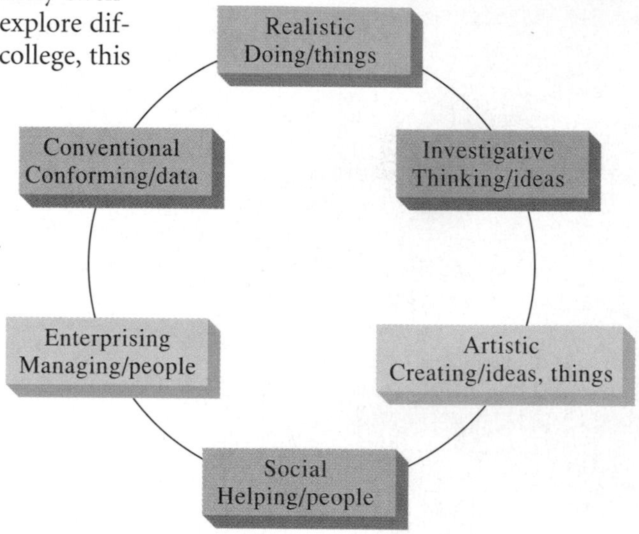

Figure **14.5**
Holland's Model of Personality Types and Career Choices

Personality Types

Personality type theory *is John Holland's (1987) view that it is important for individuals to select a career that matches up well with their personality type.* Holland believes that when individuals find careers that fit their personality, they are more likely to enjoy the work and stay in the job longer than if they'd taken a job not suited to their personality. Holland proposed six basic career-related personality types: realistic, investigative, artistic, social, enterprising, and conventional (see figure 14.5):

- *Realistic.* They like the outdoors and working in manual activities. They often are less social, have difficulty in demanding situations, and prefer to work alone. This personality type matches up best with jobs in labor, farming, truck driving, construction, engineer, and pilot.
- *Investigative.* They are interested in ideas more than people, are rather indifferent to social relationships, are troubled by emotional situations, and are often aloof and intelligent. This personality type matches up well with scientific, intellectually oriented professions.
- *Artistic.* They are creative and enjoy working with ideas and materials that allow them to express themselves in innovative ways. They value nonconformity, freedom, and ambiguity. Sometimes they have difficulties in social relationships. Not many jobs match up with the artistic personality type. Consequently, some artistic individuals work in jobs that are their second or third choices and express their artistic interests through hobbies and leisure.
- *Social.* They like to work with people and tend to have a helping orientation. They like doing social things considerably more than engaging in intellectual tasks. This personality type matches up with jobs in teaching, social work, and counseling.

personality type theory
John Holland's view that it is important to match an individual's personality with a particular career.

WWW

Holland's Personality Types

Steps to Successful Career Planning

Journal of Vocational Behavior Career Development Quarterly

Journal of Counseling Psychology

"Your son has made a career choice, Mildred. He's going to win the lottery and travel a lot."

- *Enterprising.* They also are more oriented toward people than things or ideas. They may try to dominate others to reach their goals. They are often good at persuading others to do things. The enterprising type matches up with careers in sales, management, and politics.
- *Conventional.* They function best in well-structured situations and are skilled at working with details. They often like to work with numbers and perform clerical tasks rather than working with ideas or people. The conventional type matches up with such jobs as accountant, bank teller, secretary, or file clerk.

If all individuals (and careers) fell conveniently into Holland's personality types, career counselors would have an easy job. However, individuals are typically more varied and complex than Holland's theory suggests. Even Holland (1987) states that individuals rarely are pure types, and most persons are a combination of two or three types. Still, the basic idea of matching the abilities and attitudes of individuals to particular careers is an important contribution to the career development field. Holland's personality types are incorporated into the Strong-Campbell Interest Inventory, a widely used measure in career guidance.

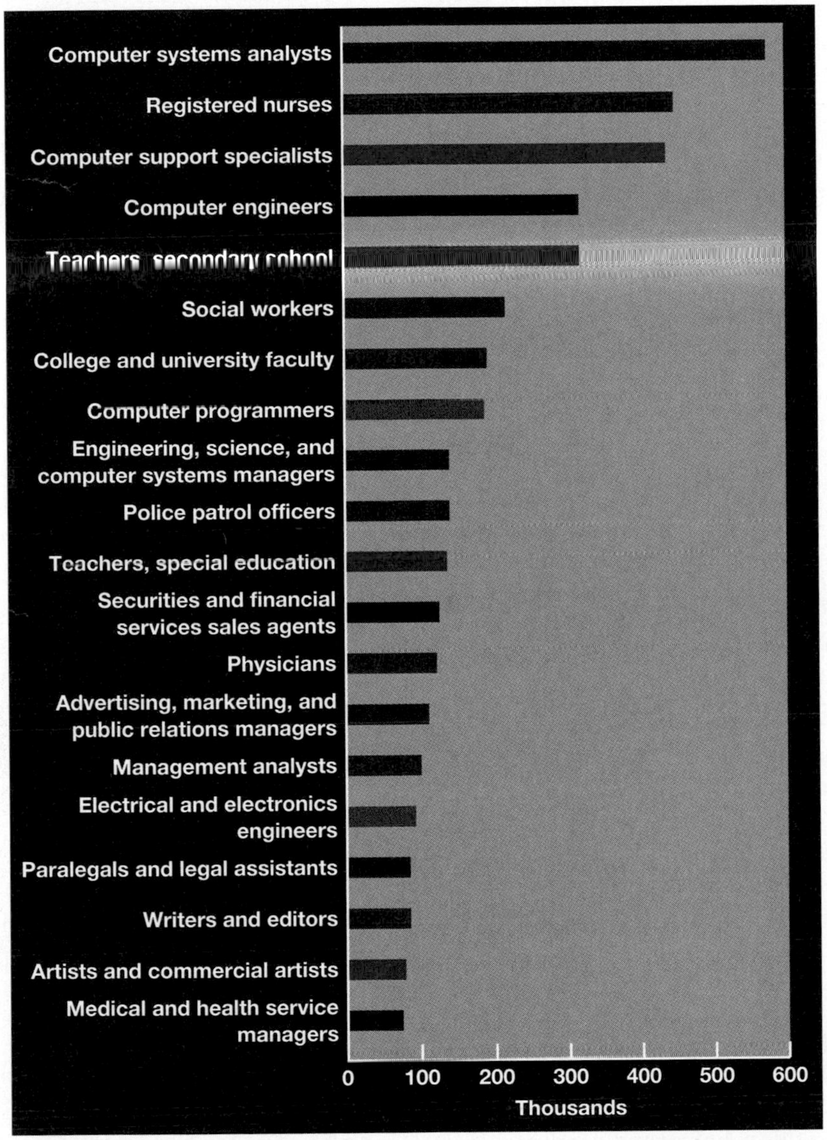

Figure **14.6**

Occupations with Fast Growth and High Pay Expected to Show the Largest Numerical Growth in Jobs from 1998 to 2008

Values and Careers

An important aspect of choosing a career is that it also match up with your values. When people know what they value most—what is important to them in life—they can refine their career choice more effectively. Some values are reflected in Holland's personality types, such as whether a person values working in career that involves helping others or in a career in which creativity is valued. Among the values that some individuals think are important in choosing a career are working with people they like, working in a career with prestige, making a lot of money, being happy, not having to work long hours, being mentally challenged, having plenty of time for leisure pursuits, working in the right geographical location, and working where physical and mental health are important.

Monitoring the Occupational Outlook

It is a good idea for individuals to keep up with the occupational outlook for various fields. An excellent source is *The Occupational Outlook Handbook,* which is revised every 2 years. The following information comes from the 2000–2001 handbook (see figure 14.6).

Service-producing industries will account for most new jobs: business, health, and professional services are projected to account for 75 percent of job growth from 1998 to 2008. Employment in computer and data-processing services is projected to grow 117 percent in this time frame, ranking it as the fastest-growing industry. Indeed, of the top four occupations with the fastest projected growth, three of the four are in the computer industry (computer systems analysts, computer support specialists, and computer engineers). Employers today

point out that no matter what their career aspirations, individuals will need computer skills to perform their job competently. The reality is that computer skills are not just nice to have—they are a must.

Jobs that require college degrees will be the fastest-growing and highest-paying. Jobs that require an associate degree from a community college are projected to increase more than 30 percent from 1998 to 2008, those that require a bachelor's degree or doctoral degree more than 25 percent, and those that require a master's degree more than 20 percent. All but a few of the highest-paying occupations require a college degree.

The labor force participation rates of women in nearly all age groups are projected to increase while that of men's is anticipated to remain unchanged. The Asian American and Latino American labor forces are expected to increase faster than other ethnic groups, by 40 and 37 percent respectively. It has been projected that by 2008, the Latino American labor force will be larger than the African American labor force.

The Skills Employers Want

Take a few minutes and think about the career you want to pursue. What do you think the profile of an ideal job candidate in this career field would be?

To begin with, computer skills are increasingly important in most careers. In one national study, the communication skils of prospective job candidates were extremely important (Collins, 1996). At the top of employers' wish lists of characteristics they desired in a future employee, oral communication skills was first, followed by interpersonal skills, analytical skills, flexibility, leadership skills, proficiency in field of study, written communication skills, and computer skills.

To determine whether a candidate has the skills to succeed at the job, employers look for evidence in the candidate's accomplishments and experiences. In particular they look for

- leadership positions
- involvement in campus organizations and extracurricular activities
- relevant experiences in internships, part-time work, or co-ops
- good grades

The ideal job candidate presents a combination of these.

Finding the Right Career

We have examined several factors—personality type and values—that are important in determining the best career for a particular person. In choosing a career, it is a good idea to have several careers in mind rather than just one. Increasingly, individuals are having more than just one career in their adult working life. Because individuals are changing jobs and careers more than in the past, it also is

Critical Thinking: Career Goal-Setting

LIKE A LONG JOURNEY, you need markers along your career path to tell you that you are on track. These are your goals, the specific things that you will do and accomplish as you move through your career development. Every dream and vision you might develop about your future career development can be broken down into specific goals and time frames. Keeping your career dreams in focus, write some of the specific work, job, and career goals you have for the next 20, 10, and 5 years. Be as concrete and specific as possible. In making up goals, start from the farthest point—20 years, and work backward. If you go the other way, you run the risk of adopting goals that are not precisely and clearly related to your dream.

CAREERS IN LIFE-SPAN DEVELOPMENT

Lilian Comas-Diaz, Clinical Psychologist

LILIAN COMAS-DIAZ received her Ph.D. from the University of Massachusetts at Amherst. She is the director of the Transcultural Mental Health Institute and maintains a private practice in clinical psychology in Washington, DC.

Lilian is the former director of the American Psychological Association's Office of Minority Affairs and the former director of the Hispanic Clinic at Yale University School of Medicine. She has a special interest in the mental health of Latinos.

> According to Lilian Comas-Diaz (1999): Latinos' experience serves as a compass in our national redefinition because their odyssey parallels the United States. Historically, some Latinos were native to this land; others arrived searching for the immigrant dream or the Golden Fleece of opportunities and freedom; and still others continue to be washed up on America's shores searching for the political and religious asylum. Their journey-paved with discrimination, socioeconomic challenge, trauma, and cultural adjustment—is emblematic of our national aspiration, *e pluribus unum* (One Out of Many).

Lilian Comas-Diaz

Her goal is to help Latinos move from trauma and stress to coping, health, and success.

Occupational Outlook

Career and Job-Hunting Resources

What Color Is Your Parachute?

Job Interviewing

Work and Family Issues

a good idea to develop skills that are important in a variety of jobs and careers, such as communication and computer skills.

Some good strategies for finding more information about a particular career are to see a career counselor, engage in personal networking (ask friends, family, and instructors if they know someone in a particular field who could be contacted for information), and scope out Internet networks and resources (extensive information about jobs and careers is available on the Internet).

Work

Work plays a powerful role in our lives. How much time to people spend in work? How can you get positive work experiences during college? What are some good strategies for nailing a job interview? What issues do dual-career couples face?

The Nature of Work

Work defines individuals in fundamental ways (Osipow, 2000). Individuals identify with their work, and work shapes their lives in many ways. It is an important influence on their financial standing, housing, the way they spend their time, where they live, their friendships, and their health.

Most individuals spend about one-third of their adult lives at work. In one recent survey, 35 percent of Americans worked 40 hours a week, but 18 percent even worked 51 hours or more per week (Center for Survey Research at the University of Connecticut, 2000). Almost half of the individuals worked more than 40 hours a week. Only 10 percent worked less than 30 hours a week.

Work creates a structure and rhythm to life that is often missed when individuals do not work for an extended period of time. When unable to work, many individuals experience emotional distress and low self-esteem.

However, some aspects of work also create stress. Four main aspects of work settings are linked with employee stress and health problems (Moos, 1986): (1) high job demands such as having a heavy workload and time pressure; (2) inadequate opportunities to participate in decision making; (3) a high level of supervisor control; and (4) a lack of clarity about the criteria for competent performance.

Getting Positive Work Experiences During College

Students can participate in cooperative education programs, internships, or part-time or summer work relevant to their field of study. This experience can be critical in helping students obtain the job they want when they graduate from college. Today's employers expect job candidates to have this type of experience. In the recent national survey of employers, almost 60% said their entry-level college hires had co-op or internship experience (Collins, 1996). Participating in these work experiences can be a key factor in whether you land the job you want when you graduate from college.

More than 1,000 colleges in the United States offer cooperative education (*co-op*) programs. A co-op is a paid apprenticeship in a career field that you are interested in pursuing. You may not be permitted to participate in a co-op program until your junior year.

"Uh-huh. Uh-huh. And for precisely how long were you a hunter-gatherer at I.B.M.?"

The Job Interview

How well you handle a job interview is a critical factor in obtaining a job. Following are some good strategies for how to get an interview and doing well in the job interview (Yate, 2001):

- Resumes are important and you will need one. They are used by employers to decide whether they want to interview you in the first place. Organize your resume, write it clearly, and don't use a lot of jargon.

- Don't wing the interview. Do your homework. Find out as much about your prospective employer as possible. What does the company/organization do? How successful is it? Employers are impressed by job candidates who have taken the time to learn about their organization. This is true whether you are interviewing for a part-time job at your college library or for a full-time job in a large corporation after you graduate from college.
- Be prepared to give positive examples of your past work experience. Interviewers anticipate that your past work behavior is a good predictor of how well you do in this new job, so the examples you give from past jobs may seal your fate.
- Anticipate what questions you will be asked in the interview. Do some practice interviews. Some typical interview questions include: What is your greatest strength? What interests you the most about this job? Why should I hire you? Also be prepared for some zingers. For example, how would you respond to these questions: Tell me something you are not very proud of? Describe a situation in which your idea was criticized? These types of questions are used by interviews to catch you off guard and determine how you handle a stressful situation.
- Ask appropriate job-related questions yourself. Review the job requirements with the interviewer
- Keep your cool. Always leave in the same mannerly and polite way you entered.
- As the interview closes, decide whether you want the job. If so, ask for it. If the job is not offered on the spot, ask when the two of you can talk again.
- That's not all. Immediately after the interview, type a follow-up letter. Keep it short, less than one page. Mail the letter within 24 hours after the interview. If you do not hear anything within five days, call the organization and ask about the status of the job.

Dual-Career Couples

The increasing career commitment on the part of women has led to new work-related issues, such as the division of work and family responsibilities in dual-career couples. As women have taken on increasing work responsibilities outside the home, there often has not been a corresponding decrease in their responsibilities at home. Although many men in dual-career families have taken on more home responsibilities, including child care, women in this type of family still have the majority of home responsibilities, including child care (Yeung & others, 2001). This combination of career and family work has some critics to label family work in this type of family "the second shift" (Hochschild & Machung, 1989).

Wives perform a far greater proportion of household tasks than their husbands even when the wife earns more money or her husband is unemployed (Greenstein, 2000). Not only do married women perform far more household labor than their husbands, they perform different types of tasks (Lennon & Rosenfield, 1994). Women still primarily do what traditionally has been thought of as "women's work"—cooking, laundry, and housecleaning. Men still primarily do what traditionally has been thought of as "men's work"—yard work, taking out the garbage, and auto maintenance.

Thus, an important issue for many women is juggling career and family work (Milke & Peltola. 2000). To read further about this issue, see the Sociocultural Worlds of Development box.

Another issue that dual-career couples face focuses on compatible job schedules and/or locations. One individual might work primarily during the day, the other in the evening or at night, in which case they rarely see each other. If one spouse receives a job offer in another geographical location, the issues of whose career takes priority or whether the couple should consider a long-distance relationship are raised.

At this point we have studied a number of ideas about career development and work. To review these ideas, see summary table 14.4. In the next chapter, we will continue our examination of early adulthood by focusing on socioemotional development.

Sociocultural Worlds of Development

Juggling Roles

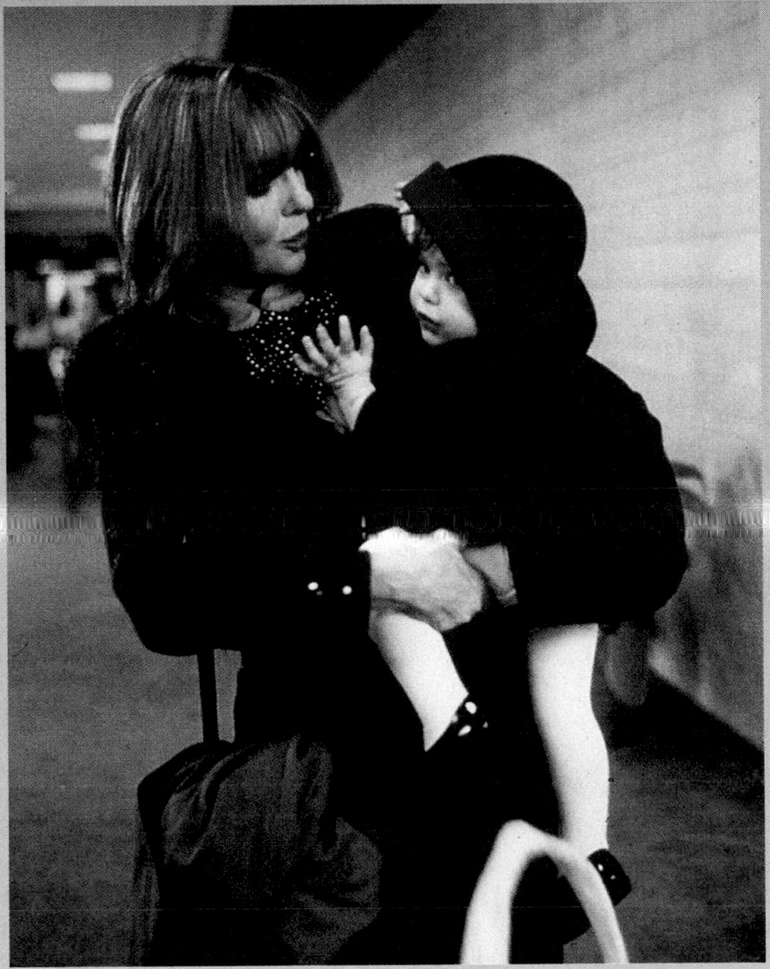

The character played by Diane Keaton (above), in the movie *Baby Boom,* lost her job when she couldn't find a way to juggle her career and family roles and still give her child adequate care and attention. Many U.S. corporations perceive flexible scheduling as an important management issue. Some individuals are turning down higher-paying jobs to take jobs with more flexibility. This is likely to be an increasing trend.

In *Juggling: The Unexpected Advantages of Balancing Career and Home for Women and Their Families,* Faye Crosby (1991) described the advantages of multiple roles for women. She also discussed ways that the stress involved in juggling the roles can be reduced. Especially noteworthy when women "jugglers" are interviewed is the lack of free minutes they have. One woman in her thirties said she would just like to have a few more minutes in the day. When asked what she would do with the additional several hours, she said that she would relax after work before she started cooking dinner, or she would go to the gym and swim. She said that yesterday when she went to pick the kids up, she had a cake in the oven and worried that she would get stuck in traffic and it would burn up. Her final comment was that she would love not to have to be somewhere at a certain time. Jugglers identify the unrelenting pace of life as a persistent problem. They speak of lacking time to relax, of pressured schedules, and of cramming weeks of work into the hours of the day.

Thus, not only do most jugglers derive a great deal of pleasure from life, they, like many other women in contemporary American society, feel stressed, stretched, and tired to the point of exhaustion. Virtually all women, especially jugglers, need competent support systems to help them cope with the multiple demands in their lives. A better national child-care policy and improved day care, as well as supportive others, can help to reduce the stress that many jugglers feel. Jugglers can build a network of adults who accept responsibility to help out, especially in times of emergency, no matter how minor.

The juggler is a real person who is striving to overcome obstacles in her path. As a society, we need to illuminate the features of our social structure that create unnecessary stress and unneeded heartache, and we need to work to change those features. We need to regard women's large-scale entry into the labor force as an unprecedented opportunity to build a better nation. As Crosby concludes, it is possible and desirable to regard the increasing number of women who are simultaneously spouse, parent, and career person as providing us all a chance to fashion social worlds that promote healthy communities, families, and individuals.

Summary Table 14.4
Careers and Work

Concept	Processes/ Related Ideas	Characteristics/Descriptions
Developmental Changes	From Fantasy to Establishing a Career	• Many young children have idealistic fantasies about a career. In the late teens and early twenties, their career thinking has usually turned more serious. By their early to mid twenties, many individuals have completed their education or training and started in a career. In the remainder of early adulthood, they seek to establish their emerging career and start moving up the career ladder.
Personality Types	Holland's View	• John Holland proposed that it is important for individuals to choose a career that is compatible with their personality type.
Values and Careers	Knowing What Is Important To You	• It is important to match up a career to your values. There are many different values, ranging from the importance of money to working in a preferred geographical location.
Monitoring the Occupational Outlook	It's a computer world	• Service-producing industries will account for the most jobs in American in the next decade. Employment in the computer industry is especially projected to grow rapidly.
	College Education	• Jobs that require a college education will be the fastest-growing and highest-paying.
	Women and Ethnic Minorities	• Labor force participation of women will increase and so will that of Latinos and African Americans.
The Skills Employers Want	Communication and Computer Skills	• In most careers today, communication skills and career skills are at the top of the list of what employers want in prospective employees.
Finding the Right Career		• Personality types and values are important in finding the right career. It is a good idea to have several careers rather than just one. Seeing a career counselor, engaging in personal networking, and scoping out Internet networks and resources are good strategies.
Work	How It Defines Us	• Work defines people in fundamental ways and is a key aspect of their identity. Most individuals spend about one-third of their adult life at work. • People often become stressed if they are unable to work but work also can produce stress, as when there is a heavy work load and time pressure.
	Positive Work Experience During College	• These might include cooperative education, internship, or part-time/summer work relevant to your field of study.
	The Job Interview	• It can be critical in getting a job and a number of positive strategies can be followed.
	Dual-Career Couples	• The increasing number of women who work in careers outside the home has led to new work-related issues. A special concern of many women is how to effectively juggle a career with family responsibilities.

Chapter Review

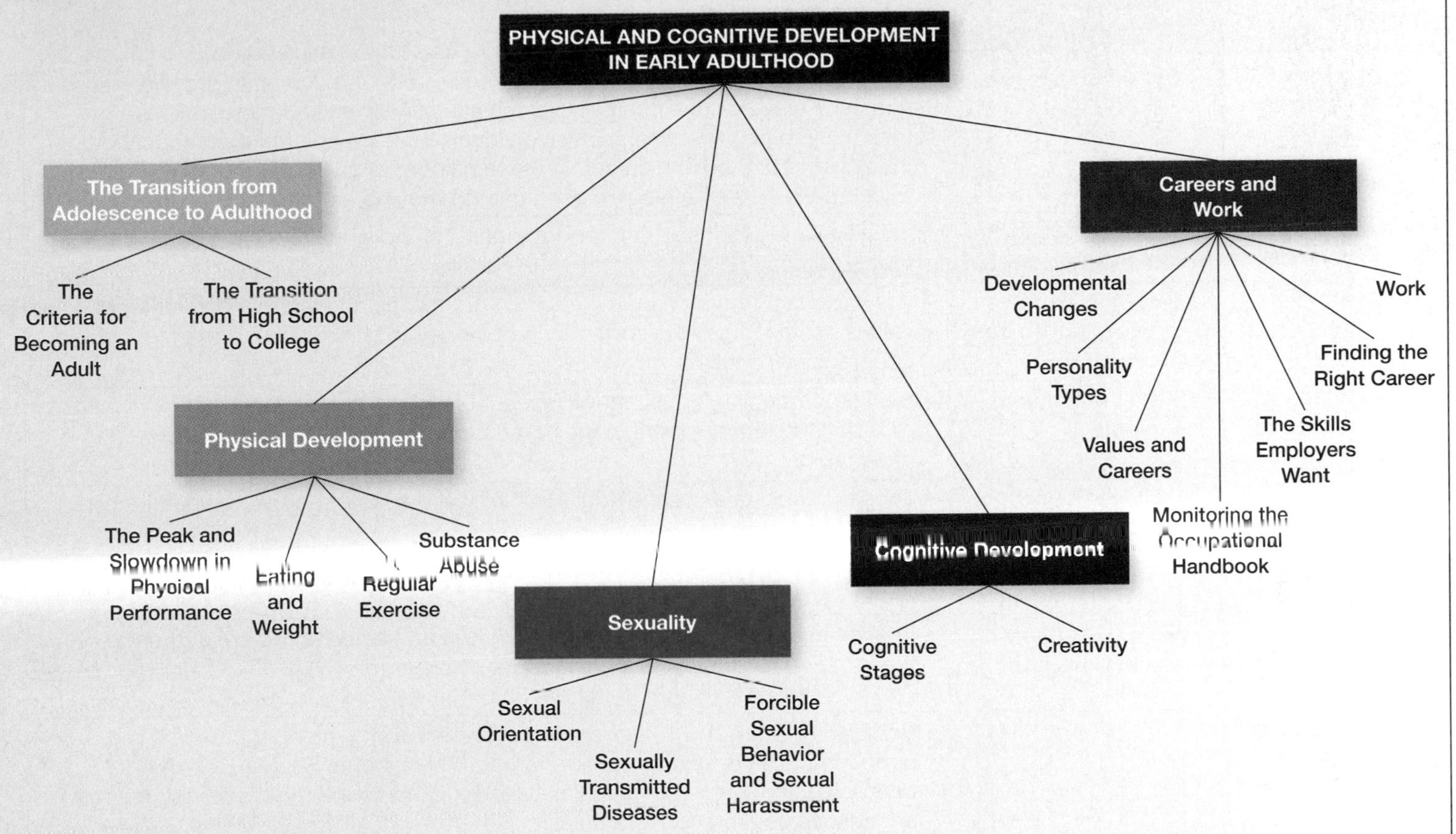

TO OBTAIN A DETAILED REVIEW OF THIS CHAPTER, STUDY THESE FOUR SUMMARY TABLES:

- Summary Table 14.1 — The Transition from Adolescence to Adulthood; Physical Development — page 423
- Summary Table 14.2 — Sexuality — page 430
- Summary Table 14.3 — Cognitive Development — page 434
- Summary Table 14.4 — Careers and Work — page 441

Key Terms

basal metabolism rate (BMR) 418
restrained eaters 419
aerobic exercise 420
addiction 422
disease model of addiction 422
life-process model of addiction 422
sexually transmitted diseases (STDs) 426
gonorrhea 426
syphilis 426
chlamydia 426
genital herpes 426
HPV 427
AIDS 427
rape 429
date or acquaintance rape 429
postformal thought 431
personality type theory 435

Key People

Robert Michael 424
Simon LeVay 425
Laura Brown 425
Jean Piaget 430
K. Warner Schaie 431
William Perry 431
Mihaly Csikszentmihalyi 433
John Holland 435
Faye Crosby 440

Taking It to the Net

1. Yvonne has always considered herself overweight, but not obese. She is 5′4″ and weighs 160 pounds. Calculate her body mass index (BMI) and use the guidelines to determine whether or not she is overweight or obese. What is your BMI?
2. Anna is working part-time in her college human resources office. She has been asked to start gathering information for a sexual harassment information booklet. What are the essential characteristics of sexual harassment and how should she communicate how the signs are identified?
3. Victor feels like he is in a real rut at work. He can't seem to find anything in his professional or personal life that interests or excites him. A friend suggested he look into "flow." What is "flow" and how can it help Victor improve his life?

Connect to www.mhhe.com/santrockld8 to research the answers and complete these exercises.

OLC Preview

To further test your knowledge of this chapter or to explore our extensive online resources that accompany *Life-Span Development*, eighth edition, please log on to the text's Online Learning Center at http://www.mhhe.com/santrockld8.com.

Chapter 15

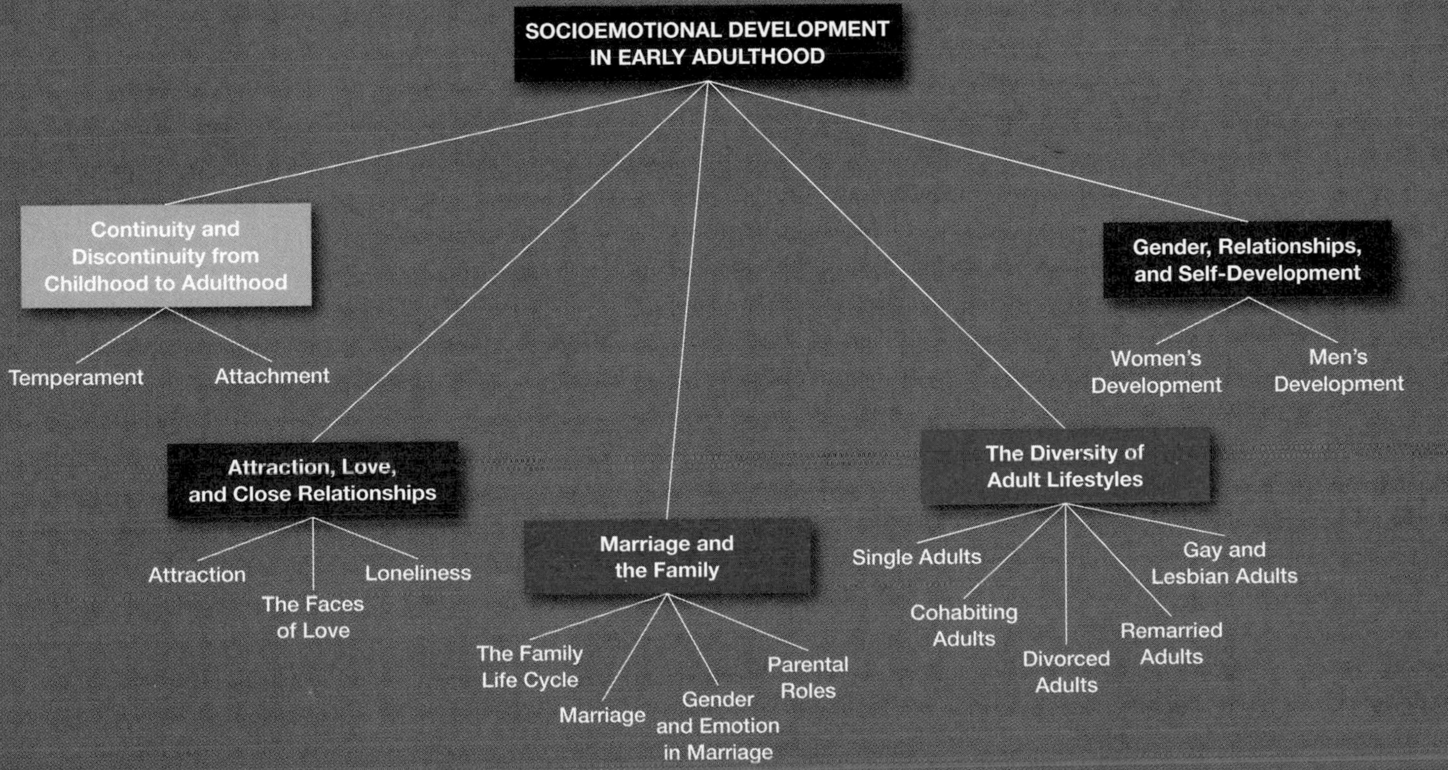
SOCIOEMOTIONAL DEVELOPMENT IN EARLY ADULTHOOD
Continuity and Discontinuity from Childhood to Adulthood
Temperament
Attachment
Attraction, Love, and Close Relationships
Attraction
The Faces of Love
Loneliness
Marriage and the Family
The Family Life Cycle
Marriage
Gender and Emotion in Marriage
Parental Roles
The Diversity of Adult Lifestyles
Single Adults
Cohabiting Adults
Divorced Adults
Remarried Adults
Gay and Lesbian Adults
Gender, Relationships, and Self-Development
Women's Development
Men's Development

Socioemotional Development in Early Adulthood

Love is a canvas furnished by nature and embroidered by imagination.

Voltaire
Pen Name of François Arovet
French Essayist, 18th Century

Images of Life-Span Development

Edith, Phil, and Sherry, Searching for Love

PHIL IS A lovesick man. On two consecutive days he put expensive ads in New York City newspapers, urging, begging, pleading a woman named Edith to forgive him and continue their relationship. The first ad read as follows:

> **Edith**
>
> I was torn two ways. Too full of child to relinquish the lesser. Older now, a balance struck, that child forever behind me. Please forgive me, reconsider. Help make a new us; better now than before.
>
> **Phil**

This ad was placed in the *New York Post* at a cost of $3,600. Another full-page ad appeared in the *New York Times* at a cost of $3,408. Phil's ads stirred up quite a bit of interest. Forty-two Ediths responded; Phil said he thought the whole process would be more private. As Phil would attest, relationships are very important to us. Some of us will go to almost any length and spend large sums of money to restore lost relationships.

Sherry is not searching for a particular man. She is at the point where she is, well, looking for Mr. Anybody. Sherry is actually more particular than she says, although she is frustrated by what she calls that "great man shortage" in this country. For every 100 men over 15 years of age who have never been married or are widowed or divorced, there are 123 women. For African Americans the ratio is 100 men for every 133 women.

William Novak (1983), author of *The Great Man Shortage,* believes it is the quality of the gap that bothers most women. He says the quality problem stems from the fact that the combination of the feminist movement and women's tendency to seek therapy when their personal relationships do not work out has made women outgrow men emotionally. He points out that many women are saying to men, "You don't have to earn all the money anymore, and I don't want to have to do all the emotional work." Novak observes that the whole issue depresses many women because society has conditioned them to assume that their lack of a marriage partner is their fault. One 37-year-old

woman told Novak, "I'm no longer waiting for a man on a white horse. Now I'd settle for the horse."

Love is of central importance in each of our lives, as it is in Phil's and Sherry's lives. Shortly, we will discuss the many faces of love, but first we will return to an issue we initially raised in chapter 1: continuity and discontinuity.

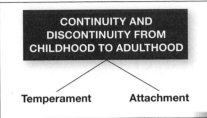

CONTINUITY AND DISCONTINUITY FROM CHILDHOOD TO ADULTHOOD

Temperament **Attachment**

Continuity and Discontinuity from Childhood to Adulthood

We no longer believe in the infant determinism of Freud's psychosexual theory, which argued that our personality as adults is virtually cast in stone by the time we are 5 years of age P. 30. But the first 20 years of life are not meaningless in predicting an adult's personality. And there is every reason to believe that later experiences in the early adult years are important in determining what the individual is like as an adult. In trying to understand the young adult's personality, it would be misleading to look only at the adult's life in present tense, ignoring the developmental unfolding of personality. So, too, would it be far off target to only search through a 30-year-old's first 5 to 10 years of life in trying to predict why he or she is having difficulty in a close relationship. The truth about adult personality development, then, lies somewhere between the infant determinism of Freud and a contextual approach that ignores the antecedents of the adult years altogether.

It is a common finding that the smaller the time intervals over which we measure personality characteristics, the more similar an individual will look from one measurement to the next. Thus, if we measure an individual's self-concept at the age of 20 and then again at the age of 30, we will probably find more stability than if we measured the individual's self-concept at the age of 10 and then again at the age of 30. Let's now explore some research findings that reflect these ideas about continuity and discontinuity.

Temperament

In chapter 7, we described *temperament* as an individual's behavioral style and characteristic emotional responses P. 182. How stable is temperament? Do young adults show the same behavioral style and characteristic emotional responses as when they were infants or young children?

Activity level is an important dimension of temperament. Is a child's activity level linked to her or his personality in early adulthood? In one longitudinal study, children who were highly active at age 4 were likely to be very outgoing at age 23, which reflects continuity (Franz, 1996). From adolescence into early adulthood, most individuals show fewer emotional mood swings, become more responsible, and engage in less risk-taking behavior, which reflects discontinuity (Caspi, 1998).

Is temperament in childhood linked with adjustment in adulthood? Here is what we know based on the few longitudinal studies that have been conducted on this topic (Caspi, 1998). Recall from chapter 7 the distinction between an easy and a difficult temperament. In one longitudinal study, children who had an easy temperament at 3 to 5 years of age were likely to be well-adjusted as young adults (Chess & Thomas, 1987). In contrast, many children who had a difficult temperament at 3 to 5 years of age were not well-adjusted as young adults. Also, other researchers have found that boys with a difficult temperament in childhood are less likely as adults to continue their formal education, whereas girls with a difficult temperament in childhood are more likely to experience marital conflict as adults (Wachs, 2000).

Inhibition is another temperament characteristic that has been studied extensively (Kagan, 2000). Researchers have found that individuals with an inhibited temperament in childhood are less likely as adults to be assertive or experience social support, and more likely to delay entering a stable job track (Wachs, 2000).

Yet another aspect of temperament involves emotionality and the ability to control one's emotions. In one longitudinal study, when 3-year-old children showed good

control of their emotions and were resilient in the face of stress, they were likely to continue to handle emotions effectively as adults (Block, 1993). By contrast, when 3-year-olds had low emotional control and were not very resilient, they were likely to show problems in these areas as young adults.

In sum, these studies reveal some continuity between between certain aspects of temperament in childhood and adjustment in early adulthood. However, keep in mind that these connections between childhood temperament and adult adjustment are based on only a small number of studies and more research is needed to verify these linkages. Indeed, Theodore Wachs (1994, 2000) recently proposed ways that linkages between temperament in childhood and personality in adulthood might vary depending on the intervening contexts in individuals' experience (see figure 15.1).

Attachment

Attachment is another topic we highlighted in chapter 7, "Socioemotional Development in Infancy" ◀ P. 186. We also described attachment in chapter 13, "Socioemotional Development in Adolescence" ◀ P. 388. Let's examine attachment in young adults and the extent to which it is linked to attachment earlier in development.

The concepts of secure and insecure attachment continue to be used to describe attachment relationships in adulthood (Cassidy & Shaver, 1999; Main, 2000; Main, Kaplan, & Cassidy, 1985; Paley & others, 2000; Ryff & Singer, 2000; Shaver & Hazan,

	Initial Temperament Trait: Inhibition	
	Child A	Child B
	Intervening Context	
Caregivers	Caregivers (parents) who are sensitive, accepting, and let child set his or her own pace.	Caregivers who use inappropriate "low level control" and attempt to force the child into new situations.
Physical Environment	Presence of "stimulus shelters" or "defensible spaces" that the children can retreat to when there is too much stimulation.	The child continually encounters noisy, chaotic environments that allow no escape from stimulation.
Peers	Peer groups have other inhibited children with common interests, so the child feels accepted.	Peer groups consist of athletic extroverts, so the child feels rejected.
Schools	School is "undermanned" so inhibited children are more likely to be tolerated and feel they can make a contribution.	School is "overmanned" so inhibited children are less likely to be tolerated and more likely to feel undervalued.
	Personality Outcomes	
	As an adult, individual is closer to extroversion (outgoing, sociable) and is emotionally stable.	As an adult, individual is closer to introversion and has more emotional problems.

Figure **15.1**

Temperament in Childhood, Personality in Adulthood, and Intervening Contexts

Varying experiences with caregivers, the physical environment, peers, and schools can modify links between temperament in childhood and personality in adulthood. The example given here is for inhibition.

1993). About 50 to 60 percent of adults in nonclinical samples are *securely attached.* These individuals provide realistic, coherent descriptions of their childhood and appear to understand how past experiences affect their current lives as adults. Approximately 25 to 30 percent of adults fall into the *insecure-dismissing* category of attachment. They don't want to discuss their relationships with their parents or do not seem invested in them. Their memories often focus on negative experiences such as being rejected or neglected by a parent. *Insecure-preoccupied* individuals make up about 15 percent of adults. In contrast to dismissing adults, preoccupied adults readily talk about their relationships but they tend to be incoherent and disorganized. They appear unable to move beyond their childhood issues with parents and often express anger toward them or ongoing efforts to please them.

Although relationships with romantic partners differ from those with parents in important ways (such as sexuality and reciprocal caregiving), romantic partners fulfill for adults some of the same needs as parents do for their children. Adults count on their romantic partners to be a secure base to which they can return and obtain comfort and security in stressful times.

Cindy Hazan and Phillip Shaver (1987; Shaver & Hazan, 1993) have examined the continuity between childhood attachment relationships and romantic relationships in a number of studies. They interview adults about their relationships with their parents as they were growing up and about their current romantic relationship. They find that the quality of childhood attachment relationships is linked with the quality of adult romantic relationships. For example, adults who report that they were securely attached to their parents are more likely to say that they have a secure attachment to their romantic partner than are adults who report having had an insecure attachment to their parents when they were growing up. In one longitudinal study, individuals who were securely attached to caregivers at 1 year of age also were likely to have secure attachments to parents and romantic partners 20 years later (Waters & others, 2000).

Adult Attachment Relationships

In sum, there appear to be some important continuities between attachment to parents as a child and attachment to parents and romantic partners as a young adult. Nonetheless, keep in mind that not all individuals fit this pattern and that attachment styles are not cast in stone (Lewis, Feiring, & Rosenthal, 2000). For example, in the longitudinal study just described and in other studies, links between earlier and later attachments are lessened by stressful and disruptive life experiences (such as the death of a parent or instability of caregiving) (Collins & Laursen, 2000; Waters & others, in press; Weinfield, 2000). Also, some individuals revise their attachment styles as they experience relationships in their adult years (Baldwin & Fehr, 1995). For example, in one study, approximately 30 percent of young adults changed their attachment style over a 4-year period (Kirkpatrick & Hazan, 1994).

Now that we have studied attachment in young adults, let's further examine the nature of young adults' social relationships.

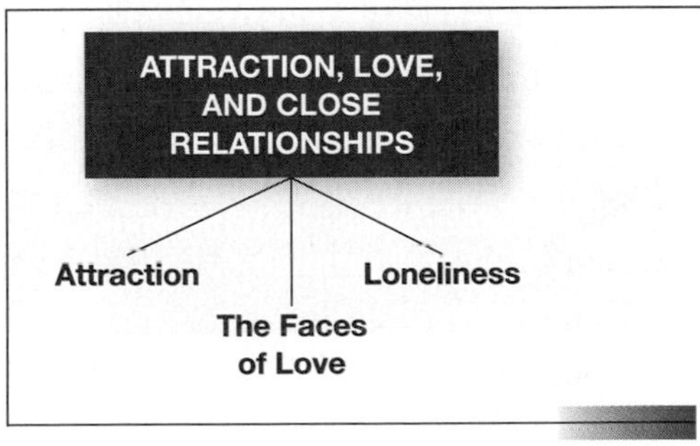

Attraction, Love, and Close Relationships

What attracts us to others and motivates us to spend more time with them? And another question needs to be asked, one that has intrigued philosophers, poets, and songwriters for centuries: What is love? Is it lustful and passionate? Or should we be more cautious in our pursuit of love, as a Czech proverb advises, "Do not choose your wife at a dance, but in the fields among the harvesters."

Of equal importance is why relationships dissolve. Many of us know all too well that an individual we thought was a marvelous human being who we wanted to spend the rest of our life with may not turn out to be so marvelous after all. But often it is said that it is better to have loved and lost than never to have loved at all. Loneliness is a dark cloud over many individuals' lives, something few human beings want to

feel. These are the themes of our exploration of close relationships: how they get started in the first place, the faces of love, intimacy, and loneliness.

Attraction

What attracts us to others and motivates us to spend more time with them? Does just being around someone increase the likelihood a relationship will develop? Do birds of a feather flock together; that is, are we likely to associate with those who are similar to us? How important is physical attraction in a relationship?

Familiarity and Similarity

Physical proximity does not guarantee that we will develop a positive relationship with another person. Familiarity can breed contempt, but familiarity is a condition that is necessary for a close relationship to develop (Bornstein & D'Agostino, 1992). For the most part, friends and lovers have been around each other for a long time; they may have grown up together, gone to high school or college together, worked together, or gone to the same social events. Once we have been exposed to someone for a period of time, what is it that makes the relationship breed friendship and even love?

Birds of a feather do indeed flock together. One of the most powerful lessons generated by the study of close relationships is that we like to associate with people who are similar to us (Berscheid, 2000). Our friends, as well as our lovers, are much more like us than unlike us (Berndt, 1996). We have similar attitudes, behavior, and characteristics, as well as clothes, intelligence, personality, other friends, values, lifestyle, physical attractiveness, and so on. In some limited cases and on some isolated characteristics, opposites may attract. An introvert may wish to be with an extravert, or someone with little money may wish to associate with someone who has a lot of money, for example. But overall we are attracted to individuals with similar rather than opposite characteristics. In one study, for example, the old adage "Misery loves company" was supported as depressed college students preferred to meet unhappy others while nondepressed college students preferred to meet happy others (Wenzlaff & Prohaska, 1989). The fact that individuals are attracted to each other on the basis of similar characteristics and attitudes is reflected in the questions that computer dating services ask their clients.

Consensual validation *provides an explanation of why people are attracted to others who are similar to them.* Our own attitudes and behavior are supported when someone else's attitudes and behavior are similar to ours—their attitudes and behavior validate ours. People tend to shy away from the unknown. We might tend, instead, to prefer people whose attitudes and behavior we can predict. And similarity implies that we will enjoy doing things with the other person, which often requires a partner who likes the same things and has similar attitudes. In one study, self-verifying evaluations were especially important in marriage (Swann, De La Ronde, & Hixon, 1994).

consensual validation
An explanation of why individuals are attracted to people who are similar to them. Our own attitudes and behavior are supported and validated when someone else's attitudes and behavior are similar to our own.

Physical Attraction

How important is *physical attraction* in a relationship? Many advertising agencies would have us believe it is the most important factor in establishing and maintaining a relationship. However, heterosexual men and women across many cultures differ on the importance they place on good looks when they seek an intimate partner. Women tend to rate as most important such traits as considerateness, honesty, dependability, kindness, and understanding; men prefer good looks, cooking skills, and frugality (Buss, 1999, 2000).

Some aspects of attractiveness vary across time in a particular culture. Consider the United States. In the 1950s, the soft, voluptuous Marilyn Monroe was the female ideal; today the ideal is the lean, athletic female.

The force of similarity also operates at a physical level. We usually seek out someone at our own level of attractiveness in both physical characteristics and social attributes. Most of us come away with a reasonably good chance of finding a "good match." Research indicates that this *matching hypothesis*—that although we might prefer a more attractive person in the abstract, in the real world we end up choosing someone who is close to our own level of attractiveness—holds up (Kalick & Hamilton, 1986).

Ask a toad what is beauty . . . he will answer that it is a female with two great round eyes coming out of her little head, a large flat mouth, a yellow belly and a brown back.

Voltaire
French Essayist, 18th Century

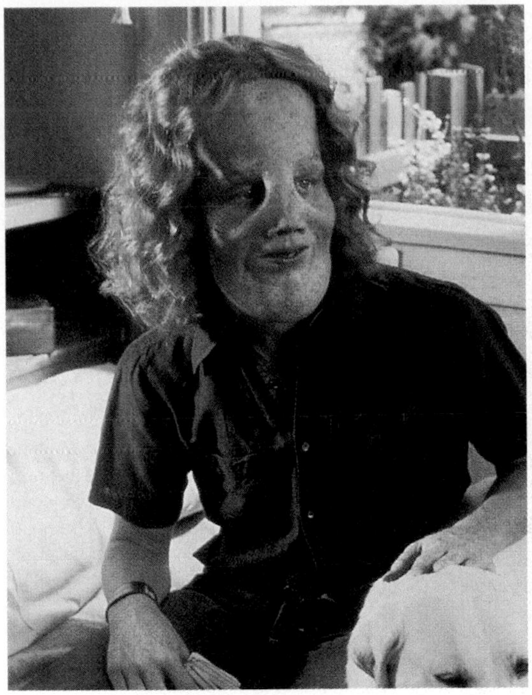

Eric Stoltz as Rocky Dennis in the movie *Mask*. Rocky was unloved and unwanted as a young child because of his grotesque features. As his mother and peers got to know him, they became much more attracted to him. *What are some of the factors that influence our attraction to others?*

Several additional points help to clarify the role of physical beauty and attraction in our close relationships. Much of the research has focused on initial or short-term encounters; researchers have not often evaluated attraction over the course of months and years. As relationships endure, physical attraction probably assumes less importance. Rocky Dennis, as portrayed in the movie *Mask*, is a case in point. His peers and even his mother initially wanted to avoid Rocky, whose face was severely distorted, but over the course of his childhood and adolescent years, the avoidance turned into attraction and love as people got to know him. As Rocky's story demonstrates, familiarity can overcome even severe initial negative reactions to a person.

Once attraction initiates a relationship, other opportunities exist to deepen the relationship to love.

The Faces of Love

Love refers to a vast and complex territory of human behavior. As you read about love, you will see that there are different types of love, such as friendship, romantic love, and affectionate love. Altruism, discussed in chapter 11, "Socioemotional Development in Middle and Late Childhood," also is classified as a type of love by some experts (Berscheid, 1988). To begin, though, we will focus on a very important theme in the lives of young adults—intimacy, which is especially important in friendship and affectionate love.

Intimacy Let's explore Erik Erikson's view of intimacy, the role of intimacy in relationship maturity, and how people juggle the motivation for intimacy and the motivation for independence.

Erikson's Stage: Intimacy vs. Isolation As we go through our adult lives, most of us are motivated to successfully juggle the development of identity and intimacy. Recall from our discussion in chapter 13 that Erik Erikson (1968) believes that identity versus identity confusion—pursuing who we are, what we are all about, and where we are going in life—is the most important issue to be negotiated in adolescence ◀ P. 382. Erikson thinks that intimacy should come after individuals are well on their way to establishing stable and successful identities. Intimacy is another life crisis in Erikson's scheme. If intimacy is not developed in early adulthood, the individual may be left with what Erikson calls "isolation." Intimacy versus isolation is Erikson's sixth developmental stage, which individuals experience in early adulthood. At this time, individuals face the task of forming intimate relationships with others. Erikson describes intimacy as finding oneself yet losing oneself in another person. If young adults form healthy friendships and an intimate relationship with another individual, intimacy will be achieved. If not, isolation will result.

We are what we love.

Erik Erikson
Danish-Born American Psychoanalyst and Author, 20th Century

An inability to develop meaningful relationships with others can harm an individual's personality. It may lead individuals to repudiate, ignore, or attack those who frustrate them. Such circumstances account for the shallow, almost pathetic attempts of youth to merge themselves with a leader. Many youths want to be apprentices or disciples of leaders and adults who will shelter them from the harm of the "out-group" world. If this fails, and Erikson believes that it must, sooner or later the individuals recoil into a self-search to discover where they went wrong. This introspection sometimes leads to painful depression and isolation. It may contribute to a mistrust of others and restrict the willingness to act on one's own initiative.

The Role of Intimacy in Relationship Maturity A desirable goal is to develop a mature identity and have positive close relationships with others. Kathleen White and her colleagues (1987) developed a model of relationship maturity that includes this goal at its highest level. Individuals are described as moving through three levels of relationship maturity: self-focused, role-focused, and individuated-connected.

The **self-focused level** *is the first level of relationship maturity, at which one's perspective on another person or a relationship is concerned only with how it affects one-*

self-focused level
The first level of relationship maturity, at which one's perspective of another or of a relationship is concerned only with how it affects oneself.

self. The individual's own wishes and plans overshadow those of others, and the individual shows little concern for others. Intimate communication skills are in the early, experimental stages. In terms of sexuality, there is little understanding of mutuality or consideration of another's sexual needs.

The **role-focused level** *is the second or intermediate level of relationship maturity, when one begins to perceive others as individuals in their own right. However, at this level, the perspective is stereotypical and emphasizes social acceptability.* Individuals at this level know that acknowledging and respecting another is part of being a good friend or a romantic partner. Yet commitment to an individual, rather than to the romantic partner role, is not articulated. Generalizations about the importance of communication in relationships abound, but underlying this talk is a shallow understanding of commitment.

role-focused level
In White's model, this is the second level of relationship maturity, at which one begins to perceive others as individuals in their own right. One's perspective is still stereotypical and emphasizes social acceptability.

The **individuated-connected level** *is the highest level of relationship maturity, when one begins to understand oneself, as well as to have consideration for others' motivations and to anticipate their needs. Concern and caring involve emotional support and individualized expressions of interest.* At this level, individuals make a commitment to specific individuals with whom they share a relationship, and they understand the personal time and investment needed to make a relationship work. In White's view, it is not until adulthood that the individuated-connected level is likely to be reached. She believes that most individuals making the transition from adolescence to adulthood are either self-focused or role-focused in their relationship maturity.

individuated-connected level
In White's model, this is the highest level of relationship maturity. One is acquiring an understanding of oneself, as well as consideration for others' motivations and anticipation of their needs. One now feels concern and caring that involve emotional support and individualized expressions of interest.

Intimacy and Independence

The early adult years are a time when individuals usually develop an intimate relationship with another individual. An important aspect of this relationship is the commitment of the individuals to each other. At the same time, individuals show a strong interest in independence and freedom. Development in early adulthood often involves an intricate balance of intimacy and commitment on the one hand, and independence and freedom on the other.

Recall that intimacy is the aspect of development that follows identity in Erikson's eight stages of development. A related aspect of developing an identity in adolescence and early adulthood is independence. At the same time as individuals are trying to establish an identity, they face the difficulty of having to cope with increasing their independence from their parents, developing an intimate relationship with another individual, and increasing their friendship commitments. They also face the task of being able to think for themselves and do things without always relying on what others say or do.

Intimate Relationships

The extent to which the young adult has begun to develop autonomy has important implications for early adulthood maturity. The young adult who has not sufficiently moved away from parental ties may have difficulty in both interpersonal relationships and a career. Consider the mother who overprotects her daughter, continues to support her financially, and does not want to let go of her. In early adulthood, the daughter may have difficulty developing mature intimate relationships and she may have career difficulties. When a promotion comes up that involves more responsibility and possibly more stress, she may turn it down. When things do not go well in her relationship with a young man, she may go crying to her mother.

The balance between intimacy and commitment, on the one hand, and independence and freedom, on the other, is delicate. Keep in mind that these important dimensions of adult development are not necessarily opposite ends of a continuum. Some individuals are able to experience a healthy independence and freedom along with an intimate relationship. These dimensions may also fluctuate with social and historical change. And keep in mind that intimacy and commitment, and independence and freedom, are not just concerns of early adulthood. They are important themes of development that are worked and reworked throughout the adult years. Next, we will explore another important aspect of adults' close relationships: romantic love.

Romantic Love

Romantic love *is also called passionate love or eros; it has strong components of sexuality and infatuation, and it often predominates in the early part of a love relationship.* Poets, playwrights, and musicians through the ages have lauded the fiery

romantic love
Also called "passionate love" or "eros," romantic love has strong sexual and infatuation components and often predominates in the early period of a love relationship.

Ellen Berscheid's Research

passion of romantic love—and lamented the searing pain when it fails. Think for a moment about songs and books that hit the top of the charts. Chances are they're about love. Well-known love researcher Ellen Berscheid (1988) says that it is romantic love we mean when we say that we are "in love" with someone. It is romantic love she believes we need to understand if we are to learn what love is all about. Berscheid (2000), believes that sexual desire is the most important ingredient of romantic love.

In our culture, romantic love is the main reason we get married. In 1967, a famous study showed that men maintained that they would not get married if they were not "in love." Women either were undecided or said that they would get married even if they did not love their prospective husband (Kephart, 1967). In the 1980s, women and men tended to agree that they would not get married unless they were "in love." And more than half of today's men and women say that not being "in love" is sufficient reason to dissolve a marriage (Bersheid, Snyder, & Omoto, 1989).

To discuss romantic love without also prominently mentioning the role that sexual arousal and desire plays in it is very much like printing a recipe for tiger soup that leaves out the main ingredient.

Ellen Berscheid
Contemporary Social Psychologist, University of Minnesota

Romantic love is especially important among college students. One study of unattached college men and women found that more than half identified a romantic partner, rather than a parent, sibling, or friend, as their closest relationship (Bersheid, Snyder, & Omoto, 1989). We are referring to romantic love when we say, "I am *in love,*" not just "I *love.*"

Romantic love includes a complex intermingling of different emotions—fear, anger, sexual desire, joy, and jealousy, for example. Obviously, some of these emotions are a source of anguish. One study found that romantic loves were more likely than friends to be the cause of depression (Berscheid & Fei, 1977).

affectionate love
In this type of love (also called "companionate love"), an individual desires to have the other person near and has a deep, caring affection for the other person.

Affectionate Love

Love is more than just passion. **Affectionate love,** *also called companionate love, is the type of love that occurs when individuals desire to have the other person near and have a deep, caring affection for the person.*

There is a growing belief that the early stages of love have more romantic ingredients, but as love matures, passion tends to give way to affection (Aron, 2000; Berscheid & Reis, 1998). Phillip Shaver (1993) describes the initial phase of romantic love as a time that is fueled by a mixture of sexual attraction and gratification, a reduced sense of loneliness, uncertainty about the security of developing another attachment, and excitement from exploring the novelty of another human being. With time, he says, sexual attraction wanes, attachment anxieties either lessen or produce conflict and withdrawal, novelty is replaced with familiarity, and lovers either find themselves securely attached in a deeply caring relationship or distressed—feeling bored, disappointed, lonely, or hostile, for example. In the latter case, one or both partners may eventually seek another close relationship.

triangular theory of love
Sternberg's theory that love has three main forms: passion, intimacy, and commitment.

When two lovers go beyond their preoccupation with novelty, unpredictability, and the urgency of sexual attraction, they are more likely to detect deficiencies in each other's caring. This may be the point in a relationship when women, who often are better caregivers than men, sense that the relationship has problems. Wives are almost twice as likely as husbands to initiate a divorce, for example (National Center for Health Statistics, 1989).

So far we have discussed two types of love: romantic (or passionate) and affectionate (or companionate). Robert J. Sternberg (1988) described a third type of love, consummate love, which he said is the strongest, fullest type of love. Sternberg proposed the **triangular theory of love:** *that love includes three types—passion, intimacy, and commitment* (see figure 15.2). Couples must experience all three types to have consummate love.

Passion, as described earlier, is physical and sexual attraction to another. Intimacy is the emotional feelings of warmth, closeness, and sharing in a relationship. Commitment is our cognitive appraisal of the

Critical Thinking

Exploring Self-Help Books on Love

HUNDREDS OF self-help books on love and relationships fill the shelves of bookstores. A lot of them have catchy titles, such as *Men Who Hate Women, and the Women They Love* and *What Every Woman Should Know About Men.* Don't choose a book for its catchy title, its glitzy advertising, or having seen the author on "Oprah."

The following are good books on developing positive relationships: *The Dance of Intimacy* by Harriet Lerner, *Getting the Love You Want* by Harville Hendrix, and *Intimate Connections* by David Burns. Go to a bookstore that has a good selection of self-help books. Look through one of these books and spend some time with it. What did you learn about relationships from the book?

relationship and our intent to maintain the relationship even in the face of problems.

Depending on which types of love are present, different patterns of love result. For example, if passion is the only ingredient (with intimacy and commitment low or absent), we are merely *infatuated.* This might happen in an affair or a fling in which there is little intimacy and even less commitment. A relationship marked by intimacy and commitment but low or lacking in passion is called *affectionate love,* a pattern often found among couples who have been married for many years. If passion and commitment are present but intimacy is not, Sternberg calls the relationship *fatuous love,* as when one person worships another from a distance.

At this point we have examined what attracts people to each other, intimacy, romantic love, and affectionate love. Let's now explore another important aspect of the lives of young adults—friendship.

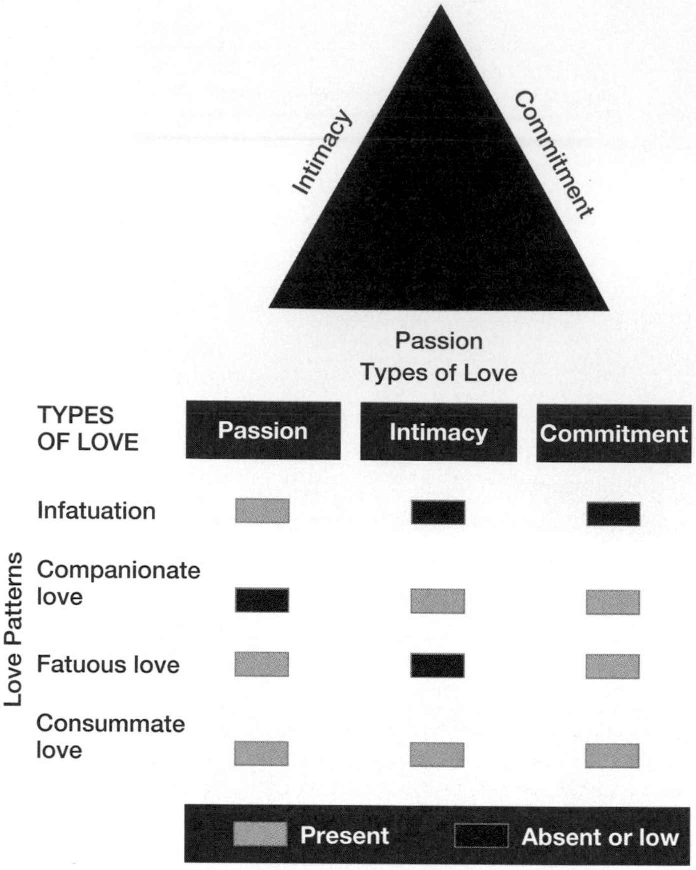

Figure 15.2
Sternberg's Triangle of Love
Sternberg identified three types of love: passion, intimacy, and commitment. Various combinations of these types of love result in these patterns of love: infatuation, affectionate love, fatuous love, and consumate love.

Friendship

Increasingly researchers are finding that friendship plays an important role in development throughout the human life span (Antonucci, 1990; Hartup, 1999) P. 332.

What Is Friendship?

In the words of American historian Henry Adams, "One friend in life is much, two are many, and three hardly possible." **Friendship** *is a form of close relationship that involves enjoyment (we like to spend time with our friends), acceptance (we accept our friends without trying to change them), trust (we assume our friends will act in our best interest), respect (we think our friends make good judgments), mutual assistance (we help and support our friends and they us), confiding (we share experiences and confidential matters with a friend), understanding (we feel that a friend knows us well and understands what we like), and spontaneity (we feel free to be ourselves around a friend).* In an inquiry of more than 40,000 individuals, many of these characteristics were given when people were asked what a best friend should be like (Parlee, 1979).

As we saw in chapter 11, friendship can serve many functions—such as companionship, intimacy/affection, support, and a source of self-esteem. In some cases, friends can provide a better buffer from stress and be a better source of emotional support than family members. This might be because friends choose each other whereas family ties are obligatory. Individuals often select a friend in terms of such criteria as loyalty, trustworthiness, and support. Thus, it is not surprising that in times of stress individuals turn to their friends for emotional support (Fehr, 1996).

friendship
A form of close relationship that involves enjoyment, acceptance, trust, respect, mutual assistance, confiding, understanding, and spontaneity.

Zick Rubin (1970) argues that liking involves our sense that someone else is similar to us; it includes a positive evaluation of the individual. Loving, he believes, involves being close to someone; it includes dependency, a more selfless orientation toward the individual, and qualities of absorption and exclusiveness.

Friendship

But friends and lovers are similar in some ways. In one study, friends and romantic partners shared the characteristics of acceptance, trust, respect, confiding, understanding, spontaneity, mutual assistance, and happiness (Davis, 1985). However, relationships with spouses or lovers were more likely to also involve fascination and exclusiveness.

As with children, adult friends usually come from the same age group. For many individuals, friendships formed in the twenties often continue through the twenties and into the thirties, although some new friends may be made in the thirties and some lost because of moving or other circumstances.

How is adult friendship different among female friends, male friends, and cross-sex friends?

Female, Male, and Female-Male Friendship As in the childhood years, there are sex differences in adult friendship. Women have more close friends and their friendships are more intimate than men's. This intimacy involves more self-disclosure and exchange of emotional support. Adult male friendships are more competitive than those of females (Antonucci, 1990; Sharkey, 1993). For example, male friends disagree with each other more. Also, when adult female friends get together, they often talk, whereas adult male friends are more likely to engage in activities, especially outdoors. Of course, adult male friends talk, but it usually is a more distant, less intimate pattern of talk. Thus, the adult male pattern of friendship often involves keeping one's distance while sharing useful information.

When women talk with their friends, they expect to be able to openly express their feelings, reveal their weaknesses, and discuss their problems. They anticipate that their friends will listen at length to what they have to say and be sympathetic. In contrast, men are less likely to talk about their weaknesses with their friends, and they want practical solutions to their problems rather than sympathy (Tannen, 1990). Later in the chapter we will further explore these differences in the talk of women and men in relationships.

Keep in mind that these differences in same-sex adult friendship often are small (Sabini, 1995). For example, many men engage in self-disclosure and provide emotional support in their friendships

But what about female-male friendship? Cross-sex friendships are more common among adults than among elementary school children, but not as common as same-sex friendships in adulthood (Fehr, 1996). Cross-sex friendships can provide both opportunities and problems. The opportunities involve learning more about common feelings and interests, and characteristics that both sexes have, as well as acquiring knowledge and understanding of beliefs and activities that historically have been reserved more for one sex than for the other. For example, in cross-sex friendships females might learn more about sports, cars, and the stock market. Males might learn more about relationships and to better appreciate art and classical music.

Problems can arise in cross-sex friendships because of the different expectations women and men have about the purpose of friendship. For example, a woman might expect a lot of sympathy from a male friend when she expresses an emotional problem to him but might instead receive back a directive solution rather than a shoulder to cry on (Tannen, 1990). Another problem that can plague an adult cross-sex friendship is unclear sexual boundaries (Swain, 1992). Men are more likely to try to turn a platonic friendship into a sexual relationship, and women often are offended by this. The ambiguity in sexual attraction can produce tension and confusion for both women and men in a cross-sex adult friendship.

Individuals who don't have friends are vulnerable to loneliness. Let's now explore what it is like to be lonely.

Loneliness

Recall that Erik Erikson (1968) believes that intimacy versus isolation is the key developmental issue for young adults to resolve. Social isolation can result in loneliness. Our society's emphasis on self-fulfillment and achievement, the importance we attach to commitment in relationships, and a decline in stable close relationships are among the reasons loneliness is common today (de Jong-Gierveld, 1987). Researchers have found that married individuals are less lonely than their nonmarried counterparts (never married, divorced, or widowed) in studies conducted in more than twenty countries (Perlman & Peplau, 1998).

Loneliness is interwoven with how people pass through life transitions. One of those transitions is the first year of college. When students leave the familiar world of their hometown and family to enter college, they especially can feel lonely. Many college freshmen feel anxious about meeting new people and developing a new social life. As one student commented:

Loneliness
Shyness

> My first year here at the university has been pretty lonely. I wasn't lonely at all in high school. I lived in a fairly small town—I knew everybody and everyone knew me. I was a member of several clubs and played on the basketball team. It's not that way at the university. It is a big place and I've felt like a stranger on so many occasions. I'm starting to get used to my life here and the last few months I've been making myself meet people and get to know them, but it has not been easy.

As this comment illustrates, freshmen rarely bring their popularity and social standing from high school into the college environment. There may be a dozen high school basketball stars, National Merit scholars, and former student council presidents in a single dormitory wing. Especially if students attend college away from home, they face the task of forming completely new social relationships.

One study found that 2 weeks after the school year began, 75 percent of 354 college freshmen felt lonely at least part of the time since arriving on campus (Cutrona, 1982). More than 40 percent said their loneliness was moderate to severe in intensity. Students who were the most optimistic and had the highest self-esteem were more likely to overcome their loneliness by the end of their freshman year. Loneliness is not reserved only for college freshmen, though. Upperclassmen are often lonely as well.

Lonely males and females attribute their loneliness to different sources, with men more likely to blame themselves, women more likely to blame external factors. Men are socialized to initiate relationships, whereas women are traditionally socialized to wait, then respond. Perhaps men blame themselves because they feel they should do something about their loneliness, while women wonder why no one calls.

How do you determine if you are lonely? Scales of loneliness ask you to respond to items like "I don't feel in tune with the people around me" and "I can find companionship when I want it." If you consistently respond that you never or rarely feel in tune with people around you and rarely or never can find companionship when you want it, you are likely to fall into the category of people who are described as moderately or intensely lonely (Russell, 1996).

If you are lonely, how can you become better connected with others? Following are some strategies:

- *Participate in activities that you can do with others.* Join organizations or volunteer your time for a cause you believe in. You likely will get to know others whose views are similar to yours. Going to just one social gathering can help you develop social contacts. When you go, introduce yourself to others and start a conversation. Another strategy is to sit next to new people in your classes or find someone to study with.
- *Be aware of the early warning signs of loneliness.* People often feel bored or alienated before loneliness becomes pervasive. Head off loneliness by becoming involved in new social activities.
- *Draw a diagram of your social network.* List whether the people in the diagram meet your social needs. If not, pencil in the people you would like to get to know.
- *Engage in positive behaviors when you meet new people.* You will improve your chances of developing enduring relationships if, when you meet new people, you are nice, considerate, honest, trustworthy, and cooperative. Have a positive attitude, be supportive of the other person, and make positive comments about him or her.
- *See a counselor or read a book on loneliness.* If you can't get rid of your loneliness on your own, you might want to contact the counseling services at

SUMMARY TABLE 15.1

Continuity and Discontinuity from Childhood to Adulthood; Attraction, Love, and Close Relationships

Concept	Processes/ Related Ideas	Characteristics/Descriptions
Continuity and Discontinuity	Both Occur	• The first 20 years are important in predicting an adult's personality, but so, too, are continuing experiences in the adult years.
	Temperament	• Activity level in early childhood is linked with being an outgoing young adult. Young adults show fewer mood swings, are more responsible, and engage in less risk-taking than adolescents. In some cases, temperament in childhood is linked with adjustment problems in early adulthood.
	Attachment	• Attachment styles in young adults are linked with their attachment history, although attachment styles can change in adulthood as adults experience relationships.
Attraction, Love, and Close Relationships	Attraction	• Familiarity precedes a close relationship. We like to associate with people who are similar to us. The principles of consensual validation and matching can explain this. • Physical attraction is usually more important in the early part of a relationship, and criteria of physical attractiveness vary across cultures and historical time.
	The Faces of Love	• Erikson theorized that intimacy versus isolation is the key developmental issue in early adulthood. White proposed a model of relationship maturity. There is a delicate balance between intimacy and commitment, on the one hand, and independence and freedom on the other. • Romantic love, also called passionate love, is involved when we say we are "in love." It includes passion, sexuality, and a mixture of emotions, not all of which are positive. • Affectionate love, also called companionate love, usually becomes more important as relationships mature. • Shaver proposed a developmental model of love and Sternberg a triarchic model of love (passion, intimacy, and commitment). • Friendship plays an important role in adult development, especially in terms of emotional support. Female, male, and female-male friendships often have different characteristics. For example, self-disclosure is more common in female friendships.
	Loneliness	• Loneliness often emerges when people make life transitions, so it is not surprising that loneliness is common among college freshmen. • A number of strategies were described to help lonely individuals become more socially connected.

your college. The counselor can talk with you about strategies for reducing your loneliness. You also might want to read a good book on loneliness. A good one is *Intimate Connections* by David Burns (1985).

At this point we have discussed many ideas about continuity and discontinuity from childhood to adulthood and attraction, love, and close relationships. To review these ideas see summary table 15.1. As we see next, among the most important social contexts in which intimacy and love are displayed are marriage and the family.

Marriage and the Family

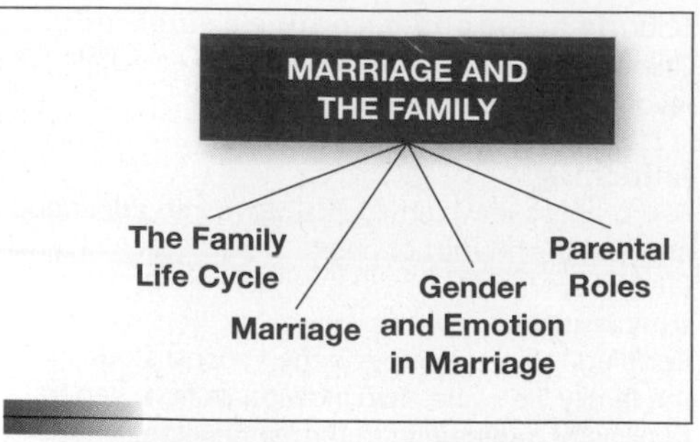

Should I get married? If I wait any longer, will it be too late? Will I get left out? Should I stay single or is it too lonely a life? If I get married, do I want to have children? How will it affect my marriage? These are questions that many young adults pose to themselves as they consider their lifestyle options. But before we explore these lifestyle options, let's examine the nature of the family life cycle.

The Family Life Cycle

As we go through life, we are at different points in the family life cycle. The stages of the family life cycle include leaving home and becoming a single adult, the joining of families through marriage (the new couple), becoming parents and a family with children, the family with adolescents, the family at midlife, and the family in later life. A summary of these stages in the family life cycle is shown in figure 15.3, along with key aspects of emotional processes involved in the transition from one stage to the next, and changes in family status required for developmental change to take place (Carter & McGoldrick, 1989).

Leaving Home and Becoming a Single Adult

Leaving home and becoming a single adult *is the first stage in the family life cycle and involves launching.* **Launching** *is the process in which youths move into adulthood and exit their family of origin.* Adequate completion of launching requires that the young adult separate from the family of origin without cutting off ties completely or fleeing in a reactive way to find some form of substitute emotional refuge. The launching period is a time for the youth and young adult to formulate personal life goals, to develop an identity, and to become more independent before joining with another person to form a new family. This is a time for young people to sort out emotionally what they will take along from the family of origin, what they will leave behind, and what they will create themselves into.

Complete cutoffs from parents rarely resolve emotional problems. The shift to adult-to-adult status between parents and children requires a mutually respectful and personal form of relating, in which young adults can appreciate parents as they are, needing neither to make them into what they are not nor to blame them for what they could not be. Neither do young adults need to comply with parental expectations and wishes at their own expense.

The Joining of Families Through Marriage: The New Couple

The **new couple** *is the second stage in the family life cycle, in which two individuals from separate families of origin unite to form a new family system.* This stage involves not only the development of a new marital system, but also a realignment with extended families and friends to include the spouse. Women's changing roles, the increasingly frequent marriage of partners from divergent cultural backgrounds, and the increasing physical distances between family members are placing a much stronger burden on couples to define their relationships for themselves than was true in the past. Marriage is usually described as the union of two individuals, but in reality it is the union of two entire family systems and the development of a new, third system. Some experts on marriage and the family believe that

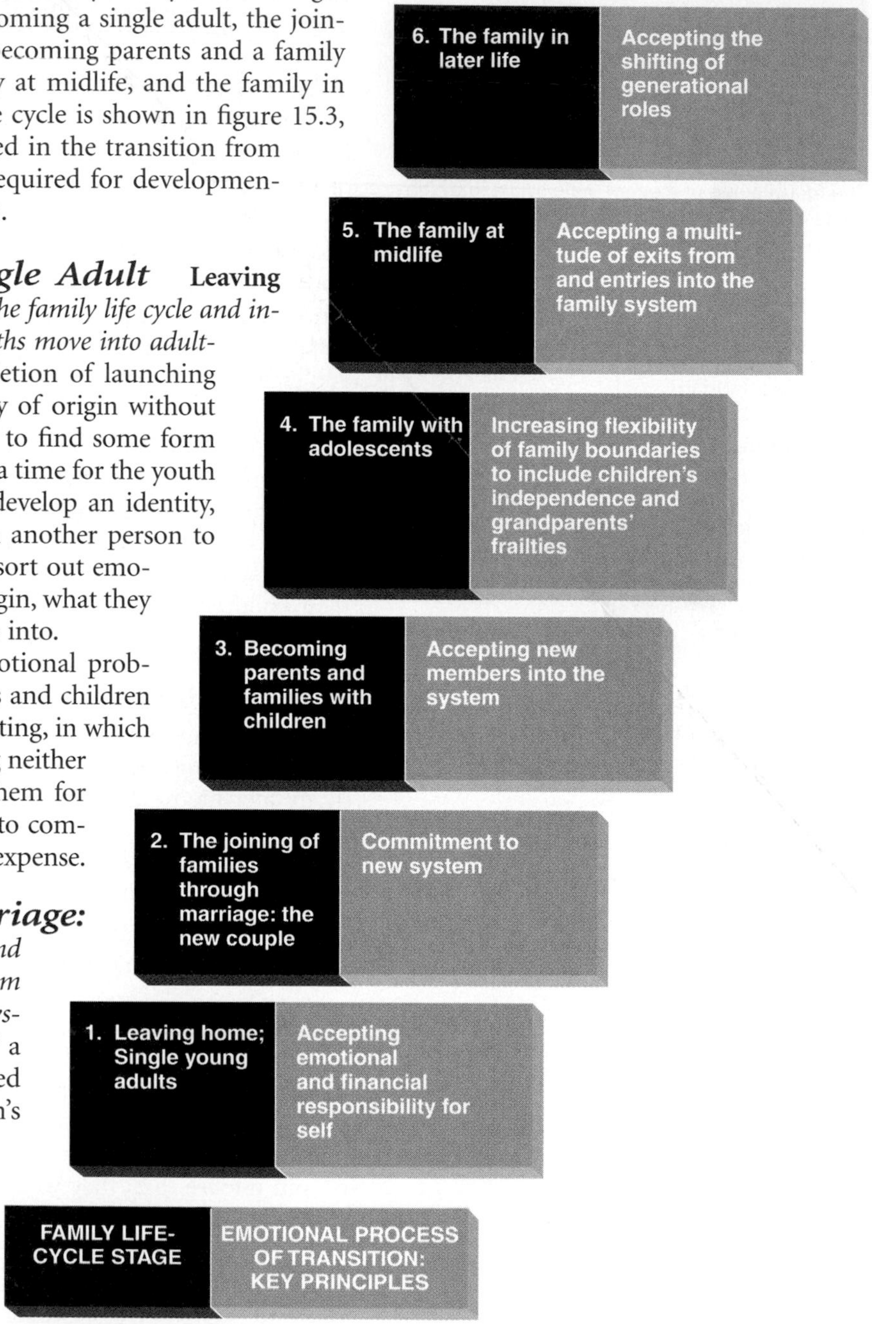

Figure **15.3**
The Family Life Cycle

leaving home and becoming a single adult
The first stage in the family life cycle and that involves launching.

launching
The process in which youths move into adulthood and exit their family of origin.

new couple
Forming the new couple is the second stage in the family life cycle. Two individuals from separate families of origin unite to form a new family system.

becoming parents and a family with children
The third stage in the family life cycle. Adults who enter this stage move up a generation and become caregivers to the younger generation.

family with adolescents
The fourth stage of the family life cycle, in which adolescent children push for autonomy and seek to develop their own identities.

family at midlife
The fifth stage in the family life cycle, a time of launching children, linking generations, and adapting to midlife developmental changes.

family in later life
The sixth and final stage in the family life cycle, involving retirement and, in many families, grandparenting.

We never know the love of our parents until we have become parents.

Henry Ward Beecher
American Clergyman, 19th Century

marriage represents such a different phenomenon for women and men that we need to speak of "her" marriage and "his" marriage. In American society, women have anticipated marriage with greater enthusiasm and more positive expectations than men have.

Becoming Parents and a Family with Children

Becoming parents and a family with children *is the third stage in the family life cycle. Entering this stage requires that adults now move up a generation and become caregivers to the younger generation.* Moving through this lengthy stage successfully requires a commitment of time as a parent, understanding the roles of parents, and adapting to developmental changes in children. Problems that emerge when a couple first assumes the parental role are struggles with each other about taking responsibility, as well as refusal or inability to function as competent parents to children. We extensively discussed this stage of the family life cycle in chapters 7, 9, and 11 ◄ P. 192, 247, and 327.

The Family with Adolescents

The **family with adolescents** *represents the fourth stage of the family life cycle. Adolescence is a period of development in which individuals push for autonomy and seek to develop their own identity.* The development of mature autonomy and identity is a lengthy process, transpiring over at least 10 to 15 years. Compliant children become noncompliant adolescents. Parents tend to adopt one of two strategies to handle noncompliance. They either clamp down and put more pressure on the adolescent to conform to parental values, or they become more permissive and let the adolescent have extensive freedom. Neither is a wise overall strategy. A more flexible, adaptive approach is best. We discussed the **family** with adolescents in chapter 13 ◄ P. 390.

The Family at Midlife

The **family at midlife** *is the fifth stage in the family cycle. It is a time of launching children, playing an important role in linking generations, and adapting to midlife changes in development.* Until about a generation ago, most families were involved in raising their children for much of their adult lives until old age. Because of the lower birth rate and longer life of most adults, parents now launch their children about 20 years before retirement, which frees many midlife parents to pursue other activities. We will discuss midlife families in greater detail in chapter 17.

The Family in Later Life

The **family in later life** *is the sixth and final stage in the family life cycle. Retirement alters a couple's lifestyle, requiring adaptation. Grandparenting also characterizes many families in this stage.* We will discuss the family in later life in chapter 20.

Marriage

Our exploration of marriage focuses on some marital trends, expectations and myths about marriage, what makes marriages work, and the benefits of a good marriage.

Marital Trends

Until about 1930, stable marriage was widely accepted as a legitimate endpoint of adult development. In the last 60 years, however, we have seen the emergence of personal fulfillment both inside and outside a marriage that competes with marriages' stability as an adult developmental goal. The changing norm of male-female equality in marriage has produced marital relationships that are more fragile and intense than they were earlier in the twentieth century (Bradbury & Fincham, 2000; Christiansen & Pasch, 1993). More adults are remaining single longer today, and the average duration of a marriage in the United States is currently just over 9 years. In 1998, the U.S. average age for a first marriage climbed to 27 years for men and 25 years for women, higher than at any point in history (see figure 15.4). However, the United States is still a marrying society. In 1998, 118 million individuals in the United States were married, about 60 percent of the total population, which is a drop of only about 5 percent since 1980. The divorce rate has begun to slow down, although it still remains high—we will discuss divorced adults later in this chapter. Even with adults

WWW

Journal of Family Psychology

Marriage and Family Therapy

remaining single for longer and divorce being a frequent occurrence, Americans still show a strong predilection for marriage—the proportion of women who never marry remained at about 7 percent throughout the twentieth century, for example.

The sociocultural context is a powerful influence on marriage. The age at which individuals marry, expectations about what the marriage will be like, and the developmental course of the marriage vary not only across historical time within a given culture, but also across cultures. For example, a new marriage law took effect in China in 1981. The law sets a minimum age for marriage—22 years for males, 20 years for females. Late marriage and late childbirth are critical efforts in China's attempt to control population growth. More information about the nature of marriage in different cultures appears in the Sociocultural Worlds of Development box.

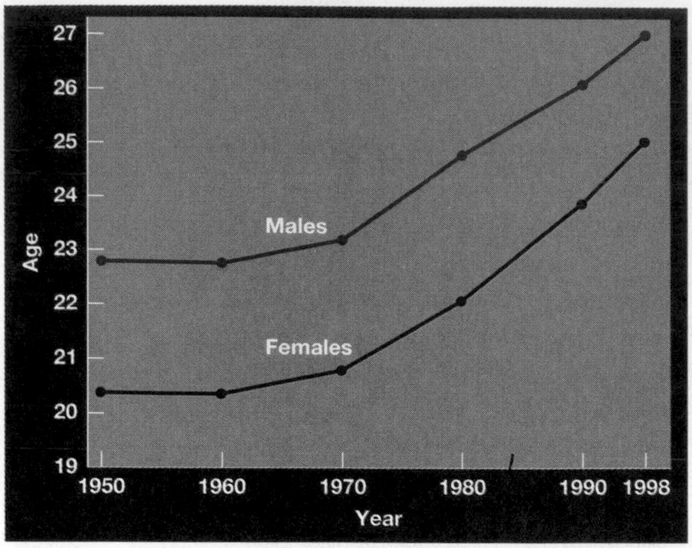

Figure **15.4**

Increase in Age at First Marriage in the United States

Shown here are average ages at first marriage in the United States. Notice that since the 1960s, the age at which this important life event occurs has steadily increased.

Marital Expectations and Myths Among the explanations of our nation's high divorce rate and high degree of dissatisfaction in many marriages is that we have such strong expectations of marriage. We expect our spouse to simultaneously be a lover, a friend, a confidant, a counselor, a career person, and a parent, for example. In one study, unhappily married couples expressed unrealistic expectations about marriage (Epstein & Eidelson, 1981).

Marriage therapists believe it is important to have realistic expectations about a marriage (Sharp & Ganong, 2000). Researchers have found that unrealistic expectations are linked with lower levels of marital satisfaction (Larson & Holman, 1994). Similarly, individuals who have highly romantic beliefs about marriage are likely to encounter disappointment as they realize that sustaining their romantic ideal is not possible (Huston, Neihuis, & Smith, 1997).

Underlying unrealistic expectations about marriage are numerous myths about marriage (Flanagan & others, 2001; Markman, 2000). A myth is a widely held belief unsupported by facts.

To study college students' beliefs in the myths of marriage, Jeffry Larson (1988) constructed a marriage quiz to measure college students' information about marriage and compared their responses with what is known about marriage in the research literature. The college students responded incorrectly to almost half of the items. Female students missed fewer items than male students, and students with a less romantic perception of marriage missed fewer items than more romantically inclined students.

What are some of the myths about marriage? They include these (Gottman & Silver, 1999):

- *Avoiding conflict will ruin your marriage.* Couples have different styles of conflict. Some avoid fights at all costs, some fight a lot, and some choose to "talk out" their differences and find solutions to problems without ever raising their voices. As long as the style works for both partners, no one style is necessarily better than the others. Couples can get into trouble if one partner wants to talk out a conflict while the other just wants to watch a favorite TV show that night.
- *Affairs are the main cause of divorce.* In most instances, it is the other way around. Marital problems send the couple on a downward trajectory, and one or both partners seek an intimate relationship outside of the marriage. In many instances, these affairs are not about sex but rather are about seeking to find friendship, support, understanding, respect, and caring.
- *Men are not biologically made for marriage.* This myth holds that men are philanderers by nature and thus ill suited for monogamy. This is sometimes called "the law of the jungle": the male of the species seeks to create as many offspring as possible and his allegiance to one mate restricts him from attaining this goal. Also involved is the view that the female's main task is tend to her young, so she seeks a

When two people are under the influence of the most violent, most insane, most delusive, and most transient of passions, they are required to swear that they will remain in that excited, abnormal, and exhausting condition continuously until death do them part.

George Bernard Shaw
Irish Playwright, 20th Century

Marriage Support

SOCIOCULTURAL WORLDS OF DEVELOPMENT

Marriage Around the World

THE TRAITS THAT people look for in a marriage partner vary around the world. In one large-scale study of 9,474 adults from 37 cultures on six continents and five islands, people varied the most on how much they valued chastity—desiring a marital partner with no previous experience in sexual intercourse (Buss & others, 1990). Chastity was the most important factor in marital selection in China, India, Indonesia, Iran. Taiwan, and the Palestinian Arab culture. Adults from Ireland and Japan placed moderate importance on chastity. In contrast, adults in Sweden, Finland, Norway, the Netherlands, and Germany generally said that chastity was not important in selecting a marital partner.

In this study, domesticity was also valued in some cultures and not in others. Adults from the Zulu culture in South Africa, Estonia, and Colombia placed a high value on housekeeping skills in their marital preference. By contrast, adults in the United States, Canada, and all Western European countries except Spain said that housekeeping was not an important trait in their partner.

Religion plays an important role in marital preferences in many cultures. For example, Islam stresses the honor of the male and the purity of the female. It also emphasizes the woman's role in childbearing, child rearing, educating children, and instilling the Islamic faith in their children.

International comparisons of marriage also reveal that individuals in Scandinavian countries marry late, whereas their counterparts in Eastern Europe marry early (Bianchi & Spani, 1986). In Denmark, for example, almost 80 percent of the women and 90 percent of the men aged 20 to 24 have never been married. In Hungary less than 40 percent of the women and 70 percent of the men the same age have never been married. In Scandinavian countries, cohabitation is popular among young adults; however, most Scandinavians eventually marry. Only 5 percent of the women and 11 percent of the men in their early forties have never been married. Some countries, such as Hungary, encourage early marriage and childbearing to offset current and future population losses. Like Scandinavian countries, Japan has a high proportion of unmarried young people. However, rather than cohabiting as the Scandinavians do, unmarried Japanese young adults live at home longer with their parents before marrying.

Based on a review of many cross-cultural studies, the following further conclusions were reached about love and marriage in the United States and Japan (Rothbaum & others, 2000). Traditionally, the Japanese family has had considerable influence on mate selection, and that influence continues to some degree today. In one-third to one-half of all marriages in Japan, initial contacts are still arranged by go-betweens (Hendry, 1995). It also is common practice for parents to investigate the background of potential spouses for children.

In the United States, personal attraction dictates mate selection more than in Japan. Japanese Americans perceive that they have more choice and independence in selecting a mate than in Japan (Markus & Kitayama, 1991).

Although romantic and passionate love are strong factors in many U.S. marriages, especially early in the marital relationship, in Japan, loyalty and commitment are more important (Dion & Dion, 1993; Yamagishi & Yamagishi, 1994). Divorce statistics bear out the emphasis on loyalty and commitment in Japan. The divorce rate in Japan is more than three times that of the United States (Kumagai, 1995). Conflict is not readily accepted in marital relations in Japan; rather, cohesion and cherishing the relationship are desired (Rothbaum & others, 2000).

(a) In Scandinavian countries, cohabitation is popular; only a small percentage of 20- to 24-year-olds are married. *(b)* Many Soviet-influenced countries encourage early marriage and childbearing to offset current and future population losses. *(c)* Islam stresses male honor and female purity.

single mate who will provide for her and her children. However, as more women have sought employment outside the home, the rate at which women have extramarital affairs has increased dramatically; women's rate of extramarital affairs now slightly exceeds that of men.

- *Men and women are from different planets.* According to a best-selling book by John Gray (1992), men and women have serious relationship problems because he is from Mars and she is from Venus. Gender differences can contribute to marital problems, but they usually don't cause them. For example, the key factor in whether wives or husbands feel satisfied with the sex, romance, and passion in their marriage is the quality of the couple's friendship.

What makes marriages work? What are the benefits of having a good marriage?

What Makes Marriages Work John Gottman (1994; Gottman & Notarius, 2000; Gottman & Silver, 1999; Gottman & others, 1998) has been studying married couples' lives since the early 1970s. He uses extensive methods to study what makes marriages work. Gottman interviews couples about the history of their marriage, their philosophy about marriage, and how they view their parents' marriages. He videotapes them talking to each other about how their day went and evaluates what they say about the good and bad times of their marriages. Gottman also uses physiological measures to measure their heart rate, blood flow, blood pressure, and immune functioning moment by moment. He also checks back in with the couples every year to see how their marriage is faring. Gottman's research represents the most extensive assessment of marital relationships available. Currently he and his colleagues are following 700 couples in seven different studies.

Unlike most approaches to helping couples, mine is based on knowing what makes marriages succeed rather than fail.

John Gottman
Contemporary Psychologist, University of Washington

John Gottman's Ideas

In his research, Gottman has found that seven main principles determine whether a marriage will work or not:

- *Establishing love maps.* Individuals in successful marriages have personal insights and detailed maps of each other's life and world. They aren't psychological strangers. In good marriages, partners are willing to share their feelings with each other. They use these "love maps" to express not only their understanding of each other but also their fondness and admiration.
- *Nurturing fondness and admiration.* In successful marriages, partners sing each other's praises. More than 90 percent of the time, when couples put a positive spin on their marriage's history, the marriage is likely to have a positive future.
- *Turning toward each other instead of away.* In good marriages, spouses are adept at turning toward each other regularly. They see each other as friends and this friendship acts as a powerful shield against conflict. The friendship doesn't keep arguments from occurring, but it can prevent differences of opinion from overwhelming a relationship. In these good marriages, spouses respect each other and appreciate each other's point of view even though they might not agree with it.
- *Letting your partner influence you.* Bad marriages often involve one spouse who is unwilling to share power with the other. Although power-mongering is more common in husbands, some wives also show this problem. A willingness to share power and to respect the other person's view is a prerequisite to compromising.
- *Solving solvable conflicts.* Gottman has found two types of problems that occur in marriage: (1) perpetual and (2) solvable. Perpetual problems include spouses differing on whether to have children and one spouse wanting sex far more frequently than the other. Solvable problems include not helping each other reduce daily stresses and not being verbally affectionate. Unfortunately, more than two-thirds of marital problems fall into the perpetual category—those that won't go away. Fortunately, marital therapists have found that couples often don't have to solve their perpetual problems for the marriage to work. In his research, Gottman has found that resolving conflicts works best when couples start out solving the problem with a soft rather than a harsh approach, make an effort to make and receive repair attempts, regulate their emotions, compromise, and are

Careers in Life-Span Development

Andrew Christensen, Clinical Psychologist

ANDREW CHRISTENSEN obtained his Ph.D. in clinical psychology at the University of Oregon and is currently a professor at UCLA, where he teaches, conducts research, and engages in couples therapy. Among the courses he teaches are abnormal psychology, communication and conflict in couples and families, and couples therapy. Andrew is one of the world's leading experts on couples therapy. He strives to improve the communication and problem-solving abilities of a couple who are having difficulties in their relationship. According to Andy, "Marriage is obviously a milestone in most people's developmental course, typically paving the way for even greater milestones: namely, the appearance of children."

Andrew Christensen conducting couples therapy.

tolerant of each other's faults. Conflict resolution is not about one person making changes, it is about negotiating and accommodating each other.

Work, stress, in-laws, money, sex, housework, a new baby: These are among the typical areas of marital conflict. Even in happy marriages, these areas are often hot buttons in a relationship. When there is conflict in these areas, it usually means that a husband and wife have different ideas about the tasks involved, their importance, or how they should be accomplished. If the conflict is perpetual, no amount of problem-solving expertise will fix it. The tension will decrease only when both partners feel comfortable living with the ongoing difference. However, when the issue is solvable, the challenge is to find the right strategy for dealing with it. Strategies include these:

a. Scheduling formal griping sessions about stressful issues
b. Learning to talk about sex in a way that both partners feel comfortable with
c. Creating lists of who does what to see how household labor is divided up

- *Overcoming gridlock.* One partner wants the other to attend church, the other is an atheist. One partner is a homebody, the other wants to go out and socialize a lot. Such problems often produce gridlock. Gottman believes the key to ending gridlock is not to solve the problem, but to move from gridlock to dialogue and be patient.
- *Creating shared meaning.* The more partners can speak candidly and respectfully with each other, the more likely it is that they will create shared meaning in their marriage. This also includes sharing goals with one's spouse and working together to achieve each other's goals.

The Benefits of a Good Marriage Now that you know what makes a marriage work, are there any benefits to having a good marriage? There are. An unhappy marriage increases an individual's risk of getting sick by approximately one-third and can even shorten a person's life by an average of 4 years (Gove, Style, & Hughes, 1990). On the other hand, individuals who are happily married live longer, healthier lives than divorced individuals or those who are unhappily married (Cotten, 1999).

What are the reasons for these benefits of a happy marriage? People in happy marriages likely feel less physically and emotionally stressed, which puts less wear and tear on a person's body. Such wear and tear can lead to numerous physical ailments, such as high blood pressure and heart disease, as well as psychological problems such as anxiety, depression, and substance abuse.

Gender and Emotion in Marriages

Wives consistently disclose more to their partners than husbands do (Becker & Moen, 1998; Peplau & Gordon, 1985). And women tend to express more tenderness, fear, and sadness than their partners. A common complaint expressed by women in a marriage is that their husbands do not care about their emotional lives and do not express their own feelings and thoughts. Women often point out that they have to literally

pull things out of their husbands and push them to open up. Men frequently respond either that they are open or that they do not understand what their wives want from them. It is not unusual for men to protest that no matter how much they talk it is not enough for their wives. Women also say they want more warmth as well as openness from their husbands. For example, women are more likely than men to give their partners a spontaneous kiss or hug when something positive happens. Overall, women are more expressive and affectionate than men in marriage, and this difference bothers many women (Fox & Murry, 2000).

CAREERS IN LIFE-SPAN DEVELOPMENT

Janis Keyser, Parent Educator

JANIS KEYSER is a parent educator and teaches in the Department of Early Childhood Education at Cabrillo College in California. In addition to teaching college classes and conducting parenting workshops, Janis also has co-authored a book with Laura Davis (1997), *Becoming the Parent You Want To Be: A Sourcebook of Strategies for the First Five Years.*

Janis also writes as an expert on the iVillage web site (http://www.parentsplace.com). And she co-authors a nationally syndicated parenting column, "Growing Up, Growing Together." She is the mother of three, stepmother of five, grandmother of 12, and great-grandmother of 6.

Janis Keyser (right), conducting a parenting workshop.

Parental Roles

For many adults, parental roles are well planned and coordinated with other roles in life and developed with the individual's economic situation in mind. For others, the discovery that they are about to become parents is a startling surprise. In either event, the prospective parents may have mixed emotions and romantic illusions about having a child. Parenting consists of a number of interpersonal skills and emotional demands, yet there is little in the way of formal education for this task (Brooks, 1996). Most parents learn parenting practices from their own parents—some they accept, some they discard. Husbands and wives may bring different viewpoints of parenting practices to the marriage. Unfortunately, when methods of parents are passed on from one generation to the next, both desirable and undesirable practices are perpetuated.

The needs and expectations of parents have stimulated many myths about parenting:

- The birth of a child will save a failing marriage.
- As a possession or extension of the parent, the child will think, feel, and behave like the parents did in their childhood.
- Children will take care of parents in old age.
- Parents can expect respect and get obedience from their children.
- Having a child means that the parents will always have someone who loves them and is their best friend.
- Having a child gives the parents a "second chance" to achieve what they should have achieved.
- If parents learn the right techniques, they can mold their children into what they want.
- It's the parents' fault when children fail.
- Mothers are naturally better parents than fathers.
- Parenting is an instinct and requires no training.

In earlier times, women considered being a mother a full-time occupation. Currently, there is a tendency to have fewer children, and, as birth control has become common practice, many individuals choose when they will have children and how many children they will raise. The number of one-child families is increasing, for example. Giving birth to fewer children and reduced demands of child care free a significant portion of a woman's life span for other endeavors. Three accompanying changes are that (1) as a result of the increase in working women, there is less maternal investment in the child's development; (2) men are apt to invest a greater amount

of time in fathering; and (3) parental care in the home is often supplemented by institutional care (day care, for example) P. 194.

As more women show an increased interest in developing a career, they are not only marrying later, but also having children later (Grolnick & Gurland, 2001). What are some of the advantages of having children early or late? Some of the advantages of having children early are these: The parents are likely to have more physical energy (for example, they can cope better with such matters as getting up in the middle of the night with infants and waiting up until adolescents come home at night); the mother is likely to have fewer medical problems with pregnancy and childbirth; and the parents may be less likely to build up expectations for their children, as do many couples who have waited many years to have children. By contrast, there are also advantages to having children late: The parents will have had more time to consider their goals in life, such as what they want from their family and career roles; the parents will be more mature and will be able to benefit from their life experiences to engage in more competent parenting; and the parents will be better established in their careers and have more income for child-rearing expenses.

At this point we have discussed a number of ideas about marriage and the family. To review these ideas see summary table 15.2. Now that we have explored marriage and the family, we will turn our attention to other life styles, which have become increasingly prominent in America.

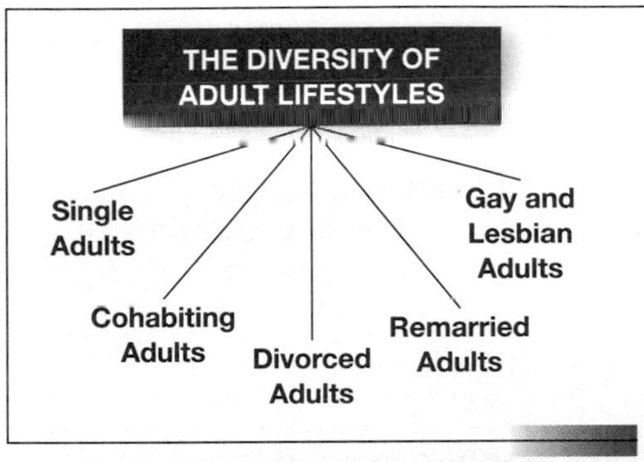

The Diversity of Adult Lifestyles

Today's adult lifestyles are diverse. We have single-career families; dual-career families; single-parent families, including mother custody, father custody, and joint custody; the remarried or stepfamily; the kin family (made up of bilateral or intergenerationally linked members); and even the experimental family (individuals in multi-adult households—communes—or cohabiting adults). And, of course, there are many single adults.

Single Adults

There is no rehearsal. One day you don't live alone, the next day you do. College ends. Your wife walks out. Your husband dies. Suddenly, you live in this increasingly modern condition, living alone. Maybe you like it, maybe you don't. Maybe you thrive on the solitude, maybe you ache as if in exile. Either way, chances are you are only half prepared, if at all, to be sole proprietor of your bed, your toaster, and your time. Most of us were raised in the din and clutter of family life, jockeying for a place in the bathroom in the morning, fighting over the last piece of cake, and obliged to compromise on the simplest of choices—the volume of the stereo, the channel on the TV, for example. Few of us grew up thinking that home would be a way station in our life course.

There has been a dramatic rise in the percentage of single adults. In 1998, more than 46 million adult Americans (24 percent of the total American adults) who never had been married lived alone (U.S. Bureau of the Census, 2000). This is three times the percentage in 1970 (8 percent). As shown in figure 15.5 being single in the age period of the early thirties had shown a similar increase.

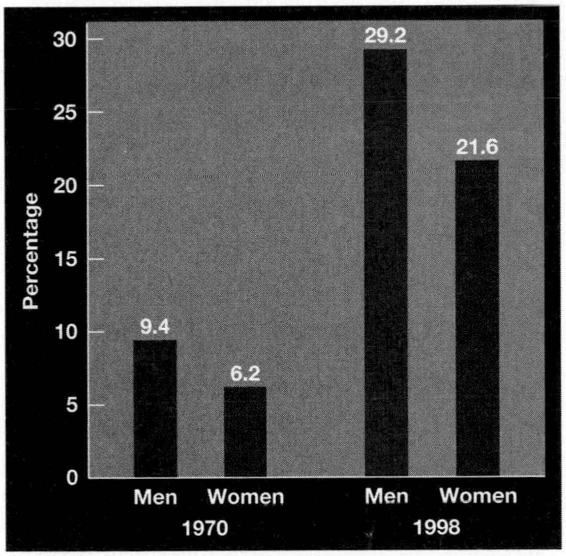

Figure **15.5**

Percentage Increase in Single Adults 30 to 34 Years of Age in 1970 and 1998

In less than three decades, the percentage of single adults 30 to 34 years of age more than tripled.

A history of myths and stereotypes is associated with being single, ranging from the "swinging single" to the "desperately lonely, suicidal" single. Of course, most single adults are somewhere between these extremes.

What are some of the advantages of being single? They include time to make decisions about one's life course, time to develop personal resources to meet goals, freedom to make autonomous decisions and pursue one's own schedule and interests, opportunity to explore new places and try out new things, and availability of privacy.

Common problems of single adults focus on intimate relationships with other adults, confronting loneliness, and finding a niche in a society that is marriage oriented. Many single adults cite personal freedom as one of the major advantages of being a single adult. One woman who never married

SUMMARY TABLE 15.2
Marriage and the Family

Concept	Processes/ Related Ideas	Characteristics/Descriptions
The Family Life Cycle	Six Stages	• There are six stages in the family life cycle: leaving home and becoming a single adult; the joining of families through marriage—the new couple; becoming parents and a family with children; the family with adolescents; the midlife family; and the family in later life.
Marriage	Trends in Marriage	• Even though adults are remaining single longer and the divorce rate is high, we still show a strong predilection for marriage. • The age at which individuals marry, expectations about what the marriage will be like, and the developmental course of marriage may vary not only across historical time within a culture, but also across cultures.
	Marital Expectations and Myths	• Unrealistic expectations and myths about marriage contribute to marital dissatisfaction and divorce. • Among the marital myths are that avoiding conflict will ruin a marriage, men are not biologically made for marriage, and men and women are from different planets.
	What Makes Marriages Work	• Gottman has conducted the most extensive research on what makes marriages work. • In his research these principles characterize good marriages: establishing love maps, nurturing fondness and admiration, turning toward each other instead of away, letting your partner influence you, solving solvable conflicts, overcoming gridlock, and creating shared meaning.
	Benefits of a Good Marriage	• They include better physical and mental health and a longer life.
Gender and Emotion in Marriage	Linkages	• Overall, women are more expressive and affectionate in marriage, and this difference bothers many women.
Parental Roles	Diversity, Myths, Realties, and Trends	• For some, the parental role is well planned and coordinated. For others, there is surprise and sometimes chaos. • There are many myths about parenting, among them the myth that the birth of a child will save a failing marriage. • Families are becoming smaller, and many women are delaying childbirth until they have become well established in a career. • There are some advantages to having children earlier in adulthood, and some advantages to having them later.

commented, "I enjoy knowing that I can satisfy my own whims without someone else's interferences. If I want to wash my hair at two o'clock in the morning, no one complains. I can eat when I'm hungry and watch my favorite television shows without contradictions from anyone. I enjoy these freedoms. I would feel very confined if I had to adjust to another person's schedule."

Some adults never marry. Initially, they are perceived as living glamorous, exciting lives. But once we reach the age of 30, there can be increasing pressure to settle down and get married. If a woman wants to bear children, she might feel a sense of urgency when she reaches 30. This is when many single adults make a conscious decision to marry or to remain single. As one 30-year-old male recently commented, "It's real. You are supposed to get married by 30—that is a standard. It is part of getting on with your life that you are supposed to do. You have career and who-am-I concerns in your twenties. In your thirties, you have to get on with it, keep on track,

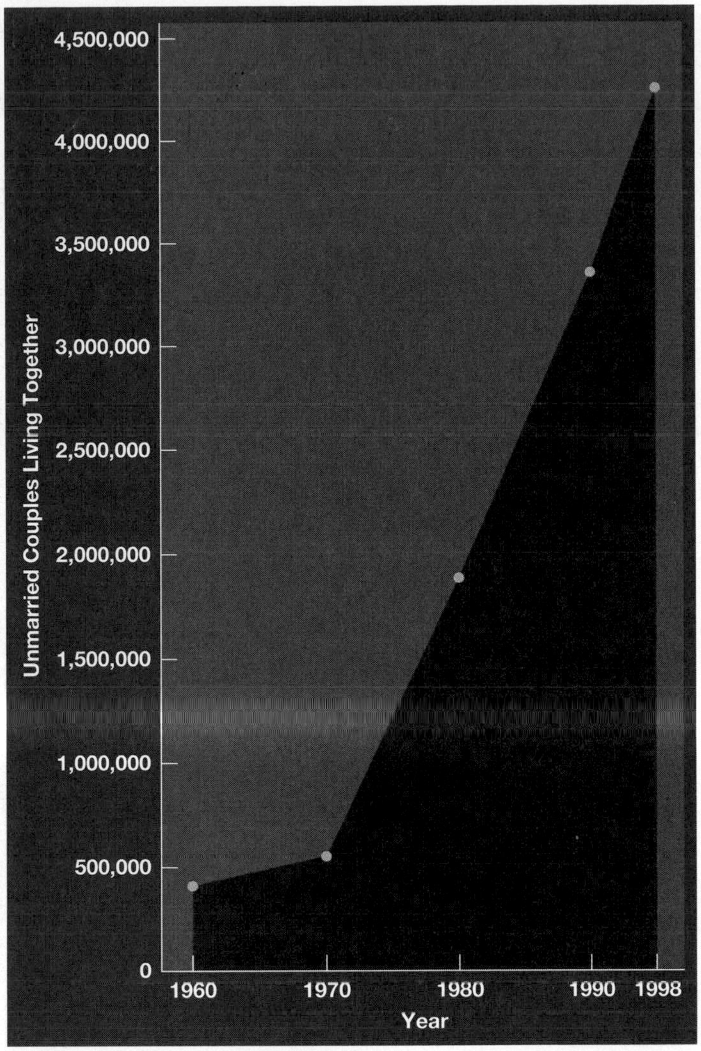

Figure **15.6**

The Increase in Cohabitation in the United States

Since 1970, there has been a dramatic increase in the number of unmarried adults living together in the United States.

make headway, financially and familywise." But, to another 30-year-old, getting married is less important than buying a house and some property. A training manager for a computer company, Jane says, "I'm competent in making relationships and being committed, so I don't feel a big rush to get married. When it happens, it happens."

Cohabiting Adults

Cohabitation refers to living together in a sexual relationship without being married. Cohabitation has undergone considerable changes in recent years (Crooks & Bauer, 1999) (see figure 15.6). There has been a significant increase in both the number of adults who engage in this lifestyle and acceptance of what once was considered unconventional (Nock, 1995). In 1996, 6.75 percent of all couples in the United States were cohabiting. Twenty-five percent of individuals 19 to 24 years old and 42 percent of individuals 25 to 29 years old have cohabited at least once. These arrangements tend to be short-lived, with one-third lasting less than a year (Hyde & DeLamater, 1999). Less than 1 out of 10 lasts 5 years.

A number of couples view their cohabitation not as a precursor to marriage but rather as an ongoing lifestyle. These couples prefer the informality of living together to the more official aspects of marriage. They like being together because they want to, not because they are bound by a legal contract.

When unmarried adults cohabit, they can feel less pressure to live up to the expectations attached to being a "wife" or a "husband." Relationships in cohabitation tend to be more equal than in marriage (Wineberg, 1994). Also, there is less stigma attached to dissolving a cohabitation relationship than there is to divorce.

Although cohabitation offers some advantages, it also can produce some problems. Disapproval by parents and other family members can be severe, placing emotional strain on the cohabiting couple. Some cohabiting couples can have difficulty owing property jointly. Without a clear, written contract, legal rights on the dissolution of the relationship are less certain than in a divorce.

Some individuals believe that cohabitation improves their chances for choosing a partner with whom they will have a stable and happy marriage. Others believe just the opposite—that living together before marriage will have a more negative impact on future marriage. Which viewpoint is right?

Some researchers have found no differences in marital quality between individuals who earlier cohabited and those who did not (Newcomb & Bentler, 1980; Watson & DeMeo, 1987). Other researchers have found lower rates of marital satisfaction in couples who lived together before getting married (Booth & Johnson, 1988). For example, in one study of 13,000 individuals, married couples who cohabited prior to their marriage reported lower levels of happiness with and commitment to their marital relationship than their counterparts who had not previously cohabited (Nock, 1995). Also, in one study, living together prior to marriage was more likely to lead to divorce than when a couple did not live together prior to marriage (DeMaris & Rao, 1992).

In sum, researchers have not found that cohabitation leads to greater marital happiness and success. Rather, they have discovered either that it leads to no differences or evidence that cohabitation is not good for a marriage.

Divorced Adults

Divorce has become epidemic in our culture P. 256. The number of divorced adults rose from 4.3 million individuals (3 percent of the adult population) in 1970 to 19.4 million individuals (10 percent of the population) in 1998. Until recently, the divorce rate was increasing annually by 10 percent, although the rate of increase is now slowing. While divorce has increased for all socioeconomic groups, those in disadvantaged groups have a higher incidence of divorce. Youthful marriage, low educational level, and low income are associated with increases in divorce. So too is premarital pregnancy. One study revealed that half of the women who were pregnant before marriage failed to live with the husband for more than 5 years (Sauber & Corrigan, 1970).

If a divorce is going to occur, it usually takes place early in a marriage, peaking in the fifth to tenth years of marriage (National Center for Health Statistics, 2000) (see figure 15.7). Some partners in a troubled marriage might stay in it and try to work things out. If after several years these efforts don't improve the relationship, they might seek a divorce.

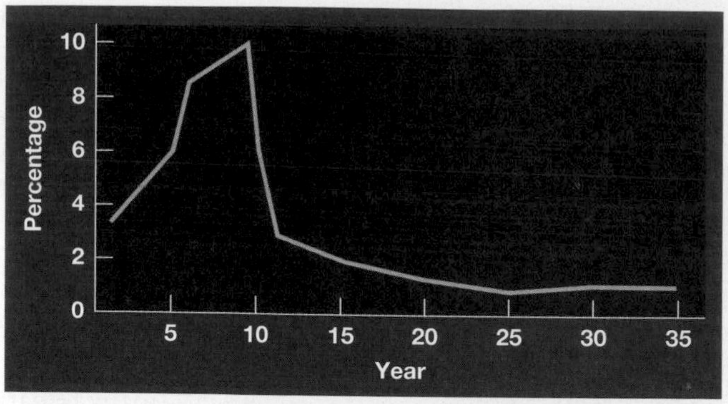

Figure 15.7
The Divorce Rate in Relation to Number of Years Married
Shown here is the percentage of divorces as a function of how long couples have been married. Notice that most divorces occur in the early years of marriage, peaking in the fifth to tenth years of marriage.

Many adults, even those who initiated the divorce, experience changes and challenges in their lives following marital dissolution (Amato, 2000; Hetherington, 2000). Both divorced women and divorced men complain of loneliness, diminished self-esteem, anxiety about the unknowns in their lives, and difficulty in forming satisfactory new intimate relationships.

The stress of separation and divorce places both men and women at risk for psychological and physical difficulties (Chase-Lansdale, 1996; Hetherington & Stanley-Hagan, 1995). Separated and divorced women and men have higher rates of psychiatric disorders, admission to psychiatric hospitals, clinical depression, alcoholism, and psychosomatic problems, such as sleep disorders, than do married adults. There is increasing evidence that stressful events of many types—including marital separation—reduce the immune system's capabilities, rendering separated and divorced individuals vulnerable to disease and infection. In one study, the most recently separated women (1 year or less) were more likely to show impaired immunological functioning than women whose separations had occurred several years earlier (1 to 6 years) (Kiecolt-Glaser & Glaser, 1988). Also in this study, unhappily married individuals had immune systems that were not functioning as effectively as those of happily married individuals.

Custodial parents have concerns about child rearing and overload in their lives. Noncustodial parents register complaints about alienation from or lack of time with their children. Men show only modest declines in income following a divorce but women reveal a significant decline in income following a divorce, with estimates of the decline ranging from 20 to 35 percent. For divorced women, the financial decline means living in a less desirable neighborhood with fewer resources, less effective schools, and more deviant peer groups for their children. Nonetheless, the economic decline for women following a divorced has diminished as increasing numbers of women have a better education and job.

WWW

Psychological Aspects of Divorce
Divorced and Remarried Parents
Remarried Adults' Resources
Stepfamily Interventions

Remarried Adults

In chapter 11, we discussed stepfamilies with a special emphasis on the effects of living in a stepfamily on children's development P. 329. Here we will continue our exploration of stepfamilies with a stronger focus on the relationships of remarried adults. On average, divorced adults remarry within 4 years after their divorce, with men doing this sooner than women.

Stepfamilies come in many sizes and forms. The custodial and noncustodial parents and stepparent all might have been married and divorced, in some cases more than once.

These parents might have residential children from prior marriages and a large network of grandparents and other relatives. Regardless of their form and size, the newly reconstituted families face some unique tasks. The couple must define and strengthen their marriage and at the same time renegotiate the biological parent-child relationships and establish stepparent-stepchild and stepsibling relationships (Coleman, Ganong, & Fine, 2000; Cox & Marter, 2001; Hetherington, 1995).

The complex histories and multiple relationships make adjustment difficult in a stepfamily (Coleman, Ganong, & Weaver, 2001; Lauer & Lauer, 1999; Shomberg, 1999; Thomson & others, 2001). The difficulty of adjusting to life in a stepfamily is born out by the data: only one-third of stepfamily couples stay remarried (Gerlach, 1998).

Why do remarried adults find it so difficult to stay remarried? For one thing, many remarry not for love but for financial reasons, for help in rearing children, and to reduce loneliness. They also might carry into the stepfamily negative relationship patterns that resulted in the failure of an earlier marriage. Remarried couples also experience more stress in rearing children than parents in never-divorced families (Ganong & Coleman, 1994).

Among the strategies that help remarried couples cope with the stress of living in a stepfamily are these (Visher & Visher, 1989):

- *Have realistic expectations.* Allow time for loving relationships to develop, and look at the complexity of the stepfamily as a challenge to overcome.
- *Develop new positive relationships within the family.* Create new traditions and ways of dealing with difficult circumstances that work. Allocation of time is especially important with all of the people involved. In this regard, the remarried couple needs to allot time alone for each other.

Gay and Lesbian Relationships

Gay and Lesbian Adults

Researchers have found that gay and lesbian relationships are similar—in their satisfactions, loves, joys, and conflicts—to heterosexual relationships (Hyde & DeLamater, 1999; Peplau, Veniegas, & Campbell, 1996). For example, like heterosexual couples, gay and lesbian couples need to find a balance in their relationships that is acceptable to both partners in terms of romantic love, affection, how much autonomy is acceptable, and how equal the relationship will be. Lesbian couples especially place a high priority on equality in their relationships (Kurdek, 1995). In one study, gay and lesbian couples listed the areas of conflict in order of frequency: finances, driving style, affection and sex, being overly critical, and household tasks (Kurdek, 1995). The components of this list are likely to be familiar to heterosexual couples as well.

What are the research findings regarding the development and psychological well-being of children raised by gay and lesbian couples?

There are a number of misconceptions about homosexual couples. For example, many people think that one partner is masculine and the other feminine in a homosexual relationship. This appears to be true only in a small percentage of cases. Indeed, some researchers have found that gay and lesbian couples are more flexible in their gender roles than heterosexual individuals are (Marecek, Finn, & Cardell, 1988). Another misconception is that homosexual couples have a huge amount of sex. Again, this is true only of a small segment of the gay male population, and it is uncommon among lesbians. Yet another misconception about homosexual couples is that they don't get involved in long-term relationships. Researchers have found that homosexuals prefer long-term, committed relationships (Peplau, 1991; Peplau & Spalding, 2000). About half of committed gay male couples do have an open relationship that allows the possibility of sex (but not affectionate love) outside of the relationship. Lesbian couples usually do not have this open relationship.

One aspect of relationships in which heterosexual and homosexual couples differ involves the obstacles that make it difficult to end a relationship (Peplau & Spalding, 2000). In this regard, the legal and social context of marriage creates barriers to breaking up that to not usually exist for same-sex partners (Peplau & Spalding, 2000).

Increasingly, gay and lesbian couples are creating families that include children. This is controversial to many heterosexual individuals who view a gay or lesbian family as damaging to the development of a child. However, researchers have found that

children growing up in gay or lesbian families are just as popular with their peers and there are no differences in the adjustment and mental health of children living in these families when they are compared with children in heterosexual families (Hyde & DeLamater, 1999). Also, the overwhelming majority of children growing up in a gay or lesbian family have a heterosexual orientation (Patterson, 1996, 2000).

Gender, Relationships, and Self-Development

GENDER, RELATIONSHIPS, AND SELF-DEVELOPMENT

- Women's Development
- Men's Development

In chapters 9 and 11, we discussed a number of ideas about gender development in children P. 243 and 320. Also, earlier in this chapter we explored gender in friendship, gender and family work, and the mother's and the father's roles. Here we will further examine gender by focusing on some issues involving gender, relationships, and self development.

Women's Development

Jean Baker Miller (1986) has been an important voice in stimulating the examination of psychological issues from a female perspective. She believes that the study of women's psychological development opens up paths to a better understanding of all psychological development, male or female. She also concludes that when researchers examine what women have been doing in life, a large part of it is active participation in the development of others. In Miller's view, women often try to interact with others in ways that will foster the other person's development along many dimensions—emotionally, intellectually, and socially.

Gender and Communication
Women's Issues
Gender and Society

Most experts believe it is important for women to not only maintain their competency in relationships but to be self-motivated, too (Donelson, 1998). Miller believes that through increased self-determination, coupled with already developed relationship skills, many women will gain greater power in the American culture. And as Harriet Lerner (1989) concludes in her book *The Dance of Intimacy,* it is important for women to bring to their relationships nothing less than a strong, assertive, independent, and authentic self. She believes competent relationships are those in which the separate "I-ness" of both persons can be appreciated and enhanced while still staying emotionally connected to each other.

Understanding the other's ways of talking is a giant leap across the communication gap between women and men, and a giant step toward opening lines of communication.

Deborah Tannen
Contemporary Sociologist, Georgetown University

Deborah Tannen (1990) analyzed the talk of women and men. She reported that a common complaint that wives have about their husbands is, "He doesn't listen to me anymore." Another is, "He doesn't talk to me anymore." Lack of communication, while high on women's lists of reasons for divorce, is much less often mentioned by men.

Tannen distinguishes between rapport talk and report talk. *Rapport talk* is the language of conversation and a way of establishing connections and negotiating relationships. *Report talk* is public speaking, which men feel more comfortable doing. Men hold center stage through such verbal performances as story telling, joking, or imparting information. Men learn to use talking as a way of getting and keeping attention. By contrast, women enjoy private speaking more, talk that involves discussing similarities and matching experiences. It is men's lack of interest in rapport talk that bothers many women.

"You have no idea how nice it is to have someone to talk to."

Women's dissatisfaction with men's silence at home is captured in a typical cartoon setting of a breakfast table at which a husband and wife are sitting. He's reading the newspaper; she's glaring at the back of the newspaper. Another cartoon shows a husband opening a newspaper and asking his wife, "Is there anything you want to say to me before I begin reading the newspaper?" The reader knows there isn't, but that as soon as

he starts reading the paper, she will think of something. *To him, talk is for information.* So when his wife interrupts his reading, it must be to inform him of something he needs to know. So, since this is the case, she might as well tell him what she thinks he needs to know before he starts reading. *But for her, talk is for interaction.* She believes saying things is a way to show involvement; listening is a way to show caring and interest.

The problem, then, may not be an individual man, or even men's styles alone, but the difference between women's and men's styles. If so, both men and women can make adjustments. A woman can push herself to speak up without being invited, or begin to speak even at the slightest pause in talk. The adjustment should not be just one-sided. Men can learn that women who are not accustomed to speaking up in groups are not as free as they are to do so. By understanding this reluctance on the part of women, men can make them feel more comfortable by warmly encouraging and allowing them to speak rather than hogging public talk.

Men's Development

The Men's Bibliography

Psychological Study of Men and Masculinity

Male Issues

The male of the species—what is he really like? What are his concerns? According to Joseph Pleck's (1981, 1995) *role-strain* view, male roles are contradictory and inconsistent. Men not only experience stress when they violate men's roles, they also are harmed when they *do* act in accord with men's roles (Levant, 1996). The following are some of the areas where men's roles can cause considerable strain (Levant & Brooks, 1997; Philpot & others, 1997).

- *Health.* Men live 8 to 10 years less than women do. They have higher rates of stress-related disorders, alcoholism, car accidents, and suicide. Men are more likely than women to be the victims of homicide. In sum, the male role is hazardous to men's health.
- *Male-female relationships.* Too often, the male's role involves images that men should be dominant, powerful, and aggressive and should control women. Also, the male role has involved looking at women in terms of their bodies rather than their minds and feelings. Earlier, we described Deborah Tannen's (1990) concept that men show too little interest in rapport talk and relationships. And the male role has included the view that women should not be considered equal to men in work, earnings, and many other aspects of life. Too often these dimensions of the male role have produced men who have disparaged women, been violent toward women, and been unwilling to have equal relationships with women.
- *Male-male relationships.* Too many men have had too little interaction with their fathers, especially fathers who are positive role models. Nurturing and being sensitive to others have been considered aspects of the female role, and not the male role. And the male role emphasizes competition rather than cooperation. All of these aspects of the male role have left men with inadequate positive, emotional connections with other males.

To reconstruct their masculinity in more positive ways, Ron Levant (1995) believes, every man should (1) reexamine his beliefs about manhood, (2) separate out the valuable aspects of the male role, and (3) get rid of those parts of the masculine role that are destructive. All of this involves becoming more "emotionally intelligent"—that is, becoming more emotionally self-aware, managing emotions more effectively, reading emotions better (one's own emotions and others'), and being motivated to improve close relationships.

At this point we have discussed a number of ideas about diversity of adult lifestyles and gender, relationships, and self-development. To review these ideas, see summary table 15.3. This concludes our coverage of early adulthood. In the next section, we will turn our attention to development in middle adulthood, beginning with physical and cognitive changes in chapter 16.

Summary Table 15.3
The Diversity of Adult Lifestyles; Gender, Relationships, and Self-Development

Concept	Processes/ Related Ideas	Characteristics/Descriptions
The Diversity of Adult Lifestyles	Single Adults	• Being single has become an increasingly prominent lifestyle. Myths and stereotypes about singles abound, ranging from "swinging single" to "desperately lonely, suicidal single." • There are advantages and disadvantages to being single, autonomy being one of the advantages. • Intimacy, loneliness, and finding a positive identify in a marriage-oriented society are concerns of single adults.
	Cohabiting Adults	• Cohabitation is an increasing lifestyle for many adults. Cohabitation offers some advantages as well as problems. • Cohabitation does not lead to greater marital happiness but rather to no differences or differences suggesting that cohabitation is not good for a marriage
	Divorced Adults	• Divorce has increased dramatically, although its rate of increase has begun to slow. • Divorce is complex and emotional. In the first year following divorce, a disequilibrium in the divorced adult's behavior occurs, but by several years after the divorce, more stability has been achieved. The divorced displaced homemaker may encounter excessive stress. • Men do not go through a divorce unscathed either.
	Remarried Adults	• Stepfamilies are complex and adjustment is difficult. Only about 1/3 of remarried adults stay remarried.
	Gay and Lesbian Adults	• One of the most striking findings about gay and lesbian couples is how similar they are to heterosexual couples. There are a number of misconceptions about homosexual couples. • Researchers have found that the children are gay and lesbian parents are as well adjusted as those of heterosexual couples. • The overwhelming number of children in gay and lesbian families grow up to be heterosexual.
Gender, Relationships, and Self-Development	Women's Development	• Many experts believe that it is important for females to retain their competence and interest in relationships, but also to direct more effort into self-development. • Tannen distinguishes between rapport talk, which many women prefer, and report talk, which many men prefer.
	Men's Development	• Men have been successful at achieving but the male role involves considerable strain. • It is possible to talk about the "male experience," but there is diversity among males, just as there is diversity among females.

Chapter Review

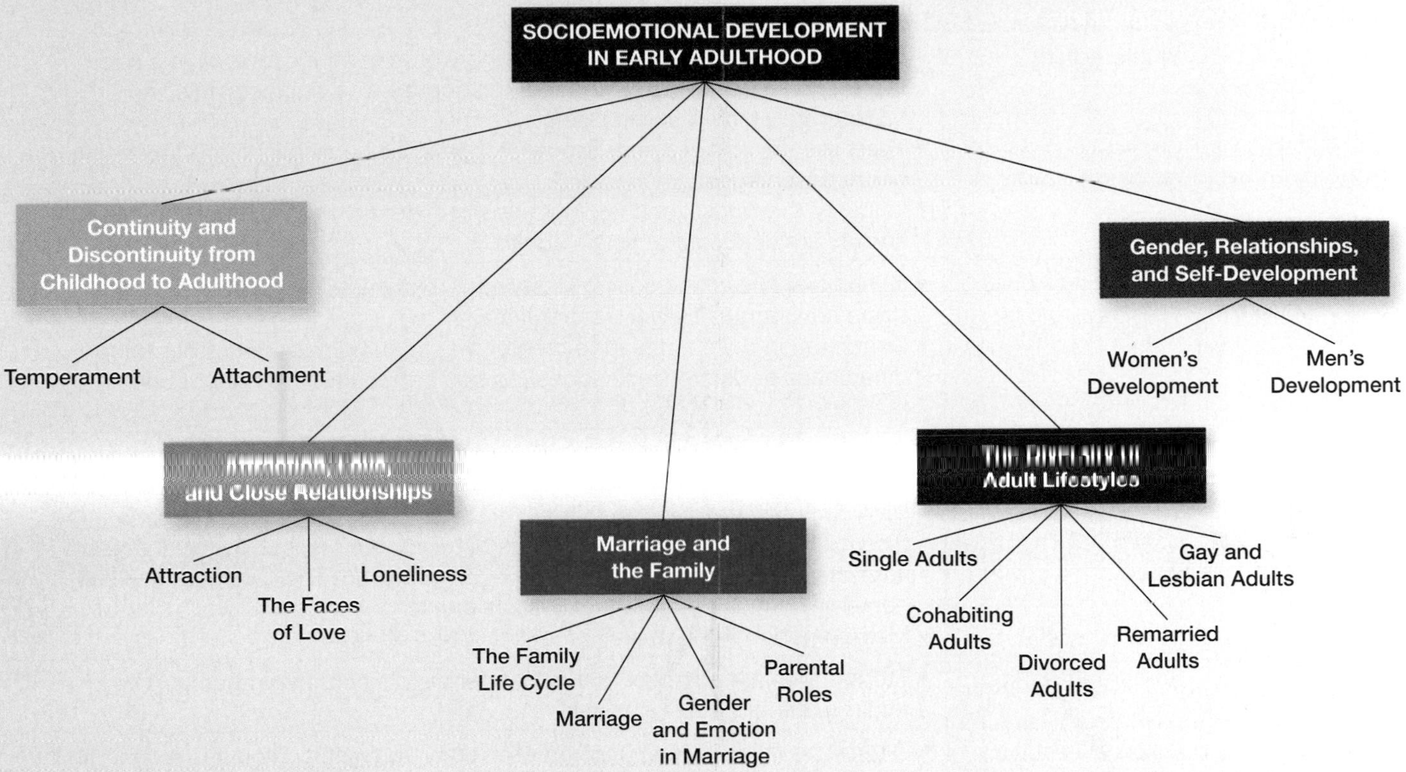

TO OBTAIN A DETAILED REVIEW OF THIS CHAPTER, STUDY THESE THREE SUMMARY TABLES:

- Summary Table 15.1 Continuity and Discontinuity from Childhood to Adulthood; Attraction, Love, and Close Relationships — page 456
- Summary Table 15.2 Marriage and the Family — page 465
- Summary Table 15.3 The Diversity of Adult Lifestyles; Gender, Relationships, and Self-Development — page 471

Key Terms

consensual validation 449
self-focused level 450
role-focused level 451
individuated-connected level 451
romantic love 451
affectionate love 452
triangular theory of love 452
friendship 453
leaving home and becoming a single adult 457
launching 457
new couple 457
becoming parents and a family with children 458
family with adolescents 458
family at midlife 458
family in later life 458

Key People

Theodore Wachs 447
Cindy Hazan and Phillip Shaver 448
Erik Erikson 450
Kathleen White 450
Ellen Berscheid 452
Robert J. Sternberg 452
Zick Rubin 453
John Gottman 461
Jean Baker Miller 469
Harriet Lerner 469
Deborah Tannen 469
Joseph Pleck 470

Taking It to the Net

1. What, according to psychologist Judith Wallerstein, are the nine psychological tasks necessary to make a good marriage?
2. Yolanda, who is divorced with two young children, is contemplating a marriage proposal from her boyfriend Dana, also divorced with one young child. She is concerned about the potential issues that may arise from this union. What should Yolanda consider before making this decision about her future?
3. Darren's lifespan psychology professor recently joined an APA division that specializes in men's issues, and is now considering offering such a specialized course himself. What is the division and what are their concerns and goals?

Connect to www.mhhe.com/santrockld8 to research the answers and complete these exercises.

OLC Preview

To further test your knowledge of this chapter or to explore our extensive on line resources that accompany Life-Span Development, eighth edition, please log on to the text's Online Learning Center at http://www.mhhe.com/santrockld8.com.

Section 8

Middle Adulthood

Generations will depend on the ability of every procreating individual to face his children.

Erik Erikson
American Psychologist, 20th Century

In middle adulthood, what we have been forms what we will be. For some of us, middle age is such a foggy place, a time when we need to discover what we are running from and to and why. We compare our life with what we vowed to make it. In middle age, more time stretches before us, and some evaluations, however reluctant, have to be made. As the young-old polarity greets us with a special force, we need to join the daring of youth with the discipline of age in a way that does justice to both. As middle-aged adults, we come to sense that the generations of living things pass in a short while and, like runners, hand on the torch of life. Section 8 consists of two chapters: "Physical and Cognitive Development in Middle Adulthood" (chapter 16) and "Socioemotional Development in Middle Adulthood" (chapter 17).

Chapter 16

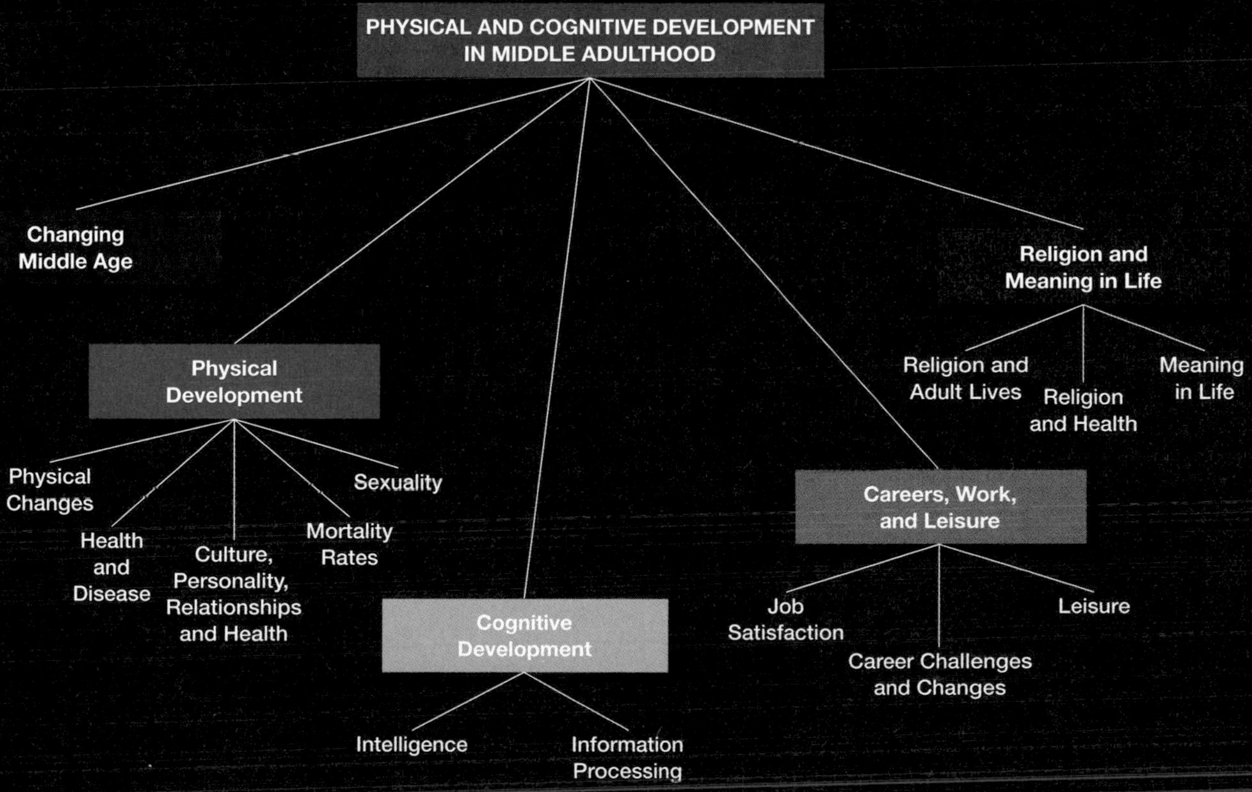

PHYSICAL AND COGNITIVE DEVELOPMENT IN MIDDLE ADULTHOOD
Changing Middle Age
Physical Development
Physical Changes
Health and Disease
Culture, Personality, Relationships and Health
Mortality Rates
Sexuality
Cognitive Development
Intelligence
Information Processing
Careers, Work, and Leisure
Job Satisfaction
Career Challenges and Changes
Leisure
Religion and Meaning in Life
Religion and Adult Lives
Religion and Health
Meaning in Life

Physical and Cognitive Development in Middle Adulthood

When more time stretches before one, some assessments, however reluctantly and incompletely, begin to be made.

James Baldwin
American Novelist, 20th Century

Images of Life-Span Development

Time Perspectives

OUR PERCEPTION of time depends on where we are in the life span. We are more concerned about time at some points in life than others (Schroots, 1996). Jim Croce's song "Time in a Bottle" reflects a time perspective that develops in the adult years:

If I could save time in a bottle
the first thing that I'd like to do
is save every day till eternity passes
away
just to spend them with you. . . .
But there never seems to be enough
time
to do the things you want to do once
you find them.
Looked around enough to know that
you're the one
I want to go through time with

—Jim Croce, "Time in a Bottle"

Jim Croce's song connects time with love and the hope of going through time with someone we love. Love and intimacy are important themes of adult development. So is time. Middle-aged adults begin to look back to where they have been, reflecting on what they have done with the time they have had. They look toward the future more in terms of how much time remains to accomplish what they hope to do with their lives.

When young adults look forward in time to what their lives might be like as middle-aged adults, too often they anticipate that things will go downhill. However, like all periods of the human life span, for most individuals there usually are positive and negative features of middle age.

Interest in middle age is essentially a phenomenon of the late twentieth century and early twenty-first century. As you read in chapter 1, in 1900 the average life expectancy was 47 years of age ◀ P. 8. It only has been since a much larger percentage of people began living to older ages that it made any sense to label, describe, and investigate a period in the human life span called "middle adulthood."

In this chapter, we will explore how middle age is changing and then turn to a number of physical and cognitive changes that take place in middle age.

CHANGING MIDDLE AGE

Changing Middle Age

Each year, for $8, about 2.5 to 3 million Americans who have turned 50 become members of the American Association for Retired Persons (AARP). There is something incongruous about so many 50-year-olds joining a retirement group when hardly any of them are retired. Indeed, many of today's 50-year-olds are in better shape, more alert, and more productive than their 40-year-old counterparts from a generation or two earlier. As more people lead healthier lifestyles and medical discoveries help to stave off the aging process, the boundaries of middle age are being pushed upward. It looks like middle age is starting later and lasting longer for increasing numbers of active, healthy, and productive people. June Reinisch (1992), director of the Kinsey Institute for Research in Sex, Gender, and Reproduction at Indiana University, recently said, "I'm 49 this year. I wear clothes that my mother would never have thought of wearing when she was this age. When skirts went up, my skirts went up" (p. 42).

Sigmund Freud and Carl Jung studied midlife transitions around the turn of the twentieth century, but "midlife" came much earlier back then. As we just mentioned, in 1900 the average life expectancy was only 47 years of age; only 3 percent of the population lived past 65. Today, the average life expectancy is 77; 12 percent of the U.S. population is older than 65. As a much greater percentage of the population lives to an older age, the midpoint of life and what constitutes middle age or middle adulthood are getting harder to pin down. In only one century, we have added 30 years to the average life expectancy. Statistically, the middle of life today is about 38 years of age—hardly any 38-year-olds, though, wish to be called "middle-aged"! What we think of as middle age comes later—anywhere from 40 to about 60 or 65 years of age. And as more people live longer, the 60 to 65 years upper boundary will likely be nudged upward. When the American Board of Family Practice asked a random sample of 1,200 Americans when middle age begins, 41 percent said it was when you worry about having enough money for health-care concerns, 42 percent said it was when your last child moves out, and 46 percent said it was when you don't recognize the names of music groups on the radio anymore (Beck, 1992).

WWW

Network on Successful Midlife Development

Exploring Middle Age

Although middle adulthood has been a relatively neglected period of the human life span (except for pop psychology portrayals of the midlife crisis), this age period is beginning to be given more attention by life-span developmentalists (Willis & Reid, 1999). One reason for the increased attention is that in the next several decades the largest cohorts in U.S. history will move through the middle-age years. From 1990 to 2015, the middle-aged U.S. population is projected to increase from 47 million to 80 million, a 72 percent increase. Because of the size of these baby-boom cohorts (recall from chapter 2 that a *cohort* is a group of people born in a particular year or time period), the median age of the U.S. population will increase from 33 years in 1990 to 42 years in 2050, reflecting the movement of "baby boomers" through middle age. The baby boomers are of interest to developmentalists not only because of their increased numbers but also because they are the best educated and most affluent cohorts in history to pass through middle age.

middle adulthood
The developmental period beginning at approximately 40 years of age and extending to about 60.

Though the age boundaries are not set in stone, we will consider **middle adulthood** *as the developmental period that begins at approximately 40 years of age and extends to about 60 years of age.* However, as we just pointed out, for many increasingly healthy adults, middle age is starting later and lasting longer. Remember from our discussion in chapter 1 that we have not only a chronological age, but biological, psychological, and social ages.

For many people, middle adulthood is a time of declining physical skills and expanding responsibility; a period in which people become more conscious of the young-old polarity and the shrinking amount of time left in life; a point when indi-

viduals seek to transmit something meaningful to the next generation; and a time when people reach and maintain satisfaction in their careers.

But these characteristics don't describe everybody in middle age. As life-span expert Gilbert Brim (1992) commented, middle adulthood is full of changes, twists, and turns; the path is not fixed. People move in and out of states of success and failure.

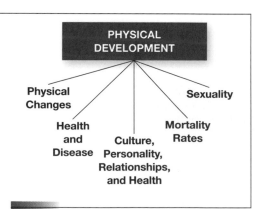

Physical Development

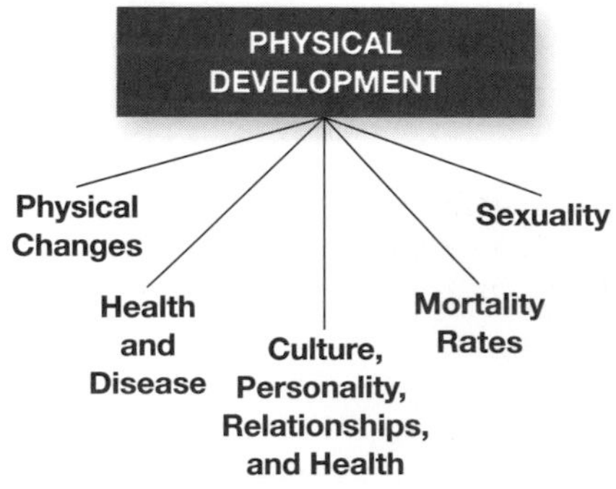

I am 56 years old at the time I am writing this book. When I was a college student and my father was 56 years old, I thought he was really old. I could not conceive of myself ever being that old! But it happened, and now I've got a few gray hairs. I'm wearing reading glasses while I'm typing this sentence. I can't run as fast as I could, although I still run 10 to 15 miles every week to keep my body from falling apart. What physical changes accompany this change to middle adulthood?

Physical Changes

Unlike the rather dramatic physical changes that occur in early adolescence and the sometimes abrupt decline in old age, midlife physical changes are usually gradual

Famous actor Sean Connery as a young adult in his 20s (left) and as a middle-aged adult in his 50s (right). *What are some of the most outwardly noticeable signs of aging in the middle adulthood years?*

(Merrill & Verbrugge, 1999) ◄ P. 349. Although everyone experiences some physical change due to aging in the middle adulthood years, the rates of this aging vary considerably from one individual to another. Genetic makeup and lifestyle factors play important roles in whether chronic disease will appear and when.

Noticeble Visible Signs One of the most visible signs of physical changes in middle adulthood is physical appearance. The first outwardly noticeable signs of aging usually are apparent by the forties or fifties.

The skin begins to wrinkle and sag because of a loss of fat and collagen in underlying tissues. Small, localized areas of pigmentation in the skin produce aging spots, especially in areas that are exposed to sunlight, such as the hands and face. Hair becomes thinner and grayer due to a lower replacement rate and a decline in melanin production. Fingernails and toenails develop ridges and become thicker and more brittle.

Since a youthful appearance is stressed in our culture, many individuals whose hair is graying, whose skin is wrinkling, whose bodies are sagging, and whose teeth are yellowing strive to make themselves look younger. Undergoing cosmetic surgery, dying hair, purchasing wigs, enrolling in weight reduction programs, participating in exercise regimens, and taking heavy doses of vitamins are common in middle age. One study found that middle-aged women focus more attention on facial attractiveness than do older or younger women (Nowak, 1977). In this same study, middle-aged women were more likely to perceive the signs of aging as having a negative effect on their physical appearance. In our culture, some aspects of aging in middle adulthood are taken as signs of attractiveness in men. Similar signs may be perceived as unattractive in women. Facial wrinkles and gray hair symbolize strength and maturity in men but may be perceived as unattractive in women.

> *Middle age is when your age starts to show around your middle.*
>
> Bob Hope
> *American Comedian, 20th Century.*

Height and Weight Individuals lose height in middle age, and many gain weight. Adults lose about one-half inch of height per decade beginning in their forties. (Memmler & others, 1995). On the average, body fat accounts for about 10 percent of body weight in adolescence; it makes up 20 percent or more in middle age.

Being overweight is a critical health problem in middle adulthood. For individuals who are 30 percent or more overweight, the probability of dying in middle adulthood increases by about 40 percent. Obesity increases the probability that an individual will suffer a number of other ailments, among them hypertension and digestive disorders.

In one recent large-scale study of middle-aged individuals, 7 of 10 said that they are overweight (Brim, 1999). Nearly half of the individuals over the age of 45 said they are less fit than they were 5 years ago.

Strength, Joints, and Bones As we saw in chapter 14, maximum physical strength often is attained in the twenties ◄ P. 416. Peak functioning of the body's joints also usually occurs in the twenties. Muscle strength decreases noticeably by the mid forties. A loss of strength especially occurs in the back and legs. It is estimated that about 10 to 15 percent of maximum strength is lost from age 35 to 60. The cushions for the movement of bones (such as tendons and ligaments) become less efficient in the middle adult years, a time when many individuals experience joint stiffness and more difficulty in movement.

Maximum bone density occurs by the mid to late thirties, from which point there is a progressive loss of bone. The rate of this bone loss begins slowly but accelerates in the fifties. Women experience about twice the rate of bone loss as men. By the end of midlife, bones break more easily and heal more slowly.

Vision Accommodation of the eye—the ability to focus and maintain an image on the retina—experiences its sharpest decline between 40 and 59 years of age. In par-

ticular, middle-aged individuals begin to have difficulty viewing close objects, which means that many individuals have to wear glasses with bifocal lenses. The eye's blood supply also diminishes, although usually not until the fifties or sixties. The reduced blood supply may decrease the visual field's size and account for an increase in the eye's blind spot. And there is some evidence that the retina becomes less sensitive to low levels of illumination. In one study, the effects of illumination level on the work productivity of individuals in early and middle adulthood were studied (Hughes, 1978). The workers were asked to look for 10 target numbers printed on sheets of paper that had a total of 420 numbers printed on them. Each of the workers performed the task under three different levels of illumination. While increased levels of illumination increased performance for both age groups, the performance of middle-aged workers improved the most.

Middle age is a mix of new opportunities and expanding resources accompanied by declines in physical abilities.

Lois Verbrugge
University of Michigan

Hearing Hearing can also start to decline by the age of 40. Sensitivity to high pitches usually declines first. The ability to hear low-pitched sounds does not seem to decline much in middle adulthood, though. And men usually lose their sensitivity to high-pitched sounds sooner than women do. However, this sex difference might be due to men's greater exposure to noise in occupations such as mining, automobile work, and so on (Olsho, Harkins, & Lenhardt, 1985).

Women's Health in Middle Age

Men's Health in Middle Age

Cardiovascular System The heart and coronary arteries change in middle adulthood. The heart of a 40-year-old pumps only 23 liters of blood per minute. The heart of a 20-year-old pumps 40 liters under comparable conditions. Just as the coronary arteries that supply blood to the heart narrow during middle adulthood, the level of cholesterol in the blood increases with age. At age 20, it is 180 milligrams. At age 40, 220 mg. At age 60, it is 230 mg and begins to accumulate on the artery walls, which are also thickening. The net result: Arteries are more likely to become clogged. This increases the pressure on the arterial walls, which in turn pushes the heart to work harder to pump blood, thus making a stroke or heart attack more likely. Blood pressure, too, usually rises in the forties and fifties (Siegler & others, 1999). At menopause, a woman's blood pressure rises sharply and usually remains above that of a man through life's later years.

Sleep Some aspects of sleep become more problematic in middle age. The total number of hours slept usually remains the same as in early adulthood, but beginning in the forties, wakeful periods are more frequent and there is less of the deepest type of sleep (stage 4). The amount of time spent lying awake in bed at night begins to increase in middle age, and this can produce a feeling of being less rested in the morning (Katchadourian, 1987).

Women	Men
1. Arthritis	1. Hypertension
2. Hypertension	2. Arthritis
3. Sinus problems	3. Hearing impairments

***Figure* 16.1**

Leading Chronic Disorders for Women and Men in Middle Age

Health and Disease

Health In middle adulthood, the frequency of accidents declines and individuals are less susceptible to colds and allergies than in childhood, adolescence, or early adulthood. Indeed, many individuals live through middle adulthood without having a disease or persistent health problem. However, as we see next, disease and persistent health problems become more common in middle adulthood for other individuals.

Chronic disorders **Chronic disorders** *are characterized by a slow onset and long duration.* Chronic disorders are rare in early adulthood, increase in middle adulthood, and become common in late adulthood. Arthritis is the leading chronic disorder in middle age, followed by hypertension.

The most common chronic disorders in middle age vary for females and males (see figure 16.1). Men have a higher incidence of fatal chronic conditions (such as coronary heart disease, cancer and stroke); women have a higher incidence of nonfatal ones (such as arthritis, varicose veins, and bursitis).

chronic disorders
Disorders that are characterized by slow onset and long duration. They are rare in early adulthood, they increase during middle adulthood, and they become common in late adulthood.

Culture, Personality, Relationships, and Health

Emotional stability and personality are related to health in middle adulthood. In the Berkeley Longitudinal Study, as individuals aged from 34 to 50, those who were the most healthy were also the most calm, the most self-controlled, and the most responsible (Livson & Peskin, 1981). Let's now explore the role of culture in cardiovascular disease and two personality profiles that are associated with health and illness.

Behavioral Medicine

Controlling Anger and Developing Life Skill

Culture and Cardiovascular Disease Culture plays an important role in coronary disease. Cross-cultural psychologists believe that studies of migrant ethnic groups help shed light on the role culture plays in health. As ethnic groups migrate, the health practices dictated by their cultures change while their genetic predispositions to certain disorders remain constant (Ilola, 1990). The Ni-Hon-San Study (Nipon-Honolulu-San Francisco), part of the Honolulu Heart Study, is an ongoing study of approximately 12,000 Japanese men in Hiroshima and Nagasaki (Japan), Honolulu, and San Francisco. In the study, the Japanese men living in Japan have had the lowest rate of coronary heart disease, those living in Honolulu have had an intermediate rate, and those living in San Francisco have had the highest rate. Acculturation provides a valuable framework for understanding why the Japanese men's cholesterol level, glucose level, and weight all increased as they migrated and acculturated. As the Japanese men migrated farther away from Japan, their health practices, such as diet, changed. The Japanese men in California, for example, ate 40 percent more fat than the men in Japan.

Conversely, Japanese men in California have much lower rates of cerebrovascular disease (stroke) than Japanese men living in Japan. Businessmen in Japan tend to consume vast quantities of alcohol and to chain-smoke, both of which are high-risk factors for stroke. As a result, stroke was the leading cause of death in Japan until it was surpassed by cancer in 1981. However, death rates from stroke for Japanese American men are at the same level as those of White American men. Researchers suspect that this level is related to a change in behavior. That is, Japanese American men consume less alcohol and smoke less than their counterparts in Japan. To read more about cultural factors in health, see the Sociocultural Worlds of Development box.

Type A behavior pattern
A cluster of characteristics—being excessively competitive, hard-driven, impatient, and hostile—thought to be related to the incidence of heart disease.

Type B behavior pattern
Being primarily calm and easygoing.

Type A/Type B Behavioral Patterns In the late 1950s a secretary for two California cardiologists, Meyer Friedman and Ray Rosenman, observed that the chairs in their waiting rooms were tattered and worn, but only on the front edges. The cardiologists had noticed the impatience of their cardiac patients, who often arrived exactly on time for an appointment and were in a great hurry to leave. Subsequently they conducted a study of 3,000 healthy men between the ages of 35 and 59 over a period of 8 years (Friedman & Rosenman, 1974). During the 8 years, one group of men had twice as many heart attacks or other forms of heart disease as anyone else. And autopsies of the men who died revealed that this same group had coronary arteries that were more obstructed than those of other men. Friedman and Rosenman described the coronary disease group as characterized by **Type A behavior pattern,** *a cluster of characteristics—being excessively competitive, hard-driven, impatient, and hostile—thought to be related to the incidence of heart disease.* Rosenman and Friedman labeled the behavior of the other group, who were *relaxed and easygoing,* **Type B behavior pattern.**

Type Z behavior

However, further research on the link between Type A behavior and coronary disease indicates that the association is not as strong as Friedman and Rosenman believed (Suls & Swain, 1998; Williams, 1995, 2001). Researchers have examined

Sociocultural Worlds of Development

Health Promotion in African Americans, Latinos, Asian Americans, and Native Americans

There are differences within ethnic groups as well as among them. This is just as true of health among ethnic groups as it is of, say, family structure. The spectrum of living conditions and lifestyles within an ethnic group are influenced by social class, immigrant status, social and language skills, occupational opportunities, and such social resources as the availability of meaningful support networks—all of which can play a role in an ethnic minority member's health.

Prejudice and racial segregation are the historical underpinnings for the chronic stress of discrimination and poverty that adversely affects the health of many African Americans. Support systems, such as an extended family network, may be especially important resources to improve the health of African Americans and help them cope with stress (Boyd-Franklin, 1989).

Some of the same stressors mentioned for African Americans are associated with migration to the United States by Puerto Ricans, Mexicans, and Latin Americans. Language is often a barrier for unacculturated Latinos in doctor-patient communications. In addition, there is increasing evidence that diabetes occurs at an above-average rate in Latinos, making this disease a major health problem that parallels the above-average rate of high blood pressure among African Americans (Gardner & others, 1984).

Asian Americans are characterized by their broad diversity in national backgrounds and lifestyles. They range from highly acculturated Japanese Americans, who may be better educated than many White Americans and have excellent access to health care, to the many Indochinese refugees who have few economic resources and may be in poor health.

Cultural barriers to adequate health care include a lack of financial resources and poor language skills. In addition, members of ethnic minority groups are often unfamiliar with how the medical system operates, confused about the need to see numerous people, and uncertain about why they have to wait so long for service (Snowden & Cheung, 1990).

Other barriers may be specific to certain cultures, reflecting differing ideas regarding what causes disease and how it should be treated. For example, there are Chinese herbalists and folk healers in every Chinatown in the United States. Depending on their degree of acculturation to Western society, Chinese Americans may go to either a folk healer or a Western doctor first, but generally they will consult a folk healer for follow-up care. Chinese medicines are usually used for home care.

Native Americans view Western medicine as a source of crisis intervention, quick fixes for broken legs, or cures for other symptoms. They do not view Western medicine as a source for treating the causes of disease or for preventing disease. For example, they are unlikely to attend a seminar on preventing alcohol abuse. They also are reluctant to become involved in care that requires long-term hospitalization or surgery.

Health-care professionals can increase their effectiveness with ethnic minority patients by improving their knowledge of patients' attitudes, beliefs, and folk practices regarding health and disease. Such information should be integrated into Western treatment rather than ignored at the risk of alienating patients.

the components of Type A behavior, such as hostility, competitiveness, a strong drive to accomplish goals, and impatience, to determine a more precise link with coronary risk. The Type A behavior component most consistently associated with coronary problems is hostility (Faber & Burns, 1996; Räikkönen & others, 1999). People who are hostile outwardly or turn anger inward are more likely to develop heart disease than their less angry counterparts (Allan & Scheidt, 1996). Such people have been called "hot reactors" because of their intense physiological reactions to stress. Their hearts race, their breathing quickens, and their muscles tense up. Redford Williams (1995), a leading behavioral medicine researcher, believes that such people can develop the ability to control their anger and develop more trust in others, which he thinks can reduce their risk for heart disease.

All men should strive to learn before they die what they are running from, and to, and why.

James Thurber
American Novelist, 20th Century

Hardiness

Hardiness *is a personality style characterized by a sense of commitment (rather than alienation), control (rather than powerlessness), and a perception of problems as challenges (rather than threats).* In the Chicago Stress Project, male business managers 32 to 65 years of age were studied over a 5-year period. During the 5

hardiness
A personality style characterized by a sense of commitment (rather than alienation), control (rather than powerlessness), and a perception of problems as challenges (rather than threats).

years, most of the managers experienced stressful events, such as divorce, job transfers, the death of a close friend, inferior performance evaluations at work, and working at a job with an unpleasant boss. In one study, managers who developed an illness (ranging from the flu to a heart attack) were compared with those who did not (Kobasa, Maddi, & Kahn, 1982). The latter group was more likely to have a hardy personality. In another study, whether or not hardiness along with exercise and social support buffered stress and reduced illness in executives' lives was investigated (Kobasa & others, 1985). When all three factors were present in an executive's life the level of illness dropped dramatically. This suggests the power of multiple buffers of stress, rather than a single buffer, in maintaining health (Maddi, 1998).

Health and Social Relationships In chapter 15, "Socioemotional Development in Early Adulthood," we saw that being in a happy marriage is linked with getting sick less, having less physical and emotional stress, and living longer than being in an unhappy marriage ◄ P. 462. These results hold for middle-aged as well as young adults.

Researchers also have revealed links between health in middle age and earlier pathways of relationships (Ryff & Singer, 2000). In one recent longitudinal study, individuals who were on a positive relationship pathway from childhood to middle age had significantly fewer biological problems (cardiovascular disease, physical decline) than their counterparts who were on a negative relationship pathway (Ryff & others, in press). In another longitudinal study, adults who experienced more warmth and closeness with their parents during childhood had fewer diagnosed diseases (coronary artery disease, hypertension, ulcer, alcoholism) than those who did not experience warmth and closeness with their parents in childhood (Russek & Schwartz, 1997). These studies reflect continuity in development over many years in the human life span. Thus, health in middle age is related to the current quality of social relationships and to the pathways of those relationships earlier in development.

So far we have examined many aspects of health and disease in middle age. Next, we will explore the main causes of death in middle age.

Cause of Death
1. Heart disease
2. Cancer
3. Cerebrovascular disease
4. Accidents
5. Pulmonary disease

Figure **16.2**
Leading Causes of Death in Middle Adulthood

Mortality Rates

Infectious disease was the main cause of death until the middle of the twentieth century. As infectious disease rates declined and more individuals lived through middle age, chronic disorders increased.

Chronic diseases are now the main causes of death for individuals in middle adulthood (Merrill & Verbrugge, 1999). Heart disease is the leading cause of death in middle age, followed by cancer and cerebrovascular disease. In the first half of middle age, cancer claims more lives than heart disease; this reversed in the second half.

Figure 16.2 shows the leading causes of death in middle age. Men have higher mortality rates than women for all of the leading causes of death.

So far we have considered many aspects of physical development in middle adulthood, including health, disease, and mortality rates. Next, we will turn our attention to another aspect of physical development that changes in middle adulthood—sexuality.

Sexuality

What kind of changes characterize the sexuality of women and men as they go through middle age? **Climacteric** *is a term that is used to describe the midlife transition in which fertility declines.* Let's explore the substantial differences in the climacteric of women and men.

climacteric
The midlife transition in which fertility declines.

Menopause Most of us know something about menopause. But is what we know accurate? Stop for a moment and think about your knowledge of menopause. What is menopause? When does it occur? Can it be treated? Most of us share some

assumptions about menopause—we might think that it is a disease, that it involves numerous complaints, that women who are undergoing menopause deeply regret losing their reproductive capacity, their sexuality, and their femininity, and that they become deeply depressed. Are these assumptions accurate?

Menopause *is the time in middle age, usually in the late forties or early fifties, when a woman's menstrual periods cease completely.* The average age at which women have their last period is 52. A small percentage of women—10 percent—go through menopause before 40. There is a dramatic decline in the production of estrogen by the ovaries. Estrogen decline produces some uncomfortable symptoms in some menopausal women—"hot flashes," nausea, fatigue, and rapid heartbeat, for example. Some menopausal women report depression and irritability, but in some instances these feelings are related to other circumstances in the woman's life, such as becoming divorced, losing a job, caring for a sick parent, and so on (Dickson, 1990; Gannon, 1998).

menopause
The complete cessation of a woman's menstruation, which usually occurs in the late forties or early fifties.

Menopause: Information and Resources

National Institute of Aging: Menopause

Medline: Menopause

The comments of the following two women reveal the extensive variation menopause may bring. One woman commented, "I had hot flashes frequently for almost 6 months. I didn't get as embarrassed as some of my friends who also had hot flashes, but I found the 'heat wave' sensation uncomfortable." Another woman commented, "I am constantly amazed and delighted to discover new things about my body, something menstruation did not allow me to do. I have new responses, desires, sensations, freed and apart from the distraction of menses [periods]."

In a recent large-scale study of Americans in midlife, almost two-thirds of postmenopausal women said they felt relief that their periods had stopped (Brim, 1999). Only 1 percent said they felt "only regret" that they no longer had their period. Just over 50 percent of middle-aged women said they did not have hot flashes at all.

Why, then, do so many individuals have the idea that menopause is such a big deal? Why do we have so many erroneous assumptions—that menopausal women will lose their sexuality and femininity, that they will become deeply depressed, and that they will experience extensive physical pain? Much of the research on menopause is based on small, selective samples of women who go to physicians or therapists because they are having problems associated with menopause. These women are unrepresentative of the large population of women in the United States.

The problem of using a small, selective sample was reflected in popular author Gail Sheehy's (1991) book *The Silent Passage.* Sheehy writes about her own difficult experiences and reports the frustrations of a few women she chose to interview. Although Sheehy dramatically overstates the percentage of women who have serious problems with menopause, she does not overstate the stigma attached to menopause or the inadequate attention accorded it by the medical community (which is male-dominated).

Researchers have found that almost 50 percent of Canadian and American women have occasional hot flashes, but only 1 in 7 Japanese women do (Lock, 1998). *What factors might account for these variations?*

Cross-cultural studies reveal wide variations in the menopause experience (Avis, 1999). For example, hot flashes are uncommon in Mayan women (Beyene, 1986). Asian women report fewer hot flashes than women in Western societies (Payer, 1991). It is difficult to determine the extent to which these cross-cultural variations in the menopause experience are due to genetic, dietary, reproductive, or cultural factors.

Our portrayal of menopause has been much more positive than its usual portrayals in the past. While menopause overall is not the negative experience for most women it was once thought to be, the loss of fertility is an important marker for women—it means that they have to make final decisions about having children. Women in their thirties who have never had children sometimes speak about being "up against the biological clock" because they cannot postpone questions about having children much longer.

Hormone Replacement Therapy There are two main types of hormone replacement therapy: estrogen alone (estrogen replacement therapy, or ERT) and estrogen combined with a progestin (combined hormone replacement therapy, or

New Choices in Hormone Replacement Therapy

SERMS

Evista

HRT) (Avis, 1999). Currently, estrogen alone is not recommended for women who still have a uterus, because of the risk ERT creates for endometrial cancer. The combination of estrogen with a progestin prevents an excess of estrogen from building up and reduces the risk of endometrial cancer.

A positive outcome of using HRT is its prevention of bone loss (Lindsay & Cosman, 1990). However, if HRT is stopped, bone loss resumes. HRT also has been cited in news reports as having a protective effect for cardiovascular disease, but the research evidence regarding this link is still unclear (Avis, 1999).

One of the primary potential risks of using HRT is breast cancer, although the evidence regarding this link also is unclear—several studies have shown no risk, several others a small risk (Barrett-Connor, 1994; Schairer & others, 2000). Scientists also do not know the long-term effects of regular use of HRT for 20 or 30 years. An alternative to HRT is selective estrogen receptor modulators (SERMS) (Rifkind & Rossouw, 1998). Recently, a SERMS drug called Evista was approved by the Federal Drug Administration for the prevention and treatment of bone loss in women (Eli Lilly, 2000).

Despite the risks of HRT, many women use it because of its benefits, and it is recommended by the American Geriatric Association for postmenopausal women. This association recommends that women should actively participate in decision making about HRT.

Hormonal Changes in Middle-Aged Men Do men go through anything like the menopause that women experience? That is, is there a male menopause? During middle adulthood, most men do not lose their capacity to father children, although there usually is a modest decline in their sexual hormone level and activity. Men experience hormonal changes in their fifties and sixties, but nothing like the dramatic drop in estrogen that women experience. Testosterone production begins to decline about 1 percent a year during middle adulthood, and sperm count usually shows a slow decline, but men do not lose their fertility in middle age. What has been referred to as "male menopause," then, probably has less to do with hormonal change than with the psychological adjustment men must make when they are faced with declining physical energy and family and work pressures. Testosterone therapy has not been found to relieve such symptoms, suggesting that they are not induced by hormonal change.

In middle age, men's testosterone levels gradually drop, which can reduce their sexual drive. Their erections are less full and less frequent, and require more stimulation to achieve them. Researchers once attributed these changes to psychological factors, but increasingly they find that as many as 75 percent of the erectile dysfunctions in middle-aged men stem from physiological problems. Smoking, diabetes, hypertension, and elevated cholesterol levels are at fault in many erectile problems in middle-aged men (Crooks & Baur, 1999).

Recently, the most attention in helping individuals with a sexual dysfunction has focused on Viagra, a drug designed to conquer impotence. Its success rate is in the range of 60 to 80 percent, and its prescription rate has outpaced such popular drugs as Prozac (antidepressant) and Rogaine (baldness remedy) in first-year comparisons (Padma-Nathan, 1999). Viagra also is being taken by some women to improve their sexual satisfaction. However, Viagra is not an aphrodisiac; it won't work in the absence of desire. The possible downside of Viagra involves headaches in 1 of 10 men, seeing blue (because the eyes contain an enzyme similar to the one on which Viagra works in the penis, about 3 percent of users develop temporary vision problems ranging from blurred vision to a blue or green halo effect), and blackouts (Viagra can trigger a sudden drop in blood pressure). Also, scientists do not know the long-term effects of taking the drug, although in short-term trials it appears to be a relatively safe drug.

Sexual Attitudes and Behavior Although the ability of men and women to function sexually shows little biological decline in middle adulthood, sexual activity usually occurs on a less frequent basis than in early adulthood. Career in-

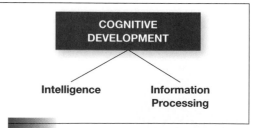

AGE GROUPS	FREQUENCY OF SEX: Not at all	A few times per year	A few times per month	2–3 times a week	4 or more times a week
Men					
18–24	15	21	24	28	12
25–29	7	15	31	36	11
30–39	8	15	37	33	6
40–49	9	18	40	27	6
50–59	11	22	43	20	3
Women					
18–24	11	16	32	29	12
25–29	5	10	38	37	10
30–39	9	16	36	33	6
40–49	15	16	44	20	5
50–59	30	22	35	12	2

Figure **16.3**

The Sex in America Survey: Frequency of Sex at Different Points in Adult Development

terests, family matters, energy level, and routine may contribute to this decline. In the recent Sex in America survey, frequency of having sex was greatest for individuals aged 25 to 29 years old (47 percent had sex twice a week or more) and dropped off for individuals in their fifties (23 percent of 50- to 59-year-old males said they had sex twice a week or more, while only 14 percent of the females in this age group reported this frequency) (Michael & others, 1994). Figure 16.3 shows the age trends in frequency of sex from the Sex in America survey.

Medline: Middle-Age Sexuality

Midlife Male Hormone Changes

A spouse or live-in partner makes all the difference in whether sexual activity occurs, especially for women over 40 years of age. In one recent study conducted by the MacArthur Foundation, 95 percent of women in their forties with partners said that they have been sexually active in the last 6 months, compared with only 53 percent of those without partners (Brim, 1999). By their fifties, 88 percent of women living with a partner have been sexually active in the last 6 months, but only 37 percent of those who are neither married nor living with someone say they have had sex in the last 6 months.

At this point we have discussed a number of ideas about changing middle age and physical development in middle adulthood. To review these ideas, see summary table 16.1. Next we will study the possibility of cognitive change in middle adulthood.

Cognitive Development

COGNITIVE DEVELOPMENT

Intelligence — **Information Processing**

We have seen that the decline in many physical characteristics in middle adulthood is not just imagined. Middle-aged adults might not see as well, run as fast, or be as healthy as in their twenties and thirties. But what about their cognitive skills? In chapter 14, "Physical and Cognitive Development in Early Adulthood," we saw that cognitive abilities are very strong in early adulthood ◄ P. 431. Do they decline as we enter and move through middle adulthood? To answer this question we will explore the possibility of cognitive changes in intelligence and information processing.

Intelligence

Our exploration of possible changes in intelligence in middle adulthood focuses on the concepts of fluid and crystallized intelligence, the Seattle Longitudinal Study, and cohort effects.

Summary Table 16.1
Changing Middle Age; Physical Development

Concept	Processes/ Related Ideas	Characteristics/Descriptions
Changing Middle Age	Its Nature	• The age boundaries of middle age are not set in stone. As more people live to an older age, what we think of as middle age seems to be occurring later. • Developmentalists are beginning to study middle age more probably because of the dramatic increase in the number of individuals entering this period of the life span. • Middle age involves extensive individual variation. With this variation in mind, we will consider middle adulthood to be entered at about 40 and exited at approximately 60 years of age.
Physical Development	Physical Changes	• Midlife changes are often gradual. Genetic and lifestyle factors play important roles in whether chronic diseases will appear and when. • Among the physical changes are outwardly noticeable changes in physical appearance (wrinkles, aging spots); height (decrease) and weight (increase), strength, joints, and bones; vision; hearing; cardiovascular system; and sleep.
	Health and Disease	• In middle age, the frequency of accidents declines and individuals are less susceptible to colds and allergies. • Chronic disorders rarely appear in early adulthood, increase in middle adulthood, and become more common in late adulthood. Arthitis is the leading chronic disorder in middle age, followed by hypertension. Men have more fatal chronic disorders, women more non-fatal ones in middle age.
	Culture, Personality, Relationships, and Health	• Culture plays an important role in coronary disease. • The Type A behavior pattern has been proposed as having a link with heart disease, but it primarily is the hostility dimension of the pattern that is consistently associated with heart disease. • Hardiness is a buffer of stress and is related to reduced illness. • Health in middle age is linked to the current quality of social relationships and to developmental pathways of relationships.
	Mortality Rates	• In middle age, the leading causes of death, in order, are heart disease, cancer, and cerebrovascular disease.
	Sexuality	• *Climacteric* is the midlife transition in which fertility declines. • Menopause is a marker that signals the end of childbearing capability, usually arriving in the late forties and early fifties. The vast majority of women do not have serious physical or psychological problems related to menopause. • Hormone replacement therapy (HRT), which consists of a combination of estrogen and progestin, reduces bone loss in women. It is unclear whether HRT is linked with breast cancer or cardiovascular disease. The American Geriatric Association recommends HRT in postmenopausal women. • Men do not experience an inability to father children in middle age, although their testosterone drops off. A male menopause, like the dramatic decline in estrogen in women, does not occur. • Sexual behavior occurs less frequently in middle adulthood than in early adulthood. Nonetheless, a majority of middle-aged adults show a moderate or strong interest in sex.

crystallized intelligence
Accumulated information and verbal skills, which increase with age, according to Horn.

fluid intelligence
The ability to reason abstractly, which steadily declines from middle adulthood on, according to Horn.

Fluid and Crystallized Intelligence John Horn believes that some abilities begin to decline in middle age while others increase (Horn & Donaldson, 1980). Horn argues that **crystallized intelligence,** *an individual's accumulated information and verbal skills, continue to increase in the middle adulthood years,* while **fluid intelligence,** *one's ability to reason abstractly, begins to decline in the middle adulthood years* (see figure 16.4).

Horn's data were collected in a cross-sectional manner. Remember from chapter 2, "The Science of Life-Span Development," that this involves assessing individuals of different ages at the same point in time P. 51. For example, a cross-sectional study might assess the intelligence of different groups of 40-, 50-, and 60-year-olds in a single evaluation, such as 1980. The average 40-year-old and the average 60-year-old were born in different eras, which produced different economic and educational opportunities. For example, as the 60-year-olds grew up they likely had fewer educational opportunities, which probably influenced their scores on intelligence tests. Thus, if we find differences between 40- and 60-year-olds on intelligence tests when they are assessed cross-sectionally, these differences might be due to cohort effects related to educational differences rather than to age.

By contrast, remember from chapter 2 that in a longitudinal study, the same individuals are studied over a period of time P. 52. Thus, a longitudinal study of intelligence in middle adulthood might consist of giving the same intelligence test to the same individuals when they are 40, 50, and 60 years of age. As we see next, whether data on intelligence are collected cross-sectionally or longitudinally can make a difference in what is found about intellectional decline.

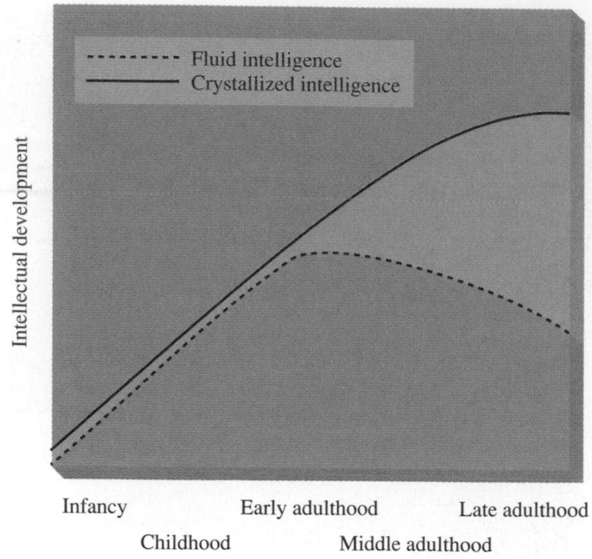

Figure 16.4
Fluid and Crystallized Intellectual Development Across the Life Span
According to Horn, crystallized intelligence (based on cumulative learning experiences) increases throughout the life span, but fluid intelligence (the ability to perceive and manipulate information) steadily declines from middle adulthood.

The Seattle Longitudinal Study K. Warner Schaie (1983, 1996) is conducting an extensive study of intellectual abilities in the adulthood years. Five hundred individuals initially were tested in 1956. New waves of participants are added periodically. The main focus in the Seattle Longitudinal Study has been on individual change and stability in intelligence. A psychometric, measurement-based approach, described in chapter 10, "Physical and Cognitive Development in Middle and Late Childhood," is used.

The main mental abilities tested include these:

- Vocabulary (ability to understand ideas expressed in words)
- Verbal memory (ability to encode and recall meaningful language units, such as a list of words)
- Number (ability to perform simple mathematical computations such as addition, subtraction, and multiplication)
- Spatial orientation (ability to visualize and mentally rotate stimuli in two- and three-dimensional space)
- Inductive reasoning (ability to recognize and understand patterns and relationships in a problem and use this understanding to solve other instances of the problem)
- Perceptual speed (ability to quickly and accurately make simple discriminations in visual stimuli)

As shown in figure 16.5, the highest level of functioning for four of the six intellectual abilities occurred in the middle adulthood years (Willis & Schaie, 1999). For both women and men, peak performance on vocabulary, verbal memory, inductive reasoning, spatial orientation was attained in middle age. For only two of the six abilities—numerical ability and perceptual speed—were there declines in middle age. Perceptual speed showed the earliest decline, actually beginning in early adulthood.

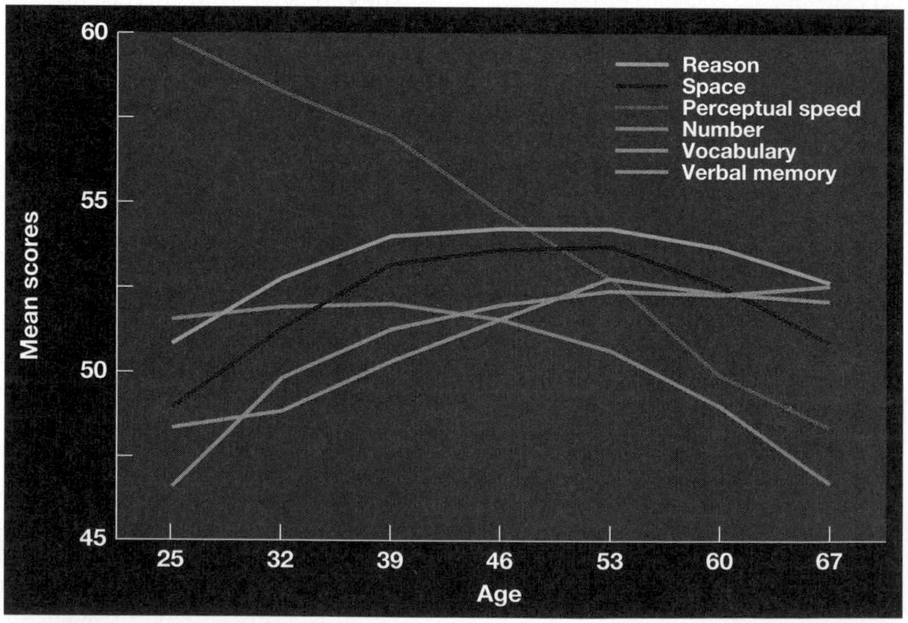

Figure 16.5
Longitudinal Changes in Six Intellectual Abilities from Age 25 to Age 67

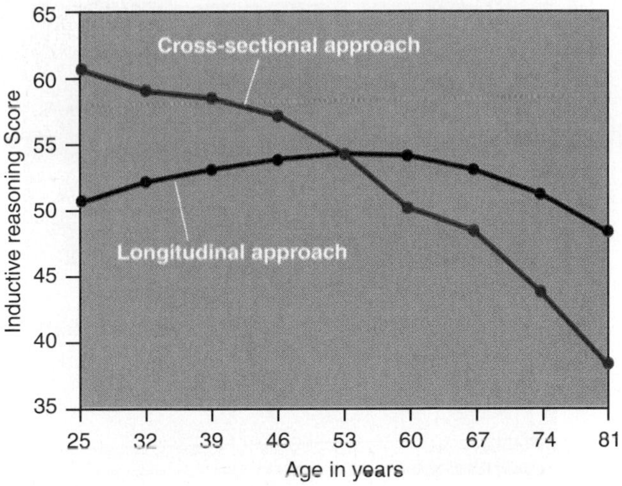

Figure **16.6**
Cross-Sectional and Longitudinal Comparisons of Intellectual Change in Middle Adulthood

When Schaie (1994) assessed intellectual abilities both cross-sectionally and longitudinally, he found decline more likely in the cross-sectional than in the longitudinal assessments. For example, as shown in figure 16.6, when assessed longitudinally, inductive reasoning increased until toward the end of middle adulthood, when it began to show a slight decline. By contrast, when assessed cross-sectionally, inductive reasoning showed a consistent decline in the middle adulthood years.

Interestingly, in terms of John Horn's ideas that were discussed earlier, middle age was a time of peak performance for both some aspects of crystallized intelligence (vocabulary) and fluid intelligence (spatial orientation and inductive reasoning) for the participants in the Seattle Longitudinal Study.

Thus, in Shaie's view, it is in middle adulthood, not early adulthood, that people reach a peak in their cognitive functioning for many intellectual skills.

Information Processing

Recall from our discussion of theories of development in chapter 2 and in a number of child development and adolescence chapters (8, 10, and 12), we also examined the information-processing approach to cognition Pp. 38, 220, 288, and 368. Among the information-processing changes that take place in middle adulthood are those involved in speed of processing information, memory, expertise, and practical problem-solving skills.

Speed of Information Processing As we saw in Schaie's (1994, 1996) Seattle Longitudinal Study, perceptual speed begins declining in early adulthood and continues to decline in middle adulthood. A common way to assess speed of information is through a reaction-time task, in which individuals simply press a button as soon as they see a light appear. Middle-aged adults are slower to push the button when the light appears than young adults are. However, keep in mind that the decline is not dramatic—under 1 second in most investigations. Also, for unknown reasons, the decline in reaction time is stronger for women than for men (Salthouse, 1994).

Memory In Schaie's (1994, 1996) Seattle Longitudinal Study, verbal memory peaked in the fifties. However, in some other studies, verbal memory has shown a decline in middle age, especially when assessed in cross-sectional studies. For example, in several studies, when asked to remember lists of words, numbers, or meaningful prose, younger adults outperformed middle-aged adults (Salthouse, 1991; Salthouse & Skovronek, 1992). Although there still is some controversy about whether memory declines in the middle adulthood years, most experts conclude that it does decline (Salthouse, 2000). However, some experts argue that studies that have concluded there is a decline in memory during middle age often have compared young adults in their twenties with older middle-aged adults in their late fifties and even have included some individuals in their sixties (Schaie, 2000). In this latter view, memory decline in the early part of middle age either is nonexistent or minimal, not occurring until the latter part of middle age or late adulthood.

Memory decline is more likely to occur when individuals don't use effective memory strategies, such as organization and imagery. By organizing lists of phone numbers into different categories or imagining the phone numbers represent different objects around the house, memory in middle adulthood can improve.

WWW
K. Warner Schaie
Midlife Baby-Boomer Characteristics

Expertise **Expertise** *involves having an extensive, highly organized knowledge and understanding of a particular domain.* Individuals can have expertise in areas as diverse as physics, art, or knowledge of wine. Developing expertise and becoming an "expert"

expertise
Having an extensive, highly organized knowledge and understanding of a particular domain.

SUMMARY TABLE 16.2
Cognitive Development in Middle Adulthood

Concept	Processes/ Related Ideas	Characteristics/Descriptions
Intelligence	Crystallized and Fluid	• Horn argued that crystallized intelligence (accumulated information and verbal skills) continues to increase in middle adulthood whereas fluid intelligence (ability to reason abstractly) declines.
	The Seattle Longitudinal Study	• Schaie found that, when assessed longitudinally, intellectual abilities are less likely to decline and are even more likely to improve than when assessed cross-sectionally in middle adulthood. • The highest level of four intellectual abilities (vocabulary, verbal memory, inductive reasoning, and spatial ability) occurred in middle age.
Information Processing	Speed of Information Processing	• Speed of information processing, often assessed through reaction time, declines in middle adulthood.
	Memory	• Although Schaie found that verbal memory increased in middle age, some researchers have found that memory declines in middle age. • Memory is more likely to decline in middle age when individuals don't use effective strategies.
	Expertise	• Expertise involves having an extensive, highly organized knowledge and and understanding of a domain. Expertise often increases in the middle adulthood years.
	Practical Problem Solving	• This often increases through the forties and fifties as individuals accumulate practical experience.

in a field usually is the result of many years of experience, learning, and effort. Because it takes so long to attain, expertise often shows up more in the middle adulthood than in the early adulthood years (Clancy & Hoyer, 1994; Hoyer, Rybash, & Roodin, 1999).

Strategies that distinguish experts from novices include these:

- Experts are more likely to rely on their accumulated experience to solve problems.
- Experts often process information automatically and analyze it more efficiently when solving a problem in their domain than a novice does.
- Experts have better strategies and short-cuts to solving problems in their domain than novices do.
- Experts are more creative and flexible in solving problems in their domain than novices are (Csikszentmihalyi, 1997).

Practical Problem Solving A final difference in the information processing of middle-aged and young adults involves solving practical problems.

Nancy Denney (1986, 1990) assessed practical problem-solving abilities in adults by observing such circumstances as how they handled a landlord who would not fix their stove and what they did if a bank mistakenly did not deposit a check in their account. She found that the ability to solve such practical problems increased through the forties and fifties as individuals accumulated practical experience.

At this point we have studied a number of ideas about cognitive development in middle adulthood. To review these ideas, see summary table 16.2.

Stephen J. Hawking is a world-renowned expert in phyics. Hawking authored the best-selling book, *A Brief History of Time.* Hawking has a neurological disorder that prevents him from being able to walk or talk. He communicates with the aid of a voice-equipped computer. *What distinguishes experts from novices?*

Next, we will continue our discussion of development in middle adulthood by focusing on career development, work, and leisure.

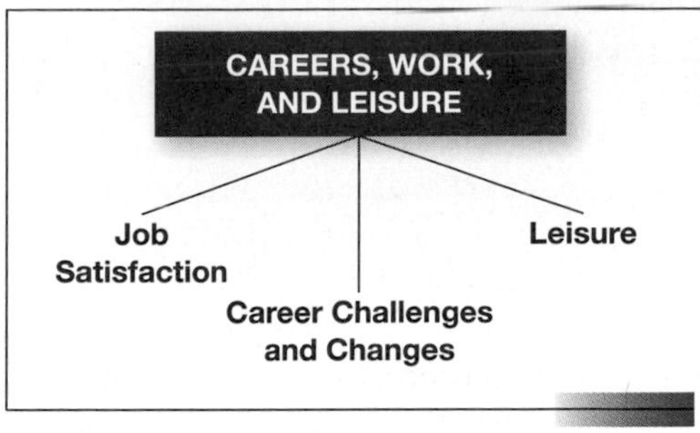

Careers, Work, and Leisure

Are middle-aged workers as satisfied with their jobs as young adult workers?

Job Satisfaction

Work satisfaction increases steadily throughout the work life—from age 20 to at least age 60, for both college-educated and non-college-educated adults (Rhodes, 1983) (see figure 16.7). This same pattern has been found for both women and men. Satisfaction probably increases because as we get older we get paid more, we are in higher positions, and we have more job security. There is also a greater commitment to the job as we get older. We take our jobs more seriously, have lower rates of avoidable absenteeism, and are more involved with our work in middle adulthood than in early adulthood. Younger adults are still experimenting with their work and still searching for the right occupation. They may be inclined to seek out what is wrong with their current job rather than focusing on what is right about it. For the most part, researchers have found the highest levels of physical and psychological well-being in people who are doing as much paid work as they would like to do (House, 1998; House & others, 1992).

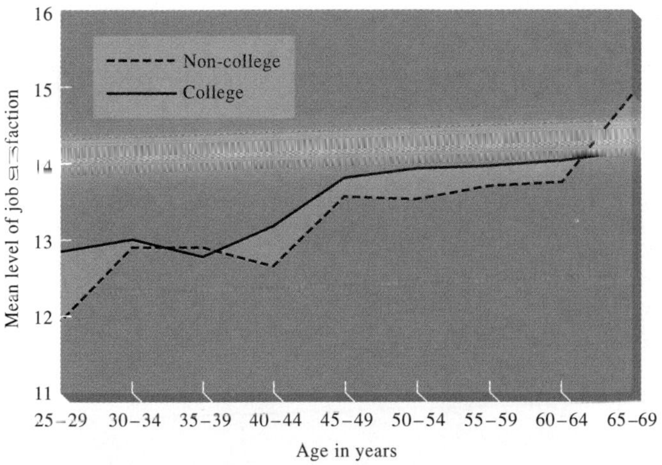

Figure 16.7

Age and Job Satisfaction

Job satisfaction increases with age, for both college- and non-college-educated adults. Among the reasons for increased satisfaction are more income, higher-status jobs, greater job security, and stronger job commitment.

Career Challenges and Changes

The current middle-aged worker faces several important challenges in the twenty-first century (Avolio & Sosik, 1999). These include the globalization of work, rapid developments in information technologies, downsizing of organizations, and early retirement.

Globalization has replaced the traditional white male workforce with employees of different ethnic and national backgrounds. The proliferation of computer technology compels middle-aged adults to become increasingly computer literate to maintain their work competence. To improve profits, many companies are restructuring and downsizing. One of the outcomes of this is to offer incentives to middle-aged employees to retire early—in their fifties, or in some cases even forties, rather than their sixties.

Some midlife career changes are self-motivated, others are the consequence of losing one's job (Moen, 1998; Moen & Wethington, 1999). Some individuals in middle age decide that they don't

WWW

Is It Time to Change Jobs?

Women and Work in Midcareer

want to do the same work they have been doing for the rest of their lives (Hoyer, Rybash, & Roodin, 1999). One aspect of middle adulthood involves adjusting idealistic hopes to realistic possibilities in light of how much time individuals have before they retire and how fast they are reaching their occupational goals (Levinson, 1978, 1997). If individuals perceive that they are behind schedule, if their goals are unrealistic, they don't like the work they are doing, or their job has become too stressful, they could become motivated to change jobs.

Critical Thinking: The Balance and Imbalance of Work, Family, and Leisure in Our Lives as We Develop

MOST OF US would like to balance work, family, and leisure activities in some fashion. Clearly, though, some individuals give priority to one or two of these to the exclusion of the other or others. Further, our commitment to and balancing of these activities may shift as we develop and see new possibilities for growth or we become dissatisfied with our earlier priorities (Clausen, 1993). Think about your own life. How balanced or unbalanced is your life in terms of work, family, and leisure? Do you think your commitment to these areas of your life will change in the future? If so, how?

Leisure

As adults, not only must we learn how to work well, but we also need to learn how to relax and enjoy leisure. With the kind of work ethic on which America is based, it is not surprising to find that many adults view leisure as boring and unnecessary. But even Aristotle recognized leisure's importance in life, stressing that we should not only work well but use leisure well. He even described leisure as better because it was the end of work. How can we define leisure? **Leisure** *refers to the pleasant times after work when individuals are free to pursue activities and interests of their own choosing—hobbies, sports, or reading, for example.*

leisure
The pleasant times after work when individuals are free to pursue activities and interests of their own choosing.

What is leisure in middle adulthood like? When Mark became 40 years old, he decided that he needed to develop some leisure activities and interests. He bought a personal computer and joined a computer club. Now Mark looks forward to coming home from work and "playing with his toy." At the age of 43, Barbara sent her last child off to college and told her husband that she was going to spend the next several years reading the many books she had bought but had never found time to read. Mark and Barbara chose different leisure activities, but their actions suggest that middle adulthood is a time when leisure activities assume added importance. For example, some developmentalists believe that middle adulthood is a time of questioning how time should be spent and of reassessing priorities (Gould, 1978).

Leisure can be an especially important aspect of middle adulthood because of the changes many individuals experience at this point in the adult life span (Mannell, 2000; McGuire, 2000). The changes include physical changes, relationship changes with spouse and children, and career changes. By middle adulthood, more money is available to many individuals, and there may be more free time and paid vacations. These mid-life changes may produce expanded opportunities for leisure. For many individuals, middle adulthood is the first time in their lives when they have the opportunity to diversify their interests.

In one recent study, 12,338 men 35 to 57 years of age were assessed each year for 5 years regarding whether they took vacations or not (Gump & Matthews, 2000). Then, the researchers examined the medical and death records over 9 years for men who lived for at least a year after the last vacation survey. Compared with those who never took vacations, men who went on annual vacations were 21 percent less likely to die over the 9 years and 32 percent less likely to die of coronary heart disease. The qualities that lead men to pass on a vacation tend to promote heart disease, such as not trusting anyone to fill in while you are gone or fearing that you will

Sigmund Freud once commented that the two things adults need to do well to adapt to society's demands are to work and to love. To his list we add "to play." In our fast-paced society, it is all too easy to get caught up in the frenzied, hectic pace of our achievement-oriented work world and ignore leisure and play. *Imagine your life as a middle-aged adult. What would be the ideal mix of work and leisure? What leisure activities do you want to enjoy as a middle-aged adult?*

get behind in your work and someone will replace you. These are behaviors that sometimes have been described as part of the Type A behavioral pattern.

Adults at midlife need to begin preparing psychologically for retirement. Constructive and fulfilling leisure activities in middle adulthood are an important part of this preparation (Kelly, 1996). If an adult develops leisure activities that can be continued into retirement, the transition from work to retirement can be less stressful.

So far in our discussion of development in middle adulthood, we have explored many facets of people's lives. One final area that needs to be examined is religion and meaning in life.

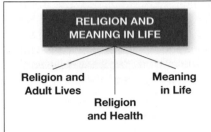

RELIGION AND MEANING IN LIFE

Religion and Adult Lives | Religion and Health | Meaning in Life

Religion and Meaning in Life

What role does religion play in our development as adults?

Religion and Adult Lives

In the recent MacArthur Study of Midlife Development, more than 70 percent of the individuals said they are religious and consider spirituality a major part of their lives (Brim, 1999). However, that does not mean they are committed to a single religion or house of worship. About one-half said they attend religious services less than once a month or never. In another study, about three-fourths of Americans said that they pray (*Religion in America*, 1993).

Religion also is an important aspect of people's lives around the world—98 percent of respondents in India, 88 percent in Italy, 72 percent in France, and 63 percent in Scandanavia say that they believe in God (Gallup, 1987).

WWW

Exploring the Psychology of Religion

Psychology of Religion Journals

Mental Health, Religion, and Culture

Females have consistently shown a stronger interest in religion than males have (Bijur & others, 1993). Compared to men, they participate more in both organized and personal forms of religion, are more likely to believe in a higher power or presence, and are more likely to feel that religion is an important dimension of their lives.

A series of recent studies have found that Americans are becoming less committed to particular religious denominations (such as Baptist or Catholic). They are more tolerant of other faiths and more focused on their own spiritual journeys (Paloutzian, 2000). This change may be partly generational, a consequence of postwar baby boomers' emphasis on experimentation and independent thinking that is reflected in a fluid religious orientation.

At the same time that many Americans show a strong interest in religion and believe in God, they also reveal a declining faith in mainstream religious institutions, in religious leaders, and in the spiritual and moral stature of the nation (*Religion in America,* 1993; Sollod, 2000).

In thinking about religion and adult development, it is important to consider the role of individual differences. Religion is a powerful influence in some adults' lives, whereas it plays little or no role in others' lives (Myers, 2000). Further, the influence or religion in people's lives may change as they develop. In John Clausen's (1993) longitudinal investigation, some individuals who had been strongly religious in their early adult years became less so in middle age; others became more religious in middle age.

Religion and Health

How might religion be related to physical health? to coping and happiness?

Religion and Physical Health What might be some of the effects of religion on physical health? One example is cults or religious sects that encourage behaviors that are damaging to health (Stotland, 1999). For example, some religious sects ignore sound medical advice or refuse pain-relieving medication (Koenig, 1992). For individuals in the religious mainstream, there is generally either no link between

religion and physical health or a positive effect. For example, in one review, five studies documented that religious commitment had a protective influence on blood pressure or hypertension rates (Levin & Vanderpool, 1989). Also, a number of studies have confirmed a positive association of religious participation and longevity (Gartner, Larson, & Allen, 1991).

Why might religion promote physical health? There are several possible answers (Hill & Butter, 1995):

- *Lifestyle issues.* For example, religious individuals have lower drug use than their nonreligious counterparts (Gartner, Larson, & Allen, 1991).
- *Social networks.* The degree to which individuals are connected to others affects their health. Well-connected individuals have fewer health problems. Religious groups, meetings, and activities provide social connectedness for individuals (Collins & others, 1993).
- *Coping with stress.* Religion offers a source of comfort and support when individuals are confronted with stressful events (Pargament, 1990). Although research has not clearly demonstrated prayer's positive effect on physical health, some investigators argue that prayer might be associated with such positive health-related changes as a decrease in the perception of pain and reduced muscle tension (McCullough, 1995).

It also has been stressed that religious organizations might have a stronger influence on physical health by providing more health-related services. For example, they could sponsor community-based health education and health-testing programs.

Coping What is the relation between religion and the ability to cope with stress? Some psychologists have categorized prayer and religious commitment as defensive coping strategies, arguing that they are less effective in helping individuals cope than are life-skill, problem-solving strategies. However, recently researchers have found that some styles of religious coping are associated with high levels of personal initiative and competence, and that even when defensive religious strategies are initially adopted, they sometimes set the stage for the later appearance of more-active religious coping (Pargament & Park, 1995; Tan, 2000). In one recent study, depression decreased during times of high stress when there was an increase in collaborative coping (in which people see themselves as active partners with God in solving problems) (Brickel & others, 1998). Also, in general, an intrinsic religious orientation tends to be associated with a sense of competence and control, freedom from worry and guilt, and an absence of illness, whereas an extrinsic orientation tends to be associated with the opposite characteristics (Ventis, 1995).

Instead of disintegrating during times of high stress, religious coping behaviors appear to function quite well in these periods (Bergin, 2000; Koenig, 1998). In one study, individuals were divided into those who were experiencing high stress and those with low stress (Manton, 1989). In the high-stress group, spiritual support was significantly related to personal adjustment (indicated by low depression and high self-esteem). No such links were found in the low-stress group. In a study of 850 medically ill patients admitted to an acute-care hospital, religious coping was related to low depression (Koenig & others, 1992). In John Clausen's (1993) analysis of individuals in the Berkeley Longitudinal Studies, the more-competent women and men in middle age were more likely than their less-competent counterparts to have a religious affiliation and involvement.

In sum, various dimensions of religiousness can help some individuals cope more effectively with their lives (Miller & Thorensen, 1999; Paloutzian, 2000). Religious

CAREERS IN LIFE-SPAN DEVELOPMENT

Alice McNair, Pastoral Counselor

ALICE MCNAIR is a pastoral counselor in Mocksville, North Carolina. She has a doctorate in pastoral counseling from Northwestern University. Prior to her present position, Alice was director of the Pastoral Ministries Institute near Washington, D.C. She also is an ordained Baptist minister. She works with adolescents and adults, providing individual, marital, and family counseling.

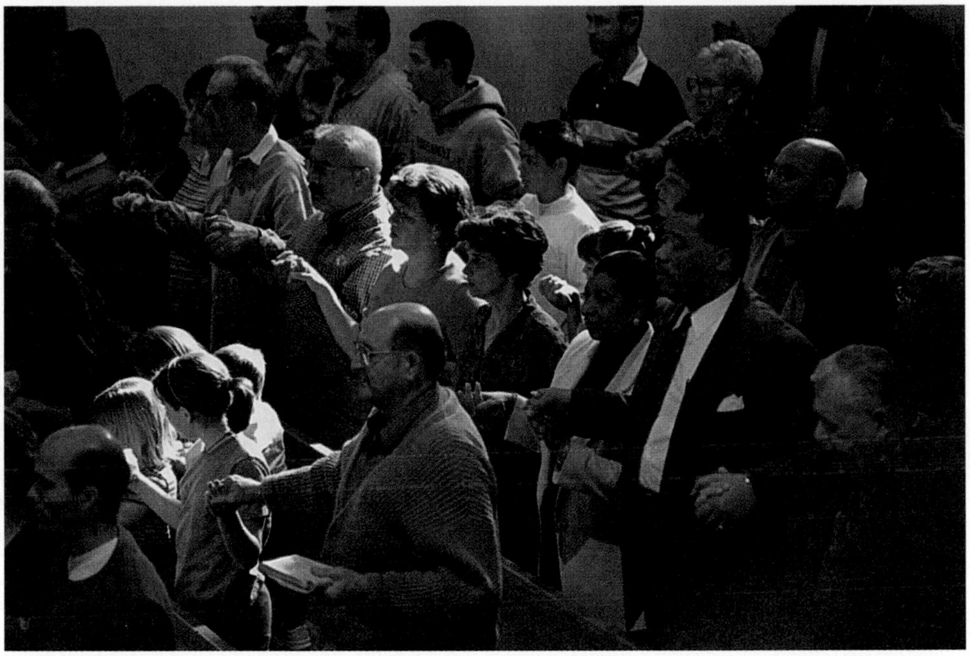

What roles do religion and spirituality play in the lives of middle-aged adults?

beliefs can shape a person's psychological perception of pain or disability. Religious cognitions can play an important role in maintaining hope and stimulating motivation toward recovery. Because of its effectiveness in reducing distress, religious coping can help prevent denial of the problem and thus facilitate early recognition and more appropriate health-seeking behavior. Religion also can forestall the development of anxiety and depression disorders by promoting communal or social interaction. Houses of religious worship are a readily available, acceptable, and inexpensive source of support for many individuals, especially the elderly. The socialization provided by religious organizations can help prevent isolation and loneliness (Koenig & Larson, 1998).

Happiness Are people who have a meaningful faith happier than those who do not? Reviews of the happiness literature suggest that happy people do tend to have a meaningful religious faith (Diener & Diener, 1998). Remember, though, that knowing that two factors correlate does not mean that one causes the other (just as in the case of religion and mental disorder co-occurring in a few individuals). A number of researchers have found that religiously active individuals report greater happiness than do those who are religiously inactive (Diener & others, 1999). However, we don't know whether this connection means that faith enhances happiness or whether happiness induces faith.

Meaning in Life

Austrian psychiatrist Victor Frankl's mother, father, brother, and wife died in the concentration camps and gas chambers in Auschwitz, Poland. Frankl survived the concentration camp and went on to write about meaning in life. In his book *Man's Search for Meaning* (1984), Frankl emphasized each person's uniqueness and the finiteness of life. He believes that examining the finiteness of our existence and the certainty of death adds meaning to life. If life were not finite, says Frankl, we could spend our life doing just about whatever we please because time would continue forever.

Summary Table 16.3
Careers, Work, and Leisure; Religion and Meaning in Life

Concept	Processes/ Related Ideas	Characteristics/Descriptions
Careers, Work, and Leisure	Job Satisfaction	• Work satisfaction increases steadily throughout life—from age 20 to at least age 60—for both college-educated and non-college-educated adults.
	Career Challenges and Changes	• The current middle-aged worker faces such challenges as the globalziation of work, rapid developments in information technologies, downsizing of organizations, and early retirement. • Midlife job or career changes can be self-motivated or forced on individuals.
	Leisure	• We not only need to learn to work well, but we also need to learn to enjoy leisure. Midlife may be an especially important time for leisure because of the physical changes that occur and because of preparation for an active retirement.
Religion and Meaning in Life	Religion and Adult Lives	• Religion is an important dimension of many Americans' lives, as well as the lives of people around the world. Females show a stronger interest in religion than males do. It is important to consider individual differences in religious interest.
	Religion and Health	• In some cases, religion can be negatively linked to physical health, as when cults or religious sects restrict individuals from obtaining medical care. In mainstream religions, religion usually shows either a positive association or no association with physical health. • Religion can play an important role in coping, for some individuals. Happy people tend to have a meaningful religious faith, but it is important to remember that the link is correlational, not causal.
	Meaning in Life	• Frankl believes that examining the finiteness of our existence leads to exploration of meaning in life. • Faced with death of older relatives and less time to live themselves, many middle-aged individuals increasingly examine life's meaning.

Frankl said that the three most distinct human qualities are spirituality, freedom, and responsibility. Spirituality, in his view, does not have a religious underpinning. Rather, it refers to a human being's uniqueness—to spirit, philosophy, and mind. Frankl proposed that people need to ask themselves such questions as why they exist, what they want from life, and what the meaning of their life is.

It is in middle adulthood that individuals begin to be faced with death more often, especially the deaths of parents and other older relatives. Also faced with less time in their life, many individuals in middle age begin to ask and evaluate the questions that Frankl proposed.

At this point we have discussed a number of ideas about careers, work, and leisure, and religion and meaning in life. To review these ideas, see summary table 16.3.

Chapter Review

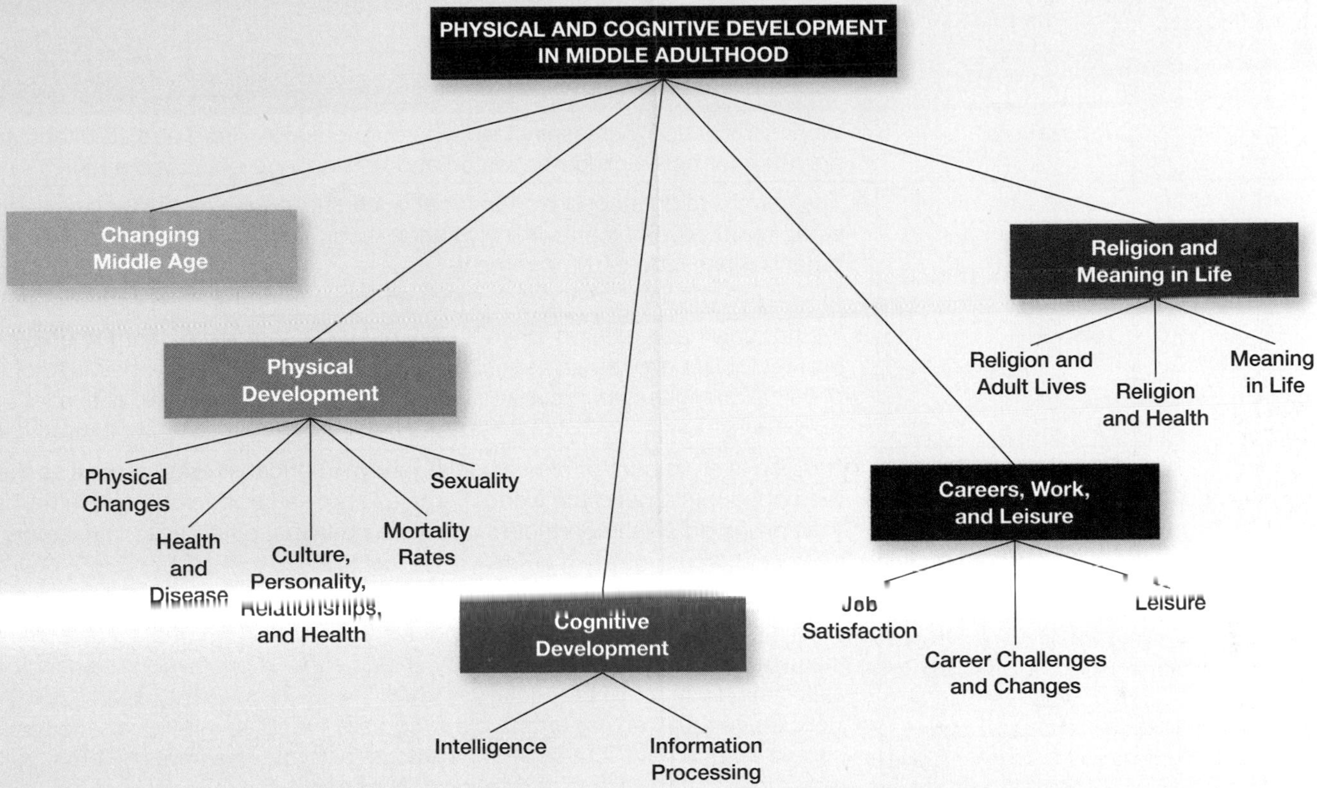

TO OBTAIN A DETAILED REVIEW OF THIS CHAPTER, STUDY THESE THREE SUMMARY TABLES:

- Summary Table 16.1 Changing Middle Age; Physical Development page 488
- Summary Table 16.2 Cognitive Development in Middle Adulthood page 491
- Summary Table 16.3 Careers, Work, and Leisure; Religion and Meaning in Life page 497

Key Terms

middle adulthood 478
chronic disorders 481
Type A behavior pattern 482
Type B behavior pattern 482
hardiness 483
climacteric 484
menopause 485
crystallized intelligence 488
fluid intelligence 488
expertise 491
leisure 493

Key People

Gilbert Brim 479
Lois Verbrugge 480
Meyer Friedman and Ray Rosenman 482
John Horn 488
K. Warner Schaie 489
Nancy Denney 491
John Clausen 495
Victor Frankl 496

Taking It to the Net

1. Clarissa's 60-year-old grandmother expressed concern about how she would pay for her medical care in her old age. Clarissa urged her to begin a regular exercise program that will benefit her later in life. How does regular exercise benefit people in their later years? What evidence can Clarissa cite to convince her grandmother of her theory?
2. Advances in health and hygiene mean that Americans tend to live longer. What do we need to know about how to cultivate physical health and productivity in America's aging population?
3. Harry can't decide whether to to theological seminary to study for the ministry, or to go to medical school. Recent polls indicate that his interests are not necessarily incompatible. What are people reporting about the role of religion in mental and physical health?

Connect to www.mhhe.com/santrockld8 to research the answers and complete these exercises.

OLC Preview

To further test your knowledge of this chapter or to explore our extensive online resources that accompany *Life-Span Development*, eighth edition, please log on to the text's Online Learning Center at http://www.mhhe.com/santrockld8.com.

Chapter 17

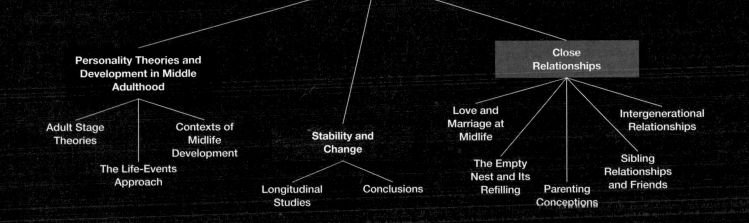

- SOCIOEMOTIONAL DEVELOPMENT IN MIDDLE ADULTHOOD
  - Personality Theories and Development in Middle Adulthood
    - Adult Stage Theories
    - The Life-Events Approach
    - Contexts of Midlife Development
  - Stability and Change
    - Longitudinal Studies
    - Conclusions
  - Close Relationships
    - Love and Marriage at Midlife
    - The Empty Nest and Its Refilling
    - Parenting Conceptions
    - Sibling Relationships and Friends
    - Intergenerational Relationships

Socioemotional Development in Middle Adulthood

The generations of living things pass in a short time, and like runners hand on the torch of life.

Lucretius
Roman Poet, 1st Century B.C.

Images of Life-Span Development

Middle-Age Variations

FORTY-FIVE-YEAR-OLD Sarah feels tired, depressed, and angry. She became pregnant when she was 17 and married Ben. They stayed together for 3 years, and then he left her for another woman. Sarah went to work as a salesclerk to help make ends meet. She remarried 8 years later to Alan, who had two children of his own from a previous marriage. Sarah stopped working for several years, but then Alan started going out on her. She found out about it from a friend. Sarah stayed with Alan for another year. Finally he was gone so much that she could not take it anymore and decided to divorce him. Sarah went back to work again as a salesclerk; she has been in the same position for 16 years now. During those 16 years, she has dated a number of men, but the relationships never seemed to work out. Her son never finished high school and has drug problems. Her father just died last year, and Sarah is trying to help her mother financially, although she can barely pay her own bills. Sarah looks in the mirror and does not like what she sees. She sees her past as a shambles, and the future does not look rosy, either.

Forty-five-year-old Wanda feels energetic, happy, and satisfied. She graduated from college and worked for 3 years as a high school math teacher. She married Andy, who had just finished law school. One year later, they had their first child, Josh. Wanda stayed home with Josh for 2 years, then returned to her job as a math teacher. Even during her pregnancy, Wanda stayed active and exercised regularly, playing tennis almost every day. After her pregnancy, she kept up her exercise habits. Wanda and Andy had another child, Wendy. Now, as they move into their middle-age years, their children are both off to college, and Wanda and Andy are enjoying spending more time with each other. Last weekend they visited Josh at his college, and the weekend before they visited Wendy at her college. Wanda continued working as a high school math teacher until 6 years ago. She had developed computer skills as part of her job and taken some computer courses at a nearby college, doubling up during the summer months. She resigned her math teaching job and took a job with a computer company, where she has already worked her way into management. Wanda looks in the mirror and likes what she sees. She sees her past

as enjoyable, although not without hills and valleys, and she looks to the future with zest and enthusiasm.

As with Sarah and Wanda, there are individual variations in the way people experience middle age. Let's now examine personality theories and development in middle age, including further ideas about individual variation.

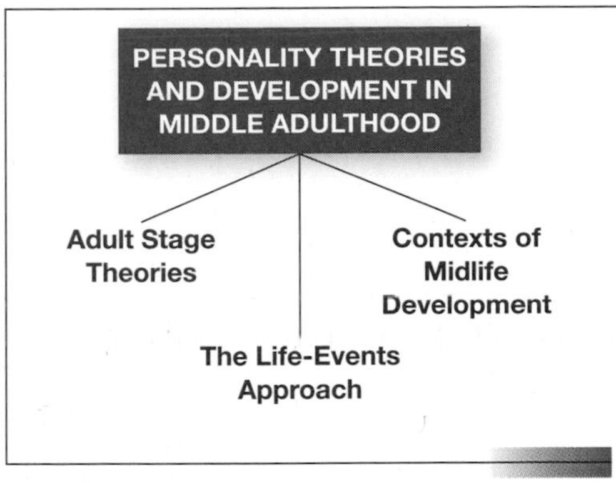
PERSONALITY THEORIES AND DEVELOPMENT IN MIDDLE ADULTHOOD
Adult Stage Theories
Contexts of Midlife Development
The Life-Events Approach

Personality Theories and Development in Middle Adulthood

What is the best way to conceptualize middle age? Is it a stage or a crisis? How pervasive are midlife crises? How extensively is middle age influenced by life events? Is personality linked with the contexts, such as the point in history in which individuals go through midlife, their culture, and their gender?

Adult Stage Theories

Adult stage theories have been plentiful, and they have contributed to the view that midlife is a crisis in development. Two prominent adult stage theories are Erik Erikson's life-span view and Daniel Levinson's seasons of a man's life.

Biological generativity
Adults conceive and give birth to infants.
Parental generativity
Adults provide nurturance and guidance to children.
Work generativity
Adults develop skills that are passed down to others.
Cultural generativity
Adults create, renovate, or conserve some aspect of the culture that survives.

Figure **17.1**
Four Paths to Developing Generativity

Erikson's Stage of Generativity Versus Stagnation Erikson (1968) believes that middle-aged adults face a significant issue in life—generativity versus stagnation, which is the name Erikson gave to the seventh stage in his life-span theory P. 34. Generativity encompasses adults' desire to leave a legacy of themselves to the next generation. Through generativity, the adult achieves a kind of immortality by leaving one's legacy to the next generation. By contrast, stagnation (sometimes called "self-absorption") develops when individuals sense that they have done nothing for the next generation.

Middle-aged adults can develop generativity in a number of different ways (Kotre, 1984). Through biological generativity, adults conceive and give birth to an infant. Through parental generativity, adults provide nurturance and guidance to children. Through work generativity, adults develop skills that are passed down to others. And through cultural generativity, adults create, renovate, or conserve some aspect of culture that ultimately survives. Figure 17.1 shows these four different ways middle-aged adults can develop generativity.

Through generativity, adults promote and guide the next generation by parenting, teaching, leading, and doing things that benefit the community (Pratt & others, 2001). Generative adults commit themselves to the continuation and improvement of society as a whole through their connection to the next generation. Generative adults develop a positive legacy of the self and then offer it as a gift to the next generation (Bradley, in press).

Does research support Erikson's theory that generativity is an important dimension of middle age? Yes, it does. In one study, Carol Ryff (1984) examined the views of women and men at different ages across adulthood. The middle-aged adults especially were concerned about generativity and guiding younger adults. In another study, having a positive identity was linked with generativity in middle age (Vandewater,

Ostrove, & Stewart, 1997). In another study, women developed generativity through different aspects of their lives (Peterson & Stewart, 1996). Generative women with careers found gratification through work; generative women who had not worked in a career experienced gratification through parenting.

In one recent modification of Erikson's theory, it was proposed that Erikson's three adult stages—involving intimacy (early adulthood), generativity (middle adulthood), and integrity (late adulthood)—are best viewed as developmental phases within identity. In this view, identity remains the central core of the self's development across all of the adult years (Whitbourne & Connolly, 1999).

Levinson's Seasons of a Man's Life In *The Seasons of a Man's Life* (1978), clinical psychologist Daniel Levinson reported the results of extensive interviews with forty middle-aged men. The interviews were conducted with hourly workers, business executives, academic biologists, and novelists. Levinson bolstered his conclusions with information from the biographies of famous men and the development of memorable characters in literature. Although Levinson's major interest focused on midlife change, he described a number of stages and transitions in the life span, ranging from 17 to 65 years of age, which are shown in figure 17.2.

Levinson emphasizes that developmental tasks must be mastered at each of these stages. In early adulthood, the two major tasks to be mastered are exploring the possibilities for adult living and developing a stable life structure. Levinson sees the twenties as a *novice phase* of adult development. At the end of one's teens, a transition from dependence to independence should occur. This transition is marked by the formation of a dream—an image of the kind of life the youth wants to have, especially in terms of a career and marriage. The novice phase is a time of reasonably free experimentation and of testing the dream in the real world.

From about the ages of 28 to 33, the man goes through a transition period in which he must face the more serious question of determining his goals. During the thirties, he usually focuses on family and career development. In the later years of this period, he enters a phase of *Becoming One's Own Man* (or BOOM, as Levinson calls it). By age 40, he has reached a stable location in his career, has outgrown his earlier, more tenuous attempts at learning to become an adult, and now must look forward to the kind of life he will lead as a middle-aged adult.

According to Levinson, the change to middle adulthood lasts about 5 years (ages 40 to 45) and requires the adult male to come to grips with four major conflicts that have existed in his life since adolescence: (1) being young versus being old, (2) being destructive versus being constructive, (3) being masculine versus being feminine, and (4) being attached to others versus being separated from them. Seventy to 80 percent of the men Levinson interviewed found the midlife transition tumultuous and psychologically painful, as many aspects of their lives came into question. According to Levinson, the success of the midlife transition rests on how effectively the individual reduces the polarities and accepts each of them as an integral part of his being.

Because Levinson interviewed middle-aged males, we can consider the data about middle adulthood more valid than the data about early adulthood. When individuals are asked to remember information about earlier parts of their lives, they may distort and forget things. The original Levinson data included no females, although Levinson (1987, 1996) reported that his stages, transitions, and the crisis of middle age hold for females as well as males. Levinson's work included no statistical analysis. However, the quality and quantity of the Levinson biographies are outstanding in the clinical tradition.

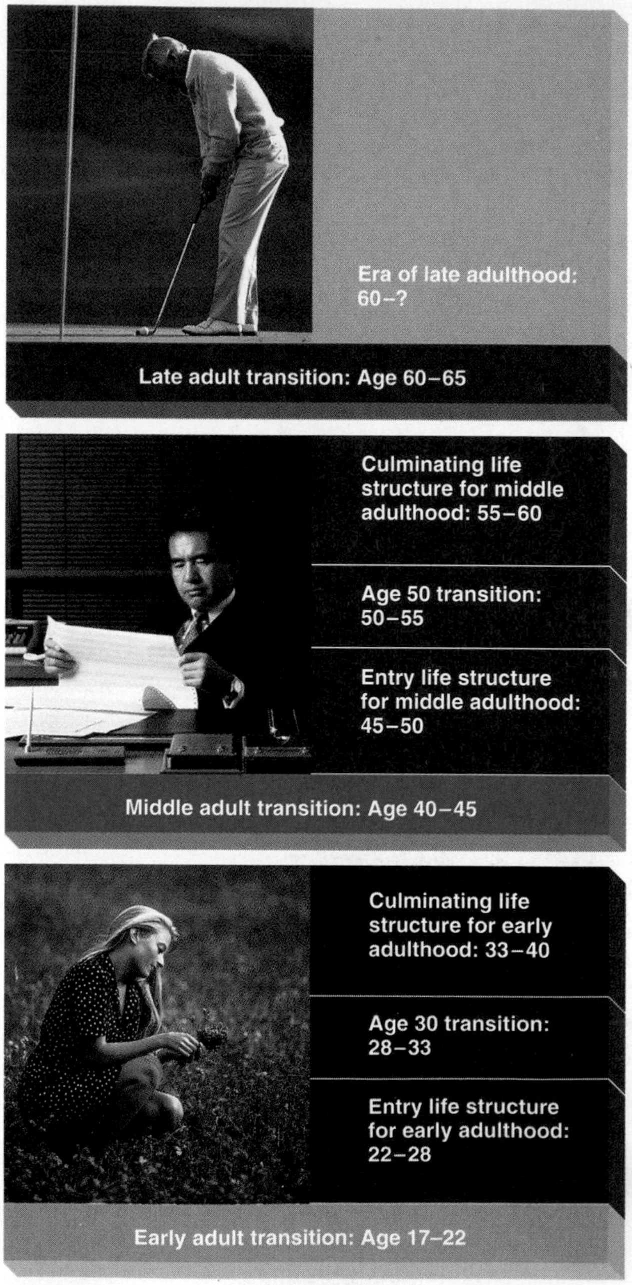

Figure **17.2**
Levinson's Periods of Adult Development

Michaelangelo (1475–1574), the great Renaissance sculptor, painter, architect, and poet hit a terrifying lull at age 40 after a brilliant earlier career. Free of unworthy patronage, he revived his career with his work on the Medici Chapel.

Julia Child, America's master chef, ate her first bite of French food at 37. It was not until her fifties that her books and TV show gained her fame and fortune.

Paul Gauguin (1848–1903), the famous French artist, was a Parisian stockbroker early in his adult years. At age 35, Gauguin left his wife and five children and absorbed himself in the life of an artist; at 43, he left France to live in Tahiti.

How Pervasive Are Midlife Crises? Levinson (1978) views midlife as a crisis, believing that the middle-aged adult is suspended between the past and the future, trying to cope with this gap that threatens life's continuity. George Vaillant (1977) concludes that just as adolescence is a time for detecting parental flaws and discovering the truth about childhood, the forties are a decade of reassessing and recording the truth about the adolescent and adulthood years. However, while Levinson sees midlife as a crisis, Vaillant believes that only a minority of adults experience a midlife crisis:

> Just as pop psychologists have reveled in the not-so-common high drama of adolescent turmoil, just so the popular press, sensing good copy, had made all too much of the mid-life crisis. The term mid-life crisis brings to mind some variation of the renegade minister who leaves behind four children and the congregation that loved him in order to drive off in a magenta Porsche with a 25-year-old striptease artiste. . . . As with adolescent turmoil, mid-life crises are much rarer in community samples. (pp. 222–223)

Midlife Crisis

Vaillant's study—called the "Grant Study"—involved a follow-up of Harvard University men in their early thirties and in their late forties who initially had been interviewed as undergraduates. In Vaillant's words, "The high drama in Gail Sheehy's best-selling *Passages* was rarely observed in the lives of the Grant Study men" (p. 223).

A recent study by 3,032 American from 25 to 72 years of age by the MacArthur Foundation found support for the idea that midlife crises have been exaggerated (Brim, 1999). The individuals from 40 to 60 years of age were less nervous and worried than those under 40. The middle-aged adults reported a growing sense of control in their work and more financial security. The middle-aged adults also indicated a greater sense of environmental mastery—the ability to handle daily responsibilities—and autonomy than their younger counterparts. In another recent study of 2,247 individuals, midlife crises were very few (Siegler & Costa, 1999). And in yet another study, adults experienced a peak of personal control and power in middle age (Clark-Plaskie & Lachman, 1999). Adult development experts are virtually unanimous in their belief that midlife crises have been exaggerated (Reid & Willis, 1999; Whitbourne & Connolly, 1999).

Middle age is such a foggy place.

Roger Rosenblatt
American Writer, 20th Century

In sum,

- The stage theories place too much emphasis on crises in development, especially midlife crises.
- There often is considerable individual variation in the way people experience the stages, a topic that we will turn to next.

Individual Variations

Stage theories especially focus on the universals of adult personality development. They try to pin down stages that all individuals go through in their adult lives. These theories do not adequately address individual variations in adult development. In one extensive study of a random sample of 500 men at midlife, it was concluded that there is extensive individual variation among men (Farrell & Rosenberg, 1981). In the individual variations view, middle-aged adults interpret, shape, alter, and give meaning to their lives.

The ability to set aside unproductive worries and preoccupations is believed to be an important factor in functioning under stress. In Vaillant's (1977) Grant Study, pervasive personal preoccupations were maladaptive in both the work and the marriages of college students over a 30-year period after leaving college. Some individuals in the Grant Study had personal preoccupations, while others did not.

"Goodbye, Alice. I've got to get this California thing out of my system."

The Life-Events Approach

Age-related stages represent one major way to examine adult personality development. A second major way to conceptualize adult personality development is to focus on life events. In the early version of the life-events approach, life events were viewed as taxing circumstances for individuals, forcing them to change their personality (Holmes & Rahe, 1967). Such events as the death of a spouse, divorce, marriage, and so on were believed to involve varying degrees of stress, and therefore likely to influence the individual's development.

The MacArthur Foundation Study of Midlife Development

Today's life-events approach is more sophisticated (Cui & Vaillant, 1996; Hultsch & Plemons, 1979; McLeod, 1996). The **contemporary life-events approach** *emphasizes that how life events influence the individual's development depends not only on the life event, but also on mediating factors (physical health, family supports, for example), the individual's adaptation to the life event (appraisal of the threat, coping strategies, for example), the life-stage context, and the sociohistorical context* (see figure 17.3). If individuals are in poor health and have little family support, life events are likely to be more stressful. One individual may perceive a life event as highly stressful, another individual may perceive the same event as a challenge. And a divorce may be more stressful after many years of marriage when adults are in their fifties than when they have only been married several years and are in their twenties (Chiriboga, 1982). Adults may be able to cope more effectively with divorce today than in the 1950s because divorce has become more commonplace and accepted in today's society.

contemporary life-events approach Emphasizes that how a life event influences the individual's development depends not only on the life event, but also on mediating factors, the individual's adaptation to the life event, the life-stage context, and the sociohistorical context.

Though the life-events approach is a valuable addition to understanding adult development, like other approaches to adult development, it has its drawbacks (Dohrenwend & Dohrenwend, 1978). One of the most significant drawbacks is that the life-events approach places too much emphasis on change. It does not adequately recognize the stability that, at least to some degree, characterizes adult development. Another drawback is that it may not be life's major events that are the primary sources of stress, but our daily experiences (Pillow, Zautra, & Sandler, 1996). Enduring a boring but tense job or marriage and living in poverty do not show up on scales of major life events. Yet the everyday pounding we take from these living conditions can add up to a highly stressful life and eventually illness. Some psychologists believe we can gain greater insight into the source of life's stresses by focusing more on daily hassles and daily uplifts (Lazarus & Folkman, 1984).

If a man does not keep pace with his companions, perhaps it is because he hears a different drummer. Let him step to the music he hears, however measured or far away.

Henry David Thoreau
American Essayist, 19th Century

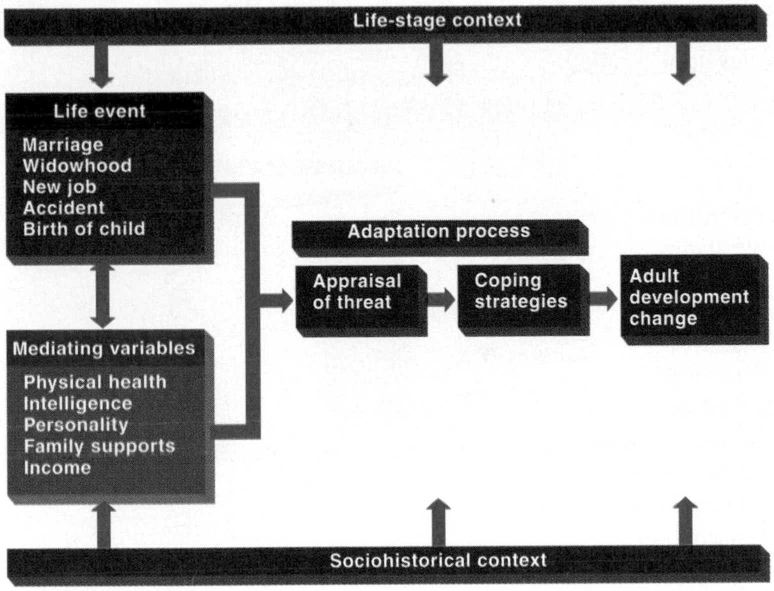

Figure **17.3**

A Contemporary Life-Events Framework for Interpreting Adult Developmental Change

In one study of 210 Florida police officers, the day-to-day friction associated with an inefficient justice system and distorted press accounts of police work were more stressful than responding to a felony in progress or making an arrest (Spielberger & Grier, 1983). In another study, the most frequent daily hassles of college students were wasting time, concerns about meeting high standards, and being lonely (Kanner & others, 1981). Among the most frequent uplifts of the college students were entertainment, getting along well with friends, and completing a task. In this same study, the most frequent daily hassles of middle-aged adults were concerns about weight and the health of a family member, while their most frequent daily uplifts involved relating well with a spouse or lover, or a friend (see figure 17.4). And the middle-aged adults were more likely than the college students to report that their daily hassles involved economic concerns (rising prices and taxes, for example). Critics of the daily-hassles approach argue that some of the same problems involved with life-events scales occur when daily hassles are assessed (Dohrenwend & Shrout, 1985). For example, knowing about an adult's daily hassles tells us nothing about physical changes, how the individual copes with hassles, and how the individual perceives hassles.

Contexts of Midlife Development

As people live through middle age, they do so in a number of contexts. Among those are historical contexts (cohort effects), gender, and culture.

Historical Contexts (Cohort Effects) Some developmentalists believe that changing historical times and different social expectations influence how different cohorts—remember that these are groups of individuals born in the same year or time period—move through the life span. Bernice Neugarten (1964) has been emphasizing the power of age-group or cohort since the 1960s. Our values, attitudes, expectations, and behaviors are influenced by the period in which we live. For example, individuals born during the difficult times of the Great Depression may have a different outlook on life than those born during the optimistic 1950s, says Neugarten.

Daily hassles	% of Times Checked*	Daily uplifts	% of Times Checked*
1. Concerns about weight	52.4	1. Relating well with your spouse or lover	76.3
2. Health of a family member	48.1	2. Relating well with friends	74.4
3. Rising prices of common goods	43.7	3. Completing a task	73.3
4. Home maintenance	42.8	4. Feeling healthy	72.7
5. Too many things to do	38.6	5. Getting enough sleep	69.7
6. Misplacing or losing things	38.1	6. Eating out	68.4
7. Yard work or outside home maintenance	38.1	7. Meeting your responsibilities	68.1
8. Property, investment, or taxes	37.6	8. Visiting, phoning, or writing someone	67.7
9. Crime	37.1	9. Spending time with family	66.7
10. Physical appearance	35.9	10. Home (inside) pleasing to you	65.5

* The "% of times checked" figures represent the mean percentage of people checking the item each month averaged over the nine monthly administrations.

Figure **17.4**

The Ten Most Frequent Daily Hassles and Uplifts of Middle-Aged Adults over a 9-Month Period

Activity/event	Appropriate age range	% who agree (late '50s study) Men	% who agree (late '50s study) Women	% who agree (late '70s study) Men	% who agree (late '70s study) Women
Best age for a man to marry	20–25	80	90	42	42
Best age for a woman to marry	19–24	85	90	44	36
When most people should become grandparents	45–50	84	79	64	57
Best age for most people to finish school and go to work	20–22	86	82	36	38
When most men should be settled on a career	24–26	74	64	24	26
When most men hold their top jobs	45–50	71	58	38	31
When most people should be ready to retire	60–65	83	86	66	41
When a man has the most responsibilities	35–50	79	75	49	50
When a man accomplishes most	40–50	82	71	46	41
The prime of life for a man	35–50	86	80	59	66
When a woman has the most responsibilities	25–40	93	91	59	53
When a woman accomplishes most	30–45	94	92	57	48

Figure **17.5**

Individuals' Conceptions of the Right Age for Major Life Events and Achievements: Late 1950s and Late 1970s

Neugarten (1986) believes that the social environment of a particular age group can alter its **social clock**—*the timetable according to which individuals are expected to accomplish life's tasks, such as getting married, having children, or establishing themselves in a career.* Social clocks provide guides for our lives; individuals whose lives are not synchronized with these social clocks find life to be more stressful than those who are on schedule, says Neugarten. She argues that today there is much less agreement than in the past on the right age or sequence for the occurrence of major life events. For example, the age at which people get married, have children, become parents, go to school, and retire varies more than in previous decades.

social clock
The timetable according to which individuals are expected to accomplish life's tasks, such as getting married, having children, or establishing themselves in a career.

One study found that, between the late 1950s and the late 1970s, there was a dramatic decline in adults' beliefs that there is a "right age" for major life events and achievements (Passuth, Maines, & Neugarten, 1984) (see figure 17.5). And in one study, Australian adults were asked the same questions about the best age for experiencing various life circumstances as Neugarten had asked American adults (Peterson, 1996). The Australian adults advocated later ages for marriage and grandparenthood, a younger age for leaving school, and a broader age range for retiring. In general, the Australians endorsed a wide age range for experiencing of life circumstances.

Trying to tease out universal truths and patterns about adult development from one birth cohort is complicated because the findings may not apply to another birth cohort. Most of the individuals studied by Levinson and Vaillant, for example, were born before and during the Great Depression. What was true for these individuals may not be true for today's 40-year-olds, born in the optimistic aftermath of World War II, or the post-baby-boom generation as they approach the midlife transition. The midlife men in Levinson's and Vaillant's studies might have been burned out at a premature age rather than reflect a normal developmental pattern of less stress (Rossi, 1989).

Gender Contexts Critics say that the stage theories of adult development have a male bias (Deutsch, 1991). For example, the central focus of stage theories is on career choice and work achievement, which historically have dominated men's life

Critics say the stage theories of adult development have a male bias by emphasizing career choice and achievement, and that they do not adequately address women's concerns about relationships, interdependence, and caring. The stage theories assume a normative sequence of development, but as women's roles have become more varied and complex, determining what is normative is difficult. *What kinds of changes have taken place in middle-aged women's lives in recent years?*

choices and life chances more than women's. The stage theories do not adequately address women's concerns about relationships, interdependence, and caring (Gilligan, 1982). The adult stage theories have also placed little importance on childbearing and child rearing. Women's family roles are complex and often have a higher salience in their lives than in men's lives. The role demands that women experience in balancing career and family are usually not experienced as intensely by men.

One of the problems in making stage theory comparisons of males and females is the assumption of a normative sequence of development by the stage theories. That is, the stage theories assume that most people will encounter a given developmental stage at more or less the same time: graduation from high school and college, getting married, starting a family, becoming grandparents, and retiring, for example. However, our contemporary life challenges many of these "normative" experiences. Many women are returning to college to obtain an education and further their career a number of years after starting a family. Many other women are delaying marriage and childbearing until after they have successfully established a career. Yet other women continue in the tradition of women earlier in this century by getting married, having children, and not pursuing a career outside the home. As the roles of women have become more complex and varied, defining a normative sequence of development for them has become difficult, if not impossible.

Many women who are now at midlife and beyond experienced a role shift in their late twenties, thirties, or beyond (Fodor & Franks, 1990). As they were engaging in traditional roles, the women's movement began and changed the lives of a substantial number of traditionally raised women and their families. Changes are still occurring for many midlife women. There is an increasing number of late-life divorces. And in an America obsessed with youth and beauty, there is a double standard of aging: Women must stay young, while men are allowed to age. In one study, most midlife women wanted to be at least 10 years younger (Rossi, 1980).

Basic changes in social attitudes regarding labor force participation, families, and gender roles have begun to broaden the opportunities available for women in middle adulthood as well as other life-span periods (Moen & Wethington, 1999). The effects of these changes are the most far-reaching for the baby-boom cohort now entering midlife. The employment patterns across the life span for women now in their middle adult years now more closely resemble those of males. (Contemporary Research Press, 1993).

Is midlife and beyond to be feared by women as a loss of youth and opportunity, a time of decline? Or is it a new prime of life, a time for renewal, for shedding preoccupations with a youthful appearance and body, and for seeking new challenges, valuing maturity, and enjoying change?

In one study, the early fifties were indeed a new prime of life for many women (Mitchell & Helson, 1990). In the sample of 700 women aged 26 to 80, women in their early fifties most often described their lives as "first-rate." Conditions that distinguished the lives of women in their early fifties from those of women in other age periods included more "empty nests," better health, higher income, and more concern for parents. Women in their early fifties showed confidence, involvement, security, and breadth of personality.

In sum, the view that midlife is a negative age period for women is stereotypical, as so many perceptions of age periods are (Huyck, 1999). Midlife is a diversified, heterogeneous period for women, just as it is for men.

Cultural Contexts We have already seen that midlife crises are less pervasive in the United States than is commonly believed (Chiriboga, 1989). How common are midlife crises in other cultures? There has been little cross-cultural research on middle adulthood, and adult stage theories, such as Levinson's, have not been

tested in other cultures. In many cultures, though, especially nonindustrialized cultures, the concept of middle age is not very clear, or in some cases is absent. It is common in nonindustrialized societies to describe individuals as young or old, but not as middle-aged (Grambs, 1989). And some cultures have no words for "adolescent," "young adult," or "middle-aged adult."

Consider the Gusii culture, located south of the equator in the African country of Kenya. The Gusii divide the life course differently for females and males (LeVine, 1979):

Females
1. Infant
2. Uncircumcised girl
3. Circumcised girl
4. Married woman
5. Female elder

Males
1. Infant
2. Uncircumcised boy
3. Circumcised boy warrior
4. Male elder

Gusii dancers perform on habitat day in Nairobi, Kenya. Movement from one status to another in the Gusii culture is due primarily to life events, not age. The Gusii do not have a clearly labeled midlife transition.

Thus, movement from one status to the next is due primarily to life events, not age, in the Gusii culture. While the Gusii do not have a clearly labeled midlife transition, some of the Gusii adults do reassess their lives around the age of 40. At this time, these Gusii adults examine their current status and the limited time they have remaining in their lives. Their physical strength is decreasing and they know they cannot farm their land forever, so they seek spiritual powers by becoming ritual practitioners or healers. As in the American culture, however, a midlife crisis in the Gusii culture is the exception rather than the rule.

What is middle age like for women in other cultures? It depends on the modernity of the culture and the culture's view of gender roles. Some anthropologists believe that middle age has more advantages in many nonindustrialized societies than in industrialized nations like the United States (Brown, 1985). As women reach middle age in many nonindustrialized societies, three changes take place that improve their status. First, they are often freed from cumbersome restrictions that were placed on them when they were younger. For example, in middle age they enjoy greater geographical mobility. Child care has ceased or can be delegated, and domestic chores are reduced. Commercial opportunities, visitation of relatives living at a distance, and religious opportunities provide an opportunity to venture forth from the village. A second major change brought on by middle age is a woman's right to exercise authority over specified younger kin. Middle-aged women can extract labor from younger family members. The work of the middle-aged woman tends to be administrative, delegating tasks and making assignments to younger women. The middle-aged woman also makes important decisions for certain members of the younger generation: what a grandchild is to be named, who is ready to be initiated, and who is eligible to marry whom. A third major change brought on by middle age in nonindustrialized societies is the eligibility of the woman for special statuses and the possibility that these provide recognition beyond the household. These statuses include the vocations of midwife, curer, holy woman, and matchmaker.

At this point we have studied a number of ideas about personality theories and development in middle adulthood. To review these ideas, see summary table 17.1. Next, we will explore another important topic in personality development during the adult years: stability and change.

Stability and Change

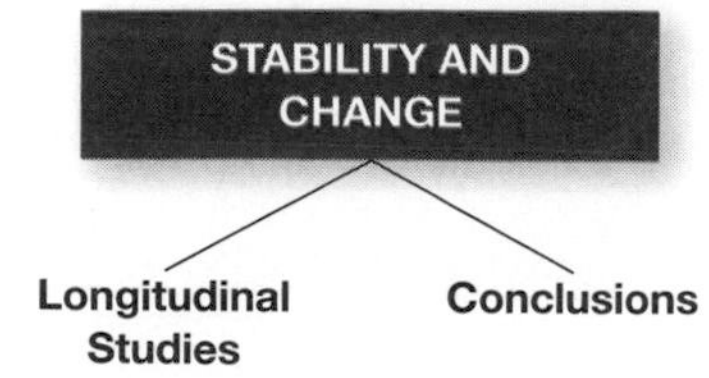

Recall from chapter 1 that an important issue in life-span development is the extent to which individuals show stability in their development versus the extent to which they change P. 20. A number of longitudinal studies have addressed the stability-change issue as they have assessed individuals at different points in their adult lives.

Summary Table 17.1
Personality Theories and Development in Middle Adulthood

Concept	Processes/ Related Ideas	Characteristics/Descriptions
Adult Stage Theories	Erikson's Theory	• Erikson says that the seventh stage of the human life span, generativity vs. stagnation, occurs in middle adulthood. • Four types of generativity are biologial, parental, work, and cultural.
	Levinson's Theory	• Developmental tasks should be mastered at different points in development. • Changes in middle age focus on four conflicts: being young vs. being old, being destructive vs. being constructive, being masculine vs. being feminine, and being attached to others vs. being separated from them. • Levinson proposed that a majority of Americans, especially men, experience a midlife crisis.
	How Pervasive Are Midlife Crises?	• For the most part, midlife crises have been exaggerated.
	Individual Variations	• There is considerable individual variation in development during the middle adulthood years.
The Life-Events Approach	Early Version	• Life events produce taxing circumstances that create stress in people's lives.
	Contemporary Version	• How life events influence the individual's development depends not only on the life event, but also on mediating factors, adaptation to the event, the life-stage context, and the sociohistorical context.
Contexts of Midlife Development	Historical Contexts (Cohort Effects)	• Neugarten believes that the social environment of a particular cohort can alter its social clock—the timetable according to which individuals are expected to accomplish life's tasks, such as getting married, having children, and establishing a career.
	Gender Contexts	• Critics say that the adult stage theories are male biased because they place too much emphasis on achievement and careers. The stage theories do not adequately address women's concerns about relationships. • Midlife is a heterogeneous period for women, as it is for men. For some women, midlife is the prime of their lives.
	Cultural Contexts	• In many nonindustrialized societies, a woman's status often improves in middle age. • In many cultures, the concept of middle age in not clear. • Most cultures distinguish between young adults and old adults.

Longitudinal Studies

We will examine four longitudinal studies to help us understand the extent to which there is stability or change in adult development: Neugarten's Kansas City Study, Costa and McCrae's Baltimore Study, the Berkeley Longitudinal Studies, and Helson's Mills College Study.

Neugarten's Kansas City Study One of the earliest longitudinal studies of adult personality development was conducted by Bernice Neugarten (1964). Known as the "Kansas City Study," it involved the investigation of individuals 40 to 80 years of age over a 10-year period. The adults were given personality tests, they filled out questionnaires, and they were interviewed.

Neugarten concluded that both stability and change characterized the adults as they aged. The characteristics that showed the most stability were styles of coping (such as avoiding problems or tackling them head on), being satisfied with life, and

being goal-directed. In terms of change, as individuals aged from 40 to 60 they became more passive and were more likely to be threatened by the environment.

Costa and McCrae's Baltimore Study Another major study of adult personality development continues to be conducted by Paul Costa and Robert McCrae (1995, 1998). They focus on what are called the **big five factors of personality,** *which consist of emotional stability (neuroticism), extraversion, openness to experience, agreeableness, and conscientiousness* (see figure 17.6).

big five factors of personality
Emotional stability (neuroticism), extraversion, openness to experience, agreeableness, and conscientiousness.

Using their five-factor personality test, Paul Costa and Robert McCrae (1995, 2000) studied approximately a thousand college-educated men and women aged 20 to 96, assessing the same individuals over a period of many years. Data collection began in the 1950s to the mid 1960s and is ongoing. Costa and McCrae concluded that considerable stability occurs in the five personality factors—emotional stability, extraversion, openness, agreeableness, and conscientiousness.

In one recent study, McCrae and his colleagues (1999) found consistent age trends in personality in a number of different cultures. In Germany, Croatia, Italy, Portugal, and Korea, older adults scored lower on extraversion and openness to experience than younger adults. In these countries, the older adults scored higher in agreeableness and conscientiousness than younger adults. Similar patterns of age changes also were found in a study of Chinese and American adults (Yang, McCrae, & Costa, 1998). Few cultural variations were found in these studies.

The Big Five
Paul Costa's Research

In another recent study, 285 adults from the United States (the Midwest) and 450 adults from China (Bejing) who were 20 to 87 years of age were given the California Psychological Inventory (CPI) (Labouvie-Vief & others, 2000). The CPI is a standardized personality test in which individuals respond to a large number of items that reflect a number of personality traits by saying whether the items are like them or not like them. Analysis of the results indicated that older adults were less extraverted and less flexible than their younger adult counterparts. The older adults were more likely to show self-control and engage in normative behavior than younger adults were. The age changes were more pronounced for the Chinese than for the American adults.

Berkeley Longitudinal Studies By far the longest-running longitudinal inquiry is the series of analyses called the Berkeley Longitudinal Studies. Initially, more than 500 children and their parents were studied in the late 1920s and early 1930s. The book *Present and Past in Middle Life* (Eichorn & others, 1981) profiles these individuals as they became middle-aged. The results from early adolescence through a portion of midlife did not support either extreme in the debate over

Emotional Stability	Extraversion	Openness	Agreeableness	Conscientiousness
• Calm or anxious	• Sociable or retiring	• Imaginative or practical	• Softhearted or ruthless	• Organized or disorganized
• Secure or insecure	• Fun-loving or somber	• Interested in variety or routine	• Trusting or suspicious	• Careful or careless
• Self-satisfied or self-pitying	• Affectionate or reserved	• Independent or conforming	• Helpful or uncooperative	• Disciplined or impulsive

Figure **17.6**
The Big Five Factors of Personality

Critical Thinking

Are There Distinct Subphases Within Middle Adulthood?

According to a leading expert on adult development, Ravenna Helson, middle age goes on for a long time and has distinguishable phases. For example, she believes that many 40-year-olds and 55-year-olds have different worlds and orientations. Think about the descriptions of middle age in this chapter and the previous chapter. Break middle adulthood into two subphases and describe what they would be like. What age boundaries would they involve? Or is there too much individual variation for clear delineation of middle-adulthood subphases?

whether personality is characterized by stability or change. Some characteristics were more stable than others, however. The most stable characteristics were the degree to which individuals were intellectually oriented, self-confident, and open to new experiences. The characteristics that changed the most included the extent to which the individuals were nurturant or hostile and whether they had good self-control or not.

John Clausen (1993), one of the researchers in the Berkeley longitudinal studies, believes that too much attention has been given to discontinuities for all members of the human species, as exemplified in the adult stage theories. Rather, he believes that some people experience recurrent crises and change a great deal over the life course, while others have more stable, continuous lives and change far less.

Helson's Mills College Study Another longitudinal investigation of adult personality development was conducted by Ravenna Helson and her colleagues (Helson, 1997, Helson, Mitchell, & Moane, 1984; Helson & Wink, 1992). They initially studied 132 women who were seniors at Mills College in California in the late 1950s. In 1981, when the women were 42 to 45 years old, they were studied again. Helson and her colleagues distinguished three main groups among the Mills women: family-oriented, career oriented (whether or not they also wanted families), and those who followed neither path (women without children who pursued only low-level work). Despite their different college profiles and their diverging life paths, the women in all three groups experienced some similar psychological changes over their adult years. However, the women in the third group changed less than those committed to career or family. Between the ages of 27 and the early forties, there was a shift toward less traditionally feminine attitudes, including greater dominance, greater interest in events outside the family, and more emotional stability. This may have been due to societal changes from the 1950s to the 1980s rather than to age changes.

During their early forties, many of the women shared the concerns that stage theorists such as Levinson found in men: concern for young and old, introspectiveness, interest in roots, and awareness of limitations and death. However, the researchers in the Mills College study concluded that rather than being in a midlife crisis, what was being experienced was *midlife consciousness.* They also indicated that commitment to the tasks of early adulthood—whether to a career or family (or both)—helped women learn to control their impulses, develop interpersonal skills, become independent, and work hard to achieve goals. Women who did not commit themselves to one of these lifestyle patterns faced fewer challenges and did not develop as fully as the other women (Rosenfeld & Stark, 1987).

In the Mills study, some women moved toward becoming "pillars of society" in their early forties to early fifties. Menopause, caring for elderly parents, and an empty nest were not associated with an increase in responsibility and self-control (Helson & Wink, 1992).

At age 55, actor Jack Nicholson said, "I feel exactly the same as I've always felt: a slightly reined-in voracious beast." Nicholson felt his personality had not changed much. Some others might think they have changed more. *How much does personality change and how does it stay the same through adulthood?*

Conclusions

What can we conclude from the series of longitudinal studies about constancy and change in personality during the adult years?

Humans are adaptive beings (Helson, 2000). We are resilient throughout our adult lives. But we do not become entirely new

Summary Table 17.2
Stability and Change

Concept	Processes/ Related Ideas	Characteristics/Descriptions
Longitudinal Studies	Neugarten's Kansas City Study	• Both stability and change were found. Styles of coping, life satisfaction, and being goal-directed were the most stable. • Individuals became more passive and feared the environment more as they aged through middle adulthood.
	Costa and McCrae's Baltimore Study	• The big five personality factors are emotional stabilty, extraversion, openness to experience, agreeableness, and responsibility. • In Costa and McCrae's longitudinal study, these factors showed considerable stability.
	Berkeley Longitudinal Studies	• The extremes in the stability-change argument were not supported. • The most stable characteristics were intellectual orientation, self-confidence, and openness to new experiences. The characteristics that changed the most were nurturance, hostility, and self-control.
	Helson's Mills College Study	• In this study of women, there was a shift toward less traditional feminine characteristics from age 27 to the early forties, but this might have been due to societal changes. • In their early forties, women experienced many of the concerns that Levinson described for men. However, rather than a midlife crisis, this is best called midlife consciousness.
Conclusions	Their Nature	• The longitudinal studies portray adults as becoming different but still remaining the same. • Amid change, there is still some underlying coherence and stability. • Some people change more than others.

personalities either (Hy & Loevinger, 1996). In a sense we become different but we are still the same. Amid change is some underlying coherence and stability. And some people change more than others (Jones & Meredith, 1996; Ruth & Coleman, 1996).

At this point we have studied a number of ideas about stability and change. To review these ideas, see summary table 17.2. Next, we will continue to explore socioemotional development in middle age by focusing on close relationships.

Close Relationships

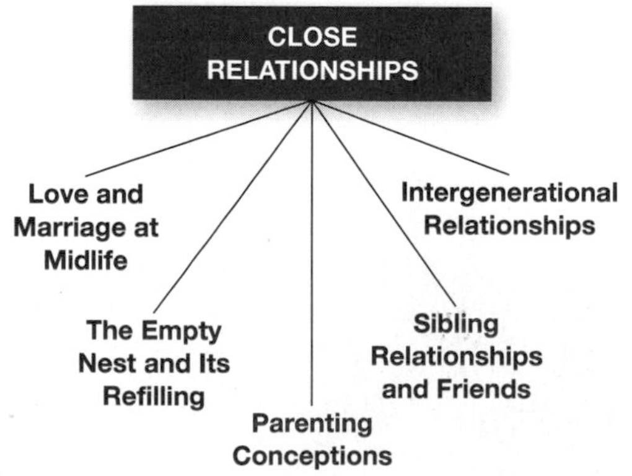

Attachment and love are important to our well-being throughout our lives. What are they like in middle age?

Love and Marriage at Midlife

Our exploration of love and marriage at midlife initially focuses on the increase in affectionate love that often takes place at midlife and the nature of marriage and divorce at this point in adulthood.

Affectionate Love Remember from chapter 15 that two major forms of love are romantic love and affectionate love ◄ P. 452. The fires of romantic love are strong in early adulthood. Affectionate or companionate love increases during middle adulthood. That is, physical attraction, romance, and passion are more important in new relationships, especially in early adulthood. Security, loyalty, and

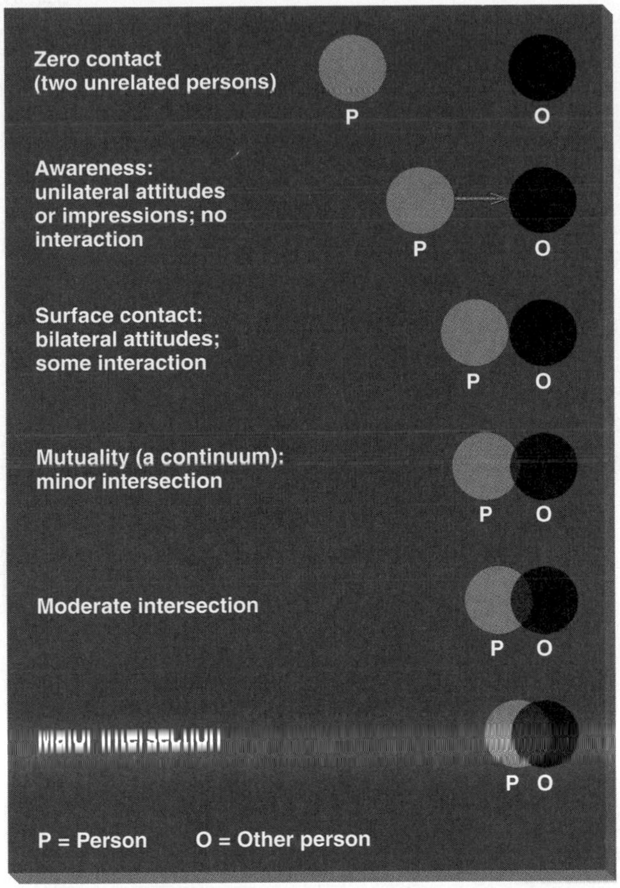

Figure 17.7
The Development of Relationships

One view of how close relationships develop states that we begin a relationship with someone at a zero point of contact *(top)* and then gradually move from a surface relationship into more intense, mutual interaction, sharing ourselves more and more with the other person as the relationship develops. At the final stage, a major intersection, we are probably experiencing affectionate or companionate love *(bottom)*.

"Thus ends another evening of dancing on the edge of the volcano."

mutual emotional interest become more important as relationships mature, especially in middle adulthood. Some developmentalists believe mutuality plays a key role in the maturity of relationships. This occurs when partners share knowledge with each other, assume responsibility for each other's satisfaction, and share private information that governs their relationship (Levinger, 1974). For example, as indicated in figure 17.7, we begin a relationship with someone at a zero point of contact. Then we gradually move from a surface relationship into more-intense, mutual interaction, sharing ourselves more and more with the other individual as the relationship deepens. At the final stage, a major intersection, we are probably experiencing affectionate or companionate love.

To explore the nature of age and sex differences in satisfying love relationships, in one study 102 happily married couples in early adulthood (average age 28), middle adulthood (average age 45), and late adulthood (average age 65) were interviewed (Reedy, Birren, & Schaie, 1981). Passion and sexual intimacy were more important in early adulthood. Feelings of affection and loyalty were more important in later-life love relationships. Young adult lovers also rated communication as more characteristic of their love than their older counterparts. Aside from the age differences, however, there were some striking similarities in the nature of satisfying love relationships. At all ages, emotional security was ranked as the most important factor in love, followed by respect, communication, help and play behaviors, sexual intimacy, and loyalty. Clearly, there is more to satisfying relationships than sex. The findings in this research also suggested that women believe emotional security is more important in love than men do.

Marriage and Divorce Even some marriages that were difficult and rocky during early adulthood turn out to be better adjusted during middle adulthood. Although the partners may have lived through a great deal of turmoil, they eventually discover a deep and solid foundation on which to anchor their relationship. In middle adulthood, the partners may have fewer financial worries, less housework and chores, and more time with each other. Partners who engage in mutual activities usually view their marriage as more positive at this time.

Most individuals in midlife who are married voice considerable satisfaction with being married. In one recent large-scale study of individuals in middle adulthood, 72 percent of those who were married said their marriage was either "excellent" or "very good" (Brim, 1999). Possibly by middle age, many of the worst marriages already have dissolved.

Are there any differences in the factors that predict whether couples will divorce in midlife compared to when they were younger adults? In chapter 15, "Socioemotional Development in Early Adulthood," we described John Gottman's extensive research on the factors that make a successful marriage ◀ P. 461. In a 14-year longitudinal study, Gottman and Robert Levenson (2000) recently found that couples who divorce in midlife tend to have a profile like the couple played by Annette Bening and Kevin Spacey in the movie *American Beauty:* cool and distant, with suppressed emotions. The midlife divorcing couples were alienated and avoidant. They were the kind of people you see in a restaurant who aren't talking with each other. It is a distant relationship with little or no laughter, love, or interest in each other. One of the divorcing midlife parents often feels like his or her life is "empty." The researchers found that when divorce occurs among younger adults (often in the first 7 years of a marriage) it is characterized by heated emotions that tend to burn out the marriage early. The young divorcing couples frequently were volatile and expressive, full of disappointment that they let each other know about.

Divorce in middle adulthood may be more positive in some ways, more negative in others, than divorce in early adulthood. For mature individuals, the perils of divorce can be fewer and less intense than for younger individuals. They have more resources, and they can use this time as an opportunity to simplify their lives by disposing of possessions, such as a large home, which they no longer need. Their children are adults and may be able to cope with their parents' divorce more effectively. The partners may have attained a better understanding of themselves and may be searching for changes that could include the end to a poor marriage.

In contrast, the emotional and time commitment to marriage that has existed for so many years may not be lightly given up. Many midlife individuals perceive this as failing in the best years of their lives. The divorcer might see the situation as an escape from an untenable relationship, but the divorced partner usually sees it as betrayal, the ending of a relationship that had been built up over many years and that involved a great deal of commitment and trust.

Annette Bening and Kevin Spacey together in the movie, *American Beauty. How is their profile similar to what researchers have found in couples who divorce in midlife?*

The Empty Nest and Its Refilling

An important event in a family is the launching of a child into adult life, to a career or family independent of the family of origin. Parents face new adjustments as disequilibrium is created by a child's absence. In the **empty nest syndrome,** *marital satisfaction decreases because parents derive considerable satisfaction from their children and the children's departure leaves parents with empty feelings.* Parents who live vicariously through their children might experience the empty nest syndrome, but most parents do not experience less marital satisfaction after their children have left home. Rather, for most parents marital satisfaction increases during the years after child rearing. With their children gone, marital partners have time to pursue career interests and more time for each other.

empty nest syndrome
A decrease in marital satisfaction after children leave home, because parents derive considerable satisfaction from their children.

In today's uncertain economic climate, the refilling of the empty nest is becoming a common occurrence as adult children return to live at home after an unsuccessful career or a divorce. And some individuals don't leave home at all until their middle to late twenties because they cannot financially support themselves. The middle generation has always provided support for the younger generation, even after the nest is bare. Through loans and monetary gifts for education, and through emotional support, the middle generation has helped the younger generation. Adult children appreciate the financial and emotional support their parents provide them at a time when they often feel considerable stress about their career, work, and lifestyle. And parents feel good that they can provide this support.

However, as with most family living arrangements, there are both pluses and minuses when adult children return to live at home. Many parents have developed expectations that their adult children would be capable of supporting themselves. And adult children had expectations that they would be on their own as young adults. In one study, 42 percent of middle-aged parents said they had serious conflicts with their resident adult children (Clemens & Axelson, 1985). One of the most common complaints voiced by both adult children and their parents is a loss of privacy. The adult children complain that their parents restrict their independence,

cramp their sex lives, reduce their rock music listening, and treat them as children rather than adults. Parents often complain that their quiet home has become noisy, that they stay up late worrying when their adult children will come home, that meals are difficult to plan because of conflicting schedules, that their relationship as a married couple has been invaded, and that they have to shoulder too much responsibility for their adult children. In sum, when adult children return home to live, a disequilibrium in family life is created, which requires considerable adaptation on the part of parents and their adult children. This living arrangement usually works best when there is adequate space, when parents treat their adult children more like adults than children, and when there is an atmosphere of trust and communication.

Parenting Conceptions

What is your relationship with your parents like? How do you perceive your parents? Do you think of them as emotional providers? financial supporters? Do you know how they became who they are? Has your perception of your parents changed as you have grown older? Several research studies recently have addressed how our relationships with and perception of our parents can change as we grow from adolescence through the adult years.

In a study of 73 women and men 50 to 60 years of age, many of the middle-aged parents said that as their children became adults they gained a new sense of appreciation for their commitment and influence as parents (Berquist, Greenberg, & Klaum, 1993). Other middle-aged parents expressed a sense of lost opportunity and said they wished they had better relationships with their adult children. When middle-aged parents mention disappointment regarding their adult children's development, they often say that they wish they had spent more time with them. Many men in the United States regret that they did not have a meaningful parenting experience.

In a longitudinal study that spans more than two decades, 30 college-educated women were interviewed about their identity development (Josselson, 1996). For all of the women, now in their forties, their relationship with their mother continues to be a part of their lives. The identity of the middle-aged women was frequently cast against the background of their mothers. In their early thirties, half of the women listed their mother as the person they felt closest to or second closest to among all the people in their lives. In their early forties, their mother often had been surpassed in importance by their spouse and sometimes their children on the list of "people you feel closest to," but their mother still frequently appeared in the second or third position.

In another study, individuals were interviewed at different points in adolescence and adult development, asking them about their perceptions of their parents (Labouvie-Vief & others, 1995). Younger individuals and those over the age of 60 primarily described their parents as providers of emotional and financial support. In contrast, during middle adulthood they were more likely to mention their parents' uniqueness and showed an awareness of the conditions that shaped their parents into the persons they were. These findings suggest that during middle adulthood we restructure our perceptions of our parents.

Sibling Relationships and Friendships

Sibling relationships also persist over the entire life span for most adults (Teti, 2001; White, 2001). Eighty-five percent of today's adults have at least one living sibling. Sibling relationships in adult-hood may be extremely close, apathetic, or highly rivalrous. The majority of sibling relationships in adulthood have been found to be close (Cicirelli, 1991). Those siblings who are psychologically close to each other in adulthood tended to be that way in childhood. It is rare for sibling closeness to develop for the first time in adulthood (Dunn, 1984).

Friendships continue to be important in middle adulthood just as they were in early adulthood (Antonucci, 1989). It takes time to develop intimate friendships, so friendships that have endured over the adult years are often deeper than those that have just been formed in middle adulthood.

Intergenerational Relationships

With each new generation, personality characteristics, attitudes, and values are replicated or changed. As older family members die, their biological, intellectual, emotional, and personal legacies are carried on in the next generation. Their children become the oldest generation and their grandchildren the second generation. As adult children become middle-aged they often develop more positive perceptions of their parents (Field, 1999). In one recent study, conflicts between mothers and daughters decreased across the life course in both the United States and Japan (Akiyama & Antonucci, 1999).

For the most part, family members maintain considerable contact across generations (Allen, Blieszener & Roberto, 2000; Bengtson, 2001). As we continue to stay connected with our parents and our children as we age, both similarity and dissimilarity across generations are found. For example, similarity between parents and an adult child is most noticeable in religion and politics, least in gender roles, lifestyle, and work orientation.

What are the most common conflicts that arise in relationships between parents and adult children? In one recent study, they included communication and interaction style (such as "He is always yelling" and "She is too critical"), habits and lifestyle choices (such as sexual activity, living arrangements), child-rearing practices and values (such as decisions about having children, being permissive or controlling), politics, religion, and ideology (such as lack of religious involvement) (Clarke & others, 1999). In this study, there were generational differences in perception of the main conflicts between parents and adult children. Parents most often listed habits and lifestyle choices; adult children cited communication and interaction style.

A consistent finding in intergenerational research is that parents and their young adult children differ in the way they describe their relationship. For example, in one recent study, middle-aged parents were especially likely to report that the relationship was closer (Acquilino, 1999). Another recent study found that parents continued to give more favorable evaluations of their relationships with adult children across 17 years in a longitudinal study (Giarrusso & Du Feng, 1999).

The relationship between parents and their adult children is related to the nature of their earlier relationship. In one recent study, individuals who felt trusted by their parents in adolescence reported greater closeness to their parents in early adulthood (Jacobs & Tanner, 1999). Also in this study, daughters who had experienced long-term lack of trust during adolescence were more alienated from their parents as young adults than sons who had similar experiences.

Gender differences also characterize intergenerational relationships. In one study, mothers and their daughters had much closer relationships during their adult years than mothers and sons, fathers and daughters, and fathers and sons (Rossi, 1989). Also in this study, married men were more involved with their wives' kin than with their own. And maternal grandmothers and maternal aunts were cited twice as often as their counterparts on the paternal side of the family as the most important or loved relative.

Careers in Life-Span Development

Lillian Troll, Professor of Psychology and Life-Span Development and Researcher on Families and Aging Women

LILLIAN TROLL has been a leading figure in the field of adult development and aging. She graduated from the University of Chicago with a joint major in psychology and premedicine. During World War II she dropped out of graduate school to work in Washington, where she helped develop the array of Army screening and achievement tests. After the war she became a suburban housewife and mother, following her husband's career moves from city to city. For a decade, the closest Lillian came to a career in life-span development was founding a nursery school in New Jersey.

Many years later, after her divorce, Lillian returned to the University of Chicago and, in 1967, completed a Ph.D. in life-span development. She then began teaching and conducting research on generations in the family and women's development, first at Wayne State University in Detroit and then, as a 60-year-old grandmother, at Rutgers University Psychology Department. In 1986 she retired and moved to California, where she continued research at the University of California at San Francisco, by collaborating with Colleen Johnson on a longitudinal study of the "oldest old" (people over 85).

Lillian Troll (*left*) with participants in a study of aging women.

Intergenerational Connections
Intergenerational Programs and Projects
William Acquilino's Research
The Sandwich Generation

SOCIOCULTURAL WORLDS OF DEVELOPMENT

Intergenerational Relationships in Mexican American Families—The Effects of Immigration and Acculturation

IN THE LAST several decades, increasing numbers of Mexicans have immigrated to the United States, and their numbers are expected to increase. The pattern of immigration usually involves separation from the extended family. It may also involve separation of immediate family members, with the husband coming first and then later bringing his wife and children. Initially isolated, especially the wife, they experience considerable stress due to relocation and the absence of family and friends. Within several years, a social network is usually established in the ethnic neighborhood.

As soon as some stability in their lives is achieved, Mexican families may sponsor the immigration of extended family members, such as a maternal or paternal sister or mother who provides child care and enables the mother to go to work. In some cases the older generation remains behind and joins their grown children in old age. The accessibility of Mexico facilitates visits to and from the native village for vacations or at a time of crisis, such as when an adolescent runs away from home.

Three levels of acculturation often exist within a Mexican American family (Falicov & Karrer, 1980). The mother and the grandparents may be at the beginning level, the father at an intermediate level, and the children at an advanced level. The discrepancies between acculturation levels can give rise to conflicting expectations within the family. The immigrant parents' model of child rearing may be out of phase with the dominant culture's model, which may cause reverberations through the family's generations. For example, the mother and grandparents may be especially resistant to the demands for autonomy and dating made by adolescent daughters, and so may the father. And in recent years an increasing number of female youth leave their Mexican American homes to further their education, an event that is often stressful for families with strong ties to Mexican values.

As children leave home, parents begin to face their future as a middle-aged couple. This may be difficult for many Mexican American middle-aged couples because their value orientations have prepared them better for parenting than for relating as a married couple. Family therapists who work with Mexican Americans frequently report that a common pattern is psychological distance between the spouses and a type of emotional separation in midlife. The marital partners continue to live together and carry on their family duties but relate to each other only at a surface level. The younger generation of Mexican Americans may find it difficult to accept their parents' lifestyle, may question their marital arrangement, and may rebel against their value orientations. Despite the intergenerational stress that may be brought about by immigration and acculturation, the majority of Mexican American families maintain considerable contact across generations and continue to have a strong family orientation.

What is the nature of intergenerational relationships?

Middle-aged adults play an important role in intergenerational relationships (Richards, Bengtson, & Miller, 1989; Williams & Nussbaum, 2001). They have been described as the "sandwich" generation (Hammer, Neal, & Brockwood, 1999). Their situation has been labeled the "generation squeeze" or "generational overload." The demands they face, as both children of elderly parents and parents of adolescents or young adults, have implications for individual life-course development and for the family systems to which they belong (Sorensen & Zarit, 1996). While middle-aged adults are guiding and financially supporting their adolescents, they may have to support elderly parents who no longer have a secure base in times of emotional difficulties or financial problems. Instead, the older parents may need affection and financial support from their middle-aged children. These simultaneous pressures from adolescents or young adult children and aging parents may contribute to stress in middle adulthood. When adults immigrate to another country, intergenerational stress may also be increased. To read about the role of immigration and

Summary Table 17.3
Close Relationships

Concept	Processes/ Related Ideas	Characteristics/Descriptions
Love and Marriage at Midlife	Affectionate Love	• Affectionate love increases in midlife, especially in marriages that have endured many years.
	Marriage and Divorce	• A majority of middle-aged adults who are married say that their marriage is good or excellent. • Researchers recently have found that couples who divorce in midlife are more likely to have a cool, distant, emotionally suppressed relationship, whereas divorcing young adults are more likely to have an emotionally volatile and expressive relationship. • Divorce is a special concern. In one recent study, divorce in middle age had more positive emotional effects for women than for men, while marriage had more positive emotional effects for men than for women.
The Empty Nest and Its Refilling	Their Nature	• Rather than decreasing satisfaction as once thought, the empty nest increases it. • An increasing number of young adults are returning home to live with their parents.
Parenting Conceptions	Middle-Aged Individuals	• In middle age, many individuals say they wish they had spent more time with their children, fathers wish they had been better parents, and mothers are important to many women. During middle age, many individuals restructure their perceptions of parents and parenting.
Sibling Relationships and Friendships	Their Nature	• Sibling relationships continue throughout life. Some are close, others are distant. • Friendships continue to be important in middle age.
Intergenerational Relationships	Their Nature	• Continuing contact across generations in families usually occurs. • Mothers and daughters have the closest relationships. • The middle-aged generation has been called the "sandwich" or "squeezed" generation because it is caught between obligations to children and obligations to parents. • The middle-aged generation plays an important role in linking generations.

acculturation in intergenerational relationships among Mexican Americans, see the Sociocultural Worlds of Development box.

However, recent analyses suggest that fewer middle-aged adults are "sandwiched" between multiple roles as caregiver to a parent and to their own children than often is reported in the media (Hoyer, Rybash, & Roodin, 1999). In one large-scale study, a large majority of middle-aged children did not have responsibility of providing direct care for their parents (Rosenthal, Martin-Matthews, & Matthews, 1996). When this type of responsibility was required, it most often was assumed by daughters in their mid to late fifties who did not simultaneously have direct child-care or child-rearing responsibilities. In another study, the point at which some adult children have to take responsibility of caring for their parents usually coincided with the launch of their own adult children who were beginning their own careers and families (Soldo, 1996).

At this point we have discussed a number of ideas about close relationships. To review these ideas, see summary table 17.3. This chapter concludes our coverage of middle adulthood. In the next section of the book, we will continue our journey through the human life span by focusing on late adulthood.

In case you're worried about what's going to become of the younger generation, it's going to grow up and start worrying about the younger generation.

Roger Allen
American Writer, 20th Century

Chapter Review

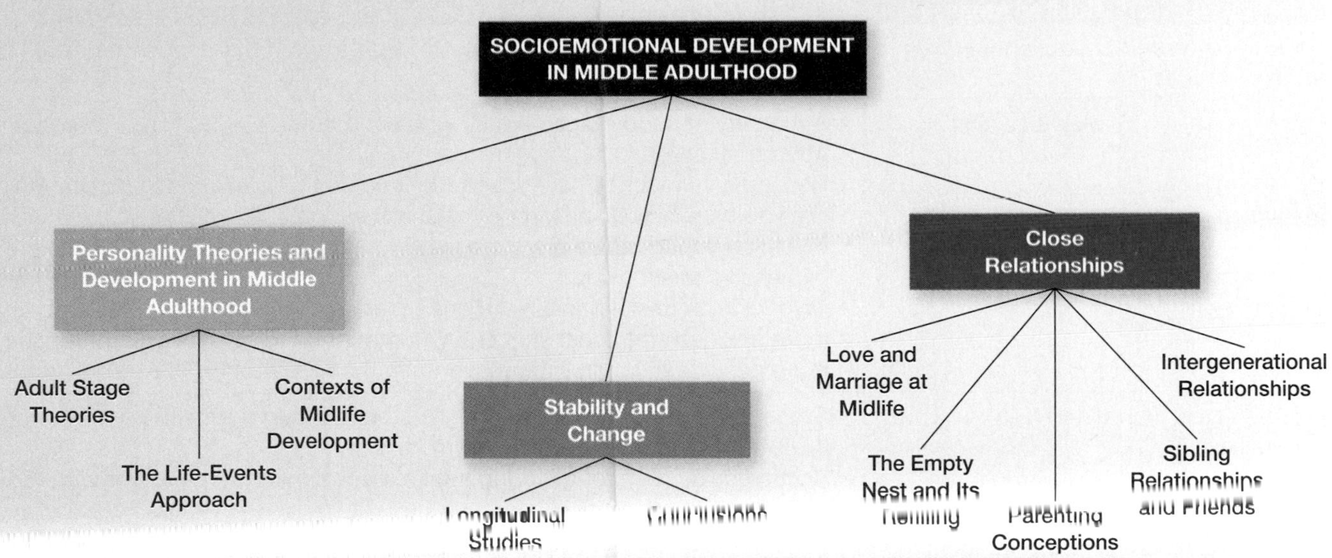

TO OBTAIN A DETAILED REVIEW OF THIS CHAPTER, STUDY THESE THREE SUMMARY TABLES:

- Summary Table 17.1 Personality Theories and Development in Middle Adulthood page 510
- Summary Table 17.2 Stability and Change page 513
- Summary Table 17.3 Close Relationships page 519

Key Terms

contemporary life-events approach 505
social clock 507
big five factors of personality 511
empty nest syndrome 515

Key People

Erik Erikson 502
Carol Ryff 502
Daniel Levinson 503
George Vaillant 504
Bernice Neugarten 506
Paul Costa and Robert McCrae 511
John Clausen 512
Ravenna Helson 512

Taking It to the Net

1. What did psychologist Daniel Goleman find out about how Erik Erikson and his wife Joan dealt with his seventh developmental stage, generativity vs. stagnation in their own lives?
2. Maurice and his wife, Jean, are struggling with the "empty nest syndrome," now that their last child has married and moved out. Edward and his wife, Kerry, wish they had that problem. Their oldest son has moved back in with them at age 30. Over dinner, both couples debate the issue. What words of advice can you offer to each couple?

Connect to www.mhhe.com/santrockld8 to research the answers and complete these exercises.

OLC Preview

To further test your knowledge of this chapter or to explore our extensive online resources that accompany *Life-Span Development,* eighth edition, please log on to the text's Online Learning Center at http://www.mhhe.com/santrockld8.com

Section 9

Late Adulthood

To be seventy years young is sometimes far more cheerful and hopeful than to be forty years old.

Oliver Wendell Holmes, Sr.
American Physician, 19th Century

The rhythm and meaning of human development eventually wend their way to late adulthood, when each of us stands alone at the heart of the earth and suddenly it is evening. We shed the leaves of youth and are stripped by the winds of time down to the truth. We learn that life is lived forward but understood backward. We trace the connection between the end and the beginning of life and try to figure out what this whole show is about before it is out. Ultimately, we come to know that we are what survives of us. Section 9 contains three chapters: "Physical Development in Late Adulthood" (chapter 18), "Cognitive Development in Late Adulthood" (chapter 19), and "Socioemotional Development in Late Adulthood" (chapter 20).

Chapter 18

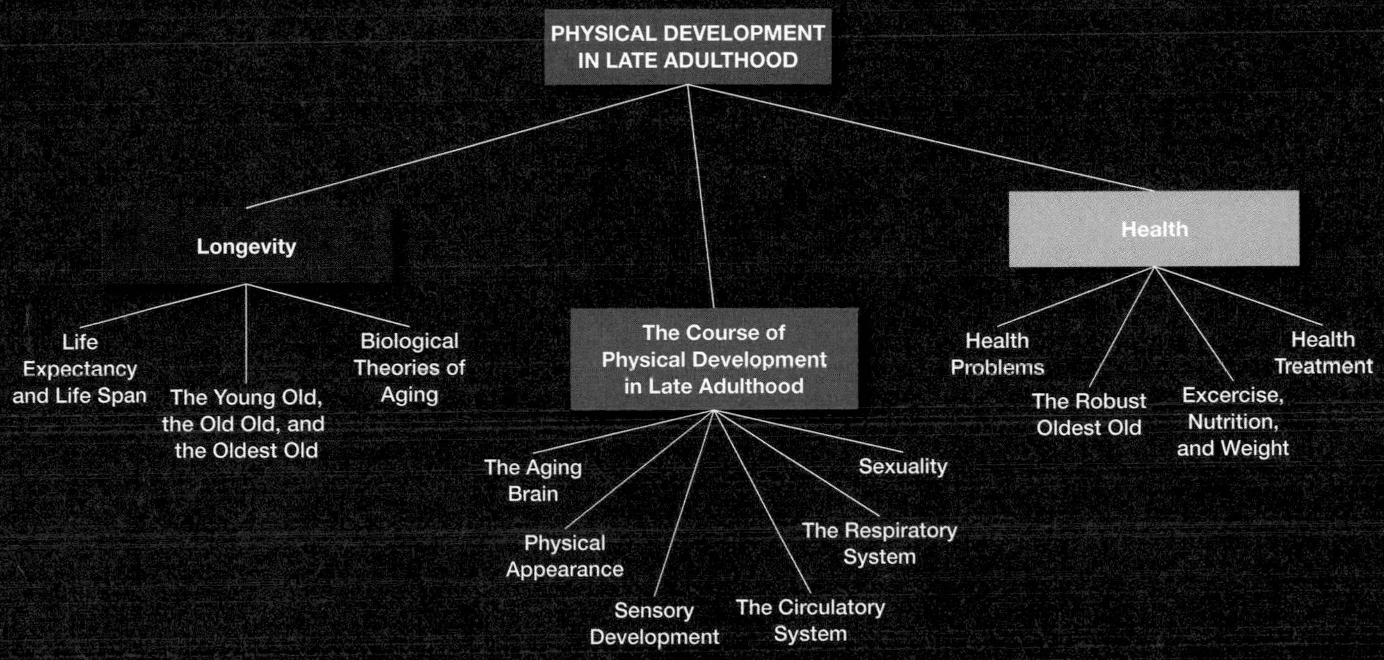
PHYSICAL DEVELOPMENT IN LATE ADULTHOOD
Longevity
Life Expectancy and Life Span
The Young Old, the Old Old, and the Oldest Old
Biological Theories of Aging
The Course of Physical Development in Late Adulthood
The Aging Brain
Physical Appearance
Sensory Development
The Circulatory System
The Respiratory System
Sexuality
Health
Health Problems
The Robust Oldest Old
Excercise, Nutrition, and Weight
Health Treatment

Physical Development in Late Adulthood

Each of us stands alone at the heart of the earth pierced through by a ray of sunlight: And suddenly it is evening.

Salvatore Quasimodo
Italian Poet, 20th Century

Images of Life-Span Development

Learning to Age Successfully

JONATHAN SWIFT said, "No wise man ever wished to be younger." Without a doubt, a 70-year-old body does not work as well as it once did. It is also true that an individual's fear of aging is often greater than need be. As more individuals live to a ripe *and* active old age, our image of aging is changing. While on the average a 75-year-old's joints should be stiffening, people can practice not to be average. For example, a 75-year-old man might *choose* to train for and run a marathon; an 80-year-old woman whose capacity for work is undiminished might *choose* to make and sell children's toys.

Consider 85-year-old Sadie Halperin, who has been working out for 11 months at a rehabilitation center for the aged in Boston. She lifts weights and rides a stationary bike. She says that before she started working out, about everything she did—shopping, cooking, walking—was a major struggle. Sadie says she always felt wobbly and held on to a wall when she walked. Now she walks down the center of the hallways and reports that she feels wonderful. Initially she could lift only 15 pounds with both legs; now she lifts 30 pounds. At first she could bench-press only 20 pounds; now she bench-presses 50 pounds. Sadie's exercise routine has increased her muscle strength and helps her to battle osteoporosis by slowing the calcium loss from her bones, which can lead to deadly fractures (Ubell, 1992).

Eighty-five-year-old Sadie Halperin doubled her strength in exercise after just 11 months. Before developing an exercise routine, she felt wobbly and often had to hold on to a wall when she walked. Now she walks down the middle of hallways and says she feels wonderful.

The story of Sadie Halperin's physical development and well-being raise some truly fascinating questions about life-span development, which we will explore in this chapter. They include:

Why do we age, and what, if anything, can we do to slow down the process? How long can we live? What chance do you have of living to be 100? Do older adults have sex? Can certain eating habits and exercise help us live longer?

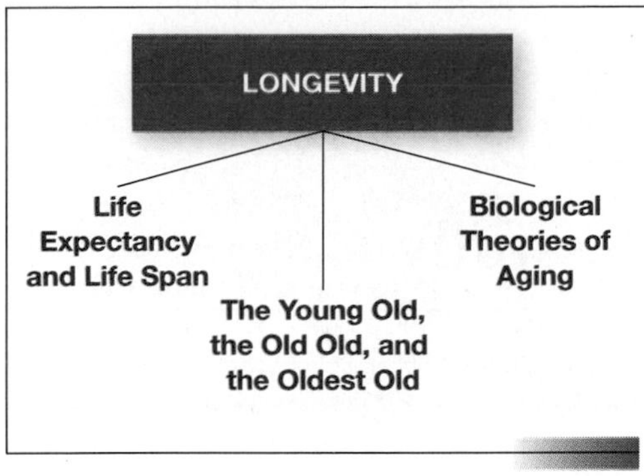

Longevity

In his eighties, Linus Pauling argued that vitamin C slows the aging process. Aging researcher Roy Walford fasts two days a week because he believes undernutrition (not malnutrition) also slows the aging process. What do we really know about longevity?

Life Expectancy and Life Span

We are no longer a youthful society. Remember from chapter 1 that, as more individuals live to older ages, the proportion of individuals at different ages has become increasingly similar P. 8. Indeed, the concept of a period called "late adulthood" is a recent one—until the twentieth century most individuals died before they were 65.

Although a much greater percentage of persons live to an older age, the life span has remained virtually unchanged since the beginning of recorded history. **Life span** *is the upper boundary of life, the maximum number of years an individual can live. The maximum life span of human beings is approximately 120 years of age.* **Life expectancy** *is the number of years that will probably be lived by the average person born in a particular year.* Improvements in medicine, nutrition, exercise, and lifestyle have increased our life expectancy an average of 30 additional years since 1900.

life span
The upper boundary of life, the maximum number of years an individual can live. The maximum life span of human beings is about 120 years of age.

life expectancy
The number of years that will probably be lived by the average person born in a particular year.

The life expectancy of individuals born today in the United States is 77 years (80 for women, 74 for men). We will have more to say about the gender difference in life expectancy shortly. There is still a gap (7 years) between the life expectancy of Whites (77 years) and African Americans (70 years) in the United States, but the gap is narrowing. In 1970 the gap was 8 years (U.S. Bureau of the Census, 2000).

How does the United State fare in life expectancy compared to other countries around the world? Considerably better than some, a little worse than some others. For example, Australia has the highest life expectancy at birth today (80 years) while Afghanistan and Kenya have very low ones (47 years). Differences in life expectancies across countries are due to such factors as health conditions and medical care throughout the life span.

Aging Links
Aging Research Center

Also, the percentage of older adults varies across countries. The country with the largest percentage of its population 65 years and older is Sweden (16 percent). Twelve percent of the U.S. population today is 65 and over, whereas in Afghanistan and Kenya it is only 3 percent (Central Intelligence Agency, 1999). Why does the United States have a lower percentage of people reaching old age than countries like Sweden? Suggested reasons include high birth rates in America's low-income, poverty population and less effective health care throughout the life span.

To me old age is always fifteen years older than I am.

Bernard Baruch
American Statesman, 20th Century

The figures given above are for life expectancy at birth. When individuals in the United States reach 65, how long can they expect to live? Today, they can expect to live an average of 18 more years (20 for females, 16 for males) (U.S. Bureau of the Census, 2000). This is 7 more years than in 1900 and 4 more years than in 1960.

Centenarians In 1980, there were only 15,000 centenarians in the United States. In the year 2000, there were 77,000, and it is projected that this number will increase to 834,000 in 2050. Because of the increase in centenarians, they are now being studied more often. One view is that "the older you get, the sicker you get." However, researchers are finding that could be a myth. Recent research on 100-year-olds reveals that many of them have been quite healthy in their old age (Perls, 1999).

Clearly, genes play an important role in surviving to an extreme old age. But there are other influencing factors as well.

In the ongoing New England Centenarian study, researchers so far have examined 169 individuals who are 100+ years of age (Perls, Lauerman, & Silver, 1999). The centenarians are a robust group. Among the characteristics of the 169 who made it to 100, only 3 have had cancer. A disproportionate number of them are women who have never been married.

A misconception is that to live to be 100, an individual has to live a stress-free life. But in the New England study, a majority of the centenarians have had difficult lives, such as surviving the Holocaust and living in extreme poverty as an immigrant to the United States (Perls, Lauerman, & Silver, 1999). What has contributed to their survival is their ability to cope successfully with stress.

In one study, 1,200 centenarians were interviewed about many aspects of their lives (Segerberg, 1982). Through their eyes, life looks like this:

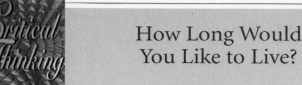

- Mary Butler said that finding something to laugh about every day is important. She believes a good laugh is better than a dose of medicine anytime.
- Elza Wynn concluded that he has been able to live so long because he made up his mind to live. He was thinking about dying when he was 77, but decided he would wait awhile.
- Anna Marie Robertson ("Grandma") Moses commented that she felt older at 16 than at any time since then. Even now that she's very old, she never thinks about being old.
- Billy Red Fox believes that being active and not worrying are important keys to living to be 100. At 95, he switched jobs to become a public relations representative. Even at 100, Billy travels 11 months of the year, making public appearances and talking to civic clubs.
- Duran Baez remarried at 50 and went on to have fifteen more children. At 100 years of age, he was asked, "Do you have any ambition you have not yet realized?" Duran replied, "No." He said that he had lived the kind of life he expected, raising a good family, never doing any harm to anybody, staying honest all his life, and finding out that people really do like him. Duran says, "That's enough for the time being."

What about you? What chance to you have of living to be 100? To find out, turn to figure 18.1. According to the items in figure 18.1, among the most important factors in longevity are heredity and family history, health (weight, diet, smoking, and exercise), education, personality, and lifestyle. To read further about living to a very old age, see the Sociocultural Worlds of Development box.

The rapid growth in the 85+ and 100+ age categories suggest that some potentially important change might lie ahead, such as these:

- Even if it is still an option, retiring at 65 might be too young for many of tomorrow's older adults.
- Increasing health and longer productivity of the elderly might offset some of the economic burden that planners have long assumed will exist for a graying America.
- Society's dismal view of old age might get a needed push toward a more positive image.

Sex Difference in Longevity Is there a sex difference in how long people live? Today, the life expectancy for females is 80 years of age, while for males it is 74. Beginning at age 25, females outnumber males; this gap widens during the remainder of the adult years. By the time adults are 75 years of age, more than 61

Critical Thinking

How Long Would You Like to Live?

In 1726, Jonathan Swift wrote about Gulliver traveling to many lands. In one land, Gulliver found the Struldbrugs—people who were immortal. Even though they never died, they continued to age, becoming blind, crippled, immobile, in constant pain, and begging for their death. Gulliver's world was a world of science fiction, but it raises interesting issues about how long we would like to live and what we want our lives to be like when we become old. How long would you like to live? Why? Describe the oldest person you know. What is he or she like?

New England Centenarian Study

Life Expectancy Calculator

Those wishing long lives should advertize for a couple of parents, both belonging to long-lived families.

Oliver Wendell Holmes, Sr.
American Physician, 19th Century

The following test gives you a rough guide for predicting your longevity. The basic life expectancy for males is age 73, and for females is 80. Write down your basic life expectancy. If you are in your fifties or sixties, you should add ten years to the basic figure because you have already proved yourself to be a durable individual. If you are over age sixty and active, you can even add another two years.

Basic Life Expectancy ______

Decide how each item below applies to you and add or subtract the appropriate number of years from your basic life expectancy.

1. Family history
   - Add five years if two or more of your grandparents lived to 80 or beyond. ______
   - Subtract four years if any parent, grandparent, sister, or brother died of heart attack or stroke before 50. ______
   - Subtract two years if anyone died from these diseases before 60. ______
   - Subtract three years for each case of diabetes, thyroid disorder, breast cancer, cancer of the digestive system, asthma, or chronic bronchitis among parents or grandparents. ______
2. Marital status
   - If you are married, add four years. ______
   - If you are over twenty-five and not married, subtract one year for every unwedded decade. ______
3. Economic status
   - Add two years if your family income is over $60,000 per year. ______
   - Subtract three years if you have been poor for the greater part of your life. ______
4. Physique
   - Subtract one year for every ten pounds you are overweight. ______
   - For each inch your girth measurement exceeds your chest measurement deduct two years. ______
   - Add three years if you are over forty and not overweight. ______
5. Exercise
   - Add three years if you exercise regularly and moderately (jogging three times a week). ______
   - Add five years if you exercise regularly and vigorously (long-distance running three times a week). ______
   - Subtract three years if your job is sedentary. ______
   - Add three years if your job is active. ______
6. Alcohol
   - Add two years if you are a light drinker (one to three drinks a day). ______
   - Subtract five to ten years if you are a heavy drinker (more than four drinks per day). ______
   - Subtract one year if you are a teetotaler. ______
7. Smoking
   - Subtract eight years if you smoke two or more packs of cigarettes per day. ______
   - Subtract two years if you smoke one to two packs per day. ______
   - Subtract two years if you smoke less than one pack. ______
   - Subtract two years if you regularly smoke a pipe or cigars. ______
8. Disposition
   - Add two years if you are a reasoned, practical person. ______
   - Subtract two years if you are aggressive, intense, and competitive. ______
   - Add one to five years if you are basically happy and content with life. ______
   - Subtract one to five years if you are often unhappy, worried, and often feel guilty. ______
9. Education
   - Subtract two years if you have less than a high school education. ______
   - Add one year if you attended four years of school beyond high school. ______
   - Add three years if you attended five or more years beyond high school. ______
10. Environment
    - Add four years if you have lived most of your life in a rural environment. ______
    - Subtract two years if you have lived most of your life in an urban environment. ______
11. Sleep
    - Subtract five years if you sleep more than nine hours a day. ______
12. Temperature
    - Add two years if your home's thermostat is set at no more than 68° F. ______
13. Health care
    - Add three years if you have regular medical checkups and regular dental care. ______
    - Subtract two years if you are frequently ill. ______

Your Life Expectancy Total ______

Figure **18.1**

Can You Live to Be 100?

Sociocultural Worlds of Development
Aging in Russia, Ecuador, and Kashmir

IMAGINE THAT you are 120 years old. Would you still be able to write your name? Could you think clearly? What would your body look like? Would you be able to walk? To run? Could you still have sex? Would you have an interest in sex? Would your eyes and ears still function? Could you work?

Has anyone ever lived to be 120 years old? Supposedly. In three areas of the world, not just a single person but many people have reportedly lived more than 130 years. These areas are the Republic of Georgia in Russia, the Vilcabamba valley in Ecuador, and the province of Hunza in Kashmir (in northern India). Five people over 100 years old (centenarians) per 100,000 people is considered normal. But in the Russian region where the Abkhasian people live, approximately 400 centenarians per 100,000 people have been reported. Some of the Abkhasians are said to be 120 to 170 years old (Benet, 1976).

However, on closer inspection these claims have not been supported (Medvedev, 1974). Indeed, we really do not have documentation of anyone living more than 120 years. In the case of the Abkhasians, birth registrations and other documents, such as marriage certificates and military registrations, are not available. In most instances, the ages of the Abkhasians is based on their recall of important historical events and interviews with other members of the village (Benet, 1976). In the Russian villages where people have been reported to live a long life, the elderly experience unparaleled esteem and honor. Centenarians are given special positions in the community, such as the leader of social celebrations. Thus there is a strong motivation to give one's age as older than one really is. One individual who claimed to be 130 years of age used his father's birth certificate to escape army duty during World War I. Later it was discovered that he only was 78 years old (Hayflick, 1975).

Eighty-seven year-old José Maria Roa is from the Vilcabamba region of Ecuador, which also is renowned for the longevity of its inhabitants. Selakh Butka, who says he is 113 years old, is shown with his wife (*upper left*), who says she is 101. The Butkas live in the Georgian Republic of Russia, where reports of unusual longevity have surfaced. *Why are scientists skeptical about their ages?*

percent of the population is female; for those 85 and over, the figure is almost 70 percent female. Why? Social factors such as health attitudes, habits, lifestyles, and occupation are probably important. For example, men are more likely than women to die from the leading causes of death in the United States, such as cancer of the respiratory system, motor vehicle accidents, suicide, cirrhosis of the liver, emphysema, and coronary heart disease. These causes of death are associated with lifestyle. For example, the sex difference in deaths due to lung cancer and emphysema occurs because men are heavier smokers than women.

However, if life expectancy is influenced extensively by the stress of work, the sex difference should be narrowing, because so many more women have entered the labor force. Yet in the last 40 years, just the opposite has occurred. Apparently, self-esteem and work satisfaction outweigh the stress of work when the longevity of women is at issue.

One-hundred-year-old Iva Blake is among the oldest old in America. Adapting to her changing circumstances, she still tends to her garden from a wheelchair. *What are some characteristics of the oldest old?*

The sex difference in longevity is also influenced by biological factors. In virtually all species, females outlive males. Women have more resistance to infections and degenerative diseases. For example, the female's estrogen production helps to protect her from arteriosclerosis (hardening of the arteries). And the X chromosome women carry may be associated with the production of more antibodies to fight off disease.

The Young Old, the Old Old, and the Oldest Old

Late adulthood, which begins in the sixties and extends to approximately 120 years of age, has the longest span of any period of human development—50 to 60 years. The combination of the lengthy span with the dramatic increase in the number of adults living to older ages has led to increased interest in differentiating the late adulthood period. Most of the demarcations involve two subperiods, although exact agreement on the age cutoffs for the subperiods has not been reached. Some developmentalists distinguish between the *young old* or *old age* (65 to 74 years of age) and the *old old* or *late old age* (75 years and older) (Charness & Bosman, 1992). Yet others distinguish the *oldest old* (85 years and older) from younger older adults (Pearlin, 1994).

Many experts on aging, however, prefer to talk about such categories as the young old, old old, and oldest old in terms of *function* rather than age. In chapter 1 we described age not only in terms of chronological age, but also in terms of biological age, psychological age, and social age ◀ P. 18. Thus, in terms of functional age—the person's actual ability to function—an 85-year-old might well be more biologically and psychologically fit than a 65-year-old (Neugarten & Neugarten, 1987). With this concept of functional age and its implication for individual differences in aging in mind, as you will see next, there still are some significant differences when the old age group segment still in their sixties is compared with the 85-and-older age group (Suzman & others, 1992).

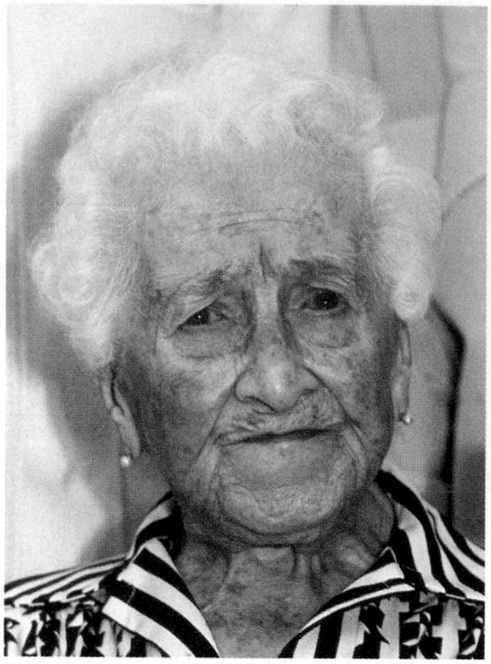
(a)

(b)

(a) Frenchwoman Jeanne Louise Calment, recently died at the age of 122. Greater ages have been claimed, but scientists say the maximum human life span is about 120. *(b)* Heredity is an important component of how long we will live. For example, in figure 18.1, you were able to add 5 years to your life expectancy if two or more of your grandparents lived to 80 or beyond. And if you were born a female, you get to start out with a basic life expectancy that is 7 years older than if you were born a male. The three sisters shown above are all in their eighties.

The oldest old are much more likely to be female. They also have a much higher rate of morbidity and a far greater incidence of disability than do the young old. Today's oldest old are much more likely to be living in institutions, less likely to be married, and more likely to have low educational attainment. Their needs, capacities, and resources are often different from those of their young old counterparts.

When thinking about the differentiation of late adulthood into subperiods, remember that every period or subperiod of development is heterogeneous. Even the oldest old are a heterogeneous, diversified group (Roberts, Dunkle, & Haug, 1994). Many of the oldest old function effectively, although others have outlived their social and financial supports and depend on society for their daily living. Almost one-fourth of the oldest old are institutionalized and many report some limitation of activity or difficulties in performing personal-care activities. A significant number are cognitively impaired.

A substantial portion of the oldest old function effectively. Society's preoccupation with the disability and mortality of the oldest old has concealed the fact that the majority of older adults aged 80 and over continue to live in the community. More than one-third of older adults 80 and over who live in the community report that their health is excellent or good; 40 percent say they have no activity limitation (Suzman & others, 1992).

In one study of successful aging, physical performance (based on tests of balance, gait, lower-body strength and coordination, and manual dexterity) in 70- to 78-year-old women and men was related to participation in moderate and/or strenuous exercise activity and emotional support from social networks (Seeman & others, 1995). Shakespeare's image of the oldest old in *As You Like It*—"mere oblivion, sans teeth, sans taste, sans everything"—clearly is not supported by the increasing research evidence that describes a more optimistic picture of a substantial portion of people in their eighties and older (Garfein & Herzog, 1995).

Biological Theories of Aging

Even if we stay remarkably healthy through our adult lives, we begin to age at some point. Life-span experts even argue that biological aging actually begins at birth (Schaie, 1997). What are the biological explanations of aging? Intriguing explanations of why we age are provided by three biological theories: cellular clock theory, free-radical theory, and hormonal stress theory.

cellular clock theory
Leonard Hayflick's theory that the maximum number of times that human cells can divide is about 70 to 80. As we age, our cells have less capability to divide.

WWW

What Causes Aging?

Telomeres Research

Research on Telomeres and Telomerase

Genetic Studies of Aging

Cellular Clock Theory

The **cellular clock theory** *is Leonard Hayflick's (1977) view that cells can divide a maximum of about 75 to 80 times and that as we age, our cells become increasingly less capable of dividing.* Hayflick found that cells extracted from older adults, in their fifties to seventies, divided fewer than 75 to 80 times. Based on the ways cells divide, Hayflick places the upper limit of the human life span at about 120 years. Thus, we rarely live to the end of our life-span potential.

In the last decade, scientists have added an extension to cellular clock theory (Warner & Hodes, 2000) Hayflick did not know why cells die. Recently, scientists have found that the answer might lie at the tip of chromosomes (Bodner & others, 1998; Martin & Buckwalter, 2001; Shay & Wright, 2000). *Telomeres* are DNA sequences that cap chromosomes. Each time a cell divides, the telomeres become shorter and shorten (see figure 18.2). After about 70 to 80 replications, the telomeres are dramatically reduced and the cell no longer can reproduce. Researchers also have found that injecting the enzyme *telomerase* into human cells grown in the laboratory can subtantially extend the life of the cells beyond the approximately 75 to 80 normal cell divisions (Shay & Wright, 1999). In one recent study, age-related telomere erosion was linked with an impaired ability to recover from stress and an increased rate of cancer formation (Rudolf & others, 1999).

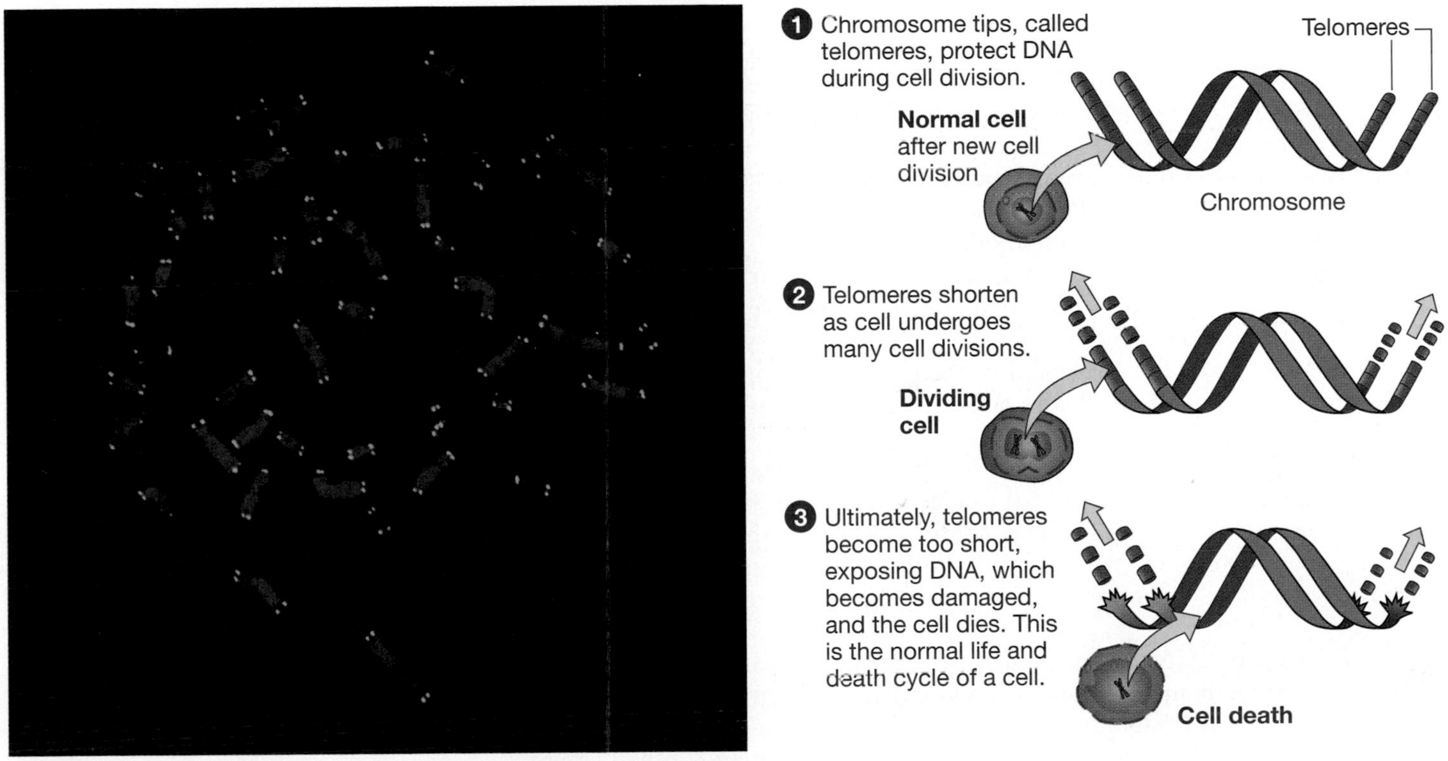

Figure **18.2**

Telomeres and Aging

The photograph shows actual telomeres lighting up the tips of chromosomes.

Free-Radical Theory A second microbiological theory of aging is **free-radical theory,** *which states that people age because inside their cells normal metabolism produces unstable oxygen molecules known as free radicals. These molecules ricochet around the cells, damaging DNA and other cellular structures.* Like all organisms, cells generate waste when they metabolize energy. The problematic by-products of this process include these free-radical oxygen molecules. As the free radicals bounce around inside of cells, their damage can lead to a range of disorders, including cancer and arthritis (Hauck & Bartke, 2001; Knight, 2000).

free-radical theory
A microbiological theory of aging that states that people age because inside their cells normal metabolism produces unstable oxygen molecules known as free radicals. These molecules ricochet around inside cells, damaging DNA and other cellular structures.

Hormonal Stress Theory The first two biological theories of aging—cellular clock and free-radical—focus on changes at the cellular level. A third biological theory of aging emphasizes changes at the hormonal level. **Hormonal stress theory** *states that aging in the body's hormonal system can lower resilience to stress and increase the likelihood of disease* (Finch & Seeman, 1999). The hypothalamic-pituitary-adrenal (HPA) axis is one of the body's main regulatory systems for responding to external stress and maintaining the body's internal equilibrium. Note that *hypothalamic* refers to the the hypothalamus in the brain, *pituitary* to the body's master gland located near the hypothalamus, and *adrenal* to the two adrenal glands that sit just above the kidneys. Hormonal stress theory emphasizes that with aging, the hormones stimulated by stress that flow through the HPA system remain elevated longer than when individuals were younger. These prolonged, elevated levels of stress-related hormones are associated with increased risks for many diseases, including cardiovascular, disease, cancer, diabetes, and hypertension.

hormonal stress theory
The theory that aging in the body's hormonal system can lower resilience to stress and increase the likelihood of disease.

Which of these three biological theories best explains aging? That question has not been answered yet. It might turn out that all of these biological processes are involved in aging.

At this point we have examined a number of ideas about longevity. A review of these ideas is presented in summary table 18.1.

The Course of Physical Development in Late Adulthood

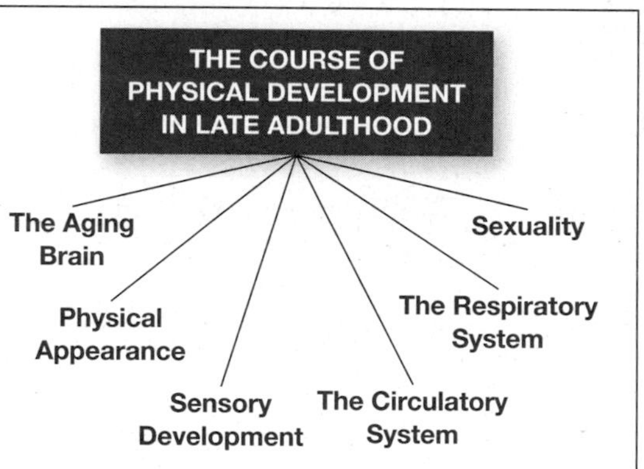

Although there are inevitable age-associated increases in the risks of physical disability, the actual onset of such problems is not uniform. Acknowledgment of considerable variability in rates of decline in functioning has generated increased attention to factors involved in the successful maintenance of functional abilities with age (Birren, 1996; Whitbourne, 2000). One analysis involved the MacArthur Research Network on Successful Aging Study, a three-site longitudinal study of successful aging in women and men aged 70 to 79 years of age. In this study, physical performance (such as walking efficiency, maintaining balance, and repeatedly standing up and sitting down) did decline with age, but there was considerable individual variation (Seeman & others, 1994). The physical performance of older adults in poor health from low-income backgrounds was inferior to that of their higher-income, healthy counterparts. A majority of the older adults also maintained their physical performance over a 3-year period in their seventies, and some even improved their performance in this time frame.

As we discuss the nature of physical development in older adults, keep in mind this emphasis on successful aging (Rowe & Kahn, 1998). We will chronicle age-related changes in physical decline, but we will also stress new developments in aging research that underscore how bodily powers decline slowly and that sometimes even lost function can be restored. In one survey, disabilities among the elderly had declined almost 15 percent from 1982 to 1994 (Manton, Corder, Stallard, 1997). Exercise, fewer smokers, and improvements in medical care account for much of the decline in disability (Suzman, 1997).

Summary Table 18.1
Longevity

Concept	Processes/ Related Ideas	Characteristics/Descriptions
Life Expectancy and Life Span	Distinctions	• Life expectancy refers to the number of years that will probably be lived by an average person born in a particular year. Life span is the maximum number of years any member of a species can live. • Life expectancy has dramatically increased, life span has not.
	Centenarians	• An increasing number of people are living to be 100 years or older. • Many of these people are healthy for most of their older years and seem to cope with stress effectively.
	Sex Difference in Longevity	• Females live about 6 years longer on average than males do. • The sex difference is likely due to biological and social factors.
The Young Old, the Old Old, and the Oldest Old	Their Nature	• The young old are 65 to 74 years of age, the old old are 75 years and older, and the oldest old are 85 years and older. • The needs, capacities, and resources of the oldest old are often different from when they were younger. • Significant numbers of the oldest old function effectively and are in good health. • A number of experts believe that when the terms *young old, old-old,* and *oldest old* are used, they should refer to functional age, not chronological age. Some 85-year-olds function far better than some 65-year-olds.
Biological Theories of Aging	Cellular Clock Theory	• Hayflick proposed that cells can divide a maximum of about 75 to 80 times and that as we age, our cells become less capable of dividing. In the last decade, scientists have found that telomeres likely are involved in explaining why cells lose their capacity to divide.
	Free-Radical Theory	• People age because unstable oxygen molecules called free radicals are produced in cells.
	Hormonal Stress Theory	• Aging in the body's hormonal system can lower resilience to stress and increase the likelihood of disease.

The Aging Brain

What are some general findings about the aging brain? How much plasticity and adaptiveness does the aging brain retain?

The Aging Brain's Plasticity and Adaptiveness

For decades it was believed that no new brain cells are generated after the early childhood years. However, researchers recently discovered that adults continue to grow new brain cells throughout their lives (Gould & others, 1999).

Even in the late adulthood years, the brain has remarkable repair capability, losing only a portion of its ability to function. The adaptive nature of the brain in older adults was demonstrated in one study (Coleman, 1986). From the forties through the seventies, the growth of dendrites (the receiving part of the neuron or nerve cell) increased. But in very old people (in their nineties), dendritic growth no longer was taking place. Thus, dendritic growth might compensate for the possible loss of neurons through the seventies but not in the nineties. Lack of dendritic growth in the elderly could be due a lack of environmental stimulation.

Stanley Rapaport (1994), chief of the neurosciences laboratory at the National Institute on Aging, compared the brains of younger and older people engaged in the

same tasks. The older brains literally rewired themselves to compensate for losses. If one neuron was not up to the job, neighboring neurons helped to pick up the slack. Rapaport concluded that as brains age, they can actually shift responsibilities for a given task from one region to another.

An intriguing ongoing investigation of the brain involves nearly 700 nuns in a convent in Mankato, Minnesota (Griener, Snowden, & Griether, 1999; Snowden, 1995, 1997).

The nuns are the largest group of brain donors in the world. Examination of the nuns' donated brains, as well as others, has led neuroscientists to believe that the brain has a remarkable capacity to change and grow, even in old age. The Sisters of Notre Dame in Mankato lead an intellectually challenging life, and brain researchers recently have found that stimulating the brain with mental exercises can cause neurons to increase their dendritic branching (see figure 18.3).

The capacity of the brain to change offers new possibilities for preventing and treating brain diseases:

- The onset of Alzheimer's disease symptoms might be delayed for years. The more educated people are, the less likely they are to develop Alzheimer's. This probably occurs because intellectual activity develops surplus brain tissue that compensates for tissue damaged by the disease.
- Older individuals might recover better from strokes. Even when areas of the brain are permanently damaged by stroke, new message routes can be created to get around the blockage or to resume the function of that area.

Figure **18.3**

The Brains of the Mankato Nuns

Top: Sister Marcella Zachman *(left)* finally stopped teaching at age 97. Now, at 99, she helps ailing nuns exercise their brains by quizzing them on vocabulary or playing a card game called Skip-Bo, at which she deliberately loses. Sister Mary Esther Boor *(right)*, also 99 years of age, is a former teacher who stays alert by doing puzzles and volunteering to work the front desk. *Below:* A technician holds the brain of a deceased Mankato nun. The nuns donate their brains for research that explores the effects of stimulation on brain growth.

Physical Appearance

In chapter 16, "Physical and Cognitive Development in Middle Adulthood," we pointed out some changes in physical appearance that take place ◄ P. 480. In late adulthood, these changes become more pronounced. The changes are most noticeable in the form of facial wrinkles and age spots.

We also get shorter when we get older. From 30 to 50 years of age, men lose about ½ inch in height, then might lose another ¾ inch from 50 to 70 years of age. The height loss for women could be as much as 2 inches from 25 to 75 years of age (Hoyer, Rybash, & Roodin, 1999).

Our weight usually drops after we reach 60 years of age. This likely occurs because we lose muscle, which also gives our bodies a more "sagging" look. The good news is that exercise and appropriate weight lifting can help to reduce the decrease in muscle mass and improve the older person's body appearance. We will have more to say about this later in this chapter.

Sensory Development

Sensory changes in late adulthood involve vision, hearing, taste, smell, touch, and pain.

Vision In late adulthood, the decline in vision that began for most of us in early or middle adulthood becomes more pronounced (Kosnick & others, 1989). Night driving is especially difficult, to some extent because tolerance for glare diminishes. Dark adaptation is slower, meaning that older individuals take longer to recover their vision when going from well-lighted rooms to semidarkness. The area of the visual field

becomes smaller, suggesting that a stimulus's intensity in the peripheral area of the visual field needs to be increased if the stimulus is to be seen. Events taking place away from the center of the visual field may not be detected.

This visual decline often can be traced to reduction in the quality or intensity of light reaching the retina. In extreme old age, these changes may be accompanied by degenerative changes in the retina, causing severe difficulty in seeing. Large print books and magnifiers may be needed in such cases.

In one recent study, sensory functioning in more than 500 adults 70 to 102 years of age was compared with competence in everyday activities (Marsiske, Klumb, & Baltes, in press). Sensory acuity, especially in vision, was related to whether and how well elderly adults bathed and groomed themselves, completed household chores, engaged in intellectual activities, and watched TV.

One vision problem associated with aging is *cataracts,* which are cloudy, opaque areas in the lens of the eye that prevent light from passing through. This causes blurred vision. Surgery to remove cataracts is usually very successful and currently is the most common operation on individuals 65 years and older in the United States.

Another vision problem related to aging is *glaucoma,* a disease that involves a hardening of the eyeball because of fluid buildup in the eye. If untreated, glaucoma can destroy vision. It is a problem for 1 percent of individuals in their seventies and 10 percent of individuals in their nineties. Special eye drops can be used to treat glaucoma.

Yet another vision problem that is linked with aging is *macular degeneration,* a disease involving deterioration of the retina. This affects 1 in 25 individuals from 66 to 74 years of age and 1 in 6 who are older. Macular degeneration is difficult to treat and is a leading cause of blindness in older adults. If the disease is detected early, it can be corrected with a laser.

Hearing Although hearing impairment can begin in middle adulthood, it usually does not become much of an impediment until late adulthood (Fozard, 2000). Even then, some but not all hearing problems may be corrected by hearing aids. Only 19 percent of individuals from 45 to 54 experience some type of hearing problem, but from 75 to 79 the figure has reached 75 percent (Harris, 1975). It has been estimated that 15 percent of the population over the age of 65 is legally deaf, usually due to the degeneration of the cochlea, the primary neural receptor for hearing in the inner ear (Olsho, Harkins, & Lenhardt, 1985). Wearing two hearing aids that are balanced to correct each ear separately can sometimes help hearing-impaired adults.

Earlier we indicated that life-span developmentalists are increasingly making distinctions between the young old or old age (ages 65 to 74) and the old old or late old age (75 years and older). This distinction is important in considering the degree of decline in various perceptual systems. As indicated in figure 18.4, the decline in the perceptual systems of vision and hearing is much greater in late old age than in yound old age (Charness & Bosman, 1992).

Smell and Taste Most older adults lose some of their sense of smell or taste, or both (Schiffman, 1996). These decrements can reduce their enjoyment of food and their life satisfaction. One negative outcome for a decline in the sense of smell is less ability to detect smoke from a fire. Smell and taste losses often begin around 60 years of age. Compounds that stimulate the olfactory nerve have been added to foods to increase intake by elderly individuals. Also, there is less decline in smell and taste in healthy older adults than in their less healthy counterparts.

Many older adults often prefer highly seasoned foods (sweeter, spicier, saltier) to compensate for their diminished taste and smell (Hoyer, Rybash, & Roodin, 1999). This can lead to eating more low-nutrient, highly seasoned "junk food."

Touch Changes in touch are associated with aging (Gescheider, 1997). One study found that, with aging, individuals could detect touch less in the lower extremities (ankles, knees, and so on) than in the upper extremities (wrists, shoulders,

Perceptual System	Old Age (65–74 years)	Late Old Age (75 years and older)
Vision	There is a loss of acuity even with corrective lenses. Less transmission of light occurs through the retina (half as much as in young adults). Greater susceptibility to glare occurs. Color discrimination ability decreases.	There is a significant loss of visual acuity and color discrimination, and a decrease in the size of the perceived visual field. In late old age, people are at significant risk for visual dysfunction from cataracts and glaucoma.
Hearing	There is a significant loss of hearing at high frequencies and some loss at middle frequencies. These losses can be helped by a hearing aid. There is greater susceptibility to masking of what is heard by noise.	There is a significant loss at high and middle frequencies. A hearing aid is more likely to be needed than in old age.

Figure **18.4**

Vision and Hearing Decline in Old Age and Late Old Age

and so on) (Corso, 1977). For most older adults, a decline in touch sensitivity is not problematic (Hoyer, Rybash, & Roodin, 1999).

Pain Older adults are less sensitive to pain and suffer from it less than younger adults (Harkins, Price, & Martinelli, 1986). Although decreased sensitivity to pain can help older adults cope with disease and injury, it can be harmful if it masks injury and illness that need to be treated.

The Circulatory System

Not long ago it was believed that cardiac output—the amount of blood the heart pumps—declines with age even in healthy adults. However, we now know that when heart disease is absent, the amount of blood pumped is the same regardless of an adult's age. In fact, some experts on aging argue that the healthy heart may even become stronger as we age through the adult years, with capacity increasing, not decreasing (Fozard, 1992).

In the past, a 60-year-old with a blood pressure reading of 160/90 would have been told, "For your age, that is normal." Now medication, exercise, and/or a healthier diet might be prescribed to lower blood pressure. Most experts on aging recommend that consistent blood pressures at 160/90 and above should be treated to reduce the risk of heart attack, stroke, or kidney disease (Lakatta, 1992). Blood pressure can rise with age because of illness, obesity, anxiety, stiffening of blood vessels, or lack of exercise. The longer any of these factors persist, the worse the individual's blood pressure gets (Rowe & Kahn, 1998).

The Respiratory System

Lung capacity drops 40 percent between the ages of 20 and 80, even without disease (Fozard, 1992). Lungs lose elasticity, the chest shrinks, and the diaphragm weakens. The good news, though, is that older adults can improve lung functioning with diaphragm-strengthening exercises.

Sexuality

Aging does induce some changes in human sexual performance, more so in the male than in the female. Orgasm becomes less frequent in males, occurring in every second to third act of intercourse rather than every time. More direct stimulation usually is needed to produce an erection. In the absence of two circumstances—actual disease and

the belief that old people are or should be asexual—sexuality can be lifelong. Even when actual intercourse is impaired by infirmity, other relationship needs persist, among them closeness, sensuality, and being valued as a man or a woman (Johnson, 1996).

Such a view, of course, is contrary to folklore, to the beliefs of many individuals in society, and even to many physicians and health-care personnel. Fortunately, many older adults have gone on having sex without talking about it, unabashed by the accepted and destructive social image of the dirty old man and the asexual, undesirable older woman.

In one study of older adults in their sixties, many were still having sex (Wiley & Bortz, 1996). The women rated kissing as one of the most satisfying sexual activities, while the men rated oral sex as the most satisfying. In another study of more than 1,200 elderly people (mean age = 77), almost 30 percent had participated in sexual activity in the past month (Matthias & others, 1997). Two-thirds of the elderly adults were satisfied with their current level of sexual activity.

Various therapies for older adults who report sexual difficulties have been effective. In one study, sex education—which consisted largely of simply giving sexual information—led to increased sexual interest, knowledge, and activity in the elderly (White & Catania, 1981).

At this point we have discussed a number of ideas about the course of physical development in late adulthood. To review these ideas, see summary table 18.2. Next, we will study the nature of health in late adulthood.

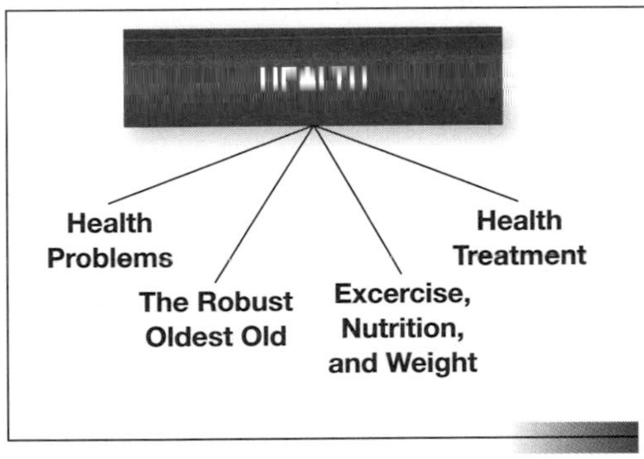

Health

How healthy are older adults? What types of health problems do they have? As we discuss the health of older adults, you will see that there are more healthy older adults than we used to envision.

Health Problems

As we age, the probability increases that we will have some disease or illness. For example, though many are still quite healthy overall, the majority of adults still alive at 80 years of age or older are likely to have some type of impairment.

In chapter 16, "Physical and Cognitive Development in Middle Adulthood," we defined *chronic disorders* as disorders with a slow onset and a long duration ◀ P. 481. Chronic diseases are rare in early adulthood, increase in middle adulthood, and become more common in late adulthood. As shown in figure 18.5, arthritis is the most common chronic disorder in late adulthood, followed by hypertension. Older women have a higher incidence of arthritis and hypertension, and are more likely to have visual problems, but are less likely to have hearing problems than older men are.

Although adults over the age of 65 often have a physical impairment, many of them can still carry on their everyday activities or work. Chronic conditions associated with the greatest limitation on work are heart conditions (52 percent), diabetes (34 percent), asthma (27 percent), and arthritis (27 percent). Low income is also strongly related to health problems in late adulthood. Approximately three times as many poor as nonpoor older adults report that their activities are limited by chronic disorders.

How many of us older persons have really been prepared for the second half of life, for old age, and eternity?

Carl Jung
Swiss Psychoanalyst, 20th Century

Causes of Death in Older Adults Nearly three-fourths of all older adults die of heart disease, cancer, or cerebrovascular disease (stroke). Chronic lung diseases, peneumonia and influenza, and diabetes round out the six leading causes of death among older adults. If cancer, the second leading cause of death in older adults, were completely eliminated, the average life expectancy would rise by only 1 to 2 years. However, if all cardiovascular and kidney diseases were eradicated, the average life expectancy of older adults would increase by approximately 10 years. This in-

Summary Table 18.2
The Course of Physical Development in Late Adulthood

Concept	Processes/ Related Ideas	Characteristics/Descriptions
The Aging Brain	Overview	• The brain occupies less of the cranial cavity after 50 years of age. • We lose some neurons as we age, but how many is debated. • The aging brain retains considerable plasticity and adaptiveness.
	Plasticity and Adaptiveness	• Growth of dendrites can take place in older adults. • The brain has the capacity to virtually rewire itself to compensate for loss in older adults.
Physical Appearance	Its Nature	• The most obvious signs of aging are wrinkled skin and age spots on the skin. • People get shorter as they age, and their weight often decreases after age 60 because of loss of muscle.
Sensory Development	Vision	• The visual system declines, but the vast majority of older adults can have their vision corrected so they can continue to work and function in the world.
	Hearing	• Hearing decline often begins in middle age but usually does not become much of an impediment until late adulthood. • Hearing aids can diminish hearing problems for many older adults.
	Smell and Taste	• These can decline, although the decline is minimal in healthy older adults.
	Touch	• Changes in touch sensitivity are associated with aging, although this does not present a problem for most older adults.
	Pain	• Sensitivity to pain decreases in late adulthood.
Circulatory System	Its Nature	• When heart disease is absent, the amount of blood pumped is the same regardless of an adult's age. • High blood pressure no longer is just accepted but rather is treated with medication, exercise, and/or a healthy diet. • Blood pressure can rise in older adults due to a number of factors, which can be modified.
Respiratory System	Its Nature	• Lung capacity does drop, but older adults can improve lung functioning with diaphragm-strengthening exercises.
Sexuality	Its Nature	• Aging in late adulthood does include some changes in sexual performance, more for males than females. Nonetheless, there are no known age limits to sexual activity.

crease in longevity is already under way as the number of strokes among older adults has declined considerably in the last several decades. The decline in strokes is due to improved treatment of high blood pressure, a decrease in smoking, better diet, and an increase in exercise.

Arthritis **Arthritis** *is an inflammation of the joints accompanied by pain, stiffness, and movement problems. Arthritis is especially common in older adults.* This disorder can affect hips, knees, ankles, fingers, and vertebrae. Individuals with arthritis often experience pain and stiffness, as well as problems in moving about and performing routine daily activities. There is no known cure for arthritis. However, the symptoms of arthritis can be reduced by drugs, such as aspirin, range-of-motion exercises for the afflicted joints, weight reduction, and, in extreme cases, replacement of the crippled joint with a prosthesis.

arthritis
Inflammation of the joints that is accompanied by pain, stiffness, and movement problems; especially common in older adults.

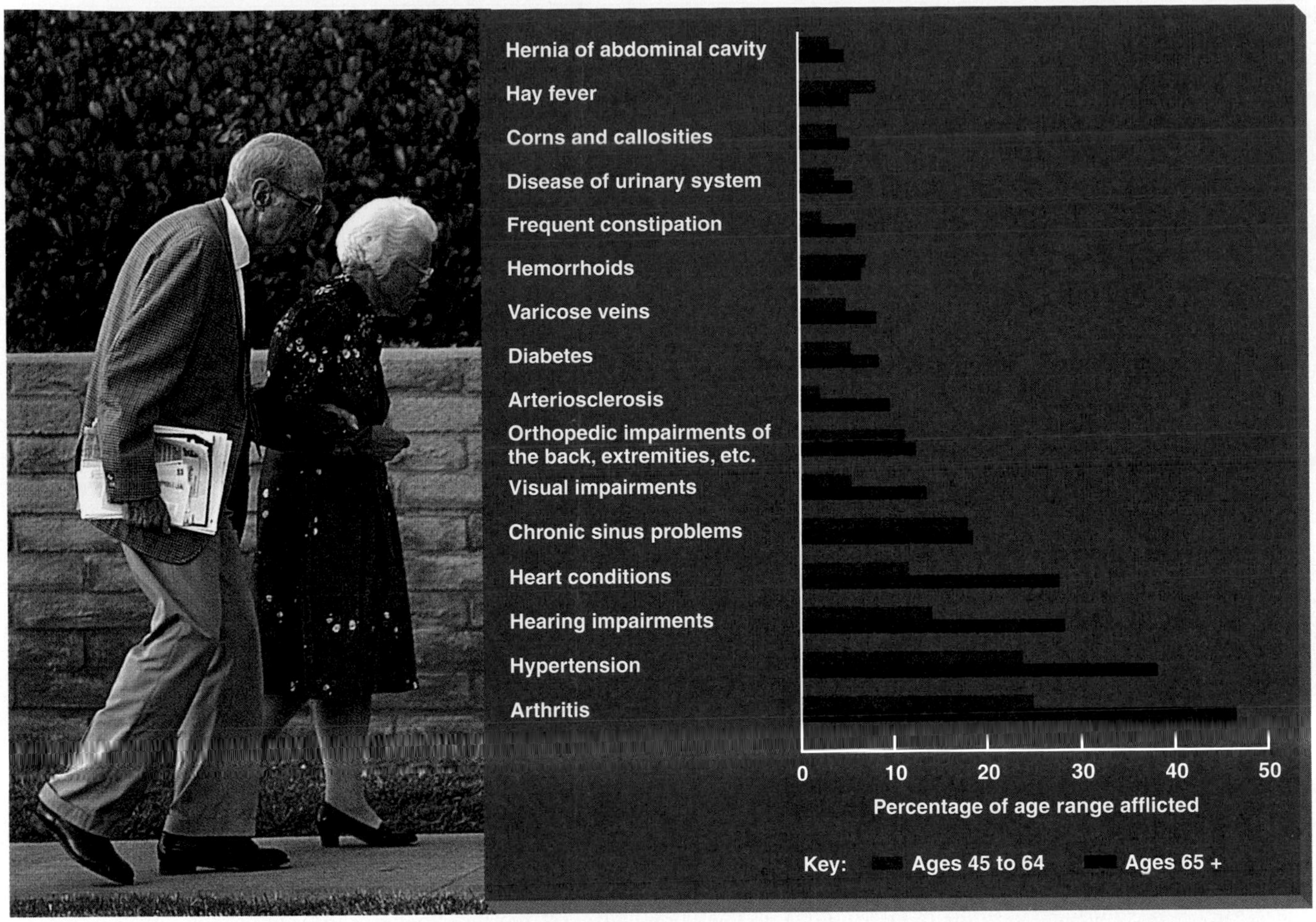

Figure **18.5**

The Most Prevalent Chronic Conditions in Middle and Late Adulthood

osteoporosis
A disorder of aging that involves an extensive loss of bone tissue and is the main reason many older adults walk with a marked stoop. Women are especially vulnerable to osteoporosis.

Arthritis
Osteoporosis

Osteoporosis Normal aging involves some loss of bone tissue from the skeleton. However, in some instances loss of bone tissue can become severe. **Osteoporosis** *is an aging disorder involving an extensive loss of bone tissue. Osteoporosis is the main reason many older adults walk with a marked stoop. Women are especially vulnerable to osteoporosis, the leading cause of broken bones in women.* Approximately 80 percent of the osteoporosis cases in the United States occur in females, 20 percent in males. Almost two-thirds of all women over the age of 60 are affected by osteoporosis. Osteoporosis is more common in White, thin, and small-framed women. This aging disorder is related to deficiencies in calcium, vitamin D, estrogen depletion, and lack of exercise. To prevent osteoporosis, young and middle-aged women should eat foods rich in calcium, get more exercise, and avoid smoking. Calcium-rich foods include dairy products (low-fat milk and low-fat yogurt, for example) and certain vegetables (such as broccoli, turnip greens, and kale). Estrogen replacement therapy may also be recommended for middle-aged women at especially high risk for developing osteoporosis, except those with a family history of breast cancer. Alternate drugs such as Fosimax can be used to reduce the risk of osteoporosis. Older women should also get bone density checks.

A program of regular exercise might have the potential to prevent osteoporosis as much or more than estrogen replacement therapy. In one study, women aged 50 to 70 who were not on estrogen replacement therapy lifted weights twice a week (Nelson & others, 1994). Their risk of osteoporosis and resulting broken bones was

sharply reduced, while their balance and muscular strength improved. The weight-lifting program included three sets of eight repetitions on machines to strengthen muscles in the abdomen, back, thighs, and buttocks.

Accidents Accidents are the seventh leading cause of death among older adults. Injuries resulting from a fall at home or during a traffic accident in which an older adult is a driver or an older pedestrian is hit by a vehicle are common. Each year, approximately 200,000 adults over the age of 65 (most of them women) fracture a hip in a fall. Half of these older adults die within 12 months, frequently from pneumonia. Because healing and recuperation are slower in older adults, an accident that is only a temporary setback for a younger person may result in long-term hospital or home care for an older adult. In one study, an exercise program reduced the risk of falls in elderly adults (Province & others, 1995).

The Robust Oldest Old

Our image of the oldest old (eighties and older) is predominantly of being disabled and frail. The implications of the projected rapid growth of the oldest old population have often been pessimistic—an expensive burden of chronic disability in which the oldest old often require the everyday help of other persons. However, as we discussed earlier in this chapter, the oldest old are a heterogeneous group, and until recently this diversity has not been adequately recognized. Although almost one-fourth of the oldest old are institutionalized, the majority live in the community and remain independent (Suzman & others, 1992).

Because so much attention has been given to chronic disabilities of the oldest old, those who have aged successfully have gone virtually unnoticed and unstudied. An increased interest in successful aging is producing a more optimistic portrayal of the oldest old than in the past (Perls, Lauerman, & Silver, 1999; Rowe & Kahn, 1998). Health service researchers are discovering that a relatively large portion of people in old age are low-cost users of medical services; a small percentage account for a large fraction of expenditures, and this usually occurs in the last year of life, a period that is expensive at any age. A surprisingly large portion of the oldest old not only do not require personal assistance on a daily basis but also are physically robust, and some who are not initially robust recover their robustness. In a longitudinal study of a national sample of adults 80 years and older, 33 percent were classified as robust based on the following criteria: no difficulty in walking $^{1}/_{4}$ mile, stooping, crouching, kneeling, lifting 10 pounds, or walking up 10 steps without resting (Suzman & others, 1992). About three-fourths of the robust older adults had no hospitalizations and had fewer than six doctor visits in the previous 12 months.

In this and other studies of very old adults, a sizable portion of individuals are free of disability, able to cope with their disabilities free of assistance, or able to recover their functioning over time (Harris & others, 1989). Cataract surgery and a variety of rehabilitation strategies can improve the functioning of the oldest old. Later in this chapter we will discuss how exercise programs can improve strength and mobility in older persons. For example, in one study, 8 weeks of leg-strength training markedly improved the walking ability of nursing home residents who averaged 90 years of age (Fiatarone & others, 1990). Promising approaches for preventing or intervening in osteoporosis include calcium supplementation, estrogen replacement, and other hormone therapies.

In sum, earlier portraits of the oldest old have been stereotypical. A substantial subgroup of the oldest old are robust and active. And there is cause for optimism in the development of new regimens of prevention and intervention.

Exercise, Nutrition, and Weight

An important aspect of preventing health problems in older adults and improving their health is to encourage individuals to exercise more and to develop better nutritional habits.

WWW
Exercise and Aging

All we know about older adults indicates that they are healthier and happier the more active they are. Several decades ago, it was believed that older adults should be more passive and inactive to be well adjusted and satisfied with life. In today's world, we believe that while older adults may be in the evening of their life span, they are not meant to passively live out their remaining years.

Exercise Although we may be in the evening of our lives in late adulthood, we are not meant to live out our remaining years passively. Everything we know about older adults suggests they are healthier and happier the more active they are. The possibility that regular exercise can lead to a healthier late adulthood, and possibly extend life, has been raised.

In one study, the cardiovascular fitness of 101 older men and women (average age = 67 years) was examined (Blumenthal & others, 1989). The older adults were randomly assigned to an aerobic exercise group, a yoga and flexibility control group, and a waiting list control group. The program lasted 4 months. Prior to and following the 4-month program, the older adults underwent comprehensive physiological examinations. In the aerobic group, the older adults participated in three supervised exercise sessions per week for 16 weeks. Each session consisted of a 10-minute warm-up, 30 minutes of continuous exercise on a stationary bicycle, 15 minutes of brisk walking/jogging, and a 5-minute cool-down. In the yoga and flexibility control group, the older adults participated in 60 minutes of supervised yoga exercises at least twice a week for 16 weeks. Over the 4-month period, the cardiovascular fitness—such as peak oxygen consumption, cholesterol level, and blood pressure—of the aerobic exercise group significantly improved. In contrast, the cardiovascular fitness of the yoga and waiting list groups did not improve.

In another study, exercise literally meant a difference in life or death for middle-aged and older adults (Blair, 1990). More than 17,000 men and women were studied at the Aerobic Institute in Dallas, Texas. Sedentary participants were more than twice as likely to die during the 8-year time span of the study than those who were moderately fit. Examples of exercise programs included running 2 miles in 20 minutes twice a week or walking 3 miles in 45 minutes twice a week. In yet another study, changes in level of physical activity and cigarette smoking were associated with risk of death during the middle and late adulthood years (Paffenbarger & others, 1993). Beginning moderately vigorous sports activity from the forties through the eighties was associated with a 23 percent lower risk of death, quitting cigarette smoking with a 41 percent lower death risk.

Gerontologists increasingly recommend strength training in addition to aerobic activity and stretching for older adults (Damush & Damush, 1999; Everard & others, 1999; Hikida & others, 2000; Hortobagyi & others, 2001; Messier & others, 2000; Rubenstein & others, 2000). The average person's lean body mass declines with age—about 6.6 pounds of lean muscle are lost each decade during the adult years. The rate of loss accelerates after age 45. Also, the average percentage ratio of muscle to fat for a 60- to 70-year-old woman is 44 percent fat. In a 20-year-old woman the ratio is 23 to 24 percent. Weight lifting can preserve and possibly increase muscle mass in older adults. And in one study, it also reduced depression in the elderly (Singh, Clements, & Fiatarone, 1997).

Exercise is an excellent way to maintain health. Researchers continue to document its positive effects in older adults (Burke & others, 2001; Evans, 2000; Kabitsis & others, 1999; Prohaska & Peters, 1999; Wang, Bashore, & Friedman, 1995). Exercise helps people to live independent lives with dignity in late adulthood. At 80, 90, and even 100 years of age, exercise can help prevent elderly adults from falling down or even being institutionalized. Being physically fit means being able to do the things you want to do, whether you are young or old. More about researchers' investigations into exercise's positive benefits for health is shown in figure 18.6.

Nutrition and Weight Seventeenth-century English philosopher and essayist Francis Bacon was the first author to recommend scientific evaluation of diet and longevity. He advocated a frugal diet. Does a restricted intake of food increase longevity or could it possibly even extend the human life span?

Scientists have accumulated considerable evidence that food restriction in laboratory animals (in most cases rats) can increase the animals' life span (Gurdal, Friedman, & Johnson, 1995; Hadley & others, 2001; Kirk, 2001). Animals fed diets restricted in calories, although adequate in protein, vitamins, and minerals, live as much as 40 percent longer than animals given unlimited access to food. And chronic problems such as kidney disease appear at a later age. Diet restriction also delays biochemical alterations such as the age-related rise in cholesterol observed in both humans and animals. Whether similar very low-calorie diets (in some instances the animals eat 40 percent less than normal) can stretch the human life span is not known. Most nutritional experts do not recommend very low-calorie diets for older adults; rather, they recommend a well-balanced, low-fat diet that includes the nutritional factors needed to maintain good health.

Leaner men do live longer, healthier lives. In one recent study of 19,297 Harvard alumni, those weighing the least were less likely to die over the past three decades (Lee & others, 1993). The men were divided into five categories according to body mass index (a complex formula that takes into account weight and height). As body mass increased, so did risk of death. The most overweight men had a 67 percent higher risk of dying than the thinnest men. For example, the heaviest men (such as 181 pounds or more for a 5-foot-10-inch man) also had 2½ times the risk of death from cardiovascular disease. Currently, these researchers are studying the relation of body mass index to longevity in women and predict similar results to the study with men.

Figure **18.6**

The Jogging Hog Experiment

Jogging hogs reveal the dramatic effects of exercise on health. In one investigation, a group of hogs was trained to run approximately 100 miles per week (Bloor & White, 1983). Then, the researchers narrowed the arteries that supplied blood to the hogs' hearts. The hearts of the jogging hogs developed extensive alternate pathways for blood supply, and 42 percent of the threatened heart tissue was salvaged compared to only 17 percent in a control group of nonjogging hogs.

The Growing Controversy over Vitamins and Aging For years, most experts on aging and health argued that a balanced diet was all that was needed for successful aging; vitamin supplements were not recommended. However, an increasing number of research studies raise questions about the practice of not recommending vitamin supplements for middle-aged and older adults. The new research suggests the possibility that some vitamin supplements—mainly a group called "antioxidants," which includes vitamin C, vitamin E, and betacarotene—help to slow the aging process and improve the health of older adults.

Roy Walford's Views

Caloric Restriction and Aging Research

The theory is that antioxidants counteract the cell damage caused by free radicals, which are produced both by the body's own metabolism and by environmental factors such as smoking, pollution, and bad chemicals in the diet. When free radicals cause damage (oxidation) in one cell, a chain reaction of damage follows. Antioxidants act much like a fire extinguisher, helping to neutralize free-radical activity. For example, people who took vitamin E supplements for 2 years significantly reduced their risk of heart disease—by up to 40 percent (Rimm & others, 1993). However, cancer and heart disease benefits of vitamin E and betacarotene were not confirmed in a large-scale study of male smokers 50 years old and older in Finland (Alpha-Tocopherol, Beta-Carotene Cancer Prevention Study

CAREERS IN LIFE-SPAN DEVELOPMENT

Deborah Radomski, Geriatric Nurse

GERIATRIC NURSES seek to prevent or intervene in the chronic or acute health problems of older adults. They take courses in schools of nursing and obtain one or more degrees in nursing. Geriatric nurses take courses in biological sciences, nursing care, and mental health. They also experience supervised training in geriatric settings. They might work in hospitals, nursing homes, schools of nursing, or with geriatric medical specialists or psychiatrists in a medical clinic or in private practice.

Deborah Radomski is a geriatric nurse who works in a different context. She is a telemedic for Geriatric Associates of America, a Texas organization that provides health care to nursing homes. In a typical 8-hour day, she handles about 120 calls from nurses working with older adult patients.

Deborah obtained her undergraduate nursing degree from Lamar University and her master's degree in nursing from the University of Texas. She worked in various nursing positions at different hospitals before assuming her current telemedic job. Nursing homes especially use her services to inquire about such matters as dietary recommendations, exercise activities, illnesses, drugs, and medical emergencies. However, Deborah says there is only so much she can do over the phone. For example, if an older adult is in acute respiratory distress, she tells the caller to immediately take the person to the hospital.

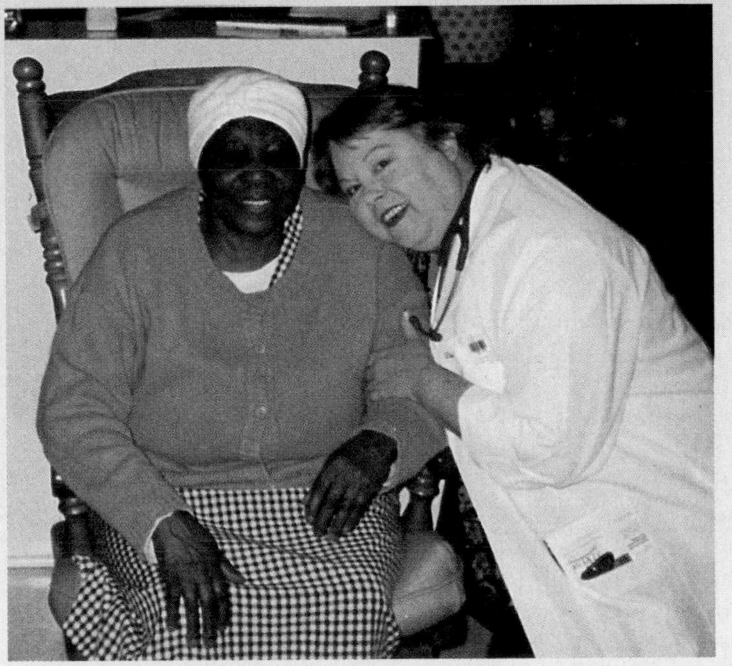

Deborah Radomski (right) with one of her patients. Most of her work, though, now involves telemedicine.

Group, 1994). Vitamin E users did have a significant reduction in prostate cancer in this study.

There is no evidence that antioxidants can increase the human life span, but some aging and health experts believe they can reduce a person's risk of becoming frail and sick in the later adult years. However, there are still a lot of blanks and uncertainties in what we know (Stern, 1993). That is, we don't know which vitamins should be taken, how large a dose should be taken, what the restraints are, and so on. Critics also argue that the key experimental studies documenting the effectiveness of the vitamins in slowing the aging process have not been conducted. The studies in this area so far have been so-called population studies that are correlational rather than experimental in nature. Other factors—such as exercise, better health practices, and good nutritional habits—might be responsible for the positive findings about vitamins and aging rather than vitamins per se. Also, the free radical theory is a theory and not a fact, and is only one of a number of theories about why we age.

With these uncertainties in mind, some aging experts still recommend vitamin supplements in the following range (Blumberg, 1993): 250 to 1000 mg of vitamin C, 100 to 400 IU of vitamin E, and 15 to 30 mg of beta-carotene.

Now that we have considered older adults' health problems and the roles of exercise and nutrition, let's turn our attention to the health treatment available to older adults.

Health Treatment

What is the quality of nursing homes and other extended-care facilities for older adults? What is the nature of the relationship between older adults and health-care providers?

Care Options Only about 5 percent of adults 65 years of age and over reside in a nursing home at any point in time in our society. However, as older adults age, their probability of being in a nursing home or other extended care facility increases. Twenty-three percent of adults 85 years of age and older live in nursing homes or other extended care facilities.

Because of the inadequate quality of many nursing homes and the escalating costs of nursing home care, many gerontologists and geriatric specialists (*geriatrics* is the branch of medicine dealing with the health problems of the aged) believe alternatives to nursing homes need to be considered (Castle, 2001). These alternatives include home health care, day-care centers, and preventive medicine clinics. The alternatives are potentially less expensive than hospitals and nursing homes. They also are less likely to engender feelings of depersonalization and dependency that occur so often among residents of institutions (Greene & others, 1995).

Giving Options for Control and Teaching Coping Skills

An important factor related to health, and even survival, in a nursing home is the patient's feelings of control and self-determination. In a classic study, a group of older nursing home residents were encouraged to make more day-to-day choices and thus feel they had more responsibility for and control over their lives (Rodin & Langer, 1977). They began to decide such matters as what they ate, when their visitors could come, what movies they saw, and who could come to their rooms. A similar group in the same nursing home was told by the administrator how caring the nursing home was and how much the staff wanted to help, but these older nursing home residents were given no opportunities to take more control over their lives. Eighteen months later, the residents given responsibility and control were more alert and active, and said they were happier, than the residents who were only encouraged to feel that the staff would try to satisfy their needs. And the "responsible" or "self-control" group had significantly better improvement in their health than did the "dependent" group. Even more important was the finding that after 18 months only half as many nursing home residents in the "responsibility" group had died as in the "dependent" group. Perceived control over one's environment, then, may literally be a matter of life or death.

Ellen Langer (1989) argues that it is extremely important for aging individuals to understand that they can *choose* the way they think. She believes that most people do things out of habit. When people no longer know why they are doing something, these habits assume a mindless quality. Although there is nothing wrong with doing something out of habit, to change a habit people need to become mindful of why they are engaging in the habit. In her research, Langer (1989) has shown that one reason people act old (as by not making decisions or not carrying heavy things) is not that their bodies force them to act this way but rather that they have stored

WWW

Trends in Health and Aging

Health and Aging: Cross-Cultural Comparisons

Ellen Langer *(left)* and Judith Rodin conducted a classic study of perceived control in nursing homes. *Was their study a correlational or an experimental study? How did they set up the study? What were the results?*

mental images of how old people act and then base their actions on these mental images. She demonstrated that when people were induced to think of themselves as younger, they showed many outward changes, such as a better posture and quicker gait. More basic changes also occurred, such as having a more positive outlook, better memory, and improved eyesight.

In another study, Richard Schulz (1976) gave nursing home residents different amounts of control over visits they received from local college students. Having control over the visits, or at least advance information about them, made the nursing home residents more active, happier, and healthier. This probably occurred because control makes life less stressful by making it more predictable. When the experiment ended, so did the visits by the college students. In a follow-up 2 years later, the nursing home residents who had been given control over scheduling of visits—and then had the visits, and the control, taken away—were doing worse psychologically than the others (Schulz & Hanusa, 1978). In sum, loss of control may even be worse than lack of control in some cases.

How can a psychological factor, such as the feeling of control, have such dramatic effects on health? Judith Rodin (1990) says that individuals who believe they have a high degree of control are more likely to feel that their actions can make a difference in their lives. Thus, they are more likely to take better care of themselves by eating healthier foods and exercising. In contrast, those who have reduced feelings of control are likely to feel that what they do will not make a difference. So they do not even bother to try to make a difference. Rodin also believes that the perception of control can have a direct effect on the body. For example, being in control reduces stress and its stress-related hormones. When stress-related hormones remain elevated, there is more wear and tear on the body. High blood pressure, heart disease, arthritis, and certain types of ulcers have all been linked with excessive stress.

Following up on this line of thinking, Rodin (1983) measured stress-related hormones in several groups of nursing home residents. Then, she taught the residents coping skills to help them deal better with day-to-day problems. They were taught how to say no when they did not want something, without worrying whether they would offend someone. They were given assertiveness training, and learned time management skills. After the training, the nursing home residents had greatly reduced levels of cortisol (a hormone closely related to stress that has been implicated in a number of diseases). The cortisol levels of the "assertive training" residents remained lower, even after 18 months. Further, these nursing home residents were healthier and had a reduced need for medication, compared to residents who had not been taught the coping skills. In sum, Rodin's research shows that simply giving nursing home residents options for control and teaching them coping skills can change their behavior and improve their health.

The Older Adult and Health-Care Providers The attitudes of both the health-care provider and the older adult are important aspects of the older adult's health care (Greene & Adelman, 2001). Unfortunately, health-care providers too often share society's stereotypes and negative attitudes toward the elderly (Nussbaum, Pecchioni, & Crowell, 2001). In a health-care setting, these attitudes can take the form of avoidance, dislike, and begrudged tolerance rather than positive, hopeful treatment. Health-care personnel are more likely to be interested in treating younger persons who more often have acute problems with a higher prognosis for successful recovery. They often are less motivated to treat older persons, who are more likely to have chronic problems with a lower prognosis for successful recovery.

Not only are physicians less responsive to older patients, but older patients, but older patients often take a less active role in medical encounters with health-care per-

Summary Table 18.3
Health

Concept	Processes/ Related Ideas	Characteristics/Descriptions
Health Problems	Health Problems and Causes of Death in Older Adults	• As we age, our probability of disease or illness increases. • Chronic disorders are rare in early adulthood, increase in middle adulthood, and become common in late adulthood. The most common chronic problem is arthritis. • Nearly three-fourths of older adults die of heart disease, cancer, or stroke.
	Arthritis, Osteoporosis, and Accidents	• Arthritis is especially common in older adults. • Osteoporosis is the main reason many older adults walk with a stoop; women are especially vulnerable. • Accidents are usually more debilitating to older than to younger adults.
The Robust Oldest Old	Cause for Optimism	• Early portraits of the oldest old were too negative; there is cause for optimism in the development of new regimens and interventions.
Exercise, Nutrition, and Weight	Exercise	• The physical benefits of exercise have clearly been demonstrated in older adults. • Aerobic exercise and weight lifting are both recommended if the adults are physically capable of them.
	Nutrition and Weight	• Food restriction in animals can increase the animals' life span, but whether this works with humans is not known. In humans, being overweight is associated with an increased mortality rate. • Most nutritional experts recommend a well-balanced, low-fat diet for older adults, but do not recommend an extremely low-calorie diet.
	The Growing Controversy Over Vitamins and Aging	• The controversy focuses on whether vitamin supplements—especially the antioxidants vitamin C, vitamin E, and beta-carotene—can slow the aging process and improve older adults' health.
Health Treatment	Care Options	• Although only 5 percent of adults over 65 reside in nursing homes, 23 percent of adults 85 and over do. The quality of nursing homes varies enormously. Alternatives to nursing homes are being proposed.
	Giving Options for Control and Teaching Coping Skills	• Simply giving nursing home residents options for control and teaching coping skills can change their behavior and improve their health.
	The Older Adult and Health-Care Providers	• The attitudes of both the health-care provider and the older adult patient are important aspects of the older adult's health care. Too often health-care personnel share society's negative view of older adults.

sonnel than do younger patients (Woodward & Wallston, 1987). Older adults should be encouraged to take a more active role in their own health care (Hummert & Nussbaum, 2001).

At this point we have discussed a number of ideas about health in older adults. To review these ideas, see summary table 18.3. In the next chapter, we will continue our examination of late adulthood by exploring the cognitive development of older adults.

Chapter Review

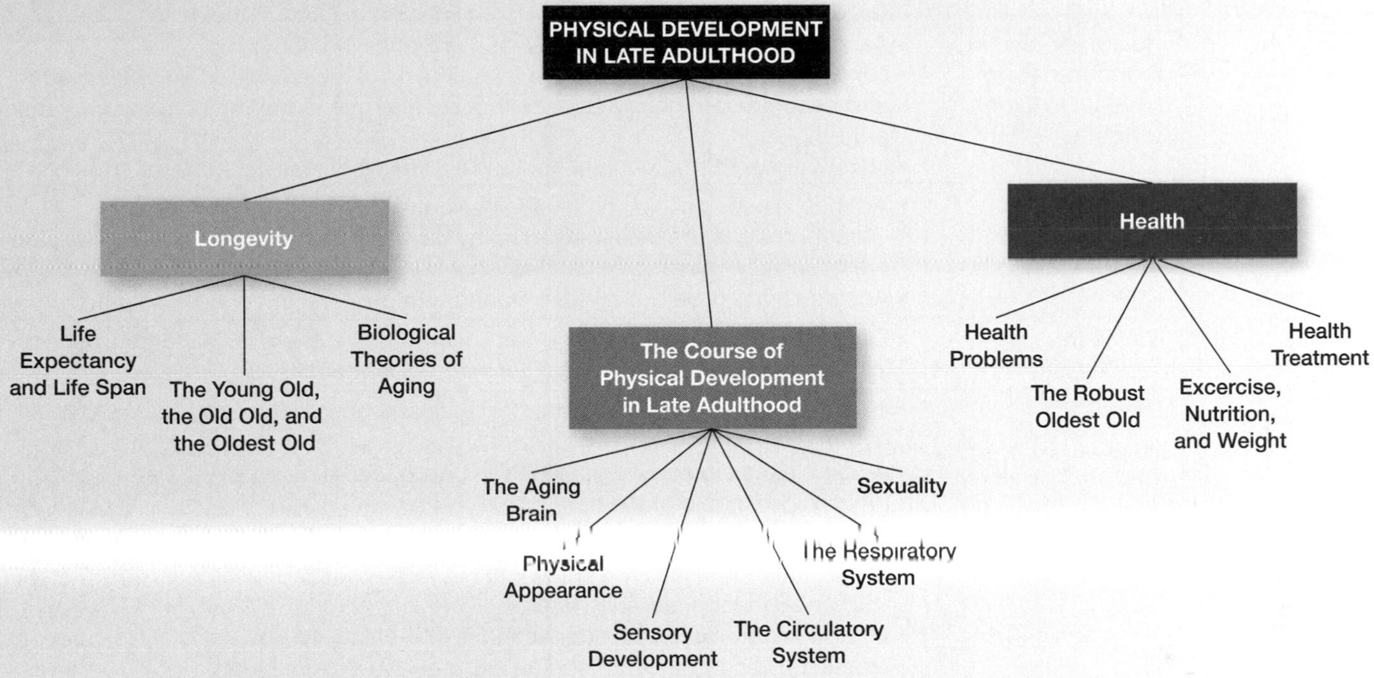

TO OBTAIN A DETAILED REVIEW OF THIS CHAPTER, STUDY THESE THREE SUMMARY TABLES:

- Summary Table 18.1 Longevity page 534
- Summary Table 18.2 The Course of Physical Development in Late Adulthood page 539
- Summary Table 18.3 Health page 547

Key Terms

life span 526
life expectancy 526
cellular clock theory 532
free-radical theory 533
hormonal stress theory 533
arthritis 539
osteoporosis 540

Key People

Stanley Rapaport 534
Ellen Langer 545
Richard Schultz 546
Judith Rodin 546

Taking It to the Net

1. Do you think you will live to be 100? Investigate your chances of being a centenarian by reading the results from an ongoing Harvard University Medical School study.
2. Sixty year old Jack knows that regular exercise is important to maintain a healthy heart. But will exercise alone guarantee Jack a long and healthy life?
3. Lucinda's eighty-year-old grandfather has moved in with the family. Lucinda is concerned about his eating habits as he is frail and thin, and says he has no appetite. What can Lucinda do to make his meals attractive and appetizing to him?

Connect to www.mhhe.com/santrockld8 to research the answers and complete these exercises.

OLC Preview

To further test your knowledge of this chapter or to explore our extensive online resources that accompany *Life-Span Development*, eighth edition, please log on to the text's Online Learning Center at http://www.mhhe.com/santrockld8.com.

Chapter 19

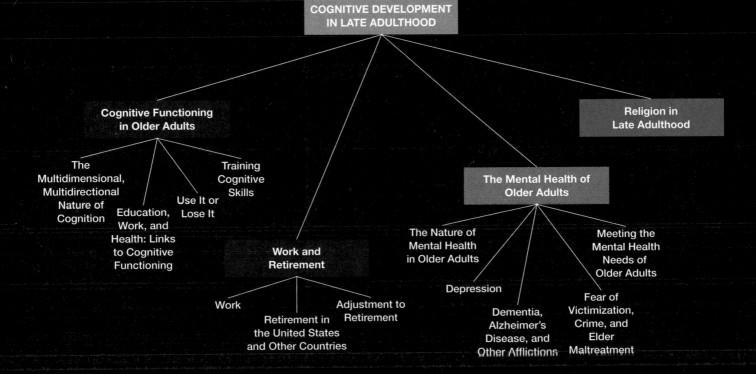

COGNITIVE DEVELOPMENT IN LATE ADULTHOOD

- **Cognitive Functioning in Older Adults**
  - The Multidimensional, Multidirectional Nature of Cognition
  - Education, Work, and Health: Links to Cognitive Functioning
  - Use It or Lose It
  - Training Cognitive Skills
- **Work and Retirement**
  - Work
  - Retirement in the United States and Other Countries
  - Adjustment to Retirement
- **The Mental Health of Older Adults**
  - The Nature of Mental Health in Older Adults
  - Depression
  - Dementia, Alzheimer's Disease, and Other Afflictions
  - Fear of Victimization, Crime, and Elder Maltreatment
  - Meeting the Mental Health Needs of Older Adults
- **Religion in Late Adulthood**

Cognitive Development in Late Adulthood

The night hath not yet come: We are not quite cut off from labor by the failing light; some work remains for us to do and dare.

Henry Wadsworth Longfellow
American Poet, 19th Century

Images of Life-Span Development

Sister Mary

SISTER MARY was born in 1892 in Philadelphia. She died in 1993 at 101 years of age. Mary was a remarkable woman who had high cognitive test scores even after she reached 100 years of age (Snowden, 1997). What is more remarkable is that she maintained this high level of cognitive competence despite having extensive neurofibrillary tangles and senile plaques, which are classic neurological characteristics of Alzheimer's disease.

Sister Mary taught full-time until she was 77 years old. Then for several years more she worked part-time as a math teacher and teacher's aide. She finally retired at 84, although she once commented that she never really retired: "I only retire at night."

Only 4 feet, 6 inches tall, and weighing only about 85 pounds, Sister Mary spent the last years of her life in the convent she had entered when she was a young girl. In her so-called retirement, she continued to give talks about various life and religious issues and to be active in the community. She was also an avid reader, often seen poring over newspapers and books with her magnifying glass.

Sister Mary was known for her great attitude. She had a wide smile and a warm, hearty laugh. When she asked her doctor if he was secretly giving her medicine to keep her alive and healthy, he replied that it was her wonderful attitude that was doing the trick.

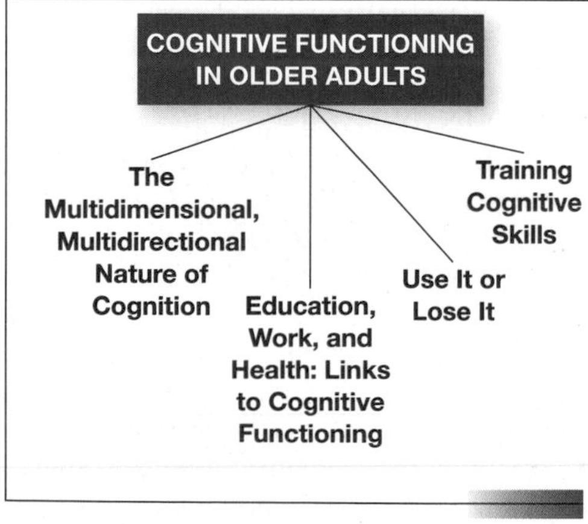

Cognitive Functioning in Older Adults

At the age of 70, John Rock invented the birth control pill. At age 76, Anna Mary Robertson Moses, better known as Grandma Moses, took up painting and became internationally famous, staging fifteen one-woman shows throughout Europe. At age 89, Arthur Rubinstein gave one of his best performances at New York's Carnegie Hall. When Pablo Casals was 95, a reporter asked him, "Mr. Casals, you are the greatest cellist who ever lived. Why do you still practice six hours a day?" Mr. Casals replied, "Because I feel like I am making progress" (Canfield & Hansen, 1995).

The Multidimensional, Multidirectional Nature of Cognition

In thinking about the nature of cognitive change in adulthood, it is important to consider that cognition is a multidimensional concept. It is also important to consider that while some dimensions of cognition might decline as we age, others might remain stable or even improve.

Cognitive Mechanics and Cognitive Pragmatics

Paul Baltes (1993, 1996, 2000) clarified the distinction between those aspects of the aging mind that show decline and those that remain stable or even improve. He makes a distinction between "cognitive mechanics" and "cognitive pragmatics." Using computer language as an analogy, **cognitive mechanics** *are the hardware of the mind and reflect the neurophysiological architecture of the brain developed through evolution. Cognitive mechanics involve the speed and accuracy of the processes involving sensory input, visual and motor memory, discrimination, comparison, and categorization.* Because of the strong influence of biology, heredity, and health on cognitive mechanics, their decline with aging is likely.

cognitive mechanics
The "hardware" of the mind, reflecting the neurophysiological architecture of the brain as developed through evolution. Cognitive mechanics involve speed and accuracy of the processes involving sensory input, visual and motor memory, discrimination, comparison, and categorization.

cognitive pragmatics
The culture-based "software" of the mind. Cognitive pragmatics include reading and writing skills, language comprehension, educational qualifications, professional skills, and also the type of knowledge about the self and life skills that help us to master or cope with life.

Conversely, **cognitive pragmatics** *are the culture-based software programs of the mind. Cognitive pragmatics include reading and writing skills, language comprehension, educational qualifications, professional skills, and also the type of knowledge about the self and life skills that help us to master or cope with life.* Because of the strong influence of culture on cognitive pragmatics, their improvement into old age is possible. Thus, while cognitive mechanics may decline in old age, cognitive pragmatics may actually improve (see figure 19.1).

Now that we have examined the distinction between cognitive mechanics and cognitive pragmatics, let's explore some of the more specific cognitive processes that reflect these two general domains, beginning with these aspects of cognitive mechanics: sensory/motor and speed of processing.

Sensory/Motor and Speed-of-Processing Dimensions

In the Berlin Study of Aging, the key factors that accounted for age differences in intelligence were visual and auditory acuity (Lindenberger & Baltes, 1994). Thus, sensory functioning was a strong late-life predictor of individual differences in intelligence. It is also now well accepted that the speed of processing information declines in late adulthood (Earles & Salthouse, 1995; Salthouse, 1996, 2000; Silwinski & Buschke, 1999).

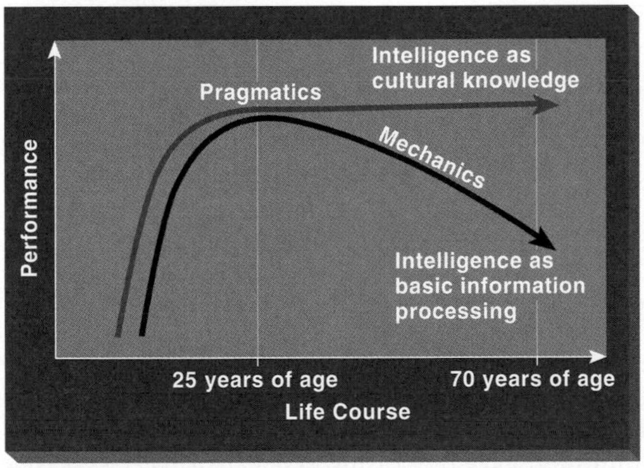

Figure **19.1**

Theorized Age Changes in Cognitive Mechanics and Cognitive Pragmatics

Baltes argues that cognitive mechanics decline during aging, whereas cognitive pragmatics do not. Cognitive mechanics have a biological/genetic foundation; cognitive pragmatics have an experiential/cultural foundation.

Although speed of processing information slows down in late adulthood, there is considerable individual variation in this ability. And it is not clear that this slowdown affects our lives in substantial ways. For example, in one experiment, the reaction time and typing skills of typists of varying ages were studied (Salthouse, 1984). The older typists usually had slower reactions, but they actually typed just as fast as the younger typists. Possibly the older typists were faster when they were younger and had slowed down, but the results in another condition suggested that something else was involved. When the number of characters that the typists could look ahead at was limited, the older typists slowed considerably; the younger typists were affected much less by this restriction. Thus, the older typists had learned to look farther ahead, allowing them to type as fast as their younger counterparts.

Memory

Memory does change during aging, but not all memory changes with age in the same way (Balota, Dolan, & Duchek, 2000; Luszcz & Bryan, 1999). The main dimensions of memory and aging that have been studied include episodic memory, semantic memory, cognitive resources (such as working memory and perceptual speed), memory beliefs, and noncognitive factors such as health education, and socioeconomic factors (Smith, 1996).

(a) Grandma Moses, known in her time as the "grand old lady of American art," took up painting at the age of 78 and continued to paint past her hundredth birthday. *(b)* Dr. Benjamin Spock, who became famous for his child-rearing advice, released his last book, *A Better World for Our Children,* in 1994 at the age of 89.

Episodic Memory **Episodic memory** *is the retention of information about the where and when of life's happenings* (Tulving, 2000). For example, what was it like when your younger sister or brother was born, what happened to you on your first date, what were you doing when you heard that the Persian Gulf War had begun, and what did you eat for breakfast this morning?

episodic memory The retention of information about the where and when of life's happenings.

Younger adults have better episodic memory than older adults. Older adults think that they can remember older events better than more recent events, typically reporting that they can remember what happened to them years ago but can't remember what they did yesterday. However, researchers consistently have found that, contrary to such self-reports, in older adults the older the memory, the less accurate it is. This has been documented in studies of memory for high school classmates, foreign language learned in school over the life span, names of grade school teachers, and autobiographical facts kept in diaries (Kausler, 1994; Smith, 1996).

Semantic Memory **Semantic memory** *is a person's knowledge about the world. It includes a person's fields of expertise (such as knowledge of chess, for a skilled chess player); general academic knowledge of the sort learned in school (such as knowledge of geometry), and "everyday knowledge" about meanings of words, famous individuals, important places, and common things (such as who Nelson Mandela and Mahatma Gandhi are). Semantic memory appears to be independent of an individual's personal identity with the past.* For example, you can access a fact—such as "Lima is the capital of Peru"—and not have the foggiest idea of when and where you learned it.

semantic memory A person's knowledge about the world—including a person's fields of expertise, general academic knowledge of the sort learned in school, and "everyday knowledge."

Does semantic memory decline during aging? Older adults do often take longer to retrieve semantic information, but usually they can ultimately retrieve it. For the most part, episodic memory declines more in older adults than semantic memory (Parkin & Walter, 1992).

Cognitive Resources: Working Memory and Perceptual Speed One view of memory suggests that a limited number of cognitive resources can be devoted to any cognitive task. Two important cognitive resource mechanisms are working memory and perceptual speed. **Working memory** *is the concept of short-term memory as a place for mental work. Working memory is like a mental "workbench" that allows*

working memory The concept currently used to describe short-term memory as a place for mental work. Working memory is like a "workbench" where individuals can manipulate and assemble information when making decisions, solving problems, and comprehending written and spoken language.

individuals to manipulate and assemble information when making decisions, solving problems, and comprehending written and spoken language (Baddeley, 2000). Researchers have found declines in working memory during the late adulthood years (Light, 2000; Light, Zelinski, & Moore, 1982; Oberauer & others, 2001; Salthouse, 1994, 2000).

Perceptual speed is another cognitive resource that has been studied by researchers on aging. Perceptual speed is the ability to perform simple perceptual-motor tasks such as deciding whether pairs of two-digit or two-letter strings are the same or different or the time required to step on the brakes when the car directly ahead stops. Perceptual speed shows considerable decline in late adulthood, and it is strongly linked with decline in working memory (Salthouse, 2000).

explicit memory
Memory of facts and experiences that individuals consciously know and can state.

implicit memory
Memory without conscious recollection; involves skills and routine procedures that are automatically performed.

Explicit and Implicit Memory Researchers also have found that aging is linked with changes in explicit memory. **Explicit memory** *is memory of facts and experiences that individuals consciously know and can state.* Explicit memory also is sometimes called declarative memory. Examples of explicit memory include being at a grocery store and remembering what you wanted to buy or recounting the events of a movie you have seen. **Implicit memory** *is memory without conscious recollection; it involves skills and routine procedures that are automatically performed.* Implicit memory is sometimes called procedural memory. Examples of implicit memory include unconsciously remembering how to drive a car, swing a golf club, or type on a computer.

Implicit memory is less likely to be adversely affected by aging than explicit memory (Schugens & others, 1997; Tulving, 2000). Thus, older adults are more likely to forget what items they wanted to buy at a grocery store (unless they wrote them down on a list and brought it with them) than they are to forget how to drive a car. Their perceptual speed might be slower in driving the car, but they remember how to do it.

Memory Beliefs An increasing number of studies are finding that people's beliefs about memory play an important role in their actual memory (Cavanaugh, 2000). That is, what people tell themselves about their ability to remember matters. For example, some older adults might believe that their memory and other cognitive skills are inadequate and therefore avoid learning how to use a computer or shy away from a training course in strategies for learning and retaining new information.

In one recent study, individuals with low anxiety about their memory skills and high self-efficacy regarding their use of memory in everyday contexts showed higher memory performance than their high-anxiety/low-self-efficacy counterparts (McDougall & others, 1999). Other researchers also are finding that positive or negative beliefs about one's memory skills are related to actual memory performance (Kwon, 1999). Some critics, though, argue that memory beliefs do not have a significant impact on memory (Schaie, 2000).

Noncognitive Factors Health, education, and socioeconomic status can influence an older adult's performance on memory tasks. Although such noncognitive factors as good health are associated with less memory decline in older adults, they do not eliminate memory decline.

One criticism of research on memory and aging is that it has relied primarily on laboratory tests of memory. The argument is that such tasks are contrived and do not represent the everyday cognitive tasks performed by older adults. If researchers used more everyday life memory tasks, would memory decline be found in older adults? A number of researchers have found that using more familiar tasks reduces age decrements in memory but does not eliminate them. Younger adults are better than older adults at remembering faces, routes through town, grocery items, and performed activities. In one recent study, young adults (20 to 40 years old) remembered news content in print, audio, and TV format better than old adults (60 to 80 years old) (Frieske & Park, 1999).

Cognitive Psychology Laboratory
Timothy Salthouse's Research

Conclusions About Memory and Aging Some, but not all, aspects of memory decline in older adults. The decline occurs primarily in episodic and working

memory, not in semantic memory. A decline in perceptual speed is associated with memory decline. Successful aging does not mean eliminating memory decline, but reducing it and adapting to it. As we will see later in this chapter, older adults can use certain strategies to reduce memory decline.

Older adults might not be as quick with their thoughts or behavior as younger adults, but wisdom may be an entirely different matter. This older woman shares the wisdom of her experiences with a classroom of children.

Wisdom Does wisdom, like good wine, improve with age? What is this thing we call "wisdom"? **Wisdom** *is expert knowledge about the practical aspects of life that permits excellent judgment about important matters.* This practical knowledge involves exceptional insight into human development and life matters, good judgment, and an understanding of how to cope with difficult life problems. Thus, wisdom, more than standard conceptions of intelligence, focuses on life's pragmatic concerns and human conditions (Baltes, Staudinger, & Smith, 1995; Baltes & Staudinger, 1998, 2000). This practical knowledge system can take many years to acquire, accumulating through intentional, planned experiences and accidental experiences. However, recent research has found no age differences in wisdom, with young adults showing as much wisdom as older adults (Baltes & Staudinger, 2000).

Wisdom involves solving practical problems. Fredda Blanchard-Fields (1996) reviewed the research on everyday problem solving in older adults. She concluded that, in contrast to research demonstrating a decline in older adults' ability to solve abstract problems, older adults' competency in problem solving is most evident in everyday types of situations.

Of course, not all older adults solve practical problems in competent ways. In one study, only 5 percent of adults' responses to life-planning problems were classified as wise, and the wise responses were equally distributed across the early, middle, and late adulthood years (Smith & Baltes, 1990).

wisdom
Expert knowledge about the practical aspects of life that permits excellent judgment about important matters.

Fredda Blanchard-Field's Research

Education, Work, and Health: Links to Cognitive Functioning

Education, work, and health are three important influences on the cognitive functioning of older adults. They are also three of the most important factors involved in understanding why cohort effects need to be taken into account in studying the cognitive functioning of older adults (P. 52).

With the ancient is wisdom; and in the length of days understanding.
Job 12:12

Education Successive generations in America's twentieth century have been better educated. Not only were today's older adults more likely to go to college when they were young adults than were their parents or grandparents, but more older adults are returning to college today to further their education than in past generations. Educational experiences are positively correlated with scores on intelligence tests and information processing tasks, such as memory (Verhaeghen, Marcoen, & Goossens, 1993).

Older adults might seek more education for a number of reasons. They might want to better understand the nature of their aging. They might want to learn more about the social and technological changes that have produced dramatic changes in their lives. They might want to discover relevant knowledge and to learn relevant skills to cope with societal and job demands in later life. They might recognize that they need further education to remain competitive and stay in the workforce. Earlier in this century, individuals made career choices in adolescence and young adulthood and never wavered from those choices throughout their adult years. Today, that is not always the pattern. Technological changes have meant that

Critical Thinking: A Challenging Intellectual Life in Old Age

MAINTAINING a challenging intellectual life through late adulthood has served many individuals well. In this text, we presented photographs and descriptions of Grandma Moses and Benjamin Spock to illustrate the cognitive capabilities of older adults. In one study, curiosity in older adults was related to their longevity (Swan & Carmelli, 1996). Curiosity was measured when the adults were 70 years of age. Five years later, the curious older adults were more likely to still be alive than their less curious counterparts.

Can you think of other older adults who have made significant contributions in late adulthood? One such African American is Gwendolyn Brooks (1917–2001), Pulitzer Prize–winning poet and novelist, who recently was awarded the highest honor given by the U.S. government for intellectual development in the humanities—National Endowment for the Humanities 1994 Jefferson Lectureship. Try to come up with the names and contributions of other older adults who, like Gwendolyn Brooks, have continued to make their intellectual mark on our society. Also spend some time reading about the lives of these individuals and evaluate how their intellectual interests contributed to their life satisfaction in old age.

some of the occupations of 15 years ago no longer exist. And some of today's occupations could not even be identified 15 years ago. Finally, older adults may seek more education to enhance their self-discovery and the leisure activities that will enable them to make a smoother adjustment to retirement.

Work Successive generations have also had work experiences that include a stronger emphasis on cognitively oriented labor. Our great-grandfathers and grandfathers were more likely to be manual laborers than were our fathers, who are more likely to be involved in cognitively oriented occupations. As the industrial society continues to be replaced by the information society, younger generations will have more experience in jobs that require considerable cognitive investment. The increased emphasis on information processing in jobs likely enhances an individual's intellectual abilities.

In one recent study, substantive complex work was linked with higher intellectual functioning in older adults (Schooler, Mulatu, & Oates, 1999). This research is consistent with findings in a wide range of disciplines, including animal-based neurobiology studies, which strongly suggest that exposure to complex environments increases intellectual functioning throughout the life course (Kempermann, Kuhn, & Gage, 1997).

> *It is always in season for the old to learn.*
>
> Aeschylus
> *Greek Playwright, 5th Century B.C.*

Health Successive generations have also been healthier in late adulthood as better treatments for a variety of illnesses (such as hypertension) have been developed. Many of these illnesses have a negative impact on intellectual performance (Hultsch, Hammer, & Small, 1993; Park, in press). In one study, hypertension was related to decreased performance on the WAIS (Wechsler Adult Intelligence Scale) by individuals over the age of 60 (Wilkie & Eisdorpher, 1971). In one recent study, physical health and physical activity were positively related to cognitive performance in older adults (Anstey & Smith, 1999). The older the population, the more persons with health problems. Thus, some of the decline in intellectual performance found for older adults is likely due to health-related factors rather than to age per se.

K. Warner Schaie (1994) concluded that some diseases are linked to cognitive dropoffs—these diseases include heart disease, diabetes, and high blood pressure. Schaie does not believe the diseases directly cause mental decline. Rather, the lifestyles of the individuals with the diseases might be the culprits. For example, overeating, inactivity, and stress are related to both physical and mental decay (Christensen & others, 1996).

In chapter 18, "Physical Development in Late Adulthood," we found that exercise is linked with longevity ◀ P. 542. Might exercise also help older adults think more clearly while they are living longer? In one recent study, 124 individuals 60 to 75 years of age whose primary activity was sitting around the house were tested for their level of aerobic endurance and their level of cognitive functioning (Kramer & others, 1999). Cognitive functioning was assessed by tasks on working memory, planning, and scheduling. Half the group was randomly assigned to engage in yoga-type stretching activities and the other half was randomly assigned to start walking three times a week. After 6 months, the walkers averaged a mile in 16 minutes, a minute faster than at the beginning, and the stretchers had become more flexible. When their cognitive functioning was retested after 6 months, the walkers scored up to 25 percent higher on the cognitive tests than the stretchers. Other researchers have found that aerobic exercise is related to improved memory and reasoning (Clarkson-Smith & Hartley, 1989). Walking or

any other aerobic exercise appears to get blood and oxygen pumping to the brain, which can help people think more clearly.

Related to the idea that health status is an important factor in the cognitive functioning of older adults is the **terminal drop hypothesis.** *It states that death is preceded by a decrease in cognitive functioning over approximately a 5-year period prior to death.* Thus, distance from death in a subsequently deceased population should be correlated with performance on tests of cognitive functioning if they were administered during the critical 5-year period (Riegel & Riegel, 1972). In investigations that compare older and younger adults, many more of the older adults than the younger adults are likely to be within 5 years of their death. The chronic diseases these older adults may have are likely to decrease their motivation, alertness, and energy to perform competently when they are given tests of cognitive functioning. Thus, the negative findings for older adults in some investigations that compare older adults with younger adults may be due in part to age from death rather than simply age from birth. One issue in considering terminal drop is in keeping with our emphasis on assessing a number of aspects of cognitive functioning rather than general intelligence alone. In one study, the terminal drop hypothesis was supported for tests of vocabulary, but not for numerical facility and perceptual speed (White & Cunningham, 1989).

terminal drop hypothesis
The hypothesis that death is preceded by a decrease in cognitive functioning over approximately a 5-year period prior to death.

Use It or Lose It

Changes in cognitive activity patterns might result in disuse and consequent atrophy of cognitive skills. This concept is captured in the adage "Use it or lose it." In a recent analysis of participants in the Victoria Longitudinal Study, when middle-aged and older adults participated in intellectually engaging activities it served to buffer them against cognitive decline (Hultsch & others, 1999). This also was found in another longitudinal study over a 45-year time frame (Arbuckle & others, 1998).

According to cognitive aging expert Marilyn Albert (1999), the mental activities that likely benefit the maintenance of cognitive skills in older adults are reading books, doing crossword puzzles, and going to lectures and concerts.

Training Cognitive Skills

If cognitive skills are atrophying in late adulthood, can they be retrained? There are essentially two main conclusions that can be derived from research: (1) There is plasticity, and training can improve the cognitive skills of many older adults; and (2) there is some loss in plasticity in late adulthood (Baltes, 1995).

As evidence of plasticity and the effectiveness of cognitive training, Sherry Willis and K. Warner Schaie (1986) studied approximately 400, adults, most of whom were older adults. Using individualized training, they improved the spatial orientation and reasoning skills of two-thirds of the adults. Nearly 40 percent of those whose abilities had declined returned to a level they had reached 14 years earlier.

Mnemonics can also be used to improve older adults' cognitive skills. **Mnemonics** *are techniques designed to make memory more efficient.* In the fifth century B.C., the Greek poet Simonides attended a banquet. After he left, the building collapsed, crushing the guests and maiming their bodies beyond recognition. Simonides was able to

mnemonics
Techniques designed to make memory more efficient.

Careers in Life-Span Development

Sherry Willis, Professor of Human Development and Researcher

Sherry Willis obtained her Ph.D. from the University of Texas at Austin and has been a professor of human development at Pennsylvania State University since 1972. She is one of the leading experts on cognitive development in adults. Sherry has shown that older adults can be trained to improve their reasoning ability. She especially believes it is important for adults to use their cognitive abilities and believes that maintaining an active mental life is important.

Sherry Willis, Professor of Human Development and Researcher (*right*), assessing the cognitive skills of aging adults.

Although the memory of older adults may show some decline, some activities can be used to improve their memory. *What kind of strategies can older adults use to retain or improve their memory?*

identify the bodies using a memory technique. He generated vivid images of each individual and pictured where they had sat at the banquet. The *method of loci,* Simonides' technique, was used in one study to improve the memory of older adults (Kliegl & Baltes, 1987). The method of loci involved practice with a map of forty Berlin landmarks. The older adults were also trained to use *chunking*—organizing items into meaningful or manageable units—to improve their memory of Berlin landmarks. Strategies for remembering telephone numbers, Social Security numbers, and license plate numbers are common examples of how chunking can help people remember large amounts of information in our everyday lives.

Using the method of loci and chunking, the elderly adults could recall more than 32 of the 40 Berlin landmarks. Later they were able to apply what they had learned in their method of loci and chunking training to recall long lists of digits. One 69-year-old woman correctly recalled 120 digits presented in intervals of eights. Such results suggest substantial memory capacity in healthy, mentally fit older adults. In another study, the method of loci was again effective in improving the memory of older adults (Kliegl, Smith, & Baltes, 1990). In yet another study, older adults benefited from mnemonic instruction, but not as much as younger adults (Verhaeghen & Marcoen, 1996).

In a 7-year-longitudinal study, Sherry Willis and Carolyn Nesselroade (1990) examined the effectiveness of cognitive training on the maintenance of fluid intelligence with advancing age (recall from chapter 16 that fluid intelligence involves the ability to reason abstractly). The older adults were taught strategies for identifying the rule or pattern required in problem solutions. Adults in their seventies and eighties performed at a higher level than they had in their late sixties following the cognitive training, which consisted of the trainer modeling the use of correct strategies in solving tasks, individual practice on training items, feedback about correct solutions of practice problems, and group discussion.

In a recent study, cognitive training helped remediate cognitive decline in elderly adults and enhanced the performance of individuals who were not showing decline (Saczynski, Willis, & Schaie, 1999). In this study, leisure activities and more time spent in communication were linked with positive cognitive training effects.

At this point, we have discussed a number of ideas about cognitive functioning in late adulthood. A summary of these ideas is presented in summary table 19.1.

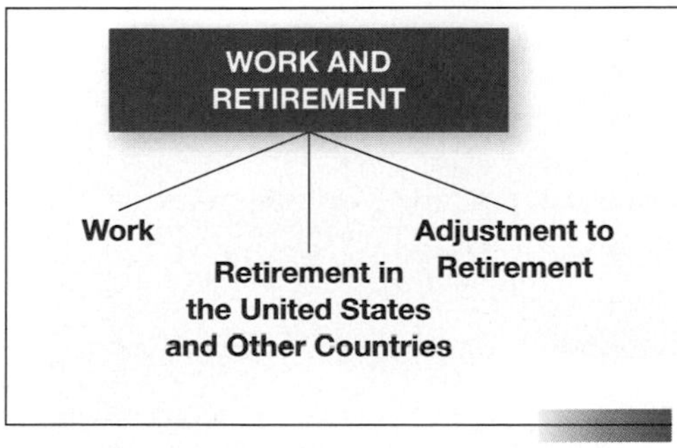

Work and Retirement

What percentage of older adults continue to work? How productive are they? Who adjusts best to retirement? What is the changing pattern of retirement in the United States and around the world? These are some of the questions we now examine.

Work

In the beginning of the twenty-first century, the percentage of men over the age of 65 who continue to work full-time is less than at the beginning of the twentieth century. The decline from 1900 to 2000 has been as much as 70 percent. An important change in older adults' work patterns is the increase in part-time work (Elder & Pavalko, 1993). The percentage of older adults who work part-time has steadily increased since 1960s. Aging and work expert James House (1998) believes that many middle-aged workers would like to do less paid work while many older adults would like to do more.

Summary Table 19.1

Cognitive Functioning in Older Adults

Concept	Processes/ Related Ideas	Characteristics/Descriptions
The Multidimensional, Multidirectional Nature of Cognition	Cognitive Mechanics and Cognitive Pragmatics	• Baltes emphasizes a distinction between cognitive mechanics (the neurophysiological architecture, including the brain) and cognitive pragmatics (the culture-based software of the mind). • Cognitive mechanics are more likely to decline in older adults than are cognitive pragmatics.
	Sensory/Motor and Speed of Processing Dimensions	• Researchers have found that these dimensions decline in older adults.
	Memory	• Younger adults have better episodic memory than older adults. Regarding semantic memory, older adults have more difficulty retrieving semantic information, but they usually can eventually retrieve it. • Researchers have found declines in working memory and perceptual speed in older adults. • Older adults are more likely to show declines in explicit than in implicit memory. • An increasing number of studies are finding that people's beliefs about memory play an important role in their memory performance. • Noncognitive factors such as health, education, and socioeconomic status are linked with memory in older adults.
	Wisdom	• Wisdom is expert knowledge about the practical aspects of of life that permits excellent judgments about important matters. • Although theorists propose that older adults have more wisdom, researchers usually find that younger adults show as much wisdom as older adults.
Education, Work, and Health: Links to Cognitive Functioning	Education	• Successive generations of Americans have been better educated. • Education is positively correlated with scores on intelligence tests. Older adults may return to education for a number of reasons.
	Work	• Successive generations have had work experiences that include a stronger emphasis on cognitively oriented labor. • The increased emphasis on information processing in jobs likely enhances an individual's intellectual abilities.
	Health	• Poor health is related to decreased performance on intelligence tests in older adults. • Exercise is linked to higher cognitive functioning in older adults. • The terminal drop hypothesis states that death is preceded by a decrease in cognitive functioning over a 5-year period prior to death.
Use It or Lose It	Use and Disuse	• Researchers are finding that older adults who engage in cognitive activities, especially challenging ones, have higher cognitive functioning that those who don't use their cognitive skills.
Training Cognitive Skills	Its Nature	• There are two main conclusions that can be derived from research on training cognitive skills in older adults: (1) There is plasticity, and training can improve the cognitive skills of many older adults; and (2) there is some loss in plasticity in late adulthood.

Some individuals maintain their productivity throughout their lives. Some of these older workers work as many or more hours than younger workers. In the National Longitudinal Survey of Older Men, good health, a strong psychological commitment to work, and a distaste for retirement were the most important characteristics related to continued employment into old age (seventies and eighties) (Parnes & Sommers, 1994). The probability of employment also was positively correlated with educational attainment and being married to a working wife.

Especially important to think about is the large cohort of baby boomers—78 million people who will begin to reach traditional retirement age in 2010. Because this cohort is so large, we are likely to see increasing numbers of older adults continue to work (Yeats, Folts, & Knapp, 1999).

Cognitive ability is one of the best predictors of job performance in the elderly (Park, in press). And older workers have lower rates of absenteeism, fewer accidents, and increased job satisfaction, compared with their younger counterparts (Warr, 1994). This means that the older worker can be of considerable value to a company, above and beyond the older worker's cognitive competence. Changes in federal law now allow individuals over the age of 65 to continue working. Also, remember from our discussion earlier in the chapter that substantively complex work is linked with a higher level of intellectual functioning (Schooler, Mulatu, & Oates, 1999). This likely is a reciprocal relation; that is, individuals with higher cognitive ability likely continue to work as older adults, and when they work in substantively complex jobs, this likely enhances their intellectual functioning (Schooler, 2001).

Age and Discrimination in Employment
Exploring Mandatory Retirement
Working Options
Volunteering and Older Adults

An increasing number of middle-aged and older adults are embarking on a second or a third career (Moon & Wethington, 1999). In some cases, this is an entirely different type of work or a continuation of previous work but at a reduced level. Many older adults also participate in unpaid work—as a volunteer or as an active participant in a voluntary association. These options afford older adults opportunities for productive activity, social interaction, and a positive identity.

Ninety-two-year-old Russell "Bob" Harrell *(right)* puts in 12-hour days at Sieco Consulting Engineers in Columbus, Indiana. A highway and bridge engineer, he designs and plans roads. James Rice (age 48), a vice president of client services at Sieco, says that "Bob" wants to learn something new every day and that he has learned many life lessons from being around him. Harrell says he is not planning on retiring. *What are some variations in work and retirement in older adults?*

Significant numbers of retirees only partially retire, moving to part-time employment by either reducing the number of hours they work on their career jobs or by taking on new (and frequently lower-paying) jobs (Han & Moen, 1998). Self-employed men are especially likely to continue paid employment, either on the same job or on a new job. Nearly one-third of the men who take on a part-time job do not do so until 2 years after their retirement (Burkhauser & Quinn, 1989).

In a recent survey, 80 percent of baby boomers said that they expect to work during the retirement years (Roper Starch Worldwide, 2000). The main reason they plan to work when they get older is to engage in part-time work for interest or enjoyment (35 percent), followed by income (23 percent), desire to start a business (17 percent), and the desire to try a different field of work (5 percent). In another recent survey, nearly 70 percent of current employees said that they expect to work for pay once they retire, mainly because they enjoy working and want to stay active and involved (Anthony Greenwald & Associates, 2000).

In summary, age affects many aspects of work (Cleveland & Shore, 1996). Nonetheless, many studies of work and aging—such as evaluation of hiring and performance—reveal inconsistent results. Important contextual factors, such as age composition of departments or applicant pools, occupations, and jobs, all affect decisions about older workers. It also is important to recognize that agist stereotypes of workers and of tasks can limit older workers' career opportunities and can encourage early retirement or other forms of downsizing that adversely affect older workers.

SOCIOCULTURAL WORLDS OF DEVELOPMENT
Work and Retirement in Japan, the United States, England, and France

ARE A LARGER percentage of older adults in Japan in the labor force than in the United States and other industrialized countries? What are the attitudes of older Japanese adults toward work and retirement compared to their counterparts in other industrialized countries? To answer these questions, the Japanese Prime Minister's Office conducted national surveys of adults 60 years of age and older in four industrialized nations—Japan, the United States, England, and France. A much larger percentage of the men over 60 in Japan were in the labor force (57 percent) than in the United States (33 percent), England (13 percent), and France (8 percent).

When asked, "What do you think is the best age to retire?" a majority of the older men in England and France said 60 years of age. In sharp contrast, only 14 percent of the older men in Japan and 16 percent of the older men in the United States chose such an early age to retire. Another question the older men in the four countries were asked was, "Where should an older person's income come from?" In Japan and the United States, the proportion of older men who favored saving while working was at least twice that advising reliance on social security. In contrast, older adult men in France and England favored reliance on social security.

The marked differences in the rate of employment among those over 60 in Japan and the United States, compared to England and France, are mainly due to attitudes and values about work, and about reliance on oneself (and on relatives, in the case of Japan) rather than on the government and its social security system.

Retirement in the United States and Other Countries

A retirement option for older workers is a late-twentieth-century phenomenon in America (Atchley, 1996). Recall from our earlier discussion that a much higher percentage of older Americans worked full-time in the early 1900s than today. The Social Security system, which establishes benefits for older workers when they retire, was implemented in 1935. On the average, today's workers will spend 10 to 15 percent of their lives in retirement.

In 1967, the Age Discrimination Act made it a federal policy to prohibit the firing of employees because of their age before they reach the mandatory retirement age. In 1978, Congress extended the mandatory retirement age from 65 to 70 in business, industry, and the federal government. In 1986, Congress voted to ban mandatory retirement for all but a few occupations, such as police officer, firefighter, and airline pilot, where safety is an issue. Federal law now prohibits employers from firing older workers, who have seniority and higher salaries, just to save money. As mandatory retirement continues to lessen, older workers will face the decision of when to retire rather than be forced into retirement.

Although the United States has extended the retirement age upward, early retirement continues to be followed in large numbers. In many European countries—both capitalist and former Communist bloc—officials have experimented with various financial inducements designed to reduce or control unemployment by encouraging the retirement of older workers. West Germany, Sweden, Great Britain, Italy, France, Czechoslovakia, Hungary, and Russia are among the nations that are moving toward earlier retirement. Nonetheless, currently in the Netherlands, there is an effort to recruit retired persons to reenter the workforce because of low unemployment in the country. More information about cultural variations in retirement appears in the Sociocultural Worlds of Development box.

AARP
Exploring Retirement
Baby Boomers and Retirement
Health and Retirement

Adjustment to Retirement

Who adjusts best to retirement? Older adults who adjust best to retirement are healthy, have adequate income, are active, are better educated, have an extended social network including both friends and family, and usually were satisfied with their lives before they retired (Gall, Evans, & Howard, 1997; Moen & Quick, 1998; Palmore & others, 1985). Older adults with inadequate income and poor health, and who must adjust to other stress that occurs at the same time as retirement, such as the death of a spouse, have the most difficult time adjusting to retirement (Stull & Hatch, 1984).

Flexibility is also a key factor in whether individuals adjust well to retirement. When people retire, they no longer have the structured environment they had when they were working, so they need to be flexible and discover and pursue their own interests (Eisdorfer, 1996). Cultivating interests and friends unrelated to work improves adaptation to retirement (Zarit & Knight, 1996).

Individuals who view retirement planning only in terms of finances don't adapt as well to retirement as those who have a more balanced retirement plan (Birren, 1996). It is important not only to plan financially for retirement, but to consider other areas of your life as well (Choi, 2001). What are you going to do with your leisure time? What are you going to do to stay active? What are you going to do socially? What are you going to do to keep your mind active?

Individuals who retire involuntarily are more unhealthy, depressed, and poorly adjusted than those who retire voluntarily (Swan, 1996). Options for control and self-determination are important aspects of older adults' mental health, the topic of our next section. Before we turn to that section, though, you can review our discussion of work and retirement by reading summary table 19.2.

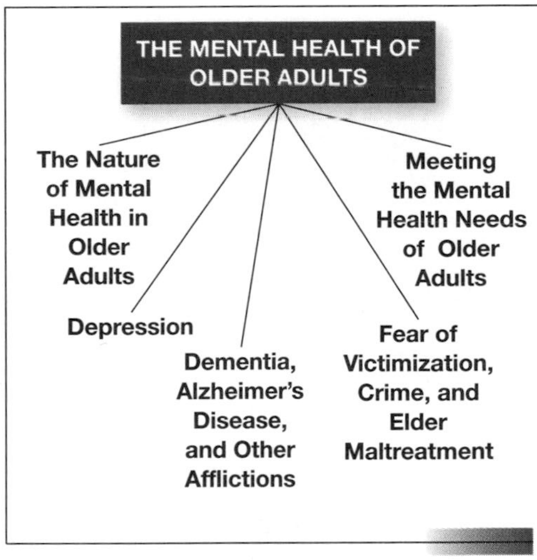

The Mental Health of Older Adults

What is the nature of mental health among older adults? What are the common mental health problems? What are the most effective mental health treatments for older adults?

The Nature of Mental Health in Older Adults

Although a substantial portion of the population can now look forward to a longer life, that life may unfortunately be hampered by a mental disorder in old age (Baltes & Horgas, 1998; Smyer & Qualls, 1996). This prospect is both troubling to the individual and costly to society. Mental disorders make individuals increasingly dependent on the help and care of others. The cost of mental health disorders in older adults is estimated at more than $40 billion per year in the United States. More important than the loss in dollars, though, is the loss of human potential and the suffering (Burns, Roth, & Christie, 1996). Although mental disorders in older adults are a major concern, older adults do not have a higher incidence of mental disorders than younger adults (Busse & Blazer, 1996).

Depression

major depression
A mood disorder in which the individual is deeply unhappy, demoralized, self-derogatory, and bored. The person does not feel well, loses stamina easily, has poor appetite, and is listless and unmotivated. Major depression is so widespread that it has been called the "common cold" of mental disorders.

Major depression *is a mood disorder in which the individual is deeply unhappy, demoralized, self-derogatory, and bored. The individual with major depression does not feel well, loses stamina easily, has a poor appetite, and is listless and unmotivated.* Major depression has been called the "common cold" of mental disorders. Estimates of depression's frequency among older adults vary, although there is no evidence that depression is more common in older adults than in younger adults (Callahan & Wolinsky, 1995). Among the most common predictors of depression in older adults are earlier depressive symptoms, poor health, loss events such as death of a spouse, and low social

Summary Table 19.2
Work and Retirement

Concept	Processes/ Related Ideas	Characteristics/Descriptions
Work	History and Change	• Today, the percentage of men over 65 who continue to work full-time is less than at the beginning of the twentieth century. • An important change in older adults' work patterns is the increase in part-time work. • Some individuals continue a life of strong work productivity throughout late adulthood.
Retirement in the United States and Other Countries	United States	• A retirement option for older workers is a late-twentieth-century phenomenon in the United States. The United States has extended the mandatory retirement age upward, and efforts have been made to reduce age discrimination in work-related circumstances.
	Cross-Cultural Comparisons	• While the United States has moved toward increasing the age for retirement, many European countries have lowered it.
Adjustment to Retirement	Its Nature	• Individuals who are healthy, have adequate income, are active, are better educated, have an extended social network of friends and family, and are satisfied with their lives before they retire adjust best to retirement.

support (Gatz, 1989). In one longitudinal study, widows showed elevated depressive symptoms up to 2 years following the death of a spouse (Turvey & others, 1999). In this longitudinal study, depression was likely to increase as older adults' health worsened (Fonda & Norgard, 1999). However, good social support and being socially integrated in the community helped to buffer the effects of declining health on depression in these individuals.

Depression is a treatable condition, not only in young adults but in older adults as well (Haynie & others, 2001). Unfortunately, as many as 80 percent of older adults with depressive symptoms receive no treatment at all. Combinations of medications and psychotherapy produce significant improvement in almost 4 out of 5 elderly adults with depression (Koenig & Blazer, 1996).

Major depression can result in not only sadness, but also suicidal tendencies. Nearly 25 percent of individuals who commit suicide in the United States are 65 years of age or older (Church, Siegel, & Fowler, 1988). The older adult most likely to commit suicide is a male who lives alone, has lost his spouse, and is experiencing failing health.

Dementia, Alzheimer's Disease, and Other Afflictions

Among the most debilitating of mental disorders in older adults are the dementias (Santacruz & Swagerty, 2001; Zarit & Downs, 1999). In recent years, extensive attention has been focused on the most common dementia, Alzheimer's disease. Other afflictions common in older adults are multi-infarct dementia and Parkinson's disease.

Dementia Web

Exploring Dementia

Dementia Research and Treatment

Dementia Caregivers

Dementia **Dementia** *is a global term for any neurological disorder in which the primary symptoms involve a deterioration of mental functioning.* Individuals with dementia often lose the ability to care for themselves and can lose the ability to recognize familiar surroundings and people (including family members) (Epstein & Connor, 1999; Hawranik & Strain, 2001; Laurin & others, 2001).

dementia
A global term for any neurological disorder in which the primary symptoms involve a deterioration of mental functioning.

(a) (b) (c)

Famous individuals who developed Alzheimer's disease: *(a)* Former president Ronald Reagan was diagnosed with the disorder at age 83; *(b)* actress Rita Hayworth died of Alzheimer's at age 68—her struggle focused attention on the disease; and *(c)* World Champion boxer Sugar Ray Robinson had Alzheimer's when he died at age 67.

It is estimated that 20 percent of individuals over the age of 80 years of age have dementia. More than seventy types or causes of dementia have been identified (Skoog, Blennow, & Marcusson, 1996).

The most common form of dementia is **Alzheimer's disease,** *a progressive, irreversible disorder that is characterized by gradual deterioration of memory, reasoning, language, and eventually physical functioning.* More than 50 percent of dementias involve Alzheimer's disease. Approximately 10 to 20 percent of dementias stem from vascular disease (Epstein & Connor, 1999).

Alzheimer's disease
A progressive, irreversible brain disorder characterized by a gradual deterioration of memory, reasoning, language, and, eventually, physical function.

Alzheimer's.com
Alzheimer's Resources
Alzheimer's Disease and Education Center

Alzheimer's Disease

Approximately 2.5 million people over the age of 65 in the United States have Alzheimer's disease. It has been predicted that Alzheimer's disease could triple in the next 50 years, as increasing numbers of people live to older ages. Because of the increasing prevalence of Alzheimer's disease, researchers have stepped up their efforts to discover the causes of the disease and find more effective ways to treat it (Bonde & Lange, 1998; Davis, 1999).

Because of differences in onset, Alzheimer's also is now described as *early-onset* (initially occurring in individuals younger than 65 years of age) or *late-onset* (which has its initial onset in individuals 65 years of age and older). Early-onset Alzheimer's disease is rare (about 10 percent of all cases) and generally affects people 30 to 60 years of age.

As Alzheimer's disease progresses, the brain deteriorates and shrinks. Figure 19.2 provides a comparison of the normally aging brain of a healthy individual and the brain of an individual with Alzheimer's disease.

Causes and Treatments

Alzheimer's disease is currently perceived as a puzzle with many pieces (Siegfried, 1995). For a number of years, scientists have tried to discover which piece of the puzzle is the cause of Alzheimer's disease. Today some scientists argue that the best strategy might be not to search for a single cause of Alzheimer's but to discover how to put all of the pieces together.

Alzheimer's disease was first diagnosed in 1906 by the German doctor Alois Alzheimer, but serious research on the disease did not begin until the 1950s, as Alzheimer's became more clearly distinguished from other types of dementia. In the 1970s, it was discovered that Alzheimer's involves a deficiency in the important brain messenger chemical acetylcholine, which plays an important role in memory

(Hodges, 2000). Aricept is the main drug currently used to treat Alzheimer's, and it works by blocking chemicals that ordinarily cut acetylcholine apart.

Efforts to identify the cause of Alzheimer's have not yet been successful. What scientists now believe is that Alzheimer's disease is a complex unraveling of neural structure and function that likely involves many different molecular and cellular dimensions (Smith & others, 1995).

Alzheimer's disease might have a genetic basis in some individuals. ApoE4, an abnormal gene on chromosome 19, results in excess levels of a blood protein that carries cholesterol through the body. It has been estimated that the ApoE4 gene could play a role in as many as one-third of the cases of Alzheimer's disease. ApoE4 is associated with plaque formation in individuals with Alzheimer's disease (Holtzmann & others, 1999).

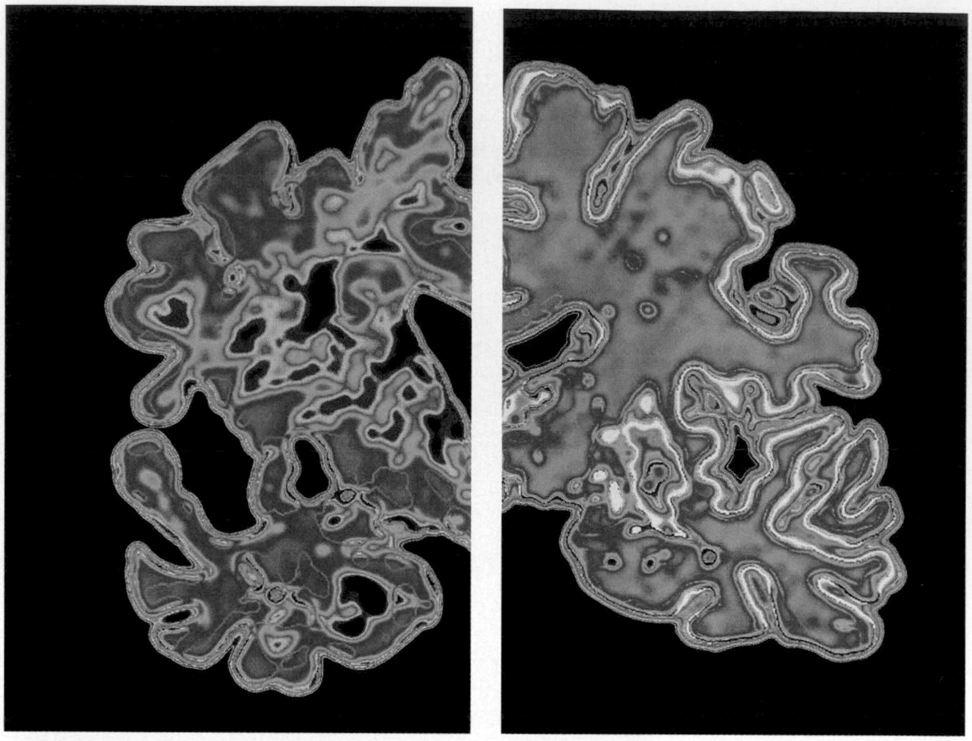

Figure 19.2

Two Brains: Normal Aging and Alzheimer's Disease

The brain image on the left is from a brain ravaged by Alzheimer's disease. The brain image on the right is from a brain of a normal aging individual. Notice the deterioration and shrinking in the Alzheimer's brain.

One of the main characteristics of Alzheimer's disease is the increasing number of *tangles* (tied bundles of protein that impair the functioning of neurons) and *plaques* (deposits that accumulate in the brain's blood vessels). In the Images of Life-Span Development section at the beginning of this chapter, we described how Sister Mary was functioning quite well despite having tangles and plaques in her brain. The formation of tangles and plaques is a normal part of aging. However, in Alzheimer's disease these are much more pervasive.

Early Detection of Alzheimer's Disease Special brain scans, such as MRI (magnetic resonance imaging) can detect changes in the brain that are fairly typical of early Alzheimer's disease even before symptoms develop (Weatherford, 1999). In addition, certain spinal fluids give early signals of Alzheimer's disease. Recently a sophisticated urine test called the neural thread protein test has predicted the occurrence of Alzheimer's in some individuals 2 years before symptoms (such as memory loss) appeared. When positive, the urine test allows preventive measures to be initiated that delay the cognitive decline of Alzheimer's disease.

Stages There is a predictable, progressive decline in physical, cognitive, and social functioning when individuals have Alzheimer's disease (Morris & others, 2001). Most Alzheimer's patients, once diagnosed, live approximately 8 years and progress from early problems of memory loss and declining intellectual function to later stages in which hospitalization in a near vegetative state ensues (Weatherford, 1999). Figure 19.3 shows the main characteristics of Alzheimer's disease at different points of disease progression and the accompanying diagnosis.

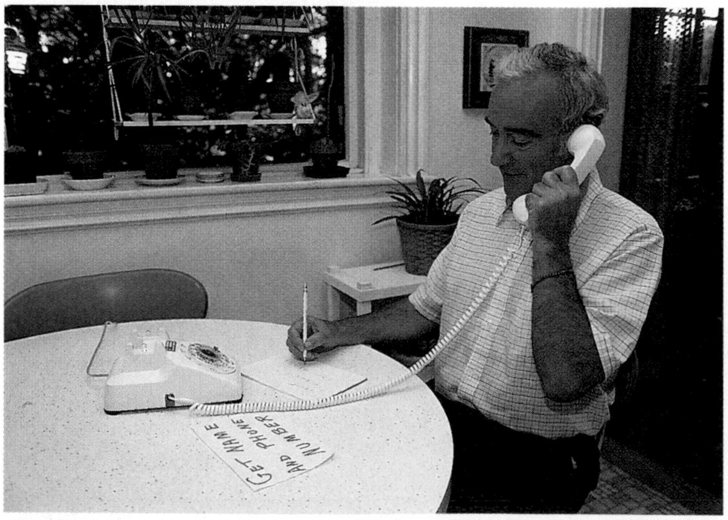

Memory loss is a common characteristic of Alzheimer's disease. Written reminders, like those shown here, can help individuals with Alzheimer's remember daily tasks.

Stage	Characteristics	Diagnosis
Stage 1	No complaints about memory and no evidence of memory deficits when interviewed.	Normal
Stage 2	Complaints of memory deficit, most often when forgetting where familiar objects have been placed and forgetting names of people formerly known well.	Normal for age
Stage 3	Clear-cut deficits in memory appear; for example, word- and name-finding deficits become more apparent, and the person might read a passage in a book and retain little of the information. Many individuals do not deteriorate any further than this pre-Alzheimer's stage and thus do not develop the disease.	Possible incipient Alzheimer's disease
Stage 4	Decreased knowledge of current and recent events; decreased ability to travel, handle finances, and so on; inability to perform complex tasks; flattening of affect and withdrawal from challenging situations.	Mild Alzheimer's disease
Stage 5	Individuals can no longer survive without some assistance, cannot recall a major relevant aspect of their current lives during an interview (such as their telephone number, address, or names of close relatives, (such as grandchildren).	Moderate Alzheimer's disease
Stage 6	Might occasionally forget the name of their spouse, are largely unaware of all recent events and experiences in their lives, generally are unaware of their surroundings, and require some assistance for daily living. They might become delusional, show obsessive behavior, and display anxiety, agitation, and apathy.	Moderately severe Alzheimer's disease
Stage 7	All verbal abilities are lost, and frequently there is no speech at all, only grunting. They require assistance in eating and toileting. They also lose their basic motor skills, such as the ability to walk.	Severe Alzheimer's disease

Figure **19.3**

Stages in the Progression of Alzheimer's Disease

Caring for Individuals with Alzheimer's Disease A special concern is caring for Alzheimer's patients. Psychologists believe that the family can be an important support system for the Alzheimer's patient, but this support can have costs for the family, who can become emotionally and physically drained by the extensive care required for a person with Alzheimer's (Lefley, 1996; Yale, 1999). For example, depression has been reported in 50 percent of family caregivers for Alzheimer's patients (Redinbaugh, MacCallum, & Kiecolt-Glaser, 1995). Respite care has been developed to help people who have to meet the day-to-day needs of Alzheimer's patients. This type of care provides an important break away from the burden of providing chronic care.

Multi-Infarct Dementia **Multi-infarct dementia** *involves a sporadic and progressive loss of intellectual functioning caused by repeated temporary obstruction of blood flow in cerebral arteries.* The result is a series of mini-strokes. The term *infarct* refers to the temporary obstruction of blood vessels. It is estimated that 15 to 25 percent of dementias involve the vascular impairment of multi-infarct dementia.

multi-infarct dementia
Sporadic and progressive loss of intellectual functioning caused by repeated temporary obstruction of blood flow in cerebral arteries.

Multi-Infarct Dementia
National Parkinson Foundation
World Parkinson Disease Foundation
Resources for Parkinson's Disease
Stages in Parkinson's Disease

Multi-infarct dementia is more common among men with a history of high blood pressure. The clinical picture of multi-infarct dementia is different than for Alzheimer's disease, many patients recover from multi-infarct dementia, whereas Alzheimer's disease shows a progressive deterioration. The symptoms of multi-infarct dementia include confusion, slurring of speech, writing impairment, and numbness on one side of the face, arm, or leg (Hoyer, Rybash, & Roodin, 1999). However, after each occurrence, there usually a rather quick recovery, although each succeeding occurrence is usually more damaging. Approximately 35 to 50 percent of individuals who have these transient attacks will have a major stroke within 5 years unless the underlying problems are treated. Especially recommended for these individuals are exercise, improved diet, and appropriate drugs, which can slow or stop the progression of the underlying vascular disease.

Parkinson's Disease Another dementia is **Parkinson's disease,** *a chronic, progressive disease characterized by muscle tremors, slowing of movement, and partial facial paralysis.* Parkinson's disease is triggered by degeneration of dopamine-producing neurons in the brain. Dopamine is a neurotransmitter that is necessary for normal brain functioning. Why these neurons degenerate is not known. The main treatment for Parkinson's disease involves the drug L-dopa, which is converted by the brain into dopamine. However, it is difficult to determine the correct level of dosage of this drug, and too much of it can produce schizophrenic symptoms.

Parkinson's disease
A chronic, progressive disease characterized by muscle tremors, slowing of movement, and partial facial paralysis.

Now that we have explored the nature of dementia, let's turn our attention to another problem that many elderly face: the fear of victimization and crime.

Muhammed Ali, one of the world's leading sports figures, has Parkinson's disease.

Fear of Victimization, Crime, and Elder Maltreatment

Some of the physical decline and limitations that characterize development in late adulthood contribute to a sense of vulnerability and fear among older adults. For some elderly adults, the fear of crime may become a deterrent to travel, attendance at social events, and the pursuit of an active lifestyle. Almost one-fourth of older adults say they have a basic fear of being the victim of a crime. However, in reality, possibly because of the precautions they take, older adults are less likely than younger adults to be the victim of a crime. However, the crimes committed against the elderly are likely to be serious offenses, such as armed robbery (Cohn & Harlow, 1993). The elderly are also victims of nonviolent crimes such as fraud, vandalism, purse snatching, and harassment. Estimates of the incidence of crimes against the elderly may be low because older adults may not report crimes, fearing retribution from criminals or believing the criminal justice system cannot help them.

Elder maltreatment can be perpetrated by anyone, but it is primarily carried out by family members. As with child maltreatment, elder maltreatment can involve neglect or physical abuse. The elderly are most often abused by their spouses. A special concern is the burden older women carry in facing possible physical violence. In one study of 614 cases of abuse in Hillsborough County, Florida, 37 percent involved physical assault, most of the abused were women, they were most likely to be living with their spouse, and they were

Exploring Elder Abuse
Elder Abuse Resources

Careers in Life-Span Development

Jan Weaver, Director of the Alzheimer's Association of Dallas

Dr. Jan Weaver joined the Alzheimer's Association, Greater Dallas Chapter, as Director of Services and Education in 1999. Prior to that time, she served as associate director of education for the Texas Institute for Research and Education on Aging and director of the National Academy for Teaching and Learning About Aging at the University of North Texas. As a gerontologist, Dr. Weaver plans and develops services and educational programs that address patterns of human development related to aging. Among the services of the Alzheimer's Association that Jan supervises are a resource center and helpline, a family assistance program, a care program, support groups, referal and information, educational conferences, and community seminars.

Dr. Weaver recognizes that people of all ages should have an informed and balanced view of older adults that helps them perceive aging as a process of growth and fulfillment rather than a process of decline and dependency. Her recent publications include editing a special issue of *Educational Gerontology,* published in 1999, that addresses the importance of aging education throughout the life span. Dr. Weaver earned her Ph.D. in sociology, with an emphasis in gerontology, from the University of North Texas in 1996.

Jan Weaver, giving a lecture on Alzheimer's disease.

most likley to be over 60 years of age (VandeWeerd & Paveza, 1999). The perpetrators were most likely to be male spouses. Elderly women also were more likely than elderly men to suffer property damage and robbery, but in these cases the perpetrator was most likely to be a young male (18 to 29 years of age) who was not related to the victim.

Meeting the Mental Health Needs of Older Adults

Older adults receive disproportionately fewer mental health services (Sadovy & others, 1996). One estimate is that only 2.7 percent of all clinical services provided by psychologists go to older adults, although individuals aged 65 and over make up more than 11 percent of the population. The proportion of community mental health services rendered to older adults has remained relatively stable—at or about 4 percent in the 1970s and 1980s (Lebowitz, 1987).

Psychotherapy can be expensive. Although reduced fees and sometimes no fee can be arranged in public hospitals for older adults from low-income backgrounds, many older adults who need psychotherapy do not get it (Knight & others, 1996). It has been said that psychotherapists like to work with young, attractive, verbal, intelligent, and successful clients (called YAVISes) rather than those who are quiet, ugly, old, institutionalized, and different (called QUOIDs). Psychotherapists have been accused of failing to see older adults because they perceive that older adults have a poor prognosis for therapy success, they do not feel they have adequate training to treat older adults, who may have special problems requiring special treatment, and they may have stereotypes that label older adults as low-status and unworthy recipients of treatment (Knight & others, 1996; Sarason & Sarason, 1996).

There are many different types of mental health treatment available to older adults. Some common mechanisms of change that improve the mental health of older adults are (Gatz, 1989): (1) fostering a sense of control, self-efficacy, and hope; (2) establishing a relationship with a helper; (3) providing or elucidating a sense of meaning; and (4) promoting educative activities and the development of skills.

How can we better meet the mental health needs of the elderly? First, psychologists must be encouraged to include more older adults in their client lists, and the elderly must be convinced that they can benefit from therapy. Second, we must make mental health care affordable: Medicare currently pays lower percentages for mental health care than for physical health care, for example.

Margaret Gatz *(right)* has been a crusader for better mental health treatment of the elderly. She believes that mental health professionals need to be encouraged to include more older adults in their client lists and that we need to better educate the elderly about how they can benefit from therapy. *What are some common mechanisms of change that can be used to improve the mental health of older adults?*

Religion in Late Adulthood

RELIGION IN LATE ADULTHOOD

In chapter 16, we described religion and meaning in life with a special focus on middle age, including links between religion and health ◀ P. 474. Here we will continue our exploration of religion by describing its importance in the lives of many older adults.

In many societies around the world, the elderly are the spiritual leaders in their churches and communities. For example, in the Catholic church, more popes have been elected in their eighties than in any other 10-year period of the human life span.

The religious patterns of older adults have increasingly been studied (Kimble & others, in press; Levin, 1994). In one analysis, both older African Americans and older Whites attended religious services several times a month, said religion was important

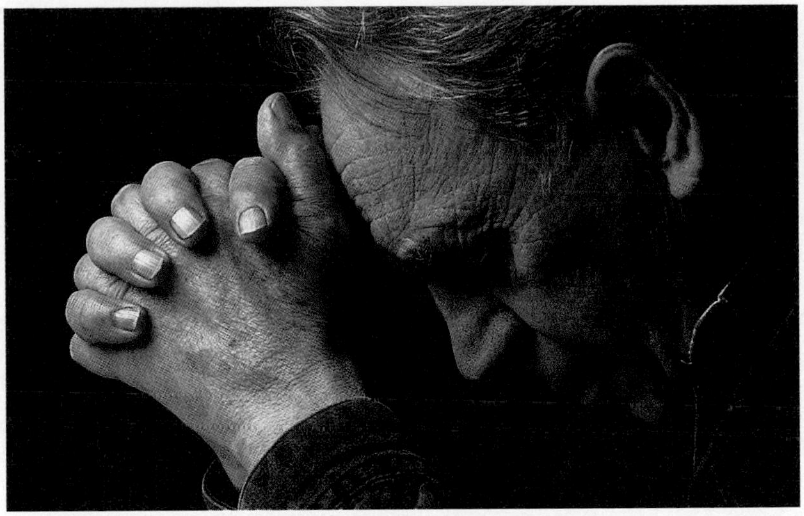

During late adulthood, many individuals increasingly engage in prayer. *How might this be linked with longevity?*

in their lives, read religious materials, listened to religious programming, and prayed frequently (Levin, Taylor, & Chatters, 1994). Also, in this analysis, older women had a stronger interest in religion than did older men.

When the significance of religion in people's lives has been assessed, individuals over 65 years of age are more likely than younger people to say that religious faith is the most significant influence in their lives, that they try to put religious faith into practice, and that they attend religious services (Gallup & Bezilla, 1992). In another survey, compared to younger adults, adults in old age were more likely to have a strong interest in spirituality and to pray (Gallup & Jones, 1989).

Is religion related to a sense of well-being and life satisfaction in old age? In one study of 836 older persons, it was. Religious practices—such as prayer and scripture reading—and religious feelings were associated with a sense of well-being, especially for women and individuals over 75 years of age (Koenig, Smiley, & Gonzales, 1988). In one study, older adults' self-esteem was highest when they had a strong religious commitment and lowest when they had little religious commitment (Krause, 1995). In another study, a commitment to religion was linked with health and well-being in young, middle-aged, and older African American adults (Levin, Chatters, & Taylor, 1995). And in one recent study of low-income Latinos in San Diego, a strong religious orientation was associated with better health (Cupertino & Haan, 1999).

WWW
Spirituality and Health in Older Adults

Religion can provide some important psychological needs in older adults, helping them face impending death, find and maintain a sense of meaningfulness and significance in life, and accept the inevitable losses of old age (Fry, 1999 Koenig & Larson, 1998). Socially, the religious community can provide a number of functions for older adults, such as social activities, social support, and the opportunity to assume teaching and leadership roles. Older adults can become deacons, elders, or religion teachers, assuming leadership roles they might have been unable to take on before they retired (Cox & Hammonds, 1988).

Might praying or meditating actually be associated with longevity? In one recent study, they were (McCullough & others, 2000). Nearly 4,000 women and men 65 years and older, mostly christians, were asked about their health and whether they prayed or meditated. Those who said they rarely or never prayed had about a 50 percent greater risk of dying during the 6-year study compared with those who prayed or meditated at least once a month. In this study, the researchers controlled for many factors known to place people at risk for dying, such as smoking, drink-

SUMMARY TABLE 19.3
The Mental Health of Older Adults and Religion in Late Adulthood

Concept	Processes/ Related Ideas	Characteristics/Descriptions
The Mental Health of Older Adults	Its Nature	• At least 10 percent of older adults have mental health problems sufficient to require professional help.
	Depression	• Depression has been called the "common cold" of mental disorders. However, a majority of older adults with depressive symptoms never receive mental health treatment.
	Dementia, Alzheimer's Disease, and other Afflictions	• Dementia is a global term for any neurological disorder in which the primary symptoms involve a deterioration of mental functioning. • Alzheimer's disease is by far the most common dementia. This progressive, irreversible disorder is characterized by gradual deterioration of memory, reasoning, language, and eventually physical functioning. • Special efforts are being made to discover the causes of Alzheimer's and effective treatments of it. Some experts believe Alzheimer's is a puzzle with many pieces. • Special brain scans, analysis of spinal fluids, and a sophisticated urine test are being used to detect Alzheimer's before its symptoms appear. • Alzheimer's disease involves a predictable, progressive decline. • An important concern is caring for Alzheimer's patients and the burdens this places on caregivers. • In addition to Alzheimer's disease, other types of dementia are multi-infarct dementia and Parkinson's disease.
	Fear of Victimization, Crime, and Elder Abuse	• Some of the physical decline and limitations that characterize development in late adulthood contribute to a sense of vulnerability and fear among older adults. Almost one-fourth of older adults say they have a basic fear of being the victim of a crime. • Older women are more likely than older men to be victimized or abused.
	Meeting the Mental Health Needs of Older Adults	• A number of barriers to mental health treatment in older adults exist; older adults receive disproportionately less mental health treatment. • There are many different ways to treat the mental health problems of the elderly.
Religion in Late Adulthood	Its Nature	• Many elderly are spiritual leaders in their church and community. • Religious interest increases in old age and is related to a sense of well-being in the elderly.

ing, and social isolation. It is possible that prayer and meditation lower the incidence of death in older adults because they reduce stress and dampen the body's production of stress hormones such as adrenaline. A decrease in stress hormones is linked with a number of health benefits, including a stronger immune system (McCullough & others, 2000).

At this point we have discussed a number of ideas about the nature of older adults' mental health and religion in later life. To review these ideas, see summary table 19.3. In the next chapter, we will continue our discussion of late adulthood, focusing on older adults' socioemotional development.

Chapter Review

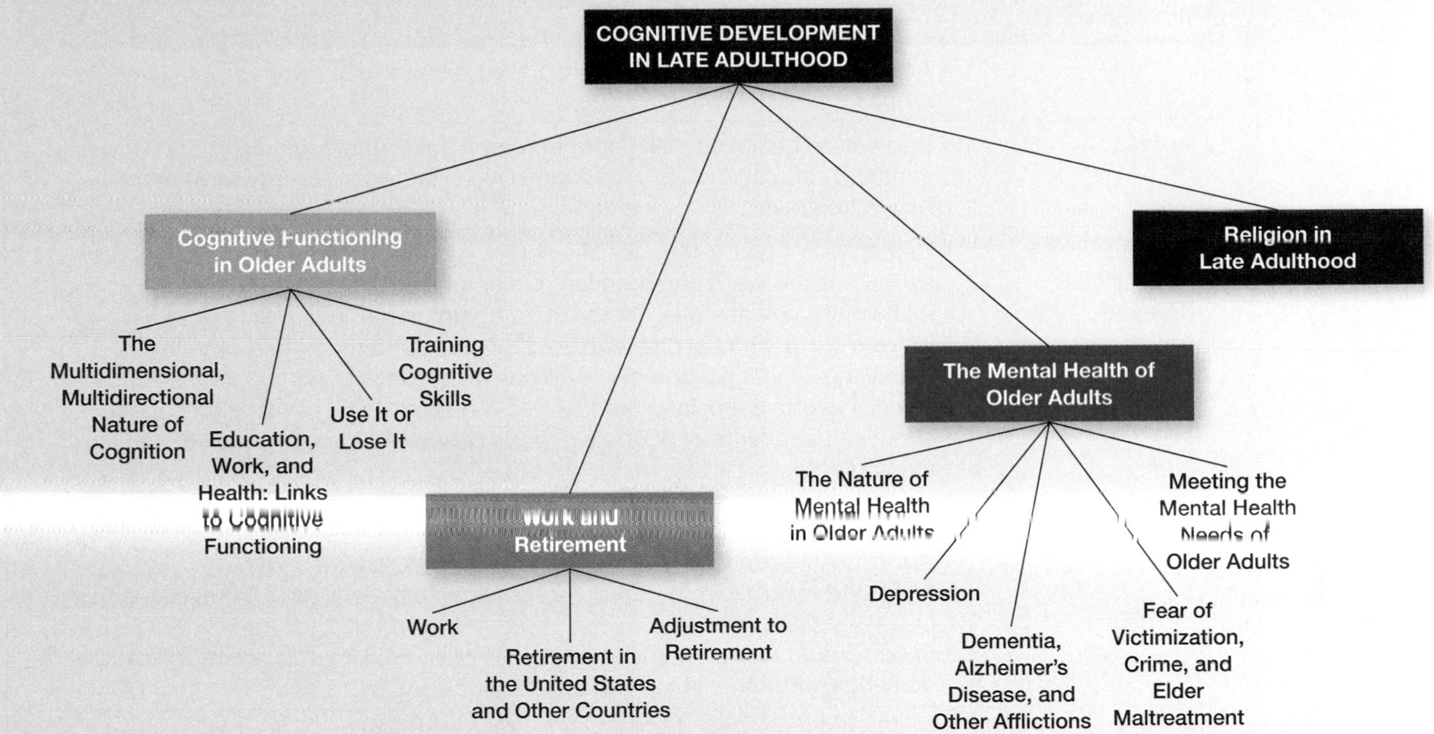

TO OBTAIN A DETAILED REVIEW OF THIS CHAPTER, STUDY THESE THREE SUMMARY TABLES:

- Summary Table 19.1 Cognitive Functioning in Older Adults page 559
- Summary Table 19.2 Work and Retirement page 563
- Summary Table 19.3 The Mental Health of Older Adults and Religion in Late Adulthood page 571

Key Terms

cognitive mechanics 552
cognitive pragmatics 552
episodic memory 553
semantic memory 553
working memory 553
explicit memory 554
implicit memory 554
wisdom 555
terminal drop hypothesis 557
mnemonics 557
major depression 562
dementia 563
Alzheimer's disease 564
multi-infarct dementia 567
Parkinson's disease 567

Key People

Paul Baltes 552
Fredda Blanchard-Fields 555
K. Warner Schaie 556
Marilyn Albert 557
Sherry Willis 558

Taking It to the Net

1. Jasper's 65-year-old father thinks he was passed over for a promotion because of his age. How can Jasper investigate whether his father has a legal claim based on age discrimination against his company? What rights do older workers have in their jobs?
2. Angela is interested in finding out more about how causes, nature, and treatment of depression change over the lifespan. Her Aunt Sadie has become very depressed as she has gotten older. What can Angela find out about the extent of depression in the elderly population and why it often goes undiagnosed, the causes, and the best treatment regimens.
3. Juan's grandfather has just been diagnosed with Alzheimer's disease. What does Juan and his family need to know about caring for his grandfather's physical needs? What legal and financial issues may need to be considered by Juan's family to help them better deal with this situation?

Connect to www.mhhe.com/santrockld8 to research the answers and complete these exercises.

OLC Preview

To further test your knowledge of this chapter or to explore our extensive online resources that accompany *Life-Span Development,* eighth edition, please log on to the text's Online Learning Center at http://www.mhhe.com/santrockld8.com.

Chapter 20

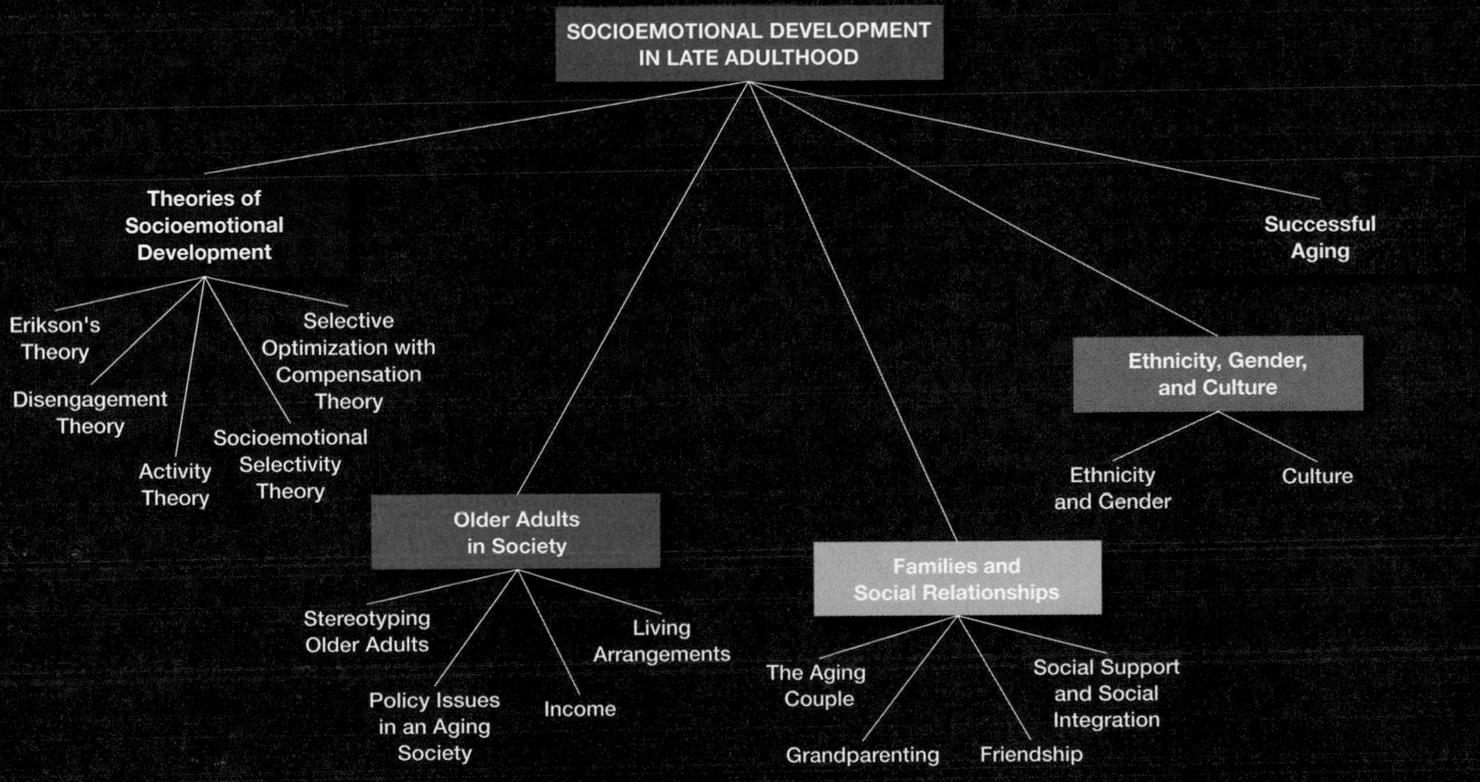

SOCIOEMOTIONAL DEVELOPMENT IN LATE ADULTHOOD
Theories of Socioemotional Development
Erikson's Theory
Disengagement Theory
Activity Theory
Socioemotional Selectivity Theory
Selective Optimization with Compensation Theory
Older Adults in Society
Stereotyping Older Adults
Policy Issues in an Aging Society
Income
Living Arrangements
Families and Social Relationships
The Aging Couple
Grandparenting
Friendship
Social Support and Social Integration
Ethnicity, Gender, and Culture
Ethnicity and Gender
Culture
Successful Aging

Socioemotional Development in Late Adulthood

I am the family face;
Flesh perishes, I live on,
Projecting trait and trace
Through time to times anon, And leaping from place to place
Over oblivion.

Thomas Hardy
English Novelist and Poet, 19th Century

Images of Life-Span Development

Bob Cousy

BOB COUSY was a star player on Boston Celtics teams that won numerous National Basketball Association championships. At age 68, he still sometimes plays 18 holes of golf in the morning and three sets of tennis in the afternoon. Says Cousy:

> I still thrive on competition, and when I feel those competitive juices flowing, I've got to find an outlet. Of course, at 68, it is not going to be playing basketball. Basketball's not a sport you grow old with. Sure, I can manage a few from the free-throw line, but being in shape for basketball is something you lose three months after you retire from the sport. . . .
>
> Now I'm working in broadcasting. I'm a commentator for the Celtics' away games. I like it because I'm controlling my own destiny.

In addition to his work as a broadcaster for the Celtics, Cousy enjoys spending time with his wife, family, and close friends.

Bob Cousy's life as an older adult reflects some of the themes of socioemotional development in older adults that we will discuss in this chapter. These include the important role that being active plays in life satisfaction, adapting to changing skills, and the positive role of close relationships with friends and family in an emotionally fulfilling life.

Bob Cousy, as a Boston Celtics star when he was a young adult (*left*) and as an older adult (*right*). *What are some changes he has made in his life as an older adult?*

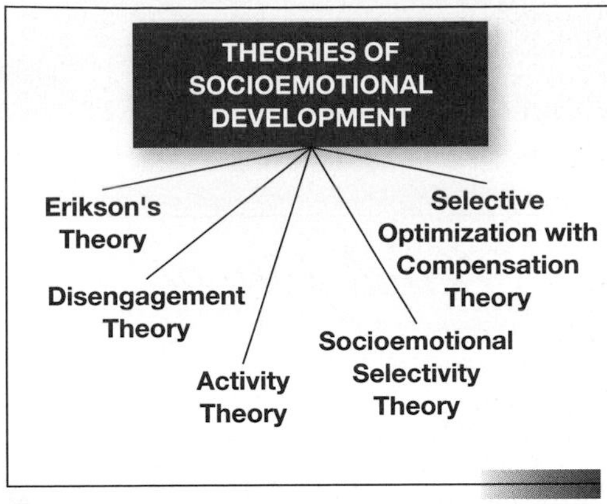

Theories of Socioemotional Development

We will look at the main theories of socioemotional development that focus on late adulthood: Erikson's theory, disengagement theory, activity theory, socioemotional selectivity theory, and selective optimization with compensation theory.

Erikson's Theory

We initially described Erik Erikson's (1968) eight stages of the human life span in chapter 2, and as we explored different periods of development in this book we examined the stages in more detail P. 33. Here we will discuss his final stage.

Integrity versus despair *is Erikson's eighth and final stage of development, which individuals experience during late adulthood. This involves reflecting on the past and either piecing together a positive review or concluding that one's life has not been well spent.* Through many different routes, the older adult may have developed a positive outlook in each of the preceding periods. If so, retrospective glances and reminiscences will reveal a picture of a life well spent, and the older adult will be satisfied (integrity). But if the older adult resolved one or more of the earlier stages in a negative way (being socially isolated in early adulthood or stagnated in middle adulthood, for example), retrospective glances about the total worth of his or her life might be negative (despair). Figure 20.1 portrays how positive resolutions of Erikson's eight stages can culminate in wisdom and integrity for older adults.

integrity versus despair
Erikson's eighth and final stage of development, which individuals experience in late adulthood. This involves reflecting on the past and either piecing together a positive review or concluding that one's life has not been well spent.

Robert Peck's Reworking of Erikson's Final Stage

Robert Peck (1968) reworked Erikson's final stage of development, integrity versus despair, by describing three developmental tasks, or issues, that men and women face when they become old. **Differentiation versus role preoccupation** *is Peck's developmental task in which older adults must redefine their worth in terms of something other than work roles.* Peck believes older adults need to pursue a set of valued activities so that time previously spent in an occupation and with children can be filled. **Body transcendence versus body preoccupation** *is Peck's developmental task in which older adults must cope with declining physical well-being.* As older adults age, they may experience a chronic illness and considerable deterioration in their physical capabilities. For men and women whose identity has revolved around their physical well-being, the decrease in health and deterioration of physical capabilities may present a severe threat to their identity and feelings of life satisfaction. However, while most older adults experience illnesses, many enjoy life through human relationships that allow them to go beyond a preoccupation with their aging body. **Ego transcendence versus ego preoccupation** *is Peck's developmental task in which older adults must recognize that while death is inevitable and probably not too far away, they feel at ease with themselves by realizing that they have contributed to the future through the competent rearing of their children or through their vocation and ideas.*

differentiation versus role preoccupation
One of the three developmental tasks of aging described by Peck, in which older adults must redefine their worth in terms of something other than work roles.

body transcendence versus body preoccupation
A developmental task of aging described by Peck, in which older adults must cope with declining physical well-being.

ego transcendence versus ego preoccupation
A developmental task of aging described by Peck, in which older adults must come to feel at ease with themselves by recognizing that although death is inevitable and probably not too far away, they have contributed to the future through the competent raising of their children or through their vocations and ideas.

Life Review

Life review is prominent in Erikson's final stage of integrity versus despair. Life review involves looking back at one's life experiences, evaluating them, interpreting them, and often reinterpreting them. Distinguished aging researcher Robert Butler (1975) believes the life review is set in motion by looking forward to death. Sometimes the life review proceeds quietly, at other times it is intense, requiring considerable work to achieve some sense of personality integration. The life review may be observed initially in stray and insignificant thoughts about oneself and one's life history. These thoughts may continue to emerge in brief intermittent spurts or become essentially continuous. One 76-year-old man commented, "My life is in the back of my mind. It can't be any other way. Thoughts of the past play on me. Sometimes I play with them, encouraging and savoring them; at other times I dismiss them."

CONFLICT AND RESOLUTION	CULMINATION IN OLD AGE
Old Age Integrity vs. despair: wisdom	Existential identity; a sense of integrity strong enough to withstand physical disintegration.
Middle Adulthood Generativity vs. stagnation: care	Caring for others, and empathy and concern.
Early Adulthood Intimacy vs. isolation: love	Sense of complexity of relationships; value of tenderness and loving freely.
Adolescence Identity vs. confusion: fidelity	Sense of complexity of life; merger of sensory, logical, and aesthetic perception.
School Age Industry vs. inferiority: competence	Humility; acceptance of the course of one's life and unfulfilled hopes.
Early Childhood Initiative vs. guilt: purpose	Humor; empathy; resilience.
Toddlerhood Autonomy vs. shame: will	Acceptance of the cycle of life, from integration to disintegration.
Infancy Basic trust vs. mistrust: hope	Appreciation of interdependence and relatedness.

Figure **20.1**

Erikson's View of How Positive Resolution of the Eight Stages of the Human Life Span Can Culminate in Wisdom and Integrity in Old Age

In Erikson's view, each stage of life is associated with a particular psychosocial conflict and a particular resolution. In an amplification of his ideas in his eighties, Erikson (1988) described how the issue from each of the earlier stages can mature into the many facets of integrity and wisdom in old age. At right, Erikson is shown with his wife Joan, an artist.

Life reviews can include sociocultural dimensions, such as culture, ethnicity, and gender. Life reviews also can include interpersonal, relationship dimensions, including sharing and intimacy with family members or a friend. And life reviews can include personal dimensions, which might involve the creation and discovery of meaning and coherence. These personal dimensions might unfold in such a way that the pieces do or don't make sense to the older adult (Kenyon, Ruth, & Mader, 1999). In the final analysis, each person's life review is to some degree unique.

As the past marches in review, the older adult surveys it, observes it, and reflects on it (Butler, 1996; Cully, LaVoie, & Gfeller, 2001). Reconsideration of previous experiences and their meaning occurs, often with revision or expanded understanding taking place. This reorganization of the past may provide a more valid picture for the individual, providing new and significant meaning to one's life. It may also help prepare the individual for death, in the process reducing fear.

As the life review proceeds, the older adult may reveal to a spouse, children, or other close associates unknown characteristics and experiences that previously had been undisclosed. In return, they may reveal previously unknown or undisclosed truths. Hidden themes of great meaning to the individual may emerge, changing the nature of the older adult's sense of self. Successful aging, though, doesn't mean thinking about the past all of the time. In one study, older adults who were obsessed about the past were less well adjusted than older adults who integrated their past and present (Wong & Watt, 1991).

Disengagement Theory

disengagement theory
The theory that to cope effectively, older adults should gradually withdraw from society.

Disengagement theory *states that to cope effectively, older adults should gradually withdraw from society.* This theory was proposed almost half a century ago (Cumming & Henry, 1961). In this view, older adults develop increasing self-preoccupation, decrease their emotional ties with others, and show less interest in society's affairs. By following these strategies of disengagement, it was believed, older adults would enjoy enhanced life satisfaction.

The theory generated a storm of protest and met with a quick death. We mention it because of its historical relevance. Although not formally proposed until 1961, it summarized the prevailing beliefs about older adults in the first half of the twentieth century.

Activity Theory

activity theory
The theory that the more active and involved older adults are, the more likely they are to be satisfied with their lives.

Activities Resources for Older Adults

Activity theory *states that the more active and involved older adults are, the more likely they will be satisfied with their lives.* Thus, activity theory is the exact opposite of disengagement theory. Researchers have found strong support for activity theory, beginning in the 1960s and continuing into the twenty-first century (Neugarten, Havighurst, & Tobin, 1968; Rook, 2000). These researchers have found that when older adults are active, energetic, and productive, they age more successfully and are happier than if they disengage from society.

Activity theory suggests that many individuals will achieve greater life satisfaction if they continue their middle-adulthood roles into late adulthood. If these roles are stripped from them (as in early retirement), it is important for them to find substitute roles that keep them active and involved.

Socioemotional Selectivity Theory

socioemotional selectivity theory
The theory that older adults become more selective about their social networks. Because they place a high value on emotional satisfaction, older adults often spend more time with familiar individuals with whom they have had rewarding relationships.

Socioemotional selectivity theory *states that older adults become more selective about their social networks. Because they place a high value on emotional satisfaction, older adults often spend more time with familiar individuals with whom they have had rewarding relationships.* Developed by Laura Carstensen (1991, 1995, 1998), this theory argues that older adults deliberately withdraw from social contact with individuals peripheral to their lives while they maintain or increase contact with close friends and family members with whom they have had enjoyable relationships. This selective narrowing of social interaction maximizes positive emotional experiences and minimizes emotional risks as individuals become older.

Socioemotional selectivity theory challenges the stereotype that the majority of older adults are in emotional despair because of their social isolation. Rather, older adults consciously choose to decrease the total number of their social contacts in favor of spending increasing time in emotionally rewarding moments with friends and family. That is, they systematically hone their social networks so that available social partners satisfy their emotional needs.

Is there research evidence to support life-span differences in the composition of social networks? Longitudinal studies reveal far smaller social networks for older adults than for younger adults (Lee & Markides, 1990; Palmore, 1981). In one study of individuals 69 to 104 years of age, the oldest participants had fewer peripheral social contacts than the relatively younger participants but about the same number of close emotional relationships (Lang & Carstensen, 1994).

Recent research paints a distinctly positive picture of aging in the emotion domain.

Laura Carstensen
Contemporary Psychology, Stanford University

Socioemotional selectivity theory also focuses on the types of goals that individuals are motivated to achieve (Carstensen, Isaacowitz, & Charles, 1999). It states that two important classes of goals are (1) knowledge-related and (2) emotional. This theory emphasizes that the trajectory of motivation for knowledge-related goals starts relatively high in the early years of life, peaking in adolescence and early adulthood and then declining in middle and late adulthood (see figure 20.2). The emotion trajectory is high during infancy and early childhood, declines from middle childhood

through early adulthood, and increases in middle and late adulthood.

One of the main reasons given for these changing trajectories in knowledge-related and emotion-related goals involves the perception of time. As older adults perceive that they have less time left in their lives, they are motivated to spend more time seeking emotion-related goals rather than knowledge-related goals. Because striving for knowledge is so important from late adolescence to middle age, it is pursued relentlessly even at the cost of emotional satisfaction.

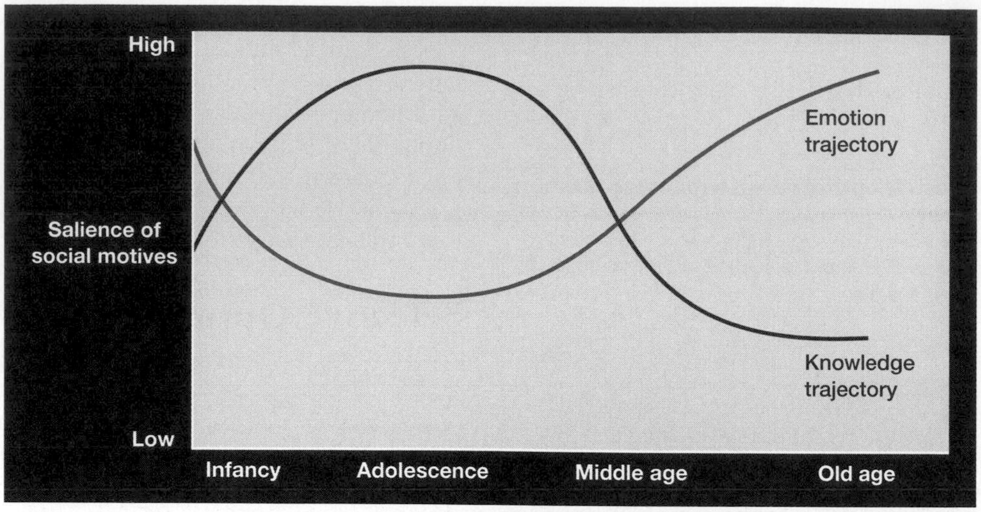

Figure **20.2**

Idealized Model of Socioemotional Selectivity Through the Life Span

In Carstensen's theory of socioemotional selectivity, the motivation to reach knowledge related and emotion-related goals changes across the life span.

Researchers have found that across diverse samples (Norwegians, Catholic nuns, African Americans, Chinese Americans, and European Americans) older adults report better control of their emotions and fewer negative emotions than younger adults (Carstensen, Gottman, & Levensen, 1995; Lawton & others, 1992). Compared to younger adults, the feelings of older adults mellow. Emotional life is on a more even keel with fewer highs and lows. It may be that although older adults have less extreme joy, they have more contentment, especially when they are connected in positive ways with friends and family (Harlow & Cantor, 1996).

In one study of individuals from early adulthood through late adulthood, emotions in everyday life were studied by giving subjects electronic pagers to carry for

What are the main ideas involved in socioemotional selectivity theory?

a week and record their emotions at each of the 35 random times they were paged (Carstensen, Pasupathi, & Mayr, 1998). Positive emotions (such as joy) were maintained in across adulthood. Negative emotions (such as anger) were highest in early adulthood and lowest in late adulthood. In sum, researchers have found that the emotional life of older adults is more positive than once believed (Carstensen, 1998; Ryan & La Guardia, 2000).

Next, we will explore a recently proposed theory that, like socioemotional selectivity theory, focuses on what is necessary for the realization of developmental goals.

selective optimization with compensation theory
The theory that successful aging is related to three main factors: selection, optimization, and compensation.

Selective Optimization with Compensation Theory

Selective optimization with compensation theory *states that successful aging is linked with three main factors: selection, optimization, and compensation.* Selection is based on the concept that older adults have a reduced capacity and loss of functioning, which require a reduction in performance in most life domains. Optimization suggests that it is possible to maintain performance in some areas through continued practice and the use of new technologies. Compensation becomes relevant when life tasks require a level of capacity beyond the current level the older adult's performance potential. Older adults especially need to compensate in circumstances with high mental or physical demands, such as when thinking about and memorizing new material very fast, reacting quickly when driving a car, or running fast. When older adults develop an illness, the need for compensation is obvious.

Selective optimization with compensation theory was proposed by Paul Baltes and his colleagues (Baltes & Baltes, 1990; Mariske & others, 1995). They describe the life of the late Arthur Rubinstein to illustrate their theory. When he was interviewed at 80 years of age, Rubinstein said that three factors were responsible for his ability to maintain his status as an admired concert pianist into old age. First, he mastered the weakness of old age by reducing the scope of his performances and playing fewer pieces (which reflects *selection*). Second, he spent more time at practice than earlier in his life (which reflects *optimization*). Third, he used special strategies, such as slowing down before fast segments, thus creating the image of faster playing (which reflects *compensation*).

The process of selective optimization with compensation is likely to be effective whenever loss is prominent in a person's life. Loss is a common dimension of old age, although there are wide variations in the nature of the losses involved. Because of this individual variation, the specific form of selection, optimization, and compensation will likely vary depending on the person's life history, pattern of interests, values, health, skills, and resources.

In Baltes' view (1996, 2000; Baltes, Lindenberger, & Stuadinger, 1998), the selection of domains and life priorities is an important aspect of development. Life goals and priorities likely vary across the life course for most people (Cantor & Blanton, 1996).

For many individuals, it is not just the sheer attainment of goals, but rather the attainment of *meaningful* goals, that makes life satisfying. In one study, younger adults were more

Careers in Life-Span Development

Laura Carstensen, Psychology Professor and Director of Women's Studies Program

Laura Carstensen is a professor of psychology at Stanford University and also is director of the Institute for Gender and Women. She obtained her doctorate in clinical psychology from West Virginia University. Laura is a leading theorist and researcher in the socioemotional development of older adults. Her theory of socioemotional selectivity is gaining recognition as an important theory. She has conducted a number of research studies on adult development and aging, which have been supported by grants from the National Institute of Aging.

Laura Carstensen (*right*), in a caring relationship with an older woman.

likely to assess their well-being in terms of accomplishments and careers, whereas older adults were more likely to link well-being with good health and the ability to accept change. And as you read earlier in our discussion of emotional selectivity theory, emotion-related goals become increasingly important for older adults (Carstensen, 1998).

In one cross-sectional study, the personal life investments of 25- to 103-year-olds, were assessed (Staudinger, 1996; Staudinger & Fleeson, in press) (see figure 20.3). From 25 to 34 years of age, participants said that they personally invested more time in work, friends, family, and independence, in that order. From 35 to 54 and 55 to 65 years of age, family became more important than friends to them in terms of their personal investment. Little changed in the rank ordering of persons 70 to 84 years old, but for participants 85 to 105 years old, health became the most important personal investment. Thinking about life showed up for the first time on the most important list for those who were 85 to 105 years old. Other researchers have found similar ratings of life domains across the life span (Heckhausen, in press).

One point to note about the study just described is the demarcation of late adulthood into the subcategories of 70 to 84 and 85 to 105 years of age. This fits with our comments on several occasions that researchers increasingly do not study late adulthood as a homogeneous category.

At this point, we have studied a number of theories of socioemotional development that pertain to late adulthood. To review these ideas, see summary table 20.1. Let's now turn our attention to how older adults are viewed in society.

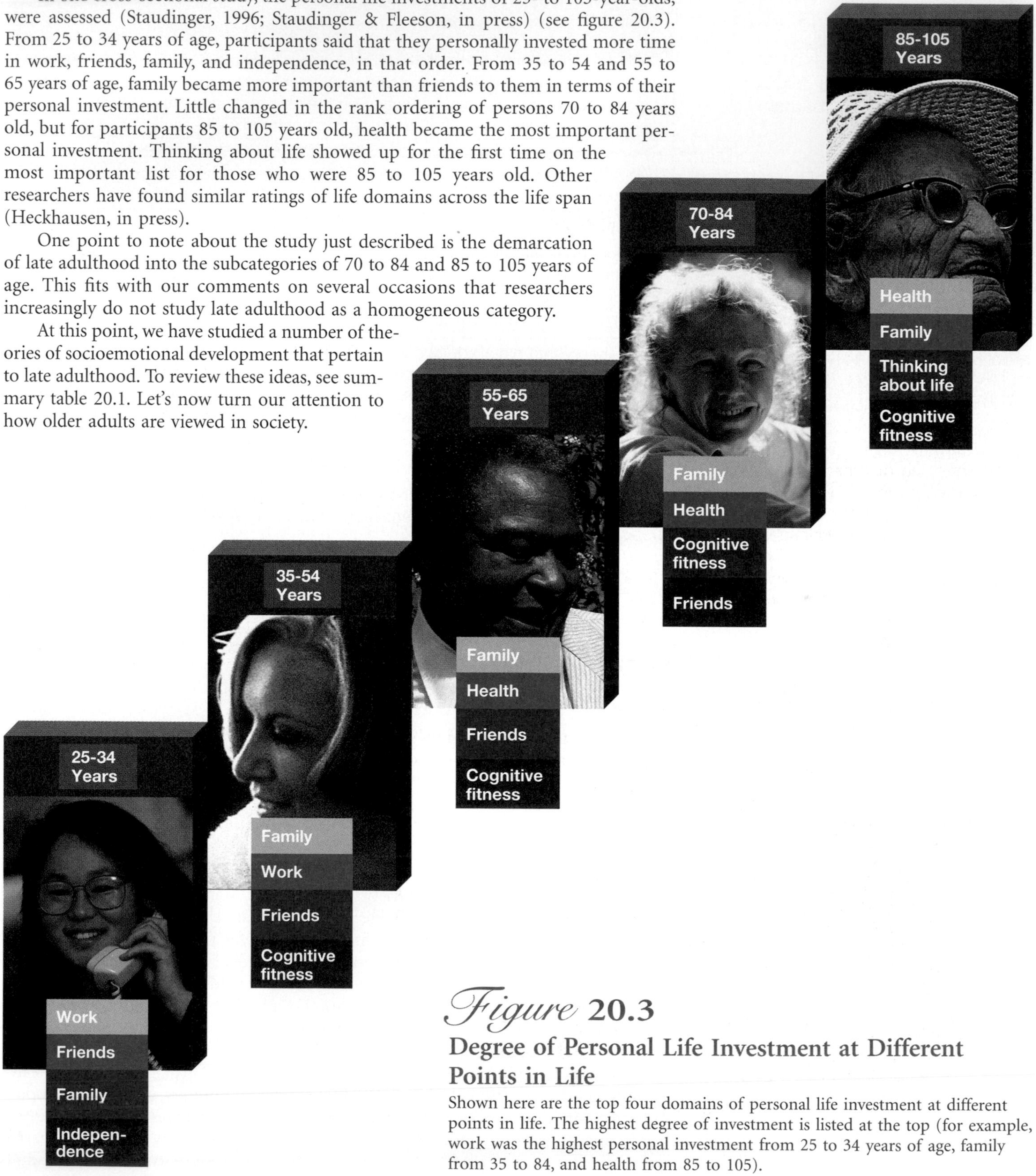

Figure 20.3

Degree of Personal Life Investment at Different Points in Life

Shown here are the top four domains of personal life investment at different points in life. The highest degree of investment is listed at the top (for example, work was the highest personal investment from 25 to 34 years of age, family from 35 to 84, and health from 85 to 105).

Summary Table 20.1
Theories of Socioemotional Development

Concept	Processes/ Related Ideas	Characteristics/Description
Erikson's Theory	Integrity Versus Despair	• Erikson's eighth and final stage of development, which individuals experience in late adulthood, involves reflecting on the past and either integrating it positively or concluding that one's life has not been well spent.
	Peck's Reworking of Erikson's Final Stage	• Peck described three developmental tasks that older adults face: (1) differentiation versus role preoccupation, (2) body transcendence versus preoccupation, and (3) ego transcendence versus preoccupation.
	Life Review	• Life review is an important theme in Erikson's stage of integrity vs. despair.
Disengagement Theory	An Historical Theory	• No longer a viable view: it stated that to be satisfied with their lives older adults need to withdraw from society.
Activity Theory	A Viable Theory	• The theory that the more active and involved older adults are, the more likely they will be satisfied with their lives.
Socioemotional Selectivity Theory	Carstensen's Theory	• The theory that older adults become more selective about their social networks. Because they place a high value on emotional satisfaction, they are motivated to spend more time with familiar individuals with whom they have had rewarding relationships.
	Goals	• Knowledge-related and emotion-related goals change across the life span, with emotion-related goals being more important when individuals get older.
Selective Optimization with Compensation Theory	Baltes' Theory	• The theory that successful aging is linked with three main factors: (1) selection, (2) optimization, and (3) compensation. These are especially likely to be relevant when loss occurs.

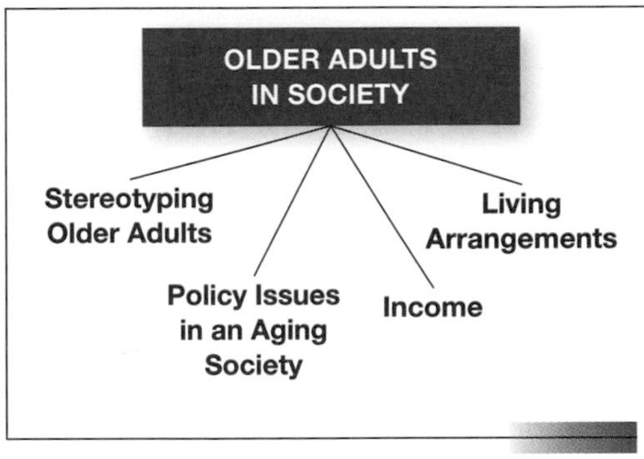

ageism
Prejudice against other people because of their age, especially prejudice against older adults.

Older Adults in Society

Are older adults stereotyped by society? What social policy issues does an aging society raise? How devastating is poverty to older adults? What are the living arrangements of older adults?

Stereotyping Older Adults

Ageism *is prejudice against others because of their age, especially prejudice against older adults.* Like sexism, it is one of society's uglier words. Many older adults face painful discrimination and might be too polite and timid to attack it (McMullin & Marshall, 2001; Perdue, 2000). Older adults might not be hired for new jobs or might be eased out of old ones because they are perceived as rigid or feebleminded, or because employing older adults is considered not cost-effective. They could be shunned socially, possibly because they are perceived as senile or boring. At other times, they might be perceived as children and described with adjectives such as "cute" and "adorable." The elderly might be edged out of their family life by children who see them as sick, ugly, and parasitic. In sum, the elderly might be perceived as incapable of thinking clearly, learning new things, enjoying sex, contributing to the community, and holding responsible jobs—inhumane perceptions to be sure, but often painfully real (McGowan, 1996).

In one study, young, middle-aged, and older adults had many of the same stereotypes of older adults (Hummert & others, 1994). Seven stereotypes of older adults

were present in all age groups: *perfect grandmother, golden ager, John Wayne conservative, severely impaired, shrew/curmudgeon, despondent,* and *recluse.* Notice that this listing includes almost the same number of positive as negative stereotypes, with only one—*severely impaired*—being a traditional stereotype of old age.

The personal consequences of negative stereotyping about aging can be serious. A physician (60 years old himself) recently told an 80-year-old: "Well, of course, you are tired. You just need to slow down. Don't try to do so much. After all you are very old." Many older adults accept this type of advice even though it is rooted in age stereotyping rather than medical records.

The increased number of adults living to an older age has led to active efforts to improve society's image of the elderly, obtain better living conditions for older adults and gain political clout. The American Association of Retired Persons (AARP), with more than 30 million members, is bigger than most countries. The Gray Panthers, with 80,000 members, pressures Congress on everything from health insurance to housing costs. These groups have developed a formidable gray lobbying effort in state and national politics.

Social Aging Resources

Social Psychology of Aging

Ageism Resources

Policy Issues in an Aging Society

The aging society and older persons' status in this society raise policy issues about the well-being of older adults. These include the status of the economy and the viability of the Social Security system, the provision of health care, supports for families who care for older adults, and generational inequity, each of which we consider in turn (Neugarten, 1988).

An important issue involving the economy and aging is the concern that our economy cannot bear the burden of so many older persons, who by reason of their age alone are usually consumers rather than producers. However, not all persons 65 and over are nonworkers and not all persons 18 to 64 are workers. And considerably more individuals in the 55 to 64 age group are in the workforce—three out of five men—than a decade ago. Thus, it is incorrect to simply describe older adults as consumers and younger adults as producers.

An aging society also brings with it various problems involving health care (Birren, 1993). Escalating health-care costs are currently causing considerable concern. One factor that contributes to the surge in health costs is the increasing number of older adults. Older adults have more illnesses than younger adults, despite the fact that many older adults report their health as good. Older adults see doctors more often, are hospitalized more often, and have longer hospital stays. Approximately one-third of the total health bill of the United States is for the care of adults 65 and over, who comprise only 12 percent of the population. The health-care needs of the elderly are reflected in Medicare, the program that provides health-care insurance to adults over 65 under the Social Security system. Of interest is the fact that the United States is the only industrialized nation that provides health insurance specifically for older adults rather than to the population at large, and the only industrialized nation currently without a national health-care system. Older adults themselves still pay about one-third of their total health-care costs. Thus, older adults as well as younger adults are adversely affected by rising medical costs.

A special concern is that while many of the health problems of older adults are chronic rather than acute, the medical system is still based on a "cure" rather than a "care" model. Chronic illness is long-term, often lifelong, and requires long-term, if not life-term, management. Chronic illness often follows a pattern of an acute period that may require hospitalization, followed by a longer period of remission, and then repetitions of this pattern. The patient's home, rather than the hospital, often becomes the center of managing the patient's chronic illness. In a home-based system, a new type of cooperative relationship between doctors, nurses, patients, family members, and other service providers needs to be developed. Health-care personnel need to be trained and be available to provide home services, sharing authority with the patient and perhaps yielding to it over the long term.

eldercare
Physical and emotional caretaking for older members of the family, whether by giving day-to-day physical assistance or by being responsible for overseeing such care.

generational inequity
The view that our aging society is being unfair to its younger members because older adults pile up advantages by receiving inequitably large allocations of resources.

Eldercare *is the physical and emotional caretaking of older members of the family, whether that care is day-to-day physical assistance or responsibility for arranging and overseeing such care.* An important issue involving eldercare is how it can best be provided (Gonyea, 1994). With so many women in the labor market, who will replace them as caregivers? An added problem is that many caregivers are in their sixties, and many of them are ill themselves. They may find it especially stressful to be responsible for the care of relatives who are in their eighties or nineties.

In one study, two distinct systems of eldercare were found: individualistic and collectivistic (Pyke & Bengtson, 1996). Individualists approached parental care-giving reluctantly and considered it a burden. They often reported that they did not have adequate time for it and they relied on formal supports. In contrast, in collectivistic families, parental caregiving was assumed by family members, who emphasized family ties.

Some gerontologists advocate that the government should provide financial support to families to help with home services or substitute for the loss of income if a worker reduces outside employment to care for an aging relative (England & others, 1991). Some large corporations are helping workers with parent-caring by providing flexible work schedules and creating more part-time or at-home jobs. Government supports have been slow to develop. One reason for their slow development is that some persons believe such government interventions will weaken the family's responsibility and thus have a negative effect on the well-being of older, as well as younger, adults.

Yet another policy issue involving aging is **generational inequity** (discussed initially in chapter 1): *the view that our aging society is being unfair to its younger members because older adults pile up advantages by receiving an inequitably large allocation of resources.* Some authors have argued that generational inequity produces intergenerational conflict and divisiveness in the society at large (Longman, 1987). The generational equity issue raises questions about whether the young should be required to pay for the old. One claim is that today's baby boomers, now in their forties and fifties, will receive lower Social Security payments than are presently being paid out, or none at all, when they reach retirement age if the economy takes a downturn.

The Gray Panthers are actively involved in pressuring Congress on everything from health insurance to housing costs. Along with the American Association for Retired Persons, they have developed a formidable gray lobbying effort in state and national politics. *What are some of the policy issues in an aging society?*

The generational equity issue sometimes also takes the form of whether the "advantaged" old population is using up resources that should go to disadvantaged children. The argument is that older adults are advantaged because they have publicly provided pensions, health care, food stamps, housing subsidies, tax breaks, and other benefits that younger age groups do not have. While the trend of greater services for the elderly has been occurring, the percentage of children living in poverty has been increasing.

Distinguished developmentalist Bernice Neugarten (1988) says it is undeniable that the large numbers of poor children are a disgrace to an affluent society like the United States. She stresses that the problem should not be viewed as one of generational equity, but rather as a major shortcoming of our broader economic and social policies. In conclusion, Neugarten envisions that we should be thinking about what a positive spirit of aging would mean to America, and to what extent this positive spirit could improve the range of options for people of all ages. Margaret Gatz (1992), an expert on aging, agrees.

Income

The elderly poor are a special concern. Recent census data suggest that although the overall number of older people living in poverty has declined since the 1960s, the percentage of older persons living in poverty has consistently remained in the 10 to 12 percent range since the early 1980s (U.S. Bureau of the Census, 2000). More than 25 percent of older women who live alone live in poverty. Also, the number of older single women just above the poverty line remains substantial. Poverty rates among ethnic minorities are two to three times higher than the rate for Whites. Combining sex and ethnicity, 60 percent of older African American women and 50 percent of older Latino women who live alone live in poverty. Also, the oldest old are the age subgroup of the elderly most likely to be living in poverty.

Many older adults are understandably concerned about their income. The average income of retired Americans is only about half of what they earned when they were fully employed. Although retired individuals need less income for job-related and social activities, adults 65 and over spend a greater proportion of their income for food, utilities, and health care. They spend a smaller proportion for transportation, clothing, pension and life insurance, and entertainment than do adults under the age of 65. Social Security is the largest contributor to the income of older Americans (38 percent), followed by assets, earnings, and pensions.

The majority of older adults face a life of reduced income. Far too few middle-aged adults adequately plan for this. For instance, middle-aged Americans who will retire in 20 to 25 years will need an income equal to 75 percent of their current annual expenditures (adjusted for inflation) to maintain their current middle-aged lifestyle.

Living Arrangements

One stereotype of older adults is that they are often residents in institutions—hospitals, mental hospitals, nursing homes, and so on. However, nearly 95 percent of older adults live in the community. Almost two-thirds of older adults live with family members—spouse, a child, a sibling, for example—while almost one-third live alone. The older people become, the greater are their odds for living alone. The majority of older adults living alone are widowed. As with younger adults, living alone as an older adult does not mean being lonely (Kasper, 1988). Older adults who can sustain themselves while living alone often have good health and few disabilities, and they may have regular social exchanges with relatives, friends, and neighbors.

For many years researchers who studied the living arrangements of older adults focused on special situations such as nursing homes, public housing, mobile-home parks, welfare hotels, or retirement communities. However, less than 10 percent of older adults live in these types of housing arrangements. Nonetheless, the quality of housing for the elderly is far from perfect. The vast majority of older adults prefer to live independently—either alone or with a spouse—rather than with a child, with a relative, or in an institution. However, too many of the elderly have inadequate housing. One recent study examined the relation between older adults' physical living environment and their self-rated health (Krause, 1996). Older adults who had the most dilapidated housing gave themselves worse health ratings than their counterparts who had better housing.

Only 5 percent of adults 65 years of age and older live in institutions, but the older adults become, the more likely they are to live in an institution. For example, 23 percent of adults 85 years and over live in institutions. The majority of the elderly adults in institutions are widows, many of whom cannot physically navigate their environment, are mentally impaired, or are incontinent (cannot control their excretory functions). Because the population is aging and because wives' life expectancies are increasing more rapidly than husbands', even greater numbers of widows are likely to be in institutions in the future.

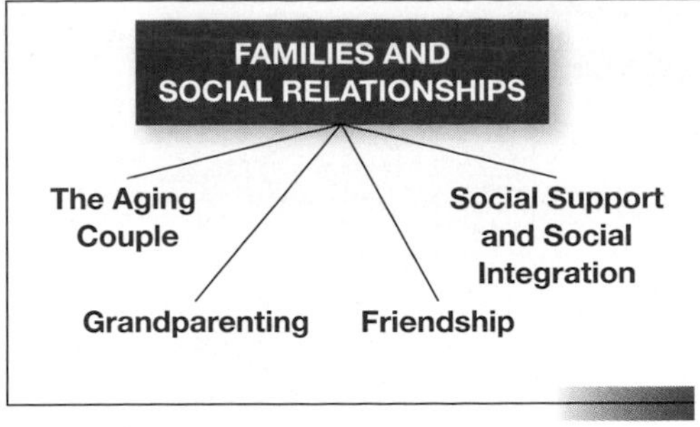

Families and Social Relationships

What are the relationships of aging couples like? What roles do grandparents play? What do friendships and social networks contribute to the lives of older adults?

The Aging Couple

The time from retirement until death is sometimes referred to as the "final stage in the marriage process." Retirement alters a couple's lifestyle, requiring adaptation. The greatest changes occur in the traditional family, in which the husband works and the wife is a homemaker. The husband may not know what to do with his time, and the wife may feel uneasy having him around the house all of the time. In traditional families, both partners may need to move toward more expressive roles. The husband must adjust from being the good provider to being a helper around the house; the wife must change from being only a good homemaker to being even more loving and understanding. Marital happiness as an older adult is also affected by each partner's ability to deal with personal conflicts, including aging, illness, and eventual death (Field, 1996).

Grow old with me!
The best is yet to be,
The last of life,
For which the first was made.

Robert Browning
English Poet, 19th Century

Individuals who are married in late adulthood are usually happier than those who are single (Lee, 1978). Marital satisfaction is greater for women than for men, possibly because women place more emphasis on attaining satisfaction through marriage than men do. However, as more women develop careers, this sex difference may not continue.

Not all older adults are married. At least 8 percent of all individuals who reach the age of 65 have never been married. Contrary to the popular stereotype, older adults who have never been married seem to have the least difficulty coping with loneliness in old age. Many of them discovered long ago how to live autonomously and how to become self-reliant.

Older Adults' Sexual Activity

Few of us imagine older couples taking an interest in sex. We might think of them as being interested in a game of bridge or a conversation on the porch, but not much else. In fact, a number of older adults date. The increased health and longevity of older adults have resulted in a much larger pool of active older adults. And the increased divorce rate has added more older adults to this pool.

Regarding their sexuality, older adults may express their sexuality differently than younger adults, especially when engaging in sexual intercourse becomes difficult. Older adults especially enjoy touching and caressing as part of their sexual relationship. When older adults are healthy, they still may engage in sexual activities. However, companionship often becomes more important than sexual activity in older adults. Older couples emphasize intimacy over sexual prowess.

Grandparenting

Let's explore these aspects of grandparenting: How satisfying is it to be a grandparent? What roles do grandparents assume and what styles do they use when they interact with their grandchildren? What is the profile of grandparenting and how is it changing?

Satisfaction with Grandparenting In one recent study, only a small minority (8 percent) of Australian grandparents said that they were more dissatisfied than satisfied with their grandparenting role (Peterson, 1999). A majority of grandparents say that grandparenting is easier than parenting. In one study, middle-aged grandparents (45 to 60 years of age) were more willing to give advice and to assume responsibility for watching and disciplining grandchildren than were older grandparents (60 years and older). Also, in another study, maternal grandparents interacted more with their grandchildren than paternal grandparents did (Bahr, 1989).

In one recent study, frequent contact with grandchildren predicted high levels of satisfaction in grandparenting for both grandmothers and grandfathers (Peter-

son, 1999). Also in this study, opportunities to observe their grandchildren's development and share in their activities were described as the best features of being a grandparent; lack of frequent contact with grandchildren was pointed to as the worst feature.

Critical Thinking: Middle-Aged Baby Boomers and Their Grandparents

BABY BOOMERS, now adults in midlife, were born in the aftermath of World War II during the high-birth-rate years from 1945 to 1960. The grandparents of baby boomers are the oldest generation now living—individuals who are 90 years old and older, born in the late nineteenth century and the early twentieth century. How are the values of today's middle-aged baby boomers similar to or different from those of their grandparents, who were influenced by the Victorian era in which women were not supposed to work outside of the home, drive a car, or enjoy sex? Compare the attitudes of these two generations about gender roles, sexuality, and other dimensions of life-span development.

Grandparent Roles and Styles What is the meaning of the grandparent role? Three prominent meanings are attached to being a grandparent (Neugarten & Weinstein, 1964). For some older adults, being a grandparent is a source of biological reward and continuity. In such cases, feelings of renewal (youth) or extensions of the self and family into the future emerge. For others, being a grandparent is a source of emotional self-fulfillment, generating feelings of companionship and satisfaction that may have been missing in earlier adult-child relationships (Sanders & Trygstad, 1993). And for yet others, being a grandparent is not as important as it is for some individuals, experienced as a remote role.

The grandparent role may have different functions in different families, in different ethnic groups and cultures, and in different situations (Kivnick & Sinclair, 1996). For example, in one study of White, African American, and Mexican American grandparents and grandchildren, the Mexican American grandparents saw their grandchildren more frequently, provided more support for the grandchildren and their parents, and had more satisfying relationships with their grandchildren (Bengtson, 1985). And in a study of three generations of families in Chicago, grandmothers had closer relationships with their children and grandchildren and gave more personal advice than grandfathers did (Hagestad, 1985).

The diversity of grandparenting was also apparent in an early investigation of how grandparents interacted with their grandchildren (Neugarten & Weinstein, 1964). Three styles were dominant—formal, fun-seeking, and distant figure. In the formal style, the grandparent performed what was considered to be a proper and prescribed role. These grandparents showed a strong interest in their grandchildren, but left parenting to the parents and were careful not to give child-rearing advice. In the

WWW

Today's Grandparent
Foundation of Grandparenting
The Grandparent Network
Adult Children and Their Elderly Parents
Grandparent Visitation Rights

What roles can grandparents play in children's development?

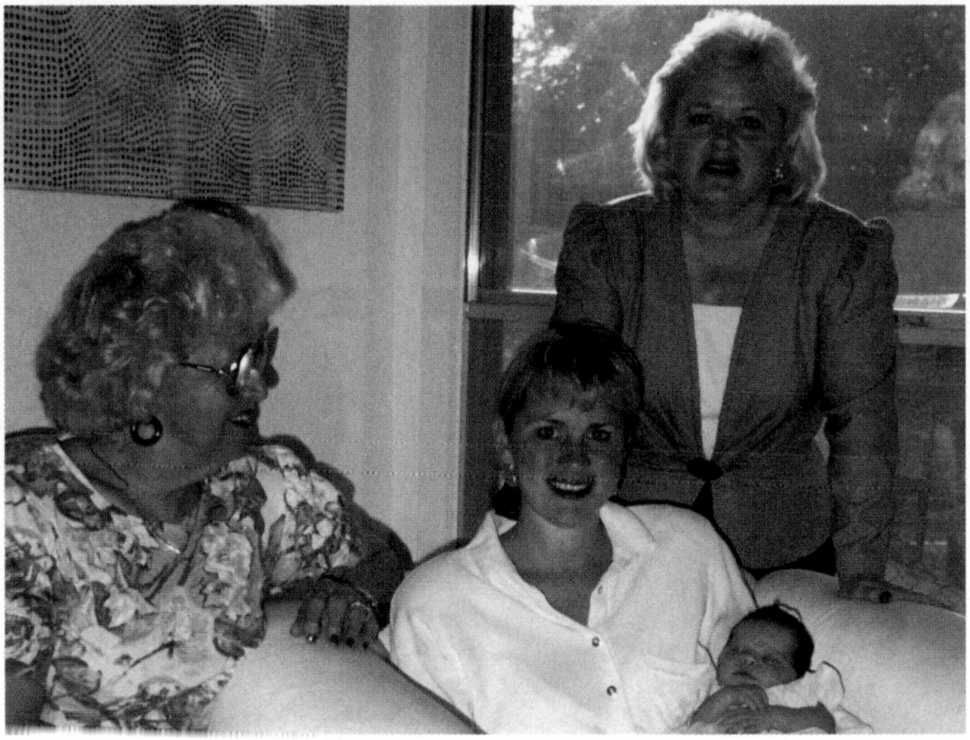

At the beginning of the twentieth century, the three-generation family was common, but now the four-generation family is common as well. Thus, an increasing number of grandparents are also great-grandparents. The four-generation family shown here is the Jordans—author John Santrock's mother-in-law, daughter, granddaughter, and wife.

fun-seeking style, the grandparent was informal and playful. Grandchildren were a source of leisure activity; mutual satisfaction was emphasized. A substantial portion of grandparents were distant figures. In the distant-figure style, the grandparent was benevolent but interaction occurred on an infrequent basis. Grandparents who were over the age of 65 were more likely to display a formal style of interaction; those under 65 were more likely to display a fun-seeking style.

The Changing Profile of Grandparents In 1997, the U.S. Bureau of the Census issued its first detailed portrait ever of many different living arrangements involving grandparents. Especially noticeable was the increasing number of grandchildren living with their grandparents (Fuller-Thompson & Minkler, 2001). In 1980, 2.3 million grandchildren lived with their grandparents, but in 1997 that figure had reached 3.9 million. Climbing divorce rates, adolescent pregnancies, and drug use are the main reason that grandparents are thrust back into the "parenting" role they thought they had shed.

Older Adults and Their Families

Almost one-half of the grandchildren who move in with grandparents are raised by a single grandmother. These families are mainly African American (53 percent). When both grandparents are raising grandchildren, the families are overwhelmingly White—63 percent when there are no parents around and 57 percent when the home has one or both of the parents.

Being embedded in a family is a positive aspect of life for many older adults.

Lillian Troll
Contemporary Developmental Psychologist, University of California at San Francisco

Grandparents who take in grandchildren are in better health, are better educated, are more likely to be working outside the home, and are younger than grandparents who move in with their children. Less than 20 percent of grandparents whose grandchildren move in with them are 65 years old or older.

In one recent study of grandparents raising their grandchildren, younger grandparents, grandchildren with physical and psychological problems, and low family cohesion were associated with stress (Sands & Goldberg-Glen, 2000).

In chapter 17, "Socioemotional Development in Middle Adulthood," we discussed the "sandwich generation," the middle generation that may be financially and time

squeezed because of having to be responsible for and care for both their children and their aging parents. In the 1997 U.S. Census report on grandparents, it was clear that not all middle-generation adults experience this generational squeeze. A majority of the grandparents who were living with their children contributed to the family income and provided child care while parents worked.

Partly because women live longer, there are more grandmothers than grandfathers (2.9 million versus 1.7 million) who live with their children. About 70 percent of the grandparents who move in with their children are grandmothers.

Only about 10 percent of the grandparents who move in with their children and grandchildren are in poverty. However, single grandmothers who move in with children who are raising children by themselves are much more likely to be in poverty (28 percent). Almost half of the grandparents who move in with their children are immigrants.

As more individuals live to an old age and as more families live in varied family structures, we can expect the nature of the grandparent's role and social interaction with grandchildren to change. Because of the aging of our society, an increasing number of grandparents are also great-grandparents. At the turn of the century, the three-generation family was common, but now the four-generation family is common. As divorce and remarriage have become more common, a special concern of grandparents is visitation privileges with their grandchildren. In the last 10 to 15 years, more states have passed laws giving grandparents the right to petition a court to legally obtain visitation privileges with their grandchildren. Now, even if a parent objects, grandparents may be permitted to spend time with their grandchildren. Whether such forced visitation rights for grandparents are in the child's best interest is still being debated.

Aging expert Lillian Troll (1994, 2000) has found in her research that older adults who are embedded in family relationships have much less distress than those who are family deprived. Next, we will consider these other aspects of social relationships in late adulthood: friendship, social support, and social integration.

Friendship

Aging expert Laura Carstensen (1997) concluded that people choose close friends over new friends as they grow older. And as long as they have several close people in their network, they seem content, says Carstensen.

In one recent study of young-old and old-old adult friendships, there was more continuity than change in amount of contact with friends (Field, 1999). There were, however, more changes in older adult male than older adult female friendships. Older men declined in number of new friends, in their desire for close friendships, and in involvement beyond family activities, while older women did not change in these areas.

The mobility of our society increases the distance between older and younger adults. Friendships with unrelated adults may help to replace the warmth, companionship, and nurturance traditionally supplied by families. In sum, friends play an important role in the support systems of older adults (Jerrome & Wenger, 1999; Troll, 1999).

What happens when older adults' friends die? One study found that one way older adults dealt with this loss was to loosen up their requirements for what they considered a friend (Johnson & Troll, 1994). Once "friends" probably meant intimate companions to them. Now they include the woman passed in the hall or the deliverer of meals on wheels.

Social Support and Social Integration

In the *social convoy* model of social relations, individuals go through life embedded in a personal network of individuals from whom they give and receive social support (Antonucci, Lansford, & Akiyama, 2001; Antonucci, Vandewater, & Lansford, 2000;

What role does social support play in the health of the elderly?

Kahn & Antonucci, 1990). Social support can help individuals of all ages cope more effectively.

Social support can improve the physical and mental health of older adults (Oxman & Hall, 2001; Reinhardt, 2001). Social support is linked with a reduction in symptoms of disease and with the ability to meet one's own health care needs (Cohen, Teresi, & Holmes, 1985). Social support also decreases the probability that an older adult will be institutionalized (Antonucci, 1990). Social support is associated with a lower incidence of depression in older adults (Joiner, 2000).

Social integration plays an important role in the lives of many older adults (Antonucci, Vandewater, & Lansford, 2000; Tarnowski & Antonucci, 1999). Being lonely and socially isolated is a significant health risk factor in older adults (Rowe & Kahn, 1997). In one study, being part of a social network was related to longevity, especially for men (House, Landis, & Umberson, 1988). And in a longitudinal study, both women and men with more organizational memberships lived longer than their counterparts with low organizational participation (Tucker & others, 1999).

Remember from our earlier discussion of socioemotional selectivity theory that many older adults choose to have fewer peripheral social contacts and more emotionally positive contacts with friends and family. Thus, although the overall social activity of many older adults decreases, this does not mean that they are emotionally distraught about this. Rather, it could reflect their greater interest in spending more time in the small circle of their friends and families where they are less likely to experience negative emotional experiences.

At this point, we have studied a number of ideas about older adults in society and families and social relationships. For a review of these ideas, see summary table 20.2. Next, we will continue our exploration of socioemotional development in late adulthood by examining ethnicity, culture, and gender.

ETHNICITY, GENDER, AND CULTURE

- **Ethnicity and Gender**
- **Culture**

Ethnicity, Gender, and Culture

What are the roles of ethnicity and gender in aging? What are the social aspects of aging in different cultures?

Ethnicity and Gender

First we will explore ethnicity in late adulthood, then gender, and finally racism and sexism.

Ethnicity Of special concern are ethnic minority older adults, especially African Americans and Latinos, who are overrepresented in poverty statistics (Hayward, Friedman, & Chen, 1996). Consider Harry, a 72-year-old African American who lives in a rundown hotel in Los Angeles. He suffers from arthritis and uses a walker. He has not been able to work for years, and government payments are barely enough to meet his needs.

Comparative information about African Americans, Latinos, and Whites indicates a possible double jeopardy for elderly ethnic minority individuals. They face problems related to *both* ageism and racism (Jackson, Chatters, & Taylor, 1993). Both the wealth and the health of ethnic minority older adults decrease more rapidly than for elderly Whites (Edmonds, 1993). Older ethnic minority individuals are more likely to become ill but less likely to receive treatment. They are also more likely to

Summary Table 20.2
Older Adults in Society; Families and Social Relationships

Concept	Processes/ Related Ideas	Characteristics/Descriptions
Older Adults in Society	Stereotyping Older Adults	• Ageism is prejudice against others because of their age. Too many negative stereotypes of older adults continue to exist.
	Policy Issues in an Aging Society	• These issues include the status of the economy and the viability of the Social Security system, the provision of health care, eldercare, and generational inequity.
	Income	• Of special concern are older adults who are in poverty. Poverty rates are especially high among older women who live alone and ethnic minority older adults.
	Living Arrangements	• Most older adults live in the community, not in institutions. Almost two-thirds of older adults live with family members.
Families and Social Relationships	The Aging Couple	• Retirement alters a couple's lifestyle and requires adaptation. Married older adults are often happier than single older adults.
	Grandparenting	• Most grandparents are satisfied with their role. There are different grandparent roles and styles. The profile of grandparents is changing, due to such factors as divorce and remarriage.
	Friendship	• There is more continuity than change in friendship for older adults, although there is more change for males than for females.
	Social Support and Social Integration	• Social support is linked with improved physical and mental health in older adults. • Older adults who participate in more organizations live longer than their counterparts who have low participation rates. Older adults often have fewer peripheral social ties but a strong motivation to spend time in relationships with close friends and family members that are rewarding.

have a history of less education, unemployment, worse housing conditions, and shorter life expectancies than their older White counterparts (Himes, Hogan, & Eggebeen, 1996). And many ethnic minority workers never enjoy the Social Security and Medicare benefits to which their earnings contribute, because they die before reaching the age of eligibility for benefits.

Despite the stress and discrimination older ethnic minority individuals face, many of these older adults have developed coping mechanisms that allow them to survive in the dominant White world (Markides & Rudkin, 1996). Extension of family networks helps elderly minority-group individuals cope with the bare essentials of living, and gives them a sense of being loved (Antonucci, Vandewater, & Lansford, 1998). Churches in African American and Latino communities provide avenues for meaningful social participation, feelings of power, and a sense of internal satisfaction. And residential concentrations of ethnic minority groups give their older members a sense of belonging. Thus, it always is important to consider individual variations in the lives of aging minorities (Whitfield & Baker-Thomas, 1999).

Gender Do our gender roles change when we become older adults? Some developmentalists believe there is decreasing femininity in women and decreasing masculinity in men when they reach the late adulthood years (Gutmann, 1975). The evidence suggests that older men do become more feminine—nurturant, sensitive, and

so on—but it appears that older women do not necessarily become more masculine—assertive, dominant, and so on (Turner, 1982). Keep in mind that cohort effects are especially important to consider in areas like gender roles. As sociohistorical changes take place and are assessed more frequently in lifespan investigations, what were once perceived to be age effects may turn out to be cohort effects (Jacobs, 1994).

One study found that time spent in committed activities by older adults had shifted in opposite ways for women and men (Verbrugge, Gruber-Baldini, & Fozard, 1996). Between 1958 and 1992, older men decreased their time in paid work and spent more doing housework, home repairs, yardwork, shopping, and child care. By contrast, older women engaged in more paid work and decreased their time in housework.

Racism and Sexism A possible double jeopardy also faces many women—the burden of *both* ageism and sexism (Lopata, 1994). The poverty rate for older adult females is almost double that of older adult males. According to Congresswoman Mary Rose Oakar, the number one priority for midlife and older women should be economic security. She predicts that 25 percent of all women working today can expect to be poor in old age. Yet only recently has scientific and political interest in the aging woman developed. For many years, the aging woman was virtually invisible in aging research and in protests involving rights for older adults (Markson, 1995). An important research and political agenda for the twenty-first century is increased interest in the aging and the rights of older adult women.

Not only is it important to be concerned about older women's double jeopardy of ageism and sexism, but special attention also needs to be devoted to female ethnic minority older adults. They face what could be described as triple jeopardy—ageism, sexism, and racism (Burton, 1996; Markides, 1995). More information about being female, ethnic, and old appears in the Sociocultural Worlds of Development box.

Culture

Old Age Across Cultures and Time

What factors are associated with whether older adults are accorded a position of high status in a culture? Seven factors are most likely to predict high status for older adults in a culture (Sangree, 1989):

- Older persons have valuable knowledge.
- Older persons control key family/community resources.
- Older persons are permitted to engage in useful and valued functions as long as possible.
- There is role continuity throughout the life span.
- Age-related role changes involve greater responsibility, authority, and advisory capacity.
- The extended family is a common family arrangement in the culture, and the older person is integrated into the extended family.
- In general, respect for older adults is greater in collectivistic cultures (such as China and Japan), than in individualistic cultures (such as the United States). However, some researchers are finding that this collectivistic/individualistic difference in respect for older adults is not as strong as it used to be and that in some cases older adults in individualistic cultures receive considerable respect (Antonucci, Vandewater, & Lansford, 2000).

Cultures vary in the prestige they give to older adults. In the Navajo culture, older adults are especially treated with respect because of their wisdom and extensive life experiences. *What are some other factors that are linked with respect for older adults in a culture?*

Sociocultural Worlds of Development

Being Female, Ethnic, and Old

Part of the unfortunate history of ethnic minority groups in the United States has been the negative stereotypes against members of their groups. Many have also been hampered by their immigrant origins in that they are not fluent or literate in English, may not be aware of the values and norms involved in American social interaction, and may have lifestyles that differ from those of mainstream America (Organista, 1994). Often included in these cultural differences is the role of women in the family and in society. Many, but not all, immigrant ethnic groups traditionally have relegated the woman's role to family maintenance. Many important decisions may be made by a woman's husband or parents, and she is often not expected to seek an independent career or enter the workforce except in the case of dire financial need.

Some ethnic minority groups may define an older woman's role as unimportant, especially if she is unable to contribute financially. However, in some ethnic minority groups, an older woman's social status improves. For example, older African American women can express their own needs and can be given status and power in the community. Despite their positive status in the African American family and the African American culture, African American women over the age of 70 are the poorest population group in the United States. Three of five older African American women live alone; most of them are widowed. The low incomes of older African American women translate into less than adequate access to health care. Substantially lower incomes for African American older women are related to the kinds of jobs they hold, which either are not covered by Social Security or, in the case of domestic service, are not reported even when reporting is legally required.

A portrayal of older African American women in cities reveals some of their survival strategies. They highly value the family as a system of mutual support and aid, adhere to the American work ethic, and view religion as a source of strength (Perry & Johnson, 1994). The use of religion as a way of coping with stress has a long history in the African American culture, with roots in the slave experience. The African American church came to fulfill needs and functions once met by religion-based tribal and community organizations that African Americans brought from Africa. In one study, the older African American women valued church organizations more than their male counterparts did, especially valuing the church's group activities (Taylor, 1982).

In sum, older African American women have faced considerable stress in their lives (Edmonds, 1993). In the face of this stress, they have shown remarkable adaptiveness, resilience, responsibility, and coping skills.

A special concern is the stress faced by older African American women, many of whom view religion as a source of strength to help them cope. *What are some other characteristics of being female, ethnic, and old?*

Now that we have examined many aspects of the socioemotional worlds of older adults, let's once again think about what constitutes successful aging.

SUCCESSFUL AGING

Successful Aging

For too long, older adults were perceived as always being in decline, and the positive dimensions of aging were ignored (Rowe & Kahn, 1997). Throughout our coverage of late adulthood, we have called attention to successful aging and how earlier stereotypes of aging are being overturned as researchers discover that being an older adult has many positive aspects ◀ P. 582. We indicated that once developmentalists began focusing on the positive aspects of aging rather than primarily focusing on its negative aspects, they realized there are far more robust, healthy older adults than they previously believed. In our discussion of aging, we have found that with a proper diet, an active lifestyle, mental stimulation and flexibility, positive coping skills, good social relationships and support, and the absence of disease, many of our abilities can be maintained, or in some cases even improved, as we get older. Improvements in medicine mean that increasing numbers of older adults with diseases can still lead active, constructive lives. Being active is especially important in successful aging. Thus, older adults who get out and go to meetings, participate in church activities, go on trips, and exercise regularly are more satisfied with their lives than their counterparts who disengage from society and passively live out the last part of their lives (Mannell & Dupuis, 1996). In this chapter, we have seen that older adults who are emotionally selective, optimize their choices, and compensate effectively for any losses they might encounter increase their chances of aging successfully.

WWW

Successful Aging

Growing Older Better and Longer

Successful aging also involves perceived control over the environment and a sense of self-efficacy. In chapter 18, "Physical Development in Late Adulthood," we described how perceived control over the environment had a positive effect on nursing home residents' health and longevity ◀ P. 545. In recent years, the term *self-efficacy* has often been used to describe perceived control over the environment and the ability to produce positive outcomes (Bandura, 2000; Clarke-Plaskie & Lachman, 1999). Researchers have found that many older adults are quite effective in main-

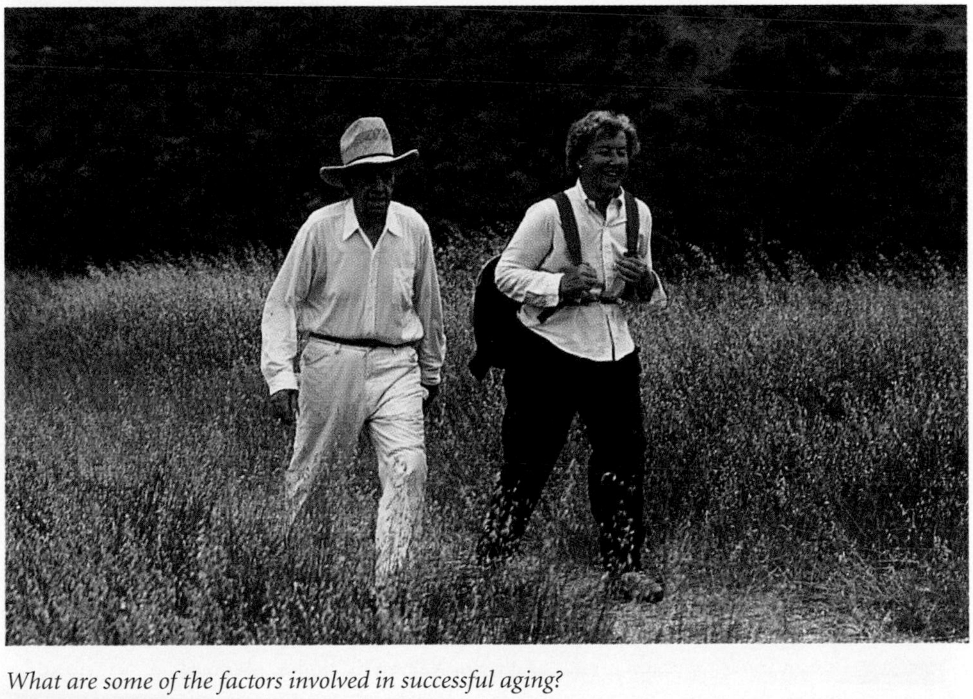

What are some of the factors involved in successful aging?

Summary Table 20.3
Ethnicity, Gender, and Culture; Successful Aging

Concept	Processes/ Related Ideas	Characteristics/Descriptions
Ethnicity, Gender and Culture	Ethnicity and Gender	• Aging minorities face special burdens, having to cope with the double burden of ageism and racism. Nonetheless, there is considerable variation in aging minorities.
		• There is stronger evidence that men become more feminine (nurturant, sensitive) as older adults than there is that women become more masculine (assertive). • Older women face a double jeopardy of ageism and sexism.
	Culture	• Historically, respect for older adults in China and Japan was high, but today their status is more variable. • Factors that predict high status for the elderly across cultures range from their valuable knowledge to integration into the extended family.
Successful Aging	A Positive Trend	• Increasingly, the positive aspects of older adults are being studied. Factors that are linked with successful aging include an active lifestyle, positive coping skills, good social relationships and support, and self-efficacy.

taining a sense of control and have a positive view of themselves (Brandstadter, Wentura, & Greve, 1993).

Examining the positive aspects of aging is an important trend in life-span development and is likely to benefit future generations of older adults. At this point, we have studied numerous aspects of ethnicity, culture, and gender, and life satisfaction and successful aging. To review these ideas, see summary table 20.3. In the next chapter, we will explore many dimensions of death and grieving.

John Glenn's recent space mission is emblematic of our rethinking of older adults in terms of successful aging.

Chapter Review

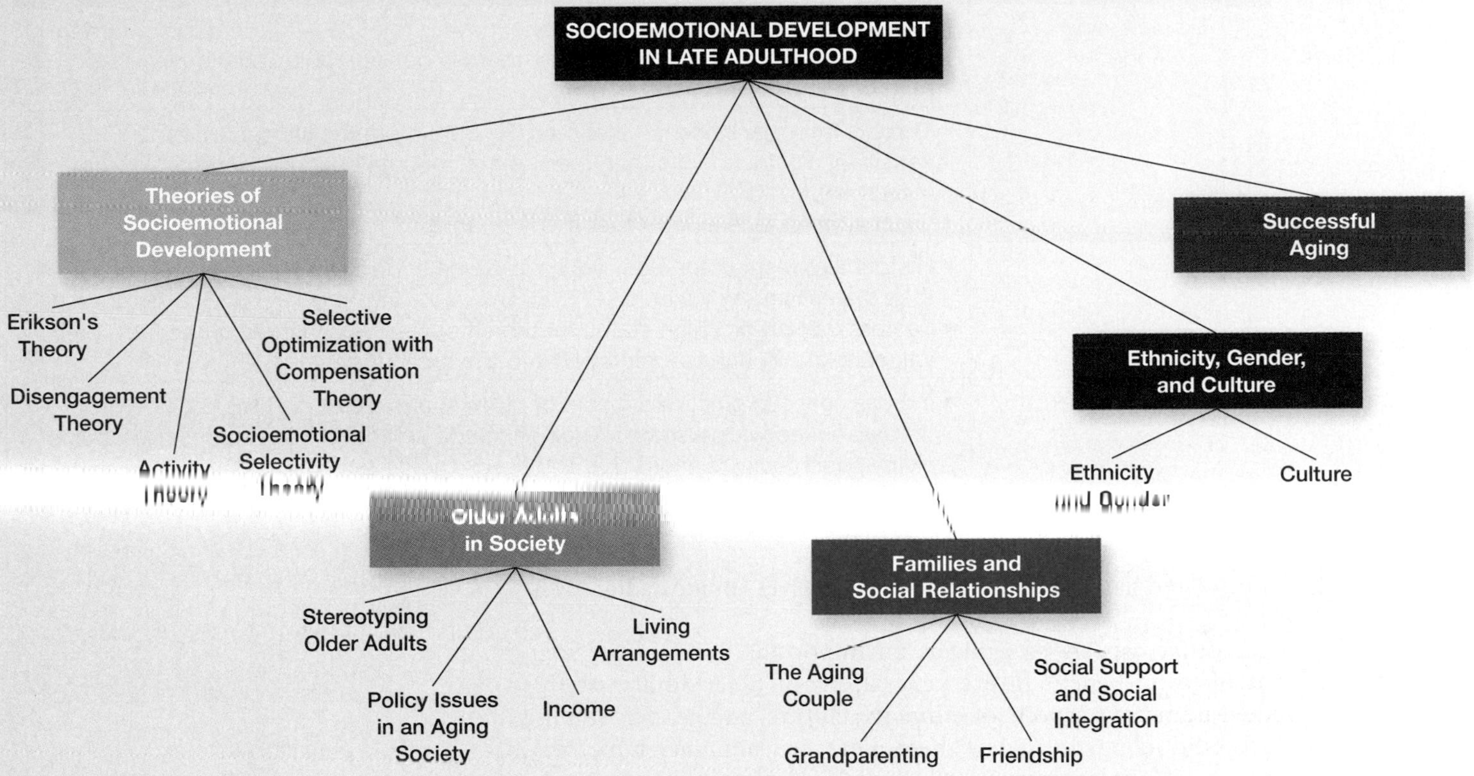

TO OBTAIN A DETAILED REVIEW OF THIS CHAPTER, STUDY THESE THREE SUMMARY TABLES:

- Summary Table 20.1 Theories of Socioemotional Development page 582
- Summary Table 20.2 Older Adults in Society; Families and Social Relationships page 591
- Summary Table 20.3 Ethnicity, Gender, and Culture; Successful Aging page 595

Key Terms

integrity versus despair 576
differentiation versus role preoccupation 576
body transcendence versus body preoccupation 576
ego transcendence versus ego preoccupation 576
disengagement theory 578
activity theory 578
socioemotional selectivity theory 578
selective optimization with compensation theory 580
ageism 582
eldercare 584
generational inequity 584

Key People

Erik Erikson 576
Robert Peck 576
Robert Butler 576
Laura Carstensen 578
Paul Baltes 580
Bernice Neugarten 584

Taking It to the Net

1. The 2000 presidential election campaign raised many key issues of debate including the viability of the Social Security program. How much do you know about your Social Security benefits? Take this quiz and follow the links to learn more about theis critical benefit's future.
2. Kristen's grandmother is getting too frail to live alone in her apartment, but does not yet need the care a nursing home provides. Is assisted living a good option for her? What are the types of assisted living facilities and what kind of services do they provide?
3. Jessica, a thirty-three year old single mother of three, has been diagnosed with breast cancer. Just as a precaution, Jessica has made arrangements for her parents to raise the children if something happens to her. What types of services and financial assistance would be available to Jessica's grandparents if they need to take on this responsibility?

Connect to www.mhhe.com/santrockld8 to research the answers and complete these exercises.

OLC Preview

To further test your knowledge of this chapter or to explore our extensive online resources that accompany *Life-Span Development,* eighth edition, please log on to the text's Online Learning Center at http://www.mhhe.com/santrockld8.com.

Section 10

Endings

Years following years steal something every day: At last they steal us from ourselves away.

Alexander Pope
English Poet, 18th Century

Our life ultimately ends—when we approach life's grave sustained and soothed with unfaltering trust or rave at the close of day; when at last years steal us from ourselves; and when we are linked to our children's children's children by an invisible cable that runs from age to age. This final section contains one chapter: "Death and Grieving" (chapter 21).

Chapter 21

- **DEATH AND GRIEVING**
  - **Defining Death and Life/Death Issues**
    - Issues in Determining Death
    - Decisions Regarding Life, Death, and Health Care
  - **Death and Sociohistorical, Cultural Contexts**
    - Changing Historical Circumstances
    - Death in Different Cultures
  - **A Developmental Perspective on Death**
    - Causes of Death and Expectations About Death
    - Attitudes Toward Death at Different Points in the Life Span
  - **Facing One's Own Death**
    - Kübler-Ross' Stages of Dying
    - Perceived Control and Denial
    - The Contexts in Which People Die
  - **Coping with the Death of Someone Else**
    - Communicating with a Dying Person
    - Grieving
    - Making Sense of the World
    - Losing a Life Partner
    - Forms of Mourning and the Funeral

Death and Grieving

Sustained and soothed
By an unfaltering trust,
approach thy grave,
Like one who wraps the
drapery of his couch
About him, and lies down
to pleasant dreams.

William Cullen Bryant
American Poet, 19th Century

Images of Life-Span Development

Princess Diana's Death

FEW DEATHS have captured the attention of the public as Princess Diana's did. Diana, Princess of Wales, died tragically in 1997 when the car she was traveling in crashed at high speed in Paris, France. Her body was subsequently returned to England and her funeral was held at Westminster Abbey. Following the funeral, which was televised around the world, the coffin was taken to the family's country estate for a private burial.

The elaborate, very formal funeral of Princess Diana is but one of many rituals of mourning. In this chapter you will read about many other types of mourning. Also, increasingly bodies are cremated rather than buried.

Death comes in many forms. For Princess Di, only 37 years old and very healthy, it was very unexpected. For many people, it occurs in old age and can be expected after a long illness.

When an individual dies, those who have had a close relationship with the deceased typically engage in a grief process that can be brief or last for many years. In Princess Di's case, her brother Earl Spencer gave a moving speech at the funeral in which he spoke of her kindness and how she would be missed. The grieving of her two sons—William and Harry, with whom she had very close, loving relationships—was especially important to their well-being. A noticeable form of grieving by William and Harry was their placement of white flowers on the coffin with a letter addressed to "Mummy."

Princess Diana's sons William and Harry placed white flowers and a letter to their mother on her coffin. *What are some ways that people mourn a death and grieve?*

After someone dies, individuals review the person's life and evaluate what they were like as a person and their contributions. Princess Di was especially remembered for her charitable work and the positive image she brought to the British royal family. At her funeral, many individuals gave tributes to her, including Elton John, who wrote and sang in her memory a special version of his song "Candle in the Wind."

DEFINING DEATH AND LIFE/DEATH ISSUES

Issues in Determining Death

Decisions Regarding Life, Death, and Health Care

Defining Death and Life/Death Issues

Is there one point in the process of dying that is *the* point at which death takes place, or is death a more gradual process? What are some decisions individuals can make about life, death, and health care?

Issues in Determining Death

Twenty-five years ago, determining if someone was dead was simpler than it is today. The end of certain biological functions, such as breathing and blood pressure, and the rigidity of the body (rigor mortis) were considered to be clear signs of death. In the past several decades, defining death has become more complex. Consider the circumstance of Philadelphia Flyers hockey star Pelle Lindbergh, who slammed his Porsche into a cement wall on November 10, 1985. The newspaper headline the next day read, "Flyers' Goalie is Declared Brain Dead." In spite of the claim that he was "brain dead," the story reported that Lindbergh was listed in "critical condition" in the intensive care unit of a hospital.

brain death
A neurological definition of death. A person is brain dead when all electrical activity of the brain has ceased for a specified period of time. A flat EEG recording is one criterion of brain death.

Brain death *is a neurological definition of death, which states that a person is brain dead when all electrical activity of the brain has ceased for a specified period of time. A flat EEG (electroencephalogram) recording for a specified period of time is one criterion of brain death.* The higher portions of the brain often die sooner than the lower portions. Because the brain's lower portions monitor heartbeat and respiration, individuals whose higher brain areas have died may continue breathing and have a heartbeat. The definition of brain death currently followed by most physicians includes the death of both the higher cortical functions and the lower brain stem functions.

Some medical experts argue that the criteria for death should include only higher cortical functioning. If the cortical death definition were adopted, then physicians could claim a person is dead who has no cortical functioning even though the lower brain stem is functioning. Supporters of the cortical death policy argue that the functions we associate with being human, such as intelligence and personality, are located in the higher cortical part of the brain. They believe that when these functions are lost, the "human being" is no longer alive. To date, the cortical definition of death is not a legal definition of death anywhere in America.

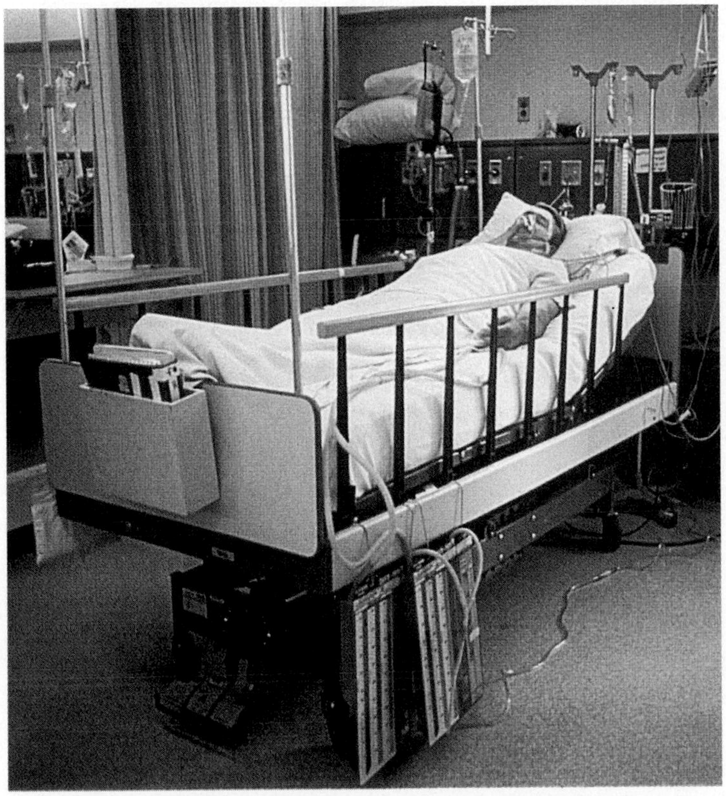

Advances in medical technology have complicated the definition of death. Controversy continues to swirl about what criteria should be used to determine when someone is dead. *What is this controversy about?*

Decisions Regarding Life, Death, and Health Care

In cases of catastrophic illness or emergency circumstances, patients might not be able to respond adequately to participate in decisions about their medical care, possibly even being comatose or irrational. To prepare for this type of situation, some individuals make choices earlier.

Natural Death Act and Advanced Directive

For many patients in a coma, it has not been clear what their wishes regarding termination of treatment might be if they still were conscious (Aiken, 2000). Recognizing that terminally ill patients might prefer to die rather than linger in a painful or vegetative state, the organization "Choice in Dying" created the Living Will. This document is designed to be filled in while the individual can still think clearly and expresses the person's desires regarding extraordinary medical procedures that might be used to sustain life when the medical situation becomes hopeless.

Physicians' concerns over malpractice suits and the efforts of people who support the Living Will concept have produced natural death legislation in many states. For example, California's Natural Death Act permits individuals who have been diagnosed by two physicians as terminally ill to sign an *advanced directive,* which states that life-sustaining procedures shall not be used to prolong their lives when death is imminent. An advanced directive must be signed while the individual still is able to think clearly. Laws in all fifty states now accept advanced directives as reflecting an individual's wishes.

Euthanasia **Euthanasia** *("easy death") is the act of painlessly ending the lives of individuals who are suffering from an incurable disease or severe disability. Sometimes euthanasia is called "mercy killing."* Distinctions are made between two types of euthanasia: passive and active. **Passive euthanasia** *occurs when a person is allowed to die by withholding available treatment, such as withdrawing a life-sustaining device.* For example, this might involve turning off a respirator or a heart-lung machine. **Active euthanasia** *occurs when death is deliberately induced, as when a lethal dose of a drug is injected.*

euthanasia
The act of painlessly ending the lives of persons who are suffering from incurable diseases or severe disabilities; sometimes called "mercy killing."

passive euthanasia
The withholding of available treatments, such as life-sustaining devices, allowing the person to die.

active euthanasia
Death induced deliberately, as by injecting a lethal dose of a drug.

Technological advances in life-support devices raise the issue of quality of life (Asch & Christakis, 1996; Jecker, 1996). Should individuals be kept alive in undignified and hopeless states? The trend is toward acceptance of passive euthanasia in the case of terminally ill patients. The inflammatory argument that once equated this practice with suicide rarely is heard today. However, experts do not yet entirely agree on the precise boundaries or the exact mechanisms by which treatment decisions should be implemented. Can a comatose patient's life-support systems be disconnected when the patient has left no written instructions to that effect? Does the family of a comatose patient have the right to overrule the attending physician's decision to continue life-support systems? These are searching questions with no simple or universally agreed-upon answers (Beckel, 1996). In one study of Canadian health-care workers, there was considerable variability in their decisions about whether to withdraw life support from critically ill patients (Cook & others, 1995).

Living Wills
Choice in Dying
Jack Kevorkian
Assisted Suicide
Exploring Euthanasia
Euthanasia Resources

The most widely publicized cases of active euthanasia involve the "assisted suicide" practiced by Jack Kevorkian, a Michigan physician. Kevorkian has assisted a number of terminally ill patients to end their lives. After a series of trials, Kevorkian was convicted of second-degree murder and given a long prison sentence.

Active euthanasia is a crime in most countries and in all states in the United States except one—Oregon. Active euthanasia is legal in the Netherlands and Uruguay. In 1994, the state of Oregon passed the Death with Dignity Act, which allows active euthansia. Through 1998, fifteen individuals were known to have died by active euthanasia in Oregon.

A recent survey of more than 900 physicians assessed their attitudes about active euthanasia (Walker, Gruman, & Blank, 1999). Most opposed active euthanasia, said that adequate pain control often eliminates the need for it, and commented that the primary role of the physician is to preserve life. They also reported that the potential for abuse in active euthanasia is substantial, and many believed that it is morally wrong.

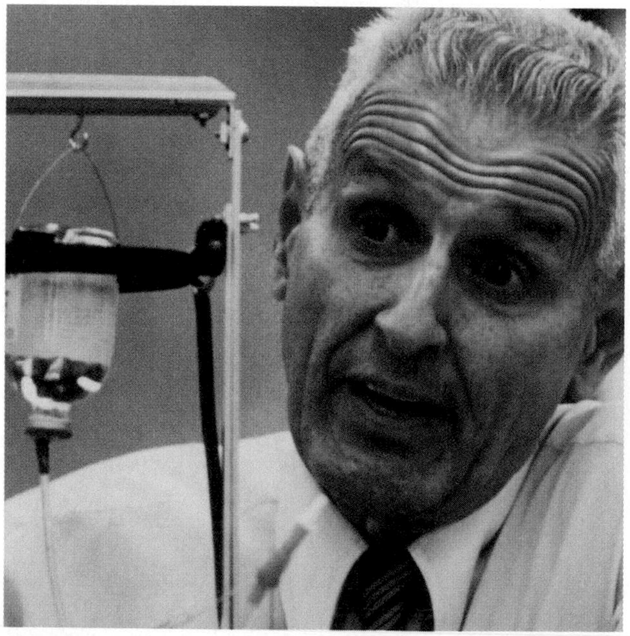
Dr. Jack Kevorkian, who assisted a number of people in Michigan as they ended their lives through active euthanasia. *Where do you stand on the use of active euthanasia?*

Needed: Better Care for Dying Individuals A recent report by a panel of experts concluded that death in America is often lonely, prolonged, and painful (Institute of Medicine, 1997). Dying individuals often get too little or too much care. Scientific advances sometimes have made dying harder by delaying the inevitable (Muth, 2000). Also, even though painkillers are available, too many people experience severe pain during the last days and months of life. The panel of experts recommended that regulations be changed to make it easier for physicians to prescribe painkillers for dying patients who need

them. The panel also pointed out that many health-care professionals have not been trained to provide adequate end-of-life care or understand how important it is.

There are few fail-safe measures for avoiding pain at end of life. Still, you can do the following (Cowley & Hager, 1995):

- Make a Living Will, and be sure there is someone who will draw your doctor's attention to it.
- Give someone the power of attorney and make sure this person knows your wishes regarding medical care.
- Give your doctors specific instructions—from "Do not resuscitate" to "Do everything possible"—for specific circumstances.
- If you want to die at home, talk it over with your family and doctor.
- Check to see whether your insurance plan covers home care and hospice care.

hospice
A humanized program committed to making the end of life as free from pain, anxiety, and depression as possible. The goals of hospice contrast with those of a hospital, which are to cure disease and prolong life.

Hospice *is a humanized program committed to making the end of life as free from pain, anxiety, and depression as possible. Hospice's goals contrast with those of a hospital, which are to cure illness and prolong life.* The hospice movement began toward the end of the 1960s in London, when a new kind of medical institution, St. Christopher's Hospice, opened. Little effort is made to prolong life at St. Christopher's—there are no heart-lung machines and there is no intensive care unit, for example. A primary goal is to bring pain under control and to help dying patients face death in a psychologically healthy way. The hospice also makes every effort to include the dying individual's family; it is believed that this strategy benefits not only the dying individual but family members as well, probably diminishing their guilt after the death.

Hospice Net

Hospice Foundation of America

Better Care for the Dying

The hospice movement has grown rapidly in the United States. Hospice advocates continue to underscore that it is possible to control pain for almost any dying individual and that it is possible to create an environment for the patient that is superior to that found in most hospitals (Hayslip, 1996).

Today more hospice programs are home-based, a blend of institutional and home care designed to humanize the end-of-life experience for the dying person. Whether the hospice program is carried out in the dying person's home, through a blend of home and institutional care, or in an institution often depends on medical needs and the availability of caregivers, including family and friends.

The widespread acceptance of hospices is evident in the more than 1,500 community groups that are involved nationally in establishing hospice programs. Hospices are more likely to serve people with terminal cancer than those with other life-threatening conditions (Kastenbaum, 2000).

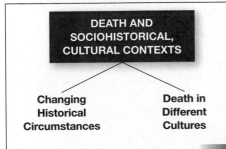

DEATH AND SOCIOHISTORICAL, CULTURAL CONTEXTS

Changing Historical Circumstances | **Death in Different Cultures**

Death and Sociohistorical, Cultural Contexts

When, where, and how people die have changed historically in the United States, and attitudes toward death vary across cultures.

Changing Historical Circumstances

We have already described one of the historical changes involving death—the increasing complexity of determining when someone is truly dead. Another historical change in death is in the age group it strikes most often. Two hundred years ago, almost one of every two children died before the age of 10, and one parent died before children grew up. Today, death occurs most often among the elderly. Life expectancy has increased from 47 years for a person born in 1900 to 97 years for someone born today (U.S. Bureau of the Census, 2000). In 1900, most people died at home, cared for by their family. As our population has aged and become more mobile, more older adults die apart from their families. In the United States today, more than 80 percent of all deaths occur in institutions or hospitals. The care of a dying older person has shifted

away from the family and minimized our exposure to death and its painful surroundings.

Dying and Medicine in America
Culture and Death
Judaism and Death
Islam and Death
Hinduism and Death

Death in Different Cultures

The ancient Greeks faced death as they faced life—openly and directly. To live a full life and die with glory was the prevailing goal of the Greeks. Individuals are more conscious of death in times of war, famine, and plague. Whereas Americans are conditioned from early in life to live as though they were immortal, in much of the world this fiction cannot be maintained. Death crowds the streets of Calcutta in daily overdisplay, as it does the scrubby villages of Africa's Sahel. Children live with the ultimate toll of malnutrition and disease, mothers lose as many babies as survive into adulthood, and it is rare that a family remains intact for many years. Even in peasant areas where life is better, and health and maturity may be reasonable expectations, the presence of dying people in the house, the large attendance at funerals, and the daily contact with aging adults prepare the young for death and provide them with guidelines on how to die. By contrast, in the United States it is not uncommon to reach adulthood without having seen someone die.

Most societies throughout history have had philosophical or religious beliefs about death, and most societies have a ritual that deals with death (see figure 21.1).

In most societies, death is not viewed as the end of existence—though the biological body has died, the spiritual body is believed to live on. This religious perspective is favored by most Americans as well. However, cultures differ in their perceptions of death and their reactions to it. In the Gond culture of India, death is believed to be caused by magic and demons. The members of the Gond culture react angrily to death. In the Tanala culture of Madagascar, death is believed to be caused by natural forces. The members of the Tanala culture show a much more

Figure **21.1**

A Ritual Associated with Death

Family memorial day at the national cemetery in Seoul, Korea.

peaceful reaction to death than their counterparts in the Gond culture. Other cultural variations in attitudes toward death include beliefs about reincarnation, which is an important aspect of the Hindu and Buddhist religions (Truitner & Truitner, 1993).

Perceptions of death vary and reflect diverse values and philosophies. Death may be seen as a punishment for one's sins, an act of atonement, or a judgment of a just God. For some, death means loneliness; for others, death is a quest for happiness. For still others, death represents redemption, a relief from the trials and tribulations of the earthly world. Some embrace death and welcome it; others abhor and fear it. For those who welcome it, death may be seen as the fitting end to a fulfilled life. From this perspective, how we depart from earth is influenced by how we have lived.

In many ways, we in the United States are death avoiders and death deniers. This denial can take many forms:

- The tendency of the funeral industry to gloss over death and fashion lifelike qualities in the dead
- The adoption of euphemistic language for death—for example, *exiting, passing on, never say die,* and *good for life,* which implies forever
- The persistent search for a fountain of youth
- The rejection and isolation of the aged, who may remind us of death
- The adoption of the concept of a pleasant and rewarding afterlife, suggesting that we are immortal
- The medical community's emphasis on the prolongation of biological life rather than an emphasis on diminishing human suffering

Even though we are death avoiders and death deniers, ultimately we face death—others' and our own.

At this point, we have discussed a number of ideas about defining death and life/death issues and death in sociocultural, cultural contexts. To review these ideas, see summary table 21.1. Next we look at a developmental perspective on death.

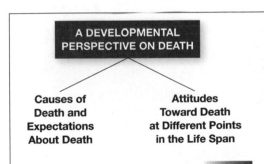

A DEVELOPMENTAL PERSPECTIVE ON DEATH

Causes of Death and Expectations About Death

Attitudes Toward Death at Different Points in the Life Span

A Developmental Perspective on Death

Do the causes of death vary across the human life span? Do we have different expectations about death as we develop through the life span? What are our attitudes toward death at different points in our development?

Causes of Death

Causes of Death and Expectations About Death

Although we often think of death as occurring in old age, death can occur at any point in the human life span. Death can occur during prenatal development through miscarriages or stillborn births. Death can also occur during the birth process or in the first few days after birth, which usually happens because of a birth defect or because infants have not developed adequately to sustain life outside the uterus. In chapter 5, "Physical Development in Infancy," we described *sudden infant death syndrome (SIDS),* in which infants stop breathing, usually during the night, and die without apparent cause. SIDS currently is the highest cause of infant death in the United States, with the risk highest at 4 to 6 weeks of age (American Academy of Pediatrics Task Force on Infant Sleep Position and SIDS, 2000).

In childhood, death occurs most often because of accidents or illness. Accidental death in childhood can be the consequence of such things as an automobile accident, drowning, poisoning, fire, or a fall from a high place. Major illnesses that cause death in children are heart disease, cancer, and birth defects, and it is not unusual for terminally ill children to distance themselves from their parents as they approach the final phase of their illness. The distancing may be due to the depression that many

Summary Table 21.1
Defining Death and Life/Death Issues: Death and Sociohistorical, Cultural Contexts

Concept	Processes/ Related Ideas	Characteristics/Descriptions
Defining Death and Life/Death Issues	Issues in Determining Death	• Twenty-five years ago, determining if someone was dead was simpler than it is today. • Brain death is a neurological definition of death, which states that a person is brain dead when all electrical activity of the brain has ceased for a specified period of time. Medical experts debate whether this should mean the higher and lower brain functions or just the higher cortical functions. • Currently, most states have a statute endorsing the cessation of brain function (both higher and lower) as a standard for determining death.
	Decisions Regarding Life, Death, and Health Care	• The Natural Death Act and advanced directive are increasingly used. • Euthanasia is the act of painlessly ending the life of a person who is suffering from an incurable disease or disability. Distinctions are made between active and passive euthanasia. • The need for more humanized care for the dying person includes the development of hospice.
Death and Sociohistorical, Cultural Contexts	Changing Historical Circumstances	• When, where, and why people die have changed historically. Today, death occurs most often among the elderly. • More than 80 percent of all deaths in the United States now occur in a hospital or an institution. • Our exposure to death in the family has been minimized.
	Death in Different Cultures	• Most societies throughout history have had philosophical or religious beliefs about death, and most societies have rituals that deal with death. • Most cultures do not view death as the end of existence—spiritual life is thought to continue. • The United States has been described as a death-denying and death-avoiding culture.

dying patients experience, or it may be a child's way of protecting parents from the overwhelming grief they will experience at the death. Most dying children know they have a terminal illness. Their developmental level, social support, and coping skills influence how well they cope with knowing they will die.

Compared to childhood, death in adolescence is more likely to occur because of motor vehicle accidents, suicide, and homicide. Many motor vehicle accidents that cause death in adolescence are alcohol-related.

Older adults are more likely to die from chronic diseases, such as heart disease and cancer, whereas younger adults are more likely to die from accidents. Older adults' diseases often incapacitate before they kill, which produces a course of dying that slowly leads to death. Of course, many young and middle-aged adults die of diseases, such as heart disease and cancer.

Younger adults who are dying often feel cheated more than do older adults who are dying (Kalish,1987). Younger adults are more likely to feel they have not had the opportunity to do what they want to with their lives. Younger adults perceive they are losing what they might achieve; older adults perceive they are losing what they have.

Attitudes Toward Death at Different Points in the Life Span

The ages of children and adults influence the way they experience and think about death. A mature, adultlike conception of death includes an understanding that death is final and irreversible, that death represents the end of life, and that all living things die. Most researchers have found that, as children grow, they develop a more mature approach to death (Wass & Stillion, 1988).

Childhood Most researchers believe that infants do not have even a rudimentary concept of death. However, as infants develop an attachment to a caregiver, they can experience loss or separation and an accompanying anxiety. But young children do not perceive time the way adults do. Even brief separations may be experienced as total losses. For most infants, the reappearance of the caregiver provides a continuity of existence and a reduction of anxiety. We know very little about the infant's actual experiences with bereavement, although the loss of a parent, especially if the caregiver is not replaced, can negatively affect the infant's health.

Even children 3 to 5 years of age have little or no idea of what death really means. They may confuse death with sleep or ask in a puzzled way, "Why doesn't it move?" Preschool-aged children rarely get upset by the sight of a dead animal or by being told that a person has died. They believe that the dead can be brought back to life spontaneously by magic or by giving them food or medical treatment. Young children often believe that only people who want to die or who are bad or careless actually die. They also may blame themselves for the death of someone they know well, illogically reasoning that the event may have happened because they disobeyed the person who died.

Discussing Death with Young Children
Grieving Children
Education About Death and Dying
Association of Death Education and Counseling

Sometime in the middle and late childhood years more realistic perceptions of death develop. In one early investigation of children's perception of death, children 3 to 5 years of age denied that death exists, children 6 to 9 years of age believed that death exists but only happens to some people, and children 9 years of age and older recognized death's finality and universality (Nagy, 1948).

In a recent review of research on children's conception of death, it was concluded that children probably do not view death as universal and irreversible until about 9 years of age (Cuddy-Casey & Orvaschel, 1997). Most children under 7 do not see death as likely. Those who do, perceive it as reversible.

An expert on death and dying, Robert Kastenbaum (1997) takes a different view on developmental dimensions of death and dying. He believes that even very young children are acutely aware of and concerned about *separation* and *loss,* just as attachment theorist John Bowlby (1980) does. Kastenbaum also says that many children work hard at trying to understand death. Thus, instead of viewing young children as having illogical perceptions of death, Kastenbaum thinks a more accurate stance is to view them as having concerns about death and striving to understand it.

Most psychologists believe that honesty is the best strategy in discussing death with children. Treating the concept as unmentionable is thought to be an inappropriate strategy, yet most of us have grown up in a society in which death is rarely discussed. In one study, the attitudes of 30,000 young adults toward death were evaluated (Shneidman, 1973). More than 30 percent said they could not recall any discussion of death during their childhood. An equal number said that, although death was discussed, the discussion took place in an uncomfortable atmosphere. Almost one of every two respondents said that the death of a grandparent was their first personal encounter with death.

In addition to honesty, what other strategies can be adopted in discussing death with children? The best response to the child's query about death might depend on the child's maturity level (Aiken, 2000). For example, the preschool child requires a less elaborate explanation than an older child. Death can be explained to preschool children in simple physical and biological terms. Actually, what young children need more than elaborate explanations of death is reassurance that they are loved and will

not be abandoned. Regardless of children's age, adults should be sensitive and sympathetic, encouraging them to express their own feelings and ideas.

Adolescence In adolescence, the prospect of death, like the prospect of aging, is regarded as a notion that is so remote that it does not have much relevance. The subject of death may be avoided, glossed over, kidded about, neutralized, and controlled by a cool, spectatorlike orientation. This perspective is typical of the adolescent's self-conscious thought; however, some adolescents do show a concern for death, both in trying to fathom its meaning and in confronting the prospect of their own demise (Baxter, Stuart, & Stewart, 1998).

Adolescents develop more abstract conceptions of death than children do. For example, adolescents describe death in terms of darkness, light, transition, or nothingness (Wenestam & Wass, 1987). They also develop religious and philosophical views about the nature of death and whether there is life after death.

You will also recall the concepts of adolescent egocentrism and personal table from chapter 12, "Physical and Cognitive Development in Adolescence"—adolescents' preoccupation with themselves and their belief that they are invincible and unique. Thus, it is not unusual for adolescents to think that they are somehow immune to death and that death is something that happens to other people but not to them.

Adulthood There is no evidence that a special orientation toward death develops in early adulthood. An increase in consciousness about death accompanies individuals' awareness that they are aging, which usually intensifies in middle adulthood. In our discussion of middle adulthood, we indicated that midlife is a time when adults begin to think more about how much time is left in their lives. Researchers have found that middle-aged adults actually fear death more than do young adults or older adults (Kalish & Reynolds, 1976). Older adults, though, think about death more and talk about it more in conversation with others than do middle-aged and young adults. They also have more direct experience with death as their friends and relatives become ill and die. Older adults are forced to examine the meanings of life and death more frequently than are younger adults.

In old age, one's own death may take on an appropriateness it lacked in earlier years. Some of the increased thinking and conversing about death, and an increased sense of integrity developed through a positive life review, may help older adults accept death. Older adults are less likely to have unfinished business than are younger adults. They usually do not have children who need to be guided to maturity, their spouses are more likely to be dead, and they are less likely to have work-related projects that require completion. Lacking such anticipations, death may be less emotionally painful to them. Even among older adults, however, attitudes toward death are sometimes as individualized as the people holding

CAREERS IN LIFE-SPAN DEVELOPMENT

Robert Kastenbaum, Geropsychologist

ROBERT KASTENBAUM became interested in aging, death, and grieving in a culture—that of the United States—whose people felt uncomfortable talking about such matters. After obtaining his doctorate at the University of Southern California, he became one of the first geropsychologists (researchers who study the psychology of aging). After years of research, he became director of a hospital for the aged and introduced new programs for providing a more stimulating and supportive institutional environment. Robert helped to plan and evaluate the National Hospice Demonstration project, which confirmed the value of patient and family-oriented care in the last phase of life. He was a cofounder of the National Caucus on Black Aging, established an interdisciplinary program in aging and human development at Arizona State University, and served for three decades as editor of the *International journal of Aging and Human Development* and *Omega: Journal of Death and Dying.* His books include *Dorian Graying: Is Youth the Only Thing That Matters?; Defining Acts; Death as Drama; The Psychology of Death;* and *Death, Society, and Human Experience.*

Now retired from Arizona State University, Robert is devoting more time to writing theater pieces that deal with themes of aging and death. He wrote the words for the operas *Dorian* (premiered in New York City) and *Closing Time* (premiered in Tucson) and, most recently, the play *Tell Me About Tigers* (premiered in English and French versions in Montreal). A strong theme in both his research and his theater pieces has been how people face critical life-and-death situations and how this is affected by the values and relationships they have been developing throughout their lives.

Robert Kastenbaum, with a poster from one of the theater pieces he wrote.

them. One 82-year-old woman declared that she had lived her life and was now ready to see it come to an end. Another 82-year-old woman declared that death would be a regrettable interruption of her participation in activities and relationships.

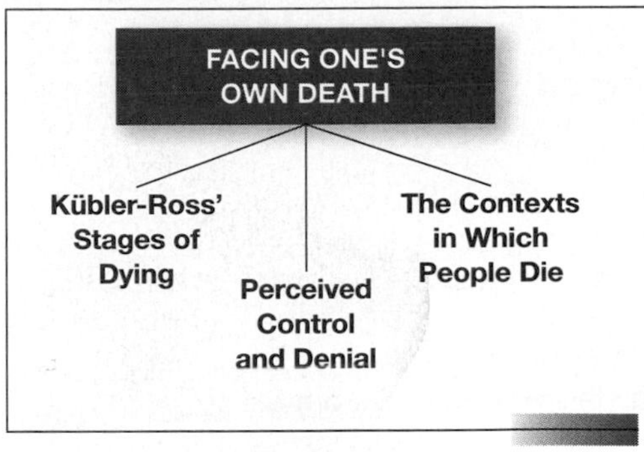

Facing One's Own Death

Knowledge of death's inevitability permits us to establish priorities and structure our time accordingly. As we age, these priorities and structurings change in recognition of diminishing future time. Values concerning the most important uses of time also change. For example, when asked how they would spend 6 remaining months of life, younger adults described such activities as traveling and accomplishing things they previously had not done; older adults described more inner-focused activities—contemplation and meditation, for example (Kalish & Reynolds, 1976).

Most dying individuals want an opportunity to make some decisions regarding their own life and death (Kastenbaum, 2000). Some individuals want to complete unfinished business; they want time to resolve problems and conflicts and to put their affairs in order. Might there be a sequence of stages we go through as we face death?

Kübler-Ross on Dying

Kübler-Ross' Stages of Dying

Elisabeth Kübler-Ross (1969) divided the behavior and thinking of dying persons into five stages: denial and isolation, anger, bargaining, depression, and acceptance. **Denial and isolation** *is Kübler-Ross' first stage of dying, in which the person denies that death is really going to take place.* The person may say, "No, it can't be me. It's not possible." This is a common reaction to terminal illness. However, denial is usually only a temporary defense and is eventually replaced with increased awareness when the person is confronted with such matters as financial considerations, unfinished business, and worry about surviving family members.

denial and isolation
Kübler-Ross' first stage of dying, in which the dying person denies that she or he is really going to die.

Anger *is Kübler-Ross' second stage of dying, in which the dying person recognizes that denial can no longer be maintained. Denial often gives way to anger, resentment, rage, and envy.* The dying person's question is, "Why me?" At this point, the person becomes increasingly difficult to care for as anger may become displaced and projected onto physicians, nurses, family members, and even God. The realization of loss is great, and those who symbolize life, energy, and competent functioning are especially salient targets of the dying person's resentment and jealousy.

anger
Kübler-Ross' second stage of dying, in which the dying person's denial gives way to anger, resentment, rage, and envy.

Bargaining *is Kübler-Ross' third stage of dying, in which the person develops the hope that death can somehow be postponed or delayed.* Some persons enter into a bargaining or negotiation—often with God—as they try to delay their death. Psychologically, the person is saying, "Yes, me, but . . ." In exchange for a few more days, weeks, or months of life, the person promises to lead a reformed life dedicated to God or to the service of others.

bargaining
Kübler-Ross' third stage of dying, in which the dying person develops the hope that death can somehow be postponed.

Depression *is Kübler-Ross' fourth stage of dying, in which the dying person comes to accept the certainty of death. At this point, a period of depression or preparatory grief may appear.* The dying person may become silent, refuse visitors, and spend much of the time crying or grieving. This behavior should be perceived as normal in this circumstance and is actually an effort to disconnect the self from all love objects. Attempts to cheer up the dying person at this stage should be discouraged, says Kübler-Ross, because the dying person has a need to contemplate impending death.

depression
Kübler-Ross' fourth stage of dying, in which the dying person comes to accept the certainty of her or his death. A period of depression or preparatory grief may appear.

Acceptance *is Kübler-Ross' fifth stage of dying, in which the person develops a sense of peace; an acceptance of one's fate; and, in many cases, a desire to be left alone.* In this stage, feelings and physical pain may be virtually absent. Kübler-Ross describes this fifth stage as the end of the dying struggle, the final resting stage before death. A summary of Kübler-Ross' dying stages is presented in figure 21.2.

acceptance
Kübler-Ross' fifth stage of dying, in which the dying person develops a sense of peace, an acceptance of her or his fate, and, in many cases, a desire to be left alone.

What is the current evaluation of Kübler-Ross' approach? According to psychology death expert Robert Kastenbaum (1998, 2000). There are some problems with Kübler-Ross' approach:

- The existence of the five-stage sequence has not been demonstrated by either Kübler-Ross or independent research.
- The stage interpretation neglected the patients' total life situations, including relationship support, specific effects of illness, family obligations, and institutional climate in which they were interviewed.

Because of the criticisms of Kübler-Ross' stages of dying, some psychologists prefer to describe them not as stages but rather as potential reactions to dying. At any one moment, a number of emotions may wax and wane. Hope, disbelief, bewilderment, anger, and acceptance may come and go as individuals try to make sense of what is happening to them. However, we should not forget Kübler-Ross' pioneering efforts:

- Her contribution was important in calling attention to people who are attempting to cope with life-threatening illnesses.
- She did much to encourage giving needed attention to the quality of life for dying persons and their families.

In facing their own death, some individuals struggle until the end, desperately trying to hang on to their lives. Acceptance of death never comes for them. Some psychologists believe that the harder individuals fight to avoid the inevitable death they face and the more they deny it, the more difficulty they will have in dying peacefully and in a dignified way; other psychologists argue that not confronting death until the end may be adaptive for some individuals (Lifton, 1977).

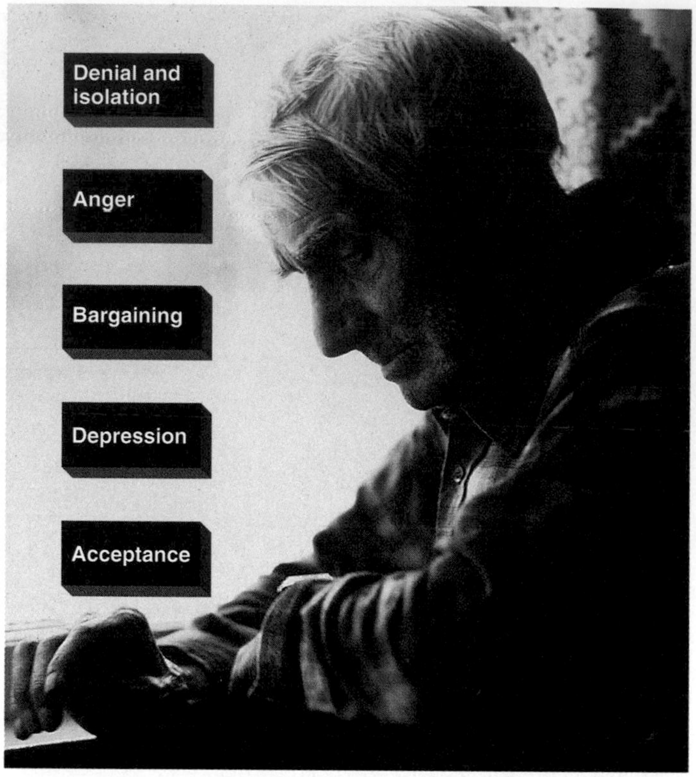

Figure 21.2

Kübler-Ross' Stages of Dying

According to Elisabeth Kübler-Ross, we go through five stages of dying: denial and isolation, anger, bargaining, depression, and acceptance. *Does everyone go through these stages, or go through them in the same order? Explain.*

Perceived Control and Denial

Perceived control and denial may work together as an adaptive strategy for some older adults who face death. When individuals are led to believe they can influence and control events—such as prolonging their lives—they may become more alert and cheerful. Remember from our discussion in chapter 18 that giving nursing home residents options for control improved their attitudes and increased their longevity (Rodin & Langer, 1977) ◀ P. 545.

Denial also may be a fruitful way for some individuals to approach death. It is not unusual for dying individuals to deny death right up until the time they die. Life without hope represents learned helplessness in its most extreme form. Denial can protect us from the torturous feeling that we are going to die.

Denial can be adaptive or maladaptive. Denial can be used to avoid the destructive impact of shock by delaying the necessity of dealing with one's death. Denial can insulate the individual from having to cope with intense feelings of anger and hurt; however, if denial keeps us from having a life-saving operation, it clearly is maladaptive. Denial is neither good nor bad; its adaptive qualities need to be evaluated on an individual basis.

Critical Thinking

Exploring Your Own Death and Dying

To explore your own death and dying, respond to the following questions and discuss your answers with several friends or family members:

- Who died in your first personal involvement with death? What do you remember about it?
- What does death mean to you?
- What aspect of your own death is the most distasteful to you?
- If you had a choice, what kind of death would you prefer?
- For whom or what would you be willing to sacrifice your own life?

The Contexts in Which People Die

For dying individuals, the context in which they die is important. More than 50 percent of Americans die in hospitals, and nearly 20 percent die in nursing homes. For some people, their final days unfortunately are spent in isolation and fear (Clay, 1997).

Summary Table 21.2
A Developmental Perspective on Death; Facing One's Own Death

Concept	Processes/ Related Ideas	Characteristics/Descriptions
A Developmental Perspective on Death	Causes of Death and Expectations About Death	• Although death is more likely to occur in late adulthood, death can come at any point in development. • The deaths of some persons, especially children and younger adults, are often perceived to be more tragic than those of others, such as very old adults, who have had an opportunity to live a long life. • In children and younger adults, death is more likely to occur because of accidents but in older adults is more likely to occur because of chronic diseases.
	Attitudes Toward Death at Different Points in the Life Span	• Infants do not have a concept of death. • Preschool children also have little concept of death, often showing little or no upset at the sight of a dead animal or person. Preschool children sometimes blame themselves for a person's death. In the elementary school years, children develop a more realistic orientation toward death. Most psychologists believe honesty is the best strategy for helping children cope with death. • Death may be glossed over in adolescence. Adolescents have more abstract, philosophical views of death than children do. • There is no evidence that a special orientation toward death emerges in early adulthood. • Middle adulthood is a time when adults show a heightened consciousness about death and death anxiety. • Older adults often show less death anxiety than middle-aged adults, but older adults experience and converse about death more. Attitudes about death may vary considerably among adults of any age.
Facing One's Own Death	Kübler-Ross' Stages of Dying	• She proposed five stages: denial and isolation, anger, bargaining, depression, and acceptance. • Not all individuals go through the same sequence. Some individuals may struggle to the end.
	Perceived Control and Denial	• Perceived control and denial may work together as an adaptive orientation for the dying individual. • Denial can be adaptive or maladaptive, depending on the circumstance.
	The Contexts in Which People Die	• Most deaths in the United States occur in hospitals; this has advantages and disadvantages. • Most individuals say they would rather die at home, but they worry that they will be a burden and they worry about the lack of medical care.

Do not go gentle into that good night Old age should burn and rave at close of day; Rage, rage against the dying of the light.

Dylan Thomas
Welsh Poet, 20th Century

Hospitals offer several important advantages to the dying individual—professional staff members are readily available, and the medical technology present may prolong life, for example, yet a hospital may not be the best place for many people to die. Most individuals say they would rather die at home (Kalish & Reynolds, 1976). Many feel, however, that they will be a burden at home, that there is limited space there, and that dying at home may alter prior relationships such as being cared for by one's children. Individuals who are facing death also worry about the competency and availability of emergency medical treatment if they remain at home. As we saw earlier in the chapter, an increasing number of people choose to die in the humane atmosphere of a hospice.

At this point we have discussed a number of ideas about a developmental perspective on death and facing one's own death. To review these ideas see summary table 21.2.

Next, we will continue our exploration of death and grieving by focusing on coping with the death of someone else.

Coping with the Death of Someone Else

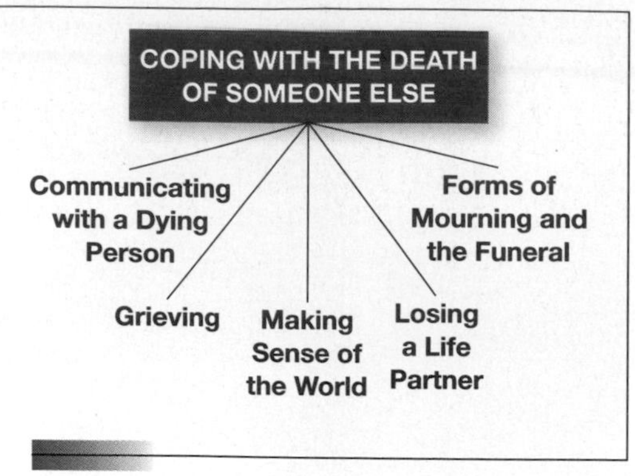

Loss can come in many forms in our lives—divorce, a pet's death, loss of a job—but no loss is greater than that which comes through the death of someone we love and care for—a parent, sibling, spouse, relative, or friend. In the ratings of life's stresses that require the most adjustment, death of a spouse is given the highest number. How should we communicate with a dying individual? How do we cope with the death of someone we love?

Communicating with a Dying Person

Most psychologists believe that it is best for dying individuals to know that they are dying and that significant others know they are dying so they can interact and communicate with each other on the basis of this mutual knowledge. What are some of the advantages of this open awareness context for the dying individual? Four such advantages are: Dying individuals can close their lives in accord with their own ideas about proper dying; dying individuals may be able to complete some plans and projects, can make arrangements for survivors, and can participate in decisions about a funeral and burial; dying individuals have the opportunity to reminisce, to converse with others who have been important individuals in their life, and to end life conscious of what life has been like; and dying individuals have more understanding of what is happening within their bodies and what the medical staff is doing to them (Kalish, 1981).

In addition to an open communication system, what are some other suggestions for conversing with a dying individual? Some experts believe that conversation should not focus on mental pathology or preparation for death but should focus on strengths of the individual and preparation for the remainder of life. Since external accomplishments are not possible, communication should be directed more at internal growth. Keep in mind also that caring does not have to come from a mental health professional only; a concerned nurse, an attentive physician, a sensitive spouse, or an intimate friend can provide an important support system for a dying individual (DeSpelder & Strickland, 1996). Figure 21.3 presents some effective strategies for communicating with a dying person.

Exploring Death and Dying
Death, Dying, and Grieving
Death and Dying Resources
Death and Dying in America
Grieving and the Loss of a Child
The Grieving Process
Grief Theories
Exploring Grief
Grief and Bereavement
Bereavement Resources

It is sweet to mingle tears with tears; griefs, where they wound in solitude, wound more deeply.

Seneca
Roman Poet, 1st Century

Grieving

Our exploration of grief focuses on dimensions of grieving, as well as cultural diversity in healthy grieving.

Dimensions of Grieving **Grief** *is the emotional numbness, disbelief, separation anxiety, despair, sadness, and loneliness that accompany the loss of someone we love.* Grief is not a simple emotional state but rather a complex, evolving process with multiple dimensions (Jacobs & others, 1987). In this view, pining for the lost person is one important dimension. Pining or yearning reflects an intermittent, recurrent wish or need to recover the lost person. Another important dimension of grief is separation anxiety, which not only includes pining and preoccupation with thoughts of the deceased person but also focuses on places and things associated with the deceased, as well as crying or sighing as a type of suppressed cry. Another dimension of grief is the typical immediate reaction to a loss discussed earlier—emotional blunting, numbness, disbelief, and outbursts of

grief
The emotional numbness, disbelief, separation anxiety, despair, sadness, and loneliness that accompany the loss of someone we love.

1. Establish your presence, be at the same eye level; don't be afraid to touch the dying person—dying individuals are often starved for human touch.
2. Eliminate distraction—for example, ask if it is okay to turn off the TV. Realize that excessive small talk can be a distraction.
3. Dying individuals who are very frail often have little energy. If the dying person you are visiting is very frail, you may not want to visit for very long.
4. Don't insist that the dying person feel acceptance about death, if the dying person wants to deny the reality of the situation; on the other hand, don't insist on denial if the dying individual indicates acceptance.
5. Allow the dying person to express guilt or anger; encourage the expression of feelings.
6. Don't be afraid to ask the person what the prognosis (expected outcome) for their illness is. Discuss alternatives, unfinished business.
7. Sometimes dying individuals don't have access to certain others; ask the dying person if there is anyone he or she would like to see that you can contact.
8. Encourage the dying individual to reminisce, especially if you have memories in common.
9. Talk with the individual when she or he wishes to talk. If this is impossible, make an appointment and keep it.
10. Express your regard for the dying individual, don't be afraid to express love, and don't be afraid to say good-bye.

Figure **21.3**
Effective Strategies for Communicating with a Dying Person

> *Everyone can master grief but he who has it.*
>
> William Shakespeare
> *English Playwright, 17th Century*

panic or extreme tearfulness. Yet another dimension of grief involves despair and sadness, which include a sense of hopelessness and defeat, depressive symptoms, apathy, loss of meaning for activities that used to involve the person who is gone, and growing desolation (Giddens & Giddens, 2000; Ringdal & others, 2001; Wiersbe, 1999). This dimension does not represent a clear-cut stage but, rather, occurs repeatedly in one context or another shortly after a loss. Nonetheless, as time passes, pining and protest over the loss tend to diminish, although episodes of depression and apathy may remain or increase. The sense of separation anxiety and loss may continue to the end of one's life, but most of us emerge from grief's tears, turning our attention once again to productive tasks and regaining a more positive view of life (Powers & Wampold, 1994).

Researchers have found that the grieving process is more like a roller-coaster ride than an orderly progression of stages with clear-cut time frames (Lund, 1996). The ups and downs of grief often involve rapidly changing emotions, meeting the challenges of learning new skills, detecting personal weaknesses and limitations, creating new patterns of behavior, and forming new friendships and relationships. Fortunately, for most individuals the roller-coaster dimensions of grief become more manageable over time, with fewer abrupt highs and lows. But many grieving spouses still report that even though time has brought them some healing, they have never gotten over the loss. They have just learned to live with it.

Long-term grief is sometimes masked and can predispose individuals to become depressed and even suicidal (Davis, 2001; Kastenbaum, 1998, 2000; Rosylyn, 2000). Good family communication can help reduce the incidence of depression and suicidal thoughts. For example, in one recent study, family members who communicated poorly with each other had more negative grief reactions 6 months later than those who communicated effectively with each other just after the loss of a family member (Schoka & Hayslip, 1999).

Cultural Diversity in Healthy Grieving Contemporary orientations on grieving emphasize the importance of breaking bonds with the deceased and the return of survivors to autonomous lifestyles. People who persist in holding on to the deceased are believed to be in need of therapy. Recent conceptual and research

analyses, however, have cast doubt on whether this uniform recommendation is always the best therapeutic advice (Stroebe & others, 1992).

Analyses of non-Western cultures suggest that beliefs about continuing bonds with the deceased vary extensively. In contrast with Western beliefs, maintenance of ties with the deceased is accepted and sustained in the religious rituals of Japan. In the Hopi of Arizona, the deceased are forgotten as quickly as possible and life is carried on as usual. Their funeral ritual concludes with a breakoff between mortals and spirits. The diversity of grieving is nowhere more clear than in two Muslim societies—one in Egypt, the other in Bali. In Egypt, the bereaved are encouraged to dwell at length on their grief, surrounded by others who relate similarly tragic accounts and express their own sorrow. By contrast, in Bali, the bereaved are encouraged to laugh and be joyful rather than be sad.

In a longitudinal study of bereavement in the Netherlands, many people tended to maintain contact with the deceased, despite the contemporary emphasis on breaking such bonds (Stroebe & Stroebe, 1991). Many of the widowed persons were not planning a major break with their pasts, but rather were integrating the loss experience into their lifestyles and trying to carry on much as before the death of a loved one. Well over halt "consulted" the deceased when having to make a decision. One widow said that she gained considerable comfort from knowing that this is exactly what her deceased husband would have wanted her to do. Similar findings have recently been reported regarding American widows (Shuchter & Zisook, in press). A similar picture emerges in another recent study of parents of sons who died in two Israeli wars, 13 and 4 years earlier (Rubin, in press). Even many years after the death of their son, the Israeli parents showed a strong involvement with and valuation of the son. They especially idealized the lost son in ways that were not present in the descriptions by a control group of parents of sons who had recently left home.

Careers in Life-Span Development

Sarah Wheeler, Certified College Grief Counselor

Sarah Wheeler has a doctorate of science in nursing and is a certified grief counselor. She teaches in the College of Nursing at the University of Illinois, Urbana campus, and also conducts grief counseling. She is especially concerned with helping families cope with their losses and strategies that nurses can use to provide support, empathy, information, and guidance.

Sarah Wheeler (*right*), conducting grief counseling.

In summary, diverse groups of people grieve in a variety of ways. The diverse grieving patterns are culturally embedded practices. Thus, there is no one right, ideal way to grieve. There are many different ways to feel about a deceased person and no set series of stages that the bereaved must pass through to become well adjusted. The stoic widower may need to cry out over his loss at times. The weeping widow may need to put her husband's wishes aside as she becomes the financial manager of her estate. What is needed is an understanding that healthy coping with the death of a loved one involves growth, flexibility, and appropriateness within a cultural context. This orientation is just beginning to appear in the fields of bereavement research and clinical practice.

Making Sense of the World

One beneficial aspect of grieving is that it stimulates many individuals to try to make sense of their world (Kalish, 1981, 1987). A common occurrence is to go over again and again all of the events that led up to the death. In the days and weeks after the death, the closest family members share experiences with each other, sometimes reminiscing over family experiences.

How might grieving vary across individuals and cultures?

Each individual may offer a piece of death's puzzle. "When I saw him last Saturday, he looked as though he were rallying," says one family member. "Do you think it might have had something to do with his sister's illness?" remarks another. "I doubt it, but I heard from an aide that he fell going to the bathroom that morning," comments yet another. "That explains the bruise on his elbow," says the first individual. "No wonder he told me that he was angry because he could not seem to do anything right," chimes in a fourth family member. So it goes in the attempt to understand why someone who was rallying on Saturday was dead on Wednesday.

When a death is caused by an accident or a disaster, the effort to make sense of it is pursued more vigorously. As added pieces of news come trickling in, they are integrated into the puzzle. The bereaved want to put the death into a perspective that they can understand—divine intervention, a curse from a neighboring tribe, a logical sequence of cause and effect, or whatever it may be.

Losing a Life Partner

Widows/Widowers
WidowNet

Those left behind after the death of an intimate partner suffer profound grief and often endure financial loss, loneliness, increased physical illness, and psychological disorders, including depression (Hungerford, 2001; Stroebe & others, 1998). How they cope with the crisis varies considerably (Fry, 1999). Widows outnumber widowers by the ratio of 5 to 1, because women live longer than men, because women tend to marry men older than themselves, and because a widowed man is more likely to remarry. Widowed women are probably the poorest group in America, despite the myth of huge insurance settlements. Many are also lonely. The poorer and less educated they are, the lonelier they tend to be. The bereaved are also at increased

risk for many health problems, including death (Corr, Nable, & Corr, 2000; Fredman, Daly, & Lazur, 1995).

Optimal adjustment after a death depends on several factors (Laz & Alberico, 1998). Women do better than men largely because, in our society, women are responsible for the emotional life of a couple, whereas men usually manage the finances and material goods. Thus, women have better networks of friends, closer relationships with relatives, and experience in taking care of themselves psychologically (Martin-Matthews, 1996). Older widows do better than younger widows, perhaps because the death of a partner is more expected for older women. For their part, widowers usually have more money than widows do, and they are much more likely to remarry (DiGiulio, 1989).

For either widows or widowers, social support helps them adjust to the death of a spouse (Boerner & Wortman, 1998; Kastenbaum, 1998). The Widow-to-Widow program, begun in the 1960s, provides support for newly widowed women. Its objective is to prevent the potentially negative effects of the loss. Volunteer widows reach out to other widows, introducing them to others who may have similar problems, leading group discussions, and organizing social activities. The program has been adopted by the American Association of Retired Persons and disseminated throughout the United States as the Widowed Person's Service. The model has since been adopted by numerous community organizations to provide support for those going through a difficult life transition that will confront the vast majority of us.

Forms of Mourning and the Funeral

In some cultures, a ceremonial meal is held; in others, a black armband is worn for 1 year following a death; and so on. Cultures vary in how they practice mourning.

What are some different forms of mourning?

Sociocultural Worlds of Development

The Family and the Community in Mourning—The Amish and Traditional Judaism

THE FAMILY and the community have important roles in mourning in some cultures. Two of those cultures are the Amish and traditional Judaism (Worthington, 1989).

The Amish are a conservative group with approximately 80,000 members in the United States, Ontario, and several small settlements in South and Central America. The Amish live in a family-oriented society in which family and community support are essential for survival. Today, they live at the same unhurried pace as that of their ancestors, using horses instead of cars and facing death with the same steadfast faith as their forebears. At the time of death, close neighbors assume the responsibility of notifying others of the death. The Amish community handles virtually all aspects of the funeral. Family members dress the body in white garments. The wearing of white clothes signifies the high ceremonial emphasis on death as final rite of passage to a new and better life. The funeral service is held in a barn in warmer months and in a house during colder months. Calm acceptance of death, influenced by a deep religious faith, is an integral part of the Amish culture. Following the funeral, a high level of support is given to the bereaved family for at least a year. Visits to the family, special scrapbooks and handmade items for the family, new work projects started for the widow, and quilting days that combine fellowship and productivity are among the supports given to the bereaved family.

The family and community also have specific and importantant roles in mourning in traditional Judaism. The program of mourning is divided into graduated time periods, each with its appropriate practices. The observance of these practices is required of the spouse and the immediate blood relatives of the deceased. The first period is *aninut,* the period between death and burial. The next two periods make up *avelut,* or mourning proper. The first of these is *shivah,* a period of 7 days, which commences with the burial. This is followed by *sheloshim,* the 30-day period following the burial, including shivah. At the end of sheloshim, the mourning process is considered over for all but one's parents. In this case, mourning continues for 11 months, although observances are minimal. The 7-day period of the shivah is especially important in mourning in traditional Judaism. The Jewish community provides considerable support during the mourning process. The mourners, sitting together as a group through an extended period, have an opportunity to project their feelings to the group as a whole. Visits from others during shivah may help the mourner deal with feelings of guilt. After shivah, the mourner is encouraged to resume normal social interaction. In fact, it is customary for the mourners to walk together a short distance as a symbol of their return to society. In its entirety, the elaborate mourning system of traditional Judaism is designed to promote personal growth and to reintegrate the individual into the community.

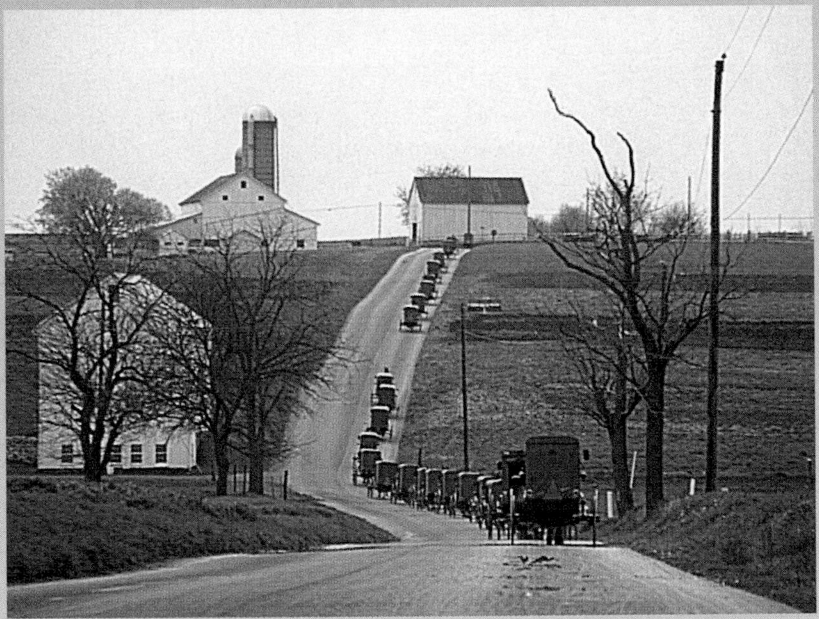

An Amish funeral procession in Pennsylvania. The funeral service is held in the barn in the warmer months and in the house during the colder months. Following the funeral, a high level of support is given to the bereaved family for at least a year.

Summary Table 21.3
Coping with the Death of Someone Else

Concept	Processes/ Related Ideas	Characteristics/Descriptions
Communicating with a Dying Person	Open Communication	• Most psychologists recommend an open communication system; this system should not dwell on pathology or preparation for death but should emphasize the dying person's strengths.
Grieving	Dimensions of Grieving	• Grief is the emotional numbness, disbelief, separation, anxiety, despair, sadness, and loneliness that accompany the loss of someone we love. • Grief is multidimensional and in some cases may last for years.
	Cultural Diversity	• There are cultural variations in grieving.
Making Sense of the World	Piecing Together Death's Puzzle	• The grieving process may stimulate individuals to strive to make sense out of their world; each individual may contribute a piece to death's puzzle.
Losing a Life Partner	Death of a Spouse, Health, and Social Support	• Usually the most difficult loss is the death of a spouse. • The bereaved are at risk for many health problems. • Social support benefits widows and widowers.
Forms of Mourning and the Funeral	Cultural Variations	• They vary from culture to culture. • The most important aspect of mourning in most cultures is the funeral. In recent years, the funeral industry has been the focus of controversy.

The funeral is an important aspect of mourning in many cultures. One consideration involves what to do with the body. Approximately 80 percent of corpses are disposed of by burial, the remaining 20 percent by cremation (Aiken, 2000; Cremation Association of America, 2000). Cremation is more popular in the Pacific region of the United States, less popular in the South. Cremation also is more popular in Canada than in the United States and most popular of all in Japan and many other Asian countries.

In one recent study, bereaved individuals who were personally religious derived more psychological benefits from a funeral, participated more actively in the rituals, and adjusted more positively to the loss (Hayslip, Edmondson, & Guarnaccia, 1999).

The funeral industry has been the source of controversy in recent years. Funeral directors and their supporters argue that the funeral provides a form of closure to the relationship with the deceased, especially when there is an open casket. Their dissenters, however, stress that funeral directors are just trying to make money; they further argue that the art of embalming is grotesque.

One way to avoid being exploited because bereavement has made us vulnerable to being talked into purchasing more expensive funeral arrangements is to purchase them in advance. However, most of us do not follow this procedure. In one survey, only 24 percent of individuals 60 and over had made any funeral arrangements (Kalish & Reynolds, 1976).

Some cultures have elaborate mourning systems. To learn about two cultures with extensive mourning systems, see the Sociocultural Worlds of Development box.

At this point, we have discussed a number of ideas about coping with the death of someone else. To review these ideas, see summary table 21.3.

Buddhist Funeral Rites

The art of living well and the art of dying well are one.

Epicurus
Greek Philosopher, 3rd Century B.C.

Chapter Review

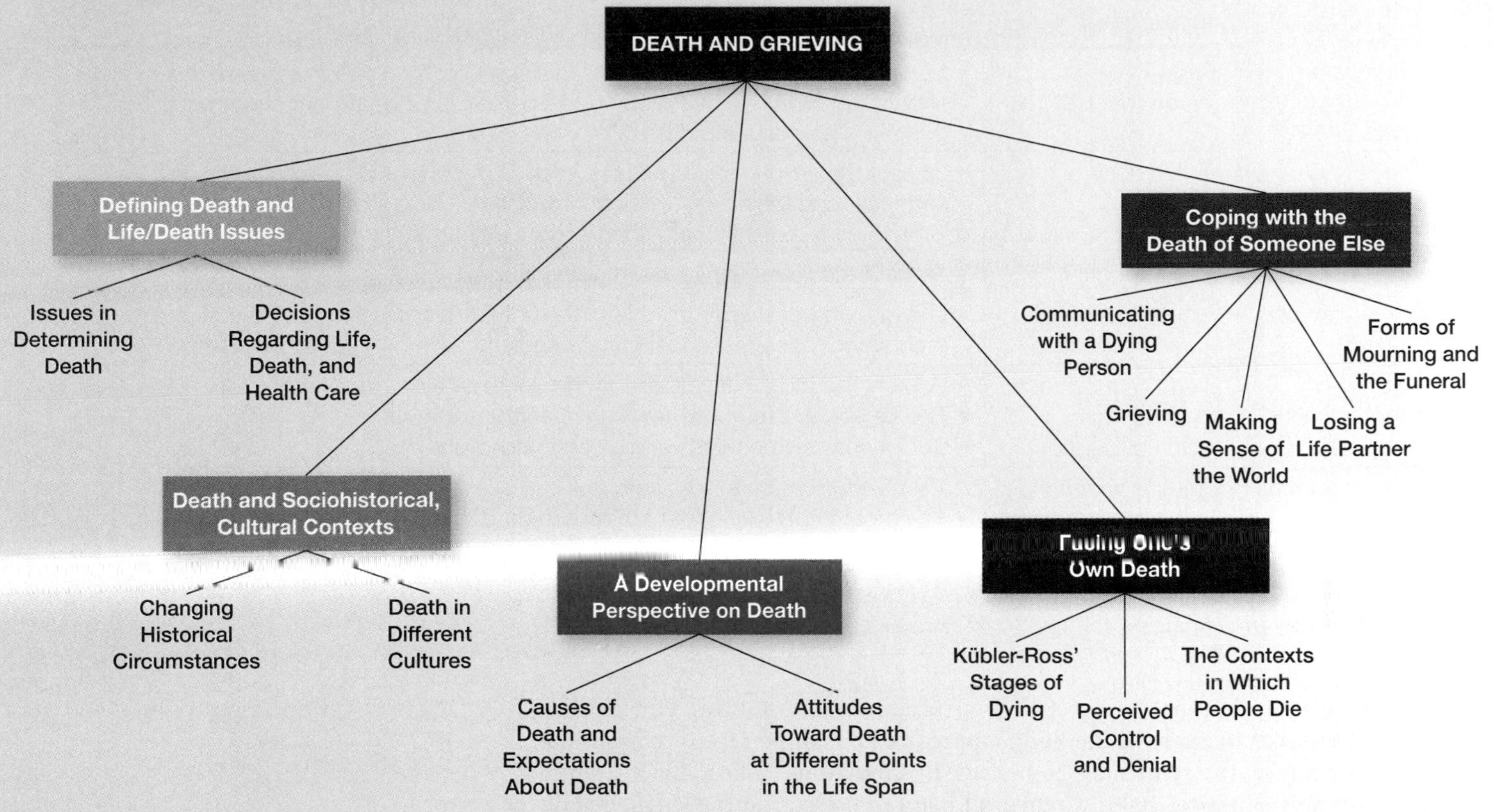

TO OBTAIN A DETAILED REVIEW OF THIS CHAPTER, STUDY THESE THREE SUMMARY TABLES:

- Summary Table 21.1 — Defining Death and Life/Death Issues: Death and Sociohistorical, Cultural Contexts — page 607
- Summary Table 21.2 — A Developmental Perspective on Death; Facing One's Own Death — page 612
- Summary Table 21.3 — Coping with the Death of Someone Else — page 619

Key Terms

brain death 602
euthanasia 603
passive euthanasia 603
active euthanasia 603
hospice 604
denial and isolation 610
anger 610
bargaining 610
depression 610
acceptance 610
grief 613

Key People

Elisabeth Kübler-Ross 610
Robert Kastenbaum 610

Taking It to the Net

1. Herman's mother has Parkinson's disease. He wants her to make some difficult end-of-life decisions while she still can. He and his mother discuss the options of a health-care power of attorney, a living will, and/or a DNR. What are the different purposes of these documents and what is the family's involvement in these decisions?
2. Letitia, a recent widow, is interested in starting a program for widowed women in her community. In order to start the process to request funding, she is exploring her options in foundation grants. As part of this process, she will need to investigate the available data on the nature and extent of widowhood in the United States today, including the age, sex, and socioeconomic status of widowed people. What type of information is available to her and her group?
3. Ellen has taken care of her mother throughout her long, lingering illness that has just been diagnosed as terminal. Ellen does not think she alone can provide the type of care necessary to take care of her mother in her final weeks. Her neighbor suggested she contact the local hospice. What does a hospice offer to families in this situation and how is it different from a nursing home?

Connect to www.mhhe.com/santrockld8 to research the answers and complete these exercises.

OLC Preview

To further test your knowledge of this chapter or to explore our extensive online resources that accompany *Life-Span Development,* eighth edition, please log on to the text's Online Learning Center at http://www.mhhe.com/santrockld8.com.

Epilogue

THE JOURNEY OF LIFE

We have come to the end of this book, I leave you with the following montage of thoughts and images that convey the power, complexity, and beauty of human development.

Life-Span Development *has been about life's rhythm and meaning, about turning mystery into understanding, and about weaving thogether a portrait of who we were, are, and will be. From the first cries of a newborn baby to the final prayers of an elderly adult, we arrive, laugh, grow, play, seek, work, question, hope, mate, quarrel, sing, achieve, and care.*

The rhythm and meaning of human development involve beginnings, when questions of whence and whither, when and how, are asked. How from so simple a beginning do endless forms develop and grow and mature? What was this organism, what is it now, and what will it become? Birth's fragile moment arrives, when the newborn is on a threshold between two worlds.

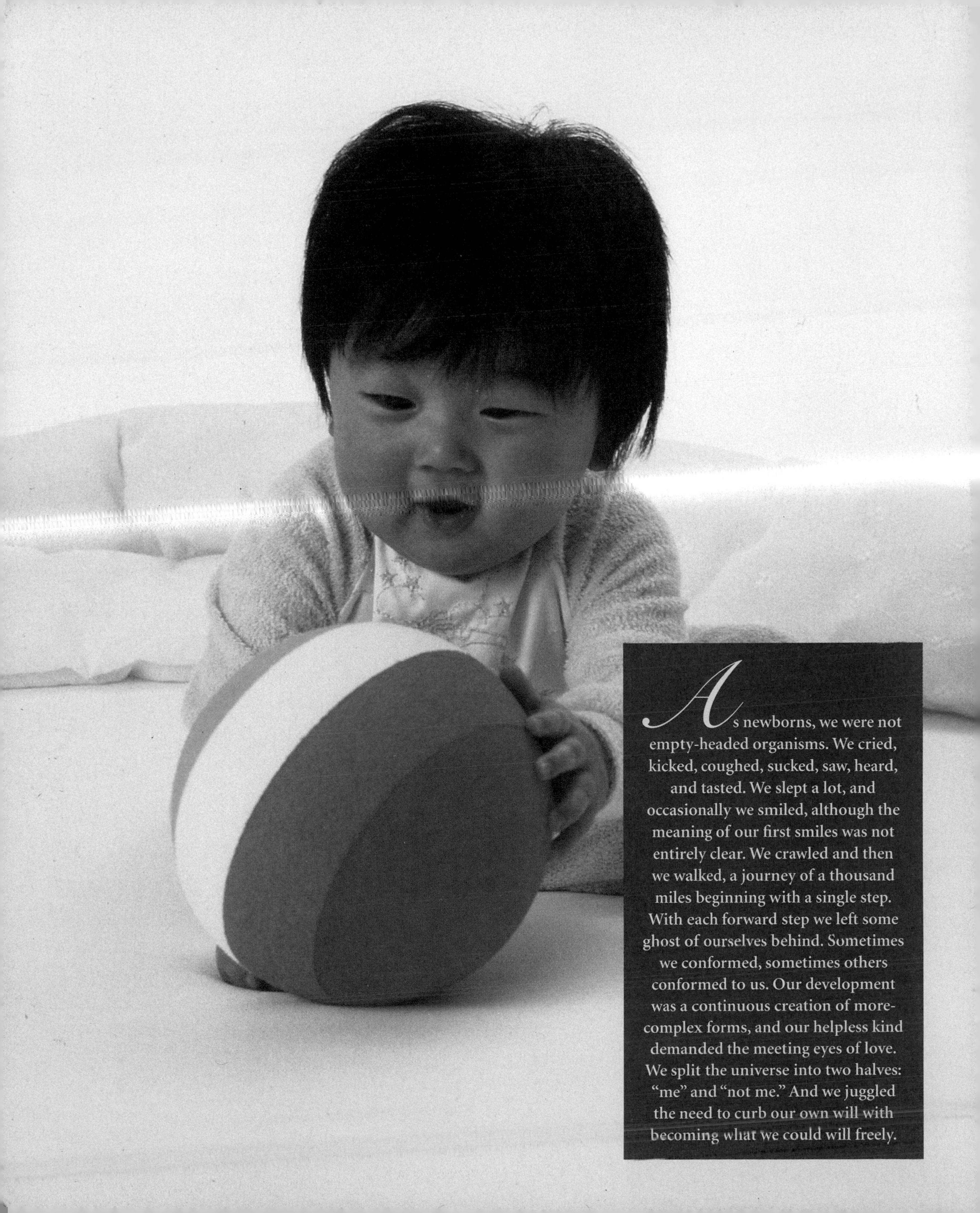

As newborns, we were not empty-headed organisms. We cried, kicked, coughed, sucked, saw, heard, and tasted. We slept a lot, and occasionally we smiled, although the meaning of our first smiles was not entirely clear. We crawled and then we walked, a journey of a thousand miles beginning with a single step. With each forward step we left some ghost of ourselves behind. Sometimes we conformed, sometimes others conformed to us. Our development was a continuous creation of more-complex forms, and our helpless kind demanded the meeting eyes of love. We split the universe into two halves: "me" and "not me." And we juggled the need to curb our own will with becoming what we could will freely.

In early childhood, our greatest untold poem was being only 4 years old. We skipped, played, and ran all the day long, never in our lives so busy, busy becoming something we had not quite grasped yet. Who knew our thoughts, which we worked up into small mythologies all our own. While our thoughts and feelings took winks, the blossoms of our heart no wind cloud touch. Our small world widened as we discovered new refuges and new people. When we said "I," we meant something totally unique, not to be confused with any other.

In middle and late childhood, we were on a different plane, belonging to a generation and a feeling properly our own. It is the wisdom of human development that at no other time are we more ready to learn than at the end of early childhood's period of expansive imagination. Our thirst was to know and to understand. Our parents continued to cradle our lives, but our growth was also being shaped by successive choirs of friends. We did not think much about the future or the past, but enjoyed the present.

In no order of things was adolescence the simple time of life for us. We clothed ourselves with rainbows and went "brave as the zodiac," flashing from one end of the world to the other. We tried on one face after another, searching for a face of our own. We wanted our parents to understand us and hoped they would give up the privilege of understanding them. We wanted to fly but found that first we had to learn to stand and walk and climb and dance. In our most pimply and awkward moments we became acquainted with sex. We played furiously at adult games but were confined to a society of our own peers. Our generation was the fragile cable by which the best and the worst of our parents' generation was transmitted to the present. In the end, there were but two lasting bequests our parents could leave us—one being roots, the other wings.

Early adulthood is a time for work and a time for love, sometimes leaving little time for anything else. For some of us, finding our place in adult society and committing to a more stable life take longer than we imagine. We still ask ourselves who we are and wonder if it isn't enough just to be. Our dreams continue and our thoughts are bold, but at some point we become more pragmatic. Sex and love are powerful passions in our lives—at times angels of light, at other fiends of torment. And we possibly will never know the love of our parents until we become parents ourselves.

In middle adulthood, what we have been forms what we will be. For some of us, middle age is such a foggy place, a time when we need to discover what we are running from and to and why. We compare our life with what we vowed to make it. In middle age, more time stretches before us and some evaluations have to be made, however reluctantly. As the young/old polarity greets us with a special force, we need to join the daring of youth with the discipline of age in a way that does justice to both. As middle-aged adults, we come to sense that the generations of living things pass in a short while and, like runners, hand on the torch of life.

The rhythm and meaning of human development eventually wend their way to late adulthood, when each of us stands alone at the heart of the earth and "suddenly it is evening." We shed the leaves of youth and are stripped by the winds of time down to the truth. We learn that life is lived forward but understood backward. We trace the connection between the end and the beginning of life and try to figure out what this whole show is about before it is over. Ultimately, we come to know that we are what survives of us.

Our life ultimately ends—when we approach life's grave sustained and soothed with unfaltering trust or rave at the close of day; when, at last, years steal us from ourselves; and when we are linked to our children's children's children by an invisible cable that runs from age to age.

I hope that this book has been not only a window to the life span of Homo sapiens but also a window to your own personal journey in life.

John W. Santrock

Glossary

A

acceptance Kübler-Ross's fifth stage of dying, in which the dying person develops a sense of peace, an acceptance of her or his fate, and, in many cases, a desire to be left alone. 610

accommodation In Piaget's theory, an individual's adjustment to new information. 61

active (niche-picking) genotype environment correlations Correlations that exist when children seek out environments they find compatible and stimulating. 86

active euthanasia Death induced deliberately, as by injecting a lethal dose of a drug. 603

activity theory The theory that the more active and involved older adults are, the more likely they are to be satisfied with their lives. 578

addiction A pattern of behavior characterized by an overwhelming involvement with using a drug and securing its supply. 422

adolescent egocentrism The heightened self-consciousness of adolescents. 367

adoption study A study in which investigators seek to discover whether, in behavior and psychological characteristics, adopted children are more like their adoptive parents, who provided a home environment, or more like their biological parents, who contributed their heredity. Another form of the adoption study is to compare adoptive and biological siblings. 74

aerobic exercise Sustained exercise (such as jogging, swimming, or cycling) that stimulates heart and lung activity. 420

affectionate love In this type of love (also called "companionate love"), an individual desires to have the other person near and has a deep, caring affection for the other person. 452

affordances Opportunities for interaction offered by objects that are necessary to perform functional activities. 145

ageism Prejudice against other people because of their age, especially prejudice against older adults. 582

AIDS Acquired immune deficiency syndrome, a primarily sexually transmitted disease caused by the HIV virus, which destroys the body's immune system. 427

altruism Unselfish interest in helping another person. 319

Alzheimer's disease A progressive, irreversible brain disorder characterized by a gradual deterioration of memory, reasoning, language, and, eventually, physical function. 573

amnion The life-support system that is a bag or envelope that contains a clear fluid in which the developing embryo floats. 95

androgyny The presence of masculine and feminine characteristics in the same individual. 324

anger Kübler-Ross's second stage of dying, in which the dying person's denial gives way to anger, resentment, rage, and envy. 610

anger cry A cry similar to the basic cry, with more excess air forced through the vocal chords (associated with exasperation or rage). 180

animism The belief that inanimate objects have "lifelike" qualities and are capable of action. 213

anorexia nervosa An eating disorder that involves the relentless pursuit of thinness through starvation. 363

Apgar Scale A widely used method to assess the health of newborns at 1 and 5 minutes after birth. The Apgar Scale evaluates infants' heart rate, respiratory effort, muscle tone, body color, and reflex irritability. 113

arthritis Inflammation of the joints that is accompanied by pain, stiffness, and movement problems; especially common in older adults. 539

assimilation The absorption of ethnic minority groups into the dominant group, which often involves the loss of some or virtually all of the behavior and values of the ethnic minority group. 35

assimilation In Piaget's theory, an individual's incorporation of new information into her or his existing knowledge. 399

associative play Play that involves social interaction with little or no organization. 262

attachment A close emotional bond between an infant and a caregiver. 186

attention deficit hyperactivity disorder (ADHD) A disability in which children consistently show one or more of the following characteristics: (1) inattention, (2) hyperactivity, and (3) impulsivity. 279

authoritarian parenting A restrictive punitive style in which parents exhort the child to follow their directions and to respect work and effort. The authoritarian parent places firm limits and controls on the child and allows little verbal exchange. Authoritarian parenting is associated with children's social incompetence. 248

authoritative parenting A parenting style in which parents encourage their children to be independent but still place limits and controls on their actions. Extensive verbal give-and-take is allowed, and parents are warm and nurturant toward the child. Authoritative parenting is associated with children's social competence. 249

autonomous morality The second stage of moral development in Piaget's theory, displayed by older children (about 10 years of age and older). The child becomes aware that rules and laws are created by people and that, in judging an action, one should consider the actor's intentions as well as the consequences. 240

B

bargaining Kübler-Ross's third stage of dying, in which the dying person develops the hope that death can somehow be postponed. 610

basal metabolism rate (BMR) The minimal amount of energy a person uses in a resting state. 209, 418

basic cry A rhythmic pattern usually consisting of a cry, a briefer silence, a shorter inspiratory whistle that is higher pitched than the main cry, and then a brief rest before the next cry. 180

basic-skills-and-phonetics approach An approach to reading instruction that stresses phonetics and basic rules for translating symbols into sounds. Early reading instruction should involve simplified materials. 302

Bayley Scales of Infant Development Scales developed by Nancy Bayley, which are widely used in the assessment of infant development. The current version has three components: a mental scale, a motor scale, and an infant behavior profile. 166

becoming parents and a family with children The third stage in the family life cycle. Adults who enter this stage move up a generation and become caregivers to the younger generation. 458

behavior genetics The study of the degree and nature of behavior's basis in heredity. 74

big five factors of personality Emotional stability (neuroticism), extraversion, openness to experience, agreeableness, and conscientiousness. 511

bilingual education An educational approach whose aim is to teach academic subjects to immigrant children in their native languages (most often Spanish) while gradually adding English instruction. 303

biological age A person's age in terms of biological health. 18

biological processes Changes in an individual's physical nature. 16

blastocyst The inner layer of cells that develops during the germinal period. These cells later develop into the embryo. 94

body transcendence versus body preoccupation A developmental task of aging described by Peck, in which older adults must cope with declining physical well-being. 576

bonding Close contact, especially psysical, between parents and their newborn in the period shortly after birth. 118

boundary ambiguity The uncertainty in stepfamilies about who is in or out of the family and who is performing or responsible for certain tasks in the family system. 329

brain death A neurological definition of death. A person is brain dead when all electrical activity of the brain has ceased for a specified period of time. A flat EEG recording is one criterion of brain death. 602

brainstorming A technique in which individuals are encouraged to come up with ideas in a group, play off each other's ideas, and say practically whatever comes to mind. 300

Brazelton Neonatal Behavioral Assessment Scale A test given several days after birth to assess

newborns' neurological development, reflexes, and reactions to people. 113

breech position The baby's position in the uterus that causes the buttocks to be the first part to emerge from the vagina. 110

bulimia nervosa An eating disorder in which the individual consistently follows a binge-and-purge pattern. 363

C

canalization The process by which characteristics take a narrow path or developmental course. Apparently, preservative forces help to protect a person from environmental extremes. 74

care perspective The moral perspective of Carol Gilligan, that views people in terms of their connectedness with others and emphasizes interpersonal communication, relationships with others, and concern for others. 319

case study An in-depth look at an individual. 49

cellular clock theory Leonard Hayflick's theory that the maximum number of times that human cells can divide is about 70 to 80. As we age, our cells have less capability to divide. 532

centration The focusing of attention on one characteristic to the exclusion of all others. 214

cephalocaudal pattern The sequence in which the greatest [illegible] occurs at the top—the head—with physical growth in size, weight, and feature differentiation gradually working from top to bottom. 126

character education A direct approach to moral education that involves teaching students a basic moral literacy to prevent them from engaging in immoral behavior and doing harm to themselves and others. 375

child-centered kindergarten Education that involves the whole child by considering both the child's physical, cognitive, and social development and the child's needs, interests, and learning styles. 226

chlamydia The most common STD. Named for Chlamydia trachomitis, an organism that spreads by sexual contact and infects the genitals of both sexes. 426

chromosomes Threadlike structures that come in 23 pairs, one member of each pair coming from each parent. Chromosomes contain the genetic substance DNA. 69

chronic disorders Disorders that are characterized by slow onset and long duration. They are rare in early adulthood, they increase during middle adulthood, and they become common in late adulthood. 481

chronological age The number of years that have elapsed since a person's birth; what is usually meant by "age." 18

climacteric The midlife transition in which fertility declines. 484

cognitive developmental theory of gender The theory that children's gender typing occurs after they have developed a concept of gender. Once they consistently conceive of themselves as male or female, children often organize their world on the basis of gender. 246

cognitive mechanics The "hardware" of the mind, reflecting the neurophysiological architecture of the brain as developed through evolution. Cognitive mechanics involve speed and accuracy of the processes involving sensory input, visual and motor memory, discrimination, comparison, and categorization. 552

cognitive moral education An approach to moral education based on the belief that students should develop such values as democracy and justice as their moral reasoning develops; Kohlberg's theory has been the basis of a number of cognitive moral education programs. 376

cognitive pragmatics The culture-based "software" of the mind. Cognitive pragmatics include reading and writing skills, language comprehension, educational qualifications, professional skills, and also the type of knowledge about the self and life skills that help us to master or cope with life. 552

cognitive processes Changes in an individual's thought, intelligence, and language. 16

cohort effects Effects that are due to a person's time of birth or generation but not to age. 52

commitment Marcia's term for the part of identity development in which adolescents show a personal investment in what they are going to do. 383

connectedness According to Cooper and her colleagues, connectedness consists of two dimensions: mutuality (sensitivity to and respect for others' views) and permeability (openness to others' views). 385

consensual validation An explanation of why individuals are attracted to people who are similar to them. Our own attitudes and behavior are supported and validated when someone else's attitudes and behavior are similar to our own. 449

conservation In Piaget's theory, awareness that altering an object's or a substance's appearance does not change its basic properties. 214

constructive play Play that combines sensorimotor/practice repetitive activity with symbolic representation of ideas. Constructive play occurs when children engage in self-regulated creation or construction of a product or a problem solution. 263

contemporary life-events approach Emphasizes that how a life event influences the individual's development depends not only on the life event, but also on mediating factors, the individual's adaptation to the life event, the life-stage context, and the sociohistorical context. 505

context The settings, influenced by historical, economic, social, and cultural factors, in which development occurs. 12

continuity-discontinuity issue The issue regarding whether development involves gradual, cumulative change (continuity) or distinct stages (discontinuity). 20

control group A comparison group in an experiment that is treated in every way like the experimental group except for the manipulated factor. 51

control processes Cognitive processes that do not occur automatically but require work and effort. These processes are under the learner's conscious control and can be used to improve memory. They are also appropriately called strategies. 288

controversial children Children who are frequently nominated both as someone's best friend and as being disliked. 330

conventional reasoning The second, or intermediate, level in Kohlberg's theory of moral development. Internalization is intermediate. Individuals abide by certain standards (internal), but they are the standards of others (external), such as parents or the laws of society. 317

convergent thinking Thinking that produces one correct answer and is characteristic of the kind of thinking tested by standardized intelligence tests. 299

cooperative play Play that involves social interaction in a group with a sense of group identity and organized activity. 262

coordination of secondary circular reactions Piaget's fourth sensorimotor substage, which develops between 8 and 12 months of age. In this substage, several significant changes take place involving the coordination of schemes and intentionality. 159

correlational research Research whose goal is to describe the strength of the relation between two or more events or characteristics. 50

creativity The ability to think in novel and unusual ways and to come up with unique solutions to problems. 299

crisis Marcia's term for a period of identity development during which the adolescent is choosing from among meaningful alternatives. 383

critical thinking Thinking that involves grasping the deeper meaning of ideas, keeping an open mind about different approaches and perspectives, and deciding for oneself what to believe or do. 288

cross-cultural studies The comparison of a culture with one or more other cultures, which provides information about the degree to which development is similar (universal) across cultures or the degree to which it is culture-specific. 12

cross-cultural studies Comparisons of one culture with one or more other cultures. These provide information about the degree to which children's development is similar, or universal, across cultures, and to the degree to which it is culture-specific. 396

cross-sectional approach A research strategy in which individuals of different ages are compared at one time. 51

crystallized intelligence Accumulated information and verbal skills, which increase with age, according to Horn. 488

cultural-familial retardation Retardation that is characterized by no evidence of organic brain damage, but the individual's IQ is between 50 and 70. 298

culture The behavior patterns, beliefs, and all other products of a group that are passed on from generation to generation. 12

culture-fair tests Tests that are designed to be free of cultural bias. 296

D

date or acquaintance rape Coercive sexual activity directed at someone with whom the perpetrator is at least casually acquainted. 429

dating scripts The cognitive models that adolescents and adults use to guide and evaluate dating interactions. 394

deferred imitation Imitation that occurs after a time delay of hours or days. 164

dementia A global term for any neurological disorder in which the primary symptoms involve a deterioration of mental functioning. 563

denial and isolation Kübler-Ross's first stage of dying, in which the dying person denies that she or he is really going to die. 610

dependent variable The factor that is measured as the result of an experiment. 51

depression Kübler-Ross's fourth stage of dying, in which the dying person comes to accept the certainty of her or his death. A period of depression or preparatory grief may appear.

development The pattern of change that begins at conception and continues through the life cycle. 6

developmental biodynamics The new perspective on motor development in infancy that seeks to explain how motor behaviors are assembled for perceiving and acting. 142

developmental quotient (DQ) An overall developmental score that combines subscores in motor, language, adaptive, and personal-social domains in the Gesell assessment of infants. 166

developmentally appropriate practice Education that focuses on the typical developmental patterns of children (age appropriateness) and the uniqueness of each child (individual appropriateness). 227

differentiation versus role preoccupation One of the three developmental tasks of aging described by Peck, in which older adults must redefine their worth in terms of something other than work roles. 576

difficult child A child who tends to react negatively and cry frequently, who engages in irregular daily routines, and who is slow to accept new experiences. 182

disease model of addiction The view that addictions are biologically based, lifelong diseases that involve a loss of control over behavior and require medical and/or spiritual treatment for recovery. 422

disengagement theory The theory that to cope effectively, older adults should gradually withdraw from society. 578

dishabituation An infant's renewed interest in a stimulus. 163

disorganized babies Babies that show insecurity by being disorganized and disoriented. 189

divergent thinking Thinking that produces many answers to the same question and is characteristic of creativity. 299

DNA A complex molecule that contains genetic information. 69

doula A caregiver who provides continuous physical, emotional, and educational support to the mother before, during, and just after childbirth. 109

Down syndrome A chromosomally transmitted form of mental retardation, caused by the presence of an extra (47th) chromosome. 76

dyslexia A category of learning disabilities involving a severe impairment in the ability to read and spell. 278

E

easy child A child who is generally in a positive mood, who quickly establishes regular routines in infancy, and who adapts easily to new experiences. 182

eclectic theoretical orientation An approach that does not follow any one theoretical approach, but instead selects and uses whatever is considered the best in many different theories. 45

ecological theory Bronfenbrenner's environmental system view of development, involving five environmental systems—microsystem, mesosystem, exosystem, macrosystem, and chronosystem. These emphasize the role of social contexts in development. 43

ecological view The view that perception functions to bring organisms in contact with the environment and to increase adaptation. 145

egocentrism The inability to distinguish between one's own perspective and someone else's (salient feature of the first substage of preoperational thought). 212

ego transcendence versus ego preoccupation A developmental task of aging described by Peck, in which older adults must come to feel at ease with themselves by recognizing that although death is inevitable and probably not too far away, they have contributed to the future through the competent raising of their children or through their vocations and ideas. 576

eldercare Physical and emotional caretaking for older members of the family, whether by giving day-to-day physical assistance or by being responsible for overseeing such care. 584

embryonic period The period of prenatal development that occurs 2 to 8 weeks after conception. During the embryonic period, the rate of cell differentiation intensifies, support systems for the cells form, and organs appear. 94

emotion Feeling or affect, that can involve physiological arousal (a fast heartbeat, for example), conscious experience (thinking about being in love with someone, for example), and behavioral expression (a smile or grimace, for example). 178

emotional intelligence A form of social intelligence that involves the ability to monitor one's own and others' feelings and emotions, to discriminate among them, and to use this information to guide one's thinking and action. 313

empty nest syndrome A decrease in marital satisfaction after children leave home, because parents derive considerable satisfaction from their children. 515

episodic memory The retention of information about the where and when of life's happenings. 553

Erikson's theory Eight stages of psychosocial development unfold throughout the human life span. Each stage consists of a unique developmental task that confronts individuals with a crisis that must be faced. 33

ethnic identity An enduring, basic aspect of the self that includes a sense of membership in an ethnic group and the attitudes and feelings related to that membership. 385

ethnicity A characteristic based on cultural heritage, nationality characteristics, race, religion, and language. 13

ethology An approach that stresses that behavior is strongly influenced by biology, tied to evolution, and characterized by critical or sensitive periods. 42

euthanasia The act of painlessly ending the lives of persons who are suffering from incurable diseases or severe disabilities; sometimes called "mercy killing." 603

evocative genotype-environment correlations Correlations that exist when the child's genotype elicits certain types of physical and social environments. 86

evolutionary psychology A contemporary approach that emphasizes that behavior is a function of mechanisms, requires input for activation, and is ultimately related to survival and reproduction. 67

experimental group A group whose experience is manipulated in an experiment. 61

experimental research Research involving experiments that permit the determination of cause. A carefully regulated procedure in which one or more of the factors believed to influence the behavior being studied are manipulated and all other factors are held constant. 50

expertise Having an extensive, highly organized knowledge and understanding of a particular domain. 491

explicit memory Memory of facts and experiences that individuals consciously know and can state. 554

F

family at midlife The fifth stage in the family life cycle, a time of launching children, linking generations, and adapting to midlife developmental changes. 458

family in later life The sixth and final stage in the family life cycle, involving retirement and, in many families, grandparenting. 458

family with adolescents The fourth stage of the family life cycle, in which adolescent children push for autonomy and seek to develop their own identities. 458

fetal alcohol syndrome (FAS) A cluster of abnormalities that appears in the offspring of mothers who drink alcohol heavily during pregnancy. 100

fetal period The prenatal period of development that begins 2 months after conception and lasts for 7 months, on the average. 96

fine motor skills Motor skills that involve more finely tuned movements, such as finger dexterity. 139

first habits and primary circular reactions Piaget's second sensorimotor substage, which

develops between 1 and 4 months of age. In this substage, infants' reflexes evolve into adaptive schemes that are more refined and coordinated. 159

fluid intelligence The ability to reason abstractly, which steadily declines from middle adulthood on, according to Horn. 488

fragile X syndrome A genetic disorder involving an abnormality in the X chromosome, which becomes constricted and, often, breaks. 76

free-radical theory A microbiological theory of aging that states that people age because inside their cells normal metabolism produces unstable oxygen molecules known as free radicals. These molecules ricochet around inside cells, damaging DNA and other cellular structures. 533

friendship A form of close relationship that involves enjoyment, acceptance, trust, respect, mutual assistance, confiding, understanding, and spontaneity. 453

G

games Activities engaged in for pleasure that include rules and often competition with one or more individuals. 263

gender The social and psychological dimension of being male or female. 13

gender The social dimension of being male or female. 243

gender identity The sense of being male or female, which most children acquire by the time they are 3 years old. 243

gender role A set of expectations that prescribes how females or males should think, act, and feel. 243

gender-role transcendence The belief that, when an individual's competence is at issue, it should not be conceptualized on the basis of masculinity, femininity, or androgyny but, rather, on a personal basis. 325

gender schema theory The theory that an individual's attention and behavior are guided by an internal motivation to conform to gender-based sociocultural standards and stereotypes. 246

gender stereotypes Broad categories that reflect our impressions and beliefs about females and males. 320

generational inequity An aging society's being unfair to its younger members because older adults pile up advantages by receiving inequitably large allocations of resources. 584

generational inequity The view that our aging society is being unfair to its younger members because older adults pile up advantages by receiving inequitably large allocations of resources. 13

genes Units of hereditary information composed of DNA. Genes act as a blueprint for cells to reproduce themselves and manufacture the proteins that maintain life. 69

genital herpes A sexually transmitted disease caused by a large family of viruses of different strains. These strains also produce other, nonsexually transmitted diseases such as chicken pox and mononucleosis. 426

genotype A person's genetic heritage; the actual genetic material. 72

germinal period The period of prenatal development that takes place in the first 2 weeks after conception. It includes the creation of the zygote, continued cell division, and the attachment of the zygote to the uterine wall. 94

gifted Having above-average intelligence (an IQ of 120 or higher) and/or superior talent for something. 298

gonads The sex glands—the testes in males and the ovaries in females. 350

gonorrhea Reported to be one of the most common STDs in the United States, this sexually transmitted disease is caused by a bacterium called gonococcus, which thrives in the moist mucous membranes lining the mouth, throat, vagina, cervix, urethra, and anal tract. This disease is commonly called the "drip" or the "clap." 426

grasping reflex A neonatal reflex that occurs when something touches the infant's palms. The infant responds by grasping tightly. 139

grief The emotional numbness, disbelief, separation anxiety, despair, sadness, and loneliness that accompany the loss of someone we love. 613

gross motor skills Motor skills that involve large muscle activities, such as walking. 139

H

habituation Repeated presentation of the same stimulus, which causes reduced attention to the stimulus. 163

hardiness A personality style characterized by a sense of commitment (rather than alienation), control (rather than powerlessness), and a perception of problems as challenges (rather than threats). 483

heteronomous morality The first stage of moral development, in Piaget's theory, occurring from approximately 4 to 7 years of age. Justice and rules are conceived of as unchangeable properties of the world, removed from the control of people. 240

hidden curriculum Dewey's concept that every school has a pervasive moral atmosphere, even if it doesn't have a program of moral education. 373

holophrase hypothesis The hypothesis that a single word can be used to imply a complete sentence; infants' first words characteristically are holophrastic. 170

hormonal stress theory The theory that aging in the body's hormonal system can lower resilience to stress and increase the likelihood of disease. 533

hormones Powerful chemical substances secreted by the endocrine glands and carried through the body by the bloodstream. 350

hospice A humanized program committed to making the end of life as free from pain, anxiety, and depression as possible. The goals of hospice contrast with those of a hospital, which are to cure disease and prolong life. 604

HPV A virus (human papillomavirus) that causes warts on people. A few types of the virus cause warts on the genitals. 427

hypothalamus A structure in the higher portion of the brain that monitors eating, drinking, and sex. 350

hypotheses Specific assumptions and predictions that can be tested to determine their accuracy. 30

hypothetical-deductive reasoning Piaget's formal operational concept that adolescents have the cognitive ability to develop hypotheses, or best guesses, about ways to solve problems, such as an algebraic equation. 366

I

identity achievement Marcia's term for adolescents who have undergone a crisis and have made a commitment. 383

identity diffusion Marcia's term for adolescents who have not yet experienced a crisis (explored meaningful alternatives) or made any commitments. 383

identity foreclosure Marcia's term for adolescents who have made a commitment but have not experienced a crisis. 383

identity moratorium Marcia's term for adolescents who are in the midst of a crisis, but their commitments are either absent or vaguely defined. 383

imaginary audience Adolescents' belief that others are as interested in them as they themselves are; attention-getting behavior motivated by a desire to be noticed, visible, and "on stage." 368

imminent justice The concept that, if a rule is broken, punishment will be meted out immediately. 241

implicit memory Memory without conscious recollection; involves skills and routine procedures that are automatically performed. 554

inclusion Educating a child with special education needs full-time in the regular classroom. 281

independent variable The manipulated, influential, experimental factor in an experiment. 51

individual differences The stable, consistent ways that people are different from each other. 291

individuality According to Cooper and her colleagues, individuality consists of two dimensions: self-assertion (the ability to have and communicate a point of view) and separateness (the use of communication patterns to express how one is different from others). 384

individualized education plan (IEP) A written statement that spells out a program tailored to a child with a disability. The plan should be (1) related to the child's learning capacity, (2) specially constructed to meet the child's individual needs and not merely a copy of what is offered to other children, and (3) designed to provide educational benefits. 281

individuated-connected level In White's model, this is the highest level of relationship maturity. One is acquiring an understanding of oneself, as well as consideration for others' motivations and anticipation of their needs. One now feels concern and caring that involve emotional

support and individualized expressions of interest. 451

indulgent parenting A style of parenting in which parents are highly involved with their children but place few demands or controls on them. Indulgent parenting is associated with children's social incompetence, especially a lack of self-control. 249

infant-directed speech Speech often used by parents (in which case it sometimes is called "parentese") and other adults when they talk to babies. It has a higher than normal pitch and involves the use of simple words and sentences. 172

infinite generativity An individual's ability to generate an infinite number of meaningful sentences using a finite set of words and rules, which makes language a highly creative enterprise. 169

information-processing approach The approach that emphasizes that individuals manipulate information, monitor it, and strategize about it. Central to information processing are the processes of memory and thinking. 38

innate goodness view The idea, presented by Swiss-born philosopher Jean-Jacques Rousseau, that children are inherently good. 7

insecure avoidant babies Babies that show insecurity by avoiding the caregiver. 189

insecure resistant babies Babies that might cling to the caregiver, then resist her by fighting against the closeness, perhaps by kicking or pushing away. 189

integrity versus despair Erikson's eighth and final stage of development, which individuals experience in late adulthood. This involves reflecting on the past and either piecing together a positive review or concluding that one's life has not been well spent. 576

intelligence quotient (IQ) A person's mental age divided by chronological age, multiplied by 100. 291

intelligence Problem-solving skills and the ability to learn from and adapt to the experiences of everyday life. 291

intermodal perception The ability to relate and integrate information about two or more sensory modalities, such as vision and hearing. 151

internalization The developmental change from behavior that is externally controlled to behavior that is controlled by internal standards and principles. 316

internalization of schemes Piaget's sixth and final sensorimotor substage, which develops between 18 and 24 months of age. In this substage, the infant's mental functioning shifts from a purely sensorimotor plane to a symbolic plane, and the infant develops the ability to use primitive symbols. 160

intimacy in friendships Self-disclosure and the sharing of private thoughts. 333

intuitive thought substage Piaget's second substage of preoperational thought, in which children begin to use primitive reasoning and want to know the answers to all sorts of questions (between 4 and 7 years of age). 214

J

justice perspective A moral perspective that focuses on the rights of the individual; individuals independently make moral decisions. 318

juvenile delinquent An adolescent who breaks the law or engages in behavior that is considered illegal. 399

K

Klinefelter syndrome A chromosomal disorder in which males have an extra X chromosome, making them XXY instead of XY. 76

kwashiorkor A condition caused by a deficiency in protein in which the child's abdomen and feet become swollen with water. 136

L

laboratory A controlled setting from which many of the complex factors of the real world have been removed. 48

language A system of symbols used to communicate with others. In humans language is characterized by infinite generativity and rule systems. 169

language acquisition device (LAD) A biological endowment, hypothesized by Chomsky, that enables the child to detect certain language categories, such as phonology, syntax, and semantics. 171

lateralization Specialization of function in one hemisphere of the cerebral cortex or the other. 128

launching The process in which youths move into adulthood and exit their family of origin. 457

learning disability A disability that involves (1) having normal intelligence or above, (2) having difficulties in at least one academic area and usually several, and (3) having no other problem or disorder, such as mental retardation, that can be determined as causing the difficulty. 278

least restrictive environment (LRE) The concept that a child with a disability must be educated in a setting that is as similar as possible to the one in which children who do not have a disability are educated. 281

leaving home and becoming a single adult The first stage in the family life cycle and that involves launching. 457

leisure The pleasant times after work when individuals are free to pursue activities and interests of their own choosing. 485

life expectancy The number of years that will probably be lived by the average person born in a particular year. 526

life-history records Records of a lifetime chronology of events and activities; often a combination of data records on education, work, family, and residence. 49

life-process model of addiction The view that addiction is not a disease but rather a habitual response and a source of gratification and security that can be understood only in the context of social relationships and experiences. 422

life span The upper boundary of life, the maximum number of years an individual can live. The maximum life span of human beings is about 120 years of age. 526

life-span perspective The view that development is lifelong, multidimensional, multidirectional, plastic, contextual, multidisciplinary, and involves growth, maintenance and regulation. 9

longitudinal approach A research strategy in which the same individuals are studied over a period of time, usually several years or more. 52

long-term memory A relatively permanent type of memory that holds huge amounts of information for a long period of time. 288

low-birthweight infant An infant born after a regular priod of gestation (the length of time between conception and birth) of 38 to 42 weeks but who weigh less than 5½ pounds. 111

M

mainstreaming Educating a child with special education needs partially in a special education classroom and partially in a regular classroom. 281

major depression A mood disorder in which the individual is deeply unhappy, demoralized, self-derogatory, and bored. The person does not feel well, loses stamina easily, has poor appetite, and is listless and unmotivated. Major depression is so widespread that it has been called the "common cold" of mental disorders. 562

marasmus A wasting away of body tissues in the infant's first year, caused by severe protein-calorie deficiency. 136

Maximally Discriminative Facial Movement Coding System (MAX) Izard's system of coding infants' facial expressions related to emotions. Using MAX, coders watch show-motion and stop-action videotapes of infants' facial reactions to stimuli. 179

meiosis The process of cell doubling and separation of chromosomes in which each pair of chromosomes in a cell separates, with one member of each pair going into each gamete. 70

memory A central feature of cognitive development, pertaining to all situations in which an individual retains information over time. 164

menarche First menstruation. 349

menopause The complete cessation of a woman's menstruation, which usually occurs in the late forties or early fifties. 485

mental age (MA) Binet's measure of an individual's level of mental development, compared with that of others. 291

mental retardation A condition of limited mental ability in which an individual has a low IQ, usually below 70 on a traditional test of intelligence, and has difficulty adapting to everyday life. 297

metacognition Cognition about cognition, or knowing about knowing. 289

middle adulthood The developmental period beginning at approximately 40 years of age and extending to about 60. 478

mitosis The process by which each chromosome in a cell's nucleus duplicates itself. 70

mnemonics Techniques designed to make memory more efficient. 573

Montessori approach An educational philosophy in which children are given considerable freedom and spontaneity in choosing activities and are allowed to move from one activity to another as they desire. 227

moral development Development regarding rules and conventions about what people should do in their interactions with other people. 240

Moro reflex A neonatal startle response that occurs in reaction to a sudden, intense noise or movement. When startled, the newborn arches its back, throws its head back, and flings out its arms and legs. Then the newborn rapidly closes its arms and legs to the center of the body. 139

multi-infarct dementia Sporadic and progressive loss of intellectual functioning caused by repeated temporary obstruction of blood flow in cerebral arteries. 567

myelination The process in which the nerve cells are covered and insulated with a layer of fat cells, which increases the speed at which information travels through the nervous system. 203

N

natural childbirth Developed in 1914 by Dick-Read, this method attempts to reduce the mother's pain by decreasing her fear through education about childbirth and relaxation techniques during delivery. 110

naturalistic observation Observations that take place out in the real world instead of in a laboratory. 48

nature-nurture issue *Nature* refers to an organism's biological inheritance, *nurture* to environmental influences. The "nature" proponents claim biological inheritance is the most important influence on development; the "nurture" proponents claim that environmental experiences are the most important. 18

neglected children Children who are infrequently nominated as a best friend but are not disliked by their peers. 330

neglectful parenting A style of parenting in which the parent is very uninvolved in the child's life; it is associated with children's social incompetence, especially a lack of self-control. 249

neo-Piagetians Developmentalists who have elaborated on Piaget's theory, believing that children's cognitive development is more specific in many respects than Piaget thought. 287

neuron Nerve cell that handles information processing at the cellular level. 127

new couple Forming the new couple is the second stage in the family life cycle. Two individuals from separate families of origin unite to form a new family system. 457

nonshared environmental experiences The child's own unique experiences, both within the family and outside the family, that are not shared by another sibling. Thus, experiences occurring within the family can be part of the "nonshared environment." 87

normal distribution A symmetrical distribution with most cases falling in the middle of the possible range of scores and a few scores appearing toward the extremes of the range. 291

O

object permanence The Piagetian term for one of an infant's most important accomplishments: understanding that objects and events continue to exist, even when they cannot directly be seen, heard, or touched. 160

onlooker play Play in which the child watches other children play. 261

operations In Piaget's theory, an internalized set of actions that allows a child to do mentally what she formerly did physically. 212

oral rehydration therapy (ORT) Treatment to prevent dehydration during episodes of diarrhea by giving fluids by mouth. 210

organic retardation Mental retardation that involves some physical damage and is caused by a genetic disorder or brain damage. 298

organogenesis Organ formation that takes place during the first 2 months of prenatal development. 96

original sin view Advocated during the Middle Ages, the belief that children were born into the world as evil beings and were basically bad. 7

osteoporosis A disorder of aging that involves an extensive loss of bone tissue and is the main reason many older adults walk with a marked stoop. Women are especially vulnerable to osteoporosis. 540

P

pain cry A sudden appearance of loud crying without preliminary moaning and a long initial cry followed by an extended period of breath holding. 180

parallel play Play in which the child plays separately from others, but with toys like those the others are using or in a manner that mimics their play. 261

Parkinson's disease A chronic, progressive disease characterized by muscle tremors, slowing of movement, and partial facial paralysis. 567

passive euthanasia The withholding of available treatments, such as life-sustaining devices, allowing the person to die. 603

passive genotype-environment correlations Correlations that exist when the natural parents, who are genetically related to the child, provide a rearing environment for the child. 86

perception The interpretation of what is sensed. 145

personal fable The part of adolescent egocentrism that involves an adolescent's sense of uniqueness and invincibility. 368

personal fable The part of adolescent egocentrism that involves an adolescent's sense of uniqueness and invincibility. 368

personality type theory John Holland's view that it is important to match an individual's personality with a particular career. 435

phenotype The way an individual's genotype is expressed in observed and measurable characteristics. 73

phenylketonuria (PKU) A genetic disorder in which an individual cannot properly metabolize an amino acid. PKU is now easily detected but, if left untreated, results in mental retardation and hyperactivity. 77

Piaget's theory Children actively construct their understanding of the world and go through four stages of cognitive development. 35

pituitary gland An important endocrine gland that controls growth and regulates other glands. 350

placenta A life-support system that consists of a disk-shaped group of tissues in which small blood vessels from the mother and offspring intertwine. 95

pluralism The coexistence of distinct ethnic and cultural groups in the same society. Individuals with a pluralistic stance usually advocate that cultural differences be maintained and appreciated. 399

popular children Children who are frequently nominated as a best friend and are rarely disliked by their peers. 330

postconventional reasoning The highest level in Kohlberg's theory of moral development. Morality is completely internalized. 317

postformal thought A form of thought, proposed as a fifth stage, that is qualitatively different from Piaget's formal operational thought. It involves understanding that the correct answer to a problem can require reflective thinking, that the correct answer can vary from one situation to another, and that the search for truth is often an ongoing, never-ending process. It also involves the belief that solutions to problems need to be realistic and that emotion and subjective factors can influence thinking. 431

postpartum period The period after childbirth when the mother adjusts, both physically and psychologically, to the process of childbirth. This period lasts for about 6 weeks or until her body has completed its adjustment and returned to a near prepregnant state. 115

practice play Play that involves repetition of behavior when new skills are being learned or when physical or mental mastery and coordination of skills are required for games or sports. Sensorimotor play, which often involves practice play, is primarily confined to infancy, while practice play can be engaged in throughout life. 262

preconventional reasoning The lowest level in Kohlberg's theory of moral development. The individual shows no internalization of moral values—moral reasoning is controlled by external rewards and punishment. 316

prepared childbirth Developed by French obstetrician Ferdinand Lamaze, this childbirth strategy is similar to natural childbirth but includes a special breathing technique to control pushing in the final stages of labor and a more detailed anatomy and physiology course. 110

pretense/symbolic play Play in which the child transforms the physical environment into a symbol. 262

preterm infant An infant born prior to 38 weeks after conception. 111

primary circular reactions A scheme based on the infant's attempt to reproduce an interesting or a pleasurable event that initially occurred by chance. 159

Project Follow Through An adjunct to Project Head Start, in which the enrichment programs are carried through the first few years of elementary school. 231

Project Head Start Compensatory education designed to provide children from low-income families the opportunity to acquire the skills and experiences important for school success. 231

proximodistal pattern The sequence in which growth starts at the center of the body and moves toward the extremities. 127

psychoanalytic theory Development is primarily unconscious and heavily colored by emotion. Behavior is merely a surface characteristic. It is important to analyze the symbolic meanings of behavior. Early experiences are important in development. 31

psychoanalytic theory of gender A theory deriving from Freud's view that the preschool child develops a sexual attraction to the opposite-sex parent, by approximately 5 or 6 years of age renounces this attraction because of anxious feelings, and subsequently identifies with the same-sex parent, unconsciously adopting the same-sex parent's characteristics. 243

psychological age An individual's adaptive capacities compared to those of other individuals of the same chronological age. 18

puberty A period of rapid skeletal and sexual maturation that occurs mainly in early adolescence. 349

Q

questionnaire A method similar to a highly structured interview except that respondents read the questions and mark their answers on paper rather than respond verbally to the interviewer. 49

R

random assignment In experimental research, the assignment of participants to experimental and control groups by chance. 51

rape Forcible sexual intercourse with a person who does not consent to it. 429

reaction range The range of possible phenotypes for each genotype, suggesting the importance of an environment's restrictiveness or richness. 73

receptive vocabulary The words an individual understands. 169

reciprocal socialization Socialization that is bidirectional; children socialize parents, just as parents socialize children. 192

reflexive smile A smile that does not occur in response to external stimuli. It happens during the month after birth, usually during irregular patterns of sleep, not when the infant is in an alert state. 180

rejected children Children who are infrequently nominated as a best friend and are actively disliked by their peers. 330

REM (rapid eye movement) sleep A recurring sleep stage during which vivid dreams commonly occur. 131

reproduction The process that, in humans, begins when a female gamete (ovum) is fertilized by a male gamete (sperm). 70

restrained eaters Individuals who chronically restrict their food intake to control their weight. Restrained eaters are often on diets, are very conscious of what they eat, and tend to feel guilty after splurging on sweets. 419

rite of passage A ceremony or ritual that marks an individual's transition from one status to another. Most rites of passage focus on the transition to adult status. 396

role-focused level In White's model, this is the second level of relationship maturity, at which one begins to perceive others as individuals in their own right. One's perspective is still stereotypical and emphasizes social acceptability. 451

romantic love Also called "passionate love" or "eros," romantic love has strong sexual and infatuation components and often predominates in the early period of a love relationship. 451

rooting reflex A newborn's built-in reaction that occurs when the infant's check is stroked or the side of the mouth is touched. In response, the infant turns its head toward the side that was touched, in an apparent effort to find something to suck. 138

S

scaffolding In cognitive development, Vygotsky used this term to describe the changing support over the course of a teaching session, with the more skilled person adjusting guidance to fit the child's current performance level. 216

scaffolding Parental behavior that supports children's efforts, allowing them to be more skillful than they would be if they relied only on their own abilities. 192

scheme In Piaget's theory, a cognitive structure that helps individuals organize and understand their experiences. 158

secondary circular reactions Piaget's third sensorimotor substage, which develops between 4 and 8 months of age. In this substage, the infant becomes more object-oriented, or focused on the world, moving beyond preoccupation with the self in sensorimotor interactions. 159

secure attachment The infant uses a caregiver as a secure base from which to explore the environment. Ainsworth believes that secure attachment in the first year of life provides an important foundation for psychological development later in life. 188

selective optimization with compensation theory The theory that successful aging is related to three main factors: selection, optimization, and compensation. 580

self-concept Domain-specific evaluations of the self. 343

self-esteem The global evaluative dimension of the self. Self-esteem is also referred to as self-worth or self-image. 343

self-focused level The first level of relationship maturity, at which one's perspective of another or of a relationship is concerned only with how it affects oneself. 450

self-understanding The child's cognitive representation of self, the substance and content of the child's self-conceptions. 238

semantic memory A person's knowledge about the world—including a person's fields of expertise, general academic knowledge of the sort learned in school, and "everyday knowledge." 553

sensation The product of the interaction between information and the sensory receptors—the eyes, ears, tongue, nostrils, and skin. 144

sensorimotor play Behavior engaged in by infants to derive pleasure from exercising their existing sensorimotor schemas. 262

sequential approach A combined cross-sectional, longitudinal design. 52

seriation The concrete operation that involves ordering stimuli along a quantitative dimension (such as length). 284

service learning A form of education that promotes social responsibility and service to the community. 376

sexually transmitted diseases (STDs) Diseases that are contracted primarily through sexual contact, which is not limited to sexual intercourse. Oral-genital and anal-genital contact also can transmit STDs. 426

sexually transmitted diseases (STDs) Diseases that are contracted primarily through sex. 357

shared environmental experiences Children's common environmental experiences that are shared with their siblings, such as their parents' personalities and intellectual orientation, the family's social class, and the neighborhood in which they live. 87

short-term memory The memory component in which individuals retain information for 15 to 30 seconds, assuming there is no rehearsal. 220

sickle-cell anemia A genetic disorder that affects the red blood cells and occurs most often in people of African descent. 77

simple reflexes Piaget's first sensorimotor substage, which corresponds to the first month after birth. In this substage, the basic means of coordinating sensation and action is through reflexive behaviors, such as rooting and sucking, which the infant has at birth. 159

slow-to-warm-up child A child who has a low activity level, is somewhat negative , shows low adaptability, and displays a low intensity mood. 182

social age Social roles and expectations related to a person's age. 18

social clock The timetable according to which individuals are expected to accomplish life's tasks, such as getting married, having children, or establishing themselves in a career. 507

social cognitive theory The theory that behavior, environment, and person/cognitive factors are important in understanding development. 40

social cognitive theory of gender A theory that emphasizes that children's gender development occurs through the observation and imitation of gender behavior and through the rewards and punishments children experience for gender-appropriate and inappropriate behavior. 244

social constructivist approach An approach that emphasizes the social contexts of learning and that knowledge is mutually built and constructed. Vygotsky's theory reflects this approach. 218

social play Play that involves social interactions with peers. 263

social policy A national government's course of action designed to influence the welfare of its citizens. 13

social smile A smile is response to an external stimulus, which, early in development, typically is in response to a face. 180

socioemotional processes Changes in an individual's relationships with other people, emotions, and personality. 16

socioemotional selectivity theory The theory that older adults become more selective about their social networks. Because they place a high value on emotional satisfaction, older adults often spend more time with familiar individuals with whom they have had rewarding relationships. 578

solitary play Play in which the child plays alone and independently of others. 261

stability-change issue The issue of whether development is best described as involving stability or as involving change. This issue involves the degree to which we become older renditions of our early experience or instead develop into someone different from who we were at an earlier point in development. 20

standardized tests Tests that require people to answer a series of questions and that have two distinct features: (1) Usually the individual's score is totaled to yield a single score, or set of scores, that reflects something about the individual; (2) the individual's score is compared to the scores of a large group of similar people to determine how the individual responded relative to others. 49

Strange Situation An observational measure of infant attachment that requires the infant to move through a series of introductions, separations, and reunions with the caregiver and an adult stranger in a prescribed order. 188

stranger anxiety An infant's fear and wariness of strangers; it needs to appear in the second half of the first year of life. 180

sucking reflex A newborn's built-in reaction of automatically sucking an object placed in its mouth. The sucking reflex enables the infant to get nourishment before it has associated a nipple with food. 138

sudden infant death syndrome (SIDS) A condition that occurs when an infant stops breathing, usually during the night, and suddenly dies without an apparent cause. 133

symbolic function substage Piaget's first substage of preoperational thought, in which the child gains the ability to mentally represent an object that is not present (between 2 and 4 years of age). 212

syphilis A sexually transmitted disease caused by the bacterium Treponema pallidum, a spirochete. 426

T

tabula rasa view The idea, proposed by John Locke, that children are like a "blank tablet." 7

telegraphic speech The use of short and precise words to communicate; young children's two- and three-word utterances characteristically are telegraphic. 170

temperament An individual's behavioral style and characteristic way of emotional response. 182

teratogen From the Greek word tera, meaning "monster." Any agent that causes a birth defect. The field of study that investigates the causes of birth defects is called teratology. 98

terminal drop hypothesis The hypothesis that death is preceded by a decrease in cognitive functioning over approximately a 5-year period prior to death. 557

tertiary circular reactions, novelty, and curiosity Piaget's fifth sensorimotor substage, which develops between 12 and 18 months of age. In this substage, infants become intrigued by the variety of properties that objects possess and by the multiplicity of things they can make happen to objects. 159

theory An interrelated, coherent set of ideas that helps to explain events and make predictions. 30

theory of mind Individuals' thoughts about how mental processes work. 222

top-dog phenomenon The circumstance of moving from the top position in elementary school to the lowest position in middle or junior high school. 371

transitivity In concrete operational thought, a mental concept that underlies the ability to logically combine relations to understand certain conclusions. It focuses on reasoning about the relations between classes. 284

triangular theory of love Sternberg's theory that love has three main forms: passion, intimacy, and commitment. 452

triarchic theory of intelligence Sternberg's theory that intelligence consists of componential intelligence, experiential intelligence, and contextual intelligence. 293

trophoblast The outer layer of cells that develops in the germinal period. These cells provide nutrition and support for the embryo. 94

Turner syndrome A chromosome disorder in females in which either an X chromosome is missing, making the person XO instead of XX, or the second X chromosome is partially deleted. 76

twin study A study in which the behavioral similarity of identical twins is compared with the behavioral similarity of fraternal twins. 74

Type A behavior pattern A cluster of characteristics—being excessively competitive, hard-driven, impatient, and hostile—thought to be related to the incidence of heart disease. 482

Type B behavior pattern Being primarily calm and easygoing. 482

U

umbilical cord A life-support system containing two arteries and one vein that connects the baby to the placenta. 95

unoccupied play Play in which the child is not engaging in play as it is commonly understood and might stand in one spot, look around the room, or perform random movements that do not seem to have a goal. 261

V

values clarification An approach to moral education that emphasizes helping people clarify what their lives are for and what is worth working for. Students are encouraged to define their own values and to understand the values of others. 375

Vygotksky's theory A sociocultural cognitive theory that emphasizes developmental analysis, the role of language, and social relations. 37

W

whole-language approach An approach to reading instruction based on the idea that instruction should parallel children's natural language learning. Reading materials should be whole and meaningful. 302

wisdom Expert knowledge about the practical aspects of life that permits excellent judgment about important matters. 555

working memory The concept currently used to describe short-term memory as a place for mental work. Working memory is like a "workbench" where individuals can manipulate and assemble information when making decisions, solving problems, and comprehending written and spoken language. 553

X

XYY syndrome A chromosomal disorder in which males have an extra Y chromosome. 76

Z

zone of proximal development (ZPD) Vygotsky's term for tasks too difficult for children to master alone but that can be mastered with assistance. 216

zygote A single cell formed through fertilization. 70

References

A

Abbassi, V. (1998). Growth and normal puberty. *Pediatrics* (Suppl.), *102* (2) 507–511.

Aboud, F., & Skerry, S. (1983). Self and ethnic concepts in relation to ethnic constancy. *Canadian Journal of Behavioral Science, 15,* 3–34.

Acquilino, W. (1999). Two views of one relationship: Comparing parents' and young adult children's reports of the quality of intergenerational relations. *Journal of Marriage and the Family, 61,* 858–870.

Acredolo, L. P., & Hake, J. L. (1982). Infant perception. In B. B. Wolman (Ed.). *Handbook of developmental psychology.* Englewood Cliffs, NJ: Prentice Hall.

Adams, R. J. (1989). Newborns' discrimination among mid- and long-wavelength stimuli. *Journal of Experimental Child Psychology, 47,* 130–141.

Addis, A., Magrini, N., & Mastroiacovo, P. (2001). Drug use during pregnancy. *Lancet, 357,* 800

Adler, T. (1991, January). Seeing double? Controversial twins study is widely reported, debated. *APA Monitor, 22,* 1, 8.

Adolph, K. (1997). Learning in the development of infant locomotion. *Monographs of the Society for Research in Child Development, 62* (3, Serial No. 251).

Ahluwalia, I. B., Tessaro, I., Grumer-Strawn, L. M., MacGowan, C., & Benton-Davis, S. (2000). Georgia's breastfeeding promotion program for low-income women. *Pediatrics, 105,* E85–E87.

Ahn, N. (1994). Teenage childbearing and high school completion: Accounting for individual heterogeneity. *Family Planning Perspectives, 26,* 17–21.

Aiken, L. (2000). *Dying, death, and bereavement* (4th ed.). Mahwah. NJ: Erlbaum.

Aiken, L. R. (2000). *Psychological testing and assessment* (10th ed). Boston: Allyn & Bacon.

Ainsworth, M. D. S. (1979). Infant-mother attachment. *American Psychologist, 34,* 932–937.

Akiyama, H., & Antonucci, T. C. (1999, November). *Mother-daughter dynamics over the life course.* Paper presented at the meeting of the Gerontological Association of America, San Francisco.

Alan Guttmacher Institute. (1998). *Teen sex and pregnancy.* New York: Author.

Alan Guttmacher Institute. (1999). *Facts in brief: Teen sex and pregnancy.* New York: Author.

Albert, M. (1999). Interview. In *Ask the scientists.* Available on the World Wide Web at http://www.pbs.org/saf/3_ask/archive/bio/103_albert.bo.htm.

Alexander, A., Anderson, H., Heilman, P. C. & others. (1991). Phonological awareness training and remediation of analytic decoding deficits in a group of severe dyslexics. *Annals of Dyslexia, 41,* 193–206.

Alexander, G. R., & Korenbrot, C. C. (1995). The role of prenatal care in preventing low birth weight. *Future of Children 5* (1), 103–120.

Allan, R., & Scheidt, S. (Eds.). (1996). *Heart and mind.* Washington, DC: American Psychological Association.

Allen, J. P., Hauser, S. T., & Borman-Spurrell, E. (1996). Attachment security and related sequelae of severe adolescent psychopathology: An eleven-year follow-up study. *Journal of Consulting and Clinical Psychology, 64,* 254–263.

Allen, J. P., Philliber, S., Herring, S., & Kuperminc, G. P. (1997). Preventing teen pregnancy and academic failure: Experimental evaluation of a developmentally based approach. *Child Development, 68,* 729–742.

Allen, K. R., Blieszener, R., & Roberto, K. A. (2000). Families in middle and later years: A review and critique of research in the 1990s. *Journal of Marriage and the Family, 62,* 911–926.

Allen, M., Brown, P., & Finlay, B. (1992). *Helping children by strengthening families.* Washington, DC: Children's Defense Fund.

Allison, J. A., & Wrightsman, L. S. (1993). *Rape: The misunderstood crime.* Newbury Park, CA: Sage.

Alpha-Tocopherol, Beta-Carotene Cancer Prevention Study Group. (1994). The effect of Vitamin E and beta-carotene on the incidence of lung cancer and other cancers in non-smokers. *New England Journal of Medicine, 330,* 1029–1035.

Amabile, T. (1993). Commentary. In D. Goleman, P. Kaufman, & M. Ray. *The Creative Spirit.* New York: Plume.

Amabile, T.M., & Hennesey, B.A. (1992). The motivation for creativity in children. In A. K. Boggiano & T. S. Pittman (Eds.), *Achievement and motivation.* New York: Cambridge.

Amato, P. R. (2000). The consequences of divorce for adults and children. *Journal of Marriage and the Family, 62,* 1269–1287.

Amato, P. R., & Booth, A. (1996). A prospective study of divorce and parent-child relationships. *Journal of Marriage and the Family, 58,* 356–365.

Amato, P. R., & Keith, B. (1991). Parental divorce and the well-being of children: A meta-analysis. *Psychological Bulletin, 110,* 26–46.

American Academy of Pediatrics. (2000). Suicide and Suicide Attempts in adolescence. *Pediatrics, 105,* 871–874.

American Academy of Pediatrics (AAP) Committee on Drugs. (1994). The transfer of drugs and other chemicals into human milk. *Pediatrics, 93,* 137–150.

American Academy of Pediatrics (AAP) Committee on Environmental Health. (1997). Environmental tobacco smoke: A hazard to children. *Pediatrics, 99,* 639–642.

American Academy of Pediatrics (AAP) Work Group on Breastfeeding. (1997). Breastfeeding and the use of human milk. *Pediatrics, 100,* 1035–1039.

American Academy of Pediatrics Task Force on Infant Positioning and SIDS. (1997). Does bed sharing affect the risk of SIDS? *Pediatrics, 100,* 272.

American Academy of Pediatrics Task Force on Infant Sleep Position and SIDS. (2000). Changing concepts of sudden infant death syndrome. *Pediatrics, 105,* 650–656.

American Association for Protecting Children. (1986). *Highlights of official child neglect and abuse reporting: 1984.* Denver: American Humane Association.

American Association of University Women. (2000). *Tech-Savvy: Educating girls in the new computer age.* Washington, DC: Author.

Amsterdam, B. K. (1968). *Mirror behavior in children under two years of age.* Unpublished doctoral dissertation, University of North Carolina, Chapel Hill.

Anderson, D.R., Huston, A.C., Schmitt, K., Linebarger, D.L., & Wright, J.C. (2001). Early childhood television viewing and adolescent behavior: The recontact study. *Monographs of the Society for Research in Child Development, 66, (1, Serial No. 264).*

Anderson, D. R., Lorch, E. P., Field, D. E., Collins, P. A., & Nathan, J. G. (1985, April). *Television viewing at home: Age trends in visual attention and time with TV.* Paper presented at the biennial meeting of the Society for Research in Child Development, Toronto.

Anderson, E., Greene, S. M., Hetherington, E. M., & Clingempeel, W. G. (1999). The dynamics of parental remarriage. In E. M. Hetherington (Ed.), *Coping with divorce, single parenting, and remarriage.* Mahwah, NJ: Erlbaum.

Anselmi, D. L. (1998). *Questions of gender.* New York: McGraw-Hill.

Anstey, K. J., & Smith, G. A. (1999). Interrelationships among biological markers of aging, health, activity, acculturation, and cognitive performance in late adulthood. *Psychology and Aging, 14,* 605–618.

Anthony Greenwald & Associates. (2000). *Current views toward retirement: A poll.* New York: Author.

Antonucci, T. (1990). Attachment, social support, and coping with negative life events. In E. M. Cummings, A. L. Greene, & K. H. Karraker (Eds.), *Life-span developmental psychology. Vol. 11: Stress and coping across the life span.* Mahwah, NJ: Erlbaum.

Antonucci, T. C. (1989). Understanding adult social relationships. In K. Kreppner & R.M. Lerner (Eds.), *Family systems and life-span development.* Hillsdale, NJ: Erlbaum.

Antonucci, T. C. (1990). Social supports and relationships. In R. H. Binstock & L. K. George (Eds.), *Handbook of aging and the social sciences.* San Diego: Academic Press.

Antonucci, T.C., Lansford, J.E., & Akiyama, H. (2001). The impact of positive and negative aspects of marital relationships and friendships on the well-being of older adults. In J.P. Reinhardt (Ed.), *Negative and positive support.* Mahwah, NJ: Erlbaum.

Antonucci, T. C., Vandewater, E. A., & Lansford, J. E. (1998). Extended family relationships. In

H. S. Friedman (Ed.), *Encyclopedia of mental health* (Vol. 2). San Diego: Academic Press.

Antonucci, T. C., Vandewater, E. A., & Lansford, J. E. (2000). Adulthood and aging: Social processes and development. In A. Kazdin (Ed.), *Encyclopedia of psychology.* Washington, DC, & New York: American Psychological Association and Oxford University Press.

Appalachia Educational Laboratory. (1998). *ADHD—Building academic success.* Charleston, WV: Appalachia Educational Laboratory.

Appelbaum, M., & Conger, R. (1996, June). *Continuity and change—What have we learned?* Paper presented at the Family Research Summer Consortium, San Diego.

Arboleda, T. (1999). *In the shadow of race.* Mahwah, NJ: Erlbaum.

Arbuckle, T. Y., Maag, U., Pushkar, D., & Chalkelsen, J. S. (1998). Individual differences in trajectory of intellectual development over 45 years of adulthood. *Psychology and Aging, 13,* 663–675.

Archer, S. L. (Ed.). (1994). *Intervention for adolescent identity development.* Newbury Park, CA: Sage.

Arendt, R., Angelopouos, J., Salvator, A., & Singer, L. (1999). Motor development of cocaine-exposed children at age two years. *Pediatrics, 103,* 86–92.

Arnett, J. D. (1995, March). *Are college students adults?* Paper presented at the meeting of the Society for Research in Child Development, Indianapolis.

Arnett, J. J. (2000). Emerging adulthood. *American Psychologist, 55,* 469–480.

Aron, A. (2000). Love. In A. Kazdin (Ed.), *Encyclopedia of psychology*. Washington, DC, & New York: American Psychological Association and Oxford University Press.

Aronson, E. (1986, August). *Teaching students things they think they already know about: The case of prejudice and desegregation.* Paper presented at the meeting of the American Psychological Association, Washington, DC.

Arshad, S.H. (2001). Food allergen avoidance in primary prevention of food allergy. *Allergy, 56* 113–116.

Asarnow, J. R., & Callan, J. W. (1985). Boys with peer adjustment problems: Social cognitive processes. *Journal of Consulting and Clinical Psychology, 53,* 80–87.

Asch, D. A., & Christakis, N. A. (1996). Why do physicians prefer to withdraw some forms of life support over others? Intrinsic attributes of life-sustaining treatments are associated with physicians' preferences. *Medical Care, 34,* 103–111.

Asher, J., & Garcia. R. (1969). The optimal age to learn a foreign language. *Modern Language Journal, 53,* 334–341.

Atchley, R. C. (1976). *The sociology of retirement.* Cambridge, MA: Schenkman.

Avis, N. E. (1999). Women's health at midlife. In S. L. Willis & J. D. Reid (Eds.), *Life in the middle: Psychological and social development in middle age.* San Diego: Academic Press.

Avolio, B. J., & Sosik, J. J. (1999). A life-span framework for assessing the impact of work on white-collar workers. In S. L. Willis & J. D. Reid (Eds.), *Life in the middle: Psychological and social development in middle age.* San Diego: Academic Press.

B

Bachman, J. (1997). *Smoking, drinking, and drug use in young adulthood: The impact of new freedoms and responsibilities.* Mahwah, NJ: Erlbaum.

Bachman, J., O'Malley, P., & Johnston, L. (1978). *Youth in transition: Vol. 6. Adolescence to adulthood—Change and stability of the lives of young men.* Ann Arbor: University of Michigan, Institute of Social Research.

Bachman, J. G., Johnston, L. D., O'Malley, P. M., & Schulenberg, J. (1996). Transitions in drug use during late adolescence and young adulthood. In J. A. Graber & J. Brooks-Gunn (Eds.), *Transitions in adolescence.* Hillsdale, NJ: Erlbaum.

Baddeley, A. (2000). Short-term and working memory. In E. Tulving & F. I. M. Craik (Eds.), *The Oxford handbook of memory.* New York: Oxford University Press.

Baer, J. S., Barr, H. M., Bookstein, F. L., Sampson, P. D., & Streissguth, A. P. (1998). Prenatal alcohol exposure and family history of alcholism in the etiology of adolescent alcohol problems. *Journal of Studies on Alcohol, 59,* 533–543.

Bagwell, C. L., Newcomb, A. F., & Bukowski, W. M. ([illegible]). [illegible] *predictor of adult adjustment: A twelve-year follow-up investigation.* Paper presented at the biennial meeting of the Society for Research on Adolescence, San Diego.

Bahr, S. J. (1989). Prologue: A developmental overview of the aging family. In S. J. Bahr & E. T. Peterson (Eds.), *Aging and the family.* Lexington, MA: Lexington Books.

Baillargeon, R. (1995). The object concept revisited: New directions in the investigation of infants' physical knowledge. In C. E. Granrud (Ed.), *Visual perception and cognition in infancy.* Hillsdale, NJ: Erlbaum.

Bakeman, R., & Brown, J. V. (1980). Early interaction: Consequences for social and mental development at three years. *Child Development, 51,* 437–447.

Baldwin, J. D., & Baldwin, J. I. (1998). Sexual behavior. In H.S. Friedman (Ed.), *Encyclopedia of mental health* (Vol. 3). San Diego: Academic Press.

Baldwin, M., & Fehr, B. (1995). On the instability of attachment ratings. *Personal Relationships, 2,* 247–261.

Balota, D. A., Dolan, P. O., & Duchek, J. M. (2000). Memory changes in healthy older adults. In E. Tulving & F. I. M. Craik (Eds.), *The Oxford handbook of memory.* New York: Oxford University Press.

Baltes, M. M., & Horgas, A. L. (1998). Aging and mental health. In H. S. Friedman (Ed.), *Encyclopedia of mental health* (Vol. 1). San Diego: Academic Press.

Baltes, P. B. (1987). Theoretical propositions of life-span developmental psychology: On the dynamics between growth and decline. *Developmental Psychology, 23,* 611–626.

Baltes, P. B. (1993). The aging mind: Potentials and limits. *Gerontologist, 33,* 580–594.

Baltes, P. B. (1995, September). Unpublished review of J. W. Santrock's *Life-Span Development,* 6th ed. (New York: McGraw-Hill).

Baltes, P. B. (1996, August). *On the incomplete architecture of human ontogenesis.* Invited award address presented at the meeting of the American Psychological Association, Toronto.

Baltes, P. B. (1996, August). *On the incomplete architecture of human ontogeny: Selection, optimization, and compensation as foundations of developmental theory*. Invited award address presented at the meeting of the American Psychological Association, Toronto.

Baltes, P. B. (2000). Life-span developmental theory. In A. Kazdin (Ed.), *Encyclopedia of psychology.* Washington, DC, & New York: American Psychological Association and Oxford University Press.

Baltes, P. B. (2000). Life-span psychology theory. In A. Kazdin (Ed.), *Encyclopedia of psychology.* Washington, DC, & New York City: American Psychological Association and Oxford University Press.

Baltes, P. B. (2000). Wisdom. In A. Kazdin (Ed.), *Encyclopedia of psychology.* Washington, DC, & New York: American Psychological Association and Oxford University Press.

Baltes, P. B., & Baltes, M. M. (1990). Psychological perspectives on successful aging: The model of selective optimization with compensation. In P. B. Baltes & M. M. Baltes (Eds.), *Successful aging: Perspectives from the behavioral sciences.* New York: Cambridge University Press.

Baltes, P. B., Lindenberger, U., & Staudinger, U. M. (1998). Life-span theory in developmental psychology. In W. Damon (Ed.), *Handbook of child psychology* (5th ed., Vol. 1). New York: Wiley.

Baltes, P. B., Reese, H. W., & Lipsitt, L. P. (1980). Life-span developmental psychology. *Annual Review of Psychology, 31,* 65–110.

Baltes, P. B., & Staudinger, U. M. (1998). Wisdom. In H. S. Friedman (Ed.), *Encyclopedia of mental health* (Vol. 3). San Diego: Academic Press.

Baltes, P. B., & Staudinger, U. M. (2000). Wisdom. *American Psychologist, 55,* 122–136.

Baltes, P. B., Staudinger, U. M., & Lindenberger, U. (1999). Lifespan psychology: Theory and application to intellectual functioning. *Annual Review of Psychology, 50,* 471–507.

Baltes, P. B., Staudinger, U. M., Maercker, A., & Smith (1995). People nominated as wise: A comparative study of wisdom-related knowledge. *Psychology and Aging, 10,* 155–166.

Bandstra, E. S., Morrow, C. E., Anthony, J. C., Haynes, V. L., Johnson, A. L., Xue, L., & Audrey, Y. (2000, May). *Effects of prenatal cocaine exposure on attentional processing in children through five years of age.* Paper presented at the joint meetings of the Pediatric Academic Societies and the American Academy of Pediatrics, Boston.

Bandura, A. (1977). *Social learning theory.* Englewood Cliffs, NJ: Prentice-Hall.

Bandura, A. (1986). *Social foundations of thought and action: A social cognitive theory.* Englewood Cliffs, NJ: Prentice Hall.

Bandura, A. (1998, August). *Swimming against the mainstream: Accentuating the positive aspects of humanity.* Paper presented at the meeting of the

American Psychological Association, San Francisco.

Bandura, A. (2000). Self-efficacy. In A. Kazdin (Ed.). *Encyclopedia of Psychology.* Washington, DC, & New York: American Psychological Association and Oxford University Press.

Bandura, A. (2000). Social cognitive theory. In A. Kazdin (Ed.), *Encyclopedia of psychology.* Washington, DC, & New York: American Psychological Association and Oxford University Press.

Banks, E. C. (1993, March). *Moral education curriculum in a multicultural context: The Malaysian primary curriculum.* Paper presented at the biennial meeting of the Society for Research in Child Development, New Orleans.

Banks, J. A. (1995). Multicultural education: Its effects on students' racial and gender role attitudes. In J. A. Banks & C. A. M. Banks (Eds.), *Handbook of research on multicultural education.* New York: Macmillan.

Banks, J. A. (1997). Approaches to multicultural education reform. In J. A. Banks & C. A. M. Banks (Eds.), *Multicultural education.* Boston: Allyn & Bacon.

Banks, M. S., & Salapatek, P. (1983). Infant visual perception. In P. H. Mussen (Ed.), *Handbook of child psychology* (4th ed., Vol. 2). New York: Wiley.

Barnett, D., Ganiban, J., & Cicchetti, D. (1999). Maltreatment, negative expressivity, and the development of type D attachments from 12 to 24 months of age. In J. I. Vondra & D. Barnett (Eds.), *Monograph of the Society for Research in Child Development, 64.* (3, Serial No. 258, 97–118).

Barr, H.M., & Streissguth, A.P. (2001). Identifying maternal self-reported alcohol use associated with fetal alcohol disorders. *Alcoholism: Clinical and Experimental Research, 25,* 283–287.

Barrett, D. E., Radke-Yarrow, M., & Klein, R. E. (1982). Chronic malnutrition and child behavior. Effects of calorie supplementation on social and emotional functioning at school age. *Developmental Psychology, 18,* 541–556.

Barrett-Connor, E. (1994). Postmenopausal estrogen and the risk of breast cancer. *Annals of Epidemiology, 4,* 177–180.

Barton, L., Hodgman, J. E., & Pavlova, Z. (1999) Causes of death in the extremely low birth weight infant. *Pediatrics, 103,* 446–451.

Bat-Chava, Y., Allen, L., Aber, J. L., & Seidman, E. (1997, April). *Racial and ethnic identity and the contexts of development.* Paper presented at the meeting of the Society for Research in Child Development, Washington, DC.

Bates, A. S., Fitzgerald, J. F., Dittus, R. S., & Wollinsky, F. D. (1994). Risk factors for underimmunization in poor urban infants. *Journal of the American Medical Association, 272,* 1105–1109.

Bates, J.E. (2001). Adjustment style in childhood as a product of parenting and temperament. In T.D. Wachs & G.A. Kohnstamm (Eds.), *Temperament in context.* Mahwah, NJ: Erlbaum.

Baum, A., Revenson, T.A., & Singer, J.E. (Eds.) (2001). *Handbook of health psychology.* Mahwah, NJ: Erlbaum.

Baum, A. S. (2000). Genetic disorders. In A. Kazdin (Ed.), *Encyclopedia of psychology.* Washington, DC, & New York: American Psychological Association and Oxford University Press.

Baumann, J. F., Hoffman, J. V., Moon, J., & Duffy-Hester, A. M. (1993). Where are teachers' voices in the phonics/whole language debate? Results from a survey of U.S. elementary classroom teachers. *Reading Teacher, 51,* 636–650.

Baumeister, A. A. (2000). Mental retardation. In M. Herson & R. T. Ammerman (Eds.). *Advanced abnormal child psychology* (2nd ed.). Mahwah, NJ: Erlbaum.

Baumeister, R. F. (1993). *Self-esteem: The puzzle of low self-regard.* New York: Plenum Press.

Baumrind, D. (1971). Current patterns of parental authority. *Developmental Psychology Monographs, 4* (1, Pt. 2).

Baumrind, D. (1991). Effective parenting during the early adolescent transition. In P. A. Cowan & E. M. Hetherington (Eds.), *Advances in family research* (Vol. 2). Hillsdale, NJ: Erlbaum.

Baumrind, D. (1999, November). Unpublished review of J. W. Santrock's *Child Development,* 9th ed. (New York: McGraw-Hill).

Baxter, G. W., Stuart, W. J., & Stewart, W. J. (1998). *Death and the adolescent.* Toronto: University of Toronto Press.

Bayley, N. (1969). *Manual for the Bayley Scales of Infant Development.* New York: Psychological Corporation.

Bayley, N. (1970). Development of mental abilities. In P. H. Mussen (Ed.), *Manual of child psychology* (3rd ed., Vol. 1). New York: Wiley.

Beagles-Roos, J., & Gat, I. (1983). Specific impact of radio and television on children's story comprehension. *Journal of Educational Psychology, 75,* 128–137.

Beal, C. R. (1994). *Boys and girls: The development of gender roles.* Boston: McGraw-Hill.

Beck, M. (1992, December 7). Middle Age. *Newsweek,* pp. 50–56.

Beckel, J. (1996). Resolving ethical problems in long-term care. *Journal of Gerontological Nursing, 22,* 20–26.

Becker, P. E., & Moen, P. (1998). *Scaling back: Dual career couples' work-family strategies.* Ithaca, NY: Cornell Employment and Family Careers Institute.

Bednar, R. L., Wells, M. G., & Peterson, S. R. (1995). *Self-esteem* (2nd ed.). Washington, DC: American Psychological Association.

Begley, S. (1997). How to build a baby's brain. *Newsweek Special Issue.* Spring/Summer, 28–32.

Behrman, R. E., Kliegman, R., & Jenson, H. B. (Eds.) (2000). *Nelson's textbook of pediatrics* (16th ed.). London: Harcourt International.

Bell, A. P., Weinberg, M. S., & Mamersmith, S. K. (1981). *Sexual preference.* New York: Simon & Schuster.

Bell, S. M., & Ainsworth, M. D. S. (1972). Infant crying and maternal responsiveness. *Child Development, 43,* 1171–1190.

Belle, D. (1999). *The after school lives of children.* Mahwah, NJ: Erlbaum.

Bellinger, D., Leviton, A., Waternaux, C., Needleman, H., & Rabinowitz, M. (1987). Longitudinal analysis of prenatal and postnatal lead exposure and early cognitive development. *New England Journal of Medicine, 316,* 1037–1043.

Belloc, N. B., & Breslow, L. (1972). Relationships of physical health status and health practices. *Preventive Medicine, 1,* 409–421.

Belsky, J. (1981). Early human experience: A family perspective. *Developmental Psychology, 17,* 3–23.

Belson, W. (1978). *Television violence and the adolescent boy.* London: Saxon House.

Bem, S. L. (1977). On the utility of alternative procedures for assessing psychological androgyny. *Journal of Consulting and Clinical Psychology, 45,* 196–205.

Benet, S. (1976). *How to live to be 100.* New York: Dial Press.

Bengtson, V. L. (1985). Diversity and symbolism in grandparental roles. In V. L. Bengtson & J. Robertson (Eds.), *Grandparenthood.* Newbury Park, CA: Sage.

Bengtson, V.L. (2001). Beyond the nuclear family: The increasing importance of multigenerational bonds. *Journal of Marriage and the Family, 63,* 1–16.

Bennett, W. (1993). *The book of virtues.* New York: Simon & Schuster.

Bennett, W. I., & Gurin, J. (1982). *The dieter's dilemma: Eating less and weighing more.* New York: Basic Books.

Benson, P. (1993). *The troubled journey.* Minneapolis: Search Institute.

Bergin, A. E. (2000). Religious values and mental health. In A. Kazdin (Ed.), *Encyclopedia of psychology.* Washington, DC, & New York: American Psychological Association and Oxford University Press.

Bergin, D. (1988). Stages of play development. In D. Bergin (Ed.), *Play as a medium for learning and development.* Portsmouth, NH: Heinemann.

Berko, J. (1958). The child's learning of English morphology. *Word, 14,* 150–177.

Berko-Gleason, J. (2000). Language: An overview. In A. Kazdin (Ed.), *Encyclopedia of psychology.* Washington, DC, & New York: American Psychological Association and Oxford University Press.

Berlin, L., & Cassidy, J. (2000). Understanding parenting. Contributions of attachment theory and research. In J. D. Osofsky & H. E. Fitzgerald (Eds.), *WAIMH handbook of infant mental health* (Vol. 3). New York: Wiley.

Berliner, D. C. (1997). Educational psychology meets the Christian right: Differing views of schooling, children, teaching, and learning. *Teachers College Record, 96,* 381–415.

Berlyne, D. E. (1960). *Conflict, arousal, and curiosity.* New York: McGraw-Hill.

Berndt, T. J. (1996). Transitions in friendship and friends' influence. In J. A. Graber, J. Brooks-Gunn, & A. C. Petersen (Eds.), *Transitions through adolescence.* Mahwah, NJ: Erlbaum.

Berndt, T. J. (1999). Friends' influence on children's adjustment. In W. A. Collins & B. Laursen (Eds.), *Relationships as developmental contexts.* Mahwah, NJ: Erlbaum.

Berndt, T. J., & Perry, T. B. (1990). Distinctive features and effects of early adolescent friendships. In R. Montemayor (Ed.), *Advances in adolescent research.* Greenwich, CT: JAI Press.

Bernier, M. O., Plu-Bureau, G., Bossard, N., Ayzac, L., Thalabard, J. C. (2000). Breastfeeding and risk of breast cancer: A metaanalysis of published studies. *Human Reproduction Update, 6*(4), 374–386.

Berquist, W. H., Greenberg, E.M., & Klaum, G. A. (1993). *In our fifties.* San Francisco: Jossey-Bass.

Berscheid, E. (1988). Some comments on love's anatomy: Or, whatever happened to old-fashioned lust? In R. J. Sternberg (Ed.), *Anatomy of love.* New Haven, CT: Yale University Press.

Berscheid, E. (2000). Attraction. In A. Kazdin (Ed.), *Encyclopedia of psychology.* Washington, DC, & New York: American Psychological Association and Oxford University Press.

Berscheid, E., & Fei, J. (1977). Sexual jealousy and romantic love. In G. Clinton & G. Smith (Eds.), *Sexual jealousy.* Englewood Cliffs, NJ: Prentice Hall.

Berscheid, E., & Reis, H. T. (1998). Attraction and close-relationships. In D.T. Gilbert, S.T. Fiske, & G. Lindzey (Eds.), *Handbook of social psychology* (4th ed., Vol. 2). New York: McGraw-Hill.

Berscheid, E., Snyder, M., & Omato, A. M. (1989). Issues in studying close relationships. In C. Hendrick (Ed.), *Close relationships.* Newbury Park, CA: Sage.

Beyene, Y. (1986). Cultural significance and physiological manifestations of menopause: A biocultural analysis. *Culture, Medicine and Psychiatry, 10,* 47–71.

Bialystok, E. (1993). Metalinguistic awareness: The development of children's representations in language. In C. Pratt & A. Garton (Eds.), *Systems of representation in children.* London: Wiley.

Bialystok, E. (1997). Effects of bilingualism and biliteracy on children's emerging concepts of print. *Developmental Psychology, 33,* 429–440.

Bialystok, E. (1999). Cognitive complexity and attentional control in the bilingual mind. *Child Development, 70,* 537–804.

Bier, J. B., Oliver, T. L., Ferguson, A., & Vohr, B. R. (1999, May). *Human milk reduces outpatient infections in low birth weight infants.* Paper presented at the meeting of the Society for Pediatric Research, San Francisco.

Bijur, P. E., Wallston, K. A., Smith, C. A., Lifrak, S., & Friedman, S. B. (1993, August). *Gender differences in turning to religion for coping.* Paper presented at the meeting of the American Psychological Association, Toronto.

Billy, J. O. G., Rodgers, J. L., & Udry, J. R. (1984). Adolescent sexual behavior and friendship choice. *Social Forces, 62,* 653–678.

Bingham, C. R., & Crockett, L. J. (1996). Longitudinal adjustment patterns of boys and girls experiencing early, middle, and late sexual intercourse. *Developmental Psychology, 32,* 647–658.

Birren, J. E. (1993). Fifteen commandments for responsible old age. In R. N. Butler & K. Kiikuni (Eds.), *Who is responsible for my old age?* New York: Springer.

Birren, J. E. (Ed.). (1996). *Encyclopedia of gerontology.* San Diego: Academic Press.

Bjorklund, D., & Bering, J.M., (2001, April). *Evolutionary developmental psychology.* Paper presented at the meeting of the Society for Research in Child Development, Minneapolis.

Bjorklund, D. F., & Rosenbaum, K. (2000). Middle childhood: Cognitive development. In A. Kazdin (Ed.), *Encylopedia of psychology.* Washington, DC, & New York: American Psychological Association and Oxford University Press.

Blachman, B. A., Ball, E., Black, R., & Tangel, D. (1994). Kindergarten teachers develop phoneme awareness in low-income inner-city classrooms: Does it make a difference? In B. A. Blachman (Ed.), *Reading and writing.* Mahwah, NJ: Erlbaum.

Black, J.E. (2001, April). *Complex and interactive effects of enriched experiences on brain development.* Paper presented at the meeting of the Society for Research in Child Development, Minneapolis.

Blair, C., & Ramey, C. (1996). Early intervention with low birth weight infants: The path to second generation research. In M. J. Guralnick (Ed.). *The effectiveness of early intervention.* Baltimore: Paul H. Brookes.

Blair, S. N. (1990, January). Personal communication. Aerobics Institute, Dallas.

Blanchard-Fields, F. (1996). Decision making and everyday problem solving. In J. E. Birren (Ed.), *Encyclopedia of gerontology* (Vol. 1). San Diego: Academic Press.

Block, J. (1993). Studying personality the long way, In D. Funder, R. D. Parke, C. Tomlinson-Keasey, & K. Widaman (Ed.), *Studying lives through time*. Washington, DC: American Psychological Association.

Block, J. H., & Block, J. (1980). The role of ego-control and ego resiliency in the organization of behavior. In W. A. Collins (Ed.), *Minnesota symposium on child psychology* (Vol. 13). Minneapolis: University of Minnesota Press.

Bloor, C., & White, F. (1983). Unpublished manuscript. University of California at San Diego, LaJolla, CA.

Blum, L. M. (2000). *At the breast: Ideologies of breastfeeding and motherhood in the contemporary United States.* Boston: Beacon Press.

Blumberg, J. (1993, June 2). Commentary in "Lowly vitamin supplements pack a big health punch." *USA Today,* p. 3D.

Blumenfeld, P. C., Pintrich, P. R., Wessles, K., & Meece, J. (1981, April). *Age and sex differences in the impact of classroom experiences on self-perceptions.* Paper presented at the biennial meeting of the Society of Research in Child Development, Boston.

Blumenthal, J., Jeffries, N. O., Castellanos, F. X., Liu, H., Zidjdenbos, A., Paus, T., Evans, A. C., Rapoport, J. L., & Giedd, J. N. (1999). Brain development during childhood and adolescence: A longitudinal MRI study. *Nature Neuroscience, 10,* 861–863.

Blumenthal, J. A., Emery, C. F., Madden, D. J., George, L. K., Coleman, R. E., Riddle, M. W., McKee, D. C., Reasoner, J., & Williams, R. S. (1989). Cardiovascular and behavioral effects of aerobic exercise training in healthy older men and women. *Journal of Gerontology: Medical Sciences, 44,* M147–157.

Blundell, J. E. (1984). Systems and interactions: An approach to the pharmacology of feeding. In A. J. Stunkdard & E. Stellar (Eds.), *Eating and its disorders.* New York: Raven Press.

Bodnar, A. G., Ouellette, M., Frolkis, M., Holt, S. E., Chiu, C.-P., Morin, G. B., Harley, C. B., Shay, J. W., & Wright, W. E. (1998). Extension of lifespan by introduction of telomerase in normal human cells. *Science, 279,* 349–352.

Boerner, K., & Wortman, C. B. (1998). Grief and loss. In H. S. Freeman (Ed.), *Encyclopedia of mental health* (Vol. 2). San Diego: Academic Press.

Bohlin, G., & Hagekull, B. (1993). Stranger wariness and sociability in the early years. *Infant Behavior and Development, 16,* 53–67.

Bolen, J. C., Bland, S. D., & Sacks, J. J. (1999, April). *Injury prevention behaviors: Children's use of occupant restraints and bicycle helmets.* Paper presented at the meeting of the Society for Research in Child Development, Albuquerque.

Bolger, K.E., & Patterson, C.J. (2001). Developmental pathways from child maltreatment to peer rejection. *Child Development, 72,* 339–351.

Bonde, M. W., & Lange, K. L. (1998). Alzheimer's disease. In H. S. Friedman (Ed.), *Encyclopedia of mental health* (Vol. 1). San Diego: Academic Press.

Bonk, C. J., & Cunningham, D. J. (1999). Searching for learner-centered, constructivist, and sociocultural components of collaborative educational learning tools. In C. J. Bonk & K. S. King (Eds.), *Electronic collaborators.* Mahwah, NJ: Erlbaum.

Bonvillian, J. D., Orlansky, M. D., & Novack, L. L. (1983). Developmental milestones: Sign language and motor development. *Child Development, 54,* 1435–1445.

Booth, A., & Crouter, A. C. (Eds.) (2000). *Does it take a village?* Mahwah, NJ: Erlbaum.

Booth, A., & Johnson, D. (1988). Premarital cohabitation and marital success. *Journal of Family Issues, 9,* 255–272.

Bornstein, M. H. (2000). Infancy: Emotions and temperament. In A. Kazdin (Ed.), *Encyclopedia of psychology.* Washington, DC, & New York: American Psychological Association and Oxford University Press.

Bornstein, M. H. (2000). Unpublished review of J. W. Santrock's *Life-Span Development,* 8th ed. (New York: McGraw-Hill).

Bornstein, M. H., & Arterberry, M. E. (1999). Perceptual development. In M. H. Bornstein & M. E. Lamb (Eds.), *Developmental psychology: An advanced textbook* (4th ed.). Mahwah, NJ: Erlbaum.

Bornstein, M. H., & Sigman, M. D. (1986). Continuity in mental development from infancy. *Child Development, 57,* 251–274.

Bornstein, R. F., & D'Agostino, P. R. (1992). Stimulus recognition and the mere exposure effect. *Journal of Personality and Social Psychology, 63,* 545–552.

Botwinick, J. (1978). *Aging and behavior* (2nd ed.). New York: Springer.

Bouchard, T. J. (1995, August). *Henuibility of intelligence.* Paper presented at the meeting of the American Psychological Association, New York, NY.

Bouchard, T. J., Lykken, D. T., McGue, M., Segal, N. L., & Tellegen, A. (1990). Source of human psychological differences. The Minnesota Study of Twins Reared Apart. *Science, 250,* 223–228.

Bower, B. (1985). The left hand of math and verbal talent. *Science News, 127,* 263.
Bowlby, J. (1969). *Attachment and loss* (Vol. 1). London: Hogarth Press.
Bowlby, J. (1980). *Attachment and loss:* Vol. 3. *Loss, sadness, and depression.* New York: Basic Books.
Bowlby, J. (1989). *Secure and insecure attachment.* New York: Basic Books.
Boyd-Franklin, N. (1989). *Black families in therapy. A multisystems approach.* New York: Guilford Press.
Boyer, K., & Diamond, A. (1992). Development of memory for temporal order in infants and young children. In A. Diamond (Ed.), *Development and neural bases of higher cognitive function.* New York: New York Academy of Sciences.
Brabeck, M. (2000). Kohlberg, Lawrence. In A. Kazdin (Ed.), *Encyclopedia of psychology.* Washington, DC, & New York: American Psychological Association and Oxford University Press.
Bracken, M. B., Eskenazi, B., Sachse, K., McSharry, J., Hellenbrand, K., & Leo-Summers, L. (1990). Association of cocaine use with sperm concentration, motility, and morphology. *Fertility and Sterility, 53,* 315–322.
Bradbury, F. D., Fincham, F. D., & Beach, S. R. H. (2000). Research on the nature and determinants of marital satisfaction: A decade in review. *Journal of Marriage and the Family, 62,* 964–980.
Brandstadter, J., Wentura, D., & Greve, W. (1993). Adaptive resources of the aging self: Outlines of an emergent perspective. *Journal of Behavioral Development, 16,* 323–349.
Bray, J. H., & Berger, S. H. (1993). Developmental Issues in Stepfamilies Research Project: Family relationships and parent–child interactions. *Journal of Family Psychology, 7,* 76–90.
Bray, J. M., Berger, S. H., & Boethel, C. L. (1999). Marriage to remarriage and beyond. In E. M. Hetherington (Ed.), *Coping with divorce, single parenting, and remarriage.* Mahwah, NJ: Erlbaum.
Brazelton, T. B. (1956). Sucking in infancy. *Pediatrics, 17,* 400–404.
Brazelton, T. B. (1983). *Infants and mothers: Differences in development.* New York: Delta.
Brazelton, T. B., Nugent, J. K., & Lester, B. M. (1987). Neonatal behavioral assessment scale. In J. D. Osofsky (Ed.), *Handbook of infant development* (2nd ed.). New York: Wiley.
Bredekamp, S. (1987). *Developmentally appropriate practice in early childhood programs serving children from birth through age 8.* Washington, DC: National Association for the Education of Young Children.
Bredekamp, S. (1997). NAEYC issues revised position statement on developmentally appropriate practice in early childhood programs. *Young Children, 52,* 34–40.
Brent, R. L., & Fawcett, L. B. (2000, May). *Environmental causes of human birth defects: What have we learned about the mechanism, nature, and etiology of congenital malformations in the past 50 years?* Paper presented at the joint meetings of the Pediatric Academic Societies and the American Academy of Pediatrics, Boston.
Bretherton, I., Stolberg, U., & Kreye, M. (1981). Engaging strangers in proximal interaction: Infants' social initiative. *Developmental Psychology, 17,* 746–755.
Brickel, C. O., Ciarrocchi, J. W., Sheers, N. J., Estadt, B. K., Powell, D. A., & Pargament, K. I. (1998). Perceived stress, religious coping styles, and depressive affect. *Journal of Psychology and Christianity, 17,* 33–42.
Brim, G. (1992, December 7). Commentary, *Newsweek,* p. 52.
Brim, O. (1999). *The MacArthur Foundation study of midlife development.* Vero Beach, FL: MacArthur Foundation.
Brislin, R. W. (2000). Cross-cultural training. In A. Kazdin (Ed.), *Encyclopedia of psychology.* Washington, DC, & New York: American Psychological Association and Oxford University Press.
Brody, G.H., & Ge, X. (2001). Linking parenting processes and self-regulation to psychological functioning and alcohol use during early adolescence. *Journal of Family Psychology, 15,* 82–94.
Brody, J. E. (1994, April 6). The value of breast milk. *New York Times,* p. C11.
Brody, N. (2000). Intelligence. In A. Kazdin (Ed.), *Encyclopedia of psychology.* Washington, DC, & New York: American Psychological Association and Oxford University Press.
Brodzinsky, D. M., Lang, R., & Smith, D. W. (1995). Parenting adopted children. In M. H. Bornstein (Ed.), *Handbook of parenting* (Vol. 3). Hillsdale, NJ: Erlbaum.
Brodzinsky, D. M., Schechter, D. E., Braff, A. M., & Singer, L. M. (1984). Psychological and academic adjustment in adopted children. *Journal of Consulting and Clinical Psychology, 52,* 582–590.
Bronfenbrenner, U. (1986). Ecology of the family as a context for human development: Research perspectives. *Developmental Psychology, 22,* 723–742.
Bronfenbrenner, U. (1995). Developmental ecology through space and time: A future perspective. In P. Moen, G. H. Elder, & K. Lüscher (Eds.), *Examining lives in context.* Washington, DC: American Psychological Association.
Bronfenbrenner, U. (1995, March). *The role research has played in Head Start.* Paper presented at the meeting of the Society for Research in Child Development, Indianapolis.
Bronfenbrenner, U. (2000). Ecological theory. In A. Kazdin (Ed.), *Encyclopedia of psychology.* Washington, DC, & New York: American Psychological Association and Oxford University Press.
Bronfenbrenner, U., & Morris, P. (1998). The ecology of developmental processes. In W. Damon (Ed.), *Handbook of child psychology* (5th ed., Vol. 1). New York: Wiley.
Brook, J. S., Brook, D. W., Gordon, A. S., Whiteman, M., & Cohen, P. (1990). The psychological etiology of adolescent drug use: A family interactional approach. *Genetic, Social, and General Psychology Monographs, 116,* 110–267.
Brooks, J. B. (1999). *The process of parenting* (5th ed.). Mountain View, CA: Mayfield.
Brooks, J. G., & Brooks, M. G. (1993). *The case for constructivist classrooms.* Alexandria, VA: Association for Supervision and Curriculum.
Brooks, M. G., & Brooks, J. G. (1999). The courage to be constructivist. *Educational Leadership, 37* (3), 12–17.
Brooks-Gunn, J., & Graeber, J. (1999). *What's sex got to do with it? The development of health and sexual identities during adolescence.* Unpublished manuscript, Columbia University, New York City.
Brooks-Gunn, J., Klebanov, P. K., & Duncan, G. J. (1996). Ethnic differences in children's intelligence test scores: Role of economic deprivation, home environment, and maternal characteristics. *Child Development, 67,* 396–408.
Brooks-Gunn, J., & Paikoff, R. (1993). "Sex is a gamble, kissing is a game": Adolescent sexuality, contraception, and sexuality. In S. P. Millstein, A. C. Petersen, & E. O. Nightingale (Eds.), *Promoting the health behavior of adolescents.* New York: Oxford University Press.
Brooks-Gunn, J., & Paikoff, R. (1997). Sexuality and developmental transitions during adolescence. In J. Schulenberg, J. Maggs, & K. Hurrelmann (Eds.), *Health risks and developmental transitions during adolescence.* New York: Cambridge University Press.
Brooks-Gunn, J., & Warren, M. P. (1989). The psychological significance of secondary sexual characteristics in 9- to 11-year-old girls. *Child Development, 59,* 161–169.
Brown, B. B. (in press). "You're going with whom?!": Peer group influences on adolescent romantic relationships. In W. Furman, B. B. Brown, & C. Feiring (Eds.), *Contemporary perspectives on adolescent romantic relationships.* Cambridge: Cambridge University Press.
Brown, J. K. (1985). Introduction. In J. K. Brown & V. Kerns (Eds.), *In her prime: A new view of middle-aged women.* South Hadley, MA: Bergin & Garvey.
Brown, L. S. (1989). New voices, new visions: Toward a lesbian/gay paradigm for psychology. *Psychology of Women Quarterly, 13,* 445–458.
Brown, R. (1973). *A first language: The early stages.* Cambridge, MA: Harvard University Press.
Brown, R. (1986). *Social Psychology* (2nd ed.). New York: Free Press.
Brown, B. B., & Lohn, M. J. (1987). Peer-group affiliation and adolescent self-esteem: An integration of ego-identity and symbolic-interaction theories. *Journal of Personality and Social Psychology, 52,* 47–55.
Brown, B. B., & Mounts, N. (1989, April). *Peer group structures in single vs. multiethnic high schools.* Paper presented at the biennial meeting of the Society for Research in Child Development, Kansas City.
Browne, A. (1993). Violence against women by male partners: Prevalence, outcomes, and policy implications. *American Psychologist, 48,* 1077–1087.
Browne, A., & Williams, K. R. (1993). Gender, intimacy, and lethal violence: Trends from 1976 through 1987. *Gender and Society, 7,* 78–98.

Brownell, K. (2000). Dieting. In A. Kazdin (Ed.), *Encyclopedia of psychology*. Washington, DC, & New York: American Psychological Association and Oxford University Press.

Brownell, K. A., & Rodin, J. (1994). The dieting maelstrom: Is it possible to lose weight? *American Psychologist, 9,* 781–791.

Brownell, K. D., & Cohen, L. R. (1995). Adherence to dietary regimens. *Behavioral Medicine, 20,* 226–242.

Bruce, J. M., Olen, K., & Jensen, S. J. (1999, April). *The role of emotion and regulation in social competence.* Paper presented at the meeting of the Society for Research in Child Development, Albuquerque.

Bruck, M., & Ceci, S. (1999). The suggestibility of young children's memory. *Annual Review of Psychology.* Palo Alto, CA: Annual Reviews.

Bruer, J. T. (1999). *The myth of the first three years.* New York: Free Press.

Bryant, J., & Bryant, J.A. (Eds.) (2001). *Television and the American family.* Mahwah, NJ: Erlbaum.

Buhrmester, D., & Carbery, J. (1992, March). *Daily patterns of self-disclosure and adolescent adjustment.* Paper presented at the biennial meeting of the Society for Research on Adolescence, Washington, DC.

Buhrmester, D., & Furman, W. (1987). The development of companionship and intimacy. *Child Development, 58,* 1101–1113.

Bulterys, M. (2001). Preventing vertical HIV transmissions in the year 2000. *Placenta, 22,* S5–S12.

Burchinal, M. (2001, April). *Using the Phase 1 data set of the NICHD Study of Early Child Care.* Paper presented at the meeting of the Society for Research in Child Development, Minneapolis.

Burchinal, M. R., Roberts, J. E., Nabors, L. A., & Bryant, D. M. (1996). Quality of center child care and infant cognitive and language development. *Child Development, 67,* 606–620.

Burke, G.L., Arnold, A.M., Bild, D., Cushman, M., Fried, O., Newman, A., & Robbins, C. (2001). Factors associated with healthy aging. *Journal of the American Geriatric Society, 49,* 254–262.

Burkhauser, R. V., & Quinn, J. F. (1989). American patterns of work and retirement. In W. Schmall (Ed.), *Redefining the process of retirement.* Berlin: Springer.

Burns, A., Roth, M., & Christie, S. (1996). The natural history of mental disorder in old age. *International Journal of Geriatric Psychiatry, 11,* 7–14.

Burns, D. (1985). *Intimate connections.* New York: William Morrow.

Burton, L., & Allison, K. W. (1995). Social context and adolescence: Alternative perspectives on developmental pathways for African-American teens. In L. J. Crockett & A. C. Crouter (Eds.), *Pathways through adolescence.* Hillsdale, NJ: Erlbaum.

Burton, L. M. (1996). The timing of childbearing, family structure, and the role of responsibilities of aging Black women. In E. M. Hetherington & E. A. Blechman (Eds.), *Stress, coping, and resilience in children and families.* Hillsdale, NJ: Erlbaum.

Burts, D. C., Hart, C. H., Charlesworth, R., Hernandez, S., Kirk, L., & Mosley, J. (1989, March). *A comparison of the frequences of stress behaviors observed in kindergarten children in classrooms with developmentally appropriate and developmentally inappropriate instructional practices.* Paper presented at the meeting of the American Educational Research Association, San Francisco.

Buss, D. (2000). Evolutionary psychology. In A. Kazdin (Ed.), *Encyclopedia of psychology.* Washington, DC, & New York: American Psychological Association and Oxford University Press.

Buss, D. M. (1995). Psychological sex differences: Origins through sexual selection. *American Psychologist, 50,* 164–168.

Buss, D. M. (1999). *Evolutionary psychology: The new science of the mind.* Boston: Allyn & Bacon.

Buss, D. M., & others. (1990). International preferences in selecting mates: A study of 37 cultures. *Journal of Cross-Cultural Psychology, 21,* 5–47.

Busse, E. W., & Blazer, D. G. (1996). *The American Psychiatric Press textbook of geriatric psychiatry* (2nd ed.). Washington, DC: American Psychiatric Press.

Butler, R. N. (1975). *Why survive? Being old in America.* New York: Harper & Row.

Butler, R. N. (1996). Global aging: Challenges and opportunities in the next century. *Aging International, 21,* 12–32.

Butterfield, L. J. (1999, May). *The Apgar legend lives.* Paper presented at the meeting of the Society for Pediatric Research, San Francisco.

Buzwell, S., & Rosenthal, D. (1996). Constructing a sexual self: Adolescents' sexual self-perceptions and sexual risk-taking. *Journal of Research on Adolescence, 6,* 489–513.

Bybee, J. (Ed.). (1999). *Guilt and children.* San Diego: Academic Press.

Byrnes, J. P. (1997). *The nature and development of decision making.* Mahwah, NJ: Erlbaum.

Byrnes, J.P. (2001). *Minds, brains, and learning.* New York: Guilford Press.

C

Cacioppo, J. T., & Gardner, W. L. (1999). Emotion. *Annual Reviews of Psychology.* Palo Alto: Annual Reviews.

Cairns, R. B. (1998). The making of developmental psychology. In W. Damon (Ed.), *Handbook of child psychology* (5th ed., Vol. 1). New York: Wiley.

Calabrese, R. L., & Schumer, H. (1986). The effects of service activities on adolescent alienation. *Adolescence, 21,* 675–687.

Callahan, C. M., & Wolinsky, F. D. (1995). Hospitalization for major depression among older Americans. *Journal of Gerontology: Medical Sciences, 50A,* M196–M202.

Cameron, J., Cowan, L., Holmes, B., Hurst, P., & McLean, M. (Eds.). (1983). *International handbook of educational systems.* New York: Wiley.

Cameron, J. R., Hansen, R., & Rosen, D. (1989). Preventing behavioral problems in infancy through temperament assessment and parental support programs. In W. B. Carey & S. C. McDevitt (Eds.), *Clinical and education applications of temperament research.* Amsterdam: Swets & Zeitlinger.

Campbell, L., Campbell, B., & Dickinson, D. (1999). *Teaching and learning through multiple intelligences* (2nd ed.). Boston: Allyn & Bacon.

Campos, J. (2001, April). *Emotion in emotional development: Problems and prospects.* Paper presented at the meeting of the Society for Research in Child Development, Minneapolis.

Campos, J. J., Langer, A., & Krowitz, A. (1970). Cardiac responses on the visual cliff in prelocomotor human infants. *Science, 170,* 196–197.

Canfield, J., & Hansen, M. V. (1995). *A second helping of chicken soup for the soul.* Deerfield Beach, FL: Health Communications.

Canfield, R. L., & Haith, M. M. (1991). Young infants' visual expectations for symmetric and asymmetric stimulus sequences. *Developmental Psychology, 27,* 198–208.

Cantor, N., & Blanton, H. (1996). Effortful pursuit of personal goals in daily life. In P. M. Gollwitzer & J. A. Bargh (Eds.), *The psychology of action: Linking cognition and motivation to behavior.* New York: Guilford.

Caplan, P. J., & Caplan, J. B. (1999). *Thinking critically about research on sex and gender* (2nd ed.). New York: Harper Collins.

Caporael, L. R. (2001). Evolutionary psychology. *Annual Review of Psychology* (Vol. 52). Palo Alto, CA: Annual Reviews.

Carlson, K. S. (1995, March). *Attachment in sibling relationships during adolescence: Links to other familial and peer relationships.* Paper presented at the meeting of the Society for Research in Child Development, Indianapolis.

Carlson, V., Cicchetti, D., Barnett, D., & Braunwald, K. (1989). Disorganized/disoriented attachment relationships in maltreated infants. *Developmental Psychology, 25,* 525–531.

Carnegie Corporation. (1989). *Turning points: Preparing youth for the 21st century.* New York: Author.

Carnegie Corporation. (1996). *Report on education for children 3–10 years of age.* New York: The Carnegie Foundation.

Carnegie Council on Adolescent Development. (1995). *Great transitions.* New York: Author.

Carstensen, L. (1997, August). *Psychology and the aging revolution.* Symposium presented at the meeting of the American Psychological Association, Chicago.

Carstensen, L. L. (1991). Selectivity theory: Social activity in life-span context. *Annual Review of Gerontology and Geriatrics, 11,* 195–217.

Carstensen, L. L. (1995). Evidence for a life-span theory of socioemotional selectivity. *Current Directions in Psychological Science, 4,* 151–156.

Carstensen, L. L. (1998). A life-span approach to social motivation. In J. Heckhausen & C. Dweck (Eds.), *Motivation and self-regulation across the life span.* New York: Cambridge University Press.

Carstensen, L. L., Gottman, J. M., & Levenson, R. W. (1995). Emotional behavior in long-term marriage. *Psychology and Aging, 10,* 140–149.

Carstensen, L. L., Isaacowitz, D. M., & Charles, S. T. (1999). Taking time seriously: A theory of socioemotional selectivity. *American Psychologist, 54,* 165–181.

Carstensen, L. L., Pasupathi, M., & Mayr, U. (1998). *Emotion experience in the daily lives of older and younger adults.* Unpublished manuscript, Dept. of Psychology, Stanford University, Palo Alto, CA.

Carter, B., & McGoldrick, M. (1989). Overview: The changing family life cycle—A framework for family therapy. In B. Carter & M. McGoldrick (Eds.), *The changing family life cycle* (2nd ed.). Boston: Allyn & Bacon.

Carter, D. B., & Levy, G. D. (1988). Cognitive aspects of children's early sex-role development: The influence of gender schemas on preschoolers' memories and preference for sex-typed toys and activities. *Child Development, 59,* 782–793.

Carter-Saltzman, L. (1980). Biological and sociocultural effects on handedness: Comparison between biological and adoptive families. *Science, 209,* 1263–1265.

Case, R. (1987). Neo-Piagetian theory: Retrospect and prospect. *International Journal of Psychology, 22,* 773–791.

Case, R. (1999). Conceptual development in the child and the field: A personal view of the Piagetian legacy. In E. K. Skolnick, K. Nelson, S. A. Gelman, & P. H. Miller (Eds.), *Conceptual development.* Mahwah, NJ: Erlbaum.

Case, R., Kurland, D. M., & Goldberg, J. (1982). Operational efficiency and the growth of short-term memory span. *Journal of Experimental Child Psychology, 33,* 386–404.

Case, R., & Mueller, M.P. (2001). Differentiation, integration, and covariance mapping as fundamental processes in cognitive and neurological growth. In J.L. McClelland & R.S. Siegler (Eds.), *Mechanisms of cognitive development.* Mahwah, NJ: Erlbaum.

Caspi, A. (1998). Personality development across the life course. In W. Damon (Ed.), *Handbook of child psychology* (Vol. 3). New York: Wiley.

Cassidy, J. (1999) The nature of the child's ties. In J. Cassidy & P. Shaver (Eds.), *Handbook of attachment.* New York: Guilford.

Cassidy, J., & Berlin, L. J. (1994). The insecure/ambivalent pattern of attachment: Theory and research. *Child Development, 65,* 971–991.

Cassidy, J., & Shaver, P. R. (Eds.) (1999). *Handbook of attachment: Theory, research, and clinical applications.* New York: Guilford.

Castle, N.G. (2001). Innovation in nursing homes. *The Gerontologist, 41, No.2,* 161–172.

Caulfield, R. A. (2001). *Infants and toddlers.* Upper Saddle River, NJ: Prentice Hall.

Cavanaugh, J. (2000, January). Commentary. *American Psychologist, 31,* p. 25.

Ceballo, R. E. (1999, April). *The psychological impact of children's perceptions of neighborhood danger and collective efficacy.* Paper presented at the meeting of the Society for Research in Child Development, Albuquerque.

Ceci, S. J. (2000). Bronfenbrenner, Urie. In A. Kazdin (Ed.), *Encyclopedia of psychology.* Washington, DC, & New York: American Psychological Association and Oxford University Press.

Ceci, S. J., Rosenblum, T., de Bruyn, E., & Lee, D. Y. (1997). A bio-ecological model of intellectual development. In R. J. Sternberg & E. Grigorenko (Eds.), *Intelligence, heredity, and environment.* New York: Cambridge University Press.

Center for Survey Research at the University of Connecticut. (2000). *Hours on the job.* Storrs: University of Connecticut, Center for Survey Research.

Centers for Disease Control and Prevention. (1999). *Sexually transmitted diseases.* Atlanta: Author.

Centers for Disease Control and Prevention. (2000). *HIV/AIDS surveillance report.* Atlanta: Author.

Centers for Disease Control and Prevention. (2000). *Status of perinatal HIV prevention: U.S. decline continues.* Atlanta: Author.

Central Intelligence Agency. (1999). *The world fact book.* Washington, DC: Author.

Charlesworth, R. (1996). *Understanding child development* (4th ed.). Albany, NY: Delmar.

Charness, N., & Bosman, E. A. (1992). Human factors and aging. In F. I. M. Craik & T. A. Salthouse (Eds.), *The handbook of aging and cognition.* Hillsdale, NJ: Erlbaum.

Chase-Lansdale, P. L. (1996, June). *Effects of divorce on mental health through the life span.* Informal talk at the family Research Summer Consortium, San Diego.

Chase-Lansdale, P.L., Coley, R.L., & Grining, C.P.L. (2001, April). *Low-income families and child care.* Paper presented at the meeting of the Society for Research in Child Development, Minneapolis.

Chattin-McNichols, J. (1992). *The Montessori controversy.* Albany, NY: Delmar.

Chauhuri, J. H., & Williams, P. H. (1999, April). *The contribution of infant temperament and parent emotional availability to toddler attachment.* Paper presented at the meeting of the Society for Research in Child Development, Albuquerque.

Chavkin, W. (2001). Cocaine and pregnancy—time to look at the evidence. *Journal of the American Medical Association, 285,* 1626–1628.

Chen, C., & Stevenson, H. W. (1989). Homework: A cross-cultural comparison. *Child Development, 60,* 551–561.

Chen, Z., & Siegler, R. E. (2000). Across the great divide: Bridging the gap between understanding of toddlers' and older children's thinking. *Monograph of the Society for Research in Child Development, 65* (2).

Chen, Z., & Siegler, R. S. (2000). Intellectual development in childhood. In R. J. Sternberg (Ed.), *Handbook of intelligence.* New York: Cambridge University Press.

Cheng, T. L., Fields, C. B., Brenner, R. A., Wright, J. L., Lomax, T., & Schedit, P. C. (2000). Sports injuries: An important cause of morbidity in urban youth. *Pediatrics, 105,* E32–33.

Cherlin, A. J., & Furstenberg, F. F. (1994). Stepfamilies in the United States: A reconsideration. In J. Blake & J. Hagen (Eds.), *Annual review of sociology.* Palo Alto, CA: Annual Reviews.

Cherlin, A. J., Furstenberg, F. F., Chase-Lansdale, P. L., Kiernan, K. E., Robins, P. K., Morrison, D. R., & Teitler, J. O. (1991). Longitudinal studies of effects of divorce in children in Great Britain and the United States. *Science, 252,* 1386–1389.

Chescheir, N. C., & Hansen, W. F. (1999). New in perinatology. *Pediatrics in Review, 20,* 57–63.

Chess, S., & Thomas, A. (1987). *Origins and evolution of behavior disorders.* Cambridge, MA: Harvard University Press.

Chess, S., & Thomas, A. (1977). Temperamental individuality from childhood to adolescence. *Journal of Child Psychiatry, 16,* 218–226.

Chi, M. T. (1978). Knowledge structures and memory development. In R. S. Siegler (Ed.), *Children's thinking: What develops?* Hillsdale, NJ: Erlbaum.

Child Trends. (1996). *Facts at a glance.* Washington, DC: Author.

Chiriboga, D. A. (1982). Adaptation to marital separation in later and earlier life. *Journal of Gerontology, 37,* 109–114.

Chiriboga, D. A. (1989). Mental health at the midpoint: Crisis, challenge, or relief? In S. Hunter & M. Sundel (Eds.), *Midlife myths.* Newbury Park, CA: Sage.

Chisholm, K. (1998). A three-year follow-up of attachment and indiscriminate friendliness in children adopted from Romanian orphanages. *Child Development, 69,* 1092–1106.

Choi, N.G. (2001). Relationship between life satisfaction and postretirement employment among older women. *International Journal of Aging and Human Development, 52,* 45–70.

Chomitz, V. R., Cheung, L. W. Y., & Lieberman, E. (1995, Spring). The role of lifestyle in preventing low birth weight. *The Future of Children, 5,* 121–138.

Chomsky, N. (1957). *Syntactic structures.* The Hague: Mouton.

Christensen, H., Korten, A., Jorm, A. F., Henderson, A. S., Scott, R., & MacKinnon, A. J. (1996). Activity levels and cognitive functioning in an elderly community sample. *Age and Aging, 25,* 72–80.

Christensen, L. (1996). *Diet-behavior relationships.* Washington, DC: American Psychological Association.

Christiansen, A., & Pasch, L. (1993). The sequence of marital conflict. *Clinical Psychology Review, 13,* 3–14.

Church, D. K., Siegel, M. A., & Fowler, C. D. (1988). *Growing old in America.* Wylie, TX: Information Aids.

Cicchetti, D. (2001). How a child builds a brain. In W.W. Hartup & R.A. Weinberg (Eds.), *Child psychology in retrospect and prospect.* Mahwah, NJ: Erlbaum.

Cicchetti, D. (2001, April). *The emergence, evolution, and future of developmental psychopathology.* Paper presented at the meeting of the Society for Research in Child Development, Minneapolis.

Cicchetti, D., Ganiban, J., & Barnet:, D. (1991). Contributions from the study of high risk populations to understanding the development of emotion regulation. In J. Garber & K. Dodge (Eds.), *The development of emotion regulation and dysregulation.* New York: Cambridge University Press.

Cicchetti, D., & Toth, S. L. (1998). Perspectives on research and practice in developmental psychology. In W. Damon (Ed.), *Handbook of child psychology* (Vol. 4). New York: Wiley.

Cicirelli, V. G. (1991). Sibling relationships in adulthood. *Marriage and Family Review, 16,* 291–310.

Clancy, S. M., & Hoyer, W. J. (1994). Age and skill in visual search. *Developmental Psychology, 30,* 545–552.

Clark, E. (2000). Language acquisition. In A. Kazdin (Ed.), *Encyclopedia of psychology.* Washington, DC, & New York: American Psychological Association and Oxford University Press.

Clark, S. D., Zabin, L. S., & Hardy, J. B. (1984). Sex, contraception, and parenthood: Experience and attitudes among urban black young men. *Family Planning Perspectives, 16,* 77–82.

Clarke, E. J., Preston, M., Raksin, J., & Bengtson, V. L. (1999). Types of conflicts and tensions between older adults and adult children. *Gerontologist, 39,* 261–270.

Clark-Plaskie, M., & Lachman, M. E. (1999). The sense of control in midlife. In S. L. Willis & J. D. Reid (Eds.), *Life in the middle.* San Diego: Academic Press.

Clarkson-Smith, L., & Hartley, A. A. (1989). Relationships between physical exercise and cognitive abilities in older adults. *Psychology and Aging, 4,* 183–189.

Clausen, J. A. (1993). *American lives.* New York: Free Press.

Clay, R. A. (1997, April). Helping dying patients let go of life in peace. *APA Monitor,* p. 42.

Clemens, A. W., & Axelson, L. J. (1985). The not-so-empty nest: The return of the fledgling adult. *Family Relations, 34,* 259–264.

Cleveland, J. N., & Shore, L. M. ([illegible]). [illegible] and employment. In J. E. Birren (Ed.), *Encyclopedia of aging* (Vol. 2). San Diego: Academic Press.

Clifford, B. R., Gunter, B., & McAleer, J. L. (1995). *Television and children.* Hillsdale, NJ: Erlbaum.

Clifton, R. K., Muir, D. W., Ashmead, D. H., & Clarkson, M. G. (1993). Is visually guided reaching in early infancy a myth? *Child Development, 64,* 1099–1110.

Cochran, S. D., & Mays, V. M. (1990). Sex, lies, and HIV. *New England Journal of Medicine, 322*(11), 774–775.

Cohen, C. I., Teresi, J., & Holmes, D. (1985). Social networks, stress, adaptation, and health. *Research on Aging, 7,* 409–431.

Cohen, G. J. (2000). *American Academy of Pediatrics guide to your child's sleep: Birth through adolescence.* New York: Villard Books.

Cohn, E., & Harlow, K. (1993, October). *Elders as victims: Randomized studies in two states.* Paper presented at the meeting of the Gerontological Association of America, New Orleans.

Coie, J. (1999, November). Unpublished review of J. W. Santrock's *Child Development,* 9th ed. (New York: McGraw-Hill).

Colby, A., Kohlberg, L., Gibbs, J., & Lieberman, M. (1983). A longitudinal study of moral judgment. *Monographs of the Society for Research in Child Development* (Serial No. 201).

Cole, M. (1999). Culture in development. In M. H. Bornstein & M. E. Lamb (Eds.), *Developmental psychology* (4th ed.). Mahwah, NJ: Erlbaum.

Coleman, M., Ganong, L., & Fine, M. (2000). Reinvestigating remarriage: Another decade of progress. *Journal of Marriage and the Family, 62,* 1288–1307.

Coleman, M., Ganong, L., & Weaver, S.E. (2001). Relationship maintenance and enhancement in remarried families. In J.H. Harvey & A. Wenzel (Eds.), *Close romantic relationships.* Mahwah, NJ: Erlbaum.

Coleman, P. D. (1986, August). *Regulation of dendritic extent: Human aging brain and Alzheimer's disease.* Paper presented at the meeting of the American Psychological Association, Washington, DC.

Coles, R. (1970). *Erik H. Erikson: The growth of his work.* Boston: Little, Brown.

Coll, C. T. G., Meyer, E. C., & Brillion, L. (1995). Ethnic and minority parenting. In M. H. Bornstein (Ed.), *Children and parenting* (Vol. 2). Hillsdale, NJ: Erlbaum.

College Board. (1996, August 22). *News from the College Board.* New York: The College Entrance Examination Board.

Collins, A. W., & Laursen, B. (2000). Adolescent relationships: The art of fugue. In C. Hendrick & S. S. Hendrick (Eds.), *Close relationships: A sourcebook.* Thousand Oaks, CA: Sage.

Collins, M. (1996, Winter). The job outlook for '96 grads. *Journal of Career Planning,* 51–54.

Collins, N. L., Dunke-Schetter, C., Lobel, M., & Scrimshaw, S. C. M. (1993). Social support and pregnancy: Psychological correlates of birth outcomes and postpartum depression. *Journal of Personality and Social Psychology, 65,* 1243–1258.

Collins, W. A., Maccoby, E. E., Steinberg, L., Hetherington, E. M., & Bornstein, M. H. (2000). Contemporary research on parenting: The case for nature and nurture. *American Psychologist, 55,* 218–232.

Collins, W.A., Maccoby, E.E., Steinberg, L., Hetherington, E.M., & Bornstein, M.H. (2001). Toward nature WITH nurture. *American Psychologist, 56,* 171–173.

Comas-Díaz, L. (1999). Foreward II. In J. D. Koss-Chioino & L. A. Vargas (Eds.), *Working with Latino youth.* San Francisco: Jossey-Bass.

Comer, J. P. (1988). Educating poor minority children. *Scientific American, 259,* 42–48.

Comer, J. P., Haynes, N. M., Joyner, E. T., & Ben-Avie, M. (1996). *Rallying the whole village: The Comer process for reforming urban education.* New York: Teachers College Press.

Committee on Drugs. (2000). Use of psychoactive medication during pregnancy and possible effects on the fetus and newborn. *Pediatrics, 105,* 880–887.

Committee on Fetus and Newborn. (2000). Prevention and management of pain and stress in the newborn. *Pediatrics, 105,* 454–461.

Committee on Pediatric AIDS. (2000). Identification and care of HIV-exposed and HIV-infected infants, children, and adolescents. *Pediatrics, 106,* 149–153.

Committee on School Health. (2000). Physical fitness and activity in schools. *Pediatrics, 105,* 1156–1157.

Committee on Sports Medicine and Fitness. (2000). Injuries in youth soccer: A subject review. *Pediatrics, 105,* 659–661.

Committee on Substance Abuse. (2000). Fetal alcohol syndrome an alcohol-related neurodevelopmental disorders. *Pediatrics, 106,* 258–261.

Commons, M.L., Sinnott, J. D., Richards, F. A., & Armon, C. (1989). *Adult development: Vol. 1. Comparisons and applications of developmental models.* New York: Praeger.

Compas, B. E., & Grant, K. E. (1993, March). *Stress and adolescent depressive symptoms: Underlying mechanisms and processes.* Paper presented at the biennial meeting of the Society for Research in Child Development, New Orleans.

Comstock, G., & Scharrar, E. (1999). *Television.* San Diego: Academic Press.

Condry, K.F., Smith, W.C., & Spelke, E.S. (2001). Development of perceptual organization. In F. Lacerda, C. von Hofsten, & M. Heimann (Eds.), *Emerging cognitive abilities in infancy.* Mahwah, NJ: Erlbaum.

Conger, R. D., & Chao, W. (1996). Adolescent depressed mood. In R.L. Simons (Ed.), *Understanding differences between divorced and intact families: Stress, interaction, and child outcome.* Thousand Oaks, CA: Sage.

Conger, R. D., & Ge, X. (1999). Conflict and cohesion in parent-adolescent relations: Changes in emotional expression. In M. J. Cox & J. Brooks-Gunn (Eds.), *Conflict and cohesion in families.* Mahwah, NJ: Erlbaum.

Contemporary Research Press. (1993). *American working women: A statistical handbook.* Dallas: Author.

Cook, D. J., Guyatt, G. H., Jaeschke, R., Reeve, J., Spanier, A., King, D., Molloy, D., Willan, A., & Streiner, D. ([illegible]). Determinants in Canadian health care workers of the decision to withdraw life support from the critically ill. *Journal of the American Medical Association, 273,* 703–708.

Cooper, C. R., & Grotevant, H. D. (1989, April). *Individuality and connectedness in the family and adolescent's self and relational competence.* Paper presented at the meeting of the Society for Research in Child Development, Kansas City.

Cooper, C. R., Grotevant, H. D., Moore, M. S., & Condon, S. M. (1982, August). *Family support and conflict: Both foster adolescent identity and role taking.* Paper presented at the meeting of the American Psychological Association, Washington, DC.

Corr, C. A., Nable, C., & Corr, D. M. (2000). *Death and dying: Life and living* (3rd ed., Belmont, CA: Wadsworth.

Corso, J. F. (1977). Auditory perception and communication. In J. E. Birren & K. W. Schaie (Eds.), *Handbook of the psychology of aging* (2nd ed.). New York: Van Nostrand Reinhold.

Costa, P. T., & McCrae, R. R. (1995). Solid ground on the wetlands of personality: A reply to Black. *Psychological Bulletin, 117,* 216–220.

Costa, P. T., & McCrae, R. R. (1998). Personality assessment. In H.S. Friedman (Ed.), *Encyclopedia of mental health* (Vol. 3). San Diego: Academic Press.

Costa, P. T., Jr., & McCrae, R. R. (2000). Contemporary personality psychology. In C. E. Coffey and J. L. Cummings (Eds.), *Textbook of geriatric neuropsychiatry.* Washington, DC: American Psychiatric Press.

Cotten, S. R. (1999). Marital status and mental health revisited: Examining the importance of risk factors and resources. *Family Relations, 48,* 225–233.

Council of Economic Advisors. (2000). *Teens and their parents in the 21st century: An examination of trends in teen behavior and the role of parent involvement.* Washington, DC: Author.

Cowan, C. P., & Cowan, P. A. (2000). *When partners become parents.* Mahwah, NJ: Erlbaum.

Cowan, C. P., Cowan, P. A., Heming, G., & Boxer, C. (1995). *Preventive interventions with parents of preschoolers on the children's adaptation to kindergarten.* Paper presented at the meeting of the Society for Research in Child Development, New Orleans.

Cowan, P. A., Powell, D. S., & Cowan, C. P. (1998). Parenting interventions: A family systems perspective. In W. Damon (Ed.), *Handbook of child psychology* (5th ed., Vol. 4). New York: Wiley.

Cowley, G. (1998, April 6). Why children turn violent. *Newsweek,* pp. 24–25.

Cowley, G., & Hager, M. (1995, December 4). Terminal care: Too painful, too prolonged. *Newsweek,* pp. 74–75.

Cox, H., & Hammonds, A. (1998). Religiosity, aging, and life satisfaction. *Journal of Religion and Aging, 5,* 1–21.

Cox, M.J., & Harter, K.S.M. (2001). The road ahead for research on marital and family dynamics. In J.P. McHale & W.S. Grolnick (Eds.), *Retrospect and prospect in the psychological study of families.* Mahwah, NJ: Erlbaum.

Craik, F. I. M., & Salthouse, T. A. (Eds.) (2000). *The handbook of aging and cognition.* Mahwah, NJ: Erlbaum.

Crawford, M., & Unger, R. (2000). *Women and gender* (3rd ed.). New York: McGraw-Hill.

Cremation Association of America. (2000). *Fact sheet.* Milwaukee. WI: Author.

Crockenberg, S. B. (1986). Are temperamental differences in babies associated with predictable differences in caregiving? In J. V. Lerner & R. M. Lerner (Eds.), *Temperament and social interaction during infancy and childhood.* San Francisco: Jossey-Bass.

Crockett, J. B., & Kauffman, J. M. (1999). *The least restrictive environment.* Mahwah, NJ: Erlbaum.

Crooks, R., & Baur, K. (1999). *Our sexuality* (7th ed.). Belmont, CA: Wadsworth.

Crosby, F. J. (1991). *Juggling.* New York: Free Press.

Croyle, R. T. (2000). Genetic counseling. In A. Kazdin (Ed.), *Encyclopedia of psychology.* Washington, DC, & New York: American Psychological Association and Oxford University Press.

Csikszentmihalyi, M. (1995). *Creativity.* New York: HarperCollins.

Csikszentmihalyi, M. (1997). *Finding flow.* New York: Basic Books.

Csikszentmihalyi, M. (2000). Creativity: An overview. In A. Kazdin (Ed.), *Encyclopedia of psychology.* Washington, DC, & New York: American Psychological Association and Oxford University Press.

Csikszentmihalyi, M., & Rathunde, K. (1998). The development of the person: An experiential perspective on the ontogenesis of psychological complexity. In W. Damon (Ed.), *Handbook of child psychology* (5th ed., Vol. 1). New York: Wiley.

Cuddy-Casey, M., & Orvaschel, H. (1997). Children's understanding of death in relation to child suicidality and homicidality. *Death Studies, 17,* 33–45.

Cui, X., & Vaillant, G. E. (1996). Antecedents and consequents of negative life events in adulthood: A longitudinal study. *American Journal of Psychiatry, 153,* 21–26.

Culatta, R., & Tompkins, J. R. (1999). *Introduction to special education.* Columbus, OH: Merrill.

Culbertson, F. M. (1991, August). *Mental health of women: An international journey.* Paper presented at the meeting of the American Psychological Association, San Francisco.

Cully, J. A., LaVoie, D., & Gfeller, J.D. (2001). Reminiscence, personality, and psychological functioning in older adults. *The Gerontologist, 41, No.1,* 89–95.

Cumming, E., & Henry, W. (1961). *Growing old.* New York: Basic Books.

Cummings, E. M. (1987). Coping with background anger in early childhood. *Child Development, 58,* 976–984.

Cupertino, A. P., & Haan, M. N. (1999, November). *Religiosity and health among elderly Latinos.* Paper presented at the meeting of the Gerontological Society of America, San Francisco.

Cushner, K. (1999). *Human diversity in action.* New York: McGraw-Hill.

Cushner, K., McClelland, A., & Safford, P. (1996). *Human diversity and education.* (2nd ed.). New York: McGraw-Hill.

Cutrona, C. E. (1982). Transition to college: Loneliness and the process of social adjustment. In L. A. Peplau & D. Perlman (Eds.), *Loneliness.* New York: Wiley.

D

D'Augelli, A. (2000). Sexual orientation. In A. Kazdin (Ed.), *Encyclopedia of psychology,* Washington, DC, & New York: American Psychological Association and Oxford University Press.

Damon, W. (1988). *The moral child.* New York: Free Press.

Damon, W. (1995). *Greater expectations.* New York: Free Press.

Damon, W. (2000). Moral development. In A. Kazdin (Ed.), *Encyclopedia of psychology,* Washington, DC, & New York: American Psychological Association and Oxford University Press.

Damon, W., & Hart, D. (1988). *Self-understanding in childhood and adolescence.* New York: Cambridge University Press.

Damon, W., & Hart, D. (1992). Self-understanding and its role in social and moral development. In M. H. Bornstein & M. E. Lamb (Eds.), *Developmental psychology: An advanced textbook* (3rd ed.). Hillsdale, NJ: Erlbaum.

Damush, T. M., & Damush, J. G. (1999). The effects of strength training on strength and health-related quality of life in older women. *The Gerontologist, 39,* 705–710.

Dapretto, M. (1999, April). *The development of word retrieval abilities in the second year of life and its relation to early vocabulary growth.* Paper presented at the meeting of the Society for Research in Child Development, Albuquerque.

Darwin, C. (1859). *On the origin of species.* London: John Murray.

Dates, J.L., & Stroman, C.A. (2001). Portrayals of families of color on television. In J. Bryant & J. A. Bryant (Eds.), *Television and the American Family.* Mahwah, NJ: Erlbaum.

Davey, R. T., Murphy, R. L., Graziano, F. M., Boswell, S. L., & Pavia, A. T. (2000). Immunologic and virologic effects of subcutaneous Interleukin 2 in combination with antiretroviral therapy. *Journal of the American Medical Association, 284,* 183–189.

Davidson, J. (2000). Giftedness. In A. Kazdin (Ed.), *Encyclopedia of psychology.* Washington, DC, & New York: American Psychological Association and Oxford University Press.

Davis, G.F. (2001). Loss and duration of grief. *Journal of the American Medical Association, 285,* 1152–1153.

Davis, K. E. (1985, February). Near and dear: Friendship and love compared. *Psychology Today,* pp. 22–29.

Davis, K. L. (1999). Alzheimer's disease: Seeking new ways to preserve brain function. *Geriatrics, 54,* 42–47.

Davis, L., & Stewart, R. (1997, July). *Building capacity for working with lesbian, gay, bisexual, and transgender youth.* Paper presented at the conference on Working with America's Youth, Pittsburgh.

Davison, G. C., & Neale, J. M. (2000). *Abnormal psychology* (8th ed.). New York: Wiley.

Davisson, M.T., Gardiner, K., & Costa, A.C. (2001). Report of the ninth international workshop on the molecular biology of human chromosome 21 and Down syndrome. *Cytogenetic Cell Genetics, 92,* 1–22.

Daws, D. (2000). *Through the night.* San Francisco: Free Association Books.

de Jong-Gierveld, J. (1987). Developing and testing a model of loneliness. *Journal of Personality and Social Psychology, 53,* 119–128.

de Wolff, M. S., & van Ijzendoorn, M. H. (1997). Sensitivity and attachment: A meta-analysis on parental antecedents of infant attachment. *Child Development, 68,* 571–591.

DeCasper, A. J., & Spence, M. J. (1986). Prenatal maternal speech influences newborn's perception of speech sounds. *Infant Behavior and Development, 9,* 133–150.

deHaan, M., & Nelson, C. A. (1999). Brain activity differentiates face and object processing in 6-month-old infants. *Developmental Psychology, 35,* 1113–1121.

DeLamater, J., & MacCorquodale, P. (1979). *Premarital sexuality.* Madison: University of Wisconsin Press.

DeLoache, J. (2001). The symbol-mindedness of young children. In W.W. Hartup & R.A. Weinberg (Eds.), *Child psychology in retrospect and prospect.* Mahwah, NJ: Erlbaum.

DeMarie, D., Abshier, D.W., & Ferron, J. (2001, April). *Longitudinal study of predictors of memory improvement over the elementary school years: Capacity, strategies, and metamemory revisited.* Paper presented at the meeting of the Society for Research in Child Development, Minneapolis.

DeMaris, A., & Rao, K. (1992). Premarital cohabitation and subsequent marital stability in the United States: A reassessment. *Journal of Marriage and the Family, 54,* 178–190.

Demetriou, A. (2001, April). *Towards a comprehensive theory of intellectual development.* Paper presented at the meeting of the Society for Research in Child Development, Minneapolis.

Dempster, F. N. (1981). Memory span: Sources of individual and developmental differences. *Psychological Bulletin, 80,* 63–100.

Denham, S. A. (1998). *Emotional development in young children.* New York: Guilford.

Denney, N. (1986, August). *Practical problem solving.* Paper presented at the meeting of the American Psychological Association, Washington, DC.

Denney, N. W. (1990). Adult age differences in traditional and practical problem solving. *Advances in Psychology, 72,* 329–349.

Derman-Sparks, L., & the A. B. C. Task Force. (1989). *Anti-bias curriculum.* Washington, DC: National Association for the Education of Young Children.

DeSpelder, L. A., & Strickland, A. L. (1996). *The last dance: Encountering death and dying* (4th ed.). Mountain View, CA: Mayfield.

Dettmer, P., Dyck, N., & Thurston, L. (2002). *Consultation, collaboration and teamwork for students with special needs (4th Ed.).* Boston: Allyn & Bacon.

Deutsch, F. M. (1991). Women's lives: The story not told by theories of development. *Contemporary Psychology, 36,* 237–238.

Dewey, C. R. (1999, April). *Day care, family, and child characteristics: Their roles as predictors and moderators of language development.* Paper presented at the meeting of the Society for Research in Child Development, Albuquerque.

Dewey, J. (1933). *How we think.* Lexington, MA: D.C. Heath.

Dibzhansky, T. G. (1997). Evolution. New York: W. H. Freeman.

Dickson, G.L. (1990). A feminist post-structuralist analysis of the knowledge of menopause. *Advances in Nursing Science, 12,* 15–31.

Diener, E., & Diener, M. B. (1998). Happiness. In H. S. Friedman (Ed.), *Encyclopedia of mental health* (Vol. 2). San Diego: Academic Press.

Diener, E., Suh, E. M., Lucas, R. E., & Smith, H. L. (1999). Subjective well-being: Three decades of progress. *Psychological Bulletin, 125,* 276–301.

Dietz, W. H., & Stern, L. (1999). *American Academy of Pediatrics guide to your child's nutrition.* New York: Villard Books.

Digest of Education Statistics. (1999). *Elementary and secondary education.* Washington, DC: U.S. Bureau of the Census, National Center for Education Statistics.

DiGiulio, R. C. (1989). *Beyond widowhood.* New York: Free Press.

DiLalla, L. F. (2000). Development of intelligence: Current research and theories. *Journal of School Psychology, 38,* 3–8.

Dion, K. K., & Dion, K. L. (1993). Individualistic and collectivistic perspectives on gender and the cultural context of love and intimacy. *Journal of Social Issues, 49,* 53–69.

Dishion, T. (2001, April). *Understanding and preventing adolescent drug use.* Paper presented at the meeting of the Society for Research in Child Development, Minneapolis.

Dishion, T. J., & Li, F. (1996, March). *Childhood peer rejection in the development of adolescent problem behavior.* Paper presented at the meeting of the Society for Research on Adolescence, Boston.

Dobzhansky, T. G. (1977). *Evolution.* New York: W. H. Freeman.

Dodge, K. A. (1983). Behavioral antecedents of peer social status. *Child Development, 54,* 1386–1399.

Dodge, K. A. (2000). Developmental psychology. In M. H. Ebert, P. T. Loosen, & B. Nurcombe (Eds.). *Current diagnosis and treatment in psychiatry.* East Norwalk, CT: Appleton & Lange.

Dohrenwend, B. S., & Dohrenwend, B. P. (1978). Some issues in research on stressful life events. *Journal of Nervous and Mental Disease, 166,* 7–15.

Dohrenwend, B. S., & Shrout, P. E. (1985). "Hassles" in the conceptualization and measurement of life stress variables. *American Psychologist, 40,* 780–785.

Donelson, F. E. (1998). *Women's experiences.* Mountain View, CA: Mayfield.

Donovan, P. (1993). *Testing positive: Sexually transmitted disease and the public health response.* New York: Alan Guttmacher Institute.

Dorn, L. D., & Chrousos, G. P. (1996, March). *Behavioral predictors of stress hormone responses.* Paper presented at the meeting of the Society for Research on Adolescence, Boston.

Dorn, L. D., & Lucas, F. L. (1995, March). *Do hormone-behavior relations vary depending upon the endocrine and psychological status of the adolescent?* Paper presented at the meeting of the Society for Research in Child Development, Indianapolis.

Downey, G., & Bonica, C. A. (1997, April). *Characteristics of early adolescent dating relationships.* Paper presented at the meeting of the Society for Research in Child Development, Washington, DC.

Doyle, J. A., & Paludi, M. A. (1998). *Sex and gender* (4th ed.). New York: McGraw-Hill.

Drew, C., & Hardman, M. L. (2000). *Mental retardation* (7th ed.). Columbus, OH: Merrill.

Drickamer, L. C., Vessey, S. H., & Miekle, D. (1996). *Animal behavior* (4th ed.). Dubuque, IA: Wm. C. Brown.

Driscoll, A. (2000). *Early childhood education, birth–8.* Boston: Allyn & Bacon.

Dryfoos, J. G. (1990). *Adolescents at risk: Prevalence and prevention.* New York: Oxford University Press.

Dunkel-Schetter, C. (1998). Maternal stress and preterm delivery. *Prenatal and Neonatal Medicine, 3,* 39–42.

Dunkel-Schetter, C. (1999, August). *Is maternal stress a risk factor for adverse birth outcomes?* Paper presented at the meeting of the American Psychological Association, Boston.

Dunkel-Schetter, C., Gurung, R.A.R., Lobel, M., & Wadhwa, P.D. (2001). Stress processes in pregnancy and birth. In A. Baum, T.A. Revenson, & J.E. Singer (Eds.), *Handbook of health psychology.* Mahwah, NJ: Erlbaum.

Dunkel-Schetter, C., Gurung, R. A. R., Lobel, M., & Wadhwa, P. D. (in press). Psychological, biological, and social processes in pregnancy: Using a stress framework to study birth outcomes. In A. Baum, T. Revenson, & J. Singer (Eds.), *Handbook of health psychology.* Mahwah, NJ: Erlbaum.

Dunn, J. (1984). Sibling studies and the developmental impact of critical incidents. In P. B. Baltes & O. G. Brim (Eds.), *Life-span development and behavior* (Vol. 6). Orlando, FL: Academic Press.

Dunn, L., & Kontos, S. (1997). What have we learned about developmentally appropriate education? *Young Children, 52* (2), 4–13.

DuRant, R. H. (1999, April). *Exposure to violence, depression, and substance use and abuse and the use of violence by young adolescents.* Paper presented at the meeting of the Society for Research in Child Development, Albuquerque.

E

Eagle, M. (2000). Psychoanalytic theory: History of the field. In A. Kazdin (Ed.), *Encyclopedia of psychology.* Washington, DC, & New York: American Psychological Association and Oxford University Press.

Eagly, A. H. (1996). Differences between women and men. *American Psychologist, 51,* 158–159.

Eagly, A. H. (2000). Gender roles. In A. Kazdin (Ed.), *Encyclopedia of psychology.* Washington, DC, & New York: American Psychological Association and Oxford University Press.

Eagly, A. H., & Crowley, M. (1986). Gender and helping behavior: A meta-analytic review of the social psychological literature. *Psychological Bulletin, 100,* 283–308.

Earles, J. L., & Salthouse, T. A. (1995). Interrelations of age, health, and speed. *Journal of Gerontology: Psychological Sciences, 50B,* P33–P41.

Eccles, J. (2000). Adolescence: Social patterns, achievements, and problems. In A. Kazdin (Ed.), *Encyclopedia of psychology.* Washington, DC, & New York: American Psychological Association and Oxford University Press.

Eccles, J. (2000). Gender socialization. In A. Kazdin (Ed.), *Encyclopedia of psychology.* Washington, DC, & New York: American Psychological Association and Oxford University Press.

Eccles, J. (2001, April). *Gender and ethnicity as developmental contexts.* Paper presented at the meeting of the Society for Research in Child Development, Minneapolis.

Edelman, M. W. (1995). *The state of America's children.* Washington, DC: Children's Defense Fund.

Edmonds, M. M. (1993). Physical health. In J. S. Jackson, L. M. Chatters, & R. J. Taylor (Eds.), *Aging in Black America.* Newbury Park, CA: Sage.

Educational Testing Service. (1992). *Cross-cultural comparison of children's learning and achievement.* Unpublished manuscript. Educational Testing Service, Princeton, N J.

Educational Testing Service. (1992, February). *Cross-national comparison of 9–13 year olds' science and math achievement.* Princeton, NJ: Author.

Egeland, B., Jacobvitz, D., & Sroufe, L. A. (1988). Breaking the cycle of abuse. *New Directions for Child Development, 11,* 77–92.

Egeren, L. V. (1999, April). *The development of the parenting alliance in first-time parents: Predictors of change patterns over the first six months.* Paper presented at the meeting of the Society for Research in Child Development, Albuquerque.

Eggebeen, D.J., & Knoester, C. (2001). Does fatherhood matter for men? *Journal of Marriage and the Family, 63,* 381–393.

Eichorn, D. H., Clausen, J. A., Haan, N., Honzik, M. P., & Mussen, P. H. (Eds.). (1981). *Present and past in middle life.* New York: Academic Press.

Eiferman, R. R. (1971). Social play in childhood. In R. Herron & B. Sutton-Smith (Eds.), *Child's play.* New York: Wiley.

Eiger, M. S. (1992). The feeding of infants and children. In R. A. Hoekelman, S. B. Friedman, N. M. Nelson, & H. M. Seidel (Eds.), *Primary pediatric care* (2nd ed.). St. Louis: Mosby Yearbook.

Eiger, M. S., & Olds, S. W. (1999). *The complete book of breastfeeding* (3rd ed.). New York: Bantam.

Eisdorfer, C. (1996, December). Interview. *APA Monitor,* p. 35.

Eisen, M.L., Quas, J.A., & Goodman, G.S. (Eds.) (2001). *Memory and suggestibility in the forensic interview.* Mahwah, NJ: Erlbaum.

Eisenberg, N. (Ed.). (1982). *The development of prosocial behavior.* New York: Wiley.

Eisenberg, N. (2000). Empathy. In A. Kazdin (Ed.), *Encyclopedia of psychology.* Washington, DC, & New York: American Psychological Association and Oxford University Press.

Eisenberg, N. (2001). Emotion-regulated regulation and its relation to quality of social functioning. In W.W. Hartup & R.A. Weinberg (Eds.), *Child psychology in retrospect and prospect.* Mahwah, NJ: Erlbaum.

Eisenberg, N., Fabes, R. A., Karbon, M., Murphy, B. C., Wosinski, M., Polazzi, L., Carolo, G., & Juhnke, C. (in press). The relations of children's dispositional prosocial behavior to emotionality, regulation, and social functioning. *Child Development.*

Eisenberg, N., Martin, C. L., & Fabes, R. A. (1996). Gender development and gender effects. In D. C. Berliner & R. C. Calfee (Eds.), *Handbook of educational psychology*. New York: Macmillan.

Eissenberg, T., Stitzer, M. L., & Hennigfield, J. E. (1999). Current issues in nicotine replacement. In D. F. Seidman & L. S. Covey (Eds.), *Helping the hard-core smoker.* Mahwah, NJ: Erlbaum.

Ekwo, E. E., & Moawad, A. (2000). Maternal age and preterm births in a black population. *Pediatric Perinatal Epidemiology, 2,* 145–151.

Elder, G. H., & Pavalko, E. K. (1993). Work careers in men's later years: Transitions, trajectories, and historical change. *Journal of Gerontology, 48,* S180–S191.

Eli Lily. (2000). *Newly approved drug therapies: Evista.* Press release, Eli Lily Corporation, Indianapolis.

Elias, M. (1998, June 23). For 50 years pediatrics has taken giant steps. *USA Today,* pp. 1, 2D.

Elicker, J. (1996). A knitting tale: Reflections on scaffolding. *Childhood Education, 72,* 29–32.

Elkind, D. (1970, April 5). Erik Erikson's eight ages of man. *New York Times Magazine.*

Elkind, D. (1976). *Child development and education: A Piagetian perspective.* New York: Oxford University Press.

Elkind, D. (1976). *Child development and education: A Piagetian perspective.* New York: Oxford University Press.

Elkind, D. (1988, January). Educating the very young: A call for clear thinking. *NEA Today,* pp. 22–27.

Ellis, E. M. (2000). *Divorce wars.* Washington, DC: American Psychological Association.

Ellis, L., & Ames, M. A. (1987). Neurohormonal functioning and sexual orientation. *Psychological Bulletin, 101,* 233–258.

Emde, R. N., Gaensbauer, T. G., & Harmon, R. J. (1976). Emotional expression in infancy: A biobehavioral study. *Psychological Issues: Monograph Series, 10* (37).

Emery, R. E. (1999). *Renegotiating family relationships* (2nd ed.). New York: Guilford Press.

Enger, E. D., Kormelink, R., Ross, F. C., & Otto, R. (1996). *Diversity of life.* Dubuque, IA: Wm. C. Brown.

England, S. E., Linsk, N. L., Simon-Rusinowitz, L., & Keigher, S. M. (1991). Paying kin for care: Agency barriers to formalizing informal care. *Journal of Aging and Social Policy, 2,* 63–86.

Enright, R. D., Lapsley, D. K., Dricas, A. S., & Fehr, L. A. (1980). Parental influence on the development of adolescent autonomy and identity. *Journal of Youth and Adolescence, 9,* 529–546.

Epstein, D. K., & Connor, J. R. (1999, Fall). Dementia in the elderly: An overview. *Generations,* pp. 9–16.

Epstein, N., & Eidelson, R. J. (1981). Unrealistic beliefs of clinical couples: Their relationship to expectations, goals, and satisfaction. *American Journal of Family Therapy, 9,* 13–21.

Erikson, E. H. (1950). *Childhood and society.* New York: W. W. Norton.

Erikson, E. H. (1968). *Identity: Youth and crisis.* New York: W. W. Norton.

Eskenazi, B., Stapleton, A. L., Kharrazi, M., & Chee, W. Y. (1999). Associations between maternal decaffeinated and caffeinated coffee consumption and fetal growth and gestational duration. *Epidemiology, 10,* 242–249.

Evans, W. (2000). Exercise strategies should be designed to increase muscle power. *Journal of Gerontology: Medical Sciences, 55A,* M309–M310.

Everard, K. M., Reed, G. R., Lach, H. W., Fisher, E. B., & Baum, M. C. (1999, November). *Aerobic, strength, and stretching exercise behavior of older adults.* Paper presented at the meeting of the Gerontological Association of America, San Francisco.

F

Faber, D., & Burns, J. W. (1996). Anger management style, degree of expressed anger, and gender influence on cardiovascular recovery from interpersonal harassment. *Journal of Behavioral Medicine, 19,* 55–72.

Fagan, J. F. (1992). Intelligence: A theoretical viewpoint. *Current Directions in Psychological Science, 1,* 82–86.

Fagot, B. I., Leinbach, M. D., & O'Boyle, C. (1992). Gender labeling, gender stereotyping, and parenting behaviors. *Developmental Psychology, 28,* 225–230.

Fagot, B. I., Rodgers, C. S., & Leinbach, M. D. (2000). Theories of gender socialization. In T. Eckes & H. M. Trautner (Eds.), *The developmental social psychology of gender.* Mahwah, NJ: Erlbaum.

Falbo, T., & Poston, D. L. (1993). The academic, personality, and physical outcomes of only children in China. *Child Development, 64,* 18–35.

Famy, C., Streissguth, A. P., & Unis, A. S. (1998). Mental illness in adults with fetal alcohol syndrome or fetal alcohol effects. *American Journal of Psychiatry, 155,* 552–554.

Fang, J., Madhaven, S., & Alderman, M. H. (1999). Low birth weight: Race and maternal nativity—Impact of community income. *Pediatrics, 103,* e5.

Fantz, R. L. (1963). Pattern vision in newborn infants. *Science, 140,* 296–297.

Farrell, M. P., & Rosenberg, S.D. (1981). *Men at mid-life.* Boston: Auburn House.

Fehr, B. (1996). *Friendship processes.* Thousand Oaks, CA: Sage.

Fein, G. G. (1986). Pretend play. In D. Görlitz & J. F. Wohlwill (Eds.), *Curiosity, imagination, and play.* Hillsdale, NJ: Erlbaum.

Feinberg, M., & Hetherington, E.M. (2001). Differential parenting as a within-family variable. *Journal of Family Psychology, 15,* 22–37.

Feiring, C. (1996). Concepts of romance in 15-year-old adolescents. *Journal of Research on Adolescence, 6,* 181–200.

Feldman, H.D. (2001, April). *Contemporary developmental theories and the concept of talent.* Paper presented at the meeting of the Society for Research in Child Development, Minneapolis.

Feldman, R., Greenbaum, C. W., & Yirmiya, N. (1999). Mother-infant affect synchrony as an antecedent of the emergence of self-control. *Developmental Psychology, 35,* 223–231.

Feldman, S. S. (1999). Unpublished review of J. W. Santrock's *Adolescence,* 8th ed. (New York: McGraw-Hill).

Feldman, S. S., & Elliott, G. R. (1990). Progress and promise of research on normal adolescent development. In S. S. Feldman & G. Elliott (Eds.), *At the threshold: The developing adolescent.* Cambridge, MA: Harvard University Press.

Feldman, S. S., Turner, R., & Aruajo, K. (1999). Interpersonal context as an influence on sexual timetables of youths: Gender and ethnic effects. *Journal of Research on Adolescence, 9,* 25–52.

Feldman, S. S., & Weinberger, D. A. (1994). Self-restraint as a mediator of family influences on boys' delinquent behavior: A longitudinal study. *Child Development, 65,* 195–211.

Ferguson, D. M., Harwood, L. J., & Shannon, F. T. (1987). Breastfeeding and subsequent social adjustment in 6- to 8- year-old children. *Journal of Child Psychology and Psychiatry, 28,* 378–386.

Ferguson, D. M., Horwood. L. J., & Beautrais, A. L. (1999). Is sexual orientation related to mental health problems and suicidality in young people? *Archives of General Psychiatry, 56,* 876–880.

Fernald, A. (2001). Two hundred years of research on the early development of language comprehension. In W.W. Hartup & R.A. Weinberg (Eds.), *Child psychology in retrospect and prospect.* Mahwah, NJ: Erlbaum.

Fernandes, O., Sabharwal, M., Smiley, T., Pastuszak, A., Koren, G., & Einarson, T. (1998). Moderate to heavy caffeine consumption during pregnancy and relationship to spontaneous abortion and abnormal fetal growth: A meta-analysis. *Reproductive Toxicology, 12,* 435–444.

Fiatarone, M. A., Marks, E. C., Meredith, C. N., Lipsitz, L. A., & Evans, W. J. (1990). High intensity strength training in nonagenarians: Effects on skeletal muscle. *Journal of the American Medical Association, 263,* 3029–3034.

Field, D. (1996). Review of *Relationships in old age* by Hansson & Carpenter. *Contemporary Psychology, 41,* 44–45.

Field, D. (1999). A cross-cultural perspective on continuity and change in social relations in old age: Introduction to a special issue. *International Journal of Aging and Human Development, 48,* 257–262.

Field, D. (1999, November). *Stability and change in relationships between older parents and their children: A 36-year longitudinal study.* Paper presented at the meeting of the Gerontological Association of America, San Francisco.

Field, T. (1990). *Infancy.* Cambridge, MA: Harvard University Press.

Field, T. (1992, September). Stroking babies helps growth, reduces stress. *Brown University Child and Adolescent Behavior Letter,* pp. 1, 6.

Field, T. (2000). Child abuse. In A. Kazdin (Ed.), [illegible] Washington, DC, & New York: American Psychological Association and Oxford University Press.

Field, T. M. (1998). Massage therapy effects. *American Psychologist, 53,* 1270–1281.

Fields, R. (1998). *Drugs in perspective* (3rd ed.). New York: McGraw-Hill.

Finch, C. E., & Seeman, T. E. (1999). Stress theories of aging. In V. L. Bengtson, & K. W. Schaie (Eds.). *Handbook of theories of aging.* New York: Springer.

Finkel, D., Whitfield, K., & McGue, M. (1995). Genetic and environmental influences on functional age: A twin study. *Journal of Gerontology, 50B,* P104–P113.

Fisch, S.M., & Truglio, R.T. (Eds.) (2001). *"G" is for growing.* Mahwah, NJ: Erlbaum.

Fitzgerald, L. (2000). Sexual harassment. In A. Kazdin (Ed.), *Encyclopedia of psychology.* Washington, DC, & New York: American Psychological Association and Oxford University Press.

Flanagan, K.M., Clements, M.L., Whitton, S.W., Portney, M.J., Randall, D.W., & Markman, H.J. (2001). Retrospect and prospect in the psychological study of marital and couple relationships. In J.P. McHale & W.S. Grolnick (Eds.), *Retrospect and prospect in the psychological study of families.* Mahwah, NJ: Erlbaum.

Flavell, J. H. (1999). Cognitive development: Children's knowledge about the mind. *Annual Review of Psychology* (Vol. 50). Palo Alto, CA: Annual Reviews.

Flavell, J. H., Friedrichs, A., & Hoyt, J. (1970). Developmental changes in memorization processes. *Cognitive Psychology, 1,* 324–340.

Flavell, J. H., & Miller, P. H. (1998). Social cognition. In W. Damon (Ed.), *Handbook of child psychology* (5th ed., Vol. 2). New York: Wiley.

Flavell, J.H., Miller, P.H., Miller, S. (2001). *Cognitive development* (4th ed.). Upper Saddle River, NJ: Prentice-Hall.

Flick, L., White, D.K., Vemulapalli, C., Stulack, B.B., & Kemp, J.S. (2001). Sleep position and the use of soft bedding during bed sharing among African American infants at increased risk for sudden infant death syndrome. *Journal of Pediatrics, 138,* 338–343.

Fodor, I., G., & Franks, V. (1990). Women in midlife and beyond. The new prime of life? *Psychology of Women Quarterly, 14,* 445–449.

Fogel, A. (2001). *Infancy* (4th ed.). Belmont, CA: Wadsworth.

Fonda, S. J., & Nogard, T. M. (1999, November). *Patterns and correlates of change in depressive symptoms among community-dwelling elderly.* Paper presented at the meeting of the Gerontological Society of America, San Francisco.

Forrest, J. D., & Singh, S. (1990). The sexual and reproductive behavior of American women, 1982–1988. *Family Planning Perspectives, 22,* 206–214.

Fox, G. L., & Murry, V. M. (2000). Gender and families: Feminist perspectives and family research. *Journal of Marriage and the Family, 62,* 1160–1172.

Fozard, J. (1992, December 6). Commentary in "W[illegible]" [illegible] pp. 14–15.

Fozard, J. L. (2000). Sensory and cognitive changes with age. In K. W. Schaie & M. Pietrucha (Eds.), *Mobility and transportation in the elderly.* New York: Springer.

Fraga, C. G., Motchnik, P. A., Shigenaga, M. K., Helbock, H. J., Jacob, R. A., & Ames, B. N. (1991). Ascorbic acid protects against endogenous oxidative DNA damage in human sperm. *Proceedings of the National Academy of Sciences of the United States, 88,* 11003–11006.

Fraiberg, S. (1959). *The magic years.* New York: Scribner's.

Frank, D. A., Augustyn, M., Knight, W.G., Pell, T., & Zuckerman, B. (2001). Growth, development, and behavior in early childhood following prenatal cocaine exposure: a systematic review. *Journal of the American Medical Association, 285,* 1613–1625.

Frankl, V. (1984). *Man's search for meaning.* New York: Basic Books.

Franz, C. E. (1996). The implications of preschool tempo and motoric activity level for personality decades later. Reported in A. Caspi, Personality development across the life course, in W. Damon (Ed.), *Handbook of child psychology,* Vol. 3 (New York: Wiley), p. 337.

Fredman, L., Daly, M. P., & Lazur, A. M. (1995). Burden among White and Black caregivers to elderly adults. *Journal of Gerontology, 50B,* S110–S118.

Fredrickson, D. D. (1993). Breastfeeding research priorities, opportunities, and study criteria: What we learned from the smoking trail. *Journal of Human Lactation, 3,* 147–150.

Freedman, J. L. (1984). Effects of television violence on aggressiveness. *Psychological Bulletin, 96,* 227–246.

Freiberg, H. J., & Driscoll, A. (2000). *Universal teaching strategies* (3rd ed.). Boston: Allyn & Bacon.

Freppon, P. A., & Dahl, K. L. (1998). Balanced instruction: Insights and considerations. *Reading Research Quarterly, 33,* 240–251.

Freud, A., & Dann, S. (1951). Instinctual anxiety during puberty. In A. Freud (Ed.), *The ego and its mechanisms of defense.* New York: International Universities Press.

Freud, S. (1917). *A general introduction to psychoanalysis.* New York: Washington Square Press.

Fried, P. A., & Watkinson, B. (1990). 36- and 48-month neurobehavioral follow-up of children prenatally exposed to marijuana, cigarettes, and alcohol. *Developmental and Behavioral Pediatrics, 11,* 49–58.

Friedman, M., & Rosenman, R. (1974). *Type A behavior and your heart.* New York: Knopf.

Friedman, M. A., & Brownell, K. A. (1998). Obesity. In H. S. Friedman (Ed.), *Encyclopedia of mental health* (Vol. 3). San Diego: Academic Press.

Friedrich, L. K., & Stein, A. H. (1973). Aggressive and prosocial TV programs and the natural behavior of preschool children. *Monographs of the Society for Research in Child Development, 38* (4, Serial No. 151).

Frieske, D. A., & Park, D. C. (1999). Memory for news in young and old adults. *Psychology and aging, 14,* 90–98.

Fry, P. S. (1999, November). *Significance of religiosity and spirituality to psychological well being of older adults.* Paper presented at the meeting of the Gerontological Society of America, San Francisco.

Fry, P. S. (1999, November). *Widows' regrets of action and inaction in coping with spousal loss: A follow-up.* Paper presented at the meeting of the Gerontological Society of America, San Francisco.

Fuller-Thomson, E., & Minkler, M. (2001). American grandparents providing extensive care to their grandchildren: Prevalence and profile. *The Gerontologist, 41, No. 2,* 201–209.

Furman, W., & Buhrmester, D. (1992). Age and sex differences in perceptions of networks of personal relationships. *Child Development, 63,* 103–115.

Furman, W., & Wehner, E. A. (in press). Adolescent romantic relationships: A developmental perspective. In S. Shulman & W. A. Collins (Eds.), *New directions for child development: Adolescent romantic relationships.* San Francisco: Jossey-Bass.

Furnival, R. A., Street, K. A., & Schunk, J. E. (1999). Too many pediatric trampoline injuries. *Pediatrics, 103* e57.

Furth, H. G., & Wachs, H. (1975). *Thinking goes to school.* New York: Oxford University Press.

G

Gadpaille, W. J. (1996). *Adolescent suicide.* Washington, DC: American Psychological Association.

Galambos, N. L., & Maggs, J. L. (1989, April). *The after-school ecology of young adolescents and self-reported behavior.* Paper presented at the biennial meeting of the Society for Research in Child Development, Kansas City.

Galambos, N. L., & Tilton-Weaver, L. (1996, March). *The adultoid adolescent: Too much, too soon.* Paper presented at the meeting of the Society for Research on Adolescence, Boston.

Galinsky, E., & David, J. (1988). *The preschool years: Family strategies that work—from experts and parents.* New York: Times Books.

Gall, T. L., Evans, D. R., & Howard, J. (1997). The retirement adjustment process: Changes in well-being of male retirees across time. *Journal of Gerontology, 52B,* P110–P117.

Gallup, G. (1987). *The Gallup poll: Public opinion 1986.* Wilmington, DE: Scholarly Resources.

Gallup, G. H., & Bezilla, R. (1992). *The religious life of young Americans.* Princeton, NJ: Gallup Institute.

Gallup, G. H., & Jones, S. (1989). *One hundred questions and answers: Religion in America.* Princeton, NJ: Gallup Institute.

Galotti, K. M., Kozberg, S. F. (1996). Adolescents' experience of a life-framing decision. *Journal of Youth and Adolescence, 25,* 3–16.

Galotti, K. M., Kozberg, S. F., & Farmer, M. C. (1990, March). *Gender and developmental differences in adolescents' conceptions of moral reasoning.* Paper presented at the meeting of the Society for Research in Adolescence, Atlanta.

Gannon, L. (1998). Menopause. In H. S. Friedman (Ed.), *Encyclopedia of mental health* (Vol. 2). San Diego: Academic Press.

Ganong, L. H., & Coleman, M. (1994). *Remarried family relationships.* Thousand Oaks, CA: Sage.

Gao, Y., Elliott, M. E., & Waters, E. (1999, April). *Maternal attachment representations and support for three-year-olds' secure base behavior.* Paper presented at the meeting of the Society for Research in Child Development, Albuquerque.

Garbarino, J. (1976). The ecological correlates of child abuse. The impact of socioeconomic stress on mothers. *Child Development, 47,* 178–185.

Garbarino, J. (1999). *Lost boys: Why our sons turn violent and how we can save them.* New York: Free Press.

Gardner, H. (1983). *Frames of mind.* New York: Basic Books.

Gardner, H. (1993). *Multiple intelligences.* New York: Basic Books.

Gardner, H. (1999). *The disciplined mind.* New York: Simon & Schuster.

Gardner, L. I., Stern, M. P., Haffner, S. M., Gaskill, S. P., Hazuda, H. P., Relethford, J. H., & Eifter, C. W. (1984). Prevalence of diabetes in Mexican Americans: Relationships to percent of gene pool derived from Native American sources. *Diabetes, 33,* 86–92.

Garfein, A. J., & Herzog, A. R. (1995). Robust aging among the young-old, old-old, and oldest-old. *Journal of Gerontology, 50B,* S77–S87.

Garmezy, N. (1985). Stress-resistant children: The search for protective factors. In J. E. Stevenson (Ed.), Recent research in developmental psychopathology. *Journal of Child Psychology and Psychiatry Book Supplement, 4,* 213–233.

Garmezy, N. (1993). Children in poverty: Resilience despite risk. *Psychiatry, 56,* 127–136.

Gartner, J., Larson, D. B., & Allen, G. D. (1991). Religious commitment and mental health: A review of the empirical literature. *Journal of Psychology and Theology, 19,* 6–25.

Gatz, M. (1989). Clinical psychology and aging. In M. Storandt & G. R. VandenBos (Eds.), *The adult years: Continuity and change.* Washington, DC: American Psychological Association.

Gatz, M. (1992). The mental health system and older adults. *American Psychologist, 47,* 741–751.

Geary, D. C., & Bjorklund, D. F. (2000). Evolutionary developmental psychology. *Child Development, 71,* 57–71.

Gelman, R. (1969). Conservation acquisition: A problem of learning to attend to relevant attributes. *Journal of Experimental Child Psychology, 7,* 67–87.

Gelman, R., & Brenneman, K. (1994). Domain specificity and cultural variation are not inconsistent. In L. A. Hirschfeld & S. Gelman (Eds.), *Mapping the Mind: Domain specificity in cognition and culture.* New York: Cambridge University Press.

Gelman, R., & Williams, E. M. (1998). Enabling constraints for congnitive development and learning. In W. Damon (Ed.), *Handbook of child psychology* (5th ed., Vol. 4). New York: Wiley.

Gerlach, P. (1998). *Stepfamily in formation.* Chicago: Stepfamily Association of Illinois.

Gescheider, G. A. (1997). *Psychophysics: The fundamentals.* Mahwah, NJ: Erlbaum.

Gesell, A. (1934). *An atlas of infant behavior.* New Haven, CT: Yale University Press.

Gesell, A.L. (1928). *Infancy and human growth.* New York: Macmillan.

Gewirtz, J. (1977). Maternal responding and the conditioning of infant crying: Directions of influence within the attachment-acquisition process. In B. C. Etzel, J. M. LeBlanc, & D. M. Baer (Eds.), *New developments in behavioral research.* Hillsdale, NJ: Erlbaum.

Giarrusso, R., & Feng, D. (1999, November). *The influence of life transitions on the intergenerational stake phenomenon.* Paper presented at the meeting of the Gerontological Association of America, San Francisco.

Gibbons, J. L. (2000). Gender development in cross-cultural perspective. In T. Eckes & H. M. Trautner (Eds.), *The developmental social psychology of gender.* Mahwah, NJ: Erlbaum.

Gibbs, J. C. (1993, March). *Inductive discipline's contribution to moral motivation.* Paper presented at the biennial meeting of the Society for Research in Child Development, New Orleans.

Gibson, E. J. (1969). *Principles of perceptual learning and development.* New York: Appleton Century Crofts.

Gibson, E. J. (1989). Exploratory behavior in the development of perceiving, acting, and the acquiring of knowledge. *Annual Review of Psychology (Vol. 39).* Palo Alto, CA: Annual Reviews.

Gibson, E.J. (2001). *Perceiving the affordances.* Mahwah, NJ: Erlbaum.

Gibson, E. J., Riccio, G., Schmuckler, M. A., Stoffregen, T. A., Rosenberg, D., & Taormina, J. (1987). Detection of the traversability of surfaces by crawling and walking infants. *Journal of Experimental Psychology: Human Perception and Performance, 13,* 533–544.

Gibson, E. J., & Walk, R. D. (1960). The "visual cliff." *Scientific American, 202,* 64–71.

Gibson, J. J. (1966). *The senses considered as perceptual systems.* Boston: Houghton Mifflin.

Gibson, J. J. (1979). *The ecological approach to visual perception.* Boston: Houghton Mifflin.

Gibson, J. H., Harries, M., Mitchell, A., Godfrey, R., Lunt, M., & Reeve, J. (2000). Determinants of bone density and prevalence of osteopenia among female runners in their second to seventh decades of age. *Bone, 26,* 591–598.

Giddens, S., & Giddens, O. (2000). *Coping with grieving and loss.* New York: Rosen.

Gilligan, C. (1982). *In a different voice.* Cambridge, MA: Harvard University Press.

Gilligan, C. (1990). Teaching Shakespeare's sister. In C. Gilligan, N. Lyons, & T. Hammer (Eds.), *Making connections: The relational worlds of adolescent girls at Emme Willard School.* Cambridge, MA: Harvard University Press.

Gilligan, C. (1992, May). *Joining the resistance: Girls' development in adolescence.* Paper presented at the symposium on development and vulnerability in close relationships, Montreal.

Gilligan, C. (1996). The centrality of relationships in psychological development: A puzzle, some evidence, and a theory: In G. G. Noam & K. W. Fischer (Eds.), *Development and vulnerability in close relationships.* Hillsdale, NJ: Erlbaum.

Gilligan, C., & Attanucci, J. (1988). Two moral orientations. In C. Gilligan, J. V. Ward, J. M. Taylor, & B. Bardige (Eds.), *Mapping the moral domain.* Cambridge, MA: Harvard University Press.

Gladue, B. A. (1994). The biopsychology of sexual orientation. *Current Directions in Psychological Science, 3,* 150–154.

Glei, D. A. (1999). Measuring contraceptive use patterns among teenage and adult women. *Family Planning Perspectives, 31,* 73–80.

Gojdamaschko, N. (1999). Vygotsky. In M. A. Runco & S. Pritzker (Eds.), *Encyclopedia of creativity.* San Diego: Academic Press.

Golbeck, S.L. (2001). *Psychological perspectives on early childhood education.* Mahwah, NJ: Erlbaum.

Goldin-Meadow, S. (1979). The development of language-like communication without a language model. *Science, 197,* 401–403.

Goldsmith, H. H. (1988, August). *Does early temperament predict late development?* Paper presented at the meeting of the American Psychological Association, Atlanta.

Goldsmith, H. H. (1994, Winter). The behavior-genetic approach to development and experience: Contexts and constraints. *SRCD Newsletter, 1, 6,* 10–11.

Goldsmith, H. H., & Gottesman, I. I. (1981). Origins of variation in behavioral style: A longitudinal study of temperament in young twins. *Child Development, 52,* 91–103.

Goldwater, P.N. (2001). SIDS: More facts and controversies. *Medical Journal of Australia, 174,* 302–304.

Goleman, D. (1995). *Emotional intelligence.* New York: Basic Books.

Goleman, D., Kaufman, P., & Ray, M. (1993). *The creative spirit.* New York: Plume.

Golombok, S., Cook, R., Bish, A., & Murray, C. (1995). Families created by the new reproductive technologies: Quality of parenting and social and emotional development of children. *Child Development, 66,* 285–298.

Gonyea, J. G. (1994). Introduction to the issue on work and eldercare. *Research on Aging, 16,* 3–6.

Goodman, G. S., & Quas, J. A. (2000). Family violence. In A. Kazdin (Ed.), *Encyclopedia of psychology.* Washington, DC, & New York: American Psychological Association and Oxford University Press.

Goodman, R. A., Mercy, J. A., Loya, F., Rosenberg, M. L., Smith, J. C., Allen, N. H., Vargas, L., & Kolts, R. (1986). Alcohol use and interpersonal violence: Alcohol detected in homicide victims. *American Journal of Public Health, 76,* 144–149.

Gottfried, A. E., Gottfried, A. W., & Bathurst K. (1995). Maternal and dual-earner employment status and parenting. In M. H. Bornstein (Ed.), *Handbook of parenting* (Vol. 3). Hillsdale, NJ: Erlbaum.

Gottlieb, G. (1991). Experiential canalization of behavioral development theory. *Developmental Psychology, 27,* 4–13.

Gottlieb, G. (2000). Nature and nurture theories. In A. Kazdin (Ed.), *Encyclopedia of psychology.* Washington, DC, & New York: American Psychological Association and Oxford University Press.

Gottlieb, G. (2001). Origin of species: The potential significance of early experience for evolution. In W.W. Hartup, & R.A. Weinberg (Eds.), *Child psychology in retrospect and prospect.* Mahwah, NJ: Erlbaum.

Gottlieb, G., Wahlsten, D., & Lickliter, R. (1998). The significance of biology for human development: A developmental psychobiological systems view. In W. Damon (Ed.), *Handbook of child psychology* (5th ed., Vol. 1). New York: Wiley.

Gottman, J. M., & Levenson, R. W. (2000). The timing of divorce: Predicting when a couple will divorce over a 14-year period. *Journal of Marriage and the Family, 62,* 737–745.

Gottman, J. M., & Notarious, C. I. (2000). Decade review: Observing marital interaction. *Journal of Marriage and the Family, 62,* 927–947.

Gottman, J. M., & Parker, J. G. (Eds.). (1987). *Conversations of friends.* New York: Cambridge University Press.

Gottman, J. M., & Silver, N. (1999). *The seven principles for making marriages work.* New York: Crown.

Gottman, J. M., Coan, J., Carrere, S., & Swanson, C. (1998). Predicting marital happiness and stability from newlywed interactions. *Journal of Marriage and the Family, 60,* 5–22.

Gottman, J. M. (1994). *Why marriages succeed or fail.* New York: Simon & Schuster.

Gould, E., Reeves, A. J., Graziano, M. S., & Gross, C. G. (1999). Neurogenesis in the neocortex of adult primates, *Science, 286*(1), 548–552.

Gould, R. L. (1978). *Transformations: Growth and change in adult life.* New York: Simon & Schuster.

Gould, S. J. (1981). *The mismeasure of man.* New York: W. W. Norton.

Gounin-Decarie, T. (1996). Revisiting Piaget, or the vulnerability of Piaget's infancy theory in the nineties. In G. G. Noam & K. W. Fischer (Eds.), *Development and vulnerability in close relationships.* Hillsdale, NJ: Erlbaum.

Gove, W. R., Style, C.B., & Hughes, M. (1990). The effect of marriage on the well-being of adults: A theoretical analysis. *Journal of Health and Social Behavior, 24,* 122–131.

Graeber, J. A., Brooks-Gunn, J., & Galen, B. R. (1999). Betwixt and between: Sexuality in the context of adolescent transitions. In R. Jessor (Ed.), *New perspectives on adolescent risk behavior.* New York: Cambridge University Press.

Graham, K.M. (2001, April). *Child survival: A right, not a need.* Paper presented at the meeting of the Society for Research in Child Development, Minneapolis.

Graham, S. (1992). Most of the subjects were white and middle class. *American Psychologist, 47,* 629–637.

Graham, S., & Harris, K. R. (1994). The effects of whole language on children's writing: A review of the literature. *Educational Psychologist, 29,* 187–192.

Grambs, J. D. (1989). *Women over forty* (rev. ed.), New York: Springer.

Grant, J. (1997). *State of the world's children.* New York: UNICEF and Oxford University Press.

Grant, J. P. (1993). *The state of the world's children.* New York: UNICEF and Oxford University Press.

Grantham-McGregor, S., Ani, C., & Fernald, L. (2001). The role of nutrition in cognitive development. In R.J. Sternberg & E.L. Grigorenko (Eds.), *Environmental effects on cognitive abilities.* Mahwah, NJ: Erlbaum.

Gray, J. (1992). *Men are from Mars, women are from Venus.* New York: HarperCollins.

Greenberg, B. S., & Brand, J. E. (1994). Minorities and the mass media. In J. Bryant & D. Zillman (Eds.), *Media effects.* Hillsdale, NJ: Erlbaum.

Greene, M.G., & Adelman, R.D. (2001). Building the physician-older patient relationship. In M.L. Hummert & J.F. Nussbaum (Eds.), *Aging, communication, and health.* Mahwah, NJ: Erlbaum.

Greene, V. L., Lovely, M. E., Miller, M. D., & Ondrich, J. I. (1995). Reducing nursing home use through community long-term care: An optimization analysis. *Journal of Gerontology: Social Sciences, 50B,* S259–S268.

Greeno, J. G., Cullins, A. M., & Resnick, L. (1996). Cognition and learning. In D. C. Berliner & R. C. Chafee (Eds.), *Handbook of educational psychology.* New York: Macmillian.

Greenough, W. T. (1997, April 21). Commentary in article, "Politics of biology." *U. S. News & World Report.* p. 79.

Greenough, W. T. (1999, April). *Experience, brain development, and links to mental retardation.* Paper presented at the meeting of the Society for Research in Child Development, Albuquerque.

Greenough, W.T. (2001, April). *Nature and nurture in the brain development process.* Paper presented at the meeting of the Society for Research in Child Development, Minneapolis.

Greenstein, T. N. (2000). Economic dependence, gender, and the division of labor in the home: A replication and extension. *Journal of Marriage and the Family, 62,* 322–335.

Griener, P. A., Snowdon, D. A., & Griener, L. H. (1999). Self-rated function, self-rated health, and postmortem evidence of brain infarcts: Finding from the Nun study. *Journal of Gerontology: Social Sciences, 54B,* S219–S222.

Grigorenko, E.L. (2001). The invisible danger: The impact of ionizing radiation on cognitive development and functioning. In R.J. Sternberg & E.L. Grigorenko (Eds.), *Environmental effects on cognitive abilities.* Mahwah, NJ: Erlbaum.

Griffiths-Joyner, F., & Hanc, J. (1999). *Running for dummies.* Foster City, CA: I D G Books.

Grolnick, W.S., & Gurland, S.T. (2001). Mothering: Retrospect and prospect. In J.P. McHale & W.S. Grolnick (Eds.), *Retrospect and prospect in the psychological study of families.* Mahwah, NJ: Erlbaum.

Gross, R. T. (1984). Patterns of maturation: Their effects on behavior and development. In M. D. Levine & P. Satz (Eds.), *Middle childhood: Development and dysfunction.* Baltimore: University Park Press.

Grossmann, K., Grossmann, K. E., Spangler, G., Suess, G., & Unzner, L. (1985). Maternal sensitivity and newborns' orientation responses as related to quality of attachment in Northern Germany. In I. Bretherton & E. Waters (Eds.), Growing points of attachment theory and research. *Monographs of the Society for Research in Child Development, 50* (1–2, Serial No. 209).

Grotevant, H. D., & McRoy, R. G. (1990). Adopted adolescents in residential treatment: The role of the family. In D. M. Brodzinsky & M. D. Schechter (Eds.), *The psychology of adoption.* New York: Oxford University Press.

Growman, W. A., Peaceman, A. M., & Socol, M. L. (2000). Cost-effectiveness of elective cesarean delivery after one low transverse cesarean. *Obstetrics and Gynecology, 95,* 745–751.

Guilford, J. P. (1967). *The structure of intellect.* New York: McGraw-Hill.

Gump, B., & Matthews, K. (2000 March). *Annual vacations, health, and death.* Paper presented at the meeting of American Psychosomatic Society, Savannah, GA.

Gunnar, M. (in press). Early adversity and the development of stress reactivity and regulation. In C. A. Nelson (Ed.). *The effects of adversity on neurobehavioral development: Minnesota Symposia on Child Psychology* (Vol. 31). Mahwah, NJ: Erlbaum.

Gunnar, M. R., Malone, S., & Fisch, R. O. (1987). The psychobiology of stress and coping in the human neonate: Studies of the adrenocortical activity in response to stress in the first week of life. In T. Field, P. McCabe, & N. Scheiderman (Eds.). *Stress and coping.* Hillsdale, NJ: Erlbaum.

Gur, R. C., Mozley, L. H., Mozley, P. D., Resnick, S. M., Karp, J. S., Alavi, A., Arnold, S. E., & Gur, R. E. (1995). Sex differences in regional cerebral glucose metabolism during a resting state. *Science, 267,* 528–531.

Gurdal, H., Friedman, E., & Johnson, M. D. (1995). Effects of dietary restriction on the change in aortic adrenocepter mediated responses during aging in Fischer 344 rats. *Journal of Gerontology: Biological Sciences, 50A,* B67–B71.

Gutmann, D. L. (1975). Parenthood: A key to the comparative study of the life cycle. In N. Datan & L. Ginsberg (Eds.), *Life-span developmental psychology: Normative life crises.* New York: Academic Press.

Guttentag, M., & Bray, H. (1976). *Undoing sex stereotypes: Research and resources for educators.* New York: McGraw-Hill.

Guyer, B. P. (2000). *ADHD: Achieving success in school and life.* Boston: Allyn & Bacon.

H

Hack, M. H., Klein, N. K., & Taylor, H. G. (1995, Spring). Long-term developmental outcomes of low birth weight infants. *Future of Children, 5,* 176–196.

Hadley, E.C., Dutta, C., Finkelstein, J., Harris, T., Lane, M., oth, G., Sherman, S., & Starke-Reed, P. (2001). Human implications of caloric restriction's effects on aging in laboratory animals. *Journal of Gerontology, 56A, Supplement,* 5–7.

Hagestad, G. O. (1985). Continuity and connectedness. In V. L. Bengston (Ed.), *Grandparenthood.* Beverly Hills, CA: Sage.

Haight, W. L., & Miller, P. J. (1993). *Pretending at home.* Albany: State University of New York Press.

Haith, M. H. (1991, April). *Setting a path for the 90s: Some goals and challenges in infant-sensory and perceptual development.* Paper presented at the Society for Research in Child Development, Seattle.

Haith, M. M., & Benson, J. B. (1998). Infant cognition. In W. Damon (Ed.), *Handbook of child psychology* (5th ed., Vol. 2). New York: Wiley.

Haith, M. M., Hazen, C., & Goodman, G. S. (1988). Expectation and anticipation of dynamic visual events by 3.5 month old babies. *Child Development, 59,* 467–479.

Hakuta, K., & Garcia, E. E. (1989). Bilingualism and education. *American Psychologist, 44,* 374–379.

Hall, R. T. (2000). Prevention of premature birth: Do pediatricians have a role? *Pediatrics, 105,* 1137–1140.

Hallahan, D. P., & Kaufman, J. M. (2000). *Exceptional learners* (8th ed.). Boston: Allyn & Bacon.

Halonen, J., & Santrock, J. W. (1999). *Psychology: Contexts and applications.* New York: McGraw-Hill.

Halpern, I. F., & Brand, K. L. (1999, April). *The role of temperament in children's emotion reactions and coping responses to stress.* Paper presented at the meeting of the Society for Research in Child Development, Albuquerque.

Hamburg, D. A. (1997). Meeting the essential requirements for healthy adolescent development in a transforming world. In R. Takanishi & D. Hamburg (Eds.), *Preparing adolescents for the 21st century.* New York: Cambridge University Press.

Hammer, L. B., Neal, M. B., & Brockwood, K. (1999, November). *Effects of work-family conflict on work attendance and performance among couple in the sandwiched generation.* Paper presented at the meeting of the Gerontological Association of America, San Francisco.

Han, S. K., & Moen, P. (1998). *Clocking out: Multiplex time use in retirement.* Bronfenbrenner Life Course Center Working Paper Series #98-03m. Ithaca, NY: Cornell University.

Hans, S. (1989, April). *Infant behavioral effects of prenatal exposure to methadone.* Paper presented at the biennial meeting of the Society for Research in Child Development, Kansas City.

Harkins, S. W., Price, D. D., & Martinelli, M. (1986). Effects of age on pain perception. *Journal of Gerontology, 41,* 58–63.

Harkness, S., & Super, E. M. (1995). Culture and parenting. In M. H. Bornstein (Ed.), *Handbook of parenting* (Vol. 3). Hillsdale, NJ: Erlbaum.

Harlow, H. F., & Zimmerman, R. R. (1959). Affectional responses in the infant monkey. *Science, 130,* 421–432.

Harlow, R. E., & Cantor, N. (1996). Still participating after all these years: A study of life task participation in later life. *Journal of Personality and Social Psychology, 71,* 1235–1249.

Harris, G., Thomas, A., & Booth, D. A. (1990). Development of salt taste in infancy. *Developmental Psychology, 26,* 534–538.

Harris, J. R. (1998). *The nurture assumption: Why children turn out the way they do: Parents matter less than you think and peers matter more.* New York: Free Press.

Harris, L. (1975). *The myth and reality of aging in America.* Washington, DC: National Council on Aging.

Harris, L. (1987, September 3). The latchkey child phenomena. *Dallas Morning News,* pp. 1A, 10A.

Harris, L. (1997). *A national poll of children and exercise.* Washington, DC: Lou Harris & Associates.

Harris, T., Koyar, M. G., Suzman, R., Kleinman, J. C., & Feldman, J. J. (1989). Longitudinal study of physical ability in the oldest old. *American Journal of Public Health, 79,* 698–702.

Hart, B., & Risley, T. R. (1995). *Meaningful differences.* Baltimore, MD: Paul Brookes.

Hart, C. H., Burts, D. C., Durland, M. A., Charlesworth, R., DeWolf, M., & Fleege, P. O. (1998). Stress behaviors and activity type participation of preschoolers in more and less developmentally appropriate classrooms: SES and sex differences. *Journal Research in Childhood Education, 12,* 176–196.

Hart, C. H., Charlesworth, R., Burts, D. C., & DeWolf, M. (1993, March). *The relationship of attendance in developmentally appropriate or inappropriate kindergarten classrooms to first-grade behavior.* Paper presented at the biennial meeting of the Society for Research in Child Development, New Orleans.

Harter, S. (1990). Self and identity development. In S. S. Feldman & G. R. Elliott (Eds.), *At the threshold: The developing adolescent.* Cambridge, MA: Harvard University Press.

Harter, S. (1998). The development of serf-representations. In W. Damon (Ed.), *Handbook of child psychology* (5th ed., Vol. 3). New York: Wiley.

Harter, S. (1999). *The construction of the self.* New York: Guilford.

Harter, S., & Marold, D. B. (1992). Psychosocial risk factors contributing to adolescent suicide ideation. In G. Noam & S. Borst (Eds.), *Child and adolescent suicide.* San Francisco: Jossey-Bass.

Harter, S., Waters, P., & Whitesell, N. (1996, March). *False self behavior and lack of voice among adolescent males and females.* Paper presented at the meeting of the Society for Research on Adolescence, Boston.

Harter, S., & Whitesell, N. (2001, April). *What we have learned from Columbine: The impact of self-esteem on suicidal and violent ideation among adolescents.* Paper presented at the meeting of the Society for Research in Child Development, Minneapolis.

Hartmann, D. P., & George, T. P. (1999). Design, measurement, and analysis in developmental research. In M. H. Bornstein & M. E. Lamb (Eds.), *Developmental psychology: An advanced textbook* (4th ed.). Mahwah, NJ: Erlbaum.

Hartshorne, H., & May, M. S. (1928–1930). *Moral studies in the nature of character: Studies in the nature of character.* New York: Macmillan.

Hartup, W. W. (1983). The peer system. In P. H. Mussen (Ed.), *Handbook of child psychology* (4th ed., Vol. 4). New York: Wiley.

Hartup, W. W. (1996). The company they keep: Friendships and their development significance. *Child Development, 67,* 1–13.

Hartup, W. W. (1999, April). *Peer relations and the growth of the individual child.* Paper presented at the meeting of the Society for Research in Child Development, Albuquerque.

Hartup, W. W. (2000). Middle childhood: Socialization and social context. In A. Kazdin (Ed.), *Encyclopedia of psychology.* Washington, DC, & New York: American Psychological Association and Oxford University Press.

Hartup, W. W., & Laursen, B. (1999). Relationships as developmental contexts: Retrospective themes and contemporary issues. In W. Andrew Collins & B. Laursen (Eds.), *Relationships as developmental contexts.* Mahwah, NJ: Erlbaum.

Hartup, W. W., & Stevens, N. (1997). Friendships and adaptation in the life course. *Psychological Bulletin, 121,* 355–370.

Hauck, S.J., & Bartke, A. (2001). Free radical defenses in the liver and kidney of human growth hormone transgenic mice. *Journal of Gerontology, 56A No.4,* B153–B162.

Hawkins, J. A., & Berndt, T. J. (1985, April). *Adjustment following the transition to junior high school.* Paper presented at the biennial meeting of the Society for Research in Child Development, Toronto.

Hawranik, P.G., & Strain, L.A. (2001). Cognitive impairment, disruptive behaviors, and home care utilization, *Western Journal of Nursing Research, 23,* 148–162.

Hayflick, L. (1975, September). Why grow old? *Stanford Magazine,* pp. 36–43.

Hayflick, L. (1977). The cellular basis for biological aging. In C. E. Finch & L. Hayflick (Eds.), *Handbook of the biology of aging.* New York: Van Nostrand.

Haynie, D. A., Berg, S., Johansson, B., Gatz, M., & Zarit, S.H. (2001). Symptoms of depression in the oldest old: A longitudinal study. *Journal of Gerontology, 56B, No.2,* P111–P118.

Hayslip, B. (1996). Hospice. In J. E. Birren (Ed.), *Encyclopedia of gerontology* (Vol. 1). San Diego: Academic Press.

Hayslip, B., Edmondson, R., & Guarnaccia, C. (1999, November). *Religiousness, perceptions of funerals, and bereavement adjustment in adulthood.* Paper presented at the meeting of the Gerontological Society of America, San Francisco.

Hayward, M. D., Friedman, S., & Chen, H. (1996). Race inequities in men's retirement. *Journal of Gerontology, 51A,* S1–S10.

Hazan, C., & Shaver, P. R. (1987). Romantic love conceptualized as an attachment process. *Journal of Personality and Social Psychology, 52,* 522–524.

Heath, S. B., & McLaughlin, M. W. (Eds.). (1993). *Identity and inner-city youth.* New York: Teacher College Press.

Heckhausen, J. (in press). *Developmental regulation in adulthood: Age-normative and sociostructural constraints as adaptive challenges.* New York: Cambridge University Press.

Helson, R. (1997, August). *Personality change: When is it adult development?* Paper presented at the meeting of the American Psychological Association, Chicago.

Helson, R., Mitchell, V., & Moane, G. (1984). Personality change in women from college to midlife. *Journal of Personality and Social Psychology, 53,* 176–186.

Helson, R., & Wink, P. (1992). Personality change in women from the early 40s to early 50s. *Psychology and Aging, 7,* 46–55.

Henderson, J. M. T., & France, K. G. (1999, April). *Sleep patterns in the first year of life: Developmental pathways.* Paper presented at the meeting of the Society for Research in Child Development, Albuquerque.

Hendry, J. (1995). *Understanding Japanese society.* London: Routledge.

Henninger, M. L. (1999). *Teaching young children* [illegible] OH: Merrill.

Herek, G. (2000). Homosexuality. In A. Kazdin (Ed.), *Encyclopedia of psychology.* Washington, DC, & New York: American Psychological Association and Oxford University Press.

Herrill, R. (1999). Sexual orientation and suicidality. *Archives of General Psychiatry, 56,* 867–884. Office of Juvenile Justice and Prevention. (1999). *Juvenile offenders and victims: 1999. National Report.* Washington, DC: Author.

Herrnstein, R. J., & Murray, C. (1994). *The bell curve: Intelligence and class structure in modern life.* New York: Free Press.

Hetherington. E. M. (1989). Coping with family transitions: Winners, losers, and survivors. *Child Development, 60,* 1–14.

Hetherington, E. M. (1993). An overview of the Virginia Longitudinal Study of Divorce and Remarriage with a focus on early adolescence. *Journal of Family Psychology, 7,* 39–56.

Hetherington, E. M. (1995, March). *The changing American family and the well-being of children.* Paper presented at the meeting of the Society for Research in Child Development, Indianapolis.

Hetherington, E. M. (1999). Social capital and the development of youth from non-divorced, divorced, and remarried families. In W. A. Collins & B. Laursen (Eds.), *Relationships as developmental contexts.* Mahwah, NJ: Erlbaum.

Hetherington, E. M. (2000). Divorce. In A. Kazdin (Ed.), *Encyclopedia of psychology.* Washington, DC, & New York: American Psychological Association and Oxford University Press.

Hetherington, E. M., Bridges, M., & Insabella, G. M. (1998). What matters? What does not? Five perspectives on the association between marital transitions and children's adjustment. *American Psychologist, 53,* 167–184.

Hetherington, E. M., & Clingempeel, W. G. (1992). Coping with marital transitions: A family systems perspective. *Monographs of the Society for Research in Child Development, 57*(2–3, Serial No. 227).

Hetherington, E. M., & Jodl, K. M. (1994). Stepfamilies as settings for child development. In A. Booth & J. Dunn (Eds.), *Stepfamilies: Who benefits? Who does not?* Hillsdale, NJ: Erlbaum.

Hetherington, E. M., Reiss, D., & Plomin, R. (Eds.). (1994). *Separate social worlds of siblings: The impact of nonshared environment on development.* Hillsdale, NJ: Erlbaum.

Hetherington, E. M., & Stanley-Hagan, M. M. (1995). Parenting in divorced and remarried families. In M. H. Bornstein (Ed.), *Children and parenting* (Vol. 4). Hillsdale, NJ: Erlbaum.

Heuwinkel, M. K. (1996). New ways of learning 5 New ways of teaching. *Childhood Education, 72,* 27–31.

Heward, W. L. (2000). *Exceptional children.* Columbus, OH: Merrill.

Higgins, A., Power, C., & Kohlberg, L. (1983, April). *Moral atmosphere and moral judgment.* Paper presented at the biennial meeting of the Society for Research in Child Development, Detroit.

Hikida, R. S., Staron, R. S., Hagerman, F. C., Wlash, S., Kaiser, E., Shell, S., & Hervey, S. (2000). Effects of [illegible] training [illegible] untrained older men. *Journal of Gerontology: Medical Sciences, 55A,* B347–B354.

Hill, C. R., & Stafford, F. P. (1980). Parental care of children: Time diary estimate of quantity, predictability, and variety. *Journal of Human Resources, 15,* 219–239.

Hill, J. O., & Trowbridge, F. L. (1998). Childhood obesity: Future directions and research priorities. *Pediatrics, 101,* 570–574.

Hill, P. C., & Butter, E. M. (1995). The role of religion in promoting physical health. *Journal of Psychology and Christianity, 14,* 141–155.

Himes, C. L., Hogan, D. P., & Eggebeen, D. J. (1996). Living arrangements of minority elders. *Journal of Gerontology. 51A,* S42–S48.

Hirsch, B. J., & Rapkin, B. D. (1987). The transition to junior high school: A longitudinal study of self-esteem, psychological symptomatology, school life, and social support. *Child Development, 58,* 1235–1243.

Hirsch-Pasek, K., Hyson, M., Rescorla, L., & Cone, J. (1989, April). *Hurrying children: How does it affect their academic, social, creative, and emotional development?* Paper presented at the Society for Research in Child Development meeting, Kansas City.

Hobel, C. J., Dunkel-Schetter, C., Roesch, S. C., Castro, L. C., & Arora, C. P. (1999). Maternal plasma corticotrophin-releasing hormone associated with stress at 20 weeks' gestation in pregnancies ending in preterm delivery. *American Journal of Obstetrics and Gynecology, 180,* S257–S263.

Hochschild, A., & Machung, A. (1989). *The second shift.* New York: Viking.

Hodapp, R. N., & Zigler, E. (1999). Intellectual development and mental retardation—Some continuing controversies. In M. Anderson (Ed.), *The development of intelligence.* Philadelphia: Psychology Press.

Hodges, J. R. (2000). Memory in the dementias. In E. Tulving & F. I. M. Craik (Ed.), *The Oxford handbook of memory.* New York: Oxford University Press.

Hodges, E. V. E., Boivin, M., Vitaro, F., & Bukowski, W. M. (1999). The power of friendship: Protection against an escalating cycle of peer victimization. *Developmental Psychology, 35,* 94–101.

Hodges, E. V. E., & Perry, D. G. (1999). Personal and interpersonal antecedents and consequences of victimization by peers. *Journal of Personality and Social Psychology, 76,* 677–685.

Hoff-Ginsberg, E., & Lerner, S. (1999, April). *The nature of vocabulary differences related to socioeconomic status at two and four years.* Paper presented at the meeting of the Society for Research in Child Development, Albuquerque.

Hoff-Ginsburg, E., & Tardif, T. (1995). Socioeconomic status and parenting. In M. H. Bornstein (Ed.), *Handbook of parenting* (Vol. 1). Hillsdale, NJ: Erlbaum.

Hoffman, L. W. (1989). Effects of maternal employment in two-parent families. *American Psychologist, 44,* 283–293.

Hoffman, L. W., & Youngblade, L. M. (1999). *Mothers at work: Effects on children's* [illegible] New York: Cambridge.

Hoffman, M. L. (1970). Moral development. In P. H. Mussen (Ed.), *Manual of child psychology* (3rd ed., Vol. 2). New York: Wiley.

Hoffman, S., Foster, E., & Furstenberg, F. (1993). Reevaluating the costs of teenage childbearing. *Demography, 30,* 1–13.

Hogan, D. M., & Tudge, J. (1999). Implications of Vygotsky's theory for peer learning. In A. M. O'Donnell & A. King (Eds.), *Cognitive perspectives on peer learning.* Mahwah, NJ: Erlbaum.

Holland, J. L. (1987). Current status of Holland's theory of careers: Another perspective. *Career Development Quarterly, 36,* 24–30.

Hollins, E. R., & Oliver, E. I. (1999). *Pathways to success in school.* Mahwah, NJ: Erlbaum.

Holmbeck, G. N. (1996). A model of family relational transformations during the transition to adolescence: Parent-adolescent conflict and adaptation. In J. A. Graber, J. Brooks-Gunn, & A. C. Petersen (Eds.), *Transitions through adolescence.* Hillsdale, NJ: Erlbaum.

Holmbeck, G. N., Paikoff, R. L., & Brooks-Gunn, J. (1995). Parenting adolescents. In M. H. Bornstein (Ed.), *Children and parenting* (Vol. 1). Hillsdale, NJ: Erlbaum.

Holmes, T. H., & Rahe, R. H. (1967). The social readjustment rating scale. *Journal of Psychosomatic Research, 11,* 213–218.

Holtzmann, D. M., Bales, K. R., Wu, S., Bhat, P., Parsadanian, M., Fagan, A. M., Chang, L. K., Sun, Y., & Pauyl, S. M. (1999). Expression of human apolipoprotein E reduces amyloid-beat deposition in a mouse model of Alzheimer's disease. *Journal of Clinical Investigation, 103,* R15–R21.

Hopkins, B. (1991). Facilitating early motor development: An intracultural study of West Indian mothers and their infants living in

Britain. In J. K. Nugent, B. M. Lester, & T. B. Brazelton (Eds.), *The cultural context of infancy: Vol. 2. Multicultural and interdisciplinary approaches to parent-infant relations* (pp. 93–143). Norwood, NJ: Ablex.

Hopkins, B., & Westra, T. (1988). Maternal handling and motor development: An intracultural study. *Genetic Psychology Monographs, 14,* 377–420.

Hopkins, B., & Westra, T. (1990). Motor development, maternal expectations, and the role of handling. *Infant Behavior and Development, 13,* 117–122.

Hopkins, J. R. (2000). Erikson, E. H. (2000). In A. Kazdin (Ed.), *Encyclopedia of psychology.* Washington, DC, & New York: American Psychological Association and Oxford University Press.

Hoppu, U., Kalliomaki, M., Laiho, K., & Isolauri, E. (2001). Breast milk—immunomodulatory signals against allergenic diseases, *Allergy, 56* 23–26.

Horn, J. L., & Donaldson, G. (1980). Cognitive development II: Adulthood development of human abilities. In O. G. Brim & J. Kagan (Eds.), *Constancy and change in human development.* Cambridge, MA: Harvard University Press.

Horney, K. (1967). *Feminine psychology.* New York: W. W. Norton.

Hortobagyi, T., Tunnel, D., Moody, J., Beam, S., & DeVita, P. (2001). Low- or high-intensity strength training restores impaired quadraceps force accuracy and steadiness in aged adults. *Journal of Gerontology, 56A, No.2,* B38–B44.

Hotchner, T. (1997). *Pregnancy and childbirth.* New York: Avon.

House, J. S. (1998). Commentary: Age, work, and well-being. In K. W. Schaie & C. Schooler (Eds.), *The impact of work on older adults.* New York: Springer.

House, J. S., Kessler, R. C., Herzog, R. C., Mero, R. P., Kinney, A. M., & Breslow, M. J. (1992). Social stratification, age, and health. In K. W. Schaie, D. Blazer, & J. S. House (Eds.), *Aging, health behaviors, and health outcomes.* Mahwah, NJ: Erlbaum.

House, J. S., Landis, K. R., & Umberson, D. (1988). Social relationships and health. *Science, 241,* 540–545.

Howes, C. (1988, April). *Can the age of entry and the quality of infant child care predict behaviors in kindergarten?* Paper presented at the International Conference on Infant Studies, Washington, DC.

Hoyer, W. J., Rybash, J. M., & Roodin, P. A. (1999). *Adult development and aging* (4th ed.). New York: McGraw-Hill.

Huebner, A. M., Garrod, A. C., & Snarey, J. (1990, March). *Moral development in Tibetan Buddhist monks: A cross-cultural study of adolescents and young adults in Nepal.* Paper presented at the meeting of the Society for Research in Adolescence, Atlanta.

Huesmann, L. R. (1986). Psychological processes promoting the relation between exposure to media violence and aggressive behavior by the viewer. *Journal of Social Issues, 42,* 125–139.

Huesmann, L. R., Eron, L. D., Klein, R., Brice, P., & Fischer, P. (1983). Mitigating the imitation of aggressive behaviors by changing children's attitudes about media violence. *Journal of Personality and Social Psychology, 44,* 899–910.

Hughes, P. C. Reported in Fozard, J. L., & Popkin, S. J. (1978). Optimizing adult development. *American Psychologist, 33,* 975–989.

Hultsch, D. F., Hammer, M., & Small, B. J. (1993). Age differences in cognitive performance in later life: Relationships to self-reported health and activity life style. *Journal of Gerontology, 48,* P1–P11.

Hultsch, D. F., Hertzog, C., Small, B. J., & Dixon, R. A. (1999). Use it or lose it: Engaged lifestyle as a buffer of cognitive decline in aging? *Psychology and Aging, 14,* 245–263.

Hultsch, D. F., & Plemons, J. K. (1979). Life events and life-span development. In P. B. Baltes & O. G. Brim (Eds.), *Life-span development and behavior.* New York: Academic Press.

Hummert, M. L., Garstka, T. A., Shaner, J. L., & Strahm, S. (1994). Stereotypes of the elderly held by young, middle-aged, and elderly adults. *Journal of Gerontology, 49,* P240–P249.

Hummert, M.L., & Nussbaum, J.F. (Eds.) (2001). *Aging, communication, and health.* Mahwah, NJ: Erlbaum.

Humpheys, K. (2000). Alcoholics Anonymous. In A. Kazdin (Ed.), *Encyclopedia of psychology.* Washington, DC, & New York: American Psychological Association and Oxford University Press.

Hungerford, T.L. (2001). The economic consequences of widowhood on elderly women in the United States and Germany. *The Gerontologist, 41, No.1,* 103–110.

Hurt, H., Malmud, E., Brodsky, N. L., & Giannetta, J. M. (1999, May). *What happens when the child with* in utero *cocaine-exposure (COC) goes to school?* Paper presented at the meeting of the Society for Pediatric Research, San Francisco.

Huston, A. (1999, August). *Employment interventions for parents in poverty: How do children fare?* Paper presented at the meeting of the Society for Research in Child Development, Boston.

Huston, A. C. (1983). Sex-typing. In P. H. Mussen (Ed.). *Handbook of child psychology* (4th ed., Vol. 4). New York: Wiley.

Huston, A. C., McLoyd, V. C., & Coll, C. G. (1994). Children and poverty: issues in contemporary research. *Child Development, 65,* 275–282.

Huston, A. C., Seigle, J., & Bremer, M. (1983, April). *Family environment and television use by preschool children.* Paper presented at the Society for Research in Child Development meeting, Detroit.

Huston, T. L., Neihuis, S., & Smith, S. (1997, November). *Divergent experiential and behavioral pathways leading to marital distress and divorce.* Paper presented at the meeting of the National Council on Family Relations, Washington, DC.

Huyck, M. H. (1999). Gender roles and gender identity in midlife. In S. L. Willis & J. D. Reid (Eds.), *Life in the middle.* San Diego: Academic Press.

Huyck, M. H., & Hoyer, W. J. (1982). *Adult development and aging.* Belmont, CA: Wadsworth.

Hy, L., & Loevinger, J. (1996). *Measuring ego development.* Hillsdale, NJ: Erlbaum.

Hyde, J. S. (1993). Meta-analysis and the psychology of women. In F. L. Denmark & M. A. Paludi (Eds.), *Handbook on the psychology of women.* Westport, CT: Greenwood.

Hyde, J. S., & DeLamater, J. D. (1999). *Understanding human sexuality* (7th ed.). New York: McGraw-Hill.

Hyde, J. S., & Plant, E. A. (1995). Magnitude of psychological gender differences: Another side of the story. *American Psychologist, 50,* 159–161.

Hyman, I.E., & Loftus, E.F. (2001). False childhood memories and eye-witness errors. In M.L Eisen, J.A. Quas, & G.S. Goodman, (Eds.) *Memory and suggestibility in the forensic interview.* Mahwah, NJ: Erlbaum.

I

Iannucci, L. (2000). *Birth defects.* New York: Enslow.

Ilola, L. M. (1990). Culture and health. In R. W. Brislin (Ed.), *Applied cross-cultural psychology.* Newbury Park, CA: Sage.

Ingelhart, R., & Rabier, J. (1986). Aspirations adapt to situations—But why are the Belgians so much happier than the French? A cross-cultural analysis of the subjective quality of life. In F. M. Andrews (Ed.), *Research on the quality of life.* Ann Arbor: University of Michigan, Institute of Social Research.

Ingersoll, E. W., & Thoman, E. B. (1999). Sleep/wake states of preterm infants: Stability, developmental change, diurnal variation, and relation with caregiving activity. *Child Development, 170,* 1–10.

Inoff-Germain, G., Arnold, G. S., Nottelmann, E. D., Susman, E. J., Cutler, G. B., & Chrousos, G. P. (1988). Relations between hormone levels and observational measures of aggressive behavior of young adolescents in family interactions. *Developmental Psychology, 24,* 124–139.

Institute for Families in Society. (1997). *Program to combat bullying in schools.* Columbia: University of South Carolina.

Institute of Medicine. (1997, June). *Approaching death: Improving care at the end of life.* Washington, DC: National Academy of Sciences.

Intons-Peterson, M. (1996). Memory aids. In D. Hermann, C. McEvoy, C. Hertzog, P. Hertel, & M. Johnson (Eds.), *Basic and applied memory research* (Vol. 2). Hillsdale, NJ: Erlbaum.

Izard, C. (2000). Affect. In A. Kazdin (Ed.), *Encyclopedia of psychology.* Washington, DC, & New York: American Psychological Association and Oxford University Press.

Izard, C. E. (1982). *Measuring emotions in infants and young children.* New York: Cambridge University Press.

J

Jackson, J. S., Chatters, L. M., & Taylor, R. J. (Eds.). (1993). *Aging in Black America.* Newbury Park, CA: Sage.

Jacobs, J. E., & Potenza, M. (1990, March). *The use of decision-making strategies in late adolescence.* Paper presented at the meeting of the Society for Research in Adolescence, Atlanta.

Jacobs, J. E., & Tanner, J. L. (1999, August). *Stability and change in perceptions of parent-child relationships.* Paper presented at the meeting of the Gerontological Association of America, San Francisco.

Jacobs, J. K., Garnier, H. E., & Weisner, T. (1996, March). *The impact of family life on the process of dropping out of high school.* Paper presented at the meeting of the Society for Research on Adolescence, Boston.

Jacobs, R. H. (1994). His and her aging: Differences, difficulties, dilemmas, delights. *Journal of Geriatric Psychiatry, 27,* 113–128.

Jacobs, S. C., Dosten, T. R., Kasl, S. V., Ostfield, A. M., Berkman, L., & Charpentier, M. P. H. (1987). Attachment theory and multiple dimensions of grief. *Omega, 18,* 41–52.

Jacobson, J. L., Jacobson, S. W., Fein, G. G., Schwartz, P. M., & Dowler, J. (1984). Prenatal exposure to an environmental toxin: A test of the multiple-effects model. *Developmental Psychology, 20,* 523–532.

Jalongo, M. R., & Isenberg, J. P. (2000). *Exploring your role: A practitioner introduction to early childhood education.* Columbus, OH: Merrill.

James, D. K., Steer, P. J., Weiner, C. P., & Gonik, B. (1999). *High risk pregnancy* (3rd ed.). London: Harcourt International.

James, M., Draycott, T., Fox, R., & Read, M. (1999). *Obstetrics and gynecology.* London: Harcourt International.

James, W. (1890/1950). *The principles of psychology.* New York: Dover.

Jecker, N. S. (1996). Ethics and euthanasia. In J. E. Birren (Ed.), *Encyclopedia of gerontology* (Vol. 1). San Diego: Academic Press.

Jeffery, H. E., Megevand, A., Page, H., & Page, M. (1999). Why the prone position is a risk factor in sudden infant death syndrome. *Pediatrics, 104,* 263–269.

Jensen, R. A. (1969). How much can we boost IQ and scholastic achievement? *Harvard Educational Review, 39,* 1–123.

Jerrome, D., & Wenger, G. C. (1999). Stability and change in late-life friendships. *Aging and Society, 19,* 661–676.

Jessor, R., Turbin, M. S., & Costa, F. (1998). Protective factors in adolescent health behavior. *Journal of Personality and Social Psychology, 75,* 788–800.

Jessor, R., Turbin, M. S., & Costa, F. (In press). Risk and protection in successful outcomes among disadvantaged adolescents. *Applied Developmental Science.*

Ji, B. T., Shu, X. O., Linet, M. S., Zheng, W., Wacholde, S., Gao, Y. T., Ying, D. M., & Jin, F. (1997). Paternal cigarette smoking and the risk of childhood cancer among offspring of nonsmoking mothers. *Journal of the National Cancer Institute, 89,* 238–244.

Jiao, S., Ji, G., & Jing, Q. (1996). Cognitive development of Chinese urban only children and children with siblings. *Child Development, 67,* 387–395.

Johnson, B. K. (1996). Older adults and sexuality. A multidimensional perspective. *Journal of Gerontological Nursing, 22,* 6–15.

Johnson, C. (1990, May). The new woman's ethics report. *New Woman,* p. 6.

Johnson, C. L., & Troll, L. E. (1994). Constraints and faciliators to friendships in late late life. *Gerontologist, 34,* 79–87.

Johnson, C. R., & Slomka, G. (2000). Learning, motor, and communication disorders. In M. Herson & R. T. Ammerman (Eds.), *Advanced abnormal child psychology* (2nd ed.). Mahwah, NJ: Erlbaum.

Johnson, D. W. (1990). *Teaching out: Interpersonal effectiveness and self-actualization.* Upper Saddle River, NJ: Prentice Hall.

Johnson, J., Dupuis, V., Musial, D., Hall, G., & Gollnick, D. (2002). *Introduction to the foundations of American Education (12th Ed.).* Boston: Allyn & Bacon.

Johnson, K., Strader, T., Berbaum, M., Bryant, D., Bucholtz, G., Collins, D., & Noe, T. (1996). Reducing alcohol and other drug use by strengthening community, family, and youth resiliency. *Journal of Adolescent Research, 11,* 36–67.

Johnson, M.E. (2001). Infants' initial "knowledge" of the world: A cognitive neuroscience perspective. In F. Lacerda, C. von Hofsten, & M. Heimann (Eds.), *Emerging cognitive abilities in infancy.* Mahwah, NJ: Erlbaum.

Johnson, M. H. (1999). Developmental neuroscience. In M. H. Bornstein & M. E. Lamb (Eds.), *Developmental psychology: An advanced textbook* (4th ed.). Mahwah, NJ: Erlbaum.

Johnson, M. H. (2000). Infancy: Biological processes. In A. Kazdin (Ed.), *Encyclopedia of psychology.* Washington, DC, & New York: American Psychological Association and Oxford University Press.

Johnson, M. K., Beebe, T., Mortimer, J. T., & Snyder, M. (1998). Volunteerism in adolescence: A process perspective. *Journal of Research on Adolescence, 8,* 309–332.

John-Steiner, V., & Mahn, H. (1996). Sociocultural approaches to learning and development: A Vygotskian framework. *Educational Psychologist, 31,* 191–206.

Johnston, C., & Leung, D.W. (2001). Effects of medication, behavioral, and combined treatments on parents' and children's attributions for the behavior of children with attention-deficit hyperactivity disorder, *Journal of Consulting and Clinical Psychology, 69,* 67–76.

Johnston, L., O'Malley, P. M., & Bachman, J. G. (1997, December). *Report of Monitoring the Future Project.* Ann Arbor: University of Michigan, Institute for Social Research.

Johnston, L., O'Malley, P., & Bachman, J. (1999, December 17). *Drug trends in 1999 among American teens are mixed.* Press release, University of Michigan, Institute of Social Research.

Johnston, L. D., Bachman, J. G., & O'Malley, P. M. (1998). Explaining recent increases in students' marijuana use: Impacts of perceived risks and disapproval, 1976 through 1996. *American Journal of Public Health, 88,* 887–892.

Johnston, L. D., O'Malley, P. M., & Bachman, J. G. (1992, January 25). *Most forms of drug use decline among American high school and college students.* News release, Institute of Social Research, University of Michigan, Ann Arbor.

Johnston, L. D., O'Malley, P. M., & Bachman, J. G. (1996). *National survey results on drug use from the Monitoring the Future Study, Vol. 2: College students.* Ann Arbor: University of Michigan, Institute of Social Research.

Johnston, L. D., O'Malley, P. M., & Bachman, J. G. (2000). *The monitoring of the future: National results on adolescent drug use.* Washington, DC: National Institute on Drug Abuse.

Joiner, T. E. (2000). Depression: Current developments and controversies. In S. H. Qualls & N. Abeles (Eds.), *Psychology and the aging revolution.* Washington, DC: American Psychological Association.

Jones, C. J., & Meredith, W. (1996). Patterns of personality change across the life span. *Psychology and Aging, 11,* 57–65.

Jones, G., Riley, M., & Dwyer, T. (2000). Breastfeeding early in life and bone mass in prepubertal children: A longitudinal study. *Osteoporosis International, 11,* 146–152.

Jones, L. (1984). White-black achievement differences: The narrowing gap. *American Psychologist, 39,* 1207–1213.

Jones, M. C. (1965). Psychological correlates of somatic development. *Child Development, 36,* [illegible].

Jones, S. E. (2000). Ethics: An overview. In A. Kazdin (Ed.), *Encyclopedia of psychology.* Washington, DC, & New York: American Psychological Association and Oxford University Press.

Josselson, R. (1996). *On becoming the same age as one's mother.* Paper presented at the meeting of the American Psychological Association, Toronto.

K

Kabitsis, C., Matsouka, O., Harahousou, Y., & Trigonis, I. (1999, November). *The effects of a physical activity program on functional ability among elderly women.* Paper presented at the meeting of the Gerontological Association of America, San Francisco.

Kagan, J. (1984). *The nature of the child.* New York: Basic Books.

Kagan, J. (1987). Perspectives on infancy. In J. D. Osofsky (Ed.), *Handbook on infant development* (2nd ed.). New York: Wiley.

Kagan, J. (1992). Yesterday's promises, tomorrow's promises. *Developmental Psychology, 28,* 990–997.

Kagan, J. (1998). The biology of the child. In W. Damon (Ed.), *Handbook of child psychology* (5th ed., Vol. 3). New York: Wiley.

Kagan, J. (1998). *The power of parents.* Available on the world wide web at: http://psychplace.com.

Kagan, J. (2000). Temperament. In A. Kazdin (Ed.), *Encyclopedia of psychology.* Washington, DC, & New York: American Psychological Association and Oxford University Press.

Kagan, J., Kearsley, R. B., & Zelazo, P. R. (1978). *Infancy.* Cambridge, MA: Harvard University Press.

Kagitcibasi, C. (1996). *Human development across cultures.* Hillsdale, NJ: Erlbaum.

Kahn, R., & Antonucci, T. C. (1980). Convoys over the life course: Attachment, roles, and social support. In P. B. Baltes & O. Brim (Eds.), *Life-span development and behavior.* San Diego: Academic Press.

Kail, R., & Pellegrino, J. W. (1985). *Human intelligence.* New York. W.H. Freeman.

Kalichman, S. (1996). *Answering your questions about AIDS.* Washington, DC: American Psychological Association.

Kalick, S. M., & Hamilton, T. E. (1986). The matching hypothesis reexamined. *Journal of Personality and Social Psychology, 51,* 673–682.

Kalish, R. A. (1981). *Death, grief, and caring relationships.* Monterey, CA: Brooks/Cole.

Kalish, R. A. (1987). Death. In G. L. Maddox (Ed.), *Encyclopedia of aging.* New York: Springer.

Kalish, R. A., & Reynolds, D. K. (1976). *An overview of death and ethnicity.* Farmingdale, NY: Baywood.

Kallio, K. D. (1999, April). *Changing conceptions of nature and nurture: Implications for theory.* Paper presented at the meeting of the Society for Research in Child Development, Albuquerque.

Kaltiala-Heino, R., Rimpela, M, Rantanen, P., & Laippala, P. (2001). Adolescent depression. *Journal of Affective Disorders, 64,* 155–166.

Kamerman, S. B. (1989). Child care, women, work, and the family: An international overview of child-care services and related policies. In J. S. Lande, S. Scarr, & N. Gunzenhauser (Eds.), *Caring for children: Challenge to America.* Hillsdale, NJ: Erlbaum.

Kamii, C. (1985). *Young children reinvent arithmetic: Implications of Piaget's theory.* New York: Teachers College Press.

Kamii, C. (1989). *Young children continue to reinvent arithmetic.* New York: Teachers College Press.

Kamphaus, R. W. (2000). Learning disabilities. In A. Kazdin (Ed.), *Encyclopedia of psychology.* Washington, DC, & New York: American Psychological Association and Oxford University Press.

Kandel, D. B. (1974). The role of parents and peers in marijuana use. *Journal of Social Issues, 30,* 107–135.

Kanner, A. D., Coyne, J. C., Schaefer, C., & Lazarus, R. S. (1981). Comparison of two modes of stress measurement: Daily hassles and uplifts versus major life events. *Journal of Behavioral Medicine, 4,* 1–39.

Kantowitz, B. H., Roediger, H. L., & Elmes, D. G. (2001). *Experimental psychology* (7th ed.). Belmont, CA: Wadsworth.

Kantrowitz, B. (1991, Summer). The good, the bad, and the difference. *Newsweek,* pp. 48–50.

Karns, J.T. (2001). Health, nutrition, and safety. In A. Fogel & G. Bremner (Eds.), *Blackwell handbook of infant development.* London: Blackwell.

Kasper, J. D. (1988). *Aging alone: Profiles and projections.* Report of the Commonwealth Fund Commission: Elderly People Living Alone. Baltimore: Commonwealth Fund Commission.

Kastenbaum, R. (1997). Unpublished review of J. W. Santrock's *Life-Span development,* 7th ed. (New York: McGraw-Hill).

Kastenbaum, R. (2000). *The psychology of death* (3rd ed.). New York: Springer.

Kastenbaum, R. J. (1998). *Death, society, and human experience* (6th ed.). Upper Saddle River, NJ: Prentice Hall.

Katchadoourian, H. (1987). *Fifty: Midlife in perspective.* New York: W. H. Freeman.

Katz, L., & Chard, S. (1989). *Engaging the minds of young children: The project approach.* Norwood, NJ: Ablex.

Kaugers, A. S., Russ, S. W., & Singer, L. T. (2000, May). *Self-regulation among cocaine-exposed four-year-old children.* Paper presented at the joint meetings of the Pediatric Academic Societies and the American Academy of Pediatrics, Boston.

Kausler, D. H. (1994). *Learning and memory in normal aging.* San Diego: Academic Press.

Keating, D. P. (1990). Adolescent thinking. In S. S. Feldman & G. R. Elliott (Eds.), *At the threshold: The developing adolescent.* Cambridge, MA: Harvard University Press.

Keener, D. C., & Boykin, K. A. (1996, March). *Parental control, autonomy, and ego development.* Paper presented at the meeting of the Society for Research on Adolescence, Boston.

Keller, A., Ford, L., & Meacham, J. (1978). Dimensions of self-concept in preschool children. *Developmental Psychology, 14,* 483–489.

Kelly, J. (2000). Sexually transmitted diseases. In A. Kazdin (Ed.), *Encyclopedia of psychology.* Washington, DC, & New York: American Psychological Association and Oxford University Press.

Kelly, J. R. (1996). Leisure. In J. E. Birren (Ed.), *Encyclopedia of gerontology* (Vol. 2). San Diego: Academic Press.

Kempermann, G., Kuhn, H. G., & Gage, F. H. (1997). More hippocampal neurons in adult mice living in an enriched environment. *Nature, 386,* 493–495.

Kennedy, G. J. (2001). *Geriatric mental health care.* New York: Guilford Press.

Kennell, J. H., & McGrath, S. K. (1999). Commentary: Practical and humanistic lessons from the third world for perinatal caregivers everywhere. *Birth, 26,* 9–10.

Kenyon, G. M., Ruth, J. R., & Mader, W. (1999). Elements of a narrative gerontology. In V. L. Bengtson, & K. W. Schaie (Eds.), *Handbook of theories of aging.* New York: Springer.

Kephart, W. M. (1967). Some correlates of romantic love. *Journal of Marriage and the Family, 29,* 470–474.

Kerig, P. K., & Lindahl, K. M. (Eds.) (2000). *Family observational coding systems.* Mahwah, NJ: Erlbaum.

Kerr, M. (2001). Culture as a context for temperament. In T.D. Wachs & G.A. Kohnstamm (Eds.), *Temperament in context.* Mahwah, NJ: Erlbaum.

Kerig, P.K., & Lindahl, K.M. (Eds.) (2001). *Family observational coding systems.* Mahwah, NJ: Erlbaum.

Kessen, W., Haith, M. M., & Salapatck, P. (1970). Human infancy. In P. H. Mussen (Ed.). *Manual of child psychology* (3rd ed., Vol. 1). New York: Wiley.

Kiecolt-Glaser, J. K., & Glaser, R. (1988). Behavioral influences on immune function. In T. Field, P. McCabe, & N. Schneiderman (Eds.), *Stress and coping across development.* Hillsdale, NJ: Erlbaum.

Kilbride, H. W., Thorstad, K. K., & Daily, D. K. (2000, May). *Preschool outcome for extremely low birth weight infants compared to their full term siblings.* Paper presented at the joint meeting of the Pediatric Academic Societies and American Academy of Pediatrics, Boston.

Kimble, M., McFadden, S. H., Ellor, J. W., & Seeber, J. J. (Eds.). (in press). *Handbook on religion, spirituality, and aging.* Minneapolis: Fortress Press.

Kimmel, A. (1996). *Ethical issues in behavioral research.* Cambridge, MA: Blackwell.

King, A. (2000). Exercise and physical activity. In A. Kazdin (Ed.), *Encyclopedia of psychology.* Washington, DC, & New York: American Psychological Association and Oxford University Press.

King, N. (1982). School uses of materials traditionally associated with children's play. *Theory and Research in Social Education, 10,* 17–27.

Kinsey, A. C., Pomeroy, W. B., & Martin, E. E. (1948). *Sexual behavior in the human male.* Philadelphia: W. B. Saunders.

Kirk, K.L. (2001). Dietary restriction and aging. *Journal of Gerontology, 56A, No.2,* B123–B129.

Kirkpatrick, L. A., & Hazan, C. (1994). Attachment styles and close relationships: A four-year prospective study. *Personal Relationships, 1,* 123–142.

Kisilevsky, B. S. (1995). The influence stimulus and subject variables on human fetal responses to sound and vibration. In J-P Lecaunet, W. P. Fifer, M. A. Krasnegor, & W. P. Smotherman (Eds.), *Fetal development.* Hillsdale, NJ: Erlbaum.

Kitchener, K. S., & King, P. M. (1981). Reflective judgment: Concepts of justification and their relationship to age and education. *Journal of Applied Developmental Psychology, 2,* 89–111.

Kivnick, H. Q., & Sinclair, H. M. (1996). Grandparenthood. In J. E. Birren (Ed.), *Encyclopedia of gerontology* (Vol. 1). San Diego: Academic Press.

Klaczynski, P. A., & Narasimham, G. (1998). Development of scientific reasoning biases: Cognitive versus ego-protective explanations. *Developmental Psychology, 34,* 175–187.

Klaus, M., & Kennell, H. H. (1976). *Maternal-infant bonding.* St. Louis: Mosby.

Klaus, M. H., Kennell, J. H., & Klaus, P. H. (1993). *Mothering the mother.* Reading, MA: Addison-Wesley.

Kliegl, R., & Baltes, P. B. (1987). Theory-guided analysis of mechanisms of development and aging through testing-the-limits and research on expertise. In C. Schooler & K. W. Schaie (Eds.), *Cognitive functioning and social structure over the life course.* Norwood, NJ: Ablex.

Kliegl, R., Smith, J., & Baltès, P. B. (1990). On the locus and process of magnification of age differences during mnemonic training. *Developmental Psychology, 26,* 894–904.

Klish, W. J. (1998, September). Childhood obesity. *Pediatrics in Review, 19,* 312–315.

Klitzing, K. V., Simoni, H., & Burgin, D. (1999, April). *Mother, father, and infant: The triad from pre-natal representations to post-natal interactions.* Paper presented at the meeting of the Society for Research in Child Development, Albuquerque.

Klonoff-Cohen, H. S., Edelstein, S. L., Lefkowitz, E. S., Srinivasan, I. P., Kaegi, D., Chang, J. C., and Wiley, K. J. (1995). The effect of passive smoke and tobacco exposure through breast milk on sudden infant death syndrome. *Journal of the American Medical Association, 293,* 795–798.

Knight, B. G., Teri, L., Wohlford, P., & Santos, J. (Eds.). (1996). *Mental health services for older adults.* Washington, DC: American Psychological Association.

Knight, J.A. (2000). The biochemistry of aging. *Advances in Clinical Chemistry, 35,* 1–62.

Kobak, R. (1999). The emotional dynamics of disruptions in attachment relationships: Implications for theory, research, and clinical intervention. In J. Cassidy & P. Shaver (Eds.), *Handbook of attachment.* New York: Guilford.

Kobasa, S., Maddi, S., & Kahn, S. (1982). Hardiness and health: A prospective study. *Journal of Personality and Social Psychology, 42,* 168–177.

Kobasa, S., Maddi, S., Puccetti, M., & Zola, M. (1985). Relative effectiveness of hardiness, exercise, and social support as resources against illness. *Journal of Psychosomatic Research, 29,* 525–533.

Kochanska, G. (1999, April). *Applying a [illegible] development.* Paper presented at the meeting of the Society for Research in Child Development, Albuquerque.

Kochhar, C. A., West, L., & Taymans, J. M. (2000). *Handbook for successful inclusion.* Columbus, OH: Merrill.

Koenig, G. (Ed.) (1998). *Handbook of religion and mental health.* San Diego: Academic Press.

Koenig, H. G. (1992). Religion and prevention of illness in later life. In K. I. Pargament, K. Maton, & R. E. Hess (Eds.), *Religion and prevention in mental health.* New York: Haworth.

Koenig, H. G., & Blazer, D. G. (1996). Depression. In J. E. Birren (Ed.), *Encyclopedia of gerontology* (Vol. 1). San Diego: Academic Press.

Koenig, H. G., Cohen, H. J., Blazer, D. G., Pieper, C., Meador, K. G., Shelp, F., Goldi, V., & DiPasquale, R. (1992). Religious coping and depression in elderly hospitalized medically ill men. *American Journal of Psychiatry, 149,* 1693–1700.

Koenig, H. G., Larson, D. B. (1998). Religion and mental health. In H. S. Friedman (Ed.), *Encyclopedia of mental health* (Vol. 3). San Diego: Academic Press.

Koenig, H. G., Smiley, M., & Gonzales, J. A. T. (1988). *Religion, health, and aging.* New York: Greenwood Press.

Koenigsberger, M. R. (2000). Advances in neonatal neurology: 1950–2000. *Review of Neurology, 31,* 202–211.

Kohl, H. W., & Hobbs, K. E. (1998). Development of physical activity behaviors among children and adolescents. *Pediatrics, 101,* 549–554.

Kohlberg, L. (1958). *The development on modes of moral thinking and choice in the years 10 to 16.* Unpublished doctoral dissertation, University of Chicago.

Kohlberg, L. (1966). A cognitive-developmental analysis of children's sex-role concepts and attitudes. In E. E. Maccoby (Ed.), *The development of sex differences.* Palo Alto, CA: Stanford University Press.

Kohlberg, L. (1969). Stage and sequence: The cognitive-developmental approach to socialization. In D. A. Goslin (Ed.), *Handbook of socialization theory and research.* Chicago: Rand McNally.

Kohlberg, L. (1976). Moral stages and moralization: The cognitive-developmental approach. In T. Lickona (Ed.), *Moral development and behavior.* New York: Holt, Rinehart & Winston.

Kohlberg, L. (1986). A current statement of some theoretical issues. In S. Modgil & C. Modgil (Eds.), *Lawrence Kohlberg.* Philadelphia: Falmer.

Kohn, M., & Golden, N.H. (2001). Eating disorders in children and adolescents. *Pediatric Drugs, 3,* 91–99

Kopp, C. B. (1992, October). *Trends and directions in studies of developmental risk.* Paper presented at the 27th Minnesota Symposium on Child Psychology, University of Minnesota, Minneapolis.

Kosnik, W., Winslow, L., Kline, D., Rasinski, K., & Sekuler, R. (1989). Visual changes in daily life through adulthood. *Journal of Gerontology: Psychological Sciences, 43,* P63–P70.

Koss, M., & Boeschen, L. (1998). Rape. In H.S. Friedman (Ed.), *Encyclopedia of mental health* (Vol. 3). San Diego: Academic Press.

Koss-Chioino, J. D., & Vargas, L. (1999). *Working with Latino Youth.* San Francisco: Jossey-Bass.

Kotler, J.A., Wright, J.C., & Huston, A.C. (2001). Television use in families with children. In J. Bryant & J. A. Bryant (Eds.), *Television and the American Family.* Mahwah, NJ: Erlbaum.

Kotlowitz, A. (1991). *There are no children here.* New York: Anchor Books.

Kotre, J. (1984). *Outliving the self: Generativity and the interpretation of lives.* Baltimore: Johns Hopkins University Press.

Kozol, J. (1991). *Savage inequalities.* New York: Crown.

Kozulin, A. (2000). Vygotsky. In A. Kazdin (Ed.). *Encyclopedia of psychology.* Washington, DC, & New York: American Psychological Association and Oxford University Press.

Kramer, A. F, Hahn, S., Cohen, N. J., Banich, M. T., McAuley, E., Harrison, C., Chason, J., Vakil, E., Bardell, L., Boileau, R., & Colcombe, A. (1999, July). Ageing, fitness, and neurocognitive function. *Nature, 400,* 418–419.

Krause, N. (1995). Religiosity and self-esteem among older adults. *Journal of Gerontology: Psychological Sciences, 50B,* P236–P246.

Krause, N. (1996). Neighborhood deterioration and self-rated health in later life. *Psychology and Aging, 11,* 342–352.

Kreppner, K. (2001). Retrospect and prospect in the study of families as systems. In J.P. McHale & W.S. Grolnick (Eds.), *Retrospect and prospect in the psychological study of families.* Mahwah, NJ: Erlbaum.

Kreutzer, M., Leonard, C., & Flavell, J. H. (1975). An interview study of children's knowledge about memory. *Monographs of the Society for Research in Child Development. 40* (1, Serial No. 159).

Krogh, S.L., & Slentz, K.L. (2001). *Early childhood education.* Mahwah, NJ: Erlbaum.

Kübler-Ross, E. (1969). *On death and dying.* New York: Macmillan.

Kuebli, J. (1994, March). Young children's understanding of everyday emotions. *Young Children,* pp. 36–48.

Kuhn, D. (1998). Afterward to Volume 2: Cognition, perception, and language. In W. Damon (Ed.), *Handbook of child psychology* (5th ed., Vol. 2). New York: Wiley.

Kuhn, D. (2000). Adolescent thought processes. In A. Kazdin (Ed.), *Encyclopedia of psychology.* Washington, DC, & New York: American Psychological Association and Oxford University Press.

Kumagai, F. (1995). Families in Japan: Beliefs and realities. *Journal of Comparative and Family Studies, 18,* 135–163.

Kupersmidt, J. B., & Coie, J. D. (1990). Preadolescent peer status, aggression, and school adjustment as predictors of externalizing problems in adolescence. *Child Development, 61,* 1350–1363.

Kupersmidt, J. B., & Patterson, C. (1993, March). *Developmental patterns of peer relations and aggression in the prediction of externalizing behavior problems.* Paper presented at the biennial meeting of the Society for Research in Child Development, New Orleans.

Kurdek, L. A. (1995). Developmental changes in relationship quality in gay and lesbian cohabiting couples. *Developmental Psychology, 31,* 86–94.

Kurtz, D. A., Cantu, C. L., & Phinney, J. S. (1996, March). *Group identities as predictors of self-esteem among African American, Latino, and White adolescents.* Paper presented at the meeting of the Society for Research on Adolescence, Boston.

Kwak, H. K., Kim, M., Cho, B. H., & Ham, Y. M. (1999, April). *The relationship between children's temperament, maternal control strategies, and children's compliance.* Paper presented at the meeting of the Society for Research in Child Development, Albuquerque.

L

Labouvie-Vief, G. (1986, August). *Modes of knowing and life-span cognition.* Paper presented at the meeting of the American Psychological Association, Washington, DC.

Labouvie-Vief, G., & Diehl, M. (1999). Self and personality development. In J. C. Kavanaugh & S. K. Whitbourne (Eds.), *Gerontology: An interdisciplinary perspective.* New York: Oxford University Press.

Labouvie-Vief, G., Diehl, M., Chiodo, L. M., & Coyle, N. (1995). Representations of self and parents across the life span. *Adult Development, 7,* 207–222.

Labouvie-Vief, G., Diehl, M., Tarnowksi, A., & Shen, J. (2000). Age differences in personality: Findings from the United States and China. *Journal of Gerontology: Psychological Sciences, 55B,* P4–P17.

Lackmann, G. M., Salzberger, U., Tollner, U., Chen, M., Carmella, S. G., & Hecht, S. S. (1999). Metabolites of a tobacco-specific carcinogen in

urine from newborns. *Journal of the National Cancer Institute, 91*, 459–465.

Ladd, G. W. (1999). Peer relationships and social competence during early and middle childhood. *Annual Review of Psychology, 50*. Palo Alto, CA: Annual Reviews.

Ladd, G.W., & Kochenderfer, B. J. (in press). Parenting behaviors and parent-child relationship: Correlates of peer victimization in kindergarten. *Developmental Psychology.*

Laible, D. J., Carlo, G., & Raffaeli, M. (2000). The differential relations of parent and peer attachment to adolescent adjustment. *Journal of Youth and Adolescence, 29*, 45–53.

Lamb, M. E. (1977). The development of mother-infant and father-infant attachments in the second year of life. *Developmental Psychology, 13*, 637–648.

Lamb, M. E. (1986). *The father's role: Applied perspectives.* New York: Wiley.

Lamb, M. E. (1994). Infant care practices and the application of knowledge. In C. B. Fisher & R. M. Lerner (Eds.), *Applied developmental psychology.* New York: McGraw-Hill.

Lamb, M. E. (2000). Attachment. In A. Kazdin (Ed.), *Encyclopedia of Psychology.* Washington, DC, & New York: American Psychological Association and Oxford University Press.

Lamb, M. E. (2000). The history of research on father involvement: An overview. *Marriage and Family Review, 29*, 23–42.

Lamb, M. E., Frodi, A. M., Hwant, C. P., Frodi, M., & Steinberg, J. (1982). Mother- and father-infant interaction involving play and holding in traditional and nontraditional Swedish families. *Developmental Psychology, 18*, 215–221.

Lamb, M. E., Hwang, C. P., Ketterlinus, R. D., & Fracasso, M. P. (1999). Parent-child relationships: Development in the context of the family. In M. H. Bornstein & M. E. Lamb (Eds.), *Developmental psychology: An advanced textbook* (4th ed.). Mahwah, NJ: Erlbaum.

Lambert, W. E., Genesee, F., Holobow, N., & Chartrand, L. (1993). Bilingual education for majority English-speaking children. *European Journal of Psychology of Education, 8*, 3–22.

Lang, F. R., & Carstensen, L. L. (1994). Close emotional relationships in late life: Further support for proactive aging in the social domain. *Psychology and Aging, 9*, 315–324.

Langer, E. (1989). *Mindfulness.* Reading, MA: Addison-Wesley.

Lapsley, D. K. (1996). *Moral psychology.* Boulder, CO: Westview Press.

Lareau, A. (1996). Assessing parent involvement in schooling: A critical analysis. In K. L. Alexander & D. R. Entwisle (Eds.), *Schools and children at risk.* Mahwah, NJ: Erlbaum.

Larson, J. (1988). The marriage quiz: College students' beliefs in selected areas of marriage. *Family Relations, 37*, 3–11.

Larson, J. H., & Holman, T. B. (1994). Premarital predictors of marital quality and stability. *Family Relations, 43*, 228–237.

Larson, R. (1999, September). Unpublished review of J. W. Santrock's *Adolescence*, 8th ed. (New York: McGraw-Hill).

Larson, R., & Richards, M. (1994). *Divergent realities: The emotional lives of mothers, fathers, and adolescents.* New York: Basic Books.

Larson, R. W., Clore, G. L., & Wood, G. A. (in press). The emotions of romantic relationships. In W. Furman, B. B. Brown, & C. Feiring (Eds), *Contemporary perspectives in romantic relationships.* New York: Cambridge University Press.

Lauer, R. H., & Lauer, J. (1999). *Becoming family: How to build a stepfamily that really works.* Augsburg, MN: Augsburg Fortress Pub.

Laurin, D., Verreault, R., Lindsay J., MacPherson, K., & Rockwood, K. (2001). Physical activity and risk of cognitive impairment and dementia in elderly persons. *Archives of Neurology, 58*, 498–504.

Lawton, M. P., Kleban, M. H., Rajagopal, D., & Dean, J. (1992). The dimensions of affective experience in three age groups. *Psychology and Aging, 7*, 171–184.

Laz, M., & Alberico, E. (1998). *Coping when your spouse dies.* New York: Liguori.

Lazar, L., Darlington, R., & Collaborators. (1982). Lasting effects of early education: A report from the consortium for longitudinal studies. *Monographs of the Society for Research in Child Development, 47.*

Lazarus, R. S., & Folkman, S. (1984). *Stress, appraisal, and coping.* New York: Springer.

Leach, C. E., Blair, P. S., Fleming, P. J., Smith, I. J., Platt, M. W., Berry, P. J., & Golding, J. (1999). Epidemiology of SIDS and explained sudden infant deaths. *Pediatrics, 104*, E43–E45.

Leadbeater, B.J.R., & Way, N. (2001). *Growing up fast.* Mahwah, NJ: Erlbaum.

Leavitt, F. (2001). *Evaluating scientific research.* Upper Saddle River, NJ: Prentice Hall.

Lebowitz, B. D. (1987). Mental health services. In G. L. Maddox (Ed.), *The encyclopedia of aging.* New York: Springer.

Lee, D. J., & Markides, K. S. (1990). Activity and mortality among aged persons over an eight-year period. *Journals of Gerontology: Social Sciences, 45*, S39–S42.

Lee, G. R. (1978). Marriage and morale in late life. *Journal of Marriage and the Family, 40*, 131–139.

Lee, I., Hsieh, C., & Paffenbarger, O. (1995). Exercise intensity and longevity in men. *Journal of the American Medical Association, 273*, 1179–1184.

Lee, I. M., Manson, J. E., Hennekens, C. H., & Paffenbarger, R. S. (1993). Bodyweight and mortality: A 27-year-follow-up. *Journal of the American Medical Association, 270*, 2823–2828.

Lefley, H. P. (1996). *Family caregiving and mental illness.* Newbury Park, CA: Sage.

Lehman, H. C. (1960). The age decrement in outstanding scientific creativity. *American Psychologist, 15*, 128–134.

Leifer, A. D. (1973). *Television and the development of social behavior.* Paper presented at the meeting of the International Society for the Study of Behavioral Development, Ann Arbor, MI.

Leith, L. M. (1998). Exercise and mental health. In H. S. Friedman (Ed.), *Encyclopedia of mental health* (Vol. 2). San Diego: Academic Press.

Lemery, K. S., Goldsmith, H. H., Klinnert, M. D., & Mrazek, D. A. (1999). Developmental models of infant and child temperament. *Developmental Psychology, 35*, 189–204.

Lenneberg, E. H., Rebelsky, R. G., & Nichols, I. A. (1965). The vocalization of infants born to deaf and hearing parents. *Human Development, 8*, 23–37.

Lennon, M. C., & Rosenfield, S. (1994). Relative fairness and the division of housework: The importance of options. *American Journal of Sociology, 100*, 506–531.

Leong, F. T. L. (2000). Cultural pluralism. In A. Kazdin (Ed.), *Encyclopedia of psychology.* Washington, DC, & New York: American Psychological Association and Oxford University Press.

Lerner, H. G. (1989). *The dance of intimacy.* New York: Harper & Row.

Lerner, J. V. (2000). Parent-child relationship: Childhood. In A. Kazdin (Ed.), *Encyclopedia of psychology*. Washington, DC, & New York: American Psychological Association and Oxford University Press.

Lerner, R. M. (1998). Theories of human development: Contemporary perspectives. In W. Damon (Ed.), *Handbook of child psychology* (5th ed., Vol. 1). New York: Wiley.

Lester, B. (2000). Unpublished review of J. W. Santrock's *Life-Span Development* (8th ed.) (New York: McGraw-Hill).

Lester, B. (2000). Unpublished review of J. W. Santrock's *Life-Span Development* (9th ed.) (New York: McGraw-Hill).

Levant, R. F., & Brooks, G. R. (1997). *Men and sex: New psychlogical perspectives.* New York: Wiley.

LeVay, S. (1991). A difference in the hypothalamic structure between heterosexual and homosexual men. *Science, 253*, 1034–1037.

Levelt, W. J. M. (1989). *Speaking: From intention to articulation.* Cambridge, MA: MIT Press.

Leventhal, A. (1994, February). *Peer conformity during adolescence: An integration of developmental, situational, and individual characteristics.* Paper presented at the meeting of the Society for Research on Adolescence, San Diego.

Levesque, J., & Prosser, T. (1996). Service learning connections. *Journal of Teacher Education, 47*, 325–334.

Levin, J. S. (1994). *Religion in aging and health.* Thousand Oaks, CA: Sage.

Levin, J. S., Chatters, L. M., & Taylor, R. J. (1995). Religious effects on health status and life satisfaction among Black Americans. *Journal of Gerontology: Social Sciences, 50B*, S154–S163.

Levin, J. S., Taylor, R. J., & Chatters, L. M. (1994). Race and gender differences in religiosity among older adults: Findings from four national surveys. *Journal of Gerontology, 49*, S137–S145.

Levin, J. S., & Vanderpool, H. Y. (1989). Is religion therapeutically significant for hypertension? *Social Science and Medicine, 29*, 69–78.

LeVine, S. (1979). *Mothers and wives: Gusii women of East Africa.* Chicago: University of Chicago Press.

Levinger, G. (1974). A three-level approach to attraction: Toward an understanding of pair relatedness. In T. Huston (Ed.), *Foundations of interpersonal attraction.* New York: Academic Press.

Levinson, D. J. (1978). *The seasons of a man's life.* New York: Knopf.

Levinson, D. J. (1987, August). *The seasons of a woman's life.* Paper presented at the meeting of the American Psychological Association, New York.

Levinson, D. J. (1996). *Seasons of a woman's life.* New York: Alfred Knopf.

Levinson, D. J. (1997). *Seasons of a woman's life.* New York: Random House.

Levy, T. M. (Ed.). (1999). *Handbook of attachment interventions.* San Diego: Academic Press.

Lewinsohn, P.M., Rohde, P., Seeley, J., & Baldwin, C. (2001). Gender differences in suicide attempts from adolescence to young adulthood. *Journal of the Academy of Child and Adolescent Psychiatry, 40,* 427–434.

Lewis, M. (1997). *Altering fate: Why the past does not predict the future.* New York: Guilford Press.

Lewis, M., & Brooks-Gunn, J. (1979). *Social cognition and the acquisition of the self.* New York: Plenum.

Lewis, M., Feiring, C., & Rosenthal, S. (2000). Attachment over time. *Child Development, 71,* 707–720.

Lewis, M., & Ramsay, D. S. (1999). Effect of maternal soothing and infant stress response. *Child Development, 70,* 11–20.

Lewis, M.D. (2001, April). *Case's neo-Piagetian model of socioemotional development.* Paper presented at the meeting of the Society for Research in Child Development, Minneapolis.

Lewis, R. (1997). With a marble and telescope: Searching for play. *Childhood Education, 36,* 346.

Lewis, R. (1999). *Human genetics* (3rd ed.). New York: McGraw-Hill.

Lieberman, E. E., Lang, J. M., Frigoletto, F., Richardson, D. K., Rengin, S. A., & Cohen, A. (1997). Epidural analgesic, intrapartum fever, and neonatal sepsis evaluation. *Pediatrics, 99,* 415–419.

Lifshitz, F., Pugliese, M. T., Moses, N., & Weyman-Daum, M. (1987). Parental health beliefs as a cause of nonorganic failure to thrive. *Pediatrics, 80,* 175–182.

Lifton, R. J. (1977). The sense of immortality: On death and the continuity of life. In H. Feifel (Ed.), *New meanings of death.* New York: McGraw-Hill.

Light, L. L. (2000). Memory changes in adulthood. In S. H. Qualls & N. Abeles (Eds.), *Psychology and the aging revolution.* Washington, DC: American Psychological Association.

Light, L. L., Zelinski, E. M., & Moore, M. (1982). Adult age differences in reasoning from new information. *Journal of Experimental Psychology: Learning, Memory, and Cognition, 8,* 435–447.

Lightwood, J. M., Phibbs, C. S., & Glantz, S. A. (1999). Short-term health and economic benefits of smoking cessation. *Pediatrics, 104,* 1312–1320.

Limber, S. P. (1997). Preventing violence among school children. *Family Futures, 1,* 27–28.

Lindenberger, U., & Baltes, P. B. (1994). Sensory functioning and intelligence in old age: A strong connection. *Psychology and Aging, 9,* 339–355.

Lindbohm, M. (1991). Effects of paternal occupational exposure in spontaneous abortions. *American Journal of Public Health, 121,* 1029–1033.

Lindsay, R., & Cosman, F. (1990). Estrogen in prevention and treatment of osteoporosis. *Annals of the New York Academy of Sciences, 592,* 326–333.

Liprie, M. L. (1993). Adolescents' contributions to family decision making. In B. H. Settles, R. S. Hanks, & M. B. Sussman (Eds.), *American families and the future: Analyses of possible destinies.* New York: Haworth Press.

Lipsitz, J. (1983, October). *Making it the hard way: Adolescents in the 1980s.* Testimony presented at the Crisis Intervention Task Force, House Select Committee on Children, Youth, and Families, Washington, DC.

Lipsitz, J. (1984). *Successful schools for young adolescents.* New Brunswick, NJ: Transaction.

Livesly, W., & Bromley, D. (1973). *Person perception in childhood and adolescence.* New York: Wiley.

Livson, N., & Peskin, H. (1981). Psychological health at age 40. Prediction from adolescent personality. In D. M. Eichorn, J. Clausen, N. Haan, M. Honzik, & P. Mussen (Eds.), *Present and past in middle life.* New York: Academic Press.

Llewellyn-Jones, D. (1999). *Fundamental of obstetrics and gynecology* (7th ed.). London: Harcourt International.

Lochman, J. J. (2000). A perception action perspective on tool use development. *Child Development, 71,* 137–144.

Lock, M. (1998). Menopause: Lessons from anthropology. *Psychosomatic Medicine, 60,* 410–419. (p. 154)

Lockman, J. J., & Thelen, E. (1993). Developmental biodynamics: Brain, body, behavior connections. *Child Development, 64,* 953–959.

Loebel, M., & Yali, A. M. (1999, August). *Effects of positive expectancies on adjustment to pregnancy.* Paper presented at the meeting of the American Psychological Association, Boston.

London, M. L., Ladewig, P. W., Olds, S. B., & Ladewig, P. W. (2000). *Maternal newborn nursing care* (4th ed.). Boston: Addison-Wesley.

Long, T., & Long, L. (1983). *Latchkey children.* New York: Penguin.

Longman, P. (1987). *Born to pay: The new politics of aging in America.* Boston: Houghton-Mifflin.

Lonner, W. J. (1990). An overview of cross-cultural testing and assessment. In R.W. Brislin (Ed.), *Applied cross-cultural psychology.* Newbury Park, CA: Sage.

Lopata, H. Z. (1994). *Circles and settings: Role changes of American women.* Albany State University of New York Press.

Lorenz, K. Z. (1965). *Evolution and the modification of behavior.* Chicago: University of Chicago Press.

Lund, D. A. (1996). Bereavement and loss. In J. E. Birren (Ed.), *Encyclopedia of gerontology* (Vol. 1). San Diego: Academic Press.

Luria, A., & Herzog, E. (1985, April). *Gender segregation across and within settings.* Paper presented at the biennial meeting of the Society for Research in Child Development, Toronto.

Luszcz, M. A., & Bryan, J. (1999). Toward understanding age-related memory loss in late adulthood. *Gerontology, 45,* 2–9.

Lutz, D. A., & Sternberg, R. J. (1999). Cognitive development. In M. H. Bornstein & M. E. Lamb (Eds.), *Developmental psychology* (4th ed.). Mahwah, NJ: Erlbaum.

Lydon-Rochelle, M., Holt, V. L., Martin, D. P., & Easterling, T. R. (2000). Association between method of delivery and maternal rehospitalization. *Journal of the American Medical Association, 283,* 2411–2416.

Lynch, E. W., & Hanson, M. J. (1993). *Developing cross-cultural competence: A guide for working with young children and their families.* Baltimore: Paul H. Brookes.

Lyon, G. R. (1996). Learning disabilities. *Future of Children,* 6(1) 54–76.

Lyon, G. R., & Moats, L. C. (1997). Critical conceptual and methodological considerations in reading intervention research. *Journal of Learning Disabilities, 30,* 578–588.

Lyon, T. D., & Flavell, J. H. (1993). Young children's understanding of forgetting over time. *Child Development, 64,* 789–800.

Lyons, N. P. (1990). Listening to voices we have not heard. In C. Gilligan, N. P. Lyons, & T. J. Hanmer (Eds.), *Making connections.* Cambridge, MA: Harvard University Press.

Lyytinen, P., Rasku-Puttonen, H., Poikkeus, A., Laakso, M., & Ahonen, T. (1994). Mother-child teaching strategies and learning disabilities. *Journal of Learning Disabilities, 27,* 186–192.

M

Maas, J. B. (1998). *Power sleep.* New York: Villard Books.

Maccoby, E. E. (1987, November). Interview with Elizabeth Hall: All in the family. *Psychology Today,* pp. 54–60.

Maccoby, E. E. (1992). The role of parents in the socialization of children: An historical overview. *Developmental Psychology, 28,* 1006–1018.

Maccoby, E. E. (1993, March). *Trends and issues in the study of gender role development.* Paper presented at the biennial meeting of the Society for Research in Child Development, New Orleans.

Maccoby, E. E. (1998). *The two sexes: Growing up apart, coming together.* Cambridge, MA: Harvard University Press.

Maccoby, E. E. (1999). The uniqueness of the parent-child relationship. In W. A. Collins, & B. Laursen (Eds.), *Relationships as developmental contexts.* Mahwah, NJ: Erlbaum.

Maccoby, E. E. (2000). Parenting and its effect on children: On reading and misreading behavior genetics. *Annual Review of Psychology* (Vol. 51). Palo Alto, CA: Annual Reviews.

Maccoby, E.E. (2001, April) *Influencing policy through research.* Paper presented at the meeting of the Society for Research in Child Development, Minneapolis.

Maccoby, E. E., & Jacklin, C. N. (1974). *The psychology of sex differences.* Palo Alto, CA: Stanford University Press.

Maccoby, E. E., & Mnookin, R. H. (1992). *Dividing the child: Social and legal dilemmas of custody.* Cambridge, MA: Harvard University Press.

MacFarlane, J. A. (1975). Olfaction in the development of social preferences in the human neonate. In *Parent-infant interaction.* Ciba Foundation Symposium No. 33. Amsterdam: Elsevier.

MacLean, W. E. (2000). Down syndrome. In A. Kazdin (Ed.), *Encyclopedia of psychology.* Washington, DC, & New York: American Psychological Association and Oxford University Press.
Maddi, S. (1998). Hardiness. In H. S. Friedman (Ed.), *Encyclopedia of mental health* (Vol. 3). San Diego: Academic Press.
Mader, S. (1999). *Biology* (6th ed.). New York: McGraw-Hill.
Maggs, J. L., Schulenberg, J., & Hurrelmann, K. (1997). Developmental transitions in adolescence: Health promotion implications. In J. Schulenberg, J. L. Maggs, & K. Hurrelmann (Eds.), *Health risks and developmental transitions during adolescence.* New York: Cambridge University Press.
Mahler, M. (1979). *Separation-individuation* (Vol. 2). London: Jason Aronson.
Main, M. (2000). Attachment theory. In A. Kazdin (Ed.), *Encyclopedia of psychology*. Washington, DC, & New York: American Psychological Association and Oxford University Press.
Main, M., Kaplan, N., & Cassidy, J. (1985). Security in infancy, childhood, and adulthood: A move to the level of representation. *Monographs of the Society for Research in Child Development, 50,* 55–64.
Main, M., & Solomon, J. (1990). Procedures for identifying infants as disorganized/disoriented during the Ainsworth Strange Situation. In M. Greenberg, D. Cicchetti, & E. M. Cummings (Eds.), *Attachment during the preschool years.* Chicago: University of Chicago Press.
Maizels, M., Rosenbaum, D., & Keating, B. (1999). *Getting to dry: How to help your child overcome bedwetting.* Cambridge, MA: Harvard Common Press.
Makrides, M., Neumann, M., Simmer, K., Pater, J., & Gibson, R. (1995). Are long-chain polyunsaturated fatty acids essential nutrients in infancy? *Lancet, 345,* 1463–1468.
Malinosky-Rummell, R., & Hansen, D. J. (1993). Long-term consequences of childhood physical abuse. *Psychological Bulletin, 114,* 68–79.
Malinowski, B. (1927). *Sex and repression in savage society.* New York: Humanities Press.
Malloy, M. H. (1999). Risk of previous very low birth weight and very preterm infants among women delivering a very low birth weight and very preterm infant. *Journal of Perinatology, 19,* 97–102.
Mandler, J. M. (1990). A new perspective on cognitive development. *American Scientist, 78,* 236–243.
Mandler, J. M. (1998). Representation. In W. Damon (Ed.), *Handbook of child psychology* (5th ed., Vol. 2). New York: Wiley.
Mandler, J. M. (2000). Unpublished review of J. W. Santrock's *Life-Span Development*, 8th ed. (New York: McGraw-Hill).
Mandler, J. M. & McDonough, L. (1995). Long-term recall in infancy. *Journal of Experimental Child Psychology, 59,* 457–474.
Mannell, R. C. (2000). Older adults, leisure, and wellness. *Journal of Leisurability, 26,* 3–10.
Mannell, R. C., & Dupuis, S. (1996). Life satisfaction. In J. E. Birren (Ed.), *Encyclopedia of gerontology* (Vol. 2). San Diego: Academic Press.
Manton, K. G., Corder, L., & Stallard, E. (1997, March 18). Chronic disability in elderly United States populations, 1982–1994. *Proceedings of the National Academy of Sciences, 94,* 2593–2598.
Manton, K. I. (1989). The stress-buffering role of spiritual support: Cross-sectional and prospective investigations. *Journal for the Scientific Study of Religion, 28,* 310–323.
Manuck, S. B., Jennings, R., Rabing, B., & Baum, A. S. (Eds.) (2001). *Behavior, health, and aging.* Mahwah, NJ: Erlbaum.
Marcia, J. (1996). Unpublished review of J. W. Santrock's *Adolescence,* 7th ed. (New York: McGraw-Hill).
Marcia, J. E. (1980). Ego identity development. In J. Adelson (Ed.), *Handbook of adolescent psychology.* New York: Wiley.
Marcia, J. E. (1994). The empirical study of ego identity. In H. A. Bosma, T. L. G. Graafsma, H. D. Grotevant, & D. J. De Levita (Eds.), *Identity and development.* Newbury Park, CA: Sage.
Marcus, D. L., Mulrine, A., & Wong, K. (1999, September 13). How kids learn. *U.S. News & World Report,* pp. 44–50.
Marecek, J., Finn, S. E., & Cardell, M. (1988). Gender roles in the relationships of lesbians and gay men. In J. P. De Cecco (Ed.), *Gay relationships.* New York: Harrington Park Press.
Margolin, L. (1994). Child sexual abuse by uncles. *Child Abuse and Neglect, 18,* 215–224.
Markides, K. S. (1995). Aging and ethnicity. *Gerontologist, 35,* 276–277.
Markides, K. S., & Rudkin, L. (1996). Race and ethnic diversity. In J. E. Birren (Ed.), *Encyclopedia of gerontology* (Vol. 2). San Diego: Academic Press.
Markman, H. J. (2000). Marriage. In A. Kazdin (Ed.), *Encyclopedia of psychology*. Washington, DC, & New York: American Psychological Association and Oxford University Press.
Markowitz, M. (2000). Lead poisoning. *Pediatrics in Review, 21,* 327–335.
Marks, M. A., & Nelson, E. S. (1993). Sexual harassment on campus: Effects of professor gender on perception of sexually harassing behaviors. *Sex Roles, 28,* 207–218.
Markson, E. W. (1995). Older women: The silent majority? *Gerontologist, 35,* 278–281.
Marsiske, M., Klumb, P., & Baltes, M. M. (in press). Everyday activity patterns and sensory functioning in old age. *Psychology and Aging.*
Marsiske, M., Lang, F. R., Baltes, P. B., & Baltes, M. M. (1995). Selective optimization with compensation. In R. A. Dixon & L. Backman (Eds.), *Compensating for psychological deficits and declines*. Hillsdale, NJ: Erlbaum.
Martin, C. L. (2000). Cognitive theories of gender development. In T. Eckes & H. M. Trautner (Eds.), *The developmental social psychology of gender.* Mahwah, NJ: Erlbaum.
Martin, E. W., Martin, R., & Terman, D. L. (1996). The legislative and litigation history of special education. *Future of Children,* 6(1), 25–53.
Martin, J.A., & Buckwalter, J.A. (2001). Biomarkers of aging. *Journal of Gerontology, 56A, No.4,* B172–B179.
Martin-Matthews, A. (1996). Widowhood and widowerhood. In J. E. Birren (Ed.), *Encyclopedia of gerontology* (Vol. 2). San Diego: Academic Press.
Matheny, A.P., & Phillips, K. (2001). Temperament and context: Correlates of home environment with temperament continuity and change. In T.D. Wachs & G.A. Kohnstamm (Eds.), *Temperament in context.* Mahwah, NJ: Erlbaum.
Matthias, R. F., Lubben, J. E., Atchison, K. A., & Schweitzer, S. O. (1997). Sexual activity and satisfaction among very old adults: Results from a community-dwelling Medicare population survey. *Gerontologist, 37,* 6–14.
Maurer, D. (2001, April). *Variations in plasticity in visual development.* Paper presented at the meeting of the Society for Research in Child Development, Minneapolis.
McAdoo, H. P. (Ed.). (1999). *Family ethnicity* (2nd ed.). Newbury Park, CA: Sage.
McBurney, D. H. (2001). *Research methods.* Belmont, CA: Wadworth.
McCall, R. B., & Carriger, M. S. (1993). A meta-analysis of infant habituation and recognition memory performance as predictors of later IQ. *Child Development, 64,* 57–79.
McCarty, M. E., & Ashmead, D. H. (1999). Visual control of reaching and grasping in infants. *Developmental Psychology, 35,* 620–631.
McCormick, C. B., & Pressley, M. (1997). *Educational psychology*. New York: Longman.
McCrae R. R., Costa P. T., et al. (1999). Age differences in personality across the adult lifespan: Parallels in five cultures. *Developmental Psychology, 35,* 466–477.
McCullough, M. E. (1995). Prayer and health: Conceptual issues, research review, and research agenda. *Journal of Psychology and Theology, 23,* 15–29.
McCullough, M. E., Hoyt, W. T., Larson, D. B., Koenig, H. G., & Thoresen, C. (2000). Religious involvement and mortality: A meta-analytic review. *Health psychology, 19,* 211–222.
McDougall, G. J., Strauss, M. E., Holston, E. C., & Martin, M. (1999, November). *Memory self-efficacy and memory-anxiety as predictors of memory performance in at-risk elderly.* Paper presented at the meeting of the Gerontological Society of America, San Francisco.
McFarlane, J., Parker, B., & Soeken, K. (1996). Abuse during pregnancy: Associations with maternal health and infant birth weight. *Nursing Research, 45,* 37–47.
McFarlane, T., Polivy, J., & Herman, C. P. (1998). Dieting. In H.S. Friedman (Ed.), *Encyclopedia of mental health* (Vol. 1). San Diego: Academic Press.
McGowan, T. G. (1996). Ageism and discrimination. In J. E. Birren (Ed.), *Handbook of gerontology* (Vol. 1). San Diego: Academic Press.
McGrath, J. E., Kelly, J. R., & Rhodes, J. E. (1993). A feminist perspective on research methodology. In S. Oskamp & M. Costanzo (Eds.), *Gender issues in contemporary society.* Newbury Park, CA: Sage.
McGrath, S., Kennell, J., Suresh, M., Moise, K., & Hinkley, C. (1999, May). *Doula support vs. epidural analgesia: Impact on cesarean rates.* Paper presented at the meeting of the Society for Pediatric Research, San Francisco.
McGuire, F. (2000). What do we know? Not much. The state of leisure and aging research. *Journal of Leisurability, 26,* 97–100.
McGuire, S. (2001). Are behavioral genetic and socialization research compatible? *American Psychologist, 56,* 171.

McHale, J. P., Lauretti, A. F., & Kuersten-Hogan, R. (1999, April). *Linking family-level patterns to father-child, mother-child, and marital relationship qualities.* Paper presented at the meeting of the Society for Research in Child Development, Albuquerque.

McKenna, J. J., Mosko, S. S., & Richard, C. A. (1997). Bedsharing promotes breastfeeding. *Pediatrics, 100,* 214–219.

McLeod, J. D. (1996). Life events, In J. E. Birren (Ed.,) *Encylcopedia of gerontology* (Vol. 1). San Diego: Academic Press.

McLoyd, V. C. (1998). Children in poverty: Development, public policy, and practice. In W. Damon (Ed.), *Handbook of child psychology* (5th ed., Vol. 4). New York: Wiley.

McLoyd, V. C. (1999). Cultural influences in a multicultural society: Conceptual and methodological issues. In A. S. Masten (Ed.), *Cultural processes in child development.* Mahwah, NJ: Erlbaum.

McLoyd, V. C. (2000). Poverty. In A. Kazdin (Ed.), *Encyclopedia of psychology.* Washington, DC, & New York: American Psychological Association and Oxford University Press.

McMillan, J. H. (2000). *Educational research* (3rd ed.). New York: HarperCollins.

McMullin, J.A., & Marshall, V. W. (2001). Ageism, age relations, and garment industry work in [illegible]

Medvedev, Z. A. (1974). The nucleic acids in the development of aging. In B. L. Strehler (Ed.), *Advances in gerontological research* (Vol. 1). New York: Academic Press.

Mehler, J., Jusczyk, P. W., Lambertz, G., Halsted, N., Bertoncini, J., & Amiel-Tison, C. (1988). A precursor of language acquisition in young infants. *Cognition, 29.* 132–178.

Melamed, B.G., Roth, B., & Fogel, J. (2001). Childhood health issues across the life span. In A. Baum, T.A. Revenson, & J.E. Singer (Eds.), *Handbook of health psychology.* Mahwah, NJ: Erlbaum.

Melby, J. N., & Vargas, D. (1996, March). *Predicting patterns of adolescent tobacco use.* Paper presented at the meeting of the Society for Research on Adolescence, Boston.

Meltzoff, A., & Gopnik, A. (1997). *Words, thoughts, and theories.* Cambridge, MA: MIT Press.

Meltzoff, A. N. (1988). Infant imitation and memory: Nine-month-old infants in immediate and deferred tests. *Child Development, 59,* 217–225.

Meltzoff, A. N. (1992, May). *Cognition in the service of learning.* Paper presented at the International Conference on Infant Studies, Miami Beach.

Meltzoff, A. N. (1999, April). *Infant memory development: Contribution of the deferred imitation paradigm.* Paper presented at the meeting of the Society for Research in Child Development, Albuquerque.

Meltzoff, A. N. (2000). Learning and cognitive development. In A. Kazdin (Ed.), *Encyclopedia of psychology.* Washington, DC, & New York: American Psychological Association and Oxford University Press.

Meltzoff, A. N., & Moore, M. K. (1999). A new foundation for cognitive development: The birth of the representational infant. In E. K. Skolnick, K. Nelson, S. A. Gelman, & P. H. Miller (Eds.), *Conceptual development.* Mahwah, NJ: Erlbaum.

Memmler, R. L., Cohen, B. J., Wood, D. L., & Schweglr, J. (1995). *The human body in health and disease* (8th ed.). Philadelphia: Lippincott Williams & Wilkins.

Meredith, N. V. (1978). Research between 1960 and 1970 on the standing height of young children in different parts of the world. In H. W. Reece & L. P. Lipsitt (Eds.),. *Advances in child development and behavior* (Vol. 12). New York: Academic Press.

Merrill, S. S., & Verbrugge, L. M. (1999). Health and disease in midlife. In S. L. Willis & J. D. Reid (Eds.), *Life in the middle: Psychological and social development in middle age.* San Diego: Academic Press.

Messier, S., Royer, T. D., Craven, T. E., O'Toole, M. L., Burns, R., & Ettinger, W. H. (2000). Long-term exercise and its effect on balance in older, oseteoarthritic adults. *Journal of the American Geriatrics Society, 48,* 131–138.

Michael, R., Gagnon, J., Laumann, E., & Kolata, G. (1994). *Sex in America.* Boston: Little, Brown.

Michael, R. T., Gagnon, J. H., Laumann, E. O., & Kolata, G. (1994). *Sex in America.* Boston: Little, Brown.

Michel, G. F. (1981). Right [illegible] consequence of infant supine head-orientation preference? *Science, 212,* 685–687.

Milke, M. A., & Peltola, P. (2000). Playing all the roles: Gender and the work-family balancing act. *Journal of Marriage and the Family, 61,* 476–490.

Miller, J. B. (1986). *Toward a new psychology of women* (2nd ed.). Boston: Beacon Press.

Miller, J. G. (1995, March). *Culture, context, and personal agency: The cultural grounding of self and morality.* Paper presented at the meeting of the Society for Research in Child Development, Indianapolis.

Miller, P.H. (2001). *Theories of developmental psychology (4th Ed.).* New York: Worth.

Miller, P. H., & Seier, W. L. (1994). Strategy utilization deficiencies in children: When, where, and why. In H. W. Reese (Ed.), *Advances in child development and behavior* (Vol. 24). New York: Academic Press.

Miller, S. A. (1998). *Developmental research methods.* (2nd ed.). Upper Saddle River, NJ: Prentice Hall.

Miller, W. R., & Thoresen, C. E. (1999). Spirituality and health. In W. R. Miller (Ed.), *Integrating spirituality into therapy.* Washington, DC: American Psychological Association.

Miller-Jones, D. (1989). Culture and testing. *American Psychologist, 44,* 360–366.

Millis, R. M. (1998). Smoking. In H.S. Friedman (Ed.), *Encyclopedia of mental health* (Vol. 3). San Diego: Academic Press.

Minuchin, P. (2001). Looking toward the horizon: Present and future in the study of family systems. In J.P. McHale & W.S. Grolnick (Eds.), *Retrospect and prospect in the psychological study of families.* Mahwah, NJ: Erlbaum.

Minuchin, P. O., & Shapiro, E. K. (1983). The school as a context for social development. In P. H. Mussen (Ed.), *Handbook of child psychology* (4th ed., Vol. 4). New York: Wiley.

Mischel, W. (1973). Toward a cognitive social learning reconceptualization of personality. *Psychological Review, 80,* 252–283.

Mischel, W. (1995, August). *Cognitive-affective theory of person-environment psychology.* Paper presented at the meeting of the American Psychological Association, New York City.

Mischel, W., & Patterson, C. J. (1976). Substantive and structural elements of effective plans for self-control. *Journal of Personality and Social Psychology, 34,* 942–950.

Mishell, D. (2000). *2000 Yearbook of obstetrics.* St. Louis: Mosby.

Mitchell, A. S. (1999, April). *The nature of sibling relationships in adolescence: A sequential analysis of verbal and nonverbal behaviors in twins and nontwins.* Paper presented at the meeting of the Society for Research in Child Development, Albuquerque.

Mitchell, V., & Helson, R. (1990). Women's prime of life: Is it the 50s? *Psychology of Women Quarterly, 14,* 451–470.

Mizes, J. S., & Miller, K. J. (2000). Eating disorders. In M. Herson & R. T. Ammerman (Eds.), *Advanced abnormal child psychology* (2nd ed.). Mahwah, NJ: Erlbaum.

[illegible], M. S. (1995). Strategy instruction, metacognition, and motivation in the elementary school classroom. In F. E. Weinert & W. Schneider (Eds.), *Memory performance and competencies.* Mahwah, NJ: Erlbaum.

Moen, P. (1998). Recasting careers: Changing reference groups, risks, and realities. *Generations, 22,* 40–45.

Moen, P., & Quick, H. E. (1998). Retirement. In H. S. Friedman (Ed.), *Encyclopedia of mental health* (Vol. 3). San Diego: Academic Press.

Moen, P., & Wethington, E. (1999). Midlife development in a life course context. In S. L. Willis & J. D. Reid (Eds.), *Life in the middle: Psychological and social development in middle age.* San Diego: Academic Press.

Monk, C., Fifer, W. P., Sloan, R. P., & Myers, M. M. (2000, May). *Individual differences in fetal cardiac reactivity are associated with maternal anxiety and infant birth eight.* Paper presented at the joint meetings of the Pediatric Academic Societies and the American Academy of Pediatrics, Boston.

Montemayor, R. (1982). The relationship between parent-adolescent conflict and the amount of time adolescents spend with parents, peers, and alone. *Child Development, 53,* 1512–1519.

Moore, C., & Lemmon, K. (2001). *The self in time.* Mahwah, NJ: Erlbaum.

Moos, R. H. (1986). Work as a human context. In M. S. Pallack & R. Perloff (Eds.), *Psychology and work: Productivity, change, and employment.* Washington, DC: American Psychological Association.

Morelli, G. A., Rogoff, B., Oppenheim, D., & Goldsmith, D. (1992). Cultural variation in infants' sleeping arrangements: Questions of independence. *Developmental Psychology, 28,* 604–613.

Morris, J.C., Storandt, M., Miller, J.P., McKeel, D., Price, J., Rubin, E.H., & Berg, L. (2001). Mild cognitive impairment represents early-stage Alzheimer's disease. *Archives of Neurology, 58,* 397–405.
Morris, L., Warren, C. W., & Aral, S. O. (1993, September). Measuring adolescent sexual behaviors and related health outcomes. *Public Health Reports, 108,* 31–36.
Morrison, G. S. (2000). *Fundamentals of early childhood education.* Columbus, OH: Merrill.
Morrongiello, B. A., Fenwick, K. D., & Chance, G. (1990). Sound localization acuity in very young infants: An observer-based testing procedure. *Developmental Psychology, 26,* 75–84.
Morrow, L. (1988, August 8). Through the eyes of children. *Time,* pp. 32–33.
Mortimer, E. A. (1997). Child health in the developing world. In R. E. Behrman, R. M. Kliegman, W. E. Nelson, & V. C. Vaughan (Eds.), *Nelson textbook of pediatrics* (14th ed.). Philadelphia: W. B. Saunders.
Moses, J., Steptoe, A., Mathews, A., & Edwards, S. (1989). The effects of exercise training on mental well-being in a normal population: A controlled trial. *Journal of Psychosomatic Research, 33,* 47–61.
Moshman, D. (1999). *Adolescent psychological development: Rationality, morality, and identity.* Mahwah, NJ: Erlbaum.
Mozingo, J. N., Davis, M. W., Droppleman, P. G., & Merideth, A. (2000). "It wasn't working": Women's experiences with short-term breast feeding. *American Maternal Journal of Nursing, 25,* 120–126.
Mueller, N., & Silverman, N. (1989). Peer relations in maltreated children. In D. Cicchetti & V. Carlson (Eds.), *Child maltreatment.* New York: Cambridge University Press.
Mullis, I. V. S. (1999, April). *Using TIMSS to gain new perspectives about different school organizations and policies.* Paper presented at the meeting of the American Educational Research Association, Montreal.
Murphy, K. R., & Davidshofer, C. O. (2001). *Psychological testing* (5th ed.). Upper Saddle River, NJ: Prentice Hall.
Murray, J. P. (2000). Media effects. In A. Kazdin (Ed.), *Encyclopedia of psychology*. Washington, DC, & New York: American Psychological Association and Oxford University Press.
Murray, L., & others. (Eds.). (1999). *Postpartum depression and child development.* New York: Guilford.
Mussen, P. H., Honzik, M., & Eichorn, D. (1982). Early adult antecedents of life satisfaction at age 70. *Journal of Gerontology, 37,* 316–322.
Muth, A. S. (Ed.)(2000). *Death and dying sourcebook: Basic consumer health information for the layperson about end-of-life care and related ethical issues.* Detroit: Omnigraphics.
Myers, D. G. (2000). *The American paradox.* New Haven, CT: Yale University Press.
Myers, D. L. (1999). *Excluding violent youths from juvenile court: The effectiveness of legislative waiver.* Doctoral dissertation, University of Maryland, College Park.

N

Naglieri, J. (2000). Stanford-Binet Intelligence Scale. In A. Kazdin (Ed.), *Encyclopedia of psychology.* Washington, DC, & New York: American Psychological Association and Oxford University Press.
Nagy, M. (1948). The child's theories concerning death. *Journal of Genetic Psychology, 73,* 3–27.
Nahas, G. G. (1984). *Marijuana in science and medicine.* New York: Raven Press.
Nash, J. M. (1997, February 3). Fertile minds. *Time,* pp. 50–54.
National and Community Service Coalition. (1995). *Youth volunteerism.* Washington, DC: Author.
National Association for the Education of Young Children. (1986). Position statement on developmentally appropriate practice in programs for 4- and 5-year-olds. *Young Children 41,* 20–29.
National Association for the Education of Young Children. (1988). NAEYC position statement on developmentally appropriate practices in the primary grades, serving 5- through 8-year-olds. *Young Children, 43,* 64–83.
National Association for the Education of Young Children. (1996). NAEYC position statement: Responding to linguistic and cultural diversity. *Young Children, 51,* 4–12.
National Center for Health Statistics. (1989, June). *Statistics on marriage and divorce.* Washington, DC: U.S. Government Printing Office.
National Center for Health Statistics. (1999, June). *National vital statistics reports* (Vol. 47, No. 19, p. 27). Atlanta: Centers for Disease Control and Prevention.
National Center for Health Statistics. (2000). *Health United States, 1999.* Atlanta: Centers for Disease Control and Prevention.
National Research Council. (1999). *Starting out right: A guide to promoting children's reading success.* Washington, DC: National Academy Press.
Negalia, J.P., Friedman, D.L., Yasui, Y., Mertens, A., Hammond, S., Stoval, S., & Donaldson, M. (2001). Second malignant neoplasms in five-year survivors of childhood cancer. *Journal of the National Cancer Institute, 93,* 618–629
Neisser, U., Boodoo, G., Bouchard, T. J., Boykin, A. W., Brody, N., Ceci, S. J., Halpern, D. F., Loehlin, J. C., Perloff, R. J., Sternberg, R., & Urbina, S. (1996). Intelligence: Knowns and unknowns. *American Psychologist, 51,* 77–101.
Nelson, C. (1999). Research description. *Institute of Child Development biennial report.* Minneapolis: Institute of Child Development.
Nelson, K. (1999). Levels and modes of representation: Issues for the theory of conceptual change and development. In E. K. Skolnick, K. Nelson, S. A. Gelman, & P. H. Miller (Eds.), *Conceptual development.* Mahwah, NJ: Erlbaum.
Nelson, M. E., Fiatarone, M. A., Moranti, C. M., Trice, I., Greenberg, R. A., & Evans, W. J. (1994). Effects of high-intensity strength training on multiple risk factors for osteoporotic fractures: A randomized controlled trial. *Journal of the American Medical Association, 272,* 1909–1914.
Nelson-LeGall, S., & Kelly, K. (2001, April). *Gender and ethnicity in the schoolroom.* Paper presented at the meeting of the Society for Research in Child Development, Minneapolis.
Neugarten, B., & Neugarten, D. (1987, May). The changing meaning of age. *Psychology Today.*
Neugarten, B. L. (1964). *Personality in middle and late life.* New York: Atherton.
Neugarten, B. L. (1986). The aging society. In A. Pifer & L. Bronte (Eds.), *Our aging society: Paradox and promise.* New York: W. W. Norton.
Neugarten, B. L. (1988, August). *Policy issues for an aging society.* Paper presented at the meeting of the American Psychological Association, Atlanta.
Neugarten, B. L., Havighurst, R. J., & Tobin, S. S. (1968). Personality and patterns of aging. In B. L. Neugarten (Ed.), *Middle age and aging.* Chicago: University of Chicago Press.
Neugarten, B. L., & Weinstein, K. K. (1964). The changing American grandparent. *Journal of Marriage and the Family, 26,* 199–204.
Newcomb, M., & Bentler, P. (1980). Assessment of personality and demographic aspects of cohabitation and marital success. *Journal of Personality Development, 4,* 11–24.
Newcomb, M. D., & Bentler, P. M. (1989). Substance use and abuse among children and teenagers. *American Psychologist, 44,* 242–248.
NICHD Early Child Care Research Network. (2000). Factors associated with fathers' caregiving activities and sensitivity with young children. *Developmental Psychology, 14,* 200–219.
Nichols, F. H., & Humenick, S. S. (2000). *Childbirth education* (2nd ed.). London: Harcourt International.
Ninio, A., & Snow, C. E. (1996). *Pragmatic development.* Boulder, CO: Westview Press.
Nock, S. (1995). A comparison of marriages and cohabitating relationships. *Journal of Family Issues, 16,* 53–76.
Nolen-Hoeksema, S. (1990). *Sex differences in depression.* Stanford, CA: Stanford University Press.
Nolen-Hoeksema, S. (1998). *Abnormal psychology.* New York: McGraw-Hill.
Nottelmann, E. D., Susman, E. J., Blue, J. H., Inoff-Germain, G., Dorn, L. D., Loriaux, D. L., Cutler, G. B., & Chrousos, G. P. (1987). Gonadal and adrenal hormone correlates of adjustment in early adolescence. In R. M. Lerner & T. T. Foch (Eds.), *Biological-psychological interactions in early adolescence.* Hillsdale, NJ: Erlbaum.
Novak, W. (1983). *The great man shortage.* New York: Rawson.
Nowak, C. A. (1977). Does youthfulness equal attractiveness? In L. E. Troll, J. Israel, & K. Israel (Eds.), *Looking ahead: A woman's guide to the problems and joys of growing older.* Englewood Cliffs, NJ: Prentice Hall.
Nugent, K., & Brazelton, T. B. (2000). Preventive infant mental health: Uses of the Brazelton scale. In J. D. Osofsky & H. E. Fitzgerald (Eds.), *WAIMH Handbook of infant mental health* (Vol. 2). New York: Wiley.
Nussbaum, J.F., Pecchioni, L., & Crowell, T. (2001). The older patient-health care provider relationship in a managed care environment. In M.L. Hummert & J.F. Nussbaum (Eds.), *Aging, communication, and health.* Mahwah, NJ: Erlbaum.

O

Oberauer, K., Demmrich, A., Mayr, U., & Kliegl, R. (2001). Dissociating retention and access in working memory. *Memory and cognition, 29,* 18–33.

Occupational Outlook Handbook (2000–2001). Washington. DC: U.S. Department of Labor.

Offer, D., Ostrov, E., Howard, K. I., & Atkinson, R. (1988). *The teenage world: Adolescents' self image in ten countries.* New York: Plenum.

Office of Juvenile Justice and Prevention. (1999). *Juvenile offenders and victims: 1999. National Report.* Washington. DC: Author.

Ogashi, K. (2001). Academic harassment. *Lancet, 357,* 396–397.

Ogbu, J., & Stern, P. (2001). Caste status and intellectual ability. In R.J. Sternberg & E.L. Grigorenko (Eds.), *Environmental effects on cognitive abilities.* Mahwah, NJ: Erlbaum.

Ogbu, J. U. (1989, April). *Academic socialization of Black children: An innoculation against future failure?* Paper presented at the meeting of the Society for Research in Child Development, Kansas City.

Olivardia, R., Pope, H. G., Mangweth, B., & Hudson, J. I. (1995). Eating disorders in college men. *American Journal of Psychiatry, 152,* 1279–1284

[illegible] (1999, August). *Bilingual infants show neither advantages nor disadvantages over monolingual infants.* Paper presented at the meeting of the American Psychological Association, Boston.

Olsho, L. W., Harkins, S. W., & Lenhardt, M. L. (1985). Aging and the auditory system. In J. E. Birren & K. W. Schaie (Eds.), *Handbook of the psychology of aging* (2nd ed.). New York: Van Nostrand Reinhold.

Olson, H. C. (2000). Fetal alcohol syndrome. In A. Kazdin (Ed.), *Encyclopedia of psychology.* Washington, DC, & New York: American Psychological Association and Oxford University Press.

Olson H. C., & Burgess, D. M. (1996). Early intervention with children prenatally exposed to alcohol and other drugs. In M. J. Guralnick (Eds.), *The effectiveness of early intervention.* Baltimore: Paul H. Brookes.

Olweus, D. (1980). Bullying among schoolboys. In R. Barnen (Ed.), *Children and violence.* Stockholm: Adaemic Litteratur.

Olweus, D. (in press). *Bullying at school: What we know and what we can do.* Oxford: Blackwell.

Orbanic, S. (2001). Understanding bulimia. *American Journal of Nursing, 101,* 35–41.

Organista, K. C. (1994). Overdue overview of elderly Latino mental health. *Contemporary Psychology, 39,* 61–62.

Osipow, S. (2000). Work. In A. Kazdin (Ed.), *Encyclopedia of psychology.* Washington, DC, & New York: American Psychological Association and Oxford University Press.

Ostrea, E. M., Whitehall, J. S., & Laken, M. A. (2000, May). *Prevalence of fetal exposure to environmental toxins: An international study.* Paper presented at the joint meetings of the Pediatric Academic Societies and the American Academy of Pediatrics, Boston.

Overton, W. F., & Byrnes, J. P. (1991). Cognitive development. In R. M. Lerner, A. C. Petersen, and J. Brooks-Gunn (Eds.), *Encyclopedia of adolescence* (Vol. 1). New York: Garland.

Oxman, T.E., Hall, J.G. (2001). Social support and treatment response in older depressed primary care patients. *Journal of Gerontology, 56B, No.1,* P35–P45.

Owen, M. (2001, April). *Family measures in the Phase 1 data set of the NICHD Study of Early Child Care.* Paper presented at the meeting of the Society for Research in Child Development, Minneapolis.

P

Padma-Nathan, H. (1999, March). *Oral drug therapy for erectile dysfunction: What have we learned from the Viagra experience?* Paper presented at the meeting of the American Psychosomatic Association, Vancouver.

Paffenbarger, O., Hyde, R. T., Wing, A. L., & Hsieh, C. (1986). Physical activity, all-cause mortality, and longevity of college alumni. *New England Journal of Medicine, 324,* 605–612.

Paffenbarger, R. S., Hyde, R. T., Wing, A. L., Lee, I., Jung, D. L., & Kampter, J. B. (1993). The [illegible] and other life style characteristics with mortality among men. *New England Journal of Medicine, 328,* 538–545.

Paikoff, R. L., Buchanan, C. M., & Brooks-Gunn, J. (1991). Hormone-behavior links at puberty, methodological links in the study of. In R. M. Lerner, A. C. Petersen, & J. Brooks-Gunn (Eds.), *Encyclopedia of adolescence.* New York: Garland.

Paley, B., Cox, M. J., Burchinal, M. R., & Payne, C. C. (2000). Attachment and marital functioning: Comparison of spouses with continuous-secure, earned-secure, dismissing, and preoccupied attachment stances. *Journal of Family Psychology, 13,* 580–597.

Palmore, E. (1981). *Social patterns in normal aging: Findings from the Duke Longitudinal Study.* Durham, NC: Duke University Press.

Palmore, E. B., Burchett, B. M., Fillenbaum, C. G., George, L. K., & Wallman, L. M. (1985). *Retirement: Causes and consequences.* New York: Springer.

Paloutzian, R. (2000). *Invitation to the psychology of religion* (3rd ed.). Boston: Allyn & Bacon.

Paludi, M. (2001). *Human development in multicultural contexts.* Upper Saddle River, NJ: Prentice-Hall.

Paludi, M. A. (1998). *The psychology of women.* Upper Saddle River, NJ: Prentice Hall.

Panchaud, C., Singh, S., Feivelson, D., & Darroch, J. E. (2000). Sexually transmitted diseases among adolescents in developed countries. *Family Planning Perspectives, 32,* 24–32.

Panofsky, C. (1999, April). *What the zone of proximal development conceals.* Paper presented at the meeting of the Society for Research in Child Development, Montreal.

Pargament, K. E., & Park, C. L. (1995). Merely a defense? Examining psychologists' stereotype of religion. *Journal of Social Issues.*

Pargament, K. I. (1990). God help me: Toward a theoretical framework of coping for the psychology of religion. In M. L. Lynn & D. O. Moberg (Eds.), *Research in the social scientific study of religion* (Vol. 2). Greenwich, CT: JAI Press.

Park, D. C. (in press). *The cognitive psychology of aging.* Cambridge, MA: Blackwell.

Parke, R. D. (1995). Fathers and families. In M. H. Bornstein (Ed.), *Children and parenting* (Vol. 3). Hillsdale, NJ: Erlbaum.

Parke, R. D. (2000). Father involvement: A developmental psychology perspective. *Marriage and Family Review, 29,* 43–58.

Parke, R. D. (2001). Parenting in the new millennium. In J.P. McHale & W.S. Grolnick (Eds.), *Retrospect and prospect in the psychological study of families.* Mahwah, NJ: Erlbaum.

Parke, R. D., & Buriel, R. (1998). Socialization in the family: Ethnic and ecological perspectives. In W. Damon (Ed.), *Handbook of child psychology* (5th ed., Vol. 3). New York: Wiley.

Parkin, A. J., & Walter, B. M. (1992). Recollective experience, normal aging, and frontal dysfunction. *Psychology and Aging, 7,* 290–298.

Parlee, M. B. (1979, April). The friendship bond: PT's survey report on friendship in America. *Psychology Today,* pp. 43–54, 113.

Parnes, H. S., & Sommers, D. G. (1994). Shunning retirement: Work experiences of men in their seventies and early eighties. *Journal of Gerontology, 49,* S117–S124.

Parten, M. (1932). Social play among preschool children. *Journal of Abnormal and Social Psychology, 27,* 243–269.

Pasch, L.A. (2001). Confronting fertility problems. In A. Baum, T.A. Revenson, & J.E. Singer (Eds.), *Handbook of health psychology.* Mahwah, NJ: Erlbaum.

Passuth, P. M., Maines, D. R., & Neugarten, B. L. (1984). *Age norms and age constraints twenty years later.* Paper presented at the annual meeting of the Midwest Sociological Society, Chicago.

Patrick, C. L. (2000). Genetic and environmental influences on the development of cognitive abilities: Evidence from the field of developmental behavior genetics. *Journal of School Psychology, 38,* 79–108.

Patterson, C. (1995). Lesbian and gay parenthood. In M. H. Bornstein (Ed.), *Handbook of parenting* (Vol. 3). Mahwah, NJ: Erlbaum.

Patterson, C. (1996). Lesbian mothers and their children: Findings from the Bay Area Families Study. In J. Laird & R. Green (Eds.), *Lesbians and gays in couples and families.* San Francisco: Jossey-Bass.

Patterson, C. J. (1995). Sexual orientation and human development: An overview. *Developmental Psychology, 31,* 3–11.

Patterson, C. J. (2000). Family relationships of lesbians and gay men. *Journal of Marriage and the Family, 62,* 1052–1069.

Patterson, G. R., DeBaryshe, B. D., & Ramsey, E. (1989). A developmental perspective on antisocial behavior. *American Psychologist, 44,* 329–355.

Pavlov, I. P. (1927). In G. V. Anrep (Trans.), *Conditioned reflexes.* London: Oxford University Press.

Payer, L. (1991). The menopause in various cultures. In H. Burger & M. Boulet (Eds.), *A portrait of the menopause.* Park Ridge, NJ: Parthenon.

Pearlin, L. I. (1994). The study of the oldest-old: Some promises and puzzles. *International Journal of Aging and Human Development, 38,* 91–98.

Peck, R. C. (1968). Psychological developments in the second half of life. In B. L. Neugarten (Ed.), *Middle age and aging.* Chicago: University of Chicago Press.

Pentz, M. A. (1994). Primary prevention of adolescent drug abuse. In C. Fisher & R. Lerner (Eds.), *Applied developmental psychology.* New York: McGraw-Hill.

Peplau, L. A. (1991). Lesbian and gay relationships. In J. C. Gonsiorek & J. D. Weinrich (Eds.), *Homosexuality: Research implications for public policy.* Newbury Park, CA: Sage.

Peplau, L. A., & Gordon, S. L. (1985). Women and men in love: Gender differences in close heterosexual relationships. In V. E. O'Leary, R. K. Unger, & B. S. Wallston (Eds.), *Women, gender, and social psychology.* Hillsdale, NJ: Erlbaum.

Peplau, L. A., & Spalding, L. R. (2000). The close relationships of lesbians, gay men, and bisexuals. In C. Hendrick and S. S. Hendrick (Eds.), *Close relationships: A sourcebook.* Thousand Oaks, CA: Sage.

Peplau, L. A., Veniegas, R. C., & Campbell, S. M. (1996). Gay and lesbian relationships. In R. C. Savin-Williams & K. M. Cohen (Eds.), *The lives of lesbians, gays, and bisexuals.* Fort Worth: Harcourt Brace.

Perdue, C. W. (2000). Ageism. In A. Kazdin (Ed.), *Encyclopedia of psychology.* Washington, DC, & New York: American Psychological Association and Oxford University Press.

Perlman, D., & Peplau, L. A. (1998). Loneliness. In H.S. Friedman (Ed.), *Encyclopedia of mental health* (Vol. 2). San Diego: Academic Press.

Perls, T. (1999, November). *An Internet-based life expectancy calculator.* Paper presented at the meeting of the Gerontological Association of America, San Francisco.

Perls, T., Lauerman, J. F., & Silver, M. H. (1999). *Living to 100.* New York: Basic Books.

Perry, C. M., & Johnson, C. L. (1994). Families and support networks among African American oldest-old. *International Journal of Aging on Human Development, 38,* 41–50.

Perry, W. G. (1970). *Forms of intellectual and ethical development in the college years.* New York: Holt, Rinehart & Winston.

Perusse, D. (1999, April). *Normal and abnormal early motor-cognitive development: A function of exposure to shared environmental risks.* Paper presented at the meeting of the Society for Research in Child Development, Albuquerque.

Peskin, H. (1967). Pubertal onset and ego functioning. *Journal of Abnormal Psychology, 72,* 1–15.

Petersen, A. C. (1979, January). Can puberty come any faster? *Psychology Today,* pp. 45–56.

Petersen, A. C. (1993). Creating adolescents: The role of context and process in developmental trajectories. *Journal of Research on Adolescence, 3,* 1–18.

Peterson, B. E., & Stewart, A. J. (1996). Antecedents and contexts of generativity motivation at midlife. *Psychology and Aging, 11,* 21–33.

Peterson, C. (1999). Grandfathers' and grandmothers' satisfaction with the grandparenting role: Seeking new answers to old questions. *International Journal of Aging and Human Development, 49,* 61–78.

Peterson, C. C. (1996). The ticking of the social clock: Adults' beliefs about the timing of transition events *International Journal of Aging and Human Development, 42,* 189–203.

Peterson, K. S. (1997, September 3). In high school, dating is a world into itself. *USA Today,* pp. 1–2D.

Peth-Pierce, R. (1998). *The NICHD Study of Early Child Care.* Washington, DC: National Institute of Child Health and Human Development.

Phillips, D., Friedman, S. L., Huston, A. C., & Weinraub, M. (1999, April). *The roles of work and poverty in the lives of families with young children.* Paper presented at the meeting of the Society for Research in Child Development, Albuquerque.

Phillips, D. A., Voran, K., Kisker, E., Howes, C., & Whitebook, M. (1994). Child care for children in poverty: Opportunity or inequity? *Child Development, 65,* 472–492.

Philpot, C. L., Brooks, G. R., Lusterman, D., & Nutt, R. L. (1997). *Bridging separate gender worlds.* Washington, DC: American Psychological Association.

Phinney, J. (2000). Ethnic identity. In A. Kazdin (Ed.), *Encyclopedia of psychology.* Washington, DC, & New York: American Psychological Association and Oxford University Press.

Phinney, J. A., & Rosenthal, D. A. (1992). Ethnic identity in adolesence. In G. R. Adams, T. P. Gullotta, & R. Montemayor (Eds.), *Adolescent identity formation.* Newbury Park, CA: Sage.

Phinney, J. S. (1989). Stages of ethnic identity development in minority group adolescents. *Journal of Early Adolescence, 9,* 34–49.

Phinney, J. S., & Alipura, L. L. (1990). Ethnic identity in college students from four ethnic groups. *Journal of Adolescence, 13,* 171–183.

Phinney, J. S., & Devich-Navarro, M. (1997). Variations in bicultural identification among African American and Mexican American adolescents. *Journal of Research on Adolescence, 7,* 3–32.

Phinney, J. S., Ong, A., & Madden, T. (in press). Cultural values and intergenerational discrepancies in immigrant and non-immigrant families. *Child Development.*

Piaget, J. (1932). *The moral judgment of the child.* New York: Harcourt Brace Jovanovich.

Piaget, J. (1952). *The origins of intelligence in children.* New York: International Universities Press.

Piaget, J. (1952a). Jean Piaget. In C. A. Murchison (Ed.). *A history of psychology in autobiography* (Vol. 4). Worcester, MA: Clark University Press.

Piaget, J. (1954). *The construction of reality in the child.* New York: Basic Books.

Piaget, J. (1962). *Play, dreams, and imitation.* New York. W. W. Norton.

Piaget, J., & Inhelder, B. (1969). *The child's conception of space* (F. J. Langdon & J. L. Lunzer, Trans.). New York: W. W. Norton.

Pick, H. L. (1997). Unpublished review of J. W. Santrock's *Child Develoment,* 8th ed. (New York: McGraw-Hill).

Pierce, K. M., Hamm, J. V., & Vandell, D. L. (1997, April). *Experiences in after-school programs and children's adjustment at school and at home.* Paper presented at the meeting of the Society for Research in Child Development, Washington, DC.

Pillow, D. R., Zautra, A. J., & Sandler, I. (1996). Major life events and minor stressors: Identifying mediational links in the stress process. *Journal of Personality and Social Psychology, 70,* 381–394.

Pinger, R. R., Payne, W. A., Hahn, D. B., & Hahn, E. J. (1998). *Drugs* (3rd ed.). New York: McGraw-Hill.

Pinker, S. (1994). *The language instinct.* New York: HarperCollins.

Plackslin, S. (2000). *Mothering the new mother: Women's feelings and needs after childbirth—A support and resource guide.* New York: Newmarket Press.

Plant, E. A., Hyde, J. S., Kelner, D., & Devine, P. G. (2000). The gender stereotyping of emotions. *Psychology of Women Quarterly, 242,* 81–92.

Pleck, J. H. (1981). *The myth of masculinity.* Beverly Hills, CA: Sage.

Pleck, J. H. (1983). The theory of male sex role identity: Its rise and fall, 1936–present. In M. Levin (Ed.), *In the shadow of the past: Psychology portrays the sexes.* New York: Columbia University Press.

Pleck, J. H. (1995). The gender-role strain paradigm. In R. F. Levant & W. S. Pollack (Eds.), *A new psychology of men.* New York: Basic Books.

Plomin, R. (1993, March). *Human behavioral genetics and development: An overview and update.* Paper presented at the biennial meeting of the Society for Research in Child Development, New Orleans.

Plomin, R., & DeFries, J. C. (1998). The genetics of abilities and disabilities. *Scientific American, 278,* 40–48.

Plomin, R., DeFries, J. C., & McClearn, G. E. (1990). *Behavioral genetics: A primer.* New York: W. H. Freeman.

Plomin, R., Reiss, D., Hetherington, E. M., & Howe, G. W. (1994). Nature and nurture: Contributions to measures of the family environment. *Developmental Psychology, 30,* 32–43.

Pollack, H.A. (2001). Sudden infant death syndrome, maternal smoking during pregnancy, and the cost-effectiveness of smoking cessation intervention. *American Journal of Public Health, 91,* 432–436.

Pollitt, E. P., Gorman, K. S., Engle, P. L., Martorell, R., & Rivera, J. (1993). Early supplementary feeding and cognition. *Monographs of the Society for Research in Child Development, 58* (7, Serial No. 235).

Pomerleau, O. (2000). Smoking. In A. Kazdin (Ed.), *Encyclopedia of psychology.* Washington, DC, & New York: American Psychological Association and Oxford University Press.

Posner, J. K., & Vandell, D. L. (1994). Low-income children's after-school care: Are there benefits of after-school programs? *Child Development, 65,* 440–456.

Posner, M. I. (1999, April). *Relating mechanisms of cognitive and emotional regulation.* Paper presented at the meeting of the Society for Research in Child Development, Albuquerque.

Potter, S. M., Zelazo, P. R., Stack, D. M., & Papageorgiou, A. N. (2000). Adverse effects of fetal cocaine exposure on neonatal auditory information processing. *Pediatrics, 105,* e40–e41.

Potvin, L., Champagne, F., & Laberge-Nadeau, C. (1988). Mandatory driver training and road safety: The Quebec experience. *American Journal of Public Health, 78,* 1206–1212.

Poulton, S., & Sexton, D. (1996). Feeding young children: Developmentally appropriate considerations for supplementing family care. *Childhood Education, 73,* 66–71.

Powers, L. E., & Wampold, B. E. (1994). Cognitive-behavioral factors in adjustment to adult bereavement. *Death Studies, 18,* 1–24.

Pratt, M. W., Danso, H.A., Arnold, M.L., Norris, J.E., & Filyer, R. (2001). Adult generativity and the socialization of adolescents. *Journal of Personality, 69,* 89–120.

Pressley, M. (1983). Making meaningful materials easier to learn. In M. Pressley & J. R. Levin (Eds.), *Cognitive strategy research: Educational applications* (pp. 239–266). New York: Springer-Verlag.

Pressley, M. (1996). Personal reflections on the study of practical memory in the mid-1990s. In D. Hermann, C. McEvoy, C. Hertzog, P. Hertel, & M. Johnson (Eds.), *Basic and applied memory research* (Vol. 2). Hillsdale, NJ: Erlbaum.

Pressley, M. (1996, August). *Getting beyond whole language: Elementary reading instruction that makes sense in light of recent psychological research.* Paper presented at the meeting of the American Psychological Association, Toronto.

Prohaska, T., & Peters, K. (1999, November). *Walking exercise behavior in younger and older adults: An evaluation of a mall walking program.* Paper presented at the meeting of the Gerontological Association of America, San Francisco.

Province, M. A., Hadley, E. C., Hornbrook, M. C., Lipitz, L. A., Miller, J. P., Mulrow, C. D., Ory, M. G., Sattin, R. W., Tinetti, M. E., & Wolf, S. L. (1995). The effects of exercise on falls in elderly patients. *Journal of the American Medical Association, 273,* 1341–1347.

Pruett, M.K., & Jackson, T.D. (2001). Perspectives on the divorce process. *Journal of the American Academy of Psychiatry and Law, 29,* 18–28.

Pyke, K. D., & Bengtson, V. L. (1996). Caring more or less: Individualistic and collectivist systems of family eldercare. *Journal of Marriage and the Family, 58,* 379–392.

R

Rabin, B. E., & Dorr, A. (1995, March). *Children's understanding of emotional events on family television series.* Paper presented at the meeting of the Society for Research in Child Development, Indianapolis.

Radford, A. (2001). Unicef is crucial in promoting and supporting breast feeding. *British Medical Journal, 322,* 555.

Räikkönen, K., Matthews, K. A., Flory, J. D., & Owens, J. F. (1999). Effects of hostility on ambulatory blood pressure and mood during daily living in healthy adults. *Health Psychology, 18,* 44–53.

Ramey, C. T., & Campbell, F. A. (1984). Preventive education for high-risk children: Cognitive consequences of the Carolina Abecedarian Project. *American Journal of Mental Deficiency, 88,* 515–523.

Ramey, C. T., Campbell, F. A., Burchinal, M., Skinner, M. L., Gardner, D. M., & Ramey, S. L. (in press). Persistent effects of early intervention on high-risk children and their mothers. *Applied Developmental Science.*

Ramey, C. T., Campbell, F. A., & Ramey, S. L. (in press). Early intervention: Successful pathways to improving intellectual development. *Journal of Developmental Neuropsychology.*

Ramey, C. T., & Ramey, S. L., (1998). Early prevention and early experience. *American Psychologist, 53,* 109–120.

Ramsay, D. S. (1980). Onset of unimanual handedness in infants. *Infant Behavior and Development, 3,* 377–385.

Rapaport, S. (1994, November 28). Interview. *U.S. News and World Report,* p. 94.

Rapport, M. D. & Chung, K. (2000). Attention deficit hyperactivity disorder. In M. Herson & R. T. Ammerman (Eds.), *Advanced abnormal child psychology* (2nd ed.). Mahwah, NJ: Erlbaum.

Rapport, M.D., Chung, K.M., Shore, G., & Issacs, P. (2001). A conceptual model of child psychopathology: Implications for understanding a deficit hyperactivity disorder and treatment effectiveness. *Journal of Clinical Child Psychology, 30,* 48–58.

Raudenbush, S. (2001). Longitudinal data analysis. *Annual Review of Psychology* (Vol. 52). Palo Alto, CA: Annual Reviews.

Ray, O. S., & Ksir, C. (1999). *Drugs, society, and human behavior* (8th ed.). New York: McGraw-Hill.

Redinbaugh, E. M., MacCallum, J., & Kiecolt-Glaser, J. K. (1995). Recurrent syndromal depression in caregivers. *Psychology and Aging, 10,* 358–368.

Reedy, M. N., Birren, J. E., & Schaie, K. W. (1981). Age and sex differences in satisfying relationships across the adult life span. *Human Development, 24,* 52–66.

Reid, J. D., & Willis, S. L. (1999). Middle age: New thoughts, new directions. In S. L. Willis & J. D. Reid (Eds.), *Life in the middle.* San Diego: Academic Press.

Reid, P. (2000). *Psychologists work in the community.* Available on the world wide web at: http://www.apa.org/students/brochure/community.html.

Reifman, A. (2001). Models of parenting and adolescent drinking. *American Psychologist, 56,* 170–171.

Reinhardt, J.P. (2001). Social support and well-being in later life. In J.P. Reinhardt (Ed.), *Negative and positive support.* Mahwah, NJ: Erlbaum.

Reinisch, J. (1992, December 7). Commentary, *Newsweek,* p. 54.

Reis, D., Neiderhiser, J. M., Hetherington, E. M., & Plomin, R. (2000). *The relationship code.* Cambridge, MA: Harvard University Press.

Religion in America. (1993). Princeton, N J: Princeton Religious Research Center.

Remafedi, G., Resnick, M., Blum, R., & Harris, L. (in press). The demography of sexual orientation in adolescents. *Pediatrics.*

Reschly, D. J. (1996). Identification and assessment of students with disabilities. In *Special education for students with disabilities.* Los Altos, Ca: The David and Lucile Packard Foundation.

Resnick, M. B., Gueorguieva, R. V., Cater, R. L., Ariet, M., Sun, Y., Roth, J., Bucciarelli, R. L., Curran, J. S., & Mahan, C. S. (1999). The impact of low birth weight, perinatal conditions, and sociodemographic factors on educational outcome in kindergarten. *Pediatrics, 104,* e74–e75.

Rest, J. (1999). *Postconventional moral thinking.* Mahwah, NJ: Erlbaum.

Reynolds, A. J. (1999, April). *Pathways to long-term effects in the Chicago Child-Parent Center Program.* Paper presented at the meeting of the Society for Research in Child Development, Albuquerque.

Rhodes, S. R. (1983). Age-related differences in work attitudes and behavior: A review and conceptual analysis. *Psychological Bulletin, 93,* 329–367.

Richards, L. N., Bengston, V. L., & Miller, R. B. (1989). The "generation in the middle": Perceptions of changes in adults' intergenerational relationships. In K. Kreppner & R. M. Lerner (Eds.), *Family systems and life-span development.* Hillsdale, NJ: Erlbaum.

Richards, M. H., & Duckett, E. (1994). The relationship of maternal employment to early adolescent daily experiences with and without parents. *Child Development, 65,* 225–236.

Rickards, T. (1999). Brainstorming. In M. A. Runco & S. Pritzker (Eds.), *Encyclopedia of creativity.* San Diego: Academic Press.

Ridgeway, D., Waters, E., & Kuczaj, S. A. (1985). Acquisition of emotion-descriptive language: Receptive and productive vocabulary norms for ages 18 months to 6 years. *Developmental Psychology, 21,* 901–908.

Riegel, K. F., & Riegel, R. M. (1972). Development, drop, and death. *Developmental Psychology, 6,* 306–319.

Rifkind, B. M., & Rossouw, J. E. (1998). Of designer drugs, magic bullets, and gold standards. *Journal of the American Medical Association, 279,* 1483–1491.

Rimberg, H. M., & Lewis, R. J. (1994). Older adolescents and AIDS: Correlates of self-reported safer sex practices. *Journal of Research on Adolescence, 4,* 453–464.

Rimm, E. B., Stampfer, M. J., Ascherio, A., Giovannucci, E., Colditz, G. A., & Willett, W. C. (1993). Vitamin E consumption and the risk of

coronary heart disease in men. *New England Journal of Medicine, 328,* 1450–1456.
Ringdal, G.I., Jordhoy, M.S., Ringdal, K., & Kaasa, S. (2001). The first year of grief and bereavement in close family members to individuals who have died of cancer. *Palliative Medicine, 15,* 91–105.
Roberts, B. L., Dunkle, R., & Haug, M. (1994). Physical, psychological, and social resources as moderators of stress to mental health of the very old. *Journal of Gerontology, 49,* S35–S43.
Roberts, W., & Strayer, J. (1996). Empathy, emotional expressiveness, and prosocial behavior. *Child Development, 67,* 471–489.
Robinson, D. P., & Greene, J. W. (1988). The adolescent alcohol and drug problem: A practical approach. *Pediatric Nursing, 14,* 305–310.
Rode, S. S., Chang, P., Fisch, R. O., & Sroufe, L. A. (1981). Attachment patterns of infants separated at birth. *Developmental Psychology, 17,* 188–191.
Rodgers, C. (2000). Gender schema. In A. Kazdin (Ed.), *Encyclopedia of psychology*. Washington, DC., and New York: American Psychological Association and Oxford University Press.
Rodgers, J. L. (2000). Birth order. In A. Kazdin (Ed.), *Encyclopedia of psychology*. Washington, DC. and New York: American Psychological Association and Oxford University Press.
Rodin, J. (1983). Behavioral medicine: Beneficial effects of self-control training in aging. *International Review of Applied Psychology, 32,* 153–181.
Rodin, J. (1990, January). Conversation with Robert Trotter. *Longevity,* pp. 60–67.
Rodin, J. (1992) *Body traps.* New York: William Morrow.
Rodin, J., & Langer, E. J. (1977). Long-term effects of a control-relevant intervention with the institutionalized aged. *Journal of Personality and Social Psychology, 35,* 397–402.
Rodriquez, J. L., Diaz, R. M., Duran, D., & Espinosa, L. (1995). The impact of bilingual preschool education on the language development of Spanish-speaking children. *Early Childhood Research Quarterly, 10,* 475–490.
Rogers, A. (1987). *Questions of gender differences: Ego development and moral voice in adolescence.* Unpublished manuscript, Department of Education, Harvard University.
Rogoff, B. (1998). Cognition as a collaborative process. In W. Damon (Ed.), *Handbook of child psychology* (5th ed., Vol. 2). New York: Wiley.
Rogoff, B. (2001, April). *Examining cultural processes in developmental research.* Paper presented at the meeting of the Society for Research in Child Development, Minneapolis.
Rogoff, B., Turkanis, C.G., & Bartlett, L. (2001). *Learning together.* New York: Oxford U. Press.
Rogosch, F. A., Cicchetti, D., Shields, A., & Toth, S. L. (1995). Parenting dysfunction in child maltreatment. In M. H. Bornstein (Ed.), *Handbook of parenting* (Vol. 4). Hillsdale, NJ: Erlbaum.
Rohner, R. P., & Rohner, E. C. (1981). Parental acceptance-rejection and parental control: Cross-cultural codes. *Ethnology, 20,* 245–260.
Rook, K. S. (2000). The evolution of social relationships in later adulthood. In S. H. Qualls & N. Abeles (Eds.), *Psychology and the aging revolution.* Washington, DC: American Psychological Association.
Roopnarine, J. L., & Johnson, J. E. (2000). *Approaches to early childhood education.* Columbus, OH: Merrill.
Roper Starch Worldwide. (2000). *Attitudes toward retirement: A poll.* New York: Author.
Rose, A. A., Feldman, J. F., McCarton, C. M., & Wolfson, J. (1988). Information processing in seven-month-old infants as a function of risk status. *Child Development, 59,* 489–603.
Rose, A. J., & Asher, S. R. (1999, April). *Seeking and giving social support within a friendship.* Paper presented at the meeting of the Society for Research in Child Development, Albuquerque.
Rose, S., & Frieze, I. R. (1993). Young singles' contemporary dating scripts. *Sex Roles, 28,* 499–509.
Rosen, K. H., & Stith, S. M. (1995). Women terminating abusive dating relationships: A qualitative study. *Journal of Personal and Social Relationships, 12,* 155–160.
Rosen, K. S., & Burke, P. B. (1999). Multiple attachment relationships within families: Mothers and fathers with two young children. *Developmental Psychology, 35,* 436–444.
Rosenblith, J. F. (1992). *In the beginning* (2nd ed.). Newbury Park, CA: Sage.
Rosenfeld, A., & Stark, E. (1987, May). The prime of our lives. *Psychology Today.* pp. 62–72.
Rosenstein, D., & Oster, H. (1988). Differential facial responses to four basic tastes in newborns. *Child Development, 59,* 1555–1568.
Rosenstock, I. (2000). Health belief model. In A. Kazdin (Ed.), *Encyclopedia of psychology.* Washington, DC. & New York: American Psychological Association and Oxford University Press.
Rosenzweig, M. (2000). Ethology. In A. Kazdin (Ed.), *Encyclopedia of psychology.* Washington, DC, & New York: American Psychological Association and Oxford University Press.
Rosenzweig, M. R. (1969). Effects of heredity and environment on brain chemistry, brain anatomy, and learning ability in the rat. In M. Monosevitz, G. Lindzey, & D. D. Thiessen (Eds.), *Behavioral genetics.* New York: Appleton-Century-Crofts.
Rossi, A. (1980). Aging and parenthood in the middle years. In P. Baltes & O. Brim (Eds.), *Life-span development and behavior* (Vol. 3). New York: Academic Press.
Rossi, A. S. (1989). A life-course approach to gender, aging, and intergenerational relations. In K. W. Schaie & C. Schooler (Eds.), *Social structure and aging.* Hillsdale, NJ: Erlbaum.
Rosylyn, A. (2000). *Complicated losses, difficult deaths: A practical guide for ministering to grievers.* New York: Resource Publications.
Roth, J., & Brooks-Gunn, J. (2000). What do adolescents need for healthy development? Implications for youth policy. *Social Policy Report, 14,* (1), 3–19.
Rothbart, M. K. (1999, April). *Developing a model for the study of temperament.* Paper presented at the meeting of the Society for Research in Child Development, Albuquerque.
Rothbart, M. K., & Bates, J. E. (1998). Temperament. In W. Damon (Ed.). *Handbook of child psychology* (5th ed., Vol. 3). New York: Wiley.
Rothbart, M. L. K. (1971). Birth order and mother-child interaction, *Dissertation Abstracts, 27,* 45–57.
Rothbaum, F., Pott, M., Azuma, H., Miyake, K., & Weisz, J. (2000). The development of close relationships in Japan and the United States: Paths of symbiotic harmony and generative tension. *Child Development, 71,* 1121–1142.
Rothstein, R. (1998, May). Bilingual education: The controversy. *Phi Delta Kappan,* 672–678.
Rovee-Collier, C. (1987). Learning and memory in children. In J. D. Osofsky (Ed.), *Handbook of infant development* (2nd ed.). New York: Wiley.
Rovee-Collier, C. (2001). Infant learning and memory. In A. Fogel & G. Bremner (Eds.), *Blackwell handbook of infant development.* London: Blackwell.
Rovee-Collier, C., Hartshorn, K., & DiRubbio, M. (1999). *Long-term maintenance of infant memory.* Unpublished manuscript, Department of Psychology. Rutgers University, New Brunswick, NJ.
Rowe, D.C. (2001). The nurture assumption persists. *American Psychologist, 56,* 168–169.
Rowe, J. W., & Kahn, R. L. (1997). *Successful aging.* New York: Pantheon Books.
Rowe, J. W., & Kahn, R. L. (1998). *Successful aging.* New York: Pantheon Books.
Rubenstein, L. Z., Josephson, K. R., Trueblood, P. R., Loy, S., Harker, J. O., Pietruszka, F. M., & Robbins, A. S. (2000). Effects of group exercise program on strength, mobility, and falls among fall-prone elderly men. *Journal of Gerontology: Medical Sciences, 55A,* M317–M321.
Rubin, D. H., Krasilnikoff, P. A., Leventhal, J. M., Weile, B., & Berget, A. (1986, August 23). Effect of passive smoking on birthweight. *The Lancet,* 415–417.
Rubin, K. (2000). Middle childhood: Social and emotional development. In A. Kazdin (Ed.), *Encyclopedia of psychology.* Washington, DC, & New York: American Psychological Association and Oxford University Press.
Rubin, K. H., Fein, G. G., & Vandenberg, B. (1983). Play. In P. H. Mussen (Ed.), *Handbook of child psychology* (4th ed., Vol. 4). New York: Wiley.
Rubin, K. H., Maioni, T. L., & Hornung, M. (1976). Free play behaviors in middle and lower social class preschoolers: Parten and Piaget revisited. *Child Development, 47,* 414–419.
Rubin, S. (in press). The death of a child is forever. The life course impact of child loss. In M. Stroebe, W. Stroebe, & R. O. Hanson (Eds.), *Handbook of bereavement.* New York: Cambridge University Press.
Rubin, Z. (1970). Measurement of romantic love. *Journal of Personality and Social Psychology, 16,* 265–273.
Ruble, D. (2000). Gender constancy. In A. Kazdin (Ed.), *Encyclopedia of psychology.* Washington, DC., and New York: American Psychological Association and Oxford University Press.
Rudolph, K. L., Chang, S., Lee, H., Gottlieb, G. J., Greider, C., & DePinho, R. A. (1999). Longevity, stress response, and cancer in aging telomerase-deficient mice. *Cell, 96,* 701–712.
Rumberger, R. W. (1995). Dropping out of middle school: A multilevel analysis of students and schools. *American Educational Research Journal, 3,* 583–625.

Runco, M. (2000). Research on the processes of creativity. In A. Kazdin (Ed.), *Encyclopedia of psychology.* Washington, DC, & New York: American Psychological Association and Oxford University Press.

Runco, M. A. (1999). Critical thinking. In M. A. Runco & S. Pritzker (Eds.), *Encyclopedia of creativity.* San Diego: Academic Press.

Russek, L. G., & Schwartz, G. E. (1997). Feelings of parental caring predict health status in midlife: A 35-year follow-up of the Harvard Mastery Study of Stress. *Journal of Behavioral Medicine, 30,* 1–13.

Russell, D. W. (1996). UCLA Loneliness Scale (Version 3): Reliability, validity, and factor structure. *Journal of Personality, Assessment, 66,* 20–43.

Ruth, J., & Coleman, P. (1996). *Personality and aging.* Cambridge, MA: Blackwell.

Rutter, M. (2001, April). *Nature, nurture, and development.* Paper presented at the meeting of the Society for Research in Child Development, Minneapolis.

Ryan, A. S. (1997). The resurgence of breastfeeding in the United States. *Pediatrics, 99,* E-12.

Ryan, R. M., & La Guardia, J. G. (2000). What is being optimized?: Self-determination theory and basic psychological needs. In S. H. Qualls & N. Abeles (Eds.), *Psychology and the aging revolution.* Washington, DC: [illegible] Psychological Association.

Ryan-Finn, K. D., Cauce, A. M., & Grove, K. (1995, March). *Children and adolescents of color: Where are you? Selection, recruitment, and retention in developmental research.* Paper presented at the meeting of the Society for Research in Child Development, Indianapolis.

Ryff, C. D. (1984). Personality development from the inside: The subjective experience of change in adulthood and aging. In P. B. Baltes & O. G. Brim (Eds.), *Life-span development and behavior.* New York: Academic Press.

Ryff, C. D., & Singer, B. (2000). Interpersonal flourishing: A positive health agenda for the new millennium. *Personality and Social Psychology Review, 4,* 30–44.

Ryff, C. D., Singer, B., Wing, E. H., & Love, G. D. (in press). Elective affinities and uninvited agonies: Mapping emotion with significant others onto health. In C. D. Ryff & B. Singer (Eds.), *Emotion, social relationships, and health.* New York: Oxford University Press.

S

Saarni, C. (1999). *The development of emotional competence.* New York: Guilford.

Saarni, C., Mumme, D. L., & Campos, J. J. (1998). Emotional development: Action, communication, and understanding. In W. Damon (Ed.), *Handbook of child psychology (5th ed., Vol. 3).* New York: Wiley.

Sabini, J. (1995). *Social psychology (2nd ed.).* New York: Norton.

Saczynski, J. S., Willis, S. L., & Schaie, K. W. (1999, November). *Cognitive training effects in normal, non-demented elderly: Associated variables and maintenance of training gains.* Paper presented at the meeting of the Gerontological Society of America, San Francisco.

Sadavoy, J., Lazarus, L. W., Jarvik, L. E., & Grossberg, G. T. (Eds.). (1996). *Comprehensive review of geriatric psychiatry* (2nd ed.). Washington, DC: American Psychiatric Press.

Sadker, M., & Sadker, D. (1994). *Failing at fairness.* New York: Touchstone.

Sagan, C. (1977). *The Dragons of Eden.* New York: Random House.

Saigal, S., Hoult, L. A., Steiner, D. L., Stoskopf, B. L., & Roenbaum, P. L. (2000). School difficulties at adolescence in a regional cohort of children who were extremely low birth weight. *Pediatrics, 105,* 325–331.

Salovy, P., & Mayer, J. D. (1990). Emotional intelligence. *Imagination, Cognition, and Personality, 9,* 185–211.

Salthouse, T. (1994). The nature of influence of speed on adult differences in cognition. *Developmental Psychology, 30,* 240–259.

Salthouse, T. (2000). Adult development and aging: Cognitive processes and development. In A. Kazdin (Ed.), *Encyclopedia of psychology.* Washington, DC, & New York: American Psychological Association and Oxford University Press.

Salthouse, T. A. (1984). Effects of age and skill in typing. *Journal of Experimental Psychology: General, 113,* 345–371.

Salthouse, T. A. [illegible] *cognitive aging.* Mahwah, NJ: Erlbaum.

Salthouse, T. A. (1994). The aging of working memory. *Neuropsychology, 8,* 535–543.

Salthouse, T. A. (1996). General and specific speed mediation of adult age differences in memory. *Journal of Gerontology, 51A,* P30–P42.

Salthouse, T. A. (2000). Adulthood and aging: Cognitive processes and development. In A. Kazdin (Ed.), *Encyclopedia of psychology.* Washington, DC, & New York: American Psychoiogical Association and Oxford University Press.

Salthouse, T. A., & Skovronek, E. (1992). Within-context assessment of working memory. *Journal of Gerontology, 47,* P110–P117.

Samour, P. Q., Helm, K. K., & Lang, C. E. (Eds.). (2000). *Handbook of pediatric nutrition* (2nd ed.). Aspen, CO: Aspen.

Samuels, M., & Samuels, N. (1996). *New well pregnancy book.* New York: Fireside.

Sanders, G. F., & Trygstad, D. W. (1993). Strengths in the grandparent-grandchild relationship. *Activities, Adaptation and Aging, 17,* 43–50.

Sandler, D. P., Comstock, G. W., Helsing, K. J., & Shore, D. L. (1989). Deaths from all causes in nonsmokers who lived with smokers. *American Journal of Public Health, 79,* 163–167.

Sands, R. G., & Goldberg-Glen, R. S. (2000). Factors associated with stress among grandparents raising their grandchildren. *Family Relations, 49,* 97–105.

Sangree, W. H. (1989). Age and power: Life-course trajectories and age structuring of power relations in East and West Africa. In D. I. Kertzer & K. W. Schaie (Eds.), *Age structuring in comparative perspective.* Hillsdale, NJ: Erlbaum.

Sanson, A., & Rothbart, M. K. (1995). Child temperament and parenting. In M. H. Bornstein (Ed.), *Handbook of parenting* (Vol. 4). Hillsdale, NJ: Erlbaum.

Santacruz, K.S., & Swagerty, D. (2001). Early diagnosis of dementia. *American Family Physician, 63,* 703–13.

Santrock, J. W. (in press). *Educational Psychology.* New York: McGraw-Hill.

Santrock, J. W., & Halonen, J. A. (1999). *Mastering the college experience.* Belmont, CA: Wadsworth.

Santrock, J. W., & Sitterle, K. A. (1987). Parent-child relationships in stepmother families. In K. Pasley & M. Thinger-Tallman (Eds.), *Remarriage and stepparenting.* New York: Guilford Press.

Santrock, J. W., Sitterle, K. A., & Warshak, R. A. (1988). Parent-child relationships in stepfather families. In P. Bronstein & C. P. Cowan (Eds.), *Fatherhood today: Men's changing roles in the family.* New York: Wiley.

Sarason, I., & Sarason, B. (1996). *Abnormal psychology* (8th ed.). Upper Saddle River, NJ: Prentice Hall.

Sarigiani, P. A., & Petersen, A. C. (2000). Adolescence: Puberty and biological maturation. In A. Kazdin (Ed.), *Encyclopedia of psychology.* Washington, DC, & New York: American Psychological Association and Oxford University Press.

Sarrel, P., & Masters, W. (1982). Sexual molestation of men by women. *Archives of Human Sexuality, 11,* 117–131.

Sauber, M., & Corrigan, E. M. (1970). *The six year* [illegible] York: Community Council of Greater New York.

Savin-Williams, R. C., & Rodriguez, R. G. (1993). A developmental, clinical perspective on lesbian, gay male, and bisexual youths. In T. P. Gullotta, G. R. Adams, & R. Montemayor (Eds.), *Adolescent sexuality.* Newbury Park, CA: Sage.

Sax, L. J., Astin, A. W., Korn, W. S., & Mahoney, K. M. (1999). *The American freshman: National norms for 1998.* Los Angeles: UCLA, Higher Education Research Institute.

Sax, L. J., Astin, A. W., Korn, W. S., & Mahoney, K. M. (2000). *The American freshman: National norms for fall 2000.* Los Angeles: UCLA, Higher Education Research Institute.

Scarr, S. (1984, May). Interview. *Psychology Today.* pp. 59–63.

Scarr, S. (1996). Best of human genetics. *Contemporary Psychology, 41,* 149–150.

Scarr, S. (2000). Day care. In A. Kazdin (Ed.), *Encyclopedia of Psychology.* Washington, DC, & New York: American Psychological Association and Oxford University Press.

Scarr, S., & Weinberg, R. A. (1978). The influence of "family background" on intellectual attainment. *American Sociological Review, 43,* 674–692.

Scarr, S., & Weinberg, R. A. (1980). Calling all camps! The war is over. *American Sociological Review, 45,* 859–865.

Scarr, S., & Weinberg, R. A. (1983). The Minnesota adoption studies: Genetic differences and malleability. *Child Development, 54,* 253–259.

Schaffer, H. R. (1996). *Social development.* Cambridge, MA: Blackwell.

Schaie, K. W., (1977). Toward a stage theory of adult cognitive development. *Aging and Human Development, 8,* 129–138.

Schaie, K.W. (1983). Consistency and changes in cognitive functioning of the young-old and old-old. In M. Bergner, U. Lehr, E. Lang, & R.

Schmidt-Scherzer (Eds.), *Aging in the eighties and beyond.* New York: Springer.
Schaie, K. W. (1993). The Seattle longitudinal studies of adult intelligence. *Current Directions in Psychological Science, 2,* 171–175.
Schaie, K. W. (1994). The life course of adult intellectual abilities. *American Psychologist, 49,* 304–313.
Schaie, K. W. (1996). *Intellectual development in adulthood: The Seattle Longitudinal Study.* New York: Cambridge University Press.
Schaie, K. W. (2000). Unpublished review of J. W. Santrock's *Life-Span Development,* 8th ed. (New York: McGraw-Hill).
Schaie, K. W., & Willis, S. L. (2001). *Adult development and aging* (5th ed.). Upper Saddle River, NJ: Prentice Hall.
Schairer, C., Lubin, J., Troisi, R., Sturgeon, S., Brinton, L., & Hoover, R. (2000). Menopausal estrogen and estrogen-progestin replacement therapy and breast cancer risk. *Journal of the American Medical Association, 283,* 485–491.
Schantz, S. (2000). Behavioral teratology. In A. Kazdin (Ed.), *Encyclopedia of psychology.* Washington, DC, & New York: American Psychological Association and Oxford University Press.
Scheer, S. D., & Unger, D. G. (1994, February). *Adolescents becoming adults: Attributes for adulthood.* Paper presented at the meeting of the Society for Research on Adolescence, San Diego.
Schiff, M., Duyme, M., Dumaret, A., & Tomkiewitz, S. (1982). How much could we boost scholastic achievement and IQ scores? A direct answer from a French adoption study. *Cognition, 12,* 165–196.
Schiffman, S. S. (1996). Smell and taste. In J. E. Birren (Ed.), *Encyclopedia of gerontology.* San Diego: Academic Press.
Schlegel, M. (2000). All work and play. *Monitor on Psychology, 31*(11), 50–51.
Schneider, B.H., Atkinson, L., & Tardif, C. (2001). Child-parent attachment and children's peer relations: A quantitative review. *Developmental Psychology, 37,* 86–100.
Schneider, W., & Pressley, M. (1997). *Memory development from 2 to 20* (2nd ed.). Mahwah, NJ: Erlbaum.
Schnorr, T. M., & others. (1991). Videodisplay terminals and the risk of spontaneous abortion. *New England Journal of Medicine, 324,* 727–733.
Schoendorf, K. C., & Kiely, J. L. (1992). Relationship of sudden infant death syndrome to maternal smoking during and after pregnancy. *Pediatrics, 90,* 905–908.
Schoka, E., & Hayslip, B. (1999, November). *Grief and the family system: The roles of communication, affect, and cohesion.* Paper presented at the meeting of the Gerontological Society of America, San Francisco.
Schooler, C. (2001). The intellectual effects of the demands of the work environment. In R.J. Sternberg & E.L. Grigorenko (Eds.), *Environmental effects on cognitive abilities.* Mahwah, NJ: Erlbaum.
Schooler, C., Mulatu, S., & Oates, G. (1999). The continuing effects of substantively complex work on the intellectual functioning of older workers. *Psychology and Aging, 14,* 483–506.
Schrag, S. G., & Dixon, R. L. (1985). Occupational exposure associated with male reproductive dysfunction. *Annual Review of Pharmacology and Toxicology, 25,* 467–592.
Schroots, J. J. F. (1996). Time: Concepts and perceptions. In J. E. Birren (Ed.), *Encyclopedia of gerontology* (Vol. 2). San Diego: Academic Press.
Schrum, L., & Berenfeld, B. (1997). *Teaching and learning in the information age.* Boston: Allyn & Bacon.
Schugens, M. M., Daum, I., Spindler, M., & Birbaumer, N. (1997). Differential effects of aging on explicit and implicit memory. *Aging, Neuropsychology, and Cognition, 4,* 33–44.
Schultz, R. (1976). Effects of control and predictability on the physical and psychological well-being of the institutionalized aged. *Journal of Personality and Social Psychology, 33,* 563–573.
Schultz, R., & Curnow, C. (1988). Peak performance and age among super athletes: Track and field, swimming, baseball, tennis, and golf. *Journal of Gerontology, 43,* P113–P120.
Schultz, R., & Hanusa, B. H. (1978). Long-term effects of control and predictability-enhancing interventions: Findings and ethical issues. *Journal of Personality and Social Psychology, 11,* 1194–1201.
Schwartz, D., & Mayaux, M. J. (1982). Female fecundity as a function of age: Results of artificial insemination in nulliparous women with azoospermic husbands. *New England Journal of Medicine, 306,* 304–406.
Schweinhart, L. J. (1999, April). *Generalizing from High/Scope longitudinal studies.* Paper presented at the meeting of the Society for Research in Child Development, Albuquerque.
Schwitzer, A.M., Rodriquez, L.E., Thomas, C., & Salami, L. (2001). The eating disorders NOS profile among college women. *Journal of American College Health, 49* 157–166.
Scott-Jones, D. (1995, March). *Incorporating ethnicity and socioeconomic status in research with children.* Paper presented at the meeting of the Society for Research in Child Development, Indianapolis.
Sears, R. R., & Feldman, S. S. (Eds.). (1973). *The seven ages of man.* Los Altos, CA: Kaufmann.
Seeman, T. E., Charpentier, P. A., Berkman, L. F., Tinetti, M. E., Guralnik, J. M., Albert, M., Blazer, D., & Rowe, J. W. (1994). Predicting changes in physical performance in a high-functioning elderly cohort: MacArthur Studies of Successful Aging. *Journal of Gerontology, 49,* M97–M108.
Segerberg, O. (1982). *Living to be 100: 1200 who did and how they did it.* New York: Scribner's.
Seidman, D. F., Rosecan, J., & Role, L. (1999). Biological and clinical perspectives on nicotine addiction. In D. F. Seidman & L. S. Covey (Eds.), *Helping the hard-core smoker.* Mahwah, NJ: Erlbaum.
Seidman, E. (2000). School transitions. In A. Kazdin (Ed.), *Encyclopedia of psychology.* Washington, DC, & New York: American Psychological Association and Oxford University Press.
Semba, R. D., & Neville, M. C. (1999). Breast-feeding, mastitis, and HIV transmission: Nutritional implications. *Nutrition Review, 57,* 146–153.
Serbin, L. A., & Sprafkin, C. (1986). The salience of gender in the process of sex-typing in three- to seven-year-old children. *Child Development, 57,* 1188–1209.
Serpell, R. (2000). Culture and intelligence. In A. Kazdin (Ed.), *Encyclopedia of psychology.* Washington, DC, & New York: American Psychological Association and Oxford University Press.
Shade, S. C., Kelly, C., & Oberg, M. (1997). *Creating culturally-responsive schools.* Washington, DC: American Psychological Association.
Sharkey, W. (1993). Who embarrasses whom? Relational and sex differences in the use of intentional embarrassment. In P. J. Kalbfleisch (Ed.), *Interpersonal communication.* Mahwah, NJ: Erlbaum.
Sharma, A. R., McGue, M. K., & Benson, P. I. (1996, March). *The emotional and behavioral adjustment of United States adopted adolescents.* Paper presented at the meeting of the Society for Research on Adolescent Development, Boston.
Sharp, E. A., & Ganong, L. H. (2000). Awareness about expectations: Are unrealistic beliefs changed by integrative teaching. *Family Relations, 49,* 71–76.
Shaver, P. (1993, March). *Where do adult romantic attachment patterns come from?* Paper presented at the biennial meeting of the Society for Research in Child Development, New Orleans.
Shaver, P. R., & Hazan, C. (1993). Adult romantic attachment: Theory and evidence. In W. H. Jones & D. Perlman (Eds.), *Advances in personal relationships.* London: Jessica Kingsley.
Shay, J. W., & Wright, W. E. (1999). Telomeres and telomerase in the regulation of cellular aging. In V. A. Bohr, B. F. Clark, & T. Stevenser (Eds.), *Molecular biology of aging.* Copenhagen, Denmark: Munksgaard.
Shay, J. W., & Wright, W. E. (2000). The use of telomerized cells for tissue engineering. *Nature Biotechnology, 18,* 22–23.
Sheehy, G. (1991). *The silent passage.* New York: Random House.
Sherwood, A., Light, K. C., & Blumenthal, J. A. (1989). Effects of aerobic exercise training on hemodynamic responses during psychosocial stress in normotensive and borderline hypertensive Type A men: A preliminary report. *Psychosomatic Medicine, 51,* 123–136.
Shields, S. A. (1991). Gender in the psychology of emotion: A selective research review. In K. T. Strongman (Ed.), *International review of studies on emotion.* (Vol.) New York: Wiley.
Shinwell, E. (2000). Neonatal pediatrics. In D. Haddad, S. A. Greene, & R. E. Olver, *Core pediatrics and child health.* London: Harcourt International.
Shiono, P. H., & Behrman, R. E. (1995, spring). Low birth weight: Analysis and recommendations. *Future of Children, 5* (1), 4–18.
Shiraev, E., & Levy, D. (2001). *Introduction to cross-cultural psychology.* Boston: Allyn & Bacon.
Shirley, M. M. (1933). *The first two years.* Minneapolis: University of Minnesota Press.
Shneidman, E. (1996). *The suicidal mind.* New York: Oxford University Press.

Shneidman, E. S. (1973). *Deaths of man.* New York: Quadrangle/New York Times.

Shomberg, E. F. (1999). *Blending families.* New York: Berkley.

Shonk, S.M., & Cicchetti, D. (2001). Maltreatment, competency deficits, and risk for academic and behavioral maladjustment, *Developmental Psychology, 37,* 3–17.

Shuchter, S., & Zisook, S. (in press). The course of normal grief. In M. Stroebe, W. Stroebe, & R. O. Hanson (Eds.), *Handbook of bereavement.* New York: Cambridge University Press.

Sieber, J. E. (2000). Ethics in research. In A. Kazdin (Ed.), *Encyclopedia of psychology.* Washington, DC, & New York: American Psychological Association and Oxford University Press.

Siegel, L. S. (1989, April). *Perceptual-motor, cognitive, and language skills as predictors of cognitive abilities at school age.* Paper presented at the biennial meeting of the Society for Research in Children, Kansas City.

Siegfried, T. (1995, April 8). Seeing big picture will be key to solving Alzheimer's puzzle. *Dallas Morning News,* p. 7D.

Siegler, I. C., & Costa, P. T. (1999, August). *Personality change and continuity in midlife:* [illegible] meeting of the American Psychological Association, Boston.

Siegler, I. C., Kaplan, B. H., Von Dras, D. D, & Mark, D. B. (1999). Cardiovascular health: A challenge for midlife. In S. L. Willis & J. D. Reid (Eds.), *Life in the Middle: Psychological and social development in middle age.* San Diego: Academic Press.

Siegler, R. S. (1998). *Children's thinking* (3rd ed.). Upper Saddle River, NJ: Prentice Hall.

Siegler, R.S. (2001). Children's discoveries and brain-damaged patients' rediscoveries. In J.L. McClelland & R.J. Siegler (Eds.), *Mechanisms of cognitive development.* Mahwah, NJ: Erlbaum.

Silverstein, L.B. (2001). Father and families. In J.P. McHale & W.S. Grolnick (Eds.), *Retrospect and prospect in the psychological study of families.* Mahwah, NJ: Erlbaum.

Silwinski, M., & Buschke, H. (1999). Cross-sectional and longitudinal relationships among age, cognition, and processing speed. *Psychology and aging, 14,* 18–33.

Simmons, R. G., & Blyth, D. A. (1987). *Moving into adolescence.* Hawthorne, NY: Aldine.

Simons, J., Finlay, B., & Yang, A. (1991). *The adolescent and young adult fact book.* Washington, DC: Children's Defense Fund.

Simonton, D. K. (1996). Creativity. In J. E. Birren (Ed.), *Encyclopedia of aging.* San Diego: Academic Press.

Singer, D. G. (1993). Creativity of children in a changing world. In G. L. Berry & J. K. Asamen (Eds.), *Children and television: Images in a changing sociocultural world.* Newbury Park, CA: Sage.

Singer, L. T., Arendt, R., Fagan, J., Minnes, S., Salvator, A., Bolek, T., & Becker, M. (1999). Neonatal visual information processing in cocaine-exposed and non-exposed infants. *Infant Behavior and Development, 22,* 1–15.

Singh, N. A., Clements, K. M., & Fiatarone, M. A. (1997). A randomized controlled trial of progressive resistance training in depressed elders. *Journal of Gerontology, 52A,* M27–M35.

Singh, S., & Darroch, J. E. (2000). Adolescent pregnancy and childbearing: Levels and trends in developed countries. *Family Planning Perspectives, 32,* 14–23.

Skadberg, B. T., Morild, I., & Markestad, T. (1998). Abandoning prone sleeping: Effect on the risk of sudden infant death syndrome. *Journal of Pediatrics, 132,* 340–343.

Skinner, B. F. (1957). *Verbal behavior.* New York: Appleton-Century-Crofts.

Skinner, B. F. (1938). *The behavior of organisms: An experimental analysis.* New York: Appelton-Century-Crofts.

Skodak, M., & Skeels, H. (1949). A final follow-up of one hundred adopted children. *Journal of Genetic Psychology, 75,* 85–125.

Skoog, I., Blennow, K., & Marcusson, J. (1996). Dementia. In J. E. Birren (Ed.), *Encyclopedia of gerontology* (Vol. 1). San Diego: Academic Press.

Slater, A. (2001). Visual perception. In A. Fogel & G. Bremner (Eds.), *Blackwell handbook of infant* [illegible]

Slee, P. T., & Taki, M. (1999, April). *School bullying.* Paper presented at the meeting of the Society for Research in Child Development, Albuquerque.

Slentz, K.L., & Krogh, S.L. (2001). *Teaching young children.* Mahwah, NJ: Erlbaum.

Slobin, D. (1972, July) Children and language: They learn the same way all around the world. *Psychology Today,* pp. 71–76.

Small, S. A. (1990). *Preventive programs that support families with adolescents.* Washington, DC: Carnegie Council on Adolescent Development.

Smith, A. D. (1996). Memory. In J. E. Birren (Ed.), *Encyclopedia of gerontology* (Vol. 2) San Diego: Academic Press.

Smith, J., & Baltes, P. B. (1990). Wisdom-related knowledge: Age-cohort differences in responses to life-planning problems. *Developmental Psychology, 26,* 494–505.

Smith, L., & Hattersley, J. (2000). *The smart guide to preventing SIDS.* New York: Smart.

Smith, M. A., Sayre, L. M., Monnier, V. M., & Perry, G. (1995). Radical aging in Alzheimer's disease. *Trends in Neuroscience, 18,* 172–176.

Smith, P. K., Morita, Y., Junger-Tas, J., Olweus, D., Catalano, R., & Slee, P. T. (Eds.). (1999). *The nature of school bullying: A cross-national perspective.* London: Routledge.

Smyer, M. A., & Qualls, S. H. (1996). *The psychology of aging and mental health.* Cambridge, MA: Blackwell.

Snarey, J. (1987, June). A question of morality. *Psychology Today,* pp. 6–8.

Snow, C. E. (1999). Social perspectives on the emergence of language. In B. MacWhinney (Ed.), *The emergence of language.* Mahwah, NJ: Erlbaum.

Snowden, D. A. (1995). *An epidemiological study of aging in a select population and its relationship to Alzheimer's disease.* Unpublished manuscript, Sanders Brown Center on Aging, Lexington, KY.

Snowden, D. A. (1997). Aging and Alzheimer's disease: Lessons from the nun study. *Gerontologist, 37,* 150–156.

Snowden, L. R., & Cheung, F. K. (1990). Use of inpatient mental health services by members of ethnic minority groups. *American Psychologist, 45,* 347–355.

Sokal, L., & Seifert, K. (2001, April). *Gender schematic development within the family context.* Paper presented at the meeting of the Society for Research in Child Development, Minneapolis.

Soldo, B. J. (1996). Cross-pressures on middle-aged adults: A broader view. *Journal of Gerontology: Psychological Sciences and Social Sciences, 51B,* S271–S273.

Sollod, R. N. (2000). Religious and spiritual practices. In A. Kazdin (Ed.), *Encyclopedia of psychology.* Washington, DC, & New York: American Psychological Association and Oxford University Press.

Sorenson, S., & Zarit, S. H. (1996). Preparation for caregiving: A study of multigeneration families. *International Journal of Aging and Human Development,* [illegible]

[illegible] Adolescent health behaviors and related factors: A review. *Public Health Nursing, 18,* 82–93.

Spearman, C. E. (1927). *The abilities of man.* New York: Macmillan.

Spear-Swerling, L., & Sternberg, R. J. (1994). The road not taken: An integrative theoretical model of reading disability. *Journal of Learning Disabilities, 27,* 91–103.

Spelke, E. S. (1979). Perceiving bimodally specified events in infancy. *Developmental Psychology, 5,* 626–636.

Spelke, E. S. (1988). The origins of physical knowledge. In L. Weiskrantz (Ed.), *Thought Without Language.* New York: Oxford University Press.

Spelke, E. S. (1991). Physical knowledge in infancy: Reflections on Piaget's theory. In S. Carey & R. Gelman (Eds.), *The epigenesis of mind: Essays on biology and cognition.* Hillsdale, NJ: Erlbaum.

Spelke, E. S., & Newport, E. L. (1998). Nativism, empiricism, and the development of knowledge. In W. Damon (Ed.), *Handbook of child psychology* (5th ed., Vol. 2). New York: Wiley.

Spelke, E. S., & Owsley, C. J. (1979). Intermodal exploration and knowledge in infancy. *Infant Behavior and Development, 2,* 13–28.

Spence, J. T., & Buckner, C. E. (2000). Instrumental and expressive traits, trait stereotypes, and sexist attitudes: What do they signify? *Psychology of Women Quarterly, 24,* 44–62.

Spence, J. T., & Helmreich, R. (1978). *Masculinity and feminity: Their psychological dimensions.* Austin: University of Texas Press.

Spence, M. J., & DeCasper, A. J. (1987). Prenatal experience with low-frequency maternal voice sounds influences neonatal perception of maternal voice samples. *Infant Behavior and Development, 10,* 133–142.

Spencer, M. B. (1990). Commentary in Spencer, M. B., & Dornbusch, S. Challenges in studying ethnic minority youth. In S. S. Feldman & G. R.

Elliott (Eds.), *At the threshold: The developing adolescent.* Cambridge, MA:

Spencer, M. B. (1999). Social and cultural influences on school adjustment: The application of an identity-focused cultural ecological perspective. *Educational Psychologist, 34,* 43–57.

Spencer, M. B., & Dornbusch, S. M. (1990). Challenges in studying minority youth. In S. S. Feldman & G. R. Elliott (Eds.), *At the threshold: The developing adolescent.* Cambridge, MA: Harvard University Press.

Spielberger, C. D., & Grier, K. (1983). Unpublished manuscript, University of South Florida, Tampa.

Sprei, J. E., & Courtois, C. A. (1988). The treatment of women's sexual dysfunctions arising from sexual assault. In R. A. Brown & J. R. Fields (Eds.), *Treatment of sexual problems in individual and couples therapy.* Great Neck, NY: PMA.

Spring, J. (1998). *American education* (8th ed.). New York: McGraw-Hill.

Spring, J. (1998). *The intersection of cultures.* New York: McGraw-Hill.

Sroufe, L. A. (2000, Spring). The inside scoop on child development: Interview. *Cutting through the hype.* Minneapolis: College of Education and Human Development, University of Minnesota.

Sroufe, L. A., Egeland, B., & Carlson, E. A. (1999). One social world: The integrated development of parent-child and peer relationships. In W. A. Collins & B. Laursen (Eds.), *Minnesota symposium on child psychology,* vol. 31. Mahwah, NJ: Erlbaum.

Sroufe, L. A., & Waters, E. (1976). The ontogenesis of smiling and laughter: A perspective on the organization of development in infancy. *Psychological Review, 83,* 173–198.

Sroufe, L. A., Waters, E., & Matas, L. (1974). Contextual determinants of infant affectional response. In M. Lewis & L. Rosenblum (Eds.), *Origins of fear.* New York: Wiley.

St. Pierre, R., Layzer, J., & Barnes, H. (1996). *Regenerating two-generation programs.* Cambridge, MA: Abt Associates.

Stallings, J. (1975). Implementation and child effects of teaching practices in Follow Through classrooms. *Monographs of the Society for Research in Child Development, 40* (Serial No. 163).

Stanhope, L., & Corter, C. (1993, March). *The mother's role in the transition to siblinghood.* Paper presented at the biennial meeting of the Society for Research in Child Development, New Orleans.

Stattin, H., & Magnusson, D. (1990). *Pubertal maturation in female development: Paths through life* (Vol. 2). Hillsdale, NJ: Erlbaum.

Staudinger, U. M. (1996). Psychologische Produktivitat und Selbstenfaltung im Alter. In M. M. Baltes & L. Montada (Eds.), *Produktives Leben im Alter.* Frankfurt: Campus.

Staudinger, U. M., & Fleeson, W. (in press). Resilence of the self in very old age. *Development and psychopathology.*

Steinberg, L. D. (1986). Latchkey children and susceptibility to peer pressure: An ecological analysis. *Developmental Psychology, 22,* 433–439.

Steiner, J. E. (1979). Human facial expressions in response to taste and smell stimulation. In H. Reese & L. Lipsitt (Eds.), *Advances in child development and behavior* (Vol. 13). New York: Academic Press.

Stern, D. N., Beebe, B., Jaffe, J., & Bennett, S. L. (1977). The infant's stimulus world during social interaction: A study of caregiver behaviors with particular reference to repetition and timing. In H. R. Schaffer (Ed.), *Studies in mother-infant interaction.* London: Academic Press.

Stern, J. S. (1993, June 2). Commentary in "Lowly vitamin supplements pack a big health punch." *USA Today,* p. 3D.

Sternberg, R. J. (1986). *Intelligence applied.* San Diego: Harcourt Brace Jovanovich.

Sternberg, R. J. (1988). *The triangle of love.* New York: Basic Books.

Sternberg, R. J. (1999). Intelligence. In M. A. Runco & S. Pritzker (Eds.), *Encyclopedia of creativity.* San Diego: Academic Press.

Sternberg, R.J., & Grigorenko, E.L. (Eds.) (2001). *Environmental effects on cognitive abilities.* Mahwah, NJ: Erlbaum.

Steur, F. B., Applefield, J. M., & Smith, R. (1971). Televised aggression and interpersonal aggression of preschool children. *Journal of Experimental Child Psychology, 11,* 442–447.

Stevenson, H. C. (1998). Raising safe villages: Cultural-ecological factors that influence the emotional adjustment of adolescents. *Journal of Black Psychology, 24,* 44–59.

Stevenson, H. C. (In press). The confluence of the "both-and" in Black racial identity theory. In R. Jones (ed.), *Advances in Black psychology.* Hampton, VA: Cobb & Henry.

Stevenson, H. G. (1995, March). *Missing data: On the forgotten substance of race, ethnicity, and socioeconomic classifications.* Paper presented at the meeting of the Society for Research in Child Development, Indianapolis.

Stevenson, H. W. (1995). Mathematics achievement of American students: First in the world by 2000? In C. A. Nelson (Ed.), *Basic and applied perspectives in learning, cognition, and development.* Minneapolis: University of Minnesota Press.

Stevenson, H. W. (2000). Middle childhood: Education and schooling. In A. Kazdin (Ed.), *Encyclopedia of psychology.* Washington, DC, & New York: American Psychological Association and Oxford University Press.

Stevenson, H. W., & Hofer, B. K. (1999). Education policy in the United States and abroad: What we can learn from each other. In G. J. Cizek (Ed.), *Handbook of educational policy*. San Diego: Academic Press.

Stotland, N. L. (1999). When religion collides with medicine. *American Journal of Psychiatry, 156,* 304–307.

Strasburger, V. C. (1995). *Adolescents and the media.* Newbury Park, CA: Sage.

Streissguth, A. P., Martin, D. C., Sandman, B. M., Kirchner, G. L., & Darby, B. L. (1984). Intrauterine alcohol and nicotine exposure: Attention and reaction time in four-year-old children. *Developmental Psychology, 20,* 533–543.

Striegel-Moore, R. H., Silberstein, L. R., & Rodin, J. (1993). The social self in bulimia nervosa: Public self-consciousness, social anxiety, and perceived fraudulence. *Journal of Abnormal Psychology, 102,* 297–303.

Stroebe, M., Gergen, M. H., Gergen, K. J., & Stroebe, W. (1992). Broken hearts or broken bonds: Love and death in historical perspective. *American Psychologist, 47,* 1205–1212.

Stroebe, M., Stroebe, W., Schut, H., & van den Bout, J. (1998). Bereavement. In H. S. Friedman (Ed.), *Encyclopedia of mental health (Vol. 1).* San Diego: Academic Press.

Stull, D. E., & Hatch, L. R. (1984). Unraveling the effects of multiple life changes. *Research on Aging, 6,* 560–571.

Stunkard, A. (2000). Obesity. In A. Kazdin (Ed.), *Encyclopedia of psychology.* Washington, DC, & New York: American Psychological Association and Oxford University Press.

Sue, S. (1990, August). *Ethnicity and culture in psychological research and practice.* Paper presented at the meeting of the American Psychological Association, Boston.

Sullivan, H. S. (1953). *The interpersonal theory of psychiatry.* New York: W. W. Norton.

Sullivan, K., & Sullivan, A. (1980). Adolescent-parent separation. *Developmental Psychology, 16,* 93–99.

Sullivan, L. (1991, May 25). U.S. secretary urges TV to restrict "irresponsible sex and reckless violence." *Boston Globe,* p. A1.

Suls, J., & Swain, A. (1998). Type A-Type B personalities. In H.S. Friedman (Ed.), *Encyclopedia of mental health* (Vol.3). San Diego: Academic Press.

Suomi, S. J. (1996, March). *Behavioral, physiological and physical changes associated with adolescence in Rhesus monkeys.* Paper presented at the meeting of the Society for Research on Adolescence, Boston.

Suomi, S. J., Harlow, H. F., & Domek, C. J. (1970). Effect of repetitive infant-infant separations of young monkeys. *Journal of Abnormal Psychology, 76,* 161–172.

Super, C., & Harkness, S. (1997). The cultural structuring of child development. In J. W. Berry, Y. H. Poortinga, & J. Pandey (Eds.), *Handbook of cross-cultural psychology:* Vol. 2. *Theory and method.* Boston: Allyn & Bacon.

Susman, E. J., Murowchick, E., Worrall, B.K., & Murray, D. A. (1995, March). *Emotionality, adrenal hormones, and context interactions during puberty and pregnancy.* Paper presented at the meeting of the Society for Research in Child Development, Indianapolis.

Sutton-Smith, B. (2000). Play. In A. Kazdin (Ed.), *Encyclopedia of psychology*. Washington, DC, & New York: American Psychological Association and Oxford University Press.

Suzman, R. (1997, March 18). Commentary, *USA Today,* p. 1A.

Suzman, R. M., Harris, T., Hadley, E. C., Kovar, M. G., & Weindruch, R. (1992). The robust oldest old: Optimistic perspectives for increasing healthy life expectancy. In R. M. Suzman, D. P. Willis, & K. G. Manton (Eds.), *The oldest old.* New York: Oxford University Press.

Swain, S. O. (1992). Men's friendships with women. In P. M. Nardi (Ed.), *Gender in intimate relationships.* Belmont, CA: Wadsworth.

Swan, G. E. (1996). Interview. *APA Monitor,* p. 35.

Swan, G. E., & Carmelli, D. (1996). Curiosity and mortality in aging adults: A 5-year follow-up of the Western Collaborative Study. *Psychology and Aging, 11,* 449–461.

Swann, W. B., De La Ronde, C., & Hixon, J. G. (1994). Authenticity and positive strivings in marriage and courtship. *Journal of Personality and Social Psychology, 66,* 857–869.

Swanson, D. P. (1997, April). *Identity and coping styles among African-American females.* Paper presented at the meeting of the Society for Research in Child Development, Washington, DC.

Swanson, D. P., Spencer, M. B., & Petersen, A. C. (1998). Identity formation in adolescence. In K. Borman & B. Schneider (Eds.), *The adolescent years: Social influence and educational challenges.* Chicago: University of Chicago Press.

T

Taddio, A., Katz, J., Ilersich, A. L., & Koren, G. (1997). Effect of neonatal circumcision on pain response during subsequent routine vaccination. *Lancet, 349,* 599–603.

Takahashi, K. (1990). Are the key assumptions of the "Strange Situation" procedure universal? A view from Japanese research. *Human Development, 33,* 23–30.

Tan, S. Y. (2000). Religion and psychotherapy: An overview. In A. Kazdin (Ed.), *Encyclopedia of psychology.* Washington, DC, & New York: American Psychological Association and Oxford University Press.

Tannen, D. (1990). *You just don't understand: Women and men in conversation.* New York: Ballantine.

Tappan, M. B. (1998). Sociocultural psychology and caring psychology: Exploring Vygotsky's "hidden curriculum." *Educational Psychologist, 33,* 23–33.

Tapper, J. (1996, March). *Values, lifestyles, and crowd identification in adolescence.* Paper presented at the meeting of the Society for Research on Adolescence, Boston.

Tarnowski, A. C., & Antonucci, T. (1999, November). *Social relationships in the United States: Historical patterns in aging across a 35-year period.* Paper presented at the meeting of the Gerontological Society of America, San Francisco.

Taub, E. (2001, April). *Adult brain plasticity.* Paper presented at the meeting of the Society for Research in Child Development, Minneapolis.

Taylor, H. G., Klein, N., & Hack, M. (1994). Academic functioning in <750 gm birthweight children who have normal cognitive abilities: Evidence for specific learning disabilities. *Pediatric Research 35,* 289A.

Taylor, S. (1999). *Health psychology* (4th ed.). New York: McGraw-Hill.

Taylor, S. P. (1982). Mental health and successful coping among Black women. In R. C. Manuel (Ed.), *Minority aging.* Westport, CT: Greenwood Press.

Tercyak, K.P., Johnson, S.B., Roberts, S.E., & Cruz, A.Z. (2001). Psychological response to prenatal genetic counseling and amniocentesis. *Patient Educational Counseling, 43,* 73–84.

Terman, D. L., Larner, M. B., Stevenson, C. S., & Behrman, R. E. (1996). Special education for students with disabilities: Analysis and recommendations. *Future of Children, 6*(1) 4–24.

Terman, L. (1925). *Genetic studies of genius: Vol. 1. Mental and physical traits of a thousand gifted children.* Standford, CA: Stanford University Press.

Tesser, A. (2000). Self-esteem. In A. Kazdin (Ed.). *Encyclopedia of psychology.* Washington, DC, & New York: American Psychological Association and Oxford University Press.

Teti, D.M. (2001). Retrospect and prospect in the study of sibling relationships. In J.P. McHale & W.S. Grolnick (Eds.), *Retrospect and prospect in the psychological study of families.* Mahwah, NJ: Erlbaum.

Teti, D. M., Sakin, J., Kucera, E., Caballeros, M., & Corns, K. M. (1993, March). *Transitions to siblinghood and security of firstborn attachment: Psychosocial and psychiatric correlates of changes over time.* Paper presented at the biennial meeting of the Society for Research in Child Development, New Orleans.

Tetreault, M. K. T. (1997). Classrooms for diversity: Rethinking curriculum and pedagogy. In J. A. Banks & C. A. Banks (Eds.), *Multicultural education* (3rd ed.). Boston: Allyn & Bacon.

Tharp, R. G. (1994). Intergroup differences among Native Americans in socialization and child cognition: An ethogenetic analysis. In P. M. Greenfield & R. Cocking (Eds.), *Cross-cultural roots of minority child development.* Mahwah, NJ: Erlbaum.

Tharp, R.G., & Gallimore, R. (1988). *Rousing minds to life: Teaching, learning, and schooling in social context.* New York: Cambridge University Press.

Thayer, J. F., Rossy, I., Sollers, J., Friedman, B. H., & Allen, M. T. (1996, March). *Relationships among heart period variability and cardiodynamic measures vary as a function of fitness.* Paper presented at the meeting of the American Psychosomatic Society, Williamsburg, VA.

Thelen, E. (1995). Motor development: A new synthesis. *American Psychologist, 50,* 79–95.

Thelen, E. (2000). Perception and motor development. In A. Kazdin (Ed.), *Encyclopedia of psychology.* Washington, DC, & New York: American Psychological Association and Oxford University Press.

Thelen, E. (2001). Dynamic mechanisms of change in early perceptual-motor development. In J.L. McClelland & R.S. Siegler (Eds.), *Mechanisms of cognitive development.* Mahwah, NJ: Erlbaum.

Thelen, E., & Smith, L. B. (1998). Dynamic systems theory. In W. Damon (Ed.), *Handbook of child psychology* (5th ed., Vol. 1.). New York: Wiley.

Thomas, A., & Chess, S. (1991). Temperament in adolescence and its functional significance. In R. M. Lerner, A. C. Petersen, & J. Brooks-Gunn (Eds.), *Encyclopedia of adolescence* (Vol. 2). New York: Garland.

Thomas, K. (1998, November 4). Teen cyberdating is a new wrinkle for parents, too. *USA Today,* p. 9D.

Thompson, P. M., Giedd, J. N., Woods, R. P., MacDonald, D., Evans, A. C., & Toga, A. W. (2000). Growth patterns in the developing brain detected by using continuum mechanical tensor maps. *Nature, 404,* 190–193.

Thompson, R. (2000). Early experience and socialization. In A. Kazdin (Ed.), *Encyclopedia of psychology.* Washington, DC, & New York: American Psychological Association and Oxford University Press.

Thompson, R. A. (1999). The individual child: Temperament, emotion, self, and personality. In M. H. Bornstein & M. E. Lamb (Eds.), *Developmental psychology: An advanced textbook* (4th ed.). Mahwah, NJ: Erlbaum.

Thomson, E., Mosley, J., Hanson, T.L., McLanahan, S.S. (2001). Remarriage, cohabitation, and changes in mothering behavior. *Journal of Marriage and the Family, 63,* 370–380.

Thorton, A., & Camburn, D. (1989). Religious participation and sexual behavior and attitudes. *Journal of Marriage and the Family, 49,* 117–128.

Thurstone, L. L. (1938). *Primary mental abilities.* Chicago: University of Chicago Press.

Tobin, J. J., Wu, D. Y. H., & Davidson, D. H. (1989). *Preschool in three cultures.* New Haven, CT: Yale University Press.

Torff, B. (2000). Multiple intelligences. In A. Kazdin (Ed.), *Encyclopedia of psychology.* Washington, DC, & New York: American Psychological Association and Oxford University Press.

Torgesen, J. K. (1999). Reading disabilities. In R. Gallimore, L. P. Bernheimer, D. L. MacMillan, D. L. Speece, & S. Vaughn (Eds.), *Developmental perspectives on children with learning disabilities.* Mahwah, NJ: Erlbaum.

Toth, S. L., Manley, J. T., & Cicchetti, D. (1992). Child maltreatment and vulnerability to depression. *Development and Psychopathology, 4,* 97–112.

Tousignant, M. (1995, April 11). Children's cure or adults' crutch? Rise of Ritalin prompts debate over the reason. *Washington Post,* p. B1.

Tout, K., & Schmidt, S. (2001, April). *Child care for infants and toddlers from low income families: A national profile.* Paper presented at the meeting of the Society for Research in Child Development, Minneapolis.

Trasler, J. (2000). Paternal exposures: Altered sex ratios. *Teratology, 62,* 6–7.

Trasler, J. M., & Doerksen, T. (2000, May). *Teratogen update: Paternal exposure-reproductive risks.* Paper presented at the joint meeting of the Pediatric Academic Societies and American Academy of Pediatrics, Boston.

Trawick-Smith, J. W. (2000). *Early childhood development: A multicultural perspective.* Upper Saddle River, NJ: Prentice Hall.

Treffers, P. E., Eskes, M., Kleiverda, G., & van Alten, D. (1990). Home births and minimal medical interventions. *Journal of the American Medical Association, 246,* 2207–2208.

Trehub, S. E., Schneider, B. A., Thorpe, L. A., & Judge, P. (1991). Observational measures of auditory sensitivity in early infancy. *Developmental Psychology, 27,* 40–49.

Triandis, H. C. (2000). Cross-cultural psychology: History of the field. In A. Kazdin (Ed.), *Encyclopedia of psychology.* Washington, DC, &

New York: American Psychological Association and Oxford University Press.
Trimble, J. E. (1989, August). *The enculturation of contemporary psychology.* Paper presented at the meeting of the American Psychological Association, New Orleans.
Troiano, R. P., & Flegal, K. M. (1998). Overweight children and adolescents: Description, epidemiology, and demographics. *Pediatrics, 101,* 497–504.
Troll, L. E. (1994). Family-embedded versus family-deprived oldest-old: A study of contrasts. *International Journal of Aging and Human Development, 38,* 51–64.
Troll, L. E. (1999). Questions for future studies: Social relationships in old age. *International Journal of Aging and Human Development, 48,* 347–351.
Troll, L. E. (2000). Transmission and transmutation. In J. E. Birren & J. J. F. Schroots (Eds.), *A history of geropsychology in autobiography.* Washington, DC: American Psychological Association.
Truitner, K., & Truitner, N. (1993). Death and dying in Buddhism. In D. P. Irish & K. F. Lundquist (Eds.), *Ethnic variations in dying, death, and grief: Diversity in universality.* Washington, DC: Taylor & Francis.
Tubman, J. G., & Windle, M. (1995). Continuity of difficult temperament in adolescence: Relations with depression, life events, family support, and substance abuse. *Journal of Youth and Adolescence, 24,* 133–152.
Tucker, J. S., Schwartz, J. E., Clark, K. M., & Friedman, H. S. (1999). Age-related changes in the associations of social network ties with mortality risk. *Psychology and Aging, 14,* 564–571.
Tulving, E. (2000). Concepts of memory. In E. Tulving & F. I. M. Craik (Eds.), *The Oxford handbook of memory.* New York: Oxford University Press.
Turecki, S., & Tonner, L. (1989). *The difficult child.* New York: Bantam.
Turk, D. C., Rudy, T. E., & Salovey, P. (1984). Health protection: Attitudes and behaviors of LPN's teachers, and college students. *Health Psychology, 3,* 189–210.
Turkheimer, E., & Waldron, M. (2000). Nonshared environment: A theoretical, methodological, and quantitative review. *Psychological Bulletin, 126,* 78–108.
Turnbull, A., Turnbull, R., Shank, M., & Leal, D. (1999). *Exceptional lives: Special education in today's schools.* Columbus, OH: Merrill.
Turner, B. F. (1982). Sex-related differences in aging. In B. B. Wolman (Ed.), *Handbook of developmental psychology.* Englewood Cliffs, NJ: Prentice Hall.
Turvey, C. L., Carney, C., Arndt, S., & Wallace, R. B. (1999, November). *Conjugal loss and syndromal depression in a sample of elders ages 70 years and older.* Paper presented at the meeting of the Gerontological Society of America, San Francisco.

U

U.S. Bureau of the Census. (1997). *U.S. census characteristics on grandparents.* Washington, DC: Author.
U.S. Bureau of the Census. (2000). *Census 2000 data.* Washington, DC: Author.
U.S. Bureau of the Census. (2000). *Death Statistics.* Washington, DC: Author.
U.S. Bureau of the Census. (2000). *Statistical abstracts of the United States.* Washington, DC: U.S. Government Printing Office.
U.S. Bureau of the Census. (2000). *Vital statistics.* Washington, DC: Author.
U.S. Department of Education. (1996). *Number and disabilities of children and youth served under IDEA.* Washington, DC: Office of Special Education Programs, Data Analysis System.
U.S. Department of Education. (1999). *Digest of education statistics.* Washington. DC: Author.
U.S. Department of Education. (2000). *Trends in educational equity for girls and women.* Washington, DC: Author.
U.S. Department of Health and Human Services. (1998). *Teen births decline.* Washington, DC: Author.
U.S. General Accounting Office. (1987, September). *Prenatal care: Medicaid recipients and uninsured women obtain insufficient care.* A report to the Congress of the United States, HRD-97-137. Washington, DC: GAO.
Ubell, C. (1992, December 6). We can age successfully. *Parade,* pp. 14–15.
Urberg, K. A., & Wolowicz, L. S. (1996, March). *Antecedents and consequences of changes in parental monitoring.* Paper presented at the meeting of the Society for Research on Adolescence, Boston.

V

Vaillant, G. E. (1977) *Adaptation to life.* Boston: Little, Brown.
Vaillant, G. E. (1992). Is there a natural history of addiction? In C. P. O'Brien & J. H. Jaffe (eds.), *Addictive states.* Cambridge, MA: Harvard University Press.
Valsiner, J. (2000). *Culture and human development.* Thousand Oaks, CA: Sage.
Van den Boom, D. (1990). Preventive intervention and the quality of mother infant interaction and infant exploration in irritable infants. In W. Koops, H. J. G. Soppe, J. L. Van der Linden, P. C. M. Molenaar, & J. J. F. Schroots (Eds.), *Developmental psychology behind the dikes: An outline of developmental psychological research in the Netherlands.* Delft, Netherlands: Uitgeverij Eburon.
van den Boom, D. C. (1989). Neonatal irritability and the development of attachment. In G. A. Kohnstamm, J. E. Bates, & M. K. Rothbart (Eds.), *Temperament in childhood.* New York: Wiley.
Van Hoorn, J., Nourot, P. M., Scales, B., & Alward, K. R. (1999). *Play at the center of the curriculum.* Columbus, OH: Merrill.
van Ijzendoorn, M. H., & Kroonenberg, P. M. (1988). Crosscultural patterns of attachment: A meta-analysis of the Strange Situation. *Child Development, 59,* 147–156.
Vandell, D. C. (2000). Parents, peer groups, and other socializing influences. *Developmental Psychology, 36,* 699–710.
Vandell, D. L., & Pierce, K. M. (1999, April). *Can after-school programs benefit children who live in high-crime neighborhoods?* Paper presented at the meeting of the Society for Research in Child Development, Albuquerque.
Vandell, D. L., & Wilson, K. S. (1988). Infants' interactions with mother, sibling, and peer: Contrasts and relations between interaction systems. *Child Development, 48,* 176–186.
Vandewater, E. A., Ostrove, J. M., & Stewart, A. J. (1997). Predicting women's well-being in mid-life: The importance of personality development and social role involvements. *Journal of Personality and Social Development, 72,* 1147–1160.
VandeWeerd, C., & Paveza, G. (1999, November). *Physical violence in old age: A look at the burden of women.* Paper presented at the meeting of the Gerontological Society of America, San Francisco.
Vaughn, S., Bos, C. S., & Schumm, J. S. (2000). *Teaching exceptional, diverse, and at-risk students in the general education classroom* (2nd ed.). Boston: Allyn & Bacon.
Ventis, W. L. (1995). The relationships between religion and mental health. *Journal of Social Issues, 51,* 33–48.
Ventura, S. J., Martin, J. A., Curtin, S. C., & Mathews, T. J. (1997, June 10). *Report of final natality statistics, 1995.* Washington, DC: National Center for Health Statistics.
Verbrugge, L. M., Gruber-Baldini, A. L., & Fozard, J. L. (1996). Age differences and age changes in activities: Baltimore Longitudinal Study of Aging. *Journal of Gerontology: Social Sciences, 51B,* S30–S41.
Verhaeghen, P., & Marcoen, A. (1996). On the mechanisms of plasticity in young and older adults after instruction in the method of loci: Evidence for an amplification model. *Psychology and Aging, 11,* 164–178.
Verhaeghen, P., Marcoen, A., & Goossens, L. (1995). Facts and fiction about memory aging: A quantitative integration of research findings. *Journal of Gerontology, 48,* P157–P171.
Vidal, F. (2000). Piaget's theory. In A. Kazdin (Ed.), *Encyclopedia of psychology.* Washington, DC, & New York: American Psychological Association and Oxford University Press.
Visher, E., & Visher, J. (1989). Parenting coalitions after remarriage: Dynamics and therapeutic guidelines. *Family Relations, 38,* 65–70.
Von Beveren, T. T. (1999). *Prenatal development and the newborn.* Unpublished manuscript, University of Texas at Dallas, Richardson.
Voyer, D., Voyer, S., & Bryden, M. P. (1995). Magnitude of sex differences in spatial abilities: A meta-analysis and consideration of critical variables. *Psychological Bulletin, 117,* 250–270.
Vygotsky, L. S. (1962). *Thought and language.* Cambridge, MA: MIT Press.

W

Wachs, T. D. (1994). Fit, context and the transition between temperament and personality. In C. Halverson, G. Kohnstamm, & R. Martin (Eds.), *The developing structure of personality from infancy to adulthood.* Hillsdale, NJ: Erlbaum.

Wachs, T. D. (2000). *Necessary but not sufficient.* Washington, DC: American Psychological Association.

Wachs, T.D., & Kohnstamm, G.A. (Eds.), *Temperament in context.* Mahwah, NJ: Erlbaum.

Wadden, T. A., Foser, G. D., Stunkard, A. J., & Conill, A. M. (1996). Effects of weight cycling on the resting energy expenditure and body composition of obese women. *Eating Disorders, 19,* 5–12.

Waddington, C. H. (1957). *The strategy of the genes.* London: Allen & Son.

Wahlsten, D. (2000). Behavioral genetics. In A. Kazdin (Ed.), *Encyclopedia of psychology.* Washington, DC, & New York: American Psychological Association and Oxford University Press.

Wakschlag, L. S., Chase-Lansdale, P. L., & Brooks-Gunn, J. (1996, March). *Not just "ghosts in the nursery": Contemporaneous intergenerational relationships and parenting in young African American families.* Paper presented at the meeting of the Society for Research on Adolescence, Boston.

Walker, C., Gruman, C., & Blank, K. (1999, November). *Physician-assisted suicide: Looking beyond the numbers.* Paper presented at the meeting of the Gerontological Society of [illegible]

Walker, L. J. (1991). Sex differences in moral development. In W. M. Kurtines & J. Gewirtz (Eds.), *Moral behavior and development* (Vol. 2). Hillsdale, NJ: Erlbaum.

Walker, L. J. (1996). Unpublished review of J. W. Santrock's *Child Development,* 8th ed. (New York: McGraw-Hill).

Walker, L. J., & Pitts, R. C. (1998). Naturalistic conceptions of moral maturity. *Developmental Psychology, 34,* 403–419.

Walsh, L. A. (2000, Spring). The Inside scoop on child development: Interview. *Cutting through the hype.* Minneapolis: College of Education & Human Development, University of Minnesota.

Walsh, W. B., & Betz, N. E. (2001). *Tests and measurement* (4th ed.). Upper Saddle River, NJ: Prentice Hall.

Walther-Thomas, C., Korinek, L., McLaughlin, V., & Wiliams, B. T. (2000). *Collaboration for inclusive education.* Boston: Allyn & Bacon.

Wang, H., Bashore, T. R., & Freidman, E. (1995). Exercise reduces age-dependent decrease in platelet protein kinase C activity and translocation. *Journal of Gerontology, 50A,* M12–M16.

Wang, X., Zuckerman, B., Kaufman, G., Pearson, C., Wang, G., Chen, C., Wise, P., Bauchner, H., & Xu, X. (2000, May). *Maternal cigarette smoking, genetic susceptibility, and birthweight.* Paper presented at the joint meeting of the Pediatric Academic Societies and the American Academy of Pediatrics, Boston.

Warner, H. R., & Hodes, R. J. (2000, Spring). Telomere length, telomerase, and aging: Hype, hope, and reality. *Generations, 24,* 48–53.

Warr, P. (1994). Age and employment. In M. Dunnette, L. Hough, & H. Triandis (Eds.), *Handbook of industrial and organizational psychology* (Vol. 4). Palo Alto, CA: Consulting Psychologists Press.

Warrick, P. (1992, March 1). The fantastic voyage of Tanner Roberts. *Los Angeles Times.* pp. El. 12,13.

Warshak, R. A. (1997, January 15). Personal communication, Department of Psychology, University of Texas at Dallas, Richardson.

Wass, H., & Stillion, J. M. (1988). Death in the lives of children and adolescents. In H. Wass, F. M. Berardo, & R. A. Neimeyer (Eds.), *Dying: Facing the facts* (2nd ed.). Washington, DC: Hemisphere.

Waterman, A. S. (1992). Identity as an aspect of optimal psychological functioning. In G. R. Adams, T. P. Gullotta, & R. Montemayor (Eds.), *Adolescent identity formation.* Newbury Park, CA: Sage.

Waterman, A. S. (1997). An overview of service-learning and the role of research and evaluation in service-learning programs. In A.S. Waterman (Ed.), *Service learning.* Mahwah, NJ: Erlbaum.

Waters, E. (2001, April). *Perspectives on continuity and discontinuity in relationships.* Paper presented at the meeting of the Society for Research in Child Development, Minneapolis.

Waters, E., Merrick, S. K., Albersheim, L. J., & Treboux, E. (1995, March). *Attachment security from infancy to early adulthood: A 20-year longitudinal study.* Paper presented at the meeting of the Society for Research in Child Development, Indianapolis.

Waters, E., Merrick, S., Albersheim, L., Treboux, D., & Crowell, J. (2000). Attachment theory from infancy to adulthood: A 20-year-longitudinal study of relations between infant Strange Situation classification and attachment representations in adulthood. *Child Development, 71,* 684–689.

Watson, J. B. (1928). *Psychological care of infant and child.* New York: W. W. Norton.

Watson, J. B., & Raynor, R. (1920). Conditioned emotional reactions. *Journal of Experimental Psychology, 3,* 1–14.

Watson, R., & DeMeo, P. (1987). Premarital cohabitation vs. traditional courtship and subsequent marital adjustment: A replication and follow-up. *Family Relations, 36,* 193–197.

Weatherford, W. (1999, October 31). Alzheimer's disease—What's new? *Dallas Morning News,* p. 4P.

Weaver, R. F., & Hedrick, P. W. (1999). *Genetics* (3rd ed.). New York: McGraw-Hill.

Webster, J., Lloyd, W. C., Pritchard, M. A., Burridge, C. A., Plucknett, L. E., & Byrne, A. (1999). Development of evidence-based guidelines in midwifery and gynaecology nursing. *Midwifery, 15,* 2–5.

Wechsler, H. (2000, March). Binge drinking in college students. *Journal of American College Health.*

Wechsler, H., Davenport, A., Sowdall, G., Moetykens, B., & Castillo, S. (1994). Health and behavioral consequences of binge drinking in college. *Journal of the American Medical Association, 272,* 1672–1677.

Wechsler, H., Lee, J. E., Kuo, M., & Lee, H. (2000). College binge drinking in the 1990s—A continuing health problem: Results of the Harvard University School of Public Health 1999 College Alcohol Study. *Journal of American College Health, 48,* 199–210

Weikart, D. P. (1993). *[Long-term positive effects in the Perry Preschool Head Start program].* Unpublished data, High Scope Foundation, Ypsilanti, MI.

Weincke, J. K., Thurston, S.W., Kelsey, K. T., Varkonyi, A., Wain, J. C., Mark, E. J., & Christiani, D. C. (1999). Early age at smoking initiation and tobacco carcinogen DNA damage in the lung. *Journal of the National Cancer Institute, 91,* 614–619.

Weinstein, N. D. (1984). Reducing unrealistic optimism about illness susceptibility. *Health Psychology, 3,* 431–457.

Weiss, S. M. (2000). Health psychology: History of the field. In A. Kazdin (Ed.), *Encyclopedia of psychology.* Washington, DC, & New York: American Psychological Association and Oxford University Press.

Weizmann, F. (2000). Bowlby, John. In A. Kazdin (Ed.), *Encylopedia of psychology.* Washington, DC, & New York: American Psychological Association and Oxford University Press.

Wellman, H. (2000). Early childhood. In A. Kazdin (Ed.), *Encyclopedia of psychology.* Washington, DC, & New York: American Psychological Association and Oxford University Press.

Wellman, H. (2001, April). [illegible] *theory of mind.* Paper presented at the meeting of the Society for Research in Child Development, Minneapolis.

Wellman, H. M. (1997, April). *Ten years of theory of mind: Telling the story backwards.* Paper presented at the meeting of the Society for Research in Child Development, Washington, DC.

Wenestam, C. G., & Wass, H. (1987). Swedish and U.S. Children's thinking about death: A qualitative study and cross-cultural comparison. *Death Studies, 11,* 99–121.

Wentworth, R. A. L. (1999). *Montessori for the millennium.* Mahwah, NJ: Erlbaum.

Wentzel, K. R., & Asher, S. R. (1995). The academic lives of neglected, rejected, popular, and controversial children. *Child Development, 66,* 754–763.

Wenzlaff, R. M., & Prohaska, M. L. (1989). When misery loves company: Depression, attributions, and responses to others' moods. *Journal of Experimental Social Psychology, 25,* 220–223.

Werker, J. F., & LaLonde, C. E. (1988). Cross-language speech perception: Initial capabilities and developmental change. *Developmental Psychology, 24,* 672–683.

Werler, M. M., Louik, C., Shapiro, S., & Mitchell, A. A. (1996). Prepregnant weight in relation to risk of neural tube defects. *Journal of the American Medical Association, 275,* 1089–1092.

Werner, E. E. (1989). High risk children in young adulthood: A longitudinal study from birth to 32 years. *American Journal of Orthopsychiatry, 59,* 72–81.

Werner, E. E., & Smith, R. S. (1982). *Vulnerable but invincible: A longitudinal study of resilient children and youth.* New York: McGraw-Hill.

Wertheimer, R. F. (1999, April). *Children in working poor families.* Paper presented at the meeting of the Society for Research in Child Development, Albuquerque.

Westin, D. (2000). Psychoanalytic theories. In A. Kazdin (Ed.), *Encyclopedia of psychology.* Washington, DC, & New York: American Psychological Association and Oxford University Press.
Whalen, C. (2000). Attention deficit hyperactivity disorder. In A. Kazdin (Ed.), *Encyclopedia of psychology.* Washington, DC, & New York: American Psychological Association and Oxford University Press.
Whalen, C.K. (2001). ADHD treatment in the 21st century. *Journal of Clinical Child Psychology, 30* 136–140.
Whitbourne, S. K. (2000). Adult development and aging: Biological processes and physical development. In A. Kazdin (Ed.), *Encyclopedia of psychology.* Washington, DC, & New York: American Psychological Association and Oxford University Press.
Whitbourne, S. K., & Connolly, L. A. (1999). The developing self in midlife. In S. L. Willis & J. D. Reid (Eds.), *Life in the middle.* San Diego: Academic Press.
White, B., Castle, P., & Held, R. (1964). Observations on the development of visually directed reaching. *Child Development, 35,* 349–364.
White, C. B., & Catania, J. (1981). Psychoeducational intervention for sexuality with the aged, family members of the aged, and people who work with the aged. *International Journal of Aging and Human Development.*
White, C. W., & Coleman, M. (2000). *Early childhood education.* Columbus, OH: Merrill.
White, K.M., Speisman, J. C., Costos, D., & Smith, A. (1987). Relationship maturity: A conceptual and empirical approach. In J. Meacham (Ed.), *Interpersonal relations: Family, peers, friends.* Basel, Switzerland: Karger.
White, L. (2001). Sibling relationships over the life course. *Journal of Marriage and the Family, 63,* 555–568.
White, N., & Cunningham, W. R. (1989). Is terminal drop pervasive or specific? *Journal of Gerontology: Psychological Sciences, 43,* P141–144.
Whitfield, K. E., & Baker-Thomas, T. (1999). Individual differences in aging minorities. *International Journal of Aging and Human Development, 48,* 73–79.
Whiting, B. B. (1989, April). *Culture and interpersonal behavior.* Paper presented at the biennial meeting of the Society for Research in Child Development, Kansas City.
Whiting, B. B., & Edwards, C. P. (1998). *Children of different worlds.* Cambridge, MA: Harvard University Press.
Whitman, T.L., Borkowski, J.G., Keogh, D.A., & Weed, K. (2001). *Interwoven lives.* Mahwah, NJ: Erlbaum.
Wickelgren, I. (1999). Nurture helps to mold able minds. *Science, 283,* 1832–1834.
Wiersbe, D. W. (1999). *Gone but not lost: Grieving the death of a child.* Grand Rapids, MI: Baker Book House.
Wilcutt, E.G., Pennington, B.F., Boada, R., Ogline, J.S., Tunick, R.A., Chhabildas, R.A., & Olson, N.A. (2001). A comparison of the cognitive deficits in reading disability and attention-deficit/hyperactivity disorder. *Journal of Abnormal Psychology, 110,* 157–172.
Wiley, D., & Bortz, W. M. (1996). Sexuality and aging—usual and successful. *Journal of Gerontology, 51A,* M142–M146.
Wilkie, F., & Eisdorfer, C. (1971). Intelligence and blood pressure in the aged. *Science, 172,* 959–962.
Williams, A., & Nussbaum, J.F. (2001). *Intergenerational communication across the life span.* Mahwah, NJ: Erlbaum.
Williams, C. R. (1986). *The impact of television: A natural experiment in three communities.* New York: Academic Press.
Williams, J. E., & Best, D. L. (1982). *Measuring sex stereotypes: A thirty-nation study.* Newbury Park, CA: Sage.
Williams, J. E., & Best, D. L. (1989). *Sex and psyche: Self-concept viewed cross-culturally.* Newbury Park, CA: Sage.
Williams, M. F., & Condry, J. C. (1989, April). *Living color: Minority portrayals and cross-racial interactions on television.* Paper presented at the Society for Research in Child Development meeting, Kansas City.
Williams, R. B. (1995). Coronary prone behaviors, hostility, and cardiovascular health. In K. Orth-Gomer & N. Schneiderman (Eds.), *Behavioral medicine approaches to cardiovascular disease prevention.* Mahwah, NJ: Erlbaum.
Williams, R.B. (2001). Hostility (among other psychosocial risk factors). In A. Baum, T.A. Revenson, & J.E. Singer (Eds.), *Handbook of health psychology.* Mahwah, NJ: Erlbaum.
Willis, S. L., & Nesselroade, C. S. (1990). Long-term effects of fluid ability training in old age. *Developmental Psychology, 26,* 905–910.
Willis, S. L., & Reid, S. L. (1999). *Life in the middle: Psychological and social development in middle age.* San Diego: Academic Press.
Willis, S. L., & Schaie, K. W. (1986). Training the elderly on the ability factors of spatial orientation and inductive reasoning. *Psychology and Aging, 1,* 239–247.
Willis, S. L., & Schaie, K. W. (1994). Assessing everyday competence in the elderly. In C. Fisher & R. Lerner (Eds.), *Applied developmental psychology.* Hillsdale, NJ: Erlbaum.
Willis, S. L., & Schaie, K. W. (1999). Intellectual functioning in midlife. In S. L. Willis & J. D. Reid (Eds.), *Life in the middle: Psychological and social development in middle age.* San Diego: Academic Press.
Wilson, B. J., & Gottman, J. M. (1996). Attention—The shuttle between emotion and cognition: Risk, resiliency, and physiological bases. In E. M. Hetherington & E. A. Blechman (Eds.), *Stress, coping, and resilience in children and families.* Hillsdale, NJ: Erlbaum.
Wilson, M. N., & Hall, F. D. (2000). Cultural diversity. In A. Kazdin (Ed.), *Encyclopedia of psychology.* Washington, DC, & New York: American Psychological Association and Oxford University Press.
Wilson-Shockley, S. (1995). *Gender differences in adolescent depression: The contribution of negative affect.* M.S. Thesis, University of Illinois at Urbana-Champaign.
Windle, W. F. (1940). *Physiology of the human fetus.* Philadelphia: W. B. Saunders.
Windridge, K. C., Cert, P. G., & Berryman, J. C. (1999). Women's experiences of giving birth after 35. *Birth, 26,* 16–23.
Wineberg, H. (1994). Marital reconciliation in the United States: Which couples are successful? *Journal of Marriage and the Family, 56,* 80–88.
Wing, R.R., & Polley, B.A. (2001). Obesity. In A. Baum, T.A. Revenson, & J.E. Singer (Eds.), *Handbook of health psychology.* Mahwah, NJ: Erlbaum.
Winner, E. (1986, August). Where pelicans kiss seals. *Psychology Today,* pp. 24–35.
Winner, E. (1996). *Gifted children: Myths and realities.* New York: Basic Books.
Winsler, A., Diaz, R. M., Espinosa, L., & Rodriquez, J. L. (1999). When learning a second language does not mean losing the first: Bilingual language development in low-income, Spanish-speaking children attending bilingual preschool. *Child Development, 70,* 349–362.
Winsler, A., Diaz, R. M., & Montero, I. (1997). The role of private speech in the transition from collaborative to independent task performance in young children. *Early Childhood Research Quarterly, 12,* 59–79.
Wintre, M.G., & Vallance, D.D. (1994). A developmental sequence in the comprehension of emotions: Intensity, multiple emotions, and valence. *Developmental Psychology, 30,* 509–514.
Witkin, H. A., Mednick, S. A., Schulsinger, R., Bakkestrom, E., Christiansen, K. O., Goodenbough, D. R., Hirchhorn, K., Lunsteen, C., Owen, D. R., Philip, J., Ruben, D. B., & Stocking, M. (1976). Criminality in XYY and XXY men. *Science, 193,* 547–555.
Wolff, R. (1993). *Good sports: The concerned parent's guide to Little League and other competitive youth sports.* New York: Dell.
Wong, C.A. (1997, April). *What does it mean to be an African-American or European-American growing up in a multi-ethnic community?* Paper presented at the meeting of the Society for Research in Child Development, Washington, DC.
Wong, D. L. (1997). *Essentials of pediatric nursing* (5th ed.). St. Louis: Mosby.
Wong, P. T. P., & Watt, L. M. (1991). What types of reminiscence are associated with successful aging? *Psychology and Aging, 6,* 272–279.
Wood, J.T. (2001). *Gendered lives.* Belmont, CA: Wadsworth.
Woodrich, D. L. (1994). *Attention-deficit hyperactivity disorder: What every parent should know.* Baltimore: Paul H. Brookes.
Woodward, N. J., & Wallston, B. S. (1987). Age and health-care beliefs: Self-efficacy as a mediator of low desire for control. *Psychology and Aging, 2,* 3–8.
Wooley, S. C., & Garner, D. M. (1991). Obesity treatment: The high cost of false hope. *Journal of the American Dietetic Association, 91,* 1248–1251.
World Health Organization. (2000, February 2). *Adolescent health behavior in 28 countries.* Geneva: Author.
Worobey, J., & Belsky, J. (1982). Employing the Brazelton scale to influence mothering: An experimental comparison of three strategies. *Developmental Psychology, 18,* 736–743.

Worthington, E. L. (1989). Religious faith across the life span: Implications for counseling and research. *Counseling Psychologist, 17,* 555–612.

Wright, J. C. (1995, March). *Effects of viewing Sesame Street: The longitudinal study of media and time use.* Paper presented at the meeting of the Society for Research in Child Development, Indianapolis.

Wright, J.C., Huston, A.C., Scantlin, R., & Kotler, J. (2001). The early window project. In S.M. Fisch & R.T. Truglio (Eds.), *"G" is for growing.* Mahwah, NJ: Erlbaum.

Y

Yale, R. (1999, Fall). Support groups and other services for individuals with early-stage Alzheimer's disease. *Generations,* pp. 57–62.

Yamagishi, T., & Yamagishi, M. (1994). Trust and commitment in the United States and Japan. *Motivation and Emotion, 18,* 129–166.

Yang, J., McCrae, R. R., & Costa, P. T. (1998). Adult age differences in personality traits in the United States and the People's Republic of China. *Journal of Gerontology: Psychological Sciences, 53B,* P375–P383.

Yates, M. (1995, March). *Political socialization as a function of volunteerism.* Paper presented at the meeting of the Society for Research in Child Development, Indianapolis.

Yeatts, D. E., Folts, W. E., & Knapp, J. (1999). Older workers' adaptation to a changing workplace: Employment issues for the 21st century. *Educational Gerontology, 25,* 331–347.

Yeung, W.J., Sandberg, J.F., Davis-Kean, P.E., & Hofferth, S.L. (2001). Children's time with fathers in intact families. *Journal of Marriage and the Family, 63,* 136–154.

Yin, Y., Buhrmester, D., & Hibbard, D. (1996, March). *Are there developmental changes in the influence of relationships with parents and friends on adjustment during early adolescence?* Paper presented at the meeting of the Society for Research on Adolescence, Boston.

Yip, R. (1995, March). *Nutritional status of U.S. children: The extent and causes of malnutrition.* Paper presented at the meeting of the Society for Research in Child Development, Indianapolis.

Young, K. T. (1990). American conceptions of infant development from 1955 to 1984: What the experts are telling parents. *Child Development, 61,* 17–28.

Young, S. K., & Shahinfar, A. (1995, March). *The contributions of maternal sensitivity and child temperament to attachment status at 14 months.* Paper presented at the meeting of the Society for Research in Child Development, Indianapolis.

Yu, V. Y. (2000). Developmental outcome of extremely preterm infants. *American Journal of Perinatology, 17,* 57–61.

Z

Zarit, S. H., & Downs, M. G. (1999, Fall). State of the art for practice in dementia: Introduction. *Generations,* pp. 6–8.

Zarit, S. H., & Knight, B. G. (Eds.). (1996). *A guide to psychotherapy and aging.* Washington, DC: American Psychological Association.

Zeskind, P. S., Gingras, J. L., Campbell, K. D., & Donnelly, K. (1999, April). *Prenatal cocaine exposure disrupts fetal autonomic regulation.* Paper presented at the meeting of the Society for Research in Child Development, Albuquerque.

Zeskind, P. S., Klein, L., & Marshall, T. R. (1992). Adults perceptions of experimental modifications of durations and expiratory sounds in infant crying. *Developmental Psychology, 28,* 1153–1162.

Zigler, E. F., & Finn-Stevenson, M. (1999). Applied developmental psychology. In M. H. Bornstein & M. E. Lamb (Eds.), *Developmental psychology: An advanced textbook* (4th ed.). Mahwah, NJ: Erlbaum.

Zigler, E. F., & Hall, N. W. (2000). *Child development and social policy.* New York: McGraw-Hill.

Zigler, E., & Styfco, S. J. (1994). Head Start: Criticisms in a constructive context. *American Psychologist, 49,* 127–132.

Zimmerman, R. S., Khoury, E., Vega, W. A., Gil, A. G., & Warheit, G. J. (1995). Teacher and student perceptions of behavior problems among a sample of African American, Hispanic, and non-Hispanic White students. *American Journal of Community Psychology, 23,* 181–197.

Zubay, G. L. (1996). *Origins of life on the earth and in the cosmos.* Dubuque, IA: Wm. C. Brown.

Credits

LINE ART AND TEXT

CHAPTER 1

Figure 1.1 Source: Data from Monroe Lerner, "When, Why, and Where People Die" in E.S. Schneidman (ed.), *Death: Current Perspectives,* 2d ed., pp. 88–91, 1980. **Figure 1.2** Source: U.S. Census Data: Social Security Administration, *The Statistical History of the United States,* 1976. **Figure 1.3** Source: Data from Kirkwood, "Comparative and Evolutionary Aspects of Longevity": in C.E. Finch and E.L. Schneider (eds.), *Handbook of the Biology of Aging,* p. 34, Van Nostrand Reinhold Company, 1985. **Lyrics (ch1)** THE GREATEST LOVE OF ALL, by Linda Creed and Michael Masser © 1977 EMI Gold Horizon Music Corp. and EMIGolden Torch Music Corp. All rights reserved. Used by permission WARNER BROS. PUBLICATIONS U.S. INC., Miami, FL 33014. **Figure 1.5** From Santrock, *Psychology 6e.* Copyright © 2000 The McGraw-Hill Companies. Reproduced with permission of The McGraw-Hill Companies. **Page 32** The Far Side® by Gary Larson © 1982 FarWorks, Inc. All Rights Reserved. Used with permission.

CHAPTER 2

Figure 2.2 From Santrock, *Child Development 9/e.* Copyright © 2001 The McGraw-Hill Companies. Reproduced with permission of The McGraw-Hill Companies. **Figure 2.3** From Santrock, *Child Development 9/e.* Copyright © 2001 The McGraw-Hill Companies. Reproduced with permission of The McGraw-Hill Companies. **Page 42** The Far Side® by Gary Larson © 1984 FarWorks, Inc. All Rights Reserved. Used with permission. **Figure 2.6** From Kopp/Krakow, *The Child,* 1982, p. 648. Reprinted by permission of Addison-Wesley Educational Publishers, Inc. **Figure 2.9** From *Children 5e* by John Santrock. Copyright © 1997 by The McGraw-Hill Companies. Reproduced with permission of The McGraw-Hill Companies. **Figure 2.10** From Santrock, *Child Development 9/e.* Copyright © 2001 The McGraw-Hill Companies. Reproduced with permission of The McGraw-Hill Companies. **Page 84** By permission of Johnny Hart and Creators Syndicate, Inc.

CHAPTER 3

Figure 3.1 With permission, from Baltes, P.B., Staudinger, U.M., & Lindenberger, U. (1999). Lifespan psychology, *Annual Review of Psychology,* Volume 50 © 1999 by Annual Reviews www.AnnualReviews.org. Also reprinted by permission of Dr. Paul B. Baltes. **Figure 3.2** From Santrock, *Child Development 9/e.* Copyright © 2001 The McGraw-Hill Companies. Reproduced with permission of the McGraw-Hill Companies. **Figure 3.3** From *Biology, 6e* by Mader S. Copyright © 1998 by The McGraw-Hill Companies. Reproduced with permission of The McGraw-Hill Companies. **Figure 3.5** From Santrock, *Children 5/e.* Copyright © 1997 by The McGraw-Hill Companies. Reproduced with permission of The McGraw-Hill Companies. **Figure 3.12** From *Biology, 6e* by Mader S. Copyright © 1998 by The McGraw-Hill Companies. Reproduced with permission of The McGraw-Hill Companies. **Figure 3.13** From Lewis, R., *Human Genetics 3e.* Copyright © 1999 by The McGraw-Hill Companies. Reproduced with permission of The McGraw-Hill Companies. **Figure 3.14** From Santrock, *Children 5/e.* Copyright © 1997 by The McGraw-Hill Companies. Reproduced with permission of The McGraw-Hill Companies.

CHAPTER 4

Figure 4.2 From Charles Carroll and Dean Miller, *Health: The Science of Human Adaptation, 5th ed.* Copyright © 1991 Wm. C. Brown Communications, Inc. Dubuque, Iowa. All Rights Reserved. Reprinted by permission. **Figure 4.3** From *Children 5e* by John Santrock. Copyright © 1997 by The McGraw-Hill Companies. Reproduced with permission of The McGraw-Hill Companies. **Figure 4.4** © 1984 by the Childbirth Association of Seattle. Reprinted from *Pregnancy, Childbirth and the Newborn: The Complete Guide* with permission of its publisher, Meadowbrook Press. **Figure 4.5** Figure from K.L. Moore, *The Developing Human: Clinically Oriented Embryology, 4/e,* 1988. Reprinted by permission of W.B. Saunders Company. **Figure 4.7** From Queenan and Queenan, *New Life: Pregnancy, Birth, and Your Child's First Year.* Copyright © 1986 Marshall Cavendish Ltd., London, England. Reprinted by permission. **Figure 4.8** From Virginia A. Apgar, "A Proposal for a New Method of Evaluation of a Newborn Infant" in *Anesthesia and Analgesia,* 32:260–267, 1975. Reprinted by permission. **Figure 4.9** Adapted from *Cultural Perspective On Child Development* by Daniel A. Wagner and Harold W. Stevenson © 1982 by W. H. Freeman and Company. Used with permission.

CHAPTER 5

Figure 5.2 From Santrock, *Child Development 9/e.* Copyright © 2001 The McGraw-Hill Companies. Reproduced with permission of The McGraw-Hill Companies. **Figure 5.3** Reprinted by permission of the publisher from *The Postnatal Development of the Human Cerebral Cortex, Vol I–VIII* by Jesse LeRoy Conel, Cambridge, Mass.: Harvard University Press, Copyright © 1939–1975 by the President and Fellows of Harvard College. **Figure 5.6** Reprinted with permission from H.P. Roffwarg, J.N. Muzio & W.C. Dement, "Ontogenetic development of human-dream sleep cycle," *Science,* 152, 1966, pp. 604–609. Copyright 1966 American Association for the Advancement of Science. **Figure 5.7** *From Children 5e* by John Santrock. Copyright © 1997 by The McGraw-Hill Companies. Reproduced with permission of The McGraw-Hill Companies. **Figure 5.8** From W.K. Frankenburg and J.B. Dodds, "The Denver Development Screening Test" in *Journal of Pediatrics,* 71:181–92. Copyright © 1967 Mosby-Year Book, Inc., St. Louis, MO. Reprinted by permission. **Figure 5.9** From Santrock, *Child Development, 9e.* Copyright © 2001 by The McGraw-Hill Companies. Reproduced with permission of The McGraw-Hill Companies. **Figure 5.11a** From "The Origin of Form" by Robert L Fantz in *Scientific American,* May 1961, p. 72. Reprinted by permission of the artist, Alex Semenoick.

CHAPTER 7

Figure 7.1 From Santrock, *Children 6e.* Copyright © 1998 by The McGraw-Hill Companies. Reproduced with permission of The McGraw-Hill Companies. **Page 184** Reprinted with special permission of King Features Syndicate. **Figure 7.3** Adapted from: M.D.S. Ainsworth & S.M. Bell (1971). Attachment, Exploration, and Separation: Illustrated by the Behavior of One-Year-Olds in a Strange Situation. *Child Development,* Vol. 41(1), 49–67. Reprinted by permission of Society for Research in Child Development. **Figure 7.4** From Jay Belsky, "Early Human Experiences: A Family Perspective," in *Developmental Psychology,* 17:3–23. Reprinted by permission of the American Psychological Association. **Figure 7.5** From *Children 5e* by John Santrock. Copyright © 1997 by The McGraw-Hill Companies. Reproduced with permission of The McGraw-Hill Companies.

CHAPTER 8

Figure 8.1 Reprinted from *Human Biology and Ecology* by Albert Damon with the permission of W.W. Norton & Company, Inc. Copyright © 1977 by W.W. Norton & Company, Inc. **Figure 8.2** From G.J. Schiner (ed.) "Performance Objectives for Preschool Children," Adapt Press, Sioux Falls, SD, 1974. **Figure 8.3** From G.J. Schiner (ed.) "Performance Objectives for Preschool Children," Adapt Press, Sioux Falls, SD, 1974. **Figure 8.5** "The Symbolic Drawings of Young Children." Reprinted courtesy of D. Wolf and J. Nove. **Page 215** © The New Yorker Collection 1989 Lee Lorenz from cartoonbank.com. All Rights Reserved. **Figure 8.10** From Santrock, *Child Development 9e.* Copyright © 2001 by The McGraw-Hill Companies. Reproduced with permission of The McGraw-Hill Companies. **Page 220** © 2001; Reprinted courtesy of Bunny Hoest and Parade Magazine. **Figure 8.11** Chen, Z., & Siegler, R. (2000). Across the great divide . . . *Monographs of the Society for Research in Child Development,* Vol. 65, No. 2, Fig 4, p. 26. Reprinted with permission. **Figure 8.12** From Jean Berko, "The Child's Learning of English Morphology," in *Word,* 1958, Vol. 14, p. 154. **Figure 8.13** From *Young Children,* 41:23–27, September 1986. Reprinted with permission from the National Association for the Education of Young Children.

CHAPTER 9

Figure 9.1 From Janet Kuebli, "Young children's understanding of everyday emotions," *Young Children,* March 1994. Reprinted with permission from the National Association for the Education of Young

Children. **Page 242** The Far Side® by Gary Larson © 1985 FarWorks, Inc. All Rights Reserved. Used with permission. **Page 248** CALVIN AND HOBBES © Watterson. Reprinted with permission of UNIVERSAL PRESS SYNDICATE. All rights reserved. **Page 265** Copyright © Martha F. Campbell

CHAPTER 10

Figure 10.1 From Santrock, *Children 6e.* Copyright © 2000 by The McGraw-Hill Companies. Reproduced with permission of The McGraw-Hill Companies. **Figure 10.2** Source: US Department of Education, Office of Special Education Programs. **Figure 10.7** Simulated items similar to those in the Wechsler Intelligence Scale for Children-Revised. Copyright 1949, 1955, 1974 by The Psychological Corporation, a Harcourt Assessment Company. Reproduced by permission. All rights reserved. "Wechsler Intelligence Scale for Children" and "WISC-R" are trademarks of The Psychological Corporation registered in the United States of America and/or other jurisdictions. **Page 294** © The New Yorker Collection 1998 Donald Reilly from cartoonbank.com. All Rights Reserved. **Page 296** © 2001 by Sidney Harris. **Figure 10.8** "Sample Item from the Raven Progressive Matrices Test," from Raven's *Standard Progressive Matrices,* Item A5. Reprinted by permission of J.C. Raven Ltd.

CHAPTER 11

Figure 11.2 From Santrock, *Psychology 6e.* Copyright © 2000 The McGraw-Hill Companies. Reproduced with permission of The McGraw-Hill Companies. **Figure 11.3** From Santrock, *Children 6e.* Copyright © 2000 by The McGraw-Hill Companies. Reproduced with permission of The McGraw-Hill Companies. **Figure 11.4** From "Gender Differences in Mathematics Performance" in *Psychological Bulletin,* 107:139–155, 1990. Copyright © 1990 by the American Psychological Association. Reprinted with permission. **Figure 11.5** From Janet S. Hyde, *Half the Human Experience: The Psychology of Women, 3d ed.* Copyright © 1985 D.C. Heath and Company, Lexington, MA. Reprinted by permission. **Page 349** From *Penguin Dreams And Stranger Things* by Berkeley Breathed. Copyright © 1985 by The Washington Post Company. By permission of Little, Brown and Company (Inc.) and International Creative Management, Inc.

CHAPTER 12

Figure 12.1 From Santrock, *Children 6e.* Copyright © 2000 by The McGraw-Hill Companies. Reproduced with permission of The McGraw-Hill Companies. **Figure 12.2** From J.M. Tanner, R.H. Whitehouse, and M. Takaishi, "Standards from Birth to Maturity for Height, Weight, Height Velocity, and Weight Velocity: British Children 1965" in *Archives of Diseases in Childhood,* 41, 1966. Copyright © British Medical Association, London, England. Reprinted by permission. **Figure 12.3** From "Growing Up" by J.M. Tanner., *Scientific American,* September 1973. Copyright © 1973 by Scientific America, Inc. All rights reserved. Reprinted by permission. **Page 357** FEIFFER © 1985 JULES FEIFFER. Reprinted with permission of Universal Press Syndicate. All rights reserved. **Figure 12.4** Source: Johnston, L.D., O'Malley, P.M., & Bachman, J.G. (2000). The monitoring of the future: National results on adolescent drug use. Washington, DC: National Institute on Drug Abuse.

CHAPTER 13

Excerpt, page 398 Reprinted by permission from *Selections from the Writings of Abdu'l-Bahß.* Copyright © 1978 by the Universal House of Justice. **Figure 13.3** From Santrock, *Children 6e.* Copyright © 2000 by The McGraw-Hill Companies. Reproduced with permission of The McGraw-Hill Companies.s. **Lyrics page 411** *Blowin' In The Wind.* Copyright © 1962, by Warner Bros. Music, Copyright Renewed 1990 by Special Rider Music. All rights reserved. International copyright secured. Reprinted by permission.

CHAPTER 14

Figure 14.1 From L.L. Langley, *Physiology of Man.* Copyright © 1971 Van Nostrand Reinhold. Reprinted by permission of L.L. Langley. **Figure 14.2** From Pate et al., *Journal of the American Medical Association,* 273:404. Copyright © 1995 American Medical Association. Reprinted by permission. **Figure 14.3** From *Sex in America* by Robert Michael, et al. Copyright © by CSG Enterprises, Inc., Edward O. Lauman, Robert Michael, and Gina Kolata. Reprinted by permission. **Figure 14.5** Reproduced by special permission of the publisher, Psychological Assessment Resources from *Making Vocational Choices: A Theory of Vocational Choices and Work Environments.* Copyright 1973, 1985, 1992 by Psychological Assessment Resources, Inc. All Rights Reserved. **Page 436** © 1985; reprinted courtesy of Bunny Hoest and Parade Magazine. **Figure 14.6** Source: *Occupational Outlook Handbook, 2000–2001,* Chart 4. **Page 438** © The New Yorker Collection 1989 Jack Ziegler from cartoonbank.com. All Rights Reserved.

CHAPTER 15

Figure 15.1 From Wachs, T.D. (1994). Fit, context and the transition between temperament and personality. In C. Halverson, G. Kohnstamm, & R. Martin (Eds.), *The developing structure of personality from infancy to adulthood* (pp. 209–222). **Figure 15.2** Source: Data from R.J. Sternberg, *The Triangle of Love,* Basic Books, New York, 1988. **Figure 15.3** Reproduced by special permission of the publisher, Psychological Assessment Resources, Inc., from *The Changing Family Life Cycle, 2d ed.* Copyright 1989 by Psychological Assessment Resources, Inc. All Rights Reserved. **Figure 15.4** Source: U.S. Bureau of the Census, 2000. **Figure 15.5** Source: U.S. Bureau of the Census, 2000. **Figure 15.6** Source: U.S. Bureau of the Census, 2000. **Figure 15.7** Source: National Center for Health Statistics, 2000. **Page 469** Copyright © 1964 Don Orehek.

CHAPTER 16

Lyrics (ch 16, page 477) © 1972, 1985 Denjac Music Co. **Page 479** FEIFFER © JULES FEIFFER. Reprinted with permission of UNIVERSAL PRESS SYNDICATE. All rights reserved. **Figure 16.1** Source: U.S. Bureau of the Census, 2000. Page 482 © The New Yorker Collection 1987 Donald Reilly from cartoonbank.com. All Rights Reserved. **Figure 16.2** Source: National Center for Health Statistics (1998). **Figure 16.3** From *Sex in America* by Robert Michael, et al. Copyright © by CSG Enterprises, Inc., Edward O. Lauman, Robert Michael, and Gina Kolata. Reprinted by permission. **Figure 16.5** Source: Schaie, K. (1994), The Life Course of Adult Intellectual Abilities, *American Psychologist,* 49, 304–313. **Figure 16.7** From *Men in Their Forties: The Transition to Middle Age* by Lois M. Tamir, 1982. Used by permission of Springer Publishing Company. **Page 492** Reprinted with special permission of King Features Syndicate.

CHAPTER 17

Page 505 © The New Yorker Collection 1984 Leo Cullum from cartoonbank.com. All Rights Reserved. **Figure 17.1** From George Levinger and Diedrick Snoek, *Attraction in Relationship: A New Look at Interpersonal Attraction.* Copyright © 1972 George Levinger and Diedrick Snoek. Reprinted by permission. **Figure 17.4** From A.D. Kener et al. in *Journal of Behavioral Medicine,* 4, 1981. Reprinted by permission of Plenum Publishers. **Figure 17.5** From D.F. Hultsch and J.K. Plemons, "Life Events and Life Span Development" in *Life Span Development and Behavior,* Vol.2 by P.B. Baltes and O.G. Brun (eds.). Copyright © 1979 Academic Press, Orlando. FL. Reprinted by permission. **Figure 17.6** From Santrock, *Psychology 6e.* Copyright © 2000 The McGraw-Hill Companies. Reproduced with permission of The McGraw-Hill Companies. **Page 514** © The New Yorker Collection 1987 Lee Lorenz from cartoonbank.com. All Rights Reserved. **Page 515** DOONESBURY © 1991 G.B. Trudeau. Reprinted with permission of Universal Press Syndicate. All rights reserved.

CHAPTER 18

Figure 18.1 From *The Psychology of Death, Dying and Bereavement* by Richard Schulz, Copyright 1978, Newberry Records, a division of Random House, Inc. Reproduced with permission of The McGraw-Hill Companies. **Figure 18.2** From *USA Today,* January 5, 1999. Copyright 1999, USA TODAY. Reprinted with permission. **Figure 18.5** Data from Advocate for the U.S. Senate Special Committee on Aging, "Aging in America," p. 50, U.S. Government Printing Office, Washington DC, 1983.

CHAPTER 19

Figure 19.3 From Reisberg et al. (1982), The global deterioration scale for assessment of primary degenerative dementia. American Journal of Psychiatry, 139, 1136–1139. Copyright 1982, the American Psychiatric Association. Copyright 1983 by Barry Reisberg, MD. Reprinted by permission.

CHAPTER 20

Figure 20.1 From "Erikson's View . . . Conflict and Resolution: Culmination in old age." Copyright © 1988 by The New York Times Co. Reprinted by permission. **Figure 20.2** From Carstenen, L., et al "The Social Context of Emotion" in the *Annual Review of Geriatrics and Gerontology* by Schaie/Lawton, 1997,17, p. 331. Used by permission of Springer Publishing Company Inc., New York 10012. **Poem, Page 612** From "Do Not Go Gentle Into That Good Night" by Dylan Thomas from *The Poems of Dylan Thomas,* copyright © 1952 by Dylan Thomas. Reprinted by permission of New Directions Publishing Corp. and David Higham Associates Limited

PHOTO CREDITS

SECTION OPENERS

1: © Bill Bachman/Photo Edit; **2:** © Petit Format/Nestle/Photo Researchers, Inc.; **3:** Northern Telecom & J. Walther Thompson Advertising; 4: © Tom Prettyman/Photo Edit, Inc.; **5:** © Tom Rosenthal/Superstock; **6:** © Butch Martin/The Image Bank; **7:** © B. Bachmann/The Image Works; **8:** © Barros & Barros/The Image Bank; **9:** © David Young-Wolff/Photo Edit, Inc.; **10:** © Dennis Stock/Magnum Photos

CHAPTER 1

Opener 1: © Joe Cornish/Stone; **p. 5 (left):** © Sygma/CORBIS; **(right):** © AP/Wide World Photos; **p. 9:** Courtesy K. Warner Schaie; **p. 11:** Courtesy of Luis Vargas; **p. 12:** © National Associate for the Education of Young Children, Robert Maust/Photo Agora; **p. 13:** © Nancy Agostini; **p. 14 (top):** © James Pozarik/Liaison Agency; **p. 14 (bottom):** Courtesy of Marian Wright Edelman, The Children's Defense Fund, photograph by Rick Reinhard; **p. 15:** © Dennis Brack Ltd./Black Star; **1.5 (top to bottom):** © Elyse Lewin/The Image Bank; © Vol. 49/PhotoDisc; © Dan Esgro/The Image Bank; © James L. Shaffer; © Michael Salas/The Image Bank; © Joe Sohm/The Image Works; John Santrock; Courtesy of Landrum Shettles; **p. 21:** © Joel Gordon 1995; **p. 22:** © Jeff Zaruba/Stone

CHAPTER 2

Opener: © John P. Kelly/The Image Bank; p. 31: Courtesy of Saundra Boyd; **pp. 32 and 34:** © Bettmann/CORBIS; © Bettmann/CORBIS; **p. 36:** © CORBIS; **p. 37:** © Yves de Braine/Black Star; **p. 38:** A.R. Lauria/Dr. Michael Cole, Laboratory of Human Cognition, University of California, San Diego; **p. 40:** © Bettmann/CORBIS; **p. 41:** Courtesy of Stanford University News Service; **p. 42:** Photo by Nina Leen/Life Magazine. © Time, Inc.; **p. 43:** Courtesy of Urie Bronfenbrenner; **p. 48:** © Richard T. Nowitz/Photo Researchers, Inc.; **2.11a:** © Photo Researchers, Inc.; **2.11b and c:** © AP/Wide World Photos; **2.11d:** © Bettmann/CORBIS; **2.11e:** © Sukie Hill Photographer; **2.11f:** © Lawrence Migdale/Photo Researchers, Inc.; **p. 56:** © McGraw-Hill Higher Education, photographer John Thoeming; **p. 57:** Courtesy of Tom Puglisi; **p. 58:** Courtesy of Pam Trotman Reid

CHAPTER 3

Opener: © Jeff Greenberg/Photo Edit; **p. 65:** © Enrico Ferorelli Enterprises; **p. 67** © Philip & Karen Smith/Stone; **p. 75:** © Joel Gordon 1989; **3.4:** © Sundstrom/Liaison International; **p. 76:** Courtesy of Holly Ishmael; **3.9:** © Andrew Eccles/Outline Press; **3.11:** © Jacques Pavlousky/Sygma/CORBIS; **p. 82:** © 1998 Brooks Kraft/Sygma/CORBIS; **p. 85:** © Enrico Ferorelli Enterprises; **p. 86:** © Elizabeth Crews/The Image Works; **p. 87:** © Vol. 28/PhotoDisc; **p. 88:** © Joel Gordon 1999

CHAPTER 4

Opener: Photo Lennart Nilsson/Albert Bonniers Forlag AB, A Child is Born, Dell Publishing Company; **p. 96:** © David Young-Wolff/PhotoEdit; **4.3 (top to bottom):** Photo Lennart Nilsson/Albert Bonniers Forlag AB, A Child is Born, Dell Publishing Company; **4.5:** Courtesy of Ann Streissguth; **p. 102:** © John Chiasson/Liaison Agency; **p. 103:** © R.I.A./Liaison Agency; **p. 104:** © Betty Press/Woodfin Camp & Associates; **p. 105:** © Alon Reininger/Contract Press Images; **p. 106:** © Charles Gupton/Stock Boston; **p. 108:** © SIU/Peter Arnold, Inc.; p. 109: Courtesy of Linda Pugh; **pp. 110 and 111:** © Charles Gupton/Stock Boston; p. 112: Courtesy of Dr. Tiffany Field; **4.7** © Comstock, Inc.; **p. 116:** © Michael Newman/Photo Edit; **p. 117:** © Tony Schanuel; **p. 118:** © James G. White Photography

CHAPTER 5

Opener : © Niki Moreschal/The Image Bank; **5.2:** Photo Lennart Nilsson/Albert Bonniers Forlag; **5.3:** Reprinted by permission of the publisher from The Postnatal Development of the Human Cerebral Cortex, Vol I-VIII by Jesse LeRoy Conel, Cambridge, Mass.: Harvard University Press, Copyright © 1939, 1975 by the President and Fellows of Harvard College; **5.4:** © 1999 Kenneth Jarecke/Contact Press Images; **5.5:** © A. Glauberman/Photo Researchers, Inc.; **p. 130 (left):** Courtesy of Steve and Cindi Binder; **5.6ab:** Courtesy of Children's Hospital of Michigan; **p. 134:** Courtesy of T. Berry Brazelton; **p. 135:** © Bruce McAllister/Image Works; **p. 136:** © Bob Dammrich/The Image Works; **p. 137:** Courtesy of The Hawaii Family Support Center, Healthy Start Program; **5.8 (left):** © Elizabeth Crews/Image Works; **(middle):** © James G. White Photography; **(right):** © Petit Format/Photo Researchers, Inc.; **5.10:** © Judith Canty/Stock Boston; **p. 144:** Courtesy of Esther Thelen; **5.11 (all):** Courtesy of Dr. Charles Nelson; **5.12:** © David Linton; **5.13:** © Enrico Ferorelli; **5.14:** © Joe McNally/Sygma/CORBIS; **5.15a:** © Michael Siluk; **5.15b:** © Dr. Melanie Spence, University of Texas; **5.16:** © Jean Guichard/Sygma/CORBIS; **5.17a-c:** From D. Rosenstein and H. Oster "Differential Facial Responses to Four Basic Tastes in Newborns," *Child Development*, Vol. 59, 1988. © Society for Research in Child Development, Inc.; **p. 152:** © Photodisc website

CHAPTER 6

Opener : © 1997 Joe Bator/Stock Market; **6.1 (both):** © Doug Goodman/Monkmeyer; **6.2:** © Denis Morcotte/Index Stock; **6.3:** Courtesy of Dr. Carolyn Rovee-Collier; **6.4:** © Enrico Ferorelli; **p. 165:** © Joe McNally/Sygma/CORBIS; **p. 167:** Courtesy of John Santrock; **p. 169:** © ABPL Image Library /Animals Animals/Earth Scenes; **p. 170:** © 1999 James Balog; **p. 171:** Courtesy of Noam Chomsky; **p. 172:** © PhotoDisc website

CHAPTER 7

Opener : © Rob Crandall/The Image Works; **p. 177:** © Andy Sacks/Stone; **p. 179:** © Andy Cox/Stone; **p. 182:** © Michael Tcherevkoff/The Image Bank; **p. 183:** © Judith Oddie/Photo Edit; **p. 185:** © G&J Images, Inc./The Image Bank; **7.2:** © Martin Rogers/Stock Boston; **7.3:** © Daniel Grogan; **p. 189:** © David Young-Wolff/Photo Edit; **p. 190:** © Penny Tweedie/Stone; **7.4:** © Comstock, Inc.; **p. 194:** © Cesar Lucas/The Image Bank; **p. 195:** Courtesy of Rashmi Nakre, The Hattie Daniels Day Care Center

CHAPTER 8

Opener: © Martin Rogers/Stone; **p. 204:** © Bob Daemmrich/The Image Works; **p. 207:** © Marc Romanelli/The Image Bank; **p. 210:** Courtesy of Barbara Deloian; **p. 211:** © William Campbell/Time, Inc.; **8.6:** © Paul Fusco/Magnum Photos; **8.8:** © Owen Franken/Stock Boston; **8.9:** © Elizabeth Crews/Image Works; **p. 217:** © James Wertsch/Washington University; **p. 218:** © Bob Daemmrich/The Image Works; **8.10 (left):** A. R. Lauria/Dr. Michael Cole, Laboratory of Human Cognition, University of California, San Diego; **(right):** © Bettmann/CORBIS; **p. 221:** © 1999 James Kamp; **p. 223:** © Nita Winter; **p. 226:** Courtesy of Anita Marie Hitchcock; **8.13 (left):** © David Young-Wolff/Photo Edit, Inc.; **8.13 (right):** © Ken Fisher/Stone; **p. 231:** © Robert Wallis/SIPA Press, Newsweek, April 17, 1989; **p. 232:** Courtesy of Yolanda Garcia; **p. 233:** © Robert Knowles/Black Star

CHAPTER 9

Opener: © Ron Chapple/FPG International; **p. 245:** © Suzanne Sasz/Photo Researchers, Inc.; **9.4:** © Peter Correz/Stone; **p. 254:** © Christopher Arnesen/Stone; **p. 256:** © 1999 Joel Gordon; **p. 258:** © Karen Kasmauski/Woodfin Camp; **p. 261:** © Richard Hutchings/Photo Edit; **p. 266:** © Claudia Parks/The Stock Market

CHAPTER 10

Opener: © Bruce Ayres/Stone; **p. 273:** © P. West/San Jose Mercury News/Sygma/CORBIS; **p. 274:** © Bob Daemmrich/Image Works; **p. 276:** © Joe McNally/Time, Inc.; **p. 277:** Courtesy of Sharon McLeod; **p.281 (left):** © David Young-Wolff/Photo Edit; **(right):** © Will McIntyre/Photo Researchers, Inc.; **10.4:** © Richard Hutchings/Photo Researchers, Inc.; **p. 286 (top & bottom):** © Archives Jean Piaget, Universite De Geneve, Switzerland; **p. 287:** © Bernheim/Woodfin Camp; **p. 289:** Courtesy of Laura Martin; **p. 291:** © Myrleen Ferguson/Photo Edit; **p. 295:** © Joe McNally; **10.8:** © Jill Cannefax/EKM-Nepenthe; **p. 299:** Courtesy of Sterling C. Jones, Jr.; **p. 302:** © Richard Howard; **p. 303:** Courtesy of Sharla Peltier; **p. 304:** © Elizabeth Crews

CHAPTER 11

Opener: © Terry Vine/Stone; **p. 312:** © Myrleen Ferguson/Photo Edit, Inc.; **p. 314:** Courtesy of Jonathan Cohen; **p. 318:** © Keith Carter Photography; **p. 326:** © Bernard Pierre Wolff/Photo Researchers, Inc.; **p. 329:** © Michael Newman/Photo Edit; **11.6:** © Suomo/The Image Bank; **p. 335:** Courtesy of Donna Smith; p. 336: © Lonnie Harp; **p. 338:** © Mike Yamashita/Woodfin Camp; **p. 339:** © John S. Abbott; **p. 340:** © Eiji Miyazawa/Black Star

CHAPTER 12

Opener: © Bob Daemmrich/Image Works; **p. 352:** © Giuseppe Molteni/The Image Bank; **p. 355:** © David Young-Wolff; **p. 356:** © Lawrence Migdale/Stock Boston; **p. 358:** © 1998 Frank Fournier; **p. 361:** © Robert Brenner/Photo Edit; **p. 363:** © Tony Freeman/Photo Edit; **12.5:** © Paul Conklin; **p. 368:** © Stewart Cohen/Stone; **p. 369:** © Susan Lapides 2001; **p. 371:** © Mark Antman/Image Works; **p. 372:** Courtesy of Armando Ronquillo;

p. 373: Courtesy of I Have a Dream - Houston, Houston, TX.; **p. 374:** © H. Yamaguchi/Gamma Liaison; **p. 376:** © Anthony Verde Photography

CHAPTER 13

Opener: © Lewin Studio, Inc./The Image Bank; **p. 385:** Courtesy of Margaret Beale Spencer; **13.2:** © Michael Melford/The Image Bank; **p. 392:** © Michael Siluk/Image Works; **p. 393:** © Tony Freeman/Photo Edit; **p. 394:** © Tessa Codrington/Stone; **p. 397:** © Daniel Laine; **p. 400:** Courtesy of El Puente Academy; **p. 402:** Courtesy of Rodney Hammond; **p. 404 (left):** © Renato Rotolo/Liaison Agency; **(right):** © Mark Richards/Photo Edit; **p. 405:** © Jim Smith/Monkmeyer

CHAPTER 14

Opener: © Jon Riley/Stone; **p. 413:** © Bettmann/CORBIS; **p. 415:** Courtesy of Grace Leaf; **p. 416:** © Alvis Upitis/The Image Bank; **p. 419:** Courtesy of Judith Rodin; **p. 420:** © Lori Adamski Peek/Stone; **p. 425:** © 1996 Rob Lewine/The Stock Market; **p. 428 (top):** © Boehringer Ingelheim International GmbH, Photo Lennart Nilsson/Albert Bonniers Forlag AB; **(bottom):** © Barry O'Rourke/The Stock Market; **p. 432 (left):** AP/Wide World Photos; **(middle):** Courtesy Nina Holton; **(right):** Courtesy of Jim Cox/The Salk Institute; **p. 433:** Courtesy Mihaly Csik[illegible] Lillian [illegible]maz-Diaz, Clinical Professor, George Washington University, Department of Psychiatry; **p. 440:** © Shooting Star

CHAPTER 15

Opener: © Gary Conner/Photo Edit, Inc.; **p. 450:** Universal (Courtesy of Kobal); **p. 454 (top):** © David Young-Wolff/Photo Edit; **(middle):** © Tony Freeman/Photo Edit, Inc.; **(bottom):** © James McLoughlin/Stone; **p. 460 (left):** © Explorer/J. P. Nacivet/Photo Researchers, Inc.; **(middle):** © Chuck Nacke/Woodfin Camp & Associates; **(right):** © Dean Press Images/Image Works; **p. 461:** © Ronald Mackechnie/Stone; **p. 462:** Courtesy of Andrew Christensen; **p. 463:** Courtesy of Janis Keyser; **p. 473:** © S. Gazin/The Image Works

CHAPTER 16

Opener: © Richard Shock/Stone; **p. 480 (left):** © Bettmann/CORBIS; **(right):** © Matthew Mendelsohn/CORBIS; **p. 485:** © 1998 Tom & Dee McCarthy/The Stock Market; **16.3:** © Larry Dale Gordon/The Image Bank; **p. 490:** © Reuters Newmedia Inc/CORBIS; **p. 493:** © Chris Cheadle/Stone; **p. 496:** © Tony Freeman/Photo Edit, Inc.

CHAPTER 17

Opener: © Myrleen Ferguson/Photo Edit, Inc.; **17.1:** © Henley & Savage/The Stock Market; **17.2 (top):** © John P. Kelly/The Image Bank; **(middle):** © Kaz Mori/The Image Bank; **(bottom):** © David DeLossy/The Image Bank; **p. 504 (all):** © Bettmann/CORBIS; **17.5 (top):** © Bettmann/CORBIS; **(bottom):** © Andy Caulfield/The Image Bank; **p. 508:** © Rhoda Sidney/Photo Edit, Inc.; **p. 509:** © Betty Press/Woodfin Camp & Associates; **p. 512:** © Bettmann/CORBIS; **p. 515:** © Everett Collection; **p. 517:** Courtesy of Lillian Troll; **p. 518:** © William Hubbell/Woodfin Camp

CHAPTER 18

Opener: © PhotoDisc website; **p. 525:** © John Goodman; **p. 529 (inset):** © John Launois/Black Star; **p. 529 (foreground):** © John Launois/Black Star; **p. 530:** © Jim [illegible] CORBIS; **p.** [illegible] **(left):** © Pascal Parrot/Sygma; **(right):** © Thomas Del Brase/The Stock Market; **18.2:** Courtesy of Dr. Jerry Shay, PhD., UT Southwestern Medical Center; **18.3 (top and bottom):** © James Balog/Stone; **18.5:** © George Gardner/Image Works; **p. 542:** © Bob Daemmrich/Stock Boston; **18.6:** Courtesy of Colin M. Bloor; **p. 544:** Courtesy of Debra Radomski; **p. 545:** Courtesy of Ellen Langer

CHAPTER 19

Opener: © A. Ramey/Photo Edit, Inc.; **p. 553 (left):** © Cornell Capa/Magnum Photos; **(right):** © Kirkland/Sygma; **p. 555:** © Elizabeth Crews; **p. 557:** Courtesy of Dr. Sherry Willis; **p. 558:** © Bill Aron/Photo Edit, Inc.; **p. 560:** © Greg Sailor; **p. 564 (all):** © Bettmann/CORBIS; **19.2 (left and right):** © Alfred Pasieka/Science Photo Library/Photo Researchers, Inc.; **p. 565:** © Ira Wyman/Sygma; **p. 567:** © AP/Wide World Photos; **p. 568:** Courtesy of Jan W. Weaver; **p. 569:** Courtesy of Donna Polisar; **p. 570:** © Bryan Peterson/The Stock Market

CHAPTER 20

Opener: © 1999 John Henley/The Stock Market; **p. 575 (left):** © AP/Wide World Photos; **(right):** Photo by Steve Lipofsky BasketballPhoto.com; **20.1:** © Sarah Putman/Picture Cube/Index Stock; **p. 579:** © Ivor Sharp/The Image Bank; **p. 580:** Courtesy of Laura Carstensen; **20.3 (bottom to top):** © PhotoDisc; © Don Klumpp/The Image Bank; © PhotoDisc; © PhotoDisc website; © Jim Richardson/CORBIS; **p. 584:** Photo by Mariou Ruiz/Time Magazine/Time, Inc.; **p. 587:** © PhotoDisc website; **p. 588:** John Santrock; **p. 590:** © Jerry Mesmer/Stone; **p. 592:** © Suzi Moore/Woodfin Camp & Associates; **p. 593:** © G. Wayne Floyd/Unicorn Stock Photos; **p. 594:** © David Young-Wolff/Photo Edit; **p. 595:** © NASA/Liaison

CHAPTER 21

Opener: © Tony Freeman/Photo Edit, Inc.; **p. 601:** © AP/Wide World Photos; **p. 602:** © Herb Snitzer/Stock Boston; **p. 603:** © Detroit News/Gamma Liaison; **p. 605:** © Patrick Ward/Stock [illegible]; **p.** [illegible] of Robert Kastenbaum; **21.2.** © Eastcott Momatiuck/Image Works; **p. 615:** Courtesy of Sara Wheeler; **p. 616:** © Phyllis Picarci/International Stock; **p. 617:** © PhotoDisc website; **p. 618:** © Hermine Dreyfuss/Monkmeyer

EPILOGUE

1: Photo Lennart Nilsson/Albert Bonniers Forlag AB, *A Child is Born,* Dell Publishing Company; **2:** © Nikki Mareschal/The Image Bank; **3:** © Barbara Feigles/Stock Boston; **4:** © Sumo/The Image Bank; **5:** © Alvin Upitis/The Image Bank; **6:** © John Kelly/The Image Bank; **7:** © Mike Mass/The Image Bank; **8:** © Dick Durrance/Woodfin Camp; **9:** © Dennis Stock/Magnum Photos

Name Index

A

Abbassi, V., 351
Aboud, F., 310
Abshier, D.W., 289
Acquilino, W., 517
Acredolo, L. P., 150
Adams, R. J., 146
Adelman, R. D., 546
Addis, A., 99
Adler, T., 66
Adolph, K., 146
Ahluwalia, I. B., 135
Ahn, N., 359
Aiken, L., 49, 602, 608, 619
Ainsworth, M. D. S., 180, 188
Akiyama, H., 517, 589
Alberico, E., 617
Albert, M., 557
Alderman, M. H., 113
Alexander, A., 279
Alexander, G. R., 106
Allan, R., 483
Allen, J. P., 7, 359
Allen, K. R., 517
Allen, M., 137
Allison, J. A., 429
Allison, K. W., 398
Amabile, T., 300
Amato, P. R., 256, 257, 467
Ames, M. A., 425
Amsterdam, B. K., 185
Anderson, D. R., 220
Anderson, E., 329
Ani, C., 136
Anselmi, D. L., 58
Anstey, K. J., 556
Antonucci, T., 453, 454, 516, 517, 589, 590, 591, 592
Antonucci, T.C., 589
Appelbaum, M., 22
Applefield, J. M., 266
Aral, S. O., 426
Arboleda, T., 383
Arbuckle, T. Y., 557
Archer, S. L., 386
Arendt, R., 102
Arnett, J. D., 414
Arnold, A. M., 542
Arnold, M. L., 502
Aron, A., 452
Aronson, E., 337
Arshad, S. H., 135
Arterberry, M. E., 152
Asarnow, J. R., 332
Asch, D. A., 603
Asher, J., 305
Asher, S. R., 330, 333
Ashmead, D. H., 142
Atchley, R. C., 561
Atkinson, L., 189
Attanucci, J., 319
Augustyn, M., 102
Avis, N. E., 485, 486
Avolio, B. J., 492
Axelson, L. J., 515

B

Bachman, J., 414, 420, 421
Baddeley, A., 554
Baer, J. S., 101
Bagwell, C. L., 393
Bahr, S. J., 586
Baillargeon, R., 161
Bakeman, R., 119
Baker-Thomas, T., 591
Baldwin, C., 406
Baldwin, J. D., 425
Baldwin, J. I., 425
Baldwin, M., 448
Balota, D. A., 552
Baltes, M. M., 536, 562, 580
Baltès, P. B., 9, 10, 20, 21, 67, 552, 557, 558, 580
Bandstra, E. S., 102
Bandura, A., 41, 68, 171, 594
Banks, E. C., 318, 337
Banks, J. A., 339
Banks, M. S., 146
Barnes, H., 337
Barnett, D., 189, 251
Barr, H. M., 101
Barrett, D. E., 136
Barrett-Connor, E., 486
Bartke, A., 533
Bartlett, L., 12
Barton, L., 111
Bashore, T. R., 542
Bat-Chava, Y., 385
Bates, A. S., 106
Bates, J. E., 182, 252
Bathurst, K., 255
Baum, A., 11
Baum, A. S., 76
Baumann, J. F., 302
Baumeister, R. F., 311
Baumrind, D., 89, 248, 390
Baur, K., 486
Baxter, G. W., 609
Bayley, N., 136, 166
Beagles-Roos, J., 267
Beam, S., 542
Beautrais, A. L., 406
Beck, M., 478
Beckel, J., 603
Becker, P. E., 462
Bednar, R. L., 312
Begley, S., 129
Behrman, R. E., 106, 113, 209
Bell, A. P., 425
Bell, S. M., 180
Belle, D., 330
Bellinger, D., 103
Belloc, N. B., 417
Belsky, J., 114, 193
Belson, W., 266
Bem, S. L., 324
Benet, S., 529
Bengston, V. L., 517
Bengtson, V. L., 584, 587
Bennett, W., 375
Bennett, W. I., 419
Benson, J. B., 286
Benson, P., 82, 377
Bentler, P., 362, 466
Berenfeld, B., 338
Berg, L., 565
Berg, S., 563
Berger, S. H., 329
Bergin, A. E., 495
Bergin, D., 262, 263
Berko, J., 225
Berko-Gleason, J., 171
Berlin, L., 189
Bering, J.M., 67
Berliner, D. C., 303
Berlyne, D. E., 261
Berndt, T. J., 311, 333, 371, 449
Bernier, M. O., 135
Berquist, W. H., 516
Berscheid, E., 449, 450, 452
Best, D. L., 322
Betz, M. E., 49
Beyene, Y., 485
Bezilla, R., 570
Bialystok, E., 304
Bier, J. B., 135
Bijur, P. E., 494
Bild, D., 542
Billy, J. O. G., 393
Bingham, C. R., 356
Birren, J. E., 514, 533, 562, 583
Bjorklund, D., 67
Bjorklund, D. F., 38, 67
Blachman, B. A., 278
Black, J. E., 131
Blair, C., 113
Blair, S. N., 542
Blanchard-Fields, F., 555
Bland, S. D., 276
Blank, K., 603
Blanton, H., 580
Blazer, D., 562, 563
Blennow, K., 564
Blieszener, R., 517
Block, J., 323, 447
Block, J. H., 323
Bloor, C., 543
Blum, L. M., 135
Blumberg, J., 544
Blumenfeld, P. C., 335
Blumenthal, J. A., 205, 420, 542
Blundell, J. E., 418
Blyth, D. A., 353
Boada, R., 278
Bodnar, A. G., 7
Boerner, K., 617
Boeschen, L., 429
Boethel, C. L., 329
Bohlin, G., 181
Bolen, J. C., 276
Bolger, K.E., 251
Bonde, M. W., 564
Bonica, C. A., 394
Bonk, C. J., 335
Bonvillian, J. D., 162
Booth, A., 7, 257, 466
Booth, D. A., 151
Borkowski, J. G., 359
Borman-Spurrell, E., 7
Bornstein, M. H., 21, 89, 152, 182, 220
Bornstein, R. F., 449
Bortz, W. M., 538
Bos, C. S., 282
Bosman, E. A., 530, 536
Botwinick, J., 18
Bouchard, T. J., 66
Bowlby, J., 43, 180, 186, 187, 608
Boyd-Franklin, N., 483
Boyer, K., 165
Boykin, K. A., 388
Brabeck, M., 318
Bracken, M. B., 79
Bradbury, F. D., 458
Brand, J. E., 264
Brandstadter, J., 595
Bray, H., 324
Bray, J. H., 329
Brazelton, T. B., 89, 114, 139, 255
Bredekamp, S., 227
Bremer, M., 264
Brenneman, K., 287
Brent, R. L., 99
Breslow, L., 417
Bretherton, I., 181
Brickel, C. O., 495
Bridges, M., 256, 257, 329
Brillion, L., 398
Brim, G., 479, 480
Brim, O., 485, 487, 504, 514
Brislin, R. W., 12
Brockwood, K., 518
Brody, G. H., 362
Brody, J. E., 135
Brody, N., 85, 293
Brodzinsky, D. M., 92
Bromley, D., 311
Bronfenbrenner, U., 43, 44, 232
Brook, J. S., 389
Brooks, G. R., 470
Brooks, J. B., 248
Brooks, M. G., 288
Brooks-Gunn, J., 185, 258, 296, 351, 352, 353, 355, 359, 364, 389, 390
Brown, B. B., 392, 394
Brown, J. K., 509
Brown, J. V., 119
Brown, L. S., 425
Brown, P., 137
Brown, R., 171, 173
Browne, A., 14, 429
Brownell, K., 419
Brownell, K. A., 418
Bruce, J. M., 239
Bruck, M., 221
Bruer, J. T., 21
Bryan, J., 552
Bryant, J., 264
Bryant, J. A., 264
Bryden, M. P., 322
Buchanan, C. M., 351
Buckner, C. E., 322, 324
Buckwalter, J. A., 532
Buhrmester, D., 393
Bukowski, W. M., 393
Bulterys, M., 104
Burchinal, M., 195
Burgess, D. M., 101
Burgin, D., 191
Buriel, R., 45, 258
Burke, G. L.,542
Burke, P. B., 190
Burkhauser, R. V., 560
Burns, A., 562
Burns, D., 456
Burns, J. W., 483
Burton, L., 398, 592
Buschke, H., 552
Buss, D., 449
Busse, E. W., 562
Butler, R. N., 576, 577
Butter, E. M., 495
Butterfield, L. J., 113
Buzwell, S., 355
Bybee, J., 238
Byrnes, J. P., 205, 366, 368

C

Cacioppo, J. T., 178
Cairns, R. B., 21
Calabrese, R. L., 377
Callahan, C. M., 562
Callan, J. W., 332
Cameron, J., 183

Campbell, B., 294
Campbell, L., 294
Campbell, S. M., 468
Campos, J., 178
Campos, J. J., 148, 178
Canfield, J., 551
Canfield, R. L., 148
Cantor, N., 579, 580
Cantu, C. L., 385
Caporael, L. R., 67
Carbery, J., 393
Cardell, M., 468
Carlo, G., 388
Carlson, E. A., 189
Carlson, K. S., 253
Carlson, V., 251
Carriger, M. S., 167
Carstensen, L., 578, 579, 580, 581, 589
Carter, B., 457
Carter, D. B., 246
Carter-Saltzman, L., 208
Case, R., 221, 288
Caspi, A., 446
Cassidy, J., 189, 388, 447
Castle, N. G., 544
Castle, P., 142
Catania, J., 538
Cauce, A. M., 58
Caulfield, R. A., 101, 126
Cavanaugh, J., 554
Ceballo, R. E., 336
Ceci, S., 44, 85, 221
Champagne, F., 368
Chance, G., 149
[illegible]
Chard, S., 335
Charles, S. T., 578
Charlesworth, R., 136, 226
Charness, N., 530, 536
Chase-Lansdale, P. L., 195, 258
Chatters, L. M., 570, 590
Chattin-McNichols, J., 227
Chavkin, W., 102
Chen, C., 341
Chen, H., 590
Chen, Z., 38, 221
Cheng, T. L., 275
Cherlin, A. J., 257, 329
Chescheir, N. C., 111, 113
Chess, S., 446
Cheung, F. K., 483
Cheung, L. W. Y., 102
Chhabildas, R. A., 278
Chi, M. T., 288
Chiriboga, D. A., 505, 508
Chisholm, K., 82
Choi, N.G., 562
Chomitz, V. R., 102
Chomsky, N., 170, 171
Christakis, N. A., 603
Christensen, H., 556
Christensen, L., 419
Christiansen, A., 458
Christie, S., 562
Chrousos, G. P., 50
Chung, K., 280
Chung, K.M., 280
Church, D. K., 563
Cicchetti, D., 129, 189, 250, 251, 252
Cicirelli, V. G., 516
Clancy, S. M., 491
Clark, E., 171
Clark, S. D., 356
Clarke, E. J., 517
Clark-Plaskie, M., 504
Clarkson-Smith, L., 556
Clausen, J. A., 49, 494, 495, 512
Clay, R. A., 117, 611
Clemens, A. W., 515
Clements, K. M., 542
Clements, M. L., 459
Cleveland, J. N., 560
Clifford, B. R., 264
Clifton, R. K., 151
Clingempeel, W. G., 329
Clore, G. L., 395
Cochran, S. D., 428
Cohen, C. I., 590
Cohen, G. J., 133
Cohen, L. R., 419
Cohn, E., 567
Coie, J., 260, 330
Colby, A., 317
Cole, M., 12
Coleman, M., 226, 468
Coleman, P., 513
Coleman, P. D., 534
Coles, R., 29
Coley, R.L., 195
Coll, C. G., 195, 398
Collins, A. W., 448
Collins, M., 437, 438
Collins, N. L., 495
Collins, W. A., 89, 252
Comas-Díaz, L., 437
Comer, J. P., 339
Commons, M. L., 431
Compas, B. E., 405
Comstock, G., 264
Condry, J. C., 264
Condry, K.F., 151
Conger, R., 22, 256, 389
Connolly, L. A., 503, 504
Connor, J. R., 563, 564
Cook, D. J., 603
Cooper, C. R., 373, 384, 389
Corder, L., 533
Corr, C. A., 617
Corr, D. M., 617
[illegible]
Corso, J. F., 537
Corter, C., 253
Cosman, F., 486
Costa, A. C., 76
Costa, F., 364, 504
Costa, P. T., 511
Cotten, S. R., 462
Courtois, C. A., 429
Cowan, C. P., 118, 192, 252
Cowan, L., 11
Cowan, P. A., 11, 118, 252
Cowley, G., 403, 604
Cox, H., 570
Cox, M.J., 468
Craik, F. I. M., 9
Crawford, M., 13, 323
Crockenberg, S. B., 183
Crockett, L. J., 356
Crooks, R., 466, 486
Crosby, F. J., 440
Crouter, A. C., 7
Crowell, T., 546
Crowley, M., 326
Croyle, R. T., 77
Cruz, A. Z., 77
Csikszentmihalyi, M., 300, 417, 433, 434, 491
Cuddy-Casey, M., 608
Cui, X., 505
Culatta, R., 278
Culbertson, F. M., 14
Cully, J. A., 577
Cumming, E., 578
Cummings, E. M., 178
Cunningham, D. J., 335
Cunningham, W. R., 557
Cupertino, A. P., 570
Curnow, C., 416
Cushman, M., 542
Cushner, K., 338, 339
Cutrona, C. E., 455

D

D'Agostino, P. R., 449
Dahl, K. L., 302, 303
Daily, D. K., 111
Daly, M. P., 617
Damon, W., 238, 242, 311, 319, 320, 375
Damush, J. G., 542
Damush, T. M., 542
Dann, S., 260
Danso, H. A., 502
Dapretto, M., 169
Darroch, J. E., 358
Dates, J. L., 264
Davey, R. T., 427
Davidshofer, C. O., 49
Davidson, D. H., 231
Davidson, J., 298
Davis, G. F., 614
Davis, K. E., 453
Davis, K. L., 564
Davis, L., 355, 463
Davis-Kean, P. E., 439
Davison, G. C., 14, 363
Davisson, M. T., 76
Daws, D., 132
DeBaryshe, B. D., 402
DeCasper, A. J., 148, 149
DeFries, J. C., 74, 84
DeHaan, M., 127
De Jong-Gierveld, J., 454
DeLamater, J., 356, 466, 468, 469
DeLoache, J., 212
De La Ronde, C., 449
DeMarie, D., 289
DeMaris, A., 466
DeMeo, P., 466
Demetriou, A., 288
Demmrich, A., 554
Dempster, F. N., 221
Denham, S. A., 239
Denney, N., 491
[illegible]
DeSpelder, L. A., 613
Dettmer, P., 282
Deutsch, F. M., 507
Devich-Navarro, M., 385
DeVita, P., 542
Dewey, C. R., 171
Dewey, J., 288, 373
Diamond, A., 165
Diaz, R. M., 217
Dickinson, D., 294
Dickson, G. L., 485
Diehl, M., 431
Diener, E., 18, 496
Diener, M. B., 496
Dietz, W. H., 134
DiGiulio, R. C., 617
DiLalla, L. F., 85
Dion, K. K., 460
Dion, K. L., 460
DiRubbio, M., 164
Dishion, T., 362
Dishion, T. J., 330
Dixon, R. L., 103
Dobzhansky, T. G., 68
Dodge, K. A., 332
Doerksen, T., 106
Dohrenwend, B. P., 505
Dohrenwend, B. S., 505, 506
Dolan, P. O., 552
Domek, C. J., 260
Donaldson, G., 488
Donaldson, M., 277
Donelson, F. E., 469
Donovan, P., 357
Dorn, L. D., 50, 350
Dornbusch, S. M., 385, 397
Dorr, A., 266
Downey, G., 394
Downs, M. G., 563
Doyle, J. A., 58, 325
Drew, C., 298
Drickamer, L. C., 50
Driscoll, A., 12, 226
Dryfoos, J. G., 356, 359, 406
Duchek, J. M., 552
Duckett, E., 255
Duncan, G. J., 296
Dunkel-Schetter, C., 103, 105
Dunkle, R., 531
Dunn, J., 516
Dunn, L., 230
Dupuis, S., 594
Dupuis, V., 12
Dutta, C., 543
Dwyer, T., 135
Dyck, N., 282

E

Eagle, M., 33
Eagly, A., 13, 323, 326
Earles, J. L., 552
Eccles, J., 13, 243, 370
Edelman, M. W., 13
Edmonds, M. M., 590, 593
Edmondson, R., 619
Edwards, C. P., 258
Egeland, B., 189, 251
Egeren, L. V., 191
Eggebeen, D. J., 493, 591
Eichorn, D., 417, 511
Eidelson, R. J., 459
Eiferman, R. R., 263
Eiger, M. S., 135
Eisdorfer, C., 556, 562
Eisen, M. L., 221
Eisenberg, N., 178, 242, 243, 323
Eissenberg, T., 422
Ekwo, E. E., 105
Elder, G. H., 558
Elias, M., 209
Elkind, D., 215, 226, 230, 238, 285, 313
Elliott, G. R., 348
[illegible]
Ellis, E. M., 11
Ellis, L., 425
Elmes, D. G., 51
Emde, R. N., 180, 181
Emery, R. E., 257
Enger, E. D., 66
England, S. E., 584
Enright, R. D., 384
Epstein, D. K., 563, 564
Epstein, N., 459
Erikson, E. H., 33, 34, 184, 185, 187, 238, 382, 386, 402, 450, 454, 502, 576, 577

F

Faber, D., 483
Fabes, R. A., 243, 323
Fagan, J., 166
Fagot, B. I., 244
Fagot, B. J., 243
Falbo, T., 254
Famy, C., 101
Fang, J., 113
Fantz, R. L., 146
Farmer, M. C., 319
Farrell, M. P., 505
Fawcett, L. B., 99
Fehr, B., 448, 453, 454
Fei, J., 452
Fein, G. G., 262, 263
Feinberg, M., 87
Feiring, C., 394, 448
Feldman, H. D., 298
Feldman, R., 192
Feldman, S. S., 348, 354, 355, 356, 359, 402
Fenwick, K. D., 149
Ferguson, D. M., 136, 406
Fernald, A., 171
Fernald, L., 136
Fernandes, O., 100
Ferron, J., 289
Fiatarone, M. A., 541, 542
Field, D., 517, 586, 589
Field, T., 7, 105, 190, 250
Fields, R., 106
Filyer, R., 502

Finch, C. E., 533
Fincham, F. D., 458
Fine, M., 468
Finkel, D., 87
Finkelstein, J., 543
Finlay, B., 137, 337, 364
Finn, S. E., 468
Finn-Stevenson, M., 232
Fisch, R. O., 150
Fisch, S. M., 265
Fitzgerald, L., 429
Flanagan, K.M., 459
Flavell, J. H., 222, 287, 289, 290
Fleeson, W., 581
Flegal, K. M., 209
Flick, L., 134
Fodor, I. G., 508
Fogel, A., 101
Fogel, J., 11
Folts, W. E., 560
Fonda, S. J., 563
Ford, L., 239
Forrest, J. D., 357
Foster, E., 359
Fowler, C. D., 563
Fox, G. L., 463
Fozard, J., 536, 537, 592
Fraga, C. G., 106
Fraiberg, S., 142
France, K. G., 132
Frank, D. A., 102
Franks, V., 508
Franz, C. E., 446
Fredman, L., 617
Fredrickson, D. D., 135
Freedman, J. L., 266
Freiberg, H. J., 12
Freppon, P. A., 302, 303
Freud, A., 260
Freud, S., 31
Fried, O., 542
Fried, P. A., 102
Friedman, D. L., 277
Friedman, E., 542, 543
Friedman, M., 482
Friedman, M. A., 418
Friedman, S., 590
Friedrich, L. K., 265
Friedrichs, A., 290
Frieske, D. A., 554
Frieze, I. R., 394
Fry, P. S., 570, 616
Fuller-Thomson, E., 588
Furman, W., 393, 394
Furnival, R. A., 276
Furstenberg, F., 329, 359
Furth, H. G., 284

G

Gadpaille, W. J., 406
Gaensbauer, T. G., 180, 181
Gage, F. H., 556
Galambos, N. L., 330, 349
Galen, B. R., 355
Gall, T. L., 562
Gallimore, R., 220
Gallup, G., 494, 570
Galotti, K. M., 319, 368
Ganiban, J., 189, 251
Gannon, L., 485
Ganong, L., 459, 468
Garbarino, J., 251, 403, 404
Garcia, E. E., 303
Garcia, R., 305
Gardiner, K., 76
Gardner, H., 288, 294, 300
Gardner, L. I., 483
Gardner, W. L., 178
Garfein, A. J., 531
Garner, D. M., 419
Garnier, H. E., 373
Garrod, A. C., 318
Gartner, J., 495
Gat, I., 267
Gatz, M., 563, 568, 584
Ge, X., 362, 389
Geary, D. C., 67
Gelman, R., 215, 287
George, T. P., 48
Gerlach, P., 468
Gescheider, G. A., 536
Gesell, A., 142
Gewirtz, J., 180
Gfeller, J. D., 577
Giarrusso, R., 517
Gibbons, J. L., 326
Gibbs, J., 318
Gibson, E. J., 145, 147, 161
Gibson, J. H., 135
Gibson, J. J., 145
Giddens, O., 614
Giddens, S., 614
Gilligan, C., 318, 319, 386, 508
Gladue, B. A., 425
Glantz, S. A., 102
Glaser, R., 467
Glei, D. A., 357
Golbeck, S. L., 226
Goldberg, J., 221
Goldberg-Glen, R. S., 588
Golden, N. H., 363
Goldin-Meadow, S., 171
Goldsmith, H. H., 74, 182
Goldwater, P. N., 133
Goleman, D., 204, 296, 300
Gollnick, D., 12
Golombok, S., 81
Gonyea, J. G., 584
Gonzales, J. A. T., 570
Goodman, G. S., 14, 148, 221
Goodman, R. A., 361
Goossens, L., 555
Gopnik, A., 161
Gottfried, A. E., 255
Gottfried, A. W., 255
Gottlieb, G., 21, 74, 88
Gottman, J. M., 310, 333, 459, 461, 514, 579
Gould, E., 534
Gould, R. L., 493
Gould, S. J., 68
Gounin-Decarie, T., 161
Gove, W. R., 462
Graeber, J., 355
Graham, K. M., 7
Graham, S., 58, 303
Grambs, J. D., 509
Grant, J., 136, 210
Grant, K. E., 405
Grantham-McGregor, S., 136
Gray, J., 461
Greenbaum, C. W., 192
Greenberg, B. S., 264
Greenberg, E. M., 516
Greene, J. W., 359
Greene, M. G., 546
Greene, V. L., 544
Greeno, J. G., 38
Greenough, W. T., 88, 130
Greenstein, T. N., 439
Greve, W., 595
Grier, K., 506
Griffith-Joyner, F., 413
Grigorenko, E. L., 85, 103, 295
Grining, C. P. L., 195
Grolnick, W.S., 464
Gross, R. T., 353
Grotevant, H. D., 82, 384
Grove, K., 58
Growman, W. A., 111
Gruber-Baldini, A. L., 592
Gruman, C., 603
Grung, R. A. R., 103
Guarnaccia, C., 619
Guilford, J. P., 299
Gump, B., 493
Gunnar, M., 82, 150
Gunter, B., 264
Gur, R. C., 322
Gurdal, H., 543
Gurin, J., 419
Gurland, S.T. 464
Gutmann, D. L., 591
Guttentag, M., 324
Guyer, B. P., 280

H

Haan, M. N., 570
Hack, M., 111, 112
Hadley, E. C., 543
Hager, M., 604
Hagestad, G. O., 587
Haight, W. L., 263
Haith, M. H., 146
Haith, M. M., 139, 148, 286
Hake, J. L., 150
Hakuta, K., 303
Hall, G., 12
Hall, J. G., 590
Hall, N. W., 13
Hall, R. T., 111
Hallahan, D. P., 282
Halonen, J., 396, 415
Hamburg, D. A., 377
Hamilton, T. E., 449
Hamm, J. V., 330
Hammer, L. B., 518, 556
Hammond, S., 277
Hammonds, A., 570
Han, S. K., 560
Hanc, J., 413
Hans, S., 102
Hansen, D. J., 252
Hansen, M. V., 551
Hansen, R., 183
Hansen, W. F., 111, 113
Hanson, M. J., 282
Hanson, T. L., 468
Hanusa, B. H., 546
Hardman, M. L., 298
Hardy, J. B., 356
Harkins, S. W., 481, 536, 537
Harkness, S., 132, 190
Harlow, H. F., 187, 260
Harlow, K., 567
Harlow, R. E., 579
Harmon, R. J., 180, 181
Harris, G., 151
Harris, J. R., 88, 252
Harris, K. R., 303
Harris, L., 275, 330
Harris, T., 543
Hart, B., 171, 311
Hart, C. H., 230
Hart, D., 238, 242, 320
Harter, K.S.M., 468
Harter, S., 310, 311, 319, 381, 406
Hartley, A. A., 556
Hartmann, D. P., 48
Hartshorn, K., 164
Hartshorne, H., 241
Harter, S., 406
Hartup, W. W., 9, 89, 192, 333, 453
Harwood, L. J., 136
Hatch, L. R., 562
Hauck, S. J., 533
Haug, M., 531
Hauser, S. T., 7, 388
Havighurst, R. J., 578
Hawkins, J. A., 311, 371
Hawranik, P. G., 563
Hayflick, L., 529, 532
Haynie, D. A., 563
Hayslip, B., 604, 614, 619
Hayward, M. D., 590
Hazan, C., 447, 448
Hazen, C., 148
Heath, S. B., 386
Heckhausen, J., 581
Hedrick, P. W., 72
Held, R., 142
Helm, K. K., 134
Helmreich, R., 324
Helson, R., 508, 512
Henderson, J. M. T., 132
Hennesey, B. A., 300
Hennigfield, J. E., 422
Henninger, M. L., 227
Henry, W., 578
Herek, G., 424
Herman, C. P., 419
Herrill, R., 406
Herzog, A. R., 531
Herzog, E., 245
Hetherington, E. M., 11, 44, 87, 88, 89, 256, 257, 329, 467, 468
Heuwinkel, M. K., 285
Heward, W. L., 282
Hibbard, D., 393
Higgins, A., 376
Hikida, R. S., 542
Hill, C. R., 327
Hill, J. O., 209, 277
Hill, P. C., 495
Himes, C. L., 591
Hirsch, B. J., 371
Hirsch-Pasek, K., 231
Hixon, J. G., 449
Hobbs, K. E., 209
Hobel, C. J., 105
Hochschild, A., 439
Hodes, R. J., 532
Hodges, E. V. E., 331
Hodges, J. R., 565
Hodgman, J. E., 111
Hofer, B. K., 12, 340
Hofferth, S. L., 439
Hoff-Ginsberg, E., 171, 258
Hoffman, L. W., 255
Hoffman, M. L., 318
Hoffman, S., 359
Hogan, D. M., 218
Hogan, D. P., 591
Holland, J. L., 435, 436
Hollins, E. R., 337
Holman, T. B., 459
Holmbeck, G. N., 389
Holmes, D., 590
Holmes, T. H., 505
Holtzmann, D. M., 565
Honzik, M., 417
Hopkins, B., 142
Hopkins, J. R., 33
Hoppu, U., 135
Horgas, A. L., 562
Horn, J. L., 488
Horney, K., 36
Hornung, M., 263
Hortobagyi, T., 542
Horwood, L. J., 406
Hotchner, T., 109
House, J. S., 492, 558, 590
Howard, J., 562
Howes, C., 195
Hoyer, W. J., 18, 19, 68, 491, 493, 519, 535, 536, 537, 567
Hoyt, J., 290
Hsieh, C., 420
Huebner, A. M., 318
Huesmann, L. R., 265, 266
Hughes, M., 462
Hughes, P. C., 481
Hultsch, D. F., 505, 556, 557
Humenick, S. S., 106
Hummert, M. L., 547, 582
Humphreys, K., 422
Hungerford, T. L., 616
Hurrelmann, K., 364
Hurt, H., 102
Huston, A., 195, 244, 264, 337
Huston, A. C., 125, 264, 265
Huston, T. L., 459
Huyck, M. H., 19, 508
Hy, L., 513
Hyde, J. S., 322, 323, 466, 468, 469
Hyman, I.E., 221

I

Iannucci, L., 99, 103
Ilola, L. M., 482
Ingelhart, R., 18
Ingersoll, E. W., 132
Inhelder, B., 212
Inoff-Germain, G., 351
Insabella, G. M., 256, 257, 329
Intons-Peterson, M., 288
Isaacowitz, D. M., 578
Isenberg, J. P., 227
Isolauri, E., 135
Issacs, P., 280
Izard, C., 178

J

Jacklin, C. N., 322
Jackson, J. S., 590
Jackson, T. D., 11
Jacobs, J. E., 368, 517
Jacobs, J. K., 373
Jacobs, R. H., 592
Jacobs, S. C., 613
Jacobson, J. L., 103
Jacobvitz, D., 251
Jalongo, M. R., 227
James, D. K., 98, 105
Jecker, N. S., 603
Jeffery, H. E., 133
Jensen, S. J., 239
Jenson, H. B., 209
Jerrome, D., 589
[illegible]
Ji, B. T., 106
Ji, G., 254
Jiao, S., 254
Jing, Q., 254
Jodl, K. M., 256, 257
Johansson, B., 563
Johnson, B. K., 538
Johnson, C., 14, 375
Johnson, C. L., 589, 593
Johnson, C. R., 278
Johnson, D., 466
Johnson, J., 12
Johnson, J. E., 226
Johnson, K., 362
Johnson, M. D., 543
Johnson, M.E., 131
Johnson, M. H., 128, 131
Johnson, M. K., 376
Johnson, S. B., 77
John-Steiner, V., 217
Johnston, C., 280
Johnston, L., 359, 360, 361, 362, 420
Joiner, T. E., 590
Jones, C. J., 513
Jones, G., 135
Jones, L., 296
Jones, M. C., 353
Jones, S., 57, 570
Jordhoy, M. S., 614
Josselson, R., 516

K

Kaasa, S., 614
Kabitsis, C., 542
Kagan, J., 21, 74, 90, 190, 195, 446
Kagitcibasi, C., 12
Kahn, R., 537, 589
Kahn, R. L., 533, 541, 590, 594
Kail, R., 291
Kalichman, S., 427
Kalick, S. M., 449
Kalish, R. A., 609, 610, 612, 613, 615, 619
Kallio, K. D., 88
Kalliomaki, M., 135
Kaltiala-Heino, R., 405
Kamphaus, R. W., 278
Kandel, D. B., 363
Kanner, A. D., 506
Kantowitz, B. H., 51
Kantrowitz, B., 237
Kaplan, B. H., 447
Karns, J. T., 210
Kasper, J. D., 585
Kastenbaum, R., 604, 608, 610, 614, 617
Katchadoourian, H., 481
Katz, L., 335
Kauffman, J. M., 282
Kaufman, J. M., 282
Kaufman, P., 204, 296, 300
Kaugers, A. S., 102
Kausler, D. H., 553
Kearsley, R. B., 195
Keating, B., 137
Keating, D. P., 368, 369
Keener, D. C., 388
Keith, B., 256
Keller, A., 239
Kelly, C., 336
Kelly, J., 14, 427
Kelly, K., 337
Kemp, J. S., 134
Kempermann, G., 556
Kennedy, G. J., 11
Kennell, H. H., 119
Kennell, J., 109, 118
Kenyon, G. M., 577
Keogh, D. A., 359
Kephart, W. M., 452
Kerig, P. K., 48
[illegible]
K[illegible], W., 139
Kiecolt-Glaser, J. K., 467, 566
Kiely, J. L., 102
Kilbride, H. W., 111
Kimble, M., 569
Kimmel, A., 57
King, A., 420
King, N., 263
King, P. M., 431
Kirk, K. L., 543
Kirkpatrick, L. A., 448
Kisilevsky, B. S., 148
Kitchener, K. S., 431
Kivnick, H. Q., 587
Klaczynski, P. A., 369
Klaum, G. A., 516
Klaus, M., 109, 119
Klaus, P. H., 109
Klebanov, P. K., 296
Klein, L., 180
Klein, N., 111, 112
Klein, R., 136
Kliegl, R., 554, 558
Kliegman, R., 209
Klish, W. J., 277
Klitzing, K. V., 191
Klonoff-Cohen, H. S., 134
Klumb, P., 536
Knapp, J., 560
Knight, B. G., 562, 568
Knight, J. A,. 533
Knight, W. G., 102
Knoester, C., 493
Kobak, R., 388
Kobasa, S., 484
Kochanska, G., 184, 252
Kochenderfer, B. J., 331
Kochhar, C. A., 282
Koenig, G., 494, 495
Koenig, H. G., 496, 563, 570
Koenigsberger, M. R., 111
Kohl, H. W., 209
Kohlberg, L., 246, 315, 316, 376
Kohn, M., 363
Kohnstamm, G.A., 182
Kontos, S., 230
Kopp, C. B., 111
Korenbrot, C. C., 106
Koss, M., 429
Kotler, J., 265
Kotler, J. A., 264
Kotlowitz, A., 309
Kotre, J., 502
Kozberg, S. F., 319, 368
Kozol, J., 336
Kozulin, A., 38
Kramer, A. F., 431
Krause, N., 570, 585
Kreppner, K., 192
Kreutzer, M., 290
Kreye, M., 181
Krogh, S.L., 227
Kroonenberg, P. M., 190
Krowitz, A., 148
Ksir, C., 422
Kübler-Ross, E., 610
Kuczaj, S. A., 239
Kuebli, J., 239, 313
Kuersten-Hogan, R., 193
Kuhn, D., 45, 289, 366, 368, 556
Kuhn, H. G., 162
Kulbok, P. A., 364
Kumagai, F., 460
Kuperminc, G. P., 388
Kupersmidt, J. B., 330
Kurdek, L. A., 468
Kurland, D. M., 221
Kurtz, D. A., 385
Kwak, H. K., 183

L

[illegible]
Labouvie-Vief, G., 431, 511, 516
Lachman, M. E., 504, 594
Lackmann, G. M., 102
Ladd, G. W., 260, 330, 331
La Guardia, J. G., 580
Laible, D. J., 388
Laiho, K., 135
Laippala, P., 405
Laken, M. A., 103
LaLonde, C. E., 149
Lamb, M. E., 119, 193, 195
Lambert, W. E., 304
Landis, K. R., 590
Lane, M., 543
Lang, C. E., 134
Lang, F. R., 578
Lang, R., 82
Lange, K. L., 564
Langer, A., 148
Langer, E. J., 545, 611
Lansford, J. E., 589, 590, 591, 592
Lapsley, D. K., 318
Lareau, A., 258
Larson, D. B., 495, 496
Larson, J., 459
Larson, R., 388, 389
Larson, R. W., 395
Lauer, J., 468
Lauer, R. H., 468
Lauerman, J. F., 527, 541
Lauretti, A. F., 193
Laurin, D., 563
Laursen, B., 192, 333, 448
LaVoie, D., 577
Lawton, M. P., 579
Layzer, J., 337
Laz, M., 617
Lazar, L., 232
Lazarus, L. W., 505
Lazarus, R. S., 505
Lazur, A. M., 617
Leach, C. E., 133
Leadbeater, B. J. R., 359
Leavitt, F., 56
Lebowitz, B. D., 568
Lee, D. J., 578
Lee, G. R., 586
Lee, I., 420
Lee, I. M., 543
Lefley, H. P., 566
Lehman, H. C., 432
Leifer, A. D., 266
Leinbach, M. D., 243, 244
Leith, L. M., 420
Lemery, K. S., 182
Lemmon, K., 238
Lenhardt, M. L., 481, 536
Lenneberg, E. H., 169
Lennon, M. C., 439
Leonard, C., 290
Leong, F. T. L., 399
Lerner, H. G., 469
Lerner, J. V., 248
Lerner, R. M., 21
Lerner, S., 171
Lester, B., 107, 114
Leung, D. W., 280
Levant, R. F., 470
Levelt, W. J. M., 9
Levenson, R. W., 514
Leventhal, A., 392
Levesque, J., 376
Levin, J. S., 495, 569, 570
Levinger, G., 514
Levinson, D. J., 493, 503, 504
Levy, D., 12
Levy, G. D., 246
Levy, T. M., 190
Lewinsohn, P. M., 406
Lewis, M., 180, 185, 190, 448
Lewis, M .D., 188
Lewis, R., 70, 76, 300
Lewis, R. J., 357
[illegible]
Lickliter, R., 74, 88
Lieberman, E., 102, 110
Lifshitz, F., 134
Lifton, R. J., 611
Light, K. C., 420
Light, L. L., 554
Lightwood, J. M., 102
Limber, S. P., 331
Lindahl, K. M., 48
Lindbohm, M., 106
Lindenberger, U., 10, 21, 67, 552, 580
Lindsay, R., 486
Lindsay J., 563
Liprie, M. L., 369
Lipsitt, L. P., 10
Lipsitz, J., 330, 371, 372
Livesly, W., 311
Livson, N., 482
Llewellyn-Jones, D., 111
Lobel, M., 103
Lochman, J. J., 152
Lockman, J. J., 143
Loebel, M., 105
Loevinger, J., 513
Loftus, E. F., 221
London, M. L., 135
Long, L., 329
Long, T., 329
Longman, P., 584
Lonner, W. J., 296
Lopata, H. Z., 592
Lorenz, K. Z., 42
Lucas, F. L., 350
Luria, A., 245
Luszcz, M. A., 552
Lutz, D. A., 162
Lydon-Rochelle, M., 111
Lynch, E. W., 282
Lyon, G. R., 278, 279
Lyon, T. D., 289
Lyons, N. P., 319
Lyytinen, P., 282

M

Maas, J. B., 133
MacCallum, J., 566
Maccoby, E. E., 13, 89, 178, 190, 244, 257, 322, 328
MacCorquodale, P., 356

MacFarlane, J. A., 150
Machung, A., 439
MacLean, W. E., 76
MacPherson, K., 563
Madden, T., 398
Maddi, S., 484
Mader, S., 88
Mader, W., 577
Madhaven, S., 113
Maggs, J. L., 330, 364
Magnusson, D., 353
Magrini, N., 99
Mahler, M., 185
Mahn, H., 217
Main, M., 189, 251, 447
Maines, D. R., 507
Maioni, T. L., 263
Maizels, M., 136
Makrides, M., 135
Malinosky-Rummell, R., 252
Malinowski, B., 36
Malloy, M. H., 111
Malone, S., 150
Mandler, J. M., 162, 165, 221
Manley, J. T., 252
Mannell, R. C., 493, 594
Manton, K. G., 533
Manton, K. I., 495
Manuck, S. B., 11
Marcia, J., 383
Marcoen, A., 555, 558
Marcus, D. L., 127
Marcusson, J., 564
Margolin, L., 251
Markides, K. S., 578, 591, 592
Markman, H. J., 459
Markowitz, M., 103
Marks, M. A., 429
Markson, E. W., 592
Marold, D. B., 406
Marshall, T. R., 180
Marshall, V. W., 582
Marsiske, M., 536
Martin, C. L., 243, 246, 323
Martin, E. W., 282
Martin, R., 282
Martinelli, M., 537
Martin-Matthews, A., 519, 617
Martin, J. A., 532
Masters, W., 429
Mastroiacovo, P., 99
Matas, L., 181
Matheny, A.P., 182
Matthews, K., 493
Matthias, R. F., 538
Maurer, D., 9
May, M. S., 241
Mayaux, M. J., 105
Mayer, J. D., 313
Mayr, U., 554, 580
Mays, V. M., 428
McAdoo, H. P., 258
McAleer, J. L., 264
McBurney, D. H., 48
McCall, R. B., 167
McCarty, M. E., 142
McClearn, G. E., 84
McClelland, A., 338, 339
McCormick, C. B., 290
McCrae, R. R., 511
McCullough, M. E., 495, 570, 571
McDonough, L., 165
McDougall, G. J., 554
McFarlane, J., 98
McFarlane, T., 419
McGoldrick, M., 457
McGowan, T. G., 582
McGrath, J. E., 14
McGrath, S., 109, 118
McGue, M., 82, 87
McGuire, F., 493
McGuire, S., 83
McHale, J. P., 193
McKeel, D., 565
McKenna, J. J., 133
McLanahan, S. S., 468
McLaughlin, M. W., 386
McLoyd, V. C., 13, 195, 337, 398
McMillan, J. H., 50
McMullin, J. A., 582
McRoy, R. G., 82
Meacham, J., 239
Medvedev, Z. A., 529
Mehler, J., 149
Melamed, B. G., 11
Melby, J. N., 362
Meltzoff, A., 161, 162, 164
Memmler, R. L., 480
Meredith, N. V., 204
Meredith, W., 513
Merrill, S. S., 480, 484
Mertens, A., 277
Messier, S., 542
Meyer, E. C., 398
Michael, R., 424, 487
Michel, G. L., 207
Miekle, D., 50
Milke, M. A., 439
Miller, J. B., 469
Miller, J. G., 318
Miller, J. P., 565
Miller, K. J., 363
Miller, P. H., 30, 221, 222, 287, 289
Miller, P. J., 263
Miller, R. B., 517
Miller, S., 222
Miller, S. A., 51, 222, 287
Miller-Jones, D., 296
Millis, R. M., 421
Minkler, M., 588
Minuchin, P., 192
Minuchin, P. O., 339
Mischel, W., 41, 241
Mishell, D., 108
Mitchell, A. S., 74
Mitchell, V., 508, 512
Mizes, J. S., 363
Mnookin, R. H., 257
Moane, G., 512
Moats, L. C., 278
Moawad, A., 105
Moely, B. E., 288
Moen, P., 462, 492, 508, 560, 562
Monk, C., 105
Montemayor, R., 389
Montero, I., 217
Moody, J., 542
Moore, C., 238
Moore, M., 554
Moore, M. K., 161, 164
Morelli, G. A., 132
Morild, I., 133
Morris, J. C., 565
Morris, L., 426
Morris, P., 43, 44
Morrison, G. S., 232
Morrongiello, B. A., 149
Morrow, L., 347
Mortimer, E. A., 136
Moses, J., 420
Moshman, D., 382
Mosko, S. S., 133
Mosley, J., 468
Mounts, N., 392
Mueller, M. P., 288
Mueller, N., 251
Mulatu, S., 556, 560
Mulrine, A., 127
Mumme, D. L., 178
Murphy, K. R., 49
Murray, J. P., 264, 266
Murray, L., 117
Murry, V. M., 463
Musial, D., 12
Mussen, P. H., 417
Muth, A. S., 603
Myers, D. L., 401

N

Nable, C., 617
Naglieri, J., 292
Nagy, M., 608
Nahas, C. G., 106
Narasimham, G., 369
Nash, J. M., 130
Neal, M. B., 518
Neale, J. M., 14, 363
Negalia, J. P., 277
Neihuis, S., 459
Neisser, U., 295
Nelson, C., 127, 162
Nelson, E. S., 429
Nelson, M. E., 540
Nelson-LeGall, S., 337
Nesselroade, C. S., 558
Neugarten, B., 15, 18, 506, 510, 530, 584
Neugarten, B. L., 507, 578, 583, 587
Neugarten, D., 530
Neville, M. C., 104
Newcomb, A. F., 393
Newcomb, M., 362
Newcomb, M. D., 466
Newman, A., 542
Newport, E. L., 161
Nichols, F. H., 106
Nichols, I. A., 169
Ninio, A., 225
Nock, S., 466
Nolen-Hoeksema, S., 14, 36
Norris, J. E., 502
Nottelmann, E. D., 350, 351
Novack, L. L., 162
Novak, W., 445
Nowak, C. A., 480
Nugent, J. K., 114
Nussbaum, J. F., 15, 517, 546, 547

O

Oates, G., 556, 560
Obach, M. S., 288
Oberauer, K., 554
O'Boyle, C., 244
Ogashi, K., 429
Ogbu, J., 337
Ogline, J. S., 278
Olds, S. W., 135
Olen, K., 239
Olivardia, R., 363
Oliver, E. I., 337
Olsho, L. W., 481, 536
Olson, H. C., 101
Olson, N. A., 278
Olweus, D., 331
O'Malley, P., 359, 360, 361, 362, 414, 420
Ong, A., 398
Orbanic, S., 363
Organista, K. C., 593
Orlansky, M. D., 162
Orvaschel, H., 608
Osipow, S., 438
Oster, H., 151
Ostrea, E. M., 103
Ostrove, J. M., 503
Overton, W. F., 366
Owen, M., 195
Owsley, C. J., 151
Oxman, T. E., 590

P

Padma-Nathan, H., 486
Paffenbarger, O., 420
Paffenbarger, R. S., 542
Paikoff, R., 351, 353, 359, 389
Paley, B., 447
Palmore, E., 578
Paloutzian, R., 494, 495
Paludi, M., 13
Paludi, M. A., 58, 325, 429
Panchaud, C., 357
Panofsky, C., 216
Pargament, K. I., 495
Park, C. L., 495
Park, D. C., 554, 556, 560
Parke, R. D., 45, 193, 258
Parker, B., 98
Parker, J. G., 333
Parkin, A. J., 553
Parlee, M. B., 453
Parnes, H. S., 560
Parten, M., 261
Pasch, L., 458
Pasch, L. A., 79
Passuth, P. M., 507
Pasupathi, M., 580
Patterson, C.J., 251
Patrick, C. L., 85
Patterson, C., 241, 330, 355, 425
Patterson, G. R., 402
Pavalko, E. K., 558
Paveza, G., 568
Pavlov, I. P., 40
Pavlova, Z., 111
Payer, L., 485
Peaceman, A. M., 111
Pearlin, L. I., 530
Peck, R. C., 576
Pecchioni, L., 546
Pell, T., 102
Peltola, P., 439
Pennington, B. F., 278
Pentz, M. A., 362
Peplau, L. A., 454, 462, 468
Perdue, C. W., 582
Perlman, D., 454
Perls, T., 526, 527, 541
Perry, C. M., 593
Perry, D. G., 331
Perry, T. B., 333
Perry, W. G., 431
Perusse, D., 87
Peskin, H., 353, 482
Peters, K., 542
Petersen, A. C., 349, 353, 385
Peterson, B. E., 503
Peterson, C., 586, 587
Peterson, C. C., 507
Peterson, K. S., 394
Peterson, S. R., 312
Peth-Pierce, R., 195
Phibbs, C. S., 102
Phillips, D., 195, 336
Phillips, K., 182
Philpot, C. L., 470
Phinney, J., 385
Phinney, J. S., 398
Piaget, J., 30, 35, 157, 158, 161, 212, 240, 260, 283
Pick, H. L., 152
Pierce, K. M., 330
Pillow, D. R., 505
Pinger, R. R., 422
Pinker, S., 170
Pitts, R. C., 240
Plackslin, S., 116
Plant, E. A., 322, 323
Pleck, J. H., 325, 470
Plemons, J. K., 505
Plomin, R., 74, 84, 85, 87, 88, 182, 350
Polivy, J., 419
Pollack, H. A., 134
Polley, B. A., 418
Portney, M.J., 459
Posner, J. K., 330
Posner, M. I., 178
Poston, D. L., 254
Potenza, M., 368
Potter, S. M., 102
Potvin, L., 368
Poulton, S., 209
Powell, D. S., 11
Power, C., 376
Powers, L. E., 614
Pressley, M., 278, 288. 290

Price, D. D., 537
Price, J., 565
Pratt, M. W., 502
Prohaska, M. L., 449
Prohaska, T., 542
Prosser, T., 376
Province, M. A., 541
Pruett, M.K., 11
Pyke, K. D., 584

Q

Qualls, S. H., 562
Quas, J. A., 14, 221
Quick, H. E., 562
Quinn, J. F., 560

R

Rabier, J., 18
Rabin, B. E., 266
Radford, A., 207
Radke-Yarrow, M., 136
Raffaeli, M., 388
Rahe, R. H., 505
Raikkonen, K., 483
Ramey, C., 113
Ramsay, D. S., 180, 207
Ramsey, E., 402
Randall, D.W., 459
Rantanen, P., 405
Rao, K., 466
Rapaport, S., 534
[illegible]
Rappaport, M. D., 280
Rathunde, K., 417
Raudenbush, S., 52
Ray, M., 204, 296, 300
Ray, O. S., 422
Raynor, R., 40
Rebelsky, R. G., 169
Redinbaugh, E. M., 566
Reedy, M. N., 514
Reese, H. W., 10
Reid, J. D., 478, 504
Reid, S. L., 21
Reifman, A., 362
Reinhardt, J. P., 590
Reinisch, J., 478
Reis, H. T., 452
Reiss, D., 88
Remafedi, G., 355
Reschly, D. J., 278
Resnick, L., 38
Revenson, T. A., 11
Reynolds, A. J., 231
Reynolds, D. K., 609, 610, 612, 619
Rhodes, J. E., 14
Rhodes, S. R., 492
Richard, C. A., 133
Richards, L. N., 517
Richards, M., 255, 388
Rickards, T., 300
Ridgeway, D., 239
Riegel, K. F., 557
Riegel, R. M., 557
Rifkind, B. M., 486
Riley, M., 135
Rimberg, H. M., 357
Rimm, E. B., 543
Rimpela, M, 405
Ringdal, G.I., 614
Ringdal, K., 614
Risley, T. R., 171
Robbins, C., 542
Roberto, K. A., 517
Roberts, B. L., 531
Roberts, S. E., 77
Roberts, W., 242
Robinson, D. P., 359
Rockwood, K., 563
Rode, S. S., 119
Rodgers, C., 243, 246
Rodgers, J. L., 253, 393
Rodin, J., 363, 419, 545, 546, 611
Rodriguez, R. G., 355
Rodriquez, J. L., 304
Rodriquez, L. E., 363
Roediger, H. L., 51
Rogers, A., 386
Rogoff, B., 12, 38, 218
Rogosch, F. A., 251
Rohde, P., 406
Rohner, E. C., 258
Rohner, R. P., 258
Role, L., 422
Roodin, P. A., 18, 68, 491, 493, 519, 535, 536, 537, 567
Rook, K. S., 578
Roopnarine, J. L., 226
Rose, A. J., 333
Rose, S., 394
Rosecan, J., 422
Rosen, D., 183
Rosen, K. H., 429
Rosen, K. S., 190
Rosenbaum, D., 137
Rosenbaum, K., 38
Rosenberg, S. D., 505
Rosenblith, J. F., 95, 142, 164
Rosenfeld, A., 512
Rosenfield, S., 439
Rosenman, R., 482
Rosenstein, D., 151
Rosenstock, I., 11
Rosenthal, D., 355
Rosenthal, D. A., 385
[illegible]
[illegible]
Rossi, A., 507, 508, 517
Rossouw, J. E., 486
Rosylyn, A., 614
Roth, B., 11
Roth, J., 364, 390
Roth, M., 562
Roth, G., 543
Rothbart, M. K., 182, 183, 252, 253
Rothbaum, F., 460
Rothstein, R., 304
Rovee-Collier, C., 162, 163, 164
Rowe, D. C., 74
Rowe, J. W., 533, 537, 541, 590, 594
Rubenstein, L. Z., 542
Rubin, D. H., 106
Rubin, E. H., 565
Rubin, K., 262, 263, 313
Rubin, S., 615
Rubin, Z., 453
Ruble, D., 246
Rudkin, L., 591
Rudy, T. E., 417
Rumberger, R. W., 373
Runco, M., 288, 300
Russek, L. G., 484
Russell, D. W., 455
Ruth, J., 513, 577
Rutter, M., 21
Ryan, A. S., 135
Ryan, R. M., 580
Ryan-Finn, K. D., 58
Rybash, J. M., 18, 68, 491, 493, 519, 535, 536, 537, 567
Ryff, C. D., 447, 484, 502

S

Saarni, C., 178, 313
Sabini, J., 454
Sacks, J. J., 276
Saczynski, J. S., 558
Sadker, D., 245
Sadker, M., 245
Safford, P., 338, 339
Sagan, C., 66
Saigal, S., 111
Salami, L., 363
Salapatek, P., 139, 146
Salovey, P., 313, 417
Salthouse, T., 8, 9, 490, 552, 554
Samour, P. Q., 134
Samuels, M., 110
Samuels, N., 110
Sandberg, J. F., 439
Sanders, G. F., 13, 587
Sandler, D. P., 421
Sands, R. G., 588
Sangree, W. H., 592
Sanson, A., 303
Santacruz, K.S., 563
Santrock, J. W., 329, 337, 396, 415
Santulli, K. A., 288
Sarason, B., 568
Sarason, I., 568
Sarigiani, P. A., 353
Sarrel, P., 429
Sauber, M., 467
Savin-Williams, R. C., 355
Sax, L. J., 415
Scantlin, R., 265
Scarr, S., 73, 74, 85, 88, 195, 296
Schaffer, H. R., 187, 192
Schaie, K. W., 8, 9, 10, 15, 21, 52, 431, 489, 490, 514, 532, 554, 556, 557, 558
Schairer, C., 486
Schantz, S., 99
Scharrar, E., 264
Scheer, S. D., 414
Scheidt, S., 483
Schiff, M., 85
Schiffman, S. S., 536
Schlegel, M., 223
[illegible]
[illegible]
Schneider, W., 290
Schnorr, T. M., 103
Schoendorf, K. C., 102
Schoka, E., 614
Schooler, C., 556, 560
Schrag, S. G., 103
Schroots, J. J. F., 477
Schrum, L., 338
Schugens, M. M., 554
Schulenberg, J., 364
Schultz, R., 416
Schumer, H., 377
Schumm, J. S., 282
Schunk, J. E., 276
Schwartz, D., 105
Schwartz, G. E., 484
Schweinhart, L. J., 231
Schwitzer, A. M., 363
Scott-Jones, D., 336, 397
Seeley, J., 406
Seeman, T. E., 531, 533
Segerberg, O., 527
Seidman, D. F., 422
Seidman, E., 370
Seifert, K., 246
Seier, W. L., 221
Seigle, J., 264
Semba, R. D., 104
Serbin, L. A., 246
Serpell, R., 296
Sexton, D., 209
Shade, S. C., 336
Shahinfar, A., 190
Shannon, F. T., 136
Shapiro, E. K., 339
Sharkey, W., 454
Sharma, A. R., 82
Sharp, E. A., 459
Shaver, P., 388, 447, 448, 452
Shay, J. W., 7, 532
Sheehy, G., 485
Sherman, S., 543
Sherwood, A., 420
Shields, S. A., 326
Shinwell, E., 111
Shiono, P. H., 106, 113
Shiraev, E., 12
Shirley, M. M., 142
Shneidman, E., 405, 608
Shomberg, E. F., 468
Shonk, S.M., 251
Shore, G., 280
Shore, L. M., 560
Shrout, P. E., 506
Shuchter, S., 615
Sieber, J. E., 57
Siegel, L. S., 167
Siegel, M. A., 563
Siegfried, T., 564
Siegler, I. C., 481, 504
Siegler, R. S., 38, 221
Sigman, M. D., 220
Silberstein, L. R., 363
Silver, M. H., 527, 541
Silver, N., 459, 461
Silverman, N., 251
Silverstein, L.B., 193
Silwinski, M., 552
Simmons, R. G., 353
Simoni, H., 191
Simons, J., 337, 364
Simonton, D. K., 432
Sinclair, H. M., 587
Singer, B., 447, 484
Singer, D. G., 267
Singer, J. E., 11
Singer, L. T., 102
Singh, N. A., 357, 358, 542
Sitterle, K. A., 329
Skadberg, B. T., 133
Skeels, H., 85
Skerry, S., 310
Skinner, B. F., 40, 171
[illegible]
[illegible]
Skovronek, E., 490
Slater, A., 146
Slee, P. T., 331
Slentz, K.L., 227
Slobin, D., 170
Slomka, G., 278
Small, S. A., 390, 556
Smiley, M., 570
Smith, A. D., 552, 553
Smith, D. W., 82
Smith, G. A., 556
Smith, J., 558
Smith, L., 47, 133
Smith, M. A., 565
Smith, R., 252, 266
Smith, S., 459
Smith, W.C., 151
Smyer, M. A., 562
Snarey, J., 318
Snow, C. E., 171, 225
Snowden, D. A., 551
Snowden, L. R., 483
Snyder, M., 452
Socol, M. L., 111
Soeken, K., 98
Soldo, B. J., 519
Sokal, L., 246
Sollod, R. N., 494
Solomon, J., 189, 251
Sommers, D. G., 560
Sorenson, S., 518
Sosik, J. J., 492
Spalding, L. R., 468
Spear, H. J., 364
Spearman, C. E., 293
Spear-Swerling, L., 303
Spelke, E. S., 148, 151, 161
Spence, J. T., 322, 324
Spence, M. J., 148, 149
Spencer, M. B., 337, 385, 386, 397
Spielberger, C. D., 506
Sprafkin, C., 246
Sprei, J. E., 429
Spring, J., 12, 336
Sroufe, L. A., 180, 181, 189, 251, 253
St. Pierre, R., 337
Stafford, F. P., 327
Stallard, E., 533
Stallings, J., 231
Stanhope, L., 253
Stanley-Hagan, M. M., 467

Stark, E., 512
Starke-Reed, P., 543
Stattin, H., 353
Staudinger, U. M., 10, 21, 67, 555, 581
Stein, A. H., 265
Steinberg, L., 89
Steinberg, L. D., 330
Steiner, J. E., 150
Stern, D. N., 192
Stern, J. S., 544
Stern, L., 134
Sternberg, R., 162, 293, 303, 452
Sternberg, R. J., 85, 295
Stern, P., 337
Steur, F. B., 266
Stevens, N., 333
Stevenson, H. C., 340
Stevenson, H. W., 12, 341
Stewart, A. J., 503
Stewart, R., 355
Stewart, W. J., 609
Stillion, J. M., 608
Stith, S. M., 429
Stitzer, M. L., 422
Stolberg, U., 181
Storandt, M., 565
Stotland, N. L., 494
Stoval, S., 277
Strasburger, V. C., 266
Strain, L. A., 563
Strayer, J., 242
Street, K. A., 276
Streissguth, A. P., 101
Strickland, A. L., 613
Striegel-Moore, R. H., 363
Stroebe, M., 615, 616
Stroman, C. A., 264
Stuart, W. J., 609
Stulack, B.B., 134
Stull, D. E., 562
Stunkard, A., 418
Styfco, S. J., 232
Style, C. B., 462
Sue, S., 399
Sullivan, A., 389
Sullivan, H. S., 392
Sullivan, K., 389
Sullivan, L., 324
Suls, J., 482
Suomi, S. J., 50, 260
Super, C., 132
Super, E. M., 190
Susman, E. J., 350
Sutton-Smith, B., 260
Suzman, R., 530, 531, 533, 541
Swagerty, D., 563
Swain, A., 482
Swain, S. O., 454
Swan, G. E., 562
Swann, W. B., 449
Swanson, D. P., 59, 385

T

Taddio, A., 150
Takahashi, K., 190
Taki, M., 331
Tan, S. Y., 495
Tannen, D., 454, 469, 470
Tanner, J. L., 517
Tappan, M. B., 37, 216, 217
Tapper, J., 392
Tardif, C., 189
Tardif, T., 258
Tarnowski, A., 590
Taub, E., 9
Taylor, H. G., 111, 112
Taylor, R. J., 570
Taylor, S., 11
Taylor, S. P., 593
Taymans, J. M., 282
Tercyak, K. P., 77
Teresi, J., 590
Terman, D. L., 280, 282
Terman, L., 298
Tesser, A., 311
Teti, D. M., 253, 516
Tetrault, M. K. T., 58
Tharp, R. G., 219, 220
Thayer, J. F., 420
Thelen, E., 47, 140, 141, 143, 144, 152
Thoman, E. B., 131, 132
Thomas, A., 151, 446
Thomas, C., 363
Thomas, K., 394
Thompson, P. M., 205
Thompson, R., 179, 182, 189, 190
Thomson, E., 468
Thorstad, K. K., 111
Thorton, A., 355
Thurston, L., 282
Thurstone, L. L., 293
Tilton-Weaver, L., 349
Tobin, J. J., 231
Tobin, S. S., 578
Tompkins, J. R., 278
Tonner, L., 183
Torff, B., 296
Torgesen, J. K., 278
Toth, S. L., 251, 252
Tousignant, M., 280
Tout, K., 195
Trasler, J., 106
Trawick-Smith, J. W., 226
Treffers, P. E., 109
Trehub, S. E., 149
Triandis, H. C., 12
Trimble, J. E., 58
Troiano, R. P., 209
Troll, L. E., 589
Trowbridge, F. L., 209, 277
Truglio, R. T., 265
Truitner, K., 606
Truitner, N., 606
Trygstad, D. W., 587
Tubman, J. G., 406
Tucker, J. S., 590
Tudge, J., 218
Tulving, E., 553, 554
Tunick, R. A., 278
Tunnel, D., 542
Turbin, M. S., 364
Turecki, S., 183
Turk, D. C., 417
Turkanis, C.G., 12
Turkheimer, E., 87
Turnbull, A., 282
Turner, B. F., 592
Turner, R., 356
Turvey, C. L., 563

U

Ubell, C., 525
Udry, J. R., 393
Umberson, D., 590
Unger, D. G., 414
Unger, R., 13, 323
Unis, A. S., 101
Urberg, K. A., 388

V

Vaillant, G. E., 422, 423, 504, 505
Vallance, D. D., 313
Valsiner, J., 12
Vandell, D. C., 252
Vandell, D. L., 192, 330
Vandenberg, B., 262
Van den Boom, D., 183, 252
Vanderpool, H. Y., 495
Vandewater, E. A., 502, 589, 590, 591, 592
VandeWeerd, C., 568
Van Hoorn, J., 260
Van Ijzendoorn, M. H., 188, 190
Vargas, D., 362
Vaughn, S., 282
Vemulapalli, C., 134
Veniegas, R. C., 468
Ventura, S. J., 109
Verbrugge, L. M., 480, 484, 592
Verhaeghen, P., 555, 558
Verreault, R., 563
Vessey, S. H., 50
Vidal, F., 36, 286
Visher, E., 468
Visher, J., 468
Von Beveren, T. T., 108
Voyer, D., 322
Voyer, S., 322
Vygotsky, L., 37, 216, 217, 260

W

Wachs, H., 284
Wachs, T. D., 182, 446, 447
Wadden, T. A., 419
Waddington, C. H., 74
Wadhwa, P. D., 103
Wahlsten, D., 74, 88
Wakschlag, L. S., 258
Waldron, M., 87
Walk, R. D., 147
Walker, C., 603
Walker, L. J., 240, 318, 319
Wallston, B. S., 547
Walsh, L. A., 253
Walsh, W. B., 49
Walter, B. M., 553
Walther-Thomas, C., 282
Wampold, B. E., 614
Wang, H., 542
Wang, X., 101
Warner, H. R., 532
Warr, P., 560
Warren, C. W., 426
Warren, M. P., 351
Warrick, P., 93
Warshak, R. A., 82, 329
Wass, H., 608, 609
Waterman, A. S., 376, 384
Waters, E., 21, 22, 180, 181, 189, 239, 448
Waters, P., 319
Watkinson, B., 102
Watson, J. B., 40, 134, 180
Watson, R., 466
Watt, L. M., 577
Way, N., 359
Weatherford, W., 565
Weaver, R. F., 72
Weaver, S. E., 468
Webster, J., 109
Wechsler, H., 362, 420, 421
Weed, K., 359
Wehner, E. A., 394
Weikart, D. P., 232
Weinberg, M. S., 425
Weinberg, R. A., 74, 85, 88, 296
Weinberger, D. A., 402
Weinstein, K. K., 587
Weisner, T., 373
Weiss, S. M., 11
Weizmann, F., 187
Wellman, H., 222, 223
Wells, M. G., 312
Wenestam, C. G., 609
Wenger, G. C., 589
Wentura, D., 595
Wentworth, R. A. L., 227
Wenzlaff, R. M., 449
Werker, J. F., 149
Werler, M. M., 105
Werner, E. E., 252, 310
Wertheimer, R. F., 336
West, L., 282
Westin, D., 33
Westra, T., 142
Wethington, E., 492, 508, 560
Whalen, C. K., 280
Whitbourne, S. K., 503, 504, 533
White, B., 142
White, C. B., 538
White, C. W., 226
White, D. K., 134
White, L., 516
White, N., 557
Whitehall, J. S., 103
Whitesell, N., 319, 406
Whitfield, K., 87, 591
Whiting, B. B., 258, 395
Whitman, T. L., 359
Whitton, S.W., 459
Wiersbe, D. W., 614
Wilcutt, E. G., 278
Wiley, D., 538
Wilkie, F., 556
Williams, A., 15, 517
Williams, C. R., 267
Williams, E. M., 287
Williams, J. E., 322
Williams, K. R., 429
Williams, M. F., 264
Williams, R. B., 482
Willis, S. L., 8, 9, 21, 478, 489, 504, 557, 558
Wilson, B. J., 310
Wilson, K. S., 192
Wilson-Shockley, S., 395
Windle, M., 406
Windle, W. F., 151
Wineberg, H., 466
Wing, R. R., 418
Wink, P., 512
Winner, E., 213, 299
Winsler, A., 217, 304
Wintre, M. G., 313
Witkin, H. A., 76
Wolff, R., 275
Wolinsky, F. D., 562
Wolowicz, L. S., 388
Wong, C. A., 274, 276, 385
Wong, K., 127
Wong, P. T. P., 577
Wood, G. A., 395
Wood, J. T., 13
Woodrich, D. L., 280
Woodward, N. J., 547
Wooley, S. C., 419
Worobey, J., 114
Worthington, E. L., 618
Wortman, C. B., 617
Wright, J. C., 264, 265
Wright, W. E., 532
Wrightsman, L. S., 429
Wu, D. Y. H., 231

Y

Yale, R., 566
Yali, A. M., 105
Yamagishi, M., 460
Yamagishi, T., 460
Yang, A., 337, 364
Yang, J., 511
Yasui, Y., 277
Yates, M., 377
Yeats, D. E., 560
Yeung, W. J., 439
Yin, Y., 393
Yip, R., 134
Yirmiya, N., 192
Young, K. T., 136
Young, S. K., 190
Youngblade, L. M., 255
Yu, V. Y., 111

Z

Zabin, L. S., 356
Zarit, S. H., 518, 562, 563
Zautra, A. J., 505
Zelazo, P. R., 195
Zelinski, E. M., 554
Zeskind, P. S., 102, 180
Zigler, E., 13, 232
Zimmerman, R. R., 187
Zimmerman, R. S., 337
Zisook, S., 615
Zubay, G. L., 66
Zuckerman, B., 102

Subject Index

A

Abecedarian Project, 86
Abstracts, 57
Acceptance of death, 610
Accidents
  late adulthood physical development, 541, 547
  middle and late childhood physical development, 276, 279
Accommodation, 35
Active euthanasia, 603
Active (niche-picking) genotype-environment correlations, 86–87, 89
Activity theory, 578, 582
Acuity, 146, 153
Adaptive behavior, 67, 69
Addiction, 422–423
"Adolescence" defined, 17
Adolescent attitudes toward death, 609
Adolescent physical and cognitive development, 347–379
  alcohol, 361–362, 365
  anorexia nervosa, 363, 365
  body image, 352–354
  bulimia nervosa, 363, 365
  character education, 375, 377
  cognitive moral education, [illegible]
  contraception, 357, 360
  critical thinking, 369–370
  culture, 374
  death, 364–365
  decision making, 368–370
  dropouts, 372–373, 377
  drug use and abuse, 359–363, 365
  eating disorders, 363
  egocentrism, 367–368, 370
  families, 362–363, 365
  formal operational thought, 365–367, 370
  gonads, 350
  health, 364–365
  height, 351, 354
  hidden curriculum, 373–375, 377
  high school dropouts, 372–373, 377
  hormones, 350–351, 354
  hypothalamus, 350
  hypothetical-deductive reasoning, 366
  imaginary audience, 368, 370
  information processing, 368–370
  junior high school, 369–371, 377
  menarche, 349
  middle school, 369–371, 377
  moral education, 373–377
  nature of, 348–349, 354
  peers, 362–363, 365
  personal fable, 368, 370
  Piaget, 365–367, 370
  pituitary gland, 350
  pregnancy, 358–360
  puberty, 349–354
  risk factors for sexual problems, 356, 360
  schools, 369–377
  service learning, 376–377
  sexual identity, 355, 360
  sexuality, 354–359
  sexually transmitted diseases (STDs), 357, 360
  sexual maturation, 351–352, 354
  smoking, 362, 365
  substance abuse, 359–363, 365
  top-dog phenomenon, 371, 377
  transition from adolescence to adulthood, 414–416, 423
  values clarification, 375–377
  weight, 351, 354
Adolescent socioemotional development, 381–409
  assimilation, 399
  attachment, 387–388, 391
  autonomy, 387–388, 391
  cliques, 392
  commitment, 383
  connectedness, 385
  crisis, 383
  cross-cultural studies, 396, 401
  culture, 385–387, 395–401
  dating, 393–395, 401
  dating scripts, 394–395
  depression, 405, 407
  emotions, 395
  Erikson, 382
  ethnic identity, 385, 387
  ethnicity, 385–386, 396–399, 401
  families, 384–385, 387–391, 401
  friendships, 392–393
  gangs, 402–405
  gender, 386–387
  identity, 382–387
  identity achievement, 383
  identity diffusion, 383
  identity foreclosure, 383
  identity moratorium, 383
  individuality, [illegible]
  juvenile delinquency, 399–405, 407
  Marcia's four statuses of identity, 383–384, 387
  parent-adolescent conflict, 388–391
  peer groups, 391–392, 401
  peers, 391–395, 401
  pluralism, 399
  prevention/intervention programs, 406–407
  rites of passage, 395–396, 401
  romantic relationships, 393–395, 401
  socioeconomic status, 397–398
  suicide, 405–407
  value conflicts, 399
  youth violence, 402–405
Adoption, 82–83
Adoption study, 74
Adult attitudes toward death, 609–610
Adult developmental changes, 432–434
Adult stage theories, 502–505, 510
Advanced directives on death, 603
Aerobic exercise, 420
Affectionate love, 452–453, 513–514, 519
Affordances, 145
Africa, bottle and breast-feeding in, 125–126
Afterbirth, 108
Age
  and happiness, 18
  late adulthood physical development, 526–534
  of mother, 105–106
Ageism, 582
Aggression and television, 265–267
AIDS
  early adulthood physical and cognitive development, 427–428, 430
  prenatal development, 104
Ainsworth strange situation, 188, 191
Alcohol
  adolescent physical and cognitive development, 361–362, 365
  early adulthood physical and cognitive development, 420–421
  prenatal development, 101
Altruism, 319–320, 327
Alzheimer's disease, 564–566, 571
Amniocentesis, 77, 80
Amnion, 95
Analgesia, 110
Anal stage, 32
Androgyny, 324
Anesthesia, 110
Anger and death, 610
Anger cry, 180
Animal research, 50, 54–55
Animism, 213
Anorexia nervosa, 363, 365
Apgar Scale, 113, 115
Arthritis, 539, 547
Assimilation
  adolescent socioemotional development, 399
  theories of development, 35
Associative play, 262
Attachment
  adolescent socioemotional development, 387–388, 391
  early adulthood socioemotional development, 447–448, 456
  infant socioemotional development, 186–191
Attendants, 109
Attention, 220, 224
Attention deficit hyperactivity disorder (ADHD), 279–281, 283
Attraction in early adulthood socioemotional development, 448–450, 456
Authoritarian parenting, 248, 250
Authoritative parenting, 249–250
Autonomous morality, 240
Autonomy in adolescent socioemotional development, 387–388, 391
Autonomy *versus* shame and doubt, 33

B

Babinski reflex, 140
Baltes' view
  evolutionary perspective, 68
  late adulthood socioemotional development, 580–582
Bandura's observational learning, 41, 45
Bargaining and death, 610
Basal metabolism rate (BMR)
  early adulthood physical and cognitive development, 418
  early childhood physical development, 209
Basic cry, 180
Bayley Scales of Infant Development, 166–168
Behavioral and social cognitive theories, 40–41, 45–47
Behavioral influences on language, 171–173
Behavior genetics, 74, 79
Bell curve, 84–85
Bem Sex-Role Inventory, 325
Berkeley Longitudinal Studies, 511, 513
Berko's study, 225–226
Big five factors of personality, 511
Bilingualism, 303–305
Binet tests, 291–292, 301
Biological age, 18
Biological beginnings, 65–91
  evolutionary perspective, 66–69
  genetic foundations, 69–77
  heredity-environment interaction, 83–89
  reproduction challenges and choices, 77–83
  twins, 65–66
Biological influences on gender, 243, 247
Biological influences on language, 170–171, 173
Biological processes, 16
Biological theories of aging, 532–534
Birth, 108–115, 120
  afterbirth, 108
  analgesia, 110
  anesthesia, 110
  Apgar Scale, 113, 115
  attendants, 109
  Brazelton Neonatal Behavioral Assessment Scale, 113–115
  breech position, 110
  cesarean delivery, 110–111
  doula, 109
  epidural block, 110
  Lamaze, 110
  low-birthweight infants, 111–113, 115
  measure of neonatal health and responsiveness, 113, 115
  methods of delivery, 109–111
  midwifery, 109
  natural childbirth, 110
  oxytocics, 110
  prepared childbirth, 110
  preterm infants, [illegible]
  process, 108–111, 115
  setting, 109
  stages of birth, 108, 115
  strategies, 109–111, 115
  transition from fetus to newborn, 108–109, 115
Birth order, 253–254, 259
Blastocyst, 94
Blinking reflex, 140
Blood tests, 78
Body growth and change
  early childhood physical development, 204–205, 208
  middle and late childhood physical development, 274, 276–277, 279
Body image in adolescent physical and cognitive development, 352–354
Body transcendence *versus* body preoccupation, 576
Bonding, 116, 118–119
Bones, 480
Bottle feeding, 125–126, 135–136
Bowlby's view of attachment, 186–187
Brain
  early childhood physical development, 205, 208
  infant physical development, 127–131
  late adulthood physical development, 534–535, 539
Brain death, 602
Brainstorming, 300–301
Brazelton Neonatal Behavioral Assessment Scale, 113–115
Breast-feeding, 125–126, 135–136
Breech position, 110
Bronfenbrenner's ecological theory of development, 43–44, 47
Bulimia nervosa, 363, 365
Bullying, 331–332, 334
Buss' view, 67, 69

C

Canalization, 74, 79
Cancer, 277–279
Cardiovascular system, 481–482
Careers, 22–25
  certified college grief counselor, 615
  child clinical psychologist, 11
  child life specialist, 277

Careers (*continued*)
child psychiatrist, 339
clinical psychologist, 117, 437, 462
college/career counselor, 415
counseling psychologist, 399
day-care director, 194–197
director, center for social and emotional education, 314
director of children's services/head start, 232
director of human subjects protection, 57
Director of the Alzheimer's Association of Dallas, 568
director of women's studies program, 580
early adulthood physical and cognitive development, 435–441
early childhood educator, 226
genetic counselor, 76
geriatric nurse, 544
health psychologist, 402
high school counselor/college advisor, 372
infant assessment specialist, 167
learning disabilities specialist, 282
middle adulthood physical and cognitive development, 492–493, 497
pediatrician, 134
pediatric nurse, 210
perinatal nurse, 109
postpartum expert, 117
professor of human development, 9, 557
professor of psychology and life-span development, 517
psychologist, 223
psychology professor, 580
researcher, 517, 557
school psychologist, 335
social worker, 251
supervisor of gifted and talented education, 299
toy designer, 223
university professor and researcher, 433
Caregiving in infant socioemotional development, 189–191, 193–195
Care options in late adulthood, 544, 547
Care perspective in middle and late childhood socioemotional development, 319
Care providers in late adulthood, 546–547
Carstenen's theory, 578–580, 582
Case studies as research method, 49, 54–55
Causes of death, 606–607, 612
Cells, 70
Cellular clock theory, 532, 534
Centenarians, 526–530
Centration in early childhood cognitive development, 214
Cephalocaudal pattern, 126, 131
Certified college grief counselor, 615
Cesarean delivery, 110–111
Character education, 375, 377
Child abuse, 249–252, 259
Child care policy, 194
Child-centered kindergarten, 226, 230, 233
Child clinical psychologist, 11
Childhood attitudes toward death, 608–609
Child life specialist, 277
Child psychiatrist, 339
Child rearing leave, 194
Chlamydia, 426
Chorionic villi sampling, 78, 80
Chromosomes
genetic foundations, 69–70, 75–76, 79
late adulthood physical development, 532
Chronic disorders in middle adulthood physical and cognitive development, 481
Chronological age, 18
Chronosystem, 44
Circulatory system, 537, 539
Classical conditioning
theories of development, 40, 47
time line, 45
Classification of attachment, 189–191
Classifying temperament, 182
Climacteric, 484
Clinical psychologist, 117
Cliques, 392
Close relationships in middle adulthood socioemotional development, 513–521
Cognitive development
adolescence. *See* Adolescent physical and cognitive development
early adulthood. *See* Early adulthood physical and cognitive development
early childhood. *See* Early childhood cognitive development
infants. *See* Infant cognitive development
late adulthood. *See* Late adulthood cognitive development
middle adulthood. *See* Middle adulthood physical and cognitive development
middle and late childhood. *See* Middle and late childhood cognitive development
Cognitive developmental theory of gender, 246
Cognitive influences on gender, 245–247
Cognitive mechanics, 552, 559
Cognitive moral education, 376–377
Cognitive pragmatics, 552, 559
Cognitive processes, 16
Cognitive social theory of development, 40–41, 45–47
Cognitive theories of development, 35–40, 46
Cohabiting adults, 466, 471
Cohort effects
middle adulthood socioemotional development, 506–507
research methods, 52–54
College, 415–416, 423, 438
College/career counselor, 415
Color, 146, 153
Commitment, 383
Communicating with a dying person, 613–614, 619
Conceptions of age, 18
Conceptual development, 161–162
Concrete operational stage, 37
Concrete operational thought, 283–288, 290
Conditioning, 162, 168
Connectedness, 385
Consensual validation, 449
Conservation, 214–215
Constructive play, 263
Context, 12
Contexts in which people die, 611–612
Continuity-discontinuity issue, 20
Continuum of sexual orientation, 425
Contraception, 357, 360
Control
death, 611–612
late adulthood physical development, 545–547
Control group as research method, 51
Control processes, 288
Conventional reasoning, 317
Convergent thinking, 299
Cooperative play, 262
Coordination of secondary circular reactions, 159
Coping
death, 613–619
late adulthood physical development, 545–547
middle adulthood physical and cognitive development, 495–496
Correlational research, 50, 54–55
Costa and McCrae's Baltimore Study, 511, 513
Counseling psychologist, 399
Cousey, Bob, 575
Creativity
early adulthood physical and cognitive development, 432–434
middle and late childhood physical and cognitive development, 299–301
Crime, fears of, 567–568, 571
Crisis in adolescent socioemotional development, 383
Critical period, 42
Critical thinking
adolescent physical and cognitive development, 369–370
middle and late childhood cognitive development, 288–290
Cross-sectional approach to research, 51–52, 54
Crying, 179–181
Crystallized intelligence, 488–489
Csikszentmihalyi's ideas, 433–434
Cultural-familial retardation, 298
Culture
adolescent physical and cognitive development, 374
adolescent socioemotional development, 385–387, 395–401, 396, 401
Baltes' view of evolution, 68
death, 605–607, 614, 618–619
early adulthood socioemotional development, 460
early childhood socioeconomic development, 250–251, 257–259
late adulthood cognitive development, 561
late adulthood physical development, 529
late adulthood socioemotional development, 592–595
middle adulthood physical and cognitive development, 482–484, 488
middle adulthood socioemotional development, 508–510, 518
middle and late childhood cognitive development, 295–297
middle and late childhood physical development, 282
middle and late childhood socioemotional development, 318, 325–326
perspectives in life-span development, 12–13
prenatal development, 98–99
theories of development, 44
Culture bias, 36
Culture-fair tests, 296
Curiosity, 159–160
Cystic fibrosis, 78

D

Daily hassles of middle-aged adults, 506
Daily uplifts of middle-aged adults, 506
Dating, 393–395, 401
Dating scripts, 394–395
Day care, 194–197
Day-care director, 194–197
Death, 601–621
acceptance, 610
active euthanasia, 603
adolescent attitudes toward, 609
adolescent physical and cognitive development, 364–365
adulthood attitudes toward, 609–610
advanced directives, 603
anger, 610
attitude toward at different points in life span, 608–610, 612
bargaining, 610
brain death, 602
causes, 606–607, 612
childhood attitudes toward, 608–609
communicating with a dying person, 613–614, 619
contexts in which people die, 611–612
control, 611–612
coping, 613–619
culture, 605–607, 614, 618–619
decisions regarding, 602–604
denial and isolation, 610–611, 612
depression, 610
determinations of death, 602, 607
developmental perspective on, 606–610, 612
early childhood physical development, 209–211
euthanasia, 603
expectations, 606–607, 610
facing one's own death, 610–613
funerals, 617–619
grief, 613
grieving, 613–615, 619
health care decisions, 602–604, 607
history, 604–605, 607
hospice, 604
husbands, 616–617, 619
Kübler-Ross' stages of dying, 610–612
late adulthood physical development, 538–539, 547
life partners, 616–617, 619
making sense of the world, 615–616, 619
middle adulthood physical and cognitive development, 484, 488
mourning, 617–619
natural death, 602–603
passive euthanasia, 603
Princess Diana, 601
spouses, 616–617, 619
wives, 616–617, 619
Decision making, 368–370
Deferred imitation, 164–165
Dementia, 563–564, 567, 571
Dendritic spreading, 128
Denial and isolation, 610–611, 612
Dependent variable, 51
Depression
adolescent socioemotional development, 405, 407
death, 610
late adulthood cognitive development, 562–563, 571
Depth perception, 147–148, 153
Determinations of death, 602, 607
Developmental biodynamics, 142–144
Developmental changes in early adulthood, 435, 441
Developmental consequences of abuse, 251–252
Developmentally appropriate practices in education, 227–230, 233
Developmental perspective on death, 606–610, 612
Developmental quotient, 166
Developmental timetable of emotions, 179, 181
Development involves growth, maintenance and regulation, 10
Development is contextual, 10
Development is lifelong, 9
Development is multidimensional, 9
Development is multidirectional, 9
Development is plastic, 9
Development is studied by a number of disciplines, 10
Development of language, 169–170, 173
Diabetes, 78
Dieting, 418–419
Differentiation *versus* role preoccupation, 576
Difficult child, 182
Director, center for social and emotional education, 314
Director of children's services/head start, 232

Director of human subjects protection, 57
Director of the Alzheimer's Association of Dallas, 568
Director of women's studies program, 580
Disabled children, 278–283
Disadvantaged children, 231–233
Disease model of addiction, 422
Diseases
- middle adulthood physical and cognitive development, 481–482, 488
- middle and late childhood physical development, 276–279
- prenatal development, 103–104

Disengagement theory, 578, 582
Dishabituation, 163–164, 168
Disorganized babies, 189
Divergent thinking, 299
Divorce
- early adulthood socioemotional development, 467, 471
- early childhood socioeconomic development, 256–257, 259
- middle adulthood socioemotional development, 514–515

DNA, 69–70
Dominant-recessive genes principle, 70–72, 79
Doula, 109
Down syndrome, 75–76
Drawings, 213
Dropouts, 372–373, 377
Drug use and abuse
- adolescent physical and cognitive development, 359–363, 365
- early adulthood physical and cognitive development, 420–423
- prenatal development, 99–103, 107

Dual-career couples, 439–441
Dyslexia, 278

E

"Early adulthood" defined, 17
Early adulthood physical and cognitive development, 413–443
- addiction, 422–423
- adult developmental changes, 432–434
- aerobic exercise, 420
- AIDS, 427–428, 430
- alcohol, 420–421
- basal metabolism rate (BMR), 418
- careers and work, 435–441
- chlamydia, 426
- college, 415–416, 423, 438
- continuum of sexual orientation, 425
- creativity, 432–434
- criteria for becoming an adult, 414
- Csikszentmihalyi's ideas, 433–434
- developmental changes, 435, 441
- dieting, 418–419
- disease model of addiction, 422
- drug use and abuse, 420–423
- dual-career couples, 439–441
- eating, 417–420, 423
- environment, 418
- exercise, 419–420, 423
- finding the right career, 437–438, 441
- Flo Jo, 413
- forcible sexual behavior, 428–430
- genital herpes, 426–427
- gonorrhea, 426
- heredity, 418
- herpes, 426–427
- high school, 415–416, 423
- Holland's personality types, 435–436, 441
- homosexuality, 424–425, 430
- HPV, 427
- interviews, 438–439, 441
- job interviews, 438–439, 441
- life-process model of addiction, 422
- obesity, 417–418
- occupational outlook, 436, 441
- peak and slowdown in physical performance, 416–417, 423
- personality type theory, 435–436, 441
- Piaget, 430–431, 434
- postformal thought, 431
- pragmatic thinking, 431, 434
- rape, 429–430
- realistic and pragmatic thinking, 431, 434
- reflective and relativistic thinking, 431, 434
- relativistic thinking, 431, 434
- restrained eating, 419
- sex in America survey, 424
- sexual harassment, 428–430
- sexuality, 424–430
- sexually transmitted diseases (STDs), 426–428, 430
- sexual orientation, 424–425, 430
- skills employers want, 437, 441
- smoking, 421–422
- substance abuse, 420–423
- syphilis, 426
- transition from adolescence to adulthood, 414–416, 423
- values, 436, 441
- weight, 417–420, 423
- work, 438–441

Early adulthood socioemotional development, 445–473
- affectionate love, 452–453
- attachment, 447–448, 456
- attraction, 448–450, 456
- becoming parents and a family with children, 458
- cohabiting adults, 466, 471
- [illegible]
- continuity and discontinuity from childhood to adulthood, 446–448, 456
- culture, 460
- diversity of adult lifestyles, 464–469, 471
- divorce, 467, 471
- emotion, 462–463, 465
- Erikson, 450
- families, 457–464
- family at midlife, 458
- family in later life, 458
- family life cycle, 457, 465
- family with adolescents, 458
- friendship, 453–454
- gay adults, 468–469, 471
- gender, 462–463, 465, 469–471
- homosexuality, 468–469, 471
- independence, 451
- individuated-connected level, 451
- intimacy, 450–451
- launching, 458
- leaving home and becoming a single adult, 457–458
- lesbian adults, 468–469, 471
- loneliness, 454–456
- love, 450–454, 456
- marital trends, 458–459
- marriage, 457–465
- men's development, 470–471
- new couple, 458
- parental roles, 463–465
- physical attraction, 449–450
- remarried adults, 467–468, 471
- role-focused level, 451
- romantic love, 451–452
- self-focused level, 450–451
- single adults, 464–466, 471
- temperament, 446–447, 456
- triangle theory of love, 452
- women's development, 469–471

Early childhood cognitive development, 203–204, 212–235
- animism, 213
- attention, 220, 224
- becoming aware the mind exists, 222
- Berko's study, 225–226
- centration, 214
- child-centered kindergarten, 226, 230, 233
- conservation, 214–215
- detecting accuracies/inaccuracies of the mind, 223
- developmentally appropriate practices in education, 227–230, 233
- disadvantaged children, 231–233
- drawings, 213
- education, 226–233
- egocentrism, 212–213
- eyewitness testimony, 221
- Head Start, 231–232
- information processing, 220–224
- intuitive thought substage, 214–215, 224
- kindergarten, 226, 230, 233
- language and thought, 217, 224
- language development, 225–226, 233
- long-term memory, 221
- memory, 220–221, 224
- Montessori approach, 226–227, 233
- morphological rules, 225–226
- operations, 212
- Piaget, 212–215, 217–220, 224
- preoperational stage of development, 212–216
- preschool, 230–231, 233
- Project Follow Through, 231–232
- Project Head Start, 231–232
- scaffolding, 216–217, 224
- short-term memory, 220–221
- social constructivist approach, 218
- strategies, 221–222, 224
- symbolic drawings, 213
- symbolic function [illegible]
- teaching, 218, 224, 228–229
- theory of mind, 222–224
- three mountains task, 213
- toy-retrieval task, 222
- understanding cognitive connections to the physical world, 222–223
- understanding the mind's active role in emotion and reality, 223
- Vygotsky's view, 216–220, 224
- zone of proximal development, 216–217, 224

"Early childhood" defined, 17
Early childhood educator, 226
Early childhood physical development, 203–211, 234–235
- basal metabolism rate (BMR), 209
- body growth and change, 204–205, 208
- brain, 205, 208
- death, 209–211
- eating, 209, 211
- energy needs, 209, 211
- fine motor skills, 206–208
- gross motor skills, 206, 208
- handedness, 207–208
- height, 204–205, 208
- illness, 209–211
- motor development, 206–208
- myelination, 205
- nutrition, 208–209, 211
- oral rehydration therapy (ORT), 210
- United States, 209–211
- weight, 204–205, 208

Early childhood socioemotional development, 237–269
- aggression and television, 265–267
- associative play, 262
- authoritarian parenting, 248, 250
- authoritative parenting, 249–250
- autonomous morality, 240
- biological influences on gender, 243, 247
- birth order, 253–254, 259
- changing family in a changing society, 254–259
- child abuse, 249–252, 259
- cognitive developmental theory of gender, 246
- cognitive influences on gender, 245–247
- constructive play, 263
- cooperative play, 262
- culture, 250–251, 257–259
- developmental consequences of abuse, 251–252
- divorce, 256–257, 259
- emotional development, 238–247
- ethnicity, 257–259
- families, 247–259
- Freud, 243–244
- games, 263–264
- gender, 243–247
- gender identity, 243
- gender role, 243
- gender schema theory, 246
- heteronomous morality, 240
- imminent justice, 241
- indulgent parenting, 249–250
- initiative *versus* guilt, 238, 240
- moral behavior, 241–242, 247
- moral development, 240–242, 247
- moral feelings, 242, 247
- nature and nurture, 252, 259
- neglectful parenting, 249–250
- onlooker play, 261
- parallel play, 261–262
- parental influences on gender, 244
- parenting, 248–256, 259
- parenting styles, 248–250, 259
- Parten's classic study of play, 261–262, 267
- peer influences on gender, 244–245
- peer relations, 259–260, 267
- personality development, 238–247
- Piaget, 240–241, 247
- play, 260–264, 267
- [illegible]
- pretense/symbolic play, 262–263
- prosocial behavior and television, 265–267
- psychoanalytic theory of gender, 243–244
- school influences on gender, 245
- self, 238–240
- self-understanding, 238–240
- sensorimotor play, 262
- sibling relationships, 253, 259
- single-parent families, 255–256
- social cognitive theory of gender, 244
- social influences on gender, 243, 247
- social play, 263
- socioeconomic variations in families, 257–259
- solitary play, 261
- teacher influences on gender, 245
- television, 264–267
- timetable of emotion language and understanding, 239–240
- types of play, 262–263, 267
- unoccupied play, 261
- working parents, 254–256, 259

Easy child, 182
Eating
- early adulthood physical and cognitive development, 417–420, 423
- early childhood physical development, 209, 211
- infant physical development, 134–135, 138

Eating disorders, 363
Echoing, 173
Eclectic theoretical orientation, 45–47
Ecological theory of development, 43–44, 46–47
Ecological view of sensory and perceptual development, 145–146, 153
Education
- early childhood cognitive development, 226–233
- late adulthood cognitive development, 555–556, 559
- middle and late childhood cognitive development, 285–286, 303–305
- middle and late childhood socioemotional development, 324–325
- perspectives in life-span development, 11–12

Education for the disabled, 280–283
Egocentrism
adolescent physical and cognitive development, 367–368, 370
early childhood cognitive development, 212–213
Ego transcendence *versus* ego preoccupation, 576
Elder abuse, 567–568, 571
Eldercare, 584
Elementary schools, 334–335, 341
Embryonic period, 94–96, 99
Emotional intelligence, 313–315
Emotions
adolescent socioemotional development, 395
early adulthood socioemotional development, 462–463, 465
early childhood socioeconomic development, 238–247
infant socioemotional development, 178–181
middle and late childhood socioemotional development, 313–315
postpartum period, 116–119
prenatal development, 105
Empty nest syndrome, 515–516, 519
Energy needs in early childhood physical development, 209, 211
Environment
early adulthood physical and cognitive development, 418
hazards in prenatal development, 102–103, 107
influences on language in infant cognitive development, 171–173
Epidural block, 110
Episodic memory, 553
Erikson
adolescent socioemotional development, 382
childhood of, 29
early adulthood socioemotional development, 450
late adulthood socioemotional development, 576–577, 582
middle adulthood socioemotional development, 502–503, 510
theories of development, 33–34, 39, 45
Erogenous zones, 32
Ethnic identity, 385, 387
Ethnicity
adolescent socioemotional development, 385–386, 396–399, 401
early childhood socioeconomic development, 257–259
late adulthood socioemotional development, 590–591, 595
middle and late childhood cognitive development, 295–297
middle and late childhood socioemotional development, 335, 337–341
perspectives in life-span development, 13
Ethological theory of development, 42–43, 45–47
Euthanasia, 603
Evocative genotype-environment correlations, 86, 89
Evolutionary perspective, 66–69
adaptive behavior, 67, 69
Baltes' view, 68
Buss' view, 67, 69
evolutionary psychology, 67–68
natural selection, 66, 69
Evolutionary psychology, 67–68
Evolution of language, 170, 173
Exercise
early adulthood physical and cognitive development, 419–420, 423
late adulthood physical development, 541–542, 547
middle and late childhood physical development, 275, 279
Exosystem, 44
Expanding, 173
Expectations of death, 606–607, 610
Experimental group, 51
Experimental research, 50–51, 54–55
Expertise, 491
Explicit memory, 554
Eyewitness testimony, 221

F

Facial expression of emotions, 179
Facing one's own death, 610–613
Fagan Test of Infant Intelligence, 167–168
Families
adolescent physical and cognitive development, 362–363, 365
adolescent socioemotional development, 384–385, 387–391, 401
early adulthood socioemotional development, 457–464
early childhood socioeconomic development, 247–259
infant socioemotional development, 191–194, 197
late adulthood socioemotional development, 586–589, 591
middle and late childhood socioemotional development, 318, 327–330, 334
Family at midlife, 458
Family in later life, 458
Family leave, 194
Family life cycle, 457, 465
Family with adolescents, 458
Fantz's experiments, 147
Fear, 567–568, 571
Fetal alcohol syndrome, 101
Fetal period, 96, 99, 108–109, 115
Fine motor skills
early childhood physical development, 206–208
infant physical development, 139, 142–143
First habits, 159
First trimester, 97
Fixation, 32
Flo Jo, 413
Fluid intelligence, 488–489
Forcible sexual behavior, 428–430
Formal operational stage, 37
Formal operational thought, 365–367, 370
Fragile X syndrome, 75–77
Free-radical theory, 533–534
Freud
early childhood socioeconomic development, 243–244
theories of development, 31–33, 39, 45
Friendship
adolescent socioemotional development, 392–393
early adulthood socioemotional development, 453–454
late adulthood socioemotional development, 589, 591
middle adulthood socioemotional development, 516, 519
middle and late childhood socioemotional development, 332–334
Funerals, 617–619

G

Games, 263–264
Gamete intrafallopian transfer (GIFT), 80
Gangs, 402–405
Gardner's eight frames of mind, 294, 301
Gay adults, 468–469, 471
Gender
adolescent socioemotional development, 386–387
early adulthood socioemotional development, 462–463, 465, 469–471
early childhood socioeconomic development, 243–247
late adulthood physical development, 527–530
late adulthood socioemotional development, 591–592, 595
middle adulthood socioemotional development, 507–508, 510
middle and late childhood socio-emotional development, 318–327
perspectives in life-span development, 13–14
Gender bias, 36
Gender identity, 243
Gender role, 243
Gender-role transcendence, 325
Gender schema theory, 246
Gender stereotypes, 320, 327
Gene-linked abnormalities, 77–79
Generational inequity
late adulthood socioemotional development, 584
perspectives in life-span development, 14–15
Generativity *versus* stagnation
middle adulthood socioemotional development, 502–503
theories of development, 34
Genes, 69–70
Genetic counselor, 76
Genetic foundations, 69–77, 70
adoption study, 74
behavior genetics, 74, 79
canalization, 74, 79
cells, 70
chromosomes, 69–70, 75–76, 79
DNA, 69–70
dominant-recessive genes principle, 70–72, 79
Down syndrome, 75–76
Fragile X syndrome, 75–77
gene-linked abnormalities, 77–79
genes, 69–70
genotype, 72, 79
Klinefelter syndrome, 75–76
male *versus* female, 73–74
meiosis, 69, 71, 79
mitosis, 69, 71, 79
molecular genetics, 74–75, 79
phenotype, 73, 79
phenylketonuria (PKU), 77–78
principles, 70–72, 79
reaction range, 73, 79
reproduction, 70
sex-linked chromosome abnormalities, 76
Sickle-cell anemia, 77–78
Turner syndrome, 75–76
twin study, 74
XYY syndrome, 75–77
Genital herpes, 426–427
Genital stage, 32–33
Genotype, 72, 79
Geriatric nurse, 544
Germinal period, 94–95, 99
Gibsons' ecological view of sensory and perceptual development, 145–146, 153
Giftedness, 298–299, 301
Gonads, 350
Gonorrhea, 426
Goodness of fit, 182–183, 186
Grammar, 302, 305
Grandparenting, 586–589, 591
Grasping reflex, 139–140
Grief, 613
Grieving, 613–615, 619
Gross motor skills
early childhood physical development, 206, 208
infant physical development, 139–142

H

Habituation, 163–164, 168
Handedness, 207–208
Happiness
and age, 18
middle adulthood physical and cognitive development, 496
Hardiness, 483
Harlow's classic "contact comfort" study, 187
Hawaii Family Support/Healthy Start Program, 137
Hazards to prenatal development, 98–107
Head Start, 231–232
Health
adolescent physical and cognitive development, 364–365
late adulthood cognitive development, 556–557, 559
late adulthood physical development, 538–547
middle adulthood physical and cognitive development, 481, 484, 488, 494–497
middle and late childhood physical development, 276–279
perspectives in life-span development, 11
Health care decisions in death, 602–604, 607
Health psychologist, 402
Hearing
infant physical development, 148–149, 153
late adulthood physical development, 536–537, 539
middle adulthood physical and cognitive development, 481
Height
adolescent physical and cognitive development, 351, 354
early childhood physical development, 204–205, 208
infant physical development, 127, 131
middle adulthood physical and cognitive development, 480
Helson's Mills College study, 512–513
Hemispheres of the brain, 128
Hemophilia, 78
Heredity, 418
Heredity-environment interaction, 83–89
Abecedarian Project, 86
active (niche-picking) genotype-environment correlations, 86–87, 89
bell curve, 84–85
evocative genotype-environment correlations, 86, 89
intelligence, 83–85, 89
Nobel prize sperm bank, 85
nonshared environmental experiences, 87–89
passive genotype-environment correlations, 86, 89
Scarr's view, 85–87, 89
shared environmental experiences, 87, 89
Heroin, 102–103
Herpes, 426–427
Heteronomous morality, 240
Hidden curriculum, 373–375, 377
High school, 415–416, 423
High school counselor/college advisor, 372
High school dropouts, 372–373, 377
Historical perspective
death, 604–605, 607
middle adulthood socioemotional development, 506–507

perspectives in life-span development, 7–8
Holland's personality types, 435–436, 441
Holophrase hypothesis, 170
Homosexuality
early adulthood physical and cognitive development, 424–425, 430
early adulthood socioemotional development, 468–469, 471
Hormonal stress theory, 533–534
Hormone replacement therapy (HRT), 485–486
Hormones
adolescent physical and cognitive development, 350–351, 354
middle adulthood physical and cognitive development, 485–486
Horney's theory of development, 36
Hospice, 604
HPV, 427
Human genome project, 79
Huntington disease, 78
Husbands and death, 616–617, 619
Hypothalamus, 350
Hypotheses, 30
Hypothetical-deductive reasoning, 366

I

Identity, 382–387
Identity achievement, 383
Identity diffusion, 383
Identity foreclosure, 383
Identity [illegible]
Identity *versus* identity confusion, 34
Illegal drugs, 102–103
Illnesses
early childhood physical development, 209–211
middle and late childhood physical development, 276–279
Imaginary audience, 368, 370
Imitation, 164, 168
Imminent justice, 241
Implicit memory, 554
Imprinting, 42
Inclusion, 281
Income in late adulthood, 585, 591
Independence
early adulthood socioemotional development, 451
infant socioemotional development, 184–186
Independent variable, 51
Individual differences
infant socioemotional development, 188–189, 191
in intelligence, 165–168
middle and late childhood cognitive development, 291
Individuality, 384–385
Individualized education plan (IEP), 281, 283
Individuated-connected level, 451
Industry *versus* inferiority, 313, 315
Industry verus inferiority, 34
"Infancy" defined, 17
Infant assessment specialist, 167
Infant cognitive development, 157–175
Bayley Scales of Infant Development, 166–168
behavioral influences on language, 171–173
biological influences on language, 170–171, 173
conceptual development, 161–162
conditioning, 162, 168
coordination of secondary circular reactions, 159
curiosity, 159–160
deferred imitation, 164–165
definition of "language," 169, 173
developmental quotient, 166
development of language, 169–170, 173
dishabituation, 163–164, 168
echoing, 173
environmental influences on language, 171–173
evolution of language, 170, 173
expanding, 173
Fagan Test of Infant Intelligence, 167–168
first habits, 159
habituation, 163–164, 168
holophrase hypothesis, 170
imitation, 164, 168
individual differences in intelligence, 165–168
infant-directed speech, 172
infinite generativity, 169
intelligence, individual differences, 165–168
internalization of schemes, 160
labeling, 173
language acquisition device (LAD), 171
language development, 168–173
learning and remembering, 162–165, 168
memory, 164–165, 168
novelty, 159–160
object performance, 160–161, 163
perceptual development, 161
Piaget, 158–163, 168
prewired language, 171, 173
primary circular reactions, 159
recasting, 172
receptive vocabulary, 169
[illegible]
schemes, 158
secondary circular reactions, 159
sensorimotor development, 158–160, 163
simple reflexes, 159
substages of sensorimotor development, 159–160, 163
telegraph speech, 170
tertiary circular reactions, 159–160
Infant-directed speech, 172
Infant physical development, 125–155
acuity, 146, 153
affordances, 145
Africa, bottle and breast-feeding in, 125–126
Babinski reflex, 140
blinking reflex, 140
bottle feeding, 125–126, 135–136
brain, 127–131
breast-feeding, 125–126, 135–136
cephalocaudal pattern, 126, 131
classification of infant states, 131–132, 138
color, 146, 153
dendritic spreading, 128
depth perception, 147–148, 153
developmental biodynamics, 142–144
early deprivation and brain activity, 130
early experience and the brain, 129
eating, 134–135, 138
ecological view of sensory and perceptual development, 145–146, 153
expectations, visual, 148, 153
Fantz's experiments, 147
fine motor skills, 139, 142–143
Gibsons' ecological view of sensory and perceptual development, 145–146, 153
grasping reflex, 139–140
gross motor skills, 139–142
Hawaii Family Support/Healthy Start Program, 137
hearing, 148–149, 153
height, 127, 131
hemispheres of the brain, 128
intermodal perception, 151–153
kwashiorkor, 136
lateralization, 128
malnutrition, 136, 138
marasmus, 136
measuring the brain's activity in research on infant memory, 129
memory, 129
moro reflex, 139–140
motor development, 138–144
neurons, 127
nutrition, 134–136, 138
pain, 149–150, 153
perception, 145, 153
perceptual-motor coupling and unification, 152–153
preferences, visual, 146, 153
proximodistal pattern, 127, 131
reflexes, 138–139
REM sleep, 131–132, 138
research, 129
rooting reflex, 138–140
sensation, 144–145, 153
sensory and perceptual development, 144–153
shared sleeping, 132–133, 138
sleep, 131–133, 138
smell, 150–151
startle reflex, 139–140
states of infancy, 131–134, 138
stepping reflex, 140
sucking reflex, 138–140
sudden infant death syndrome (SIDS), 133–134, 138
swimming reflex, 140
[illegible]
toilet training, [illegible]
tonic neck reflex, 140
touch, 149–150, 153
visual perception, 146–148, 153
weight, 127, 131
Infant socioemotional development, 177–199
Ainsworth strange situation, 188, 191
anger cry, 180
attachment, 186–191
basic cry, 180
Bowlby's view of attachment, 186–187
caregiving, 189–191, 193–195
child care policy, 194
child rearing leave, 194
classification of attachment, 189–191
classifying temperament, 182
crying, 179–181
day care, 194–197
definition of "attachment," 186–187, 191
definition of "emotion," 178
definition of "temperament," 182
developmental timetable of emotions, 179, 181
difficult child, 182
disorganized babies, 189
easy child, 182
emotional development, 178–181
facial expression of emotions, 179
family, 191–194, 197
family leave, 194
goodness of fit, 182–183, 186
Harlow's classic "contact comfort" study, 187
independence, 184–186
individual differences, 188–189, 191
insecure avoidant babies, 189
insecure resistant babies, 189
Izard's coding system, 179–181
maternal caregiving, 193–194, 197
maternity leave, 194
maximally discriminative facial movement coding system (MAX), 179
NICHD child-care study, 195–197
pain cry, 180
parental leave, 194
parent-child relationships, 178–179, 181, 183–184, 186, 191–194
paternity leave, 194
personality development, 184–186
reciprocal socialization, 192, 197
reflexive smiling, 180
scaffolding, 192
secure attachment, 188
sense of self, 184–186
slow-to-warm-up child, 182
smiling, 180–181
social contexts, 191–197
social smile, 180
stranger anxiety, 180–181
strange situation, 188
temperament, 182–184, 186, 190–191
transition to parenthood, 191–192
trust, 184, 186
Infectious diseases, 103–104
Infertility, 79–83
Infinite generativity, 169
Information processing
adolescent physical and cognitive development, 368–370
early childhood cognitive development, 220–224
middle adulthood physical and cognitive development, 490–492
middle and late childhood cognitive development, 288–290
Information-processing approach, 38–39
Initiative *versus* guilt
early childhood socioeconomic development, 238, 240
theories of development, 34
Injuries, 276, 279
Innate goodness view, 7–8
Insecure avoidant babies, 189
Insecure resistant babies, 189
Integrity, 577
Integrity *versus* despair
late adulthood socioemotional development, 576–577, 582
theories of development, 34
Intelligence
heredity-environment interaction, 83–85, 89
individual differences, 165–168
middle adulthood physical and cognitive development, 487–490
middle and late childhood cognitive development, 290–299, 301
Intelligence quotient (IQ), 291–292
Intergenerational relationships in middle adulthood socioemotional development, 517–519
Intermodal perception, 151–153
Internalization, 316
Internalization of schemes, 160
Interviews
early adulthood physical and cognitive development, 438–439, 441
research methods, 49, 54–55
Intimacy
early adulthood socioemotional development, 450–451
middle and late childhood socioemotional development, 333
Intimacy *versus* isolation, 34
Intracytoplasmic sperm injection (ICSI), 81
Intrauterine insemination (IUI), 80
Intuitive thought substage, 214–215, 224
In vitro fertilization (IVF), 80
Izard's coding system, 179–181

J

Job interviews, 438–439, 441
Job satisfaction, 492, 497
Jogging hog experiment, 543
Joints, 480
Journals, research, 54–57, 59
Junior high school, 369–371, 377
Justice perspective, 318
Juvenile delinquency, 399–405, 407

K

Kaczynski, Ted, 5
Kindergarten, 226, 230, 233
Klinefelter syndrome, 75–76
Kohlberg's theory of moral development, 315–320, 327
Kübler-Ross' stages of dying, 610–612
Kwashiorkor, 136

L

Labeling, 173
Laboratory as research method, 48
Lamaze, 110
Language acquisition device (LAD), 171
Language and thought, 217, 224
Language development
  early childhood cognitive development, 225–226, 233
  infant cognitive development, 168–173
  middle and late childhood cognitive development, 302–305
Latchkey children, 329–330
Late adulthood cognitive development, 551–573
  Alzheimer's disease, 564–566, 571
  cognitive mechanics, 552, 559
  cognitive pragmatics, 552, 559
  crime, fears of, 567–568, 571
  culture, 561
  dementia, 563–564, 567, 571
  depression, 562–563, 571
  education, 555–556, 559
  elder maltreatment, 567–568, 571
  episodic memory, 553
  explicit memory, 554
  fear, 567–568, 571
  health, 556–557, 559
  implicit memory, 554
  major depression, 562–563
  maltreatment, 567–568
  memory, 552–555, 559
  memory beliefs, 554
  mental health, 562–569, 571
  mnemonics, 557
  multidimensional and multidirectional nature, 552–555, 559
  multi-infarct dementia, 567
  nuns, 551
  Parkinson's disease, 567
  religion, 569–571
  retirement, 558–562
  semantic memory, 553
  sensory/motor and speed-of-processing dimensions, 552, 559
  terminal drop hypothesis, 557
  training cognitive skills, 557, 559
  use it or lose it, 557, 559
  victimization fears, 567–568, 571
  wisdom, 555, 559
  work, 556, 558–562
  working memory, 553–554
"Late adulthood" defined, 17
Late adulthood physical development, 525–549
  accidents, 541, 547
  age, 526–534
  arthritis, 539, 547
  biological theories of aging, 532–534
  brain, 534–535, 539
  care options, 544, 547
  care providers, 546–547
  cellular clock theory, 532, 534
  centenarians, 526–530
  chromosomes, 532
  circulatory system, 537, 539
  control, 545–547
  coping, 545–547
  course of physical development, 533–538
  culture, 529
  death, 538–539, 547
  exercise, 541–542, 547
  free-radical theory, 533–534
  gender, 527–530
  health, 538–547
  hearing, 536–537, 539
  hormonal stress theory, 533–534
  jogging hog experiment, 543
  learning to age successfully, 525–526
  life expectancy, 526–530, 534
  life span, 526–530, 534
  longevity, 526–534
  Mankato nuns, 535
  nutrition, 543, 547
  osteoporosis, 540–541, 547
  pain, 537, 539
  physical appearance, 535, 539
  prevalent chronic conditions, 540
  respiratory system, 537, 539
  sensory development, 535–537, 539
  sex differences in longevity, 527–530
  sexuality, 537–539
  smell, 536, 539
  taste, 536, 539
  telomeres, 532
  touch, 536–537, 539
  vision, 535–537, 539
  vitamins, 543–544, 547
  weight, 543, 547
Late adulthood socioemotional development, 575–597
  activity theory, 578, 582
  ageism, 582
  Baltes' theory, 580–582
  body transcendence *versus* body preoccupation, 576
  Carstenen's theory, 578–580, 582
  Cousey, Bob, 575
  culture, 592–595
  differentiation *versus* role preoccupation, 576
  disengagement theory, 578, 582
  ego transcendence *versus* ego preoccupation, 576
  eldercare, 584
  Erikson, 576–577, 582
  ethnicity, 590–591, 595
  families, 586–589, 591
  friendship, 589, 591
  gender, 591–592, 595
  generational inequity, 584
  grandparenting, 586–589, 591
  income, 585, 591
  integrity, 577
  integrity *versus* despair, 576–577, 582
  life review, 576–577, 582
  living arrangements, 585, 591
  older adults in society, 582–585, 591
  Peck's reworking of Erikson's final stage, 576, 582
  personal life investment, 581
  policy issues in an aging society, 583–584, 591
  relationships, 586–589, 591
  selective optimization with compensation theory, 580–582
  sexism, 592
  social integration, 589–591
  social relationships, 586–589, 591
  social support, 589–591
  socioemotional selectivity theory, 578–580, 582
  stereotypes, 582–583, 591
  successful aging, 594–595
  theories, 576–582
  wisdom, 577
Latency stage, 32
Lateralization, 128
Launching, 458
Learning and remembering, 162–165, 168
Learning disabilities, 278–279, 281, 283
Learning disabilities specialist, 282
Learning to age successfully, 525–526
Least restrictive environment (LRE), 281, 283
Leisure in middle adulthood physical and cognitive development, 493–494, 497
Lesbian adults, 468–469, 471
Life-events approach, 505–506, 510
Life expectancy, 526–530, 534
Life history records, 49, 54–55
Life partners, death of, 616–617, 619
Life-process model of addiction, 422
Life review, 576–577, 582
Life span, 526–530, 534
Living arrangements of late adulthood, 585, 591
Loneliness, 454–456
Longevity, 526–534
Longitudinal approach to research, 52, 54–55
Longitudinal studies
  middle adulthood physical and cognitive development, 489–490
  middle adulthood socioemotional development, 510–513
Long-term memory
  early childhood cognitive development, 221
  middle and late childhood cognitive development, 288
Lorenz's ecological theory, 43–44, 46–47
Love
  early adulthood socioemotional development, 450–454, 456
  middle adulthood socioemotional development, 513–514, 519
Low-birthweight infants, 111–113, 115

M

Macrosystem, 44
Mainstreaming, 281
Major depression, 562–563
Malnutrition, 136, 138
Maltreatment of older adults, 567–568
Mankato nuns, 535
Marasmus, 136
Marcia's four statuses of identity, 383–384, 387
Marijuana, 102
Marital trends, 458–459
Marriage
  early adulthood socioemotional development, 457–465
  middle adulthood socioemotional development, 514–515, 519
Maternal age in prenatal development, 105–106
Maternal blood tests, 78
Maternal caregiving, 193–194, 197
Maternity leave, 194
Maximally discriminative facial movement coding system (MAX), 179
Meaning in life for middle adulthood physical and cognitive development, 496–497
Meiosis, 69, 71, 79
Memory
  early childhood cognitive development, 220–221, 224
  infant cognitive development, 164–165, 168
  infant physical development, 129
  late adulthood cognitive development, 552–555, 559
  middle adulthood physical and cognitive development, 490
  middle and late childhood cognitive development, 288, 290
Memory beliefs, 554
Menarche, 349
Menopause, 484–485
Mental age (MA), 291
Mental health, 562–569, 571
Mental retardation, 297–298, 301
Mesosystem, 43
Metacognition, 289–290
Methods of delivery, 109–111
"Middle adulthood" defined, 17
Middle adulthood physical and cognitive development, 477–499
  bones, 480
  cardiovascular system, 481–482
  careers, 492–493, 497
  changing middle age, 478–479, 488
  chronic disorders, 481
  climacteric, 484
  coping, 495–496
  crystallized intelligence, 488–489
  culture, 482–484, 488
  death, 484, 488
  definition of "middle adulthood," 478
  disease, 481–482, 488
  expertise, 491
  fluid intelligence, 488–489
  happiness, 496
  hardiness, 483
  health, 481, 484, 488, 494–497
  hearing, 481
  height, 480
  hormone replacement therapy (HRT), 485–486
  hormones, 485–486
  information processing, 490–492
  intelligence, 487–490
  job satisfaction, 492, 497
  joints, 480
  leisure, 493–494, 497
  longitudinal study, 489–490
  meaning in life, 496–497
  memory, 490
  menopause, 484–485
  mortality rates, 484, 488
  personality, 482–484, 488
  physical changes, 479–481, 488
  practical problem solving, 491–492
  relationships, 484, 488
  religion, 494–497
  Seattle Longitudinal Study, 489–490
  sex survey in America, 487
  sexuality, 484–488
  sleep, 481
  social relationships, 484, 488
  speed of information processing, 490
  strength, 480
  type a behavior pattern, 482–483
  type b behavior pattern, 482–483
  vision, 480–481
  weight, 480
  work, 492–493, 497
Middle adulthood socioemotional development, 501–521
  adult stage theories, 502–505, 510
  affectionate love, 513–514, 519
  Berkeley Longitudinal Studies, 511, 513
  big five factors of personality, 511
  close relationships, 513–521
  cohort effects, 506–507
  contemporary life-events approach, 505–506
  contexts of midlife development, 506–510
  Costa and McCrae's Baltimore Study, 511, 513
  culture, 508–510, 518
  daily hassles of middle-aged adults, 506
  daily uplifts of middle-aged adults, 506
  divorce, 514–515
  empty nest syndrome, 515–516, 519
  Erikson, 502–503, 510
  friendships, 516, 519
  gender, 507–508, 510
  generativity *versus* stagnation, 502–503
  Helson's Mills College study, 512–513
  historical contexts, 506–507
  individual conceptions of the right age for major life events, 507
  individual variations, 505, 510
  intergenerational relationships, 517–519
  Levinson's seasons of a man's life, 503, 510
  life-events approach, 505–506, 510
  longitudinal studies, 510–513
  love, 513–514, 519

marriage, 514–515, 519
midlife crises, 504–505, 510
Neugarten's Kansas City Study, 510–511, 513
parenting conceptions, 516, 519
personality, 502–509, 511
relationships, 513–521
sibling relationships, 516, 519
social clock, 507
stability and change, 509–513
Middle and late childhood cognitive development, 273–274, 283–307
bilingualism, 303–305
Binet tests, 291–292, 301
brainstorming, 300–301
concrete operational thought, 283–288, 290
control processes, 288
convergent thinking, 299
creativity, 299–301
critical thinking, 288–290
cultural-familial retardation, 298
culture, 295–297
culture-fair tests, 296
divergent thinking, 299
education, 285–286, 303–305
ethnicity, 295–297
Gardner's eight frames of mind, 294, 301
giftedness, 298–299, 301
grammar, 302, 305
individual differences, 291
information processing, 288–290
intelligence, 290–299, 301
intelligence quotient (IQ), 291, [illegible]
language development, 302–305
long-term memory, 288
memory, 288, 290
mental age (MA), 291
mental retardation, 297–298, 301
metacognition, 289–290
neo-Piagetians, 287–288
normal distribution, 291
organic retardation, 298
Piaget, 283–288, 290
Raven Progressive Matrices Test, 297
reading, 302–303, 305
seriation, 284
Stanford-Binet scores, 291–292, 301
Sternberg's triarchic theory, 293–294, 301
transitivity, 284–285
triarchic theory of intelligence, 293–294, 301
types of intelligence, 292–293, 301
vocabulary, 302, 305
Wechsler scales, 292–293, 301
"Middle and late childhood" defined, 17
Middle and late childhood physical development, 273–283, 306–307
accidents, 276, 279
attention deficit hyperactivity disorder (ADHD), 279–281, 283
body growth, 274, 276–277, 279
cancer, 277–279
culture, 282
disabled children, 278–283
disease, 276–279
dyslexia, 278
education for the disabled, 280–283
exercise, 275, 279
health, 276–279
illnesses, 276–279
inclusion, 281
individualized education plan (IEP), 281, 283
injuries, 276, 279
learning disabilities, 278–279, 281, 283
least restrictive environment (LRE), 281, 283
mainstreaming, 281
motor development, 274–275, 279
obesity, 276–277, 279
proportion, 274, 279
sports, 275–276, 279
Middle and late childhood socioemotional development, 309–343
altruism, 319–320, 327
androgyny, 324
Bem Sex-Role Inventory, 325
bullying, 331–332, 334
care perspective, 319
conventional reasoning, 317
culture, 318, 325–326
education, 324–325
elementary schools, 334–335, 341
emotional development, 313–315
emotional intelligence, 313–315
ethnicity, 335, 337–341
families, 318, 327–330, 334
friends, 332–334
gender, 318–327
gender-role transcendence, 325
gender stereotypes, 320, 327
industry *versus* inferiority, 313, 315
internalization, 316
intimacy in friendships, 333
justice perspective, 318
Kohlberg's theory of moral development, 315–320, 327
latchkey children, 329–330
moral development, 314–320, 327
peers, 330–331, 334
postconventional reasoning, 317
preconventional reasoning, 316
prosocial behavior, 319–320, 327
schools, 334–341
self, 310–313, 315
self-concept, 311, 315
self-esteem, 311, 315
self-understanding, 310–311, 315
social cognition, 332, 334
socioeconomic status, 335–337, 341
stepfamilies, 329
teaching, 321
Middle school, 369–371, 377
Midlife crises, 504–505, 510
Midwifery, 109
Mitosis, 69, 71, 79
Mnemonics, 557
Molecular genetics, 74–75, 79
Montessori approach, 226–227, 233
Moral behavior, 241–242, 247
Moral development
early childhood socioeconomic development, 240–242, 247
middle and late childhood socioemotional development, 314–320, 327
Moral education, 373–377
Moral feelings, 242, 247
Moro reflex, 139–140
Morphological rules, 225–226
Mortality rates, 484, 488
Motor development
early childhood physical development, 206–208
infant physical development, 138–144
middle and late childhood physical development, 274–275, 279
Mourning, 617–619
Multidimensional and multidirectional nature in late adulthood cognitive development, 552–555, 559
Multi-infarct dementia, 567
Myelination, 205

N

Natural childbirth, 110
Naturalistic observation in research, 48
Natural selection, 66, 69
Nature and nurture, 252, 259
Nature of development, 16–22, 25
Neglectful parenting, 249–250
Neonatal health and responsiveness measures, 113, 115
Neo-Piagetians, 287–288
Neugarten's Kansas City Study, 510–511, 513
Neurons, 127
New couple, 458
NICHD child-care study, 195–197
Nicotine, 101
Nobel prize sperm bank, 85
Nonprescription drugs, 99–100, 107
Nonshared environmental experiences, 87–89
Normal distribution, 291
Novelty, 159–160
Nuns
late adulthood cognitive development, 551
late adulthood physical development, 535
Nutrition
early childhood physical development, 208–209, 211
infant physical development, 134–136, 138
late adulthood physical development, 543, 547
prenatal development, 104–105

O

Obesity, 276–277, 279, 417–418
Object performance, 160–161, 163
Observational learning, 41, 45
Observation in research, 48, 54–55
Occupational outlook, 436, 441
Oedipus complex, 32
Onlooker play, 261
Operant conditioning
theories of development, 40, 45, 47
Operations in early childhood cognitive development, 212
Oral rehydration therapy (ORT), 210
Oral stage, 32
Organic retardation, 298
Organogenesis, 96
Original sin view, 7–8
Osteoporosis, 540–541, 547
Oxytocics, 110

P

Pain
infant physical development, 149–150, 153
late adulthood physical development, 537, 539
Pain cry, 180
Parallel play, 261–262
Parent-adolescent conflict, 388–391
Parental influences on gender, 244
Parental leave, 194
Parental roles in early adulthood socioemotional development, 463–465
Parent-child relationships, 178–179, 181, 183–184, 186, 191–194
Parenting
early childhood socioeconomic development, 248–256, 259
middle adulthood socioemotional development, 516, 519
perspectives in life-span development, 11–12
Parenting styles, 248–250, 259
Parkinson's disease, 567
Parten's classic study of play, 261–262, 267
Passive euthanasia, 603
Passive genotype-environment correlations, 86, 89
Paternal factors in prenatal development, 106–107
Paternity leave, 194
Pavlov's classical conditioning, 40, 45, 47
Peck's reworking of Erikson's final stage, 576, 582
Pediatrician, 134
Pediatric nurse, 210
Peers
adolescent physical and cognitive development, 362–363, 365
adolescent socioemotional development, 391–392, 391–395, 401
early childhood socioeconomic development, 244–245, 259–260, 267
middle and late childhood socioemotional development, 330–331, 334
Perception, 145, 153
Perceptual development, 161
Perceptual-motor coupling and unification, 152–153
Perinatal nurse, 109
Periods of development, 16–18
Personal fable, 368, 370
Personality
middle adulthood physical and cognitive development, 482–484, 488
middle adulthood socioemotional development, 502–509, 511
Personality development
early childhood socioeconomic development, 238–247
infant socioemotional development, 184–186
Personality type theory, 435–436, 441
Perspectives in life-span development
adolescence, 17
age and happiness, 18
biological age, 18
biological processes, 16
careers in life-span development, 9, 11, 22–25
characteristics, 9–10
child development, 7–8
chronological age, 18
cognitive processes, 16
conceptions of age, 18
contemporary concerns, 11–15
context, 12
continuity-discontinuity issue, 20
cross-cultural studies, 12–13
culture, 12
developmental issues, 19–22
development involves growth, maintenance and regulation, 10
development is contextual, 10
development is lifelong, 9
development is multidimensional, 9
development is multidirectional, 9
development is plastic, 9
development is studied by a number of disciplines, 10
early adulthood, 17
early childhood, 17
education, 11–12
ethnicity, 13
gender, 13–14
generational inequity, 14–15
health and well-being, 11
historical perspective, 7–8
infancy, 17
innate goodness view, 7–8
late adulthood, 17
middle adulthood, 17
nature-nurture issue, 19–20
nature of development, 16–22, 25
original sin view, 7–8
parenting, 11–12
periods of development, 16–18
prenatal period, 17
psychological age, 19
science of life span development, 29–61
social age, 19
social policy, 13–15
sociocultural contexts, 12–13
socioeconomic processes, 16
stability-change issue, 20
tabula rasa view, 7–8
traditional v. life span view, 8
twentieth century, 8
why study life-span development, 6–7

Phallic stage, 32
Phenotype, 73, 79
Phenylketonuria (PKU), 77–78
Physical adjustments, 116, 119
Physical appearance, 535, 539
Physical changes, 479–481, 488
Physical development
adolescence. *See* Adolescent physical and cognitive development
early adulthood. *See* Early adulthood physical and cognitive development
early childhood. *See* Early childhood physical development
infants. *See* Infant physical development
late adulthood. *See* Late adulthood physical development
middle adulthood. *See* Middle adulthood physical and cognitive development
middle and late childhood. *See* Middle and late childhood physical development
Physiological research, 50, 54–55
Piaget, 30
adolescent physical and cognitive development, 365–367, 370
early adulthood physical and cognitive development, 430–431, 434
early childhood cognitive development, 212–215, 217–220, 224
early childhood socioeconomic development, 240–241, 247
infant cognitive development, 158–163, 168
middle and late childhood cognitive development, 283–288, 290
theories of development, 35–37, 39
Pituitary gland, 350
Placenta, 95–96
Play, 260–264, 267
Pluralism, 399
Policy issues in an aging society, 583–584, 591
Postconventional reasoning, 317
Postformal thought, 431
Postpartum expert, 117
Postpartum period, 115–120
bonding, 116, 118–119
defined, 115–116, 119
emotional adjustments, 116–119
physical adjustments, 116, 119
psychological adjustments, 116–119
Practical problem solving, 491–492
Practice play, 262
Pragmatic thinking, 431, 434
Preconventional reasoning, 316
Pregnancy, 358–360
Prenatal care, 106–107
Prenatal development, 94–107, 120
age of mother, 105–106
AIDS, 104
alcohol, 101
amnion, 95
blastocyst, 94
course of prenatal development, 94–99
culture, 98–99
diseases, 103–104
drugs, 99–103, 107
embryonic period, 94–96, 99
emotional state, 105
environmental hazards, 102–103, 107
fetal alcohol syndrome, 101
fetal period, 96, 99, 108–109, 115
first trimester, 97
germinal period, 94–95, 99
hazards to prenatal development, 98–107
heroin, 102–103
illegal drugs, 102–103
infectious diseases, 103–104
marijuana, 102
maternal age, 105–106
nicotine, 101
nonprescription drugs, 99–100, 107
nutrition, 104–105
organogenesis, 96
paternal factors, 106–107
placenta, 95–96
positive prenatal development, 107
prescription drugs, 99–100, 107
psychoactive drugs, 101, 107
second trimester, 97
smoking, 101–102
stress, 105
teratology, 98–107
third trimester, 97
trophoblast, 94
umbilical cord, 95–96
Prenatal diagnostic tests, 77–79, 83
Prenatal period, 17
Preoperational stage, 37
Preoperational stage of development, 212–216
Prepared childbirth, 110
Preschool, 230–231, 233
Prescription drugs, 99–100, 107
Pretense/symbolic play, 262–263
Preterm infants, 111, 115
Prevention/intervention programs, 406–407
Prewired language, 171, 173
Primary circular reactions, 159
Princess Diana, 601
Problems, causes and treatments, 81
Professor of human development, 9, 557
Professor of psychology and life-span development, 517
Project Follow Through, 231–232
Project Head Start, 231–232
Proportion, 274, 279
Prosocial behavior
middle and late childhood socioemotional development, 319–320, 327
television, 265–267
Proximodistal pattern, 127, 131
Psychoactive drugs, 101, 107
Psychoanalytic theories, 31–35, 39, 46
Psychoanalytic theory of gender, 243–244
Psychological adjustments in postpartum period, 116–119
Psychological age, 19
Psychological stages, 33
Psychologist, 223
Psychology professor, 580
Psychosexual stages, 33
Puberty, 349–354

Q

Questionnaires in research, 49

R

Random assignment, 51
Rape, 429–430
Raven Progressive Matrices Test, 297
Reaction range, 73, 79
Reading in middle and late childhood cognitive development, 302–303, 305
Realistic and pragmatic thinking, 431, 434
Recasting, 172
Receptive vocabulary, 169
Reciprocal socialization, 192, 197
Records of life history, 49, 54–55
Reflective and relativistic thinking, 431, 434
Reflexes, 138–139
Reflexes, simple, 159
Reflexive smiling, 180
Relationships
late adulthood socioemotional development, 586–589, 591
middle adulthood physical and cognitive development, 484, 488
middle adulthood socioemotional development, 513–521
Relativistic thinking, 431, 434
Religion
late adulthood cognitive development, 569–571
middle adulthood physical and cognitive development, 494–497
Remarried adults, 467–468, 471
REM sleep, 131–132, 138
Reproduction, 77–83
adoption, 82–83
amniocentesis, 77, 80
blood tests, 78
chorionic villi sampling, 78, 80
gamete intrafallopian transfer (GIFT), 80
infertility, 79–83
intracytoplasmic sperm injection (ICSI), 81
intrauterine insemination (IUI), 80
maternal blood tests, 78
ultrasound sonography, 77
in vitro fertilization (IVF), 80
zygote intrafallopian transfer (ZIFT), 81
Research challenges, 57–59
culture, 58–59
ethics, 57, 59
ethnicity, 58–59
gender, 58–59
Researcher, 517, 557
Research in infant physical development, 129
Research journals, 54–57, 59
Research methods, 48–57
animal research, 50, 54–55
case studies, 49, 54–55
cohort effects, 52–54
control group, 51
correlational research, 50, 54–55
cross-sectional approach, 51–52, 54
dependent variable, 51
experimental group, 51
experimental research, 50–51, 54–55
independent variable, 51
interviews, 49, 54–55
laboratory, 48
life history records, 49, 54–55
longitudinal approach, 52, 54–55
naturalistic observation, 48
observation, 48, 54–55
physiological research, 50, 54–55
principles of the experimental strategy, 51
questionnaires, 49
random assignment, 51
records of life history, 49, 54–55
sequential approach, 52, 54–55
standardized tests, 49, 54–55
surveys, 49, 54–55
tests, standardized, 49, 54–55
time span of research, 51, 54–55
Respiratory system, 537, 539
Restrained eating, 419
Retirement, 558–562
Rites of passage, 395–396, 401
Role-focused level, 451
Romantic love, 451–452
Romantic relationships, 393–395, 401
Rooting reflex, 138–140

S

Scaffolding
early childhood cognitive development, 216–217, 224
infant socioemotional development, 192
Scarr's view, 85–87, 89
Scheme, 158
School influences on gender, 245
School psychologist, 335
Schools
adolescent physical and cognitive development, 369–377
middle and late childhood socioemotional development, 334–341
Science of life span development, 29–61
research challenges, 48–59
research methods, 48–57
theories of development, 30–47
Seattle Longitudinal Study, 489–490
Secondary circular reactions, 159
Second trimester, 97
Secure attachment, 188
Selective optimization with compensation theory, 580–582
Self
early childhood socioeconomic development, 238–240
middle and late childhood socioemotional development, 310–313, 315
Self, sense of, 184–186
Self-concept, 311, 315
Self-esteem, 311, 315
Self-focused level, 450–451
Self-understanding
early childhood socioeconomic development, 238–240
middle and late childhood socioemotional development, 310–311, 315
Semantic memory, 553
Sensation, 144–145, 153
Sensorimotor development, 158–160, 163
Sensorimotor play, 262
Sensorimotor stage, 36
Sensory and perceptual development
infant physical development, 144–153
late adulthood physical development, 535–537, 539
Sensory/motor and speed-of-processing dimensions, 552, 559
Sequential approach in research, 52, 54–55
Seriation, 284
Service learning, 376–377
Setting for birth, 109
Sex differences in longevity, 527–530
Sex in America survey
early adulthood physical and cognitive development, 424
middle adulthood physical and cognitive development, 487
Sexism, 592
Sex-linked chromosome abnormalities, 76
Sexual harassment, 428–430
Sexual identity, 355, 360
Sexuality
adolescent physical and cognitive development, 354–359
early adulthood physical and cognitive development, 424–430
late adulthood physical development, 537–539
middle adulthood physical and cognitive development, 484–488
Sexually transmitted diseases (STDs)
adolescent physical and cognitive development, 357, 360
early adulthood physical and cognitive development, 426–428, 430
Sexual maturation, 351–352, 354
Sexual orientation, 424–425, 430
Shared environmental experiences, 87, 89
Shared sleeping, 132–133, 138
Short-term memory, 220–221
Sibling relationships
early childhood socioeconomic development, 253, 259
middle adulthood socioemotional development, 516, 519
Sickle-cell anemia, 77–78
Simple reflexes, 159
Single adults, 464–466, 471
Single-parent families, 255–256
Skills employers want, 437, 441
Skinner's operant conditioning, 40, 45, 47

Sleep
infant physical development, 131–133, 138
middle adulthood physical and cognitive development, 481
Slow-to-warm-up child, 182
Smell, 536, 539
Smiling, 180–181
Smoking
adolescent physical and cognitive development, 362, 365
early adulthood physical and cognitive development, 421–422
prenatal development, 101–102
Social age, 19
Social cognition, 332, 334
Social cognitive theory, 40–41, 45–47
Social cognitive theory of gender, 244
Social constructivist approach, 218
Social contexts, 191–197
Social influences on gender, 243, 247
Social integration, 589–591
Social play, 263
Social policy in life-span development, 13–15
Social relationships
late adulthood socioemotional development, 586–589, 591
middle adulthood physical and cognitive development, 484, 488
Social smile, 180
Social support, 589–591
Social worker, 251
Sociocultural contexts in life-span development, 12–13
Socioeconomic processes, 16
Socioeconomic status
adolescent socioemotional development, 397–398
middle and late childhood socioemotional development, 335–337, 341
Socioeconomic variations in families, 257–259
Socioemotional development
adolescents. *See* Adolescent socioemotional development
early adulthood. *See* Early adulthood socioemotional development
early childhood. *See* Early childhood socioemotional development
infants. *See* Infant socioemotional development
late adulthood. *See* Late adulthood socioemotional development
middle adulthood. *See* Middle adulthood socioemotional development
middle and late childhood. *See* Middle and late childhood socioemotional development
Socioemotional selectivity theory, 578–580, 582
Solitary play, 261
Speed of information processing, 490
Spina bifida, 78
Sports, 275–276, 279
Spouses, death of, 616–617, 619
Stability and change in middle adulthood socioemotional development, 509–513
Stages of birth, 108, 115
Standardized tests, 49, 54–55
Stanford-Binet scores, 291–292, 301
Startle reflex, 139–140
Stepfamilies, 329
Stepping reflex, 140
Stereotypes of older adults, 582–583, 591
Sternberg's triarchic theory, 293–294, 301
Stranger anxiety, 180–181
Strange situation, 188
Strategies
birth, 109–111, 115
early childhood cognitive development, 221–222, 224
Strength in middle adulthood physical and cognitive development, 480
Stress, 105
Substages of sensorimotor development, 159–160, 163
Substance abuse
adolescent physical and cognitive development, 359–363, 365
early adulthood physical and cognitive development, 420–423
Successful aging, 594–595
Sucking reflex, 138–140
Sudden infant death syndrome (SIDS), 133–134, 138
Suicide, 405–407
Superego, 31
Supervisor of gifted and talented education, 299
Surveys in research, 49, 54–55
Swimming reflex, 140
Symbolic drawings, 213
Symbolic function stage, 212–213, 224
Syphilis, 426

T

Tabula rasa view, 7–8
Taste
infant physical development, 151
late adulthood physical development, 536, 539
Tay-Sachs disease, 78
Teacher influences on gender, 245
Teaching
early childhood cognitive development, 218, 224, 228–229
middle and late childhood socioemotional development, 321
Telegraph speech, 170
Television, 264–267
Telomeres, 532
Temperament
early adulthood socioemotional development, 446–447, 456
infant socioemotional development, 182–184, 186, 190–191
Teratology, 98–107
Terminal drop hypothesis, 557
Tertiary circular reactions, 159–160
Tests, standardized, 49, 54–55
Theories of development
accommodation, 35
anal stage, 32
assimilation, 35
autonomy *versus* shame and doubt, 33
Bandura's observational learning, 41, 45
behavioral and social cognitive theories, 40–41, 45–47
Bronfenbrenner's ecological theory of development, 43–44, 47
chronosystem, 44
classical conditioning, 40, 45, 47
cognitive social theory, 40–41, 45–47
cognitive theories, 35–40, 46
concrete operational stage, 37
critical period, 42
cross-cultural studies, 44
culture bias, 36
definition of "hypotheses," 30
definition of "theory," 30
eclectic theoretical orientation, 45–47
ecological theory, 43–44, 46–47
Erikson, 33–34, 39, 45
erogenous zones, 32
ethological theory, 42–43, 45–47
exosystem, 44
fixation, 32
formal operational stage, 37
Freud's theory, 31–33, 39, 45
gender bias, 36
generativity *versus* stagnation, 34
genital stage, 32–33
Horney, 36
hypotheses, 30
identity *versus* identity confusion, 34
imprinting, 42
industry verus inferiority, 34
information-processing approach, 38–39
initiative *versus* guilt, 34
integrity *versus* despair, 34
intimacy *versus* isolation, 34
latency stage, 32
Lorenz's ecological theory, 43–44, 46–47
macrosystem, 44
mesosystem, 43
observational learning, 41, 45
Oedipus complex, 32
operant conditioning, 40, 45, 47
oral stage, 32
Pavlov's classical conditioning, 40, 45, 47
phallic stage, 32
Piaget, 35–37, 39
preoperational stage, 37
psychoanalytic theories, 31–35, 39, 46
psychological stages, 33
psychosexual stages, 33
sensorimotor stage, 36
Skinner's operant conditioning, 40, 45, 47
social cognitive theory, 40–41, 45–47
superego, 31
trusts *versus* mistrusts, 33
Vygotsky's theory, 37–39, 45
Theory of mind, 222–224
Third trimester, 97
Three mountains task, 213
Time span of research, 51, 54–55
Toilet training, 136–138
Tonic neck reflex, 140
Top-dog phenomenon, 371, 377
Touch
infant physical development, 149–150, 153
late adulthood physical development, 536–537, 539
Toy designer, 223
Toy-retrieval task, 222
Training cognitive skills, 557, 559
Transition to parenthood, 191–192
Transitivity, 284–285
Triangle theory of love, 452
Triarchic theory of intelligence, 293–294, 301
Trophoblast, 94
Trust, 184, 186
Trusts *versus* mistrusts, 33
Turner syndrome, 75–76
Twins, 65–66
Twin study, 74
Type a behavior pattern, 482–483
Type b behavior pattern, 482–483

U

Ultrasound sonography, 77
Umbilical cord, 95–96
United States and early childhood physical development, 209–211
University professor and researcher, 433
Unoccupied play, 261
Use it or lose it, 557, 559

V

Value conflicts, 399
Values, 436, 441
Values clarification, 375–377
Victimization fears of older adults, 567–568, 571
Vision
late adulthood physical development, 535–537, 539
middle adulthood physical and cognitive development, 480–481
Visual perception, 146–148, 153
Vitamins, 543–544, 547
Vocabulary, 302, 305
Vygotsky's view, 37–39
early childhood cognitive development, 216–220, 224
time line, 45

W

Walker, Alice, 6
Wechsler scales, 292–293, 301
Weight
adolescent physical and cognitive development, 351, 354
early adulthood physical and cognitive development, 417–420, 423
early childhood physical development, 204–205, 208
infant physical development, 127, 131
late adulthood physical development, 543, 547
middle adulthood physical and cognitive development, 480
Wisdom
late adulthood cognitive development, 555, 559
late adulthood socioemotional development, 577
Wives, death of, 616–617, 619
Work
early adulthood physical and cognitive development, 438–441
late adulthood cognitive development, 556, 558–562
middle adulthood physical and cognitive development, 492–493, 497
Working memory, 553–554
Working parents, 254–256, 259

X

XYY syndrome, 75–77

Y

Youth violence, 402–405

Z

Zone of proximal development, 216–217, 224
Zygote intrafallopian transfer (ZIFT), 81

Coping with the Death of Someone Else 613
Communicating with a Dying Person 613
Grieving 613
■ CAREERS IN LIFE-SPAN DEVELOPMENT
Sara Wheeler, Certified College Grief Counselor 615
Making Sense of the World 615
Losing a Life Partner 616
Forms of Mourning and the Funeral 617
■ SOCIOCULTURAL WORLDS OF DEVELOPMENT
The Family and the Community in Mourning—The Amish and Traditional Judaism 618

Epilogue: The Journey of Life E-1

GLOSSARY G–1
REFERENCES R–1
CREDITS C–1
NAME INDEX NI–1
SUBJECT INDEX SI–1

Fear of Victimization, Crime, and Elder Maltreatment 567

■ CAREERS IN LIFE-SPAN DEVELOPMENT
Jan Weaver, Director of the Alzheimer's Association of Dallas 568

Meeting the Mental Health Needs of Older Adults 568

Religion in Late Adulthood 569

Chapter 20

Socioemotional Development in Late Adulthood 575

■ IMAGES OF LIFE-SPAN DEVELOPMENT
Bob Cousy 575

Theories of Socioemotional Development 576

Erikson's Theory 576
Disengagement Theory 578
Activity Theory 578
Socioemotional Selectivity Theory 578

■ CAREERS IN LIFE-SPAN DEVELOPMENT
Laura Carstensen, Psychology Professor and Director of Women's Studies Program 580

Selective Optimization with Compensation Theory 580

Older Adults in Society 582

Stereotyping Older Adults 582
Policy Issues in an Aging Society 583
Income 585
Living Arrangements 585

Families and Social Relationships 586

The Aging Couple 586
Grandparenting 586
Friendship 589
Social Support and Social Integration 589

Ethnicity, Gender, and Culture 590

Ethnicity and Gender 590
Culture 592

■ SOCIOCULTURAL WORLDS OF DEVELOPMENT
Being Female, Ethnic, and Old 593

Successful Aging 594

Section 10

Endings 599

Chapter 21

Death and Grieving 601

■ IMAGES OF LIFE-SPAN DEVELOPMENT
Princess Diana's Death 601

Defining Death and Life/Death Issues 602

Issues in Determining Death 602
Decisions Regarding Life, Death, and Health Care 602

Death and Sociohistorical, Cultural Contexts 604

Changing Historical Circumstances 604
Death in Different Cultures 605

A Developmental Perspective on Death 606

Causes of Death and Expectations About Death 606
Attitudes Toward Death at Different Points in the Life Span 608

■ CAREERS IN LIFE-SPAN DEVELOPMENT
Robert Kastenbaum, Geropsychologist 609

Facing One's Own Death 610

Kübler-Ross' Stages of Dying 610

■ CRITICAL THINKING
Exploring Your Own Death and Dying 611

Perceived Control and Denial 611
The Contexts in Which People Die 611

Parenting Conceptions 516
Sibling Relationships and Friendships 516
Intergenerational Relationships 000
■ CAREERS IN LIFE-SPAN DEVELOPMENT
Lilian Troll, Professor of Psychology and Life-Span Development and Researcher on Families and Aging Women 517
SOCIOCULTURAL WORLDS OF DEVELOPMENT
Intergenerational Relationships in Mexican American Families—The Effects of Immigration and Acculturation 518

Section 9
Late Adulthood 523

Chapter 18
Physical Development in Late Adulthood 525

■ IMAGES OF LIFE-SPAN DEVELOPMENT
Learning to Age Successfully 525
Longevity 526
Life Expectancy and Life Span 526
■ CRITICAL THINKING
How Long Would You Like to Live? 527
SOCIOCULTURAL WORLDS OF DEVELOPMENT
Aging in Russia, Ecuador, and Kashmir 529
The Young Old, the Old Old, and the Oldest Old 530
Biological Theories of Aging 532
The Course of Physical Development in Late Adulthood 533
The Aging Brain 534
Physical Appearance 535
Sensory Development 535
The Circulatory System 537
The Respiratory System 537
Sexuality 537
Health 538
Health Problems 538
The Robust Oldest Old 541
Exercise, Nutrition, and Weight 541
Health Treatment 544
■ CAREERS IN LIFE-SPAN DEVELOPMENT
Deborah Radomski, Geriatric Nurse 544

Chapter 19
Cognitive Development in Late Adulthood 551

■ IMAGES OF LIFE-SPAN DEVELOPMENT
Sister Mary 551
Cognitive Functioning in Older Adults 551
The Multidimensional, Multidirectional Nature of Cognition 552
Education, Work, and Health: Links to Cognitive Functioning 555
■ CRITICAL THINKING
A Challenging Intellectual Life in Old Age 556
Use It or Lose It 557
■ CAREERS IN LIFE-SPAN DEVELOPMENT
Sherry Willis, Professor of Human Development and Researcher 557
Training Cognitive Skills 557
Work and Retirement 558
Work 558
SOCIOCULTURAL WORLDS OF DEVELOPMENT
Work and Retirement in Japan, the United States, England, and France 561
Retirement in the United States and Other Countries 561
Adjustment to Retirement 561
The Mental Health of Older Adults 562
The Nature of Mental Health in Older Adults 562
Depression 562
Dementia, Alzheimer's Disease, and Other Afflictions 563

Attachment 447
Attraction, Love, and Close Relationships 448
Attraction 449
The Faces of Love 450
CRITICAL THINKING
Exploring Self-Help Books on Love 452
Loneliness 454
Marriage and the Family 457
The Family Life Cycle 457
Marriage 458
SOCIOCULTURAL WORLDS OF DEVELOPMENT
Marriage Around the World 460
CAREERS IN LIFE-SPAN DEVELOPMENT
Andrew Christensen, Clinical Psychologist 462
Gender and Emotion in Marriage 462
Parental Roles 463
CAREERS IN LIFE-SPAN DEVELOPMENT
Janis Keyser, Parent Educator 463
The Diversity of Adult Lifestyles 464
Single Adults 464
Cohabiting Adults 466
Divorced Adults 467
Remarried Adults 467
Gay and Lesbian Adults 468
Gender, Relationships, and Self-Development 469
Women's Development 469
Men's Development 470

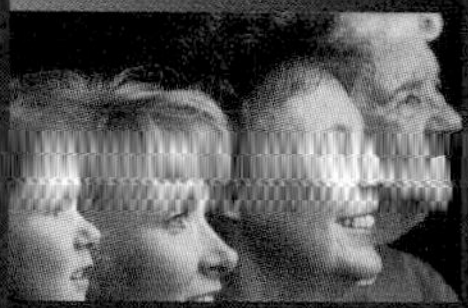

Section 8

Middle Adulthood 475

Chapter 16

Physical and Cognitive Development in Middle Adulthood 477

IMAGES OF LIFE-SPAN DEVELOPMENT
Time Perspectives 477
Changing Middle Age 478
Physical Development 479
Physical Changes 479
Health and Disease 481
Culture, Personality, Relationships, and Health 482
SOCIOCULTURAL WORLDS OF DEVELOPMENT
Health Promotion in African Americans, Latinos, Asian Americans, and Native Americans 483
Mortality Rates 484
Sexuality 484
Cognitive Development 487
Intelligence 487
Information Processing 490
Careers, Work, and Leisure 492
Job Satisfaction 492
Career Challenges and Changes 492
Leisure 493
Religion and Meaning in Life 494
Religion and Adult Lives 494
Religion and Health 494
CAREERS IN LIFE-SPAN DEVELOPMENT
Alice McNair, Pastoral Counselor 495
Meaning in Life 496

Chapter 17

Socioemotional Development in Middle Adulthood 501

IMAGES OF LIFE-SPAN DEVELOPMENT
Middle-Age Variations 501
Personality Theories and Development in Middle Adulthood 502
Adult Stage Theories 502
The Life-Events Approach 505
Contexts of Midlife Development 506
Stability and Change 509
Longitudinal Studies 510
CRITICAL THINKING
Are There Distinct Subphases Within Middle Adulthood? 512
Conclusions 512
Close Relationships 513
Love and Marriage at Midlife 513
The Empty Nest and Its Refilling 515

■ CAREERS IN LIFE-SPAN DEVELOPMENT
Rodney Hammond, Health Psychologist 402
Depression and Suicide 405

■ CRITICAL THINKING
Why Is a Course of Risk Taking in Adolescence Likely to Have More Serious Consequences Today Than in the Past? 406
The Interrelation of Problems and Successful Prevention/Intervention Programs 406

Section 7

Early Adulthood 411

Chapter 14

Physical and Cognitive Development in Early Adulthood 413

■ IMAGES OF LIFE-SPAN DEVELOPMENT
Flo Jo 413

The Transition from Adolescence to Early Adulthood 414
The Criteria for Becoming an Adult 414
The Transition from High School to College 415

■ CAREERS IN LIFE-SPAN DEVELOPMENT
Grace Leaf, College/Career Counselor 415

Physical Development 416
The Peak and Slowdown in Physical Performance 416
Eating and Weight 417

■ CAREERS IN LIFE-SPAN DEVELOPMENT
Judith Rodin, University Professor, Health Psychology Researcher, and University President 419
Regular Exercise 420
Substance Abuse 420

■ CRITICAL THINKING
Do You Abuse Drugs? 422

Sexuality 424
Sexual Orientation 424
Sexually Transmitted Diseases 426

■ CRITICAL THINKING
Sexual Behavior and Moral Choices: Privacy and Protection 427
Forcible Sexual Behavior and Sexual Harassment 428

Cognitive Development 430
Cognitive Stages 430
Creativity 432

■ CAREERS IN LIFE-SPAN DEVELOPMENT
Mihaly Csikszentmihalyi, University Professor and Researcher 433

Careers and Work 435
Developmental Changes 435
Personality Types 435
Values and Careers 436
Monitoring the Occupational Outlook 436

■ CRITICAL THINKING
Career Goal-Setting 437

■ CAREERS IN LIFE-SPAN DEVELOPMENT
Lilian Comas-Diaz, Clinical Psychologist 437
The Skills Employers Want 437
Finding the Right Career 437
Work 438
The Nature of Work 438
Getting Positive Work Experiences During College 438
The Job Interview 438

SOCIOCULTURAL WORLDS OF DEVELOPMENT
Juggling Roles 440

Chapter 15

Socioemotional Development in Early Adulthood 445

■ IMAGES OF LIFE-SPAN DEVELOPMENT
Edith, Phil, and Sherry, Searching for Love 445

Continuity and Discontinuity from Childhood to Adulthood 446
Temperament 446

Section 6

Adolescence 345

Chapter 12

Physical and Cognitive Development in Adolescence 347

■ IMAGES OF LIFE-SPAN DEVELOPMENT
The Best of Times and the Worst of Times for Today's Adolescents 347

The Nature of Adolescence 348

Puberty 349
- Puberty's Boundaries and Determinants 349
- Hormonal Changes 350
- Height, Weight, and Sexual Maturation 351
- Body Image 352

■ CRITICAL THINKING
Thinking About Puberty 353
- Early and Late Maturation 353

Adolescent Sexuality 354
- Developing a Sexual Identity 355
- The Progression of Adolescent Sexual Behaviors 356
- Risk Factors for Sexual Problems 356
- Contraceptive Use 357
- Sexually Transmitted Diseases 357
- Adolescent Pregnancy 358

Adolescent Problems and Health 359
- Substance Use and Abuse 359
- Eating Disorders 363
- Adolescent Health 364

Adolescent Cognition 365
- Piaget's Theory 365

■ CRITICAL THINKING
Piaget, Children, Adolescents, and Political Convictions 366
- Adolescent Egocentrism 367
- Information Processing 368

Schools 369
- The Transition to Middle or Junior High School 369
- Effective Schools for Young Adolescents 371
- High School Dropouts 372

■ CAREERS IN LIFE-SPAN DEVELOPMENT:
Armando Ronquillo, High School Guidance Counselor 372
- Moral Education 373

■ SOCIOCULTURAL WORLDS OF DEVELOPMENT
Cross-Cultural Comparisons of Secondary Schools 374

Chapter 13

Socioemotional Development in Adolescence 381

■ IMAGES OF LIFE-SPAN DEVELOPMENT
A 15-Year-Old Girl's Self-Description 381

Identity 382
- Some Contemporary Thoughts About Identity 382
- Identity Statuses and Development 383

■ CRITICAL THINKING
Exploring Your Identity 384
- Family Influences on Identity 384
- Cultural and Ethnic Aspects of Identity 385

Families 387
- Autonomy and Attachment 387
- Parent-Adolescent Conflict 388

■ CRITICAL THINKING
Age Trends in the Parents of Adolescents and Parent-Adolescent Relationships 389

Peers 391
- Peer Groups 391
- Friendships 392
- Dating and Romantic Relationships 392

Culture and Adolescent Development 393
- Cross-Cultural Comparisons and Rites of Passage 395
- Ethnicity 396

■ CAREERS IN LIFE-SPAN DEVELOPMENT
Teresa LaFromboise, Counseling Psychologist 399

Adolescent Problems 399
- Juvenile Delinquency 399

■ SOCIOCULTURAL WORLDS OF DEVELOPMENT
El Puente and Quantum 400

Section 5

Middle and Late Childhood 271

Chapter 10

Physical and Cognitive Development in Middle and Late Childhood 273

- IMAGES OF LIFE-SPAN DEVELOPMENT
  Jessica Dubroff, Child Pilot 273

Physical Development 274
Body Growth and Proportion 274
Motor Development 274
Exercise and Sports 275
Health, Illness, and Disease 276
- CAREERS IN LIFE-SPAN DEVELOPMENT
  Sharon McLeod, Child Life Specialist 277

Children with Disabilities 278
- CRITICAL THINKING
  Reflecting on Learning Disabilities 281
- CAREERS IN LIFE-SPAN DEVELOPMENT
  Myla Burgess, Learning Disabilities Specialist 282

Cognitive Development 283
Piaget's Theory 283
Information Processing 288
- CAREERS IN LIFE-SPAN DEVELOPMENT
  Laura Martin, Science Museum Educator and Research Specialist 289

Intelligence 290
- CRITICAL THINKING
  Should Parents Be Testing Their Own Child's IQ? 292

Creativity 299
- CAREERS IN LIFE-SPAN DEVELOPMENT
  Sterling Jones, Supervisor of Gifted and Talented Education 299

Language Development 299
- CAREERS IN LIFE-SPAN DEVELOPMENT
  Sharla Peltier, Speech Pathologist 303

Chapter 11

Socioemotional Development in Middle and Late Childhood 309

- IMAGES OF LIFE-SPAN DEVELOPMENT
  The Stories of Lafayette and Pharoah: The Tragedy of Poverty and Violence 309

Emotional and Personality Development 310
The Self 310
Emotional Development 313
- CAREERS IN LIFE-SPAN DEVELOPMENT
  Jonathan Cohen, Director of Social Emotional Learning Center 314

Moral Development 314
- CRITICAL THINKING
  Exploring Your Moral Thinking 317

Gender 320
- CRITICAL THINKING
  Rethinking the Words We Use in Gender Worlds 324

Families 327
Parent-Child Issues 327
Societal Changes in Families 328

Peers 330
Peer Statuses 330
Bullying 331
Social Cognition 332
Friends 332

Schools 334
The Transition to Elementary School 334
- CAREERS IN LIFE-SPAN DEVELOPMENT
  Donna Smith, School Psychologist 335

Socioeconomic Status and Ethnicity in Schools 335
- SOCIOCULTURAL WORLDS OF DEVELOPMENT
  The Global Lab 338
- CAREERS IN LIFE-SPAN DEVELOPMENT
  James Comer, Child Psychiatrist 339

Cross-Cultural Comparisons of Achievement 340

Section 4

Early Childhood 201

Chapter 8

Physical and Cognitive Development in Early Childhood 203

▪ IMAGES OF LIFE-SPAN DEVELOPMENT
Teresa Amabile and Her Creativity 203

Physical Development in Early Childhood 204
Body Growth and Change 204
Motor Development 206
Nutrition 208
Illness and Death 209

▪ CAREERS IN LIFE-SPAN DEVELOPMENT
Barbara Deloin, Pediatric Nurse 210

Cognitive Development in Early Childhood 212
Piaget's Preoperational Stage of Development 212
Vygotsky's Theory of Development 216
Information Processing 220

▪ CAREERS IN LIFE-SPAN DEVELOPMENT
Helen Schwe, Developmental Psychologist and Toy Designer 223

Language Development 225
Early Childhood Education 226

▪ CAREERS IN LIFE-SPAN DEVELOPMENT
Anita Marie Hitchcock, Early Childhood Educator 226

▪ CRITICAL THINKING
Observing Children in Preschool and Kindergarten 230

▪ CAREERS IN LIFE-SPAN DEVELOPMENT
Yolanda Garcia, Director of Children's Services/Head Start 232

Chapter 9

Socioemotional Development in Early Childhood 237

▪ IMAGES OF LIFE-SPAN DEVELOPMENT
Sara and Her Developing Sense of Morality and Values 237

Emotional and Personality Development 238
The Self 238
Emotional Development 239
Moral Development 240
Gender 243

Families 247
Parenting [illegible]

▪ CRITICAL THINKING
Evaluating the Parenting Styles of Both Parents 249

▪ CAREERS IN LIFE-SPAN DEVELOPMENT
Debby Troopy, Child Social Worker 251

▪ CRITICAL THINKING
Developing a Model of Intervention for Maltreating Families 252

Sibling Relationships and Birth Order 253
The Changing Family in a Changing Society 254

Peer Relations, Play, and Television 259
Peer Relations 259
Play 260
Television 264

▪ CRITICAL THINKING
Developing Parental Guidelines for Children's TV Viewing 266

Section 3

Infancy 123

Chapter 5

Physical Development in Infancy 125

- IMAGES OF LIFE-SPAN DEVELOPMENT
  Bottle- and Breast-Feeding in Africa 125

Physical Growth and Development in Infancy 126
- Cephalocaudal and Proximodistal Patterns 126
- Height and Weight 127
- The Brain 127
- Infant States 131

- CAREERS IN LIFE-SPAN DEVELOPMENT
  T. Berry Brazelton, Pediatrician 134
- Nutrition 134
- Toilet Training 136

- SOCIOCULTURAL WORLDS OF DEVELOPMENT
  A Healthy Start 137

Motor Development 138
- Reflexes 138
- Gross and Fine Motor Skills 139
- Developmental Biodynamics 142

Sensory and Perceptual Development 144
- What Are Sensation and Perception? 144
- The Ecological View 145
- Visual Perception 146
- Other Senses 148
- Intermodal Perception 151
- Perceptual-Motor Coupling and Unification 152

Chapter 6

Cognitive Development in Infancy 157

- IMAGES OF LIFE-SPAN DEVELOPMENT
  Laurent, Lucienne, and Jacqueline 157

Piaget's Theory of Infant Development 158
- The Stage of Sensorimotor Development 158
- Substages 159
- Object Permanence 160
- Evaluating Piaget's Sensorimotor Stage 161

Learning and Remembering 162
- Conditioning 162
- Habituation and Dishabituation 163
- Imitation 164
- Memory 164

Individual Differences in Intelligence 165

- CRITICAL THINKING
  Comparing Piaget's Approach with the Individual Differences Approach 166

- CAREERS IN LIFE-SPAN DEVELOPMENT
  Toosje Thyssen VanBeveren, Infant Assessment Specialist 167

Language Development 168
- What Is Language? 169
- How Language Develops 169
- Biological Influences 170
- Behavioral and Environmental Influences 171

Chapter 7

Socioemotional Development in Infancy 177

- IMAGES OF LIFE-SPAN DEVELOPMENT
  The Story of Tom's Fathering 177

Emotional and Personality Development 178
- Emotional Development 178
- Temperament 182
- Personality Development 184

Attachment 186
- What Is Attachment? 186
- Individual Differences 188
- Caregiving Styles and Attachment Classification 189
- Attachment, Temperament, and the Wider Social World 190

Social Contexts 191
- The Family 191

- SOCIOCULTURAL WORLDS OF DEVELOPMENT
  Child Care Policy Around the World 194
- Day Care 194

- CRITICAL THINKING
  Characteristics of Competent Caregivers 195

- CAREERS IN LIFE-SPAN DEVELOPMENT
  Rashmi Nakhre, Day-Care Director 195

Experimental Research 50
Time Span of Research 51
Research Journals 54
■ CAREERS IN LIFE-SPAN DEVELOPMENT
Tom Puglisi, Director of Human Subjects Protection 57
Research Challenges 57
Ethics 57
Gender 58
Ethnicity and Culture 58
■ CAREERS IN LIFE-SPAN DEVELOPMENT
Pam Reid, Educational and Developmental Psychologist 58
■ CRITICAL THINKING
Isn't Everyone a Psychologist? 59

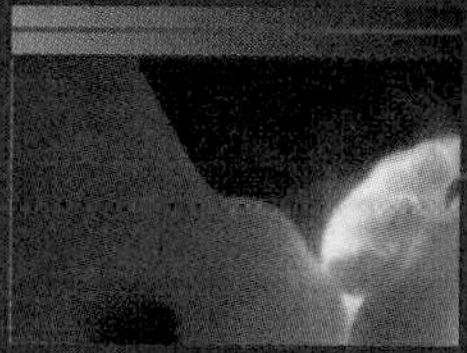

Section 2

Beginnings 63

Chapter 3

Biological Beginnings 65

■ IMAGES OF LIFE-SPAN DEVELOPMENT
The Jim and Jim Twins 65
The Evolutionary Perspective 66
Natural Selection and Adaptive Behavior 66
Evolutionary Psychology 67
Genetic Foundations 69
What Are Genes? 69
Mitosis and Meiosis 69
Genetic Principles 70
Behavior Genetics 74
Molecular Genetics 74
Chromosome and Gene-Linked Abnormalities 75
■ CAREERS IN LIFE-SPAN DEVELOPMENT
Holly Ishmael, Genetic Counselor 76
Reproduction Challenges and Choices 77
Prenatal Diagnostic Tests 77
Infertility 79
Adoption 82
Heredity-Environment Interaction 83
Intelligence 83
■ CRITICAL THINKING
The Nobel Prize Sperm Bank 85
Heredity-Environment Correlations 85
■ SOCIOCULTURAL WORLDS OF DEVELOPMENT
The Abecedarian Project 86
Shared and Nonshared Environmental Experiences 87
Conclusions About Heredity-Environment Interaction 88

Chapter 4

Prenatal Development and Birth 93

■ IMAGES OF LIFE-SPAN DEVELOPMENT
Tanner Roberts' Birth: A Fantastic Voyage 93
Prenatal Development 94
The Course of Prenatal Development 94
Cultural Beliefs About Pregnancy 98
Teratology and Hazards to Prenatal Development 98
■ CRITICAL THINKING
Interventions to Stop Pregnant Women from Smoking 102
Prenatal Care 106
Positive Prenatal Development 107
Birth 108
The Birth Process 108
■ CAREERS IN LIFE-SPAN DEVELOPMENT
Linda Pugh, Neonatal Nurse 109
Preterm Infants and Age-Weight Considerations 111
Measures of Neonatal Health and Responsiveness 113
The Postpartum Period 115
What Is the Postpartum Period? 115
Physical Adjustments 116
Emotional and Psychological Adjustments 116
■ CAREERS IN LIFE-SPAN DEVELOPMENT
Diane Stanford, Clinical Psychologist and Post-Partum Expert 117
Bonding 118

Contents

PREFACE x
TO THE STUDENT xx

Section 1
The Life-Span Developmental Perspective 3

Chapter 1
Introduction 5

- IMAGES OF LIFE-SPAN DEVELOPMENT
  How Did Ted Kaczynski Become Ted Kaczynski and Alice Walker Become Alice Walker? 5

The Life-Span Perspective 6
  Why Study Life-Span Development? 6
  The Historical Perspective 7
  Characteristics of the Life-Span Perspective 9
- CAREERS IN LIFE-SPAN DEVELOPMENT
  K. Warner Schaie, Professor of Human Development 9
  Some Contemporary Concerns 11
- CAREERS IN LIFE-SPAN DEVELOPMENT
  Luis Vargas, Child Clinical Psychologist 11
- SOCIOCULTURAL WORLDS OF DEVELOPMENT
  Women's Struggle for Equality: An International Journey 14

The Nature of Development 16
  Biological, Cognitive, and Socioemotional Processes 16
  Periods of Development 16
- CRITICAL THINKING
  Asking Questions ... What Is the Best Age to Be? 17
  Age and Happiness 18
  Conceptions of Age 18
  Developmental Issues 19

Careers in Life-Span Development 22

Chapter 2
The Science of Life-Span Development 29

- IMAGES OF LIFE-SPAN DEVELOPMENT
  The Childhoods of Erikson and Piaget 29

Theories of Development 30
- CAREERS IN LIFE-SPAN DEVELOPMENT
  Saundra Boyd, Community College Instructor 31
  Psychoanalytic Theories 31
  Cognitive Theories 35
- SOCIOCULTURAL WORLDS OF DEVELOPMENT
  Cultural and Gender Bias in Freud's Theory 36
  Behavioral and Social Cognitive Theories 40
  Ethological Theory 42
  Ecological Theory 43
- CRITICAL THINKING
  Imagine Growing Up Somewhere Else 43
  An Eclectic Theoretical Orientation 45

Research Methods 48
  Observation 48
  Interviews and Questionnaires 49
  Case Studies 49
  Standardized Tests 49
  Life-History Records 49
  Physiological Research and Research with Animals 50
  Correlational Research 50

Brief Contents

Section 1
The Life-Span Developmental Perspective 3

1 Introduction 5
2 The Science of Life-Span Development 29

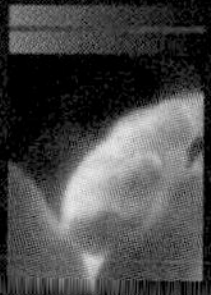

Section 2
Beginnings 63

3 Biological Beginnings 65
4 Prenatal Development and Birth 93

Section 3
Infancy 123

5 Physical Development in Infancy 125
6 Cognitive Development in Infancy 157
7 Socioemotional Development in Infancy 177

Section 4
Early Childhood 201

8 Physical and Cognitive Development in Early Childhood 203
9 Socioemotional Development in Early Childhood 237

Section 5
Middle and Late Childhood 271

10 Physical and Cognitive Development in Middle and Late Childhood 273
11 Socioemotional Development in Middle and Late Childhood 309

Section 6
Adolescence 345

12 Physical and Cognitive Development in Adolescence 347
13 Socioemotional Development in Adolescence 381

Section 7
Early Adulthood 411

14 Physical and Cognitive Development in Early Adulthood 413
15 Socioemotional Development in Early Adulthood 445

Section 8
Middle Adulthood 475

16 Physical and Cognitive Development in Middle Adulthood 477
17 Socioemotional Development in Middle Adulthood 501

Section 9
Late Adulthood 523

18 Physical Development in Late Adulthood 525
19 Cognitive Development in Late Adulthood 551
20 Socioemotional Development in Late Adulthood 575

Section 10
Endings 599

21 Death and Grieving 601
Epilogue: The Journey of Life E-1

About the Author

John W. Santrock

John Santrock received his Ph.D. from the University of Minnesota in 1973. He taught at the University of Charleston and the University of Georgia before joining the Program in Psychology and Human Development at the University of Texas at Dallas, where he currently teaches a number of undergraduate courses. In 1982, John created the life-span development course at UT–Dallas and has taught it every year since then.

John has been a member of the editorial boards of *Child Development* and *Developmental Psychology.* His research on father custody is widely cited and used in expert witness testimony to promote flexibility and alternative considerations in custody disputes. John also has authored these exceptional McGraw-Hill texts: *Psychology* (6th edition), *Child Development* (9th edition), *Children* (6th edition), *Adolescence* (8th edition), and *Educational Psychology* (1st edition).

For many years, John was involved in tennis as a player, teaching professional, and coach of professional tennis players. He has been married for more than 35 years to his wife, Mary Jo, who is a realtor. He has two daughters—Tracy, who is a technology specialist at Nortel in Raleigh, North Carolina, and Jennifer, who is a medical sales specialist at Guidant. He has one granddaughter, Jordan, age 9. Tracy recently completed the Boston Marathon, and Jennifer was in the top 100 ranked players on the Women's Professional Tennis Tour. In the last decade, John also has spent time painting expressionist art.

John Santrock, teaching in his undergraduate course in life-span development.

With special appreciation
to my parents, Ruth
and John Santrock

Life-Span Development